FROMMER'S

DOLLARWISE GUIDE TO AUSTRIA & HUNGARY

By Darwin Porter

1985-86 Edition

Published by Frommer/Pasmantier Publishers
A Division of Simon & Schuster, Inc.
1230 Avenue of the Americas
New York, New York 10020

ISBN 0-671-50943-8

Manufactured in the United States of America

Although every effort was made to ensure the accuracy of price information appearing in this book, it should be kept in mind that prices can and do fluctuate in the course of time.

CONTENTS

MAPS

Acknowledgment

The author wishes to express his appreciation to Margaret Foresman and Danforth Prince for their enormous contributions in the preparation of this guide.

INFLATION ALERT: We don't have to tell you that inflation has hit Austria and Hungary as it has everywhere else. In researching this book we have made every effort to obtain up-to-the-minute prices, but even the most conscientious researcher cannot keep up with the current pace of inflation. As we go to press, we believe we have obtained the most reliable data possible. Nonetheless, in the lifetime of this edition—particularly its second year (1985)—the wise traveler will add 15% to 20% to the prices quoted throughout these pages.

A DISCLAIMER: Although every effort was made to ensure the accuracy of the prices and travel information appearing in this book, it should be kept in mind that prices do fluctuate in the course of time, and that information does change under the impact of the varied and volatile factors that affect the travel industry.

Readers should also note that the establishments described under Readers' Selections or Suggestions have not in many cases been inspected by the author and that the opinions expressed there are those of the individual reader(s) only. They do not in any way represent the opinions of the publisher or author of this guide.

Introduction

A DOLLARWISE GUIDE TO AUSTRIA, PLUS HUNGARY

THIS BOOK IS about two small countries in Central Europe that were once the seat of a great empire. The territories and lands of both countries have been reduced by a roller-coaster ride from the heights to the depths. Austria, for example, only regained its full sovereignty as late as July 27, 1955; whereas Hungary, unsuccessful in its attempt at revolution in 1956, is still a Soviet-bloc land, having lost much of its territory, including Transylvania, to neighboring countries (in this case Rumania).

1. The Reason Why

Even after the loss of its former colonies, Austria was left with a land of scenic grandeur and soaring alpine peaks. There are those (and perhaps I join them) who say that, when taken as a whole, Austria is the most beautiful country on earth.

A great world power in the 18th and 19th centuries, Austria still preserves reminders of its past in its epic monuments and grandiose baroque buildings.

The Federal Republic of Austria consists of nine fairly autonomous provinces, called Bundesländer: Vienna (of course), Upper Austria, Lower Austria, Salzburg, Tyrol, Vorarlberg, Styria, Carinthia, and tiny Burgenland. Each of these provinces contains great geographical and cultural differences, and it is the lucky visitor who gets to see all of Austria, which, though small, takes many weeks to visit in its entirety (and even then you'll have skimmed only the surface).

Austria is a sports-oriented country (and not just for skiers). It's also rich in music and drama, in art, museums, galleries, churches, and cathedrals.

West Germany (to which it once had an ill-fated alliance in the 1930s and early 1940s) lies to the north. On the northeast is Czechoslovakia, on the east is Hungary, and on the southeast lies Yugoslavia, three countries which Austria used to dominate in part. Of course Italy is to the south, and on its west is Switzerland, with whom it often fought battles until that even tinier country fully gained its independence from Habsburg domination.

Austria is peaceful today, and if it thinks of empire, it is only nostalgically (I've talked to many Viennese who remember the last parade in their city of the Austro-Hungarian Empire). Nowadays its German-speaking populace (English is virtually a second language) are among the most hospitable and friendly in Europe.

Austria, like Switzerland, no longer sends its soldiers marching across other frontiers but is itself invaded in both summer and winter. Austria is a true biseasonal country, enjoying both a huge summer and winter tourist industry. The new invaders are tourists, and they come to seek out the grandeur of "the roof of Europe." About 75% of Austria is mountainous. Austria today has about 7.5 million in population, a people associated with gemütlichkeit, a warm, contented, friendly feeling generated by those who appreciate the good life.

This is best summed up by a popular saying in the country: "In Britain everything is allowed that is not expressly forbidden; in Germany everything is verboten that is not expressly permitted, and in Austria everything is permitted that is not expressly forbidden!"

A comparable amount of freedom and permissiveness doesn't exist in the Hungary of today, yet perhaps more than in any other country in Eastern Europe, Hungary is welcoming visitors as never before. It has made border crossings easier (visas are now granted at the frontier), and it is sprucing up its monuments and building better hotels and finer restaurants to receive the millions who cross its borders annually.

Austria itself is one of the least expensive countries of Western Europe, but Hungary is so cheap that the Austrians themselves visit it sometimes just to get their hair done.

These two countries which once formed the heart of the Austro-Hungarian Empire have long been separated by the tides of history—Austria now neutral, Hungary a part of the Warsaw Pact Nations. But—and only for the purposes of this guidebook—we will join them for a reunion once more. Vienna, now more than ever as in olden days, is the gateway to Budapest.

FROM THE ALPS TO THE DANUBE: The scenery of Austria is more varied than that of Switzerland, combining rich agricultural plains along the Danube, alpine peaks and lakes, and castles (often in ruins) that evoke the Middle Ages. All that, combined with acres and acres of vineyards, has made Austria a tourist mecca since the 19th century.

The name Austria, or Österreich, means "Eastern Empire," a designation given to the far eastern sector of the lands conquered by Charlemagne. But from prehistoric times, the part of Europe centering around present-day Austria has been a crossroads, with the Danube Valley allowing traverse both by land and water.

During the "twilight of the Habsburgs," culminating in 1918, Austria, poised between the West and the East, lost much of its territory and since then has faced international humiliation.

Memories of Hitler—who turned their country into a virtual colony of the Third Reich, in spite of the sentiment of many Austrians at the time who wanted to "amalgamate" with Nazi Germany—and of the succeeding partial Soviet occupation are still strong in the minds of many Austrians. However, despite reverses which may well be credited to the *hubris* of their rulers, Austria has recovered its spirit admirably.

This country, once reaching from czarist Russia to the Adriatic, now smaller than the state of Maine, is still a land of music. Its festivals, such as the one at Salzburg which is famous the world over, its skiing, and those monumental baroque edifices referred to hold an appeal that I, along with thousands of others, find irresistible.

Vienna is the most distinguished capital city in the German-speaking world, but although they share a common language, Austria and Germany are two very different countries. A visit to one will hardly be like a visit to the other.

Austria has one of the lowest inflation rates in Europe, and among the trio of big skiing countries, it's cheaper than either Switzerland or France.

As fat as this book is—probably the single biggest guide ever published on the hotels and restaurants of Austria—you should know that it represents only a fraction of the actual facilities available. What I'm sharing with you are my favorites. Perhaps, using the book as your seed core, you'll find dozens more on your own.

Likewise, this is the first major guide in English to describe in any detail the hotels, restaurants, shops, and nightclubs of Hungary, along with the country's many tourist attractions. And not only those found in Budapest but also in its colorful provinces, which take in the famed Danube Bend, Lake Balaton, and the Great Hungarian Plain.

THE BEST OF AUSTRIA AND HUNGARY: I have set for myself the formidable task of seeking out Austria and Hungary at their finest and condensing them between the covers of a book. The best towns, villages, cities, and sightseeing attractions are documented, as well as the best hotels, restaurants, bars, cafés, shops, and nightspots.

But the best need not be the most expensive. My ultimate aim—beyond that of familiarizing you with the offerings of Austria and Hungary—is to stretch your dollar power . . . to reveal to you that you need not pay scalper's prices for charm, top-grade comfort, and gourmet-level food.

In this guide I'll devote a lot of attention to those old tourist meccas—Vienna, Salzburg, Innsbruck, Budapest—focusing on both their obvious and their hidden treasures. But they are not the full "reason why" of this book. Important as they are, they simply do not reflect fully the widely diverse and complicated countryside of Austria and Hungary. To discover that, you must venture deep into the Tyrolean country or perhaps to the romantic windswept puszta of the Great Hungarian Plain.

2. Dollarwise—What It Means

In brief, this is a guidebook giving specific details—including prices—about Austrian and Hungarian hotels, restaurants, bars, cafés, sightseeing attractions, nightlife, and tours. Establishments in many price ranges have been documented and described, although I am constantly searching for bargains. Along with the deluxe citadels, I am more interested in the family-run *gasthof*-type place where you can often bask in gemütlich warmth but at low prices. In all cases, deluxe or budget, each establishment was measured by a strict yardstick of value. If they measured up—meaning if they were the best in their category—they were included.

Now, more than ever, one needs an accurate guidebook including tips for saving money. By careful planning and selecting from my listings, you'll find the true Austrian or Hungarian experience while remaining within a reasonable budget. This applies to independent travelers as well as those who visit Austria or Hungary on a tour. If you're one of the latter, and have already obtained your flight ticket and hotel, you'll still need a guide to direct you to restaurants, nightlife, and sightseeing attractions rarely covered on a package tour. If you're given a car, then you'll be in the market for suggestions of where to go in the country once you leave either Vienna or Salzburg, whichever is your "gateway" city.

SOME WORDS OF EXPLANATION: No restaurant, inn, hotel, nightclub, shop, or café paid to be mentioned in this book. What you read are entirely personal recommendations; in many cases the proprietors never knew their establishments were being visited or investigated for inclusion in a travel guide.

Unfortunately, although I have made every effort to be as accurate as possible, prices change, and they rarely go downward.

When checking into a hotel, always inquire about the rate and agree on it. That policy can save much embarrassment and disappointment when it comes time to settle the tab. If the prices quoted are not the same as those mentioned in this book, remember that my prices reflect those in effect at the time this edition was researched. As I said, prices change.

This guide is revised cover to cover every other year. But even in a book that appears with such frequency, it may happen that that cozy little wine tavern of a year ago has changed its stripes, blossoming out with cut-velvet walls, crystal chandeliers, and dining tabs that include the decorator's fee and the owner's new villa. It may further develop that some of the people or settings I've described are no longer there or have changed in this fast-moving world.

All that leads up to the next major point—

AN INVITATION TO READERS: Like all the books in the "Dollarwise" series, the *Dollarwise Guide to Austria plus Hungary* hopes to maintain a continuing dialogue between its author and its readers. All of us share a common aim, I'm sure, and that is to travel as widely and as well as possible, at the lowest possible cost. In achieving that goal, your comments and suggestions can be of aid to other readers.

Therefore if you come across a particularly appealing hotel, restaurant, shop, or bargain, please don't keep it to yourself. It will be good for your soul if you share your gem with others.

Comments about existing listings are always helpful. The fact that a hotel or restaurant (or any other establishment) appears in this edition doesn't mean that it will necessarily appear in future editions if readers report that its service has slipped or that its prices have not only risen drastically but unfairly.

Even if you like a place I've recommended, your comments are especially welcome, and have been known to brighten many a gray day.

Send your comments or finds—and, yes, those inevitable complaints that always arise—to Darwin Porter, c/o Frommer/Pasmantier Publishers, 1230 Avenue of the Americas, New York, NY 10020.

3. About This Book

Here's how the Dollarwise Guide to Austria plus Hungary sets forth its information:

Chapter I, directly ahead, explores the methods of "getting to" and "getting around" Austria. The most obvious means of reaching it would be by air from America, or perhaps you'll go by car after your exploration of Germany, Italy, or Switzerland. But my coverage of transportation within Austria will focus mainly on the railway lines and bargain passes.

Chapter II provides a general discussion of the country and a brief historical survey, along with a description of its people, customs, hotels, and cuisine. Special features include farmhouse holidays and castle hotels. Austria as both a summer and winter playground will be surveyed in the sports section, along with winter skiing, mountain climbing, camping, fishing, golf, and gliding, among other activities. The chapter concludes with a general ABCs of the country, from customs to postal services, from tipping to currency.

Chapter III wings in on Vienna, one of the great tourist attractions of Europe. All the deluxe hotels will be included, many of the first class, and an even wider range in the middle bracket, followed by inexpensive hotels and a large category of pensions (boarding houses). Restaurants will cover a wide range of the establishments that serve the celebrated Austrian cuisine.

Chapter IV will continue the exploration of Vienna, focusing on its sightseeing attractions, of which there are many, and its shops and nightlife. In this chapter we'll also seek out the famous cafés of Vienna, along with the wine taverns, heurigen, which are noted for their festivities and "new wine." The chapter will conclude with an ABC listing of the facts of life in Vienna, including how to get around the city (try a "horse cab").

Crisscrossed by the Danube, Lower Austria, covered in Chapter V, is a land of castles and vineyards. Hotels are generally inexpensive, of the gasthaus type, but many first-class resorts exist in such spots as Baden. The chapter explores the Wienerwald (Vienna Woods), along with the wine villages. An itinerary, with sights, food, and inns along the "Wine Road," is presented. The major winter sports and mountain-air resorts in the high peaks of Semerling and Schneeberg are described. This chapter also explores another wine district, Weinviertel, north of Vienna, lying between the Danube and Czechoslovakia. Although the chapter deals with trips on Danube paddleboat steamers, the most space is devoted to castles and abbeys in the area—some in ruins, some turned into hotels, others into sightseeing attractions. Chief among these is the Benedictine abbey at Melk, the largest in Lower Austria.

A small section, Burgenland, in Chapter VI, is devoted to this province, which is known for its gardens, castles, and fortresses. We'll visit the mysterious Neusiedler See, a shallow, saltwater lake. This chapter adds a little paprika to the book, because it is much like Hungary. Spa and castle hotels will be surveyed, along with more modest guest houses. Burgenland is one of the great bargain areas of Austria and is rich in sights.

Chapter VII, Salzburg, takes in the "city of Mozart." The annual Mozart Festival is described, along with both "Left Bank" and "Right Bank" tour notes. A full range of hotels, from deluxe to inexpensive, is surveyed, including some special ones in the environs. Likewise, restaurants range from inexpensive brewery-operated establishments (one where priests make their own beer) to first-class selections serving an international cuisine. Special restaurants in the environs, including some with terraces and belvederes overlooking the Alps, are covered. Attractions range from Mozart's birthplace to the Fortress Hohensalzburg, along with details of how to get about, including by aerial cable railway. Nightlife takes in the casino, and there's also a sports section, as the Gaisberg mountain lies on the outskirts of the city.

Chapter VIII, Land Salzburg, covers that area of sports and spas—famous the world over—which lie to the north and northeast of Salzburg. Our selection of hotels ranges from the deluxe ones at Badgastein to modest mountain lodges. The great High Alpine Highway, the Grossglockner Road, is described, with peaks at 12,000 feet and views at 8000-foot levels. A full range of towns includes hotels near Radstädter Tauern Pass, one of the most prestigious ski areas in Land Salzburg, and such famous resorts as Zell am See.

Chapter IX goes into Upper Austria, which is crossed in part by the Danube. Here the Salzkammergut, the lake country, is the most popular area with visitors. Major attention is devoted to Linz, the capital of Upper Austria, and its many sights nearby. The baroque Augustinian abbey of St. Florian, with its Bruckner organ and lavishly decorated imperial rooms, is one of the chief sights of the country. The highlights of this province emphasize attractions along the Danube. Little-known places are spotlighted, including Enns, the oldest town in Austria. The outstanding castles and abbeys of the area include Kremsmünster Abbey, founded in 777. A special section is devoted to Bad Ischl, the fashionable spa and winter sports center where Franz Joseph held summer court in the heyday of Imperial Austria. Hotels and restaurants range from elegant castles to old hotels that were the settings for operettas. Restaurants include many relatively unpublicized places known for their fish and game specialties. Some of the mountain hotels can be reached only by cable car.

Chapter X turns to Innsbruck and Tyrol, the favorite part of Austria for nearly all visiting Americans. The obvious attention goes to the capital, baroque-style Innsbruck, acclaimed by many as one of the loveliest towns of Europe. Innsbruck's sights, hotels, restaurants, shops, and nightlife are followed by such sights in the environs as the winter-sports center at Igls. The Stubai Valley is previewed, both as a summer center and a winter ski mecca, with its glacier and mountains. A section includes one of the Tyrol's most exciting events, an excursion along the Karwendel railway, traveling by electric train along the Austrian-Bavarian border. Winter sports centers such as Seefeld are surveyed. Lienz, called by many "the prettiest little city in Europe," is given a special bouquet, and Kitzbühel, one of the best known towns in Austria, is cited for exceptional ski facilities. The chapter includes information on the famous Zugspitze, from which at nearly 10,000 feet one can see Austria, the Swiss Alps, and part of Bavaria. The valleys of the Tyrol, including Achen, Tuxer, and Ziller, are surveyed, along with a full range of Tyrolean hotels and restaurants, plus shopping for such specialties as dirndls, lederhosen, woodcarvings, and those famous Tyrolean hats.

Austria's westernmost province, Vorarlberg, unfolds in Chapter XI. It's much like Switzerland. Here we'll center mainly at Bregenz, a little town on the Bodensee (Lake Constance), and we'll explore the Bregenz Forest, a land of lovely woods, alpine meadows, and highlights. For the most part, hotels and restaurants in the area are of the small, family-type operation. Stübe taverns and restaurants—some of them centuries old—are presented.

Carinthia, in Chapter XII, is the southernmost part of Austria, bordering Italy. Framed by high mountains, it's a land of lakes and narrow valleys. Its best known summer resorts lie around Wörthersee, and the most fashionable spot on the lake, Velden, has first-class hotels and boarding houses, including one of the finest in Austria, the baroque Schloss Velder. Winter sports resorts, such as Kanzelhöhe, known for its "perfect snow" and sunshine, are covered as well. The latter, on the Gerlitzen Plateau, is reached by cable car. There is a heavy emphasis on sports: boat races, waterskiing, swimming, and sailing.

The "green state," Styria, covered in Chapter XIII, in the southeastern part of the country, has Graz as its capital. The Styrian gray-and-green hunting suits are known all over the world. It is the Styrian version of the dirndl that is most popular. Its skiing terrains are covered, now that the Alpine World Skiing Championships gave them such publicity. Old Graz is cited as one of the best bargain hotels of Austria, in both restaurants and hotels. Other towns include Bad Aussee, an important spa and winter sports center, and the summer resort of Altausee, in the Styrian sector of the Salzkammergut. The province has many well-known hotels along with the relatively undocumented colorful old inns. Weinstuben are also very important here, along with cafés and pastry shops. A small number of museums are previewed, including the old buildings of the Gra Joanneum and the Styrian Folklore Museum.

In Chapter XIV we'll take a side trip to Hungary, which, along with Austria, once formed the nucleus of a great empire. But the two are vastly different countries today, one lying in the West, the other, Hungary, behind the so-called iron curtain. That curtain lifts in this chapter to reveal one of the most exciting tourist destinations in Europe. Visa requirements, transportation, whatever, will be previewed before our descent on the lively capital of Hungary, Budapest, 1000 years old. After enjoying everything here among its many attractions—ranging from the beauty of its six bridges spanning the Danube to goulash parties—we will then explore the main sightseeing targets of the country itself, ranging from the Danube Bend to Lake Balaton. We'll also explore some of the great spas of Hungary, along with the horseback-riding country of the Great Plain.

4. A Word About Cost

Austria has had a low inflation rate when compared to some of the other countries of Western Europe. With the dollar on the rise (at least as of this writing), that has made the country one of the better buys in Europe (as hordes of Germans pouring across its borders annually can testify!). Hotels and restaurants have shown only minor increases in the past two or three years, and some of the worst hikes in the cost of living for the Austrian are outside the concern of the average visitor (rising taxes, etc.).

Vienna and Salzburg are the two most expensive cities, with Innsbruck a runner-up. But one of the reasons for that is that these are the three cities the typical American visitor has heard of and therefore heads for. So I have a suggestion. If you have only a few days for Austria, don't just spend all your time in these high-priced tourist meccas, but head instead for a night or two in such old and historic cities as Graz and Linz where the hoteliers and the restaurateurs are not as tab-happy.

As for restaurants, the main meal of the day in Austria is taken at noon. That's when most restaurants, wanting to attract local business (not just the tourist), offer a fixed-price menu, often at an incredibly modest price. So when in Austria, do as the Austrians do and enjoy a most filling and reasonably priced lunch, perhaps ordering a much lighter dinner or supper when the tabs are likely to be much higher.

Sometimes, particularly if you're planning to tour a province such as the Tyrolean country, it's better to anchor into just one place in the countryside, perhaps a centrally located inn, and then branch out from there on a series of day trips. Chances are, you'll get a much better rate, especially on half-board arrangements, than you would by hotel-hopping, checking in and out of a different place every night, which is, regrettably, still the chief American way of traveling.

Because Austria is a small country you can stay put longer in one place, yet still see widely varying scenery by taking day trips. Therefore if you confine yourself to just one hotel per province and explore everything that province has to offer, you'll save more money and always experience less wear and tear on yourself than if you had to shop for a different hotel every night.

Whenever possible, try to book into a country inn on the half-board plan, which can mean amazing discounts for you. Half board means one main meal a day, along with breakfast. You're free to have lunch outside, and if you've planned your itinerary well, you can easily be back at your hotel for dinner in the evening.

If you'd like to see a part of Austria—any part, since all of them are fascinating—and economy is a major concern in your case, then there are some spots of Austria that are extremely reasonable, allowing you to keep costs bone-trimmed. Chief among these is Burgenland (see Chapter VI), a province much sought out and known to Europeans, but little known to most North Americans. Isolated, remote, almost forgotten (but not abandoned), East Tyrol is another such spot, as are certain sections of Styria and Carinthia.

Of course, if you can adjust your schedule, off-season travel can be quite a bargain in Austria. Sometimes hotel prices are lowered as much as 30%.

Costs have been rising greatly in Hungary, but after a trip through Western Europe it will come as a great relief to your pocketbook. As a quick rule of thumb, if you've traveled "second class" in most of the nations of Western Europe, you'll find that you can afford "first class" or deluxe (which exists mainly in Budapest) once you cross the border. Budapest, naturally, is the most expensive destination, and once you're out of that city into the countryside of Hungary, you'll encounter prices you haven't seen in the last decade or so.

TIME OUT FOR A COMMERCIAL: The very fact that you've purchased a guide to two small countries of Europe puts you in a special, sophisticated category of traveler—that is, those who want to explore and get to know a single country or two, as opposed to the "Grand Tour" individual who wants to do not only Belgium on Tuesday, but Rome on Wednesday, and perhaps the North Cape by Friday.

Even so, on your tour of Austria or Hungary, you come to the very doorstep of major attractions in other countries which you may want to explore. Since I had to set some limitation on the number of pages in this book, it was impossible to devote separate chapters to neighboring attractions.

I'll cite only an example or two to prove my point. For example, when you visit southern Austria you're close to the many attractions of Italy, including Venice. At Salzburg you're on the doorstep of exciting Bavaria. In Vorarlberg you're next door to Switzerland and Liechtenstein, that tiny principality left over from the Habsburg Empire.

Because of the geography of Austria, and, again, depending on which sections of that country you plan to travel in, you may want to take along some of our sister guides as traveling companions.

Specific ones that might appeal to you include:

Dollarwise Guide to Switzerland, plus Liechtenstein
Dollarwise Guide to Germany
Dollarwise Guide to Italy

5. The $25-a-Day Travel Club—How to Save Money on All Your Travels

In this book we'll be looking at how to get your money's worth in Austria and Hungary, but there is a "device" for saving money and determining value on *all* your trips. It's the popular, international $25-a-Day Travel Club, now in its 22nd successful year of operation. The Club was formed at the urging of numerous readers of the $$$-a-Day and Dollarwise Guides, who felt that such an organization could provide continuing travel information and a sense of community to value-minded travelers in all parts of the world. And so it does!

In keeping with the budget concept, the annual membership fee is low and is immediately exceeded by the value of your benefits. Upon receipt of $15 (U.S. residents), or $18 U.S. by check drawn on a U.S. bank or via international postal money order in U.S. funds (Canadian, Mexican and other foreign residents) to cover one year's membership, we will send all new members the following items:

(1) *Any two* of the following books

Please designate in your letter which two you wish to receive:

Europe on $25 a Day
Australia on $25 a Day
England and Scotland on $25 a Day
Greece on $25 a Day
Hawaii on $35 a Day
India on $15 & $25 a Day
Ireland on $25 a Day
Israel on $30 & $35 a Day
Mexico on $20 a Day
New York on $35 a Day
New Zealand on $20 & $25 a Day
Scandinavia on $25 a Day
South America on $25 a Day
Spain and Morocco (plus the Canary Is.) on $25 a Day
Washington, D.C. on $35 a Day

Dollarwise Guide to Austria and Hungary
Dollarwise Guide to Canada
Dollarwise Guide to the Caribbean (including Bermuda and the Bahamas)
Dollarwise Guide to Egypt
Dollarwise Guide to England and Scotland
Dollarwise Guide to France
Dollarwise Guide to Germany
Dollarwise Guide to Italy
Dollarwise Guide to Portugal (plus Madeira and the Azores)
Dollarwise Guide to Switzerland and Liechtenstein
Dollarwise Guide to California and Las Vegas
Dollarwise Guide to Florida
Dollarwise Guide to New England
Dollarwise Guide to the Northwest
Dollarwise Guide to the Southeast and New Orleans
Dollarwise Guide to the Southwest

(Dollarwise Guides discuss accommodations and facilities in all price ranges, with emphasis on the medium-priced.)

Dollarwise Guide to Cruises
(This complete guide covers all the basics of cruising—ports of call, costs, fly-cruise package bargains, cabin selection booking, embarkation and debarkation and describes in detail over 60 or so ships cruising in Alaska, the Caribbean, Mexico, Hawaii, Panama, Canada, and the United States.)

How to Beat the High Cost of Travel
(This practical guide details how to save money on absolutely all travel items—accommodations, transportation, dining, sightseeing, shopping, taxes, and more. Includes special budget information for seniors, students, singles, and families.)

The New York Urban Athlete
(The ultimate guide to all the sports facilities in New York City for jocks and novices.)

Museums in New York
(A complete guide to all the museums, historic houses, gardens, zoos, and more in the five boroughs. Illustrated with over 200 photographs.)

The Fast 'n' Easy Phrase Book
(The four most useful languages—French, German, Spanish, and Italian—all in one convenient, easy-to-use phrase guide.)

Where to Stay USA
(By the Council on International Educational Exchange, this extraordinary guide is the first to list accommodations in all 50 states that cost anywhere from $3 to $25 per night.)

A Guide for the Disabled Traveler
(A guide to the best destinations for wheelchair travelers and other disabled vacationers in Europe, the United States, and Canada by an experienced wheelchair traveler. Includes detailed information about accommodations, restaurants, sights, transportation, and their accessibility.)

Marilyn Wood's Wonderful Weekends
(This very selective guide covers the best mini-vacation destinations within a 175-mile radius of New York City. It describes special country inns and other accommodations, restaurants, picnic spots, sights, and activities—all the information needed for a two- or three-day stay.)

Bed & Breakfast—North America
(This guide contains a directory of over 150 organizations that offer bed & breakfast referrals and reservations throughout North America. The scenic attractions, businesses, and major schools and universities near the homes of each are also listed.)

(2) A one-year subscription to The Wonderful World of Budget Travel

This quarterly eight-page tabloid newspaper keeps you up to date on fast-breaking developments in low-cost travel in all parts of the world bringing you the latest money-saving information—the kind of information you'd have to pay $25 a year to obtain elsewhere. This consumer-conscious publication also features columns of special interest to readers: **The Traveler's Directory** (members all over the world who are willing to provide hospitality to other members as they pass through their home cities); **Share-a-Trip** (offers and requests from members for travel companions who can share costs and help avoid the burdensome single supplement); and **Readers Ask . . . Readers Reply** (travel questions from members to which other members reply with authentic firsthand information).

(3) A copy of Arthur Frommer's Guide to New York

This is a pocket-size guide to hotels, restaurants, nightspots, and sightseeing attractions in all price ranges throughout the New York area.

(4) Your personal membership card

Membership entitles you to purchase through the Club all Arthur Frommer publications for a third to a half off their regular retail prices during the term of your membership.

So why not join this hardy band of international budgeteers and participate in its exchange of travel information and hospitality? Simply send your name and address, together with your annual membership fee of $15 (U.S. residents) or $18 U.S. (Canadian, Mexican, and other foreign residents), by check drawn on a U.S. bank or via international postal money order in U.S. funds to: $25-A-Day Travel Club, Inc., Frommer/Pasmantier Publishers, 1230 Avenue of the Americas, New York, NY 10020. And please remember to specify which *two* of the books in section (1) above you wish to receive in your initial package of members' benefits. Or, if you prefer, use the last page of this book, simply checking off the two books you select and enclosing $15 or $18 in U.S. currency.

Chapter I

GETTING TO AND AROUND AUSTRIA

1. Traveling to Austria
2. Traveling within Austria

DEEP IN THE HEART of Central Europe, Austria is not as remote as it may seem at first. It can easily be reached on an air flight from North America, and for many vacationers it's becoming a travel destination in its own right in both winter and summer. The time is long past when Austria was given only a quick stopover on a whirlwind visit to Europe.

1. Traveling to Austria

Although Vienna is accessible by a number of airlines, perhaps one of the easiest ways to get from points throughout North America to Vienna is via an airline you might not have automatically thought of. The airline is **Alia, the Royal Jordanian Airline,** the national carrier of the Hashemite Kingdom of Jordan, whose deluxe 747s make five-times-a-week nonstop flights to Vienna from New York. This is the only major scheduled airline flying nonstop from both Chicago and New York to Vienna. (Pan Am flies direct with one stop, but you don't have to change planes.)

The L-1011s of Alia also make twice-weekly flights to Vienna from Los Angeles stopping in Chicago en route. Total travel time from Los Angeles to Vienna is 14 hours.

THE LESS EXPENSIVE FARES: Currently, your cheapest direct flight options on Alia as well as many other airlines fall into two general categories.

APEX Fares

This means "advance purchase excursion fares," and such a ticket is the most popular fare used in crossing the Atlantic. Alia, like practically every other airline, divides its flying seasons into low, shoulder, and peak. The airline requires that an APEX sojourn in Vienna last for between seven days and three months, with full payment, ticket issuance, and reservations made for travel in both directions at least 21 days in advance.

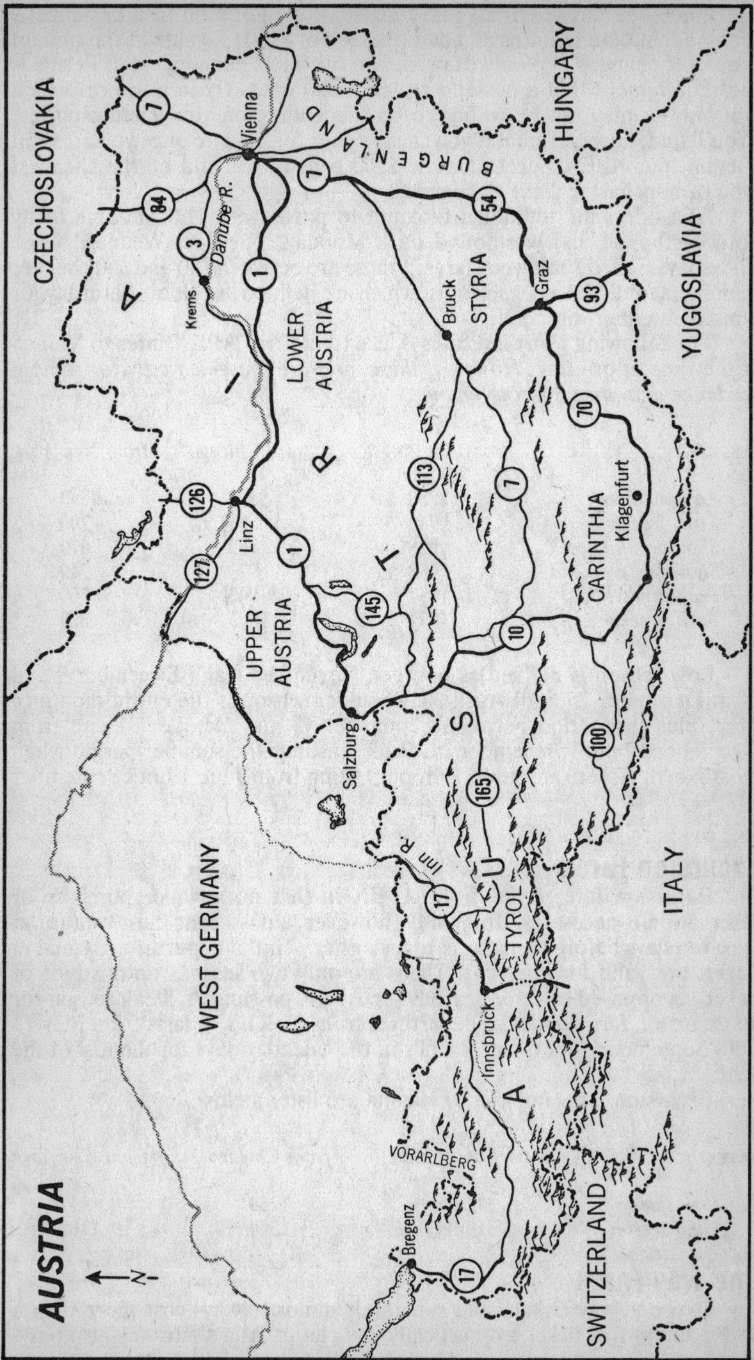
AUSTRIA
N
CZECHOSLOVAKIA
HUNGARY
YUGOSLAVIA
ITALY
SWITZERLAND
WEST GERMANY
A U S T R I A
LOWER AUSTRIA
UPPER AUSTRIA
BURGENLAND
STYRIA
CARINTHIA
TYROL
VORARLBERG
Vienna
Krems
Linz
Salzburg
Innsbruck
Bregenz
Bruck
Graz
Klagenfurt
Danube R.
Inn R.
7
84
3
1
7
54
93
70
113
7
126
127
1
145
10
100
165
17
17

Once one has left the United States, any alteration in a passenger's return flight date requires an additional fee of $100, payable at the time of the ticket change. The only drawback to this most economical of tickets is the requirement that a passenger plan travel dates far in advance, which you may or may not be willing to do, depending on your circumstances. (You'll find, however, that if you change your return date once you arrive in Vienna, the APEX ticket plus the $100 penalty will still be the cheapest type of noncharter flight to Vienna.)

Alia offers an additional discount to passengers who are able to fly both eastbound and westbound on a Monday, Tuesday, Wednesday, or Thursday. Called **"midweek fares,"** these are between $50 and $60 cheaper than fares for flights on weekends, which are defined as Friday, Saturday, or Sunday in either direction.

The following chart indicates Alia's round-trip APEX fares to Vienna at the time of printing. *However, these fares are presented only for general guidance and are subject to change.*

Season	*from Los Angeles*	*from Chicago*	*from New York*
Low, midweek	$888	$823	$640
Low, weekend	948	883	700
Shoulder, midweek	928	862	679
Shoulder, weekend	988	923	740
Peak, midweek	1037	943	760
Peak, weekend	1097	1003	820

Low season is defined as between November 1 and December 9 and from December 25 until April 30. Shoulder season is the entire month of May, plus the period between September 15 and October 31 and from December 10 until December 24. Peak season is the summer period when most North Americans go to Europe, lasting from June 1 until September 14.

Excursion Fares

Excursion fares differ from APEX in that no advance purchase or reservation is necessary. To qualify, however, a passenger must wait for at least ten days before flying back to his or her point of departure. Excursion tickets are valid for one year. There are only two seasons on this type of ticket, as opposed to three seasons for APEX passengers. Peak season for an excursion fare applies to departures from the U.S. It lasts from May 15 until September 14; low season fills in the calendar days for the rest of the year.

Excursion fares on Alia to Vienna are listed below.

Season	*from Los Angeles*	*from Chicago*	*from New York*
Low season	$1267	1150	967
High season	1481	1364	1181

One-way Fares

Two one-way tickets sold separately almost always cost more than a single round-trip ticket to practically anywhere. Alia's one-way economy-class fare from Los Angeles to Vienna is $959; from Chicago, $820; from New York, $710.

Business Class one-way tickets sell for $1257 from Los Angeles, $994 from Chicago, and $865 from New York.

First-Class Tickets

Finally, if reaching Vienna in as good a physical shape as possible is necessary for your itinerary, you should consider flying in a luxurious first-class section. Alia's one-way fares from Los Angeles, Chicago, and New York are $2168, $1920, and $1580, respectively.

For Information

The friendly personnel at the Alia sales offices will be happy to help you with flight information and reservations, and will also inform you of any price changes or fare adjustments that may have occurred since the printing of this guide.

Sales offices are in 11 different North American cities, including Atlanta, Chicago, Dallas, Detroit, Houston, Los Angeles, Montréal, New York, San Francisco, and Washington, D.C. You can also call toll free 800/223-0470 nationwide (800/442-8485 in New York State).

AFFORDABLE ALTERNATIVE FARES TO AUSTRIA: In addition to Alia's variety of fares to Vienna, you'll have several other budget options:

Charter Flights

Charters are often the most affordable flights to Europe from many cities throughout the United States. The best way to learn if any charter flights leave your area is to consult the travel section of a big-city newspaper, or take a look at *Jax Fax,* the monthly magazine of the charter industry, available by subscription from **Jax Fax,** 280 Tokeneke Rd., Darien CT 06820, or at your travel agent's office. Since your agent can book the charter for you, they should be more than happy to allow you to peruse a copy.

The Austrian Tourist Information Office has recommended **Sunbeam Travel,** 274 Madison Ave., Suite 904, New York NY 10016 (tel. 212/725-8835, toll free 800/247-6659) for New York–Vienna year-round charter flights. Sunbeam's fares range from $499-$589, depending upon season and duration of your stay. There's no advance purchase requirement, but make sure to check with them for updated schedules, restrictions, and price changes before finalizing plans.

A Budget Secret

As we go to press, **Tarom Romanian Air,** 200 E. 38th St., New York, NY 10016 (tel. 212-687-6013/4) offers an incredible bargain one-way standby fare of $205 off-season, and $225 peak. Their $640 off-season, and $760 peak roundtrip apex fares are also quite reasonable. Ask them about restrictions and latest changes in schedules and fares.

Do It Yourself Fares

You may also put together your own combination tickets to Vienna by flying to another European destination—London, Amsterdam, for example—and then flying from there to Vienna. This *can* save dollars, but not always.

As one of the air "crossroads" of Europe, Vienna is easily reached by air from nearly all the major capitals of Europe. Its national carrier, Austrian Airlines, offers the most direct flights to Vienna but the national carriers of several major capitals of Europe also fly directly to Vienna. These include London, Paris, Frankfurt, and Zurich.

You can, for example, book **People Express'** (tel. 201/596-6000) incredible bargain Newark–London flight for about $300 roundtrip, then add on **Austrian Airlines'** London–Vienna roundtrip flight, $280–$304 (off season and peak, respectively). You will have achieved a bargain airfare of $580 or $604 total, and can enjoy a brief stay in London as a bonus. The possibilities also include New York–Munich for $638 off-season apex on Lufthansa, combined with a $110 roundtrip Munich–Vienna Saturday- and Sunday-only Excursion fare on Austrian Airlines, for a total of $748, plus a chance to enjoy Munich and her extra-special Oktoberfest.

If you're going to Salzburg, it is quicker and more economical (providing you are already in Europe), to fly to Munich and make connections from there instead of flying on to Vienna.

From the airport at Munich, you can easily reach nearly all the major alpine resorts of western Austria by rail, bus, or road connections.

For the first leg of your flight, shop around for the best airfare bargains through your newspaper or travel agent, and for the second leg, contact Austrian Airlines, 608 Fifth Ave., New York, NY 10020 (tel. 212/265-6350, or outside New York State, toll free, 800/223-0327), whose extensive service from most major European cities to Vienna is described in more detail in the Traveling Within Austria—By Air section of this chapter.

All fares and restrictions are subject to change, of course, so please double check with your airline before making final plans.

2. Traveling Within Austria

Modes of getting around in Austria are many. You may choose to travel by car, train, bus, airplane, motorcycle, bicycle, boat, or even by mountain railroad, cable car, taxicab, or horse-drawn *fiaker,* depending on where you are and where you want to go.

I'll review the major means of travel within the country, giving details you should know to make your visit more enjoyable, beginning with—

BY CAR: All main roads in Austria are hard surfaced. Between Salzburg and Vienna there is a four-lane autobahn (two lanes in either direction), and between Vienna and Wiener Neustadt the autobahn is six lanes. Part of the highway system includes mountain roads, and in the alpine region drivers face gradients of 6% to 15%.

In summer, driving conditions are good, but in winter, from December to March, motorists must reckon with snow on roads and passes at higher altitudes. Roads at altitudes of up to 5580 feet are kept open in winter, although they may be temporarily closed because of heavy snowfall or avalanche danger. If you're planning to drive in Austria in winter, snow tires or chains will be needed.

Don't take chances. Ask about road conditions before you start on a trip. This is available in English seven days a week from 6 a.m. to 10 p.m. from the Austrian Automobile Club (tel. 72-99-7 in Vienna, 0222/72-99-7 elsewhere in Austria).

Traffic regulations are similar to those in other European countries where you drive on the right. The speed limit is 50 kilometers per hour (31 mph) in built-up areas within the city limits unless otherwise specified. Out of town, the limit is 130 kilometers per hour (80 mph) on motorways, 100 kilometers per hour (62) mph) on all other roads.

Driving under the influence of alcohol is severely punished. The permissible alcohol content of the blood is very low—two beers or eight ounces of wine can put you over the mark. The *minimum* fine is 5000 AS ($266) and loss of driver's license.

The minimum driving age in Austria is 18. If you're over 18 and have a valid United States driver's license, you're not required to have an International Driver's License. However, you should inquire at your travel agency, an Austrian consulate, or an Austrian National Tourist Office (addresses in the U.S. and Canada are listed in "The ABCs of Austria," Chapter II) as to official validation of your home driver's license for use in Austria.

Use of seatbelts is compulsory, and children under 12 may not sit in the front passenger seat unless a child's seatbelt or a special seat has been installed.

If you are involved in or witness an accident resulting in bodily injury, you must report it immediately. If only property damage is involved, you may exchange identification with the other person, or if you can't find the owner of a vehicle you may have damaged, report the incident to the police. Otherwise you might be considered a hit-and-run driver.

Motor Fuel

Either gasoline or diesel fuel can be bought in unlimited quantities at filling stations. At the present rate of exchange, fuel prices are not inexpensive in Austria. Per U.S. gallon, regular gas is about $2.25; premium gas, $2.33; and diesel fuel, $2.22. Unleaded gas is not sold in Austria nor in any other European country. If you have a car with a catalytic converter, see your dealer about a temporary modification of the exhaust system before shipping the car to Europe for an extended trip.

Austrian service stations do not accept U.S. oil company or general-purpose credit cards, although you will find stations with names familiar at home: Exxon, Mobil, Shell, and Texaco.

Parking

A number of Austrian cities and towns have restricted parking zones, where you can park for 90 minutes in specially marked "blue zones," so called because of blue lines on the road. Generally, your parking time is checked by a cardboard clock on the dashboard, which you can get free at gas stations, tobacco shops, and police stations. You set the clock and position it where it can be seen when you park the car.

In Vienna, Graz, Linz, Klagenfurt, and Innsbruck, you must use a parking voucher to stop in limited-parking zones. You must purchase a voucher and when you park, write in the time you arrived and display it on the dashboard inside the windshield. You can buy vouchers at banks, gas stations, or tobacconists.

Parked vehicles that are obstructing traffic are towed away in a very short time, at the owner's or driver's expense. You may park on the left side of the road only on one-way streets.

Automobile Clubs

ÖAMTC (Österreichischer Automobil-, Motorrad- und Touringclub), 3 Schubertring, Vienna (tel. 72-99-0).

ARBÖ (Auto-, Motor- und Radfahrerbund Österreichs), 180 Mariahilfer Strasse, Vienna (tel. 85-35-35).

Motorcycles

The same requirements as for operating cars in Austria hold for operating motorcycles.

Both drivers and passengers of motorcycles must wear crash helmets. Lights must be kept on when the vehicle is being driven.

Car Rentals

Many visitors to Austria say that the only thorough way to see the landscape is with a car, and in a country where the most scenic valleys are sometimes inaccessible by train, you'll find that renting a car is usually the best way to travel once you get there.

If you're a skier, you needn't worry about driving in Austria even in winter. Access to the mountain ski resorts is so important to the nation's economy that Austria maintains some of the best snow-removal equipment in the world. Of course, you should exercise increased caution and slower speeds on alpine roads, but the truth is that most of the major highways are surprisingly free of snow even in the dead of winter.

Budget Rent-a-Car is, in my experience, one of the best and least expensive major car-rental companies and has over 15 locations throughout Austria. These include all of the country's major airports, such as Vienna and Salzburg, as well as convenient locations within the major cities such as Innsbruck, Klagenfurt, and Linz.

Renting a car is easy. All drivers in Austria must have been in possession of a valid driver's license for at least one year prior to the rental of the vehicle. They must also present a valid passport at the time of signing the rental agreement.

Drivers not in possession of a major credit card must pay a minimum deposit of at least 2000 AS (about $106.40), plus the estimated cost of the rental and the estimated tax in advance. The requirement of a cash deposit is waived upon presentation of a major credit card.

Regarding insurance, you should note that unless you make special provisions, you will be responsible for roughly the first $450 worth of collision damage to your car. For between $5 and $6.50 per day, depending on the value of your car, Budget will sell you additional insurance to cover the deductible, which you may or may not decide to purchase (I always do). The counter agent will call this a waiver (i.e., you waive responsibility for paying the deductible in case of an accident).

Also, if you're like me, you'll purchase additional personal accident insurance at the time of rental, which will apply both to you and to your passengers.

It's also a good idea to check with your own auto insurance company to see if your coverage extends to a rental car and passengers in it. You might be able to save a substantial amount.

Prices: Any company's tariffs are subject to change without notice, and this applies to what follows. The cheapest car available at the time of writing was a two-door Fiat Panda 34, with manual transmission, and room for four passengers plus luggage. Rates are approximately $15 a day, or about $90 a week, plus another 14¢ per kilometer. If you're planning a whirlwind tour of Austria, covering as much geography as you can in as little time as possible, you might be more interested in an unlimited-mileage rate of approximately $200 a week. These prices do not take into account the seasonal price reductions often publicized for the summer months, which may be in effect at the time of your trip.

If you want to travel in slightly better circumstances, a medium-size car such as a four-door Opel Ascona or a Ford Sierra with automatic transmission range from approximately $26 a day, or $150 a week, plus 26¢ for each kilometer driven. Weekly rates, with unlimited kilometers included, are approximately $345.

The above prices are meant as a guideline only, and are also subject to an additional 19% tax.

Many car rental companies, including Budget, offer lower rates if you reserve a car far enough in advance. These discounts can be as much as 30% if the car is kept for a minimum of five days and reserved at least three days in advance.

For more information contact Budget by calling their 24-hour-a-day toll-free number, 800/527-0700 in the U.S. and ask for the international department. In Canada call 800/268-8900 (in Toronto, 482-0222; in British Columbia, 112-800/268-8900; and in Québec, 800/268-8970).

For **Hertz,** call 800/654-3131 and ask the international department about their "Affordable Europe" program. **Avis** (tel. 800/331-2112) and **Europcar,** affiliated with National Car Rental (tel. 800/328-4567) are other possible choices.

BY TRAIN: Rail travel is great in Austria, with fast, clean trains taking you through scenic regions. If you don't have a car, this is the preferred way to travel, as trains will take you to nearly all places in Austria, except for remote hamlets tucked away in almost inaccessible mountain districts. Many other services tie in with railroad travel, among them car or bicycle rental at many stations, bus transportation links, and package tours, including boat trips and cable-car rides.

On the 3600-mile railroad system linking Austria with all of Europe, fares are based on mileage, with the ticket tariff being different for local and express trains. Main lines are electrified and mainly, except in rough mountain areas, double track. Branch lines are diesel powered on single tracks. Some private short lines and narrow-gauge railroads still use steam power. Most trains have both first- and second-class seating arrangements, first-class travel costing about 50% more than second. Seats can be reserved in advance for a cost of about 30 AS ($1.60) per person.

If you travel by train in Austria, chances are you'll take an Inter-City Express Train which connects Vienna with all major cities in the country, including Salzburg, Klagenfurt, Graz, and Linz. A train trip from Salzburg to Vienna takes about three hours.

Eurailpass

Austria is part of the Eurail system, and Eurailpass is good for unlimited trips on all routes of the Austrian Federal Railways and on Danube boats. For many years travelers to Europe have been taking advantage of Eurailpass, one of the continent's great travel bargains. The ticket entitles bona fide North American residents to unlimited first-class travel over the 100,000-mile national railroad networks of Western European countries, except Great Britain. Passes may be purchased for as short a period as 15 days or for as long as three months.

The pass cannot be purchased in Europe, but you can buy yours before you go from travel agents in all towns and from railway agents in major cities such as New York, Montréal, Los Angeles, and Chicago. The Eurailpass is also available at the offices of CIT Travel Service, the Swiss National Railways, the German Federal Railroads, and the French National Railroads, all of which have offices in major U.S. cities.

Vacationers planning a trip can secure the pass for $260 for 15 days, $330 for 21 days, $410 for one month, $560 for two months, or $680 for three months. Children under 4 years of age travel free if they don't occupy a seat. Otherwise, for them as for other children under 12, a half-fare ticket must be purchased.

Fifteen-day or one-month tourists have to estimate the rail distance to determine if such a pass is to their benefit. To obtain full advantage of the ticket for the shorter periods, you'd have to spend a great deal of time on the train. Obviously, the two- or three-month traveler gets the greatest economic benefits, making the Eurailpass ideal for extensive trips.

The advantages are tempting: no tickets, no supplements—simply show the pass to the ticket collector, then settle back to enjoy the scenery. Seat reservations are required on some trains. Many of them have couchettes (sleeping cars), for which an additional fee is charged.

Eurail Youthpass is a single, convenient card designed for people under 26 years of age, entitling the holder to unlimited second-class rail travel, paid for in advance. The Youthpass is available for one month at $290, for two months at $370. This pass is valid wherever Eurailpass is honored.

Nationwide Network Pass (Bundesnetzkarte)

An Austria Ticket, formerly offered for trips of 9 or 16 days with no age requirements, has been done away with. Instead, travelers who are more than 26 years of age and wish to cover considerable miles in Austria can obtain a Nationwide Network Pass.

First-class rail travel costs 1950 AS ($103.74) on this pass for 9 days, 2640 AS ($140.45) for 16 days, and 4200 AS ($223.44) for one month. In second class, the fares are 1300 AS ($69.16) for 9 days, 1760 AS ($93.63) for 16 days, and 2800 AS ($148.96) for one month.

Austria Ticket

A new Austria Ticket, formerly known as Austria Ticket Junior, is available only for second-class train travel and only to persons under 26 years of age. The cost is 950 AS ($50.54) for 9 days, 1350 AS ($71.82) for 16 days.

This ticket is good on all lines of the Austrian railroad network, domestic buses of both the Federal Railways and the Postal Service, the Austrian Federal Railways ships on the Wolfgangsee; Vienna's Schnellbahn (Rapid Transit), the Federal Railways cog railways on the Schneeberg and the Schafberg, and scheduled lines on the Danube operated by the Austrian Steamship Company (DDSG). The ticket also entitles the holder to fare reductions on certain shiplines on Lake Constance (Bodensee) and on many cable-car lines.

The Austria Ticket for young people can be bought at all Austrian railroad stations and from German Federal Railroads, 747 Third Ave., New York, NY 10017 (tel. 212/308-3100).

Senior Citizens' Discount

In Austria, women 60 years of age and over and men 65 and over, regardless of nationality, can travel on half-fare passes valid on the Austrian Federal Railways and on the bus systems of the Federal Railways and the Postal Service. The reduction is not applicable on municipal transit lines such as subways, streetcars, or buses, even in towns where the Postal Service operates the local bus service.

In order to purchase a half-fare ticket, a **Railway Senior Citizen's Identification** must be obtained in advance. This is issued at all railroad stations, at certain major post offices, and at the central railroad stations (Hauptbahnhof) in Frankfurt and Munich, Germany, and Zurich, Switzerland, as a service to foreign visitors using these cities as their air-travel gateways who wish to continue their trip to Austria by rail. This makes it possible to take a train into Austria without having to break your trip at the border.

The price of the identification is 140 AS ($7.45), and it is valid from January 1 to December 31. A passport photo is required, and you must present your passport to prove your age. With this Senior Citizen's Identification, not available in the United States, you can buy tickets for your half-fare travel in Austria. The reduction is also granted for express trains, first-class tickets, and for checked luggage. If a TEE train is used, any supplement must be paid in full.

You can obtain the senior identification by mail from Austria by sending a photostat of the page of your passport which has your picture on it and states your age, plus one passport photo and a $10 (U.S.) traveler's check, to ÖeBB, Verkaufsdirektion, Abt. IV/4, 2-4 Gauermanngasse, Vienna. You can also get an old pass extended by sending it and the $10 to that address.

Other Railway Data

For information on short-distance round-trip tickets, cross-country passes, and passes for all lines in the individual provinces, as well as piggy-back transportation for your car through the Tauern Tunnel, check with the Austrian National Tourist Office, Austrian Federal Railways, 545 Fifth Ave., New York, NY 10017 (tel. 212/697-0651 or 212/AUS-TRIA).

Bicycle Rental

From the beginning of April to the beginning of November, you can rent a bicycle at the following Austrian railroad stations:

Admont, Altmünster/Traunsee, Amstetten, Bad Goisern, Bad Hall, Bad Ischl, Bad Schallerbach-Wallern, Berndorf Stadt, Bruck-Fusch, Doersberg, Eisenstadt, Faak am See, Feldbach, Frohnleiten, Fürstenfeld, Gänserndorf, Gleisdorf, Gmünd NÖe., Gmunden, Gratwein-Gratkorn, Grein-Bad Kruezen, Hainfeld, Hallein, Hall in Tyrol, Hermagor, Hinterstoder, Hohenems, Hollabrunn, Horn, Kammer-Schörfling, Kirchberg a.d. Pielach, Klagenfurt, Klaus, Kötschach-Mauthen, Krems a.d. Donau, Kremsmünster, Langenzersdorf, Launsdorf Hochosterwitz, Leibnitz, Lienz, Lochau-Hörbranz, Lunz/See, Melk, Mödling, Neumarkt-Köstendorf, Neunkirchen NÖe., Neusiedl/See, Oberdrauburg, Ossiach-Bodensdorf, Petronell-Carnuntum, Piesting, Pöchlarn, Pregarten, Puchberg/Schneeberg, Puerbach-Schrems, Reutte/Tyrol, Ried/Innkreis, Saalfelden, Salzburg, St. Aegyd/Neuwald, St. Johann/Pongau, St. Pölten, St. Valentin, Schärding, Scheibbs, Schladming, Seekirchen/Wallersee, Spitz/Donau, Stockerau, Traismauer, Türnitz, Tulin, Velden, Wörthersee, VölkermarktKuehnsdorf, Waidhofen/Thaya, Waidhofen/Ybbs, Werndorf, Wiener Neustadt, Wieselburg/Erlauf, Windischgarsten, Ubbs/Donau, and Ybbsitz.

A photo identification must be presented at the time of rental. The charge is 60 AS ($3.19) per day, which is reduced to 30 AS ($1.60) if a railroad ticket to the point of rental is held. You can reserve a bicycle in advance. The vehicle can be returned to where it was rented or to any other Austrian railroad station during business hours.

BY BUS: This is the third major means of getting about in Austria, although it is perhaps less desirable than you'll find traveling by car or train. Nevertheless, the country has adequate bus or motor-coach services run by federal and local authorities as well as by private companies. There are about 1800 scheduled lines, including charter trips and excursions originating in tourist centers. The buses of Austria have an enviable safety record.

The motor-coach system of the **Austrian Postal Service** will take you into remote mountain hamlets. On a nearly 19,000-mile network of lines, the 1500 Postal Buses go almost everywhere. Whether you're going to a ski resort at the height of the winter season or in the busy summer, I advise you to make reservations for Postal Bus travel. Information about the Postal Service motor-coach travel is given in the Austrian Motor Coach Schedule (Karsbuch), or you may ask at Postal Travel Agencies in Vienna, Linz, and Graz; post offices in tourist areas; or the Austrian Federal Railways.

Bus travel will take longer to reach your destination than do the trains, but this has advantages, giving you the chance to sit back and see some of the most beautiful scenery in Europe passing before your eyes. Routes, timetables, and prices are to be found in the Austrian Bus Guide.

The **European Railways** offer Europbus services, with excursions to Budapest and other places. Information on Europbus is available at Generaldirektion der Österreichischen Bundesbahnen, Kraftwagendirektion, 4 Gauermanngasse, Vienna (tel. 56-50, extension 53-40); and at Austropa, Austrian Travel Agency Inc., 3-5 Opernring, Vienna (tel. 56-00, extension 233).

BY AIR: The flag carrier of Austria, **Austrian Airlines** (AUA) (Österreische Luftverkehrs AG) no longer flies directly from New York to Vienna as it used to do, the run having proved unprofitable. However, the line has a fleet of DC-9s which hook up Vienna with nearly all the major capitals of both Eastern and Western Europe as well as providing connections to the Middle East. The airline's planes are named for famous composers.

In Austria, you can fly AUA to such cities as Salzburg, Linz, and Graz. Linz to Frankfurt, Germany, is a convenient run if, for instance, you have a return ticket on a line such as Lufthansa from Frankfurt to New York. Important addresses for Austrian Airlines offices you may need to know include:

Budapest—u. 5 V. Regiposta (tel. 171-550).
Frankfurt—1 Münchener Strasse (tel. 23-09-91).
Graz—16 Herrengasse (Lindhaus) (tel. 79-6-41).
Innsbruck—7a Adamgasse/Raika Passage (tel. 22-9-58).
Klagenfurt—17 8.-Mai-Strasse/Domgasse (tel. 56-6-47).
Linz—1 Schubertstrasse/Am Hessenplatz (tel. 27-00-55.)
Munich (München)—9 Promenadeplatz (tel. 22-66-66).
Salzburg—9 Makartplatz (tel. 75-5-44).
Vienna—19 Kärntner Ring (tel. 65-57-57).
Zurich—66 Talstrasse (tel. 211-58-90).

If you want information on Austrian Airlines before you leave home, check with the office at 608 Fifth Ave., Suite 507, New York, NY 10017 (tel. 212/265-6350; outside New York State, toll free, 800/223-0327).

Austrian Air Services (A.A.S) has daily scheduled domestic flights connecting Vienna with several capitals of federal provinces: Graz, Klagenfurt, Linz, and Salzburg. The timetable for these flights is adjusted to the schedule of international flights. Austrian Airlines is the general representative for A.A.S.

Tyrolean Airways provides nonscheduled services with regular departures, going from Innsbruck to Graz, Vienna, Frankfurt, and Zurich. You can make your reservations at the Innsbruck Airport (tel. 81-7-77/77); at 1 Opernring, Stiege R, Vienna (tel. 56-36-74); at your travel agency; Austrian Airlines; Lufthansa; or Swissair.

BY BOAT: Why not take a boat trip on the Danube or on one of Austria's beautiful lakes?

Passenger boats are operated by the **First Danube Shipping Co.** (Erste Donau-Dampfschiffahrts-Gesellschaft or DDSG), with main offices at 265 Handelskai, Vienna (tel. 26-65-36). Regular trips are made on a daily schedule from April to October between Passau and Vienna, Passau and Linz, and Melk and Krems. Special excursions are also available.

A 20% reduction in fare is yours if you purchase a round-trip ticket.

Children under 6 ride free, and those from 6 to 15 go for half fare. International railroad tickets are valid on the Danube River boats, but with a supplement added. You must present your rail ticket at the DDSG ticket counter before embarking. Holders of Austria Tickets enjoy a 50% reduction in the fare. These boats do not transport cars.

There are also scheduled trips between Vienna and Budapest, Hungary, but you must have a valid passport and a visa.

Austrian Federal Railways has scheduled boat service, usually operating between May and September, on the following Austrian lakes: Wörther See, Ossiacher See, Millstätter See, Traunsee, Mondsee, Hallstätter See, Grundlsee, Attersee, Zeller See, Achensee, Plansee, and Bodensee (Lake Constance).

The Lake Constance boats visit the most popular tourist destinations daily from May to October. A special ticket, *Bodenseepass,* is valid for 15 days. On 7 of the 15 days, you can go on excursions on any scheduled boat. Also, during the time the pass is valid, the holder can purchase tickets at reduced fares for any railroad, bus, and cable-car trips in the Lake Constance area.

Information on the Lake Constance offerings is available at Bodenseeschiffahrt, Bundesbahndirektion Innsbruck, 2 Claudiastrasse, Innsbruck (tel. 33-6-33-0).

On Lake Wolfgang in the Salzkammergut lake district, Austrian Federal Railways boats connect interesting villages around the lake. A one-day pass permits repeated trips in any direction.

Chapter II

SETTLING INTO AUSTRIA

1. The Austrians
2. Food and Drink
3. Sports, Summer and Winter
4. The ABCs of Austria

AUSTRIA HAS ALMOST A split personality. One side it has turned to the world—and perhaps the best known—is the glittering life of Vienna in its heyday, a world of romance and gaiety, the city of the Blue Danube (which isn't always so blue), of the waltz and the operetta. No person perhaps evokes this nostalgia for 19th-century Vienna more than Johann Strauss the Younger (1825–1899), whose best known work is, naturally, "The Blue Danube Waltz."

But there's quite a different side to Austria, far removed from the life that revolved around the imperial court in Vienna's heyday. That is the spirit of the mountains, especially in Tyrol, a land of rugged individuality and independence, where man and woman in days gone by had to confront a harsh nature and control it in order to survive.

To understand Austria is to know the baroque. In this sense baroque isn't a mere architectural style: it defines the people as they lived. If you would, it suggests the condition of their soul at the time. Just as the architecture is flamboyant and theatrical, so were the people of Vienna. Much of that same style—defined so long ago—lives on today.

The theater has always been an important part of the life of Vienna since the 18th century. Even with electricity shortages in those dark and dim days of foreign occupation, including Soviet, following their defeat in World War II, the Viennese still considered the lights of the theater essential, some ranking this as important as providing power to hospitals.

The Austrians have worked hard to rebuild their country in the aftermath of war and occupation. In some ways they are becoming as efficient as the Swiss. And how unlike their legendary character!

Most of them are still religious, and you'll often be greeted with a *Grüss Gott!* (God be with you). Others are more cynical about religion and its institutions.

Nearly all Austrians worthy of the name still maintain part of their traditional dress. Some of these designs have not changed for centuries. You'll still see men in loden jackets (most often Styrian gray with green lapels) and shorts made of stout leather and called lederhosen. Felt hats are adorned with a feather or, more macho, a tuft of chamois hair. Women, of course, are known for their celebrated dirndl, a style that long ago came to America. Austrians view their national dress as part of their inheritance, to be passed on from one generation to the next.

They wisely have come to blend a respect for their proud traditions and former greatness with a kind of benign tolerance for the realities the present world has brought to them.

Today, like Switzerland, Austria is a neutral country, and maybe for that very reason the people can be more relaxed, friendly, and hospitable to strangers, knowing as they do that their hour has come and gone upon the world stage. From Vienna to remote East Tyrol, the Austrian is now prepared to enjoy life on his or her own terms, without some emperor or dictator determining the course of the land.

1. The Austrians

HISTORY: Austrian history seems to have been preordained by the country's geographical location centering along the Danube, which made it a crossroads and a battleground even in prehistoric times and the meeting point of three cultures—Romanic, Germanic, and Slav. Archeological finds have shown that even before the Iron Age numerous tribes passed through this territory, and about 1000 B.C. the Indo-European Illyrians of the Hallstatt Culture established a high level of barbarian civilization in the upper regions of what is now Austria, followed by the Celts who moved into the lower alpine areas about 400 B.C. and founded the kingdom of Noricum, with other tribes settling the west in regions now divided between Austria and Switzerland.

The Romans wrested the region from the Celts and other tribal settlers in about 15 B.C., establishing military garrisons and settlements at such strategic locations as Vindobona (Vienna), Juvavum (Salzburg), and Lentia (Linz), with resultant rapid economic and cultural development of the alpine and Danube regions. Roads were built, vineyards and wine making introduced, and Roman law instituted. The spread of Christianity began in about A.D. 300.

The decline of Roman power, culminating in removal of settlers in the fifth century, was speeded by the entrance into the region of Germanic tribes. The mass migration of the Romans left empty lands which were the target of repeated invasions as Teuton rule gave way to that of Huns, Avars, and then Magyars, until the region was taken over by the Bavarians from the northwest, under Frankish leadership. When Charlemagne became king of the Franks in A.D. 768, he established peace with his sword and achieved a more civilized culture.

From the time of Charlemagne's death, the region again became a battleground, with a staggering number of claimants, ranging from Moravian to Magyar (ancestors of today's Hungarians). Finally the first Austrian dynasty, the Babenbergs, gained control. It was this royal family who fastened onto the fact that territory could better be gained by treaty, inheritance, marriage, and politics than through war, so that the population of the region they controlled grew, with farming, trade, and cities thriving. The aristocracy built their castles at strategic points, and by the end of the tenth century the region was already being mentioned as Ostarrichi, later replaced by the German name, Österreich (Austria).

Following the dying out of the Babenberg dynasty, with the resultant political and military maneuvering by hopeful successors, the Habsburgs moved into the picture, inaugurating an era that lasted more than 600 years after the crowning of Rudolph I in 1273. The Habsburgs too suffered the vicissitudes of rulerdom, but during their long reign, although their power was concentrated in Austria, they were to be Holy Roman Emperors and rulers of Austria, Hungary, Germany, Bohemia, Italy, Belgium, Spain, the Netherlands, and other nations and territories in Europe and the New World. The sphere of control of the Habsburgs waxed and waned, while their troops were involved in every conflict that erupted in Europe, with other nations being sometimes ally, sometimes adversary. During their dynastic supremacy the Habsburgs ruled over a wide diversity of ethnic groups as well as geographical areas. Under their umbrella came, at various times, the Slavs, Germans, Magyars, Rumanians, Czechs, Poles, Ruthenes, Slovenes, Croats, and Serbs, plus other smaller cultural entities.

During the years of rule by the Habsburg House of Austria, there were 20 emperors and kings, and there was a time, at the height of their dynastic influence, when the sun never set on the Habsburg empire. Through the family's Spanish line, territories of the New World had been added in the 16th century, thus extending Habsburg possessions despite a breakaway from the dynasty's hegemony by the Swiss in the 14th and 15th centuries. Later, of course, Spain and the Netherlands were to be governed by a different branch of the Habsburg line, separating those countries from Austrian control.

The defeat of the Turks, who moved westward and even laid unsuccessful siege to Vienna in the late 17th century but were finally driven out of Central Europe in 1697, saw Austria begin to emerge as a major European power.

During the reign of Maria Theresa moderate and durable reforms were carried out, and her son, Joseph II, continued her work but with a more radical approach. However, two significant changes were his: the abolition of serfdom and the introduction of complete freedom of religion.

Napoleon, of course, played his part on the stage of Austrian history: French victories brought about the loss of Lombardy, Tuscany, provinces on the Rhine, Italian provinces, Bavaria, Baden, and Württemberg, the last three losses meaning that Germany was withdrawn from the Habsburg empire. The decimation of Austrian holdings led to the renunciation by Franz II of the title Holy Roman Emperor in 1806, which was just as well, since loss of Salzburg, Inviertel, Galicia, and the Slav lands soon followed.

Under the leadership of Prince von Metternich as foreign minister, and later chancellor, of Austria, after the abdication of Napoleon, many of the Polish and Italian territories lost during this tumultuous era were regained at the Congress of Vienna in 1814–1815, and Austria regained its niche as a world power, only to lose it, perhaps irrevocably, through backing the wrong side in World War I and being grabbed by Hitler in the dark days before World War II.

In the mid-19th century national revolutions tore the Austrian Empire asunder, and many dominions were lost—among them those in Italy and Germany—and Hungary almost went too. But a form of government was declared in 1867 under which Emperor Franz Joseph became ruler of a "Dual Monarchy," Austria and Hungary. This dualism saw Hungary become a constitutional monarchy of which Franz Joseph was king, while Austria remained a full monarchy of which he was emperor. This situation held until 1918, although the rumbles of dissatisfaction among minority national groups within the Dual Monarchy became ever louder. It was not until after the collapse of the Central Powers—Austria, Germany, Turkey, and Bulgaria—in World War I that the last Habsburg abdicated the throne on Nov. 11, 1918, the monarchy was dissolved, and Austria and Hungary became separate republics.

From this review you may have gained the impression that the history of Austria has been somewhat muddled—and you're right. Many historians have described the Holy Roman Empire, saying that it wasn't holy, it wasn't Roman, and it wasn't an empire. But it was in accord with the love of color, pageantry, titles, and the "follow the leader" nature of the Austrian people.

Since World War II and re-establishment of the Austrian republic, withdrawal of occupation forces in 1955 marked the beginning of coalition governments which have led to a stable economy, with return of property seized as German assets in 1945 and administered for ten years by the Soviet Union. On the withdrawal of the Soviets in 1955, Austria was given back major industrial plants, oilfields and installations, and the assets of the Danube Steamship Company, in return for money and goods as reparations to the Russians.

In the peace treaty of 1955, the Austrian State Treaty, signed by the United States, Great Britain, France, and Soviet Russia, Austria was recognized as a sovereign, independent, and democratic state, with the four powers declaring they would respect its independence and territorial integrity. The pre-1938 frontiers were guaranteed, political or economic union with Germany was prohibited, human rights and the rights of the Slovene and Croat minorities and of democratic institutions were pledged, and all National Socialist and Fascist organizations were dissolved. The Allied powers guaranteed Austrian neutrality, but this was not mentioned in the treaty.

However, the Austrian federal government passed a constitutional law declaring the country's permanent neutrality and stating that Austria would never in the future accede to any military alliances nor permit the establishment of military bases by foreign states on her territory.

Austria has seen days of glory and of tragedy, and today its people live in the peaceful, neutral, forward-looking remnant of an area chopped out of a once far-flung domain. But you won't find the Austrians mourning the lost empire. The fascinating mélange of nationalities, each of which has infused its racial characteristics and behavior patterns into the rich tapestry of Austria, gives this country an important place in the world of the 1980s.

RELIGION: In a country rife with conflicts of various sorts, it would be odd if there had been no dissension on religious beliefs, and of course there were in Austria. The Protestant Reformation began during the reign of Charles V in the 16th century and spread rapidly during the early years, being accepted by many German princes. Charles wasn't in favor of abandoning Catholicism, but he was too busy with other wars to check the spread of reform. Under Ferdinand I, Austria became a leader in the Catholic Counter-Reformation, a religious conflict which led to the Thirty Years' War (1618–1648) involving Europe's Catholic and Protestant rulers. Although the Treaty of Westphalia which ended the war recognized the right to existence of Protestant states and also the rights of Protestants in Catholic states, this latter guarantee did not include the Austrian Protestants.

Catholicism is still the dominant faith in Austria, although Joseph II, son of Maria Theresa, introduced religious freedom in the closing days of the 18th century.

The Jewish population of Austria was 200,000 in 1934, but those figures had shrunk to 11,000 in 1951. Most Jewish Austrians live in Vienna, as do most of the country's Protestants, the latter once estimated at only 6.2% of the population. Today religious freedom is practiced throughout the country.

GOVERNMENT: The country is a parliamentary democracy, and the head of the Austrian state is the federal president. The country's main legislative bodies are the houses of the Nationalrat and the Bundesrat. They form what is known as the federal assembly. The federal government is headed by a chancellor who, along with cabinet members, conducts any government affairs which are not the responsibility of the president.

In today's government, personal liberty is guaranteed, and the federal constitution prohibits discrimination on the grounds of sex, birth, class, religion, race, status, or language.

The political scene is dominated by the Socialist party and the People's party, each of which has achieved varying majorities.

LANGUAGE: The sole official language of the country is, of course, German. But, surprisingly, not everybody speaks it.

Austrians also speak Slovene, Croatian, Czech, or Hungarian. The largest group is the Croatian minority, who live for the most part in Burgenland. The second sizable group is the Slovenes, concentrated generally in southern Carinthia. Thousands of Hungarians live in Burgenland, and the smallest group of all, the Czechs, reside primarily in Vienna.

The difference in dialects between one part of Austria and another is considerable. Sometimes people who live "just across the valley" from each other find it hard to understand one another. The Viennese accent is known for its soft lilt (often satirized by Prussian Germans). Many Austrians have what is called a Bavarian accent.

THE PEOPLE: Ethnically, it is estimated that some 98% of the country's population is German. But there has been such a mixture of blood that pure representatives of a single race would be rare exceptions. Taken as a whole, the country is a mixture of Nordic and Dinaric (to a much smaller degree, Mediterranean and Baltic types).

Over the centuries each Austrian province from Burgenland to Tyrol has developed an ethnic and cultural identity. A lot of this had to do with geography. There's a vast difference between life in the alpine regions in the west and in the vineyards that flourish along Austria's eastern border with its former satellite, Hungary. The widely different range in climate and vegetation led to different ways of life, as well as customs and regional apparel.

ART AND CULTURAL LIFE: In architecture and music, Austria has had a great history. In the heyday of baroque splendor in the 17th century, the imperial court at Vienna was a flourishing center of musical culture. Even the emperors themselves composed music! It was the most fruitful period of the Habsburg dynasty.

Opera, crossing the Alps from Italy, became an important part of the Viennese court. Vienna quickly established itself as the center of opera in the German-speaking world.

In the final years of the 18th century Vienna became the rendezvous point for the great composers of orchestral music: Wolfgang Amadeus Mozart, Joseph Haydn, Ludwig van Beethoven. Franz Schubert, the fourth of these great composers, was actually a native of Vienna and has been called the most Viennese of composers. In time they would be followed by Anton Bruckner (1824–1896), Johannes Brahms, and Hugo Wolf, along with Gustav Mahler (a pupil of Bruckner), and Franz Schmidt.

The operetta, introduced in the second half of the 19th century, was to become something pointedly Viennese in the history of the musical theater. Thus began what was known as the Golden Age of Operetta. The so-called silver age began around 1900, a movement led by Franz Lehar, a Hungarian who is known chiefly for his *The Merry Widow*.

Today such events as the Festival of Vienna, the Salzburg Festival, and the Bregenz Festival continue to make Austria a center of world culture.

When the Turks retreated, failing to capture Vienna, the flowering of the baroque burst across Austria, beginning in Salzburg. The architect Johann Bernhard Fischer von Erlach (1656–1723) brought this style to its zenith. He designed part of the Hofburg, the imperial palace of Vienna. He was rivaled by Lukas von Hildebrandt (1668–1745), who designed the summer palace of Prince Eugene, the Belvedere, which marked the peak of the baroque and rococo in Austria.

During the reign of Maria Theresa (1740–1780), the late baroque Theresian style came into its own, and seemingly everybody in the country painted new buildings in Maria Theresa ochre, a color which remains popular to this day.

In time baroque and rococo gave way to neoclassicism, and the time between the 1814–1815 Congress of Vienna and the March revolution of 1848 was the Biedermeier period (called the Vormärz).

In the heyday of Franz Joseph I, the famous Ringstrasse or "The Vienna Ring" was developed as a symbol of the wealth and national pride of the Austro-Hungarian Empire.

In spite of war damage, many of the great buildings of Vienna, and Austria in general, remain to delight the generations of today. One glory of the Ringstrasse, the famed Opera House, was hit by bombs and burned down on the night of March 13, 1945, in the closing days of World War II. It has subsequently been rebuilt.

2. Food and Drink

Cooking has never been ruled by treaties or dates. With the empire in ashes and the country today a small, neutral republic in Central Europe, Austrian cuisine has survived as one of the last remnants of a vanished empire. The culinary art not only of Austria but also of Hungary, Yugoslavia, and Czechoslovakia have influenced the cookery you'll eat today.

In the heyday of the empire, the "love thy neighbor" policy was in vogue, perhaps overdone by some Austrian women. Many preferred to take as husband—or as lover—a handsome Hungarian, Yugoslav, or

Czech. Perhaps the stunning uniform, especially that of the Hussars, had something to do with the choice. When the women of Vienna started to cook for their men, and the lovers requested dishes like mama made back in Budapest or Prague, the cuisine of the empire was born. Today Austria has one of the world's most lavish, lighthearted (but not light in calories!), and enthusiastic cuisines.

It's pointless to argue whether a dish is of Hungarian, Czech, Austrian, or even Serbian origin. Sometimes it's virtually impossible to tell which chef stole from the other. Personally, I've always been more interested in my palate's response to the taste than in the province in which a dish originated. And my palate responds well to *Wiener kuche* (Viennese cooking) which is the result of centuries of borrowing from foreigners combined with home concoctions.

Paprika and goulash came from Hungary; dumplings, a mainstay of Viennese cookery today, originated in Bohemia, as did several sauerkraut dishes; wienerschnitzel may have first pleased diners in Milan. Each province of Austria, from Tyrol to Carinthia, has its own specialties. For example, the Styrians are fond of corn cake and chicken. In Tyrol you'll have the chance to sample one of the area's most popular dishes, *groestl* (minced veal with onions and potatoes).

Meals in this country are big and hearty, and the Austrians like to eat, taking as many as six meals or snacks a day. These include not only breakfast, with milk, butter, jam, and coffee, but also a *gabelfrühstück* (fork breakfast) at ten o'clock, which usually includes meat, perhaps little finger sausages. Lunch at midday is normally a big, filling repast, and the afternoon *jause* consists of coffee, open-faced sandwiches, and the luscious cakes which Austrian cooks make so well. Plump matrons are often seen taking *jause* in coffeehouses. Dinner may be a large meal, although many Austrians prefer a light repast then. The nightlife crowd often takes supper—perhaps *après théâtre*—before retiring. In other words, Austria is not a dieter's delight.

Austrians eat mainly meat dishes, except for fresh fish from the lakes and rivers. Among these, my personal favorite is the salmon trout of the Salzkammergut lake district.

Wienerschnitzel (breaded veal cutlets) is Vienna's most famous meat dish outside Austria. The most authentic local recipes insist that the schnitzel be fried in lard; others prefer butter or at least a combination of the two. On one point everybody agrees: the schnitzel should have the golden-brown color of a Stradivari violin.

The main meat specialty in Austria is boiled beef, or **tafelspitz,** said to reflect "the soul of the empire." It is the *specialité de la nation.* In fact, you won't find a single discriminating Viennese who hasn't, at least once in his or her life, eaten this celebrated dish. Try it at Sacher's in Vienna, or if the price there is too high, then the boiled beef can be ordered at a much cheaper *beisel,* the cousin of a French bistro. Of course, the tafelspitz at Sacher's will probably be served to you at a table graced by a silver candelabrum. But at a beisel, the decorative note is likely to be an empty wine bottle holding a candle.

Boiled beef originated during the reign of Franz Joseph I who liked it for his midday meal. The rest of the kingdom followed his example, and before World War II the most celebrated people of Vienna ordered boiled beef at Meissl and Schadn's, the best known beef restaurant in Austria in the pre-Nazi era. There, one could choose from two dozen different cuts of beef. It became a ritual to order your favorite cut, and you had really arrived in status if the waiter knew your preference without having to ask. Alas! Meissl and Schadn's—that venerated landmark where the Austrian composer Gustav Mahler used to dine in 1897 when he was chief conductor of the Vienna State Opera—is no more. It was destroyed by Allied bombs during World War II.

Roast goose is served in Austria on festive occasions such as Christmas, but at any time of the year you can order *eine gute fettgans,* a good fat goose. After such a rich dinner, you may want to relax over some wonderful, strong coffee, followed by *schnapps.*

Soups are usually good in Austria and quite inexpensive. Among the favorites are *gulyassuppe* (a goulash soup of—you guessed it—Hungarian origin) and *leberknodlsuppe* (meat broth with round dumplings containing chicken liver). There are infinite varieties of goulashes, both Austrian and Hungarian. These are usually stews of beef or pork, spiced with paprika. The Austrian version, *Wiener gulasch,* is usually less highly seasoned with paprika than the Hungarian.

Austrian **bread,** especially that baked in the ovens of Vienna, is considered among the best in the world. It comes in all shapes, sizes, and colors, made with many different grains and flours. Strudels too come in all shapes, sizes, and flavors. I often enjoy a poppyseed yeast strudel. In the baking line, the Lily Langtry of Vienna, Katharine Schratt, an actress at the Burgtheatre, was reported to make a special old Vienna coffee cake, *alt Wiener gugelhupf,* which was so good that the Emperor Franz Joseph I fell in love with her!

Austrians generally are exceedingly fond of **desserts,** and all over the country you will have the chance to sample *Salzburger nockerln,* a taste-tempting, frothy soufflé. Viennese pastries are also renowned, including chocolate saddle of venison cake, a delightful chocolate-almond concoction.

Even if you're not addicted to eating sweets, there's a gustatory experience you mustn't miss in the city of its origin: you must have **Sacher torte** in Vienna. This dessert is known all over the world, and many gourmets claim to have the original recipe for the "king of tortes," *die echte.* Master pastry baker, Franz Sacher, created the Sacher torte for Prince von Metternich, and tourists would often ask Madame Sacher for the recipe but she never gave it to them. Where else but in Vienna would a cake lead to a lawsuit? Demel's sued the Sacher Hotel, each insisting that it had the authentic recipe. The suit became a *cause célèbre.* But the hotel and Demel's still make Sacher torte today and ship it all over the world. You decide for yourself which does it better.

Madame Sacher helped cultivate the legend of Vienna as a citadel of gourmet cuisine. In Robert E. Sherwood's play *Reunion in Vienna,* this fabulous, cigar-smoking hostess was played by Helen Westley. The spirit of Madame Sacher lives on in Vienna and in the hotel she made famous.

Beer and Wine

Austria imposes few restrictions on the sale of alcohol, so except in alcohol-free places, you should be able to order beer or wine with your meal—even if it's 9 in the morning, or earlier, when many Austrians have their first strong drink of the morning, some preferring beer to coffee as a bracer to get them trucking.

In general, Austrian wines are served when new. Most of them are consumed where they are produced and are not known outside the region where they are grown. I generally prefer the white wine to the red, and perhaps you will too.

More than 99% of all Austrian wine is produced in vineyards in eastern Austria, principally Vienna, Lower Austria, Styria, and the youngest province of the country, Burgenland.

The most famous Austrian wine, **Gumpoldskirchen,** comes from Lower Austria, not only the largest province but the biggest wine producer. The center of the Baden wine district—called in Austria the Südbahnstrecke—is the village of Gumpoldskirchen, which gives the wine its name. This white wine is heady and rich, and just a little sweet.

An outer district of Vienna, **Klosterneuburg,** an ancient abbey on the right bank of the Danube, produces what is—arguably—the finest white wine in Austria. Monks have been making wine at this Augustinian monastery for centuries.

The ancient town of Krems, on the left bank of the Danube, produces very popular table wines, including **Kremser Sandgrube.**

The Wachau district, lying to the west of Vienna, also produces some fine wines known for their delicate bouquet, including **Loibner Kaiserwein** and **Duernsteiner Katzensprung.** These wines are fragrant and fruity.

By far the best red wine, and on this there is little disagreement, is **Voslauer** from Voslau. It's strong but, even though red, not quite as powerful as Gumpoldskirchen and Klosterneuburger.

From Styria comes Austria's best known rosé, the **Schilcher,** which is slightly dry, fruity, and sparkling.

Because many Viennese visiting the heurigen outside their capital didn't want to get too drunk, they started diluting the new wine with club soda or mineral water. Thus the **spritzer** was born, a drink that has now swept Europe and North America as well. The mix is best with a very dry wine. If you use a sweetish wine, you're likely to get what Marlene Dietrich once called "weak lemonade."

In all except the most deluxe places it is possible to order a carafe of wine (called *offener wein),* which will be much less expensive in price.

Austrian beers are relatively inexpensive and quite good, and they are sold throughout the land. **Gösser,** produced in Styria, is one of the most favored brews. It comes in both light and dark. In Salzburg, the **Augustiner Bräu** is famous, and in Innsbruck, **Adambräu.** The country brews most of its own beer (Vienna is a major production center, and **Schwechater** is the finest beer made in the city.)

Two of the most famous liqueurs—beloved by the Austrians—include **slivovitz** (a plum brandy which originated in Croatia) and **barack** (made from apricots, of Hungarian origin).

Imported whisky and bourbon are likely to be lethal in price. When in Austria, it's a good rule of thumb to drink the "spirit of the land." In this case that means wine and beer. It'll be far easier on your budget than Chivas Regal or whatever it is you drink back home.

The most festive drink, in my opinion, is **bowle** (pronounced bole). Austrians, especially the Viennese, often serve this at a party. It was first made for me by the great chanteuse Greta Keller, and I've been a devotee of it ever since. She preferred the lethal method of soaking berries and sliced peaches overnight in brandy. She would then pour three bottles of dry white wine over the fruit and let it stand for another two to three hours. Before serving, she'd pour a bottle of champagne over it! In her words, "You can drink it as a cocktail, during and after dinner, and on . . . and on . . . and on!"

The Heurigen

It was in 1784 that Joseph II decreed that each vintner in the suburbs of Vienna could sell his own wine right on his doorstep to paying guests. And thus a tradition was born which has continued to this day.

Heurig means new wines or, more literally, "of this year." These taverns lie on the outskirts of Vienna, mainly in Grinzing but also in Nussdorf and Sievering. The latter two make a wine so full bodied that the legend is "one has to bite them!" Most of the heurigen are in a rustic style, with wooden benches and tables. Much of the drinking, however, takes place in vine-covered gardens in fair weather. A green branch hanging above the doorway usually designates a heurige. In some of the more old-fashioned places, on a nippy night there's a crackling fire in a colorful, often flower-bordered ceramic stove.

Schmaltzy Viennese songs are often featured. Naturally, there's likely to be not only a gypsy violin but perhaps an accordion or even a zither (remember the movie *The Third Man?).*

Many heurigen today are in fact quite elaborate restaurants; others are still simple, and it's quite acceptable in these to bring your own snacks or else drink the "new wine" with cheese and sausage you buy on the premises.

The wine is surprisingly potent, in spite of its innocent taste.

Once the Viennese came out to the wine districts just after the harvest. Nowadays the heurigen are year-round institutions.

The Ritual of Coffee Drinking

Although it may sound heretical, Turkey is credited with establishing the tradition of the famous Viennese coffeehouse. The Imperial City was successful in fending off two Turkish invasions, one in 1529 and another in 1683. The Turks, in their hasty retreat, left behind bags of coffee, and a legend was born.

It is said that the first coffeehouse opened in Vienna in the mid-17th century. The proprietor of this inaugural *Wiener kaffeehaus* was Frantz Kolschitzky, a notorious rogue.

In the heyday of Vienna, the literati gathered at the Café Central. There you might have encountered Karl Kraus, an ugly little man, almost a hunchback, who was as aggressive as his writings. Or perhaps Stefan Zweig, the man who became known throughout the world for his psychological tales such as *Amok* and *Kaleidoscope.*

In Vienna, *jause* is a 4 p.m. coffee and pastry ritual. Naturally, you select your favorite cake or pastry, the true Viennese usually preferring one he or she has been served since childhood.

Of course, one must not drink Viennese coffee in a café that doesn't have dark-wood paneling stained by the smoke of Schubert, Mozart, Suppé, Lehar, Strauss, or Beethoven, assuming that any of these gentlemen smoked.

On your second visit to a Viennese coffeehouse, the *herr obers* should know at once which table you prefer (your *stammtisch),* and how you like your coffee!

You can order your coffee several ways—everything from almost milk-pale *(verkehrt),* which is one part coffee to four parts milk, to mocha (ebony-black coffee served in a delicate demi-tasse).

Kaffee mit schlagobers is the easiest, simplest, and most traditional method of preparing coffee in Vienna. Whipped cream is served with it. You might even order *doppelschlag* (double whipped cream).

Turkish coffee is also brewed authentically in Vienna.

3. Sports, Summer and Winter

Leisure sports are an important part of life in Austria, with more people than ever pursuing some kind of sporting activity. Today there isn't a resort in the country, however small, which does not offer visitors more than one sport to enjoy. The sports opportunities provided depend, of course, on the area visited, ranging from activities suited to the sun-drenched lakes, to the wide lowlands in the east, to the alpine heights, and to the many rivers, some placid and some turbulent.

For information about sports to watch or to participate in, try the **Austrian National Tourist Office,** 1 Margaretenstrasse, Vienna (tel. 57-57-14). They can put you in touch with the right persons or organizations to help you plan your vacation if you tell them what sport or sports you are interested in.

SUMMER: The mountains and lakes provide plenty of opportunities for all kinds of sports and pastimes.

Mountaineering

With more than 70% of Austria's total area taken up by mountains of all shapes and sizes, it's no wonder that outdoor-oriented visitors find the Alps to be a paradise for walking, hiking, and mountain climbing. Paths and trails are marked and secured, guides and maps are available, and there's an outstanding system of huts to shelter you. Austria has more than 450 chair lifts or cable cars to open up the mountains for visitors.

Certain precautions are essential, foremost being to inform your innkeeper or host of the route you plan to take. Also, suitable hiking or climbing shoes and protective clothing are imperative. Camping out overnight is strongly discouraged here because of the rapidly changing mountain weather and the established system of keeping track of hikers and climbers in the mountains. More than 700 alpine huts—many of which are really full-service lodges with restaurant facilities, rooms, and dormitories—are fixed points spaced about four to five hours apart, so that you can make rest and lunch stops. Hikers are required to sign into and out of the huts and to give the destination of the day before setting off in the morning. If you don't show up at a hut as planned, search parties go into action.

If you're advised that your chosen route has difficulties, be wise. Hire a mountain guide or get expert advice from some qualified local person before braving the unknown. Certified hiking and climbing guides are based in all Austrian mountain villages and can be found by looking for their signs or by asking at the local tourist office.

Above all, *obey signs.* Even in summer, if there's still snow on the ground you could be in an area threatened by avalanches. There are other important rules to follow for your own safety if you're going walking, hiking, or mountaineering. You can obtain these from the Austrian National Tourist Offices, from bookstores in Austrian cities, at the branches of various alpine clubs, or at local tourist offices in villages throughout the Alps.

Schools of mountaineering are found in 36 resorts, in all Austrian provinces except Burgenland, with regular courses, mountain tours, and camps for all ages. Distinction is made between summer and winter mountaineering, of course.

Camping

Austria has some 400 camping sites placed in its most beautiful areas. If you want to park away from a public campground, you must have the consent of the property owner. Also, you can't park your camp trailer on or beside a public highway unless you have a traction vehicle and obey parking regulations. Some mountain roads are either closed to or not recommended for campers. For details on camping opportunities and the cost at various campsites, ask for the camping list available at the National Tourist Office.

Water Sports

Austria has no sea coast, but from Lake Constance (Bodensee) in the west to the Neusiedl See in the east, the country is rich in lakes and boasts some 150 rivers and streams.

Swimming is, of course, possible year round if you wish to use an indoor pool or to swim at one of the many health clubs in winter. Recent major developments of swimming facilities at summer resorts, especially those on the warm waters of Carinthia, where you can swim from May to October, and in the Salzkammergut lake district between Upper Austria and Salzburg province, have seen this sport increase greatly in popularity.

The beauty of Austria underwater is attested to by those who have tried **diving** in the lakes. Most outstanding, I am told, are the diving and underwater exploration possibilities in the Salzkammergut lake district and in the Weissen See in Carinthia. You can receive instruction and obtain necessary equipment at both places.

If you prefer to stay on top of the water, you can go sailing, windsurfing, or canoeing on the lakes and rivers.

The **sailing** (yachting) season lasts from May to October, with activity centered on the Attersee in the Salzkammergut district, on Lake Constance out of Bregenz, and on Lake Neusiedl, a large shallow lake in the east. Winds on the Austrian lakes can be treacherous, but a warning system and rescue services are alert. For information on sailing, get in touch with the **Austrian Sailing Association,** 12 Prinz-Eugen-Strasse, Vienna (tel. 65-84-95). A recognized sailing license, required for Lake Constance, can be acquired from the Chief District Office in Bregenz.

Most resorts on lakes or rivers where **windsurfing** can be safely enjoyed have equipment and instruction available. This sport is increasing in popularity and has been added to the curriculum of several sailing schools, especially in the area of the Wörthersee in Carinthia, warmest of the alpine lakes.

If you're interested in shooting the rapids of a swift mountain stream or just paddling around on a placid lake, don't miss the chance to go **canoeing** in Austria. Possibilities vary from slow-flowing lowland rivers such as the Inn or Mur to the wild waters of glacier-fed mountain streams suitable only for experts. Special schools for fast-water paddling operate from May to September at the village of Klaus on the Steyr River in Upper Austria, at Opponitz in Lower Austria on the Ybbs River, and at Abtenau in Salzburg province.

Austria is a **fishing** paradise, offering as it does many clear, unpolluted streams, deep rivers, and lakes. You can angle for trout, char, pike, sheat-fish (monster catfish), and pike-perch in well-stocked mountain streams. In the right-hand tributaries of the Danube, you might catch huck, a land-locked salmon which is an excellent fighter and a culinary delight, usually fished for in late fall. The waters of Wörthersee in Carinthia sometimes yield the North American big-mouth black bass with which an owner of Velden Castle once stocked the lake by accident. Intended for a pond on his estate, one barrel fell into the lake and burst, introducing the immigrants from America to a new happy home.

A Sports Potpourri

Hunters find game of all sorts both in the mountains and the lowlands of Austria. If you're a passable shot, you may want to try your skill as a Nimrod here. Who knows? You might bag a roebuck, a marmot, or a chamois in season. For wild boar, foxes, polecats, wild rabbits, and weasel, it's open season all year, but you can't hunt without a license. For the latest information on whether you can bring your sporting guns and ammunition into the country, or where you can secure such equipment, plus facts about where and how to get a hunting license, check with the National Tourist Office.

Golfing, once a pursuit only of a privileged few, has become a sport for everybody who takes the time to learn. One of the country's most outstanding 18-hole courses is at the Murhof in Styria, near Frohnleiten. Others are the Igls/Rinn near Innsbruck, Seefeld-Wildmoos, Dallach on the shores of the Wörthersee in Carinthia, Enzefeld and Wiener Neustade-Foehrenwald in Lower Austria, and the oldest of them all, Vienna-Freudenau, founded in 1901. There are numerous nine-hole courses throughout the country. The season generally extends from April to October or November.

Tennis courts are to be found at most resort hotels and at sports centers.

Ask at a local office of tourist information, at a railroad station, or at your resort hotel if you'd like to rent a bicycle. **Cycling** tracks and paths are laid out so that you can ride across the country untroubled by vehicular traffic.

For a change from land and water sports, why not take to the air? **Gliding,** for which Austria is well suited, can be arranged at many airfields, and instruction is available at Spitzerberg, some 30 miles east of Vienna; at Zell am See in Salzburg province; at Niedr-Oblarn and Graz in Styria; and at Wiener-Neustadt.

Hang-gliding has gained in popularity recently. Facilities for this dare-devil sport are spread across the country.

Hot-air **ballooning** is available at Puch near Weiz in Styria.

Personally, I'll stick to **horseback riding,** for which you can rent a mount for one ride or spend your holiday on an Austrian-style ranch.

Besides all these sports in which you can participate, Austria has a wealth of spectator sports, ranging from auto racing to soccer to boat racing to horse racing, plus much more.

Also in the world of sports to be enjoyed in summer, there's **grass skiing,** which doesn't require snow and can be practiced by those who don't care to go high into the Alps to ski on snow. Ask at the Tourist Information Office for a list of resorts providing this sport, as well as for details about centers offering summer snow skiing. As for winter snow sports, read on.

WINTER: The winter sports scene in Austria is snow-white, with the towering peaks of the Alps, snow-blanketed pastures and forests, and smooth ice on lakes providing such attractions as downhill and cross-country skiing, hot-dogging, ice skating, tobogganing, curling, bobsledding, sleigh riding, and mountaineering for the sturdy hiker.

Skiing

It may have lost world-power status with the death of the empire, but Austria today has world renown for its uphill transportation which whisks skiers to the snow slopes for their downhill ski runs. Some 3500 facilities transport passengers on rides of scenic splendor to the sites where they can begin their enjoyment of the approximately 12,500 miles of marked runs. Intricate networks cover whole mountainsides so that you don't have to take a step uphill on your own. Ski "circuses" allow skiers to move from mountain to mountain, and a ski "swing" opening up opposite sides of the same mountain ties villages in different valleys into one big ski region.

Shuttle buses, usually free for those with a valid lift ticket, take you to valley points where you board funiculars, gondolas, aerial trains, or chair lifts. Higher up, you may leave the larger conveyance and continue by another chair lift or, even higher up, by surface lift, probably by T-bar.

Austria made its way into winter sports history through the selection of Innsbruck twice for the site of the Winter Olympics. But skiing here is not the monopoly of stars. It's a popular leisure activity of young and old, mainly because of the climate and topography. Compare the vast ski area transportation network today with that of 1945, when the country had only 12 cableways, eight mountain railways, and six ski lifts.

The Austrian Ski School is noted for its fine instruction and practice techniques, available in many places: Arlberg; the posh villages of Zürs and Lech/Arlberg where jet-setters gather; the Silvretta mountains; and Hochgurgl, Obergurgl, Hochsölden, and Sölden in the Tyrolean Ötztal, to name a few. Year-round skiing is possible in the little villages of the Stubaital, through use of a cableway on the Stubai glacier, more than 10,000 feet above sea level. Known to all top skiers in the world are Kitzbühel, another lure to the jet set, as is Seefeld.

Skiing is a family sport in Europe, and ski centers usually have gentle slopes and instruction for youngsters, plus babysitting services for the very small. Many places have something extra to offer, since Austria's ski resorts have been working villages for centuries, while skiing facilities are relative newcomers. The Valley of Gastein was known for its medicinal thermal springs long before it became a ski center. The people of Schladming, in the Dachstein mountains, wore their local costumes and lodens before the first cross-country skier came to the high plateau of the little, unspoiled village of Ramsau.

Among the most attractive large-scale skiing areas are the Radstädter Tauern region and Saalbach/Hinterglemm in Salzburg province. Here, as in most of the winter sports areas, you'll find ski huts with crackling fires in the grates and hot spiced wine or perhaps *jagatee,* hot tea heavily laced with rum.

Hot-dogging is an American import to Austria and is a special kind of skiing involving acrobatics, trick skiing, artistic skiing, and ski "ballet." Organized hot-dogger activities usually occur early in the season in such places as Bad Kleinkirchheim, Badgastein, the Kitzsteinhorn near Zell am See, or the Stubai glacier.

Cross-country skiing is popular among those who want to enjoy the winter beauty in quiet. Many miles of tracks are marked for this sport, and special instructors are available.

Other Winter Sports

Tobogganing, called the *luge* in the Winter Olympics, requires no special skills and is a thrill sport for amateurs. Many towns have special runs, and some mountain roads are closed to allow sledding.

Eisschiessen is the alpine form of **curling.** Instead of stones, "sticks" are used, weighted wooden disks with handles.

You can ride horseback in the snow, but it's more romantic to go in a one- or two-horse open **sleigh** to huts in the winter forest for a mug of hot spiced wine.

Whether you wish to indulge in any of these activities in the bracing alpine air or not, at most resorts you can enjoy swimming in an indoor pool, basking in a sauna, playing tennis or ninepins, trying your skill on a rifle range, or working out in the exercise room or gymnasium.

And there's always après-ski festivity, the main drawing card for some winter vacationers.

For the spectator, there are many competitive winter sports events held at the resorts and elsewhere.

4. The ABCs of Austria

BANKING: Foreign and Austrian money can be brought into Austria without any restrictions, and there is no restriction on taking foreign money out of the country. However, Austrian schillings can only be taken out up to a limit of 15,000 AS ($798). To export more than that, you must have a special permit from the Austrian National Bank. Foreign currency and travelers checks can be exchanged at all banks, savings banks, and exchange counters at airports and railroad stations at the official exchange rate of the day as given out by the Austrian National Bank.

BANKING HOURS: In the federal provinces, banking hours vary according to the region. The exchange counters at airports and railroad stations are generally open from the first to the last plane or train, usually from 8 a.m. to 8 p.m. every day. For banking hours in Vienna, see "The ABCs of Vienna," coming up in Chapter IV.

BULLETIN: In a world of fast-changing developments, it's hard to keep abreast of late-breaking events that may affect your travel plans. For that reason, I recommend a new travel newsletter to readers who travel a lot and want "the latest word" on what's happening in Europe. *Travel Bulletin* is intended only for travel agents, but has also been recently made available to readers of the Dollarwise series. This way, you'll learn the news the agents are getting at the same time they do. This four-page newsletter is mailed first class to its subscribers every month, and is augmented by a two-page supplement seasonally on some timely subject. It is completely free of sponsors and advertisers, and seeks out bargains, particularly cut-rate air fares, as part of its "value-for-dollar" policy. You can subscribe by paying a yearly fee of $35 to Department AUS, **Travel Bulletin,** c/o Pinder Lane, 159 West 53rd St., New York, NY 10019.

CLIMATE: At the center of Europe, the temperature in Austria varies greatly depending on the location. The national average ranged from a low of 9°F in January to a high of 68°F in July. However, in Vienna the January average is 32°F, while for July it's 66°F. A New Yorker who lived in Austria for eight years told me the four seasons were "about the same." In a sub-alpine climate it's neither very, very hot nor, on the other hand, is it Siberian cold. Snow falls in the mountainous sectors by mid-November. Road conditions in winter can be very dangerous in many parts of the country. The winter air is usually crisp and clear, with many sunny days. The winter snow cover lasts from late December through March in the valleys, from November through May at about 6000 feet, and all year at above 8500 feet. The ideal times for visiting Vienna are spring and fall, which have mild, sunny days. The so-called summer season generally means from Easter until about mid-October.

CLOTHING: In spring and fall, a few warm pieces and a topcoat or raincoat are advisable. In winter you'll need a sweater and an all-purpose raincoat, as evenings are cool, especially in the mountain areas. You'll be wise to plan your wardrobe according to where you'll be staying. Vienna is fairly dressy, especially in the evening. Mountain country demands some woollies and sturdy walking shoes, and if you get into alpine activities you'd better have a heavy sweater and a down parka. Don't forget to have boots or shoes with slip-proof soles for winter walking.

CONSULATES AND EMBASSIES: The **U.S. Embassy** is at 9 Boltzmanngasse (tel. 31-55-11) in Vienna. However, for such matters as a lost passport (anything considered nonpolitical), go to the **U.S. Consulate** at 2 Friedrich Schmidt Platz (tel. 34-66-11), Vienna. The **Canadian Embassy** is at 10 Dr.-Karl-Lueger-Ring (tel. 63-36-91), also in Vienna.

CRIME: No particular caution is needed, other than what a discreet person would maintain anywhere. Compared to the rest of the world, Austria is a very safe country in which to travel.

CURRENCY: The basic unit of currency is the Austrian **schilling** (AS), which contains 100 **groschen.** There are coins with denominations of 5, 10, and 50 groschen and 1, 5, 10, 20, 25, 100, 500, and 1000 schillings, and banknotes with denominations of 20, 50, 100, 500, and 1000 schillings.

As a general guideline the price conversions in this book have been computed at the rate of 18.8 AS equals $1 U.S. (1 AS equals $.0532). As for all European countries, the international exchanges are far from stable, and this ratio might be old hat when you go to Austria. As a guide, however, I'm including the following exchanges at the rates given above.

Schilling	U.S.$	Schilling	U.S.$
1	.05	500	26.60
5	.26	600	31.92
10	.53	700	37.24
25	1.33	800	42.56
50	2.66	900	47.88
100	5.32	1000	53.20
150	7.98	1100	58.52
200	10.64	1200	63.84
250	13.30	1300	69.16
300	15.96	1400	74.48
400	21.28	1500	79.80

CUSTOMS: Austrian officials are fairly lenient (and the most tolerant people in the world if you're just arriving from one of the Communist countries where they really check your luggage!). The duty-free limit is 400 cigarettes or 80 cigars or a pound of tobacco, if you're over 17 and you come from a non-European country. However, if you fly to Austria from the continent, the limit is reduced to 200 cigarettes or 50 cigars or 250 grams of tobacco. You can also bring in two liters of wine and a liter of liquor (but only .75 liter from a country in Europe). Likewise, you're allowed ten ounces of cologne and two ounces of perfume, along with $100 worth of souvenirs. Most items such as cameras, tape recorders, portable typewriters, sports equipment, or whatever, intended for your personal use, are allowable.

Upon leaving Austria, you're allowed to bring back $400 worth of merchandise into the U.S. without paying additional tax. The duty-free limit on gifts sent home from abroad has been raised to $50.

ELECTRIC CURRENT: Austria operates on 220 volts AC, with the European 50-cycle circuit. That means that U.S.-made appliances will need an adapter-converter. Many Austrian hotels stock adapter plugs but not power converters. Electric clocks, record players, and tape recorders, however, will not work well even on converters.

GAMBLING: Casinos are found in ten locations in Austria: Vienna, Velden am Wörther See in Carinthia, Baden near Vienna, Badgastein in Salzburg province, Salzburg, Seefeld and Kitzbühel in Tyrol, Linz, and Bregenzaand Riezlern/Kleinwalsertal in Vorarlberg. Each has its own style, giving the opportunity to try your luck in a historic downtown palace, a nostalgic spa pavilion, or a rustic alpine mansion as well as in modern settings.

GUIDES: In the federal provinces, guides are available through the Provincial Tourist Boards or the various city tourist offices. For guides in the capital, see "The ABCs of Vienna" in Chapter IV.

HOLIDAYS: Bank holidays in Austria are as follows: January 1, January 6 (Epiphany), Easter Monday, May 1, Ascension Day, Whitmonday, Corpus Christi Day, August 15, October 25 (Nationalfeiertag), November 1, 8, and 25, and December 25 and 26.

INFORMATION: The **Austrian National Tourist Office,** 1 Margaretenstrasse (tel. 56-16-66-0) in Vienna dispenses information about the entire country. It cannot, however, make reservations for you. As you travel throughout the towns and villages of Austria, you'll see signs indicating a fat "i." Most often that will stand for "information," and you'll be directed to a local tourist office, where, chances are, you can obtain maps of the area and might even be assisted in finding a hotel should you arrive without a reservation.

INFORMATION (BEFORE YOU GO): Your travel agent can supply you with the information you wish, or get in touch with the **Austrian National Tourist Office,** whose U.S. representatives are at: 545 Fifth Ave., New York, NY 10017 (tel. 212/697-0651); Standard Oil Building, Suite 7023, 200 E. Randolph Dr., Chicago, IL 60601 (tel. 312/861-0100); 4800 San Felipe St., Suite 500, Houston, TX 77056 (tel. 713/850-8888); 3440 Wilshire Blvd., Suite 906, Los Angeles, CA 90010 (tel. 213/380-3309); and 1007 N.W. 24th Ave., Portland, OR 97210 (tel. 503/224-6000). In Canada: 1010 Sherbrooke St. West, Suite 1410, Montréal, PQ H3A 2R7 (tel. 514/849-3708 or 849-3709); 2 Bloor St. East, Suite 3330, Toronto, ON M4W 1A8 (tel. 416/967-3348 or 967-3380); and Suite 1220-1223, Vancouver Block, 736 Granville St., Vancouver, BC V6Z 1J2 (tel. 604/683-5808 or 683-5809).

LANGUAGE: German is, of course, the official language of Austria. But since English is taught in the high schools, it is commonly spoken throughout the country, especially in tourist regions. Certain Austrian minorities speak Slavic languages, and Hungarian is commonly spoken in Burgenland.

PASSPORTS AND VISAS: Citizens of the U.S. or Canada need only a valid passport to enter Austria. No visa is required.

PHOTOGRAPHY: You'll want to take lots and lots of pictures in Austria, as it's one of the most beautiful countries on earth. However, take along as much film as you can, because film sold in Austria, although readily available, carries a 30% tax!

RADIO: The Austrian Radio network (ÖRF) has English news broadcasts at 8:05 a.m. daily during the tourist season. "Blue Danube Radio" broadcasts daily in English from 7 to 9 a.m., noon to 2 p.m., and 6 to 7:30 p.m.

STAYING IN A PRIVATE HOME: If you want to meet the Austrian people at home, sleep in comfortable rooms at moderate rates, and travel without a set itinerary, look for signs that say *Zimmer Frei* attached to the front of a house or to a short post at the front yard gate or driveway. This means the proprietors rent rooms on a bed-and-breakfast basis to travelers. You'll encounter these signs along Austria's highways, and even more so, along some of the most scenic byways.

Such accommodations in a farmhouse or in the home of a craftsman or worker are invariably spotlessly clean and quite pleasant. Almost all of them have hot and cold running water in the bedrooms, although private bath and toilet facilities are rare. (There's usually a toilet on every floor and one bathroom in the house). A continental breakfast is served. These B&B houses are often new and have modern furniture, although you can still find comfort in, say, an old farmhouse.

Rates for such rooms vary considerably, depending on the type of accommodation provided, but on the average, the charge is $5 (U.S.) to $10 for a single with breakfast, $8 to $15 for a double. Few such homes accept advance reservations, so you just stop in and inquire. When the rooms are filled, the sign is taken down or covered. You can find help in securing accommodations of this kind through the local tourist office, in houses close to or in a town or village.

You may need a few words of basic German, as only a few such proprietors speak a little English. If you're staying for only one night, you may be asked to pay your bill in advance, and it must be paid in Austrian schillings.

Whole families or traveling parties can have the experience of staying on a farm, renting several rooms or even a wing of the house, but generally a stay of at least a week is required and advance reservation through a local tourist office or regional tourist board is necessary. The correct form of address for the local offices is *Verkehrsverein,* then the name of the town near which you wish to stay, and the name of the country, Austria. Regional boards should be addressed by writing to *Landesfremdenverkehrsamt,* followed by the name of the capital of the respective Austrian province, and the name of the country. Your reservation will be confirmed upon receipt of a deposit.

I highly recommend that you seek out such accommodations if you really want to get to know the people of the country and how they live at home. Any language barriers can be overcome sufficiently to allow you to be directed to good country inns for dining and to interesting sights in an area.

SHOPPING: A large variety of quality items is available to the shopper in Austria. You'll find jewelry, including costume jewelry, leather goods, needlepoint articles, traditional-costume-inspired fashions, knitwear, sports wear and equipment, novelties, and hunting rifles, among the many Austrian-made goods offered.

SHOPPING HOURS: In most Austrian stores, hours on weekdays are 8 a.m. to 6 p.m., 8 a.m. to noon on Saturday. Many stores close for two hours during the middle of the day.

TAXES: An 18% or 30% value added tax (VAT) is included in the list price of items sold in Austria. Tourists must pay this VAT at the time of purchase, but can obtain a tax refund on purchases totaling more than 1000 AS ($53.20) or more per store if the merchandise is taken out of the country unused. Your bill will show the VAT *(MWSt)* as a separate item or will say that the tax is part of the total price. In order to get the refund, you must fill out a form, U-34, which is available at most stores patronized by tourists. A sign will say "Tax-free Shopping." Sales personnel will help you fill out the form and will affix the store identification stamp. Keep your U-34 forms handy when you leave the country and have them validated by the Austrian Customs officer at your point of departure. You may have to prove that the merchandise is unused before Customs will validate your forms.

After returning home, mail the validated U-34 form or forms to the store where you bought the merchandise, keeping a copy of each form. The store will mail to your home address a check, bank draft, or international money order covering the amount of VAT refund due you. It sounds complicated, but if you work it right, you may get up to 23% of your shopping expenditure refunded. Information and help in expediting some steps of this process are available at the Austrian Automobile and Touring Club (ÖAMTC). Check with the Austrian National Tourist Office at one of its North American offices before you go. Ask for the OAMTC brochure "Tax-free Shopping in Austria."

TAXIS: In the large Austrian cities, taxis are equipped with officially sealed taximeters which show the cost of your trip in schillings. If a rate change has recently been instituted, there may be a surcharge added to the amount shown on the meter, pending adjustment of the taximeter. Surcharges will be posted in the cab. A supplement is charged for luggage carried in the vehicle's trunk. Zone charges or set charges for standard trips are the rule in most resort areas. Tip the driver 10% of the fare.

TIPPING: A service charge of 10% to 15% is included on hotel and restaurant bills, but it's a good policy to leave an additional 5% to 7% for waiters and 10 AS (53¢) per day for your hotel maid.

Railroad station, airport, and hotel porters get 10 AS (53¢) per piece of luggage, plus a 5-AS (26¢) tip. Your hairdresser should be tipped 10% of the bill, and the shampoo girl will be thankful for a 5-AS (26¢) gratuity. Hat-check women and toilet attendants are usually given about 5 AS (26¢).

TIME: Austria operates on Central European Time, which makes it six hours later than U.S. Eastern Standard Time. It advances its clocks one hour in summer, however.

TOBACCO: Tobacco is a state monopoly in Austria and sale is through shops and kiosks marked *Austria Tabak* as well as by vending machines, and in hotels, restaurants, cafés, and inns. A number of specialty tobacconist shops sell foreign tobacco products. Golden Smart, Belvedere, and Smart Export are some of the best known Austrian cigarette brands. In 1784 Joseph II founded the Österreichische Tabakregie, the oldest tobacco-processing concern in Europe.

YOUTH HOSTELS: Austria has about 100 youth hostels distributed throughout the provinces. Rates for bed and breakfast range from 70 AS ($3.72) to 100 AS ($5.32) per person. Accommodation and three meals a day range from 140 AS ($7.45) to 195 AS ($10.37), plus taxes (except in some exempt areas). Some hostels lock their doors between 10 p.m. and 6 a.m. to discourage late arrivals. Dormitories must be empty between 10 a.m. and 5 p.m. You must have an International Youth Hostel Federation membership card for use of Austria's youth hostels, and advance reservations are recommended.

In Austria, you can get information regarding the hostels from **Österreichischer Jugendherbergsverband,** 28 Schottenring, Vienna (tel. 63-53-53). A detailed brochure is also available at the Austrian National Tourist Office (see "Information," above) and its representatives abroad.

Chapter III

VIENNA: HOTELS AND RESTAURANTS

1. Where to Stay
2. Where to Dine

CITY OF MUSIC, cafés, waltzes, parks, pastries, and gemütlichkeit—that's Vienna. The capital city of Austria has long held an enchantment for visitors, gaining much of its charm even during times of great upheaval in the long reign of the Habsburgs and retaining it in the dark days of World Wars I and II, a charm which is present today.

Vienna is a true cosmopolitan city, with a blend throughout its history of tribes, races, and nationalities all becoming assimilated through the centuries, with countless, constant additions of foreigners of all backgrounds fusing their customs, ideas, and culture to become the witty, charming, and cynical Viennese.

From the time the Romans selected the site of a Celtic settlement for location of one of its most important Central European forts, Vindobona, the city which grew up in the Vienna Basin of the Danube has played a vital role in European history. Austria grew up around the city and developed into a mighty empire, but the Viennese character formed during the long history of the country can only be said to be a rich amalgam of the blending of cultures that have made Vienna what it still is today: a city whose people devote themselves to enjoyment of the good life.

Music, art, literature, theater, architecture, education, food, and drink (perhaps wine from the slopes where the Romans had vineyards in the first century A.D.)—all are a part of the gemütlichkeit of Vienna.

The splendor and brilliance of Habsburg Vienna was seen in the court panoply, where uniforms, decorations, gems, and precious metals made a dazzling, if sometimes tiring, show. Before some of the city's brilliance was dimmed by the fall of the empire, it was described as a "royal palace amidst surrounding suburbs."

The roster of renowned Viennese, either born in the city or spending much of their creative lives there, is endless—endless, that is, in that more names are added constantly as more Viennese make their appearance on the stage of cultural and professional life and become world renowned.

Whenever I watch the boat traffic flow past on the Danube (not so beautiful and blue as Johann Strauss described it but still an important, navigable Central European waterway), I am always a little awed at the thought of the immortal music and musical dramas which had their inception here. Mozart, Lehar, Schubert, Beethoven, the Strausses (all of them), Suppé, Gluck, Mahler, Brahms, Liszt, Hoffmann, Lanner, Haydn, Weber, Schönberg—in the music world alone these are some of the outstanding names which were known during the days of empire.

Another name familiar in Vienna toward the latter days of the Habsburgs is Biedermeier, but this is not the name of a real person but of a character in a book, and is the appellation used for a period and a style to describe avant-garde artists. The name Freud, however, is that of a real Viennese.

But I am not nostalgic for that era, because I know that talent, even genius, still burgeons in this beautiful country. Many personalities, especially theatrical, have come out of Vienna in recent decades and gone on to world acclaim: Erich von Stroheim, Hedy Lamarr, Curt Jurgens, Oskar Werner, Magda Schneider, Josef von Sternberg, Fritz Lang, G. W. Pabst, Maria Schell, Paula Wessely, and Greta Keller, to name a few.

The Viennese have always been hospitable to foreigners, but there was a time at the end of the 18th century when the emperor felt that tourists might spread pernicious ideas, and all non-Austrians were limited to a one-week stay in the capital. This of course is no longer so, nor has it been for nearly 200 years. Now you can laugh, play, feast, sightsee—enjoy all the offerings of the city to the fullest with the smiles of the Viennese welcoming you to gemütlich Vienna.

The face of the city has been altered by many occurrences—war, siege, victory, defeat, death of an empire, birth of a republic, bombing, occupation, and the passage of time—but Vienna is still the happy, cosmopolitan "Queen of the Danube."

AN ORIENTATION: First, you'll need a very good and detailed map to explore Vienna, as it covers more than 158 square miles and has some 1500 miles of streets (many of them only narrow alleyways).

Most visitors will spend all their time in the **Inner City** or Innere Stadt of Vienna, its First District. This is that famed section encircled by the Ringstrasse and the Danube Canal. Most of the city's best known churches, baroque palaces, galleries, historic monuments, hotels, and museums lie within this much-frequented district.

The **Ringstrasse** runs along the line of the old city walls for about 2½ miles. My suggestion is that you take a tram along the Ring before you do any actual exploring. That way, you'll get a feel for monumental Vienna before taking it on block by block.

The Ringstrasse on your map will come under a number of different names: sometimes it's called the Opernring, or the Schottenring, or else the Burgring or the Dr. Karl-Lueger-Ring. After an interruption by the Danube Canal, the Ringstrasse resumes with such names as the Stubenring, the Parkring, the Schubertring, and the Kärntnerring.

The **Graben,** once the southwestern frontier of Vienna, is hardly that now. Absorbed by the city, it is today a major shopping artery. But if Vienna has a "main" street, it is surely the **Kärntnerstrasse,** which is jampacked with pedestrians during the day. It extends as far as the **Karlsplatz.** Along the way, you'll find some of Vienna's best known hotels and cafés.

Beyond the Danube Canal is the Second District, with the famous

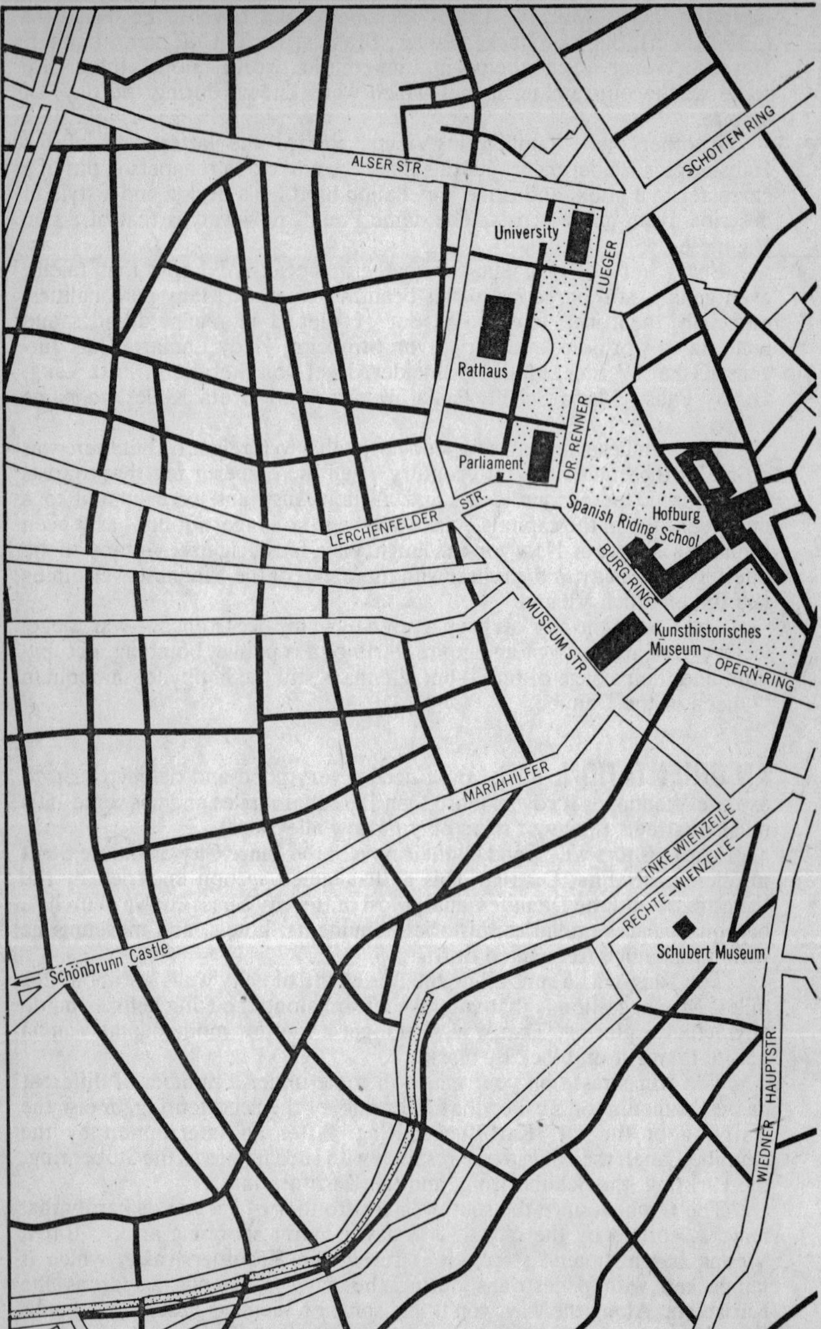
ALSER STR.
SCHOTTEN RING
University
LUEGER
Rathaus
DR. RENNER
Parliament
STR.
LERCHENFELDER
Spanish Riding School
Hofburg
BURG RING
MUSEUM STR.
Kunsthistorisches Museum
OPERN-RING
MARIAHILFER
LINKE WIENZEILE
RECHTE-WIENZEILE
Schubert Museum
Schönbrunn Castle
WIEDNER HAUPTSTR.

Danube Canal
Prater
HAUPT ALLEE
Johann Strauss Wohnung
Maria am Gestade
FRANZ JOSEF KAI
RADETZKI STR.
Radetzki Pl.
Aquincum
ROTENTURM
STUBEN RING
Stephans Pl.
St. Stephen's Cathedral
KÄRNTNER STR.
PARK RING
Stadtpark
Opera
SCHUBERT RING
AM HEUMARKT
LANDSTRASSER HAUPTSTR.
KÄRNTNER RING
Konzerthaus
Karlskirche
RENNWEG
PRINZ EUGEN
FAVORITEN STR.
Belvedere Palace
N
VIENNA

amusement park, the **Prater.** In the Third District, you'll find the **Belvedere Palace,** and in the Eighth District, **Schönbrunn Palace.**

1. Where to Stay

Finding a room in Vienna, in spite of its great number of hotels, can be a problem, especially in August and September (the latter the time of the Vienna Fair), if you should arrive without a reservation. Vienna has some of the greatest hotels in Europe, more than 300 recommendable ones with some 27,000 beds. If you arrive without a reservation in the peak visiting months, you may have to stay on the outskirts of Vienna, in the Grinzing or the Schönbrunn district, for example, and commute to the inner city by streetcar, bus, or underground.

In Vienna a five-star hotel such as the Imperial is decidedly luxurious and expensive. A four-star hotel is first class. Two- and three-star hotels are in the middle bracket, and a little one-star is the lowest of the lot, often no more than a boarding house (but often comfortable and quite clean).

THE DELUXE HOTELS: Hotel Imperial, 16 Kärntner Ring (tel. 65-17-65), is perhaps the grandest hotel in Vienna, evoking memories of the Austro-Hungarian Empire and Strauss waltzes to practically everyone who visits it. Luminaries from around the world use this as their headquarters, especially musical stars who prefer the location two blocks from the State Opera and one block from the Musikverein. Wagner stayed here with his family for a few months in 1875 (some scholars claim that he worked out key sections of both *Tannhäuser* and *Lohengrin* during that period). Other artists who have soothed their opening-night jitters in one of the rooms include Domingo, Caballé, Carreras, Fonteyn, Ormandy, Fürtwangler, and Karajan, along with the thousands of music lovers who travel to Austria to hear them.

The hotel was built in 1869 as the private residence of the Duke of Württemberg. The Italian architect Zanotti designed the facade like an almost overwhelmingly massive governmental building with a heroic frieze carved into the triangular pediment below the roofline. Surprisingly, it was converted into a private hotel in 1873. The Nazis commandeered it as their headquarters during World War II, and the Russians requisitioned it in 1945, turning it into a shadowy ghost of its former self. Since Austria regained its independence, massive expenditures have returned it to the glory of its former beauty.

On the staircase leading up from the glittering salons you'll see archways supported by graceful statues of gods and goddesses, along with two Winterhalter portraits of Emperor Franz Joseph and his wife Elizabeth. Everything is outlined against a background of polished red, yellow, and black marble, crystal chandeliers, Gobelin tapestries, and fine rugs. For many, the favorite rooms are the salons whose arched ceilings are painted with intricately designed garlands of fruit, ornate urns, griffins, and the smiling faces of sphinxes. Some of the royal suites are palatial, but all the rooms today are soundproof and air-conditioned, contain private baths, and are large enough to evoke memories of another century. A café downstairs plays Viennese music, while an intimate bar is a rendezvous point of the chic and elegant.

This is unquestionably one of the world's great hotels. The general manager is Otto Heinke, whose career has taken him to five hostelries in Canada, Monte Carlo, several Austrian ski resorts, and even a deluxe hotel in Baghdad. Generally acknowledged as one of the Europe's great hôteliers, he ably directs the staff, which includes a concierge, Erich Benesch, who is able to get tickets to musical events in town that are usually considered impossible to find.

Room rates include an automatic 15% service charge and run from 1100 AS ($58.52) to 1700 AS ($90.44) in a single, from 1700 AS ($90.44) to 2600 AS ($138.32) in a double. While these prices are nothing to sneeze at, they are nonetheless a lot less than what you'd pay for comparable service and accommodations at, for example, the Ritz in Paris or Claridge's in London.

Hotel Ambassador, Kärntnerstrasse 22 (tel. 52-75-11). This renowned hotel sits on the square with the Donner Fountain splashing water in its middle and the shop-lined Kärntnerstrasse on the other side. Mark Twain stayed here, as have a host of diplomats and celebrities, including Theodore Roosevelt. The trademark of the hotel has always been the color red, either in the silk wall coverings, the bedspreads, the upholstery, or the long carpet which is sometimes unrolled to the waiting limousine of some person known in world headlines. The wall-to-wall carpeting is, as you guessed, scarlet, relieved often by a discreet pattern of forest foliage. The public rooms have many, many chandeliers, which, in contrast to the vivid colors of everything else, appear sometimes as the most prominent furnishings. The Ambassador couldn't be better located: it's between the Opera House and St. Stephen's Cathedral.

High-season rates are in effect from April 1 to November 15 and from December 28 to January 2. At that time singles cost between 850 AS ($45.22) and 1050 AS ($55.86), and doubles range from 1400 AS ($74.48) to 1800 AS ($95.76). The rest of the year singles rent for between 720 AS ($38.30) and 850 AS ($45.22), doubles from 1250 AS ($66.50) to 1600 AS ($85.12). Sumptuous accommodations include TV, radio, air conditioning, and breakfast. This hotel, in summation, might be the ideal choice for guests who are devotees of rococo/*fin-de-siècle* decor.

Hotel Bristol, Kärntner Ring (tel. 52-95-52). You probably won't notice that this Vienna landmark looks any different from many other anonymously grand buildings in town from the outside. But connoisseurs of Austrian hotels maintain that this is a superb choice, with a decor evoking the full power of the Habsburg Empire. The hotel was constructed in 1894 next to the State Opera, in the ultimate of *fin-de-siècle* luxury, although it's been updated to give its clients the benefit of black tile baths and all the up-to-date conveniences. Many of the architectural embellishments rank as objets d'art in their own right, from the black carved marble fireplaces and the oil paintings in the salons to the corkscrew baroque columns of rare marble in the Bristol restaurant, which is, by the way, one of the chicest in Vienna. Even the chairs are beautifully crafted in a style that, depending on your mood, can be identified as either shield-back or heart-back Hepplewhite.

The *après-théâtre* ambience is a Viennese legend. The hotel's music room has a resident pianist who fills the ground floor with a collection of usually waltz-like melodies on the Grand Boesendorfer which you can hear while sipping drinks in the nearby Sirk Café, glitteringly appointed in pure art deco. On your way to the sumptuously appointed bedrooms, you'll see grandfather clocks in the corridors, most of them giving accurate time. Gerhard Paul, the general manager, is reputed to be one of the great hôteliers of Vienna.

Prices include an automatic 15% service charge. Singles cost between 1100 AS ($58.52) and 1700 AS ($90.44), while doubles go from 1700 AS ($90.44) to 2400 AS ($127.68). An extra bed can be set up in any room for an additional 300 AS ($15.96).

Hotel Sacher, 4 Philharmonikerstrasse (tel. 52-55-75). When the Sacher was built in 1876, Vienna, the empire, and the world were all very different places from what they are today. Nevertheless, much of the glory of the Habsburgs is still evoked during a walk through the public salons. The facade is appropriately grand, with enough neoclassical detailing to make a Roman feel at home, a striped awning over the sidewalk café, and flags from seven friendly nations displayed near the caryatids of the second floor.

You might sense an undercurrent of espionage here. Enough novelists have used it in settings for their spy stories to evoke that image, yet despite that, both the crowned heads of Europe and the deposed heads (especially those of Eastern European countries) have dined and lived here.

In addition to intrigue, the Sacher has produced culinary creations that still bear its name. Franz Sacher, the celebrated chef, left the world a fabulously caloric chocolate cake called the Sacher torte, which has appealed to virtually everybody over the years. The late Greta Keller, the famous Viennese chanteuse, recalled in her unpublished memoirs how Madame Sacher once twisted her ear and forced her out of the café when she caught her sipping champagne with an older crowd of opera-goers. Greta was only 12 at the time.

The Sacher, and especially its elegant coffeehouse, are the logical music-lover's choice in Vienna. You'll hear some kind of lilting classical music there in the afternoon, just as you had probably fantasized. All of the interior, by the way, is a rococo splendor. The concierge, for a fee, can probably produce "unobtainable" theater and opera tickets.

The dining hall offers fixed-price meals for between 380 AS ($20.22) and 480 AS ($25.24) (demi-pension), which will be well prepared and impeccably served. Breakfast is included in the room price of 500 AS ($26.20) for a single without bath, between 980 AS ($52.14) and 1400 AS ($74.48) for a single with private bath. A double room with private bath costs from 1700 AS ($90.44) to 2800 AS ($148.96). The reception desk is fairly flexible about making arrangements for salons, apartments, or joining two rooms together, if it is possible to do so.

Palais Schwarzenberg, 9 Schwarzenbergplatz (tel. 78-45-15), is the only hostelry of Vienna with the elite status of having been named *Relais de Campagne.* Set in a 19-acre private park right in the center of town, the hotel is unique, historical, and very, very grand. A walk around the gardens affords landscaped vistas accented with baroque staircases, balustrades ornamenting paths which stretch far away from the castle, and laughing cherubs who cavort with nymphs below arching beeches. The hotel occupies one wing of a baroque palace still owned by Prince Schwarzenberg.

It offers 43 rooms, each with authentic period furniture, many of them with views over the garden, all of them with private baths and telephones. The palace was gutted during the Nazi era but was completely reconstructed after the Soviet occupation of Vienna. Today the same ambience of high ceilings with striated marble, crystal chandeliers, mythical beasts, oval mirrors, and gilt—lots of it—fill the public rooms between painted murals of festive deities.

Pierre Roth, the general manager, supervises the two-level bar, the superb restaurant, the upkeep of the grounds, and the maintenance of the extremely well-furnished rooms. Singles cost between 960 AS ($51.07) and 1350 AS ($71.82) in low season (January 2 through March 6 and October 30 to December 25), while doubles range from 1400 AS ($74.48) to 2200 AS ($117.04). In high season, which is all the rest of the year, singles cost between 1290 AS ($68.63) and 1750 AS ($93.10), and doubles rent for 1750 AS ($93.10) to 3150 AS ($167.58). A continental breakfast is included, and an English breakfast is available for a 110-AS ($5.85) supplement. An extra bed can be set up for an additional 350 AS ($18.62).

Vienna Hilton, Am Stadtpark (tel. 75-26-52), part of the international chain, offers the predictably good service Hilton is known for with a modern format which might come as a familiar relief to you after "olde worlde" Vienna. You'll find it attached to the downtown air terminal building, where the airport bus will deliver you. The hotel, lying just beyond the Ring, offers 622 well-furnished air-conditioned rooms in what is one of the most handsome Hiltons in Europe. In fact, if you like to stay at a Hilton wherever you go, you'll love the Hilton in Vienna.

The Prinz Eugen restaurant competes with the finest dining rooms in this very competitive city. Many Viennese, by the way, like to "go to the Hilton" for a night, ignoring the more time-honored dowagers such as the Sacher and the Imperial. The hotel offers excellent fitness facilities, and since it towers over the city skyline, it affords very good views from the top floors. The Café am Park has a large open terrace where you'll want to have (Viennese) coffee.

Single rooms rent for anywhere from 1090 AS ($57.99) to 1650 AS ($87.78), while doubles range between 1470 AS ($78.20) and 2220 AS ($118.10). Breakfast is extra.

Hotel Intercontinental, 28 Johannesgasse (tel. 7505), rises imposingly in the center of Vienna close to the government buildings. Its facade is almost pure white, with big windows and a rectangular frame that can be recognized from many points within the city. It provides streamlined, deluxe, contemporary comfort, especially to the hundreds of conventioneers who use this as their headquarters. It offers more than 500 well-furnished and well-upholstered rooms, each with private bath and all the accessories you'd expect, as well as a collection of in-house feature films shown on your room's video system. A sauna, solarium, and gym await you, if you ever have time for them in the midst of your sightseeing, as does a bar area that looks like something from a sophisticated inner-city private club. It has been said that this bar, the Intermezzo, has the kind of lighting that makes every woman look attractive. Judging from what I saw of the clientele there, that would be true. Guests often move on to the Four Seasons restaurant. John F. Edmaier is the best general manager they've ever had, making the place sparkle.

Singles cost between 1590 AS ($84.59) and 1790 AS ($95.23), and doubles range between 2080 AS ($110.66) and 2280 AS ($121.30), breakfast included. All accommodations have baths, in-house movie systems, and color TVs, and are newly furnished. The Intercontinental is close to the Hilton, with which it is quite competitive.

Hotel Modul, 78 Peter-Jordan-Strasse (tel. 47-15-84). The architecture for this ultramodern hotel is nothing short of striking, particularly since it sits at the edge of one of Vienna's green areas, the Türkenschanzpark. The facade looks almost like a row of organ pipes in a gigantic cathedral. Different tiers of vertical lines rise parallel to one another in a series of glass, steel, and concrete angles, all of which shimmer under the Austrian sun. Inside you'll find 42 rooms, a trio of apartments, and manager Mario Krofta, who does everything he can to make your stay pleasant. The hotel lies in the suburb of Heurigen. Its bar and restaurant are popular but tranquil.

Singles rent for between 880 AS ($46.82) and 1060 AS ($59.39), and doubles go for 1450 AS ($77.14) to 1820 AS ($96.92), with an extra bed available for an additional 540 AS ($28.73), breakfast included.

THE UPPER BRACKET: Parkhotel Schönbrunn, 10-14 Hietzinger Hauptstrasse (tel. 82-26-76), is called by its owners "the guest house of the kaisers," which is completely true. Emperor Franz Joseph I constructed this edifice in 1907 as a guest house for his diplomatic visitors. Today it's a modern and updated hotel: the original core is still being used as public rooms, but modern wings and annexes house many of today's guests. Inside you'll find a coffeehouse furnished almost entirely in Biedermeier tables and chairs, along with a series of trendy public rooms which may or may not be to your liking. The Jagerstübl is traditionally outfitted in forest colors and white napery. A pool on the premises allows guests to release any leftover tensions from the day of sightseeing. The establishment lies 1½ miles from the West Station, and three miles from the city air terminal.

Singles rent for between 535 AS ($28.46) and 1075 AS ($57.19), while doubles cost from 990 AS ($52.67) to 1980 AS ($105.34), depending on the season. An extra bed is provided for an additional 250 AS ($13.30) to 300 AS ($15.96). Prices from April 1 to October fall into the upper regions of the prices I just listed.

Hotel Romischer Kaiser, 16 Annagasse (tel. 52-77-51), is housed in what is now a baroque national trust building which, like many of us, has seen its share of transformations. It was constructed in 1684 as the private palace of the imperial chancellor but has served both as a military academy and as a *fin-de-siècle* hotel. You'll find slightly more than two dozen romantically decorated rooms (my favorite piece has red satin upholstery over a chaise longue and white and gold paint and plenty of curlicues). In Vienna this is not only acceptable but perfectly charming. A small café on the ground floor will give you an idea of what Vienna must have been like as an imperial capital.

A single room rents for between 800 AS ($42.56) and 900 AS ($47.88) in season, 700 AS ($37.24) and 850 AS ($45.22) off-season; while doubles cost between 550 AS ($29.26) and 700 AS ($37.24) per person in season, 500 AS ($26.60) and 625 AS ($33.25) per person off-season. Every room includes breakfast, bathroom, radio, phone, mini-bar, and color TV.

Hotel König von Ungarn, 10 Schulerstrasse (tel. 52-62-20), is on a narrow street near the cathedral, a choice site. The building is a massive former private residence, painted yellow, with an angled roofline supporting three tiers of tiled gables. The walls date from the 16th century, and a hotel has been on the premises since 1815, with renovations completed in 1977. The interior is filled with interesting architectural details, such as marble columns supporting the arched ceiling of the King of Hungary restaurant, one of the finest in the city, a high-ceilinged mirrored solarium/bar area with a glass roof over the atrium, and a live tree growing out of an opening in the pavement. There are comfortable chairs, Venetian mirrors, and an atmosphere of old Vienna in the tall hinged windows overlooking views of the old town. Everywhere you'll find low-key luxury, old tradition, and modern convenience.

P. Valouch is the manager of the reception desk here. He charges from 800 As ($42.56) to 900 AS ($47.88) in a single, from 1100 AS ($58.52) to 1200 AS ($63.84) in a double. Prices include breakfast.

Hotel Kaiserpark-Schönbrunn, 11 Grunbergstrasse (tel. 83-86-10). Not everyone can walk out his or her front door and stare immediately at Schönbrunn Palace, but if you stay here that's precisely what will happen. This elegant hotel is outfitted with lots of dark paneling, red velvet, and a life-size portrait of some faded Austrian noblewoman in an off-the-shoulder décolletage. The 41 bedrooms are as comfortable as you'd expect from an establishment of this quality. Each of them has a private bath, phone, and radio (TV by request). A public swimming pool in Schönnbrunn Park is only a short walk away. K. Dietrich (no relation to Marlene), the manager, charges between 890 AS ($47.35) and 950 AS ($50.54) in a single, from 1200 AS ($63.84) to 1400 AS ($74.48) in a double. Breakfast is included in the tariffs.

Hotel Tyrol, 15 Mariahilfer Strasse (tel. 57-54-15), is a privately owned hotel which is conveniently located in the center of town near the Imperial Palace. The interior is decorated with a combination of newly installed upholstered chairs and couches with a few select pieces of antique furniture. Each of the up-to-date rooms offers a bath, phone, radio, and TV, and there's a garage in the immediate vicinity. Rates in the soundproof rooms are from 550 AS ($29.26) to 750 AS ($39.90) in a single, from 780 AS ($41.50) to 1080 AS ($57.46) in a double. An extra bed can be set up for an additional 200 AS ($10.64), and half board costs 120 AS ($6.38) per person extra.

Hotel Europa, 3 Neuer Markt (tel. 52115-94). The welcoming parapet of this glass-and-steel hotel extends over the sidewalk almost to the edge of the street. You'll find it midway between the State Opera and the main cathedral, St. Stephen's. It offers 102 comfortable rooms, a Viennese café, and a first-class restaurant, Zum Donnerbrunnen, with evening zither music. The Europa Bar is elegant, dark, and glamorous, particularly since the lighting makes the many vertical lines look almost like the architecture inside a cathedral. Bedrooms are spacious and colorful, with lots of light coming in from the large windows, baths, and air conditioning. Josef Kvasnicka, the manager, charges from 910 AS ($48.41) to 980 AS ($52.14) in a single, from 1260 AS ($67.03) to 1540 AS ($81.93) in a double, depending on the season. A deluxe corner twin-bedded room goes for 1540 AS ($81.93). Half board is available for an additional 240 AS ($12.77) per person per day. Breakfast is included in the price.

Hotel Amadeus, 5 Wildpretmarkt (tel. 63-87-38), is only two minutes away from the cathedral and within walking distance of practically everything else of musical or historical note within the city. Christa Wittenberger, the manager, maintains the 47 beds and the red-carpeted public rooms in tip-top shape. Some of the walls in the reception area are papered over with enlargements of old engravings of the Vienna of young Amadeus Mozart's era. The bedrooms offer peaceful nights, baths, phones, radios, refrigerators, and TV hookups. An elevator will carry you to your room. Singles rent for between 670 AS ($35.64) and 880 AS ($46.82), and doubles cost 1250 AS ($66.50), including breakfast.

Hotel Prinz Eugen, 14 Wiedner Gürtel (tel. 65-17-41), directs a facade of identical soundproof windows with balconies facing toward a residential section of Vienna favored by diplomats. The hotel is immediately opposite Belvedere Palace and the railroad station of Vienna South. Subways will carry you quickly to the downtown section, and there are good highway connections. Specially constructed windows keep out a surprising amount of noise. Inside you'll find a restaurant, a warmly paneled bar, and a series of conference rooms and salons that are often in demand by the local business community. The decor inside is a mixture of traditional pieces, a few antiques, some Oriental rugs, and a few glitzy touches such as glass walls with brass trim, adaptations of crystal chandeliers, and blowups of 18th-century illustrations of everyday life in Austria covering the structural supports in one of the salons. Singles rent for between 865 AS ($46.02) and 975 AS ($51.97), while doubles cost between 1280 AS ($68.10) and 1600 AS ($85.12), breakfast included. An extra bed can be set up in any room for an additional 300 AS ($15.96). Charlotte Ferstl is the director of the Prinz Eugen.

Hotel Bellevue, 5 Althanstrasse (tel. 34-56-31). The sandstone facade of this five-story hotel reminds me a little of the Flatiron Building in Manhattan, as it's set on the acute angle of a street corner one block away from the Franz-Josefs Bahnhof. The Italianate embellishments seem to converge at a point on the fifth floor where the statues of two demigods support the corner of the roofline. Inside, the many renovations have stripped the former detailing, leaving a clean series of lines, often with high ceilings, amid wood paneling and a limited number of antiques. Bedrooms are functionally furnished with low beds, utilitarian desks and chairs, and a few padded armchairs. In high season (the Christmas holidays and from April to the end of October) singles rent for 750 AS ($39.90) and doubles cost 525 AS ($27.93) per person. During the rest of the year singles cost 490 AS ($26.07); doubles, 325 AS ($17.29) per person. Breakfast is included. A sauna inside is for the use of the guests. Heinz Kores is the manager.

Hotel de France, 3 Schottenring (tel. 34-35-40), is an elegantly painted buff and white building with neoclassical trim around its windows and under the eaves. A blue awning stretches above the sidewalk café, which usually does a brisk summertime business because of its location on the Ringstrasse. Inside you'll find a series of restaurants (one of them French), salons, and bars where you'll enjoy relaxing after a day around Vienna. The 150 rooms are priced from 815 AS ($43.36) to 1115 AS ($59.32) in a single, between 1360 AS ($72.35) and 1990 AS ($105.87) in a double. Breakfast costs an additional 80 AS ($4.26), while an extra bed can be set up in any room for another 300 AS ($15.96).

Hotel Erzherzog Rainer, 27-29 Widner Hauptstrasse (tel. 65-46-46), is housed in an old-fashioned building with rows of gently curved bay windows rippling across the facade. It's only five minutes on foot to the Opera House and the Kärntnerstrasse, with a subway stop only a few steps away. The hotel has the ambience of a well-run family business, which is exactly what it is. Peter Nedomansky, the managing director, supervises the polite staff in their duties throughout the 84 well-decorated rooms. You'll find color TV, radio, and phone, and a private bath in all but a few of the cheapest singles. A booking service for opera and theater tickets operates out of the lobby, while Austrian specialties are served in the attractive restaurant, Chez Rainer. A cozy bar is modishly decorated in accents of black and brass, with brown carpeting, orange couches, and friendly service. There are other services offered, too, including ten-hour cleaning on weekdays.

High-season rates are in effect during New Year's and from April to October, inclusive, when singles cost between 685 As ($36.44) and 965 AS ($51.34), and doubles range between 1310 AS ($69.69) and 1470 AS

($78.20). The rest of the year singles are priced between 590 AS ($31.39) and 810 AS ($43.09), while doubles go from 1120 AS ($59.58) to 1260 AS ($67.03), with breakfast included. An extra bed costs 355 AS ($18.87) in high season and 315 AS ($16.76) the rest of the year.

Hotel am Parkring, 12 Parkring (tel. 52-65-24), is a luxurious hotel in the top three floors of a massive, relatively new construction on the edge of Vienna's best known city park. From many of the windows you'll have views of St. Stephen's Cathedral less than a block away and of much of the rest of Vienna laid out at your feet. All of the air-conditioned units have direct-dial phones, mini-bars, and color TVs. The Himmelstube restaurant and the Coffee-Bar give an ambience that's unmistakably Viennese, particularly with the skyline so spread out before you. You'll take an elevator from the streetside private entrance directly to your floor. E. Stockringer is the director of this up-to-date establishment.

Singles cost from 880 AS ($46.82) to 930 AS ($49.48) during high season (from April to October, inclusive) while doubles range between 1100 AS ($58.52) and 1310 AS ($69.69). During low season singles go for between 660 AS ($35.11) and 790 AS ($42.03), and doubles cost between 880 AS ($46.82) and 1060 AS ($56.39), breakfast included. An extra bed can be set up for an additional 280 AS ($14.90).

Hotel Grinzingerberg, 10 Ettingshausengasse (tel. 32-30-51). I am told that the site of this hotel is in the same area where the Turkish army camped during the siege of Vienna in 1683. Today that area is a vineyard-filled suburb called Grinzing, which is three miles from the center of town, at the edge of the Vienna Woods. The hotel operates a shuttle service to downtown for its guests. The hotel has a backyard swimming pool with machines to simulate currents. The exterior is painted yellow, in a format that looks almost like an overgrown private house. Inside you'll find a sauna, solarium, massage facilities, and a fitness room. Singles rent for between 780 AS ($41.50) and 900 AS ($47.88). Doubles cost between 980 AS ($52.14) and 1300 AS ($69.16), while triples are available for between 1150 AS ($61.81) and 1400 AS ($74.48). A generous buffet breakfast is included in the price.

Hotel Maté, 34-36 Ottakringer Strasse (tel. 43-61-33). Many of the ceilings of this dramatically modern hotel are fashioned of handcrafted hardwood planks intricately fastened together for an effect of visual interest. In one of the conference rooms the ceiling looks like an inverted topographical map of some Austrian mountain range, finished in natural wood grains. The rest of the public rooms are fitted with marble floors, comfortable upholstery, and in the case of the bar area, a combination of natural woods which frame magenta and red panels on the walls and ceilings. An indoor swimming pool has been built under a roofline that is shaped into a continuous barrel vault, with cutouts of Polynesian-style fish, potted palms, and rattan furniture. The outside of this hotel has decorative geometric designs on the streamlined facade, and there's a protective parapet big enough to shelter hundreds of persons from the rain.

Singles cost between 690 AS ($36.71) and 870 AS ($46.28) in high season (New Year's and April through October), while doubles range from 920 AS ($48.94) to 1180 AS ($62.78). During low season singles rent for between 600 AS ($31.92) and 700 AS ($37.24), and doubles range from 700 AS ($37.24) to 950 AS ($50.54), breakfast included.

A cheaper annex, at a different address, 22 Bergsteigasse (tel. 42-47-64), charges much less: from 390 AS ($20.75) to 590 AS ($31.39) in a single in high season, from 490 AS ($26.07) to 810 AS ($43.09) in a double. In low season singles cost between 300 AS ($15.96) and 520 AS ($27.66), while doubles are priced between 400 AS ($21.80) and 660 AS ($35.11). Units in the main hotel are clean, comfortable, and well maintained, each with bath, toilet, radio, phone, color TV hookup, and mini-bar.

Hotel Kummer, 71A Mariahilferstrasse (tel. 57-36-95), looks as highly ornamented as any public monument constructed during the height of the empire. Delightfully baroque, painted yellow with white trim, the facade is embellished with just about every architectural adornment you can think of, from Corinthian capitals with what look like acanthus-leaf bases to balustrades shaped like urns to four deities staring down from under the eaves. The public rooms inside, unfortunately, are not as well preserved as the exterior. Someone has replaced the old style with a streamlined modern interior which, while not as delightful as the street side, is very comfortable and perfectly satisfactory in every way. The 110 rooms, within walking distance of the Vienna West train station, are all equipped with bath and soundproof windows. The red-carpeted restaurant and the blue, green, and yellow bar area are attractive places.

Singles rent for between 865 AS ($46.02) and 915 AS ($48.69), while doubles range from 1260 AS ($67.03) to 1470 AS ($78.20), with breakfast included. Gustav Baumgartner is the personable director.

Hotel President, 23 Wallgasse (tel. 57-36-36), was designed with enough angles in the facade to allow each of the bedrooms to have an irregular shape, usually with two windows in each unit, both facing toward different skylines. The facade is white and bronze, and there's a rooftop terrace where many guests sit sipping drinks for hours in summertime, separated from the old buildings of old Vienna by an eight-story dropoff and a barrier of luxuriant green plants. Aside from the views, each of the bedrooms has a complete bath, comfortable furnishings, phone, radio, TV, air conditioning, mini-bar, and mini-safe. The Restaurant Casserole serves Viennese and international cuisine in a pleasingly informal setting every night till 11. S. Seyrling, the manager, charges 890 AS ($47.35) in a single and 1340 AS ($71.29) in a double, breakfast included. Apartments for two persons are available for 1540 AS ($81.93).

Hotel Royal, 3 Singerstrasse (tel. 52-46-31), is on one of the more prestigious streets of the old city. The outside presents a restrained dignity to the older buildings around it. The hotel lies less than a block from St. Stephen's Cathedral, on a pedestrian walkway which assures quiet evenings. Each of the 66 rooms is differently furnished, with some good reproductions of antiques and even an occasional original. The entire facility was built in 1960 and rebuilt in 1982. All units today have private baths, radios, TVs, and room service if you want it. Singles rent for 950 AS ($50.54), and doubles cost between 950 AS ($50.54) and 1300 AS ($69.16). Breakfast is included in this price, and an extra bed can be set up for an additional 250 AS ($13.30).

THE MODERATE RANGE: **Hotel Kaiserin Elisabeth,** 3 Weihburggasse (tel. 52-26-26), is perfectly located, a few blocks from the cathedral. The first thing you might notice about the interior is the surprising number of beautiful Oriental rugs, lying on top of well-maintained marble or wood floors. The main salon has a pale-blue skylight suspended above it, with mirrors and half-columns in natural wood. If you should select one of the hotel's rooms, you'll be interested to know that Richard Wagner, Franz Liszt, and Edvard Grieg all spent at least one night here. The rooms have been considerably updated since then, and although some parts of the building date from the 14th century, what you're likely to see in your private space is an up-to-date decor of polished wood, clean linen, and perhaps another Oriental rug. In the breakfast room you'll see a portrait of the Empress Maria Theresa above the fireplace. Singles rent for 340 AS ($18.09) to 430 AS ($22.88) without private bath; with private bath they cost from 680 AS ($36.18) to 770 AS ($40.96). Doubles with bath cost between 900 AS ($47.88) and 1200 AS ($63.84), including breakfast.

Ring Hotel, 1 Maria am Gestade (tel. 63-77-01). You'll notice this 15th-century structure on the Concordiaplatz, at the bottom of a flight of steps leading up to one of Vienna's older churches. In summer many of the hinged windows will be opened outward toward the square, which becomes restfully quiet every night. This hotel is a real discovery, offering rooms with bath and attractive and unusual furnishings in high season, April to October, for between 600 AS ($31.92) and 650 AS ($34.58) in a single, for 880 AS ($46.82) to 950 AS ($50.54) in a double. In low season singles rent for between 580 AS ($30.87) and 600 AS ($31.92), while doubles range from 770 AS ($40.96) to 880 AS ($46.82). Breakfast, included in the price, is taken in a vaulted breakfast room. There are many features about this place that you'd love to take home with you, including the wrought-iron lighting fixtures in the breakfast room and many of the decorative objects hanging on the walls. This is one of the best establishments in its category for value.

Hotel Mailbergerhof, 7 Annagasse (tel. 52-06-41). If you're friendly with any actors or musicians who have ever played in Vienna, chances are they stayed here, or at least had a drink in the interior courtyard. This hotel originated in the 15th century as two separate burgher's houses, which were later joined together to form the local headquarters for the Knights of Malta, the Hospitaliers. After seeing many changes, the building has been adapted as a hotel and restaurant, opening its doors to business in 1976. The 40 rooms are only a five-minute walk to either the opera or the cathedral. Each of the rooms has a private bath, color TV, radio, mini-bar, and direct-dial telephone. Accommodations are surprisingly spacious. The reception hall is tasteful, with big windows and walls covered with a refreshing green. The restaurant serves international as well as Greek specialties. Single rooms cost between 950 AS ($50.54) and 1050 AS ($55.86), and doubles rent for 1500 AS ($79.80), breakfast included.

Hotel am Stephansplatz, 9 Stephansplatz (tel. 63-56-05). You'll walk out of your door and face the front entrance to Vienna's cathedral if you stay in this 66-room hotel, with its unadorned, rather banal facade. The public rooms are done in a lukewarm mixture of modern and "traditional," with some of the bedrooms furnished with painted reproductions of rococo furniture and red-flocked wallpaper. A coffeehouse with a sidewalk café fills part of the ground floor. Maria Engelmann, the proprietor, charges 420 AS ($22.34) for a bathless single, from 690 AS ($36.71) to 790 AS ($42.03) in a single with bath or shower. Doubles cost between 895 AS ($47.61) and 1140 AS ($60.65), breakfast included. An extra bed will be provided for between 240 AS ($12.77) and 360 AS ($19.15).

Hotel Opernring, 11 Opernring (tel. 57-55-18), is a European branch of the Best Western hotel chain. It sits on the Ringstrasse, directly opposite the State Opera House. The hotel is comfortably furnished, with up-to-date furniture, such as reclining upholstered armchairs on chrome bases, wall-to-wall carpeting, and subtly patterned draperies. Aside from the decor, however, you'll quickly find that the efforts of the owner, Mrs. Susie

Riedl, more than justify this as a choice for your stay in Vienna. If you write to her far enough in advance, she will forward the schedule for both of the Vienna Opera companies, and even arrange for ticket purchases for guests who live in foreign countries. Aside from her musical skills, and her gift for wheeling and dealing, she proves to be helpful in every way.

Singles cost 90 AS ($50.54), while doubles range from 1280 AS ($68.10) to 1680 AS ($89.38). Triples are tabbed at 1680 AS ($89.38). Rates include breakfast. Between November 1 and Christmas the tariffs drop to 880 AS ($46.82) in a single, to between 980 AS ($52.14) and 1280 AS ($68.10) in a double, and to 1280 AS ($68.10) in a triple.

Hotel Albatros, 89 Liechtensteinstrasse (tel. 34-35-08), lies close to the U.S. Embassy and the Franz-Josefs Bahnhof, some distance to the north of the Rathaus. If any reader associates an albatross with bad luck, you'll need to change your thinking about this one. The clean and comfortable bedrooms are cheerfully decorated, clean, and well furnished. Singles rent for 750 AS ($39.90), doubles for between 950 AS ($50.54) and 1150 AS ($61.18), and a generous breakfast is included in the price.

Hotel Austria, 3 Wolfengasse (tel. 52-74-39). The staff of this friendly hotel always seems willing to tell you where to go in the neighborhood for a good meal or a glass of wine, and often distributes carefully typed letters explaining the medieval origins of this part of Vienna. This unpretentious family-owned establishment (Karl and Amalie Korger are the owners) sits on a small street whose name will probably be unfamiliar to many taxi drivers, although a corner building on the adjoining street, 20 Fleischmarkt, is the point where you'll turn into the narrow lane. Manager Walter Koschler maintains the comfortable furnishings in the lobby and in the chandeliered breakfast room in tip-top condition.

Single rooms without bath cost between 440 AS ($23.41) and 470 AS ($25), and singles with bath range from 660 AS ($35.11) to 700 AS ($37.24). Doubles cost between 640 AS ($34.05) and 670 AS ($35.64) without bath, from 980 AS ($52.14) to 1050 AS ($55.86) with bath, breakfast included. To reach this hotel from the Westbahnhof, take the stadtbahn, getting off at the Schwedenplatz. If you're coming from the Südbahnhof, take tram D from the Ring, then change to tram no. 1 or no. 2, and again get off at the Schwedenplatz.

Hotel Wandl, 9 Petersplatz (tel. 63-63-17). Stepping into this hotel is like stepping into a piece of another family's history since it's been in the same ownership for generations. The establishment lies quietly in the inner city and offers views of the steeple of St. Stephen's Cathedral from many of its windows, which often open onto small balconies with railings. The breakfast room is a high-ceilinged two-toned room with hanging chandeliers and lots of ornamented plaster, while the bedrooms usually offer the kind of spacious dimensions that went out of style 60 years ago. The hotel faces St. Peter's Church, in a section of Vienna you'll probably find attractive. Bathless singles cost 320 AS ($17.02), while singles with bath range between 430 AS ($22.88) and 500 AS ($26.60). Doubles cost 550 AS ($29.26) without bath, from 730 AS ($38.84) to 820 AS ($43.62) with bath. Breakfast is included. Some apartments for longer stays are offered.

Hotel Wimberger, 34-36 Neubaugürtel (tel. 93-76-36). The decorator of this 100-year-old hotel had both a good sense of color and a good sense of humor. The bedrooms are decorated in a tastefully lighthearted combination of colors that is never garish and usually a lot of fun, from the pink-tile bathrooms to the panoply of colors and designs in the well-appointed bedrooms. Even the dining room, while more subdued than the rest of the hotel, is tasteful and makes a positive statement in pure white, cream, and blue-gray. Rudolf Wimberger is today's conscientious owner of the palatial 19th-century property across the street from the Westbahnhof. On the premises you'll find an old-fashioned coffeeshop and a restaurant whose marble floor is arranged in rectangles of black and white reflecting the light from the oversize windows. Without bath, singles cost 315 AS ($16.76); doubles, 525 AS ($27.93). With private bath, singles rent for 525 AS ($27.93) and doubles for 755 AS ($40.17).

Hotel Stephanie, 12 Taborstrasse (tel. 24-24-12), is an updated hotel across the Danube Canal from the cathedral, in an area easily accessible to the rest of the city. The interior is newly appointed with royal blue or baroquely patterned green and yellow wall-to-wall carpeting, beautifully finished wall paneling in geometric designs, and gilded wall sconces. Although upon closer examination much of the decor is reproduction, the hotel still gives a hint of the rococo splendor of 19th-century Vienna. A bar area is filled with black leather armchairs on chrome swivel bases and mysteriously concealed lighting that throws an azure glow over the artfully displayed rows of bottles. All rooms have baths. During high season, April through October, singles cost from 880 AS ($46.82) to 930 AS ($49.48), and doubles from 1100 AS ($58.52) to 1310 AS ($69.69). In low season singles rent from 620 AS ($32.98) to 680 AS ($36.18), while doubles range between 760 AS ($40.43) and 840 AS ($44.69), breakfast included.

Hotel Post, 24 Fleischmarkt (tel. 52-66-87), lies in what was the slaughterhouse district in the Middle Ages and what is today an interesting section full of hotels and restaurants. The front of this hotel is constructed with a restrained dignity of gray stone with a facade of black marble covering the street level. The manager is quick to tell you that both Mozart and Haydn frequently stayed in a former inn at this address. Those composers would probably be amused to hear recordings of their music played in the coffeehouse/restaurant attached to the hotel. About half of the 105 rooms have private baths.

During high season, April through October, singles cost 560 AS ($29.79) with private bath, between 270 AS ($14.36) and 330 AS ($17.56) without. Bathless doubles range from 250 AS ($13.30) to 290 AS ($15.43) per person, and doubles with bath go for between 370 AS ($19.68) and 440 AS ($23.41) per person. In low season singles cost 490 AS ($26.07) with bath, between 240 AS ($12.77) and 280 AS ($14.90) without. Doubles rent from 315 AS ($16.76) to 380 AS ($20.22) per person with bath, between 220 AS ($11.70) and 265 AS ($14.10) per person without private bath. Breakfast is included in all room rates.

Hotel Kärntnerhof, 4 Grashofgasse (tel. 52-19-23), advertises itself as a gutbürgerlich family-oriented hotel, which, depending on your tastes, might suit you perfectly. The decor of the public rooms is tastefully arranged around red and blue Oriental rugs, well-upholstered chairs and couches with cambriole legs, and an occasional 19th-century portrait. The bedrooms are more up-to-date, usually with the original parquet floors and striped or patterned wallpaper set off by geometrically colored curtains. Many of the private baths glisten with recently tiled walls and floors. The owner of this pleasant hotel is Josef Huber, who supervises the maintenance of the 42 rooms and does what he can to be helpful, directing guests to the post office and other nearby Vienna landmarks.

Singles with and without bath cost 420 AS ($22.34) and 620 AS ($32.98) respectively. Doubles go for 630 AS ($33.52) without bath, 850 AS ($45.22) with shower, and 960 AS ($64.90) with bath. Triples and quads are available in an apartment-like format for 1220 AS ($64.90) and 1550 AS ($82.46) respectively. The cathedral, by the way, is only a four-minute walk from here.

Hotel Graben, 3 Dorotheergasse (tel. 52-15-31). Elegant is the only word I'd use to describe the facade of this inner-city hotel which housed, among other great names, Franz Kafka. The establishment lies on the Graben (which, if you don't know already, leads into the St. Stephansplatz) in a district loaded with antique dealers and on a street which insists on pedestrians only during most of the day. The hotel is graced with such architectural ornaments as carved marble fireplaces, Oriental rugs, and gilded chandeliers. In addition to the period antiques, you'll find a lot of art nouveau gracefully decorating the 46 bedrooms, half of which are equipped with baths. The rest of them have radios and telephones, and rent for 590 AS ($31.39) in a bathless single, for between 700 AS ($37.24) and 850 AS ($45.22) in a single with bath. The doubles, upon which great care has been taken by management to decorate either in art nouveau or reproduction period antiques, cost between 980 AS ($52.14) and 1080 AS ($57.46), depending on the type of bed you prefer, double or twin. Breakfast is included in the price.

Hotel Regina, 15 Rooseveltplatz (tel. 42-76-81), was established in 1896 in a format which every Viennese would instantly recognize, the "Ringstrasse" style. The facade is appropriately grand for its neighborhood, close to the Votive Church, and looks a lot like a Renaissance French palace. The tree-lined street is usually calm and quiet, especially at night, when you'll have ample opportunity to explore the red salons and the interminable corridors of this old-world hotel. Singles rent for 360 AS ($19.15) to 850 AS ($45.22), depending on the wide range of plumbing options available, while doubles cost anywhere from 880 AS ($46.82) to 1500 AS ($79.80), with an extra bed going for 250 AS ($13.30), including breakfast.

Hotel Savoy, 12 Lindengasse (tel. 93-46-46). You'll find a hotel called "the Savoy" in many European capitals, and this one is perfectly satisfactory and worthy of bearing that illustrious name. Built within walking distance of the Ringstrasse, the hotel is centered in one of Vienna's principal shopping districts known both for wholesale and retail purchases. Each of the 45 rooms is tastefully and colorfully decorated in a low-key ambience guaranteed to make you feel at home, using such cosmetic touches as the kind of ruffled bedspreads you grew up with, along with big-windowed views of a city very far from home. Each bedroom has its own private bath, as well as radio and TV (both available upon request). Garages and streetcar and bus stops are all to be found in the immediate vicinity. Singles cost 730 AS ($38.84), and doubles rent for 1060 AS ($56.39), including breakfast.

Hotel Zur Rossmühle, 12 Hauptplatz (tel. 2411), in the Vienna suburb of Tulln an der Donau, is housed in a yellow building with white trim, standing on the central square of this quiet and historic village 30 minutes from the heart of Vienna. The entrance is under a rounded arch protected with a wrought-iron gate. The interior is an attractive combination of antique furniture and crystal chandeliers in a setting which has been modernized into a well-maintained series of white stucco walls and dramatically structured floor space. The 56 bedrooms are decorated in a streamlined baroque style, with simple furniture occasionally highlighted with accents of gilt and white. Singles cost 460 AS ($24.47), while doubles rent for 350 AS ($18.62) per person daily. Half board is available for another 115 AS ($6.12) per person daily.

SOME BUDGET HOTELS: Hotel Goldene Spinne, 1a Linke Bahngasse (tel. 72-44-86), is a low-key hostelry near the city air terminal, managed by a friendly, English-speaking staff who indicate to clients where most of the monuments are within the vicinity of this inner-city location. Of its 42 units, only about a dozen contain private baths, which is not really a hardship considering the convenient placement of facilities in the halls near most of the rooms. Theophil Böck, the manager, maintains the corner building with charm. Bathless singles rent for 264 AS ($14.05), while singles with private bath cost between 345 AS ($18.35) and 380 AS ($20.22). Bathless doubles go for 490 AS ($26.07); with private bath, between 590 AS ($42.03) and 640 AS ($34.05). Triples, ideal for families, cost 710 AS ($37.77). Breakfast is included in the tariffs.

Hotel Schweizerhof, 22 Bauernmarkt (tel. 63-19-31). You'll probably stop to admire the elaborately baroque facade of this family-run hotel even if you don't plan on staying inside, but after meeting Johann Ungersböck, the pleasant manager, you'll probably choose to make this your headquarters in Vienna. To cross into the lobby, you'll walk beneath the statues of two heroic figures which strain to support the balcony above their heads. Inside you'll find clean and comfortable rooms and an elevator, and you'll discover that the Schweizerhof is convenient to most of the inner-city monuments. All rooms have private bath or shower, and rent for between 700 AS ($37.24) and 750 AS ($39.90) in a double, for 480 AS ($25.54) in a single, breakfast included.

Hotel Graf Stadion, 5 Buchfeldgasse (tel. 42-52-84), is a modestly priced hotel immediately behind the Rathaus, within a ten-minute walk from most of the downtown monuments. The facade gives a hint at this building's former elegance, particularly with the triangular or half-round ornamentation above many of the windows. Prices for the accommodations without private bath are: 250 AS ($13.30) in a single, and on a per-person basis, 220 AS ($11.70) in a double, 185 AS ($9.84) in a triple, and 175 AS ($9.31) in a quad. With private shower, singles cost 300 AS ($15.96), while doubles, triples, and quads, respectively on a per-person basis go for 250 AS ($13.30), 200 AS ($10.64), and 190 AS ($10.11). Breakfast is included in all tariffs.

Hotel Rathaus, 13 Lange Gasse (tel. 43-43-02). You'll enter the Rathaus through a wrought-iron gate, which leads you to an elevator requiring some small change for the operator, who will take you up to the hotel reception area. The corridors are attractively tiled and decorated in a functional style, as are the approximately 32 bedrooms you'll find scattered over four different floors. Half of these have private baths or toilets. Without bath, singles rent for 280 AS ($14.90), doubles for 480 AS ($25.54). With shower and toilet, singles cost 360 AS ($19.15); doubles, 600 AS ($31.92). An additional bed can transform any double into a triple for an extra 140 AS ($7.45). Breakfast is included. You'll find this to be basically a no-frills, no-nonsense type of establishment, but because it's so well-situated near the university and the Parliament, and because its prices are so reasonable, I feel it's a worthy choice.

Hotel Cottage, 12 Hasenauerstrasse (tel. 31-25-71), is in a residential part of Vienna, near the Türkenschanzpark, about a 20-minute tram ride from the heart of Vienna (take tram no. 38). This establishment is more or less like a little pension, run by Christa Reisenhofer, who charges from 650 AS ($34.58) to 850 AS ($45.22) for a single and 1100 AS ($58.52) to 1300 AS ($69.16) for a double, breakfast included. All bedrooms have bath or shower. If being in Vienna inspires you to practice your music, you'll find a grand piano in the tiny dining room.

Hotel Wolf, 10 Strossigasse (tel. 42-23-20), represents what I think is a very good hotel bargain not far from the Parliament house. You'll be only a five- to ten-minute walk from the inner city, with tram and bus stops on the street corner near the front door. The hotel charges 220 AS ($11.70) per person per day in rooms without private bath, breakfast included. The showers in the hallways are free.

Hotel Schweiger, 4 Schikanedergasse (tel. 56-42-15), is a four-minute walk south from the southern edge of the Ring, in an imposingly proportioned stone building with garlands of what look like laurel leaves carved into the facade. The bedrooms are clean, often with parquet floors, and contain functional furniture and private bathrooms. Singles cost 391 AS ($20.80) per day, while doubles rent for 651 AS ($34.63) per day, breakfast included. L. Bitterman is the English-speaking manager.

Hotel Academia, 3a Pfeilgasse (tel. 42-25-34), along with three others, has connections to the university system of Vienna. During term they're filled with scholars who live in comfortably appointed modern rooms, all with private bath. The authorities turn these buildings into hotels every summer between July 1 and September 30, so that reasonably priced lodgings can be available during the annual influx of tourists into Vienna. These hotels are one of the best bargains in town, especially since all of them are close to the university, very up-to-date, and only five minutes by streetcar no. 46 from the opera. The institutional-looking facade may evoke memories of your own college days, but you'll find the price right.

At the main 672-bed hotel, the Academia, singles cost 495 AS ($26.33), doubles go for 320 AS ($17.02) per person, and triples are charged 260 AS ($13.83) per person, with breakfast. It is here, by the way, that visitors present themselves for room rentals in the other three hotels, all of which are nearby. Among those three, the cheapest charges 380 AS ($20.22) in a single, 250 AS ($13.30) per person in a double, and 195 AS ($10.37) in a triple. At all these hotels, full- and half-board plans are available for 290 AS ($15.43) and 145 AS ($7.71) respectively. The names of the other hotels in the system are the Avis, the Aquila, and the Atlas.

Hotel-Pension Museum, 3 Museumstrasse (tel. 93-44-26). The exquisite facade of this art nouveau hotel must have been the ultimate in Viennese chic when it was first constructed across from the Imperial Museums. Enough palaces, museums, and monuments are within a five-minute walk to keep any visitor occupied for several days of sightseeing. You'll appreciate the spacious proportions inside many of the bedrooms, some of which echo they're so big—especially the ones in front on the lower floors. With private bath and toilet, and breakfast, singles cost 450 AS ($23.94) a night, doubles going for 860 AS ($45.75).

Hotel Pension Schneider, 5 Getreidemarkt (tel. 57-76-04), sits at the corner of a well-known street, the Lehargasse. The hotel is a recently constructed five-story building with panoramic windows on the ground floor and a red-tile roof; the facade is painted a baroque yellow with vertical white stripes. The interior is warmly and imaginatively decorated with well-polished 19th-century antiques and comfortably upholstered chairs, many of them chosen by owner Leopoldine Pölzl, who seems especially willing to welcome musicians from around the world. This is one of Vienna's better pensions, situated near the flower market. Singles with private bath rent for 700 AS ($37.24); doubles with private bath cost 990 AS ($52.67). Breakfast is included.

Europahaus, 429 Linzer Strasse (tel. 97-25-38). The modern annex of this baroque palace from the 17th century is used to house students in the wintertime, but when they leave for the summer the building converts to a hotel. In a large park with many mature, large trees, the site is frequently used for conventions and corporate meetings. The best feature is the price, which makes the 35-minute commute to city center worthwhile. Take tram no. 49 from the central Vienna tram station (Ring-Bellaria) to the end of the line, which is called Hütteldorf, and note that the last tram leaves at midnight. The rooms are clean and streamlined in the dormitory style you'd expect, although each has a private bath. Singles cost 285 AS ($15.16), while doubles rent for 220 AS ($11.70) per person, with breakfast. Eduard Kustrich is the director.

THE BEST OF THE PENSIONS: **Hotel-Pension Elite,** 32 Wipplingerstrasse (tel. 63-25-18), is housed in a magnificent corner building next to the Vienna stock exchange. The neighborhood is appropriately grand for this edifice which looks like a former private palace. You'll be near the university, the Burgtheatre, and the cathedral. The public rooms are tastefully furnished with a mixture of antiques and modern pieces, crystal chandeliers, lots of well-oiled paneling, green-tile fireplaces, and Oriental rugs. The establishment lives up to its name and deserves a high recommendation for good service in a refined framework. Without private shower or bath, singles cost from 450 AS ($23.94) to 600 AS ($31.92); doubles range from 700 AS ($37.24) to 900 AS ($47.88). Breakfast, which is included in the rates, is served in the elegantly upholstered and carpeted dining room. Mrs. Ida Lasar is the proprietor.

Hotel-Pension Arenberg, 2 Stubenring (tel. 52-52-91), is an old-world pension in the most prestigious section of downtown Vienna, on the Ringstrasse near all the museums and palaces, three minutes away from the air terminal and close to the canal. Rooms are soundproof and often contain Oriental rugs, interesting art, and good furniture. The entire establishment boasts only 25 rooms, with room service available during the dinner hour only. A restaurant and a disco are housed in the same building. All units have bath or shower, and cost from 490 AS ($26.07) to 530 AS ($28.20) in a single, from 780 AS ($41.50) to 820 AS ($43.62) in a double during low season. In high season, April through October and during the Christmas holidays, the charges are 580 AS ($30.87) to 660 AS ($35.11) in a single, 920 AS ($48.94) to 1060 AS ($56.39) in a double. An extra bed can be set up for an additional 240 AS ($12.77).

Pension Sacher, 1 Rotenturmstrasse (tel. 63-32-38 between 8 a.m. and 1 p.m., 46-97-693 after 4 p.m.). Although this extremely well-run hostelry has no relation to the famous hotel with the same name, the regular clients who return here year after year consider the pension's location on the Stephansplatz to be an even better address than that of the hotel. This establishment is usually very heavily booked, so it would pay to write ahead for reservations. The pension consists of eight apartments, four of them with sitting rooms and couches which could sleep a third person. All the units have private bathrooms and kitchenettes, and are serviced every day by the chambermaid. Singles rent for 470 AS ($25), doubles for between 570 AS ($30.32) and 745 AS ($39.63), with extra charges of approximately 40 AS ($2.13) to 65 AS ($3.46) per day for heat during the cold months, beginning October 1. Rates are reduced by approximately 20% for stays of more than nine days. Carl Sacher, the owner/overseer, frequently reserves his apartments up to nine months in advance. The pension is on the seventh floor of the building.

Pension Wiener, 16 Seilergasse (tel. 52-48-160). Mr. and Mrs. Thau-Ohg sold their Hotel de France a few years ago to open this tiny pension, which is in an office building in a downtown section two blocks from the cathedral. You're made to feel like a guest in a private home at this friendly, tranquil oasis with plenty of up-to-date conveniences and old-fashioned hospitality. The 30 beds are in units with private baths, radios, TVs, phones, and refrigerators. From April till October a single rents for between 650 AS ($34.58) and 690 AS ($36.71), while doubles cost 950 AS ($50.54), with breakfast served in your room.

Hotel Goldenes Einhorn, 5 Am Hundsturm (tel. 55-47-55). Much of the flavor of old Austria can be gleaned from a visit to this family-run guest house in a residential area between the cathedral and Schönbrunn Palace. The staff speaks four languages (including English), and welcomes visitors into a kind of old Vienna ambience they work hard to sustain. The reasonably priced rooms are highly recommended as a good and safe location in downtown Vienna. A bathless single goes for 205 AS ($10.91), and a double costs 410 AS ($21.81) with shower, 380 AS ($20.22) without. Breakfast is not included in the price, although guests will be directed to a nearby inexpensive coffeeshop where good Viennese morning meals are served.

Pension Pestalozzi, 3 Pestalozzigasse (tel. 72-15-51). The clients of this apartment hotel close to the Musikverein and the Konzerthaus benefit from an extremely quiet accommodation in a residential area. The highly ornamented facade conceals an updated interior decorated in pleasing shades of autumnal colors, with flame-red accents in many of the bedrooms. Barbara Bican, the attractive director, takes a great interest in developments at the Spanish Riding School. Without private bath, singles go for between 450 AS ($23.94) and 600 AS ($31.92), and doubles cost 700 AS ($37.24). With bath or shower, singles range between 650 AS ($34.58) and 1250 AS ($66.50), and doubles cost from 750 AS ($39.90) to 1300 AS ($69.16). Breakfast is included in the price.

Pension-Reimer, 18 Kirchengasse (tel. 93-61-62). Frau Margarethe Mattis is one of the best reasons to choose this attractive family-run guest house near the Mariahilfer Church. To get there, you can take tram no. 52 or 58 from the Westbahnhof or bus no. 13 if you're coming from the Südbahnhof. The interior is crafted in a reproduction rustic style, with a modicum of circa-1950 furniture. The welcome given by the management is worth many of the drawbacks, however, and the price is certainly reason in itself for taking a second look. Singles without private bath cost 190 AS ($10.11), bathless doubles rent for 160 AS ($8.51) per person, and a triple room with shower goes for 200 AS ($10.64) per person. Breakfast is not included in the price but will be served for an additional 40 AS ($2.13) per person. Frau Mattis can find you a babysitter if you need one, and she allows her guests the use of a kitchen if they want it.

Pension Nossek, 17 Graben (tel. 52-45-91), is a friendly guest house in an antique building, although the interior has been renovated. The English-speaking owners, Hans and Hilda Rakowitz, offer pleasantly furnished rooms, some of them bathless singles, and a few large double rooms, charging 280 AS ($14.90) in a bathless single, 490 AS ($26.07) in a bathless double, and from 560 AS ($29.79) to 700 AS ($37.24) in a double with bath, breakfast included. A baroque-style lounge allows clients the chance to meet other guests, while a restaurant with about a dozen tables serves satisfactory meals. The hotel occupies the second, third, and fourth floors of the building, so you'll have to go up in an elevator to get there. Front-door keys are provided to all guests, as the reception desk closes early every night.

Pension Neuer Markt, 9 Seilergasse (tel. 52-23-16), is a hotel offering no single rooms, although some of the doubles are cheap enough to serve as a single if your budget allows it. The hotel is housed in a white baroque building with an interesting elliptical facade facing a square with an ornate fountain, near the cathedral. The rooms are clean and well maintained in an updated motif of colorful carpeting, white walls, and vibrant color accents. Some of the beds are set into niches, and many of the windows are bigger than you'd expect. All units have baths, phones, and central heating. Doubles rent for between 580 AS ($30.87) and 880 AS ($46.82), while triples cost 1130 AS ($60.12), breakfast included.

Kellner's Altwienerhof, 6 Herklotzgasse (tel. 83-71-45). On foggy winter nights the amber carriage lights on the facade of this corner building almost seem to call out to the guests who eventually discover the old-world charm served here by the carload. The same family has managed this establishment for many years, welcoming visitors to the high-ceilinged reception area with the polished wood detailing and the wrought-iron space dividers. The rooms are comfortably furnished, each one different, usually with padded chairs and vibrant colors. Singles with bath cost 390 AS ($20.75) per day, while doubles with bath rent for 620 AS ($32.98), breakfast included.

Pension Dr. Geissler, 14 Postgasse (tel. 63-28-03), is an attractively informal guest house offering unpretentious lodgings at reasonable prices to visitors who will find themselves near the well-known Schwedenplatz at the edge of the Danube Canal. The bedrooms are attractively furnished with simple blond headboards, colorful draperies, and a few chairs. Singles with bath or doubles without bath rent for 550 AS ($29.26). A double with bath ranges between 650 AS ($34.58) and 800 AS ($42.56). A bathless single costs 450 AS ($23.94). These prices include breakfast.

Pension Zipser, 49 Lange Gasse (tel. 42-02-28), is attractively situated within a five-minute walk of the Rathaus. It offers 50 rooms—many overlooking a private garden—which are reached by the elevator. They have phones, wall-to-wall carpeting, and central heating, and are efficiently managed by the Austerer family. The facade is ornamented with skillfully carved shell motifs above the third floor. Much of the renovated interior is tastefully adorned with wood detailing. Without bath, singles cost 280 AS ($14.90); doubles, 510 AS ($27.13). With bath, singles go for 350 AS ($18.62); doubles, 66 AS ($35.11); and triples, 700 AS ($37.24). Breakfast is included in all the tariffs.

Pension Bellaria, 41 Kirchengasse (tel. 93-63-81). Constructed around 1910, this small pension offers comfortable single, double, and triple rooms to guests who appreciate its central location. Without private bath, singles rent for 250 AS ($13.30) and doubles for 185 AS ($9.84) per person. With private bath, singles cost 350 AS ($18.62); doubles, 285 AS ($15.16) per person; triples, 230 AS ($12.24) per person; and quads, 200 AS ($10.64) per person. Breakfast is not included in these prices but can be obtained for an additional 30 AS ($1.60) per person.

Pension Barich, 3 Barichgasse (tel. 72-12-73), might be the choice for guests who prefer quiet residential surroundings. Northeast of the Südbahnhof (train station), near the route going toward the airport, the pension offers clean, colorful, and comfortable rooms for 560 AS ($29.79) in a single, for between 800 AS ($46.82) and 880 AS ($46.82) in a double, and for 950 AS ($50.54) in a triple. All units have private bath, plus enough space to unpack in, and prices include breakfast.

Hotel Hohe Warte, 7 Steinfeldgasse (tel. 37-31-28). Tram. no. 37 runs here from downtown Vienna (get off at the last stop), along a route that you'll find to be a pleasant ride in and of itself. The setting here is attractively rural, especially those accommodations with a view of the garden. The hotel is well run by Hans Weinwurm and his family, who treat it like a large country house. Bathless singles rent for 390 AS ($20.75), while bathless doubles cost 590 AS ($31.39). Singles with bath go for 650 AS ($34.58), and doubles with bath range between 790 AS ($42.03) and 840 AS ($44.69). Breakfast is included.

2. Where to Dine

What you'll find in Vienna are restaurants of all types, serving not only the Austrian cuisine, but that of Yugoslavia, Hungary, and Czechoslovakia as well.

There are also many classic dishes of the *Wiener kuche* (Viennese kitchen) that you'll want to try. Before dining out, refer to the notes on Austrian cookery in Chapter II under "Food and Drink."

THE UPPER BRACKET: **Sacher Hotel Restaurant,** 4 Philharmonikerstrasse (tel. 52-55-75), is a famous, famous restaurant, serving the epitome of Viennese cookery. Long an enduring favorite—either before or after the opera—it has many detractors, but I'm not one of them. Seemingly all celebrities who come to Vienna eventually are seen in the red dining room, where they're likely to order the restaurant's most famous dish, tafelspitz, the Viennese boiled beef platter that was fit for an emperor. The chef serves it with a savory, herb-flavored sauce. Of course that emperor was not Franz Joseph I. Madame Sacher annoyed him by encouraging liaisons between archdukes and the attractive young members of the Vienna Opera Ballet.

Wear your finest for dinner here, and make sure you show up before 11 p.m. Count on spending about 600 AS ($31.92) for a sumptuous meal. Waiters will often suggest various Austrian wines to accompany your dinner. For dessert, the Sacher torte enjoys world renown. Some people claim that the torte was invented by the cigar-smoking owner of the hotel, Frau Anna Sacher. However, it is said to have been created in 1832 by Franz Sacher, while he served as Prince Metternich's chef. The Sacher torte is the most famous pastry in Vienna. It's primarily a chocolate sponge mixture. After it's baked, it's sliced in half and filled with apricot jam.

Zu den 3 Husaren, 4 Weihburggasse (tel. 52-11-92), is an enduring favorite among Viennese restaurants. Some consider it as much an institution as St. Stephen's Cathedral. Few social or business leaders would consider a trip to Vienna without a dinner here. Over the years, it has entertained the famous (the Duke and Duchess of Windsor) and the infamous. Just off the kärntnerstrasse, it has a large plate-glass window with plaster mannequins of the Hungarian officers who established the place after World War I. An interior view reveals Gobelin tapestries, valuable antiques, fine rugs, and masses of flowers.

The establishment is very expensive and very select, with a delectable cuisine that has been rated by practically everyone as the best traditional food in Vienna. To the background music of gypsy melodies, you dine on such dishes as lobster cream soup with tarragon, stewed rumpsteak with white cabbage and noodles, freshwater salmon with pike soufflé, breast of guinea fowl, and an array of sole dishes. The chef specializes in veal, including his deliciously flavored kalsbrücken Metternich. The place is celebrated for its repertoire of more than 40 hors d'oeuvres, which are served on a trolley rolled through its elegant precincts. A desert specialty is the Husaren pfannkuchen (Hussar's pancake), as well as a form of cheese-filled crêpe which, as if that weren't enough, has a chocolate sauce poured over it (the recipe is known only to the chef). The restaurant serves dinner nightly from 6. It's often closed for a month in parts of July and August, and also shuts down on Sunday. A la carte meals range from 300 AS ($15.96) to 600 AS ($31.92).

Palais Schwarzenberg Restaurant, 9 Schwarzenberplatz (tel. 78-45-15), has one of the most elegant backgrounds of any restaurant in the city. It lies in a famous hotel (see the previous recommendation). The owner is Prince Karl Johannes von Schwarzenberg, scion of one of the country's most aristocratic families. Take your time over an apéritif in the deluxe cocktail lounge, where the waiter will most likely recite the daily specialties of the chef. In summer you can dine on a terrace. Dining in such an imperial setting might cause you to imagine you are a Habsburg. The cuisine is refined, with many French dishes, and the service is first class and very old world. The wine cellar is superb, and chef Gerard Parachini is a man of many talents. He seasonally adjusts his menu and therefore has many specialties, including medallions of veal with crabmeat and pearl onions. Dinner ranges frm 320 AS ($17.02) to 540 AS ($28.73), and reservations are suggested. The restaurant is open all year.

Prinz Eugen Rôtisserie, Hilton Hotel, 2 Landstrasser Hauptstrasse (tel. 75-26-52), is one of the finest restaurants of Vienna. The setting is like that of an operetta version of a baronial château, filled with every comfort imaginable and certain to impress with its overlay of charm. There are three rooms, each one embellished in the style of the Belvedere Palace, itself dating from the 18th century. You might dine in a salon all in muted beige and gold, honoring the musical heritage of the Austrian capital. A second salon is the Baronial Hall, a grill, with scenes from the prince's battles adorning the walls. You'll feel like a knight in all this setting of baroque furniture and oak paneling. The waiters serve international specialties from the open grill. The final room is the Belvedere Library, the bookshelves holding hundreds of antique volumes. It has dark-wood paneling and the chef prepares such dishes as veal kidney vindobona. The grilled meats are prepared Vienna style, and the Salzburger nockerl is feather light. If you like fish, try the salmon with a watercress puree, and for dessert, the hazelnut parfait.

The service is superb, and each dish is prepared for a discriminating palate. This place is an exclusive Viennese haunt, drawing both locals and foreign patronage, each group of which seems to appreciate its excellent wine cellar. You can order from the international menu from noon to 3 p.m. and from 6 to 11 p.m., paying from 260 As ($13.83) to 320 AS ($17.02) for a set meal or from 220 AS ($11.70) to 550 AS ($29.26) on the à la carte.

Balkan Grill, 13 Brunnengasse (tel. 92-14-94), is not only the finest Balkan restaurant in Vienna (which has quite a few), but one of the best dining rooms as well. On some lists of the city's top-notch restaurants it appears at the very top. Near the west train station, it's open daily from 6:30 p.m. to midnight, serving meals for around 250 AS ($13.30) and up. Waiters are dressed in Bosnian regional garb, and the waitresses, in case you can't guess, are in Herzegovinian dress. The music, however, is soulfully Hungarian, and from time to time, Viennese as well. The cuisine is spicy and Balkan, of course, with many grill specialties. The chef is famous for his Genghis Khan flaming sword which is served with a musical flourish. In fair weather guests can also dine in a charming courtyard.

König von Ungarn (King of Hungary), 10 Schulerstrasse (tel. 52-53-19), is a beautifully decorated restaurant inside the famous inner-city hotel of the same name. The service here is superb, with a masterful assistance added by the owner, Don Pedro, who's usually on hand to guide you through the menu. If you're in doubt about what to order and Don Pedro isn't around, try the tafelspitz, the savory boiled beef dish which we've already sampled at the Sacher Hotel. It's elegantly dispensed from a trolley which makes the rounds through the richly decorated place. Other menu choices, which change frequently according to what is seasonal, include a ragoût of seafish with fresh mushrooms, tournedos with a mustard and horseradish sauce, and a stunning collection of appetizers that might include scampi in a caviar sauce. The restaurant is open daily except Saturday from 11:30 a.m. to 3 p.m and from 6:15 p.m until midnight. À la carte dinners average from 320 AS ($17.02) to 420 AS ($22.34), and considering what you get, that's not an overpriced check.

Zur Frommen Helene, 16 Breitegasse (tel. 93-46-82). If you want fish, veal, or pork, you should go elsewhere. But if you want a steak, this is the finest place to come to in Vienna. It's in an ochre-colored, turn-of-the-century house, with an art nouveau decor that offers plenty of visual distraction. It encompasses two different rooms on two different floors, both with late-19th-century memorabilia. In some cases the lamps look like jeweled tiaras hanging from chains. Part of the evening's amusement will be the unexpected flashes of flambé pans going off to different parts of the restaurant. The staff, in spite of the flames, has everything under control. In addition to steaks, they also provide a wide range of fresh salads and tempting desserts. French wine is sold by the carafe, and you may want to end your meal with an Irish coffee. Complete dinners range from 420 AS ($22.34) to 630 AS ($33.52), and are served from 6 p.m until midnight every day of the week. Reservations are suggested, and the restaurant shuts down in August for vacation.

Steirereck, 2 Rasumofskygasse (tel. 73-31-68), means "corner of Styria," which is exactly what Heinz and Grete Reitbauer have tried to create in the rustic decor of this friendly and intimate restaurant, one of the finest in the city, lying on the Danube Canal. They do the cooking themselves, turning out such specialties as traditional Viennese dishes and nouvelle cuisine selections. For example, tafelspitz might be served in the old-fashioned way or else in a more trendy manner, with a warm cranberry sauce. Other dishes are likely to include veal with Calvados and wild rice, rack of lamb Styrian style, and soufflé of trout with sorrel noodles. The menu is wisely limited and well prepared, and it usually costs 400 AS ($21.28) for a typical meal. The restaurant is closed on weekends and holidays, but open otherwise from 11 a.m. to midnight Monday to Friday.

Zum Weisser Schwan, 59 Nussdorferstrasse (tel. 34-16-50), is the most celebrated game restaurant in Vienna. Unlike most restaurants in the country, game is available here year round except when the restaurant is closed, which is on Saturday and Sunday but also from mid-July to mid-August and for part of December until January 10. It's imperative to book a table for dinner. The location is in a mellow old Viennese house with a historic courtyard more than 250 years old. The Pilsener beer here comes straight from a barrel, while the cuisine is straightforward, authentic, and without unnecessary frills. An average meal will cost 320 AS ($17.02) and could include woodcock "grandmother's style," filet of young deer with lentils, mushrooms, and bacon, or guinea fowl in a cream sauce. Other specialties include the classic partridge with red cabbage, pheasant wrapped in bacon, and young wild boar. There's also a well-stocked list of fish dishes, including perch, fogosch (a form of whitefish), and sole. A staff member will hand you a list of specialties which include virtually anything made from a goose, ranging from soup to a terrine to a well-seasoned breast.

Leupold's Kupferdachl, 7 Schottengasse (tel. 63-93-81), has been directed by the Leupold family for the past 30 years. Today it specializes in the Austrian equivalent of nouvelle cuisine, but the chef also prepares more conservatively traditional dishes. The rustically elegant interior has lots of paneling, a scattering of Oriental rugs, and a cozy ambience of powder-blue banquettes and elegantly detailed straight-backed chairs. Lunch averages around 320 AS ($17.02) to 420 AS ($22.34), while dinner costs from 420 AS ($22.34) to 520 AS ($27.66). The restaurant is open Monday to Friday from noon to 3 p.m and from 6 p.m. to mignight. On Saturday it's open only for dinner, and is closed from late July until sometime in August.

Kervansaray, 9 Mahlerstrasse (tel. 52-88-43). The historic links between Austria and the Ottoman Empire are revived in this place, which looks vaguely Turkish and has fresh fish flown in every day from the Bosphorus. The owner controls a sister establishment in Istanbul. Downstairs in the Kervansaray your meal might begin with yogurt soup or lobster bisque, to be followed by kebabs, chicken curry, or mussels marinara. A dessert sepcialty is a mango soufflé. Fish is the specialty of the upstairs Hummer Bar, which serves lobsters that are succulently fresh and very expensive. They can be cooked thermidor style or just about any way you prefer. A half lobster is priced at 400 AS ($21.28). The establishment lies only 90 yards from the Vienna State Opera, which almost assures its status as a rendezvous point for gourmets. It's also attached to one of Vienna's most elegant delicatessens, DO and Company, which ranks with Fauchon's in Paris. You can even dine on the linen-covered tables of the deli if you choose. Meal prices in the Kervansaray range from 180 AS ($9.58) to 260 AS ($13.83), while the more expensive Hummer Bar charges between 210 AS ($11.17) to 670 AS ($35.64). All these establishments close on Sunday.

Grotta Azzurra, 5 Babenbergerstrasse (tel. 56-11-44), near the Hofburg, is considered the most charming—and best—Italian restaurant in Vienna. The proprietor comes from Capri, the site of the famed Blue Grotto (hence the name of his restaurant). His birthplace also explains the nautical decor. Some of the touches, such as mosaics in sunny colors, may send you south of the border for a vacation in Italy. The owner has many regular customers, who appreciate the good food, the friendly service, and the excellent wines. The simply printed menu lists the classic Italian dishes served here, and dinner prices range from 175 AS ($9.31) to 300 AS ($15.96). The restaurant is open only five days a week, Monday to Friday, from noon to 3 p.m. and from 6:30 to 11:30 p.m. Reservations are necessary.

Landhaus Winter, 262 Alberner Hafensufahrtsstrasse (tel. 76-23-17), is a century-old country house surrounded with flowers in summer and decorated inside with powder-blue napery and rustic artifacts. It sits at the edge of the Danube Canal, providing a pleasant refuge for those Viennese who wish to escape the congestion of their city. The terrace might be particularly pleasant on a summer day, although the interior is cozily paneled and elegant. Well-prepared fish is one of the specialties here, and a selection might include perch or eel, both cooked in a number of ways, or Greenland salmon, French oysters, Portuguese mussels, and a young brook trout from local waters. Meat dishes might include medallions of roebuck, tournedos with mushrooms, lamb steak with fennel, and filet of beef in a cabbage cream sauce. Reservations are suggested, and the restaurant is closed on Sunday evening and all day Monday. À la carte meals range between 300 AS ($15.96) and 450 AS ($23.94).

Steinerne Eule, 30 Halbgasse (tel. 93-22-50), is the exclusive haunt of some of the most prestigious gourmets of Vienna. With the prices they charge—between 250 AS ($13.30) and 720 AS ($38.30) for a fixed-price meal—you can see why. À la carte dinners cost less, from 120 AS ($6.38) to 370 AS ($19.68). The chef has learned to blend an attractive synthesis of nouvelle Austrian cuisine with traditional Viennese recipes. The menu changes according to the season and the market availability. Therefore, depending on this, you might get venison terrine with fresh goose liver, cream of asparagus soup, or veal delicacies sometimes served with spinach noodles. For an innovative dessert, the chef occasionally features an avocado mousse with fresh strawberries or perhaps an apple parfait with kiwi fruit. Service is daily until midnight, except on Sunday and Monday.

Hauswirth, 20 Otto-Bauer-Gasse (tel. 57-12-61). The imposing entrance to this restaurant is under a rectangular corridor with a well-polished fan window at the far end. You'll push open the leaded-glass door to enter this art nouveau enclave which has become a stamping ground of often well-dressed habitués. The summertime gardens are lovely, but in winter you'll probably eat in a paneled ambience of dark wood and crystal chandeliers. Günter Winter is the chef and owner, and he adheres to *neue Wiener küche.* He seasonally adjusts his menu, which might include quail, venison, asparagus, lots of fresh berries, goose liver, sweetbreads, well-prepared steaks, and suckling lambs, along with a tempting array of homemade pastries. His place is open daily except Sunday and holidays from 11:30 a.m. to 3 p.m. and from 5:30 p.m. to midnight. À la carte meals range from 320 AS ($17.02) to 420 AS ($22.34) for lunch and from 420 AS ($22.34) to 600 AS ($31.92) for dinner. The cellar holds a large variety of the best of Austrian wines plus a well-chosen assortment from some of the best European vineyards.

Restaurant Fischerhaus, an der Höhenstrasse (tel. 44-13-20), in the Vienna Woods, is popular with members of Vienna's diplomatic community and the city's business elite. Former Austrian chancellor Bruno Kreisky is a regular client, and other celebrities have included Arnold Schwarzenegger, Happy Rockefeller, Robert Mitchum, and Elizabeth Taylor. Owners Erich and Pauline Kruder are natural restaurateurs, whose cellars read like an international directory of fine wines, especially those from the Napa Valley of California. Their establishment is housed in a century-old farmhouse surrounded by greenery, with an outdoor terrace and an interior with a blazing wintertime fireplace and an intriguing collection of antique firearms and hunting memorabilia. Prices range between 350 AS ($18.62) and 900 AS ($47.88) for fixed-price meals, and between 195 AS ($10.37) and 480 AS ($25.54) for à la carte dinners. Reservations are strongly suggested before heading here. The restaurant is closed from the first of November until the end of February. On Sunday it closes at 5 p.m.

Kellner's Altwienerhof, 6 Herklotzgasse (tel. 83-71-45), near Schönbrunn Palace, is a ground-floor room behind wrought-iron doors which is now one of the leading restaurants in the city, with a menu featuring an Austrian version of nouvelle cuisine. The chef also turns out a satisfying range of well-prepared traditional favorites. In a paneled room with trompe-d'oeil landscapes covering much of the wall space, you can dine on such delicacies as cold cucumber soup with shrimp, pike soufflé with crab sauce, gratinée of mussels with Riesling sauce and seaweed, a traditional tafelspitz, veal steak in a basil and tomato sauce with fresh zucchini, and fresh turbot with leafy spinach and red wine butter. The menu changes frequently. The restaurant is open Monday to Saturday from 11:15 a.m. to 3 p.m. and from 6 p.m. to midnight, and is usually closed for the last days of January and the first two weeks of February. Fixed-price lunches begin at 220 AS ($11.70), while set evening meals range from 600 AS ($31.92) to 700 AS ($37.24). À la carte meals begin at around 250 AS ($13.30), but could go as high as 750 AS ($39.90), depending on what you order.

THE MEDIUM-PRICED RANGE: Restaurant Stiebitz (Zum Schwarzen Kameel), 5 Bognergasse (tel. 63-81-25). A delicatessen against one of the walls of this popular place sells wine, liquor, and specialty meat items, although most of the action takes place among the chicly dressed clientele in the café. On a Saturday morning the café section is packed with weekend Viennese recovering from a late night out with massive doses of caffeine. Everyone stands here, drinking the beverages that the friendly uniformed waiters bring on trays, and selecting open-faced, delicately prepared sandwiches from the trays on the black countertops.

While you're here, be sure to glance through the door to the restaurant, where you'll see a perfectly preserved art deco room, once probably one of the most avant-garde rooms in Vienna when it was built in 1920. Jeweled copper chandeliers hang from beaded strings, with discreet illumination beaming through their etched-glass globes. The walls are a combination of polished paneling, yellowed ceramic tiles, and an attractively dusky plaster ceiling frieze of grape leaves. The vine theme is repeated in the machine-age marquetry in several kinds of hardwoods, which graces many of the room dividers. The restaurant contains only 11 tables, and it might be a perfect place for a nostalgic lunch or dinner in Vienna. The international cuisine features specialties such as herring filet Oslo, potato soup, Valencian paella, Roman saltimbocca, and a host of daily specials. Meals range from 225 AS ($11.97).

Hotel Astoria, 32 Kärntnerstrasse (entrance is at 1 Führichgasse) (tel. 52-65-85). The first-floor restaurant inside this hotel is one of the finest in Vienna. The foyer is filled with theatrical portraits of opera stars, and the decor inside is appropriately grand. The service is superb, and the clientele is often elegant and well-heeled. An opera menu is offered either before or after the performances at the nearby state-run institution. It costs 345 AS ($18.35), and could include prats on eggplant slices, cold cream of avocado soup, pork filet with soy sauce, followed by a dessert of kiwi salad. More expensive à la carte items could include a parsleyed filet of sole with almonds, veal, beef, and game dishes. The typically Austrian dishes include tafelspitz and kaiserschnitzel, the latter with caper sauce and buttered rice. Dessert could be a concoction of hot egriots with truffled ice cream or a cranberry parfait. À la carte meals cost from 360 AS ($19.15). Lunch is served from noon to 3 p.m. and dinner from 6 to 11:30 p.m. every day, and reservations are strongly suggested.

Franz Zimmer Schubertstüberln, 4 Schreyvogelgasse (tel. 63-71-87). Brown and white striped awnings cover the pink and white café chairs set onto a raised platform above the pink begonias and cobblestones of the quiet street outside near the Burgtheater. From looking at it, you'd never guess that the inside is as big as it is, but once you pass through the small garden entrance you'll see a series of rooms that have been elevated to a high pitch of the modern decorator's art. You'll find a room here for practically every taste, from the plushly modern bar with horseshoe-shaped banquettes to an informal eatery in rustic gemütlich. My favorite rooms are the two salons in pastel-colored high-ceilinged elegance, with immaculate linens and lots of light. Look carefully before you select an ambience here. If the first one isn't to your liking, you'll eventually find something that is. The distinguished chef has prepared several menus, allowing clients to spend very little money or quite a lot, depending on their tastes. A bistro menu, priced from 70 AS ($3.72), offers daily specials with three courses, including soup, a meat dish, and dessert, while more expensive dinners range from 300 AS ($15.96). The restaurant is open from 9 a.m. to midnight every day except Sunday, and reservations are suggested.

Abend-Restaurant Fuervogel, 21 Alserbachstrasse (tel. 34-10-392). For more than 65 years this has been a Viennese landmark, bringing Russian cuisine to a location across the street from the palace of the Prince of Liechtenstein. You'll eat in romantically Slavic surroundings with gypsy violins playing Russian and Viennese music in the background. Specialties include chicken Kiev, beef Stroganoff, veal Dolgoruki, borscht, and many other dishes that taste as if they came right off the steppes. Your hors d'oeuvres might be sakkuska, a variety platter popular in Russia. For dessert you might select a Russian ice cream called plombier. The restaurant is open every day except Sunday from 6 p.m. to 1 a.m. It's closed from mid-July until after the first week of August. An average meal will range between 200 AS ($10.65) and 500 AS ($26.60).

Ming Court, 32-34 Kärntnerstrasse (tel. 52-17-15), serves genuine Chinese food in a far eastern setting near the Vienna State Opera. The location is at the Hotel Astoria. Its entrance is around the corner at 1 Fürichgasse. An average meal costs around 300 AS ($15.96), and Korean barbecues are a specialty. The restaurant is open from 11:30 a.m. to 3 p.m. and from 5:30 p.m. to 1 a.m. every day of the year. José Chuh, the friendly owner, directs the excellent service.

Restaurant Bukarest, 7 Bräunerstrasse (tel. 52-37-63), serves Balkan—mainly Rumanian—specialties in a tunnel-like room with old vaulting, an exposed charcoal grill, and soulful gypsy music to accompany your meal. A café in front offers sidewalk tables for guests who prefer to be outdoors. Specialties include Serbian bean soup, salami, grilled sirloin steak stuffed with chopped meat, and a Jamaican pepper and garlic dish. Another dish of which the chef is proud is his mixed grill. Expect to spend from 240 AS ($12.77) per person. The restaurant serves from 11:30 a.m. to 2:30 p.m. and from 6 p.m. to midnight every day of the week except Monday.

Sailer, 14 Gersthoferstrasse (tel. 47-21-21), near the Türkenschanzpark, is tastefully decorated in an old Vienna style, with wood paneling, Biedermeier portraits, and in one of the cellar rooms, antique chairs, each hand-carved in a different design. The art nouveau exterior is lit with spots at night, revealing an interior where clients are seated on two different levels, according to their choice. Specialties of the house include deer and elk, wild boar, pheasant, and partridge, each prepared according to classic and time-honored Viennese recipes, along with a tempting collection of tortes and pastries. The third-generation owners acquiesce to the demands of an updated light cuisine with daily specials which depend on the availability of produce in the marketplace. They serve weekdays from 11:30 a.m. to 2:30 p.m. and from 6 until 11 p.m. The restaurant closes on weekends. Meals average 170 AS ($9.04) for lunch, going up to around 340 AS ($18.09) for dinner.

Restaurant Zauberlehrling, 2 Lazaristengasse (tel. 34-51-35), in Währing. Before you finish your meal in this charming and intimate restaurant it's likely that the chef will come out of the kitchen to welcome you personally. Translated, the name of the restaurant means sorcerer's apprentice, although from the quality of the Viennese and international specialties served here, it's obvious there's no neophyte back there rattling those pots and pans. Specialties include cream of snail soup with chives, appetizers with shrimp variations, medallions of veal in sherry sauce, and a series of seasonal menus featuring fish, game, and fresh vegetables. Dessert might be the Zauberlehrling Hausbombe or some equally rich concoction. An average meal will range between 250 AS ($13.30) and 320 AS ($17.02). They're open Monday through Saturday from 6 p.m. to midnight (the kitchen closes at 11 p.m.), with an annual vacation taken from mid-July to mid-August and from the day before Christmas until January 1.

Tokyo Restaurant, 1 Rauhensteingasse (tel. 52-13-33), is the leading Japanese restaurant of Vienna, with a bamboo and wood interior which has all the craftsmanship and subtlety you'd expect in the Far East. You'll find two separate rooms (or more accurately, teahouses) inside, seating from five to ten diners in each. You'll have the choice of dining in either the Japanese or Western style, selecting such specialties as sukiyaki, tempura, chicken teriyaki, or a Japanese meat fondue. The waitresses will serve you in kimonos, and will provide excellent service at reasonable prices. À la carte meals range from 150 AS ($7.98) to 300 AS ($15.96). The restaurant is open daily from noon to 3 p.m. and from 6 p.m. to midnight.

Niky's Kuchlmasterei, 6 Obere Weissgerberstrasse (tel. 72-44-18). The bill, when it comes after a long and pleasant meal, will arrive in an elaborate box suitable for jewels, along with an amusing message in German (if you can read it) which offers a tongue-in-cheek apology for cashing your check. The salad and the hors d'oeuvres bar are among the most tempting in Vienna—so much so that you might just fill up on before-dinner snacks to the point where a meal is almost redundant. All of it is encased in a decor of old stonework with modern innovations both in the architecture and the cuisine. The large menu, the well-prepared food, the welcoming, friendly ambience, and the lively crowd of loyal habitués, make it a good choice for an evening meal. Three courses average around 300 AS ($15.96). The restaurant is open Monday to Saturday from 10 a.m. to midnight.

Chez Rainer, 27 Wiedner Hauptstrasse (tel. 65-46-46), is an intimately elegant dining room attached to the attractive Hotel Erzherzog Rainer. The building was constructed in 1912, and was renovated twice since then into the clean and inviting place it is today. The well-run service includes food items such as tafelspitz with applesauce, horseradish, chives, and sauteed potatoes, a tender wienerschnitzel, and grilled fogasch with anchovy butter. Many of their specialties are based on the produce of the season, which are likely to include fresh strawberries or raspberries and, inevitably, summer vegetables. In the autumn they feature hare, deer, venison, and wild boar. Dessert might be shredded pancakes with stewed plums or a Salzburg-style soufflé. Fixed-price meals range from 230 AS ($12.24) to 450 AS ($23.94), with à la carte dinners costing from 170 AS ($9.04) to 375 AS ($19.95). A less expensive brasserie on the premises serves food until 1 a.m., offering an inexpensive quick lunch with beer on tap and tempting pastries.

Griechenbeisl, 11 Fleischmarkt (tel. 63-19-77), was established in 1450 and today is still one of the leading restaurants of Vienna. It has a labyrinthine collection of at least seven different eating areas on three different floors, all of them with low vaulted ceilings, smoky paneling, wrought-iron chandeliers, and green-vested waiters who scurry around with large trays of food. This is a long-enduring favorite with the Viennese and especially the foreign colony, who appreciate its mellow antique atmosphere and its dozens of charming touches. As you enter from the street, look down at the grate below your feet for an illuminated view of a pirate counting his gold. As you go in, be sure to see the so-called inner sanctum, with the signatures of former patrons ranging from Liszt to Mozart, from Beethoven to Molnar, from Mark Twain to Strauss.

The Pilsen beer is well chilled, and the food is bürgerlich (hearty, ample, and solidly bourgeois). The restaurant features nighttime accordion and zither music. Menu items include apricot quenelles, crêpes with poppyseed, both Hungarian and Viennese goulash, sauerkraut garni, and braised leg of venison. À la carte meals range from 300 AS ($15.96), and they're served from 10 a.m. to 12:30 a.m.

THE BUDGET RESTAURANTS: **Ofenloch,** 8 Jurrentgasse (tel. 63-88-44), is a well-reputed eating house of old Vienna in the medieval section of town. The waitresses wear Biedermeier costumes and will give you a menu that looks more like a magazine. Some of the mock medieval illustrations inside are funny, and when you get around to reading the food items you'll be prepared for the gutbürgerlich aspect of many of them. Specialties include vaillerostbraten, two kinds of schnitzel, pork, noodle, and hearty soup dishes, as well as salads and cheese platters. For smaller appetites, there's a page devoted to wurst salads and one-dish meals, any of which would go well with the wine and beer consumed in copious quantities here. It's open daily except Sunday from 10 a.m. to midnight. A robust three-course meal will cost around 150 AS ($7.98).

Restaurant Kardos, 8 Dominikaner Bastei (tel. 52-69-49), serves Hungarian and mixed-grill specialties. However, the menu is adjusted seasonally so that the chef can turn out well-prepared foods using the freshest ingredients available to him. Vegetarian meals are offered to those who prefer them, along with regional recipes familiar to many Eastern Europeans. Barack, an apéritif made from apricots, is offered, as well as piquant little rolls known as grammel. They're seasoned with pork and hot spices. The decor is brightly Hungarian, with contrasting sunny colors, elaborate pine detailing cut into country baroque patterns, and a cellar locale with gypsy music in wintertime. An average meal ranges from 170 AS ($9.04) to 200 AS ($10.64). The restaurant is open every day except Wednesday from 11 a.m. to 2:30 p.m. and from 5 p.m. to midnight. Doris Kardos, the hard-working owner, prepares some of the most elaborate food displays in Vienna.

Zwölf-Apostelkeller, 3 Sonnenfelsgasse (tel. 52-67-77), is an old wine tavern, parts of its walls predating the year 1561. You'll find rows of wooden tables under the vaulted ceilings, with illumination provided partially with the streetlights that have been set into the masonry floor. This place is popular with students, partly because of its reasonable prices and partly because of its proximity to St. Stephen's. It's so deep you feel you're entering a dungeon. The tavern is open every day from 4:30 p.m. to midnight. In addition to beer and wine, which sells for between 16 AS (85¢) and 25 AS ($1.33) for a small carafe, the establishment serves light meals and snacks. These include a roast beef platter with tartar sauce, roast pork with horseradish, and several generous salads with wurst and cheese. Plates of food range from 20 AS ($1.06) to 65 AS ($3.46).

Zum Laterndl, 12 Landesgerichtsstrasse (tel. 43-43-58), is near the university and the U.S. Consulate. This is an intimate tavern usually filled with barristers, American diplomats, members of the Austrian Parliament, and Viennese students who enjoy the establishment's atmosphere. Laterndl means lantern, and you'll see a few of these, as well as assorted hunting trophies, antique beer mugs, and all the accessories that seem to go with what was once a coaching tavern. The place is known for its wines, whose quality and modest price usually guarantee that it's a lively place. It's closed Saturday and Sunday, but open weekdays from 9 a.m. to midnight. It's also closed from the day before Christmas until January 9. Steaks are a specialty throughout the year, while fish, asparagus, mushrooms, berries, wild game, and wild goose are prominently featured on the menu only in season. Meals range between 150 AS ($7.98) and 450 AS ($23.94), the latter price charged only if you order the most expensive à la carte specialties.

Restaurant Siddhartha, 16 Fleischmarkt (tel. 53-11-97), is at the end of a covered arcade in the old city, in a crowded, clean ambience of white stucco, candlelight, fresh flowers, and vaulted ceilings. This restaurant serves only vegetarian food. It's very popular, and you'll be fortunate to get a seat on weekends during peak serving hours. Menu specialties include ratatouille, quiche Lorraine, a Siddhartha plate for two persons (mixed specialties), many curry dishes, roquefort crêpes, piccata milanese (with imitation veal), french onion soup, avocados in a cognac dressing, mushrooms Romanoff, and mangos in port. The restaurant is closed on Sunday. Fixed-price meals are available at lunchtime only, ranging from 65 AS ($3.46) to 70 AS ($3.72), while à la carte dinners cost from between 120 AS ($6.38) and 240 AS ($12.77).

Au-Restaurant, 122 Arbeiterstrandbadstrasse (tel. 23-61-10), stands in Vienna's biggest green area, the Donaupark. Appropriate to its loyal clientele of international guests, many of whom work at the nearby United Nations facilities, the menu is in German, French, and English. Every month the management features a full week of the cuisine of another culture, including Italian and Slovakian. Friday night is special, with party music, candlelit dinners, and an ambience more suited for fun than on the other nights of the week. Fixed-price meals range from 145 AS ($7.71) to 375 AS ($19.95), while à la carte dinners cost between 160 AS ($8.51) and 330 AS ($17.56). Live music is usually provided at night. The management is honest and conscientious, and the waiters are friendly and used to foreign business. The restaurant is open every day of the week from 10 a.m. to midnight.

Restaurant Anatol, 12 Würthgasse (tel. 36-11-81), offers good Viennese cookery, always with an emphasis on the light-textured creations of *die neuen Kuchen* in an art nouveau ambience. It looks like a turn-of-the-century Austrian coffeehouse, serving well-prepared French, Italian, and Austrian food in a large central room and in a smaller salon off to the side.

Fixed-price meals range from 120 AS ($6.38) while à la carte dinners go from 120 AS ($6.38) to 250 AS ($13.30). Reservations are suggested. The restaurant is open from 11 a.m. to 2 p.m. and from 5:30 p.m. until midnight every day but Tuesday.

Dubrovnik, 3 am Heumarkt (tel. 73-27-55), is a Balkan restaurant where much of the menu is in Serbo-Croatian and where the staff wears the regional garb of different provinces of Yugoslavia. It's set up in two rooms on either side of a central vestibule filled with busy waiters rushing in and out of the kitchen, which you can see through an open door at the far end. In a decor of red carpeting, a decorative fish tank, and a half-hearted pianist plunking out American show tunes, you'll see an efficient maître d' directing the show which on a good night can be gregarious and fun. The menu lists about a dozen Yugoslav national dishes, including Serbian bean soup, as well as specialties from the grill, including pork kidney and liver as well as a mixed grill. Among the fish dishes, the most exotic is the Serbian fogosch (a kind of whitefish), served with potatoes and garlic. Dessert could be baklava and both Bulgarian and Serbian cheese. The restaurant is open every day from 11:30 a.m. to 2:30 p.m. and from 6 p.m. to midnight. Meals average about 125 AS ($6.65) per person.

Figlmüller, 5 Wollzeile (tel. 52-61-77), in the inner city, is considered one of the most famous beisels in Vienna. The passageway down which it's located leads to a site which is about 500 years old. Inside, the relaxed ambience is one of good and simple Viennese cookery, with a wienerschnitzel which is by now legendary. It sprawls across (and off) your plate it's so big. You'll also find an excellent selection of Viennese sausages, along with tafelspitz and about ten fresh salads. Daily specials are written on a blackboard, and are served between 8 a.m. and 11 p.m. Monday to Friday and from 8 a.m. to 3 p.m. on Saturday. The wines are excellent, and the restaurant is usually packed at the peak serving hours. Meals cost from 75 AS ($3.99) to 145 AS ($7.71).

Gösser Bierklinik, 4 Steindlgasse (tel. 63-33-36), which is also known as the Güldene Drache (golden dragon), serves what is reportedly the finest beer in the city. It's brewed in Styria. This is an ancient rustic institution in a building which, according to tradition, dates from Roman times. An inn was opened here in the early 16th century, way back during the reign of Maximilian I. With such a tradition, naturally the decor seems strictly from the Middle Ages, and the cuisine is quintessentially Viennese. The waitresses always seem to be carrying ample mugs of Gösser beer, and are often rushed and harassed. When you finally get their attention, you can order such hearty fare as veal chops with dumplings, plus a wide variety of gutbürgerlich ribstickers. You will likely spend from 150 AS ($7.98) for a full meal. The restaurant serves from 11:30 a.m. to 11:30 p.m. daily except Sunday.

Thomaskeller, 4 Postgasse (tel. 52-74-46), lies just off the Wollzeile, in the cellars of a Dominican monastery. It's one of the finest wine taverns in Vienna, with a casual atmosphere, friendly service, and carafes of excellent wine from Haugsdorf. Gutbürgerlich food is served in a gutbürgerlich setting under a tall vaulted ceiling of dark-red brick. Flags from the different parts of "the Empire" hang above the wrought-iron wall sconces and the two antique streetlights set into the brick floor. No one puts on airs. The waiters seem to have a sense of humor, and the daily specials are written on a blackboard. You'll find bargain dining in an authentic setting. A fixed-price evening meal will cost about 70 AS ($3.72), and might include schweinbraten with sauerkraut and good apple strudel. Service is from 7 p.m. till midnight. You might prefer the lower section at the far end of the restaurant. This room is usually more popular with the locals and gives you a closer look at the drinkers and diners, both male and female, who make this their preferred hangout in the neighborhood.

Zum Weissen Rauchfangkehrer, 2 Rauhensteingasse (tel. 52-34-71), is 125 years old, the former guildhall of Vienna's chimney sweeps. In fact the name of the place, translated as the "white chimney sweep," comes from a blackened wretch who terrified his neighbor, the city baker, by falling into a drunken sleep in a kneading trough and emerging the next day like a ghost covered with flour. The interior is rustic, with pine banquettes that look vaguely like church pews, deer antlers, fancifully crafted chandeliers, and red and blue tablecloths. Stained glass is set into the dividers separating the many niches and cubbyholes, while big street-level windows let in lots of light behind the summer begonias of the windowboxes. A piano in one of the inner rooms provides nighttime music and has an ornate gilt candelabrum set on top of it. The menu offers such specialties as Viennese fried chicken, both a Tyrolean and a paprika schnitzel, veal goulash, wild game specialties, bratwurst, tafelspitz, and several kinds of strudel. You should reserve a table, and you'll certainly want to finish with the house specialty, a fabulously rich chocolate cream puff whose long German name I won't give for reasons of space. You can dine here for 150 AS ($7.98). It's open daily from noon to 3 p.m. and from 6 p.m. to 1 a.m.

Toni Wagner's Glacisbeisel, Messepalast (tel. 96-16-58), is housed inside the walls of what were once the imperial stables. The location is near the English Theater, inside a maze of palatial buildings whose entrances lie on Museumstrasse. Toni Wagner renovated this historic building in 1976, and has done a thriving business ever since. The restaurant serves one of the best wienerschnitzels I've ever tasted, as well as Viennese specialties such as rehfilet Diana (filet of venison in madeira wine and oranges with croquettes and tomatoes), plus a milk and cream strudel with vanilla sauce. In summer the restaurant seats more than 300 diners on an open-air terrace constructed right into the ramparts in what used to be a vineyard. The restaurant is open Monday to Saturday from 6 p.m. to midnight, and it closes in January. It offers a relatively low-cost and filling meal at a cost ranging upward from 170 AS ($9.04).

Melker Stiftskeller, 1 Schottengasse (tel. 63-55-30). On the edge of the courtyard at the end of a cobblestone arcade sits a peach-colored, very grand building. During the day the entrance is closed with a wrought-iron gate adorned with what looks like a bishop's insignia, although at night it opens to reveal one of the finest wine cellars in Vienna. No beer is available, but the extensive collection of wine is served in both carafes and bottles. Menu items include fried Viennese hen, pork schnitzel and pork bräten, bratwurst with sauerkraut, cavapcici (ground spicy meat), and a specialty of the chef, roast leg of pork. Simple meals range from 150 AS ($7.98). The restaurant is open daily, except Sunday and holidays, from 5 p.m. to midnight.

De Alte Schmiede, 9 Schönlaterngasse (tel. 52-34-95). Before you descend the winding metal stairway leading to this basement restaurant, you'll be rewarded with a view of the old smithy through the plate-glass window separating it from the inside stairwell. The walls of this ancient forge look like something from a Louise Nevelson sculpture, with more than 1000 antique metal-working tools hanging in orderly rows from the aged masonry walls. You might want to make a daytime excursion just for the sight of the occasional artist who still has access to the shop.

On the street level of this building you'll find a Libresso open from 11 a.m. to 7 p.m. There the friendly management serves coffee and snacks, and newspapers in many languages, including English, are available. The works of young artists are displayed. Under the high vaulted ceilings of the brick-lined cellar restaurant, Viennese specialties "in the style of grandmother" are served. These might include tafelspitz, paprika braten, two kinds of strudel, seven kinds of soup, an occasional fish dish, and good Turkish coffee. A candlelit dinner costs from 175 AS ($9.31) and is served from 5 p.m. to 1 a.m. daily except Sunday. The café is also closed on Sunday.

Augustinerkeller, 1 Augustinerstrasse (tel. 52-34-83), lies in the basement of a palace that shelters the Albertina collection in the Hofburg complex. It has a lively group of patrons from all walks of life, and sometimes they get boisterous, especially when the Schrammel music goes on late into the night. This place offers one of the best values for wine-tasting in Vienna. The ground-floor lobby lists in big letters the prices of vintage local wines by the glass. A quiet crowd of drinkers take a taste from the hundreds of bottles near the stand-up stainless-steel counter.

You walk past a brick area with a rack of chickens roasting on a spit behind a glass window. You then enter a vaulted brick room with a worn pine-board floor and wooden banquettes painted in horizontal stripes of black and lime green. This long and narrow room is usually packed with people and atmosphere, and often it features strolling accordion players. An upstairs room looks much the same as the one below, although it's less crowded, much quieter, and usually doesn't have music. Aside from the wine and beer, the establishment serves food from 10 a.m. to 11 p.m. The cooking is simple, including half a roast chicken on a spit at 50 AS ($2.66) as well as schnitzels from 45 AS ($2.39). A glass of wine (which is defined as one-eighth of a liter) begins at 10 AS (53¢), and usually costs a few more schillings at night.

Antiquitäten-Keller, 32 Magdalenenstrasse (tel. 56-95-33), offers a well-prepared but limited menu in an antique cadre of local beerhall style with nightly classical music. It's open from 6 p.m. to 1 a.m. seven days a week, with an annual closing sometime in August. Drinks cost between 20 AS ($1.06) and 25 AS ($1.33), while a main course of typical Viennese food goes for around 100 AS ($5.32). There are three rooms inside, so feel free to walk around a bit before selecting a place to sit.

Restaurant Gösser Bierhaus, 2 Stubenbastei/Wollzeile (tel. 52-48-39), is an unpretentious and plainly decorated beer restaurant midway between the Vienna Hilton and St. Stephen's. All the brew served is on tap, and is usually accompanied by simple and tasty Viennese dishes, costing between 90 AS ($4.79) and 130 AS ($6.92) for a main course. This serving is so big it can usually do as a complete meal. Hilda Koranda, the owner, is usually on the premises, opening her restaurant from 9 a.m. to 11:30 p.m. Tuesday to Saturday. Monday hours are from 3 p.m. to 11:30 p.m. She closes on Sunday. A summertime beer garden allows clients to take their meals outside.

Rathauskeller, 1 Rathausplatz (tel. 42-12-19), is decorated like a mammoth baroque beer barrel, with massively arched ceilings and stained-glass chandeliers. In the center of Vienna, in the basement of the City Hall, it serves robust, gutbürgerlich fare such as crayfish soup, Hungarian goulash soup, Serbian bean soup, grilled pike-perch, special "City Hall goulash," and veal paprika. If you have a hearty appetite, try the Bauernschmaus, which is a farmer's banquet with pork chops, sauerkraut, bread dumplings, grilled sausages, and potatoes. This establishment has four separate settings, all of them ideal for consuming massive quantities of beer which on a rowdy night seems to be the intention of many a client. If you go to the big Grinzingerkeller you can hear Viennese music after 7 p.m. The cellar is open every day except Sunday from noon to 3 p.m. and from 6 p.m. to midnight. An average three-course meal will cost about 190 AS ($10.11).

St. Urbani-Keller, 12 am Hof (tel. 63-91-02), named after the patron saint of wine-making, is one of the most historic and one of the deepest cellars in Vienna. The owner is an attractive brunette who keeps finding Roman artifacts under the foundations of the lowest levels, and who maintains the tradition of her grandfather, Carl Hipfinger, who renovated the cellar as a public gathering place in 1906. Many of the artifacts inside, from the paneling in the German Romantic style, to the fanciful wrought-iron lighting fixtures, were designed by one of Austria's most famous architects, Walcher von Molthein, who rebuilt Vienna's Kreuzenstein Castle at the beginning of the century. The cellar has brick vaulting dating from the 13th century, and sections of solid Roman walls which you can admire while listening to the folkloric music at night.

The most popular room is the one on the lowest level, so be sure to continue your descent down the steep stairs until you reach the room with the thick oak tables at the bottom. There you'll find enough art, including numerous crucifixes and a Renaissance chandelier of St. Lucretia, to keep anyone interested. Many kinds of wine are served, but the featured vintage comes from the vineyards of the owner's family. That wine has been offered as gifts to everybody from the famous General Rommel (the so-called desert fox) to the president of Austria.

The establishment is open from 6 p.m. to 1 a.m., with hot food served until midnight seven days a week. Food items include filet steak "les gourmets," entrecôte with lyonnaise potatoes, swiebelrostbraten, tafelspitz, trout meunière, veal medallions Monte Carlo, and many kinds of soup, including cream of salmon. That fare is backed up by a wide selection of cheese and crêpes for dessert. Meals cost from 200 AS ($10.64), and if you've already eaten, no one will mind if you drop in just for a drink. Watch your step on the way up or down.

Buffet Trześniewski, 1 Dorotheergasse (tel. 43-15-68). Everyone in Vienna knows about this place, from the most hurried office worker to the city's most elite hostesses. Franz Kafka lived next door and used to come here for sandwiches and beer. It's unlike any buffet you may have seen, with a crowded format of six or seven cramped tables and a rapidly moving queue of clients who jostle for space next to the glass countertops. You'll indicate to the waitress the kind of sandwich you want, and if you can't read German signs, you just point.

Most people come here for at least six or seven of the delicious finger sandwiches, which include 18 combinations of cream cheese, egg and onion, salami, mushroom, herring, green and red peppers, tomatoes, lobster, and many more. You might also want to order small glasses of fruit juice, beer, or wine with your snack. If you want something to drink, the cashier will give you a rubber token which you'll present to the woman at the far end of the counter (again, you'll jostle your way through the crowd). Each of the sandwiches costs 5 AS (26¢), while drinks range from 6 AS (32¢) to 12 AS (64¢) apiece.

The buffet is open Monday to Friday from 9 a.m. to 7:30 p.m., from 9 a.m. to 1 p.m. on Saturday. Unfortunately for summer tourists, it's closed from mid-July to mid-August.

Piaristenkeller, 45 Piaristengasse (tel. 42-91-52), is a wine tavern where the guests sit below vaulted ceilings amid ornately carved room dividers that resemble something from a high Gothic cathedral. The largest section focuses upon three wine (or beer) barrels set up like icons at the far end of the vast room. All of this is highlighted with hanging banners of different heraldic designs, swaying beneath the massive chandeliers. Formerly the cellars of a cloister, the establishment today has zither music to accompany the beer, wine, and wholesome Germanic foods served here. Meals cost from 190 AS ($10.11) and up.

Chapter IV

VIENNA: SIGHTS, SHOPS, NIGHTLIFE

"ASIA BEGINS at the Landstrasse." Prince von Metternich, the Austrian statesman who arranged the marriage of Napoleon and Marie-Louise of Austria, made that now-famous remark to suggest the power and influence of the far-flung Austrian Empire whose destiny was linked with that of the Habsburgs from 1273 to 1918.

After deliverance from the dreaded plague and the equally dreaded Turks, Vienna entered into a great period of power and prosperity which reached the zenith of empire under the long reign of Maria Theresa from 1740 to 1780. Many of the sights I'll describe shortly are traced directly to that great empress of the Age of Enlightenment. She welcomed Mozart to her court at Schönbrunn when he was only six years old, a child prodigy indeed.

At the collapse of the Napoleonic Empire, Vienna took over Paris's long-held position as "the center of Europe." The crowned heads of Europe met for the now-legendary Congress of Vienna in 1814–1815. But so much time was devoted to galas that a remark made by Prince de Ligne became famous in its day: "The Congress doesn't make progress, it dances."

In this chapter we'll explore this legendary city of gemütlichkeit, beginning first with its many sightseeing attractions—most of which are a holdover from its days of empire—and going on to take in its many shopping possibilities as well as its exciting nightlife and cafés, plus practical facts which will help you enjoy your Vienna visit.

GETTING AROUND IN VIENNA: Whether you want to visit historical buildings or the Vienna Woods, museums, theaters, the Prater, or the heurigen, the **Vienna Transport** (Wiener Verkehrsbetriebe), with its network of facilities covering hundreds of miles, can take you there—by U-Bahn (underground), Stadtbahn (metropolitan), streetcar, or bus.

Vienna has a uniform rate, allowing the same tickets to be used on all these means of transportation as well as on the Schnellbahn (Rapid Transit) of the Austrian Federal Railways and on some connecting private bus lines.

There are no conductors on most buses and streetcars, which means you must have the correct change, 24 AS ($1.28), when you get your ticket at a vending machine at the station or aboard the vehicle you choose. A ticket from the machine will be stamped with the date and time of purchase. It's wiser to buy your tickets in advance at a Tabak-Trafik (tobacconist shop) or at an advance-sales office. Here you can get reduced-fare tickets in blocks of five, costing 12 AS (64¢) per ticket. Tickets purchased in advance must be stamped before you start your ride by the machine on conductorless streetcars or at the platform barriers of the underground or Stadtbahn. Once a ticket is stamped, it may be used for any one trip in one direction, including changes.

You can ride directly into the inner city on the underground U-1 or on city bus 1-A, 2-A, or 3-A. The underground runs from 6 a.m. to midnight seven days a week and the buses from 7 a.m. to 8 p.m. Monday to Friday, 7 a.m. to 3 p.m. on Saturday.

Further information, all types of tickets, and free maps of the transportation system are available at Vienna Transport's main offices at the Karlsplatz (tel. 57-31-86) or at St. Stephen's Square underground stations (tel. 52-42-27) Monday to Friday from 8 a.m. to 6 p.m., on Saturday, Sunday, and holidays from 8:30 a.m. to 4 p.m.

Three-Day Vienna Ticket

One of the city's best deals for tourists is Vienna Transport's Special Sightseeing Pass, a three-day rover ticket costing 83 AS ($4.42). You can use not only the public transportation network (underground, Stadtbahn, streetcars, and buses), which covers hundreds of miles, but also the Schnellbahn in the Vienna area and buses carrying the letter "B," for as many rides as you like.

The three-day ticket is available at Vienna Public Transport Information Centers at the following locations:

Karlsplatz (tel. 57-31-86), open Monday through Friday from 7 a.m. to 6 p.m., on Saturday, Sunday, and holidays from 8:30 a.m. to 4 p.m.

Stephansplatz (tel. 52-42-27), open the same days and hours as Karlsplatz.

Praterstern (tel. 24-93-02) and Kagran Center (tel. 23-23-97), open Monday through Friday from 10 a.m. to 6 p.m.

All advance-sales offices of Vienna Public Transport, open Monday from 6 a.m. to noon, Tuesday and Wednesday from 6:30 a.m. to 12:30 p.m., Thursday and Friday from 12:30 to 6:30 p.m.

Opernpassage Tourist Information (in the pedestrian underpass next to the Opera / Kärntner Ring / Karlsplatz) daily from 9 a.m. to 7 p.m.

You can also get the three-day ticket at tourist information offices: Vienna West (on the Autobahn from Salzburg, Autobahnstation Wien-Auhof) and Vienna South (on the Autobahn from Graz, exit Zentrum, 149 Triester Strasse).

Other places selling the tickets are at the airport in the arrival hall next to where you pick up your baggage; at the DDSG landing pier, Reichsbrücke; and at the information offices of the Austrian Travel Agency (Österreichisches Verkehrburo) at the main railway stations. The one at Westbahnhof is found in the upper hall and at Südbahnhof in the lower hall.

The three-day ticket is valid on three consecutive days including the day it is stamped.

1. What to See

Vienna stands today, as it always has, as a crossroads between West and East (it's only 44 miles from the Iron Curtain). After New York and Geneva, it's the third city of the United Nations. It's also the home of many international organizations.

You can spend a week here and you'll have just touched the attractions of this multifaceted international city. I'll skim only the highlights, and even seeing what's listed below will take more than a week of some fast-paced walking.

THE INNER CITY: *Inner Stadt,* the inner city, is the tangle of streets of the old town from which Vienna grew in the Middle Ages. Much of your exploration will be confined to this area. It is encircled by the boulevards of "The Ring" and the Danube Canal. The main street of the inner city is the Kärntnerstrasse, most of which is a pedestrian mall. The heart of Vienna is the Stephansplatz, the square on which St. Stephen's Cathedral sits.

RINGSTRASSE: In 1857, seeing no further need for the old walls which had girdled old town Vienna for several centuries, Emperor Franz Joseph ordered them torn down and replaced by a series of grand buildings and a wide promenade. Ringstrasse, or Ring Boulevard, was laid out between 1858 and 1865, an elegant horseshoe curve 2½ miles long, one of the grand boulevards of Europe, overhung with leafy trees. The emperor got his wish—a boulevard worthy of an empire that controlled some 50 million people.

A cross-section of architectural styles was used in constructing the buildings on the Ringstrasse, ranging from Greek to Gothic. The street names change eight times around the boulevard, and along it you'll pass the Stadtpark, the State Opera House, the Burggarten, the Hofburg Palace, the Volksgarten, the Parliament, the Rathaus, the Burgtheater, the University of Vienna, and the Museum of Fine Arts. The Viennese call this pastiche of architecture *Ringstrassenstil.* They refer to the Ringstrasse simply as "The Ring."

You can circle the boulevard in one of the Viennese red trolleycars, but some people walk from one end to the other. If you wish to do that, the starting point is Aspernplatz by the Danube Canal. Along the way—for a rest—you can stroll into one of the parks (perhaps the Stadtpark), where you might hear Viennese music in summer as you relax at an outdoor café.

THE PALACES OF VIENNA: On your sightseeing tour of Vienna, I suggest that you start with the once-royal palaces, perhaps first—

Schönbrunn Palace

A Habsburg palace of 1441 rooms, Schönbrunn (tel. 83-36-46) was designed by those masters of the baroque, the von Erlachs. It was built between 1695 and 1700, ordered by Emperor Leopold I for his son, Joseph

I, with Leopold directing the architects to design a palace whose grandeur would surpass that of Versailles. However, Austria's treasury, drained by the cost of wars, would not support the ambitious undertaking, and the original plans were never carried out.

When Maria Theresa became empress, she had the original plans changed greatly, and Schönbrunn looks today much as she conceived it, with delicate, feminine rococo touches designed for her by the Italian, Pacassi. It was the imperial summer palace during Maria Theresa's 40-year reign, from 1740 to 1780, being considered by the empress as a fit place for her 16 children, six of whom did not live to grow up. Schönbrunn was the scene of great ceremonial balls and lavish banquets. During the 1814–1815 Congress of Vienna, fabulous receptions were held here. At the age of six, Mozart performed in the Hall of Mirrors before Maria Theresa and her court, and the empress held secret meetings with her chancellor, Prince Kaunitz, in the Chinese Room.

Franz Joseph was born at Schönbrunn, and the palace was the setting for much of the lavish court life carried on when he was emperor. He spent the last years of his life at Schönbrunn. The last of the rulers of the House of Habsburg, Karl I, signed his abdication document here on Nov. 11, 1918.

Napoleon, then Emperor of France, stayed here in 1806. A melancholy footnote to the connection between the arrogant Bonapartes and the House of Habsburg is revealed in the brief life history of the son of the Emperor Napoleon and his second wife, Marie-Louise, daughter of Franz I of Austria. The boy, hailed by his father as "King of Rome" but officially known as the Duke of Reichstatt, lived at Schönbrunn—but not entirely from choice. The Austrian minister of foreign affairs, Metternich, who had for his own Machiavellian reasons arranged the marriage of Napoleon and Marie-Louise, ordered what was tantamount to imprisonment for the young duke—house arrest at Schönbrunn. The palace was no doubt the best of all possible worlds in which to be incarcerated, but the "King of Rome" was still in custody there upon his death in one of the splendid guest rooms at the age of 21.

Schönbrunn Palace was damaged in World War II by Allied bombs and by occupation troops, but restoration has obliterated the scars.

In complete contrast to the grim, forbidding-looking Hofburg, Schönbrunn Palace, done in "Maria Theresa ochre," has **formal gardens,** laid out in 1705, embellished by the Gloriette, a marble summerhouse topped by a stone canopy on which the imperial eagle is mounted. The so-called Roman Ruins consist of a collection of marble statues and fountains, dating from the late 18th century when it was fashionable to simulate the ravaged grandeur of Rome. The park, which can be visited until sunset daily, was laid out by Ferdinand of Hohenburg and contains many lovely fountains and heroic statues, often depicting Greek mythological characters.

The **State Apartments** are the most stunning display within Schönbrunn Palace. Much of the interior ornamentation is in 14-karat gold, and many porcelain tile stoves are in evidence. Of the 45 rooms which you can visit, particularly fascinating is "The Room of Millions," decorated with Indian and Persian miniatures and considered to be the grandest rococo salon in the world. Much of the palace is in the rococo style, done in reds, white, and gold. You get to see the apartments once lived in by Franz Joseph and his ill-fated empress, Elizabeth, and the lavish rooms in which guests of the royal family were housed. Three of the rooms in Franz Joseph's quarters were decorated by the painter Joseph Rosa. You'll be shown the bleak chamber and the spartan iron bedstead in which the aging Franz Joseph died in 1916.

Among statistics you'll be told as you tour the palace, you learn that there are 139 kitchens but a shortage of private bathrooms. In fact not even Franz Joseph, the emperor, had a private bath.

Guided tours lasting 45 minutes are narrated in English from 9 a.m. to noon and from 1 to 5 p.m. in summer. The palace closes at 4 p.m. in winter. Admission is 35 AS ($1.86).

Well worth seeing is the **Schlosstheater,** or Palace Theater, which is still the setting for performances in summer. Marie Antoinette appeared on its stage in pastorals during her happy youth, and Max Reinhardt, the celebrated theatrical impresario, launched an acting school here.

Adjacent to the palace is the **Wagenburg,** or coach house (tel. 82-32-44), with a fine display of imperial coaches from the 17th, 18th, and 19th centuries. The coronation coach of Karl VI, which was pulled by eight white stallions, is here. It was hauled out for a total of seven Habsburg coronations. Also to be seen are coaches ridden in by Franz Joseph and his wife Elizabeth, and by Napoleon and his wife Marie-Louise. The grim funeral coach of Franz Joseph is also on display. The children's phaeton you will see was built for Napoleon's son. The Wegenburg is open from 10 a.m. to 5 p.m. (until 4 p.m. in winter), costing 15 AS (80¢) for admission. It's closed Monday.

The oldest zoo in Europe, **Tiergarten Schönbrunn** (tel. 82-12-36), dating from 1752, is in the grounds of Schönbrunn Palace, open daily from 9 a.m. to 6 p.m. Maria Theresa liked to take breakfast in the middle of the zoo.

The Schönbrunn botanical gardens are also open to visitors.

To reach the palace, take the underground U-4 green line to the Schönbrunn stop.

Hofburg Palace

The winter palace of the Habsburgs, known for its vast, impressive courtyards, the Hofburg (tel. 57-55-54) sits in the heart of Vienna. To reach it (you can hardly miss it), head up the Kohlmarkt into Michaelerplatz, which is decorated with two enormous fountains embellished with statuary. This complex of imperial edifices, the first of which was constructed in 1279, grew and grew as the empire did, so that today the Hofburg Palace is virtually a city within a city. The earliest parts were built around a courtyard, the **Swiss Court,** named for the Swiss mercenaries who used to perform guard duty here. This most ancient part of the palace is at least 700 years old.

Hofburg's complexity of styles, not always harmonious, is the result of each emperor's having added to it according to his own tastes and taking away some of the work of his predecessors. So grand were the architect's plans for the 20th-century changes that the empire had ended before they could be carried out. The palace, which has withstood three major sieges and a great fire, is called simply "*die Burg,*" or "the palace," by Viennese. Of its more than 2600 rooms, fewer than two dozen are open to the public.

The Imperial Treasury, **Schatzkammer** (tel. 52-63-99), reached by a staircase from the Swiss Court, is considered the greatest treasury in the world. It is divided into two sections: the Imperial Profane and the Sacerdotal Treasuries. One part displays the crown jewels and other imperial riches, and the other, of course, contains ecclesiastical treasures.

The most outstanding exhibit in the Schatzkammer is the imperial crown which dates from 962. It is so big that even though padded, it was likely to slip down over the ears of a Habsburg at a coronation. Studded with emeralds, sapphires, diamonds, and rubies, this 1000-year-old symbol of sovereignty is a priceless treasure, a fact recognized by Adolph Hitler who had it taken to Nürnberg in 1938 (the American army returned it to Vienna after World War II ended). Also on display is the imperial crown which was worn by the Habsburg rulers from 1804 to the end of the empire. You will see the saber of Charlemagne and the holy lance from the ninth century, a sacred emblem of imperial authority which in medieval times was thought to be the weapon that pierced the side of Christ on the cross. The Agate Bowl was once believed to be the Holy Grail.

Among great Schatzkammer prizes is the Burgundian Treasure seized in the 15th century, rich in vestments, oil paintings, gems, and robes. This loot is highlighted by artifacts connected with the Order of the Golden Fleece, that romantic medieval order of chivalry. You will also see the coronation robes of the imperial family, some of which date from the 12th century. The cradle of the "King of Rome," son of Napoleon and his Austrian second wife Marie-Louise, is in the Empire style in silver, pearl, and gilt.

Schatzkammer is open Monday, Wednesday, and Friday from 10 a.m. to 3 p.m., on Tuesday and Thursday from 1 to 5 p.m., and on Sunday from 9 a.m. to 1 p.m. It's closed on Saturday. Admission is 25 AS ($1.33). The treasury may not actually be open at the time of your visit, as it is being massively restored. However, while it is closed, some of its exhibits may be seen in the Museum of Fine Arts.

The Hofburg complex also includes the **Reichskanzleitrakt,** or Imperial Chancellery, where the emperors and their wives and children lived on the first floor. To reach the **Kaiserappartements** (Imperial Apartments), you enter via the rotunda of the Michaelerplatz. The apartments are richly decorated with tapestries, many from Aubusson. The court tableware and silver are magnificent, revealing the pomp and splendor of a bygone era. Leopoldinischer Trakt, or Leopold's apartments, date from the 17th century. You can't visit the quarters once occupied by Maria Theresa as they are now used by the president of Austria.

These Imperial Apartments seem to be more closely associated with Franz Joseph than with any other emperor, probably because of his long reign. His wife, Elizabeth of Bavaria, lived here too when she wasn't traveling, which actually was most of the time until her fatal stabbing by an assassin in Switzerland. Elizabeth believed in keeping fit and had a room where she worked out. She was a vain empress, refusing to sit for portraits after she turned 30. You'll see the "iron bed" of Franz Joseph, who claimed he slept like his own soldiers. Maybe that explains why his wife spent so much time elsewhere!

Guided tours of the Kaiserappartements, lasting half an hour, are conducted in English in summer from 8:30 a.m. to 4:30 p.m., to 1 p.m. on Sunday and holidays. Admission is 20 AS ($1.06).

Construction of **Die Burgkapelle** (Palace Chapel) in the Gothic style started in 1447 during the reign of Emperor Frederick III, but it was subsequently massively renovated in a rich baroque style. From 1449 it was the private chapel of the royal family. Today the Burgkapelle is the scene of the Hofmusikkapelle, an ensemble consisting of the Vienna Boys' Choir and members of the Vienna State Opera chorus and orchestra, performing works by classical and modern composers. Masses (performances) are held every Sunday and on religious holidays at 9:15 a.m. from January 1 to May 25, June 1 to June 29, September 21 to December 25, and December 28. Written applications for reserved seats should be sent at least eight weeks in advance of the time you wish to attend. The cost per seat ranges from 40 AS ($2.13) to 90 AS ($4.79). For reservations, write to **Verwaltung der Hofmusikkapelle,** A-1010 Vienna, Hofburg. If you failed to reserve in advance, you may be lucky enough to secure tickets from a block sold at the Burgkapelle box office every Friday from 5 p.m. on, but the queue starts lining up at least a half hour before that. Or you might settle for standing room (it's free).

The Vienna Boys' Choir boarding school is at Palais Augarten, 1 Obere Augartenstrasse.

Neue Burg, called the New Château, was the most recent addition to the Hofburg complex. Construction was started in 1881 and continued until work was halted in 1913. The palace was the residence of Archduke Franz Ferdinand, the nephew and heir apparent of Franz Joseph, whose assassination at Sarajevo set off the chain of events that led to World War I.

Neue Burg now houses four museums. One collection devoted to arms and armor is considered second only to that of the Metropolitan Museum in New York. It is in the **Waffensammlung** on the second floor of the New Château. You'll see crossbows, swords, helmets, and pistols, plus armor dating from the era of Maximilian and Charles V in the 15th and 16th centuries. Some of the exhibits, such as scimitars, were captured from the Turks as they fled the scene of their losing sieges of Vienna. Of bizarre interest is the armor worn by the little Habsburg princes, who had to learn the martial arts at a very early age.

Waffensammlung is open Tuesday through Friday from 10 a.m. to 3 p.m. and on Saturday and Sunday from 9 a.m. to 1 p.m. It's closed Monday. Admission is 25 AS ($1.33).

Another section, called **Musikinstrumentensammlung,** is devoted to old musical instruments, mainly from the 17th and 18th centuries but with some from the 16th. Some of the instruments, especially pianos and harpsichords, were played by Brahms, Liszt, Mahler, and Beethoven. The hours and admission charge are the same as for the Collection of Arms and Armor.

The **Ephesos-Museum,** or Museum of Ephesian Sculpture (tel. 93-45-41), is also in Neue Burg, with the same hours and price as those for the preceding collections. Here the prize exhibit is the 11 marble reliefs of Ephesus once owned by the co-regent with the Emperor Marcus around A.D. 161. The remains of a good-size marble frieze from the mausoleum of Lucius Verus depicts battle scenes from the Roman wars with the Parthians.

Visit the **Museum für Völkerkunde** (Ethnographical Museum) (tel. 93-45-41) if for no other reason than to see "Montezuma's treasure," three flamboyant feather robes which the mighty Aztec emperor is supposed to have given Cortés when the Spanish conquistador went to Mexico. The museum is open from 10 a.m. to 1 p.m. on Monday, Thursday, and Friday, to 5 p.m. on Wednesday, and from 9 a.m. to 1 p.m. on Sunday. Closed Tuesday. Admission is 15 AS (80¢).

Also in the Hofburg complex is the **Österreichische Nationalbibliothek,** or Austrian National Library (tel. 52-52-42), entrance on Josefplatz where you'll see an equestrian statue of Joseph II. The royal library of the Habsburgs was established in the 14th century, but the present building was constructed between 1722 and 1726. It was ordered by Karl VI and designed by those masters of the baroque, the von Erlachs. The Great Hall is a thing of ornate splendor, with frescoes by Daniel Gran. Part of the collection here belonged to Prince Eugene of Savoy during his lifetime. Many of the texts in the library date from the Middle Ages and even the Dark Ages. There's also a collection of thousands of rare autographs of both the famous and the forgotten.

The library may be visited daily, except Sunday and holidays, May to September from 10 a.m. to 4 p.m. (off-season from 11 a.m. to noon). Admission is 20 AS ($1.06).

The **Albertina** (tel. 52-42-32), entrance at 1 Augustinerstrasse, is another Hofburg museum, this one showing the development of graphic arts since the 14th century. Housing one of the world's greatest graphic collections, the museum was named for a son-in-law of Maria Theresa. The most outstanding exhibit in the Albertina is the Dürer collection, although what you will see are copies, the originals being shown only on special occasions. See, in particular, Dürer's *Praying Hands,* which has been reproduced throughout the world. The some 20,000 drawings and more than 250,000 original etchings and prints include work by such artists as Poussin, Fragonard, Rubens, Rembrandt, Michelangelo, and Leonardo da Vinci. Prince Eugene of Savoy collected many of the graphics displayed here.

The Albertina is open Monday, Tuesday, and Thursday from 10 a.m. to 4 p.m., until 6 p.m. on Wednesday, and until 2 p.m. on Friday. On weekends it's open from 10 a.m. to 1 p.m. (except closed on Sunday in July and August). Admission is 15 AS (80¢).

Augustinerkirche (Church of the Augustians), 3 Augustinerstrasse (tel. 52-33-38), was constructed in the 14th century as part of the Hofburg complex to serve as the parish church of the imperial court. In the latter 18th century it was stripped of its baroque embellishments and returned to the original Gothic features. The Chapel of St. George, dating from 1337, which you enter from the right aisle, is a mausoleum in which are 54 urns containing the hearts of Habsburgs. The chapel is open from Easter till the end of September from 2 to 2:30 p.m. on Monday and from 10 a.m. to 12:30 p.m. Tuesday through Friday. It's closed weekends and holidays. The tomb of the favorite daughter of Maria Theresa, Maria Christina, is also here, but there's no body in it. The princess is actually buried in the Capuchin Crypt, which I will describe later in this section under "Tombs of the Habsburgs." The richly ornamented empty tomb here was designed by Canova and is considered one of his masterpieces.

This church is a place of death but also of life. Maria Theresa married François of Lorraine here in 1736, and the Augustinerkirche was the site of other royal weddings: Marie Antoinette to Louis XVI of France in 1770, Marie-Louise of Austria to Napoleon in 1810 (by proxy—he didn't show up), and Franz Joseph to Elizabeth of Bavaria in 1854. Some of the great church music of Vienna is performed at this church on Sunday morning.

A bittersweet nostalgia seems to permeate the **Spanische Hofreitschule** (Spanish Riding School), a reminder of the fact that horses were an important part of both imperial and everyday life for many centuries, with their care and training a matter of pride and honor. The school is in the white, crystal-chandeliered ballroom in an 18th-century building of the Hofburg complex, designed by J. E. Fishcher von Erlach. There I always marvel at the skill and beauty of the sleek Lipizzaner stallions as their adept trainers put them through their paces in a show which is the same now as it was four centuries ago. These are the world's most famous and most classically styled equine performers. Many North Americans have seen them in the States, but to watch the Lipizzaners move to the music of Johann Strauss or a Chopin polonaise in their "airs above the ground" dressage in this, their home setting in Vienna, is a pleasure you should not miss.

Performances usually take place on Sunday at 10:45 a.m. and on Wednesday at 7 p.m., except in January, February, July, August, and December. Between mid-April and June and in September and October, short performances are held at 9 a.m. on Saturday. Reservations must be made in advance, as early as possible. Order your tickets for the Sunday show from the Spanish Riding School, 1 Michaelerplatz (tel. 52-18-36), or through your travel agency. Tickets for Wednesday and Saturday shows can be made only through a booking or travel agency. Prices for seats are 120 AS ($6.38) to 350 AS ($18.62); for standing room, 80 AS ($4.26) to 90 AS ($4.79); for short performances, 70 AS ($3.72). Children under 3 are not admitted, but those from 3 to 6 can attend free with adults.

Training sessions may be visited daily except Sunday in February, except Sunday and Monday from March till June and September till November. Tickets with no advance reservations for the training sessions can be purchased at door 3, Josefplatz, costing 35 AS ($1.86) for adults, 10 AS (53¢) for children.

Stallburg, which you enter at 2 Reitschulgasse, is a combination art gallery and stables for the Spanish Riding School, a somewhat unusual association. The structure in the Hofburg complex was begun in 1558 and was once the home of Emperor Maximilian. It consists of three floors of galleries opening onto a Renaissance-style courtyard. Maximilian II transformed the ground floor into stables for his horses, and despite heavy damage from Allied bombs in 1945, restoration has since allowed the stabling here of the Spanish Riding School's Lipizzaners. You may visit the stables Wednesday and Saturday from 2 to 4 p.m., on Sunday and holidays with performances from 12:15 to 12:45 p.m. (on those days with no performances from 10 a.m. to noon). Cost of the visit is 10 AS (53¢).

Tombs of the Habsburgs

Kaisergruft (Capuchin Crypt), Neuer Markt (tel. 52-68-53), was the burial place of the imperial family of Habsburgs for some three centuries. The vault is below the Kapuziner Church which was built between 1622 and 1632. Capuchin friars guard the final resting place of the Habsburgs, where 12 emperors, 16 empresses, and dozens of archdukes are entombed. But only their bodies are here. Their hearts are in urns in the St. George Chapel of the Augustinerkirche in the Hofburg complex, and their entrails are similarly enshrined in a crypt below St. Stephen's Cathedral.

Most outstanding of the imperial tombs is the double sarcophagus of Maria Theresa and her consort, the Emperor Francis I (François of Lorraine). Before she joined him on a permanent basis, the empress used to descend into the tomb by elevator to visit the gravesite of her beloved Francis. The "King of Rome," that ill-fated son of Napoleon and Marie-Louise of Austria, was buried here in a bronze coffin after his death at the age of 21. (Hitler managed to anger both the Austrians and the French by having the body of Napoleon's son transferred to Paris in 1940.)

Emperor Franz Joseph was interred here in 1916, a frail old man who outlived his time and died just before the final collapse of his empire. His wife, Empress Elizabeth, was buried in the crypt following her assassination in Geneva in 1898, as was their son, Archduke Rudolf, who committed suicide at Mayerling. Archduke Franz Ferdinand, heir apparent to Franz Joseph at the time of his assassination at Sarajevo, and Karl I, the last of the Habsburg rulers, were not entombed in the Kaisergruft. Karl I was buried in Madeira where he lived in exile after the fall of the Habsburgs. Countess Fuchs, the governess who practically reared Maria Theresa, lies in the crypt although she was not a Habsburg. (The empress bestowed this burial honor on the countess.)

The crypt may be visited daily from 10 a.m. to 4 p.m. for 20 AS ($1.06) admission. To find the Kaisergruft, head for Neuer Markt. The entrance is to the left of Kapuziner Church.

Belvedere Palace

Lying to the southeast of Schwarzenberg Palace on a slope above Vienna, approached through a long garden with a huge circular pond, Belvedere Palace was designed by Johann Lukas von Hildebrandt, who is considered the last major Austrian baroque artist. Built as a summer home for Prince Eugene of Savoy, Belvedere consists of two palatial buildings the design of which foretokens the rococo. The pond reflects the sky and the palace buildings, which are made up of a series of interlocking cubes. The interior is dominated by two great, flowing staircases.

Unteres Belvedere (Lower Belvedere), entrance at 6 Rennweg, was the only part lived in by Prince Eugene, known for his brilliant military strategy and a professor to Frederick the Great. The prince resided here from the time of its construction, complete with Orangery, which took from 1714 to 1716. He never lived in **Oberes Belvedere** (Upper Belvedere), which was started in 1721 and completed in 1723. It is entered at 27 Prinz-Eugen-Strasse.

The Gold Salon in Lower Belvedere, one of the most beautiful rooms in the palace, was selected by Prince Eugene as the site of his death. The legendary conqueror of the Turks breathed his last in 1736 in the salon in an elaborate baroque bed. Following his death, the Habsburgs took over the palace. Anton Bruckner, the composer, lived in Upper Belvedere until his death in 1896, and the palace was once the residence of Archduke Franz Ferdinand who was slain in 1914. In May 1955 the peace treaty recognizing Austria as a sovereign state was signed in Upper Belvedere by foreign ministers of the four powers which occupied this country at the close of World War II—France, Great Britain, the United States, and the Soviet Union.

Today visitors can come to the splendid baroque palace, enjoying the superb view of the Wienerwald (Vienna Woods) from the terrace and passing the regal formal French-style garden to go between Unteres and Oberes Belvedere to see the art collections now open to the public in both.

Lower (Unteres) Belvedere has a wealth of sculptural decorations and houses the **Österreichlisches Barokmuseum** (Museum of Baroque Art). Here are displayed the original sculptures from the Neuer Markt fountain, the work of George Raphael Donner who died in 1741. During his life, Donner dominated the development of Austrian sculpture of the 18th century, well founded in Italian art. On the fountain, four figures represent the four major tributaries of the Danube. Works by Franz Anton

Maulbertsch, an 18th-century painter, are also exhibited. Maulbertsch, strongly influenced by Tiepolo, was considered the most original and the greatest Austrian painter who lived in his century. He was best known for his iridescent colors and flowing brushwork.

Another section is the **Museum mittelalterlicher österreichischer Kunst** (Museum of Medieval Austrian Art) in the Orangery. Here you'll see works from the Gothic period. One Tyrolean Romanesque crucifix dates from the 12th century. Outstanding works include seven panels by Rueland Frueauf, scenes from the life of the Madonna.

Upper (Oberes) Belvedere was turned into **Österreichische Galerie des 19. and 20. Jahrhunderts** (the Austrian Gallery of 19th- and 20th-Century Art) (tel. 78-41-58-0) in 1954. In a large salon decorated in red marble you can see the 1955 peace treaty, mentioned above. Many paintings of the Biedermeier period in Austria are in this gallery. The west wing is devoted to art turned out during the long reign of Franz Joseph. Among outstanding works is *The Entrance of Charles V into Antwerp,* painted by Hans Makart. Also on display are many pictures by Gustav Klimt, who died at the end of World War I at the very collapse of the Austro-Hungarian Empire. Klimt was a founder of the Secession movement in art. See *Adam and Eve,* one of his most celebrated works. Klimt's student, Egon Schiele, who also died in 1918, is represented. *Death and the Girl* is one of his better known paintings.

The work of one of Austria's most noted artists, Oscar Kokoschka, can be seen here. Although most of the painter's life was spent in Britain to which he fled when the Nazis entered Vienna in 1938, becoming a naturalized citizen of the United Kingdom, Kokoschka is viewed as the greatest contemporary Austrian artist. He attempted to express psychological confusion and the solitude of women and men. The artist died in 1980.

Belvedere Palace is open daily from 10 a.m. to 4 p.m., until 1 p.m. on Friday. On Sunday and holidays, hours are from 9 a.m. to noon. It's closed Monday and most holidays. Admission is 15 AS (80¢). One-hour guided tours in English are conducted in summer.

THE MUSEUMS OF VIENNA: There are those who say that all of the inner city of Vienna is virtually a museum. That's true. Much of the city is to be enjoyed by strolling through its streets enjoying the monuments and squares, but in some cases you'll want to find out what's behind those grandiose facades, what hidden treasures they protect. The many buildings actually operating as museums will let you do just that.

Admission to all municipal museums is free throughout the year. Children up to the age of 14 are admitted free to most national museums. From September 1 to April 30, admission is free on Saturday, Sunday, and public holidays; from October 1 to March 31 at the Museum of Fine Arts (Kunsthistorisches Museum) and the Museum of Military History (Heeresgeschichtliches Museum).

If your schedule allows for a visit to only one, make it the—

Kunsthistoriches Museum

The Museum of Fine Arts, the Kunsthistoriches, 1 Maria-Theresian-Platz, across from the Hofburg Palace (tel. 93-45-41), is housed in a huge building which contains many of the fabulous art collections gathered up by the Habsburgs when they added new territories to their empire. Acquisitions range from the art of ancient Greece and Egypt up to the 20th century. The museum is rich in works of Dutch, German, Flemish, French, and Italian painters, with representation of many of the greatest European masters, such as Velásquez and Titian.

Among notable works from the German, Dutch, and Flemish schools are Roger van der Weyden's crucifixion triptych, a Memling altarpiece, and Jan van Eyck's portrait of Cardinal Richelieu. But it is the works of Pieter Brueghel the Elder for which the museum is renowned. This 16th-century Flemish master is known for his sensitive yet vigorous landscapes. He did many lively studies of the life of the peasants, and his pictures today are almost a storybook of life in his time. See especially his *Massacre of the Innocents* and *The Hunter in the Snow,* one of his most celebrated works. Don't confuse this artist with his son, Pieter Brueghel the Younger, also an artist.

Many visitors go to the gallery which displays the work of Van Dyck especially to see his *Venus in the Forge of Vulcan.* Rubens, naturally, comes in for a big, lavish display. You'll see his *Self-Portrait* and *Woman with a Cape,* for which he is said to have used the face of his second wife, Helen Fourment. Rubens brings a robust Flemish enthusiasm to the museum's galleries in both religious and allegorical works. Great pride is, of course, taken in the Rembrandt collection, which includes two remarkable self-portraits as well as a moving portrait of his mother and one of his son Titus. Holbein the Younger, who lived in England, painted *Jane Seymour,* third wife of Henry VIII.

For me, other than revisiting the works of Brueghel, the thrill of any trip to Vienna is seeing the Kunsthistoriches Museum's aggregation of the works of Albrecht Dürer, the German painter and engraver (1471–1528), known for his imaginative art and his painstakingly detailed workmanship. Here you will see his noted *Blue Madonna.* He was also known for his realistic landscapes as best seen in *Martyrdom of 10,000 Christians.* Dürer was a true Renaissance man.

The glory of the French, Spanish, and Italian schools is also to be seen in this Vienna museum, having often come into Habsburg hands as "gifts." Represented are Titian by his *A Girl with a Cloak,* Veronese by the *Adoration of the Magi,* Caravaggio by his *Virgin of the Rosary,* Raphael by *Virgin in a Country Scene,* and Tintoretto by his painting of Susanna caught off guard in her bath when the Peeping Tom elders came along. One of my all-time favorite painters is Il Giorgione, and here I can gaze long at his *Trio of Philosophers.* If you have only a short time to spend in this museum, I suggest that you skip many galleries if necessary just to see the work of Velásquez, the 17th-century Spanish artist often referred to as a "painter's painter." Some of his pictures of the court of Philip IV of Spain are exhibited.

One whole section of galleries is devoted to the works of ancient Egypt, Greece, and Rome. Don't miss seeing the tiny Egyptian hippopotamus. There is a noteworthy assemblage of cameos in onyx, some of which belonged to Emperor Augustus. There are also Etruscan antiquities on display.

In a sculpture and applied arts section, you can drool over the celebrated gold salt celler by Benvenuto Cellini, which was made for Francis I and is a Renaissance goldwork masterpiece. Here you'll also see a large collection of tapestries, some going back to early medieval times, and ivory horns from the ninth century. Perhaps you'll fancy a rococo breakfast service which was used by Maria Theresa and her big brood of young Habsburgs. Finally, there's a numismatic exhibit, with many medals left over from the Austro-Hungarian Empire.

The museum is open from 10 a.m. to 3 p.m. Tuesday to Friday, from 9 a.m. to 1 p.m. on Saturday, Sunday, and holidays. It's also open from 7 to 9 p.m. on Tuesday and Friday; closed Monday. Admission is 25 AS ($1.33).

On Maria-Theresian-Platz where the Kunsthistoriches Museum is situated stands a glorious concoction, a memorial constructed in 1888 to honor the long reign of Maria Theresa, with everybody from the Prince of Liechtenstein to Mozart clustered at the feet of the empress.

Uhrenmuseum der Stadt Wien

The Municipal Clock Museum, 2 Schulhof (tel. 63-22-65), has a wide-ranging assemblage of timepieces, some ancient, some modern, some in between. Housed in what was once the Obizzi town house, the museum dates from 1690 and displays clocks of all shapes and sizes. Clock collectors from all over Europe and America come to gaze and perhaps to covet. See Rutschmann's astronomical clock made in the 18th century. There are many cuckoo clocks and a gigantic timepiece which was once mounted in the tower of St. Stephen's.

The museum is open Tuesday to Friday from 10 a.m. to 4 p.m., on Saturday from 2 to 6 p.m., and on Sunday and holidays from 9 a.m. to 1 p.m. Admission is free.

Historisches Museum für Stadt Wien

The Historical Museum of Vienna, on the Karlsplatz (tel. 42-804), is a fascinating but apparently little-visited collection. History buffs seek it out, however, finding here the full panorama of the history of the old city unfolded, beginning with the settlement of prehistoric tribes in the Danube basin. Roman relics, artifacts from the reign of the dukes of Babenberg, and a wealth of leftovers from the Habsburg sovereignty are here, as well as arms and armor from various eras. A scale model shows Vienna as it looked in the Habsburg heyday. You'll see pottery and ceramics from the Roman era forward, 16th-century stained-glass windows, mementos of the Turkish sieges of the city in 1529 and 1683, and even Biedermeier furniture. There's also a section on Vienna "between the wars."

The museum is open Tuesday to Friday from 10 a.m. to 4 p.m. (till 7 p.m. on Thursday), on Saturday from 2 to 6 p.m., and on Sunday from 9 a.m. to 5 p.m. No admission is charged.

Akademie der bildenden Künste

When I'm in Vienna, I always make at least one visit to this academy of fine arts, 3 Schillerplatz (tel. 57-95-16), to see the *Last Judgment* triptych by the incomparable Hieronymus Bosch. In this work, the artist conjured up all the demons of the nether regions for a terrifying view of the suffering and sins that mankind must go through. There's more here than that, however, and you'll have the opportunity to see many Dutch and Flemish paintings, some from as far back as the 15th century, although the academy is noted for its 17th-century art. The gallery boasts works by Van Dyck, Rembrandt, Botticelli, and a host of other artists. There are several works by Lucas Cranach the Elder, outstanding being his *Lucretia,* completed in 1532, which some say is as enigmatic as *Mona Lisa*. Rubens is represented here by more than a dozen oil sketches. You can see Rembrandt's *Portrait of a Woman* and scrutinize Guardi scenes from 18th-century Venice.

Hours are from 10 a.m. to 2 p.m. on weekdays (except Wednesday, when the gallery is open from 10 a.m. to 1 p.m. and from 3 to 6 p.m.). On weekends it's open from 9 a.m. to 1 p.m. It's closed Monday. Admission is 10 AS (53¢).

Niederösterreichisches Landesmuseum

That polysyllabic name simply identifies the Museum of Lower Austria, 9 Herrengasse (tel. 63-57-11), housed in a 17th-century palace. Exhibits trace the story of life in Vienna from prehistoric times. Roman objets d'art, folkloric artifacts, Viennese antiques, regional costumes, and ecclesiastical works of art, including an altarpiece from Roggencorf, vie for attention here.

The museum is open from 9 a.m. to 5 p.m. daily, from noon to 5 p.m. on Sunday; closed on Monday. Admission is 15 AS (80¢).

Österreichisches Museum für Volkskunde

The Austrian Museum of Folklore, 15-19 Laudongasse (tel. 43-24-93), dating from the late 19th century, brings vividly to life the domestic affairs of the Austrian people of earlier times. You'll see how people lived in the remote east Tyrol and all the way to Lake Constance through some completely furnished farmhouse rooms, much baroque and religious art, and regional dress, among the exhibits. Artifacts depict a way of life—much of it already gone—made meaningful through well-arranged displays. Many painted chests, porcelain stoves, old toys and puppets reveal how people lived. The biggest and most impressive crib collection in the country is here, as well as a fascinating toboggan display.

Open from 9 a.m. to 3 p.m. daily, from noon to 3 p.m. on Saturday, and from 1 to 3 p.m. on Sunday, the museum is closed on Monday. Admission charge is 15 AS (80¢).

Österreichisches Museum für angewandte Künst

The Museum of Applied Art, 5 Stubenring (tel. 72-56-96), has a rich collection of tapestries, some from the 16th century. Of special interest is a Persian carpet depicting *The Hunt*. The most outstanding assemblage of Viennese porcelain in the world is here, as are some 13th-century Limoges enamels. Exhibits include much Biedermeier furniture and other antiques, glassware and crystal, and large collections of lace and textiles. One hall is devoted to art nouveau.

You can see these displays of applied art from 10 a.m. to 4 p.m. daily, until 6 p.m. on Thursday, and until 1 p.m. on Sunday. The museum is closed on Monday and Saturday. Entrance costs 15 AS (80¢).

Museum Moderner Künst

The Museum of Modern Art, 1 Fürstengasse (tel. 34-12-59), was opened in 1979 in a building which is virtually an architectural museum display item. Built between 1698 and 1711, the edifice, one of the most splendid in Vienna, was the home of the Prince of Liechtenstein. It is lavish with baroque adornment on the first floor. On the second floor, reached by elevator, there's a collection of early modern art, especially rich in German Expressionism.

Hours are daily from 10 a.m. to 6 p.m. (except Tuesday when it's closed). Admission is 15 AS (80¢).

Heeresgeschichtliches Museum

Vienna's Museum of Military History in the Armory, 18 Objekt, Arsenalstrasse (tel. 78-23-03), is the oldest state museum building in Vienna, constructed from 1849 to 1856. Mostly, of course, the military history of the Habsburgs—their glittering triumphs and their defeats—is delineated. A glass case in the center of the Hall of Glory (Ruhmeshalle) contains the six orders of the House of Habsburg which Franz Joseph wore on all public occasions. The colors are faded and the pins and other fasteners almost worn away from use. I find fascinating the Sarajevo room, with mementos of the assassination of Archduke Franz Ferdinand and his wife on June 28, 1914, the event which ignited the smoldering kindling and set off the deadly bonfire of World War I. The archduke's blood-stained uniform is displayed, along with the bullet-scarred car in which the royal couple rode on that fateful day. Many exhibits relating to the navy of the Austro-Hungarian Empire may be seen. You'll also view frescoes depicting important battles, including those fought with the Turks in and around Vienna.

The museum is open daily from 10 a.m. to 4 p.m. (except Friday when it's closed). A 15-AS (80¢) admission fee is charged.

THE CHURCHES OF VIENNA: The houses of worship are so inviting that even nonbelievers may want to attend on their Vienna visit, if not for the rich baroque decoration of crystal chandeliers and trompe l'oeil ceilings, then for the magnificent music of Mozart, Bach, Haydn, perhaps Bruckner. Many former Gothic churches have a massive baroque overlay, although some have been relieved of this decoration and put back to their original simpler style. If you spent a week visiting the churches of Vienna you still wouldn't have seen them all. If your stay here is relatively brief, I suggest you look at the first two recommended below, and then see others if you have more time. I'll begin with the king of them all—

St. Stephen's Cathedral

Lying in the very heart of the city on Stephansplatz, a bustling intersection where legend has it that if you wait long enough you'll see anybody you're looking for in the city, St. Stephen's Cathedral (tel. 53-25-61-563) was founded in the 12th century in what even in the Middle Ages was the town's center. The church was the result of a new basilica being built on the site of a Romanesque sanctuary.

Stephansdom, the German name for this church, was virtually destroyed in a 1258 fire which swept Vienna, and toward the dawn of the 14th century the Romanesque basilica gave way to a Gothic building. The cathedral suffered terribly in the Turkish siege of 1683 but then was allowed to rest until the Russian bombardments of 1945, with the Germans bringing more destruction when they continued to fire on Vienna from the outskirts as they fled the city. During these most recent depredations the wooden roof of St. Stephen's was heavily bombed, but it has been replaced with a steel structure. The steeple, rising to some 450 feet, has come to symbolize the very spirit of Vienna. Reopened in 1948 after restoration from war damage, today the cathedral is considered one of the greatest Gothic structures in Europe, rich in woodcarvings, altars, sculptures, and paintings.

The west door, in the Romanesque style, called Giants' Doorway *(Riesentor),* is one of the oldest parts of the main building, having been spared from the 1258 fire. It is richly embellished with statuary. The mammoth bell of St. Stephen's, Pummerin, or Boomer Bell, largest in the country, was originally cast from cannons left behind by the fleeing Turks after their failed siege of 1683. I'm sure the bell was sufficiently blessed to remove any heretical taint from the metal. Or perhaps some tinge remained, to be released in the fire of 1945, for the bell fell and shattered then, since replaced by a bell donated by Upper Austria.

The 352-foot-long cathedral is inextricably linked with Viennese and Austrian history. It was here that Mozart was buried in 1791 in a "pauper's funeral," and it was on the cathedral door that Napoleon posted his farewell edict in 1805.

The pulpit of St. Stephen's was carved from stone by Anton Pilgrim, his enduring masterpiece. But the chief treasure of the cathedral is the carved wooden Wiener Neustadt altarpiece dating from 1447, richly painted and gilded, found in the Virgin's Choir. See also the curious tomb of Emperor Frederick III in the Apostles' Choir. Made of a pinkish Salzburg marble in the 17th century, the tomb is carved with hideous little hobgoblins trying to enter and wake the emperor from his eternal sleep. The entrance to the catacombs or crypt is on the north side next to the Capistran pulpit. You can visit it from 10 a.m. to 4:30 p.m. for 20 AS ($1.06). In the crypt you'll see the funeral urns which contain the entrails of 56 members of the Habsburg family. (As I said earlier, the hearts are inurned in the St. George Chapel of the Augustinerkirche and the bodies entombed in the Capuchin Crypt of the Kapuziner Church.)

You can climb the south tower of St. Stephen's, 344 steps, which dominates the Viennese skyline and from which you have a view of the Vienna Woods. Called Alter Steffl (Old Steve), the tower with its needle-like spire was built between 1350 and 1433. From it, watch-keepers of earlier days kept vigil over the city. So well known is Old Steve that the Viennese refer to the entire cathedral as Alter Steffl. If you're game to climb the tower, you can do so from March to mid-November from 9 a.m. to 3:30 p.m., and until 5 p.m. in other months, for a fee of 15 AS (80¢).

The north tower (Nordturm) was never finished to match the south one, but was crowned with a Renaissance tower in 1579. You can reach it by elevator during the hours St. Stephen's is open, between 8 a.m. and 5 p.m., at a charge of 25 AS ($1.33). You view a panoramic sweep of the city and the Danube.

St. Maria am Gestade

This church at Passauer Platz, the Church of Our Lady of the Riverbank, was once just that, with an arm of the Danube flowing by it, making it a favorite place of worship for fishermen. But the river was redirected, and now the church draws people by its beauty. A Romanesque church on this site was rebuilt in Gothic style between 1394 and 1427. The western facade is in the flamboyant Gothic style, with a seven-sided Gothic tower surmounted by a dome which culminates in a lacelike crown. This tower has long been an Old Town landmark.

The church's most remarkable treasure is in the Chapel of St. Clement, an altarpiece made in 1460. See the panels depicting the Coronation of the Virgin and the Annunciation. In the interior are many pieces of Gothic statuary and superb woodcarving.

St. Maria am Gestade was much damaged during Turkish sieges, both in 1529 and 1683. In World War II, stained glass from the 14th century which had survived the Turks was damaged by modern man.

Church of the Teutonic Order

Die Deutschordenkirche and its treasury, Schatzkammer des Deutschen Ordens, both at 7 Singerstrasse (tel. 52-11-656), will stir thoughts of the Crusades in the minds of history buffs, but the relics of vanished glory may make some visitors wish they had been among the nobility of the Middle Ages.

The Order of the Teutonic Knights was a German society founded in 1190 in the Holy Land, and this is the church they built in Vienna in 1395. The building did not share in the baroque madness that swept the city following the Counter-Reformation, so you see it pretty much as it was originally, a Gothic church dedicated to St. Elizabeth. A choice feature is the 16th-century Flemish altarpiece standing at the main altar which is richly decorated with woodcarving, much gilt, and painted panel inserts. Many knights of the Teutonic Order are buried here, their heraldic shields still mounted on some of the upper walls.

In the treasury of the knights on the second floor of the church, you'll see mementos such as seals and coins illustrating the history of the order, as well as a collection of arms, vases, gold, crystal, and precious stones. These were very wealthy knights. Also on display are the charter given to the Teutonic Order by Henry IV of England and medieval paintings. A curious exhibit is a Viper Tongue Credenza, said to have the power to detect poison in food and render it harmless.

The treasury can be visited from 10 a.m. to noon and from 3 to 5 p.m. except on Monday. Admission is 15 AS (80¢).

St. Peter's Church

Called Peterskirche, this church dominates Peterplatz. It's the second-oldest church in Vienna, but the spot on which it stands may well be the *oldest* Christian church site. Many places of worship have stood here, the first believed to date from the second half of the fourth century. Charlemagne is credited with having founded a church on the site (late eighth or early ninth century).

The present St. Peter's, the most lavishly decorated baroque church in Vienna, was designed in 1702 by Gabriel Montani. Von Hildebrandt, the noted architect who designed the Belvedere Palace, is believed to have finished the building in 1708. The fresco in the dome is a masterpiece by J. M. Rottmayr, depicting the Coronation of the Virgin. The church contains many frescoes and much gilded stucco, plus altarpieces which are the work of many well-known artists of the time.

St. Rupert's Church

The oldest church in Vienna, Ruprechtskirche, stands at Ruprechtsplatz where it has been since 740, although much that you see now, such as the aisle, is newer—from the 11th century. It's believed that much of the masonry from a Roman shrine on this spot was used in the present church. The tower and nave are Romanesque, the rest Gothic.

St. Rupert is the patron saint of salt merchants of the Danube. I wonder if he was watching when the dread Gestapo of Hitler's Third Reich set up headquarters during World War II in a hotel close by. The grim reminder of Nazi inhumanity to man was demolished in 1945.

The church is not always open to the public, so if you really want to see it, I suggest you attend service on Sunday.

Church of St. Charles

Construction on Karlskirche, opening onto Karlsplatz, dedicated to St. Charles Borromeo, was begun in 1716 by order of Emperor Charles VI. Black plague swept Vienna in 1713, and the emperor made a vow to build the church if the disease would abate. Work on the structure was begun by that master of the baroque, Johann Bernard Fischer von Erlach, who labored from 1716 to 1722. His son Joseph Emanuel completed it between 1723 and 1739. The lavishly decorated interior was given to the people by the father and son leaders in the baroque field.

The well-known ecclesiastical artist, J. M. Rottmayr, painted many of the frescoes inside the church from 1725 to 1730. The green copper dome of Karlskirche is a lofty 236 feet high, a dramatic landmark on the Viennese skyline. Two columns, spin-offs from Trajan's Column in Rome, flank the front of the church, and there is also a statue in place by Henry Moore.

The Church of the Jesuits

Built at the time of the Counter-Reformation, the Jesuitenkirche at Dr. Ignaz-Seipel-Platz is rich in baroque embellishments, which is no surprise as it was constructed between 1627 and 1631 when the baroque craze in churches was sweeping the city. This was the university church, dedicated to the Assumption of the Virgin and built by order of the emperor, Frederick III.

In 1705 Andrea Pozzo, a Jesuit at a time when the influence of his order in Austria was at its zenith, created the trompe l'oeil painting on the ceiling which gives the illusion of a dome.

Church of St. Michael

Michaelerkirche on Michaelerplatz can date some of its Romanesque portions to the early 1200s. The exact date of the chancel is not known, but it is probably from the mid-14th century. Over its long history this church has felt the hand of many architects and designers, resulting in a medley of styles, not all harmonious. Perhaps only the catacombs would be recognized by droppers-in from the Middle Ages.

Most of the present look of St. Michael's dates from 1792, when the facade was done in the neoclassical style typical of the time. The spire, however, is from the 16th century. The main altar is richly decorated in baroque style, and the altarpiece, entitled *The Collapse of the Angels,* is the last major baroquc work done in Vienna. The year was 1781.

Church of the Minorites

If you're tired of baroque ornamentation, visit Minoritenkirche on Minoritenplatz, a church of the Friar Minor Capuchins, a Franciscan order also called the Minorite friars (inferior brothers, so called to emphasize their humility). This church, begun in 1250 but not completed until early in the 14th century, had its tower damaged by the Turks in their two sieges of Vienna, and then it fell prey to baroque architects and designers in the 18th century. But in 1784 Ferdinand von Hohenberg ordered that the baroque be removed and the simple lines of the original Gothic church returned, complete with Gothic cloisters. Inside you'll see a mosaic copy of da Vinci's *The Last Supper.*

Church of the Piarist Order

Work on Piaristenkirche, on Jodok-Fink-Platz, which is more popularly known as Piaristenplatz, was launched in 1716 by the Roman Catholic teaching congregation known as Piarists (fathers of religious schools), but the church was not consecreated until 1771. Some of the designs submitted during that long period are believed to have been drawn by von Hildebrandt, the noted architect who designed the Belvedere Palace, but many builders had a hand in things during the decades between construction start and consecration.

Despite the time lag and the many alterations during construction, this church is noteworthy for its fine, classic facade. Frescoes by F. A. Maulbertsch, done in 1752, adorn the inside of the circular cupolas.

Church and Court of the Scots

Heinrich, a Babenberg ruler who died in 1177, during his reign founded a "monastery of the Scots," Schottenhof in Freyung, in 1155. The monks were in fact Irish, but who was inclined to point out an error to a medieval monarch? So Schottenhof was and still is the "Courtyard of the Scots" and Schottenkirche the "Church of the Scots." Although it suffered much damage in the late Middle Ages, the church always bounced back and has survived massive alterations done in the 17th century, plus a major facelift which gave it its present appearance in 1880, the heyday of the empire. In the art gallery in the abbey, you'll see paintings showing Vienna in the Middle Ages.

Kirche am Hof

This most exuberantly baroque of all Vienna's churches is called "The Church of the Nine Choirs of Angels." With the Germanic penchant for expressing a name by stringing all the words together, I'm glad they simply call this church by its am Hof location rather than using a literal translation.

The church was constructed between 1386 and 1403 by Carmelite monks in the Gothic style. However, when the Jesuits took it over early in the time of the Counter-Reformation, they made many architectural changes, so that today it bears a simple baroque facade which was completed in 1692. In a chapel inside the church you can see a fresco by Franz Anton Maulbertsch, perhaps the greatest and most original of the 18th-century Austrian painters.

Kirche am Hof has a place in history. It was here that Franz II, seeing the end of the Holy Roman Empire approaching, proclaimed the Austrian Empire in 1804. It was well that he did. Just two years later the Holy Roman Empire, brought forth with great fanfare in 962, ceased to exist.

VIENNA WOODS: Yes, dear reader, there really are Vienna Woods. They weren't simply dreamed up by Johann Strauss as the subject of musical tales in waltz time. The Wienerwald is a land of gentle paths and trees several thousand acres in size in a delightful hilly landscape. If you stroll through this pleasant area, a weekend playground for the Viennese, you'll be following in the footsteps of Strauss and Schubert. Beethoven, when his hearing was failing, claimed that the chirping birds, trees, and leafy vineyards of the Wienerwald made it easier for him to compose.

A round trip through the woods, which lie to the south and west of Vienna, takes about 3½ hours by car, a distance of some 50 miles. You leave the city on the Eichenstrasse. Even if you don't have a car, the woods can be visited relatively easily on your own. Board trolleycar no. 1 near the State Opera House, going to Schottenring. There you must switch to tram no. 38 (the same ticket is valid) going out to Grinzing, the village that is the site of the famous heurigen, or wine taverns. At Grinzing you can board a bus that goes through the Wienerwald to Kahlenberg (see below). The whole trip costs about 35 AS ($1.86) and takes about 1½ hours each way. You might rent a bicycle nearby to make your own exploration of the woods.

Many of the attractions of the Wienerwald will be described in Chapter V, "Lower Austria."

When you go to the Vienna Woods by public transportation, after you reach Grinzing (if you can resist the heurigen), you board bus no. 38A up the hill to **Kahlenberg** on the northeasternmost spur of the Alps (1585 feet). If the weather is fair and clear, you can see all the way to Hungary and Czechoslovakia from here. At the top of the hill is the small Church of St. Joseph where King John Sobieski of Poland stopped to pray before leading his troops to the defense of Vienna against the Turks. For one of the best of all views overlooking Vienna, go to the right of the Kahlenberg restaurant. From the terrace there, you'll have a panoramic sweep, including the spires of St. Stephen's.

Many Austrian visitors from the country, a hardy lot, walk along a footpath to the suburb of Nussdorf and Heiligenstadt, perhaps along the very path Beethoven trod when he lived there. At Nussdorf, it's possible to take a trolleycar, designated D, which will return you to the heart of Vienna.

THE PARKS OF VIENNA: When the weather is fine, the typical Viennese shuns city parks in favor of the Wienerwald, brought to the notice of the world by Johann Strauss in his celebrated work, "Tales of the Vienna Woods." But if you're an aficionado of parks, you'll find some magnificent ones in Vienna, where there are more than 4000 acres of garden and parks within the city limits and no fewer than 770 sports fields and playgrounds. You can, of course, visit Schönbrunn Park and Belvedere Park when you tour those once-royal palaces.

Of the parks of Vienna, tastefully laid out by municipal authorities, I will highlight only the most popular, beginning with—

Stadtpark: This lovely garden is on the site of the slope where the Danube used to overflow into the inner city, before the canal was constructed. It can be reached from the Ring or from Lothringer-Strasse. Many memorial statues stand in the park, perhaps the best known being the one to Johann Strauss, Jr., composer of operettas and waltzes, including "The Blue Danube Waltz." (His father was also a noted musician.) Here too are monuments to Franz Schubert and to Hans Makart, a well-known artist whose work you'll see in churches and museums. You may wonder who some of the musicians and artists so memorialized were, as their fame has not survived.

The Kursalon, an elegant café-restaurant, sits at the south end of the Stadtpark. Here you can sit at a garden table and often enjoy a concert of Viennese music as you sip the local wine.

Volksgarten: Next to the Burgtheater, visited elsewhere in this book, the people's park was laid out on the site of the old city wall fortifications and can be entered from Dr.-Karl-Lueger-Ring. It's the oldest public garden in Vienna, dating from 1820. Here too there are many monuments. One to Franz Grillparzer, the poet, was sculptured in 1889. A memorial to the assassinated Empress Elizabeth dates from 1907. Construction of the so-called Temple of Theseus, a copy of the Theseion in Athens, was begun in 1820.

Burggarten: From the Burgring, you can enter this former garden of the Habsburg emperors, built soon after the Volksgarten was completed. There is a monument to Mozart in this park as well as an equestrian statue of Franz I, beloved husband of Maria Theresa. The only open-air statue of Franz Joseph in all Vienna is here. The Burggarten lies next to the Neue Hofburg. There's a statue of Goethe at the park entrance.

Botanischer Garten: Exotic plants from all over the world, many extremely rare, are found in this garden at 14 Rennweg (tel. 73-12-58), next to Belvedere Park, from which it can also be entered. The botanical garden grew out of a place where medicinal herbs were planted on orders from Maria Theresa. The garden may be visited from mid-April until the first of October from 9 a.m. to dusk, but always call before going if the weather is inclement as the garden may be closed. No admission is charged.

Donaupark: The entrance to this, the Danube Park laid out in 1964 between the Danube and the Old Danube which was diverted from its original course, is on Wagramer Strasse. The 247-acre park was converted from a garbage dump by municipal authorities. It's visited mainly by those who wish to go up to the 828-foot tower where there is a rotating café-restaurant, offering superb vistas of the city. There's an observation platform at 560 feet. Two express elevators take people to the top of the tower for 30 AS ($1.60) per person. The café revolves quickly, the restaurant taking more time. The tower is open from 9 a.m. till midnight (from 10 a.m. till 11 p.m. in winter). For information, phone 23-53-68.

The Prater

Since 1766, when Emperor Joseph II opened the Prater to the public, this extensive tract of woods and meadowland lying between the Danube River and the Danube Canal has been Vienna's favorite recreation area. Joseph, son and co-ruler of Maria Theresa, a liberal reformer and humanist, didn't always come up with changes everybody liked, but when he declared that "everybody shall be allowed to walk, ride, and drive in the Prater at their pleasure," he came up with a winner. Before that the area had been used mostly as a hunting preserve, riding ground, and general pleasance for the aristocracy. People still hunted in the wooded section until the reign of Franz Joseph.

Perhaps the coming of too many people drove all the game away, because from the time it was opened to the public, a collection of booths, amusements, and restaurants sprang up in the Prater and drew many visitors. In its early years it was a gathering place for the carriage trade too. Even the emperor and empress came here—when they could get in!

The Prater is considered the birthplace of the waltz. It was first heard here in 1820, introduced by Johann Strauss (the elder) and Josef Lanner. However, it was under Johann Strauss the Son, who became known as "the king of the waltz," that this music form reached its greatest popularity.

The best known part of the huge park is at the end nearest the entrance from the Ring. Here you'll find the **Riesenrad,** the giant ferris wheel, one of the landmarks of Vienna, constructed in 1897, 220 feet at its highest point. If you saw the film *The Third Man,* you may recall this ferris wheel in the scene where it appeared that Orson Welles was going to murder Joseph Cotten.

Just beside the Riesenrad is the terminus of the Lilliputian railroad, the 2.6-mile narrow-gauge line which operates in summer using vintage steam locomotives. The amusement park, right behind the ferris wheel, has all the typical entertainment facilities—roller coasters, merry-go-rounds, tunnels of love, games arcades, whatever.

The Prater is not a fenced-in park, but not all amusements are open all year. The season lasts from March or April until October, but the Riesenrad operates from the beginning of March until November 1. A ride on it costs 25 AS ($1.33) for adults, 10 AS (53¢) for children. Some of the more than 150 booths and restaurants stay open in winter, including the pony merry-go-round and the gambling places.

The **Prater Museum** (tel. 24-94-32), called Wurstelprater by the Viennese, has historical exhibits, including carousel figures and posters, illustrating the 200-year history of the park. In the Planetarium building near the ferris wheel, the museum is open on Saturday, Sunday, and public holidays from 2 till 7 p.m. Admission is free.

The Prater is also a sports center with swimming pools, riding schools, and race courses here and there between woodland and meadows. International soccer matches are held in the Prater stadium.

To reach the Prater, take either streetcar A or B from the Ring. If you drive here, don't forget to observe the "No Entry" and "No Parking" signs which apply from 3 p.m. on daily. The place is usually jammed on Sunday afternoon in summer. I suggest you schedule your visit at some other time.

HOMES OF FAMOUS MEN: Many of the residences once occupied by celebrated personages in Vienna, most often composers, have been made into museums and opened to the public. It's a privilege for the music lover to see the rooms once lived and worked in by his or her particular favorites. But dwelling places of noted persons outside the music world are also preserved. For instance, you may visit the apartment where the originator of psychoanalysis wrote of his revolutionary studies.

If you're a Beethoven fancier and want to see where this genius lived, you'll have to do a bit of footwork, as he seems never to have stayed long in one place. He was evicted from several of his dwellings because of a habit he had of composing at 3 o'clock in the morning. His music may have been heavenly, but it probably came off as pretty hellish to neighbors who preferred to spend the night hours sleeping.

You can visit one of his residences where the landlord was tolerant (or the neighbors hard of hearing!), the **Pasqualati House,** 8 Mölkerbastei (tel. 63-70-665). The building dates from the 1790s, and Beethoven lived there—on and off—from 1804 to 1819. He is known to have composed his Fourth, Fifth, and Seventh Symphonies here, as well as *Fidelio* and the *Moonlight Sonata,* among other works.

There isn't much to see except some family portraits and the composer's scores, but you may feel it's worth the climb to the fourth floor (there's no elevator). You may visit the apartment Tuesday to Friday from 10 a.m. to 6 p.m., on Saturday from 2 to 6 p.m., and on Sunday from 9 a.m. to 1 p.m. No admission is charged.

Haydns Wohnhaus (Haydn's House), 19 Haydngasse (tel. 56-13-07), is where Franz Josef Haydn conceived and wrote his magnificent later oratorios *The Seasons* and *The Creation.* He lived here from 1797 until his death in 1809. Haydn gave lessons to Beethoven here. There's also a room in this house, which is a branch of the History Museum of Vienna, honoring Johannes Brahms. Hours are from 10 a.m. to 6 p.m. Tuesday to Friday, from 2 to 6 p.m. on Saturday, and from 9 a.m. to 1 p.m. on Sunday. There's no admission charge.

The **Mozart-Erinnerungsräume,** or Mozart Memorial, is at 5 Domgasse (tel. 52-40-732), in a 17th-century house, called the House of Figaro because Mozart composed his opera *The Marriage of Figaro* here. The composer's life in this house from 1784 to 1787 was a relatively happy period in what was otherwise a rather tragic life. It was here that he often played chamber music concerts with Haydn, whose home we have just visited. Later, Mozart was not to have such a fancy address as this one on Domgasse. Over the years he lived in a dozen houses in all, which became more squalid as he aged. He died in poverty and was given a pauper's burial at St. Stephen's Cathedral in 1791.

The Domgasse apartment has been turned into a museum. Hours are from 10 a.m. to 4 p.m. Tuesday to Friday, 2 to 6 p.m. on Saturday, and 9 a.m. to 1 p.m. on Sunday.

Schuberts Geburthaus (Schubert's birthplace) is at 54 Nussdorferstrasse (tel. 34-59-924). The composer, son of a poor schoolmaster, was born in 1797 in a house built earlier in that century. Many Schubert mementos are on view. The house is open from 10 a.m. to 4 p.m. Tuesday to Friday, from 2 to 6 p.m. Saturday, and from 9 a.m. to 1 p.m. Sunday. Schubert's last residence was in his brother's house, 6 Kettenbruckengasse (tel. 57-39-072), and the room in which he died at the early age of 31 has been made into a memorial. Admission is free.

"The king of the waltz," Johann Strauss, Jr., lived at the **Johann-Strauss-Wohnung,** 54 Praterstrasse (tel. 24-01-21), for a number of years, composing "The Blue Danube Waltz" here in 1867. Now part of the History Museum of Vienna, the house is open Tuesday to Friday from 10 a.m. to 4 p.m., on Saturday from 2 to 6 p.m., and on Sunday from 9 a.m. to 1 p.m. There is no charge for admission.

The **Sigmund Freud apartment,** 19 Berggasse (tel. 31-15-96), with its dark furniture (only part of it original), lace curtains, and collection of antiquities, gives you the feeling that the doctor might walk in at any moment and tell you to make yourself comfortable on the couch. His velour hat, dark walking stick with ivory handle, and other mementos are to be seen in the study and waiting room he used during his life here from 1891 to 1938. When Hitler staged his takeover of Austria, the so-called Anschluss, Freud fled these quarters to seek safety in London.

You may visit the apartment from 9 a.m. to 1 p.m. Monday to Friday, from 9 a.m. to 3 p.m. on weekends. Admission costs 25 AS ($1.33) for adults, 15 AS (80¢) for children.

2. Where to Shop

Visitors find much of interest to buy or just to look at in Vienna's shops, where you'll see handicrafts produced in a long-established tradition of skilled workmanship. Popular for their beauty, quality, and reasonable prices are petit-point items, hand-painted Wiener Augarten porcelain, work of gold- and silversmiths, handmade dolls, ceramics, enamel jewelry, wrought-iron articles, leathergoods, and many other items of value and interest.

The main shopping streets are in the city center (first district). Here you'll find **Kärntnerstrasse,** between the Opera House and Stock-im-Eisen-Platz; the **Graben,** between Stock-im-Eisen-Platz and Kohlmarkt; **Kohlmarkt,** between the Graben and Michaelplatz; and **Rotensturmstrasse,** between Stephansplatz and Kai. There are also **Mariahilferstrasse,** between Babenbergerstrasse and Schönbrunn, one of the longest streets in Vienna; **Favoritenstrasse,** between Sütdiroler Platz and Reumannplatz; and **Landstrasser Hauptstrasse.**

Shops are normally open Monday through Friday from 9 a.m. to 6 p.m. and on Saturday from 9 a.m. to noon. Small shops close at noon for lunch. Railroad station shops in the Westbahnhof and the Südbahnhof are open from 7 a.m. to 11 p.m., offering groceries, smoker's supplies, stationery, books, and flowers. These two stations also have hairdressers, public baths, and photo booths.

Vienna's antique shops hold what seems to be a limitless treasure trove, and you can find valuable old books, engravings, etchings, and paintings in secondhand shops, bookshops, and picture galleries.

The state-owned **Dorotheum,** 19 Dorotheergasse (tel. 52-31-29), is the oldest auction house in Europe, dating from 1707 when it was founded by the emperor, Joseph I, as an auction house for the poor people of Vienna. If you're interested in what is being auctioned off, you give a small fee to a *Sensal,* one of the licensed bidders, and he or she will bid in your name. The Dorotheum is also the scene of many art auctions, and there are 16 subsidiaries in other districts, plus large private galleries and antique dealers.

You may find a little of everything at the **Flohmarkt** or flea market, in the vicinity of the Naschmarkt, near the Kettenbrückengasse underground station. It is held every Saturday from 8 a.m. to 6 p.m. except on public holidays. Naturally it's customary to haggle over the price, and the Viennese have perfected that skill.

The **Naschmarkt** itself is a vegetable and fruit market, the "Covent Garden of Vienna," which has a lively scene every day. To visit it, head south of the Opera district. It's at Linke and Rechte Wienzeile.

Ö. W. (Österreichische Werkstatten), 6 Kärntnerstrasse (tel. 52-24-18), is a big, well-run store that sells hundreds of handmade art objects from Austria. You'll find an especially good selection of pewter, along with enameled jewelry, glassware, brass, baskets, ceramics, and serving spoons fashioned from deer horn and bone. Be sure to keep wandering through this place, as there are three floors and a friendly staff. Even if you skip the other stores of Vienna, check this one out.

Trachten Schlössl, 2 Kohlmarkt (tel. 63-92-34), is one of Vienna's most fabulous women's clothing stores, where the decor is as elegant as the garments. The dozen or so saleswomen are charming and very helpful. It opened as recently as 1982 in a three-story town house where the in-house fitters (all three of them) work in rooms opening off the wrought-iron stairwell connecting the three floors. You'll see the most exotic Biedermeier sofas and chairs in Vienna against a background of marble floors, wood paneling, and pink- and cream-colored walls. Many of the clothes are custom-made, and include suits in Austrian suede or English tweed. Austrian and English winter coats are sold, along with lots of accessories, including scarves and umbrellas. The clothes are not as expensive as you might think, with suits generally ranging upward from 2000 AS ($106.48).

Lanz, 10 Kärntnerstrasse (tel. 52-24-56), is a prominent branch of a well-known Austrian chain store which specializes in regional clothing. It has a rustically elegant format of wood paneling and brass chandeliers. Most of their stock is for women, although they do offer a limited selection of men's jackets. Clothes for toddlers begin at sizes appropriate for a six-month-old child, while women's apparel begins at size 36 (American size 7). A well-made suede skirt usually costs around 4500 AS ($239.40), although less expensive dirndls are available too.

Gerold and Co., 31 Graben (tel. 52-22-35), is the best bookstore in Vienna for English-language publications. The sales personnel are very helpful, and you can often pick up many titles not readily available elsewhere.

J. and L. Lobmeyer, 26 Kärntnerstrasse (tel. 52-21-89). If during your exploration of Vienna you should happen to admire a crystal chandelier, there's a good chance that it was made by this company. It was designated in the early 19th century as a purveyor to the Imperial Court of Austria, and it has maintained an elevated position ever since. The company is credited with designing and creating the first electric chandelier in 1883. It has also designed chandeliers for the Vienna Opera, the Metropolitan Opera in New York, even the Assembly Hall in the Kremlin.

Behind its art nouveau facade on the main shopping street of town, you'll see at least 50 chandeliers of all shapes and sizes. The store also sells hand-painted Hungarian porcelain, along with complete breakfast and dinner services. They'll also engrave your family crest on a wine glass if you want it, or sell you one of the uniquely modern pieces of sculptured glass from the third-floor showroom. The second floor is a museum of some of the outstanding pieces the company has made since it was established in 1823. The least expensive item in the store sells for 200 AS ($10.64). It's a paperweight.

Mary Kindermoden, 14 Graben (tel. 52-79-03), is—at last!—an inexpensive store specializing only in children's clothing with a regional twist. If you've thought about buying your nephew a pair of lederhosen or a dirndl for your niece, this is the place to go. In the heart of the old city, near St. Stephen's Cathedral, the establishment has two floors of well-made garments which even include lace swaddling clothes for a christening. Most garments are for children aged 10 months to 14 years, although lederhosen (which are adorable if you can get junior to wear them) range from children 10 months to 8 years. The most expensive pair in the store costs 450 AS

($23.94). The staff speaks English and seems to know how to deal with children.

J. Jolles Werkstätte, 5 Fassziehergasse (tel. 93-01-11). Petit-point embroidery is a famous Viennese craft, and much of the merchandise you'll see here comes from private homes where women create it on a piecemeal basis. Some of the handbags are exceptional, and some truly outstanding wall hangings and tapestries are on sale as well. Some of the goods are produced on the premises, with a total output so large that the establishment is said to be the major producer in Europe. Closed Saturday.

Albin Denk, 13 Graben (tel. 52-44-39), is the oldest remaining porcelain store doing continuous business since its establishment in 1702. Its clients have included the Empress Elizabeth, who saw the shop in almost the same format you'll see it in today. The decor of the three low-ceilinged rooms is beautiful, as are the thousands of objects from Meissen, Dresden, and other regions contained therein. With such a wealth of riches it's hard to make a selection, but the amusing staff will help you.

Mädler, 24 Mariahilferstrasse (tel. 93-32-39), has been *the* name in leather wear in Vienna since 1973. The firm was originally established in Leipzig in 1850, and now has branches in chic districts throughout Europe. Suitcases and handbags are traditional favorites here. All of Mädler's goods have style, flair, and durability.

3. Vienna After Dark

Come to the cabaret . . . or the heurigen or the disco or the casino—whatever turns you on in the nightlife scene. Vienna has a little bit of everything and a lot of some late-evening entertainment activities to pursue after you've been to the theater or opera and perhaps topped it off with a fine dinner. Now you're ready to play. You can dance, go to shows, gamble, listen to music, and smile a lot in gemütlich nighttime Wien.

Liquor costs pretty much the same in all the clubs, although sometimes a cover charge is imposed, especially when live entertainment is offered. Often it's only 125 AS ($6.65), but it may be higher if you go for erotic specialties. Financially, it's better to drink beer in nightspots than hard liquor as the latter is expensive—from 75 AS ($3.99) for scotch.

FASHIONABLE BARS: The **Eden Bar,** 2 Liliengasse (tel. 52-74-50), is perhaps the top chic rendezvous spot in Vienna, drawing local society figures as customers. It's open from 10 p.m. to 4 a.m., but if you show up much before midnight you may have the place to yourself. The Eden is a popular *après-théâtre* stop, and if there's a foreign celebrity in Vienna, he or she is likely to visit here. A live band plays for dancing.

New Splendid Bar, 3 Jasomigrottstrasse (tel. 63-15-15), rivals the Eden as a fashionable watering spot and keeps the same hours—10 p.m. to 4 a.m.—making it a good place to drop in for a nightcap. A live band, usually from Milan or some other place "south of the border," plays for dancing in this three-tiered room. The New Splendid also attracts celebrities.

DISCO: **Queen Anne,** 12 Johannesgasse (tel. 52-02-03). Lots of colorful people have dropped into the Queen Anne nightclub and disco (the leading one in town), including Joan Fontaine, German playboy Gunther Sachs, the Princess of Auersperg, and Jimmy Page of Led Zeppelin. It recently celebrated its ninth year as one of Vienna's foremost "hot spots." The club has a big collection of the latest Stateside and Italian records, as well as occasional musical acts performed by singers ranging from Mick Jagger lookalikes to jungle imitations of Watusi dancers. The evergreen doors with brass trim open from 9 p.m. to 3 a.m. Drinks begin at 75 AS ($3.99).

Take Five, 3 Annagasse (tel. 52-32-76), is one of the city's leading discos, with an international clientele. Mostly recorded music is played at this nightspot just off the Kärntnerstrasse. Open from 10 p.m. to 3:30 a.m., the disco charges 10 AS (53¢) at the door.

Atrium, 10 Schwarzenbergplatz (tel. 65-35-94), was Vienna's first disco. For a long time it was the "in" place for university students, but a more diversified crowd is now found at this disco-cum-wine tavern. Customers can savor the smoke-gets-in-your-eyes atmosphere from 8 p.m. to 2 a.m. The entrance charge is 25 AS ($1.33).

It's called **Scotch Dancing,** but except perhaps for the whisky you might drink, there's not much Scottish ambience at this disco at 10 Parkring (tel. 52-94-17). The place has a hodgepodge decor—everything from nautical gear to Tyrolean artifacts. The bar is on the ground level, but it's in the candlelit cellar that you'll find the action. Customers are an international crowd in their late 20s and early 30s, usually. Although not as chic as it once was, the place is still quite popular most nights. It's open from 8 p.m. to 2 a.m. Sunday to Tuesday, to 4 a.m. Wednesday to Saturday. There's no cover charge.

Capt'n Cook, 23 Franz-Josefs-Kai (tel. 63-13-81), is one of the top discos in Vienna, with one of the city's best DJs. During peak time, Friday and Saturday, it's open from 8 p.m. to 4 a.m., closing at 2 a.m. from Sunday to Thursday. This is a large, comfortable place where you can sit at the bar if you prefer.

Chattanooga, 29a Graben (tel. 52-41-86), offers one of the most popular sidewalk cafés along the Graben in summer. Inside, the decor of its restaurant is like that of a railroad car in the Gay '90s, with formally dressed waiters working feverishly behind glass counters. Aside from drinks such as beer at 22 AS ($1.17), they serve cheeseburgers and simple meals from 50 AS ($2.66) to 150 AS ($7.98). The real reason for coming here, however, is the disco downstairs. You'll get a modernized view of the generous proportions of old Vienna in the wide mirrored staircase leading to the half-rounded room with its maroon velvet niches. Stylized white tree trunks sprout from the floor to the sophisticated decor of the ceiling (displays are likely to change for certain musical acts). The entrance fee is usually between 20 AS ($1.06) and 30 AS ($1.60). Drinks start at 70 AS ($3.72) for a Coke. The club is open from 8 p.m. to 2 a.m. weekdays, to 4 a.m. on Saturday and Sunday. Its location on the Graben puts it in the very center of the city.

Sowieso, 1 Grashofgasse (tel. 52-12-36), contains two restaurants, a disco, and a backgammon club. Specialties in the restaurant include spare ribs, chili con carne, and an additional 15 dishes as part of the daily menu. The first restaurant is open from 5 p.m. to 2 a.m, while the disco and the second restaurant are open from 8 p.m. to 4 a.m. The gambling club opens at 5 p.m., closing at 4 a.m. Whisky in all sections begins at 75 AS ($3.99).

JAZZ: Right next door to Take Five, described above, is the **Tenne,** 3 Annagasse (tel. 52-57-08), where live groups play jazz music for listening or for dancing on a floor with a circle of boxes hovering above. Tenne has a log cabin ambience with lots of farm equipment, such as ox yokes, making up the decor. Waitresses wear tight-fitting dirndls. Admission is usually 15 AS (80¢).

EROTIC NIGHTCLUBS: **Casanova,** 6 Dorotheergasse (tel. 52-98-45), is considered *the* leading nightclub of Vienna. The top bands of Europe perform here. If you're an unattached male, many girls will find you interesting—if the price is right. The club is open from 9 p.m. to 4 a.m., with erotic shows presented at 9:30 p.m. and at 12:30 a.m. Each show lasts two hours and is aimed at increasing the pulse rates of the audience. Expect to spend from 300 AS ($15.96) for a seat.

Moulin Rouge, 11 Walfischgasse (tel. 52-21-30), was for years the leading nightclub of Vienna, but there's serious competition for that slot today. If you're window-shopping, you can see pictures of the "artists" who will later disrobe for you during a show. However, in the pictures you view from the sidewalk the girls are stark naked, so there's no surprise awaiting you if you decide to go into the club's lavishly decorated room which has two tiers of seating. You'll spend from 300 AS ($15.96) for a seat. Drinks are expensive, but some visitors feel impelled to buy a whole bottle of scotch, which skyrockets the expenditure. The per-drink charge for scotch is 160 AS ($8.51). Beer by the mug is 100 AS ($5.32). Girls come in all shades here. If you're a halfway presentable single male and willing to pay the price, you won't have to wait long for companionship.

Another leading nightclub, **Renz,** 50 Zirkusgasse (tel. 24-31-35), is a bit out of the way, being near the Prater. The art of disrobing is practiced to perfection here, with ecdysiastic artistes from all over the world and in all skin hues likely to be featured. Sometimes, even, a renowned headliner (with clothes on) will appear on stage. You'll be charged from 300 AS ($15.96) for a seat.

GAY: **Why Not?** at 22 Tiefer Graben (tel. 66-11-58) draws not only the gay crowd but also a large number of straight couples, who, for reasons known only to themselves, like to hang out in a homosexual ambience. You can make merry here until 4 a.m.

SONG AND DANCE: **Fledermaus,** 2 Spiegelgasse (tel. 52-84-38), is one of my favorite clubs in Vienna, and it might get to be yours too. George Dimou, an old hand at show business, runs this place, presenting first-rate entertainment at honest prices. Prepare to make an evening of it when you come here, as some shows last up to 3½ hours or more, with breaks between some of the acts for dancing. Fledermaus is sort of a "Catch a Rising Star" place for young Viennese singers who hope to be discovered through appearances here. It's open from 10 p.m. to 4 a.m. Monday through Saturday. If you want a companion, bring your own—there are no pickups here.

GAMBLING: **Spiel-Casino Wien,** Estherhazy Palace, 41 Kärntnerstrasse (tel. 52-48-36), which opened in 1968, is the most expensive casino in Austria. Its admission is 130 AS ($6.92), but that entry fee provides you with 150 AS ($7.98) in gambling chips. You'll need to show your passport to get in (and they're strict about that!). The casino itself is one flight above street level. The minimum stake at any game is 50 AS ($2.66). You can charge up to $600 worth of chips to a Diner's Club credit card, providing you do so over a three-day period. You'll see gaming tables for baccarat, roulette, blackjack, and chemin de fer. The club opens at 7 p.m.

THE HEURIGEN: These wine taverns on the outskirts of Vienna were introduced in Chapter II, under "Food and Drink." These gardens of vintners lie principally in Grinzing (the most popular district) or in Sievering, Neustift, Nussdorf, or Heiligenstadt. They have been celebrated in operettas, films, and song.

In some of the more basic taverns the schilling-wise Viennese bring their own *heurigenpackerl,* a picnic composed mainly of cold cuts, cheese, some chicken, always a sausage, and hard-boiled eggs. But many of these so-called heurigen have grown into elaborate restaurants.

If you don't want to pack your own lunch or dinner and still want to economize, you can bring along inexpensively priced picnic packages sold at many a deli in Vienna. However, you can bring your own lunch into only the simpler worker's type of wine cellars, where the proprietor is content just to sell wine. Often his wife and family prepare food which they'd like to sell, however.

The most-visited section, **Grinzing,** lies at the edge of the Vienna Woods. Once it was a separate village until it was overtaken by the ever-increasing city boundaries of Vienna. Much of Grinzing remains unchanged, as it looked in the days when Beethoven lived nearby and composed music. It's a district of crooked old streets and houses with thick walls which are built around inner courtyards that are often grape arbors sheltering gemütlich Viennese wine-drinkers on a summer night. The playing of zithers and accordions lasts long into the night.

Which brings up another point. If you're a motorist, don't drive out to the heurigen. Police patrols are very strict, and you're not to be apprehended with more than 0.8% alcohol in your bloodstream. It's much better to take public transportation. For example, to go to Grinzing from the heart of Vienna takes only about half an hour.

Take trolley line No. 38 to Grinzing; No. 41 to Neustift am Wald, or trolley car no. 38, the same as for Grinzing, to Sievering, which is also reached by bus 39. Heiligenstadt is reached by underground line U-4.

At a typical heurige you can spend an evening, ordering a liter of wine and snacks, for about 250 AS ($13.30).

I'll lead off with some of my favorites, although you may find dozens more on your own.

Figlmüller, 55 Grinzingerstrasse (tel. 32-42-57), in Grinzing, is a Biedermeier-style heurige restaurant, which is much larger than its already-recommended sister restaurant in Vienna. Its menu is very big, always featuring Viennese-style specialties, well prepared and relatively inexpensive at between 70 AS ($3.72) and 150 AS ($7.98) for a meal. It's open from 5 p.m. to midnight Monday to Saturday, and is closed Sunday and holidays and from Christmas until the end of April. The wienerschnitzel here is so large it almost falls off your plate, and the potpourri salad offers copious amounts of 11 kinds of vegetables and greens.

Grinzinger Hauermandl, 20 Cobenzlgasse (tel. 32-20-444), in Grinzing, is a rustic inn where many of the guests are lively Viennese escaping their city for an evening in the suburbs. You'll enter through a garden where you'll notice a gypsy wagon perched on the roof. The farm-style cookery includes noodle soup with liver dumplings, as well as a selection of dishes so hearty they could fortify you for a day's work in the vineyards. A quarter liter of wine (about two glasses) costs around 25 AS ($1.33), while à la carte meals range from 130 AS ($6.92) to 240 AS ($12.77).

Altes Presshaus, 15 Cobenzlgasse (tel. 32-23-93), in Grinzing, is the oldest heurige in Grinzing, with an authentic cellar which you should ask to see. The interior is filled with wood paneling and antique furniture, giving the place lots of character. It's closed Sunday and during all of November and December, and every Thursday until 5 p.m. The garden terrace blooms throughout most of the summer. Meals cost from 130 AS ($6.92) to 240 AS ($12.77); wine from 25 AS ($1.33).

Mayer, 2 am Pfarrplatz (tel. 37-1-287), in Heiligenstadt, is a historic house, some 130 years old when Beethoven composed sections of his Ninth Symphony while living here in 1817. Today Viennese music replaces the melodies that may have filled the house during Ludwig's era. However, the same kind of fruity dry wine is still sold to guests in the shady courtyard of the well-kept rose garden. Menu items, aside from the new wine, include grilled chicken, savory pork, and a lavish buffet of well-prepared country-style food. Reservations are suggested. It's open daily from 4 p.m. to midnight. The owner, Franz Mayer, spends part of his time working with the Austrian Ministry of Agriculture. Meals cost from 150 AS ($7.98).

Alt Sievering, 63 Sieveringer Strasse (tel. 32-58-88), is one of several attractive heurigen in this pleasant suburb of Vienna. The owner, Walter Slupetzky, serves not only excellent new wine, but prepares such specialties as game, lamb, fish, soufflés, dessert pancakes, strudels, and cakes. A fixed-price meal, which you can eat in summer under the trees, costs around 65 AS ($3.46), while à la carte meals range from 150 AS ($7.98). The restaurant is open from 9 a.m. to 11 p.m. except Tuesday and Wednesday. If you prefer beer, the house keeps three different types on tap.

Killerman, 22 Sonnbergstrasse (tel. 86-81-81), in Perchtoldsdorf, wasn't a heurige until Luki and Marina Killerman transformed a century-old building into the attractive establishment you see today. The tasteful interior is painted in clear colors, the service is friendly and efficient, and the food is a savory blend of fleckerln with ham, roast veal, all kinds of country meats, sauerkraut, fresh salads, and noodles, much of it embellished with heaps of butter and sour cream. Reservations are suggested. It's closed Sunday and Monday and from the day before Christmas until the end of the first week of January, as well as during most of July and August. The cost of a meal is from 150 AS ($7.98).

Heuriger Zimmerman, 3-5 Armbrustergasse (tel. 37-22-11), in the Heiligenstadt/Nussdorf sector, has a pleasant interior of brick, stucco, heavy beams, and paneling. One of the rooms looks onto an arbored courtyard, with a flagstone floor and simple tables and wooden benches. The ample buffet is placed on a trestle table with red napery, and usually costs between 65 AS ($3.46) and 180 AS ($9.58), not counting your drinks. It's open every day from 5 p.m. to midnight except on Sunday and holidays. It's also closed in August.

COFFEEHOUSES, TEAROOMS, AND CAFÉS: The café has been called the most traditional Viennese institution. Today they come in all shapes and sizes. Many, frankly, are modern, while others have clung more to their traditional past. Some Viennese still use the café as their living room, where they meet and entertain their friends, especially if their apartments are too small. Others, however, have deserted the café completely, preferring to stay home these days and watch television.

In theory at least you're never rushed, even if you occupy a table for hours and order only one cup of coffee. Your coffee is always brought with a glass of water on the side. Most Viennese order a pastry to go with their coffee. Even though service is included in your tab, it is customary to leave an extra tip.

It's also possible to order simple meals in most of these establishments recommended. You can almost always get a hearty bowl of goulash soup, and if not that, certainly sausage and hard-boiled eggs, along with good bread and cheese.

Café Demel, 14 Kohlmarkt (tel. 63-55-16). The windows of this much-venerated establishment are filled with fanciful spun-sugar creations of characters from folk legends. When I was last there, Lady Godiva's five-foot tresses sheltered a miniature village of Viennese dancers. Inside you'll find a splendidly baroque Viennese landmark of black marble tables, cream-colored embellished plaster walls, elaborate half paneling, and crystal chandeliers covered with white milkglass globes. Dozens of different pastries are offered every day, including pralinentorte, giselatorte, sandtorte, neopolitanertorte, nelsontorte, as well as cream-filled horns (kugelhupfs), plus a mammoth variety of elegantly salty small sandwiches made of smoked salmon, egg salad, caviar, or shrimp among other ingredients.

You'll select what you want from the glass cases before going in to seat yourself on one of the bentwood chairs or paisley-covered loveseats. The counterwoman will give you a ticket which you'll keep. Another waitress will bring the confection to your table, along with whatever beverage you select. At the end of your visit you'll pay the waitress for the bill she'll calculate from the ticket stubs you've accumulated from the counterwoman. If you want to be traditional, ask for an Einspanner, which is a glass of espresso with a "hat" of frothy whipped cream. Salads range from 40 AS ($2.13), and snacks such as ratatouille cost 75 AS ($3.99). Coffee goes for 38 AS ($2.02), and pastries begin at 30 AS ($1.60).

Café Landtmann, 4 Dr. Karl-Lueger-Ring (tel. 63-06-21), is one of the great cafés of the Ringstrasse, with a history that goes back more than 110 years and a view overlooking the Burgtheater. It has traditionally drawn a colorful mixture of politicians, journalists, and actors, and was recently renovated at the cost of half a million dollars (some of the funds came from an urban-renewal kitty). The original chandeliers and the prewar chairs have been refurbished, and you can read Austrian and foreign newspapers in a spot which some VIP probably just vacated. An hour here, where you'll spend around 75 AS ($3.99) for two coffees and a pastry, might be an attractive way to spend part of a day in Vienna, although full meals are served if you want them. The café is open every day from 8 a.m. to midnight.

Café Hawelka, 1 Dorotheergasse (tel. 52-82-30). Just off the Graben, this is one of the most famous rendezvous points in Vienna for poets, artists, and the literati. In fact if you yearn for a view of the kind of café where someone plotted a revolution in the 19th century, this is it. Trotsky used to meet here with radical cronies for long cups of coffee, and from the decor of marble-topped tables and black Thonet chairs, you could easily imagine that the secretive conversations going on around you would be good material for a spy story. The setting is unmistakably Middle European, with smoke-stained places between the dark paneling and unusual artistic statements in mismatched black and gold frames.

Waiters in formal dress or in shirt sleeves and suspenders scurry from the well-stocked bar area with drinks on small silver trays. If the service is slow (which it usually is) you can amuse yourself by reading the bulletin board at the far end of the room, listing nearly every underground artistic event going on in Vienna.

On some nights you're likely to see Frau Hawelka herself, a small, gray-haired lady who usually leaves at midnight. She'll ask you if you'd like a tiny glass of her pear brandy and one of her homemade dumplings, buchteln. How could you possibly say no? The café is open daily except Tuesday until 2 a.m.

Café Imperial, 16 Kärntner Ring (tel. 65-17-65), is associated with the glittering hotel covered earlier in this guide. "Imperial Toast" is a very good snack here, and if you want a main meal you can always order tafelspitz, which the Emperor Joseph preferred to all other dishes. Meals begin at 190 AS ($10.11), which you can enjoy under the kind of ornate crystal chandeliers that Vienna has made famous.

Café Mozart, 2 Albertiner Platz (tel. 52-27-07). There are at least five Mozart cafés in Vienna, but this one is the most famous of all of them. It attracts affluent members of the business community, along with opera singers and university professors. There's been a café named Mozart on this spot since 1794, although the current establishment was founded in 1840. In 1980 it was renovated into the plushly streamlined format you see today, which is certainly elegant but without the baroque detailing you might have hoped for. You'll be served by a black-vested waiter while you're seated on one of the dark-pink velvet-covered banquettes. The tablecloths and napery are pink. A silhouette of the composer himself rests above the front door. Coffee costs 25 AS ($1.33), and you can also order a wienerschnitzel with salad for 100 AS ($5.32). The menu is in English. Scenes from *The Third Man,* that thriller starring Orson Welles and Joseph Cotton, were shot here.

Café/Restaurant Prückel, 24 Stubenring (tel. 52-61-15), was one of the last "Ringstrassencafés" built in Vienna. The year was 1955 when Austria had just gained its independence from foreign domination. Open from 9 a.m. until 10 p.m., the café offers stacks of recent international newspapers, comfortable chairs, and friendly waiters who serve snacks, desserts, beverages, or else full meals. A large bridge room accommodates card players who sometimes spend the day here. The owner, Christl Sedlar, offers 20 different kinds of coffee, including my favorite, kaffee Maria Theresia, which is a large black coffee with orange liqueur and whipped cream.

Café Tirolerhof, 8 Tegetthoffstrasse (tel. 52-78-33), is convenient after you've viewed the Albertina collection or been to the Spanish Riding School. Under management by the same family for the past 60 years, it's open Monday to Saturday from 7 a.m. to 9 p.m. and from 9:30 a.m. to 8 p.m. on Sunday. They offer very good apple strudel here, costing from 20 AS ($1.06), and coffee at 28 AS ($1.49) a cup.

Café/Restaurant Arabia, 5 Kohlmarkt (tel. 52-83-15), serves specialties such as asparagus in season, venison, fresh strawberries, and delectable Viennese pastries. Centrally located, the café is open from 7 a.m. to 8 p.m. every day of year. An average meal costs between 90 AS ($4.79) and 110 AS ($5.85).

Café Carrousel, 3 Krugerstrasse (tel. 52-73-97), in the middle of the city, a few blocks from the Vienna State Opera, offers 220 seats in a modernized art nouveau format of bright colors, bentwood chairs, and an occasional statue of a merry-go-round horse. A sidewalk terrace under Victorian globe lights extends the seating capacity of the restaurant. The menu features the usual café drinks, such as coffee, tea, wine, and beer, plus good Viennese cookery with a few international dishes thrown in for variety.

Café Josefinum, 33-35 Währingerstrasse (tel. 43-33-35), is outside the old city, about ten blocks behind the Votivkirche. Part of the Hotel Atlanta, it has a coffeeshop decor of glass, stainless steel, lime-green accents, and lots of wood detailing. In addition to its excellent coffee with whipped cream, the café also sells health products, fruit and vegetable juices, good Austrian wines, and set meals from 130 AS ($6.92). It's open from 8 a.m. to 11 p.m.

Demmer's Teehaus, 1 Auerspergstrasse (tel. 43-15-68), serves 30 different kinds of tea, plus dozens of pastries, cakes, toasts, and English sandwiches. This is under the same management as the excellent Buffet Trzensniewski, previously recommended. However, the teahouse gives you a chance to sit down and enjoy your drink and snack. Teas begin at 25 AS ($1.33). The establishment is open Monday to Friday from 9 a.m. to 6 p.m., from 9:30 to 12:30 p.m. on Saturday.

CULTURAL VIENNA: The cultural life of Vienna is set to music. This has been true for a couple of centuries or so, with the city being a lure to composers and librettists, musicians and music lovers even up to today. There's plenty of room for music in Vienna, and you can find places to enjoy everything from chamber music to pop, from waltzes to jazz. You'll find small discos and large concert halls, as well as musical theaters. And if you should (how could you?) tire of tuneful, atonal, or whatever musical sounds, then there's drama from classical to modern to avant garde, among other attractions. Below I'll describe just a few of the better known spots for cultural recreation. There are many others for you to find on your own if you're in Vienna long enough.

The four state theaters—Staatsoper (State Opera House), Volksoper, Burgtheater (National Theater), and the Akademietheater—are all reached by the same phone number, 53-24-0. The season is generally from September until June. Tickets for all state theater performances, including the opera, are available by writing to the **Österreichischer Bundestheaterverband,** 1 Goethegasse, A-1010 Vienna, at least two weeks to two months in advance. Otherwise you can purchase your ticket at the box office, the **Bundestheaterkasse,** 3 Hanuschgasse, which is open from 9 a.m. to 5 p.m. on weekdays and from 9 a.m. to noon on Sunday.

A highlight of the cultural season is the **Vienna Festival,** usually from May 20 to June 20. During this important European event, Vienna is likely to stage at least 1000 performances. This is not just a music festival—theater and other activities are offered too. For instance, Clown Town at the Prater draws entertainers from all over the continent. The State Opera is the centerpiece of the festival. The Theater an der Wien is the official festival house, and there's a good chance you'll get to see Beethoven's *Fidelio* here.

The Major Halls

If your German is halfway passable, try to see a play by Arthur Schnitzler if one is being staged during your visit. This mild man, who died in 1931, was the most characteristically Viennese of the Austrian writers. Through his works he gave the Imperial City the charm and style more often associated with Paris. Whenever possible I attend a revival of one of his plays, such as *Einsame Weg* (The Solitary Path) or *Professor Bernhardi.* My favorite is *Reigen,* on which the film *La Ronde* was based. Schnitzler's plays are often performed at the Theater in der Josefstadt (see below).

The **Staatsoper,** or State Opera House, is considered one of the three most important in the world, and the upkeep is apparently a necessity to the Austrians, as its operation is estimated at a cost to the taxpayers of some million schillings a day! When the opera house, at 2 Opernring, was originally built in the 1860s, criticism of the structure so upset one of the architects, Eduard van der Mull, that he killed himself. At the end of World War II, despite other pressing needs such as for public housing, Vienna started restoration work on the opera house in 1945, finishing it in time to celebrate the country's independence from occupation forces in 1955.

With the Vienna Philharmonic Orchestra in the pit, some of the leading opera stars of the world perform here. In their day, Richard Strauss and Gustav Mahler worked as directors. Daily performances are given from the first of September until the end of June. Standard prices are from 400 AS ($21.80) to 1200 AS ($63.84), but these may vary for special events. Guided tours of the Staatsoper are conducted at 9, 10, and 11 a.m. and at 1, 2, and 3 p.m. in summer, usually at 3 p.m. in winter.

Volksoper, 78 Währingerstrasse, the folk opera house, presents lavish productions of Viennese operettas and other musicals from the first of September until the end of June on a daily schedule. Tickets are generally from 140 AS ($7.45) to 440 AS ($23.41).

Burgtheater, the National Theater, 2 Dr.-Karl-Lueger-Ring, produces classical plays in German. Work started on the original structure in 1874, but the theater was destroyed during World War II and has since been rebuilt. It is the dream of every German-speaking actor to appear here.

Akademietheater, 3 Lisztstrasse, the largest theatrical concern in Europe, specializes in contemporary works. The Burgtheater company often performs here.

Theater an der Wien, 6 Linke Wienzeile (tel. 57-71-51), opened on the night of June 13, 1801, and ever since that time fans have been able to enjoy both opera and operetta presentations here. This was the site of the première of Beethoven's *Fidelio* in 1805 in fact the composer once lived in this building. The world première of *Die Fledermaus* was also given here. Invariably, every year an article appears in some newspaper proclaiming that Theater an der Wien was the site of the première of Mozart's *The Magic Flute.* However, considering that the first performance of that great work by Mozart was in 1791 while this theater did not exist until 1801, that première would have been a neat trick. During the years of occupation after World War II, when the Staatsoper was being restored after heavy damages, the Vienna State Opera made Theater an der Wien its home.

Operetta fans can still enjoy productions here in summer when other theaters are closed. Franz Lehar's *The Merry Widow* is presented annually from mid-July until the end of August. Tickets for performances cost from 90 AS ($4.79) to 225 AS ($11.97).

Schlosstheater at Schönbrunn Palace, mentioned earlier, is a gem of a theater in a regal setting, which opened in 1749 for the entertainment of the court of Maria Theresa. The architecture is a medley of baroque and rococo, and there's a large, plush box where the imperial family sat to enjoy the shows. Today anyone who has the price of a ticket—generally from 100 AS ($5.32) to 250 AS ($13.30)—can see a show if he or she is in Vienna in the summer. Opéra comique is often presented.

Other Theaters

The **Volkstheater,** 1 Neustiftgasse (tel. 93-27-76), opened in 1889 and has a long tradition of a classical repertoire, from Ibsen to Strindberg. Modern plays and comedies are also presented.

The **Vienna English Theatre,** 12 Josefsgasse (tel. 42-12-60), is the only English-speaking theater on the continent. It was established in 1963 and proved so popular that it's been around ever since. Many international celebrities have appeared on the stage of this neobaroque theater building, and many British actors perform here. Princess Grace of Monaco played here, before her tragic death, in a performance to raise money for charity. Occasionally works of American playwrights are presented.

Theater in der Josefstadt, 26 Josefstädter Strasse (tel. 42-51-27), is a typically Viennese theater, which presents, among other works, contemporary social comedies and classical plays. Under the aegis of Max Reinhardt, who took it over in 1924, this became one of the most outstanding theaters in the German-speaking world.

Count yourself fortunate if you get to hear a concert by the Wiener Philharmoniker at the **Musikverein,** 3 Dumbastrasse (tel. 65-81-90). The box office is at 6 Karlsplatz.

Konzerthaus, 20 Lothringerstrasse (tel. 72-12-11), is another major concert hall, this one with a trio of auditoriums. The "Concert House" was built just before the outbreak of World War I.

4. The ABCs of Vienna

AIRPORT: Vienna's international airport is **Wien Schwechat,** about 12 miles from the city center, which can be reached either by bus or by train. There is a regular bus service between the airport and the City Air Terminal (Wien Mitte), at the Hotel Hilton. Buses run every 30 minutes from 6 to 8 a.m. and every 20 minutes from 8 a.m. to 7:20 p.m., and to accommodate flights arriving after 7:20 p.m. The one-way fare is 48 AS ($2.55). There's also a service between the airport and the railroad stations, Westbahnhof and Südbahnhof, leaving Westbahnhof every 30 minutes between 6 a.m. and 7 p.m. (reaching Südbahnhof 15 minutes later) and starting from the airport every 30 minutes between 7 a.m. and 7 p.m. A train service runs between the airport and the City Air Terminal and Wien Nord (Praterstern) from 7:30 a.m. to 8:30 p.m. Trains run about every hour. A minibus service will shuttle you between the airport and your hotel. Seats may be reserved at the airport, at your hotel, or with your airline. A one-way taxi ride from the airport into the inner city is likely to cost from $21. Therefore it's better to take the bus. An official Tourist Information Office in the arrival hall of the airport is open October to May daily from 9 a.m. to 10 p.m., June to September from 9 a.m. to 11 p.m.

AMERICAN EXPRESS: You'll find the Vienna American Express office at 21-23 Kärntnerstrasse (tel. 52-05-44-0).

BABYSITTING: Phone 95-11-35 or 65-28-93 for information about baby-sitters (most of whom speak English). Call only Monday to Friday from 8 a.m. to 2:30 p.m.

BANKS AND EXCHANGE OFFICES: The open hours of Vienna banks and savings banks are 8 a.m. to 3 p.m. on Monday, Tuesday, Wednesday, and Friday, to 5:30 p.m. on Thursday (branch offices are closed from 12:30 to 1:30 p.m.). Monday through Saturday you can change money in many travel agencies, and daily in the exchange offices of the Westbahnhof from 7 a.m. to 10 p.m., and the Südbahnhof from 6:30 a.m. to 10 p.m. At the airport the exchange windows are open from 6:30 a.m. to 11 p.m.; in the City Air Terminal (Wien Mitte) from 8 a.m. to 12:30 p.m. and from 2 to 6 p.m.; and in the Tourist Information Office in the Opernpassage from 8 a.m. to 7 p.m.

CHURCH SERVICES: For information on services held by the religious group of your choice, call the following numbers: Roman Catholic (tel. 53-25-61); Evangelist (tel. 52-83-92 or 52-83-93); Jewish, with a temple at 4 Seitenstättengasse (tel. 63-45-16); Anglican, 17-19 Jaurèsgasse (tel. 73-15-75); or Methodist (tel. 37-72-45).

CLOTHING: For concerts and theaters, dark suits and cocktail dresses are recommended. For specially festive occasions such as opera premières, receptions, and balls, tails and dinner jackets are the preferred dress for men and evening dresses for women. You can rent men's evening wear, as well as carnival costumes, from several places in Vienna, which you will find in the telephone directory classified section (the yellow pages in the U.S.) under "Kleiderleihanstalten." I've learned that it's a good idea to take a light topcoat when I go out in the evening, even in summer, and I advise my women companions to carry or wear a stole or some other wrap.

DRIVING AND TRAFFIC REGULATIONS: In general, Austria's traffic regulations do not differ much from those of other countries where you drive on the right. In Vienna the speed limit is 50 kilometers about 30 miles per hour. Honking car horns is forbidden everywhere in the city. From December 15 to March 30, between 8 p.m. and 5 a.m., parking is prohibited on all streets where streetcars run. You are allowed a maximum stop of ten minutes even though parking is forbidden. In limited-parking areas you may park on weekdays between 8 a.m. and 6 p.m. only if you have a valid ticket, allowing parking for up to 1½ hours. The parking tickets may be obtained from the ticket offices of the Vienna Public Transport, from many gasoline stations, from tobacconists, and from most bank branches. The tickets are canceled by having marked on them the year, month, date, and time of day. *Warning:* The "No Parking" signs with the additional sign "Kurzparkzone" (limited-parking zone) are only displayed at the beginning and end of the zones. Special maps indicating location of hotels, one-way streets, and parking facilities in the first district are available at the official tourist offices. If you have car trouble, 24-hour service is offered by ARBÖ (tel. 78-25-25) and ÖAMTC (tel. 95-40).

DRUGSTORES: Chemist's shops are open Monday through Friday from 8 a.m. to noon and 2 to 6 p.m. on Saturday from 8 a.m. to noon. At night and on Sunday you'll find the names of shops whose turn it is to be open at those times listed on a sign outside every shop.

EMERGENCIES: If you're faced with an emergency in Vienna, help is available. Depending on the nature of the situation, you may call: fire brigade (tel. 122), police (tel. 133), or ambulance (tel. 144).

GUIDES: Licensed guides for sightseeing tours in and around Vienna are available through the Vienna Guide Service, A-1130 Vienna, 1-3/9/9 (only written orders). Rates are 720 AS ($38.30) for a half day, 1440 AS ($76.61) for a full day.

HORSE-DRAWN CARRIAGES: Vienna's *fiakers,* or horse-drawn carriages, have transported people around the inner city for some 300 years. You can clip-clop along in one for about 20 minutes at a cost of 300 AS ($15.96). In the first district you'll find a fiaker for hire at the following sites: north side of St. Stephen's, on Heldenplatz near the Hofburg, on Josefplatz, and in front of the Albertina on Augustinerstrasse.

INFORMATION: The official **Tourist Information Office,** in the Opernpassage, the pedestrian underpass next to the opera (tel. 43-16-08), is open daily from 9 a.m. till 7 p.m. The **Austrian Information Office,** 1 Margaretenstrasse, corner of Wiedner Hauptstrasse (tel. 57-57-14), is open Monday through Saturday from 9 a.m. till noon.

LOST PROPERTY: A lost property office is maintained at 22 Wasagasse (tel. 31-66-11-0), open Monday through Friday from 8 a.m. to 1 p.m. Items found on trains are taken to the central lost property office at Westbahnhof. Things left on buses and streetcars are passed on to the Wasagasse office after three days. If you miss something as soon as you get off the bus, you can pick it up at the Wiener Stadtwerke (Verkehrsbetriebe) (tel. 65-9-30-0) without waiting the three days.

MEDICAL SERVICE: A list of doctors can be found in the telephone directory under "Ärzte." All emergency calls for a physician on weekends from 7 p.m. Friday to 7 a.m. Monday and on holidays should be made to Ärztlicher Notdienst (tel. 56-35-11). Of course, your hotel or embassy can give you the name of an English-speaking doctor or dentist. For emergencies, telephone 55-00.

POST AND TELEGRAPH OFFICES: Addresses for both these facilities can be found in the telephone directory under "Post." Post offices are generally open Monday through Friday from 8 a.m. to 6 p.m. The central post office, 19 Fleischmarkt, and all railroad station post offices are open at night and on Sunday. Postage stamps are available at all post offices and at tobacco shops, and there are stamp vending machines outside most post offices. For information, phone 83-21-01. The central telegraph office is at 1 Börseplatz.

RAILROAD STATIONS: Vienna has two main railway stations, the **Südbahnhof** and the **Westbahnhof.** The Sübahnhof, Südtirolerplatz, 1100 Vienna (tel. 22-21-55-3 for train information), services all trains heading south, which includes parts of eastern Italy, all of Yugoslavia, and the southern provinces of Styria, Carinthia, Burgenland, and Weiner Neustadt. The Westbahnhof, Europaplatz, 1150 Vienna (for train information, telephone 22-21-55-2), services all trains heading west, including those to Salzburg, Innsbruck, all of Germany, and any connections to Italy that are made through Salzburg via the Brenner Pass. In addition, another number gives train information for both stations: 22-27-20-0.

TAXIS: Taxi stands are marked by signs, or you can call for a radio cab by phoning 31-30, 43-69, 62-82, or 91-01. Fares are indicated on an officially calibrated taxi meter. The fare for trips outside the Vienna area, for instance to the airport, should be agreed on with the driver in advance. Count on spending about $6 for a trip within the city center.

TOURS: The two Vienna sightseeing companies, **Cityrama Sightseeing Tours** and **Vienna Sightseeing Tours**, offer a wide range of trips for visitors. If sufficient notice is given, you can be picked up at your hotel for all but the mini-tours.

Cityrama conducts nonstop tours lasting about 1½ hours each at 9:45 a.m. and 2:45 p.m. daily from Stephansplatz and at 10 a.m. and 3 p.m. daily from Johannesgasse.

Vienna Sightseeing Tours (Wiener Rundfahrten), 4/11 Stelzhamergasse (tel. 72-43-83), offers many tours, ranging from a 1½-hour **Vienna—Getting Acquainted** trip to a two-day luxury excursion to Budapest and a flight across the Alps to Innsbruck. The getting-acquainted tour, costing 130 AS ($6.92) for adults, 50 AS ($2.66) for children, is a favorite with visitors who are pressed for time and yet want to see the most important sights of the city. It takes you past the historic buildings of the Ringstrasse—the Opera House, Hofburg, museums, the House of Parliament, City Hall, Burgtheatre, the university, and the Votive Church—and into the heart of Vienna to St. Stephen's Cathedral, as well as Belvedere Palace, St. Charles Church, and the Musikverein (Vienna Philharmonic Orchestra building). Tours leave the Opera House daily at 9 and 10:30 a.m. and at 3 and 4:30 p.m.

Another popular excursion, lasting about three hours, **Vienna Woods Impressions**, leaves from the Opera House and takes you to the picturesque towns of Perchtoldsdorf and Mödling, passing by the Höldrichsmühle, where Franz Schubert composed many of his beloved *Lieder*, going to the Abbey of Heiligenkreuz, a center of Christian culture since medieval times. The commemorative chapel in the village of Mayerling reminds visitors of the tragic suicide of Crown Prince Rudolph, only son of Emperor Franz Joseph, and his mistress. The tour also takes you for a short walk through Baden, the spa once a favorite summer resort of the aristocracy. Tours start and end at the Opera House, leaving at 1 p.m. daily and costing 200 AS ($10.64) for adults, 50 AS ($2.66) for children.

A **Grand City Tour**, which includes a visit to Schönbrunn and Belvedere Palaces, leaves the Opera House daily at 9:30 and 10:30 a.m. and at 2:30 p.m., lasting approximately three hours and costing adults 250 AS ($13.30); children, 100 AS ($5.32).

A visit to the **Spanish Riding School**, where the world-renowned Lipizzaner horses are trained, is offered daily Tuesday through Saturday, leaving the Opera House at 9:30 a.m., except in July and August. The charge is 300 AS ($15.96) for adults, 100 AS ($5.32) for children. On some Saturdays there's a special short performance by the Lipizzaners, for which a 50 AS ($2.66) supplement is charged. Also on this tour, you will take a short stroll through the old city and visit the Museum of Fine Arts.

In July and August, when the riding school is closed, a **Tour of the Habsburgs** replaces that excursion, Tuesday through Sunday at 9:30 a.m. and lasting three hours. The price of this tour is also 300 AS ($15.96) for adults, 100 AS ($5.32) for children. You'll visit the Imperial Apartments, Capuchins' Crypt with its sumptuous tombs of the Habsburgs, and the Museum of Fine Arts.

Perhaps you'll have time to make an eight-hour trip along the Danube, going to Wachau by bus and boat and tasting the wines produced in this area since Roman times. From the end of March until October 31 this tour leaves daily at 9:30 a.m., cutting the schedule to every Thursday and Sunday from November 1 to March 31. The price is 700 AS ($37.24) for adults, 300 AS ($15.96) for children.

Chapter V

LOWER AUSTRIA

1. The Wienerwald
2. Baden
3. Wiener Neustadt
4. Semmering
5. The Southeast Corner
6. The Marchfeld
7. The Weinviertel
8. The Wachau-Danube Valley
9. The Nibelungengau
10. The Ybbs and Erlauf Valleys
11. The Ötscher Mountains
12. The Waldviertel

"THE CRADLE of Austria's history," Lower Austria, or Niederösterreich, is the biggest of the nine federal states which make up the country today. This province, crisscrossed by the Danube, is in fact named *Lower* Austria because the great river flows east into it. It may seem to you more like *Upper* Austria because of its geographic location, much of it being north of the rest of the country. The 7402 square miles of the state are bordered on the north and east by Czechoslovakia, on the south by the province of Styria, and on the west by Upper Austria. It lies virtually on the doorstep of Vienna, the state capital of this province of 1½ million living souls as well as being the nation's capital.

This historic nucleus of the Austria of today was once a heavily fortified land, as some 550 fortresses and castles—many still standing but often in ruins—testify. The medieval dynasties of the Kuenringers and the Babenbergers had their hereditary estates here, and it was through Lower Austria that the legendary Nibelungen passed. Many monasteries and churches, ranging from the Romanesque and Gothic eras up to the much later baroque abbeys, are found here.

The province is filled with vineyards, and in summer it's rich in festivals, not only of music and operetta but also of classical and contemporary theater.

It's relatively inexpensive to travel in Lower Austria, with a drop of at least 30% below the prices you encounter in Vienna, just visited, or in such places as Salzburg and Innsbruck which will be explored further on in this book. This price differential explains why many people, especially those from other Austrian provinces, visit in Vienna but stay at one of the neighboring towns in Lower Austria. Parking is also accessible in the outlying towns. However, you mustn't expect always to have a private bath if you want to check into an old inn.

Lower Austria is divided into five distinct districts, the best known being the **Wienerwald** (Vienna Woods) completely surrounding Vienna.

Another district, **Alpine Lower Austria**, lies about an hour's drive south of Vienna. With mountains up to 7000 feet high, this area has been greatly developed in the past few years and has a system of mountain railways, chair lifts, and cable cars, as well as hundreds of miles of hiking paths.

The **foothills of the Alps,** beginning about 30 miles west of Vienna, comprise a district extending to the borders of Styria and Upper Austria. This area has some 50 open-air swimming pools that are busy in summer and nine chair lifts which go up to the higher peaks, such as Otscher and Hochkar, each around 6000 feet.

A celebrated section is the **Waldviertel-Weinviertel,** a viertel being a traditional division of Lower Austria. The viertels in this case are the woods (*wald*) and wine (*wein*) areas. They contain thousands of miles of marked hiking paths and, of course, many mellow old wine cellars.

Another district, **Wachau-Nibelungengau,** is of historical and cultural significance. In fact it's considered one of the most historic valleys in Central Europe. It is a land of castles and palaces, of abbeys and monasteries. For centuries it has also been known for its wine making. Lying on both banks of the Danube, this area begins about 40 miles west of Vienna.

Some 60% of the grape harvest of Austria is produced in Lower Austria, stretching from the rolling hillsides of the Wienerwald to the terraces of the Wachau. Many visitors to the country like to take a "wine route" through the province, stopping off at cozy taverns to sample the vintages from Krems, Klosterneuburg, Dürnstein, Langenlois, Retz, Gumpoldskirchen, Poysdorf, and other spots.

Lower Austria has 12 spa resorts, of which Baden is the most celebrated. Innkeepers make families with children especially welcome at these resorts. Most hotels accommodate children up to 6 years old free. Between ages 7 and 12, they are given 50% reductions on the listed prices for adults. Many towns and villages have facilities designed especially for the amusement of children.

In short, Lower Austria is a good place to go for a family holiday.

1. The Wienerwald

The Vienna Woods—romanticized in operetta, literature, and the Strauss waltz—have already been introduced in the sightseeing section of Vienna. The woods stretch all the way from Vienna's city limits to the foothills of the Alps to the south.

You can hike through the woods along marked paths or else drive through at a leisurely pace, stopping off at country towns to sample the wine and the local cuisine, usually hearty, filling, and reasonable in price. The woods are filled with wine taverns and cellars, and on weekends with Viennese and a horde of foreign tourists, principally German. I advise you to make any summer visit on a weekday. Perhaps the best time of year to go is September and October, the months when the grapes are harvested from the terraced hills.

If you don't want to go on your own, a popular tour out of Vienna will take you to the Wienerwald and Mayerling. It goes through the Vienna Woods to the Castle of Liechtenstein and the old Roman city of Baden, with an excursion to Mayerling where Crown Prince Rudolf and his mistress died violent deaths. You'll also go to the Cistercian Abbey of Heiligen-Höldrichsmühle-Seegrotte. A boat ride on Seegrotte, the largest subterranean lake in Europe, is included.

This tour is operated by **Vienna Sightseeing Tours,** 4 Stelzamergasse (tel. 72-46-83). It runs from April 1 to October 30 at 9:30 a.m. and 2:30 p.m., taking about four hours. The cost is 350 AS ($18.62) for adults, 130 AS ($6.92) for children. The price includes admission fees and a guide.

KLOSTERNEUBURG: Lying on the northwestern outskirts of Vienna within easy reach of the capital, Klosterneuburg is an old market town in the major wine-producing center of Austria. The Babenbergs founded the town practically at the gates of Vienna in the eastern foothills of the Vienna Woods, making it an ideal spot to enjoy the countryside and also to participate in the cultural and entertainment activities of Vienna, seven miles southeast.

A Roman stronghold occupied the site of the town in the first century A.D.

Klosterneuberg Abbey (Stift Klosterneuberg) which lies to the east of the Upper Town is considered the most significant abbey in the country and is the major sightseeing attraction of the town. The abbey church dates from 1114, but the first of the Gothic west towers was not constructed until the end of the 14th century. The abbey has magnificent stained-glass windows, also dating from that century. The altar of the church is from 1181 and contains more than 50 biblical scenes in enamel. The most outstanding exhibit in Stift Klosterneuberg is the altarpiece by Nicolas of Verdun in the Chapel of St. Leopold. The abbey apartments are richly furnished with many empire antiques.

The abbey may be visited daily from 9:30 to 11 a.m. and from 1:30 to 4 p.m. On Sunday it's open only in the afternoon. Admission is 30 AS ($1.60).

The abbey came into its glory when the ruling family of Austria, the Babenbergs, moved here from Melk and built a grand residence, remnants of which are preserved in the Albrechtsberger alley. After the royal residences were moved to Vienna the abbey declined in power and prestige, but it was revived in the 18th century by Emperor Charles VI, who came up with an ambitious architectural scheme—to build a pompous residence and monastic edifice which would rival El Escorial, the celebrated palace built by Philip II of Spain on the outskirts of Madrid. This grandiose building scheme was never completed, but the monastery was finally finished in the 19th century, looking as you will see it today.

The abbey has an old restaurant, Stiftskeller, where you can dine well at moderate prices. The restaurant has a historic wine cellar. If you don't choose to eat here, you can patronize one of several heurigen in the district, enjoying good wine and simple country food.

Austrians and tourists gather in Klosterneuberg annually to celebrate St. Leopold's Day on November 15.

Food and Lodging

Schlosshotel Martinschloss, 34-36 Martinstrasse (tel. 7426), is the historic baroque castle on the banks of the Danube that was owned by the Trapp family (did you see *The Sound of Music*?) between 1924 and 1938. Before that the 1766 castle was held by a British naval officer, Sir John Whitehead, who developed the world's first submarine torpedo from experiments he performed in the castle's swimming pool. The castle was renovated after the Second World War, as the Russians had virtually ruined it during their occupation. Today it's a comfortable and glamorous hotel, and most of its well-furnished bedrooms contain private baths. Singles range from 650 AS ($34.58) to 1330 AS ($70.46), while doubles cost from 540 AS ($28.73) to 900 AS ($47.88) per person, with breakfast included.

Hotel/Restaurant Josef Buschenreiter, 188 Wiener Strasse (tel. 2385), is a modern white-walled hotel with metal window frames and a mansard roof above the balcony on the fourth floor. A terrace on the roof and an indoor swimming pool provide diversion to the hotel guests, who will also find a contemporary bar area in contrasting earth-colored patterns. Singles range from 440 AS ($23.41) to 510 AS ($27.13), while doubles cost between 360 AS ($19.15) and 420 AS ($22.34) per person, depending on the plumbing. Breakfast is included, and half board can be arranged for an additional 100 AS ($5.32) per person daily.

Pension Alte Mühle, 36 Mühlengasse (tel. 7788), is housed in an uncomplicated two-story building with a red tile roof and a facade of yellow paint and iron balconies. The breakfast room is simple to the point of being spartan, although a comfortable restaurant and café in the same building has upholstered banquettes and a sunny modern decor of bright colors and conservative designs. The Veit family, the owners, charge between 310 AS ($16.49) and 410 AS ($21.81) in a single and between 230 AS ($12.24) and 370 AS ($19.68) per person in a double, with breakfast included. Half board is offered for an additional 110 AS ($5.85) per person daily.

PERCHTOLDSDORF: This old market town with colorful buildings, referred to locally as Petersdorf, is one of the most visited spots in Lower Austria when the Viennese make the wine tour. You'll find many heurigen, where you can sample local wines and enjoy good, hearty cuisine. Perchtoldsdorf is not as well known as Grinzing, which is actually within the city limits of Vienna, but many discriminating visitors find it less touristy. It has a Gothic church, and part of its defense tower is from the early 16th century. A vintners' festival is held annually in early November. Local growers make a "goat" from grapes for this festive occasion which attracts many Viennese.

MÖDLING: The Viennese use this place as a resort. Quite old, it lies at the beginning of the Brühl Valley and still has a medieval core, the Hauptplatz. The Rathaus (town hall) dates from 1548. Beethoven wrote his *Missa Solemnis* here in 1818.

About a 15- to 18-minute drive from Mödling is **Schloss Liechtenstein.** The castle was built originally in the 12th century, but that one was largely demolished in one of the Turkish sieges. Construction on the present schloss began in 1820. You can visit a relic of the old castle, however, a Romanesque chapel dating from 1165.

Another popular excursion from Mödling is to **Schloss Laxenburg,** a short drive to the east. In the complex, surrounded by a baroque park, are an old castle from the 14th century and a new one. The Neues Schloss, once used by the Habsburgs as a summer residence, has been turned over to an institute. Yet another mock Gothic castle from the 19th century has been converted into a restaurant. Mainly, however, the place is visited for its park, once the hunting ground of the dukes of Austria but now the home of protected wild game. True to the baroque ideal, the park is studded with statuary and "temples."

Food and Lodging

Hotel/Restaurant Babenbergerhof, 6 Babenbergergasse (tel. 2246), is a three-story rectangular building painted a deep Maria Theresa ochre with a garden restaurant extending out behind it. On a summer night the management stretches lights below the large trees in the garden, while in winter the indoor ambience is one of well-maintained modernity. Rooms are comfortably furnished and well maintained. Singles range from 185 AS ($9.84) to 300 AS ($15.96), while doubles go from 360 AS ($19.15) to 750 AS ($39.90). Prices include breakfast.

Föhrenhof, 12 Meiereigasse (tel. 2256), at Mödling-Vorderbrühl, is a sprawling country house hotel and restaurant, with terracotta paint between the elaborate half-timbering. In summertime the management places wooden tables and chairs on the outdoor terrace in a protected angle of the building. The interior focuses around a massive stone fireplace and the many rural artifacts which adorn the white stucco walls. Singles cost 450 AS ($23.94) per day, while doubles range between 635 AS ($33.78) and 800 AS ($42.56), with breakfast included. Rooms are neat and immaculate.

HINTERBRÜHL: Instead of staying in Mödling, you might prefer to drive to the neighboring hamlet of Hinterbrühl, where you'll find a good hotel and food. The village is only a 20-minute drive from Vienna. This is no more than a cluster of bucolic homes, much favored by the Viennese who want to escape the city for a long weekend. Hinterbrühl holds memories of Schubert, who wrote *Am Brunnen vor dem Tore* here.

Food and Lodging: **Hotel/Restaurant Höldrichsmühle,** 34 Gaadner Strasse (tel. 6274), has been painted a pastel pink since the era when Schubert stayed here, and it still has much of its old allure. Singles, all comfortably furnished, range from 315 AS ($16.75) to 600 AS ($31.92), while doubles cost between 335 AS ($17.82) and 425 AS ($22.61) per person, with breakfast included. Prices depend on the plumbing and the size of the accommodation. The restaurant connected to the hotel is one of the best in the village. Viennese often make the 20-minute ride from the heart of the city to eat under the linden trees of the restaurant's terrace. In winter they find the Biedermeier-filled interior cozy and inviting. Specialties of the chef include fresh trout, roast veal with corn salad, an array of venison dishes in season, and many varieties of fish, including eel. Reservations are suggested, and à la carte meals range from 120 AS ($6.38) to 300 AS ($15.96), while fixed-price dinners cost from 145 AS ($7.71) to 360 AS ($19.15).

GUMPOLDSKIRCHEN: From Mödling, you can take the wine road, or *weinstrasse,* to Gumpoldskirchen, a vine-growing town celebrated for its Gumpoldskirchner wine, a Viennese favorite. Along the main street are heurigen. Like Perchtoldsdorf, this village is preferred by many Viennese to Grinzing. Go to any of the wine taverns whose doors are open, and chances are you'll be served not only delectable white wine of the town but food as well, all at reasonable prices.

Where to Dine

Weinstadl, 42 Jubiläumsstrasse (tel. 62218), is a rustically cozy establishment with wood tables, big flasks of local wine, and a friendly reception given by the unpretentious staff. The room here is vast, usually with live music, in a building that in olden days was used to store the abundant harvests that came from this region. You can sit in an upper level if it's open on the night you happen to visit, which might be a good idea since the music near the bandstand can be rather loud. The chef is known for his grills, turning out an especially good tournedos. The produce is most often super fresh, and the food is attractively prepared and well presented. The restaurant is closed from January 10 to February 10 and on Sunday. It's open only in the evening, and reservations are suggested. À la carte meals range from 120 AS ($6.30) to 300 AS ($15.96).

Weinbergschenke, Pfaffstätten (tel. 88540), is not the kind of place to dress up for a high-society evening on the town. The ambience is low key, informal, and gutbürgerlich, with copious amounts of the local wine consumed by the hearty clientele. Whether you appreciate the noise level will depend a great deal on your degree of joviality. The food is well prepared, wholesome, and filling, the fare consisting of country specialties made with pork, ham, beef, and veal. A small carafe of wine costs 20 AS ($1.06), but few guests settle for such a modest amount. À la carte meals range from 85 AS ($4.52) to 195 AS ($10.37). The restaurant is closed on Monday.

GUNTRAMSDORF: In your search for a charming place to stay in the Wienerwald, with the atmosphere typical of the area, the following recommendation near Gumpoldskirchen might be considered. The hamlet lies at the very doorstep of the Wienerwald.

Food and Lodging

Jagdhof, 41 Hauptstrasse (tel. 52-2-25). The limited numbers of rooms here are tastefully decorated and comfortable. The hotel is identified by a wrought-iron bracket hanging over the front door with a medieval-style sign announcing the locale. Singles go for 340 AS ($18.09) and up, while doubles, depending on the size, cost from 520 AS ($27.66) to 570 AS ($30.32), with breakfast included. All units have private bath.

Much of the reputation of the establishment, however, revolves around its well-known restaurant. Under the vaults of an old farmhouse, it reeks of rustic atmosphere, and has a cuisine which is so well prepared that many of the clients return again and again. Menu items include Canadian salmon with dill sauce, rack of lamb with beans and cabbage, and a tender array of veal dishes. Dessert might be an unusual ice cream flavored with kiwi, lemon, and vodka. The restaurant is closed Monday and occasionally on Sunday, depending on the season. À la carte meals range between 120 AS ($6.38) and 330 AS ($17.56).

TULBINGER-KOGEL: This is a small hamlet a short drive from Vienna whose main virtue seems to be its wooded rolling hills and the autumn foliage, which can be spectacular. Dozens of Viennese make the drive here to escape the congestion of their capital. When they do, they often choose to stay at the following recommendation.

Berghotel Tulbinger-Kogel (tel. 7391) sprawls like an 18th-century château across a wide vista of forested land. Its walls are white, and the symmetrically sloping roofline comprises a single row of prominent gables. An outbuilding with surrounding balconies provides modern accommodations as well as a calm and beautiful view of the nearby region. Prices per person, based on double occupancy, range from 180 AS ($9.58) to 395 AS ($21.01), with a single supplement of 150 AS ($7.98) per person daily.

HEILIGENSTADT: Once a fairly remote and isolated wine-growing village, Heiligenstadt is really a suburb of Vienna today. It is visited chiefly for its connection with Beethoven, who came here hoping that a sulfur spring to which miraculous powers were attributed could help him recover his hearing. In 1802, the composer wrote a letter, the "Testament of Heiligenstadt," in the house at 6 Probusgasse, which painfully documents his hopelessness about his rapidly approaching deafness. This house is open from 10 a.m. to 4 p.m. on weekdays, from 2 to 6 p.m. on Saturday, and from 9 a.m. to 1 p.m. on Sunday. Closed Monday.

For a few months in 1817, Beethoven lived at 2 Pfarrplatz in a 17th-century house which has been turned into a heurige.

HEILIGENKREUZ: This most ancient Cistercian abbey in Austria, dating from 1135, lies in the village of the Sattelbach about ten miles to the west of the spa in Baden. Called the Abbey of the Holy Cross, the church, founded by Leopold III, was built in the 12th century, but there has been an overlay of Gothic and baroque in subsequent centuries, with some stained glass from the 14th century still in place. The abbey was once ravished by the Turks, but much of the complex was reconstructed in the 17th and 18th centuries. However, the Romanesque and Gothic cloisters date from 1220, with some 300 pillars of red marble, a striking display. There's also a gallery of Teutonic baroque paintings and a library.

Some of the dukes of Babenberg were buried in the 1240 chapter house, including Duke Friedrich II, the last of his line, who died in 1246.

Tours are offered from 9 to 11:30 a.m. and from 1:30 to 6:30 p.m. (until 4:30 p.m. in winter), except on Sunday and public holidays when hours are from 11 to 11:30 a.m. and from 1:30 to 5:30 p.m. Admission is 25 AS ($1.33).

MAYERLING: This beautiful spot in the heart of the Wienerwald, to the west of Baden and 2½ miles from Heiligenkreuz, was the setting in 1889 for a grim tragedy which altered the line of succession of the Austro-Hungarian Empire and shocked the world. On a snowy night, Archduke Rudolf, only son of Emperor Franz Joseph and Empress Elizabeth, and his mistress, Maria Vetsera, were found dead in the hunting lodge at Mayerling and called suicide victims.

Rudolf was locked into an unhappy marriage, and neither his father nor Pope Leo XIII would allow, through annulment, breaking the matrimonial bonds. At the time of his death Rudolf was 30 years old. He had met Maria at a German embassy ball when she was only 17. Because of the young archduke's liberal leanings and sympathy for certain Hungarian partisans, he was not popular with his country's aristocracy, which of course gave rise to lurid speculation about the deaths, not only in the press but also in books and in films, as to whether the couple actually killed themselves or were the victims of cleverly designed assassination.

Franz Joseph, grief stricken at the loss of his only son, ordered the hunting lodge torn down and had built the Carmelite nunnery which still occupies the lodge site.

As it turned out, if Rudolf had lived he would have succeeded to the already-tottering Habsburg throne in 1916 in the middle of World War I, shortly before the collapse of the empire.

Food and Lodging

Marienhof (tel. 379) advertises itself as the cozy guest house in the midst of the hunting territory most preferred by Crown Prince Rudolf. It's a long three-story structure with white stucco walls and a brown tile roof with matching shutters, somewhat removed from the other buildings of the village. The contemporary interior has rustic touches, usually arranged by Johann and Cäcilia Hanner. The bedrooms tend to be smallish, but are comfortable and cheerful. With half board included, the per-person rates are around 400 AS ($21.28) daily.

2. Baden

Czar Peter the Great of Russia is credited with ushering in the golden age of Baden as a spa around the dawn of the 18th century. The Soviet army used the resort city as its headquarters from the end of World War II to the end of the Allied occupation of Austria in 1955. But there's not much Russian about Baden, the dowager empress of health spas in Europe.

The Romans, who didn't miss many of the natural attractions in sections of Europe into which they moved, began in A.D. 100 to visit and enjoy what they called Aquae, with its 15 thermal springs whose temperatures are up to 95° Fahrenheit. You can still see the Römerquelle (Roman spring) in the Kurpark which is the center of Baden today.

This lively casino town and spa in the eastern sector of the Vienna Woods was at its most fashionable in the early part of the 18th century, but its appeal for royalty, aristocracy, sycophants, musicians, and intellectuals continued for much of the 19th century. For years the resort was the summer residence of the Habsburg court. In 1803, when he was still Francis II of the Holy Roman Empire, the monarch (who became Francis I of Austria when the vast empire originated by Charlemagne ended in 1806) began annual summer moves to Baden, a practice which ended only at his death in 1835.

Where the court went, there went the most outstanding musicians and artists of the age. Even before the spa was "discovered" by Emperor

Francis, however, Mozart spent time in Baden, and it is here that he is said to have composed his *Ave Verum*. Schubert is supposed to have done creative work at this spa, and Beethoven, who lived in Baden for three summers, worked on his Ninth Symphony in this peaceful town surrounded by forests and vineyards.

At **Beethoven's house,** 10 Rathausgasse, a little museum has been set up, open from 9 a.m. to 11 a.m. and from 3 to 5 p.m. daily, except Thursday, in summer. In winter it's open only on Tuesday, Thursday, and Saturday. Admission is 10 AS (53¢).

During the Biedermeier era (mid to late 19th century), Baden became known for its Schönbrunn yellow (Maria Theresa ochre) Beidermeier buildings which still contribute to the spa city's charm. The Kurpark, Baden's center, is handsomely laid out and beautifully maintained. Public concerts performed here keep alive the magical music of the great Austrian composers.

The bathing house complex was constructed over the location of more than a dozen sulfur springs. In the complex are some half dozen bath establishments, plus two outdoor thermal springs.

Emperor Karl made this town the Austrian army headquarters in World War I, but a certain lightness of heart persisted in the Austrians and in the life of Baden. It was the presence of the Russians during post–World War II years that brought about the lowest ebb in the resort's fortunes. The Soviets did little to encourage luxurious spa resort vacations and casino gambling.

Among sights in Baden there's a celebrated death mask collection at the **Städtisches Rollet Museum,** 1 Weikersdorfer (tel. 3-51-23). The Trinity column at the Hauptplatz commemorates the lifting of the plague that swept over Vienna and the Wienerwald in the Middle Ages.

The resort (officially named Baden bei Wien to differentiate it from other Badens *not* near Vienna) is some 15 miles from the capital city. An old and rather flamboyant streetcar is the best—or at least, the most romantic—way to go. However, the resort is also connected to Vienna by rail and bus lines.

FOOD AND LODGING: **Clubhotel Baden** (Schloss Weikersdorf), 9-11 Schlossgasse (tel. 4071), has all the massive beams you'd expect in such an old building, along with arched and vaulted ceilings which are sculpted into unusual sinuous patterns. The oldest part of the hotel has an Italianate loggia stretching toward the manicured gardens, and an inner courtyard with stone arcades and a flagstone pavement. Even the rooms in the newer section have repeated the older section's arches and high ceilings, with a constant reappearance of ornate chandeliers and antique (or reproduction) furniture. The nearby sports facility has an indoor swimming pool, tennis courts, a sauna, a whirlpool, and massage facilities. On the premises you'll find a charming baroque bar with a serving area that resembles a piece of fine furniture and two restaurants. Accommodations are handsomely furnished and most comfortable. Singles range from 520 AS ($27.66) to 720 AS ($38.30), while doubles cost between 380 AS ($20.22) and 580 AS ($30.87) per person daily. Breakfast is included in these rates, and all units contain private bath. Half board is offered for an additional 120 AS ($6.38) per person.

Hotel Gutenbrunn, 22 Pelzgasse (tel. 48171). If what you want is an elegant old-world hotel with lots of original architectural features, this might be the one for you. The pink-and-white facade has a hexagonal tower at one of its corners, and a slate roof capped with a baroque steeple. The interior has a skylit reception area with a double tier of neoclassical loggias, all of them focusing on the hanging chandelier in the center. Rooms are well furnished and maintained. Singles rent for between 600 AS ($31.92) and 850 AS ($45.22), while doubles cost between 930 AS ($49.48) and 1800 AS ($95.76), with breakfast included. You'll find a sauna and a swimming pool on the premises, plus a restaurant which provides half board for an additional 160 AS ($8.51) per person daily. The hotel is connected to the city spa facilities by an underground tunnel.

Kurhotel Herzoghof, 5 Theresiengasse (tel. 2117), is an elegant inner-city hotel with a cream-colored facade, pleasing and complicated indentations, and lots of 19th-century detailing. The garden terrace is dotted with potted plants and neoclassical statues, while the interior has much of the stained glass, wrought iron, and embellished moldings that were part of the original design. The antique-filled bedrooms rent for between 450 AS ($23.94) and 800 AS ($42.56) in a single and between 1000 AS ($53.20) and 1200 AS ($63.84) in a double, with breakfast included. Half board is obligatory for guests who stay for extended periods, at an additional 165 AS ($8.79) per person daily. All accommodations contain private baths.

Hotel Sauerhof zu Rauhenstein, 11-13 Weilburgstrasse (tel. 41251). Ludwig von Beethoven once took Karl Maria von Weber to lunch here. Today it's considered a place where comfort and a sense of history go hand in hand. It was formerly a recreational center for Austria's imperial officers. Today the exterior has been restored to its former grandeur. It rambles across a wide expanse of lawn in a three-story neoclassical format of steeply sloping slate roofs and discreetly restrained detailing. Few of the original furnishings remain, although the updated sunny bedrooms are comfortably furnished in conservative pieces. Just outside the complex you'll find two tennis courts, a jogging course, and a nearby golf course. Under the brick vaulting of one of the older sections, the management has installed a 40-foot swimming pool. Singles range from 720 AS ($38.30) to 1140 AS ($60.65), while doubles cost between 1060 AS ($56.39) and 1560 AS ($82.99), with breakfast included. All accommodations have private bath, and half board is offered for an additional 195 AS ($10.37) per person.

Parkhotel, 5 Kaiser-Franz-Ring (tel. 44386), is an elegantly up-to-date hotel in the middle of an inner-city park dotted with trees and formal statuary. Each of the sunny bedrooms has its own loggia and private bath. A heated indoor swimming pool, two Finnish saunas, a restaurant, and a coffeeshop are on the premises, as well as private parking and a beautiful outdoor terrace. Singles range from 800 AS ($42.56) to 900 AS ($47.88), while doubles cost between 625 AS ($33.25) and 700 AS ($37.24) per person daily, with breakfast included.

Krainerhütte (tel. 44511) stands five miles west of Baden at Helenental, on its own tree-filled grounds. It's a large A-frame chalet, with generously proportioned rows of wooden balconies stretching across its front. The interior has well-worked wooden surfaces and more detailing than you'd expect in a modern hotel. Singles rent for between 580 AS ($30.87) and 850 AS ($45.22) with breakfast included. Doubles cost from 500 AS ($26.60) to 700 AS ($37.24) per person, also with breakfast. On the premises you'll find an indoor swimming pool, an outdoor tennis court, a sauna, and an exercise room.

Badner Stüberl, 19 Gutenbrunnstrasse (tel. 41232), an old-fashioned coffeehouse in the center of the older section of Baden, is filled with black and red upholstery and unusually designed lighting fixtures. Specialties of the house include generous proportions of a Stroganoff dish which is searched out by visitors from Vienna, along with a green salad garnished with chicken, and pork and beef steaks grilled to savory tenderness. Frau Ackerl, the experienced chef, prepares many of the noodles and desserts herself. À la carte meals range from 95 AS ($5.05) to 285 AS ($15.16). The establishment is closed Tuesday.

READER'S RESTAURANT SELECTION: "We arrived on an autumn day when the sign was out for game, but **Cholerakapelle,** 40 Helenental (tel. 4213), from all reports, is good all year round. The location is in the tranquil Helenental valley, to the west of Baden. We also saw many local people dining here—not just tourists—which we took for a good sign. When in doubt as to what to order, try a most delectable wienerschnitzel which is very similar to what the Italians call a veal cutlet milanese. The service is excellent, and the staff is most hospitable. Naturally, one of the fine wines of the Vienna Woods should accompany your meal, which will most likely cost around 225 AS ($11.97)" (Nick Phillips, Miami, Fla.).

NIGHTLIFE: The major attraction, of course, is the **Casino in Spa Park** (tel. 4496), which opens daily at 4 p.m. Here you can play roulette, blackjack, and baccarat. On Wednesday night, and also on Saturday and Sunday, many Viennese come down to Baden for a night of gambling, drinking, and eating. They are often most fashionably dressed.

3. Wiener Neustadt

When you head south from Vienna on the Südautobahn, Wiener Neustadt, a former imperial city, might be your first stopover. Called Allzeit Getreue because of its loyalty to the throne, this thriving business city between the foothills of the Alps and the edge of the Pannonian lowland has a strong historical background.

Unfortunately, Wiener Neustadt was a popular target for Allied bombs during World War II, because it lay at the point where the routes from Vienna diverge, one going to the Semmering pass and the other to Hungary via the Sopron gate. The presence here of a military academy which turned out officers for the Austrian army for some 200 years may have been an added attraction to bombers. German Gen. Erwin Rommel, "the desert fox," was the academy's first commandant during the Nazi era. At any rate, bomb the city the Allies did—more than any other town in the country. It's estimated that some 60% of its buildings were leveled.

The town was founded in 1192, when its castle was built by Duke Leopold V of the ruling house of Babenberg. He had it constructed as a citadel to ward off attacks of the Magyars from the east. From 1440 to 1493 Austrian emperors lived at this fortress in the southeast corner of what is now the old town. Maximilian I, called "the last of the knights," was born here in 1459 and lies buried in the Church of St. George in the castle. It was Maria Theresa who in 1752 ordered that the structures comprising the castle be turned into a military academy.

You can visit the **Church of St. George** (St. Georgskirche) daily from 8 a.m. to 4 p.m. The gable of the church is adorned with more than 100 heraldic shields of the habsburgs. It's noted for its handsome interior, decorated in the late Gothic style.

Neukloster, a Cistercian abbey, was founded in 1250 and reconstructed in the 18th century. The New Abbey Church (Neuklosterkirche), on Ungargasse near the Hauptplatz, is Gothic with a beautiful choir. It contains the tomb of the Empress Eleanor of Portugal, wife of Friedrich III and mother of Maximilian I. Mozart's *Requiem* was first presented here in 1793.

Liebfrauenkirche, on the Domplatz, was once the headquarters of an episcopal see. It's graced by a 13th-century Romanesque nave, but the choir is Gothic. The west towers have been rebuilt.

In the town is a **Recturm,** a tower in the Gothic style said to have been built with the ransom money paid for Richard the Lionhearted.

FOOD AND LODGING: **Hotel Corvinus,** Ferdinand Porsche Ring (tel. 4134), is a dramatically designed modern hotel with a color scheme of white and weathered bronze. It sits in a quiet neighborhood near the city park. Its 68 rooms have all of the modern comforts in a decor of patterned bedspreads and solid colors. Inside you'll find an ultramodern bar area, a parasol-covered sun terrace, and a lightheartedly elegant restaurant with big sunny windows. Singles cost 660 AS ($35.11), while doubles rent for 900 AS ($47.88), with breakfast included. Children under 12 stay in their parents' room for free, although there's an extra breakfast charge.

Hotel/Restaurant Forum, 2 Heimkehrerstrasse (tel. 4918), is a comfortable 37-room hotel near the railway and bus stations. Bedrooms are cheerfully papered and usually high-ceilinged, while the outdoor terrace restaurant and the indoor bar area are attractive gathering spots. Doubles cost 600 AS ($31.92) per night, while singles go for 300 AS ($15.96).

Hotel Zentral, 27 Hauptplatz (tel. 3169), is an unpretentious hotel on the baroque square in the center of town. It has an inviting restaurant on the ground floor, with lots of contrasting kinds of decorative wood paneling. Upstairs are comfortable bedrooms, sometimes with furniture stenciled with regional designs. Singles cost 260 AS ($13.83) to 370 AS ($19.68), while doubles range between 240 AS ($12.77) and 300 AS ($15.96) per person daily, with breakfast included.

Restaurant Porsche, at the Volkswagen-Porsche workshop (tel. 35-91-44). Years ago a garage mechanic opened a small restaurant above his shop so that his clients would have a place to wait. Today the shop is the biggest Volkswagen-Porsche workshop in the city, and the restaurant has evolved into a high-quality and popular eatery filled with garage and racecar memorabilia (the silverware, for example, is engraved with the initials V.W.). The daily menus are solid, hearty, and what the Austrians call "honest." The savory and uncomplicated selections include veal steak Ticino style, a nourishing beef soup, and a wide range of generously served gutbürgerlich dishes. The restaurant doesn't "run" on Saturday. Fixed-price meals cost around 70 AS ($3.72), while à la carte dinners range from 80 AS ($4.26) to 200 AS ($10.64).

Witetschka, 1 Allerheiligenplatz (tel. 3109). This small and tasteful restaurant was long ago used by Austrian Protestants as a meeting place. Today it's a trendy hangout on one of the city's most beautiful squares. Much of the menu is devoted to café items, such as ice cream, elaborate pastries (try the crêpes Suchard, if you're fond of chocolate), and coffee drinks. Coffee is priced from 14 AS (75¢) to 25 AS ($1.33), pastries from 19 AS ($1.01). It's closed Sunday.

4. Semmering

One of the best known places for skiing in Austria, Semmering, at an elevation of 3200 feet sheltered by forests of firs and mountain ranges, is just over an hour by car or train from Vienna. It's a cool spot in summer and a choice location for winter sports when snow blankets the area. The resort, built on terraces, is perched around the Semmering pass which divides Lower Austria from Styria.

An international resort, called by the Austrians a *kurort,* a fresh-air spot rather than a mineral springs spa, Semmering is considered by doctors to be ideal for the health of patients, and there are many rest homes in the vicinity.

In winter guests can ski on the Raxalpe and the Schneeberg, two of the highest mountains in Lower Austria. They are separated by the Höllental, or Valley of Hell. This misnamed valley is really a lovely, wild spot, lying to the northwest of Semmering. The Schwarza River creates the gap between the two mountains.

If you don't want to stay right in Semmering, you'll also find accommodations in **Puchberg** and **Reichenau,** which is like a summer spa. It has a direct cable-car hookup which will take you up to the Rax.

Puchberg, at the foot of the Schneeberg, is a quiet, tranquil place which has a rack railway to take you right into the mountain range. It will take a full day for an excursion up to Schneeberg. The train from Puchberg climbs to the Hochschneeberg terminus in about an hour and 20 minutes. A hotel (see below) is perched on the mountainside. From the terminus, you can go by foot to the Kaiserstein (6760 feet), from which you're rewarded with a vista of the Alps and a panoramic sweep of the Raxalpe, a limestone massif which attracts many climbers. It is riddled with tunnels. From its upper belvedere you can see a sweep of the Semmering mountains to the south, the Kaiserstein to the north, and the Valley of Hell, also to the north.

Departures from Puchberg on the mountain railway in summer are at 9 a.m. and again at 11:30 a.m. The return trip is made at 2:30 and 5:30 p.m. The fare, likely to change by the time you read this, was 125 AS ($6.65) the last time I was there.

FOOD AND LODGING: **Kurhaus Dr. Stühlinger** (tel. 447) receives guests in an imposing four-story building with large arched windows on the ground floor, horizontal rows of wooden balconies, and a landscaping which makes it seem taller than it actually is. You'll enter through the grand loggia extending off the front of the building. The public rooms are elegant and modern, filled with curved lines and big windows. A covered swimming pool and a host of health facilities are available, sometimes for an extra charge, to guests. The rooms are clean and filled with 1950s-style wooden furniture and lots of natural light. Because of the health treatments which usually go with a room at this establishment, full board is encouraged. With all meals included, singles rent for between 585 AS ($31.12) and 790 AS ($42.03), while doubles cost 630 AS ($33.52) per person daily.

Pension Daheim (tel. 382) is a gracefully embellished chalet with green shutters and a series of gables that look out over the valley below. The interior is filled with pleasant wooden furniture and warmly patterned fabrics. The establishment is directed by the Hahnl-Steeger family, who charge between 160 AS ($8.51) and 250 AS ($13.30) per person in either a single or double room. Prices depend on the plumbing and the view.

Hotel/Pension Belvedere, 60 Hochstrasse (tel. 270), is a four-story building with a gabled roofline and a series of arches repeating themselves in the ground-floor windows and in the second-floor loggias. A formal garden grows abundantly off to one side, while a café with parasols has been placed near the stone walls of the ground floor. On the premises you'll find a small swimming pool and sauna. Rooms with private bath range from 310 AS ($16.49) to 335 AS ($17.82) per person daily, while bathless units cost around 225 AS ($11.97) per person. The Englschall family are your congenial hosts.

Gartenhotel Alpenheim, 55 Villenstrasse (tel. 322), is a well-designed chalet with a modern annex extending toward the downhill side of a forested hill. You'll find an indoor swimming pool, as well as a comfortable bar area with plushly upholstered chairs and lots of rustic details. Singles range from 380 AS ($20.22) to 460 AS ($24.47), while doubles cost between 350 AS ($18.62) and 420 AS ($22.34) per person daily. All units have phone, radio, and a TV outlet. Half board costs an additional 65 AS ($3.46) per person. The Steiner family will give you a hearty welcome.

Haus Mayer, Fremdenheim (tel. 251), is a small, family-run hotel in a chalet format of wooden balconies and a gently sloping roof. The inside is as cozily simple and rustic as you'd expect. Doubles with bath cost 195 AS ($10.37) per person daily, while singles without bath rent for 170 AS ($9.04), breakfast included. Guests have use of a big garden near the hotel.

At Puchberg

Forellenhof Wanzenböck, 20 Losenheim (tel. 22-05-11). From the front, you'll see a curved series of windows capped with a sloped roof and an upper-level terrace. A more conventional modern wing stretches off to the side, accented with flagstone walls and blue-green fir trees. The interior has wrought-iron wall sconces, pine paneling with arched niches for religious art, and lots of hunting trophies. The earth-toned bedrooms are filled with comfortable contemporary furniture. An in-house swimming pool has imaginative metal cutouts of giant fish fastened to one of the brown tile walls. As the name of the hotel would imply, the Wanzenböck family are the owners. They charge 215 AS ($11.44) per person in a bathless chamber, 280 AS ($14.90) per person in a unit with bath. Half board is offered for another 100 AS ($5.32) per person daily. A sauna is on the premises.

Hotel Puchbergerhof (tel. 2278) is a mellow old building with a stucco facade highlighted with golden illustrations, slate gables, and honey-colored wooden shutters. The backyard is filled with flowers and well-kept greenery, while the simple interior has wooden paneling which, on the wall areas, is sometimes stenciled with regional designs. The cozy bedrooms sometimes have wooden ceilings and an occasional carved headboard. The 40 rooms range from 175 AS ($9.31) to 255 AS ($13.57) in a single and between 240 AS ($12.77) and 265 AS ($14.10) in a double, with breakfast included. Edith Resch-Stickler, the charming hostess, works hard to make her guests comfortable.

Berghaus Hochschneeberg (tel. 2257) is a solidly built masonry house which can be reached only by a cog railway on a path up through alpine meadows. The hotel is perched over a steep cliff, and might be an ideal place to get away from it all. There are only two trains a day from the terminal at Puchberg which go to a station (Hochschneeberg) five minutes away from the hotel. They leave at 9 a.m. and at noon. On Friday and Saturday there's a train at 3:45 p.m. as well. The ride to the hotel takes an hour and a half. Guests are received from April 1 to October 30. Josef Schanner charges 335 AS ($17.82) in a double and 170 AS ($9.04) in a single. Half board costs an additional 205 AS ($10.91). However, in this isolated spot you'll probably want to take full board at 235 AS ($12.50) extra.

At Reichenau

Kurhotel Ferienhotel Marienhof (tel. 995) is a pastel-colored château-like building with a spacious renovated interior and a big indoor swimming pool. Most of the public rooms are outfitted in rustically modern touches which detract from any sense of history, although one of the entrance halls still retains some of its baroque touches. Singles range from 420 AS ($22.34) to 430 AS ($22.88), while doubles go from 370 AS ($19.68) to 385 AS ($20.48) per person, with breakfast included.

Alpenhotel Knappenhof (tel. 3633) is an alpine chalet covered with yellow stucco and wooden slats. Its shutters are forest green, and from the parasol-dotted sun terrace you'll have a view of the rock-covered mountains in the distance. Aside from the sauna and indoor swimming pool there's a choice of a wide range of health facilities, including underwater massage and diet therapy. The bedrooms are filled with simple blond furniture and cheerful warm colors. Singles range from 240 AS ($12.77) to 340 AS ($18.09), while doubles cost between 230 AS ($12.24) and 340 AS ($18.09). In winter there's an additional charge of 35 AS ($1.86) daily for heat.

Gasthof Flackl (tel. 3291) is a simple country chalet-style hotel with pleasant balconies covered with summertime flowers. Inside you'll find a green ceramic oven, chalet chairs, wooden ceilings, and a clean terracotta floor. The Flackl family charges between 180 AS ($9.58) and 440 AS ($23.41) in a single and between 145 AS ($7.71) and 275 AS ($14.63) per person in a double, with breakfast included. Prices, of course, depend on the plumbing. In summertime and during the Christmas holidays the management adds 30 AS ($1.60) per person to the rates cited above.

5. The Southeast Corner

You might want to consider anchoring in the very southeast corner of Lower Austria, at the doorway to Burgenland. There are several good spots to select from, all off the beaten track and all with good food and reasonable prices. Places I'll recommend are patronized by Austrians and are hardly known to foreigners. All of them are easily reached by driving south from Wiener Neustadt. They are to the east of Semmering.

First, I'll take you to—

KIRCHSCHLAG: In summer, visitors are drawn by the healthy climate and scenic location of this little market town. You'll see the ruins of a castle and a church which was fortified against border skirmishes. Passion Plays are presented at the theater in summer every five years. The next performance will be given in 1985.

Food and Lodging

Hotel Post, 2 Günser Strasse (tel. 2216), is an elegantly embellished symmetrical two-story hotel with baroque detailing painted around each of its windows. It was built more than 100 years ago as a tavern, and was recently updated so that it can continue its function as a place of good food and wine. My favorite room has a high ceiling of light-grained pine and well-sanded beams supporting chandeliers with pink lampshades. The bedrooms are modern, simple, and attractive. They range between 210 AS ($11.17) and 230 AS ($12.24) per person, in a single or a double, with breakfast included. Half board is offered for another 75 AS ($3.99) per person daily, and all accommodations contain private baths.

Under the same management, **Rendezvous** lives up to its name, proving to be one of the most popular gathering points in Kirchschlag. It's at 11 Wiener Strasse (tel. 2319). In a belle-époque decor of hanging lamps, brick walls, striped wallpaper, and wooden accents, the place serves drinks to both a youngish crowd of locals and tourists. Food is available as well.

BAD SCHÖNAU: This small spa has baths said to be helpful to persons with circulatory troubles. Outside the town is Krumbach Castle (2000 feet), a medieval fortress which saw action in the Turkish siege of Austria in 1683.

Food and Lodging

Kurhotel Bad Schönau, 1 Am Kurpark (tel. 2585). One of its facades is designed like a futuristic opera house, with sleek horizontal lines of arched windows looking out over a sun terrace and jets of water. It stretches over a wide expanse of green lawns and has evenly spaced balconies leading into comfortable bedrooms with lots of light. An indoor swimming pool is covered with a slanted roof and has a full wall of big windows. On the premises you'll find a wide range of massage and health facilities, as well as dining and drinking areas that are inviting and appealing. Per-person room prices range from 500 AS ($26.60) to 515 AS ($27.40) in a single or double, with breakfast included. All accommodations contain private baths.

MÖNICHKIRCHEN: On the road from Vienna to Graz where good accommodations are not as plentiful as one might wish, the following recommendation—roughly at the halfway point in your trip—might be handy either for food or lodging or both.

Food and Lodging

Hotel Pension Robert Reidinger (tel. 242) is a boxy, recently constructed cement building with flower-covered rows of balconies separated one from another with masonry dividers. Inside you'll find comfortable rooms, a sauna, an elevator, and a quiet location guaranteed to afford you a pleasant night's rest. Singles range from 205 AS ($10.91) to 240 AS ($12.77), while doubles cost between 175 AS ($9.31) to 260 AS ($13.83) per person, with breakfast included. Half board is offered for another 80 AS ($4.26) per person daily. The hotel is closed from mid-November until just before Christmas.

6. The Marchfeld

When you travel through Lower Austria in the autumn, you see signs at little inns advertising wild game on the menu, with such graphics as a defenseless stag depicted cornered by hunting dogs. Or you might see pheasant and quail strung up for proper aging. A lot of this game comes from the Marchfeld, a rich agricultural plain lying to the east of Vienna in the direction of the Iron Curtain. The Marchfeld, called "the fertile granary of Austria," was under Soviet domination during the Allied occupation years.

The "fertile granary" lies roughly between the River March and the Danube, which, with all due respect to Strauss, is a muddy brown rather than a beautiful blue. The plain lies on the border between Lower Austria and the Slovakia section of Communist Czechoslovakia. The Marchfeld is not one of the scenic sections of Austria, but it is historically significant, having been a battleground on many occasions. Here the Austrians fought the Magyars (Hungarians), the Turks, and even the forces of Napoleon.

While you're still based in Vienna, you can explore much of this area on a long morning's drive, leaving the city on the right bank of the Danube via Route 9 and heading toward Bratislava in Czechoslovakia. You'll have to have a visa as well as your passport if you cross the border.

On your drive, a good stopover might be—

FISCHAMEND: I suggest you explore in the morning and return to this town for lunch, as it's the site of the oldest fish restaurant in Austria. Many Viennese make culinary pilgrimages here to partake of its cuisine (see below). A market town with an early 16th-century tower, Fischamend lies on the Fischa River.

Where to Dine

Fischrestaurant Merzendorfer (tel. 314) is supposed to be the oldest restaurant in Austria specializing in fish, all of which are deliciously and conscientiously prepared. If you've wanted to try eel (with fennel or dill sauce, for example) or fish from the Danube, as well as carp, Serbian-style fogasch, trout, sheat-fish, or pike-perch with anchovy butter, this is the place to come. You might begin your meal with an Austrian roe soup. The restaurant is small, pleasant, cozy, with an outdoor terrace filled with plants in summer. Lunch is served from 11 a.m. to 2 p.m. while dinner is offered from 5:30 to 10 p.m. The restaurant is closed Sunday evening, all day Monday, and from the day before Christmas until January 6. It's also closed during all of August. À la carte meals begin at 225 AS ($11.97).

For your next sightseeing stop, you might take a look at some Roman ruins by driving to—

PETRONELL: In an open-air museum (not very spruced up) you can see the remains of several houses built in Roman times, along with some interesting mosaics.

Nearby are the partially excavated ruins of **Carnuntum,** a Roman city of some 45,000 inhabitants, maybe more, which thrived between the second and the fourth centuries A.D. Signs direct you to the ruins of two amphitheaters, where plays are presented in summer. The smaller and older of the two was surpassed by the one built in the second century which held an estimated 10,000 spectators. Near it are the ruins of a triumphal arch, also built in the second century.

North of Petronell, in an attractive park, is the 17th-century **Traun Castle,** home of the counts of Traun. In 1955 when Austria regained its sovereignty, the Danube Museum was opened here, displaying artifacts depicting the history of the river as a strategic route ever since Roman days. You'll also see a history of invaders of the area, ranging from the Turks to the army of Napoleon.

Admission to the castle is 25 AS ($1.33). Hours are 9 a.m. to 5 p.m. daily except Monday.

BAD DEUTSCH–ALTENBURG: The **Museum Carnuntinum** stands in this spa town, a neighbor of Petronell. Near the spa complex, the museum contains the most interesting of the Roman artifacts excavated at Carnuntum. Museum hours are 9 a.m. to 5 p.m. Admission is 25 AS ($1.33).

ROHRAU: Four miles on from Petronell is Rohrau, where a 16th-century castle houses one of the most important private art collections in Austria. Called the **Harrach Gallery,** it has an impressive aggregation of art and is particularly rich in paintings from the Spanish baroque period. The gallery is open to the public April through November daily except Monday from 10 a.m. to 5 p.m. Admission is 30 AS ($1.60).

Music lovers come to Rohrau because it was where Joseph Haydn, son of a wheelwright, was born in 1732. Haydn wrote some 104 symphonies, perfecting the classical sonata form. The **Haydn House,** a modest thatched cottage, contains mementos, including original scores. It's open daily except Monday from 10 a.m. to 5 p.m., charging an admission of 15 AS (80¢).

Even if you're not going on to Czechoslovakia, you might want to continue toward the border to the old town of—

HAINBURG: As nations developed and boundaries between countries were fixed, border towns naturally became defensive citadels. Hainburg was no exception. Its great moment in history was long ago, during the Middle Ages, but it still has a ruined castle and some fortified gateways, and part of the 13th-century wall that circled the town still stands. The Wiener Tor gateway is also from the 13th century. There are many vintage houses, in Gothic, Renaissance, and the ubiquitous baroque style.

Haydn attended school in this town, which lies between two cone-shape hills overlooking the Danube. A fountain is dedicated to the composer.

GROSSENZERSDORF: If you don't want to drive back to Vienna for the night, you can stay in this hamlet north of the Danube, in an area immediately east of the capital city. The village is partially enclosed by its former fortified wall, and nearby battlefields haunt the communal memory —at Aspern in 1809 Napoleon suffered his first defeat in the field, and through this sector the Red army and the retreating Nazis fought in the closing weeks of World War II in Europe.

Food and Lodging

Hotel am Sachsengang (tel. 2901) is a rambling, recently constructed building with a gently sloping roof and an elegantly crafted wood-trimmed interior. The indoor swimming pool is sunny and spacious, with scattered café tables to permit you to take coffee beside the water. An outdoor terrace faces a tree-lined canal. The hotel has a sauna and elaborate conference facilities, although that needn't get in the way of the attention paid to individual guests. Singles range from 650 AS ($34.58) to 760 AS ($40.43), while doubles go from 830 AS ($44.17) to 1000 AS ($53.20), with breakfast included. Half board is offered for an additional 200 AS ($10.64) per person daily (see separate restaurant review).

Taverne, Hotel am Sachsengang (tel. 2901), is an elegant restaurant dotted with wood detailing and handsomely rustic touches, and is a part of the best known hotel in the village. Many of the featured dishes come in puff pastry, including Hungarian fogosch and rack of lamb. Other specialties include veal parma, wild venison, and a wide range of desserts, all of them served on blue-and-white porcelain. Fixed-price meals range from 190 AS ($10.11) to 460 AS ($24.47), while à la carte meals cost anywhere from 195 AS ($10.37) to 360 AS ($19.15).

Farther along, still on the north bank of the Danube, you can visit—

ECKARTSAU: This tiny hamlet has had its moment in history. It was to an imperial hunting lodge here that Emperor Karl I and the royal family fled in the last days of the empire, when the Habsburg sovereignty collapsed in 1918. The baroque-style lodge was built in 1722. You are allowed to stroll through the baroque gardens and some display rooms, run by the Federal Forestry Administration and open daily except Monday from 9 a.m. to 5 p.m. Admission is 25 AS ($1.33).

DEUTSCH-WAGRAM: Should you become fascinated by the Marchfeld, you can drive along a more northerly route from Vienna, reaching the village of Deutsch-Wagram in about 20 minutes. Many memories of Napoleon are here, especially at the hotel recommended below.

Food and Lodging

Hotel Marchfelderhof (tel. 2243) is a beautiful hotel with lots of atmosphere, covered as it is with historic artifacts, valuable paintings, and carefully worked rustic detailing. It was established in 1912, and is today directed by the Bocek family, who charge 235 AS ($12.50) for a bathless single and between 420 AS ($22.34) and 480 AS ($25.54) in a double, depending on the plumbing. Only a few of the units have private baths.

You'll find a disco, a souvenir shop, a restaurant (see below), and an art nouveau café on the premises.

Restaurant Marchfelderhof (tel. 2243) is one of the best restaurants in the region. It has a gemütlich and cozy decor of polished wood, hunting artifacts, warmly tinted textiles, and oil paintings which add an elegant and rustically appropriate note. Some of the accessories, such as a mandolin and a coal miner's lamp hanging from the ceiling, add a lighthearted touch. A garden terrace with a cherub-capped fountain is pleasant on a summer afternoon, while the musical entertainment of the evening sometimes includes a live harpist. Specialties on any given night might be avocado sections with oysters in a spicy sauce, filet of wild venison, all the meat dishes you can think of, and a satisfying array of desserts. Portions are more than generous. The restaurant is closed Monday, and reservations are suggested. Fixed-price meals range from 135 AS ($7.18) to 420 AS ($22.34), while à la carte dinners cost from 120 AS ($6.38) to 460 AS ($24.47).

7. The Weinviertel

The Weinviertel, or wine district, referred to in my introduction, lies to the north of Vienna, a rich wine-growing territory between the Danube and the closely guarded Austria-Czechoslovakia border. On one of the most pleasant drives to be made in the environs of Vienna, you not only go through the vineyard district but you also pass many castles, often in ruins, which evoke the tumultuous Middle Ages.

You can stop in somnolent old market towns that seem light years removed from bustling Vienna. Many of the little towns have beautiful churches, and scenic views abound. The people who inhabit the district appear to lead relaxed and peaceful lives.

Your tour might take you to—

KORNEUBURG: This town, like Vienna, has a landmark column commemorating deliverance from the plague. It also has the Augustinerkirche, a rococo church built in 1773. A tower from the 15th century crowns the Rathaus (town hall).

A short distance from the town center is a castle fortress, **Burg Kreuzenstein,** rebuilt after being virtually demolished by the Swedes in 1645. Reconstruction was launched in 1874 and carried on into the 20th century. Some objets d'art are on exhibit. The castle is open daily except Monday from 9 a.m. to 5 p.m. for a 25-AS ($1.33) admission charge. You can enjoy the café and restaurant on the premises from which a fine vista unfolds.

From Korneuburg, I suggest that you continue on to the little town of—

EGGENBURG: One of the most beautiful little towns in the Weinviertel, Eggenburg, lying on the Schmida, was encircled by fortified walls in the 15th century. You can still see the defense towers and gates. Its castle, now in ruins, evokes thoughts of past grandeur. The parish church, dedicated to St. Stephen, has two Romanesque towers. On the main square, the Hauptplatz, stands a pillory dating from the 16th century. It's only there to look at today. Look for the **Gemaltes Haus** (painted house). The Krahuletz Museum, which has some prehistoric relics, is only of minor interest.

Towns near the border might intrigue you. One is—

RETZ: This well-known wine village lies near the Thaya Valley, almost in the Bohemian hills of Czechoslovakia. Retz is distinguished by fortified towers and ramparts, two gate towers dating from the 13th century. The center of this wine district town is the main square, or Hauptplatz, where a stately column dedicated to the Holy Trinity stands. The houses on the square are much photographed. The Rathaus (town hall) was reconstructed in the 16th century. The church, a Gothic Dominican structure, is noteworthy. The town also has an 18th-century windmill.

Many Viennese drive to Retz, mostly on Sunday, to take tours of the **wine cellars** of the town. Tours are conducted at 1:30 p.m. on weekdays and at 10 and 11 a.m. and 2 and 3 p.m. on Sunday. Each takes about an hour and costs 30 AS ($1.60). For advance information on these tours, telephone 23-79.

If you head east along the Thaya River, you come to—

LAA: This 13th-century town, very near the Czechoslovakia border, was once heavily fortified. Some of its walls still stand, and there's an ancient fortress. Also, there is an early Gothic parish church and a castle where you can see an armor collection from the 15th century.

Close by are some wine-growing towns, including **Poysdorf,** which is quite near the Iron Curtain.

On your way back to Vienna from Laa, you might enjoy a stopover at—

MISTELBACH: This charming old town, not far from Czechoslovakia, is in the northeast corner of Austria. Its Gothic-style parish church is from the 15th century. The *karner* (charnel house or bone house) is even older, from the 12th century. Mistelbach also has a baroque castle, built in 1725.

Food and Lodging

Zur Goldenen Krone, 15 Oberhofer Strasse (tel. 27-295). Walter Heindl is the engaging owner of this wine tavern and hotel. The outside has a faded ochre facade and tall, old-fashioned windows which let in lots of light. Singles range from 210 AS ($11.17), while doubles cost between 170 AS ($9.04) and 200 AS ($10.64) per person daily. The wood-paneled restaurant has a wall-size illustration of one of Austria's royal families, and lots of comfortably intimate nooks and crannies. Specialties include game and veal dishes, all of them cooked in a regional style. À la carte meals range from 85 AS ($4.52) to 175 AS ($9.31).

8. The Wachau-Danube Valley

If you plan to journey along the Danube, I recommend taking a paddleboat steamer in summer. You can travel by armchair, lounging on the deck along this longest river in Central Europe. (The Volga holds "longest river" title for the continent.)

If you're really "doing the Danube," as some travelers do, you can begin your trip at Passau, West Germany, and go all the way to the Black Sea and across to the Crimean Peninsula, stopping over at Yalta, scene of the famous, now controversial, meeting of Roosevelt, Churchill, and Stalin. However, the Vienna to Yalta portion of the trip alone takes nearly a week and few travelers have that kind of time to devote to it.

Therefore most visitors limit themselves to a more restricted look at the Danube, taking one of the many popular trips offered in Vienna. If you go westward on the river, your first stop might well be at **Klosterneuburg,** which was previewed as an excursion in the environs of Vienna (see Chapter IV under sightseeing attractions).

Cityrama Sightseeing, 1 Börsegasse (tel. 63-66-19) in Vienna, offers Wachau-Danube Valley tours from May 1 to October 31 on Monday, Wednesday, Friday, and Sunday, lasting about eight hours and costing 800 AS ($42.56) per person. The tour takes you from Vienna to Krems, with the boat trip on the river lasting about two hours. You have lunch on board, arriving soon after at Melk Abbey. From there, a bus takes you to Dürnstein before your return to Vienna.

Of course, you can do a Wachau-Danube Valley land tour in your own car. Some of the sights lie a few miles from the river, so if you're a serious sightseer an automobile will give you far more freedom to explore on your own.

Actually, the Wachau is that part of the Danube Valley lying between Krems and Melk, about 50 miles to the west of Vienna. It's possible to reach this far-western tip of the Wachau, where many visitors come to see Melk Abbey, by train; a one-way, second-class fare from Vienna costs 150 AS ($7.98). You can also take a river trip between Melk and Krems for 125 AS ($6.65) one way.

Scenic experts consider the Wachau one of the most beautiful parts of Austria, where competition for top rating is keen. Throughout this part of the Danube Valley you'll pass ruins of castles which are reminiscent of the Rhine Valley.

Stopovers along your route by car could include some of the following places, beginning with—

TULLN: This is one of the most ancient towns in Austria, originally being the naval base, Comagena. Later a center for the Babenbergs, who ruled Austria before the Habsburgs, Tulln, on the right bank of the Danube, is called "the flower town" because of the masses of blossoms you'll see in spring and summer. It is the place, according to the saga of the Nibelungen, where Kriemhild, the Burgundian princess of Worms, met Etzel, king of the Huns.

The twin-towered parish church (*pfarrkirche*) grew out of a 12th-century Romanesque basilica dedicated to St. Stephen, as was the cathedral in Vienna. Its west portal is from the 13th century. A Gothic overlay added in its early centuries gave way in the 18th century to the baroque craze that swept the country. A 1786 altarpiece commemorates the martyrdom of St. Stephen. Ogival vaulting was used in the chancel and the nave. Adjoining the church is the **karner** (charnel house or bone house). This funereal chapel is actually the major sight of Tulln, considered the finest of its kind in the entire country. Built in the mid-13th century in the shape of a polygon, it is richly decorated, with capitals and arches. The Romanesque dome is adorned with frescoes.

Food and Lodging

Hotel/Restaurant Römerhof Stoiber, 66 Langenlebarnerstrasse (tel. 2954), was built in 1973. It has a simple modern facade of white walls and unadorned windows, with a prominent sign announcing its name in big letters. The interior is warmly outfitted with earth colors, a macramé wall hanging, and hanging lighting fixtures. A wood-ceilinged restaurant serves well-prepared meals in an attractively rustic setting. The comfortable bedrooms rent for 320 AS ($17.02) in a single and 500 AS ($26.60) in a double, with breakfast included. All units have private baths. Specialties of the hotel's restaurant include wienerschnitzel, veal cutlets in a barbecue sauce, and roast or grilled pork dishes. Complete meals average around 180 AS ($9.58).

Farther along you come to—

TRAISMAUER: This old market town hardly merits a stopover, but it does have a ring of town walls, partially preserved, and a Renaissance castle that was once the property of the archbishops of Salzburg. Its Wiener Tor dates from the 16th century.

A drive of about seven miles will take you to a more interesting spot, the—

HERZOGENBURG MONASTERY: Founded in the early 12th century by a German bishop from Passau, this Augustinian monastery has a long history with some illustrious highlights. The present complex of buildings comprising the church and the abbey was reconstructed in the baroque style. That master of baroque, Fischer von Erlach, designed some of the complex. The art painted in the high altar of the church is by Daniel Gran, and the most outstanding art owned by the abbey is a series of 16th-century paintings on wood, displayed in a room devoted to Gothic art. The monastery is known for its library containing more than 80,000 works.

Guided tours lasting an hour take visitors through the monastery from the first of April until the end of October from 9 a.m. to noon and from 1 to 5 p.m. for an admission of 25 AS ($1.33). There's a wine tavern in the complex where you can drink the product of local grapes.

ST. PÖLTEN: Most guidebooks omit St. Pölten, which is today mainly an industrial town and rail link on the line from Linz to Vienna. But this is not only an important rail junction, it's also a city of culture and tradition, its origins going back to the time it was a Roman village known as Aelio Cetio. It lies on the left bank of the River Traisen which connects to the Danube 12½ miles to the north, passing along Traismauer, visited above.

The cultural heyday of St. Pölten, an episcopal see in the province which lies in the foothills of the Alps, was the 18th century, but many devotees today appreciate its special treasures. Daniel Gran, the painter, and Jakob Prandtauer, the architect, lived here and some of their works remain. These two loom large in the art and architectural annals of Austria.

For your tour of the old town, head for the Domplatz, which, as its name indicates, is dominated by a **cathedral** of early Gothic style. The present structure supplanted a Romanesque church built on the site in the mid-12th century. However, some of the original edifice remains. One of the cathedral's towers is crowned by a baroque onion-shape dome. Prandtauer worked on designs for the interior, and there are ceiling paintings by Gran.

The second most important square in the old town is the Rathausplatz where you will of course find the Rathaus (town hall), dating from the 16th century, and also a colony of baroque houses. To the north of the square is a Franciscan church known for outstanding altarpieces by Kremser Schmidt, the noted baroque artist from Krems (see below).

Another interesting sight is the **Institute of the English Maidens** (Institut der Englischen Fraulein) on the Linzerstrasse. The charming baroque building dates from 1715. A portrait of the Virgin by Lucas Cranach the Elder is exhibited in one of the altars.

Food and Lodging

Hotel Pittner (Zum Roten Krebs), 18 Kremmer Gasse (tel. 2060). There's been a hotel on this site since 1514, although the building as you'll see it today was built in 1870 and rebuilt in 1912. It's seen many imperial guests below its formal facade, and it remains a proudly elegant establishment with parquet floors, vaulted corridors, and wrought-iron chandeliers. The hotel has 90 rooms, only 17 of which have private baths. The Viennese cuisine served in the high-ceilinged dining room is outstanding. Singles range from 230 AS ($12.24) to 380 AS ($20.22), while doubles go from 210 AS ($11.17) to 300 AS ($15.96) per person, with breakfast included.

Back along the Danube, continue on to one of the major sightseeing targets of the Wachau-Danube Valley—

KREMS: In the eastern part of the Wachau on the left bank of the Danube lies Krems, a city some 1000 years old. The city today encompasses Stein and Mautern, once separate towns (see my recommendation of a restaurant in Mautern).

Krems is a mellow town of courtyards, old churches, and ancient houses in the heart of the vineyard country, with some partially preserved town walls. Just as the Viennese flock to Grinzing and other suburbs to sample new wine in heurigen, so do the people of the Wachau come here to taste the vintners' products which are new in Krems earlier in the year than in the Vienna area.

The most interesting part of Krems today is what was once the little village of **Stein.** Narrow streets are terraced above the river, and the single main street, Steinlanderstrasse, is flanked with houses, many from the 16th century. The Grosser Passauerhof, 76 Steinlanderstrasse, is a Gothic structure decorated with an oriel. Another house, at 84 Steinlanderstrasse, which combines Byzantine and Venetian elements among other architectural influences, was once the imperial toll house. In a troubled era, the aristocrats of Krems barricaded the Danube and extracted heavy fines from the river traffic. Sometimes the fines were more than the hapless victims could pay, so the townspeople just confiscated the cargo.

The parish church (*pfarrkirche*) of Krems is somewhat overadorned, rich with gilt and statuary. Construction on this, one of the oldest baroque churches in the province, began in 1616. In the 18th century Martin Johann Schmidt painted many of the frescoes you'll see inside the church. In the Altstadt, or old town, the **Steiner Tor,** a 1480 gate, is a landmark. The town's Rathaus (town hall), from 1549, has an oriel.

The **Historisches Museum der Stadt Krems** (Historical Museum of Krems) is in a restored Dominican monastery. The abbey is in the Gothic style from the 13th and 14th centuries. It has a painting gallery displaying the works of Martin Johann Schmidt, a well-known 18th-century artist better known as Kremser Schmidt (mentioned earlier).

The complex also has an interesting **Weinbaumuseum** (wine museum) where artifacts, many quite old, gathered from the vineyards along the Danube are exhibited.

The historical museum is open from around Easter until the middle of November. Hours are 9 a.m. to noon and 2 to 5 p.m. (9 a.m. to noon on Sunday). It's closed on Monday. Admission is 25 AS ($1.33).

Food and Lodging

Parkhotel Krems, 19 Edmund-Hofbauer-Strasse (tel. 32-66), is a large, glass-walled hotel with a wooden canopy stretching out over the front entrance. After registering in a simply paneled modern reception area, you'll be able to choose between a meal in the airy café or on its terrace, the restaurant, or in what is my personal favorite, the Wachauer-Keller. This room caters as much to the local population as to the hotel guests, and has a rustically timbered decor of chalet chairs, red-checked curtains, and red tablecloths. The waitresses, all of whom wear regional garb, will bring you local and Austrian specialties which include fish from the Danube and wine from the Wachau district. Singles cost 475 AS ($25.27) while doubles rent for 385 AS ($20.48) per person, with breakfast included. All units contain private baths.

Hotel/Restaurant Am Förthof, 8 Donaulände (tel. 33-45), in the Stein sector of the city, is a big-windowed building with white stucco walls between each of its flower-covered wooden balconies. A rose garden surrounds the base of an al fresco café, while the inside is decorated with Oriental rugs and a scattering of antiques amid the newer furniture. On the grounds is an outdoor swimming pool bordered in stone. The high-ceilinged bedrooms rent for between 385 AS ($20.48) and 470 AS ($25) in a single and between 280 AS ($14.90) and 365 AS ($19.42) per person in a double, with breakfast included. All units have private baths. Half board is offered for another 100 AS ($5.32) per person daily.

Restaurant Bacher (tel. 29-37), at Mautern, 2½ miles away from Krems, is a friendly restaurant with an elegant dining room and a well-kept garden. Liesl Wagner, the engaging owner, cooks à la Paul Bocuse, serving an imaginative array of the freshest possible ingredients. Specialties include crabmeat salad with nut oil, zucchini stuffed with fish, and two kinds of sauces, plus a changing collection of creatively prepared foods. Dessert might be beignets with apricot sauce and vanilla ice cream. She has won awards for her cuisine, as her enthusiastic clientele will tell you. À la carte meals range from 150 AS ($7.98) to 395 AS ($21.01). Reservations are strongly advised, and the restaurant is closed Monday and Tuesday from November to March. A limited number of bedrooms, each attractively furnished, are offered for 310 AS ($16.49) in a single and for between 250 AS ($13.30) and 310 AS ($16.49) per person in a double.

DÜRNSTEIN: Less than five miles from Krems is the loveliest town along the Danube, Dürnstein, which draws throngs of tour groups in summer. Terraced vineyards mark this as another Danube wine town. Once fortified, the walls are partially preserved.

The ruins of a castle fortress, 520 feet above the town, are a link with the crusades. It was here that Leopold V, the Babenberg duke ruling the country at that time, held Richard the Lionhearted of England prisoner in 1193. It seems that Richard had insulted the powerful Austrian duke in Palestine during one of the frequent religious forays of the Middle Ages to get the Holy Sepulcher and its appurtenances into Christian custody. The story goes that when Richard was trying to get back home, his boat went on the rocks in the Adriatic and he tried to sneak through Austria disguised as a peasant. Somebody probably turned stool pigeon, but at any rate, the English monarch was arrested and imprisoned by Leopold.

For quite some time nobody knew exactly where Richard was incarcerated in Austria, but his loyal minstrel companion, Blondel, had a clever idea. He went from castle to castle, playing on his lute and singing Richard's favorite songs, particularly where it seemed as though somebody important might be held prisoner. The tactic paid off, the legend says, and at Dürnstein Richard heard the voice of the minstrel singing and took up the lyrics in reply. This discovery forced Leopold to transfer the English king to another castle, this one in the Rhineland Palatinate, but by then everybody knew where he was, so Leopold set a high ransom on the Plantagenet head which was eventually met, and Richard was set free.

The castle was demolished by the Swedes in 1645, but you can visit the ruins if you don't mind a vigorous climb (allow an hour). The castle isn't so much, but the view of Dürnstein and the Wachau is more than worth the effort.

Back in the town, take in the principal artery, Hauptstrasse, which is flanked by richly embellished old residences. Many of these date from the 1500s and have been well maintained through the centuries. In summer the balconies are filled with flowers.

The 15th-century *pfarrkirche* (parish church) also merits a visit. The building was originally an Augustinian monastery and was reconstructed in baroque when this style swept Austria. The church tower is considered the finest one in baroque in the whole country. There is also a splendid church portal. Kremser Schmidt, the noted baroque painter mentioned earlier, did some of the altar paintings.

Food and Lodging

Richard Löwenherz (tel. 222) is built into what was once an abbey. Classified today as one of Austria's "Romantik" hotels, it's filled with antiques, Renaissance sculpture, and elegant chandeliers. The vaulting of some of the ceilings rests on exposed stone columns, while the paneling in other rooms is well polished and mellow. An arbor-covered sun terrace with restaurant tables extends toward the Danube, and will give you a chance to see the other residents of the hotel enjoying the view. Best of all, the hotel offers a swimming pool where you'll be able to see the reflection of the apse of a medieval church in its waters. The spacious bedrooms, especially those in the balconied modern section, are tastefully filled with lighthearted furniture and cheerful, unobtrusive colors. Singles range from 480 AS ($25.54) to 880 AS ($46.82), while doubles cost between 850 AS ($45.22) and 1150 AS ($61.18), with breakfast included. The restaurant offers excellent local wines as well as fish from the Danube among its many regional specialties.

Hotel Schloss Dürnstein (tel. 212). The baroque tower of this Renaissance castle rises above one of the most colorful parts of the Danube. It used to be owned by the princes of Starhemberg, but today it's one of the best furnished hotels in Austria, with a series of intricate architectural details. Inside you'll see white ceramic stoves, immaculately maintained vaulted ceilings, parquet floors, Oriental rugs, gilt mirrors, and oil portraits of elaborately dressed courtiers. Below the ochre facade of one of the wings, an ivy-covered wall borders the water of a swimming pool. The real beauty of the grounds, however, is found on the shady terrace a stone's throw from the river whose traffic stimulated the construction of this building more than 350 years ago.

The restaurant is outfitted with velvet armchairs with cambriole legs. Here you'll be served well-prepared dishes from the kitchen of an experienced chef. With half board included, regular singles cost between 880 AS ($46.82) and 1060 AS ($56.39), while doubles range between 670 AS ($35.64) and 900 AS ($47.88) per person. One of the hotel's elegant rooms, with rare antiques, beautiful upholstery, and beds worthy of either Napoleon or one of his wives, costs between 1000 AS ($53.20) and 1200 AS ($63.84) per person nightly. The hotel is open only from March 25 until the end of November, with a 10% reduction made for visits during March and most of April and November.

Gartenhotel Pfeffel (tel. 206) is a black-roofed, white-walled hotel whose angularity is partially concealed by the well-placed shrubbery growing around it. Most of the pleasant rooms have private balconies. The public rooms are invitingly furnished with contemporary pieces, usually clustered around a wintertime fireplace. Leopold Pfeffel, the congenial owner, charges between 370 AS ($19.68) and 600 AS ($31.92) in a single and between 190 AS ($10.11) and 370 AS ($19.68) per person in a double, with breakfast included. Half board is included for an additional 125 AS ($6.65) per person.

Gasthof-Pension Sänger Blondel (tel. 253) is a lemon-colored, charmingly old-fashioned hotel with green shutters and clusters of flowers gathered at the windows. Its name is derived from the faithful minstrel who searched the countryside until he found Richard the Lionhearted imprisoned at Dürnstein. Aside from the good and reasonably priced restaurant, Sänger Blondel offers 36 rooms to travelers, costing between 270 AS ($14.36) and 450 AS ($23.94) in a single and between 210 AS ($11.17) and 355 AS ($18.87) per person in a double, with breakfast included.

After exploring Dürnstein most visitors rush on to Melk, but if you have more time to spend in this beautiful area there are other sights in the immediate vicinity. These include—

WEISSENKIRCHEN: This is a celebrated wine town in the heart of the vineyards of Wachau which lie along the Danube. You'll see many old houses, but Weissenkirchen's main attraction is its fortified Gothic **pfarrkirche,** or parish church, from the 15th century. The builders had the church fortified in 1531, fearing that the Turks would take Vienna and pose a threat to areas to the west of the capital. From one of the belvederes here you have an excellent view of the Danube Valley. A car ferry crosses the river here.

The **Wachaumuseum** (Wachau Museum) also merits a visit. The Teisenhofer-Hof, once a patrician house, was also fortified in the 16th century. It has a charming courtyard and arcades extending out to support a canopied gallery. The museum is devoted to the history of the region. It's open from the first of April to the end of October from 10 a.m. to 5 p.m., except Monday. Admission is 20 AS ($1.06).

Weissenkirchen has some of the finest food in the Wachau (see below), so you may want to schedule a luncheon stop here.

Food and Lodging

Raffelsbergerhof (tel. 2201), at Weissenkirchen, is the former headquarters of one of the river's traffic controllers. It's been renovated to its Renaissance integrity, and converted into a tastefully decorated hotel, with a pretty garden and contemporary touches in the comfortable bedrooms. The Anton family, your hosts, charge between 280 AS ($14.90) and 355 AS ($18.87) per person in a single or double. The place is closed from November until April.

Florianihof (tel. 3212), at Wösendorf, is a beautifully old-fashioned house decorated with taste and rustic furniture. Specialties of the house include such gutbürgerlich dishes as blutwurst and sauerkraut, zucchini and chicken cream soup, and cabbage noodles with ham. Reservations are suggested, and the establishment is closed Wednesday from June until October and Wednesday and Thursday from November until May. À la carte meals range from 130 AS ($6.92) to 275 AS ($14.63).

JOCHING: If you feel the prices are too high in Weissenkirchen, you can turn off the main Wachau route deep into vineyard country to the little hamlet of Joching, where you'll find the following establishment.

Where to Dine

Jamek (tel. 2235) is named after its owner, Joseph, who, in addition to fermenting excellent wine, is also a good cook. The restaurant is in an old house covered with flowers. Someone will bring you a different glass for each of the wines you order, along with an excellent cuisine which includes what is reputed to be the best blutwurst in the region, as well as sauerkraut, goose, duck, venison, pork dishes, black bread, veal schnitzel, filet of lamb with basil, and zucchini in a cream sauce flavored with dill. You might prefer on a warm day to eat in the flowering garden, although the inside is also cozy. À la carte meals range from 250 AS ($13.30) to 300 AS ($15.96), and reservations are suggested. Jamek is closed for all of December and January and for the first week of July. Otherwise, it's open Tuesday to Saturday from 11 a.m. to 11 p.m.

Back along the wine route, you might consider a stopover in—

SPITZ: Southward along the Danube in the direction of Melk is Spitz, a sleepy little market town celebrated for its grapes and characterized by its terraced vineyards. It is at its most beautiful in spring when hundreds of fruit trees are in bloom.

Spitz has the ubiquitous ruined castle and is noted for its ancient houses, many owned by vintners. Balconies of the houses are filled with masses of geraniums in spring and summer. A walk along the Schlossgasse will permit you to see some of the town's finest buildings. The Gothic *pfarrkirche* (parish church) is from the 15th century. The well-known baroque painter, Kremser Schmidt, worked on the altar.

Food and Lodging

Hotel Wachauer Hof (tel. 303) is a large gabled building with white walls and a pleasant situation near vineyards and other buildings. Attractively furnished singles rent for between 200 AS ($10.64) and 220 AS ($11.70), while doubles go for between 350 AS ($18.62) and 480 AS ($25.54), with breakfast included. The staff is friendly and helpful.

From here, a car ferry will take you and your vehicle over to the Danube's right bank.

SCHÖNBÜHEL: On the right bank of the Danube in one of the most idyllic settings of the Wachau, some three miles before you reach Melk, stands the castle of Schönbühel, built in the early 1800s. It was erected on a rocky ledge commanding a view of the valley and of Melk. An architect was allowed to create a fantasy of onion-shape domes and "pepperpot" towers on the castle.

Finally, you arrive at one of the chief sightseeing goals of every pilgrim to Austria—

MELK: Some 55 miles from Vienna on the right bank of the Danube, Melk marks the west terminus of the Wachau. **Melk Abbey,** one of the finest baroque buildings in the world, and the **Stiftskirche,** or abbey church, are the major attractions today. However, Melk has been an important place in the Danube Basin since establishment of a Roman fortress on a promontory looking out onto a tiny "arm" of the Danube. Melk also figures in the *Nibelungenlied,* in which it is called Medelike.

The rock-strewn bluff where the abbey now stands overlooking the river was the seat of the Babenbergs who ruled Austria from 976 until the Habsburgs took over. In the 11th century Leopold III of the House of Babenberg presented Melk to the Benedictine monks, who turned it into a fortified abbey. It became known as a center of learning and culture, and its influence spread all over Austria. However, it did not fare well during the Reformation, and it felt the fallout from the 1683 Turkish invasion, although it was spared from direct attack when the armies of the Ottoman Empire were repelled at the outskirts of Vienna. The abbey structure was razed by fire, but reconstruction began in 1702, just in time to be given the full baroque treatment.

Most of the design of the present abbey was by the celebrated baroque architect Jakob Prandtauer. Its marble hall, called the Marmorsaal, contains pilasters coated in red marble stucco. A richly painted allegorical picture on the ceiling is the work of Paul Troger, whose work is distinguished by his blue coloring. The library, rising two floors, again with a

Troger ceiling, contains some 80,000 volumes. The Kaisergang, or emperors' gallery, 650 feet long, is decorated with paintings of the rulers of Austria, the most notable of which is the prominently displayed likeness of Maria Theresa.

Despite all this adornment in the abbey, it still takes second place in lavish glory to the Stiftskirche, the golden abbey church. Richly embellished with marble and frescoes, the church has an astonishing number of windows. Many of the paintings are by Johann Michael Rottmayr, but Troger also had a hand in decorating the church.

Guided tours of the abbey complex are from 9 to 11:30 a.m. and from 1 to 4 p.m. in April and May, till 5 p.m. in summer. Otherwise, the hours are from 11 a.m. to 2 p.m. Admission is 35 AS ($1.86).

Everybody heads for the terrace for the view of the river. Napoleon probably used it for a lookout when he made Melk his headquarters during his campaign against Austria.

Food and Lodging

Hotel Stadt Melk, 1 Hauptplatz (tel. 2475), is a four-story beflowered hotel with a gabled roof, white stucco walls, and a position just below the yellow baroque walls of the town's palace. The pleasant restaurant has leaded-glass windows in round bull's-eye patterns of greenish glass, while the simply furnished bedrooms are clean and comfortable. There's a sauna on the premises. Singles rent for 370 AS ($19.68) per person, while doubles go for between 260 AS ($13.83) and 340 AS ($18.09) per person daily, with breakfast included. Half board is another 140 AS ($7.45) per person daily.

9. The Nibelungengau

Austrians call one section of the Danube Valley the Nibelungengau, a name which brings a nostalgic "Once upon a time . . ." feeling even to those only vaguely familiar with the legend of Siegfried and his struggle to steal the treasure of the Nibelungen, a tribe of dwarfs, and awaken the enchanted princess, Brunhild. The *Nibelungenlied* is that German epic poem, probably written about A.D. 1200, which set down household legends that had been centuries in the making. After the gold hoard was taken from the dwarfs, the name Nibelungen was given to the followers of Siegfried, the Burgundian kings who acquired the treasure after Siegfried's death.

In Teutonic tradition, the epic of the Nibelungen enjoys a renown equaled only by that of King Arthur in England.

The Nibelungengau is that part of the Danube Valley lying beyond the Wachau to the west. Here you'll find—

PÖCHLARN: This river town, which still has remnants of its medieval walls, is today a focal point of tourist attention in June. Visitors from all over Europe and America come to attend a festive pageant, complete with bonfires, which briefly turns back the clock to the Middle Ages. In the *Nibelungenlied,* Pöchlarn was Bechelaren, where the margrave, Rüdiger, entertained the Burgundian kings who were going east to face the king of the Huns (really Attila). The Erlauf River flows into the Danube at Pöchlarn.

Two miles north of the town stands **Hohenstein Castle** at Arstetten. The baroque chapel here, a parish church since the 17th century, contains the tombs of two people who figured prominently and tragically in the history of the 20th century—Archduke Franz Ferdinand, heir to the throne of Austria, and his wife. Their assassinations at Sarajevo (now a Yugoslavian city) on June 28, 1914, touched off events that led to World War I.

MARBACH: A ferry connects this little village with the right bank of the Danube. Summer tourists visit it, but otherwise it's a fairly sleepy little market town.

However, from here you can take a steep, 2¼-mile drive up to—

MARIA TAFERL: At this little summer resort, a fantastic view of the Nibelungengau unfolds. The hamlet is known for its pilgrimage church, designed by Jakob Prandtauer, the architect of Melk Abbey. A Celtic sacrificial stone can be seen outside.

If you'd like to anchor in this bucolic little spot, I have the following recommendations—

Food and Lodging

Hotel Krone (tel. 325) has an elegantly detailed pseudo-baroque facade stretching out in two separate wings, each of them with a modernized mansard roof. The interior has a paneled bar area where you might decide to have a pre-dinner drink below the light from the brass chandeliers, plus an opulent dining room with a splendid view of the Danube. Bedrooms are rustic and comfortable, costing between 270 AS ($14.36) and 420 AS ($22.34) per person, based on double occupancy. Occupants of singles pay a 40-AS ($2.13) supplement. An indoor swimming pool, a rooftop sun terrace, and a whirlpool and sauna are part of the facilities.

Hotel Kaiserhof (tel. 325), under the same management as its sister hotel, the Krone, has a large outdoor swimming pool within sight of the twin baroque towers of a nearby church. The facade is pleasantly simple, with attractive shrubbery and colorful flowerboxes, an imposing entrance area, and a summertime cold buffet which is sometimes served on the spacious lawns outside. An outdoor terrace offers panoramic views of the Danube. Prices are the same as for the Hotel Krone.

Terrassenhotel Rose (tel. 304) is a cozy-looking gabled house with illustrations painted onto the front and wooden balconies near a few of the windows. A small swimming pool sits partially above ground level in the backyard, while the interior is paneled, timbered, and filled with an occasional hunting trophy. The 100 comfortable rooms cost between 230 AS ($12.24) and 260 AS ($13.83) per person daily, with breakfast included.

PERSENBEUG: Near the end of the Nibelungengau is Persenbeug, a market town across the river from Ybbs with a bridge connecting the towns. Persenbeug was built in 1617 at a loop of the Danube on a rocky ledge overlooking the river. Persenbeug Castle, a Habsburg imperial residence, was the birthplace of "the last of the Habsburgs," Karl I, who died in exile in Madeira in 1922. The river you can see from here has been dammed by a power station.

If you take the bridge across the dam, you'll arrive at—

YBBS: On the right bank of the Danube, this old town lies near the mouth of the Ybbs River. You can still see the remains of its medieval walls. The town, which may or may not have grown up on the site of a Roman fort, has a Gothic church.

10. The Ybbs and Erlauf Valleys

In the far-western section of Lower Austria are two little-known—at least to North Americans—valleys containing a number of charming old towns and villages as well as beautiful scenery. To explore the Erlauf Valley, called "one of the few backwaters left in Europe," you can head south from Ybbs, going toward the celebrated Styrian resort of Mariazell.

Your first stop along this route might be at the brewery town of **Wieselburg,** which has an old church and castle.

If you continue along the same route, soon you'll reach **Pürgstall,** which also has an old church and castle.

In a short time you'll reach **Scheibbs,** which is bigger than Wieselburg or Pürgstall. Remnants of the town walls have survived ever since the Middle Ages, and a tower gate and some houses date from the Renaissance. The parish church is in the Gothic style, and—you guessed it—there's a castle, this one from the 16th century.

From Scheibbs, you can drive to **Gaming,** a little summer resort noted for its former Carthusian monastery, Marienthorn, built in 1330 and dissolved by order of Emperor Joseph II in 1782. The church, from 1332, is in the "high Gothic" style.

At Erlauf Lake you can take a road which connects with the upper part of the Ybbs Valley. I recommend heading for **Lunz am See,** a market town and small summer resort on Lunzer lake. It has a celebrated Gothic parish church from the early years of the 16th century.

Along the Ybbs River, about 6½ miles from Lunz, lies **Göstling,** a very tiny summer resort. Many travelers pass through, going another 5¼ miles to Lassing where they connect with the **Hochkar Alpine Road.** This is less than 6 miles long and reaches a height of 4720 feet. At the end of the road you can go the rest of the way by chair lift almost to the summit of Hochkar at 5931 feet. From this vantage point you'll have a panoramic view of the countryside.

Your chief target in the Ybbs Valley should be—

MAIDHOFEN AN DER YBBS: This mellow old place in the lower part of the valley got its city charter in 1288. The early economy of the town was based on work in the forges with iron mined in the Erzberg. Many houses here are from the 1400s and 1500s. Gables and oriels were common in early house construction, as were arcaded courtyards.

The Rathaus, or town hall, has such an arcaded court. The parish church, built in 1510, is in late Gothic style. The **stadtturm** (tower) was erected in 1542 to commemorate the town's victory over the Turks. The exact moment of the Turkish defeat, shortly before noon, was "frozen for eternity" in the tower's clock dial. A nearby castle was the summer home of the Baron von Rothschild for some years of the 19th century.

The pilgrimage church of **Sonntagberg,** rising five miles north of the town, is the most distinguishing landmark to be seen in the Ybbs Valley. The church was built in 1706 by Jakob Prandtauer, the noted baroque architect.

Nearby, you might want to stay at one of the most idyllic stopovers in this part of the country—

NEUHOFEN AN DER YBBS: This "cradle of Austria" is so called because of a document discovered here in 996 in which the oldest spelling of the word *Österreich* is used. This, of course, is the German word for Austria.

Food and Lodging

Gasthof-Pension Kothmühle (tel. 2112) is directed by the Scheiblauer family, who run this light-hearted hotel with friendliness and sensitivity. It's built in a pleasant balconied format of white walls and surrounding parklands, with a gemütlich bar area and a changing repertoire of folkloric musicians who seem to be as funny as they are musical. You'll recognize the hotel from the outside by the antique water wheel which sits drydocked on the front lawn, surrounded by flowerbeds. There's also a sauna, plus indoor and outdoor exercise facilities. With half board included, the per-person rates range from 285 AS ($15.16) to 305 AS ($16.23).

STEINAKIRCHEN AM FORST: For one of the most spectacular accommodations not just in the valley but in all of Austria, consider the following 12th-century castle, which lies in a forest setting in the foothills of the Alps with a superb view of the Danube Valley.

Ernegg, the site of the castle, is a satellite of Steinakirchen, lying about ten miles south of the Vienna/Salzburg motorway (take the Ybbs exit). It's about a 90-minute drive from Vienna. By railroad, take the train to Amstetten.

Food and Lodging

Schloss Ernegg (tel. 214), on the outskirts of Steinakirchen am Forst. It's hard to imagine a more idyllic hotel: it's isolated from the nearest village, which is one mile away. From the outside it looks like a cross between a medieval fortress and a baroque pleasure palace, and once you're inside you'll realize that it's actually a bit of both. Constructed originally in the 12th century, it has an inner courtyard whose three floors of arcades rest on chiseled granite columns, elaborate public rooms whose salmon-colored walls reflect off the white tile ceramic stoves, and an impressive collection of rugs, antiques, and oil paintings. The dining room has a high ceiling, pink napery, well-prepared food, and a collection of hunting trophies.

There are only 20 bedrooms in the castle open to the public. The hotel maintains a private stable, whose horses are available for the use of guests. You'll also find tennis courts and a heated swimming pool in the nearby village. A nine-hole golf course is on the grounds. Clay pigeon shooting and trout fishing can be arranged nearby. The daughter of the last Count of Auersperg is today in charge of the hotel, charging between 360 AS ($19.15) and 500 AS ($26.60) per person daily, based on double occupancy with half board included. Occupants of singles pay a supplement of 75 AS ($3.99) daily. The castle is open from the first of May until October. In July and August there's an additional supplement of 120 AS ($6.38) per person daily.

AMSTETTEN: This is a busy commercial town of light industry on the Ybbs River, but it makes a convenient stopover in this part of the province, as it has some fine accommodations and good food. Its parish church is from the 14th century.

Food and Lodging

Hotel Hoffman, 2-4 Bahnhofstrasse (tel. 2516), is an imposing 19th-century hotel, constructed with a combination of Victorian and baroque elements which render it grandly imperial in a faded sort of way. It has a square cupola above a complicated roofline, plus well-embellished laurel wreaths crowning the top of the single third-floor lunette window. Some of the inside rooms still have rustic timbers and old-fashioned decor, although the bedrooms have been modernized into a slickly contemporary format. Near the train station, the hotel has a country-style dance bar which is popular with local residents on weekends. Singles range from 220 AS ($11.70) to 270 AS ($14.36), while doubles go from 400 AS ($21.28) to 650 AS ($34.58), with breakfast included. There's a parking garage on the premises.

Hotel/Restaurant Gürtler, 13 Rathausstrasse (tel. 2765), is an inner-city hotel with boldly outlined windows and a simple stucco facade. The interior has paneling, wrought-iron detailing, and strong colors which look pleasingly accommodating to the drinkers and diners who congregate in the restaurant. The contemporary bedrooms have patterned wallpaper and comfortable beds. The friendly atmosphere is what makes this place successful. Singles rent for between 200 AS ($10.64) and 235 AS ($12.50), while doubles cost between 360 AS ($19.15) and 465 AS ($24.74), with breakfast included. Streetside rooms tend to be noisy, so get a unit facing the courtyard if available. The restaurant serves well-prepared specialties which include, for example, grilled and pan-fried seafish, plus a daily menu that often has nouvelle cuisine touches. Try the pork cutlet with a spicy orange and apricot sauce, a variety of velvety-smooth cream soups, and a tempting list of pastries. À la carte meals range from 110 AS ($5.85) to 220 AS ($11.70), while fixed-price meals go from 60 AS ($3.19) to 170 AS ($9.04). The restaurant is closed on Monday.

Paradiesgartl (Schlemmer) (tel. 2694) has green shrubs surrounding it and a Mediterranean ambience of relaxed conviviality. The food is well prepared and attractively served. Desserts are made fresh daily (the strudel is divine). Main courses are likely to include roast ham, veal, fish, and pork dishes. À la carte meals range from 65 AS ($3.46) to 100 AS ($5.32).

St. Georg's Stub'n (tel. 332), in St. Georgen (Ybbsfelde), is a country-style rendezvous point for local gourmets. The menu is unusual, emphasizing light recipes that have been strongly influenced by nouvelle cuisine. The menu changes almost daily, although staples of the establishment include the chef's gourmet salad, polenta noodles, rack of lamb local style, and a host of other specialties, culminating with a piece of apple strudel. Fixed-price meals range from 145 AS ($7.71) to 420 AS ($22.34), while à la carte meals range between 100 AS ($5.32) and 220 AS ($11.70). The place is closed on Thursday.

HAAG: Sometimes called Stadt Haag, this is my most remote recommendation in the province. It lies in the far-western reaches of Lower Austria.

Actually, it's not inconvenient, being just off the autobahn to Linz. You might prefer to stop here instead of going on into busy Linz. Haag is only a short drive from Amstetten (visited above), and it may well suit your taste if you're looking for an overnight stay in an "undiscovered" Austrian village.

Food and Lodging

Gasthof Schafelner, 11 Hauptplatz (tel. 2411), is a lime-green baroque confection of a building, with it's white trim and steeply sloping tile roof. The interior has elegantly upholstered straight-back chairs clustered beneath the vaulted arches of the dining room, and a less formal weinstube paneled in wood with chairs that might be called "country Biedermeier." Restaurant specialties include mousse of smoked trout, lamb sausages on lentils, homemade herb noodles with fresh mushrooms, saddle of venison with bread dumplings and cranberries, filet of veal with morels and roast potatoes, roast duck with red cabbage and potato dumplings, and sweetbreads in Austrian white wine sauce. Desserts might include soufflé of cottage cheese in orange sauce and coffee mousse with rum sauce. An average meal will cost 300 AS ($15.96). The restaurant serves Tuesday till Sunday from 11 a.m. to 3 p.m. and from 6 p.m. to midnight. It's closed for part of January.

A limited number of rooms are available, costing between 145 AS ($7.71) and 200 AS ($10.64) per person, in singles or doubles, with breakfast included. Only four of the accommodations have private showers.

11. The Ötscher Mountains

To the south of St. Pölten, lying between the Eisenerz Alps and the Vienna Woods, are alpine foothills known as the Ötscher mountains or massif. The Austrians jealously guard for themselves this popular area, which is unspoiled and certainly not yet overbuilt or filled with tourist lures. If you appreciate beautiful scenery and a tranquil way of life, you'll enjoy this area.

After leaving St. Pölten, the first stop will be—

LILIENFELD: This was once a huge Cistercian abbey in the Traisen Valley, founded by one of the Babenberg dukes named Leopold in 1202 when Romanesque was in flower, but many baroque architects worked on it through the years. The tomb of that Leopold is here. Lilienfeld has one of the most celebrated libraries in Lower Austria, dating from 1704. Inside the abbey is an art gallery, and the cloisters have 13th-century pillars of red marble. Some of the stained glass is from the 14th century. The abbey church is Gothic. A park surrounds the complex.

Tours are conducted from 8 to 11 a.m. and from 2 to 5 p.m. for a fee of 25 AS ($1.33).

At **Freiland,** an industrial town at the confluence of the Turnitz and the Traisen, you can take one of the area's most scenic drives, which takes you to—

ST. AEGYD: You pass many sawmills as you go through the Unrecht Traisen Valley before reaching this little summer resort in a setting of mountains and forests.

A good place to anchor in the Ötscher mountains is at—

LACKENHOF: A short drive from Lunz Lake is Lackenhof, just a village but in a setting that's beautiful in both summer and winter.

Food and Lodging

Hotel Jagdhof (tel. 300) is a tall chalet-style hotel set into a gently sloping alpine meadow. Many of the comfortable bedrooms have flowered balconies and a cozy decor of wood paneling and big windows. The public rooms include attractively rustic artifacts, a country-style fireplace, and a beamed dining room with pink napery. The ski lifts are a few steps from the hotel, and summertime tennis courts and swimming pools are close. A sauna is on the premises. The Borbath family charges between 375 AS ($19.95) and 470 AS ($25) in a single and between 325 AS ($17.29) and 435 AS ($23.14) per person in a double, with half board included. Prices depend on the plumbing and the season.

ANNA BERG: This small hamlet lies at the top of a pass. It is known for its church of pilgrimage dating from the 14th century. The church later received, as did every other building in Austria, a baroque overlay.

12. The Waldviertel

To the north of the Wachau and the "land of the Nibelungen" lies the Waldviertel, not to be confused with the already-visited Weinvertel. That was a trip to the land of the grapes. In the Waldviertel you'll meet forests. From Krems, in the Danube Valley, you can begin your exploration of this history-rich region, much of which can be visited in a day's sightseeing trip and return to Krems or nearby Dürnstein for the superior food and lodging as night falls.

The area abounds with castles, many in ruins. Two rivers, the Thaya and the Kamp, cross it. Waldviertel means forest sector, and the region lives up to its name, with many wooded uplands as well as river valleys.

Your first stop might be at—

LANGENLOIS: Standing at the top of the Valley of Kamp, Langenlois, six miles from Krems, is known for vineyards from which a good, dry white wine called Schluck is made. In this old market town, complete with Gothic church, you should visit the old buildings of the Altstadt (old town), taking in, among other attractions, a column built in the 13th century to commemorate deliverance from the plague. Many houses dating from the 16th century have arcaded courtyards. Others are from the 17th and 18th centuries, and you'll note differences in building styles. Often the houses are richly painted in pastels, including Maria Theresa ochre.

From Langenlois, the road heads north through the Kamp Valley to—

GARS AM KAMP: This market town, perched on the east bank of the river, enjoys a modest summer visitor traffic. The Rathaus (town hall) is from the late 16th century.

A much more appealing destination is the romantic town of—

HORN: The major business hub of the eastern Waldviertel, Horn has many buildings of historic interest, including a castle built in the Middle Ages which was given a much later architectural overlay. Armed with a good map, you can set out on many excursions from Horn, especially if you're interested in castles.

Rosenburg Castle, built in 1614, has a large courtyard where tournaments were held when knighthood was in flower. Apartments of the edifice, which stands on a rocky slope, contain antiques and much weaponry. Visitors are allowed through only on conducted tours, from 9 a.m. to noon and from 1 to 5 p.m., except Friday. Admission is 25 AS ($1.33).

Even more important is the nearby **Abbey of Altenburg,** founded in 1144. Reconstruction on this Benedictine religious house began in 1650 and lasted for almost a century. The design of the abbey was the masterpiece of Joseph Mungenast. As the taste for baroque swept the land during that time, the abbey was of course not spared, with the result that some parts of the facade, with onion-shape domes, appear Byzantine. The lowest point in the abbey's history was when it was used as a barracks for Soviet soldiers during 1945 and 1946.

The abbey cupola was frescoed by the noted baroque painter Paul Troger, whose work I have already mentioned in this chapter. In the crypt are macabre paintings illustrating *The Dance of Death*. The abbey church and its buildings are open April through October from 9 a.m. to noon and from 1 to 5 p.m. for an admission of 30 AS ($1.60). You pay another 20 AS ($1.06) to see the treasury of the abbey, with antiques, objects in gold and silver, and statuary.

From Fuglau, a road leads to **Greillenstein Castle,** which dates from the 14th century although the present structure is more 16th century. Contained within is a Criminal Law Museum, with exhibits of instruments of torture. The property has been the traditional seat of the counts of Kuefstein. You can visit the castle April through October from 9 a.m. to noon and from 1 to 5 p.m. Admission is 30 AS ($1.60).

For your final visit in the Waldviertel, I suggest—

ZWETTL: Much of the old city walls, studded with towers and gates, can still be seen in this major hub of traffic and business lying at a loop of the Kamp River near the Ottenstein Dam in the northern sector of the Waldviertel. Two miles northeast of the town lies **Zwettl Abbey,** a Cistercian religious house founded in 1138, now an architectural mélange of Romanesque, Gothic, and baroque. Its choir, in the late Gothic style, is one of its chief treasures. The cloister is intriguing, with both Romanesque and Gothic touches. The church, whose baroque tower pierces the sky, was built in the 14th century but now has 18th-century overlays. Paul Troger, the noted painter, did pictures on the altarpieces.

The abbey complex is open from the first of May until mid-September from 10 a.m. to noon and from 2 to 5 p.m. The rest of the year the hours are the same except that closing is at 4 p.m. On Sunday it opens at 11 a.m. Admission is 25 AS ($1.33).

Chapter VI

BURGENLAND

1. Eisenstadt
2. Lake Neusiedl
3. Drassburg
4. Forchtenstein
5. Bernstein
6. Bad Tatzmannsdorf
7. Heiligenkreuz

THE EASTERNMOST and the newest province of Austria, Burgenland is a little border region between East and West which came into being in 1921, formed of German-speaking border areas of what had been Hungary in the Austro-Hungarian Empire and for centuries before that. It's the start of a large, flat steppe (*puszta*) that reaches almost to Budapest, but it also lies practically on the doorstep of Vienna. The province shares a western border with Styria and Lower Austria, and its long eastern boundary separates it from its former fatherland, Hungary.

This area has suffered greatly from wars over the centuries—from tribal ages through long years when it was a part of the Roman Central European country Pannonia, to efforts to add it to the Ottoman Empire, and up to the war-torn times in this century. Burgenland joined Austria after a vote of its citizens in the aftermath of World War I, although when the vote was taken in 1919, its capital, Ödenburg, now called Sopron, chose to remain with Hungary. This accounts for the narrow corridor between the northern and southern parts of the province. The Hungarian city of Sopron actually lies to the west of Lake Neusiedl (Neusiedler See, in German), an important part of Burgenland. Sopron represents a far penetration of what used to be called the Iron Curtain into Austria. The Russians occupied Burgenland from 1945 to 1955, and few of its citizens seemed sorry to see them depart.

Called "the vegetable garden of Vienna," Burgenland is mostly an agricultural province, also growing such products as wheat and fruit. It is noted for its wines, producing more than one-third of all the wine made in Austria. The province is a point where the vast Hungarian plain gradually modulates into the foothills of the eastern Alps, 29% of its area being covered by forest and 7% of its agricultural lands composed of vineyards. Its Pannonian climate means hot summers with little rainfall, but the winters are moderate. For the most part you can enjoy sunny days from early spring until late autumn.

Besides the 2% of the Burgenland population that is Hungarian, many other citizens of the province are not typically Austrian. Some 10% belong to the Croat ethnic group which settled here in the 16th century after fleeing their southern Slav homes before the advance of Turkish armies which brought fear and pillage through the countryside in their path. For hundreds of years the Croats, Hungarians, and German-speaking people have lived together in this area, but the ethnic and religious variety is still reflected in customs, language, dress, legends, folk songs, and folklore. Many Burgenlanders interested in maintaining their traditions wear the traditional garb of their ancestors on Sunday.

This mixture of ethnic stock has resulted in a regional cookery that is among the best in Europe. It has of course been heavily influenced by its eastern neighbors, especially Hungary, as you'll appreciate when you savor goulashes and strudels, as well as goose dishes. Much wild game lives in the wooded areas of Burgenland and is often featured on menus.

The capital of Burgenland, **Eisenstadt,** is a small provincial city which was for many years the home of Joseph Haydn, and the composer is buried here. Each summer there's a festival at **Mörbisch,** using **Lake Neusiedl** (Neusiedler See) as a theatrical backdrop. Neusiedl is the only steppe lake in Central Europe. If you're here in summer, you'll most certainly want to explore it by motorboat. Lots of Viennese are attracted to Burgenland on weekends for sailing and/or birdwatching.

Accommodations in this province are extremely limited, but they're among the least expensive in the country. It's relatively unknown to North Americans, which I consider a pity and recommend that you add it to your itinerary. Like Lower Austria, Burgenland contains many fortresses and castles, often in ruins, but you'll find a few castle hotels in the romantic style, as well as some rather high-class spa establishments with all the modern amenities. **Bad Tatzdammsdorf** is the most important spa in the province, with the best facilities. Or perhaps you'll prefer to settle into a *gasthof*-type place. The spa season in Burgenland lasts from April to October.

This small province is connected to Vienna by both train and bus services. It's estimated that you can drive through it in about 2½ hours. You can also travel between Eisenstadt, capital of the province, and Lake Neusiedl by bus.

1. Eisenstadt

In the early 1920s when Burgenland joined Austria it was a province without a capital, its former seat of government, Ödenburg (now the far-western Hungarian city of Sopron), having voted to remain a part of Hungary. In 1924, realizing that they needed a provincial capital, Burgenlanders agreed on Eisenstadt for the honor. This small town at the foot of the Leitha mountains is only 25 miles southeast of Vienna, at the beginning of the great Hungarian plain. The town is surrounded by vineyards and forests and has lots of fruit trees. It's a convenient stopover for exploring Lake Neusiedl, six miles to the east.

Even before assuming its new role, however, Eisenstadt was not unknown. Mainly it was renowned as the place where the great composer Joseph Haydn lived and worked while under the patronage of the Esterhazys, a powerful family who ruled Eisenstadt and its surrounding area. For a good part of his life (1732–1809) Haydn divided his time between Eisenstadt and the Esterhazy Castle in Hungary. Prince Esterhazy eventually gave the composer his own orchestra and a concert hall in which to perform.

Schloss Esterhazy, the Eisenstadt château of the Esterhazy princes in which Haydn worked, was built on the site of a medieval castle. The Esterhazy clan was a great Hungarian family with vast estates. They claimed descent from Attila the Hun. The Esterhazys helped the Habsburgs gain control in Hungary. So great was their loyalty to Austria that when Napoleon offered the crown of Hungary to Nic Esterhazy in 1809, he refused it.

The schloss, built around an inner courtyard, was designed by the Italian architect Carlone, and fortified because of its strategic position. Carlone started work on the castle in 1663, but subsequently it was remodeled by many other architects, resulting in sweeping alterations to its appearance. In the late 18th and early 19th centuries it was given a baroque pastel facade. On the first floor, the great baronial hall was made into the Haydnsaal, where the composer conducted the orchestra Prince Esterhazy had provided for him and often performed his own works before the Esterhazy court. The walls and ceilings of this concert hall are elaborately decorated, but the floor is of bare wood, which, it is claimed, is the cause of the room's acoustical perfection.

Today, much of the castle is used by officials in administering the affairs of Burgenland, but the Haydnsaal is open to the public. Guided tours, lasting 25 minutes, are conducted through it from the first of June until the end of December. Tours leave from 9 a.m. to 5 p.m. (from 10 a.m. to 4 p.m. in winter). Admission is 25 AS ($1.33).

Haydn House, 21 Haydngasse, the little Eisenstadt home of the composer from 1766 to 1778, has been made into a museum honoring its former tenant, and the hours are the same as those for the Haydnsaal at the castle. Although he appeared in court nearly every night, Haydn actually lived very moderately when he was at home. However, the home wasn't exactly bleak, as he had a little flower-filled courtyard. The museum has collected mementos of Haydn's works and also some mementos of Liszt, his fellow composer.

If you want to pay your final respects to the memory of Haydn, follow Hauptstrasse, which will connect you to Esterhazystrasse leading to the **Bergkirche** (Church of the Calvary), containing Haydn's tomb, built of white marble.

Until 1954 only the composer's headless body was here. His skull was in the Music Museum in Vienna, where curious spectators were actually allowed to feel it. Haydn's head was stolen a few days after his death and did not get back together with his body for a total of 145 years! The story of how the head traveled from one owner to another—eventually even being sold—before finally, I hope, coming to rest with the other part of Haydn's remains at Eisenstadt is long and complicated.

To honor another composer, Franz Liszt, you can leave Eisenstadt going south on the road to the small village of **Raiding.** There the **Liszt Geburthaus,** or Franz Liszt birthplace, is now a museum containing many mementos of the composer's life, including an old church organ he used to play. Liszt's father worked as a bailiff for the princes of Esterhazy, and this was his home when little Franz was born in 1811. The museum is open from Easter until the end of October from 9 a.m. to noon and from 1 to 5 p.m., charging an admission of 15 AS (80¢).

Near Eisenstadt at **St. Margarethen** is an outdoor sculpture gallery with monumental stone art at a quarry. Sculptors have done carvings on the site instead of taking the material for their artwork back to their studios.

FOOD AND LODGING: **Rosenberger Hotel Burgenland,** Schubertplatz (tel. 521), is a dramatically designed contemporary hotel with a modified mansard roof, white stucco walls, and big windows. The comfortable bedrooms have lots of light, wood-grained headboards, and simple furniture. A swimming pool, a sauna, two restaurants, and a café are on the premises. With breakfast included, singles rent for between 490 AS ($26.07) and 570 AS ($30.32), while doubles range from 720 AS ($38.30) to 830 AS ($44.17), depending on the season. All accommodations have private bath, TV, radio, and mini-bar.

One of the best restaurants in Burgenland is the in-house **G'wû·stöckl,** open daily from noon to 2:30 p.m. and from 6 to 11 p.m. Dotted with antiques, it specializes in such dishes as cabbage soup, veal steak with fresh vegetables, and a host of other platters strongly influenced by the kitchen of nouvelle cuisine. Fixed-price meals range from 155 AS ($8.25) to 500 AS ($26.60), while à la carte meals go from 120 AS ($6.38) to 275 AS ($14.63). Reservations are suggested.

Parkhotel Mikschi, 38 Haydngasse (tel. 4361), is a modern hotel in the center of town. Its prominent balconies shelter big windows and look out over a sunny garden. Inside, the contemporary public rooms have wintertime fireplaces encased in modern brick and copper hearths. Singles rent for 590 AS ($31.39), while doubles go for 790 AS ($42.03), with breakfast included. All rooms have modern baths, refrigerators, phones, and wall-to-wall carpeting.

Hotel Eder Zum Goldenen Adler, 25 Hauptstrasse (tel. 2645), is a cozily decorated family-style guest house filled with wooden furniture, deer antlers, and hanging iron chandeliers. A garden terrace is surrounded with a thick wall of greenery, while the simple bedrooms are clean and comfortable. Singles rent for between 200 AS ($10.64) and 250 AS ($13.30), while doubles range between 155 AS ($8.25) and 250 AS ($13.30) per person, with breakfast included.

2. Lake Neusiedl

This lake, called Neusiedler See in German, is a true steppe lake lying in the northern part of Burgenland. It has been described as strange and mysterious, and is certainly like no lake familiar to North Americans. It was part of a body of water that once blanketed all of the Pannonian Plain. Today it's only about six feet deep at its lowest point, and the wind can shift the water dramatically, causing parts of the lake to become dry at times. A broad belt of reeds encircles the huge expanse of lake, about 115 square miles. It's roughly between 4¼ and 9¼ miles wide, and about 22+ miles long. If you're tall enough you could walk across it, but I'm not recommending that!

Because of the curvature of the earth, the middle of the lake is about 80 feet higher than the longitudinal axis. The Neusiedler See possesses no natural outlets. Its water is slightly salty, and the plants and animal life here are unique in Europe. This is the meeting place of alpine, Baltic, and Pannonian flora and fauna. Some 200 different species of birds inhabit the lake area, resting on its reeds, including the Rust stork.

Destinations along the lake include:

ILLMITZ: This old *puszta* (steppe) village lying on the east side of the lake has grown into a town which does a slight tourist business in summer. This is steppe country, and a tourist brochure issued by the town pictures the most characteristic part of the landscape, a traditional rural Hungarian-type well with long wooden poles which are used to draw up water.

Leaving Illmitz and heading toward the border, you come to the village of **St. Andrä bei Frauenkirchen,** where you'll see thatch houses. The little town is known for its basket-weaving, so you might want to drive here for a shopping expedition.

A short drive farther will take you to **Andau,** which became the focus of world attention in 1956 during the Hungarian uprising. It was through this point, almost on the border, that hundreds of Hungarians dashed to freedom in the West, fleeing the grim massacres of Budapest.

From the town you can see the closely guarded border, with its forbidding barbed-wire fences and watchtowers on the Communist side, where guards are prepared to shoot Hungarians who might attempt to escape. This is not a particularly happy place for a vacation, but it's a fascinating piece of geography between the East and the West.

What makes the place intriguing, however, is that the surrounding marshy area of this remote sector of Austria, called **Seewinkel,** is a haven for birds and contains much rare flora, plus many small *puszta* animals. This is a large natural wildlife sanctuary. You'll see a few windmills and expanses of reeds which are used to make roofs and shelters.

This area, very different from the celebrated Austria of alpine and Wienerwald lore, is little known to North Americans, and therefore a visit here can qualify as an offbeat adventure. For devotees of geography, it's a fine part of Central Europe for exploration, with sights you won't see elsewhere.

READERS' FOOD AND LODGING SELECTIONS: "**Heurigenrestaurant/Pension Rosenhof,** 1 Floriangasse (tel. 2232). Our friends from Boulder recommended this cozy guest house which is part of a baroque building with plenty of charm and atmosphere. The Haider family welcomed us with a sunny smile, and placed us in a cozy double room with private bath and all the modern comforts. The best part about it was the meal in the hotel's restaurant, which was loaded with what looked like local residents who seemed to enjoy the Hungarian specialties and regional fare as much as we did. Of course, music accompanied our meal. Our room cost 300 AS ($15.96) for two persons with breakfast included. I understand that some of the larger accommodations are more expensive" (Mr. and Mrs. Thomas Athebauer, Denver, Colo.). . . . "**Gasthof Zentral** (tel. 2312). We stopped here not imagining it would be as pleasant as it turned out. Since the weather was sunny, the maître d'hôtel seated us in the shade of the garden terrace, where lots of plants added a lush note to our meal. My husband ordered fish, and was happy with his choice, while I decided to try one of the Hungarian specialties, which proved to be tasty and well seasoned. Meals cost from 150 AS ($7.98) per person. The Kroiss family, your hosts, treated us with sensitivity and respect. We didn't ask about the rooms" (Mrs. J. R. Daley, Chicago, Ill.).

HALBTURN: North of St. Andrä, if you go through Frauenkirchen you reach the hamlet of Halbturn, which lies within a stone's throw of the Austria-Hungary border. Here you'll find a lovely baroque concoction designed by the architect Lukas von Hildebrandt, which was used as a summer palace by Empress Maria Theresa and her large brood. It's surrounded by well-laid-out park grounds forming a handsome setting for this landmark of luxurious imperial living, standing in curious contrast to the sparsely settled, bleak villages in the far-western extremities of Hungary.

This was originally a hunting lodge which was destroyed by the Turks during the siege of 1683 and rebuilt by Hildebrandt in the 18th century. It was again partially burned in 1949 in the postwar era when it was part of the Soviet-occupied zone. In the central hall is a ceiling painted by F. A. Maulbertsch, done in 1765 and considered his masterpiece.

Visits are possible from 9 a.m. to noon and from 1 to 5 p.m. for an admission of 25 AS ($1.33).

PODERSDORF: If you head west from Frauenkirchen, you reach Podersdorf am See, one of the finest places for swimming on the mysterious lake, as its shoreline is relatively free of reeds. This attracts visitors, and the little town has become a modest summer resort. The parish church in the village is from the late 18th century. You'll see many storks nesting atop chimneys, and some of the cottages have thatch roofs. The Viennese like to drive out here on a summer Sunday to go for a swim and also to purchase wine from the local vintners.

Food and Lodging

Haus Atilla, 1 Strandplatz (tel. 415), sits directly on the water. Its tastefully designed light-grained balconies are discreetly concealed with a brake of verdant trees. The bedrooms are comfortable, clean, and tastefully filled with livable furniture. In the basement you'll find a well-stocked wine cellar where a member of the Karner family might take you for a visit. Apartments rent for between 300 AS ($15.96) and 390 AS ($20.75) per person daily, with breakfast included.

Gasthof Seewirt, 1 Strandplatz (tel. 415), under the same management, stands close to the Haus Atilla. This pleasant hotel sits at the edge of the lake, with a wide expanse of deserted marshland close by. The bedrooms are comfortable and tasteful, while the public rooms include a rustically modern restaurant, a café terrace, and an indoor sauna. Singles range from 215 AS ($11.44) to 230 AS ($12.24), while doubles go from 215 AS ($11.44) to 350 AS ($18.62) per person daily.

Hotel Martinshof, 91 Seestrasse (tel. 288), is a comfortably proportioned two-story building, sprawling across an expanse of flower-dotted lawn near the lake. The bedrooms are clean, appealing, and modern, with smallish windows opening onto sun balconies. The Lentsch family, the proprietors, charge between 270 AS ($14.36) and 310 AS ($16.49) per person, depending on the plumbing and the season, with breakfast included. Half board costs an additional 60 AS ($3.19) per person.

Haus am Heideboden (tel. 247). If you're looking for an unassuming country restaurant, this family-run establishment at the edge of town might be for you. Impeccably clean, and attracting a loyal crowd of local residents, it serves such specialties as turkey schnitzel, roast goose, ham Maria Theresa, and Hawaiian-style steak, along with seasonal wild game and a wide variety of fresh salads. Many of the wines are produced in the region. A meal at this friendly place will cost between 85 AS ($4.52) and 210 AS ($11.17). Reservations are suggested.

Zur Goldenen Traube (tel. 388) is a big woodsy building designed to hold dozens of happy diners and drinkers. The food inside is as solid and wholesome as anything you'll find in the region, and it's served in copious portions and is usually well seasoned and tasty. Menu items include liver and noodle soup, ham, rump steak Café de Paris, and a variety of schnitzels. Reservations are suggested, and à la carte meals range from 90 AS ($4.79) to 255 AS ($13.57).

KITTSEE: On to the north in the direction of Bratislava, Czechoslovakia, is the Austrian border town of Kittsee, where a Count Esterhazy (of the same family that ruled in Eisenstadt and sponsored the composer Haydn there) had a baroque castle erected, beginning in 1730. Toward the southeast sector of the village is the Czechoslovakian frontier.

En route to Bratislava is a colony of residential houses with a startling name for this area—**Chicago.** It's considered the most easterly village west of the Iron Curtain. It was named by an emigré who likened the pace of construction to what he'd known as a laborer in Chicago, Illinois.

NEUSIEDL AM SEE: At the top of Lake Neusiedl on the north bank lies this popular stopover, which is likely to be crowded on summer weekends. Water sports prevail here, and sailboats can be rented. The parish church, in the Gothic style, is noted for its "ship pulpit." A watchtower from the Middle Ages still stands guard over the town, although it's no longer manned. Many vineyards cover the nearby acreage. If you plan to be here on a weekend in summer, I advise you to make a reservation ahead.

Food and Lodging

Hotel Wende, 40-42 Seestrasse (tel. 8111). This pleasant and well-groomed hotel has a series of wooden balconies set into a stucco L-shaped building with fieldstone detailing on the ground floor. A glass-walled clubhouse with surrounding verandas extends toward the back lawn, with summertime chairs, a sauna, and an indoor swimming pool. You'll be able to eat in an outdoor terrace under colorful parasols, or in the adjoining restaurant which is so well known that many of the guests come from throughout the region. Specialties include turkey schnitzel, wild game dishes, and if it appeals to you, an elegant and bountiful buffet where the uniformed chefs practically wait at attention while you select from a wide range of beautifully decorated dishes. Meals range from 100 AS ($5.32) to 350 AS ($18.62). Rooms, each comfortable and well furnished, go from 280 AS ($14.90) to 315 AS ($16.75) per person in a bathless unit and between 370 AS ($19.68) and 500 AS ($26.60) per person in accommodations with bath. Half board is offered for an additional 110 AS ($5.85) per person daily.

Hotel Till Eulenspiegel, 36 Seestrasse (tel 439), is a white-painted hotel with natural wood trim, lots of detailing, and a lighthearted ambience partially created by the kindly owners, Anna and Stefan Frischmann. A garden terrace behind well-kept shrubbery serves meals and drinks under the shade of an ancient tree. The hotel is about a mile from the lake, near the city tennis courts and the public indoor swimming pool. It's closed from November until April. Per-person rates in a double are 190 AS ($10.11), while singles cost 300 AS ($15.96), with breakfast included.

Gasthof Zur Traube, 9 Hauptplatz (tel. 423). On a sunny day this looks like a gingerbread house from a regional folk tale. Brightly painted, with white walls and red and yellow trim, it has a double gable, stone corner mullions, and a gilt-and-black sign welcoming guests under the broad arch of the entrance. A walled garden in back is a winning combination of massive beams and modern lighting fixtures. Inside, the red and gold restaurant has a vaulted ceiling of white stucco and wrought-iron detailing. Pleasantly furnished singles range from 230 AS ($12.24) to 250 AS ($13.30), while doubles cost between 200 AS ($10.64) and 230 AS ($12.24) per person daily, with breakfast included. Franz Rittsteuer and his family are your hosts.

Neusiedler Csárda, 1 Obere Wiesen (tel. 383), is constructed with lots of overhanging eaves and a series of stucco arches that look like something straight from a farm on the Great Plain of Hungary. Rüdiger and Herta Rennke maintain 18 horses for the use of hotel guests, which might be the main reason to choose to stay here. Each of the rooms has a private bath, costing 250 AS ($13.30) per person in a double, with a supplement of 70 AS ($3.72) for single occupancy. Breakfast is included in the price, and half board is another 100 AS ($5.32) per person. The hotel offers a wide range of week-long riding and hunting packages, which are usually more economical than sojourns priced on a per-day rate.

WEIDEN AM SEE: This little summer resort set on the lakeside lies due southeast of Neusiedl am See. I recommend considering it as an alternative stopover as its attractions are practically identical.

Food and Lodging

Seepark Weiden (tel. 80322). If you're planning on traveling with a family, this might be one of the most ideal choices on the lake. Some of the accommodations are in a format of cozy guest cottages painted in different colors and set like row houses at the edge of the water. Other buildings have pleasant balconies and front verandas, looking not unlike something you might find among the colonial buildings of the Caribbean. Activities include many water sports such as windsurfing, along with tennis, bicycling, and other pleasures that a family might enjoy together. Weekly rates can include the rental of a motorboat, but if all you want is a room with breakfast, then doubles range from 375 AS ($19.95) to 465 AS ($24.74), while singles cost between 200 AS ($10.64) and 240 AS ($12.77). It's open only in the summer.

PURBACH AM SEE: If you take the road south from the area around the northern tip of Lake Neuseidl, your first stopover might be in this little resort village which has some decent accommodations. Purbach is also a market town, and you can buy Burgenland wine in the shops. Some of the town walls, built against invading Turks, still stand.

Food and Lodging

Gasthof am Spitz (tel. 5519). The main building of this hotel has unusual baroque embellishments rounding out the angular sections of the frontal gable. When you enter you'll see unusual stucco detailing in the rounded columns of the restaurant and bar area, lots of weathered timbers and ceiling beams, and a scattering of antiques and good carpets on the marble floors. The Hölzl-Schwarz family are your efficient hosts here, charging between 250 AS ($13.30) and 370 AS ($19.68) in a single and between 225 AS ($11.97) and 250 AS ($13.30) per person in a double. Many of the accommodations have panoramic views of the lake. The adjoining restaurant, rustically decorated, is one of the best places in the region for Burgenland cookery. Specialties include chicken soup, bacon salad, lamb cutlets with potatoes and spinach, and an array of local wines. À la carte meals range from 90 AS ($4.79) to 240 AS ($12.77). Reservations are suggested, and the gasthof is closed every Monday between September and Easter.

Nikolauszeche (tel. 5514). In a niche high above the rest of the baroque decor, someone has placed a statue that looks more like the Madonna than the namesake of this establishment, Saint Nicholas. The food, however, is authentically regional, attracting a wide cross section of Austrians, many of whom travel from Vienna. Once here, they can order the rich bouillon or cabbage soup, the Hungarian fogosch, and the chef's special ham crêpes, plus selecting from a well-chosen wine list. The gypsy music can sometimes be overwhelming. If you seek privacy and quiet, you can gravitate to an interior courtyard, finding a quiet corner for an intimate conversation. The restaurant is closed Wednesday, and à la carte meals range from 75 AS ($3.99) to 240 AS ($12.77). Reservations are suggested.

Leaving Purbach and taking the road south toward Eisenstadt, you can veer off on a secondary road southeast along the lakeshore to our final destinations, which are also provided with limited accommodations. The first stopover is at—

RUST: This little, colorfully named summer resort—famous for its stork nests built on chimneys throughout the town—stands right on the lakeshore. The heart of Rust is an old town section that is well preserved and immaculately ready for your inspection. Its walls were built in 1614 as protection against the Turks.

The little resort has a gemütlich atmosphere, especially on weekends. Summers tend to be hot, and the water of the lake is warm. Sailboats and windsurfers are rented for touring the Neusiedler See, where the shallowness of the waters relieves you of much fear of drowning, except for small children.

No one has ever designated it as such, so far as I've learned, but Rust might be called the capital of the Burgenland lake district. The town lies in a rich setting of vineyards which produce the celebrated Burgenlander grape. If it's available, you should try the Blaufränkisch, a red wine which seems to be consumed entirely either locally or by the Viennese, who flock to the area and often return home with the back seats of their cars filled with bottles of the wine of the region. Sometimes you can go right up to the door of a vintner's farmhouse, especially if a green bough is displayed, and sample wine and buy it on the spot, as at a heurige.

On my last visit in August, the taverns in the town had lively gypsy music. Some local residents, when the wine is in their blood, like to dance in regional costume wearing high boots. You're left with the distinct impression that you're in Hungary.

Food and Lodging

Seehotel Rust (tel. 381) is a well-designed modern hotel set on a grassy lawn at the edge of the lake. It has an appealing series of connected balconies, rounded towers that look vaguely medieval, and a series of recessed loggias set into the slope of the roofline. The ceiling beams of the big-windowed restaurant sweep dramatically up toward the central lighting fixture, while a series of floor-mounted lamps curves over many of the immaculate tablecloths like spokes of an umbrella. Food items include tafelspitz with chive sauce, calf brains with a honey vinegar, watercress soup, and sole meunière.

On the premises of the hotel are a dramatically modern indoor swimming pool, a sauna, two tennis courts, and a graceful bar area. The pleasant bedrooms are decorated with a combination of white plaster and blond wood. A gypsy band sometimes provides the evening's entertainment. À la carte meals in the restaurant range from 160 AS ($8.51) to 380 AS ($20.22). Bedrooms cost between 790 AS ($42.03) and 820 AS ($43.62) in a single and between 585 AS ($31.12) and 620 AS ($32.98) per person in a double, with full board included.

Hotel Sifkovits, 8 Am Seekanal (tel. 276), is a dramatically designed hotel with a concrete and stucco facade fashioned into sloping rows of well-planted balconies. An older wing has a less daring format of red tile roofs and big windows which sometimes cover entire wells. The bedrooms get a lot of sun and are comfortably streamlined. Other facilities include a sauna, an exercise room, a café, a sun terrace, and outdoor tennis courts. With half board included, singles range from 215 AS ($11.44) to 510 AS ($27.13), while doubles cost from 215 AS ($11.44) to 460 AS ($24.47) per person. Prices, of course, depend on the season and the accommodation. A reduction of 25 AS ($2.39) per person is made for guests who want only bed and breakfast.

Eselmühle (tel. 2223) at St. Margarethen is an interesting and fun establishment built around a defunct water wheel. It's about two miles from the center of Rust, and you'll probably find that the food is worth traveling the distance. You'll be greeted with the strains of live Hungarian music, which will certainly whet your appetite for the country-style hors d'oeuvres. These might include paprika-flavored pork, thinly sliced ham, and smoked eel. Soups include classic Burgenland varieties, often heavily spiced, and a delectable Hungarian fish soup called halaszle. Marinated meat dishes include sauerbraten with homemade noodles and sauerkraut. Many of the clients are local residents, who pay between 110 AS ($5.85) and 360 AS ($19.15) for fixed-price meals and between 85 AS ($4.52) and 250 AS ($12.77) for à la carte dinners. Reservations are suggested, and the restaurant is open every day until midnight.

MÖRBISCH: Our final stopover along the lake, near the Hungarian border, is this charming little, typical Burgenlander lakeside hamlet. There's a small bathing beach and mineral springs, the water of which is bottled for sale. The town fills up in August when the lakeside outdoor theater presents operettas such as *The Merry Widow.* Wine-tasting festivals are also a Mörbisch feature, especially on Sunday when the Viennese flock here and, with luck, manage to drive home safely.

With such excitement and festivity, it's hard to accept that the grim, closely guarded Hungarian border is so near by.

Food and Lodging

Hotel Steiner (tel. 8218) has an attractively simple cream-colored facade with one recessed balcony covered with flowers. With 110 beds, it's big enough usually to have an empty room, but quiet enough to afford relaxing comfort. The Steiner family, your hosts, rent rustically modern bedrooms, where singles range from 355 AS ($18.87) to 400 AS ($21.28) and doubles from 300 AS ($15.96) to 400 AS ($21.28) per person, depending on the plumbing and the season. On the premises are a sauna, a heated swimming pool, and an appealing restaurant.

South of Eisenstadt lies one of the most romantic and charming accommodations in all of Burgenland. It's at—

3. Drassburg

Hotel Schloss Drassburg (tel. 2220). Parts of this castle date from the 14th century, although what you'll see today is an 18th-century facade of ochre paint and white trim. It's owned by the Baroness Maria von Patzenhofer, who rents about 30 of the bedrooms to paying guests. The vaulted interior is lavishly equipped, usually in an antique style with a heavy emphasis on the baroque. Near the Hungarian border and some ten miles south of Eisenstadt, the estate includes about two dozen acres of parkland designed by Le Nôtre, the landscape architect of Versailles.

The water of the indoor swimming pool surrounds a few of the masonry columns that support the overhead vaulting. There's also an outdoor pool, plus tennis courts. Persons interested in horseback riding often book in here for long weekends, although even overnight guests can rent a horse from a nearby stable. Singles range from 550 AS ($29.26) to 670 AS ($35.64), while doubles cost between 450 AS ($23.94) and 570 AS ($30.32) per person. All units contain private baths. An elegant breakfast costs an additional 100 AS ($5.32) per person.

4. Forchtenstein

After leaving the lake district, you can head south from Eisenstadt toward the narrow "waistline" of the province, a small corridor between north and south Burgenland created when Ödenburg, then the capital (now the Hungarian far-western frontier city of Sopron), voted to remain with the fatherland and be ruled by Budapest. Many of the people of Forchtenstein grow fruit.

Visitors come here chiefly to get a look at **Forchtenstein Castle,** lying nine miles southeast of Wiener Neustadt in Lower Austria. From a belvedere here you can see as far as the great plain of Hungary. The castle was constructed on a rock on orders of the counts of Mattersdorf in the 13th century. The Esterhazy family had it greatly expanded around 1636.

The castle saw action in the Turkish sieges of Austria, both in 1529 and in 1683. You can see a handsome collection of armory here, some captured from the fleeing Turks. But they didn't all get away. Turkish prisoners carved out of the rock the castle cistern, more than 450 feet deep. There's also a display of "memorabilia of the hunt," as it is described here.

The castle may be visited from 10 a.m. to 5 p.m. (to 4 p.m. in winter). Admission is 25 AS ($1.33).

In the first part of summer, Viennese actors perform **Grillparzer** plays here.

FOOD AND LODGING: **Gasthof Sauerzapf,** 9 Rosalienstrasse (tel. 42-05-17), is a long grange-like building with two stories of weathered stucco, renovated windows, and a roofline that's red on one side and black on another. The updated interior is cozy and appealing, albeit simple, and is kept immaculately. Franz Sauerzapf and his family charge 150 AS ($7.98) in a single and between 140 AS ($7.45) and 170 AS ($9.04) per person in a double, with breakfast included. Prices depend on the plumbing and the season. The gasthof is closed in October. The in-house restaurant serves good food and a full array of local wines.

Gasthof Zur Rosalienkapelle, 12 Rosalia (tel. 32-45-11). The view from the rooms of this family-run stucco guest house encompasses all of the valley and many square miles of forested hills. Inside you'll find a late 1950s-style decor. In keeping with that spirit, you'll even find a jukebox in the striped and wood-paneled bar area. Hubert Wutzlhofer, the owner, charges between 135 AS ($7.18) and 160 AS ($8.51) per person, in either a single or a double, with breakfast included. Prices depend on the plumbing and the accommodation.

Reisner (tel. 3139) serves garden-fresh vegetables in a rustic setting, with especially good steaks. The main dining room is perfectly acceptable, but my favorite is the cozily rustic stüberl, which seems to be preferred by the locals as well. You might enjoy trout filet served with a savory ragoût of tomatoes, zucchini, potatoes, and basil, or the gently sauteed sweetbreads with beans and a yogurt-vinaigrette dressing over cabbage. A la carte meals range from 80 AS ($4.26) to 300 AS ($15.96). The restaurant is closed on Wednesday, and reservations are suggested otherwise.

5. Bernstein

This little market village lying in the Valley of the Tauchen is known for its castle, which ranks along with the just-visited Drassburg Castle for providing the most dramatic accommodations in Burgenland (see below).

Bernstein is also known for its serpentine stone, a jet-green stone sometimes called Bernstein jade. Workers polish the stone here, and it can be purchased in the shops, although much of it is shipped around the world. It's shaped into ornaments of many different types.

Hotel Burg Bernstein (tel. 220). Initially constructed during the era of Charlemagne (around A.D. 800), most of the castle you will see today was built in the 13th century, with thick stone walls and towers, plus small windows along the outer walls. The owners were so preoccupied with defending themselves from invaders that they even surrounded the 120-meter-deep well with a defensive stone tower.

In 1953 this rich piece of history was converted into a hotel and furnished with antiques appropriate to its status as a historic monument. Its dining room has a stone floor and a lushly ornate baroque ceiling. The bedrooms are baronial, even the singles, and are filled with beautiful pieces of craftsmanship.

The castle is said to have a resident ghost. Its long-ago former owner, a medieval lord, Graf Uilaky, reportedly returned home from a siege somewhere in Hungary only to discover his wife in bed with one of the male servants. He slashed out the heart of the hapless servant, but for his adulterous wife he showed he was no women's liberation advocate. He sealed her up in her bedroom and left her there to die of thirst and starvation. Her "ghost" is still reported to roam the place on dark nights.

Singles cost 450 AS ($23.94) while doubles go for 800 AS ($42.56), with breakfast included. For guests staying more than three days, half board is available for around 500 AS ($26.60) per person daily.

6. Bad Tatzmannsdorf

The best known spa of the province, nine miles south of Bernstein, lies in a heavily forested valley. Its springs and baths, said to be beneficial to certain cardiac patients and for female ailments, have been used for centuries. Many wealthy Hungarians from Budapest spent part of their summers here in earlier, freer times.

Naturally, the resort has a Kurpark, where on a summer evening entertainment is likely to be presented. There's also an open-air museum where many ancient structures moved from the surrounding valley have been placed on exhibit.

FOOD AND LODGING: **Parkhotel** (tel. 287) is constructed in a modern format of several different beige and white sections connected together in a flowering garden. Many of the rooms have private balconies, which open into the comfortable and pleasing sleeping areas with lots of paneling and tasteful furniture. The public rooms are padded and upholstered with built-in banquettes in buff-colored velvet near big windows, while an outdoor café affords a relaxing get-away on a warm day. The Anderle family are the distinguished owners of this hotel, charging between 270 AS ($14.36) and 400 AS ($21.28) in a single and between 605 AS ($32.19) and 760 AS ($40.43) for a double, with breakfast included. Half and full board are offered only for stays of seven days or more.

Hotel Zum Kastell, 6 Joseph Haydnplatz (tel. 428). On a summer day, all the guests of this attractive, modern hotel gather on the sun terrace or on one of the private balconies attached to their bedrooms. Many of the private accommodations are decorated in firecracker colors such as hot orange and autumn browns. Seats in the dignified restaurant are usually fashioned in a banquette format around round tables, with cluster chandeliers hanging near the arched windows. A less formal restaurant is cozily outfitted with terracotta tiles and upholstered wooden chairs. Many of the summertime guests have moved in for a week or more as part of their annual vacations, but if you want to stay for just a night, singles rent for between 315 AS ($16.75) and 380 AS ($20.22), while doubles range from 315 AS ($16.75) to 345 AS ($18.35) per person, with breakfast included.

Hotel/Pension Sonnenhof, 33 Parkstrasse (tel. 417), is a big-windowed, balconied hotel set on a hillside with a view of a collection of old farmhouses in the distance. Maria Janisch is the kindly owner of this simple but well-maintained establishment, charging between 180 AS ($9.58) and 235 AS ($12.50) per person in a double, with breakfast included. Half board is offered for another 85 AS ($4.52) per person daily.

7. Heiligenkreuz

If you're looking for a tranquil hideaway, this is it! No one will ever find you in this, one of the most remote places recommended in this guide (not to be confused with Heiligenkreuz, the Cistercian Abbey west of Baden). This little town lies in the far-southern tip of Burgenland, right next to the Hungarian frontier, near the confluence of the Raab and the Lafnitz. There are many thatch houses in the area, which is known and treasured by the Austrians. If a North American turns up here, it's considered a rarity.

Heiligenkreuz is near a battle site where General Montecuccoli defeated the Turks in 1664, a fact honored by Maria Rainer Rilke, the noted German epic poet, in *The Cornet*.

If you should get bored in this peaceful town, you can head for nearby Hungary or Yugoslavia, although a visa is required to enter either country.

FOOD AND LODGING: **Gasthof Edith Gibiser** (tel. 216) is one of my favorite hotels in the region. Thanks partly to the concerned service given by the namesake of the hotel (whom everyone calls Edith), it's a pleasant and well-maintained place to stay during your tour of Burgenland. The exterior is a symmetrical white country-style villa with comfortable horizontal lines and pink and white detailing around each of the rectangular windows. The interior is tastefully paneled in a format of modern rusticity. Rooms are comfortably and attractively furnished, with singles ranging from 175 AS ($9.31) to 255 AS ($13.57), while doubles cost between 170 AS ($9.04) and 240 AS ($12.77) per person, with breakfast included.

The adjoining restaurant serves well-prepared meals on beautiful china, and is usually filled with flowers. Specialties of the house include cabbage soup, fried pike-perch, and steak cordon rouge (stuffed with goose liver and served with fresh mushrooms). Meals cost between 60 AS ($3.19) and 340 AS ($18.09). The restaurant is open all day long every day of the week (except Monday during the period from November until May).

Chapter VII

SALZBURG

1. Where to Stay
2. Where to Dine
3. What to See
4. Where to Shop
5. The Cafés of Salzburg
6. Salzburg After Dark
7. Practical Facts

A BAROQUE CITY on the banks of the Salzach River, Salzburg, set against a mountain backdrop, is the beautiful capital of the Austrian province of Land Salzburg. The city and the river were so named because many of the early residents earned their living in the salt mines in the region. The site of Salzburg was once the Roman town of Juvuvum.

This "heart of the heart of Europe" is the city of Mozart, who was born here in 1756. The composer's association with the city beefs up tourism even today, providing major revenue to the area.

This fact carries a certain irony, because Mozart wasn't all that appreciated in Salzburg in his lifetime. But since his death almost 200 years ago, his image seems to be everywhere. A square bears his name. A statue in its center honors him. A music academy is named for him. And of course his music dominates the Salzburg Festival. Too bad he couldn't have been more honored when he was still around to enjoy it. He died in Vienna on December 6, 1771, and the sad truth is that the body of the 35-year-old musical genius was carried in a pauper's hearse to a common grave in the cemetery of St. Mark's in the Austrian capital.

The old town of Salzburg lies on the left bank of the river where a monastery and bishopric were founded in 700. From that start, Salzburg grew in power and prestige, becoming an archbishopric in 798. In the heyday of the prince-archbishops, the city became known as the "German Rome." The little province known as **Land Salzburg,** of which Salzburg is the capital, still occupies much the same space in the mountains of west-central Austria as shown on maps of the Middle Ages designated as "church lands." It was in the Holy Roman Empire, a part of Germany until it was joined to Austria in 1816 after the Congress of Vienna.

Salzburg is a city of 17th- and 18th-century houses and for the most part, with a worldwide reputation for the grandeur of its architecture. Much of that work was done by those masters of the baroque, Fischer von Erlach and Lukas von Hildebrandt.

As well as being the scene of the celebrated Salzburg Festival, this is where Max Reinhardt staged Hugo von Hoffmannsthal's miracle play *Everyman* (*Jedermann,* in German) in 1920, an event which has become a tradition.

Salzburg lies a short distance from the Austria–West Germany frontier, so it's convenient for exploring many of the nearby sightseeing attractions of Bavaria. On the northern slopes of the Alps, the city is at the intersection of traditional European trade routes and is well served today by air, autobahn, and railroad.

AN ORIENTATION: Most visitors head for the *old town*, which lies on the left bank of the Salzach, that part stretching from the river to the Mönchsberg. This is a section of narrow streets (many from the Middle Ages) and slender houses. This part of Salzburg is in complete contrast with the town constructed by the Prince Bishops, which lies between the Neutor and the Neugebäude. The bishops created a town of magnificent buildings and large, airy squares.

The heart of the old section, on the left bank of the Salzach, is the **Residenzplats,** with its splendid Unterberg marble baroque fountain.

The newer part of town is on the right bank of the Salzach, below the **Kapuzinerberg,** which is the right bank counterpart of the Mönchsberg. This peak rises 2090 feet, and is a lovely woodland.

Mönchsberg itself, to the west of Hohensalzburg, is a mountain ridge slightly less than two miles long. It rises over the old town.

1. Where to Stay

Some of the finest accommodations, particularly the schloss hotels or even converted farmhouse pensions, lie on the outskirts of Salzburg, within an easy drive of the city. However, for the most part they're suitable only for motorists. If you don't have a car, then you may want to consider one of the hostelries right in the city—within walking distance of all the major sightseeing attractions. If you're driving, you may want to read Chapter VIII before selecting a hotel. Since the hotels of Salzburg are often very crowded in the summer (and are impossibly booked during the Salzburg Festival in August), many travel-wise Europeans reserve one of the less expensive accommodations in "Land Salzburg," from which they then drive into Salzburg.

THE DELUXE CHOICES: **Hotel Bristol,** 4 Markartplatz (tel. 73-5-57). The bar of this 19th-century hotel has terrazzo floors and Oriental rugs in an ambience of concealed lighting, light-grained paneling, and discreet piano music. The bedrooms range from upper-class functional to opulently baroque, with embellished ceilings and crystal chandeliers. The armchairs in the public rooms are comfortably upholstered in brown leather, which affords a vantage point for the enormous paintings, some of which should probably be in a museum.

The cream-colored baroque facade of the hotel encompasses a view of the Hohensalzburg Fortress and the Mirabell Gardens. As you'd expect from such an elegant hotel, each of the rooms has its own bath. Singles cost between 900 AS ($47.88) and 1450 AS ($77.14), while doubles range between 1700 AS ($90.44) and 2600 AS ($138.32), with breakfast included.

During high season, which is at Easter, for a few days in mid-June, and from late July till early September, the hotel requests that guests take half

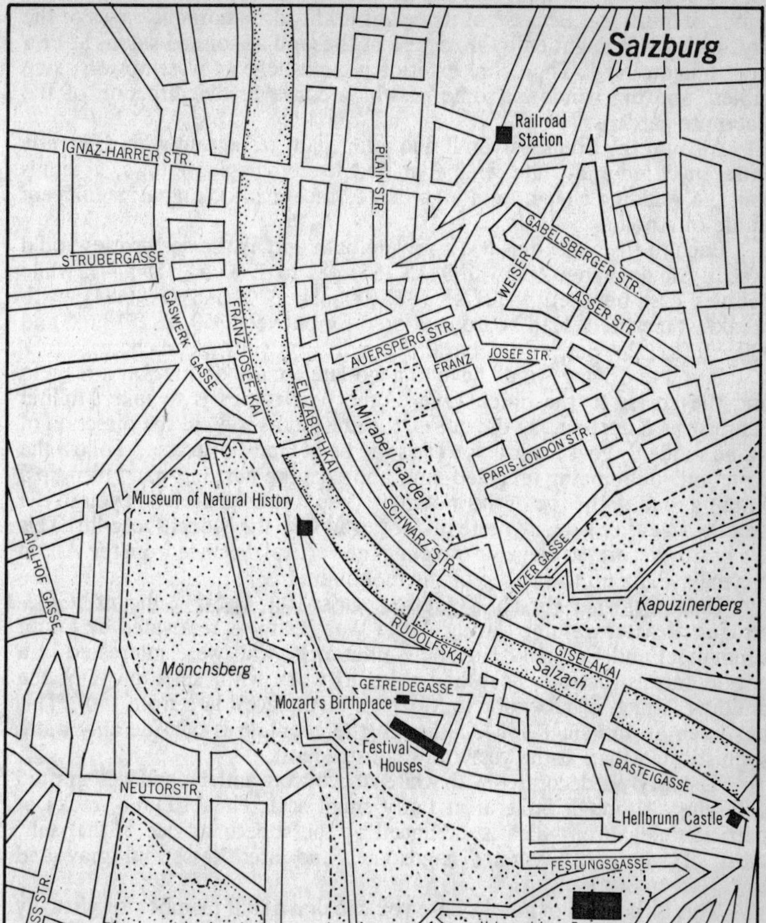
Salzburg
Railroad Station
IGNAZ-HARRER STR.
PLAIN STR.
STRUBERGASSE
GABELSBERGER STR.
WEISER
LASSER STR.
GASWERK GASSE
FRANZ-JOSEF-KAI
AUERSPERG STR.
FRANZ JOSEF STR.
ELIZABETHKAI
Mirabell Garden
PARIS-LONDON STR.
Museum of Natural History
SCHWARZ STR.
LINZER GASSE
AIGLHOF GASSE
Kapuzinerberg
RUDOLFSKAI
GISELAKAI
Salzach
Mönchsberg
GETREIDEGASSE
Mozart's Birthplace
Festival Houses
BASTEIGASSE
NEUTORSTR.
Hellbrunn Castle
FESTUNGSGASSE
MOSS STR.
Hohensalzburg Fortress
SINNHUBSTR.
LEOPOLDSKRON STR.
N
W
E
S

board. At that time singles range from 1850 AS ($98.42) to 2300 AS ($122.36), while doubles go from 3000 AS ($159.60) to 3600 AS ($191.52).

Hotel Schloss Mönchstein, 26 Am Mönchsberg (tel. 41-36-30), is a Teutonic-style manor house on top of a rocky outcropping high above the center of Salzburg. Because of its height it affords panoramic views of the city, which you might enjoy from one of the well-appointed salons after a day of sightseeing. The ochre exterior is a pastiche of watchtowers, step gables, and big windows, some of which curve in the direction of the elaborate gardens.

Also on the premises you'll find an elegant restaurant with discreetly patterened red-and-white wallpaper and leaded-glass windows, a tennis court, a wedding chapel, and a garden terrace overlooking a magnificent statue of Apollo.

Each of the bedrooms has a private bath and all the accessories you'd expect. Singles range from 1150 AS ($61.18) to 1700 AS ($90.44), while doubles cost between 1350 AS ($71.82) and 3700 AS ($196.84), with breakfast included. Half board is offered for between 350 AS ($18.62) and 400 AS ($21.28) per person extra, depending on your menu choice.

If you're driving, you'll have to negotiate a maze of one-way streets to find the access to the hotel. One of the best routes is to take Müllner Hauptstrasse north along the quays, turning left as soon as the direction of traffic suddenly goes against you (this will be at Ganshofstrasse). Follow the direction you're being funneled into, and take the next left-hand turn up a winding road to the top of the mountain (you'll see signs leading you to the hotel). An easier way, if you're on foot, is to take the Mönchsberg-lift. This is a grimly decorated elevator traveling the vertical distance from the Anton Neymayr Platz up to the top of the mountain.

Hotel Goldener Hirsch, 37 Getreidegasse (tel. 41-5-11), means "Golden Hart." After a slump during World War II, it was renovated by Count Emmanuel and Countess Harriet Walderdorff, who were interested in a period reconstruction. They had a lot to work with, since parts of the building (which is next door to Mozart's birthplace) date from 1407. This has been an inn since 1564, although the clientele is considerably more sophisticated than at the year of its construction.

The lobby is decorated with white stucco, stag antlers, and well-crafted detailing. Although built on a fairly small scale, it absolutely reeks of patrician elegance, which is enhanced by the superb service of the staff, most of whom are young, handsome, and are dressed in gray and forest-green Styrian suits.

This is the kind of hotel where you can dial a staff member for virtually anything from flowers to theater tickets. The dining room is rustic, vaulted, and elegant. Well-furnished rooms range from 1200 AS ($63.84) to 1450 AS ($77.14) in a single and from 1750 AS ($93.10) to 2050 AS ($109.06) in a double. All prices are slightly higher at the time of the Salzburg Festival.

Hotel Kobenzl, Salzburg-Gaisberg (tel. 20-2-75), is a country-style inn on Gaisberg mountain, about seven miles from the heart of Salzburg. If your intention is to stay outside of the crowded city, this might be a good choice. Its exterior has half-timbered detailing, fieldstone masonry, big windows with a panoramic view over Salzburg, and weathered wooden balconies. The air here is mountain pure, the amenities are top-notch, and the decor is tasteful and attractive.

The Herzog family prepares a savory cuisine, which has appealed to everybody from Werner von Braun to Austrian President Kreisky. A swimming pool is on the premises, and a public bus runs to and from the city. Management closes down certain sections of the hotel, including the restaurant, after October 31, but reopens everything by March. Per-person rates range from 800 AS ($42.56) to 1150 AS ($61.18) in single or double rooms, with some triple apartments available for around 2600 AS ($138.32).

Hotel Österreichischer Hof, 5-7 Schwarzstrasse (tel. 7-25-41), is a palatial white hotel on the less crowded right bank of the Salzach. It has a magnificent view across the water to the old town, plus an interior decor of wrought iron, very grand staircases, potted palms, Biedermeier and Victorian antiques, big windows, and Oriental rugs. Built about a century ago, it has attracted a clientele that has numbered some of the most powerful figures in Europe.

Among the restaurants inside, my favorite is the wood-paneled Zirbelzimmer, whose craftsmanship is admirable. Other facilities include a piano bar and a garden terrace. The 130 well-furnished rooms range from 520 AS ($27.66) to 1300 AS ($69.16) in a single and from 1150 AS ($61.18) to 2500 AS ($133) in a double, with breakfast included.

Schloss-Hotel Klessheim, Siezenheim (tel. 31-1-77), is a yellow neoclassical villa which was built originally for the brother of Franz Joseph in 1882. After Hitler took over Austria, he ordered that the palace be fixed up for him to have as a private retreat, perhaps intending to journey over from Berchtesgaden, but these plans never worked out. It was later used as a vacation home for top-ranking military brass during the American occupation of Austria. Among others, it received Richard Nixon.

Open only in summer, it contains more than two dozen rooms, about 16 of which have private bath. It has a nine-hole golf course, a swimming pool, a tennis court, and a large surrounding park. On the outskirts of Salzburg, it lies less than four miles from the center. Bed and breakfast costs from 500 AS ($26.60) to 900 AS ($47.88) in a single and between 810 AS ($43.09) and 1700 AS ($90.44) for a double. Half board is offered for an additional 170 AS ($9.04) per person daily.

FIRST-CLASS HOTELS: **Hotel Fondachhof,** 46 Gaisbergstrasse, Salzburg-Parsch (tel. 20-9-06), is one of the most pleasing hotels at the foot of Gaisberg. It was built as a manor house 200 years ago in a baroque format of mustard-yellow walls, white trim, and a steep red-tile roof. It was made into a hotel in 1950, and today affords quiet and secluded lodgings to guests in summertime only (from April to October). Many of the bedrooms look down on a gazebo set close to the flowered sun terrace. On the grounds you'll find sculpted fountains, a heated swimming pool, and a sauna. Many of the accommodations are furnished with antiques, while the architectural detailing inside includes stone columns and decorative ceramic stoves. Singles range from 600 AS ($31.92) to 1000 AS ($53.20), while doubles cost between 1250 AS ($66.50) and 2150 AS ($114.38), with breakfast included. Prices depend on the season.

Maria Theresien Schlössl, 87 Morzgerstrasse, Salzburg-Hellbrunn (tel. 41-2-44). An archbishop ordered this castle built in the early part of the 17th century, and there's still a vague feeling of the ecclesiastical in the proportions of the lemon-colored baroque facade with curved gables. It became a hotel about three years before Hitler annexed Austria. Lying on the southern outskirts of the city, it's more a manorial home than an actual castle. In fact it was once an outbuilding of the neighboring Hellbrunn Palace. It's set in spacious park-like grounds, through which guests wander freely, inspecting the well-manicured gardens. There are about 30 bedrooms, some dozen of which have private bath. The friendly and helpful staff serves good food, which includes both German and French specialties. Well-furnished singles range from 400 AS ($21.28) to 800 AS ($42.56), while doubles cost between 450 AS ($23.94) and 1400 AS ($74.48), depending on the plumbing and the season. Prices include breakfast.

Hotel Kasererhof, 6 Alpenstrasse (tel. 21-2-65), is composed of two mustard-colored baroque buildings connected with a low passageway. The main building was built in 1642 on land that had previously belonged to an archbishop. A nearby chapel, which is part of the hotel, was constructed 35 years later, and is still filled with museum-caliber pieces from the 18th century. The public rooms are outfitted with cozily contrasting patterns of flowered upholstery over Oriental rugs. The Günther-Strohbichler family do everything they can to make a visitor's stay pleasant. They charge between 780 AS ($41.50) and 1100 AS ($58.52) in a single and between 1380 AS ($73.42) and 2050 AS ($109.06) in a double.

Hotel Winkler, 7 Franz-Josef-Strasse (tel. 7-35-13), can be recognized by the huge sign stretching above the honeycomb concrete of its rectangular facade. The contemporary bedrooms are outfitted with discreet colors, big windows, and romantic touches which sometimes include gilded headboards in baroque patterns. Singles range from 720 AS ($38.30) to 900 AS ($47.88), while doubles cost between 600 AS ($31.92) and 800 AS ($42.56) per person, with breakfast included. Half board is offered for an additional charge of 160 AS ($8.51) per person. The hotel is outside the old town, near many 19th-century buildings, in a commercial section. It accepts tour groups, who have their own dining room.

THE MIDDLE RANGE: **Hotel Stieglbräu,** 14 Rainerstrasse (tel. 77-6-92), is a comfortable, contemporary hotel within a five-minute walk of the main train station, in the Mirabell section of Salzburg. Facilities include two pleasant restaurants and a salad bar for light snacks. The 50 bedrooms are simply furnished, with big windows, clean sheets, snug beds, and private baths. The hotel has its own parking lot, which will solve at least one of your problems in traffic-congested Salzburg. Singles range from 450 AS ($23.94) to 550 AS ($29.26), while doubles go from 750 AS ($39.90) to 920 AS ($48.94), with breakfast included.

Hotel Mozart, 27 Franz-Josef-Strasse (tel. 72-2-74), angles itself around a street corner a few blocks south of the train station. It's facade of beige stucco contains modern weatherproof windows which let in plenty of light to fill the simply furnished bedrooms, each of which has its own private bath and phone. Singles cost 800 AS ($42.56), while doubles go for 1200 AS ($63.84). A limited number of triples is available for 1400 AS ($74.48), with breakfast included.

Hotel Pitter, 6-8 Rainerstrasse (tel. 78-5-71), has an impressive gray stucco facade which angles around a curve in the street on which it sits. The lower floors have restrained neoclassical detailing around their windows, although the upper stories are adorned with nothing more elaborate than the well-maintained white paint protecting them from the winter rains. The huge lobby area has beautifully polished square columns of red porphyry, a sea-green ceiling, and a marble floor. One of the three inviting restaurants contains a sympathetic wood-paneled bar, while a daytime café provides a place to read the local newspapers. The Fellner family with their two sons are the genteel owners of this hotel, where attractively furnished singles or doubles rent for 530 AS ($28.20) to 720 AS ($38.30) per person, depending on the season.

Hotel Restaurant Gablerbräu, 8 Linzer Gasse (tel. 83-4-41), is an inviting hotel built in three six-story sections. The end sections are rust colored with white trim, while the center part has been painted a beige pink, with arched windows on the ground floor and wrought-iron detailing on its imposing facade. Inside you'll find three pleasant restaurants: one with vaulted ceilings and green and yellow murals, another covered with wrought-iron detailing, and a third—the least formal of all—which is a beer hall. Not far from the right bank's Markartplatz, the hotel offers well-appointed rooms for between 330 AS ($17.56) and 600 AS ($31.92) in a single and from 320 AS ($17.02) to 530 AS ($28.20) per person in a double, with breakfast included. All prices depend on the season and the plumbing.

Flughafen Hotel, 105 Innsbrucker Bundesstrasse (tel. 87-1-23), might be the ideal choice if you're arriving on a late flight into Salzburg. Close to the airport, it has comfortable and modern bedrooms, many with views of the city. The public rooms are tastefully appointed in leather, wood, and chrome, with colorful carpeting, while the good restaurant serves well-prepared food in a verdant setting of lots of plants and big windows. Singles cost between 400 AS ($21.28) and 550 AS ($29.26), while doubles range from 630 AS ($33.52) to 970 AS ($51.60), with breakfast included. Half board is offered for another 180 AS ($9.58) per person daily.

Hotel Kasererbräu, 33 Kaigasse (tel. 42-4-45), has a distressed stucco facade and baroque ornamentation around each of its windows. It's in one of the old town's most colorful neighborhoods, a few blocks from the cathedral. The building has sections dating from the 13th century, plus a collection of baroque and Biedermeier furniture that goes well with the Oriental rugs and embellished plaster ceilings. The dining room is rustically alpine, while some of the bedrooms have painted regional furniture covered with provincial floral motifs. Singles range from 400 AS ($21.28) to 640 AS ($34.05), with doubles costing from 820 AS ($43.62) to 1300 AS ($69.16), breakfast included. Prices depend on the plumbing and the season, and half board is offered for another 125 AS ($6.65) per person daily.

Hotel Johann Strauss, 37 Makartkai (tel. 34-6-19), is an ochre-colored hotel on a pedestrians-only square near the river. You might want to rest after a day of sightseeing on its flower-covered terrace which offers a view of the old town. The simple contemporary bedrooms have patterned carpeting in autumnal colors and private baths. The dining room is pleasant and not overly decorated, serving well-prepared food. Depending on the plumbing and the season, singles range from 280 AS ($14.90) to 690 AS ($36.71), while doubles go from 580 AS ($30.87) to 1150 AS ($61.18), breakfast included.

Hotel Wolf-Dietrich, 7 Wolf-Dietrich-Strasse (tel. 71-2-75), is composed of two neoclassical town houses joined together with an updated ground-floor facade. The lobby area is covered in Oriental rugs, with unbroken modern paneling accented with brass detailing. The smallish bedrooms are appealing and cozy, while parts of one of the two restaurants are outfitted in alpine carving and graceful pine detailing. An indoor swimming pool is covered with mirrors and unusual murals of Neptune chasing a sea nymph. Comfortably furnished doubles cost between 950 AS ($50.54) and 1150 AS ($61.18), while singles range from 450 AS ($23.94) to 700 AS ($37.24), with breakfast included.

Hotel Auersperg, 61 Auerspergstrasse (tel. 71-7-57), is a rectangular building with a gently sloping roof and a prominent curved wall of big windows, behind which is a restaurant. The establishment lies between the rail station and the Kapuzinerberg, within a three-minute walk of the center of town. Pleasantly equipped singles range from 390 AS ($20.75) to 720 AS ($38.30), while doubles go from 365 AS ($19.42) to 565 AS ($30.06) per person, with breakfast included, the prices depending on the season and the plumbing.

Hotel Stein, at Staatsbrücke (tel. 74-3-46). You'd never know it by looking at its renovated stucco and stone exterior, but there has been an inn on this site since 1399. The interior is the kind of spacious and airy place where you'll feel at ease. The big-windowed bedrooms are conservatively furnished in comfortable chairs and sofas. One of my favorite parts about this place is its rooftop terrace, where you can sip coffee or wine while listening to the splashing of a fountain as you take in the baroque buildings of old town. With breakfast included, singles range from 410 AS ($21.81) to 620 AS ($32.98), while doubles go from 650 AS ($34.58) to 1070 AS ($56.92).

Hotel Europa, 31 Rainerstrasse (tel. 73-2-93), is a concrete building rising from a tree-dotted area across the street from the main station. On the 14th floor you'll find a panoramic restaurant serving an international cuisine, while a less expensive snackbar on the ground floor might be a good stopover for lunch. The contemporary bedrooms are tastefully decorated, with vivid color schemes whose tones are sometimes repeated on the ceilings. Each of the 104 rooms has its own private bath, as well as radio and mini-bar. A TV is available on request. Singles range from 800 AS ($42.56) to 980 AS ($52.14), while doubles cost between 1180 AS ($62.78) and 1570 AS ($83.82), with breakfast included. Half board is offered for an additional 175 AS ($9.31) per person daily.

Hotel Drei Kreuz, 9 Vogelweiderstrasse (tel. 72-7-90), has a ground-floor series of aluminum-framed windows set into the kind of porous rock that Salzburg is built of. The upper floors are a two-toned combination of yellow stucco and terracotta colored panels. At the reception area you'll be greeted with a friendly smile and a wall-size illustration of a view of medieval Salzburg. The restaurant has some of the most massive beams I've seen in this part of Austria, along with a cozy bar and a gemütlich decor of rustic tables and chairs. The bedrooms are tasteful and well furnished. The name of the hotel derives from the three crosses of the Kapuzinerberg nearby, which was the site for public executions centuries ago. Well-furnished singles range from 600 AS ($31.92), while doubles cost 900 AS ($47.88), breakfast included.

BUDGET HOTELS: **Hotel Elefant,** 4 Sigmund-Haffner-Gasse (tel. 43-3-97), is a well-established family-run hotel near the Rathaus in the old city. You'll see a pink-and-white marble checkerboard floor in the lobby, as well as a friendly poodle and a 400-year-old marquetry cabinet. One of my favorite rooms is the vaulted restaurant, where high wooden banquettes separate the tables from one another and where the chairs are comfortably curved like horseshoes. The well-furnished and high-ceilinged bedrooms rent for between 320 AS ($17.02) and 410 AS ($21.81) in a single and 550 AS ($29.26) and 1050 AS ($55.86) in a double, depending on the plumbing and the season. Breakfast is included in the price.

Hotel Fuggerhof, 9 Eberhard-Fugger-Strasse (tel. 20-4-79), is a family-run boarding house on the south slope of the Kapuzinerberg. From the outside it looks like the secluded mountain home of a wealthy industrialist, with three stories of curved walls, stone detailing, and cone-shaped roofs. A kidney-shaped swimming pool is set among pine trees near the hotel's entrance. The furnishings are comfortably rustic, often painted in regional designs or richly grained with baroque carvings. Each of the bedrooms has a private bath, phone, and radio. Herta Kammerhofer, your congenial hostess, charges between 720 AS ($38.30) and 825 AS ($43.98) in a single and between 420 AS ($22.34) and 630 AS ($33.52) per person in a double, breakfast included.

Hotel Weisse Taube, 9 Kaigasse (tel. 41-7-83). The reception area lies behind a stone-trimmed wrought-iron and glass door a few steps from the Mozartplatz. It's ideally located for sightseeing but not for private car parking. Constructed in 1365, it's been owned by the Haubner family since 1904. Some of the public rooms maintain the massive ceiling beams of their original construction, but the 30 bedrooms are for the most part renovated and comfortably streamlined. Singles range from 375 AS ($19.95) to 610 AS ($32.45), while doubles go from 610 AS ($32.45) to 1100 AS ($58.52), with breakfast included. Prices, of course, depend on the season and on the plumbing. On the premises you'll find a sauna, an elevator, a television room, and a bar.

Hotel Garni Reiter, 8 Mirabellplatz (tel. 77-6-17), is a recently constructed hotel whose interior is filled with well-executed wood paneling and neutral-colored carpeting. You'd think the building was older than it is, except for the construction dates carved into some of the ceiling beams (1974 and 1977). The hotel is well situated on the Mirabellplatz, about five pedestrian minutes from the old city. The bedrooms are unpretentious and outfitted in autumnal colors of beiges, yellows, and browns. Singles rent for 550 AS ($29.26), while doubles cost 880 AS ($46.82), with breakfast and free parking included.

Hotel Blaue Gans, 43 Getreidgasse (tel. 41-3-17), has an ash-colored facade and a convenient location in the old city near the underground garages of the Mönchsberg. On the ground floor you'll find an informal beer hall. The narrow sidewalk outside is barely wide enough to walk three persons abreast. The bedrooms are simple and comfortable, with brightly colored carpeting and wood-grained furniture. Singles rent for between 250 AS ($13.30) and 360 AS ($19.15), while doubles cost between 500 AS ($26.60) and 720 AS ($38.30), breakfast included. Prices depend on the plumbing and the season.

Hotel Neutor, 8 Neutorstrasse (tel. 44-1-54), presents a gray and white elliptical facade, lots of windows, and one of the most modern formats of all the hotels in Salzburg. Views from the contemporary bedrooms (where you'll usually find a padded quilt covering the comfortable bed) include the Mönchsberg and the Untersberg. The dining room has red, white, and blue vertical stripes on the draperies, the colors repeated on the laminated wood chairs. Per-person rates range from 320 AS ($17.02) to 380 AS ($20.22). All units contain private baths.

PENSIONS: A pension or boarding house in Salzburg does not necessarily indicate economy. They can be luxurious, rated five stars, or of a more modest class, comparable to (but often better than) a third-class hotel. I'll lead off with the most expensive. If you're on a strict budget, read from the bottom of the list.

Haus Ingeborg, 9 Sonnleitenweg (tel. 21-7-49), is a small and luxurious alpine-style chalet in a secluded area northeast of the old town. It has a slope-roofed facade of reddish-colored wood and white stucco. The interior is outfitted with well-crafted details such as exposed ceiling beams, a riserless staircase of glowing hardwood, and a geometrically paneled ceiling. Some of the bedrooms are furnished with special accessories such as baronial beds. On the premises you'll find an outdoor swimming pool and a sauna. All the handsomely equipped bedrooms contain private baths as well. Singles rent for between 1000 AS ($53.20) and 1200 AS ($63.84), while doubles cost between 1450 AS ($77.14) and 2050 AS ($109.06), with breakfast included. Fritz and Inge Oberrauch are your hosts, and they keep their place open from the first of March until the end of October.

Haus Arenberg, 8 Blumensteinstrasse (tel. 77-1-74). Staying in a place like this gives you the chance to enjoy the best of the Austrian countryside while being a short car ride from the old city. Surrounded with a fieldstone foundation, the establishment rises two balconied stories in a format of white stucco and wood detailing. Parts of the interior are completely covered in blond paneling, while the panoramic breakfast room is accented with hunting trophies and Oriental rugs. The view from the comfortable bedrooms usually encompasses the nearby city. All units have private baths. Singles cost from 550 AS ($29.26) to 660 AS ($35.11), while doubles range from 880 AS ($46.82) to 1040 AS ($55.33), depending on the season. Breakfast is included in the price.

Dr. Wührer's Haus Gastein, 25 Ignaz-Rieder-Kai (tel. 22-5-65), is a dignified chalet on the banks of the Salzach in a residential section half a mile southeast of the center. It has a pleasantly flowered garden and a large back lawn which Sophia Wührer (who is a doctor of philosophy) maintains in good condition. The spacious and comfortable bedrooms rent for 1000 AS ($53.20) to 1100 AS ($58.52) in a single and between 750 AS ($39.90) and 850 AS ($45.22) per person in a double. All accommodations contain private bath and phone.

Pension Wolf, 7 Kaigasse (tel. 43-4-50), near the Mozartplatz, dates from 1429. It's built of stucco with big shutters, and in a location that couldn't possibly be more ideal. Red polished stone steps lead to the wood-ceilinged first-floor reception area. This hotel is usually full, even in off-season, so make reservations way in advance. The interior is rustically cozy, with a few baroque touches, such as an embellished ceiling, which make it inviting and appealing. The sunny bedrooms rent for 580 AS ($30.87) in a single and for 450 AS ($23.94) per person in a double, breakfast included.

Pension Am Eschenbach, 21 Hellbrunner Strasse (tel. 20-3-47). One of the best parts about this country-style guest house is the welcome provided by the kindly owner, Elisabeth Elwischger. The public rooms are filled with an eclectic mixture of 19th-century paintings, formal sculpture, and cozy contemporary furniture. The high-ceilinged bedrooms have painted designs on the furniture and are outfitted in cheerful colors. Singles cost around 350 AS ($18.62), while doubles range from 630 AS ($33.52) to 680 AS ($36.18). There are some apartments and a bungalow available for up to five persons as well. Breakfast is included in the price.

Pension Helmhof, Lieferinger Hauptstrasse (tel. 33-0-79), is an appealingly rustic stucco chalet with flowered balconies and a stone-trimmed sun terrace. Rooms are comfortably furnished and well kept, and the staff is most hospitable. Singles cost from 310 AS ($16.49) to 350 AS ($18.62), while doubles range from 420 AS ($22.34) to 550 AS ($29.26), with breakfast included. Prices depend on the plumbing.

Hotel Pension am Dom, 17 Goldgasse (tel. 42-7-65), is a rustically decorated family-run guest house a few steps from the Residenzplatz. The Bachleitner family, your hosts, charge between 640 AS ($34.05) and 750 AS ($39.90) in a single and between 400 AS ($21.28) and 410 AS ($21.81) per person in a double, with breakfast included. All units have private baths.

Pension Adlerhof, 25 Elisabethstrasse (tel. 75-2-36). Only the second and third floors of this guest house near the train station retain their original baroque embellishments. The windows of the first and fourth floors have been stripped and recovered with polished marble and gray stucco. The result is a pastiche of styles which eventually reveals a cozy interior with high ceilings. It's filled with wooden furniture that has occasional painted designs over parts of it, plus lots of folkloric touches which include an occasional hunting trophy. The Pregartbauer family charges from 210 AS ($11.17) to 310 AS ($16.49) in a single and from 360 AS ($19.15) to 550 AS ($29.26) in a double, breakfast included. Prices depend on the season and the plumbing.

Hotel/Pension Goldene Krone, 48 Linzer Gasse (tel. 06-2-22). My favorite part of this family-run guest house is the ivy-covered walls of its big sun terrace, where a member of the Egger family might serve you coffee after a tiring day in the city. Only a few minutes from the Staatsbrücke, the hotel offers comfortably outfitted bedrooms with patterned carpeting and wooden furniture. Singles rent for between 310 AS ($16.49) and 385 AS ($20.48), while doubles cost between 440 AS ($23.41) and 620 AS ($32.98); a few triples go for 810 AS ($43.09). Breakfast is included in these rates. Prices depend on the plumbing and the season.

Food and Lodging at Anif

Romantik Hotel Schlosswirt (tel. 21-75) is the kind of country inn many urbanites dream about. It's on the outskirts of Anif, four miles from the center of Salzburg and a half mile from the autobahn's exit at Salzburg-Süd. It was founded in 1607, and with its flagstone floors, thick walls, and a pleasing collection of local artifacts and hunting trophies, has done a thriving business ever since. It's so well known that Austrians sometimes drive all the way from Innsbruck to dine here.

The bedrooms, whether in the main building or in the L-shaped annex, are furnished mainly with Biedermeier furniture, with patterned wallpaper and flowerboxes at the windows. If you're a late riser, be warned that traffic beginning at 7 a.m. might disturb you if you're housed in the annex, which is right on the highway.

All rooms have private bath and are well equipped. Singles range from 500 AS ($26.60) to 640 AS ($34.05), while doubles go from 850 AS ($45.22) to 1100 AS ($58.52), depending on the season. Rooms come with a generous breakfast buffet with wurst, cheese, and coddled eggs.

Dinner is an elegant experience. Menu items include matjes herring with dill, an array of wild game in season, duckling in orange sauce, and many traditional fish dishes. A kindly English-speaking hostess in regional dress will help you with translations. Fixed-price meals begin at 220 AS ($11.70), with à la carte dinners costing from 250 AS ($13.30) to 400 AS ($21.28).

Hotel Friesacher (tel. 20-75) is an elegant, elongated chalet with a hipped roof, a long expanse of gables, and natural-grained wooden balconies covered with flowers. It has an older building a few steps away, which serves as a well-furnished annex to the main hotel, with flowering lawns scattered in between. The entrance hall to the main building has an intriguing variety of blue-gray and rust-colored marble covering the floor, and a wooden ceiling muting the light from the big windows. Throughout the hotel you'll find unusual artifacts, intimate corners, and friendly service provided by the Friesacher family. Each of the spacious bedrooms has its own bath, renting for between 450 AS ($23.94) and 500 AS ($26.60) in a single and for between 650 AS ($34.58) and 740 AS ($39.37) in a double. Apartments are offered for around 1000 AS ($53.20).

Food and Lodging at Aigen

Gasthof/Pension Doktorwirt, 9 Glaserstrasse (tel. 22-9-73), is a green-shuttered chalet with prominent gables, a red tile roof, and white stucco walls. It lies on the southern edge of Salzburg, within ten minutes by car from the old city. The adjoining restaurant produces many of the sausages it serves, as well as a collection of tempting pastries. The decor is rustic, sunny, and pleasant, with lots of wood detailing. On the premises is an outdoor swimming pool with a view of the mountains. The cozy bedrooms rent for between 400 AS ($21.28) and 425 AS ($22.61) in a single and for between 600 AS ($31.92) and 640 AS ($34.05) in a double, breakfast included. By car, exit from the autobahn at Salzburg-Süd, or if you don't have a car you can reach the place from the center of Salzburg by taking city bus line "E," which has buses running every ten minutes.

Food and Lodging at Bergheim

Hotel Gasthof Gmachl (tel. 52-1-24) lies four miles from the center of Salzburg. It looks like a private chalet home of a prosperous business person, with an interior embellished with carved stone and octagonal ceiling panels. In one of the public rooms, a massive hearth burns under a stone and stucco overhang. The 60 beds are contained in interesting and cozy rooms, some of them with sloping paneled ceilings and lots of homey individualized touches. On the premises you'll find three sand tennis courts, an indoor heated swimming pool, a sauna, and 2½ miles away, a riding stable (for which you will have to pay extra, of course). Singles rent for 530 AS ($28.20) to 795 AS ($42.29), while doubles cost between 800 AS ($42.56) and 1070 AS ($56.92), with breakfast included. Half board is included for an additional 200 AS ($10.64) per person daily.

2. Where to Dine

Salzburg has a wide range of restaurants in all price ranges. But two special desserts you'll have to sample while there include the famous Salzburger nockerln, a light mixture of stiff egg whites, as well as the elaborate confection known as the Mozart-Kugeln, with bittersweet chocolate, hazelnut nougat, and marzipan. You'll also want to taste the beer in any one of the numerous Salzburg breweries.

THE UPPER BRACKET: **Restaurant Alt-Salzburg,** 2 Bürgerspitalgasse (tel. 41-4-76), is one of the bastions of intensely formal Austrian service. The predominant colors are red and white, in a wood-ceilinged room crafted to reveal part of the chiseled rock of Mönchsberg. The crystal here shines from dozens of polishings; the waiters are formally dressed (often better than the clients), and the food choices include specialties such as a very tender T-bone steak with rosemary, breast of chicken farmer's style, filet of sole poached and served in a sabayon of vegetables, and medallions of venison in a cream sauce with cranberries. The restaurant is open from 11:30 a.m. until 2 p.m. and from 6:30 to 11 p.m. (till midnight during August). It's closed in February. Meals generally cost from 320 AS ($17.02). The restaurant doesn't open on Sunday, and reservations are suggested on the other nights of the week.

Goldener Hirsch, 37 Getreidegasse (tel. 41-5-11). Even if this restaurant only served the clients of its adjoining hotel (see my hotel recommendation) it would still attract the brightest luminaries of the international music and business community. The fact is, however, that dozens of the fans of this place journey far and wide to eat in the authentically renovated ambience of an inn established in 1407. It's staffed with a superb team of chefs and waiters in an atmosphere of elegantly restrained rusticity. Specialties include parfait of smoked trout in a mustard dill sauce, grilled hare, veal in saffron sauce, and many more dishes, all beautifully served and impeccably prepared. À la carte meals range from 210 AS ($11.17) to 480 AS ($25.54). The restaurant is open every day, and reservations are suggested.

G'würzmühl, 1 Leopoldskronstrasse (tel. 46-3-56). Sixty years ago this cozy restaurant was used as a spice mill (that's what its name means in German). Now it's American owned, offering an imaginative array of specialties such as a concoction of lobster and crabmeat in a dill cream sauce with buttered rice, along with trout dumplings, mock turtle soup, two kinds of schnitzel, peppersteak Madagascar, and veal chop Du Barry. The kitchen will also serve a children's menu as well. The restaurant, charging from 350 AS ($18.62) and up for a meal, is open every day except Tuesday from 11:30 a.m. to 3 p.m. and from 6 p.m. to midnight. In August it remains open every day. The location is about five minutes from the center of town.

Zum Eulenspiegel, 2 Hagenauerplatz (tel. 43-1-80), is housed in a white- and peach-colored building at one end of a quiet cobblestone square in the old city. Inside you'll find five rooms on three different levels, all of them rustically but elegantly decorated. Management seems to have no problem with allowing clients to pick their favorite rooms, so feel free to look around. A bar area on the ground floor might be a pleasant place for an apéritif.

After that, you'll climb a stone staircase whose stucco walls are loaded with unusual art objects. The menu features a table d'hôte priced between 310 AS ($16.49) and 370 AS ($19.68). It might include cream of zucchini soup, along with many classic dishes such as tafelspitz, salzburger nockerln, and perch filet. À la carte meals cost approximately the same as the set dinners. The restaurant is open from 11:30 a.m. to 2 p.m. and from 6 to 11 p.m.; however, the bar is open from 10 a.m. to midnight daily. Renate and Helmuth Wienerroither, who go on vacation in February, are the polite and friendly owners of the place.

THE MIDDLE RANGE: **Restaurant Zinnkrug,** 1 Lederergasse (tel. 76-6-11), offers one of the best dining rooms in Salzburg, with a menu prepared by one of the city's most talked-about chefs, Gerhart Royer. Its fourth-floor location provides a fine view over the river, with meals served not in pewter pots (which is what the restaurant's name means in English), but on fragile china, beautifully presented by an experienced staff. Fresh lake fish is a specialty, as well as a salad named after the famous French chef Paul Bocuse. Other recommendable dishes include fresh poached trout and any of their pork dinners. Reservations are strongly suggested. Open every day, they serve surprisingly inexpensive fixed-price meals, costing from 65 AS ($3.46) for a very simple repast to 100 AS ($5.32). However, most diners may want to order à la carte, paying from 185 AS ($9.84) to 350 AS ($18.62) for dinner.

Stiftskeller St. Peter (Peterskeller), 1-4 St. Peter-Bezirk (tel. 41-2-68). There's a legend that says that Mephistopheles met with Faust in this tavern, which isn't that far-fetched considering that it was established by Benedictine monks in A.D. 803. In fact it's the oldest restaurant in Austria, and is housed in the abbey of the church which supposedly brought Christianity to Austria. Aside from a collection of baroque banqueting rooms, open only for special occasions, the establishment contains an inner courtyard with vaults cut from the living rock, a handful of dignified wood-paneled rooms, and a brick-vaulted cellar with a tile floor and rustic chandeliers.

In addition to the wine fermented from the abbey's vineyards, the tavern serves such menu items as cheese soup with white wine and ham, filet of pork in a roquefort cream sauce with rice, roast duckling, and a combination plate of sausages, pork chops, semolina dumplings, potatoes, and sauerkraut. An unusual dessert might be curd dumplings with plum jam. Meals cost from 150 AS ($7.98) to 250 AS ($13.30), and the restaurant is open every day of the week all day until 1 a.m., and hot food is served until midnight. It's closed on Monday from the first of November until just before Easter.

Restaurant Hohensalzburg, in the Hohensalzburg Schloss (tel. 41-7-80), offers a chance to dine at the former stronghold of the prince-archbishops of Salzburg (see the sightseeing attractions). The restaurant is in the castle, which is perched on a block of Dolomite rock. You are 400 feet above the Salzach, and naturally you'll have a panoramic view.

Three times a week this gutbürgerlich restaurant is host to a folkloric music group which performs every Tuesday, Thursday, and Friday from 8:30 to 10:30 p.m. The rest of the week, clients enjoy such specialties as grilled pork, grilled steak with pearl onions and pepperoni, veal dishes, schnitzels, fish, and fowl. The restaurant, charging from 170 AS ($9.04) to 280 AS ($14.90) for a typical meal, is open from March until the end of October from 10 a.m. to 8 p.m. (until 11 p.m. at the time of the festival in July and August).

Daimler's Rôtisserie, 17 Giselakai (tel. 73-2-18). My favorite seats in this interesting restaurant are those in the window niches, where you'll have a view over most of Salzburg. The place has a kind of low-key elegance that's relaxed and informal, and especially appealing when accompanied by the specialties of the house, which include trout soup with salmon dumplings, lamb and game dishes, pork filet with mint-flavored butter, and a small but select range of stylishly presented other courses. You help yourself to the cheese and salad buffet, after selecting a wine from the rôtisserie's extensive list. Desserts are appropriately caloric. The friendly and attractive personnel will serve you à la carte meals, ranging from 130 AS ($6.92) to 300 AS ($15.96) for a typical repast. Reservations are suggested, and the restaurant is closed on Sunday.

Jedermann Grill and Café (Hotel Winkler), 7 Franz-Josef-Strasse (tel. 73-5-13), near the station, is outfitted in a modern format of orange tablecloths, exposed brick, and hanging lamps. The frequently changing daily specials include continental dishes, plus an occasional piece of exotica such as an Indian fish ragoût and Viennese specialties such as tafelspitz, pork filet with almonds and homemade gnocchi, smoked trout with horseradish, and something called a Jedermann-Spiess (a skewer of pork, beef, and veal, served with tomatoes and a hollandaise sauce). An adjoining bar might be an attractive place for a before-dinner drink. The restaurant is open every day, with meals beginning at 150 AS ($7.98).

Restaurant K & K (Stiegl-Bräu-Keller), 2 Waagplatz (tel. 41-1-56), is on a giant square in the old city, with three different sections, each with a separate ambience. From the street you'll see an elaborate wrought-iron and gilt bracket holding a sign. You'll go down a massive stone staircase to reach the cellar bierkeller, which is a marvel of another time's masonry (it was built 900 years ago). The stube on the ground floor is candlelit, with a wood-paneled ambience which seems to be the host to intimate groups of two, three, and four diners conversing quietly together.

Upstairs is the restaurant, which is divided by a flagstone-covered hallway into three separate eating areas, with dozens of stone accents crafted from both the porous rocks of Salzburg and beautiful slabs of salmon-colored marble. The diners here tend to be better dressed, and the atmosphere is slightly more formal. Caged trout swim frantically below the wrought-iron barrier of their aerated stone tank. The three restaurants serve warm food from 11 a.m. to 2 p.m. and from 6 to 10 p.m. They're also open for drinks and snacks from 9 a.m. till midnight in summer and from 10 a.m. to midnight in winter. Fixed-price meals range from 110 AS ($5.85) to 240 AS ($12.77). Menu items in the three restaurants include such specialties as perch, trout, roast filet of beef in a cognac cream sauce with fresh mushrooms and green peppercorns, tafelspitz, and breast of chicken in a curry cream sauce, along with grilled lamb and an array of seafood.

THE BUDGET RANGE: **Weinhaus Moser,** 3 Wiener Philharmoniker Gasse (tel. 41-3-16), is a smoke-stained winehouse with vaulted ceilings, paneling that looks polished from the backs of generations of drinkers, and the most unusual collection of overhead chandeliers in Salzburg. You'll also see a green ceramic oven, friendly uniformed waiters, and if you stop in before noon, groups of senior citizens sitting around gossiping as they drink coffee.

Menu items include typical Austrian dishes such as zander (pike-perch), tafelspitz, veal filet with spätzle, seasonal wild game, schnitzels, peppersteak with zucchini, and salzburger nockerl. Set meals begin at 70 AS ($3.72), while à la carte dinners range between 100 AS ($5.32) and 130 AS ($6.92). Warm food is served from 11 a.m. to 2:30 p.m. and from 5:30 p.m. until midnight (on Saturday, from 10 a.m. to 2:30 p.m.). From July 25 until the end of August the wine house is open all day from 11 a.m. to midnight, but it's closed on Sunday.

Hotel Stadtkrug, 20 Linzer Gasse (tel. 73-5-45), is a rustic and attractive restaurant which is part of a hotel on a narrow street in the old city. The layout is unusual, with a kitchen opening off the hotel's reception area and with a dining room that contains a stone staircase leading from the back to the large arched window in front. Wooden tables are set on two tiers, illuminated by gilded wooden chandeliers with pink shades. The fixed-price meals are a good bargain at 70 AS ($3.72) and 100 AS ($5.32), with a long list of à la carte specialties, usually priced at 185 AS ($9.84) and up. These include mixed grills, goulash, peppersteaks, and salzburger nockerl. One of the featured specialties is trout meunière, the ingredients of which come from the exposed trout tank that bubbles in the entrance vestibule. There are also daily blackboard specials. The restaurant is open from 11 a.m. to 11 p.m. seven days a week.

Restaurant Zum Mohren, 9 Judengasse (tel. 42-3-87). A statue of an exotic-looking Moor sits atop the wrought-iron sign announcing the entrance to this restaurant. The house that contains it was built in 1423, with much of the original masonry still showing. You'll have to descend a flight of gray stone steps to reach the three distinctly different eating areas, the best of which is on the right as you enter. The ceilings are made either of vaulted stucco or of well-crafted paneling. You'll see many replicas of Moors, with or without a gold earring, either in bas-relief or in full-rounded sculpture. A third area, on the left as you enter, is more cave-like, with an orange ceramic stove and a low ceiling.

The staff is friendly yet attractively formal. Meals range from 250 AS ($13.30) and up, and might include entrecôte Parisian style, filet mignon with broccoli and béarnaise sauce, grilled lamb chops, a good selection of cheese, and lots of rich desserts. The restaurant is open every day from 11 a.m. to midnight, and the chef stops serving hot food after 11 p.m.

Sternbräu, 23 Griesgasse (tel. 42-1-40). You'll enter this establishment through a cobblestone arched passageway leading off a street in the old city. The place seems big enough to have fed half of the old Austro-Hungarian army, in a series of rooms that lead one after another in varying degrees of formality. The Hofbräustübl is a rustic fantasy of square masonry columns with a massive format of hand-hewn beams and wood paneling. The other rooms have such accessories as sea-green tile stoves, marble columns, and oil paintings.

In addition to the different rooms, you'll also be able to eat in the chestnut-shaded beer garden, which is usually packed on a summer's night, or else under the weathered arcades of an inner courtyard. Daily specials, which are served by a battalion of aproned waiters, include typically Austrian dishes such as wienerschnitzel, some trout recipes, cold marinated herring, Hungarian goulash, hearty peasant soups, and lots of other gutbürgerlich selections. À la carte meals begin at 110 AS ($5.85), and the restaurant is open from 8 a.m. to midnight every day.

Mundenhamer Bräu, 2 Rainerstrasse (tel. 75-6-93). As you enter this warm-hued paneled restaurant, you'll pass by an elongated stainless-steel counter which almost looks like something from a delicatessen. There are several different seating areas, of which my favorite is the big-windowed section with a view of a city park. Through an open door you'll be able to see the energetic staff working in the very clean kitchens. They do set meals for 140 AS ($7.45), along with à la carte dinners for around 180 AS ($9.58). Menu items include Salzburger cream schnitzel, paprika cutlets, mushroom ragoüt, and a specialty of the house called Mundenhamer potpourri, a mixed grill for two persons. The menu is in English, and the portions are large. The restaurant lies near the main train station.

Hotel Weisses Kreuz, 6 Bierjodlgasse (tel. 43-3-22), has a facade of stone blocks that are almost hidden on a very small, village-style street just south of the cathedral. A grape arbor shelters the front terrace, where summertime tables have been set out for relaxed guests. The cuisine is both Viennese and Balkan, and includes Serbian bean soup, boiled beef, wienerschnitzel, mutton chops, roast beef in a cream and onion sauce, and peppersteak. More exotic specialties include Serbian goulash soup, moussaka, fried mincemeat loaf Serbian style with pickled peppers, and Dalmatian steak with Serbian rice and stuffed cabbage, along with a Serbian-style risotto. An average meal costs from 140 AS ($7.45), and the restaurant is open from 11 a.m. to midnight.

Schloss Stube Mirabell, 4 Auerspergstrasse (tel. 73-7-73). In a distant wing of the magnificent pink and white baroque palace giving this restaurant its name, you'll find a small and intimate square dining room with a high vaulted ceiling and a pictorial mural of a medieval city. A tiny beer garden is set on the cobblestones in front, separated from the sidewalk by an attractive row of potted ivy and evergreen trees. The clientele tends to be a silent crowd of older local residents at certain times of the day. The price is right: from 50 AS ($2.66) for a fixed-price meal, plus 18 AS (96¢) for a mug of beer. Warm food is served from noon till 2 p.m. and from 6:30 to 9 p.m., although the establishment opens at 10 a.m. for drinks. It serves only from Monday to Friday.

3. What to See

The old town lies between the left bank of the Salzach River and the ridge known as Mönchsberg, which rises to a height of 1650 feet and is the site of Salzburg's gambling casino. The main street of the old town is **Getreidegasse,** a narrow little thoroughfare lined with five- and six-story burghers' buildings. Most of the houses along the street are from the 17th and 18th centuries. Mozart was born at no. 9 (see below). Many lacy-looking wrought-iron signs are displayed, and a lot of the houses have carved windows.

You might begin your tour at the **Mozartplatz,** with its outdoor cafés. From here you can walk to the even more spacious **Residenzplatz,** where torchlight dancing is staged every year, along with outdoor performances.

The **Residenz** (former archepiscopal residence), on the west side of the Residenzplatz, just north of the Domplatz, was the seat of the Salzburg prince-archbishops after they no longer felt the need of the protection afforded in the gloomy Hohensalzburg Fortress on Mönchsberg (see below). The Residenz dates from 1120, but work on the series of palaces in its present form, which comprised the ecclesiastical complex of the ruling church princes, began in the late 1500s and continued until about 1782. The lavish rebuilding was originally ordered by Archbishop Wolfgang (sometimes called "Wolf") Dietrich. The Residenz fountain, from the 17th century, is one of the largest and most impressive baroque-style fountains to be found north of the Alps.

The child prodigy, Mozart, often played in the Conference Room for guests. In 1867 Emperor Franz Joseph received Napoleon III here, and in 1871 Kaiser Wilhelm I was also a state guest at the Residenz. More than a dozen state rooms, each richly decorated, are open to the public. Conducted tours are given through these rooms daily from June 1 until the end of September at 10 and 11 a.m. and at 2, 3, and 4 p.m.; from October to May at 10 and 11 a.m. and at 2 and 3 p.m.; on Saturday, Sunday, and holidays at 10 and 11 a.m. Admission is 15 AS (80¢) for adults, free for children.

On the second floor you can visit the **Residenzgalerie** (tel. 41-5-61/2770), an art gallery founded in 1789, now containing works mainly from the 16th to the 19th centuries displayed in 15 historical rooms. The some 200 paintings on exhibit include the art of Rembrandt, Rubens, Brueghel, Titian, Waldmüller, Maulbertsch, Poussin, Bordone, Troger, Vernet, Makart, Rottmayr, and Barbieri, among others. Gallery hours are 10 a.m. to 5 p.m. daily. Admission is 15 AS (80¢) for adults, free for children.

Concerts are often presented in the Residenz ballroom, and official receptions are held here. Special art exhibitions are frequently arranged in the sumptuous salons.

Across from the Residenz stands the celebrated **Glockenspiel,** with its 35 bells. You can hear this 18th-century carillon at 7 a.m., 11 a.m., and 6 p.m. Conducted tours are offered weekdays at 10:45 a.m. and at 5:45 p.m. from November 1 to March 15 for 5 AS (26¢) for adults, 3 AS ($16¢) for children.

At the south side of the Residenzplatz, where it flows into the **Domplatz** centered by a 1771 statue of the Virgin, stands the Dom, the **Salzburg cathedral,** surrounded by a trio of large open squares, world-renowned for its 4000-pipe organ. The original building from 774 was superseded by a late-Romanesque structure erected from 1181 to 1200. When this edifice was destroyed by fire in 1598, Prince-Archbishop Wolf Dietrich followed up the start of work on the Residenz by commissioning construction of a new cathedral, which was built between 1614 and 1655 and consecrated in 1628 by Paris Lodron, considered the most artistic of the prince-archbishops who ruled the Salzburg see. Dietrich's dream was to build a cathedral bigger than St. Peter's in Rome, but that grandiose scheme was never carried out. Nevertheless, this baroque cathedral can hold as many as 10,000 people.

Considered the "most perfect" Renaissance building in the Germanic countries, the cathedral has a lavishly ornamented marble facade and twin symmetrical towers. Its mammoth bronze doors date from 1628. The interior is in rich baroque with elaborate frescoes. In the cathedral you can see the Romanesque font at which Mozart was baptized. The dome was damaged during World War II and restored by 1959. In the crypt, traces of the old Romanesque cathedral which once stood on this spot have been unearthed. These excavations can be viewed by the public Easter to October daily from 9 a.m. to 5 p.m. Admission is 10 AS (53¢) for adults, 7 AS (37¢) for children.

The authority who dreamed what proved to be an impossible dream—to build the Salzburg cathedral on a scale larger than St. Peter's in Rome—Wolf Dietrich, mentioned above, had some other setbacks in his career as an ecclesiastic. The vigorous prince-archbishop fathered about a dozen children by his mistress, Salome Alt. A Renaissance man who was once closely allied with the Medici, Dietrich was imprisoned in 1612 for "misconduct" and sentenced to Hohensalzburg Fortress where he died five years later.

The treasure of the cathedral and a parade of the "arts and wonders" of the archbishops collected in the 17th century are displayed in the **Dom Museum,** open from mid-May to mid-October weekdays from 10 a.m. to 5 p.m., on Sunday and holidays from noon to 5 p.m. Admission is 20 AS ($1.06) for adults, 5 AS (26¢) for children 6 to 15.

The allegorical play *Everyman,* by Hoffmannsthal, is performed in the Domplatz at the Salzburg Festival. Based on my experience, if you attend a performance of this miracle play, bring your raincoat.

Stiftskirche St. Peter is the church of St. Peter's Abbey and Benedictine Monastery, founded by St. Rupert in 696. The church, once a Romanesque basilica with three aisles, was completely overhauled in the 17th and 18th centuries in an elegant baroque style. The west door dates from 1240. The tomb of St. Rupert is here. The church is richly adorned with art treasures, some altar paintings being by Kremser Schmidt. The Salzburg Madonna in the left chancel is from the early 15th century. You'll see a marble epitaph for Archbishop Wolfgang Dietrich's father.

St. Peter's Cemetery (Petersfriedhof, in German) lies at the stone wall that merges into the rock called Mönchsberg. Many of the aristocratic families lie buried here as well as many other noted persons, including Nannerl Mozart, sister of Wolfgang Amadeus. Four years older than her better known brother, Nannerl was also an exceptionally gifted musician. You can see the Romanesque Chapel of the Holy Cross and St. Margaret's Chapel, dating from the 15th century. The cemetery and its chapels are rich in nostalgia, monuments to a way of life long vanished.

Conducted tours are given through the early Christian catacombs in the rock above the cemetery every 30 minutes May to September from 10 a.m. to noon and 1 to 5 p.m., and every hour October to April from 11 a.m. to noon and 1:30 to 3:30 p.m. The tour costs 7 AS (37¢) for adults, 5 AS (26¢) for children.

The Kollegienkirche, or Collegiate Church, opening onto Universitälsplatz, an open-air marketplace, was built between 1694 and 1707 for the University of Vienna, designed by the great baroque architect Fischer von Erlach. There is no university in this area today, although part of the former seat of learning is a fine library and reading room. This is von Erlach's finest and largest Salzburg church and one of the most celebrated baroque churches in Austria (and that's saying a lot). Altar paintings are by Rottmayr.

The **Hohensalzburg Fortress,** stronghold of the ruling prince-archbishops before they moved "downtown" to the Residenz to live, towers 400 feet above the Salzach River on a rocky Dolomite ledge. The massive fortress crowns the Mönchsberg and literally dominates Salzburg. Work on Hohensalzburg began in 1077 and was not finished until 1681, during which time many builders of widely different tastes and purposes had a hand in the construction. This largest completely preserved castle left in Central Europe has bastions for the cannons needed in the strife-torn Middle Ages when the odor of sanctity was often mixed with the odor of gunpowder. Functions of defense and state were combined in this fortress for six centuries.

The elegant state apartments once lived in by the prince-archbishops and their courts are on display. Coffered ceilings and much intricately constructed ironwork are of interest. See, in particular, an early 16th-century porcelain stove in the Golden Room.

A **Burgmuseum** which has been installed is distinguished mainly by its collection of medieval art. Plans and prints tracing the growth of Salzburg are on exhibit, as well as instruments of torture and many Gothic artifacts. The Salzburger Stier, or Salzburg bull, is an open-air barrel organ built in 1502 which plays melodies by Mozart and his friend Haydn for daily concerts following the Glockenspiel chimes. The **Rainermuseum** has displays of arms and armor. The late Gothic, beautiful St. George's Chapel, dating from 1501, has marble reliefs of the apostles.

Conducted tours of the Hohensalzburg Fortress and museums are given every 15 minutes May to September from 9 a.m. to 5:30 p.m., and every 30 minutes October to April from 9:30 a.m. to 3:30 p.m. Admission is 25 AS ($1.33) for adults, 7 AS (37¢) for children 6 to 15.

You should visit Hohensalzburg even if you're not interested in the fortress, just for the experience of the view from the terrace. From the Reck watchtower you get a panoramic sweep of the Alps. Also, the

Kuenberg bastion has a fine view of the domes and towers of Salzburg, looking from here like a riot of baroque architecture.

There are several ways to reach the fortress. If you're athletic you can climb the stone steps leading to it, or you can come afoot or by car from Kapitelplatz by way of Festungsgasse or else from Mönchsberg via the Schartentor. I like to take the funicular from Festungsgasse at the station in back of the cathedral. The round trip costs 16 AS (85¢) for adults, 8 AS (43¢) for children, and it runs every ten minutes during daylight hours (the trip takes six minutes).

West of Hohensalzburg Fortress is **Mönchsberg.** This heavily forested ridge extending for some 1½ miles rising above the old town has fortifications dating from the 15th century. Several panoramic vistas can be seen from it, and a lovely view of Salzburg is possible from Mönchsberg Terrace just in front of the Grand Café Winkler where the casino is located. Three express elevators from along Gslättengasse take you to the terrace daily May 1 to September from 7 a.m. till 3 a.m., October 1 to April 30 from 7 a.m. till 2:30 a.m. Fare is 7 AS (37¢) each way for adults or 12 AS (64¢) for a round trip. Children's fare is 3.50 AS (21¢) each way or 6 AS (32¢) round trip.

The **Mozart Museum,** Mozart's Geburtshaus (Mozart's birthplace), 9 Getreidegasse, is a typical old burgher's house which frankly is not a great sight but nevertheless attracts practically all visitors to Salzburg to see it. Leopold Mozart lived on the third floor of this structure from 1747 to 1773, and it was here that Wolfgang Amadeus was born on Jan. 27, 1758, a date all Salzburgers remember.

The apartment contains a number of mementos. The child prodigy Mozart, who began composing at the age of four, wrote his early works here. You can see the small violin on which he played and his childhood spinet.

You can visit this birthplace of Salzburg's most renowned citizen in June and September from 9 a.m. to 7 p.m., in July and August from 8:30 a.m. to 7:30 p.m., and October to May from 9 a.m. to 6 p.m. Admission is 25 AS ($1.33) for adults, 10 AS (53¢) for children.

It's also possible to visit **Mozart's Wohnhaus,** his residence, at 8 Makartplatz, the Mozart family home from 1773 to 1787. The house was rebuilt after World War II damage. All that remains of the original are the entrance and the Tanzmeistersaal (dance master's hall), which is the site of chamber music recitals during the festival. The house is open to visitors June 1 to September 30, Monday to Saturday from 10 a.m. to 4 p.m. Admission is 20 AS ($1.06) for adults, 10 AS (53¢) for children.

Mirabell Gardens, on the right bank of the river, laid out by Fischer von Erlach and now a public park, are the finest baroque gardens in Salzburg. They are studded with statuary and reflecting pools. Some of the marble balustrades and urns were also designed by von Erlach. There's a natural theater, Landestheatre. As you wander in the gardens at your leisure, be sure to visit the bastion with fantastic marble baroque dwarfs and other figures, by the Pegasus Fountain in the lavish garden west of Schloss Mirabell (coming up). From the gardens is an excellent view of Hohensalzburg Fortress. The marble statues make Mirabell Gardens virtually an open-air museum.

Mirabell Palace (Schloss Mirabell) was built originally as a luxurious private residence called Altenau. Prince-Archbishop Wolfgang Dietrich had it constructed in 1606 for his mistress and mother of his children, Salome Alt. Not much remains of the original grand structure. Lukas von

Hildebrandt rebuilt the schloss in the first quarter of the 18th century, and it was modified after a great fire in 1818. The official residence of the mayor of Salzburg is now in the palace, which is like a smaller edition of the Tuileries in Paris. The ceremonial marble "angel staircase" with sculptured cherubs, carved by Raphael Donner in 1726, leads to the Marmorsaal, a marble and gold hall now used for concerts and weddings. Candlelit chamber music concerts are staged here.

Admission is free to both the gardens and the palace, which lie just off the Makartplatz.

You can also visit **Salzburger Barockmuseum** in the orangery in the Mirabell Gardens. Here European art of the 17th and 18th centuries is displayed, with works by Giordano, Rottmayr, Bernini, and Straub, among other artists in the Rossacher collection. Hours all year are 9 a.m. to noon and 2 to 5 p.m. Tuesday to Saturday, 9 a.m. to noon on Sunday and holidays. Admission is 20 AS ($1.06) for adults, 10 AS (53¢) for children.

The **Friedhof St. Sebastian** (St. Sebastian Cemetery) in Linzergasse was commissioned by Prince-Archbishop Wolf Dietrich in 1595, to be laid out like an Italian *campo santo*. Tombs of Mozart's wife, who endured many hardships, and of his father, Leopold, are here. In the middle of the cemetery is St. Gabriel's Chapel, wherein lies the mausoleum of the now-notorious Dietrich. The interior of his sarcophagus is lined with multicolored porcelain.

To reach the cemetery, you take steps modeled after those in the Italian style up from **St. Sebastian's Church.** The original late Gothic edifice dated from the early 16th century. It was rebuilt and enlarged in 1749, decorated in the rococo style. Destroyed by fire in 1818, it was later reconstructed. The 1752 rococo doorway remains from the old church building. Paracelsus, the Renaissance doctor and philosopher who died in 1541, is entombed here.

Nonnberg Convent, reached by a flight of steps at the end of the Kargasse, founded about 700 as a Benedictine nunnery by St. Rupert, is the oldest existing convent on earth. St. Rupert's niece, St. Erentrudis (or Ehrentrude), was the first abbess. The convent is a storehouse of treasures, with elaborate woodcarvings. There's also a museum of sacred relics. In the abbey church, in late Gothic style, is the tomb of St. Erentrudis. The St. John Chapel over the gateway displays a Gothic altarpiece from the late 15th century. An underground passage leads from the convent to Hohensalzburg Fortress.

The **Franciscan Church** (Franziskanerkirche), near the Domplatz, was built to replace St. Mary's parish church which was destroyed by fire in 1167. The present edifice was consecrated in 1223, the Romanesque nave dating from that year. In the 17th century the house of worship was rebuilt, and now is one of the most interesting churches of Salzburg stylistically, having Romanesque and Gothic styles as well as rococo and baroque elements in its architecture and decoration. On Sunday the finest church music in Salzburg is played here.

Leopoldskron Palace, in the suburb of Riedenberg, is set in lovely grounds which are now a pleasure park. It can be reached on foot from the heart of Salzburg, about a 30-minute walk to the southwest on the Leopoldskroner Weiher. The palace was built by a prince-archbishop in 1737 and at the time was considered the most significant rococo schloss in Austria. The great impresario Max Reinhardt lived here from the end of World War I until Hitler annexed the country. This was one of the settings used in filming *The Sound of Music*. The palace, currently occupied by a studies group, is not open to the public. The spacious park, with a lake and an open-air theater, is private property.

The **Festspielhaus,** or Festival Hall, was once the stables for the court, designed by Wolf Dietrich and built in 1607. Today it's the center for the major musical events of Salzburg, cultural activity reaching its peak at the August festival. Standing near Kollegienkirche on Universitätsplatz, the small old hall has superb ceiling paintings by Rottmayr. The modern hall seats 2300 spectators. The major concerts and big operas are performed here during the festival. Many outstanding Austrian artists contributed works to decorate the modern Festival Hall.

Guided tours are given Monday to Friday at 11 a.m. and 3 p.m. and on Saturday at 11 a.m. in April, May, and June; Monday to Friday at 11 a.m. and 3 p.m. in September; Monday to Friday at 3 p.m. and on Saturday at 11 a.m. from October to March; and Monday to Saturday at 2 p.m. during the Easter Festival. There are no guided tours in July and August. Admission is 15 AS (80¢) for adults, 7 AS (37¢) for children.

On the right bank of the Salzach at 26 Schwarzstrasse is the **Mozarteum,** founded almost a century after the composer's birth. In the building (constructed just before World War I) the first Mozart festival took place in 1922. There are two concert halls and a vast library of works about and by the composer. In the garden is the **Magic Flute House,** a little wooden structure in which Mozart composed *The Magic Flute* in 1791. It was shipped here from the Nachtmarkt in Vienna. In 1970 the Mozarteum was designated as the College of Music and the Performing Arts.

The Magic Flute House may be visited Monday to Friday July 1 to August 1 from 11 a.m. to noon for 10 AS (53¢) per person.

Also on the right bank is the "other hill" of Salzburg, the **Kapuzinerberg,** a forested area rising more than 2000 feet. Today this area is a lovely park. A Capuchin friary was built here in the closing year of the 16th century, constructed inside an old fortification from the Middle Ages. On the south side of the hill is a handsome street, Steingasse, from medieval times, and the Steintor, which was once a gate in the walls of Salzburg. The author of "Silent Night," Joseph Mohr, was born here in 1792.

From vantage points on the Kapuzinerberg you can see into Bavaria.

IN THE ENVIRONS: The environs of Salzburg are outstanding, and to explore them fully you'll need to refer to the information contained in Chapter VIII of this book, "Land Salzburg." The area is a setting of beautiful old romantic castles, charming villages, glacial lakes, salt mines, ice caves, and some of the most spectacular alpine scenery in Europe. But before going on to Land Salzburg, I'll describe a few attractions to be found right on the doorstep of the city.

Schloss Hellbrunn (Hellbrunn Palace), about three miles south of the city, is a popular spot for outings from Salzburg. It's at the end of Hellbrunnerstrasse off Alpenstrasse. Also to be seen here is the Alpenzoo. The palace dates from the early 17th century, built as a hunting lodge and summer residence for Prince-Archbishop Marcus Sitticus. The zoo was formerly the palace deer park.

The palace **gardens,** the oldest baroque formal gardens in all Europe, are known for their trick fountains. As you walk through, take care. You may be showered when and from a source you least suspect. In some of the contrived fountain play, spurts of water shoot out from unlikely spots, such as from antlers. More than 100 figures in a mechanical theater are set in motion by a clockwork movement to the music of an organ, powered by water.

The rooms of the schloss are furnished and decorated in 18th-century style. See, in particular, the banqueting hall with its *trompe l'oeil* ceiling. There's also a domed octagonal room that was used as a music room and reception hall.

The **Salzburg Folklore Museum** is housed in the Monatsschlosschen, the original hunting lodge of Schloss Hellbrunn. Mementos of life in Land Salzburg are on display.

Conducted tours of the castle, trick fountains, and folklore museum are given from 9 a.m. to 4 p.m. April 1 to April 15, to 5 p.m. April 16 to April 30 and September 1 to September 15; to 5:30 p.m. May to August. From September 16 to September 30, hours are 9 a.m. to noon and 1 to 4:30 p.m., to 4 p.m. in October. Admission is 30 AS ($1.60) for adults, 17 AS (90¢) for children. The gardens, orangery, and pheasantry may be visited free.

Castle concerts, together with a visit to the trick fountains and the historic wine cellar, are given on Wednesday and Saturday (occasionally on Monday) in July and August, beginning at 7:30 p.m. Adults pay 160 AS ($8.51), and children 80 AS ($4.26).

In the same setting, a natural gorge forms the **Stone Theater** where the first opera performed in the German-speaking world was presented in 1617. A Hellbrunn Festival is held in the gardens, palace, and theater in August.

In 1961 the **Alpenzoo** was opened, stretching around the western slope of the hill, with low fences allowing the public close views of the mainly alpine animal zoo denizens. As this was the deer park for the prince-archbishops, there are still large herds of stags and their families grazing on their ancestral acres. The zoo is open all year. Visiting hours are 8:30 a.m. to 5 p.m. October to March, to 6 p.m. April to September. Admission costs 25 AS ($1.33) for adults, 5 AS (26¢) for children.

It's only about a 20-minute drive from the heart of Salzburg to Hellbrunn Palace, and if the weather is good, many visitors prefer to walk the three miles. If you drive, turn off Alpenstrasse at the Mobil gas station. Or you can take an "H" bus, which makes the run in about 18 minutes.

About ten miles east from the center of Salzburg is **Gaisberg,** which at 4250 feet is one of the best places for views of the Salzburg Alps. Much of the road leading here is hewn out of rock. You can take a bus to the Gaisbergspitz or summit from which you see almost a full panorama. On a clear day you can see into Chiemsee in West Germany and to the Dachstein massif. In summer the bus leaves Mirabellplatz by St. Andrew's Church at 9 a.m. or at 11 a.m. The trip takes about an hour and costs 100 AS ($5.32).

To reach **Untersberg,** about 7½ miles from Salzburg, you head south out of the city toward Berchtesgaden in West Germany, the retreat of Hitler during his days of power. At the St. Leonhard junction, turn right and drive to the platform of a cable-car station. The funicular goes to the Untersberg summit (6020 feet), from which you have a panoramic view of the Salzburg Alps. A marked path leads to the Salzburger Hochtron (6100 feet), highest Austrian peak in the Untersberg massif.

Funicular service March 1 to June 30 and September 16 to October 31 is from 9:15 a.m. to 4:45 p.m., July 1 to mid-September from 8:30 a.m. to 5:30 p.m., and December 25 to February 28 from 10 a.m. to 4 p.m. The fare is 125 AS ($6.65).

The **Church of Maria Plain,** about 2½ miles north of Salzburg, is the most important pilgrimage church in the vicinity of the city. Construction on the twin-towered baroque church started in 1671, and it's lavishly embellished. To reach Maria Plain you head out Plainstrasse, eventually turning right onto Plainwegberg. If you take the tram it's about 45 minutes further on foot. Many people prefer the view from here at night.

From Maria Plain you can continue on about nine miles northwest to another pilgrimage church at **Oberndorf.** This village lying on the Salzach River is where Joseph Mohr wrote the carol "Silent Night" on Christmas Eve in 1818. A memorial chapel was built here in 1937.

Mattsee, 14 miles from Salzburg, is a small resort for city residents, on the shores of Niedertruner See, Obertrumer See, and Grabensee. Many tombstones from the 14th century have been found in the cloister of a 13th-century collegiate church here. To get to Mattsee, head out on Plainstrasse and the Itzlinger Hauptstrasse. You'll go through the hamlets of Bergheim, Lengfelden, and Elixhausen to reach it.

4. Where to Shop

Salzburg, being a much smaller city, obviously doesn't have the wide range of merchandise that Vienna does. However, if you're not going on to the Austrian capital, you may want to patronize some of the establishments recommended below, most of them opening at 9 a.m. and staying open until 6 p.m. Note that a number of them, especially the smaller places, take a one- or two-hour break for lunch. The stores also close down on Saturday afternoon and all day on Sunday.

Good buys in Salzburg include souvenirs of Land Salzburg, dirndls, lederhosen, petit-point, and all types of sports gear. Getreidegasse is a main shopping thoroughfare, but you'll also find some intriguing little shopkeepers on the Residenzplatz.

Original Trachten Wenger, 2 Munzgasse (tel. 41-3-59), is one of the best shops in Salzburg for elegantly traditional clothing. The gracious and sophisticated owner, Edith Hagn, will direct her in-house fitter to alter any garment within two hours, so you can buy it in the morning and wear it that evening at dinner. Dozens of well-made dirndls, skirts, and women's coats hang from racks in this well-furnished store. Couturier made-to-order garments can be created from patterns and individualized fabrics. The English-speaking staff includes attractive women who do everything they can to be of assistance. Accessories include umbrellas, belts, scarves, and gloves. The store is near the river in the old town.

Jahn-Markl, 3 Residenzplatz (tel. 42-6-10), is a small and elegant store with a forest-green facade trimmed with brass and wrought-iron detailing. In the center of the old town, it carries lederhosen for both men and women, leather skirts, and a full line of traditional Austrian coats and blazers. The less expensive items are usually sold off the racks that stretch high above the clients' heads. More expensive items are usually made to order in four weeks and can be mailed anywhere in the world for an additional charge. Some children's clothing is available as well, along with hats, belts, and gloves.

Salzburger Heimatwerk, Am Residenzplatz (tel. 44-1-19), is one of the best places in town to buy native Austrian handicrafts. It's a dignified stone building in the least crowded section of the Residenzplatz, with a discreet (and hard to see) sign announcing its location. Items for sale include Austrian and silver garnet jewelry, painted boxes, candles, woodcarvings, copper and brass ceramics, tablecloths, and patterns for cross-stiched samplers in alpine designs. A special section sells dressmaking materials such as cotton, silk, and wool fabrics in Tyrolean designs, with dressmaker patterns that can be adapted for the eventual size of the garment. A dirndl pattern I recently saw cost only 185 AS ($9.84). Wherever you go in this interesting store, be sure to keep exploring until you've seen every room.

Sporting Goods Dschulnigg, 8 Griesgasse (tel. 42-3-76), is an upper-crust emporium for clothes, guns, fishing equipment, overcoats for both men and women, intricately patterned sweaters in alpine colors, a collection of fur-lined hats, and many kinds of sporting goods. Queen Elizabeth II and Prince Phillip have been photographed on a shopping expedition here. You can get hunting rifles in Austria without a license (but not pistols or revolvers), although the Customs officers back home might present a problem. Be sure to climb to the second floor if you're interested.

Slezak, 8 Makartplatz (tel. 73-5-68), near Mozart's house, sells gloves, skirts, leather goods, umbrellas, suitcases, sweaters, belts, and leather and suede jackets for men, and has a good selection of all these items mentioned.

Schatz-Konditorei, 3 Getreidegasse (tel. 42-7-92). Already covered in the café section of this chapter, this establishment is an excellent pastry shop and one of the few in Salzburg that will mail cakes to foreign clients. The specialty of the store is the highly acclaimed Mozart-Kugeln, a concoction of pistachio, marzipan, and hazelnut nougat, dipped in chocolate. It might make a nice present for the friends or relatives you left behind. Packages of this gourmet delight will be air-mailed to North America, ranging in price from $14.20 to $23.60, depending on the size of the package.

Gollhofer Herrenmode, 10 Getreidegasse (tel. 42-1-75), is a large store selling quality clothing for men and women. It has a high-ceilinged spacious format with lots of modern paneling and a collection of merchandise that includes sports jackets, leather garments, and women's shoes. This is more of a large downtown store than an intimate boutique.

Brüder Fritsch, 42 Getreidegasse (tel. 47-5-51), sells leather goods to an up-market clientele. The contents of the store are expensive, filling two floors. Both Celine and Gucci are represented here.

Musikhaus Pühringer, 13 Getreidegasse (tel. 43-2-67), is a store selling recorders, classical records, and tapes, plus Mozart recordings by many different artists from many different countries. The store is appropriately located a few buildings away from Mozart's birthplace. It also sells guitars made in Germany, Italy, and Japan.

Lobmeyr, 20 Schwartzstrasse (tel. 73-1-81), is the Salzburg branch of the famous store in Vienna. Among a wide range of crystal goblets and elegant china, it includes some of the prettiest breakfast services I've seen, many of them made in Hungary.

Lanz, 4 Schwartzstrasse (tel. 74-2-72), is a well-stocked store across the river from the old town. The format is rustically modern, with one of the widest collections of long-skirted dirndls in town, in dozens of different fabrics and colors. The only men's clothing are loden-colored overcoats. The store also sells dirndls for little girls, women's shoes, and hand-knitted sweaters.

J. B. Neumüller, 3 Rathausplatz (tel. 41-4-29). In wintertime this store sells children's toys. In summer the stock changes, the shelves filling up with handcrafted souvenirs such as mugs, cowbells, and rustic art objects.

5. The Cafés of Salzburg

Cynics in the festival city sometimes complain that there isn't a lot to do in Salzburg except drink endless cups of thickened coffee while waiting for someone at the next table to be brilliant about art or music.

But that isn't the perception of everyone. A hometown friend of mine told me that the peak emotional experience of her trip to Europe happened while seated at a café table in the Mozartplatz. The combination of the baroque setting, the strains of a string orchestra, the Austrian pastry half eaten on her plate, and the companionship of a close friend made her realize that she was suddenly living her fantasy of what culture, art, and beauty are all about.

Don't leave Salzburg without some significant time in one of the world-famous cafés of the inner city. Descriptions of some of my favorites immediately follow.

Café Tomaselli, 9 Alter Markt (tel. 44-4-88), was established in 1703. It opens onto the cobblestone pavement of one of the most charming squares of Salzburg. Aside from the summertime chairs placed outdoors, you'll find a high-ceilinged square room with many tables, lots of what look like elegant conversations, and small crystal lighting fixtures. Another more formal room to the right of the entrance has oil portraits of well-known 19th-century Salzburgers in oval frames hung one above another. The crowd is chic, many of them with wintertime fur coats and jewelry. A waiter will probably show you a pastry tray filled with 40 different kinds of cakes, which you are free to order or not as you see fit. Other menu items include omelets, wursts, ice cream, and a wide range of drinks. Pastries cost around 30 AS ($1.60), omelets from 55 AS ($2.93), a sherry from 30 AS ($1.60), and coffee from 30 AS ($1.60) also. The café is open from 7 a.m. to 9 p.m., from 8 a.m. to 9 p.m. on Sundays and holidays.

Café Winkler (Restaurant am Mönchsberg), 32 am Mönchsberg (tel. 41-2-15). To some residents of Salzburg the inconvenience of getting to this mountaintop café is simply not worth the trouble. But if you want to take the antiquated elevator from the Anton Neumayer Platz for a round-trip fare of 15 AS (80¢), you'll be rewarded with a panoramic view of Salzburg and a well-prepared cuisine from the kitchens of Manfred Brugger.

Café items include beer from 20 AS ($1.06), omelets from 65 AS ($3.46), soup from 35 AS ($1.86), and whiskey from 70 AS ($3.72). Featured on the restaurant menu are such dishes as wienerschnitzel, filet of veal à la folie, mushroom terrine with celery hearts, and trout dumplings with wild rice. Fixed-price meals range from 170 AS ($9.04) to 480 AS ($25.54), while à la carte items range from 125 AS ($6.65) to 260 AS ($13.83). For full meals, reservations are suggested. From September until the middle of July the restaurant is closed on Monday.

Kaffeehäferl, 6 Universitätsplatz (tel. 43-2-49), is constructed in an arcaded gray and white format of stucco walls set onto columns made of the porous rock that supports many of the buildings of Salzburg. This establishment attracts members of the business and art communities of the city. The interior is more modern and simpler than you'd expect, yet there's lots of visual interest from the masses of ceramic pots displayed in cases on one of the far walls. A specialty of the house is fleckerl with ham, which is served in addition to the wide selection of coffee, wine, and pastries. Coffee costs from 30 AS ($1.60), with the price the same for the average pastry. The café is open Monday to Friday from 9 a.m. to 7 p.m., on Saturday to 6 p.m., and on Sunday in summertime from noon to 6 p.m. (in winter, Sunday hours are from 2 to 6 p.m.).

Schatz-Konditorei, 3 Getreidegasse (tel. 42-7-92), is the kind of oldtime Austrian confectioner that you probably fantasized about before leaving home. The cobblestones in front of its 19th-century wood-and-glass facade are from the 14th century. Almost everything is made from traditional recipes, my favorite of which is the well-known Mozart-Kugeln, a combination of pistachio, marzipan, and hazelnut nougat, all of it dipped in chocolate. Clients are free to try any of the pastries with coffee at an indoor café table or to purchase them for consumption elsewhere. A pastry with a cup of coffee or chocolate costs between 40 AS ($2.13) and 60 AS ($3.19). Management will also mail some kinds of their pastries, including the Mozart-Kugeln, around the world. They're open from 8:30 a.m. to 6:30 p.m. weekdays, from 8 a.m. to 1:30 p.m. on Saturday. During festival performances in summer they're open full time on Saturday.

Konditorei Ratzka, 45 Imbergstrasse (tel. 70-9-19), is a small shop ten minutes from the center of town. Herwig Ratzka is the owner and pastry chef, and by all accounts he's a master at his craft. He uses the freshest ingredients to produce about 30 different pastries every day. Since the cakes are made fresh every day, much of the selection is gone by late afternoon. So for an insight into what's for sale, go early in the day. Prices begin at 30 AS ($1.60). Mr. Ratzka requests that clients not smoke in the shop, which is open Wednesday to Friday from 8 a.m. to 12:30 p.m. and from 1:30 to 5 p.m. (on Sunday, from 9 a.m. to 5 p.m.). It's closed on Monday and Tuesday and for two weeks in January, two weeks in June, and two weeks in September.

Café Glockenspiel, Mozartplatz (tel. 41-4-03). Its location on one of the most colorful squares of Salzburg has made this café the most popular and the most frequented in the city. Management keeps about 100 tables with well-maintained white armchairs in front of the café. If the day is warm enough, you might want to spend an afternoon in one of the chairs, particularly on the days when there is live chamber music. Immediately after entering you'll find yourself face to face with a glass case filled with every high calorie delight west of Vienna.

The rooms opening on either side are upholstered in gray and pink, with big arched windows overlooking the statue in the square. A restaurant upstairs, with an even bigger pastry case than the one downstairs, is tastefully decorated in browns and beiges, with a big balcony, if you choose to sit there. Food items include daily specials, with main courses ranging from 75 AS ($3.99), which are likely to include fried plaice, spaghetti bolognese with green salad, and other offerings. Most people, however, come here for the drinks and pastries. Coffee costs 30 AS ($1.60); tea, 20 AS ($1.06); and beer, 30 AS ($1.60). There are many varieties of coffee, including Maria Theresa, which has orange liqueur in it.

Café Bazar, 3 Schwartzstrasse (tel. 74-2-78), is as deeply entrenched into Salzburg's social life as practically anything else in town. It has a regular clientele which includes persons from all walks of Austrian life, many of whom usually sit in the same section of the café and order practically the same item every time they visit.

It's housed in a pink stucco, palace-like building with many baroque features across the river from the main section of the old town. The inside is high ceilinged and vaguely art deco, with light-grained wooden walls covered with marquetry designs.

You'll occasionally see someone with a Franz-Joseph mustache wearing a gray flannel Styrian suit with loden trim, but a growing number of the clients are young, trendy, and fashionable, and would probably be much at home at a café in London or Paris. A waitress in a frilly apron carries a pastry tray around the room, while the formally dressed waiters perform a correct service.

Menu items include an array of salads, sandwiches, and omelets, usually priced at around 25 AS ($1.33) to 40 AS ($2.13). Coffee or a gin and tonic ranges from 25 AS ($1.33) to 45 AS ($2.39), respectively, while pastries go from 18 AS (96¢) to 30 AS ($1.60). It's closed on Sunday.

Café Papageno, 14 Pfeifergasse (tel. 41-1-06), is a gemütlich hangout for an under-26 crowd. It's named after the comic character from Mozart's *Magic Flute,* whose statue stands in the nearby Papageno-Platz. The inside has wooden ceilings, comfortable banquettes, and a crowd of young people in couples or groups. The ambience is welcoming, and the food items include snacks such as hamburgers and salads from 25 AS ($1.33) and menus from 45 AS ($2.39). Beer costs from 17 AS (90¢).

6. Salzburg After Dark

FESTIVAL: By the time you read this, assuming it's 1984, the **Salzburg Festival**—one of the premier music attractions of Europe—will have celebrated its 64th season. Or if you're reading this in 1985, its 65th season. The composer Richard Strauss founded the festival, aided by the director Max Reinhardt and the writer Hugo van Hofmannsthal. Details on this festival are available by writing the Austrian National Music Festivals, Suite 207, 545 Fifth Ave., New York, NY 10017 (tel. 212/697-0656) before the middle of May. After that, direct inquiries to the box office of the Salzburg Festival, Festspielhaus, A 5010 Salzburg, Austria (or telephone 4-24-51 for information).

Regrettably, tickets are in great demand, and there never are enough of them. Don't arrive expecting to get into any of the major events unless you've already purchased tickets. Travel agents can often get tickets for you, and you can also go to branches of the Austrian Tourist Office at home or abroad. Hotel concierges, particularly at the deluxe and first-class hotels of Salzburg, always have some tickets on hand, but they most often ask outrageous prices for them, depending on the particular performance you wish to attend. At first-night performances of the major productions, remember that evening dress is *de rigueur.*

An annual event is Hofmannsthal's morality play *Everyman,* which last year was staged outside the cathedral in the Domplatz. Concerts are likely to be conducted in the Rittersaal of the Residenz Palace (Mozart also conducted here) and in the marble salon of Mirabell Palace (Mozart's father, Leopold, conducted here). The Salzburg Marionette Theater (see below) also presents performances. Ballet is likely to be performed by the Vienna State Opera Ballet with the Vienna Opera Chorus and the Vienna Philharmonic. Operas (certainly Mozart, and most likely Richard Strauss and Beethoven) are also accompanied by the Vienna Philharmonic. International soloists—such big names as Luciano Pavarotti—are invited annually, and the London Symphony or the Berlin Philharmonic are also likely to be invited.

Tickets begin at 65 AS ($3.46) for standing room at one of the serenade concerts, going up to 2500 AS ($133) for the choice opera seats.

Most performances begin at 8 in the evening or slightly later, and these annual events overshadow any nightlife you might find in Salzburg, where clubs rise and fall fairly rapidly.

OTHER CONCERTS: As mentioned, the **Salzburger Marionetten Theater,** 24 Schwarzstrasse (tel. 7-24-06), presents shows of operas and operettas, running from Easter through September (there are also special shows at Christmas). These puppets perform both opera and ballet and are a delight to both adults and children. Usually they present Mozart operas. Seats are likely to range from 180 AS ($9.58) to 300 AS ($15.96). The theater was founded in 1913, and since that time has been one of the most unusual—and enjoyable—theatrical entertainments in Salzburg. You may forget that marionettes are on stage, it's that realistic.

The **Salzburger Landestheater,** 22 Schwarzstrasse (tel. 7-40-86), doesn't play for summer visitors, but if you're in Salzburg from September until some time in June, you can see its regular repertoire of operas (not just Mozart) and operettas. On my last visit, for example, I saw a thrilling performance of Giuseppe Verdi's *La Traviata.*

All year round you can go to the tourist office in Salzburg and pick up a list of musical events that are being presented when you're there, even if you should arrive in January. In fact the annual **Mozart Week** is in January. Summer chamber music concerts are most often offered at the Residenz and Mirabell Palace.

Music, especially organ concerts, is also presented at the **Mozarteum,** 26 Schwarzstrasse (tel. 7-31-54).

If you're not a music lover, you may prefer some casino action instead.

CABARET: If you'd like to see a mildly erotic show with lots of girls, the leading choice is the **Casanova Cabaret and Nightclub,** 23 Linzergasse (tel. 71-90-64), open from 9 p.m. to 4 a.m. and seating 70. It accepts most major credit cards, and you should count on spending from 600 AS ($31.92).

DISCOS: Discos are still alive, but not doing that well in Salzburg. Sometimes admission fees of about 30 AS ($1.60) are charged, and drinks begin at 60 AS ($3.19) to 75 AS ($3.99).

One of the leading discos is in the suburb of Anif, just outside the city limits. It's the **Friesacher Stadl,** 57 Anif (tel. 24-11), a substantial-looking country house set about 100 yards away from a busy highway in Anif. You'll enter a dimly lit and smoke-stained room loaded with paneling, wooden tables, and rustic artifacts. The bar area, which is usually a good place to meet people, stretches toward the small dance floor, where many of the couples dance in each other's arms, even to the disco/folkloric music. This is a popular rendezvous point for Salzburg and all its suburbs. A burly-looking man will greet you at the door, and there's rarely a cover charge.

Other leading discos include **Golden Black,** 3 Lederergasse (tel. 76-7-28), which is open from 9 p.m. to 4 a.m. daily, except Monday. Seating 100, it plays what the Austrians call "plattenmusik." There's more disco dancing at the **Old Grenadier,** 2 Ursulinenplatz (tel. 4-37-18), which is usually open daily except Sunday from 9:30 p.m. to 4 a.m. You might also try the gyrations at **Disco-Tyrol,** 4 Wolf-Dietrich-Strasse (tel. 7-62-79), which is open from 9 p.m. to 3 a.m. It can squeeze in as many as 250, most often a very international crowd.

LATIN AMERICAN MUSIC AND DINING: **Mexicano Keller** (Hotel Blaue Gans), 43 Getreidegasse (tel. 42-4-91), is a popular evening spot in

Salzburg, offering Latin American music and Mexican food. The cuisine includes both enchiladas and chili con carne at 80 AS ($4.26) each, along with five different steak dishes, including carne asada Acapulco at 150 AS ($7.98). Fondue Mexicano is another specialty, served for two persons at 440 AS ($23.41). Sangría costs 25 AS ($1.33) and up, depending on how much you order. The decor looks like a combination of an Austrian wine cellar and a ranch south of the (American) border, with a vaulted stone ceiling and rustic ranchero-style banquettes. The cellar is closed on Wednesday.

FOLK DANCING: If you like folk dancing, you can go to the **Sternbräu** beer gardens on any Friday night. Refer to my restaurant recommendations for more detailed information.

GAMBLING: If you're interested in either losing or winning a fortune, you can head for the **Spiel-Casino** which sits along with the Café Winkler on Mönchsberg (tel. 45-6-56). You can reach it by an elevator at the bottom of the hill. The entrance is Mussolini-style grand, and as you enter you'll find gaming tables where you can play roulette, baccarat, and blackjack, as well as the inevitable slot machines. The casino might be a way to pass a few evening hours in Salzburg, if only for the sake of the view from the top.

You must take your passport because they're very strict about this—no exceptions are allowed. Frankly, if you don't speak German it may be difficult to follow the action. The casino is open from 7 p.m. to 2 a.m. weekdays, with late closings of 4 a.m. on Saturday and Sunday. In exchange for an entrance fee of 130 AS ($6.92), the management will give you gaming tokens worth 150 AS ($7.98).

Casino Fallenegger, 14 Bayerhamerstrasse (tel. 71-1-69), at George Town, is a wide-ranging entertainment complex on the northeast bank of the Salzach River. Its facilities include a summertime athletic complex, seven outdoor tennis courts, and an inviting collection of sun terraces with waiter service. Also on the premises are two restaurants, a disco, two indoor tennis courts, a sauna, and several bars. You'll enter the site through a central courtyard, which is closed on one side by shrubbery and a rustic post-and-lintel construction capped with a sign that looks like something from the American Southwest.

One of the bars has a forest-green decor, Oriental rugs, and a pleasantly masculine well-appointed ambience of green leather and polished wood. Other places to have a drink overlook the indoor tennis courts. Drinks are also served in a pine-walled billiard room, where the upper walls are covered in romantically patterned wallpaper. Something called the Zirbenstube serves gutbürgerlich food in a rustic, pleasantly woodsy atmosphere, while another restaurant has a high wood-covered ceiling, Oriental rugs, and an inviting bar area. Drinks throughout the complex range from 40 AS ($2.13) to 80 AS ($4.26), while meals in the restaurant go from 250 AS ($13.30) to 400 AS ($21.28).

A rustic disco (the Casino-Alm) is one of the oldest surviving ones in Salzburg, founded in 1955. Its cozily rustic format of sloped ceilings and open fireplaces sometimes gets crowded in the evening. Drinks cost from 70 AS ($3.72) to 105 AS ($5.59), and it's open every day except Sunday from 9 p.m. to 3 a.m. You'll find adjoining rooms and offshoot areas attached to many of the places described.

A BEER GARDEN: Casinos not for you? My recommendation for one of the most enjoyable and authentic evenings in Salzburg is to pay a gemütlich visit to the **Augustiner Bräustüble,** 4-6 Augustinergasse (tel. 3-12-46), the most famous beer gardens in Salzburg. Augustinian fathers run the place, and in winter guests retreat inside to one of several large beer halls, but in fair weather the beer-drinking fraternity spills out into the leafy chestnut garden to "taste the brew." The brew, incidentally, is excellent, and it's served daily from 3 to 11 p.m. Don't get the impression that this is some gloomy monk's den either. The activity gets loud and raucous, especially when the young men from Munich invade on their summer tours south from neighboring Bavaria. The very fine brew goes for only 30 AS ($1.60) a mug. This place has been known to squeeze in some 2200 beer-drinkers on the busiest night ever recorded. If you want, some cold snacks are available, but beer is king here.

7. Practical Facts

USEFUL INFORMATION: The **City Tourist Office** is at 7 Auerspergstrasse (tel. 74-6-20 or 71-5-11). The **Land Tourist Office,** where you can get information on the Land Salzburg province, is at 1 Mozartplatz, opposite the Mozart monument (tel. 41-5-61).

You'll find the main **railway station** at 17 Südtiroler Platz (tel. 70-5-51). **Flughafen Salzburg,** the airport, is at 95 Innsbrucken Bundestrasse (tel. 45-3-23).

Information on various problems or answers to **emergency** needs are available by telephone as follows: police—133; fire—122; ambulance—144. The **Medical Emergency Center,** at 8a Paris-Lodron-Strasse (tel. 75-3-50), is open from 7 a.m. Saturday to 7 a.m. Monday and on public holidays.

For information on medical **doctors, specialists, and dentists,** call Ärztekammer für Salzburg, 2 Schrannengasse (tel. 71-3-72 or 71-3-28); Österr. Dentistenkammer, 22 Bergstrasse (tel. 73-9-06).

Drugstores are open Monday to Friday from 8 a.m. to 12:30 p.m. and from 2:30 to 6 p.m. on Saturday from 8 a.m. to noon. For night or Sunday service, shops display a sign giving the address of the nearest pharmacy open.

Banks are open Monday to Friday from 8 a.m. to noon and from 2 to 4:30 p.m. Money can be changed at the main railway station daily from 7 a.m. to 10 p.m. and at the airport from 9 a.m. to 4 p.m.

The **American Express** office, 5 Mozartplatz (tel. 42-5-01), is open Monday to Friday from 9 a.m. to 5:30 p.m., on Saturday from 9 a.m. to noon.

The main **post office** is at 9 Residenzplatz (tel. 44-1-21). The post office at the main railway station is open all year 24 hours a day.

If you need help from the **U.S. Consul,** you'll find the Consular Agency of the United States of America at 67 Gaisbergstrasse (tel. 22-9-05), open Monday to Friday from 9 a.m. to noon.

Lost something? Try the Police Headquarters and **Lost Property Office,** 1 Churfürststrasse (tel. 44-5-57).

Parking: To park downtown, try the City Center parking facility in Mönchsberg, open day and night. The cost is about 90 AS ($4.79). On the right bank there's the Mirabell car park on Mirabellplatz, open from 7 a.m. to midnight. The Raiffersen facility, 13-15 Schwarzstrasse, keeps the same hours as Mirabell. There are attended car-parking facilities at Hellbrunn, Franz-Josef-Kai, Glockingasse, and the airport.

Car breakdown service needed? Try SAMTC (Salzburg Automobile Service), 102 Alpenstrasse (tel. 20-5-01/24), 6 a.m. to 8 p.m. daily; or ARBÖ (Motorists Association), 9 Münchner Bundesstrasse (tel. 33-6-01), 6:30 a.m. to 7 p.m. daily.

If you need to wash clothes, you'll find **"laundrettes"** available: Constructa, 10 Kaiserschutzenstrasse, opposite the main railway station (tel. 76-2-53); and Norge, 16 Paris-Lodron-Strasse (tel. 76-3-81).

TRANSPORTATION: **City buses:** A quick, comfortable service is provided through the center of the city from the Nonntal car park to Sigmundsplatz, the city center car park. Fares are 9 AS (48¢) for one ride for an adult, 4 AS (21¢) for a child, and an additional 4 AS (21¢) per bag. You can purchase a ten-ride ticket at 70 AS ($3.72) for an adult, 35 AS ($1.86) for a child. A five-ride ticket is sold at 35 AS ($1.86) for an adult, 17.50 AS (93¢) for a child.

These reduced-fare tickets may be purchased at the local railway station (opposite the main railway station), at the ticket counter of the cable train up to Hohensalzburg Fortress, from conductors of the lift to Mönchsberg, and in 91 tobacco shops in the city which are specially marked.

For **information** on all bus transportation, telephone 71-2-10. *Be warned:* Buses stop running at 11 p.m.

Taxis: You'll find taxi ranks scattered at key points all over the city center and in the suburbs. Salzburg Funktaxi-Vereinigung (radio taxis) office is at 27 Rainerstrasse (tel. 76-1-11). To order a taxi in advance, telephone 74-4-00. Taxi fares are high.

Horse-drawn cabs (fiacres): At Residenzplatz. Four persons pay 240 AS ($12.77) for a half-hour ride, 460 AS ($24.47) for an hour's jaunt.

TOURS: A **City Sightseeing Tour** is offered daily at 9:30 a.m., 11 a.m., noon, and 3 p.m. from Mirabellplatz, taking about two hours and costing 140 AS ($7.45). This tour highlights both the old and modern parts of the city, beginning with Mirabell Palace, passing the Congress Hall, Mozarteum, and Landestheater. You cross the main bridge to the left bank of the Salzach River and go past the oldest bakery, the Horse Pond, the Festival Hall, St. Peter's Church, the Salzburg Cathedral, the Residenz, and on to Hellbrunn Palace where you're given a guided tour through the trick fountains garden.

You must take your passport along for the afternoon **excursion to Berchtesgaden and Königsee.** The trip, beginning daily at 2 p.m. and returning about 6 p.m. from April 1 to October 31, costs 170 AS ($9.04). You leave from Mirabellplatz and tour neighboring Bavaria, going past Hellbrunn and Anif Palaces en route to Hintereck (3000 feet), from which you have a good view of Hitler's "Eagle's Nest." The guide explains matters of interest about Der Fuhrer's aerie. The tour takes you down to Königsee where you can make a brief cruise on the lake if you wish. Next you go to Berchtesgaden, formerly a salt-mining town and now a popular summer resort, before returning to Salzburg.

Another interesting half-day trip is an afternoon **excursion to the lake district, Salzkammergut,** which leaves Mirabellplatz daily at 2 p.m. from April 1 to October 31, returning around 6 p.m. The cost is 170 AS ($9.04).

You're driven through the outskirts of Salzburg, passing the pilgrimage church of Maria Plain and going to Mondsee, warmest of the lakes in the Salzkammergut area, and into Upper Austria. You stop for tea at the celebrated White Horse Inn in the market town of St. Wolfgang, also visiting the 15th-century church there. This scenic tour brings you back to Salzburg via the summer resort of Ruschl.

A *Sound of Music Tour* leaves from the American Express office, 5 Mozartplatz (tel. 42-5-01), daily except Sunday all year, at 9:30 a.m. and 2:30 p.m., costing 200 AS ($10.64) and lasting three hours. The tour revitalizes the celebrated movie **The Sound of Music,** which shows how the Trapp family escaped from Austria when the Nazis took over, making their way to the United States. On this tour you're shown palaces, squares, and other settings that were used in the film.

Another, slightly longer **Mountain Picnic Tour,** arranged by Bob's Special Tours, 21 Schiesstattstrasse (tel. 98-33-77), provides a lot for your money. For just 200 AS ($10.64), plus your lunch cost (see below), from mid-May through September you can be picked up at your hotel or pension free, in time to leave Salzburg on the tour at 9 a.m. or 2 p.m. You'll be returned after about four hours either to the old town (Neutor) or the main railway station. The trip takes you past the major *Sound of Music* sites, including Schloss Leopoldskron, through the Bavarian Alps for a one-hour stop at Berchtesgaden, where you will get to enjoy an indoor or outdoor concert (depending on the weather). You'll go to remote, peaceful Untersberg Nature Park.

Participation in the picnic is optional, but for only 30 AS ($1.60) you get a variety of cheese and cold cuts, fresh vegetables and fruit, and dark farmer's bread, with lemon tea. Picnic time is at noon for the morning tour, at 5 p.m. for the afternoon trek. If the weather is inclement, you have lunch for 30 AS ($1.60) at a cozy mountain inn.

On the tour route are Anif, the West German border, Marktschellenberg, Berchtesgaden, Bischofswiesen, Bayerisch Gmain, and Grossgmain. You must take your passport on this tour.

You can make reservations for the Mountain Picnic Tour at the reception desk of your hotel or pension or at ticket office Polzer, 4 Residenzplatz; Salzburger Landesreisebüro, 13 Schwarzstrasse; or Neubaur travel and ticket office, 14 Getreidegasse in the arcade.

There are numerous other tour possibilities, including full-day excursions to Grossglockner Glacier and other points of interest, but a shorter one I think you might enjoy is a **Tour of the Salt Mines,** offered Monday, Wednesday, and Saturday from June 1 to September 15, leaving Mirabellplatz at 8:30 a.m. and returning about noon. You must have your passport with you.

You go through the Salzach Valley and cross the West German border at Hangender Stein into Bavaria. The route follows the Königsee Ache Valley, and you get a unique view of the Hoher Göll and Watzmann Mountains. To enter the old salt mine, you put on miner's garb and board the mine tramway. About 700 yards into the mountain, you see how the salt—the "white gold" that was the economic mainstay of this area for centuries—was extracted. After you cross the underground salt lake, you take a chute and then continue back to daylight by tram.

Chapter VIII

LAND SALZBURG

1. Badgastein
2. Bad Hofgastein
3. The Pongau
4. The Tennengau
5. The Pinzgau
6. The Grossglockner Road
7. Zell am See
8. The Flachgau
9. The Lungau

THE GEOGRAPHIC BORDERS of Land Salzburg may appear to be a fantasy—the work of a mapmaker gone haywire—but actually the boundaries of this lofty province in the high Alps follow the dictates of Mother Nature. Craggy mountains, deep valleys, winding rivers, lakes, and rolling foothills, plus a little political expediency, all had their effect on the cartographers' pens. This Bundesland (state, or province) of Austria takes in some 2762 square miles. It's known for its beautiful waterfalls, including the Krimml Falls, the most important cataracts in the eastern Alps.

This is a land of both summer and winter sports, with such celebrated spas as Badgastein and such renowned ski resorts as Zell am See, Kaprun, and Saalbach. You can select resorts right on the lakeside or else mountain hotels at celestial levels. You'll be better suited to the activities of this province if you're athletic.

Instead of staying in Salzburg, especially during the crowded, hotel-scarce months of festival time, you might prefer to anchor into one of the resorts described below and commute to the province's capital city. You'll find the prices far cheaper and the living much easier if you don't mind the drive. (You won't necessarily have to go into the city *every* day.)

Accommodations are wide ranging. If you want deluxe, you'll find it. If you want a mountain hut or just a *zimmer* (room) in one of the local houses—usually perched in some idyllic spot—these are available too. A few castle hotels, some of the finest accommodations in Austria, are found in Land Salzburg, to suit those who have traditional and romantic tastes and don't always demand the latest in plumbing fixtures.

The terrain directly around Salzburg is flat, but most of Land Salzburg is mountainous. Always inquire about local weather conditions before embarking for a day's sightseeing, particularly if you're going to be traversing one of those lofty alpine highways. The highest mountain range in Austria, the Hohe Tauern, lies on the southern fringe of Land Salzburg.

Because many of the alpine highways are feats of engineering, requiring enormous investment of capital and paralyzingly expensive upkeep, tolls are charged. They're not excessive, but are vital to keeping some scenic splendors open to the public.

Of course, Land Salzburg is a skier's paradise. The season begins about ten days before Christmas and usually lasts until Easter or beyond, depending on snow conditions. Skiing on some of the lofty plateaus is possible all year long.

Kaprun, Saalbach, and Zell am See are celebrated resorts, long established *and* expensive. However, in the true spirit of the *Dollarwise* guides, I've sought out less familiar and even undiscovered places—many known only to the Austrians and an occasional German tourist—for this book. Many establishments we'll visit, particularly the smaller, off-the-beaten-track resorts, are making their debut in a guide (in any language).

Long cut off from the rest of the world but now accessible because of modern engineering achievements, some of the sections of Land Salzburg still cling tenaciously to their traditions. Old costumes and folklore still flourish in the province, although who can say whether the present generation—heavily influenced by U.S. styles, music, or whatever—will want to keep the traditional ways alive into the next century?

The quickest way to reach the province of Land Salzburg is to fly into Salzburg, then go by train, bus, or private car to one of the resorts. If you're really in a hurry, you can take an air taxi from the capital to either Zell am See or Badgastein.

Many excursions leave from Salzburg and go into Land Salzburg, but frankly I think it's much more fun if you do it on your own. Most of the people involved in tourist services speak English, and you can travel in relative security and comfort, perhaps making discoveries of your own. You might even prefer to take a Postal Bus which goes to *all* regions, even if you don't have a private car.

Of course, during your tour of Land Salzburg, you can easily stray toward the West German frontier. In many places you'll be very near the border, and in fact in your exploration you might have to cross that border once or twice. That should pose no problem. Often, if you don't look suspicious, the border guards will wave you across without even looking at your passport.

One of the most interesting sections to explore in west-central Austria is the Salzkammergut lake country. This is a narrow-waisted corridor in Land Salzburg between Bavaria and Upper Austria. Parts of it will be explored in other sections of this guide. Essentially, it's a land for those who like clear alpine air and blue mountain lakes, the country of *The Sound of Music.*

Salzkammergut, incidentally, means "domain of the salt office." Many parts of the area grew rich from mining salt—and also gold.

1. Badgastein

The premier spa of Austria and one of the great spa towns of Europe—that's Badgastein. The local tourist industry is said to have been founded by Frederick, Duke of Styria, who came here in the 15th century for treatment of a gangrenous wound. The duke was healed, and the word spread. Badgastein had made its way onto the medieval tourist map.

In more modern times, royalty and aristocrats put it back on the spa map when they flocked here around the turn of the century to "take the waters." And good waters they are—radioactive springs with healing properties. The curative effect of Badgastein's springs is not only due to their natural heat from deep under the earth but also to the radium emanation called radon.

Badgastein lies on the north slope of the Tauern massif in one of the most dramatically beautiful spots in all of Austria. The spa town climbs steep hillsides split by the foaming waters of the tumbling Gasteiner Ache. Hotels, many with water piped in directly from the Ache, adorn the steep slopes formed by the cascading waterfall. The spa's indoor swimming pool is carved into a rock filled with the radon waters.

With its pristine alpine air, skiing equaling that of St. Moritz in Switzerland, 18 hot springs for thermal hydrotherapy, and a mountain tunnel which has been called "the world's only natural giant sauna," Badgastein is considered by many people to be the pinnacle of mountain spa resorts.

Those who want to "take the cure" in the natural sauna go to **Böckstein,** two miles to the south, where the thermal galleries (underground passageways) are in an abandoned goldmine. A small train takes those seeking treatment to the various chambers.

Badgastein began its resort existence as a summer retreat, but is now also a center for winter sports. It contains the finest hotels in Land Salzburg province, and a big convention center attracts large crowds from many places.

Besides the delightful natural scenery of the town and its environs, you can see the **Nikolauskirche,** a 15th-century church with well-preserved Gothic frescoes, a late Gothic stone pulpit, and baroque altars and tombs.

In summer there are things to do other than swimming in thermal baths or taking advantage of concomitant activities. There are saunas, massages, gymnastics, and sunning in the solarium. You can go golfing (on a nine-hole course), play tennis, ride horseback, go on mountain outings, or make excursions, perhaps in a fiacre (horse-drawn trap). Cableways and chair lifts (see below) are not only for winter sports crowds. In summer they'll take you to places from which you can view the magnificent world of the Hohe Tauern.

There's quite a lot of evening entertainment in Badgastein, both in summer and in winter, with cabaret, theater, folkloric events, and other activities.

In winter, however, most visitors are drawn here for the fine skiing possibilities, with three principal areas for skiers, where world championships and world-cup races are held. In 1958 Graukogel, one of the main areas, was the site of the world championships for skiers.

Graukogel (7330 feet), to the east of the valley, is reached by bus from Badgastein. A chair lift takes skiers to the halfway station, from which they go the rest of the way by drag lift. Expert European skiers prefer these slopes in the afternoon.

On the west side of the valley rises **Stubnerkogel** (7380 feet), reached by a four-seat gondola. However, it takes a chair lift and a couple of drag lifts to reach the top station.

Kreuzkogel (8800 feet) is at **Sportgastein,** which lies five miles up the valley to the south of the village of Böckstein, site of the tunnel sauna mentioned above. It's about a 20-minute bus ride from the heart of

Badgastein. A chair lift will take you to the halfway station, with a drag lift taking you on up to Kreuzkogel's top station. Sportgastein offers high-altitude bowl skiing. Besides the well-equipped skiing facilities here, including cross-country runs, you can also enjoy indoor horseback riding or trekking, indoor tennis on sandy courts, alpine curling, ice skating, and walks on beautiful winter paths away from traffic.

UPPER BRACKET HOTELS: **Grand Hotel de l'Europe** (tel. 3337). Even though it was opened in 1906, it wasn't completed until three years later, which was probably the time it took to finish the marble columns and majestic symmetrical facade. Emperor Franz Joseph and Wilhelm II came here often, making it one of the leading hotels of Badgastein until its decline during the Russian occupation and the years that followed.

It was eventually closed in 1969, but on New Year's Eve of 1982, Liza Minelli reopened the glamorously renovated hotel with a gala act that's still talked about in the region. Today the hotel is outfitted with elegant velvet walls, masses of crystal chandeliers, and dozens of original paintings by Austrian artists. The Wiener Saal is filled with art nouveau murals and cuisine prepared by the well-known chef, Jörg Wörther.

A more rustic restaurant, the Ritterstüberl, has stained-glass windows and well-prepared food. A Biedermeier building nearby offers guest apartments and another restaurant, the Vinothek, in the 16th-century cellars below ground level. Singles range from 950 AS ($50.54) to 1900 AS ($101.08), while doubles go from 1300 AS ($69.16) to 2450 AS ($130.34), with breakfast included. Children under 12 stay free in their parents' room.

Hotel Elisabethpark (tel. 2551). The ceilings of this hotel are as varied and unusual as anything else you are likely to find in Austria. They include sections covered with heavily textured knotty pine as well as rooms crowned with Moorish patterns of geometric greens and reds. One of the sitting rooms has a white ceiling with iridescent gray-blue wallpaper and elegant marble detailing around the windows. The public rooms stretch on and on, which is not surprising since this hotel is a vast, sprawling collection of buildings, with a white exterior, lots of balconies, and a never-ending series of hallways that are often decorated with unusual paintings, hunting trophies, and regional antiques. A thermally heated swimming pool on the premises, a sauna, and a host of massage therapies are part of the health facilities here. In well-furnished rooms, summertime tariffs range from 850 AS ($45.22) to 1300 AS ($69.16) per person, while wintertime rates go from 850 AS ($45.22) to 1500 AS ($79.80) per person, including full board.

Der Kaiserhof (tel. 2544). You'll discover the yellow facade of this opulent hotel in a woodland setting, a short stroll away from the heart of the spa. This is a sister to the Grand Hotel. Der Kaiserhof dates from 1909, with all the exterior and interior detailing you'd expect from a fin de siècle palace. It lies along the tree-shaded Kaiser-Wilhelm II Promenade, named after the German emperor who loved to stroll along here with his entourage.

The 76 rooms are individually decorated with period furniture and their own private baths. Some of them also contain private balconies, and even the ones that don't have windows big enough to take in a panoramic sweep of the Gasteiner Valley and the mountains beyond.

In addition to the grand salons, the hotel has a cluster of tiny sitting rooms, each with a distinctive character, usually with overstuffed chairs, select antiques (some of them with imperial associations), and high ceilings. The excellent food served in the deluxe dining room includes both Viennese cookery and international specialties. Singles range from 1150 AS ($61.18) to 1500 AS ($79.80), while doubles go between 1130 AS ($60.12) and 1400 AS ($74.48) per person, with full board included. Prices depend on the season, of course.

Parkhotel Bellevue (tel. 2571) offers a vast expanse of covered balconies turned toward the most scenic part of the nearby mountains. Viewed from the downhill side, it looks like a glittering collection of windows and extensions, with a generous covering of ivy over the foundations of many of them. The hotel includes a 400-year-old alpine hut near the ski slopes, with a rustic bar area and a smoke bonnet supported by carved wooden posts. In the main building an elegant series of public rooms is colorfully and tastefully filled with Oriental rugs, painted ceilings, and comfortable niches.

The bedrooms are spacious, well furnished, and sunny, usually with big balconies and beautiful lighting fixtures. An American-style bar offers live music, while an indoor thermal swimming pool is graced with copies of ancient Roman sculptures. A full range of massage therapies are available for an additional fee. Per-person rates, based on double occupancy, range from 750 AS ($39.90) to 1150 AS ($61.18) per day, with full board included, the tariffs depending on the season and the plumbing. Residents of single rooms pay an additional supplement of 100 AS ($5.32) per day. Prices are slightly higher between December 20 and January 6.

Hotel Weismayr (tel. 2594) sits prominently in the center of town, rising grandly in a series of milk-white stories, each embellished with neoclassical ornamentation. The roof is fashioned of green copper, while the street level has been modernized to include cafés and kiosks. The main sitting room is a blend of browns and reds, with Oriental rugs, comfortable settees, wing chairs, and high ceilings. The elegant high-ceilinged dining room is decorated in shades of blue and white. A terrace café is dotted with blue parasols and verdant plants, with a sunny exposure that might be an ideal place for a midday coffee. Well-furnished singles range between 700 AS ($37.24) and 800 AS ($42.56), while doubles cost between 600 AS ($31.92) and 700 AS ($37.24) per person daily. The hotel is sometimes closed during part of April and May and for all of November.

Hotel Wildbad (tel. 2443) stands out from the collection of buildings around it because of its dark-yellow facade and its flat-roofed construction of big windows and prominent balconies. Views from the wood-detailed bedrooms usually offer splendid vistas of the valley. The public rooms are pleasant and up to date. On the premises you'll find a sauna and a range of physical therapy services, as well as a terrace sundeck with chaise longues and café tables. In the center of the village, close to the indoor thermal pools and the ski lifts, the hotel charges between 500 AS ($26.60) and 710 AS ($37.77) in a single and between 590 AS ($31.39) and 675 AS ($35.91) per person in a double, with full board included.

Hotel Habsburgerhof, Kaiser-Wilhelm-Promenade (tel. 2561) is a comfortable hotel built in 1964 on a sunny hillside somewhat removed from the center of town. Each of the contemporary bedrooms faces southwest, and each one has a wood-covered private balcony with a view of the valley and the resort. Inside you'll find a heated swimming pool, a sauna, a flowered café terrace, and an elegantly modern panoramic dining room. The immaculately clean bedrooms rent for 670 AS ($35.64) to 880 AS

($46.82) in a single and between 1180 AS ($62.78) and 1650 AS ($87.78) in a double. Half or full board is available for an extra 180 AS ($9.58) to 240 AS ($12.77) per person daily.

MIDDLE-BRACKET HOTELS: **Hotel Salzburgerhof** (tel. 2037) sits amid towering pine trees on a rise above the rest of the spa town. It looks like a 19th-century balconied building with a later series of stories added on top, one of which holds an indoor swimming pool. Much of the interior, including the reception area and bar, is covered with paneling and small accents of vivid color. Anny and Helmut Lercher, the owners, charge between 600 AS ($31.92) and 830 AS ($44.17) per person, with half board included, depending on the season. The hotel is closed between October 1 and December 17.

Hotel Straubinger (tel. 2012) is a 360-year-old traditional hotel in the center of town where Franz Joseph, the emperor, used to stay. Inside you'll find an American bar, two dining rooms, a sun terrace, a reading room with a small library, and a massage service. The food is well prepared, and the service, directed by Karl-Michael Rödhamer, is friendly and professional. In well-furnished rooms, singles range from 500 AS ($26.60) to 770 AS ($40.96), while doubles cost between 960 AS ($51.07) and 1440 AS ($76.61), with full board included.

Kurhotel Miramonte (tel. 2377) sits on the landscaped side of an alpine hill, with a panoramic view of the valley from the hotel's downhill side. It's surrounded with wooden balconies in their full natural grain, which contrasts prettily with the white walls of the superstructure. A big terrace has sun umbrellas jutting up from the extended roof of the second floor. Inside, the public rooms are elegantly simple, with Oriental rugs that cover even the tile floors of the rustic bar and weinstube area. Sauna, massage services, and hydrotherapy services are available for an additional fee. Singles range from 580 AS ($30.87) to 840 AS ($44.69), depending on the plumbing and the season, while doubles (all of which contain private bath) cost between 680 AS ($36.18) and 840 AS ($44.69) per person daily, including full board.

Hotel Grüner Baum (tel. 25160) is a complex of six chalet-style buildings surrounding a grassy area in the Kötschach Valley on the outskirts of Badgastein. The oldest building has, during its long history, offered hospitality to Kaiser Wilhelm and to the Empress Elisabeth, the former Shah of Iran, and Arturo Toscanini, Arthur Schopenhauer, Charles Laughton, and King Ibn Saud. The oldest parts of the building are exquisitely crafted of local woods, sometimes with charmingly elaborate regional carving, with hunting trophies beneath the beamed ceilings.

The hotel sits at the starting point for four kilometers of cross-country ski trails, and will rent equipment to guests. It has a beginner's slope nearby, with a T-bar lift, as well as facilities for bowling, curling, shooting, and boccia, plus both indoor and outdoor heated swimming pools. There's a dancing bar as well as organized weekly activities.

The bedrooms are cozily rustic, with wood paneling and sometimes a recessed sleeping alcove in some of the singles. With full board included, per-person prices, based on double occupancy, range from 540 AS ($28.73) to 1100 AS ($58.52), depending on the season and the plumbing. The supplement for occupants of a single ranges between 25 AS ($1.33) and 60 AS ($3.19), again depending on the plumbing and the season.

Hotel Germania (tel. 2247) is a six-story, high-ceilinged hotel set onto a hillside with a view of the valley. Its cream-colored salons are filled with cozy easy chairs and Oriental rugs, while its bar and dining area are outfitted in an inviting series of low-slung chairs and hanging contemporary lamps. A more formal dining room has about the biggest arched windows in Badgastein, gilt and crystal chandeliers, and clean white napery. An indoor swimming pool is on the premises. Singles range from 420 AS ($22.34) to 960 AS ($51.07), while doubles cost between 400 AS ($21.28) and 880 AS ($46.82) per person, with full board included.

Hotel Savoy (tel. 2588) is a roadside hotel with dramatic terraces and big expanses of glass covering some of the windows. Inside is a covered swimming pool, a sauna, and a graceful series of public rooms with high ceilings, crystal chandeliers, and attractive antiques. Some of the floors have marble coverings, others contain Oriental rugs, and most of the rooms are tastefully filled with pleasing fabrics and colors. Tennis courts are nearby. With full board included, singles range from 620 AS ($32.98) to 720 AS ($38.30), while doubles go from 510 AS ($27.13) to 720 AS ($38.30) per person, depending on the season.

Hotel Krone (tel. 2330) is designed like an Italian villa, with arched windows on the ground floor and French windows opening onto iron balconies on the front, sides, and back. The high-ceilinged interior alternates light-grained paneling with white plaster walls, and a refreshing series of colors are used in the pink- and green-accented dining room. Pleasantly furnished singles range from 360 AS ($19.15) to 420 AS ($22.34), from 360 AS ($19.15) to 390 AS ($20.75) per person in a double.

Schillerhof (tel. 2581) sits in a clearing on the side of a forested hill above Badgastein. Its symmetrical construction encompasses wings on either side of the main section, which is covered with horizontal rows of wooden balconies. The interior has big windows, warmly tinted public rooms, and a panoramic restaurant. An outdoor swimming pool is flanked with chiseled stone walls, while the bedrooms are sometimes covered with light-grained planking. With half board included, per-person rates in a double range upward from 560 AS ($29.79) in a room with bath, and from 440 AS ($23.41) in units without bath. Residents of singles pay an additional supplement of between 60 AS ($3.19) and 120 AS ($6.38) per day, depending on the plumbing.

Meranhaus (tel. 2328). An engraving in the Biedermeier-furnished lobby shows a view of the hotel shortly after it was built as a summer retreat in 1828 for Archduke Johann. Today the hotel has been expanded, elongated, and enlarged, although much of the original charm remains. My favorite room is the pine-covered sitting salon, with a green ceramic stove, a vivid Oriental rug, and round-framed portraits. Several of the bedrooms are filled with delicate Victorian-era chairs and good settees and dressers, some of which, if they could talk, would remember the visit of Empress Elisabeth during the summer of 1886. The hotel is closed from early October till just before Christmas and during most of April. Per-person rates for rooms with private bath range from 600 AS ($31.92) to 700 AS ($37.24), depending on the season, although accommodations without bath are cheaper.

BUDGET HOTELS: **Hotel Mozart** (tel. 2686) is an unusual hotel designed in the 19th century with stone half-rounded projections extending toward the front, a long veranda on the ground floor, and a gabled mansard roof on top of which someone later added an additional story. The inside has beautifully patterned Oriental rugs in muted colors covering the floor of the wood-paneled lobby area, as well as crystal chandeliers hanging from the detailed plaster ceiling. Even the reception desk has a band of intricately carved hardwood, just above a pen-and-ink illustration of a medieval Austrian city. Some of the 70 comfortably furnished rooms have private bath, although there are thermally heated baths on each floor, costing 70 AS ($3.72) each time you use one. Bed and breakfast ranges from 185 AS ($9.84) to 320 AS ($17.02) per person, depending on the plumbing and season.

Kurhaus Alpenblick (tel. 2087) is a beige and wood-covered chalet with a wing stretching off to one side containing a comfortable collection of balconied bedrooms. These are decorated in an eclectic collection of furniture, which includes Oriental rugs, heavy simple wooden headboards, richly upholstered chairs, and big windows with views of the mountains. In the timbered and beamed dining room, well-prepared meals are served by a friendly staff. A swimming pool is outside on the grounds near a small mountain stream. The 58 rooms rent for between 300 AS ($15.96) and 525 AS ($27.93) in a single, and for 300 AS ($15.96) to 500 AS ($26.60) per person in a double, with breakfast included, tariffs depending on the season and plumbing.

Kurhaus Orania (tel. 2124) is a comfortable and pleasant family-run stucco and wood chalet. It has a large yellow-and-black sign announcing its presence two minutes away from the train station. The interior is a cozy combination of exposed wood, clean napery, rustic artifacts, and contrasting patterns of brightly colored fabrics. The unpretentious bedrooms range from 190 AS ($10.11) to 260 AS ($13.83), depending on the season and the plumbing. Half and full board are available for an additional 85 AS ($4.52) and 170 AS ($9.04) respectively. The Röck family are your congenial hosts.

Ullrichshaus Badgastein (tel. 2753) is composed of two futuristic white-walled buildings set in a grassy meadow near a rushing alpine stream. The interior is pleasantly rustic, with gaily striped red and green draperies and carpets, and lots of exposed-wood and wrought-iron detailing. Close to the train station, the hotel has an indoor swimming pool with its own therapy center, and in addition to the cozy rooms, a series of apartments with kitchenettes. Accommodations for one person (the most expensive of which contain kitchens) range from 335 AS ($17.82) to 360 AS ($19.15), while units for two persons cost from 480 AS ($25.54) to 600 AS ($31.92). An extra bed can be set up in many of the doubles or apartments for another 120 AS ($6.38) per day. A pleasant restaurant is in the main building in case you don't feel like cooking.

Haus Gerke (tel. 2378) is a graceful old chalet-style hotel, with a hip-roofed upper section covered with green and white shutters and weathered planking, plus a lower section embellished with yellow stucco and gray masonry. The inside is filled with Oriental rugs, high ceilings with hanging painted chandeliers, marble fireplaces, and oil paintings. The bedrooms have 1950s-style wood-grained furniture and comfortable beds, some of which are recessed into curtained sleeping compartments. Singles range from 230 AS ($12.24) to 300 AS ($15.96), while doubles cost between 410 AS ($21.81) and 610 AS ($32.45), depending on the plumbing and the season. Breakfast is included in the price.

THE LEADING CAFÉ: **Restaurant Gastein,** in the Kongresshaus (tel. 2982), is a popular café designed in a decor that's best called international. Except for the language of the menu, you'll find it easy to forget where you are, since a place this modern could as easily be an upper-class establishment in Sydney, New York, or South Africa. Still, it's a relaxing place for a midafternoon cup of coffee and perhaps a pastry or ice cream. Coffee costs from 20 AS ($1.06) to 30 AS ($1.60), with pastries beginning at 30 AS ($1.60). It's open all day every day of the week.

AFTER DARK: The center of nightlife—and the chicest spot to be seen at the spa and winter sports center—is the **Spiel-Casino Badgastein** (tel. 21-21). Here you can play roulette, baccarat, and blackjack, but you'll need a passport to get in. The summer season lasts from June 1 until mid-September, and the winter season is from Christmas until the end of January. The casino opens daily at 5 p.m.

At the height of the season, most of the clubs charge about 75 AS ($3.99) for a drink.

One of the most popular discos in town is at the already-recommended **Hotel Weissmayr.** This place attracts a generally young and affluent crowd.

Another popular disco, **Mahlhäusl,** is beneath the Hotel Söntgen (tel. 22-35), a three-minute walk from the Cure and Congress Centre. This is an intimate rendezvous point, attracting a young crowd.

If you want more conventional dancing, head for the **Hotel Elisabethpark,** already recommended. This is an elegant nightlife retreat, and most of its patrons are well dressed.

Another elegant choice on the après-ski circuit is the also recommended **Parkhotel Bellevue,** where guests often linger in its alpine tavern, enjoying drinks, candlelight, and an open fire. Its American bar has live music in season, a band playing for dancing couples.

READER'S NIGHTLIFE SELECTIONS: "Nightlife in Badgastein is likely to be unpredictable, depending on the time you're there. Among discos, I prefer **Baders-Blockhaus.** However, if you're seeking an intimate atmosphere with an open fire and amusing companions, try the **Zipfer-Bierstube**" (Loretta Smithey, Charlotte, N.C.).

2. Bad Hofgastein

Lying five miles from Badgastein, halfway to Dorfgastein (coming up), is another resort, Bad Hofgastein (2850 feet), an old established spa and long a rival of Badgastein for the tourist schilling.

Bad Hofgastein is tinier than Badgastein, but it's almost as charming, and in general its hotels are less expensive. The little resort is actually almost a satellite of the larger spa, for the radioactive waters of Badgastein are pumped to its neighbor. Some hardy visitors like to follow a marked footpath between the two towns, the trip taking about 2½ hours. As a resort unit, Badgastein and Bad Hofgastein welcome at least as many visitors as does Salzburg—maybe more.

The **pfarrkirche** (parish church) of this tiny village is late Gothic, dating from the end of the 15th century, although it has a baroque altar. Some sights, such as old houses with turrets, evoke thoughts of the gold-mining days in the Gastein Valley. In the 16th century the nearby goldmines made Bad Hofgastein the rival of Salzburg in wealth. A rich mining family lived at the 15th-century **Weitmoserschlössl,** which has now been converted into a restaurant.

The most popular ski area hereabouts is the **Schlossalm,** which can be reached by mountain railway (board a train in the parking section). Skiers or just plain sightseers are transported to Kitzstein, where a chair lift takes over. Expect long lines of prospective passengers in the height of the season. The Schlossalm area has two chair lifts and eight drag lifts.

Bad Hofgastein, about 55 miles south of Salzburg, is on the town railway and federal road 167 and is served by Postal Buses.

UPPER BRACKET HOTELS: Kur- und Sporthotel Moser (tel. 209), on the main square of town, has sections dating back to the 12th century. You'd never know it from a quick glance at the facade, which is pleasantly balconied with yellow accents above the red street-level awnings. The interior, however, is vaulted and cozy, with lots of old exposed wood, heavy beams, Oriental rugs, and a tapestry. The furnishings are rustic and regional, with lots of homey touches such as racks of pewter above the banquettes of the dining room. The sunny bedrooms rent for 555 AS ($29.53) to 800 AS ($42.56) in a single, while the per-person rates in a double range from 565 AS ($30.06) to 765 AS ($40.70), with full board included. Prices, of course, depend on the season and the plumbing. All doubles contain private baths.

Grand Park Hotel (tel. 356) rises majestically in a contemporary adaptation of a chalet. It's in its own birch-filled park, with a swimming pool and lawn chairs on the grassy lawns around it. The interior is filled with stone and polished-wood accents, plush carpets, and modern touches of bright colors and polished brass, all of which combine for a pleasant feeling of well-being. An indoor pool under a soaring timbered roof is only one of the many sports and health-oriented facilities. Handsomely furnished singles range from 480 AS ($25.54) to 1200 AS ($63.84), while doubles cost between 540 AS ($28.73) and 1250 AS ($66.50) per person with full board included. The hotel is open all year.

Hotel Carinthia (tel. 8374) is a large solid-looking chalet, with flowered balconies on all sides and regional-style painted detailing on the corner mullions and around some of the windows. The interior has elegant and unusual touches, such as brass sheathing above the stone curves of the fireplace, the tucked-away corner bar, and the luminous modern chandeliers in the high-ceilinged dining room. The colors of the spacious bedrooms are coordinated in pleasing combinations such as reddish violet with beiges and browns in a contemporary decor of style and comfort. In addition to the indoor swimming pool the hotel has a wide range of massage and hydrotherapy regimes. Singles range from 700 AS ($37.24) to 780 AS ($41.50), while doubles cost from 630 AS ($33.52) to 720 AS ($38.30) per person, with full board included.

Hotel Palace Gastein (tel. 7150) was constructed in 1967 in a sprawling stone-trimmed design where double sets of black-accented windows alternate repeatedly with recessed balconies. An ornamental pool reflects the lights from the windows of the high-ceilinged covered swimming pool, whose waters are thermally heated. The public rooms stretch on and on in an invitingly contemporary format of straight lines, light-grained paneling, and big sunny windows.

In addition to frequent barbecue parties held on the brick-covered terrace, the manager stages a monthly "candlelight gala," which usually tends to be a lot of fun. Clients will find a free hotel bus making frequent trips to the ski slopes, as well as a free kindergarten supervised by a trained nurse. The cuisine is well prepared as well. Comfortably furnished singles range from 565 AS ($30.06) to 1150 AS ($61.18), while doubles go from 565 AS ($30.06) to 1050 AS ($55.86) per person, with full board included.

Hotel Norica, Bachbauergasse (tel. 8391), is dramatically designed in such a way that the flowered balconies angle themselves directly toward the sun. A spacious sun terrace whose surface area is almost as big as that of the hotel itself is verdantly covered with potted shrubs. A rounded hearth inside illuminates the unusual art objects and striped banquettes of one of the public rooms, while the dining room is carpeted with plush stripes of two shades of violet.

An in-house disco, a curved bar, tennis, and indoor pool, and a wide range of sports offer plenty of distractions. The light-toned bedrooms have wood accents, modern baths, and rent for between 350 AS ($18.62) and 840 AS ($44.69) per person, based on double occupancy, with a supplement of between 95 AS ($5.05) and 180 AS ($9.58) for occupants of single rooms. Breakfast is included in the price, and half board is offered for an additional fee of between 120 AS ($6.38) and 150 AS ($7.98), depending on the season.

MODERATE AND BUDGET HOTELS: **Hotel Sendlhof** (tel. 3510) is a family-run hotel with six big-windowed floors, each surrounded with balconies and potted flowers. An outdoor heated swimming pool lies across the lawn. The interior has heavily recessed rectangular designs in the ceiling's paneling, large windows with attractive pink or red curtains, cozy fireplaces with masonry detailing, and lots of extra touches such as ceramic stoves and painted detailing below some of the massive arches. Management sometimes provides live zither music in the evening.

The bedrooms are elegant and cozy, each of them with lots of exposed wood and a private bath. Singles range from 575 AS ($30.59) to 690 AS ($36.71), while doubles cost between 500 AS ($26.60) and 685 AS ($36.44) per person, with half board included. Most of the units have private balconies. However, for the few that do not the charges range from 460 AS ($24.47) to 575 AS ($30.59) per person, with half board included.

Hotel Astoria (tel. 377) is a generously proportioned five-story building with a simple white and wood-balconied facade and an interior that has been renovated into a contemporary format of streamlined furniture and warmly inviting colors. An indoor swimming pool is encircled with molded tangerine-colored furniture. Per-person rates range from 580 AS ($30.87) to 750 AS ($39.90), depending on the season and the plumbing. Prices include full board.

Kurhaus St. Georg (tel. 500) is approached by a long, curved road that stops in front of the arches of the ground floor. The building is solidly constructed of painted concrete, with recessed balconies, wood trim, big windows, and pleasing proportions, against an alpine backdrop of forested mountains. The comfortable bedrooms each have private baths and balconies, renting for between 490 AS ($26.07) and 700 AS ($37.24), with half board included. Prices are per person per day and depend on the season.

Kurhotel Österreichischer Hof (tel. 2160). One of the many charming aspects about this family-run hotel is the regionally styled portal, which is surrounded with yellow and gold painted detailing, a theme repeated around many of the chalet's windows. A balconied extension with the same detailing stretches out behind. Both sections have the added benefit of angled stone buttresses reaching as high as the second-floor windows. The interior contains a heated pool, a range of massage therapy rooms, warmly tinted public rooms, and simple and attractive bedrooms, many of them with wood paneling. Sometimes they're surprisingly spacious, and often have good views over the valley. Singles range from 430 AS ($22.88) to 700 AS ($37.24), while doubles go from 450 AS ($23.94) to 645 AS ($34.31) per person, depending on the plumbing and season. Half board is included.

Kurhotel Germania, 14 Kurpromenade (tel. 232). Although this is a recently built hotel, it has some beautifully maintained Victorian antiques (including an exquisite collection of armchairs) filling some of the big-windowed public rooms. If your unit has a balcony—and many of the pleasant and sunny bedrooms here do—you'll have a view of the houses and barns of the valley below. The facade of the hotel rises in a symmetrical series of white walls and wooden balconies, with summertime parasols adding accents of color to the white walls. A full range of massage and hydrotherapy services are available inside. With full board included, singles range from 640 AS ($34.05) to 695 AS ($36.97) while per-person prices in a double go from 610 AS ($32.45) to 660 AS ($35.11). Tariffs depend on the plumbing.

Kur- and Sporthotel Alpina, 11-17 Parkstrasse (tel. 84750), looks like a double chalet, with symmetrical rooflines that peak above rows of wooden balconies. The interior is as tasteful and warm as anything you'll find in town, with attractive color schemes of amber and brown. A heavily beamed modern ceiling covers the illuminated waters of the heated indoor swimming pool, while the lobby area is lit with pin spotlights shining from the ceiling beams. The sunny bedrooms rent for between 350 AS ($18.62) and 400 AS ($21.28) in a single and for between 310 AS ($16.49) and 370 AS ($19.68) per person in a double, breakfast included. The hotel is closed between the end of October and the middle of December.

Kurhotel Völserhof, Kurpromenade (tel. 8288), rises five balconied stories above a flowering garden near the edge of town. In summertime the areas above the windows of the second-floor restaurant are covered with masses of red flowers, while the arched windows on the ground floor are surrounded with meticulously painted regional designs. Much of the interior alternates areas of white with full-grained areas of wood, some of which have been embellished with patterns of sky blue, gold, and yellow, especially on some of the ceilings. The city's recreation center is a five-minute walk from the hotel, and the terminus of the funicular is ten minutes away. The Lang family, your hosts, close the hotel from mid-October to mid-December. Doubles rent for around 500 AS ($26.60) to 600 AS ($31.92) per person daily, with breakfast included.

Kurpark Hotel, 17-21 Kurgartenstrasse (tel. 8436), is a wood and stucco alpine-style house discreetly concealed behind the leaves of the trees that grow close around it. The garden terrace is one of the establishment's main social centers on a sunny day. Inside, the public rooms are filled with angular furniture and neutral colors, while the bedrooms tend to be covered with flowered wallpaper and furnished with modern pieces. An annex nearby offers bathless rooms at lower rates. Doubles rent for between 500 AS ($26.60) and 650 AS ($34.58) per person if bathless, and between 615 AS ($32.72) and 780 AS ($41.50) per person with private bath. Full board is included in these prices, and residents of single rooms are charged a supplement of 60 AS ($3.19). Units with balcony require an additional charge of 25 AS ($1.33).

THE LEADING CAFË: **Cafë Weitmoser-Schlössl** (tel. 601) is near the departure point of the Schlossalmbahn, and because of its position on a steep hillside, affords a good view of the valley below. Parts of it date from the 14th century, although today you'll just be grateful for the warmth of the place in winter and for the shaded terrace surrounded by mountain ash trees in summer. Whether you decide to have coffee, tea, snacks, or afternoon schnapps, you'll find a full array of these items, as well as a lot of other clients who seem to sample a bit of everything. Coffee costs between 18 AS (96¢) and 30 AS ($1.60), while pastries range between 30 AS ($1.60) and 40 AS ($2.13). It's closed on Monday.

AFTER DARK: For your big night on the town, you can take a free taxi from Bad Hofgastein to Badgastein to gamble at the **casino,** already recommended here.

Otherwise, you can stay right in Bad Hofgastein, dancing at its discos, enjoying open fires in its taverns, or else dancing more formally at the hotels that import live bands in season. The tourist office will always tell you the latest information about which hotels or clubs are likely to have nightlife at any given time, as schedules and programs fluctuate.

Most drinks cost around 75 AS ($3.99), and no one forces more on you unless you want them.

Among the hotels, one of the best centers for après-ski life is the **Hotel Norica** (see above). You can just drop in for a drink at its bar, or else patronize one of its restaurants, including the Schneckenthurm-Häusl, the Egghaus-Stübl, or the Kitscher Grill. The young at heart will go below to the Vision, a disco. There's also nightly dancing to a band at the **Palace Gastein** (see above).

For your afternoon après-ski drink, I'd suggest the **Café Weitmoserschlössl,** which is installed in the 15th-century castle (already mentioned) that was once the home of a gold-mining family.

READER'S NIGHTLIFE SELECTIONS: "On my last ski vacation, I found that the **Tennistreff,** in addition to its tennis and squash courts, also offers folk singing and, on some nights, jazz. If you're hungry, the waiter will bring you the alpine version of a pizza. If you still like disco, you might also try **Manfred's,** an intimate bar and a tiny dance floor lying near the river. For dancing, you might also try the **Glucknerkeller**" (Ellen Freeport, New York, N.Y.).

3. The Pongau

Badgastein and Bad Hofgastein, already explored, are part of a section of Land Salzburg known as the Pongau. It's one of several parts of an alpine valley called Salzach. The Pongau basin, heart of the Salzach Valley, lies between Werfen and Golling downstream and between Taxenbach and Lend upstream. The Pinzgau section (coming up) of the Salzach Valley is in the southwest.

The Pongau's most frequented tourist route is through the **Gastein Valley,** of which Badgastein and Bad Hofgastein are a part. For many centuries the Gastein Valley has been celebrated for its hot springs, and in more recent times it has also become known as a winter sports center, this phase of activity developing mainly after World War II. As a consequence, many old spas such as Badgastein suddenly find themselves overrun with skiers in winter.

The **Radstädter Tauern** region is the second most popular section of the Pongau. It sprawls across five mountains and four valleys, with a mammoth expanse of skiable terrain from St. Johann to Obertauern. In between, you'll find that Wagrain, Flachau, Altenmarkt, and Radstadt are all well provided with hotels. Unlike in some parts of Austria, you might find a car convenient in the Radstädter Tauern. However, most of it can be reached by lifts and runs.

One of the major attractions of the Pongau to which I'd like to introduce you first is most often visited on day trips from Salzburg. It is the—

EISRIESENWELT: Some 30 miles south of Salzburg by train is the "World of the Ice Giants," the largest known ice caves in Europe. The caves, opening at some 5500 feet up, stretch for about 26 miles, although only a portion of that length is open to the public. You'll see fantastic ice formations at the entrance, extending for half a mile.

To reach the Eisriesenwelt, head for Werfen, a village of no particular distinction except being the center for exploring the ice caves. If you come by train from Salzburg, you can take a taxibus from Werfen's Hauptplatz (main square), going 3½ miles by mountain road to the same point you'll reach if you're traveling in your own car, rising from 1600 feet to 3000 feet. You have to take a cable car to the entrance of the caves, which involves a 15-minute walk along a shady path with stunning views to the lower station. The round-trip cable-car ride costs 60 AS ($3.19) for adults, 30 AS ($1.60) for children to this point.

Tours begin at the Dr. Fritz Oedl Haus at 5141 feet, from which a cable car takes you to the actual entrance for 50 AS ($2.66) for adults, 25 AS ($1.33) for children. Tours take about two hours and cost 55 AS ($2.93) per person for adults, 30 AS ($1.60) for children. Conducted tours are given every hour from May to October from 9:30 a.m. to 4 p.m. In July and August the schedule is accelerated if demand justifies it. For information, phone 0-64-68/248.

Eisriesenwalt is on the western cliffs of the Hochkogel, towering over the Salzach Valley. You can imagine you're in the kingdom of the Ice Queen as you pass through this underground ice wonderland, which looks as if fairies had decorated their frozen precincts, adorning them with icy figures that look almost man-made and with frozen waterfalls. The climax of this chill underworld tour is the spectacular Ice Palace. It's too bad visitors can't explore the entire 26-mile length of the cave, but such a venture is extremely dangerous and cannot be permitted.

Allow about 5½ hours for the entire trip from Werfen and back. Dress warmly, and wear shoes appropriate for hiking.

I recommend making the drive as far up toward the caves as you can go even if you don't want to go underground, as the scenery along the way is truly splendid.

DORFGASTEIN: This pleasant alpine village (2750 feet) in the Gastein Valley is both a winter and a summer resort, its tranquil ambience attracting many who shun the more commercial atmosphere of Badgastein and Bad

Hofgastein. You'll find an assortment of hotels and gasthof-type places here, as well as an open-air swimming pool heated by solar energy.

Dorfgastein is popular with Austrian families who, in winter, can park the small fry all day at a ski kindergarten while the grownups enjoy the ski runs and slopes. In fact the resort has many faithful habitués who resent its increasing popularity.

The village has a **parish church** (*pfarrkirche*) "updated" in the baroque style but originally built in the 14th century.

You can take a bus from the heart of the village to the lower station of the chair lift, the trip taking less than an hour. The lift takes you to Wengeralm, and from there you can go by another lift to Kreuzkogel (6690 feet).

Food and Lodging

Hotel/Restaurant Römerhof (tel. 209) has four floors of well-built wood and stucco, designed like an expanded version of a chalet. Constructed in 1966, it sits near the site of a 12th-century tower which served after 1421 as a shelter for men and horses. The Hasenauer family maintains accommodations considerably more comfortable than those written about in the medieval annals.

The interior is decorated with wood beams, wrought-iron embellishments, and rustic furniture. The exterior walls of the pleasant, wood-paneled, pink-upholstered restaurant are covered with painted floral designs in gold, yellow, and light blue. A public swimming pool and the departure point for the cable cars are each a five-minute walk from the hotel. Per-person rates, with breakfast included, range from 300 AS ($15.96) to 420 AS ($22.34) in a single and from 260 AS ($13.83) to 380 AS ($20.22) in a double. Prices depend on the season and the plumbing.

Hotel Kirchenwirt (tel. 251) is a large, cozy, and tastefully decorated chalet-style hotel a few steps from the village church. Its wood-paneled restaurant can be viewed through the arched stucco windows of the ground floor, while the public rooms are filled with Oriental rugs, comfortable chairs, and a dramatically coffered ceiling.

The bedrooms are spacious and comfortable, often with unusual shapes and many wood accents. The bar area is den-like and intimately rustic, with provincial artifacts hanging from the walls. The building has its own elevator and is maintained by the Köstinger family. Per-person rates range from 325 AS ($17.29) to 350 AS ($18.62), with breakfast included. Prices depend on the season and the plumbing.

Après-Ski

When darkness falls on the slopes, the after-dark circuit starts buzzing. Nightlife (and there is some) is fairly restrained, taking place for the most part in the lounges and bars of the hotels, many of which have open blazing fires.

The most popular place seems to be the **Hotel Kirchenwirt,** already recommended. Its nighttime diversion is the K-Keller, which has an open burning fireplace and dancing to disco music. In season the place becomes very gemütlich.

Also popular is the **Hotel Romenhof,** which was just recommended. It not only has two lounge bars, but two stüberls as well. The Hasenauer family maintains a lively, friendly atmosphere.

The cost of an evening out in Dorfgastein is usually much cheaper than in Badgastein and Bad Hofgastein, with most drinks costing from 65 AS ($3.46).

GOLDEGG: Lying on a small lake dominated by a castle from the 14th century, Goldegg, reached by going through Schwarzach, is about an 18-minute bus ride from St. Veit im Pongau. Schwarzach is at the western end of the Pongau. Goldegg, both a winter and a summer sports resort, is known also for its peat baths.

The castle, once owned by the counts of Galen, now shelters the **Pongau Folk Museum,** where you can see displays of old rural utensils and a collection of tools used in early day occupations. Guided tours are conducted May 1 until the end of September every Thursday at 3, 4, and 5 p.m. and April 30, only one tour a week is conducted, every Thursday at 2 p.m. Adults are charged 15 AS (80¢); children, 8 AS (43¢). For information, phone 81-71.

Food and Lodging

Hotel Gesinger Zur Post (tel. 8103) consists of two country-style buildings, both with flowered balconies and window boxes, plus a pleasant lakeside location with a view of the mountains. The interior is outfitted with painted regional furniture, polished pine paneling, homey detailing, and lots of comfort. Under the rafters of what was probably a barn the hotel has installed a dancing nightclub, complete with hanging lanterns and lots of intimate corners. Raimund and Hertha Gesinger, your congenial hosts, do everything they can to make guests comfortable. The cozy bedrooms are equipped with spacious private baths, and usually have enclosed sleeping compartments behind full-length curtains. Per-person rates, double occupancy, range from 425 AS ($22.61) to 700 AS ($37.24), depending on the season. Occupants of singles pay a supplement of 35 AS ($1.86) daily.

Hotel Zum Bierführer (tel. 8102) is a pleasingly rustic inner-village chalet with elaborate wrought-iron grillwork covering the ground-floor windows and evenly spaced rows of balconies. Inside, the public rooms are covered with a combination of paneling, ornate plaster, and 19th-century memorabilia, while the spacious and sunny bedrooms have hardwood floors and painted regional furniture. On the premises you'll find a sauna and outdoor tennis courts. Per-person rates in double rooms, with half board included, range from 280 AS ($14.90) to 420 AS ($22.34), depending on the season and plumbing. Occupants of singles pay a supplement of 35 AS ($1.86) per day.

Hotel/Pension Neuwirt (tel. 8114) sits on the side of a hill in the center of the village. The approach road to the hotel will take you around the back side of a miniature religious shrine. The ground-floor windows are big enough to let lots of light flood into the public rooms. Many guests sit on a sun terrace built into stone columns above the downhill side of the building. The interior has lots of country-style charm, heavy ceiling beams, and hand-painted murals set into wooden frames carved into naïve patterns. The Mayr family, your hosts, charge between 385 AS ($20.48) and 550 AS ($29.26) per person in a double, depending on the plumbing and the season. These prices include full board. Singles pay a surcharge of 20 AS ($1.06) per day.

Hotel Lärchenhof, 24 Weng (tel. 8169), is pleasantly surrounded with weathered balconies and green lawns. A white-walled extension in back is the only part of this rustic hotel without wood trim. The ground-floor restaurant has lots of exposed light-grained wood and big windows, while elsewhere on the premises is a dancing bar along with a rustic drinking area adorned with cut saplings stripped of their bark and nailed into rustic table dividers. The cozy bedrooms rent for 335 AS ($17.82) to 435 AS ($23.14) per person, depending on the season, with half board included.

Hotel Seehof (tel. 8137) is filled with the kind of rustic artifacts and local painted furniture that many of us could spend weeks looking for in antique shops. It sits on the lake, which reflects the chalet's forest-green shutters and the many flowerpots on the hotel's balconies. The bedrooms are contemporary and warm, often with private balconies and sloping paneled ceilings. The modern baths are tiled in autumnal colors, with wood detailing and big mirrors. An outdoor sun terrace sits under the angle of the house, with red-and-white checked tablecloths and sun parasols. In summer many guests enjoy the private lakeside beach, while in winter the hotel rents ski equipment for the nearby slopes. A sauna is on the premises. Each of the accommodations has its own private bath, renting for between 435 AS ($23.14) and 660 AS ($35.11) per person, depending on the season, with half board included. An in-season disco, filled with a decor of rustic beams and farmer's implements, affords a pleasant place for a drink.

WAGRAIN: At 2750 feet, Wagrain, in the vicinity of Salzburg, lies in a sunny valley amid lush green meadows and forests in summer and fine ski runs in winter. It's the hometown of the poet Karl-Heinrich Waggerl. This tiny resort is in the three-valley ski round point of Flachau-Wagrain-St. Johann, with open skiing ground protected against avalanches.

From mid-December to mid-April some 60 miles of mechanically prepared downhill runs are open, suitable for everybody from beginners to intermediates, and there's a ski school in the area. Three chair lifts and 11 drag lifts are available. The top station that can be reached is at 6600 feet. You can go to Flachau, the neighboring resort, by chair lift.

For nonskiers Wagrain offers rambling trails, tobogganing, folkloric evenings, Austrian curling, and horse-drawn sleigh rides in winter. Summer visitors can use the chair lifts for sightseeing, and they can swim in a heated outdoor pool or take advantage of one of the four tennis courts.

Food and Lodging

Hotel Alpina, 108 Kirchboden (tel. 337), is a white stucco chalet with balconies and a low-lying extension that stretches off down the hillside. One of the public rooms contains a white brick fireplace with a large metallic hood—a pleasant place for a drink if a fire is burning. On the premises is a rustic bar, as well as a sauna and an indoor pool with big glass windows looking out onto the snow-covered hillside. Your hosts, the Wiesbacher family, rent their sunny bedrooms from 575 AS ($30.59) to 865 AS ($46.02) for a single, and between 345 AS ($18.35) and 800 AS ($42.56) per person in a double, with half board included. The hotel is closed from early October until the beginning of December, with special discounts available between early December and Christmas.

Hotel Wagrainerhof (tel. 204). Local residents say that you can tell what time it is by the direction of the shadows that fall from the ornate eaves of this enlarged chalet. You'll enter through a pointed arch into which some craftsman has skillfully inserted a door of patterned brass. Inside you'll find a high-quality series of cozy rooms with thick carpeting, burnished paneling, and unusual art objects sitting in niches. A rustic bar often has live music, while the gemütlich restaurant is filled with homey touches. Finally, the in-house café has standing brass lamps and a cross-beam ceiling. In the center of the village, the hotel is owned by the Rötzer family, who charge from 515 AS ($27.40) to 635 AS ($33.78) per person, with half board included.

Alpengasthof Kirchboden (tel. 202) is a solidly constructed chalet with cutout patterns on its three tiers of balconies, arched windows on its ground floor, and a flowered sun terrace with red and yellow parasols. The interior is covered in many areas with natural-grained wood, while some of the thick beams are reinforced with wrought-iron straps. A fieldstone fireplace is capped with a timbered mantelpiece and a sloping stucco chimney stretching upward. The view encompasses most of the village of Wagrain. With half board included, per-person rates range from 350 AS ($18.62) to 560 AS ($29.79), depending on the season and the exposure. All rooms have private bath.

The adjoining restaurant is excellent. The well-prepared specialties tend to be regional (palatschinken, pariser schnitzel), along with good appetizers and a fine selection of cheese). Fixed-price meals cost from 85 AS ($4.52) to 115 AS ($6.12), while á la carte ranges from 105 AS ($5.59) to 280 AS ($14.90).

Alpenhof Edelweiss (tel. 447) blends gracefully into the sloping hillside on which it sits. It has all the balconies and wood trim you'd expect in a mountain chalet, as well as a raised sun terrace with summertime parasols. About 300 yards above the village, the hotel has an interior filled with overhead beams and panels, modern adaptation of chalet chairs, and an indoor swimming pool. Each of the contemporary bedrooms has its own private bath, and some of them contain balconies with southern exposure. Per-person rates, half board included, range from 335 AS ($17.82) to 550 AS ($29.26), depending on the season.

Gasthof Grafenwirt (tel. 230) is a pleasant three-story villa with white walls and lots of ivy growing up the side. A walled garden is a pleasant place for a summertime drink. The inside is accented with lots of recently applied paneling, rustic artifacts, and brightly contrasting patterns. The smallish bedrooms have painted furniture and a minimum of other decoration, but are comfortable nevertheless. Singles range from 190 AS ($10.11) to 285 AS ($15.16), while doubles go from 155 AS ($8.25) to 250 AS ($13.30) per person, breakfast included.

The in-house restaurant is one of the better ones in the region. Colorfully decorated with pretty chandeliers and wrought-iron accents, it serves standard Austrian specialties such as liver noodle soup, beef goulash, and Tyrolean-style liver. Fixed-price meals range from 85 AS ($4,52) to 120 AS ($6.38), while á la carte meals cost between 75 AS ($3.99) and 300 AS ($15.96). Half or full board can be arranged for residents of the hotel.

Gasthof Enzian (tel. 502), built in 1974–1975, is a chalet hotel with big balconies, lots of wood trim, and panoramic windows looking out over the green area around it. The bedrooms usually have white walls, autumnal colors, patterned curtains, and wood trim around the windows and around the rim of the ceilings. A few steps away, two smaller buildings constructed in the same style hold more accommodations. The 32 bedrooms rent for between 200 AS ($10.64) and 360 AS ($19.15) in a single, between 200 AS ($10.64) and 300 AS ($15.96) per person in a double, with breakfast included.

FLACHAU: This member of the trio of resorts which includes Wagrain and St. Johann im Pongau is just five miles southwest of Altenmarkt, in a lovely position in the Enns Valley, on the motorway. From the village, you can go by chair lift to Griesskareck at 6530 feet.

Flachau, known heretofore mainly to Europeans, is just beginning to attract skiers. Hence the prices are fairly reasonable.

Food and Lodging

Hotel Pongauerhof (tel. 242). The balconies of this stucco-and-wood chalet only extend part of the way across the facade, interrupted as they are with an extension stretching toward the front. This allows the cheerful bedrooms inside to be more spacious than those in the other hotels in the region, although the walls between them might not be as thick. The public rooms are busily filled with contrasting patterns and designs, with lots of new paneling and hanging light fixtures. Per-person rates range from 500 AS ($26.60) to 560 AS ($29.79), with half board included.

The in-house restaurant is often sought out by the local residents. Snails are a specialty of the chef, who also prepares a full line of snacks, including pizzas and various salads (often without lettuce). Full meals are also available, and main courses are likely to include pork wienerschnitzel and marinated roast pork (sometimes garnished with a cabbage salad). A wide variety of Austrian beer is on tap as well. Fixed-price meals range from 105 AS ($5.59) to 145 AS ($7.71), while à la carte dinners go from 120 AS ($6.38) to 245 AS ($13.03).

Hotel Alpenhof (tel. 205) has a pleasing exterior design, where the balconies have thick timbers running vertically up the front of the solidly constructed chalet. In summertime the café terrace offers a resting point in the shadows of the flowers on these balconies. In winter guests usually prefer to bathe in the sunny indoor pool or enjoy the rustic wood-covered interior. The contemporary bedrooms are simple and sunny, renting for between 360 AS ($19.15) and 730 AS ($38.84), with half board included. Prices depend on the plumbing, the exposure, the season, and whether or not the unit has a balcony. The restaurant is especially worth the visit. Specialties of the house include grilled filet of pork in a cream sauce, as well as roast marinated pork and an array of veal dishes. For clients not on the board plan, à la carte meals range from 105 AS ($5.59) to 310 AS ($16.49).

Hotel Tauernhof (tel. 3110) has two almost identical chalet-like sections connected by a glassed-in series of public rooms. The proportions are generous and comfortable, with a rustic decor of heavy timbers, hanging lamps, warm colors, and indoor fireplaces. On the premises you'll find a bowling alley, an indoor pool, a dancing bar, a sauna, outdoor tennis courts, and an inviting restaurant. Per-person rates in a double range from 570 AS ($30.62) to 775 AS ($41.23), with half board included. Occupants of a single are charged a supplement of 70 AS ($3.72) per day.

Forellenhof (tel. 273) is a wood-and-stucco chalet with a gently sloping roof and a pleasing facade of recessed balconies and symmetrical detailing.

From the café sun terrace, clients can look at the pink and white walls of the onion-domed church next door. The interior is attractive and cozy, with lots of handcrafted paneling and dozens of extra touches, such as stained-glass inserts, hanging ornate lamps, and an occasional niche containing a statue. Under the heavy overhead beams of the ceiling you can enjoy well-prepared regional cuisine. An octagonal indoor swimming pool is sheltered below a wooden ceiling that is supported by an unusual series of curved laminated beams. A sauna and a whirlpool are also on the premises. The sunny bedrooms rent for between 360 AS ($19.15) and 775 AS ($41.23), with half board included. Prices depend on the season and the exposure, and all units contain private bath. Residents of singles pay a surcharge of 60 AS ($3.19). The Krauthauf family are your conscientious hosts.

ST. JOHANN IM PONGAU: The third of the three-valley trio of summer and winter resorts, including Wagrain and Flachau, St. Johann im Pongau (there's a larger St. Johann in Tyrol) lies 38 miles from Salzburg on the sun-drenched terrace on the right bank of the river. The town's twin-towered **parish church** (*pfarrkirche*) was built in 1855, but use of the site for a house of worship dates from the year 924.

The winter sports season here lasts from December to April. There are some 52 lifts and cable cars in the tri-resort area, plus some 60 miles of prepared runs. This best known ski lift network in the Salzburg mountains is called Drei-Täler-Skischaukel, or three-valley ski swing.

If you're a nature lover, St. Johann is a good base for many excursions, such as to the **Grossarlbach Valley** to the south of the town and to the mouth of **Wagrainer Tal** to the north.

Just three miles south of St. Johann im Pongau is the most important gorge of the eastern Alps, the spectacular **Liechtensteinklamm,** which attracts more visitors to its three-quarter-mile length than any other such site. A path has been blasted through the gorge, and during about a 45-minute trek you can climb up a mammoth cauldron with rock walls some 1000 feet high. At its tiny waist the gorge is only 12½ feet wide. A tunnel leads to the waterfall with a drop of about 200 feet at the gorge's end.

To reach the Liechtensteinklamm, go three miles by road to Grossarl. The road to the gorge is marked. From there, count on about an hour by foot. The gorge may be visited from May 10 to the first Sunday in October from 8 a.m. to 5 p.m. Admission is 20 AS ($1.06).

Food and Lodging

Hotel Prem, 1 Premweg (tel. 6320), is a comfortably proportioned yellow stucco house styled like the home of a wealthy farmer. It sits in the middle of town, near all the sports facilities, with a nearby annex that holds the overflow from the main hotel. You'll recognize this place by the red and white horizontally striped shutters, which look almost like racing stripes, especially to the skiers who stay here in winter. The hotel is about three buildings away from the Haumbaumlifte chair lift. Inside, the public rooms are cozy, with a regional decor that includes a ceramic stove and well-oiled paneling. The hotel is frequently booked throughout the winter. Year-round prices range from 230 AS ($12.24) to 410 AS ($21.81) in a single and from 215 AS ($11.44) to 390 AS ($20.75) per person in a double, breakfast included.

Alpengasthof Hahnbaum-Alm (tel. 6133) is a small, family-run guest house set on an alpine hill with a sweeping view of the valley and the knife-edged mountains beyond. The interior is rustically outfitted with wood detailing, big windows, and a kind of homey ambience that only a small hotel can provide. Franz and Veronika Reischl, the hosts, charge 210 AS ($11.17) per person with breakfast included, or 280 AS ($14.90) per person with half board. Each of the units has its own bath.

Pension Monika, 2 Liechtensteinkammstrasse (tel. 411), a ten-minute walk from the train station at the southern edge of St. Johann, has weathered pine siding and a double row of balconies festooned with flowers. The sunny interior has lots of wood trim and simple comfortable furniture. The cuisine is prepared by the owners themselves, the Rudolf Wedl family, who charge between 200 AS ($10.64) and 220 AS ($11.70) for a single and between 170 AS ($9.04) and 195 AS ($10.37) per person in a double, breakfast included.

Speckbacher Stuben, 31 Speckbacher Strasse (tel. 2843), is a cozy, rustic restaurant with a loyal following. Specialties include regional fare such as cabbage and bacon soup, pork chops, lamb chops, and an array of schnitzels. Fixed-price meals range from 105 AS ($5.59) to 195 AS ($10.37), while à la carte dinners go from 110 AS ($5.85) to 275 AS ($14.63). Reservations are suggested, and the restaurant is closed on Monday and from mid-April to mid-May and for all of November.

KLEINARL: This tiny resort in the vicinity of Wagrain lies in the Kleinarl Valley, which is free of fog and wind. The home of Annemarie Moser, Olympic and world ski champion, Kleinarl was developed as a ski resort, with a cable car, triple chair lift, and ten drag lifts taking people to ski runs and slopes of the Tauern motorway ski station of Kleinarl-Flachauwinkel-Zauchensee (6560 feet). Tobogganing, curling, rides in horse-drawn sleighs, and walks along a footpath to **Jägersee,** a lake, are other attractions.

Food and Lodging

Hotel Tauernhof (tel. 247) is an appealingly designed chalet. It and its nearby annex blend gracefully into the wooded hillside behind them. A flagstone-covered sun terrace behind the main house is within view of the masses of summer flowers climbing over the balconies, the slate steps leading inside, and the wrought-iron detailing accenting the entranceway. The honey-colored timbers supporting the interior's ceilings are sometimes carved and otherwise crisscrossed into angled patterns. A covered swimming pool indoors is flanked by big mirrors, while a nearby sauna allows guests the time to reheat themselves after a day on the ski slopes. With half board included, per-person rates range from 340 AS ($18.09) to 480 AS ($25.54), depending on the season. All units have private bath, balcony, and phone. Accommodations with southern exposure require an additional supplement of 25 AS ($1.33) per person, and occupants of singles are charged an extra 60 AS ($3.19) per day.

Après-Ski

Everybody heads for the **Café Annemarie,** named after Annemarie Moser, the Olympic champion, five times world champion, and six times World Cup winner in the downhill. Ski fans pack in here to see her large collection of trophies, which are on display behind a huge glass window. These range from the first cup she won in the local ski race to the crystal balls from her World Cup triumphs to her Olympic Gold Medal she won in Lake Placid in 1980. The café also has good pastries, coffee, and drinks, costing around 65 AS ($3.46).

RADSTADT: Between the Dachstein massif in the north and Radstädter Tauern to the south lies Radstadt, at the beginning of the 13½-mile Radstädter Tauern Road to the pass, which has been used since Roman days as a way north through the mountains.

The town, built by a prince-archbishop of Salzburg, has many handsome patrician houses. Some other features of its past, including town walls, have been preserved. The skyline is distinguished by a trio of large towers built in the 16th century. Its **pfarrkirche** (parish church) is from the 14th and 15th centuries. In the churchyard stands a late Gothic **Schustersäule** (cobbler's column) from 1513.

Radstadt, for a long time a summer resort, now has been developed as a winter sports attraction. Many excursions from here are possible to the satellite resorts of Altenmarkt, Filzmoos, and Obertauern (coming up).

Food and Lodging

Sporthotel Weissenbacher (tel. 590) is skillfully landscaped into the side of an alpine meadow. A flight of stone-trimmed stairs will lead you first to the raised sun terrace, with its views of the many flowers surrounding the balconies, and then into the well-decorated public rooms. These are awash with comfortable niches, mellow paneling, and rustic conviviality. A full range of sporting pastimes lies within a short distance of the hotel. One of the foremost attractions is a network of some 15 kilometers of freshwater streams in the region, which are said to be filled with an angler's dream of eel, trout, and carp. Per-person rates, with half board included, range from 375 AS ($19.95) to 580 AS ($30.87), depending on the season. All the accommodations contain private baths.

The in-house restaurant is one of the best in the village. Filled with hunting trophies and covered with old paneling, it serves specialties that are both regional and Italian, ranging from 90 AS ($4.79) to 145 AS ($7.71) for fixed-price meals and from 110 AS ($5.85) to 320 AS ($17.02) on the à la carte menu. Reservations are suggested.

Gasthof Stegerbräu (tel. 313). It's hard to miss this ample guest house with a gently sloping roof. The shutters have diagonal stripes, which give part of the facade a chevron effect. A hand-painted mural of medieval villagers covers three stories of wall space in colors of sky blue, gold, and black. The elegant interior has flagstone floors, coffered ceilings, and more murals, plus a tradition which the owners say is 600 years old. Maria Weissenbacher, the English-speaking hostess, charges between 350 AS ($18.62) and 370 AS ($19.68) per person, double occupancy, with half board included. Residents of singles pay an additional charge of 25 AS ($1.33) per day.

Gasthof Pertill, 4 Schwemmberg (tel. 471), is a small, family-run inn set on the side of a mountain 300 yards above Radstadt. The view from the sun terrace encompasses the village and the valley that contains it. The inside is as rustic and cozy as you'd expect. The Kocher family charges

180 AS ($9.58) per person for bed and breakfast, and 290 AS ($15.34) per person with half board included, in units with private bath.

Berggasthof Seitenalm (tel. 490) is a well-designed complex of chalets two miles (via good roads) from the center of Radstadt. The main building has a dining room whose high ceiling is supported by massive vertical timbers. For skiers who want to be close to the slopes, or for mountain climbers in summer, the hotel rents rooms in its rustic Kurzenhof, which is about a mile and a half away near the hotel's T-bar lift. An outdoor swimming pool and nearby horseback riding provide distraction, along with fishing, hiking, shooting, and table tennis. You'll also find a sauna on the premises.

The romantic bedrooms are individually decorated with good taste and lots of homemade touches. Sometimes in summer you might want to eat in the country-style Grill Hut, assembled from logs notched together, while zither music accompanies your meal. Three generations of the Arnold family, the owners, charge between 235 AS ($12.50) and 260 AS ($13.83) per person, breakfast included.

ALTENMARKT: Some two miles west of Radstadt lies this sleepy provincial hamlet, sometimes called Altenmarkt in Pongau (2790 feet). It's popular with Austrian families who come here to take advantage of the good accommodations available at reasonable prices and to enjoy swimming, skiing, and other sports typical of the region.

Of interest is the **parish church** *(pfarrkirche)* with an 18th-century statue of the Virgin.

Food and Lodging

Hotel Urbisgut (tel. 7227) is a symmetrical double chalet connected with a balconied center section. The exterior walls have been decorated in some areas with regional painted designs. The cozy interior has painted furniture in some of the bedrooms and a bar area that sometimes is one of the most active and convivial places in nighttime Altenmarkt. Emma and Bartl Bittersam, the convivial owners of this place, charge between 340 AS ($18.09) and 420 AS ($22.34) per person, double occupancy, with half board included. Occupants of singles pay a supplement of 45 AS ($2.39) per day.

Hotel Alpenhof (tel. 606614) has two almost identical sections, each capped by a gently sloping roof and surrounded with weathered balconies of darkly textured wood. Inside is a rustically cozy series of public rooms, dotted with stucco arches and beamed ceilings. The nightclub downstairs, Gamsbar, has disco music and an inviting ambience. The sunny bedrooms are comfortably and simply furnished, while an on-the-premises covered swimming pool has big windows and a view of the mountains. Singles range from 470 AS ($25) to 565 AS ($30.06), while doubles cost between 425 AS ($22.61) and 540 AS ($28.73) per person, with half board included. Full board is available for an additional 50 AS ($2.66) per person daily.

Gasthof Markterwirt (tel. 420) is one of my favorite places in town, located in a three-story chalet with weathered facing and white shutters. It's next door to the village's baroque church. Aside from having cozy and comfortable rooms, the gasthof serves as one of the village's social centers. The café has big windows and a woodsy modern decor, where you might want to stop for coffee even if you're just driving through town. The

Kellerstüberl has a vaulted ceiling, cozy ambience, and painted designs on the white plaster. In addition, the Alte Küche, the main dining room, and the Gaststube, as well as the outdoor sun terrace, are inviting places to stop for a drink or a meal. The Schneider family, your hosts, charge between 240 AS ($12.77) and 300 AS ($15.96) per person in a single or double with breakfast included.

Lebzelter Stub'n (tel. 503) is an accommodating restaurant whose prices are low enough for a large family and whose specialties are so varied that guests can enjoy a different dish every day of the week. Wednesday, for example, is fondue day. Tuesday is strudel day. In addition to that, the restaurant serves thick and savory steaks, tafelspitz, tiroler Gröst'l (sauteed potatoes, onions, boiled meat, and bacon), blutwurst, lamb, fish, and venison dishes. A member of the Kohlmayr family is always on the premises, serving, in addition to everything else, pizzas priced between 60 AS ($3.19) and 100 AS ($5.32). À la carte meals range from 75 AS ($3.99) to 350 AS ($18.62). The restaurant is open every day of the week from 11 a.m. to 11 p.m., but closes in May and again in October.

FILZMOOS: A still-unspoiled resort 50 miles south from Salzburg, Filzmoos (3465 feet) lies at the foot of the 8000-foot Bischofmütze, a section of the Dachstein massif.

Filzmoos is a good starting point for many excursions, as well as for walking tours. In winter you can ride in horse-drawn sleighs (ask at your hotel), practice curling and ice skating, and go skiing. The resort has a good ski school, along with 16 ski lifts and many fine slopes, some of which are suitable for beginners, others for the most experienced of skiers. From here you can try the Dachstein Glacier runs about 7½ miles away, via the scenic Höhenstrasse.

Ski areas include Rossbrand (5250 feet), which lies to the south of Filzmoos. This section is serviced by a drag lift. Rettenstein (5380 feet), to the north of the resort, is the second most popular area. Its drag lift is in two stages. The third ski section is Grossberg (4590 feet), also to the north of Filzmoos, served by a chair lift. It has runs for all grades of skiers.

You'll find the innkeepers here, for the most part, friendly and hospitable.

Food and Lodging

Sporthotel Filzmooserhof (tel. 232) is the balconied chalet between the village church and the public swimming pool. Sports enthusiasts will find lots to do, since the public facilities for golf, mini-golf, and tennis are close at hand, as well as access to the ski slopes. One of the hotel's exterior walls has a hand-painted illustration of a man carrying a child across a stream, which guests can study while sipping coffee on the sun terrace. The interior is cozy, rustic, and filled with sunny colors. Half-board prices in summer range from 360 AS ($19.15) to 540 AS ($28.73). In winter the Webinger family charges between 515 AS ($27.40) and 720 AS ($38.30), also with half board included.

The adjoining restaurant is one of the better establishments in the village, serving international dishes such as scampi, steak, and schnitzel, and a collection of regional dishes which, even if you speak German, you'll have difficulty translating. The staff will help you, especially with the names of some of the Bosnian dishes, which include a well-prepared sour cream soup with potatoes. Fixed-price meals range from 90 AS ($4.79) to 145 AS ($7.71), while à la carte dinners go from 75 AS ($3.99) to 250 AS ($13.30). Both the restaurant and the hotel are closed from Easter till mid-May and from mid-October until mid-December.

Hotel Alpenkrone (tel. 280). One of the best times to view this hotel is in summer, when masses of alpine flowers cluster in the meadow nearby. Constructed in two parts, the chalet-style hotel has balconies facing the jagged mountains and an interior decoration which makes ample use of light-grained wood paneling. The doors to the bar area are wrought of straps and plates of solid iron, strong enough to keep anyone in (or out) for a long time. The dancing bar is a popular local hangout. Singles range from 290 AS ($15.34) to 400 AS ($21.28), while doubles cost from 265 AS ($14.10) to 370 AS ($19.68) per person with full board included. Half board costs 20 AS ($1.06) less per person daily.

Hotel Hanneshof (tel. 276). The bedrooms in this comfortable chalet-style hotel have windows as big as those in any hotel in town, as well as spacious balconies, lots of paneling, and a series of colorful public rooms designed around open hearths and ornate wrought-iron chandeliers. The hotel was constructed in 1974, with careful attention to all the modern amenities, including a big indoor pool and a sauna. Well-furnished singles cost 480 AS ($25.54), while doubles rent for 420 AS ($22.34) per person, breakfast included.

Alpenhotel Wurzer (tel. 220). The Wurzer family are your hosts in this family-run hotel near the village church. From the front the hotel looks like an old-fashioned slope-roofed chalet, with one end of the facade devoted to a country baroque painted design of what might be called the tree of life. The more contemporary backside looks out over a rolling grassy lawn. Constructed in 1959, the hotel is full of beautifully crafted paneling and cozy public rooms. Per-person rates with half board included range from 270 AS ($14.36) to 440 AS ($23.41), depending on the season. Accommodations with private balcony go for a supplement of 25 AS ($1.33) per person. Tariffs, otherwise, depend on the season and plumbing.

Après-Ski

In season live bands are brought in, and there is the inevitable collection of discos. The **Hotel Alpenkrone,** already recommended, is one of the most popular stops on the after-dark circuit. Young skiers especially are drawn to its Königskeller disco, where all drinks cost about 65 AS ($3.46). Also you might ask about the next "fondue evening."

The also-recommended (see above) **Sporthotel Filzmooserhof** may attract you if you like your music live. A band plays for dancing until 3 a.m.

Another one of the hotels just recommended, the **Hanneshof,** has the Kaminstube, which also offers disco dancing.

OBERTAUERN: This winter and summer resort at 5930 feet lies at the top of an old Roman road which divides Land Salzburg from Carinthia (see Chapter XII). The unspoiled resort is about 60 miles from Salzburg. It can be reached by train from Radstadt or else by Postal Bus. A car isn't really necessary here, as you can easily get around on skis in winter and on foot in summer. The people of Obertauern are friendly, and the tourist office is exceptionally helpful.

In the vicinity is the **graveyard of the nameless ones,** the burial place of bodies recovered from the mountain area over the centuries, most of them victims of avalanches. The cemetery is near the Tauern Pass and dates from the 16th century.

One of the newest ski resorts in Land Salzburg, Obertauern has become an international sports center, with both ski and chair lifts, plus a cable car. A ski school is in business, with state-qualified instructors, and there are children's ski courses, plus a ski kindergarten.

The elevation at the top of the pass ensures that the snow is good and the season extra long. You can ski from November until the end of May at this "snow-proof" resort, with its ski circus. It's easier on one side, steep on the other, letting you ski all around the village.

Food and Lodging

Alpenhotel Perner (tel. 236). There's so much variety to the many sections of this mountainside hotel that it almost gives the impression of a long series of balconied railroad cars strung together. The interior is appealingly outfitted with hewn beams and timbers, often with carved detailing, as well as unusual accents such as stained-glass insets and both stone and wrought-iron embellishments.

The public swimming pool is connected to the hotel via an underground passage, and covered tennis courts are close nearby. The friendly and engaging owners of this place are Erich and Maria Perner. High-season rates, with full board included, range from 840 AS ($44.69) to 870 AS ($46.28) for singles and from 720 AS ($38.30) to 800 AS ($42.56) per person for doubles. Clients wishing half board can deduct 40 AS ($2.13) from these tariffs. The dancing bar sees a lot of wintertime action, often with live music.

Hotel Kristall (tel. 323) has a chalet-style facade and a two-story balconied extension angling attractively off to one side. The contemporary interior has lots of rustic touches, including a fireplace whose hood is fashioned from curved and textured stucco. The bedrooms usually have good views of the mountains, pleasing wooden furniture, and springtime colors in the curtains, bedspreads, and wall-to-wall carpeting. Guests enjoy well-prepared meals under the coffered ceiling of a panoramic dining room. With breakfast included, per-person rates range from 370 AS ($19.68) to 400 AS ($21.28), double occupancy. All units have private baths. Occupants of a single pay a surcharge of 40 AS ($2.13) daily.

Clubhotel Kärntnerland (tel. 271) is a cream-colored balconied building with painted embellishments in regional patterns covering its stucco walls. It sees itself as more of a private club than a resort hotel, with attentive service provided by the Günter Kanduth family. Inside you'll find a library, an open hearth, and two restaurants, one of them a rustic keller and the other a high-ceilinged paneled room with comfortable upholstered armchairs and colorful napery. The bedrooms are warmly intimate, often with contrasting patterns and cozy colors. High-season rates, with half board included, range from 420 AS ($22.34) to 580 AS ($30.87) in singles and between 480 AS ($25.54) and 580 AS ($30.87) per person in a double, depending on the plumbing.

Berghotel Pohl (tel. 209) is a white-walled chalet with wooden balconies in front of two of its four stories. An extension on the ground floor has oversize glass windows, behind which is the small but elegant restaurant. A rustically modern bar area has red accents and lots of wood, while the smallish bedrooms have simple and comfortable furniture. The hotel is in the heart of the ski-lift station, a short distance from the center of the village. High-season rates range from 480 AS ($25.54) to 530 AS ($28.30) per person, plus another 50 AS ($2.66) if you want half board.

Hotel Kohlmayr (tel. 282). As you approach this well-run hotel it looks like a pleasantly situated chalet, with stucco walls and several rows of wooden balconies with matching shutters. You'll soon realize, however, that the entire construction rests on top of a glass-walled foundation that contains the heated swimming pool with its view of the mountains. The rest of the hotel is tastefully and rustically filled with paneling, cozy bric-a-brac, and pleasing colors. Also on the premises are a sauna and a fitness room. The spacious sunny bedrooms look out over an alpine vista, and are sometimes divided into two sections with a full-length curtain which you can close if you plan to sleep late. With breakfast included, doubles rent for between 480 AS ($25.54) and 600 AS ($31.92) per person, while singles range between 480 AS ($25.54) and 660 AS ($35.11), depending on the season.

Hotel Edelweiss (tel. 245). Once you sit down at the bar in this imaginatively decorated hotel you're likely never to leave. That's because the bar stools hang from a ceiling beam like children's swings and, in addition, mold themselves to the contours of your back. Other niches within the hotel's public rooms include Hitchcock-style rocking chairs placed beside the rustic fireplace, whose semicircular metallic bonnet exposes the flames to three sides of the room. A heated swimming pool and sauna are pleasant places to relax in before dinner in the restaurant or the brasserie, which might be followed by nighttime dancing. The contemporary bedrooms are sunny and filled with autumnal colors. They rent for 540 AS ($28.73) to 1000 AS ($53.20) in a single and between 515 AS ($27.40) and 960 AS ($51.07) per person in a double. These prices include half board, and are likely to be cheaper in summer. Full board is available for another 65 AS ($3.46) per person daily.

Après-Ski

Nightlife is very limited, but there is some. Many skiers, mostly European, go to bed by ten so they'll have an early chance on the slopes. Prices of most drinks average around 65 AS ($3.46).

One of the best places for after-dark diversions is the **Alpenhotel Perner,** already recommended. In their "Stage Coach," a dance band keeps the joint jumping.

The **Hotel Edelweiss,** again recommended previously, also occasionally has dancing to live music.

But the most fun is likely to be found at the **Gasthof Taverne,** where a ski expert, Mr. Oberhumer, and his sons welcome you in a real gemütlich atmosphere. They feature Tyrolean music and dancing. The place has plenty of atmosphere (it was actually converted from a stable).

4. The Tennengau

The Tennengau, named for the Tennen massif, is one of the divisions of the Salzach Valley to the south of Salzburg. It's characterized by rolling hills and many woodlands. Often you'll see waterfalls, of which those outside the town of Golling are the most visited.

As you leave Salzburg going south on the left bank of the Salzach River you'll pass through Anif, a section already previewed in the environs of Salzburg (Chapter VII). You'll find some excellent, old romantic accommodations in Anif, if you'd like to live on the immediate outskirts of the provincial capital.

If you don't want to stay in the Tennengau region, you might consider it as a day's exploration from Salzburg, its chief sight being the Dürrnberg Salt Mines outside Hallein. However, if you'd like to anchor in the district—in either summer or winter—the town that is most blessed with accommodations in a wide range of prices is Abtenau (sometimes called Bad Abtenau), which for decades has been known mainly as a winter ski business.

Much of the Tennengau area, especially the houses with their gables and window boxes of geraniums, will remind you of Bavaria.

HALLEIN: The second-largest town in Land Salzburg, Hallein, once a center for processing the salt from the mines of Dürrnberg, was a prize possession of the prince-archbishops of Salzburg. Today it's an industrial town on the Salzach River, and tourists pass through it on the way to the Dürrnberg mines.

On the north side of the Hallein parish church are the former home and tomb of the man who composed the music for Father Joseph Mohr's Christmas carol "Silent Night," Franz-Xaver Gruber, a schoolteacher, who died in 1863.

The **Dürrnberg Salt Mines** are the big lure, forming one of the most popular attractions in Land Salzburg. On guided tours, visitors toboggan downhill into the mines on polished tree trunks and are shown through large underground salt chambers. One of the highlights is traversing a salt lake on a raft. For a finale, you're allowed to ride on mining trucks through deep galleries until you emerge again into the light of day. An underground museum traces the history of salt mining back into remote time.

Tours are conducted daily May to October from 8 a.m. to 5 p.m., lasting about 1½ hours. Admission is 85 AS ($4.52) for adults, 45 AS ($2.39) for children.

Hallein is connected to Salzburg, ten miles away, by both train and bus service. From here there's a cable railway to Dürrnberg, although many Germans and Austrians prefer to walk to the mines, the trip taking about an hour. Cable railway fare for a round trip is 55 AS ($2.93) per person.

GOLLING: The major attraction drawing visitors to Golling, 7½ miles south of Hallein, is the **Gollinger Wasserfall** (Golling waterfall), two miles outside the little resort, plus about an hour's walk in addition. The waterfall is between Golling and Kuchl, 17 miles from Salzburg.

Visits to the wasserfall, which tumbles down more than 500 feet over a rock wall, are from May to October daily, a tour taking about an hour. Admission is 8 AS (43¢) for adults, 5 AS (26¢) for children.

You can also visit the **Salzach Gorge** near Golling. It's an hour's walk from Golling up to Pass Luez. You can visit the gorge from May to October daily. Allow about an hour. Adults are charged 10 AS (53¢); children, 8 AS (43¢).

In Golling you can visit the castle with its chapel and folklore collection. You'll see remains of cave bears, fossils, and copies of rock drawings, plus views of the village in old pictures. Visiting hours are June to September on Wednesday and Saturday from 9 a.m. to noon. Admission is 15 AS (80¢) for adults, 8 AS (43¢) for children.

Many visitors use Golling as a base for enjoying the varied sports facilities in the nearby mountains.

Food and Lodging

Hotel Stern (tel. 220) sits in a row of picture-book houses in the center of the village. It has arched windows on the ground floor, three floors of embellished windows above that, and a wrought-iron bracket holding a sign out over the street. The interior is filled with rustically modern furniture, while the bedrooms are cozy and comfortable. Singles range from 300 AS ($15.96) to 385 AS ($20.48), while doubles go from 260 AS ($13.83) to 380 AS ($20.22) per person, with half board included.

Many of the region's gourmets know about the in-house restaurant. Its specialties include dried alpine beef, sliced wafer-thin and served with pearl onions and pickles, filet steak, filet Stroganoff, and an Austrian version of the Italian saltimbocca (veal schnitzel stuffed with ham and served with a savory sauce). There's also an array of seafood which includes mussels prepared in several different ways. Fixed-price meals range from 80 AS ($4.26) to 115 AS ($6.12), while à la carte dinners cost from 85 AS ($4.52) to 330 AS ($17.56). The restaurant is closed every Monday and between October and April, and reservations are suggested otherwise.

OBERALM: The main reason for visiting this little hamlet, which lies near Hallein and Salzburg, is to stay at the castle hotel recommended below.

However, if you're sightseeing in the area you might want to stop to see the **parish church** *(pfarrkirche),* which is Romanesque with Gothic extensions. It has a magnificent high altar from 1707 by J. G. Mohr. The church is embellished with baroque furnishings and has heraldic tombstones. See the funereal shield from 1671.

Food and Lodging

Schloss Haunsperg (tel. 2662) is an early 14th-century castle, decorated with the towers and interior ornamentation you'd expect. The outside is restrained, with a grayish-pink covering of stippled stucco with white trim. A small but ornate baroque chapel adjoining the hotel has a wrought-iron gate separating the vestibule from the inner sanctuary, along with plenty of gilt embellishments. The public rooms include a series of vaulted corridors, each furnished with antiques and rustic chandeliers, several salons with parquet or flagstone floors, and a collection of antiques. My favorite is the second-floor music salon. Many of the accommodations are divided into suites of two or three rooms plus private bath, along with some doubles with bath also. The cost per person ranges between 460 AS ($24.47) and 770 AS ($40.96), breakfast included. A tennis court is on the premises.

ABTENAU: A small town nestling at the foot of the Kogel, Abtenau is known for its Gothic church. The little town, 30 miles from Salzburg, can be reached by bus from Golling in the Salzach Valley. It does mostly a summer business, but some winter trade has been developing. The minor spa is closed in winter.

Summer holiday visitors enjoy the mountain landscape through which to tour, strolling on forest paths, canoeing, playing tennis, horseback riding, swimming, and watching cheerful folkloric entertainment. You can hire guides for climbs in the Tennengebirge, but allow a whole day for this activity. A chair lift goes from Abtenau to the Karkogel at 3950 feet.

During the winter months guests often assist in feeding the deer. Abtenau offers skiing, tobogganing, horse-sledge rides, ice skating, and swimming in a covered pool.

There are some 60 miles of quiet hiking trails and fitness runs.

Food and Lodging

Windhofer's Hotel/Restaurant Post (tel. 209) has lots of rustic artifacts scattered throughout its country-style interior, including an ox yoke positioned below a hay-filled manger hanging from the ceiling of the intimate bar area. The Windhofer family has positioned an old iron-and-wood postal cart in the lobby, which is today filled with flowers. Summer guests might enjoy the terrace below the balconies of the pleasant chalet, whose smallish bedrooms are comfortable and clean. A covered swimming pool is nearby. A member of the family will sometimes organize bus excursions to sights in the area.

With half board included, per-person rates range from 430 AS ($22.88) to 380 AS ($20.22) per day, with occupants of singles paying a supplement of 45 AS ($2.39).

Breakfasts are buffet style and generous, but the evening meals are particularly inviting and well prepared, served in a gemütlich room with a big ceramic stove and lots of niches. Specialties include rumpsteak Tyrol, Indian-style veal, onion-flavored roast of beef, and fresh salads. À la carte meals range from 70 AS ($3.72) to 240 AS ($12.77).

Gasthof Roter Ochs (tel. 259) sits on the village's central square, across from the church. The sides of the building are covered with red, gold, and gray geometric illustrations, while the front has paintings of village characters who appear to be dancing and leaping over the sides of the wooden balconies. The public rooms are modern and rustic, while some of the comfortable bedrooms have carved headboards and rustic furniture. Live folkloric music and dancing are part of the entertainment provided in the Tiroler Keller which, except for the electronic musical instruments, looks like the inside of a log cabin high up in the mountains. You'll find a wide variety of accommodations, ranging from bathless singles to more elaborate units with private bath, phone, radio, mini-bar, and balcony. Per-person prices range from 335 AS ($17.82) to 635 AS ($33.78), based on double occupancy, with half board included. Tariffs depend on the accommodation and season. Singles pay a supplement of 75 AS ($3.99) per day.

Sporthotel Gasthof Moisl (tel. 232) is a prosperous-looking building in the middle of the town, with a backside dotted with short masonry columns and carriage lamps and a front side covered with regional paintings, wooden balconies, and heavily overhanging eaves. The interior is filled with heavy coffered ceilings, curved half timbering, rounded stucco columns, and an unusually shaped central fireplace in the baroque style. A scattering of carved regional antiques adds to the appeal of the hotel, along with an inviting collection of bar and restaurant areas. On the premises is an indoor shooting range, plus an indoor swimming pool with a big-windowed view of the rest of the village, along with a bowling alley and fitness room. Singles range from 350 AS ($18.62) to 800 AS ($42.56), while doubles cost between 315 AS ($16.75) and 830 AS ($44.17) per person, with half board included.

Gasthof Weisses Rössl (tel. 302). You'll be impressed with the glass and wrought-iron doors guarding the entrance to this place. They add an appeal to the skillfully lit beamed ceiling of the entrance hall of this chalet-style hotel. The bedrooms are filled with alpine furniture, most of it painted in forest green and blue-gray, with doorways decorated to match. The Eder family are your hosts in this pleasant hotel, where each of the accommodations has a private bath, renting for 360 AS ($19.15) per person, based on double occupancy, with half board included. Single occupancy carries a 30-AS ($1.60) surcharge. The hotel also rents apartments by the week in a building down the street, charging 4000 AS ($212.80). Management says it doesn't care how many people lodge there.

Gasthof/Pension Galler (tel. 269) was originally a village house with a flagstone roof, yellow walls, lime-green shutters, and masses of flowers. Years ago someone added a modern white-walled extension which today dominates the smaller building, but also provides additional accommodations. The comfortable bedrooms rent for between 250 AS ($13.30) and 310 AS ($16.49) per person, based on double occupancy, with breakfast included. Half board is another 40 AS ($2.13) per person daily.

PUCH-THURNBERG: This small spa catering mainly to Europeans lies at an altitude of 2600 feet, 7½ miles south of Salzburg. Here you can breathe in mountain air full of ozone and clear the city pollution from your lungs. Puch-Thurnberg is known for its ultramodern curative and rehabilitation therapies.

Food and Lodging

Kurhotel Vollererhof (tel. 3231) sits imposingly on a hillside with its balconies turned toward one of the most panoramic views in the region. A parasol-dotted sun terrace is surrounded by fir trees, which come close to the sides of the hotel except in those areas covered with well-tended lawns. The indoor swimming pool is angled toward the view, which swimmers can see through large windows. The public rooms are elegant and tasteful, with a kind of restrained dignity to many of the high ceilings and cozy niches.

The bedrooms have chaise longues near the wooden railings of their balconies. A toboggan run and a small ski lift are on the hotel's grounds. Another building, the Landhaus, charges slightly lower rates for its rooms. For accommodations in their two buildings the Eberlein family charge between 555 AS ($29.53) and 1100 AS ($58.52) per person, with full board included. Prices depend on the season and the accommodation.

5. The Pinzgau

The Pinzgau section of Land Salzburg stretches east from the Gerlos Pass to the Gastein Valley, with the Salzach River flowing through. To the south lies Hohe Tauern and to the north the Kitzbühel alpine region.

This is a very special area for skiing, especially the twin villages of **Saalbach** and **Hinterglemm,** which lie at the end of a valley ringed by a horseshoe of mountains laced with more than 40 ski lifts. The chief resort of the Pinzgau, **Zell am See,** is treated separately (see below). Another outstanding ski resort in the Upper Pinzgau region is **Kaprun.** The celebrated **Grossglockner Road** begins in Pinzgau (see below).

The Austrians call the Upper Pinzgau Valley the Oberpinzgau. This was one of the most isolated regions of the country until massive hydroelectric works opened it to the world. But the Upper Pinzgau areas, from a touristic point of view, isn't as lively as the resorts, such as Saalfelden, of the Mittelpinzgau, or Middle Pinzgau. This area runs along the **Steinernes Meer,** or "sea of stone," marking the frontier of Bavaria, part of West Germany.

LOFER: Ideally situated in a setting of forests, valleys, and mountain rivers, Lofer is an old market town, with a **Bauerntheater** (peasant theater) and a Gothic-style **pfarrkirche** (parish church). The church tower dominates the town with its two onion-shape domes. Many of the houses are decorated with oriels, as much of the architecture was inspired by nearby Bavaria.

Lofer is both a health resort and a ski center, offering friendly hospitality as well as native tradition and rural charm. It's known for its peat-water and mud baths and its Kneipp cures. The fog-free area around Loper is suitable for walking in both summer and winter. There are a tennis court, skating rink, miniature golf course, and enclosed swimming pool.

A ski school is operated here, and there are nine T-bar lifts. A chair lift will deliver you to the Sonnegg-Loderbühel at 3290 feet and the upper station of the Loferer Alm, 4600 feet. Rising in the background of the town are the Loferer Steinberge and the Reiter Steinberge.

A popular excursion is to the pilgrimage church, **Maria Kirchenthal** (see St. Martin, below). You can also visit the **Lamprechtsofen Cavern** on the road from Lofer to Weissbach, about 37 miles from Salzburg by bus. A guided tour takes about 40 minutes. Admission is 20 AS ($1.06) for adults, 10 AS (53¢) for children.

Food and Lodging

Haus Gertraud in der Sonne (tel. 203) is a wood-covered chalet with red and white shutters. It's set high on a mountainside, in a solitary position among fir trees which gets a lot of sunshine. Access to the hotel can be made via a winding alpine road, where Haus Gertraud is the last stop. The Blüm family maintains a private rope tow up a beginner's ski slope, or advanced skiers can reach more challenging slopes at the nearby ski lift.

In winter or summer a terrace provides a wooden deck where guests can usually get a suntan. The colorful and cozy interior has a rustic bar area with rows of exposed shingles serving as a roof and evenly spaced rows of honey-colored planks covering the walls of many of the bedrooms. Singles range from 450 AS ($23.94) to 615 AS ($32.72), while doubles cost between 440 AS ($23.41) and 700 AS ($37.24) per person, with full board included.

Hotel Gasthof Post (tel. 3030) is a gracefully painted chalet with two-dimensional colored embellishments surrounding each of the facade's windows. It also has intricately carved wooden balustrades serving as the balcony railings and lots of flowers. Guests rarely check out of this place without having coffee on the street-level sun terrace, where a view of the village street life is presented just beyond the summer barrier of yellow marigolds. The decor inside contains lots of aged wood and a few well-placed ceramic stoves.

The comfortable bedrooms rent for between 350 AS ($18.62) and 600 AS ($31.92) per person, based on double occupancy, with half board included. Prices depend on the plumbing and the season. Single renters pay a supplement of 70 AS ($3.72) per day.

The adjoining restaurant is charmingly filled with all the rustic detailing you'd expect in such an old house, coupled with a gemütlich feeling. Specialties of the house include a ragoût of fresh venison, trout, pork cutlets, and a tempting array of fish and meat dishes priced at between 95 AS ($5.05) and 255 AS ($13.57) for a full à la carte dinner and at about 120 AS ($6.38) for a fixed-price meal.

Hotel Bräu (tel. 2070) has a lemon-colored facade, white neoclassical ornamentation around each of the windows, and voluptuously curved wrought-iron balconies on the second floor. It's in the center of the village. If you don't see it as you approach it on the narrow flagstone-covered sidewalk, you'll recognize it by the ornate curved bracket (it's shaped like the garlanded head of a mythical bird) extending out over the pavement. Parts of the hotel were constructed in 1639, and from a view of the antiques inside it's easy to get a sense of the era of its construction.

The modern parts of the hotel have made every effort to offset the antique appearance of the older sections. A persimmon- and lime-colored bar area is an unusual study in modern design, while the entrance hall is covered with marble floors and discreet geometric designs. The bedrooms are usually filled with painted alpine furniture and a romantic selection of colors. Per-person rates, based on double occupancy, range from 480 AS ($25.54) to 700 AS ($37.24), with half board included. Singles pay a supplement of 100 AS ($5.32). Prices depend on the season.

The garden restaurant is one of the most charming places in town for a meal, and you can easily move into the rustic dining room when it turns cold. Specialties include a delectable soup of smoked trout, roast pork in a gorgonzola cream sauce served with green spätzle, and tafelspitz, while desserts might include a variety of fresh strudels. À la carte meals range from 85 AS ($4.52) to 300 AS ($15.96). Fixed-price dinners cost from 110 AS ($5.85).

Hotel St. Hubertus (tel. 266). You'd never guess that this beautifully painted chalet is as big as it is, but actually it stretches for dozens of yards behind the regional designs and balconies of its facade. The spotlessly clean interior has ceilings almost universally made of wood—at least in the public rooms—and a simple attractive decor of wooden chairs with upholstery in autumnal colors. Each of the comfortable bedrooms has its own private bath, and many of them contain balconies. With half board included, doubles rent for between 360 AS ($19.15) and 470 AS ($25) per person, while singles cost between 385 AS ($20.48) and 470 AS ($25), depending on the season. The Grissesman family will give you a fine welcome.

ST. MARTIN BEI LOFER: This tiny hamlet is visited for its pilgrimage church, a large baroque edifice in a romantic setting called **Maria Kirchenthal.** The building was designed by the renowned master of the baroque J. B. Fischer von Erlach. The church has a museum displaying votive pictures from the 17th to the 19th centuries.

The church, one mile west of the village, is reached by a toll road, a passenger car costing 35 AS ($1.86) both ways, or you can make an hour's walk from Lofer (see above).

The **Vorderkaser Gorge** can be visited from St. Martin. A 1½-mile road connects the gorge with the Mittelpinzgau Road near the Vorderkaser bus stop. The gorge may be seen daily from the first of May until the end of October. A visit costs adults 18 AS (96¢); children, 10 AS (53¢).

Where to Stay

Schlossparkappartement (tel. 249). The bedrooms here are sunny, big windowed, and spacious, with brightly patterned area rugs laid over wall-to-wall carpeting and comfortable contemporary furniture. On the grounds are a supermarket, a covered swimming pool, a large park, and two tennis courts. The exterior is chalet-style modern, built in two identical overlapping sections. The accommodations consist of apartments for two to five persons. Depending on the apartment and the season, a unit for two or three guests costs between 300 AS ($15.96) and 470 AS ($25), an apartment for two to four, between 420 AS ($22.34) and 620 AS ($32.98), while an apartment for up to five ranges from 500 AS ($26.60) to 750 AS ($39.90).

SAALBACH: This internationally celebrated tourist resort, at an elevation of 3290 feet, places emphasis on relaxation, recreation, and sports—both summer and winter.

From spring until late in the autumn many quiet walks or more extended hikes are possible, as well as mountaineering, riding, bowling, mini-golf, and tennis. You can swim in a nearby lake, where surfing and sailing are also possible. There are some 160 miles of well-laid-out footpaths. A kindergarten caters exclusively to children of holiday-makers.

Saalbach has seen rapid growth as a winter sports resort in recent years, with numerous lifts in close proximity to the center of town. There's one cable car big enough to carry 100 passengers, along with 40 tow and chair lifts. Tobagganing is popular too, as are ski-bobbing, sleigh rides, and curling in the clear, alpine winter. Many cross-country ski tracks emanate from here.

Saalbach is a twin resort to **Hinterglemm,** which lies about an eight-minute car ride to the west, at the head of the valley. Often the region is spoken of as a unit—the Saalbach-Hinterglemm ski area. The resorts are linked by a lift system and a ski bus. The area has a surprising variety of well-groomed slopes and deep-snow runs. The major lift, the Schattberg cableway, leaves from the heart of Saalbach, taking skiers to the top station (6560 feet) where there's an excellent restaurant with a suntrap terrace and a panoramic vista. Of course summer visitors can also take the cableway to enjoy the scenery.

The Saalbach-Hinterglemm visitors' racing course is available to enthusiasts from Tuesday to Sunday between 10 a.m. and noon and 2 and 4 p.m., with slaloms, giant slaloms, and parallel slaloms being held. Both resorts have ski schools and provide ski circus runs.

Saalbach has fine shops where you can find traditional Austrian clothing as well as chic apparel for dress or sports. Local arts and crafts shops are also of interest to visitors.

Saalbach can be a good center for exploring the neighboring resorts of Kaprun and Zell am See.

The Resort Hotels

Hotel Sonnleiten (tel. 402) is a multi-sectioned balconied hotel with a series of gently sloping rooflines and a format that looks like a greatly expanded chalet. It's on the ski slopes a short distance above the village, and parts of the hotel are attractively angled to create a varied facade of many different planes. Some sections of the interior have high modern ceilings supported by massive sloping beams. Management often has a fire going, even in summertime, near the curved bar.

The dining room is large, with a paneled ceiling and graceful wooden chairs. On the premises you'll find tennis courts and an outdoor swimming pool which management heats in winter so that you can have a dip and roll around in the snow afterward (many guests do!). With half board included, singles range from 700 AS ($37.24) to 940 AS ($50.01), while doubles cost between 650 AS ($34.58) and 900 AS ($47.88) per person, depending on the season and the exposure of the room. All of the accommodations contain private bath. Full board is an additional 100 AS ($5.32) per person daily.

Hinterhag (tel. 291) is an unusual and appealing hotel set on the side of an alpine hill a short distance from the center of town. It's composed of at least five different sections, all of them balconied and built in a chalet style, connected into an architectural unit that might be your headquarters during your stay in Saalbach. In addition to a large collection of paneled and timbered public rooms, the hotel maintains a combination art nouveau café and art gallery. When I was last there the paintings were a dreamy collection of pastel-tinted water colors, but the collection changes frequently.

The story of the construction of this oft-expanded hotel is documented in photographs on one of the walls of the public rooms. The cuisine is the finest at the resort (see the dining recommendations coming up). The varieties of lighthearted activities for wintertime guests bring repeat business. The bedrooms have lots of exposed wood and an occasional wry touch, such as a nun's head extending over a bed's headboard, seemingly looking down at whatever might be happening inside. Sepp and Evi Fersterer, both avid skiers, are your hosts. They charge between 850 AS ($45.22) and 1200 AS ($63.84) per person, with half board included, depending on the season. The hotel is closed between April 1 and July 1 and from September 30 until mid-December.

Hotel Glemmtalerhof (tel. 3637) rises six stories, all of them in a chalet style, above the central street of the village. The street level of the hotel contains a few small shops as well as the front entrance. Inside you'll find gemütlich and cozy public rooms, sometimes accented with fireplaces and lots of exposed wood. A covered swimming pool has big windows and sun chairs, while the public tennis courts are a few buildings away. The decorator here used a combination of knotty-pine paneling and conservatively modern accessories for an attractive and appealingly rustic format. The bedrooms are the kinds of places where you'll be tempted to linger. They're covered with mellow pine and invitingly lit. A coffeeshop, two bars, a nightclub, and a choice of restaurants are part of the facilities. Depending on the season, singles range from 650 AS ($34.58) to 880 AS ($46.82), with doubles costing from 600 AS ($31.92) to 910 AS ($48.41) per person, with half board included. The hotel has a dozen family apartments.

Hotel Bauer (tel. 213) presents lots of visual distraction. You'll see a mixture of colors and patterns, all of them invitingly cozy. In summer many guests sit on the flowered terrace in front, while in winter they move into the happily cluttered public rooms, which are large, containing lots of niches for secluding oneself with a book or a friend. In the center of town, the hotel maintains a chalet-style annex a few minutes away, closer to the ski slopes. The annex contains rooms similar to the ones in the main buildings, as well as a snackbar which skiers find convenient. Singles range from 675 AS ($35.81) to 935 AS ($49.74), while doubles cost between 625 AS ($33.25) and 890 AS ($47.35) per person, with half board included.

Hotel Saalbacher Hof (tel. 7111) has one of the prettiest chalet-style facades in town. It's embellished with heraldic paintings, masses of summertime flowers, and on top of the lower of the two sloping rooflines, an open-sided stork's tower supported by a single stout post. The interior is dignified, restrained, and baronial, with a big stone fireplace in the attractively formal main salon, acres of chestnut-colored paneling, and pleasingly bold Oriental rugs. A wide grassy lawn with a view of the onion dome of the village church leads down to the outdoor heated swimming pool.

The Dschulnigg family provides live music for dancing at five o'clock tea and in the evening. You'll find three different restaurant and bar areas, my favorite of which has masonry walls and hanging lamps shaped like enormous pewter double-handled tankards. The accommodations in a nearby annex are similar to the ones in the main house. Per-person rates, based on double occupancy, range from 650 AS ($34.58) to 1130 AS ($60.12), with half board, heating, and taxes included. Prices vary according to the season.

Berger's Sporthotel (tel. 577). If you arrive in midwinter, the ambience is almost like that of a giant house party which almost never ends, the guests of which tend to be refugee urbanites celebrating their once-a-year vacation. On the premises are a boutique and dress shop, a small heated indoor swimming pool, a two-tiered restaurant and disco with a central marble-covered dance floor, a stüberl, and a cellar bar with live music, dark colors, and intimate lighting. In the center of the village, the hotel can be recognized by its wooden balconies and its big yellow sign. Per-person rates range from 600 AS ($31.92) to 1140 AS ($60.65), with half board included. Prices depend on the season, and each of the comfortable and brightly colored bedrooms has its own bath.

Hotel Kristiana (tel. 253) is one of my favorite hotels in Saalbach. It has a facade that bristles with jutting balconies, the horizontal supports of which have been intricately cut into pleasing patterns. On one corner, just above the sun terrace, an artist has executed a series of etched panels designating what might be the different seasons in Saalbach.

The interior is a rustic fantasy of carved beams and well-polished paneling, several open fireplaces, and comfortable, well-planned rooms, each with its own private bath. A sauna is on the premises, while tennis courts and an indoor swimming pool are just around the corner. Johann Breitfuss and his family are your accommodating hosts at this pleasant hotel. Per-person rates range from 570 AS ($30.32) to 870 AS ($46.28), based on double occupancy, with half board included. Singles pay a surcharge of 120 AS ($6.38) daily. Prices depend on the season.

Alpenhotel Saalbach (tel. 666) is a big modern hotel with a design reminiscent of a chalet. It has painted detailing around some of the windows on the lower floors, lots of wooden balconies, and a facade divided into several different sections. A disco in the basement is one of the attractions, as well as a cozy, well-furnished interior. This includes a prosperous-looking collection of rustic artifacts, several fireplaces (one of which juts pleasantly into the room and is capped with a conical stucco chimney), a popular bar with enough unusual details and enough people to make you want to linger, and a cellar with regional folk music.

A long narrow indoor pool capped with what looks like hand-hewn ceiling beams is part of the sports facilities, along with a sauna, exercise room, a whirlpool, and a solarium. Apartments are available for extended stays, sleeping between two and six guests. For shorter stays, singles range from 490 AS ($26.07) to 1300 AS ($69.16) daily, while doubles go from 425 AS ($22.61) to 1180 AS ($62.78) per person. Prices depend on the season. The Thomas family are your hosts.

Hotel Panther (tel. 7319). When the flowers are out in full force the balconies of this hotel are stunning. Even when they're not the exterior is invitingly rustic, with solidly constructed wooden balconies, heavy overhanging eaves, and an open-sided tower, ideal for a stork's nest, crowning the roof. One of the village's popular discos is reached by a separate entrance clearly marked on the outside of the building.

The interior is generously covered with well-crafted paneling, tile floors, and Oriental rugs. Some of the ceiling beams have concealed lighting fixtures, giving the lobby and bar area a dramatic lift. One of the salons has white walls, a massive beamed ceiling, and an unusual painted sculpture of a warrior with a shield, along with beautifully crafted cane-backed chairs.

The hotel is only a few steps from the cable car and within skiing distance from the bottom of the slopes. The Rottner family are your hosts, charging between 550 AS ($29.26) to 935 AS ($49.74) per person, based on double occupancy, with half board included. Prices depend on the plumbing and season. A single room carries a supplement of 35 AS ($1.86) per day.

Hotel Kristall (tel. 377) is a pleasant family-style chalet in the center of Saalbach. Its five stories contain well-furnished bedrooms, many of them wallpapered in light patterns of gray and white, with furniture that sometimes looks as if it came from a private home. The public rooms are either rustic and heavily timbered or filled with modern and flamboyant colors and big windows. One area looks like a Victorian pub complete with globe lights. On the premises you'll find an indoor pool, a sauna, a fitness room, and frequent live entertainment. The Lettner family charges between 750 AS ($39.90) and 1000 AS ($53.20) per person daily, with half board included. Singles pay a daily supplement of 50 AS ($2.66).

Gasthof Unterwirt (tel. 274) has a modern balconied addition set at right angles to the main house. The overall effect is pleasant and relaxed, a feeling helped by the rustic decor of the ceiling beams, ceramic tile stoves, and full-grained paneling. Paul Kröll and his family are the accommodating owners, charging between 420 AS ($22.34) and 850 AS ($45.22) in a single and between 400 AS ($21.28) and 750 AS ($39.90) per person in a double, with half board included. Prices depend on the season, the plumbing, and the exposure.

Hotel "Haus Wolf" (tel. 3460). If you're interested in ski lessons, this might be an ideal hotel since the local ski school makes its headquarters here. The hotel is right beside the Reiterkogel cable car in a pleasant chalet with wooden balconies and a first-floor sun terrace. The interior is covered with wood paneling, some of it crafted into curved and geometric designs.

The vertical columns supporting the ceilings are made either of wood or stone, while many of the homey touches include shelves with hand-painted plates just below ceiling level.

In winter fires burn beneath copper-sheathed chimneys, and guests often congregate in one of the several bars and restaurants. A smaller annex provides comfortable accommodations, often filled with painted furniture, a short distance away. Per-person rates range from 420 AS ($22.34) to 700 AS ($37.24), depending on the plumbing and the season. Residents of singles pay a surcharge of 65 AS ($3.46) per day. Half board is included in the above prices.

Where to Dine

Hinterhag-Alm, at the Hotel Hinterhag (tel. 291), is considered by some gourmets to be among the best restaurants in Austria. The award-winning chef, Peter Huber, uses ingredients from the mountains that wouldn't ordinarily be used anywhere else. One example is a local variety of stinging nettles which, when properly prepared, makes a delicious flavoring for dumplings, salads, and soups. Some of his recipes are updated versions of very old local dishes. He uses large quantities of cabbage, reaching perfection in the cabbage soup. Dandelion greens, which are used in salads, as you'd expect, also might turn up in a honeyed dessert parfait. Specialties also include whortleberry omelets, sometimes suggested as an appetizer, as well as mountain-style roast mutton flavored with thyme. The restaurant is closed from April 1 till June 15 and for all of October and November. À la carte meals range from 125 AS ($6.65) to 375 AS ($19.95). Reservations are suggested.

Restaurant Ingonda (tel. 5753) is a recently constructed alpine-style building constructed partly of logs. Included inside are a coffeehouse and a paneled restaurant, not too big, which serves an international menu. Featured dishes are likely to include scampi, steaks, fondues, filet of pike-perch (served with cabbage-flavored butter), and an assortment of savory soups. À la carte meals range from 130 AS ($6.92) to 390 AS ($20.75).

Après-Ski

Saalbach is one of the liveliest centers in Land Salzburg for après-ski and nightlife.

First, for coffee, tea, or pastries, you might drop in at one of the many cafés in town. In Saalbach, the **Café Bauer** (tel. 213) is popular, as is the **Café Bernhofer.** In Hinterglemm, try the **Café Glemmtalerhof** (tel. 7135).

The **Saalbacher Fassl** (tel. 7309) is another café-restaurant, and it has dance music and is open every day from 10 a.m. to 10 p.m. It's beyond the Hochalm lift at Hinterglemm.

The **Kristall Keller,** to the right of the entrance to the already-recommended Hotel Kristall, draws an attractive young crowd to its lively bar where in high season a live band plays for dancing. In addition its Bacchus Weinstube is considered "the meeting point in Saalbach."

The **Hotel Panther,** also recommended previously, shelters one of the most popular discos in the village. It's the Zum Herrn Karl, an American-style music bar which shows video films daily.

If you want more local entertainment, consider the Kuhstall Bar at the also recommended **Alpenhotel.** It only has a two-man Tyrolean band, but they manage to sound like a dozen musicians and they keep the place lively. The setting is rustic with beamed ceilings.

One of my favorite spots is the **Hotel-Gasthof Neuhaus,** where a two-man Zigeuner band entertains the skiers after a hard day on the slopes. This is one of the friendliest places on the nighttime circuit of Saalbach.

Among the major hotels, the Sportkeller Night Club Disco at the recommended **Sporthotel** is very festive for those who like their après-ski with a good band and a good drink (maybe more than one). Sportsmen are very fond of the place.

The après-ski crowd shuttles back and forth between Saalbach and Hinterglemm, and after a few drinks the resorts merge into one.

In Hinterglemm, a good spot is the Knappenhof Knappenkeller of the **Knappenhof Tirolerhof** (tel. 529). Grilled food is served until 3 a.m., and most often there is live music for your dancing and entertainment pleasure. Sometimes Tyrolean music is interspersed between the more modern sounds.

Also at Hinterglemm, the **Hotel Glemmtalerhof,** also recommended, has perhaps the most gemütlich atmosphere of any place in the village. The Almbar, a small, intimate disco, stays open very late, and the Glemmerkeller Apéritif Bar is just the place to order a fondue any time before midnight. The show room, however, is Harlekin Dancing, where well-known international bands often appear in season.

If you're seeking a rustic, charming setting, try the previously recommended **Landhaus Wolf** at Hinterglemm. Some of the most attractive and fun-loving people in the area gather here around the fire. The decor might be called "Come to the Stable."

In recent years the nightlife prices of Saalbach and Hinterglemm have almost caught up with the high tariffs of Zell am See, and you're likely to spend from 75 AS ($3.99) for a drink in most of the taverns and clubs recommended above. There is rarely a cover charge, unless a name band happens to appear.

SAALFELDEN: An old market town in the Middle Pinzgau, Saalfelden is set against a background of towering mountains. Lying in a broad valley formed by the Saalbach River, this is a good center for touring the **Steinernes Meer,** or "sea of stone," a karistic limestone plateau which the Austrian government has turned into a nature reserve.

Although Saalfelden is primarily a summer resort, winter sports areas in the mountains are within easy reach.

The town has a **pfarrkirche** (parish church) with a Gothic crypt beneath the choir and a late Gothic triptych in the presbytery.

At **Ritzen Castle,** which dates from 1650, a local museum (Heimatmuseum) is devoted to life in the Pinzgau region. Here you'll see a rich collection of Christmas cribs by the artist Xandl Schläffer, exhibited in four rooms. Another hall displays a collection of pictures and ecclesiastical art. The museum is open Wednesday, Saturday, and Sunday from 2 to 4 p.m. (daily in high season). Admission is 18 AS (96¢) for adults and 8 AS (43¢) for children.

Food and Lodging

Hotel Dick (tel. 2215) is a long four-story building with unusual geometric designs around the windows and heraldic paintings on the white front section. The reception hall has Louis XIII–style chairs and dark paneling, while the rest of the interior has coffered ceilings, bright colors, and high ceilings. In the back yard a heated swimming pool is the gathering place in summer. The featured bedroom has 18th-century furniture and a painted ceiling, but the other units contain pleasant furniture quite a bit newer.

Doubles rent for between 400 AS ($21.28) and 460 AS ($24.47) per person, with half board included. Singles go for an additional 60 AS ($3.19) surcharge per night. Prices depend on the season, and all the accommodations are equipped with private bath. The adjoining restaurant serves unusual specialties, such as Japanese goulash, plus a wide variety of the freshest possible fish. Someone told me that the chef goes out to catch them himself in his free time.

Restaurant Schatzbichl, 82 Ramseiden (tel. 3281), is an alpine-style country house known for its cuisine. The recipes are usually derived from formulas used for generations by the area's grandmothers, and are served by local waitresses dressed in colorful regional garb. Specialties are often placed in a copper pan directly onto your table, while members of your party dig in with forks and serving spoons.

You might enjoy kasfarfeln (thick consommé with cheese, onions, chives, and dumplings) or schottnocken (served in a big pot with spätzle, smoked cheese, chives, and onions), or finally my favorite, erdäpfelgröstl (a big pot with potatoes, broth, sausages, onions, and chives).

You can get here by car, because the restaurant lies off a road dug into the valley of Maria Alm. But if you're adventurous, you can walk here in an hour and a half from Maria Alm, which might make a pleasant midday excursion. Be sure to call ahead for a reservation. À la carte meals range from 85 AS ($4.52) to 210 AS ($11.17). The restaurant is closed in April and November.

LEOGANG: This is really an off-the-beaten-track little hamlet known principally to the Austrians and Bavarians. In the general vicinity of Saalfelden, it's so undiscovered that you can enjoy quietness and tranquility here. Leogang is both a summer and a winter resort, lying at an elevation of 2750 feet, in the Middle Pinzgau. Many day excursions are possible from here, including one to the "sea of stone" mentioned above.

Food and Lodging

Hotel Krallerhof (tel. 246) is designed in a combination of antique rural styles (which include painted baroque detailing around some of the windows) and late 20th-century adaptations such as an A-frame roof over part of the front section. The result is a pleasing combination of old and new, with an interesting sprinkling of contemporary sculpture thrown in. Because of its isolation from other buildings in the village, you'll be able to imagine that the sun terrace stands at the edge of a virtual wilderness, which goes as far as the dramatic peaks of the nearby Leoganger Steinberge.

The popular double-tiered nightclub inside is appealingly decorated with lofty ceilings, gently sloping exposed stairways, and hand-carved paneling. Regional live music can often be heard. The bedrooms usually have checked curtains and wood ceilings. They rent for between 400 AS ($21.28) and 765 AS ($40.70) per person, based on double occupancy, with half board included. Prices depend on the plumbing, the room assignment, and the season. Singles pay a daily supplement ranging between 50 AS ($2.66) and 70 AS ($3.72). On the premises is an indoor and outdoor swimming pool, plus a ski school and a small ski lift for beginners.

KAPRUN: Both a summer resort and a winter ski center as are most towns in the area, Kaprun is known for its high glacier skiing. The town is hardly the most attractive or the most atmospheric in Land Salzburg, but serious skiers don't seem to mind that. It's about a 12-minute run from Zell am See, which is easily reached by bus.

The surrounding area takes in the Valley of Kaprun and its magnificent dams. It includes an ascent to the Kitzsteinhorn (9612 feet), which can be quite complicated, involving Postal Buses, funiculars, and cableways. Always have your routes outlined at the tourist office with a detailed area map before you set forth. An English-speaking staff member there will supply the best possible routing and provide you with the most up-to-date hours, costs, and types of services likely to be available at the time of your visit. Also, you can learn about weather conditions from that source. For example, after mid-October, tours to the valley of the dams may not be possible. However, a visit to Kitzsteinhorn is an attraction in both summer and winter.

The **Kitzsteinhorn** will probably be first on your list of things to see. To reach the summit, you can go by cable car, transferring to the Salzburger Hütte at the Restaurant Alpincenter, where you can enjoy lunch with a view. The Alpincenter (8020 feet), incidentally, is the largest ski area in Austria.

You can also reach the mountain by taking the underground funicular and changing at the Alpincenter. Don't forget that traffic gets very heavy here in winter.

The bottom station of this glacier railway is at an elevation of 2784 feet and the top one is at 9087 feet. Not only can you ski from the Alpincenter, but you can also take glacier and mountain tours.

It's best to purchase a day ticket—round trip, naturally—for both the cable railway and the glacier lift, costing 300 AS ($15.96), as the railway goes only to the second platform of the cableway. You get off the train at that station and board a cableway which will swing west, coming to a stop near the summit of Kitzsteinhorn. This station is called the Gletscherbahn.

You'll find the Panoramatunnel cut through the mountains, as well as the Aussichtsrestaurant (talk about dining with a view!). You'll also be able to see Grossglockner, the neighboring mountain and the highest in Austria at 12,340 feet. The tunnel measures some 1000 feet on the south side of the mountain, opening onto a panoramic gallery from which the view of Grossglockner is possible.

The **Kapruner Tal,** or Valley of Kaprun, is visited in summer to see its dams, which form a dramatic mountain sight. These dams, constructed in tiers, were originally built as part of the World War II recovery act, the U.S.-financed Marshall Plan. Experts from all over the world come here to study these hydroelectric constructions, considered brilliant feats of engineering genius. Trips are possible from the middle of May until around the middle of October, depending on weather conditions.

From Kaprun you can take a road to see the mammoth wall of the Limbergsperre (Limberg Dam). At the Gletscherbahn cable-car station, you can go all the way to the Kitzsteinhorn, already described. From the Limbergstollen car park, you can take a shuttle bus to the lower station of the Lärchwand funicular. At the upper platform you'll have a magnificent view of the Limberg Dam rising nearly 400 feet. The dam holds back water to form the Upper Mooserboden reservoir.

You can go along the valley by Postal Bus, passing through some 1½ miles of tunnels, to the Mooser Dam. A view of the Wasserfallboden lake reservoir (5480 feet) is possible from here. The reservoir holds more than 18,500 million gallons of water.

You can see the two dams, the Moosersperre and the Drossensperre, which combine to form the Mooserboden reservoir, capable of holding nearly 19 million gallons of water. These hydroelectric plants have reservoirs surrounded by glaciers of the Glockner range.

An inclusive ticket to visit the plants costs 150 AS ($7.98) in high season, 130 AS ($6.92) in off-season. This covers the cost of transport from the Limbergstollen or Kesselfall car parks as far as Mooserboden and back. The ice-covered peaks of the High Tauern can be seen from the dams.

Food and Lodging

Sporthotel Kaprun (tel. 625) is a large chalet with a gently sloping roof and flowered balconies. It's near the cableway stations at the southern exit of Kaprun. Built in 1977, it has an attractively simple format of paneled ceilings, big windows, and spacious public rooms. These include a sauna, a children's playroom, and a game room. You'll also find exercise machines and table tennis tables nearby, plus at least one bar area.

The bedrooms are modern, and some areas are covered with paneling. With half board included, per-person rates in a double range from 400 AS ($21.28) to 580 AS ($30.87), while singles carry a daily supplement of 60 AS ($3.19).

Menu items in the adjoining restaurant read like a "Who's Who" of international geography. They include recipes from the Pacific (veal steak Hawaii), the Far East (Chinese fondue), and India (a range of curry dishes). If you like steak tartare, it's succulent here. Steaks are also elegantly presented at your table in a copper pan. À la carte meals range from 85 AS ($4.52) to 300 AS ($15.96), while fixed-price dinners cost from 115 AS ($6.12) to 135 AS ($7.18).

Hotel zur Burgruine (tel. 306) is a rambling, three-story building set on a hillside, with a design somewhat like that of a chalet. Its public rooms have high ceilings with huge timbers crisscrossing it, beautifully notched and skillfully joined together. The decor includes knotty-pine big-bottomed chairs and stippled stucco. On the premises is an indoor pool with a rustic ceiling, plus a sauna, an exercise room, and a large restaurant whose specialties are well-flavored grilled meats. A member of the Heinze family will be glad to tell you about excursions in the region. Rooms range in price from 325 AS ($17.29) to 745 AS ($39.63) in a single and between 325 AS ($17.29) and 625 AS ($33.25) per person in a double, according to the season and plumbing, with half board included.

Hotel Orgler (tel. 205) is a cream-colored house with flowered balconies in the middle of the village. Slightly isolated from its neighbors, it offers peace, quiet, and a pleasantly rustic interior of high ceilings, heavy beams, and chalet-style furniture. A sauna, a solarium, and a day café are all on the premises, as well as a sunny dining room. Each of the bedrooms has its own bath, and many of them contain their own balconies as well. Per-person rates in a double range from 460 AS ($24.47) to 520 AS ($27.66), depending on the season, with half board included. Occupants of singles pay a 30 AS ($1.60) daily surcharge.

Gasthof zur Mühle (tel. 254) is a white-walled chalet with wooden balconies and five floors of unpretentiously cozy rooms. On a quiet road in an isolated part of the village, it contains a sauna, table tennis facilities, and a comfortable TV room. It's owned and operated by the Nindl family, who charges between 320 AS ($17.02) and 465 AS ($24.74) per person in a double, with half board included. The single surcharge is 45 AS ($2.39) daily. A covered swimming pool in a nearby hotel is available to guests at zur Mühle.

Gasthof Hotel Tauernhof (tel. 235). Elise Mayerhofer and her family run this L-shaped chalet with the painted illustrations and the prominent balconies. Constructed in the recent past, the establishment contains comfortable bedrooms, a restaurant, and a wine cellar. With half board included, doubles cost between 290 AS ($15.34) and 400 AS ($21.28) per person. Singles pay a daily surcharge of 30 AS ($1.60).

Barbarahof (tel. 7248) is adjacent to its sister hotel, the Tauernhof. The windows of its frontal bedrooms are gently angled to allow more of the sunlight to penetrate behind the flowered balconies. Inside you'll find a covered swimming pool, a sauna, a separate breakfast room, a fitness room, and an elevator. Each of the accommodations has a private bath, phone, TV, and radio. Per-person rates in a double range from 420 AS ($22.34) to 500 AS ($26.60) depending on the season, with half board included. Singles carry a daily surcharge of 60 AS ($3.19).

Grabner's Gasthof Gletscherblick (tel. 293) is a small, family-run guest house with flowered balconies and a sunny terrace. A bus stops in front of the house to transport guests to the village. Inside the gasthof you'll find gutbürgerlich cookery, a kellerbar, and a café. The comfortable bedrooms are clean, with lots of exposed wood. Singles rent for 375 AS ($19.95), and doubles range between 340 AS ($18.09) and 375 AS ($19.95) per person, depending on the plumbing, with half board included.

Krefelderhütte (tel. 621-361) is a mountain lodge in lonely isolation above the village at 7545 feet. It's an elongated three-story house with wood siding and a hipped and gabled roof. It sits next to a rocky outcropping near the ski slopes, with an amiable direction provided by the Rattensberger family. Simply furnished doubles rent for 150 AS ($7.98) per person. Half board costs an additional 50 AS ($2.66) per person, a super-bargain. The hotel is closed in June and October, and almost constantly booked during Easter, Christmas, and New Year's.

Alpincenter (tel. 300) is a sturdily built wood-and-concrete hotel near the terminus of the ski lift on top of the mountain. The interior is modern and rustic, with lots of heavy exposed beams, a central fireplace with curved stools pulled up in a circle around it (the smoke is funneled up through a chimney), and a series of clean and attractive public rooms, usually filled with sports enthusiasts. This hotel makes week-long offers in wintertime that include a seven-day ski pass, but for the daily rate half board ranges from 395 AS ($21.01) to 445 AS ($23.67) per person, with single occupants paying a daily surcharge of 60 AS ($3.19).

Kesselfall Alpenhaus (tel. 202) is a beautifully detailed alpine chalet built at the bottom of a steep semi-forested cliff. It's one of the few chalets in the region with a stone sheathing over its ground floor. The plant-covered balconies have balustrades with heart-shaped cutouts, which, in addition to the lime-green shutters, give almost a fairyland aspect to this house. The bedrooms often have patterned wall-to-wall carpeting wooden furniture partially painted with alpine flora. Singles range from 230 and AS ($12.24) to 245 AS ($13.03), while doubles cost between 210 AS ($11.17) and 225 AS ($11.97) per person, with breakfast included.

Après-Ski

Kaprun has its own relatively modest nightlife, but should you ever get bored you can always take the shuttle bus over to Zell am See for much more excitement. Nightlife reaches its peak in Kaprun on Friday and Saturday nights, and on other nights you might like to turn in with a good book . . . or whatever.

The **Sporthotel Kaprun,** already recommended, is the scene of the most action, offering dancing to either disco records (often the latest hits from the U.S.) or else live bands, often imported from Italy. You might begin your evening with a Chinese fondue dinner or an Indonesian-style rijsttafel, that ceremonial feast of the Dutch colonists.

Your evening in Kaprun might begin relatively modestly—and early—by dropping into **Morokutti** (if you can find a seat) for one of those mouthwatering Austrian pastries. Sometimes the **Nindl Café** has folkloric evenings and dancing, which you'll definitely want to see and participate in.

You can also attend tea dances in the late afternoon at the **Baum tavern,** later enjoying disco action at the **Salzburger Keller.**

Many skiers like to spend their evening sitting and drinking around an open fire. Nearly all hotels and pensions welcome outside guests.

Drink prices are about the same in all these establishments, beginning at 65 AS ($3.46).

MARIA ALM: The village of Maria Alm, three miles east of Saalfelden at an elevation of 2600 feet, is both a summer and a winter resort. Lying at the foot of the Steineres Meer, the karstic limestone plateau called the "sea of stone," now a nature reserve, Maria Alm holds many attractions for warm weather visitors, including chair-lift rides to heights presenting glorious alpine vistas, a 35-mile network of marked pathways for walks in shady woods and across wide romantic grassways, tennis, and mini-golf.

The surrounding mountains attract skiers in winter. Together with Hintermoos and Hinterthal, Maria Alm forms a large avalanche-free winter sports area, with continuous snow cover from the beginning of December to the end of April.

The church spire in Maria Alm rises to 276 feet.

Food and Lodging

Hotel Norica (tel. 491) is a four-story roadside chalet, with all the balconies and rustic detailing you'd expect. The cozy interior is comfortable, filled with alpine-style timbers (some of them decorative), knotty paneling, and conference facilities. A heated indoor swimming pool and a sauna, along with a wind-sheltered sun terrace, are part of the facilities. The location of this hotel, near the ski lifts, makes it ideal for skiers. Each of the rooms has a large bath. Singles range from 720 AS ($38.30) to 915 AS

($48.69), while doubles cost between 600 AS ($31.92) and 800 AS ($42.56) per person, with half board included.

The adjoining restaurant is definitely an above-average place at which to eat. Menu items include scampi Café de Paris, peppersteak Madagascar, filet Stroganoff, and roast pork Singapore style. Fixed-price meals range from 115 AS ($6.12) to 180 AS ($9.58), while à la carte dinners cost between 95 AS ($5.05) and 290 AS ($15.34). The restaurant is open seven days a week, and reservations are a good idea.

Restaurant Arcade, 9 Hinterthal (tel. 828-235), is a small and intimate restaurant loaded with personalized touches. The decor, both inside and out, is one of regionally inspired handiwork. The clientele is local and loyal, although the establishment draws a large number of vacationers as well. Menu items include delicately flavored specialties such as watercress soup, filet of beef in a paprika-rosemary sauce, trout in a Riesling sauce, and turbot with a chive sabayon. Dessert items are too lengthy to list, but one of the most popular is a walnut parfait. À la carte meals range from 130 AS ($6.92) to 335 AS ($17.82), while fixed-price dinners cost between 335 AS ($17.82) and 600 AS ($31.92). Reservations are important. The restaurant is closed during all of May and from early October until just before Christmas.

MAISHOFEN: This is actually a little satellite outpost of Zell am See where you might choose to anchor if you want to stay in the area, yet escape the frenetic pace that overtakes the larger resort in the height of both the winter and the summer seasons. Maishofen has convenience and tranquility, with all the sights and attractions of Zell am See at its doorstep.

Food and Lodging

Gasthaus Schloss Kammer (tel. 8202). From the outside this place looks more like a prosperous bourgeois house than a castle. But for romantics, a small room in the main building might be a perfect hideaway. Most of them get lots of sun and are furnished with antiques or reasonably good copies, along with some baroque fireplaces or ceramic stoves. You can stay here for 275 AS ($14.63) for complete board. Or, especially if you're a family, the Neumayer family will rent you an apartment in a neighboring annex, suitable for two to six persons, costing between 540 AS ($28.73) and 980 AS ($52.14) daily.

In the main hotel the public rooms have unusual old photographs and lots of carved statues. The dining room is one of the most sought after in the region. Most of its plaster ceiling is supported by massive stone columns and old vaulting. A green ceramic stove provides heat to offset the winter winds blowing against the small-paned windows. The noodles are homemade, accompanying such main dishes as roast pork, roast venison, goulashes, and a variety of tempting stews. À la carte meals range from 75 AS ($3.99) to 185 AS ($9.84). The restaurant is closed on Tuesday.

BRUCK AN DER GROSSGLOCKNERSTRASSE: The starting point for Grossglockner Road (coming up) is at this little mountain resort, which becomes a lure to skiers when the snow falls. In summer the Grossglocknerstrasse brings lots of vehicular traffic through the village, standing at an elevation of 2485 feet. Bruck's **parish church** *(pfarrkirche)* is from the 19th century.

From here visitors go up to **Schloss Fischhorn** for one of the most celebrated views in the area. Another excursion is to **Taxenbach,** 7½ miles away. Some 15 minutes from that point, you reach **Kitzloch Gorge,** where you can take an hour's tour from May 1 until the end of October, costing adults 25 AS ($1.33); children, 8 AS (43¢).

Food and Lodging

Hotel Lukashansl (tel. 458) has an unusual facade of white stucco with beige detailing and avocado-colored shutters. The windows are small and are surrounded with detailing in country baroque. A member of the Peter Mayr family has cultivated a grape arbor near the café terrace, which is separated from the road by a row of potted shrubs. A recently built annex with flowered balconies juts off to one side of the main building with parking space beside it. Half-board rates range from 360 AS ($19.15) to 385 AS ($20.48) per person, based on double occupancy, while singles cost 460 AS ($24.47). The hotel is especially popular in winter.

RAURIS: Motorists entering the Rauris Valley from Taxenbach come upon Rauris, which was a goldmining town in the Middle Ages. Many of the elegant old houses in the town are from that era.

The **Rauris Museum** exhibits popular art and artifacts left over from the goldmining heyday of the town. The collection is in honor of Rojacker, founder of the Sonnblick Observatory. The museum is open all year, with guided daily visits from 10 a.m. Admission is 15 AS (80¢) for adults and 7 AS (37¢) for children.

Rauris (2600 feet) is a summer excursion and a winter ski resort. You can take chair lifts to the Kreuzboden at 4280 feet and the Jack-Hochalm at 4820 feet.

Food and Lodging

Sporthotel Rauriserhof (tel. 213) is a large, recently built hotel which, if you could see it from the air, looks like two huge chalets connected by a central corridor and a series of low-lying sports facilities. The outdoor tennis courts are a few steps away, and immediately next to them are two indoor tennis courts. Other facilities include a sauna, a swimming pool, a bowling alley, and at the end of a tiring day of sports and play, a collection of cozily paneled bars, backgammon rooms, crackling fireplaces, and intimate corners. The place is fun, interesting, and could be a central point for a prolonged stay exploring the region's footpaths.

Well-furnished singles range from 385 AS ($20.48) to 720 AS ($38.30), while doubles cost between 515 AS ($27.40) and 810 AS ($43.09) per person, with half board included. The in-house restaurant is worth a special trip. Aside from its Austrian specialties, international fare includes snails, crabmeat soup, and entrecôte Café de Paris. Gutbürgerlich selections feature well-prepared game, schnitzels, roasts, and pork cutlets in vodka sauce. Fixed-price meals range from 85 AS ($4.52) to 135 AS ($7.18), while à la carte dinners cost between 95 AS ($5.05) and 325 AS ($17.29). It's open every day.

Restaurant Schüttgut, Wörth (tel. 403), is authentic enough to make you feel like one of the prosperous local farmers. The restaurant used to be a rough-timbered farm building, constructed in the 16th century, until it was transformed into this charming establishment run by Anton Hubers and his pretty wife. The service is personalized, and you are likely to feel a gemütlich warmth before the end of your meal. Specialties are wholesome, filling, and regional. À la carte meals range from 75 AS ($3.99) to 165 AS ($8.79). It's open every day.

MITTERSILL: The major town of the Upper Pinzgau region (Oberpinzgau), Mittersill, at an elevation of 2590 feet, is at the intersection of ancient trade routes, with buildings rich in tradition. Surrounded by three lakes and 30 miles of alpine brooks, with many beautiful paths for summer walking and hiking, the town is also a popular winter sports center.

Skiers can go to the main skiing area of Pass Thurn-Kitzbühel, where one ski pass allows use of any of the 56 ski lifts and a ski bus.

The glaciers of Hohe Tauern south of the village are part of the national park system, which you can visit.

Mittersill has two churches built in the baroque style in the mid-18th century. Schloss Mittersill, from the 16th century, is privately owned and cannot be visited.

There's a local **museum** in the Felber Tower, where a varied collection of Pinzgau peasant furnishings is exhibited, as well as many minerals, tools, and other artifacts. It also shows ecclesiastical art. The museum is open from June 1 until the end of September Monday to Friday from 9 a.m. to 5 p.m., on Saturday and Sunday from 1 to 5 p.m. Admission is 18 AS (96¢) for adults, 8 AS (43¢) for children.

Food and Lodging

Hotel Schloss Mittersill (tel. 4523). The Gothic chapel attached to this prosperous-looking house is frequently used for marriage ceremonies, which eventually spill over into the main hotel. The hotel is about a 20-minute walk from the center of the village and is easily accessible by car. You'll recognize it by its patterned red and white shutters and its roofline with three tiers of small-windowed gables. The public rooms are appropriately baronial, with vaulted ceilings and thick walls pierced with triple sets of arched Gothic windows. A library/sitting room has stone detailing and paneling darkened long ago by frequent polishing. My favorite room has a massively timbered ceiling, pure-white walls, graceful proportions, a baronial stone fireplace, and lots of hunting trophies.

Each of the bedrooms is individually furnished, sometimes with built-in closets of knotty pine. Singles range from 270 AS ($14.36) to 720 AS ($38.30), while doubles cost between 420 AS ($22.34) and 1170 AS ($62.24) per room, including breakfast. Half board goes for another 130 AS ($6.92) per person daily.

Gasthof Bräurup (tel. 216) is a historical white-walled house with four floors of wood-grained shutters and a surrounding grassy lawn. The interior has rustic touches which include lots of burnished paneling, ceramic stoves with unusual hand-painted illustrations, shelves of antique pewter, and a scattering of colorful regional antiques. The bedrooms are usually large and furnished with big windows and more furniture than you'd expect. The elevator is large enough to accommodate wheelchairs.

My favorite room is the richly paneled rectangular restaurant with the hand-carved baroque finials at the corner of the walls and ceiling. In the center is a round panel bristling with sheaves of grain carved into the glowing hardwoods. The inn is in the center of the village. Per-person rates in double rooms range from 275 AS ($14.63) to 435 AS ($23.14), with half board included. Singles pay a daily surcharge of 35 AS ($1.86).

Hotel/Restaurant Pass Thurn (tel. 34611), built in an area convenient to skiers, is large, balconied, imposing, and covered on the outside with wood detailing. The rustically elegant interior has a collection of painted armoires and chests in the public rooms that deserve a second look, a heavily beamed two-story bar and restaurant in a separate building, and cozy eating and drinking areas where you'll run into sports enthusiasts. Depending on the season, per-person rates in a double range from 325 AS ($17.29) to 475 AS ($25.27), with half board included. Residents of a single pay a daily surcharge of 40 AS ($2.13). All units contain private baths.

NEUKIRCHEN AM GROSSVENEDIGER: Lying near Wald in Pinzgau at an elevation of 2800 feet, in a setting of alpine woods and meadows, fields and forest paths, Neukirchen's sunny terraces afford a view of 15 mountain peaks, including the Grossvenediger, the Kleinvenediger, and the Geiger. Many alpine hikes can be arranged by the Oberpinzgau school of mountaineering.

The village has a late Gothic church with a 14th-century fresco. You can also see the **Castle Hochneukirchen** here, dating from the 16th century. The present schloss was built on the site of a much older structure that was destroyed.

Like nearly all resorts in Land Salzburg, Neukirchen is a ski center in winter and a holiday resort in summer.

Food and Lodging

Hotel Gassner (tel. 232) is a large hotel built chalet style in two sections joined together by a series of balconied rooms. A sun terrace rests on massive stone columns above a parking lot, and the hotel is slightly outside the central part of the village. The interior is contemporary and rustic, with lots of comfortable banquettes and full-grained polished planking decorating the ceilings and walls. The indoor pool is big enough to swim laps in, while the spacious bedrooms are simple, cozy, and comfortable. Also on the premises is a sauna, and the hotel has easy access to the nearby ski slopes. Usually a crackling fire will be waiting for you after your return from a winter's day outdoors. Per-person rates in doubles range from 275 AS ($14.63) to 410 AS ($21.81), with half board included. Prices vary according to the plumbing and the season. Occupants of singles pay a supplement of 35 AS ($1.86) daily.

Gasthof/Pension Kammerlander (tel. 231) is a large, four-story hotel with a concrete exterior, painted white, wraparound balconies, and heavy overhanging eaves. Not far from the village church, the gasthof is owned by the Kammerlander family, who do everything they can to welcome guests to their comfortable hotel. The interior includes masonry detailing, lots of wood, unusual art objects, and a comfortably inviting restaurant and bar area with red tablecloths, hanging lamps, and well-prepared Austrian-style food. Per-person rates, double occupancy, range from 275 AS ($14.63) to 450 AS ($23.94), with half board included. Occupants of singles pay a supplement ranging between 40 AS ($2.13) and 60 AS ($3.19) daily. Prices depend on the plumbing, the season, and the room assignment.

Alpengasthof Rechtegg (tel. 324). The Kröll family are your friendly hosts at this hillside chalet, where the views from the windows are spectacular. The panoramic restaurant on the downhill side has a well-planted sun terrace on top, and someone has accommodatingly built a rooftop covered platform for any happenstance stork who feels like living there. The public rooms are cozy and sunny, while the bedrooms look like something from a private home, with combinations of knotty pine and textured white walls that are pleasing. With half board included, rooms with private bath rent for 265 AS ($14.10) to 350 AS ($18.62) per person, while bathless units go for 195 AS ($10.37) to 265 AS ($14.10) per person, depending on the season.

WALD IM OBERPINZGAU: Wald, a summer and winter resort at a 2900-foot elevation, occupies one of the most beautiful sites in the Upper Pinzgau. The village lies at the junction of the old road from the Gerlos Pass, and from it you can see the glacial peaks of the Grossvenediger massif. In its churchyard you'll see gravestones carved out of rare minerals.

In summer, Wald is a good center for easy footpaths and climbs in the national park at certain times of year. From here, you can enjoy alpine hunting and trout fishing. Also, a hang-gliding school may attract you.

Skiing and other sports lure winter visitors. A ski school prepares you to try the 25 miles of slopes. About 18 major lifts reach three skiing areas where snow is virtually guaranteed well past Easter. Skiing is possible at elevations ranging from 4800 feet to 6500 feet. There are also any number of easy footpaths. Hotels here can organize toboggan runs, riding, horse-sleigh rides, and curling.

Food and Lodging

Jagdschloss Graf Recke (tel. 417). This elegant red-roofed mansion was built in 1926 as the personal hunting lodge of the Silesian family of the Count von der Recke. At the time they owned the hunting rights in what is today the nearby Austrian National Park of Hohe Tauern. The best time to see this place might be in summer, when a thick layer of wildflowers covers the grounds around it. A curved swimming pool lies just beyond the stone foundation. The famous guests who stayed here in the 1920s and 1930s would make a long (and perhaps notorious) list, although today the hunting trophies that fill the interior are the only reminder of their presence. An indoor pool, sauna, and the proximity to the miles of footpaths in the region, along with the dozens of ski lifts all around, are part of the benefits of this well-run hotel.

With half board included, singles rent for between 500 AS ($26.60) and 750 AS ($39.90), while doubles cost between 445 AS ($23.67) and 660 AS ($35.11) per person, depending on the plumbing and the season. Some of the suites and apartments inside are more expensive. An extra bed can be set up in any room for an additional fee which almost matches the per-person rate for the room itself.

The handsome restaurant is worth a detour, especially if you're fond of game or freshly caught fish. Many of the fish are caught in the nearby wilderness. Fixed-price meals range from 110 AS ($5.85) to 335 AS

($17.82), while à la carte dinners cost between 120 AS ($6.38) and 315 AS ($16.75).

Walderwirt and Märzenhof (tel. 8216). Everyone has a choice in life, and in this case you'll be able to choose between two different buildings on either side of the street. The older of the two was built in 1770, and still maintains the vaulted ceilings, heavy timbers, and some of the painted antiques of the year of its construction. The modern section has streamlined wooden balconies, an indoor pool, tennis courts, lots of paneling, and an open fireplace whose massive hanging chimney is made of small plates of iron riveted together.

Bedrooms cost approximately the same in the two buildings, and they're connected by an underground passage in case you can't decide which you like better. Per-person rates, based on double occupancy, range from 360 AS ($19.15) to 650 AS ($34.58) with half board included, depending on the season and the plumbing.

The restaurant is contained in the older section. It has old paneling, smallish windows, and a ceramic stove. The food comes in copious quantities, and is the kind of gutbürgerlich fare you'll probably want to wash down with a few beers. Many of the cheese selections come from the region. Fixed-price meals cost between 85 AS ($4.52) and 145 AS ($7.71), while à la carte dinners range from 80 AS ($4.26) to 250 AS ($13.30).

KRIMML: This village in the far-western extremity of Land Salzburg is visited mainly by those wishing to explore **Krimml Falls.** The German name for this scene of iridescent splendor is Krimmler Wasserfälle. These falls, the highest in Europe, are spectacular, dropping 1250 feet in three stages. They lie to the south of the Gerlos Pass, which connects the Salzach Valley in Land Salzburg with the Siller Valley in the Tyrolean country. Krimml, mainly a summer resort, is the best base for exploring the falls. The village is in a heavily forested valley called Krimmler Ache, between the Kitzbühel Alps and the Hohe Tauern.

If you're coming from Salzburg, figure on some 95 miles by train. There's also bus service from Zell am See. If you're traveling by car you have a choice of leaving your vehicle at the car park at the south of the village and making a 30-minute walk to the lower falls, or taking the Gerlos Pass toll road, open from June 1 to September 30. The toll is 8 AS (43¢) for adults and 4 AS (21¢) for children. Visits to the falls are possible from May until October.

Most visitors allow about 3½ hours to explore the entire falls area. On a sunny day, try to visit the Wasserfälle around noon when they are at their most spectacular. On summer nights the waterfalls are likely to be floodlit on Wednesday, depending on weather conditions.

Wear good, sturdy shoes, and since viewing points are always shrouded in spray, a raincoat will come in handy.

After you've seen the lower falls, if you want to see the second stage, count on another 12-minute walk. From there it's only a five-minute jaunt to the third and final stage for viewing the cataracts. There are also paths leading to the fourth and fifth viewing points. The middle part of the falls can be seen at the sixth and seventh lookouts. At the Bergerblick, you'll have your greatest view of the waterfalls, reached by continuing another 20 minutes from the seventh viewing point. If you wish, you can go on to the Schettbrücke (4800 feet) for a look at the upper cascades.

Krimml is also visited in winter, because good skiing is offered at Gerlosplatte (5600 feet), seven miles away. The waterfalls lie under a deep ice layer during the winter.

If you like to drive along high alpine roads, you can take the Gerlos Road leading from the Krimml Waterfalls to the Gerlos Pass where it joins the road to Zell an Ziller in Tyrol. A single trip costs passenger cars a toll of 80 AS ($4.26).

Food and Lodging

Gastehaus Hanke (tel. 279) is a contemporary, solidly built two-story chalet. It has white walls, wood balconies, and heavy overhanging eaves. The tasteful interior has much wood paneling and lots of cozy touches. The bedrooms are warmly modern and rustic. An indoor heated swimming pool is on the premises. A café and restaurant with painted detailing around the windows and a busy sun terrace are in a separate building. Comfortably furnished singles cost 290 AS ($15.34); doubles, 265 AS ($14.10) per person; triples, 215 AS ($11.44) per person. Some three-person apartments are available for 550 AS ($29.26). Breakfast is included in these prices, and each unit contains a private bath.

Alpengasthof Krimmler Tauernhaus (tel. 313). The location of this wood-sided hotel couldn't be more idyllic. It's built on the grassy flatlands of a high alpine valley. Two streams rush by at a safe distance on either side of the green shuttered building, whose only neighbors are a few barns and storage sheds. This is the perfect place to get away from urban mania and everything that goes with that.

The interior is charming, with a timbered restaurant decorated with red-and-white checked curtains, musical instruments, and an antique polychrome crucifix hanging from the old paneling on the walls. You'll be tempted to spend your days outdoors, and there are plenty of nearby footpaths to accommodate you. Half board costs 325 AS ($17.29) per person. Few of the rooms have a private bath. Adolf and Franziska Geisler are your hosts.

Hotel Klockerhaus (tel. 208) is a peaceful double chalet with wooden balconies, gently sloping rooflines, and a central section two stories high. The restaurants inside are timbered, covered with natural-grained pine, and filled with chalet-style chairs and tables. The spacious bedrooms are outfitted with regionally painted furniture with flowered panels set into natural pine frames. Per-person rates in a double range from 265 AS ($14.10) to 360 AS ($19.15), with half board included. Singles pay a daily supplement of 35 AS ($1.86). Prices depend on the plumbing and the season.

Gasthof Schönmoosalm (tel. 272) is a roadside hotel consisting of two chalets joined together in the middle like Siamese twins. The airy dining room has a coffered ceiling, tile floor, and pink napery. The hotel is small, containing only 22 beds, but the location is quiet and sunny, and the accommodations have a view of the mountains. The Eder family, your hosts, charge 265 AS ($14.10) per person in winter and 210 AS ($11.17) per person in summer, with breakfast included.

Gasthof Krimmlerfälle (tel. 203) is a pretty four-story house with sea-green shutters and wood siding covering the third and fourth floors. In summertime the balconies are covered with pink and red flowers. The dining room is laid out below a wooden ceiling whose planks are arranged in a circular pattern above the modern upholstered chairs. The simple and unpretentious rooms are tasteful, filled with extra-graceful touches, and very comfortable. They range in price from 315 AS ($16.75) in a single and from 275 AS ($14.63) per person in a double, with breakfast included. Your congenial hosts are the Schöppl family.

6. The Grossglockner Road

Grossglocknerstrasse, the longest and most splendid alpine highway in Europe, and one of the outstanding tourist attractions on the continent, will afford you one of the greatest drives of your life.

The hairpin turns and bends of the Grossglockner Road have been called "the stuff Grand Prix is made of." It's believed that this was the same route through the Alps used by the Romans, although this was forgotten until 1930 when engineers building the highway discovered remains of the work of their road-building predecessors done some 19 centuries earlier. The highway, representing engineering genius, was finished in 1935. It was the one that such countries as Switzerland and France copied years later when they built their own alpine highways.

It runs for nearly 30 miles, beginning at Bruck an der Grossglocknerstrasse (see above) at 2483 feet, via Fusch/Grossglocknerstrasse, and heading toward Ferleiten, Hochmais, and Fuschtörl through Hochtortunnel, where the highest point is 8220 feet, to Guttal and Heiligenblut (4267 feet) in Carinthia.

The actual mountain part of the road stretches for some 13½ miles, usually at about 6500 feet. It has a maximum gradient of 12%.

Many visitors prefer to take the bus over this spectacular stretch, but if you feel that your driving is good enough, you can do it by private car. Because of the high altitudes, the road is only passable from mid-May to mid-November. Always check with some authority about the road conditions before considering such a drive, especially in spring and autumn. A single trip in a passenger car costs a toll of 250 AS ($13.30). The toll is collected either at Ferleiten or at Heiligenblut. In summer there is regular Postal Bus service running from such places as Zell am See and Salzburg.

After leaving Bruck, you enter the Fuscher Valley going south, and along the way you'll be rewarded with breathtaking alpine scenery. Four miles from the Hochtortunnel on the north side, you can branch off onto the Edelweiss-Strasse, going along for about 1½ miles to the car park at the **Edelweiss-Spitze** (8433 feet). Here you'll see a panorama of 37 10,000-foot peaks. At Edelweiss-Spitze is an observation tower, going up to more than 8450 feet.

One of the interesting detours along the road is to the stone terrace of the **Franz-Josefs-Höhe.** It's named for the emperor who once had a mansion constructed here in the foothills of the Pasterze Glacier. The stretch from Gletscherstrasse to Franz-Josefs-Höhe (7770 feet) is some five miles long, branching off near Guttal. This road lies above the Pasterze Glacier, opposite the Grossglockner (12,430 feet). The Pasterze, incidentally, is the largest glacier in the eastern Alps, 5½ miles long.

If you're traveling in spring and autumn, it might not be possible to take detours to the Edelweiss-Spitze or the Franz-Josefs-Höhe if heavy snow falls. If you do take the side trip to the latter site, avoid arriving there around midday. On a bright sunny day in summer the place is literally mobbed. It has an outstanding view of the majestic Grossglockner.

It's possible to descend from Freiwandeck to Pasterze Glacier by taking a funicular from May until the end of September. Service is every hour from 8 a.m. to 4 p.m. at a cost of 50 AS ($2.66) for a round-trip ticket.

7. Zell am See

Founded by monks around the middle of the eighth century, the old part of Zell am See lies on the shore of the Zeller See (Lake Zell), with a backdrop of mountains. Zeller See is a deep glacial lake filled with clear blue alpine water. The town today is the most important resort in the Middle Pinzgau, a district that has already been previewed. Zell is popular and fashionable in both summer and winter. It's also a center for those who'd like to get an early start and travel the celebrated Grossglockner alpine highway, described above.

Unlike most resorts in Land Salzburg, Zell am See has some old buildings worth exploring. These include **Kastnerturm,** or the constable's tower, the oldest building in town, dating from the 12th century. It was once used as a grain silo.

The town's **parish church** *(pfarrkirche)* is an 11th-century Romanesque-style structure. It has, however, a late Gothic choir from the 16th century.

Castle Rosenberg is also from the 16th century. It was once an elegant residence of South Bavaria. Today it houses the Rathaus (town hall), a gallery, and a folklore museum. There's a tower at each of the four corners, and a round tower. Old costumes are displayed in the museum, and many artifacts on exhibit show the traditional way of life in earlier Land Salzburg. The museum is open Monday, Wednesday, and Saturday from 4 to 6 p.m., charging no admission.

Zell is as well equipped for summer and for winter sports as are the competitive resorts of Kaprun and Saalbach.

For winter visitors, snow conditions in the Zell area are usually ideal from December all the way to the end of April. Zell am See attracts beginner and intermediate skiers but, surprisingly, more nonskiers it seems—people who like the attractions of the resort in winter and the bustling life even if they never take to the slopes. They do take the chair lift (sans skis) for the magnificent alpine scenery. Skiing is possible at elevations ranging from 3000 feet to 9000 feet.

Sports fans gravitate to the Kur- und-Sportzentrum, an arena northwest of the resort housing a mammoth indoor swimming pool as well as a sauna and an ice rink. Sometimes in cold weather, the lake is frozen over. Aircraft, presumably lightweight ones, have been known to land on the Zeller See in the dead of winter.

Although known as a winter sports center, Zell am See seems to attract even more visitors in the peak summer months. **Lake Zell,** which has been called "the cleanest" lake in Europe, is warm, maintaining an average temperature of some 70° Fahrenheit in summer. The lake is 2½ miles long and 1 mile wide. Motorboats can be rented for tours. You can go along a footpath from the town to the bathing station at Seespitz, the walk taking about half an hour.

Schmittenhöhe, at 6450 feet, towers to the west of Zell am See. You can go up the mountain in four different ways, with even more choices for ways to descend. In summer the hardy and hearty have been known to climb it in four hours. I suggest, however, that you take the cableway. The view from here is one of the finest in the Kitzbühel Alps, the majestic glacial peaks of the Grossglockner range being only part of the celestial heights you'll see on your excursion. You can have lunch at the Burghotel at the upper station.

From the west side of Zell am See you can take a four-seater cableway to the middle station. From here you can connect with several lifts that will take you to the upper platform. A sun terrace at the upper station is popular in both summer and winter. (Don't be surprised to see bare breasts even in February.)

It's about one mile up Schmittenhöhe. Figure on about 1¾ hours for your round trip, plus another 18 minutes by cable car. In summer service is every half hour. A round trip costs 150 AS ($7.98) per adult.

You can also take the Sonnalm cableway (entrance near the Schmittenhöhe terminus) to Sonnalm at 4540 feet. You'll find another restaurant here. From Sonnalm, it's possible to go by chair lift to Sonnkogel (6020 feet) and by drag lift to Hochmais (5665 feet). From the eastern part of Lake Zell you can take the chair lift up to Ronachkopf (4875 feet).

From Zell am See you can also take a funicular to Kaprun (see above), at the foot of the Kitzsteinhorn, for glacier and year-round skiing. In fact some of the most spectacular excursions possible from Kaprun can be made easily on tours from Zell am See (refer to the Kaprun description for more details).

Food and Lodging

Hotel Salzburger Hof, 11 Auerspergstrasse (tel. 2828). You'll get a glimpse of the handcrafted interior of this hotel through the glass doors leading inside. A polychrome wood statue of what might be an archbishop is fastened to a background of carved pine in the lobby. The most elegant piece of wrought iron in town serves as the entrance to the dining room.

In the salon a blazing fire is housed in an unusual brick-lined stucco fireplace, which guests enjoy under heavily timbered ceilings. The Holleis family maintains the pleasant outdoor garden with its sun terrace. You'll recognize the hotel by its chalet design and its location near the lake. A sauna and heated indoor swimming pool are on the premises.

With half board included, per-person rates in a double range from 520 AS ($27.66) to 1020 AS ($54.26), depending on the season. Singles cost an additional 90 AS ($4.79) per day. All units contain a private bath.

Hotel Zum Hirschen (tel. 2447). The Pacalt family are the congenial and hard-working owners of this balconied hotel with its white walls, wood trim, and central location. You'll enter from the street through a double doorway angled into a corner of the building, whose recently renovated interior has lots of wood accents, a central heating stove in white stucco and dark-green tiles, along with a combination of modern furniture that blends well with the exquisite painted armoire in the main salon. A covered heated swimming pool has an unusual border of smooth river rocks, with a sauna and steambath close at hand. Per-person rates in a double range from 530 AS ($28.20) to 1020 AS ($54.26), with half board included. Singles pay a surcharge of 50 AS ($2.66) daily.

Restaurant Zum Hirschen is connected to the hotel. The setting is one of elegantly light-grained paneling, immaculate napery, and wholesome rusticity. Specialties include fresh lavarits from the nearby lake, mountain game, and homemade pâté. If that doesn't appeal to you, you might try creamed chipped veal with the Swiss-style rösti, a range of schnitzels and pork dishes, as well as roast veal in a burgundy sauce or perhaps entrecôte

Café de Paris. The chef also prepares that traditional Franz Joseph favorite, tafelspitz. The service is friendly and efficient. À la carte meals range from 180 AS ($9.58) to 500 AS ($26.60).

Hotel Porschehof (tel. 7248) is a charming chalet in a woodsy area a few minutes' drive from the center of town. The main salon inside has a gently vaulted ceiling, painted chests, and wrought-iron lighting fixtures. You'll find several attractive fireplaces, my favorite of which has a pleasingly scaled fieldstone construction with an arch for the fire itself and a tapering pyramid for the chimney. The rest of the building's detailing includes ceramic ovens, beamed ceilings, rustically alpine dining room chairs, and the kind of inviting bar area where you can enjoy a drink before dinner. On the premises are a solar-heated indoor pool, a sauna, a fitness room, and massage facilities. Rates range from 420 AS ($22.34) to 660 AS ($35.11) per person, based on double occupancy, and half board pension costs another 90 AS ($4.79) per person daily. Singles pay a supplement of 35 AS ($1.86) per day. Each of the units has a private bath, and almost all of the accommodations contain private balconies.

Clima Seehotel, 1 Esplanade (tel. 2504), is an imposing building with a crescent-shaped terrace above the curved windows of the panoramic first floor. The hotel sits directly on the water, with several floors of white walls, yellow window trim, and at least one well-placed skylight. The bedrooms behind the mansard-style gables on the top floor have an especially good view. Per-person rates, based on double occupancy, range from 600 AS ($31.92) to 830 AS ($44.17), with a supplement of 130 AS ($6.92) daily charged for single occupancy. Half board costs another 50 AS ($2.66) per person daily.

Schmittenhöhe (tel. 2376). The ski lifts leading to the top of this mountain will deposit you a few steps from the door of this cozy hotel. The only buildings nearby are the isolated village church and those connected with the ski lifts, so much of your nighttime activity will be centered within the hotel. The format is pleasant, well furnished, warm, and intimate, with blazing masonry fireplaces, lots of paneling, good food, and superb views from the romantic bedrooms. An "Ice Bar" and a buffet attract lots of daytime visitors as well. The hotel is owned by the Grand Hotel in the middle of Zell am See, an edifice closed during most of 1984. At the Schmittenhöhe, singles range from 465 AS ($24.74) to 750 AS ($39.90), while doubles cost between 420 AS ($22.34) and 675 AS ($35.91) per person, half board included. Prices depend on the plumbing and the season.

Hotel St. Hubertushof, Thumersbach (tel. 3130), is a large sprawling hotel that's designed like a collection of balconied chalets clustered in a single unit. The sober and elegant decor attracts many repeat visitors, and the staff is efficient and friendly. The flat-roofed dance bar which juts forward into the parking lot is one of the area's popular nightspots. The hotel is in one of the sunniest spots of the resort. Its bedrooms are large, comfortable, and rustic. Josef and Erna Hollaus, your hosts, charge between 300 AS ($15.96) and 540 AS ($28.73) in a single and between 290 AS ($15.34) and 540 AS ($28.73) per person in a double, with half board included. The hotel is closed between November 1 and mid-December.

The menu in the adjoining restaurant includes specialties from around the world, as well as a few regional grandmother-style recipes. Meals are well prepared and beautifully served, and might be followed by one of the chef's flaming desserts. Fixed-price meals range from 95 AS ($5.05) to 180 AS ($9.58), while à la carte dinners cost between 85 AS ($4.52) and 300 AS ($15.96).

Hotel St. Georg, 10 Schillerstrasse (tel. 3533), will greet you with one of the prettiest facades in town. Roughly half of the front is devoted to finely drawn country baroque designs around the windows. The other half of the exterior has flowered balconies, curved yellow awnings, and a graceful parapet covered with thick cedar shingles.

The rustically romantic interior is tastefully filled with beamed ceilings, concealed lighting, antique wrought iron, and old painted chests. In one of the salons, a pair of polychrome statues of barely remembered saints give a quiet benediction to the conversations on the velvet settees. On the premises are an indoor swimming pool, a sauna, and several cozy bars.

The restaurant has vaulted plaster ceilings, hunting trophies, elegant wrought-iron wall sconces with yellow shades, and a circular open fireplace which acts as a focal point for the entire room. For visitors not on the board plan, à la carte meals range from 110 AS ($5.85) to 350 AS ($18.62), and might include oxtail soup, a ragoût of fresh mussels, local fresh fish from the Zellersee, and medallions of fresh crayfish. With half board included, singles range from 650 AS ($34.58) to 950 AS ($50.54), while per-person rates in a double go from 625 AS ($33.25) to 950 AS ($50.54), also with half board included. Prices depend on the season, and each unit has a private bath.

Sporthotel Alpin (tel. 3576) is a contemporary chalet whose balconies almost completely surround it. It was designed in such a way that cars can drive up to the front entrance on a concrete platform cantilevered above the hillside slope. The elegant and sporty interior has big sunny windows, a warmly tinted decorative scheme with wine-colored accents, and lots of intricately beamed ceilings. On the premises are a large indoor pool, a sauna, and massage facilities.

Since the hotel lies slightly outside the village, it has both an excellent view of the lake and easy accessibility to the ski lifts. The well-proportioned doubles contain private bath, radio, phone, color TV, and mini-bar. With half board included, they rent for 620 AS ($32.98) to 760 AS ($40.43) per person, and occupants of the singles pay a daily supplement of 140 AS ($7.45).

The handsome restaurant has a black and red tartan carpet, immaculate napery, lots of plants, and big windows. Specialties include both Austrian and international foods which range from wild game to scampi to nouvelle cuisine dishes. If you happen to be around during one of the suckling pig banquets or one of the elaborate farmer's buffets, a uniformed chef will stand behind the heavily laden table to assist you. Fixed-price meals range from 145 AS ($7.71) to 335 AS ($17.82), while à la carte dinners cost between 145 AS ($7.71) and 370 AS ($19.68). Reservations are suggested.

Hotel Waldhof (tel. 2853) is a recently built country-style hotel with lots of weathered planking and balconies. Just outside the sun terrace you'll find an outdoor pool. A warmly decorated cellar bar, filled with alpine-style timbers and colored lights, often has dancing with live music both at 5 p.m. and later in the evening. The other public rooms are tastefully filled with Oriental rugs, big windows, and wood accents. The hotel, run by Joseph Loferer and his family, is about five minutes from the center of town. It charges between 550 AS ($29.26) and 700 AS ($37.24) per person in a double, including half board. Singles pay a daily surcharge of 80 AS ($4.26).

Hotel/Restaurant Neue Post (tel. 3773). One of the best parts of this hotel is the dozens of details carved into the wood of the heavy ceilings of both the public rooms and the bedrooms. The interior has cozy wintertime fireplaces and huge hanging chandeliers fashioned of wrought iron and gilt. The outside of the building has lots of balconies, an enlarged central gable, and a painted design under the side of the roof peak. The spacious bedrooms rent for between 550 AS ($29.26) and 830 AS ($44.17) per person, with half board included. All units have private bath. Prices depend on the season, the size, and the exposure. The supplement for single occupancy is 80 AS ($4.26) a day.

Sporthotel Lebzelter (tel. 2411) is a pretty balconied hotel with subdued ornamentation around its windows and shutters, and under the overhang of the eaves. Sections of the hotel are 500 years old, with the best view of the oldest parts in the vaulted stone cellar, which the Schandlbauer family has converted into a bar. Details inside include an old-fashioned stove made of a combination of plaster and green ceramic tiles, chalet-style chairs, lots of paneling, and rustic artifacts. My favorite room is the Sport-Stüberl, whose attractive clientele somehow looks even better in the reflected glow from the polished wood paneling. Per-person rates, based on double occupancy with half board included, range from 390 AS ($20.75) to 540 AS ($28.73), depending on the season and the plumbing. Singles pay a surcharge of 40 AS ($2.13) per day.

Gasthof Schütthof (tel. 7391) has a central location and a large floor plan. It rises five floors above one of the village's main streets. The only interruption in the three horizontal rows of balconies is a central bay window jutting out from the facade, the front of which has gray and white painted designs and the name of the hotel. The interior has wrought-iron chandeliers, lots of paneling, and a cozy format of big windows and exposed wood. With half board included, per-person rates in a double range from 255 AS ($13.75) to 330 AS ($17.56), while singles cost between 365 AS ($19.42) and 390 AS ($20.75). The above prices apply to bathless units. Accommodations with bath go for another 35 AS ($1.85) per day.

Après-Ski

Zell am See has one of the liveliest après-ski scenes in Land Salzburg. No one puts on airs here, and the clubs and taverns are very informal and getmütlich, with most hard drinks costing from 65 AS ($3.46) to 75 AS ($3.99).

Perhaps the friendliest place after the sun sets is the already-recommended **Sporthotel Lebzelter.** Many times the word "keller" or "cellar" is used in Austria to evoke the atmosphere of a real cellar when it's merely the mock. But at the Lebzelter the cellar is genuine, with a vaulted stone ceiling. Attractive young skiers, mainly European, gravitate here at night, enjoying the booze.

Hotel Waldhof, also recommended, has a typical tavern with regional artifacts. Often a local musician—attired in lederhosen and red stockings—will play for skiers (the women invariably wear pants) who like to dance on the small floor.

A typical Austrian stüberl is found at the **Gasthof Alpenblick,** lying in the satellite hamlet of Schüttdorf on the road to Kaprun. Zither music is usually played for your enjoyment here every evening in season.

The major disco action is usually at the **Pinzgauer Diele,** where you can dance until the wee hours.

In addition to the above-mentioned establishments, there are countless taverns willing to welcome you around their open fire and give you a mug of chilled beer or something more potent.

8. The Flachgau

One of the chief attractions of the Flachgau district is **Wolfgangsee** (Lake Wolfgang) which lies mainly in Land Salzburg, although its major center, St. Wolfgang, is in Upper Austria. The chief Land Salzburg resort on the lake is St. Gilgen. Many people visit Lake Wolfgang on day trips from Salzburg, as it lies within easy commuting distance.

The most celebrated lake in the Salzkammergut, Wolfgangsee is 6 miles long and 1¼ miles wide. The northwest shores are fairly inaccessible.

The Flachgau is a relatively flat area in the environs of Salzburg, dividing Styria, another Austrian province, from Bavaria in West Germany. This section, unlike many of the districts of Land Salzburg to which I've previously introduced you, is strictly a summer resort area for those who enjoy lakeside holidays.

FUSCHL AM SEE: Fuschlsee, of all the lakes in Land Salzburg, is closest to the festival city. It lies to the east of the provincial capital. Salzburgers frequent it heavily, particularly on summer weekends. You may choose to stay in Fuschl am See as an alternative to Salzburg at any time of the year but especially during the festival season. From here you can explore Wolfgangsee.

Lake Fuschl is ringed by woodland. In fact sections bordering the lake comprise a nature reserve. The lake is only 2½ miles long and less than a mile wide. It lies to the northwest of Lake Wolfgang. Fuschl, strictly a summer resort, lies on the eastern strip of the lake.

Food and Lodging

Parkhotel Waldhof (tel. 342) is a first-class chalet hotel with a sprawling facade of flower-bedecked balconies as well as a curved series of bay windows. The interior is graced with lots of wood detailing, stone columns, acres of knotty-pine paneling, leaded windows set in diamond-shaped panes, and crackling exposed fireplaces. On the premises and grounds are a shooting gallery with rifles set on stationary tripods, a high-ceilinged swimming pool, a sauna, a grassy lawn with frontage on the lake, massage facilities, and table tennis. Guests go on guided nature walks which invariably end up with the guide leading his charges to his local tavern.

Each of the individually furnished bedrooms has its own bath, as well as a collection of elegantly comfortable furniture. With full board included, per-person rates range from 465 AS ($24.74) to 600 AS ($31.92) in a single and from 465 AS ($24.74) to 760 AS ($40.43) in a double. There are two rustic and comfortable guest houses nearby. With breakfast included, singles at these places cost between 220 AS ($11.70) and 295 AS ($15.69), while doubles range between 140 AS ($7.45) and 295 AS ($15.69) per person. Breakfast is served in the guest house while half board—arranged for an additional 130 AS ($6.92) per person—can be enjoyed in the hotel's main dining room. All three establishments are directed by members of the Ebner family.

Sporthotel Leitner and **Stefanihof** (tel. 208) are two hotels both owned by the Leitner family. Both establishments charge the same rates for their comfortable rooms. The older of the two is a hip-roofed, green-shuttered building with a prominent dining room jutting out toward the lake. The more modern of the two has a streamlined format of modern windows and a few wood-trimmed balconies. Singles range from 290 AS ($15.34) to 555 AS ($29.53), while doubles cost between 275 AS ($14.63) and 575 AS ($30.59) per person, with full board included. Prices depend on the plumbing and the season.

Gasthof Zum Mohren (tel. 228) is a large, prosperous-looking building with a stippled stucco facade of climbing roses, and smooth bands around and between each of the green-shuttered windows. The cozy interior has much rustic detailing, including several areas for drinking and dining. Established in 1846, it combines tradition with modern comfort. Jakobu and Emmy Schmidlechner, the owners, will welcome you to one of their attractively furnished rooms. For half board, and depending on the season, they charge from 425 AS ($22.61) to 475 AS ($25.27) in a single and from 400 AS ($21.28) to 550 AS ($29.26) per person in a double. Some units contain hot and cold running water; others have private baths.

Brunnwirt (tel. 236) is one of the region's leading restaurants, serving light and well-prepared meals to vacationing gourmets from as far away as Vienna. Housed in a 15th-century building loaded with atmosphere, it receives a healthy business from urbanites who motor here on the autobahn. The cuisine is light textured and inspired by Austrian regional recipes. The kitchen staff is directed by Frau Brandstätter, who insists on a strictly fresh list of ingredients.

Specialties include game dishes, veal, lamb, and a range of other foodstuffs which appear on the frequently changing daily menu. Portions are generous. Herr Brandstätter will probably help you select a wine, and the clientele seems to have a good time. Fixed-price meals cost from 175 AS ($9.31) to 475 AS ($25.27), while à la carte dinners range from 135 AS ($7.18) to 400 AS ($21.28). The restaurant is closed all day Tuesday and on Wednesday until 6 p.m. It has an annual closing during the first two weeks of February and for the first two weeks of October.

HOF BEI SALZBURG: About 15 minutes from Salzburg on Lake Fuschl is this resort which has long drawn the aristocrats of Salzburg because of its private hunting and fishing preserves. There's a nine-hole golf course. You can fish for trout or rent boats for a tour of the lake. The setting is one of mountains, woods, and alpine lake water. From here it's easy to explore not only Fuschlsee but also Wolfgangsee and Mondsee.

Like the suburb of Anif (see Chapter VII), Hof bei Salzburg might be considered for its traditional and romantic accommodations, especially at festival time in August when hotel rooms are virtually impossible to obtain in Salzburg.

Food and Lodging

Hotel Schloss Fuschl (tel. 253). The main section of this castle built in 1450 has the porportions of a city building, with a simple facade of unadorned windows and a height that's taller than its width or depth. It was the former hunting lodge of the prince-archbishops of Salzburg, who cultivated the exquisite gardens on the peninsula jutting into Lake Fuschl and who, over the course of time, gradually transformed it from a semi-fortress into a luxurious pleasure palace.

Among its former guests were Nehru, Eleanor Roosevelt, and Khrushchev. In World War II, von Ribbentrop selected the schloss as his headquarters. Later, Mussolini came here to meet with Nazi leaders.

The interior is dotted with elegant, sometimes baronial fireplaces, along with timbered ceilings, stone columns, and handcrafted stonework. The swimming pool, dedicated to the mythical figure of Diana, is constructed under the plastered vaulting of the ground floor.

According to the price you want to pay, you can rent either a modern room inside the hotel, part of a cozy bungalow on the surrounding grounds, or a luxurious suite fit for a prince and studded with valuable antiques. Singles range from 1200 AS ($63.84) to 1300 AS ($69.16), while doubles go from 1800 AS ($95.76) to 2280 AS ($120.30). An apartment or a two-person bungalow costs between 3600 AS ($191.52) and 3900 AS ($207.48). All accommodations contain private bath and include a buffet-style breakfast. Half and full board are available for an additional 360 AS ($19.15) and 720 AS ($38.30) respectively.

The restaurant is one of the most frequented and highly praised in Austria, with a clientele that includes many of the country's leading politicians and industrialists. Designated long ago as a Relais de Campagne, it has several elegant rooms from which to choose, all decorated in excellent taste with dozens of antiques and paintings, along with charmingly authentic details. One of the rooms is entirely outfitted in pale blue and pink, not unlike a Viennese pastry. The view encompasses much of the lake and sometimes a vista of Salzburg.

Menu items from the handwritten carte include lobster terrine with caviar, homemade noodles with goose-liver pâté, and summer truffles, plus a host of seasonally adjusted specialties. Josef Illinger is the chef, Martin Adlgasser is the wine steward, and their combined efforts produce meals which are known throughout the region. Reservations are almost essential. À la carte meals range from 200 AS ($10.64) to 575 AS ($30.59), while fixed-price dinners go for 375 AS ($19.95) to 850 AS ($45.22).

Jagdhof am Fuschlsee (tel. 372) was an outbuilding of a nearby feudal castle. Originally a 16th-century farmhouse, it's in the authentic style that many 20th-century Austrian buildings are modeled after. The public rooms have evenly spaced timbers supporting the massive ceiling beams, with many contemporary and practical updates such as comfortable chairs, hanging lights, tile floors, and glass display cases. Part of the decoration consists of masses of hunting trophies and some 1000 pipes. Management has also added two bowling alleys.

Per-person rates range from 480 AS ($25.24) to 540 AS ($28.73) in a single and from 720 AS ($38.30) to 900 AS ($47.88) in a double. All the comfortably furnished bedrooms have private bath, so prices depend on the season. Half board is available for another 150 AS ($7.98) per person.

The dining room is filled with rustic artifacts, heavy beams, and a loyal and conservative clientele. A specialty of the chef is pike terrine with green sauce, which could be followed by a wide variety of fish and game dishes. Fixed-price meals range from 110 AS ($5.85) to 195 AS ($10.37), while à la carte dinners go for 130 AS ($6.92) to 330 AS ($17.56). Reservations are suggested.

Gasthof/Pension Nussbaumer (tel. 275) is a recently constructed country hotel, set against an alpine meadow, with a big asphalt parking lot on two sides. On the premises are an indoor heated pool, a sauna, and comfortable public rooms with honey-colored ceiling paneling, inviting banquettes, and lots of sunny windows. An elevator is part of the conveniences, as well as outdoor tennis courts, and a grassy children's playground. The hotel sits just beside a wintertime ski lift. Per-person rates, based on double occupancy, range from 360 AS ($19.15) to 375 AS ($19.95), with half board included. The supplement in a single is 60 AS ($3.19) daily.

OBERTRUM: Lying on the northern part of Lake Obertrum, about ten miles to the north of Salzburg, Obertrum is a popular holiday resort, offering bathing in the lake, water sports, sailing, fishing, tennis, horseback riding, and in winter, ice sports. It's also a good center for many hikes and excursions in a beautiful district.

Incidentally, the lake virtually joins Mattsee and Grabensee, separated only by narrow tongues of land.

Food and Lodging

Braugasthof Sigl (tel. 212). This hotel, along with the nearby brewery, has been owned by the same family since 1775. In the center of the village, it's housed in a distinguished-looking hip-roofed building with lots of chimneys, a row of gables, and a distinctive yellow-and-white facade. In summer, flowers bloom in the boxes near the rounded tower at one of the corners and also in the arched windows on the ground floor.

The interior has a very old carved clothing chest, along with a sprinkling of other antiques. The comfortable bedrooms usually have conservative furnishings and a scattering of homey touches. The hotel is open only in the summertime, charging between 200 AS ($10.64) and 230 AS ($12.24) for a single and between 190 AS ($10.11) and 240 AS ($12.77) for a double, breakfast included.

If you're a beer lover, you'll gravitate to the earthy, unpretentious restaurant adjoining this hotel. You'll have a chance to sample each of the beers brewed in the region, as well as a solid country-style cooking that goes with the brew. Management features week-long specials of, for example, wild game, depending on the season and the availability of ingredients. Desserts are satisfyingly rich, often containing their share of schnapps. Fixed-price meals range from 70 AS ($3.72) to 105 AS ($5.59), while à la carte dinners go from 65 AS ($3.46) to 230 AS ($12.24).

Gasthof Neumayr, 8 Dorfplatz (tel. 302), is a centrally located, hip-roofed guest house with a facade of yellow stucco, forest-green shutters, and an arched entryway leading into a rustically old-fashioned interior. The hotel has 30 rooms, mainly with private shower. The per-person rate is 250 AS ($13.30) in a single and from 220 AS ($11.70) in a double.

The food served in the rustic stube is good enough to attract diners from Salzburg. Specialties of the establishment include fish, especially trout. For an appetizer, you may prefer the matjes herring or liver noodle soup. Other main dishes include an onion-flavored roast beef. À la carte meals range from 70 AS ($3.72) to 220 AS ($11.70), while fixed-price dinners go from 75 AS ($3.99) to 135 AS ($7.18). The restaurant is closed every Tuesday from November to March.

ST. GILGEN: This leading lakeside resort of Land Salzburg lies at the western edge of Wolfgangsee. In the summer it's filled mainly with

Austrians and Germans enjoying the indoor swimming pool and bathing beach.

Once St. Gilgen was one of the strongholds of the prince-archbishops of Salzburg, and in a sense the aristocratic tradition continues even today, as many of the fashionable and wealthy from Salzburg maintain mountain villas here. Parties at festival time tend to be lavish. You're lucky if you get an invitation.

The town has many Mozart connections. In the vicinity of the Rathaus (town hall) is the house in which Anna Maria Pertl was born in 1720. She was to become Mozart's mother. After the composer's sister, Nannerl, married Baron Berchtold zu Sonnenberg, she also settled in St. Gilgen. The **Mozart Fountain,** built in 1927, stands on the main square in front of the town hall.

Food and Lodging

Parkhotel Billroth (tel. 217), a mile from town, sits imposingly on its own spacious grounds. One wing was designed in a white-walled villa style, with the main section looking more like an overblown chalet. The view from the bedrooms and from the parasol-dotted sun terrace takes in the lake and the mountains beyond. The hotel has its own lakeside beach, with a floating sun raft ideal for bathing (especially since it's connected to the shoreline). It has its own outdoor tennis courts and easy access to the ski lifts. Some of the public rooms are baronial, with dark paneling, Oriental rugs, and wide, gently sloping staircases. Bathless rooms rent for 265 AS ($14.10) to 470 AS ($25) per person, while units with private bath cost between 300 AS ($15.96) and 590 AS ($31.39) per person. Prices depend on the accommodation and the season. Breakfast is included in the above prices.

Hotel Zur Post, 8 Mozartplatz (tel. 239), is the comfortably proportioned hotel on the main square of town. It was established in 1415, and aside from the charm of the thick walls and heavy timbers, it has a high level of comfort and efficient and friendly service directed by the Hinterberger family. The interior has been updated so frequently it's difficult in some places to see the original building. Everything is nonetheless comfortable, clean, and pleasant. Someone has painted murals of village life under some of the ceiling's vaults, while parts of some of the wood ceilings are ornately decorated with paint and inlays. A swimming pool with a lake scene on the far wall is part of the lure.

The well-furnished bedrooms rent for 230 AS ($12.24) to 450 AS ($23.94) per person, with breakfast included. Prices depend on the plumbing and the season. The hotel is closed from early November till December 10.

The in-house restaurant is worth a stopover. Aside from its view over the center of the resort, it has a romantic ambience with a ceramic tile oven along with good food such as farmer's-style goulash, pork cutlets, and an exotic rumpsteak served with mandarin orange slices and kiwi à la nouvelle cuisine. À la carte meals range from 75 AS ($3.99) to 300 AS ($15.96).

Hotel Radetzky-Hof (tel. 232) is a centrally located house that's easy to recognize thanks to its orange shutters and its lighthearted designs painted onto a gray-and-white facade. The interior is simple and elegant, in good taste, and filled with comfortable, pleasing chairs and colors. Some of the ceilings are timbered, others are vaulted, but there's usually lots of exposed wood and a cozy feeling of well-being. The per-person rate in a single or double room is 360 AS ($19.15), with breakfast included.

Grossgasthof/Hotel Kendler (tel. 223) is a contemporary chalet set onto a well-maintained lawn. Many of the pleasant bedrooms inside have their own balconies, and most of them contain private baths. The main salon has a high beamed ceiling, a massive ornate chandelier, and cozy easy chairs scattered over a collection of intricately patterned Oriental rugs. Singles with bath range from 360 AS ($19.15) to 470 AS ($25), while doubles with bath rent for 435 AS ($23.14) per person, with half board included.

Café/Pension Nannerl (tel. 368). An 18th-century name deserves an 18th-century ambience, and that's exactly what you'll see in this charming old-style coffeehouse which happens to be named after Mozart's sister. The furnishings are something you might have found in a wealthy farmer's house around 1801, and the food served includes the most delicious (and most caloric) in the repertoire of Austrian pastries, including Sacher torte, poppy tart, and Malakoff tart, each mouthwatering, each baked fresh every day and served in generous slices. Pastries range from 20 AS ($1.06) to 30 AS ($1.60), while coffee costs between 15 AS (80¢) and 25 AS ($1.33).

STROBL: The flower gardens along the shore of Lake Wolfgang make this small resort a potent lure in summer. Strobl lies on the southeast side of the lake, almost opposite St. Gilgen at the western end. For a relatively undiscovered little lakeside village it has much appeal, mainly because of its romantic setting. The road to St. Wolfgang in Upper Austria branches off here.

Food and Lodging

Hotel Stadt Wein (tel. 381) is a long modern hotel with floor-length windows and stone detailing. The interior is attractively outfitted in dramatic and tasteful colors (the bar is painted forest green) and occasional rustic details such as a ceramic stove in the dining room. The sunny and airy singles rent for between 400 AS ($21.28) and 470 AS ($25), half board included. Doubles cost between 815 AS ($43.36) and 890 AS ($47.35), with half board included for both occupants. Prices depend on the season, and all the units contain private baths.

Parkhotel Seethurn (tel. 202). One side of this big balconied hotel faces the edge of the village, whose occupants sometimes admire the elaborate regional designs painted on part of the facade. The other end looks out over a well-maintained lawn area. The roof of the swimming pool is supported with massive laminated timbers, while the rest of the public rooms are elegantly and rustically laid out with wood furniture, big fireplaces, and coffered ceilings. P. E. Wicher, the talented director of this hotel, does everything he can to make guests feel at home. Per-person rates, with half board included, range from 550 AS ($29.26) to 750 AS ($39.90), depending on the season and the view. All accommodations contain private baths.

EUGENDORF: If you're touring in the Flachgau, you'll find good food at the following recommendation.

Landgasthof Holznerwirt (tel. 8205). Johann and Eveline Bimminger are the genteel owners of this hip-roofed chalet near the onion dome of the village church. They pride themselves on serving a traditional menu of such specialties as three kinds of roast, tafelspitz, and veal dishes. A rustic buffet at 190 AS ($10.11) per person includes stews, warm cabbage salads, an array of meats, and assorted breads. Full meals cost around 155 AS ($8.25). If you're touring in the area, it makes a fine dining choice.

9. The Lungau

A heavily forested district in the southeastern part of Land Salzburg, Lungau can be visited easily on a day trip. The section is beginning to develop as a winter sports center now that the Tauern highway has opened up the valley. However, in spite of its at times sun-drenched slopes, the Lungau is one of the chilliest parts of Austria in winter.

TAMSWEG: The principal town of the Lungau, whose people show a healthy respect for tradition, is Tamsweg, with a 1570 Rathaus (town hall) and a baroque pfarrkirche (parish church). This was once a Roman town, and some ruins remain. The pilgrimage **Church of St. Leonard,** enclosed by defensive walls, is a Gothic edifice known for its stained glass, including a unique "golden window."

You can visit the **Lungauer Folklore Museum,** which has fine pieces of provincial furniture and collections of paintings and weapons. The museum is open May to October daily except Monday from 10 a.m. to noon and from 2 to 5 p.m. Guided tours are given every hour. Admission is 20 AS ($1.06) for adults, 10 AS (53¢) for children.

From Tamsweg, you might want to visit **Moosham Castle** at Unternberg, first mentioned in documents in 1256. This was formerly a fortress of the prince-archbishops of Salzburg. Its most outstanding feature is the lower courtyard. Its schloss chapel has a late Gothic triptych. A folkloric museum in the castle is open January 1 until mid-June and from mid-September until the end of October daily except Monday from 10 a.m. to 3 p.m. In summer it's open from 10 a.m. to 4 p.m. Admission is 30 AS ($1.60).

MAUTERNDORF: This is an old market town going back 1000 years and today both a summer resort center and a mecca for skiers in winter. It lies on a highway to the northwest of the Tauern Pass. From here you can take a cableway to Speiereckhütte (6805 feet).

Mauterndorf Castle, erected on the ruins of a fort which stood here in Roman times, dates from 1253, although parts of it were extended in the 14th and 15th centuries. It contains a chapel with frescoes from the 14th century and a winged altarpiece, circa 1450. You can visit the keep, a local museum, and the galleries June 1 to September 30 from 10 a.m. to noon and from 4 to 6 p.m. They're closed Tuesday and Friday. Admission is 25 AS ($1.33).

Mauterndorf's **pfarrkirche** (parish church) has a sumptuous baroque altar from 1702.

Food and Lodging

Hotel Elisabeth (tel. 365). The position of this hotel at the edge of the village marks the beginning of acres of farmland, most of which you can see from the windows of your well-furnished bedrooms. The hotel is one of the most elegant in town, outfitted like a private home with lots of balconies, a pleasing hip-roofed design, and alpine-style furniture. The hospitable hosts, members of the Spreitzer family, charge between 520 AS ($27.66) and 800 AS ($42.56) for a single and between 500 AS ($26.60) and 775 AS ($41.23) per person for a double, with half board included. All accommodations contain private baths.

On the premises you'll find a sauna, an indoor pool, a dancing bar, and a hairdresser. The in-house restaurant offers a wide range of flambés and fondues, as well as Austrian and international specialties. Fixed-price meals range from 120 AS ($6.38) to 145 AS ($7.71), while à la carte dinners cost between 115 AS ($6.12) and 270 AS ($14.36).

Hotel Post (tel. 316), the most atmospheric choice in town, is a four-story gray building with a dignified facade and solid proportions. The interior has lots of rustic 19th-century touches, such as vaulted ceilings, Oriental rugs, flagstone floors, green tile ovens, and regional antiques. The dining room is elegant, with immaculate napery and leather-upholstered chairs. In summer guests retreat to a courtyard garden. Depending on the plumbing and season, singles range from 350 AS ($18.62) to 460 AS ($24.47), and doubles from 300 AS ($15.96) to 490 AS ($26.07) per person, these tariffs including full board.

Gasthof Steffner-Wallner and **Hotel Kernwirt** (tel. 214 and 7048) are two cozy hotels, both owned by the Steffner-Wallner family and charging roughly the same rates. The interiors of both hotels are rustically and pleasingly outfitted with painted furniture and lots of plants. Per-person rates, based on double occupancy, range from 240 AS ($12.77) to 345 AS ($18.35), with half board included. All units contain private baths. Singles pay a daily surcharge of 40 AS ($2.13).

Gasthof/Pension Neuwirt (tel. 268) is announced by its wrought-iron bracket extending over the pavement in front of the mustard-colored facade. The bedrooms inside are cozy, colorful, and warm. Per-person rates in doubles range from 220 AS ($11.70) to 475 AS ($25.27), depending on the season, the plumbing, and the room assignment. Half board is included in the above prices. On the premises are a swimming pool and table tennis facilities.

MARIAPFARR: This little town, at an elevation of 3675 feet, becomes lively in winter when it fills up with skiers. Mariapfarr lies in an area of Austria renowned for its variety of runs and for attracting cross-country skiers. There are some 80 miles of beautifully placed tracks. It's possible to rent heavy skis and boots on the spot in the town's shops.

Mariapfarr has long been known for its pilgrimage church, dating from the 13th and 14th centuries. This Gothic **pfarrkirche** (parish church) is decorated with wall paintings and has an exceptional winged altar in the late Gothic style. Its 14th-century frescoes include Saint Mary, Protectress with Man of Sorrows, the only known representation of its kind.

Food and Lodging

Hotel Haus Carinth (tel. 235). Karl-Peter Dindl is the accommodating owner of this pleasantly isolated double chalet. Both wings of the hotel have hip roofs, balconies, and impressive views. The interior has all the rustic comfort you'd expect, as well as an invitingly dark decor of masonry, wood wall coverings, and comfortable furniture. On the premises are a children's outdoor pool and a sauna. Per-person rates, based on double occupancy, range from 345 AS ($18.35) to 540 AS ($28.73), with half board included. Singles rooms cost approximately 30% more than the per-person rate in a double.

Chapter IX

UPPER AUSTRIA

1. Linz
2. The Mühlviertel
3. Attersee and Mondsee
4. St. Wolfgang and Bad Ischl
5. Hallstatt
6. The Traunsee
7. Wels
8. The Southeast Corner
9. Steyr and Enns
10. Stops Along the Danube
11. Schärding and Braunau

TOO OFTEN NEGLECTED by North Americans who may be unaware of its charms, Upper Austria contains some of the country's most beautiful scenery. It is a land of mountains, scenic valleys, and lakes, with Styria and Land Salzburg to its south and Bavaria on the west. Its northern parts border the Bohemian forest in Czechoslovakia. Its eastern neighbor is Lower Austria, traditionally called its twin. The Austrian name of this province is Bundesland–Ober Österreiche, since it lies nearer to the source of the Danube, which cuts across both provinces, than does Lower Austria.

Upper Austria has three different types of landscape. In the north are the granite and gneiss hills which are separated in the center of the province by the Valley of the Danube. There are also the limestone Alps and the Salzkammergut lake district, about a 30-minute drive from Linz, which crosses into Upper Austria. Here you'll find the most breathtaking scenery in the entire area. You can center at the Attersee, the Mondsee, the Traunsee, and the Wolfgangsee, part of the latter being in Land Salzburg.

Boating is fine on these lakes *(sees)*, but if you like to swim, know that the *see* water here is not as warm as you'll find in Carinthia (Chapter XII). There are farms and fruit trees in the lake district. The cider of the region is excellent and competes with wine for popularity among the local inhabitants.

Except for Linz, the provincial capital, Upper Austria is a choice location for nature-lovers. Most of its towns are small, and although there's much industry, it doesn't blight the province with grime. Industrial installations are often discreetly hidden away as is usually the case in Switzerland.

Bad Ischl, once a retreat of the Austrian imperial court, is perhaps the most fashionable spa attraction. Most of the hotels are in the Salzkammergut region, but in all towns and villages you can find one or two moderately priced to inexpensive inns. There are few deluxe accommodations, although several old castles have been turned into "romantik" lodging places. Most of the hotels around the lakes are open only in summer months, and May is an ideal time to visit. These areas tend to be overrun with visitors, especially Germans, in the peak months of July and August.

The ski areas of Upper Austria are not much known to the North Americans visiting this country, as they lie for the most part in the southeast corner. The Dachstein is another major ski area. If you like to ski and don't demand massive facilities and a lot of après-ski festivity, you'll find the emerging ski resorts of this province far less expensive than such more celebrated resorts as those in the Tyrol and Zell am See in Land Salzburg.

If you're coming into the region, you can fly to the Linz international airport served by planes from main points in Europe or to Salzburg, from which train service is good into Upper Austria. To remote places where trains don't go, and excellent local Postal Bus service takes over. If you're driving, you can reach the province easily by the autobahn from Vienna.

It's also possible to take steamer service on the Danube between Passau in West Germany and Linz, but these boats operate only in summer. By steamer, you can continue on from Linz along the Danube into Lower Austria, to Vienna, and on to Budapest or even the Black Sea, as mentioned earlier. At certain times of the year you can make an excursion on the Danube leaving from the Linz marina.

1. Linz

This provincial capital of Upper Austria, about 100 miles northwest of Vienna, is the third-largest city in the country after Vienna and Graz. It is the biggest port on the Danube, which widens out considerably here to become a majestic thoroughfare. Three bridges connect Linz with the suburb of **Urfahr,** on the left bank of the river. If you enter the country from Passau, West Germany, Linz might be your gateway to Austria.

Linz was the site of a Roman castle and settlement, Lentia, in the first century A.D., and by the Middle Ages it had become a thriving center of trade through its position on the river. Emperor Friedrich III lived here from 1489 to 1493. The city now lies also on a direct rail route between the Adriatic and Baltic Seas. It was here that Austria's first railroad terminated. Because of these factors, Linz became an industrial and manufacturing center, with blast furnaces and steel factories. These were built up rapidly after Hitler seized Austria in 1938, and the Nazis also established chemical plants here. This industrial upsurge led to massive destruction by Allied bombs, with reconstruction being started after 1945.

Like Frankfurt in West Germany, Linz became known in the days of the empire for its trade fairs. It has been the seat of a bishop since 1785. Its heyday, at least with the aristocracy, came in the 18th century, after which it experienced a cultural decline.

Linz today, however, is one of the leading cultural centers of Austria, although nowhere near the level of Vienna and Salzburg. The city's name appears in numerous Germanic songs, and many notable figures have come from or been connected with Linz, including native son Anton Bruckner, the composer. Mozart composed and dedicated a symphony to the city, and

Beethoven wrote his Eighth Symphony here. Franz Schubert described with pleasure his holidays in Linz. Goethe, who had a romance with a Linz fräulcin, dedicated one of his most lyrical works "to the beautiful girls of Linz."

Napoleon lived here three times—in 1800, 1805, and 1809. The first steel airplane was constructed at Linz by the Schiessl brothers.

THE SIGHTS: The most popular shopping district in the city is the **Landstrasse,** filled with boutiques, sometimes with Victorian embellishments on the buildings.

The **Hauptplatz** was the original marketplace and is now one of the biggest and most beautiful squares in all Europe, with baroque and rococo facades surrounding it. On the east side is the rathaus (city hall). In the heart of the square stands the **Trinity Column,** like the celebrated column in Vienna, built in 1723 to mark deliverance in the case of Linz from plague, fire, and invasion by the Turks. This marble column, the Dreifaltigkeitssaule, rises 85 feet.

Martinskirche, or St. Martin's Church, is the most ancient church in Austria in its original form. It was constructed by Charlemagne in the eighth century, near the castle on the remains of a Roman wall. Mention was first made of the church in written records in 788. St. Martin's is considered a good example of Carolingian architecture. Frescoes inside the church date from the 15th century, and it also contains masterpieces of baroque art. This edifice is in dramatic contrast with the ultramodern buildings that surround it.

The concert hall, called **Bruckner Haus** in honor of Anton Bruckner, the Linz-born composer, has an elliptical facade of glass and steel with a wooden interior where a raised dais accomodates an orchestra whose conductors have included Leonard Bernstein and Herbert von Karajan. Concerts presented in this acoustically perfect hall have been transmitted throughout the world. The building was constructed from 1969 to 1973 as a cultural and conference center.

The most popular place of pilgrimage from Linz is to **Pöstlingberg,** three miles northwest of the city on the north bank of the Danube, up a very steep hill. You can get there by going out Rudolfstrasse on the left bank of the river and taking a turn right onto Hagenstrasse. If you don't have a car, take the electric railway.

Pöstlingberg has a botanical garden with exotic tropical plants, and the summit terrace is a riot of blooming flowers in summer. A defensive tower now houses a grotto with a miniature railway, which makes a hit with children. The pilgrimage church is visited because of an 18th-century carved wood Pietà, but most tourists make the ascent mainly to take in the view over thc Danubc Valley. Linz is spread out below. The panorama stretches all the way to the foothills of the Alps and to the Bohemian forest in Czechoslovakia.

The **Landhaus,** southwest of the Hauptplatz, is one of the most important landmark buildings of Linz and headquarters of the government of Upper Austria. The original structure was built in the latter 16th century with an arcaded courtyard around a fountain. The Landhaus was rebuilt in the early 19th century. In the 17th century this was the city's university, where Johann Kepler, noted astronomer and mathematician, taught and developed the theory of planetary motion. The present university of Linz, on the north bank of the Danube, bears Kepler's name.

The **Minoritenkirche,** or Church of the Minorite Brothers, is Gothic, dating from the 13th century, but with a rococo overlay done in 1758. An art masterpiece inside is the high altar by Bartolomeo Altomonte, depicting the Annunciation. There are three red marble side altars.

The **Schloss** (castle), standing high above the river, was the residence of Emperor Friedrich III when he and his court resided in Linz in the 15th century. It was built for the emperor and rebuilt after a fire in the early 19th century. Today it houses the Provincial Museum of Upper Austria, which has exhibits ranging from prehistoric artifacts from the Roman era to the provincial art of the province. Weaponıy is also displayed, and you'll see much popular art and folkloric exhibitions showing how the people of Upper Austria used to live. There's a gallery of paintings, none outstanding, from the 19th century. Many Gothic and Renaissance interiors have been reproduced. A railway museum is also to be seen at the castle.

You can visit the parts of the castle open to the public Wednesday through Saturday from 10 a.m. to 1 p.m. and from 2 to 6 p.m., from 9 a.m. to 1 p.m. on Sunday. It's closed Monday and Tuesday.

Alter Dom on Domgasse, the biggest baroque church in the city and formerly the cathedral of Linz, was constructed by the Jesuits around the latter part of the 17th century. You mustn't judge this church by its relatively simple exterior. The inside warms up considerably with pink marble columns, an intricately carved pulpit, and much statuary. The high altar is a concoction bedecked with marble images. Bruckner was the organist of this church for 12 years, and the annual Bruckner festival is centered here. Two other composers who worked in Linz are honored at the same time—Mozart, who composed his Linz symphony (No. 36 in C, K.425) here, and Beethoven, who wrote his Eighth in Linz.

The **Neue Galerie der Stadt Linz** (new gallery) is in the industrial suburb on the left bank, Urfahr, already referred to. Paintings shown are mostly by Austrian and German artists of the 19th century. You can visit daily from 10 a.m. to 6 p.m., to 1 p.m. on Sunday, and to 10 p.m. on Thursday. Admission is 15 AS (80¢).

Priesterseminarkirche, or seminary church, is a small place of worship dedicated to the Holy Cross. Dating from the early part of the 18th century, the building plans were the work of Johann Lukas von Hildebrandt, the celebrated architect. The church is worth a visit just to see its richly decorated interior.

EXCURSIONS: Of possible short trips out of Linz, the most popular is to the **Abbey of St. Florian,** about a 12-mile trek. The abbey, largest in Upper Austria, is one of the major attractions of the province, an outstanding example of baroque architecture.

Augustinians have occupied a building of some sort on this site since the 11th century, although the structures you see today are baroque, having been under construction from 1686 to 1751. St. Florian was a Christian martyr, killed by being drowned in the Enns River around 304. As a saint he is often called upon by the faithful to protect their homes against flood and fire. The abbey was constructed over his grave.

The greatest composer of church music in 19th-century Austria, Anton Bruckner, a native of Linz born near the present abbey site in 1824, became the organist at St. Florian as a young man and composed many of his world-renowned masterpieces here. Although he went on to greater fame in Vienna, he was granted his wish to be buried at the abbey church underneath the organ he loved so well at St. Florian. You can visit the crypt, as well as the room where the composer lived for about a decade.

Carlo Carlone was originally in charge of rebuilding the abbey in the baroque style, the job being started in 1686, and the progress was continued by others.

The western exterior of the abbey is crowned with a trio of towers. The doorway is especially striking. As you enter the inner court, you'll see the celebrated **Fountain of the Eagle.** In the library, said to contain some 140,000 books and manuscripts, you'll see allegorical ceiling frescoes by Bartolomeo Altomonte. The marble salon honors Prince Eugene of Savoy for his heroic defense of Vienna against a major siege by the Turks. Naturally the ceiling paintings here depict the Austrian victory over the "infidels."

The **Altdorfer Gallery** is the most outstanding feature of the abbey, surpassing even the imperial apartments. Well-known works of Albrecht Altdorfer, born in 1480, a master of the Danube school of painting, are displayed. Altdorfer was a warm, romantic contemporary of Dürer, to whom he is often compared. He did more than a dozen paintings for the abbey's Gothic church, his panels depicting, among other scenes, the martyrdom of St. Sebastian.

The **imperial apartments,** called the Kaiserzimmer, are reached by climbing a splendid staircase. Once Pope Pius VI stayed here. A whole host of royalty has occupied these richly decorated quarters, and you're allowed to visit the royal bedrooms of the emperor and empress.

The **abbey church,** designed by Carlone, has twin towers rising to 260 feet. The decoration is rich—maybe too rich. It's distinguished by columns of pink marble, quarried near Salzburg. Lavish stucco decoration was used in the interior, and the pulpit is in black marble. The choir stalls are heavily gilded and rich with ornamentation and carving. You should allow about an hour for a tour.

You must go with a guide to visit the abbey. Tours are conducted April to October at 10 and 11 a.m. and 1:30, 3, and 4 p.m. Otherwise, you must write to the abbey for permission to visit. Admission is 30 AS ($1.60).

One of the most macabre outings from Linz is to **Mauthausen,** 16 miles down the Danube from the provincial capital, the village of the quarries that once supplied the granite for paving stones of Vienna. The Nazis used the quarries, about two miles northwest of the village, as a concentration camp in World War II. It was also an extermination center, where Austria's Jewish population was dramatically and horrifyingly reduced in number in the darkest days of the war. Not only were Austrian Jews exterminated at this camp but thousands of other so-called "undesirables" were also annihilated—homosexuals, gypsies, whatever.

The government of Austria does not hide the scene and reminder of these atrocities. The camp's site was declared a national monument in 1949, and often schoolchildren are brought here and given descriptions of what went on in this notorious camp. Various countries who lost citizens have erected memorials outside the camp to honor the dead. It's believed that the Nazis killed some 200,000 victims here, although exact figures are not available. It may have been more.

You can visit the huts where the condemned, most of whom almost surely knew their ultimate fate, were kept. You are also led down the infamous "Stairway of Death" which the prisoners took on their last walk. To visit the ghastly site is a shattering experience, but still people come here to be painfully reminded of a cruel and savage era.

It takes about 1½ hours to take a tour of the camp, which is open April 1 to mid-October from 8 a.m. to noon and from 12:30 to 4 p.m. (to 3 p.m. off-season). It's closed from mid-December to February 1. Admission is 20 AS ($1.06).

Besides traveling to Mauthausen from Linz, you can visit the site via commuter train from Vienna, the ride taking about 45 minutes.

WHERE TO STAY: **Hotel Schillerpark,** 2-4 Rainerstrasse (tel. 55405), is the most prestigious modern hotel in town. It's in a futuristic mirrored building at the entrance to the downtown's pedestrian zone, about ten minutes on foot from the rail station. Inside you'll find a gambling casino (the center of nightlife in Linz), two bars, an elegant restaurant, a sauna, and a solarium. The lobby area is covered with slabs of polished marble, while the bedrooms are airy, sunny, and tastefully filled with streamlined furniture. Singles cost 1000 AS ($53.20), while doubles rent from 1350 AS ($71.82), with breakfast included. Each of the units has a private bath.

Tourotel, 9 Untere Donaulande (tel. 75075), is one of Linz's most prominent "skyscrapers," rising many stories above the ground in the center of the city. On the premises you'll find all the facilities of a large urban hotel, including a range of bars and restaurants, an indoor pool, and bedrooms with all the modern comforts. International bands often play at the hotel's nightclub. Singles cost 950 AS ($50.54); doubles, 1200 AS ($63.84). Weekend rates are about 40% less.

Domhotel, Baumbachstrasse (tel. 278441), is especially attractive for motorists, who'll find parking in the rear courtyard. The hotel is reached on a narrow one-way street in the center of town near the cathedral. It has a modern bar on the ground floor, a sauna, and a friendly English-speaking management directed by Mrs. Agnes Daane, along with large, comfortable bedrooms. Someone is usually on hand to help you with your luggage onto the elevator. Singles range from 540 AS ($28.73) to 620 AS ($32.98), while doubles cost around 1110 AS ($59.05), with breakfast included. All accommodations have private bath, phone, and radio.

Hotel/Restaurant Zur Lokomotive, 40 Weingartshofstrasse (tel. 54555), has a severe facade with practical, unadorned windows. Its interior is clean but stark, and it's very much of a no-frills kind of hostelry which provides shelter. Singles range from 350 AS ($18.62) to 470 AS ($25), while doubles go from 530 AS ($28.20) to 700 AS ($37.24), with breakfast included.

Hotel Ebelsberger, 485 Wiener Strasse (tel. 42125), stands in the suburb of Ebelsberg, and is easy to locate because of its vivid pink facade. The interior is woodsy and elegant, with thick curtains, lots of handcrafted paneling, thick beams, and an upper-class ambience of well-being and fine cuisine. The bedrooms are papered in romantically flowered patterns, and each of them has its own bath. The 40 rooms rent for 750 AS ($39.90) in a single and for 910 AS ($48.41) in a double, breakfast included. A station wagon will pick you up at the airport if you arrange it in advance.

Hotel Prielmayerhof, 33 Weissenwolffstrasse (tel. 274131), is housed in a five-story distinguished-looking building slightly outside the center of town. It can be reached from the main train station by public bus. Its exterior is painted a vivid terracotta with white trim, while its streamlined and comfortable interior has been renovated into a tasteful modern format of white walls and exposed wood. Singles rent for 625 AS ($33.25), while doubles cost 780 AS ($41.50), breakfast included.

Hotel Wolfinger, 19 Hauptplatz (tel. 273291), is housed in a historic building on what is said to be the largest and best preserved baroque square in Europe. Its entrance is through an arcade a short distance from the Danube. If you take one of the front rooms, you'll see old-fashioned trams running through the center of the square. The reception desk is one flight above ground level. The management is casual, and the decor includes lots of homey touches which help to make the place a friendly oasis.

Parking is a problem, but management told me that police allow cars headed toward the hotel to traverse the pedestrian-only square to park in the inner courtyard. Doubles rent for 550 AS ($29.26) to 675 AS ($35.91), while singles cost between 310 AS ($16.49) and 395 AS ($21.01), with breakfast included. Prices usually depend on the plumbing. The adjoining restaurant is one of my favorites in Linz (see my restaurant recommendations).

Hotel Mercure, 39 Wankmüllerhofstrasse (tel. 42361), lies about a mile and a half from the center, close to the Linz exit from the autobahn. Built in an attractively up-to-date format of big windows and sand-colored walls, the hotel offers modern comfort in warmly tinted rooms with all the conveniences. The public rooms are filled with padded and upholstered banquettes and include an elegant futuristic bar area. Singles cost 620 AS ($32.98), while doubles rent for 765 AS ($40.70). An extra bed can be set up in any room for an additional 320 AS ($17.02). All these prices include breakfast.

Hotel Zum Schwarzen Bären, 9-11 Herrenstrasse (tel. 272803), is housed in a two-tone building that you'll have to look for carefully, as it's hidden on a narrow street in the old section. The unpretentious interior of "The Black Bear" is outfitted in a rustically modern decor of chalet chairs, parquet floors, and unusual configurations of decorative ceiling beams. The comfortable bedrooms have their own private baths. Doubles rent for between 420 AS ($22.34) and 550 AS ($29.26), with breakfast included. Singles cost between 275 AS ($14.63) and 365 AS ($19.42). Half board is offered for another 95 AS ($5.05) per person. Richard Tauber, by the way, was born on this site in 1891.

Hotel Mühlviertlerhof, 24-26 Graben (tel. 272268), has only 18 rustic and cozy rooms, all of them with private bath, phone, and color TV. The Zangerle family are the hosts, maintaining their centrally located hotel with charm and efficiency. Rooms are immaculately kept and comfortable. Rates depend on the plumbing, with singles ranging from 320 AS ($17.02) to 600 AS ($31.92) and doubles going for 400 AS ($21.28) to 460 AS ($24.47) per person.

WHERE TO DINE: **Allegro,** 68 Schillerstrasse (tel. 669800), is an elegant restaurant near the vegetable markets at the train station. In addition to the live music that the management sometimes provides, the menu is set up like the movements of a concerto, labeled "overture," "intermezzo," "theme and variations," along with "finale." A first course might be the house specialty of jamosala, mint sauce, and tonic (they call it "Allegretto"). Other introductory items include smoked salmon, pampas-style peppered ham, several kinds of salad, and snails. Main courses might be a steak potpourri or one of several fresh fish dishes. One of the best desserts is the homemade strudel. Fixed-price meals range from 105 AS ($5.59) to 340 AS ($18.09), while à la carte goes from 100 AS ($5.32) to 265 AS ($14.10). The restaurant is closed on Sunday and for the first two weeks of August.

Schloss Puchenau, Puchenau (tel. 221515). There's a local legend that mentions a castle ghost, yet he (or she) certainly doesn't seem averse to the idea of a tastefully decorated restaurant in its former abode. From certain parts you'll be able to see the Danube, while head chef Max Eidlhuber prepares a collection of tempting specialties. You'd better phone ahead for reservations, since it's located in a nearby satellite village of Linz. Fixed-price meals are usually priced from 180 AS ($9.58) to 455 AS ($24.21), while à la carte dinners cost from 140 AS ($7.45) to 350 AS ($18.62). The restaurant is closed on Sunday and sometimes on Thursday.

Restaurant Donautal, 105 Obere Donaulande (tel. 75169). The expanse of the muddy waters of the Danube dominates the view from the inside of this lovely restaurant. It's five minutes by taxi from the center of town, between a wooded hillside and the riverbank. The terrace offers chairs beneath a 200-year-old chestnut tree. The restaurant has been managed by the Kirchmayr-Emhof family for more than 120 years. It specializes in traditional Austro-Hungarian cookery, including a collection of family-owned recipes served here for generations. A trout tank keeps the fish alive until the last possible moment. Fixed-price meals range from 120 AS ($6.38) to 385 AS ($20.48), while à la carte dinners go from 110 AS ($5.85) to 280 AS ($14.90). It's closed all day Monday and after 3 p.m. on Sunday, and reservations are suggested.

Restaurant Primo Piano, Hotel Wolfinger, 19 Hauptplatz (tel. 273291). The menu is handwritten on a large sheet of handmade paper. The restaurant is one floor above ground level in this historic hotel building on the baroque main square of Linz, with a view over the spires of the two churches and the fountain in the center. The napery is dark pink, the carpeting is black, and an upright piano sits against one wall with a bowler hat and a piece of ragtime sheet music on top.

The rest of the room might be art nouveau or art deco, depending on where you look. However, if you gaze at the center of the plaster ceiling, the triple-cherub motif is pure baroque. Menu items include three kinds of spaghetti, onion soup, trout meunière, peppersteak, veal piccata, saltimbocca, and excellent desserts. Meals range upward from 180 AS ($9.58). The restaurant is open every day of the week for lunch and dinner, but on Sunday only coffee and drinks are served.

Restaurant Niccolai, 7 Klammstrasse (tel. 79028). For years Linzers joked that this was the only pizzeria in town directed by a real Italian. This cozy restaurant, however, offers much more than pizza, even though there are a dozen kinds of this pie, ranging from fish to meat to cheese to just about everything good in the Mediterranean repertoire. You might want to try the Italian-style pastas (the tortellini à la casa is good), saltimbocca, a range of fish dishes, and a variety of tempting cheese and dessert. À la carte meals range from 80 AS ($4.26) to 305 AS ($16.23). The restaurant shuts down on Sunday.

Wachauer Weinhaus, 29 Pfarrgasse (tel. 74618). A baroque bas-relief of an ecstatic saint adorns the corner of this building near the old cathedral. The sign announcing this historic place is part of a wrought-iron bracket hanging over the cobblestone sidewalk. The smallest portion of any wine sold here is a quarter liter, which experience has taught me is about two full wine stems worth. The wines from the Wachau region are featured, including five different kinds of white, four kinds of red, and one rosé, each priced from 18 AS (96¢) to 25 AS ($1.33) per quarter liter. The establishment serves food from a limited menu priced from 115 AS ($6.12). Food items might include bean or goulash soup, bratwursts, half a grilled hen, or free access to a self-service buffet. It's open daily except Sunday from 10 a.m. to closing.

Restaurant Stieglbräu zum Klosterhof, 30 Landstrasse (tel. 73373). If you're not sure where you want to sit inside this large homey restaurant, you'll see photographs of the various eating areas posted in the vestibule. In some of the rooms formally dressed waiters serve food under formally high ceilings, while in other rooms blue-jeaned youths in leather jackets, along with a scattering of older people, fill the air with smoke and loud talk. A bubbling aquarium in the pink and white stone vestibule usually swarms with live trout. The place was once the library of Kremsmünster Abbey, and some of the elaborate darkened trim still remains beside an impressive collection of deer antlers. Meals cost around 150 AS ($7.98) and could include several kinds of schnitzels, half a hen cooked Viennese style, daily specials, Serbian bean soup, peppersteak, and for dessert, a salzburger nockerl.

Ursulinenhof, 31 Landstrasse (tel. 74686), is the kind of restaurant that can feed an army in a gemütlich setting, and is willing to do so from 9 a.m. to midnight every day of the year. Menu items include soups, a wide range of salads, tafelspitz, all kinds of roasts, a selection of cheeses, pastries, and an assortment of diet-conscious foods. For anyone who wants to drink, the menu shows an illustration of the size of the glass, along with the price, for at least seven different kinds of beer. A fixed-price meal is around 110 AS ($5.85), while an à la carte dinner begins at 165 AS ($8.79).

Hotel/Restaurant Mühlviertlerhof, 24-26 Graben (tel. 272269). In the heart of the old town you'll find a pleasant restaurant on the ground floor of this already-recommended hotel. There's more than one dining area, the biggest of which has wrought-iron hanging lamps and table dividers, vivid colors that could almost be Spanish, and heavy half-timbering between the renovated stucco walls. Fresh flowers are usually on the tables. Set meals range from 75 AS ($3.97) to 90 AS ($4.79), which usually include gutbürgerlich, seasonally adjusted menus as well as tafelspitz, several veal dishes, wild game, a knödelplatte, farmer's goulash, with a dessert specialty known as topfenstrudel. All the food, including the noodles, dumplings, and sausages, are handmade by the kitchen staff. À la carte meals range upward from 125 AS ($6.65).

Wienerwald, 22 Promenade (tel. 71419), is a branch of the famous chain restaurant that does more than any other to offer gemütlich ambience and rustic settings on a mass scale. This particular branch has a dark, woodsy interior with big arched windows overlooking a summertime beer garden. Menu items include a quarter or half a fried chicken priced around 40 AS ($2.13) to 75 AS ($3.99), plus a variety of schnitzels, goulashes, steaks, and braised beef with potato noodles. The staff also offers a children's menu, as well as beer and wine. Full meals average around 160 AS ($8.51), but it's easily possible to dine for less.

THE CAFÉS OF LINZ: **Café Traxlmayr,** 16 Promenade (tel. 73353), is an old-style coffeehouse of the variety you imagined died at the end of World War I. It's next to a baroque palace on a wide ornamental boulevard, in a beige and brown building. Its outdoor sun terrace is protected by thick privets and geraniums in classical-style pots. It even has a fountain designed like a little boy playing with two gurgling fish set into a wall out in front. The first thing you'll notice inside are the formally dressed staff (black and white tie are *de rigeur*), scurrying around with trays of coffee and cakes. The decor includes 1890s-style round marble tables, big mirrors, and crystal and gilt chandeliers. A rack of Austrian and foreign-language newspapers gives this place all the trappings of a Viennese coffeehouse, with elaborate pastries priced from 20 AS ($1.06) to 30 AS ($1.60) and coffee from 21 AS ($1.11) to 26 AS ($1.38). During cold weather, management serves some hot dishes such as goulash soup.

Café-Konditorei Fritz Wagner, 15 Landstrasse (tel. 271765). The orange-and-brown facade of this small shop might not be too impressive, but the Linzer torte and the other pastries sold inside are heavenly. Owned by the same family for more than 80 years, the coffeeshop maintains a limited number of outdoor café tables during the summer, with more than 40 more seats available indoors. It's open Monday to Friday from 8 a.m. to 7 p.m. and on Saturday from 8 a.m. to 1 p.m. (closed Sunday). Linzer torte can be mailed to any country in the world. The three sizes cost 40 AS ($2.13), 90 AS ($4.79), and 140 AS ($7.45). Peter Wagner is the third-generation owner.

Café-Konditorei Tautermann, 14 Klammstrasse (tel. 79680). The pastries from this small shop have won gold medals from contests held in places as far away as Brussels. You'll be able to buy fabulous-looking and tasting pastries, some of them with kiwi or regional fruits, from the ground-floor display cases. If you climb a simple flight of stairs you can order coffee in a sunny upstairs room with a view of the spire of the cathedral. The café is open from 9 a.m. to 8 p.m. every day of the week but Tuesday. Aside from pastries, the upstairs also serves the Linzer torte along with ice cream and small cold dishes. Coffee costs from 21 AS ($1.19), pastries from 20 AS ($1.06).

Philipp Wrann, 6 Hofgasse (tel. 73288), is a well-known chain of pastry shops that specialize in the Linzer torte, that heavenly concoction of butter, nuts, chocolate, and in this case, gooseberry jam instead of raspberry jam, along with honey pies, candies, cakes, and chocolates. The company, which began in 1646, maintains five shops in Linz. Coffee is from 21 AS ($1.11); pastries, from 20 AS ($1.06) to 30 AS ($1.60).

Café am Park, Hotel Schillerpark, 2-4 Rainerstrasse (tel. 55405), seems to be the hottest place to go on a Sunday afternoon in Linz. If there's an equivalent of a sit-down singles bar, where everyone, and grandmother too, goes to watch, this is it. It's a big L-shaped room filled with belle-époque globe lights, mille-fleur carpeting in autumnal colors, upholstered bentwood chairs, and curtained glass windows overlooking the busy pedestrian traffic outside. You can get all the beverages you'd expect, as well as light snacks and wholesome meals, priced at around 160 AS ($8.51).

WHERE TO SHOP: **O. Ö. Heimatwerk,** 31 Landstrasse (tel. 73377), is an airy, sunny store with a stone floor, lots of handcrafted pine shelving, and a vaulted stucco ceiling dotted with pin spotlights. The entrance is under an arcade, although the shop windows face the busy pedestrian walkway of Linz's main shopping districts. Items for sale include local handicrafts such as pewter, intricately patterned silver, rustic ceramic pots, slippers, dresses, and a collection of dress-making fabrics in regional patterns, many of them in polka-dot.

Trachten Feichtinger, 9 Herrengasse (tel. 72884), has a decor of tasteful stucco curves and shiny wood floors. Its inventory includes a good selection of dirndls, suede skirts and jackets, and a full range of regional clothing, including sizes for men and women, girls and boys. This shop is open from 8 a.m. to noon and from 2 to 6 p.m. weekdays, and on Saturday from 8 a.m. to noon.

2. The Mühlviertel

This is a district of the Mühl River with pleasant hills for exploring. The Mühl is a small river that flows into the Danube at a point above Linz. The district, or viertel, lies between the Upper Austrian capital and the heavily guarded border of Czechoslovakia. To visit the district, leave Linz on the road to Bad Leonfelden (coming up). The road you'll take is lofty at certain points, reaching an elevation of 2800 feet, and you'll see places where the hills have been quarried for granite. The tourist office in Linz will outline a route for you through these hills, the entire round trip lasting some 4½ hours—longer if you want to take your time.

If you're touring and would like to stop over, the chief town of the Mühlviertel is—

FREISTADT: Once a thriving little town on the route followed by salt traders from the alpine districts to reach Bohemia, Freistadt lies in the northeastern section of the Mühlviertel. Remnants of the town's watchtowers, gates, and fortified walls can still be seen. On the large, rectangular main square, the **Hauptplatz,** you'll find the church of St. Catherine, dating from the 14th century. A baroque overlay was added in the 17th century, but the church was rebuilt in the Gothic style. An onion-shape dome crowns the parish church.

Schloss Freistadt, with a 175-foot high keep, shelters the **Mühlviertler Heimathaus,** a provincial museum known for its collection of decorated glass engraved with gold.

Food and Lodging

Gasthof Deim (Zum Goldenen Hirschen), 8 Böhmergasse (tel. 2258). The outside of this hotel has a dramatic series of neoclassical pilasters, corner mullions, and triangular window pediments, all clustered close together and accented with contrasting colors of reddish-brown and white. The interior ceilings are usually vaulted, with stone ribs supported by massive masonry columns. Furnishings are simple, and collections of hunting trophies and wrought-iron implements hang from the plaster walls. The cozy bedrooms have the kind of color schemes you can live with (mustards and russets) and lots of exposed wood. A garden sun terrace offers summertime drinks. With half board included, singles rent for 290 AS ($15.34) to 385 AS ($20.48), while doubles cost between 540 AS ($28.73) and 700 AS ($37.24), depending on the plumbing.

KEPERMARKT: On the left bank of the Feldaist, north of the Danube, is the old town of Kepermarkt, about six miles south of Freistadt. A visit to the two towns can be ideally combined in a half-day excursion from Linz. Kepermarkt lies between the Mühlviertel and the Waldviertel, which was explored in the chapter on Lower Austria.

Kepermarkt is visited chiefly for its **Church of St. Wolfgang,** a Gothic edifice known for its altarpiece in the chancel, back of the main altar. You may be staggered at the size of it, as it appears to be about 42 feet high, with life-size figures. The carved part is of natural limewood. It's not only big, it's also beautiful to look at. Regrettably, the sculptor of this handsome work, dating from the latter part of the 15th century, is unknown. Otherwise he would have earned a place for himself in books devoted to ecclesiastical art. It is believed that the altarpiece was originally painted, but this is not the case today.

BAD LEONFELDEN: A small spa 13 miles to the west of Freistadt, Bad Leonfelden is known for its mud baths and the Kneipp treatment. It's mostly familiar only to Europeans, but you might want to make it a center for exploring Upper Austria if you book at one of the accommodations listed below. The spa has a pilgrimage church dating from the latter part of the 18th century.

A chair lift will take you to **Sternberg,** at 3590 feet the loftiest point in the Mühlviertel. Once there you'll find a lookout tower and a panoramic sweep of the area. The spa has been customarily visited by summer travelers, but lately some winter skiers have been seeking it out.

You'll find prices reasonable here.

Food and Lodging

Gasthof Böhmertor (tel. 231) was designed in a modern format using lots of glass and steel, with a balconied section containing comfortable bedrooms. The large indoor pool and the sauna are bigger than you'd ordinarily expect. A range of massage facilities are also offered. The restaurants and bars inside are wood paneled and cozy, with hanging lamps and lots of color. Singles range from 240 AS ($12.77) to 310 AS ($16.49), while doubles cost from 410 AS ($21.81) to 575 AS ($30.59), with breakfast included.

Pension Angel, 132 Kurhausstrasse (tel. 429), offers clean, simple rooms and a friendly oldtime management which does everything it can to make your stay comfortable. There's a swimming pool on the premises, as well as an elevator, plus 54 beds in comfortable bedrooms, mainly with private bath. Singles cost from 280 AS ($14.90), while doubles range from 250 AS ($13.30) to 300 AS ($15.96) per person, with breakfast included.

NEUFELDEN: Lying in the Grosse Mühl Valley, Neufelden has been a market town since the 13th century. Today it's known by the Austrians primarily as a little holiday resort in the Mühlviertel. The town has some lovely baroque buildings as well as a parish church from the 15th century. A wildlife park containing many different birds of prey is to the west of the town.

Food and Lodging

Mühltalhof (tel. 258). Many of the balconies of this charming hotel look out over an artificial lake that comes close to the hotel's flowered sun terrace. A private beach extends right to the stone wall at the water's edge.

On the premises are tennis courts, a children's playground, and a sauna. The inside is gracefully decorated with tasteful furniture, coffered ceilings, and lots of extra touches. This hotel is a good choice for families traveling with children, especially since the relaxed management does what it can to make your holidays pleasant. Each of the comfortable rooms has its own bath. Singles cost from 410 AS ($21.81) to 475 AS ($25.27), while doubles range from 350 AS ($18.62) to 420 AS ($22.34) per person, with half board included. Prices depend on the season and the accommodation.

AIGEN: A little market town enjoying a modest claim as a summer resort, Aigen lies in a forested area in the northwestern corridor of the Mühlviertel. From the resort, you can visit **Schlagl** (1845 feet), an abbey built in 1218 and reconstructed centuries later. Its formerly Gothic church now flowers in the baroque style.

Aigen is surrounded by some of the most beautiful scenery in Upper Austria. From some of the panoramic belvederes you can look into Czechoslovakia.

Food and Lodging

Sporthotel Almesberger (tel. 213). The Gruber family will be your hosts in this modern hotel complex which wraps itself around two sides of a grassy area with a fountain in the middle. The interior is cozily outfitted with wooden beams and timbers, tasteful upholstery, and rustic furniture. The spacious bedrooms often have wood-covered ceilings and attractively contrasting patterns. Per-person rates, based on double occupancy, range from 365 AS ($19.42) to 540 AS ($28.73), with single occupants paying a daily surcharge of 30 AS ($1.60). Half board is included in the above prices.

3. Attersee and Mondsee

The noted Salzkammergut, to the northeast of Salzburg, is the most explored part of Upper Austria, although portions of it spill into other provinces. In fact the parts we are about to consider are more often visited from Salzburg than from Linz.

Our first stopovers will be at a warm lake and a cold one. First, the cold one—

ATTERSEE: The largest lake in the Austrian Alps, Attersee comes alive in summer with the sporting crowd, when visitors flock to the resort town that bears the lake's name. Frankly, in my opinion the lake is too cold almost all the time for swimming (although polar bear club members may disagree), but it's a great draw to boaters in summer. An Austrian sailing club has its headquarters here.

Those interested in fishing will be attracted to the lake's clear alpine waters, as it holds trout, char, and in little tributaries, brook trout. At many guest houses along the shore you can have for dinner the fish you caught.

The blue-green *see* is 12½ miles long and about 1½ miles wide, with many orchards growing on its uplands. The government has built a road around the entire body of water. From the southern part of the lake, to the west of Burgau, you can take a 12-minute walk to a beautiful gorge, the

Burggrabenklamm, with a waterfall, one of the most scenic sights along the Attersee.

Food and Lodging

Hotel Oberndorfer (tel. 364) is a long, multi-sectioned hotel with a one-story extension stretching all the way to the edge of the lake. From the far edge of the sun terrace you can see the village church on the other side of the hotel. The bedrooms are sunny, carpeted, and comfortable, while the public rooms have more than their share of wood paneling and wrought iron. Well-furnished singles rent for 270 AS ($14.36) to 410 AS ($21.81), while doubles go for between 355 AS ($18.87) and 540 AS ($28.73), with breakfast included. Rates depend on the season and the room assignment, and half board costs another 110 AS ($5.85) per person daily.

NUSSDORF AM ATTERSEE: This is a little lakeside village next to the better known holiday resort, Attersee, just recommended. Nussdorf, in a central position on the lake, is a small holiday place enjoying mainly a summer trade. There are tennis courts, a sailing school, boats for rent, fishing, and folkloric concerts.

Food and Lodging

Bräugasthof Aichinger (tel. 8007) is a pleasant four-story rectangular building with a long garden stretching through flowering trees to a sunny lawn. A wellhouse with constantly flowing water is the first thing you'll see from the quiet street on the hotel's downhill side. Inside, the builders added stone accents, such as a rounded column to support the vaults of the breakfast room, as well as a dome-capped green tile oven studded with ceramic rosettes. The comfortable and practical bedrooms are outfitted with every comfort. Singles rent for 230 AS ($12.24) to 275 AS ($14.63), while doubles cost between 200 AS ($10.64) and 255 AS ($13.57) per person, with breakfast included. Prices depend on the season and the plumbing.

WEISSENBACH AM ATTERSEE: You'll find this tiny lakeside hamlet and mini-holiday resort on the southeastern corner of the lake. From here you can take a heavily forested, scenic road to a pass at **Weissenbach Sattel,** which has a chapel. Along this road you'll have a view of the Weissenbachklamm Gorge.

Food and Lodging

Hotel Post (tel. 240) is a balconied, white-walled hotel set at the edge of the lake. It's surrounded by trees, with a sun terrace stretching up to the edge of the water. Long rows of green-shuttered windows look out over iron railings onto the water. Modern furniture fills the tastefully appointed bedrooms, some of which have Oriental rugs as floor coverings. In one of the public rooms stands a big ceramic oven with painted tiles. On the premises are tennis courts, two bowling alleys, sailing facilities, a sauna, and waterskiing equipment. Single rooms range from 515 AS ($27.40) to 625 AS ($33.25), while doubles cost between 360 AS ($19.15) and 515 AS ($27.40) per person, with full board included. Prices depend on the season, and all units contain private baths.

UNTERACH AM ATTERSEE: This lakeside hamlet is so small it doesn't appear on most maps, but it occupies one of the loveliest positions on the lake. It's on the right bank, across from Weissenbach, and it can be a base for exploring either Attersee or Mondsee.

Food and Lodging

Hotel Georgshof (tel. 501) is a wood-and-stucco chalet set on a hillside. If you walk out onto the backyard's sun terrace, you'll realize that the hotel is actually bigger than it appears from the road. The exteriors of many of the windows are embellished with regional designs in yellow and brown. Inside you'll find a timbered and stuccoed bar area with chalet chairs and an angled serving area with alpine-style barstools. An indoor pool has a high ceiling and tile walls and floors. The bedrooms are spacious and comfortable. The Hollenwöger family, your hosts, charge between 330 AS ($17.56) and 370 AS ($19.68) for a single and between 320 AS ($17.02) and 370 AS ($19.68) per person in a double, including breakfast.

SEEWALCHEN AM ATTERSEE: At the northern extremity of Lake Atter (Attersee) is this small hamlet and holiday resort. It offers sailing and other water sports, but the main reason I'm recommending it is because of the following accommodation, one of the most pleasant stopovers in the Salzkammergut.

Food and Lodging

Gasthof Häupl (tel. 2249) is one of the most elegant hotels in the region. From the street side it has a pleasingly simple facade of white walls and a steeply sloped series of rooflines with long rows of interconnected gables. From the lake side the design literally blossoms into masses of flowers, set into boxes which hang from the handcrafted wooden balconies. The interior looks like a tastefully opulent private house. The paneling that covers many of the rooms glows softly in the reflected light from the wall sconces. In the light-grained bar the ceiling is crafted around baroque patterns and curves.

Well-furnished singles range from 600 AS ($31.92) to 1050 AS ($55.86), while doubles cost from 900 AS ($47.88) to 1340 AS ($71.29). These prices include breakfast and use of the sauna.

The rustic dining room is said to be one of the best in the region. It's accented with graceful curves of wrought iron, and the chef prepares such delicacies as roast goose with baby vegetables in a savory sauce. This could be followed by a dessert parfait of fresh prunes in a caramel sauce. Frau Häupl, whose family has run this place for the past seven generations, does most of the cooking, assisted by an able collection of chefs. Fixed-price meals range from 180 AS ($9.58) to 660 AS ($35.11), while à la carte dinners cost from 140 AS ($7.45) to 430 AS ($22.88). The restaurant is closed Monday and in the period between October and April.

MONDSEE: "Moon Lake," or Mondsee, is considered one of the warmest lakes in the Salzkammergut. It's a crescent-shaped body of water which was named for the moon as long ago as Roman times. The Salzburg–Vienna autobahn runs along the south shores of this, the third-largest lake in the

Salzkammergut district. In the background you can see the **Drachenwand** mountain and also the **Schafberg.**

The lake is sparsely settled, and if you want to find accommodations, you should head for the village which bears the lake's name, Mondsee, lying in the northwest corner. The village is popular in summer as a resort, with sailing schools and bathing beaches operating on the *see.*

A Benedictine abbey once was situated in Mondsee, dating from 748. However, Emperor Joseph II ordered the abbey dissolved in 1791, so the abbey church became the **parish church** *(pfarrkirche),* still a point of interest in the village. It's a 15th-century structure with an added baroque exterior, but its crypt is from the 11th century. The church was richly decorated by Meinrad Guggenbichler, a sculptor born in 1649. He designed seven of the more than dozen altars.

Part of the abbey is now the **Schloss Mondsee** (see below). The castle is adjacent to the church. The wedding scene in *The Sound of Music* was filmed here.

The town also has a small local museum, the **Heimatmuseum,** open from the first of May until the end of October from 9 a.m. to 5 p.m. daily, charging 20 AS ($1.06). Local artifacts of life in the province in other days are displayed in what used to be chapels of the abbey. The history of the abbey is traced, and other works by Guggenbichler are displayed.

You may also visit the **Mondseer Rauchhaus,** or smokehouse, a rustic wood chalet flanked by outbuildings. Farmers from the district came here to dry their crops. There is no chimney above the vaulted hearth. The smokehouse is open April until the end of October from 8 a.m. to 6 p.m. Admission is 18 AS (96¢) for adults, 10 AS (53¢) for children.

Food and Lodging

Hotel/Restaurant Plomberg (tel. 2912) might remind you of a wealthy private home. It's dotted in dozens of places—even the bedrooms—with Oriental rugs, thick curtains, and lots of tasteful accessories which range from wrought-iron detailing to unusual art objects. The hotel sits above a stone wall that edges onto the lake. It's surrounded by deciduous trees and prosperous-looking villas. Bed and breakfast ranges from 440 AS ($23.41) to 660 AS ($35.11) per person daily.

The hotel doesn't offer full- or half-board plans, because most of the guests make their own plans during the day. These activities may or may not include a meal in the in-house restaurant, which serves outstanding food often considered among the best in Upper Austria. Karl and Monika Eschlböck devote more time to the restaurant than to anything else about their establishment. It's divided into several cozy dining rooms, decorated with Oriental rugs and accented with heavy timbers and an occasional antique.

Mr. Eschlböck was an apprentice at Troisgros in France and carries much of that establishment's expertise into his own restaurant. The menu is long and includes unusual adaptations of Austrian recipes as well as such items as veal liver with tomatoes, a salad of mache and duck breasts, lotte with a mousseline sauce, an array of veal dishes, roebuck Corsican style, crab soup, and carp with a finely chopped mixture of gruyère, carrots, fennel, and potatoes. À la carte meals range from 120 AS ($6.38) to 540 AS

($28.73), while fixed-price dinners go from 455 AS ($24.21) to 830 AS ($44.17). Reservations are important.

Seehotel Lackner, 33 Gaisberg (tel. 2359), is a rambling white hotel with balconies facing the lake and flowerboxes blossoming toward the street. The sun terrace has a covering of gray flagstones, while the interior is a rustic ensemble of modern furniture and wood accents. Comfortably furnished singles range from 430 AS ($22.88) to 485 AS ($25.80), while doubles cost between 360 AS ($19.15) and 450 AS ($23.94) per person, with half board included. Prices depend on the season and the plumbing.

Grossgasthof Leitnerbräu (tel. 2219) has been owned by many generations of the Marschallinger family. You'll recognize it by its natural stucco facade with the white and pink geometric detailing around the windows. A wrought-iron bracket extends out over the candy-striped awning, holding a depiction of two lions drinking happily from a barrel. The interior is cheerfully rustic, with a green ceramic stove in the restaurant and a scattering of painted antique furniture. Per-person rates range from 340 AS ($18.09) to 370 AS ($19.68), with half board included. All accommodations contain private bath and are usually spacious and sunny. The hotel is closed in November.

Gasthof Weisses Rössl, 5 Marktplatz (tel. 2224). If you haven't learned the geography of Austria yet, the newspaper-like menu will help you to at least identify the most popular dishes of each of the regions. These are often among the cheaper selections on the menu and are featured, one specialty per region, below each of the province's heraldic symbols. The menu also offers grilled specialties, three kinds of trout dishes, and an array of recipes served directly at the table in a copper pan. À la carte meals range from 120 AS ($6.38) to around twice that much, depending on what you order. The restaurant serves every day but Monday from October to May.

Castello Bar and Restaurant (tel. 388). At a recent party here the hostess requested that the guests show up in Rolls-Royces, and the resulting traffic jam is still talked about in the region. The restaurant is housed in a château beside the lake, with a setting that someone once described as something from an operetta. In fact many of the clients are high-rollers in the rarefied atmosphere of the Salzburg music world, and the intrigue that develops every year below the vaulted ceilings of the bar might be more interesting than what actually happens on stage.

Countess Almeida is the colorful owner of this place. She personally supervises the preparation of various specialties, which are eventually served in the flamboyantly decorated dining room. The centerpiece is a pair of polychrome statues dressed like savages, who stand guard from on top of the dessert table. The simple menu includes seven kinds of soup, a wide range of appetizers, and an array of local fish from the nearby lake, plus a range of about ten different meat dishes. Meals cost from 300 AS ($15.96). Reservations are necessary.

Café Frauenschuh (tel. 2312) is an establishment so famous that it's known by sweet tooths throughout the region for its delectable pastries and chocolates. In the middle of the village, it offers racks of fruited and chocolate-covered confections which you can eat on the spot or buy by the dozen to (supposedly) distribute among your friends back at the hotel. Coffee costs around 20 AS ($1.06), while pastries run the range between 18 AS (96¢) and 30 AS ($1.60). The café is open every day of the week except Wednesday between October and April.

4. St. Wolfgang and Bad Ischl

The next two resorts, quite different in character, lie a short distance apart in the Salzkammergut.

St. Wolfgang lies on the Wolfgangsee, already visited in Chapter VIII, Land Salzburg. St. Gilgen in that province is a rival for St. Wolfgang, lying on the same lake but in Upper Austria. The province boundary crosses the lake.

Bad Ischl, once the summer residence of Emperor Franz Joseph, is the most fashionable spa in the lake district.

ST. WOLFGANG: In the midst of mountains in the Salzkammergut, Wolfgangsee is considered one of the most romantic lakes in Austria. Mountains and *see* join harmoniously to provide the setting for St. Wolfgang, a little holiday resort on the northeastern side of the lake below the Schafberg. Here in summer you can enjoy private bathing and other water sports, as well as frequenting the beach cafés. Hiking is possible in many directions.

There's also winter skiing in the hills, with snow from December to mid-March. The ski slopes are free of avalanches. You'll find facilities here for skating, curling, and horse sleighrides. Folkloric dancing is often presented as well.

In summer the resort is overrun with tourists, but there are two car parks at the entrance to the town. At certain times of the year I find it better to go to St. Wolfgang by boat, leaving from the landing stage at **Gschwendt** on the southern rim of the lake. Departures from mid-May to mid-October are usually hourly. The round-trip fare is 35 AS ($1.86).

St. Wolfgang is the site of the celebrated **White Horse Inn** (see below), and the landscape has been called operetta-like, which is natural as the inn was the setting for Ralph Benatzky's operetta *White Horse Inn,* which brought glory to the town.

Long before it was a holiday resort, St. Wolfgang was a renowned pilgrimage center, having been so since the 12th century. The **Church of St. Wolfgang** is said to stand on the spot where St. Wolfgang built a hermitage on a rocky spur of land. The church, from the latter 15th century, is highlighted by the Michael Pacher altarpiece, a magnificent work from 1481, pictured in many Gothic art books. Pacher's altarpiece is luxuriantly adorned with panel paintings and masterfully carved figures. The main panel depicts the Coronation of the Virgin. Thomas Schwanthaler designed the double altar of the patron saint, Wolfgang, and John the Baptist.

You can visit the church May to September from 9 a.m. to 5 p.m., until 6 p.m. on Sunday and public holidays. Otherwise, its hours are from 10 a.m. to 4 p.m., from 11 a.m. on Sunday. Admission is 10 AS (53¢).

The most popular excursion from St. Wolfgang is to **Schafberg,** the view from the top being one of the best known and most sought in Upper Austria. Legend has it that you can see 13 lakes of the Salzkammergut from here, but I have never been able to do so. However, you're almost sure to have a good view of Mondsee and Attersee (which I've just introduced you to), and of course the entire Wolfgangsee. On a clear day you can see as far as the Berchtesgaden Alps of Hitler fame. As a backdrop to the view, you can gaze at the peaks of the Hollengebirge and the Dachstein with its glacier caps.

The whole trip to Schafberg takes about 4½ hours, nearly half by rack rail which operates from May to October. Once there, allow for about 30 minutes' walking. Departures are hourly mid-May to mid-June from 8:30 a.m. to 4:30 p.m., mid-June to mid-September from 7 a.m. to 6:25 p.m., and mid-September to mid-October from 8:30 a.m. to 6:20 p.m. A round trip costs 150 AS ($7.98).

There's a hotel on the summit of the mountain, which rises to 5850 feet.

Food and Lodging

The **White Horse Inn** (Weissen Rössl) (tel. 2306). A popular play *(Im Weissen Rössl am Wolfgangsee)* was written in 1896 and adapted for the Berlin stage by a group of actors and directors who returned here to rewrite it in 1930. Actually, there has been an inn on this site since 1474, with continual ownership by the Peter family since 1712.

This scene of the famous operetta absolutely reeks of romance and atmosphere. Its stippled yellow facade conceals a collection of carved antiques which are clustered into intimate conversational groupings. The public rooms are large and sunny, usually covered with wood and upholstered with pleasant and cheerful colors. The indoor pool has wall-to-wall paneling and direct access to the wide lakeside sun terrace with its view of the village church.

On the premises are private tennis courts, a gymnasium, a sauna, sailing, waterskiing, and windsurfing facilities. In the evening the management usually provides live piano or zither music. With half board included, singles rent for 500 AS ($26.60) to 900 AS ($47.88), while doubles cost between 570 AS ($30.32) and 1030 AS ($54.80) per person.

Hotel Appesbach (tel. 2209). The entrance is through an arched portico covered with ivy, which brings you into a pleasant family-run hotel with plenty of character. About a mile from the center of town, the establishment is a collection of what looks like three separate yellow buildings with green shutters. They are joined together into a rambling complex set directly on the lake. The surrounding lawn area contains table-tennis tables, outdoor chairs, and children's toys. Tennis courts are a short distance away. The hotel has a small private beach and facilities for sailboat rentals as well. It's closed in winter, reopening for business in April. Doubles with breakfast cost 720 AS ($38.30), while singles go for 440 AS ($23.41).

Sporthotel Wolfgangerhof (tel. 2237) is a modern balconied guest house with two elongated sections set at right angles to one another. A summertime café has been set up under a tree just outside the entrance. Inside you'll find a bar and several restaurants, as well as a swimming pool, sauna, and facilities for renting either bicycles or ski equipment. Per-person rates in doubles range from 300 AS ($15.96) to 400 AS ($21.28), half board included. The supplement in a single is 60 AS ($3.19) daily. Prices depend on the season and the plumbing.

Seehotel Cortisen (tel. 376) is separated from the lake only by a solid stone wall which supports a sun terrace and a short expanse of well-maintained lawn. From the street side the first thing you'll see are the illustrations of regionally dressed couples that cover parts of the facade.

Inside, the decor is rustically elegant, with well-crafted woodwork, richly patterned Oriental rugs, and lots of antique knickknacks.

The cozy bedrooms often have private balconies and are tastefully furnished with lots of well-detailed pieces. The Ballner family are your hosts at this pleasant oasis. They charge between 275 AS ($14.63) and 400 AS ($21.28) per person, based on double occupancy with breakfast included. Singles pay a daily surcharge of 50 AS ($2.66). Prices depend on the exposure of your room and the season. Half board costs another 125 AS ($6.65) per person daily. The hotel shuts down on Halloween for the winter months.

Hotel Tirol (tel. 3269) is a lakeside chalet that rises four flower-covered stories above a grassy area which serves as a combination beach, sun terrace, and café. The interior has lots of rustic ceiling beams and cozy alpine-style furniture, while many of the comfortable bedrooms have carved headboards, paneled closet doors, and lots of atmosphere. The bar area is especially inviting, with the bottles arranged in a wood, brick, and stucco combination that looks almost like a converted hearth. With half board included, per-person rates, based on double occupancy, range from 335 AS ($17.82) to 430 AS ($22.88) in accommodations without private bath. With bath, supplements range from 120 AS ($6.38) to 155 AS ($8.25) daily, and singles pay yet another daily surcharge of 120 AS ($6.38).

Hotel Post, Eibenstein, and Gästehaus Gastberger (tel. 2346, 2342, and 2218) are a complex of three imposing buildings linked by a common management and a shared dining room inside the Hotel Post. That dining room has a beamed ceiling and a rustically elegant decor that was partially installed when the hotel was built in 1574. The front of the Post has country-baroque detailing around the windows and lots of balconies.

The Eibenstein is a forbidding-looking castle with red and white chevron-patterned shutters, while the Gästehaus looks like a sprawling, greatly expanded lakeside chalet. Room prices are the same in the three hotels. Per-person rates in doubles range from 280 AS ($14.90) to 350 AS ($18.62), depending on the season. All the hotels are closed in winter. Tariffs include breakfast, and half board costs another 120 AS ($6.38) per day. Singles carry a daily surcharge of 30 AS ($1.60). Occupants of the three hotels have access to two indoor pools and a sauna.

Hotel Belvedere (tel. 302) is a cozy chalet-style hotel with a lakeside location and an interior filled with a scattering of Victorian antiques and ceramic stoves. One of the most pleasant places on the premises is the rustic covered café-terrace with a view of the lake. The hotel is open year round. Singles rent for 180 AS ($9.58) to 335 AS ($17.82), while doubles cost between 165 AS ($8.79) and 310 AS ($16.49) per person, with breakfast included. Prices depend on the plumbing and the season.

Hotel Eden, 40 Michael Pacher Strasse (tel. 2326), is a recently constructed building with long rows of wooden balconies and a location on a hillside at the upper end of the village. The comfortable bedrooms are simply furnished, renting for 400 AS ($21.28) per person in a double and from 440 AS ($23.41) in a single.

Gasthof/Pension Zimmerbräu (tel. 204) has the kind of facade that will make you want to stop in for coffee. A big-windowed restaurant extends partly into the street, while someone has installed lots of gingerbread under the eaves. You'll get a sense of some seaside town from the sun terrace of the two rustic beach huts whose foundations are built right into the lake. These also are accented with gingerbread and a wholesome sense of another era. The interior of the main hotel is simply and attractively furnished, with the kinds of floors that are easy to keep clean. The per-person rate in a double is 455 AS ($24.21), while singles rent for 480 AS ($25.54), with half board included.

BAD ISCHL: The spa of Bad Ischl, one of the country's most fashionable watering places and the summer seat of Emperor Franz Joseph for more than 60 years, can be reached coming from Salzburg–Munich by leaving the motorway at Mondsee, heading along a well-constructed federal highway through the Salzkammergut, along Wolfgangsee and Mondsee. It's a 25-mile drive after you turn off the autobahn. Bad Ischl is easily accessible by daily bus and train service also. The spa establishments provide brine-sulfur mud baths for a variety of ailments.

The town, constructed on a peninsula between the Traun River and its tributary, the Ischl, still reflects a certain imperial conceit in its architecture, much of it left over from the heyday of the Austro-Hungarian Empire. The spa went into a decline after Franz Joseph stopped coming here in the first year of World War I, ending a practice he started in 1848 at the very beginning of his reign.

During imperial days the court was a magnet to musicians and artists, who depended on patronage from royalty and aristocracy for their bread and butter—and wine and caviar. Among those who made their way to Bad Ischl were Johann Strauss, Oscar Straus, Meyerbeer, Brahms, Bruckner, Lehar, Kálmán, Tauber, and Waldmüller.

Bad Ischl has surprisingly chic shopping even today, as you'll note if you go along the **Pfarrgasse.** This street comes to an end at the **Esplanade,** a shaded promenade where the most famous figures in Europe once strolled. The smart set of the 19th century shunned the sun. Wealthy salt merchants once lived along this promenade, and Maximilian, ill-fated Emperor of Mexico, was born in a royal dwelling here in 1832.

The former **Pump Room,** dating from 1831, is in the middle of town on the Ferdinand-Auböck-Platz. Many of the buildings seen on the platz are in the Biedermeier style. The 1753 parish church was rebuilt when Maria Theresa was empress.

Many riverside walks are possible at this spa, and you'll see lovely gardens and villas which attract viewers. **Lehar Villa** stands on the opposite bank of the Traun. Franz Lehar, the composer best known for his creation *The Merry Widow,* lived here from 1912 until his death in 1948. The villa is now a museum.

The most important attraction of the town is the **Kaiservilla,** or imperial villa, in Kaiserpark, to the north of town. This is where Franz Joseph lived, being drawn to the area by his love of hunting. The **Gray Saloon** where the Empress Elisabeth lived is one of the highlights of a tour of the villa. Elisabeth left this room on July 16, 1898, to begin her trip to Switzerland where an assassin awaited her.

Guided tours of the Kaiservilla are conducted from the first of May until mid-October from 9 a.m. to noon and from 1 to 5 p.m. Off-season it's open only on weekends from noon to 4 p.m. Admission is 50 AS ($2.66).

Empress Elisabeth used to retreat to a tiny palace built of marble and called **Marmorschlössl.** It evokes memories of Marie Antoinette's use of the

Petit Trianon at Versailles. To visit Marmorschlössl, open from the first of May until the end of October from 9:30 a.m. to 5 p.m., a separate fee of 15 AS (80¢) is charged.

For a view of the overall area, you can take a chair lift to the **Siriuskogel** (1960 feet). Another tour is south of the spa to the **salt mine** which has hour-long conducted tours.

The tourist office at 6 Bahnhofstrasse (tel. 35-20) will give you complete directions and information about all the sights in the immediate environs if you'd like to stay in the spa and make some day trips.

Food and Lodging

Kurhotel Bad Ischl (tel. 4271), in the center of town, is a futuristic-looking hotel easy to recognize because of its multi-sectioned design of jutting angles and recessed balconies. Painted a dazzling white, the hotel has a streamlined interior with neutral colors and lots of sunny, light-filled spaces. It was built between 1974 and 1976 with all the modern conveniences, including an underground garage, a hairdressing salon, an indoor mineral water bath, a sauna, and a glistening collection of restaurants, plus massage and therapy facilities. A heated corridor leads directly to the famous spa. Singles rent for 815 AS ($43.36) to 875 AS ($46.55), while doubles cost between 755 AS ($40.17) and 815 AS ($43.36) per person, with half board included. Each of the accommodations has a private bath, phone, radio, color TV, and private balcony. Harald Rehbock is the well-trained manager.

Sport- und Golfhotel (tel. 324172). If you're tired of pseudo-romantic chalets and traditional architecture, this might be the place for you. Outside of town, it's designed almost like a Mayan pyramid, with an A-shape frame separated into evenly spaced rows of big windows and weathered balconies. The dramatic interior has well-placed Oriental statues, glistening modern accents, textured walls of marble and concrete aggregates, and wooden ceilings pierced with skylights and stained into a variety of decorator colors including vivid green and purple.

The bedrooms are spacious, livable, and filled with rattan furniture from the Philippines. Best of all, you'll occasionally see unusual pieces of furniture built around 18th-century patterns with beautifully crafted inlays and painted designs. An indoor pool is long enough to swim laps in, with lots of sun from the full-view windows. One of the area's most modern tennis facilities is only about 100 yards from the hotel, while a golf course is close at hand.

Gerda Pirktl is the conscientious manager. Rates for a single range from 560 AS ($29.79) to 800 AS ($42.56), while doubles cost between 480 AS ($25.54) and 870 AS ($46.28) per person, with breakfast included. Half board is an additional 120 AS ($6.38) per person daily. Prices depend on the season, and all accommodations contain private baths.

Hotel Schenner, 9 Schulgasse (tel. 2327), is owned and managed by a family with the same name. Its interior is outfitted with stone detailing and plenty of exposed wood, as well as a conservatively rustic format that includes lots of wrought iron and a few hunting trophies. You'll recognize the building by its painted corner mullions and country baroque window detailing. A parasol-dotted sun terrace sits on the grass of the back lawn. The pleasant bedrooms are decorated in a comfortable selection of autumnal colors and usually have oversize tile bathrooms. Singles range from 435 AS ($23.14) to 590 AS ($31.39), while per-person rates in a double go from 415 AS ($22.08) to 510 AS ($27.13), with half board included. Prices depend on the season and the plumbing.

Hotel Goldenes Schiff, 3 Stifterkai (tel. 4241), is a leisurely five-minute walk from the spa facilities. It sits directly on the river, housed in a simple white building taller than it is wide. The riverfront rooms usually contain balconies, while even those facing the street have an invitingly cozy decor of modern furniture and sunny colors accented with lots of exposed wood. The restaurants are outfitted with refreshing touches of green, blue, and red, and all have pleasant combinations of rough-sawed planking and smoothly polished wood. Josef and Christine Gruber are the congenial owners. They charge between 410 AS ($21.81) and 625 AS ($33.25) per person in a wide range of singles, doubles, as well as apartments, all with half board included.

Goldenes Hufeisen, 13 Pfarrgasse (tel. 3653). From the street side this family-run hotel has a simple and restrained facade of pastel-colored stucco and white trim. From the garden side the building opens onto a green area with big sunny windows and parallel rows of wood-railed balconies. The beer garden adjoining the establishment is staffed with businesslike hausfraus and shaded with big trees. The bedrooms are comfortable and clean. An annex holds the overflow from the main hotel and lies about three minutes away. Both buildings are in the center of the spa. The Abpurg family charge between 315 AS ($16.75) and 390 AS ($20.75) for a single, while doubles range from 550 AS ($29.26) to 730 AS ($38.84) per room, with half board included. Prices depend on the season and the plumbing.

Hotel Goldener Stern, 30 Kreuzplatz (tel. 3530), has one of the most memorable facades at the spa, covered with turquoise-colored stucco, white trim, and a white-walled rectangular tower jutting out from the corner. It's in the center of town, and while some of the public rooms have been renovated into an unpretentious and streamlined format of clean lines and modern paneling, the simple bedrooms retain much of their rustic allure. They're usually filled with painted furniture and wall-to-wall carpeting. Singles range from 485 AS ($25.80) to 500 AS ($26.60), while doubles cost anywhere from 825 AS ($43.89) to 860 AS ($45.75), with half board included. Prices depend on the season.

Weinhaus Attwenger (tel. 3327) is the rustically decorated wine tavern which, it's said, used to be a favorite of Bruckner and Lehar. It's very much an old-style decor that many more modern establishments try to duplicate. Even so, many summertime clients enjoy the riverside sun terrace where on a pleasant day the savory coffee and delectable pastries seem even more tempting. If you want a full meal, the menu includes a wide range of Austrian and international dishes. These feature medallions of veal chef's style, mussels in a savory sauce, and several kinds of fish. À la carte meals range from 120 AS ($6.38) to 335 AS ($17.82). Reservations might be a good idea.

Konditorei-Café Zauner (tel. 3310) is the pastry shop and coffeehouse that anyone with a sense of history usually heads for after viewing the summer playgrounds of the former Habsburg monarchs. The only Austrian coffeehouse more famous than this is Demel in Vienna. The imperial court used to order their pastries here, and it used to be said that the easiest way to listen to the heartbeat of the empire during July and August was to eavesdrop on a nearby table at Zauner.

You can buy pastries from the gold and white rococo showroom (which has been renovated to handle the flood of summer tourists) or eat at the small round-topped tables in an elegant series of inner rooms. Menu items include sandwiches and salads as well as an extensive assortment of exquisitely prepared pastries. The café is open every day in summer between 8:30 a.m. and 6 p.m. From October to March it closes on Tuesday. Many of the items can be mailed as gifts. Coffee costs 20 AS ($1.06), while pastries range between 18 AS (96¢) and 30 AS ($1.60).

BAD GOISERN: This little spa town can be visited as an excursion from Bad Ischl, only six miles away, or else it can be used as a base for exploring this part of Upper Austria. Because it's much less well known than Bad Ischl, its prices are quite reasonable. Its little spa hotels offer good value for your schillings. The sulfurous spring waters of the spa contain iodine.

The resort attracts mainly Austrians and Germans who know of its quiet location in the Traun Valley. It's most popular in summer because of its good-size open-air swimming pool, but it does some winter business, being convenient to a toboggan run and ski lifts. Hikers like to base here, from where they can go up **Hochkalmberg** mountain (more than 6000 feet high) in 4½ hours and **Predigstuhl** (4190 feet) in 3 hours.

Food and Lodging

Kurhotel Jodschwefelbad (tel. 305) is a sprawling hotel and sanitorium with a modern format and a 100-year-old history in the treatment of rheumatic and skin disorders, especially psoriasis. Maintaining resident dermatologists on the premises, the hotel offers clean and modern accommodations to patients and tourists alike. A range of outdoor activities is in the region, and a thermally heated outdoor pool is on the premises. With half board included, singles rent for 570 AS ($30.32) to 745 AS ($39.63), while doubles go for between 475 AS ($25.27) and 650 AS ($34.58) per person, with half board included. Prices depend on the plumbing and the season.

Hotel Agatha-Wirt (tel. 342) is a romantic country-style hotel that was built in 1517. Today it has a humor-loving and friendly direction by the descendants of the family who bought it 200 years ago. It's designed with a steep hipped roof, lots of flowers, stone detailing around the entrance arch, and painted highlights around the corner mullions. The functional bedrooms inspire lingering and are suitable for other than just a good night's sleep. The headboards are often carved into regional patterns, and sometimes several kinds of wood are joined together for color contrast. If you're a light sleeper, avoid the units facing the street. Tennis, swimming, and ski facilities are all nearby. Per-person rates, with half board included, range from 285 AS ($15.16) to 490 AS ($26.07), depending on the plumbing and the season. The hotel is usually closed for the first part of December.

Hotel/Café Goiserermühle (tel. 206). The second floor of this square-based building is capped with a pyramid-shaped roof which comes to a point high above the immaculate lawns. The building is capped with a series of gables and a small tower surrounded by chimneys. The rooms have been renovated with all the modern comforts, costing 230 AS ($12.24) in a single and from 210 AS ($11.17) per person in a double, with half board included. The in-house restaurant serves well-seasoned steaks, schnitzels, and fish (especially trout) in a homey and rustic setting. Fixed-price meals range from 100 AS ($5.32) to 110 AS ($5.85), while à la carte dinners cost between 95 AS ($5.05) and 220 AS ($11.70).

5. Hallstatt

Hallstatt, a small market town south of Bad Ischl, considered one of the most beautiful villages in Austria, is my favorite place in this province. It stands on the left bank of the dark, brooding Hallstättersee in the Salzkammergut, on the southernmost tip of the province, right at the border of Land Salzburg (see Chapter VIII) and Styria (see Chapter XIII). You may well drive through a part of Styria to reach the lake, going via Bad Aussee.

To reach Hallstatt you take a road through a tunnel in the mountain. Park your car in the car park and then go by foot past waterfalls to the traffic-free town. There are several large cascades in the area.

Hallstättersee is a narrow lake, about 5 miles long and 1½ miles wide at its broadest expanse, almost completely surrounded by mountains. Its waters are so dark they're often called black.

Now a modern town, Hallstatt is considered the oldest still-inhabited village in Europe, owing its importance and its longevity to the local deposits of salt. Its perch against a mountain on a rocky terrace overlooking Hallstättersee seems like a curious place to build a town, but this was the site of an early Iron Age culture dating from 800 to 400 B.C. Many Iron Age relics have been unearthed in the area. The mining of salt from the mountain behind Hallstatt was known among pre-Celtic tribes of 1000 B.C. It died out in medieval times but was revived by the Habsburgs and continues today.

THE SIGHTS: The town of Hallstatt gave its name to one of the most important eras of prehistory. Some 1000 tombs have been excavated in the area, which Austrians refer to as a "cradle of civilization." The 1000 graves were of prehistoric people, who constructed huts on piles in the lake. Many of the artifacts excavated here—dating back to Neolithic times—are displayed in the **Museum of Prehistory,** 56 Seistrasse, open from the first of April until the end of October from 10 a.m. to 5 p.m. Admission is 25 AS ($1.33).

The center of this beautifully situated village, with views of the Dachstein mountain massif, is the Market Square, which contains 16th-century buildings. The lakeside terrace is from the 18th century. Hallstatt's streets are narrow and often steep.

You can visit the **pfarrkirche** (parish church), which is romantically situated, the churchyard bordering the dark waters of the lake. The house of worship is a large structure from the latter part of the 15th century. It has a squat tower, but its unusually designed roof with overhanging eaves evokes thoughts of Oriental buildings. The church's most outstanding art treasure is a big altarpiece, the gift of a salt merchant (obviously a rich one). Ten years in the making, beginning in 1505, the altarpiece depicts the Virgin between St. Catherine and St. Barbara.

Visitors can also go to the **Chapel of St. Michael,** a Gothic church next to the parish church. The cemetery was so small that this *karner* (charnel house or bone house) had to be used, starting in the 17th century. Some 12 to 15 years after a body had been buried in the ground the bones were transferred to the charnel house. Some skulls bear markings of the date of their owners' deaths. Other signs reveal the age of the dead, and sometimes markings show the cause of death.

The **Heimatmuseum** (local museum) is open from the first of May until the end of September from 9 a.m. to 6 p.m., charging an admission of 25 AS ($1.33). The museum is in the oldest secular building in the village, the 14th-century **Hallstatt-Markt.** It contains exhibits of artifacts and details the history of the region.

Numerous cable cars and lifts are found in the town and surrounding area, as well as many walking paths or hiking trails. Mountain climbing is also possible, as Dachstein (9900 feet) is in the vicinity, and the Dachstein Giant Ice Caves can be visited, although actually the mountain is more easily reached from nearby Obertraun (see below) than from Hallstatt. You can enjoy fishing on the Hallstättersee and in the Traun River, sailing, rowing, motorboating, swimming, and tennis. In winter Hallstatt is also a sports center, with snow from November to April. There are no fog problems. You can go skiing, sledding, curling, and ice skating, or hike along pleasant winter footpaths.

"Salt Mountain"

Lying above Hallstatt to the northwest is **Salzberg** (salt mountain), not to be confused with Salzburg, the city. The salt mines are still active and can be visited. Archeologists are constantly digging in this area and have unearthed many interesting finds.

To reach the mountain, you take the cableway from Lahn and make about a 20-minute walk after getting off. The funicular runs between 8 a.m. and 4 p.m., a round trip costing 55 AS ($2.93). Guided tours of the mines are conducted from the first of May to the end of September from 9 a.m. to 6 p.m., but you can't start the tour after 4:30 p.m. Admission is 70 AS ($3.72) for adults and 40 AS ($2.13) for children over 5. (children under 5 are not admitted). Dress warmly, and be sure to wear strong walking shoes for the 2¾-hour mine tour.

There's a restaurant and snackbar with a terrace and a belvedere letting you take in the view. Hikers go all the way from here to the **Iron Age cemetery,** a trip taking about 1½ hours. If you like to hike, the tourist office will outline a series of walks in the area. One goes along the Echerntal to **Waldbachstrub** at the top of the valley, with lovely waterfalls. You can also climb to the **Tiergartenhütte,** which has a small inn, and on to the **Wiesberghaus,** 6180 feet. After that, only the hardy continue to the **Simony-Hütte** at 7230 feet, where there's another small inn lying at the foot of the Hallstatt Glacier. From Simony-Hütte, mountain climbers go up the **Hoher Dachstein,** the loftiest peak in the massif (9820 feet), the climb taking 3½ hours.

The Dachstein Caves

These caves are among the most spectacular natural attractions of Upper Austria. To reach them, you can drive to Obertraun, where a sign in the vicinity will direct you to the lower station of the cableway that takes you to the caves. The cableway will deposit you at the intermediate platform (4430 feet) on the Schönbergalm. From here it's about a 20-minute walk to the entrance to the caves.

Among the many attractions is the **Giant Ice Cave,** where even in summer the temperature is about 30° Fahrenheit. Be sure to dress for the cold. Among the ice cave's breathtaking features are the frozen waterfalls. You'll also see the so-called King Arthur's Cave and the Great Ice Chapel.

The ice cave is open from the first of May until mid-October from 8:30 a.m. to 4:30 p.m., a guided tour costing 45 AS ($2.39). If you also wish to visit the **Mammoth Cave,** a combined ticket costs 60 AS ($3.19). The Mammoth Cave has large galleries (subterranean passageways) cut through the rock by some ancient underground torrent. It takes about 1½ hours to go on a conducted tour of these caves. You're allowed to visit only a small part of the network of caves, which totals 23 miles in length, with a drop of 3870 feet.

It's possible to go from the Schönbergalm station by cableway to the upper platform at a height of 6920 feet. This is the **Hoher Krippenstein,** which offers an excellent panoramic view of the Dachstein massif. A chapel erected in the 1950s commemorates the accidental deaths here of 13 teachers and students. A round trip to Krippenstein costs 165 AS ($8.79). Service is about every hour from 8 a.m. to 5 p.m. You may have to queue up in summer when many visitors make the trip.

From Krippenstein you can take a cable car down to **Gzaidalm** (5880 feet).

Another cave can be visited in the area of Hallstatt, the **Koppenbrüllerhöhle,** or Koppenbrüller Cave. A torrent crosses the cave, and its activity causes continual enlargement of the cavern. The Austrians have made galleries which you can traverse for a glimpse of these turbulent underground waters.

The Koppenbrüller Cave is reached from Gasthaus Koppenrast, two miles upstream from Obertraun. You have to go on foot for about an hour. Guided tours, lasting an hour, are conducted through the cave from the first of May until the end of September from 9 a.m. to 5 p.m. for a charge of 45 AS ($2.39).

The south wall of the Dachstein can also be explored. Take a cable car known as the Gletscherbahn (glacier road) up to **Hunerkogel.** To reach the cable car, leave from Schladming, going ten miles via Ramsau on a toll road costing 25 AS ($1.33) per person. The 12-minute cable-car ride, leaving from 8 a.m. to 5 p.m., costs 175 AS ($9.31) per person for a round trip. At the upper belvedere (8840 feet) a magnificent view spreads out before you. You'll be able to see the Grossglockner as well as the Salzkammergut Alps. At Hunerkogel it's possible to ski in summer on the Schladminger Gletscher (small glacier).

FOOD AND LODGING: **Seehotel Grüner Baum** (tel. 263) has a churchside location in a quiet spot between the lake and a baroque fountain in the center of town. It's capped with a hipped roof of hammered copper (one of the only ones in town) and has an ochre-colored facade with white, heavily bordered windows. Its simple and comfortable rooms are accented with wood trim and often get lots of sunshine. The hotel's sun terrace extends out over the water on a pier, where you can go swimming or simply lie on a chaise longue with a drink if you want to. Later in the day you can sample local lake fish in the restaurant or on the terrace. The hotel is closed between mid-October and May. The rest of the year it charges between 250 AS ($13.30) and 430 AS ($22.88) for a single and between 455 AS ($24.21) and 865 AS ($46.02) for a double, with breakfast included. Prices depend on the plumbing and the accommodation.

Grillgasthof Zauner (tel. 246) is a local institution dedicated to serving copious amounts of well-prepared food to a loyal collection of local residents as well as to the armies of tourists who pass through. The establishment is divided into a series of tastefully rustic dining rooms, my favorite of which has a high beamed ceiling, paneling arranged into a series of repeating squares, and a host of hunting trophies. Menu items include fresh fish from the nearby lake, grilled meats, Austrian and Balkan specialties, and an occasional Indian dish. Sepp Zauner (the king of the grill) is the hard-working owner.

Single rooms range from 285 AS ($15.16) to 310 AS ($16.49), while doubles cost between 465 AS ($24.74) to 515 AS ($27.40), depending on the season, with breakfast included. If you want to take advantage of the restaurant, room plus half board costs around 400 AS ($21.28) per person daily.

Hotel Krippenstein (tel. 7129). Rarely have I seen such an inhospitable spot for a hotel—it stands on a rocky bluff which you can reach after taking three stages of cableways. It's billed as the tourist attraction with the highest elevation in all of Upper Austria. It looks like a concrete fortress as you approach it from the lichen-covered rocks below. In wintertime it's ideally suited for skiers, although the views of the glacier in summer are well worth the trip here. The 80 beds rent for between 380 AS ($20.22) and 420 AS ($22.34) for a single, while per-person rates in a double range from 420 AS ($22.34) to 485 AS ($25.80), depending on the season, with half board included.

Under the same management is the **Schönnberghaus** (tel. 27223). This might be the ideal departure point for excursions to the ice caves of the Dachstein massif. At the end of the first stage of the Dachstein cableway, it's built entirely of wood, and offers a sunny terrace, a 100-seat restaurant, and 40 beds. Your neighbors in the next room might be one of the youth groups who sometimes rent out large blocks of beds for nature excursions. With half board included, the per-person rate is around 320 AS ($17.02) daily.

OBERTRAUN: This is a small village which because of its location is often overrun with visitors. It opens directly onto Hallstättersee at an elevation of about 1960 feet. Obertraun is one of the most popular places to begin many sightseeing excursions in the district, especially to the Dachstein. For a rundown on tours, refer to the Hallstatt description (see above).

Skiers, including many from Great Britain, come here in winter to take advantage of several ski lifts in the area and to enjoy the slopes of the Krippenstein mountain mentioned above. Only the most dedicated skiers will wish to stay at Obertraun, as there is little après-ski activity here. Nonskiers will definitely want to seek out more exciting resorts in the winter. As a summer center, however, it's far livelier, being such a fine excursion base.

Food and Lodging

Gasthof Zum Sarstein (tel. 331) is a pleasant roadside guest house with a pale-yellow facade in a verdant setting surrounded by trees. A café offers midday refreshment. The comfortable rooms rent for between 180 AS ($9.58) and 200 AS ($10.64) for a single and between 360 AS ($19.15) and 400 AS ($21.28) in a double, with breakfast included. Half board is available for another 90 AS ($4.79) per person daily.

GOSAU: This little village can be a happy alternative to staying at Hallstatt, as its prices are much more reasonable. Relatively little known, Gosau lies six miles west of Hallstättersee in the vicinity of the Gschütt Pass. Because it's in a ski region the village attracts winter business. Some of the Dachstein ski tours leave from here.

Gosau is also an ideal base for some summer touring. A road running south for about five miles leads to the Gosausee (Lake of Gosau), a mountain lake at 3060 feet, encircled by steep rock walls. From here you can see the Gosau Glacier and the Dachstein (9820 feet), surrounded by glaciers. The best view is from the lower lake.

It's popular to board a funicular going up to Gablonzer Hütte (5200 feet), where you can enjoy snacks as you take in the view. The surrounding ski area is called the Swieselalm. A panoramic vista takes in the Hohe Tauern. Adventurers can climb to the top of Grosser Donnerkogel in about 2½ hours.

Food and Lodging

Sommerhof (tel. 258) is separated from the road by a generous parking lot and a gracefully curved series of stone-flanked steps. From the sun terrace you can study the gold and white floral designs decorating the facade. You can also compare the artist's rendition to the masses of real flowers growing from the balconies. The interior has coffered wood ceilings painted in regional patterns, well-placed stone columns under beautifully illustrated arches, and cozy, well-furnished bedrooms, all of which contain private baths. Many of the local residents who come here to socialize in the evening still wear regional garb. With half board included, per-person rates range from 335 AS ($17.82) to 450 AS ($23.94), depending on the season and the plumbing.

Pension Koller (tel. 207). The architecture of this Victorian-style building isn't the only unusual aspect about it. It sits on an expanse of lawn into which has been set a slate-ringed swimming pool. In the background rises a knife-edged series of jagged mountains, whose heights look even more forbidding because of the smooth grounds around the house. The hotel is built with arched loggias, recessed balconies, a series of hipped and gabled roofs, and a feudal-style tower covered with cedar shingles. Forests come almost to the back door, but from the front the view is uninterrupted for several hundred feet. Inside you'll find winter fireplaces giving off a welcome warmth, plus a cozy weinstube. The Koller family charges between 310 AS ($16.49) and 400 AS ($21.28) per person, with half board included, depending on the season and the room assignment.

6. The Traunsee

One of the biggest lakes in the Salzkammergut, the Traunsee is about 7½ miles long and some 2 miles wide at its broadest expanse, and lies to the east of the two major lakes already explored: the Attersee and the Mondsee. Three mountain peaks—Traunstein, Hochkogel, and Eriakogel—make a silhouette which Austrians call *Schlafende Griechin* (sleeping Greek girl). Some sections of the Salzkammergut road run along the western edge of the lake.

The most dramatic part of this road is from Ebensee, at the southwestern tip of the lake, to Trauenkirchen. This spectacular corniche had to be hewn out of rock. The Traunsee is ringed with a number of resorts, the chief town being Gmunden. There's lake steamer service in summer. To reach this lake from Bad Ischl (see above), you drive northeast along the Traun River.

Your first stopover along the Traunsee will be at—

EBENSEE: This resort town on the southern Traunsee lakeside draws visitors by its scenic splendors and its mild, constant climate. It's a good base for excursions into the mountains or along the lake.

For summer visitors there are natural bathing beaches, trips to the **Gassi Stalactite Cavern,** windsurfing, diving, fishing, and boating. In winter the alpine plateau in the nearby Hollengebirge massif offers 15½ square miles of ski area with practice slopes, descents into the valley, and ski hikes. This avalanche-free region has snow from December until April. There are eight ski lifts.

You can reach Ebensee by road from Bad Ischl (see above) or by train.

Food and Lodging

Hotel Post (tel. 208) is set far back from the street where it stands in the center of town near the Rathaus. Because it's designed like a chalet, many of the rooms have private balconies. The tasteful interior gives the impression of being older than it actually is. Parts of it have vaulted ceilings, lots of exposed wood, and unusual wall murals showing idyllic scenes of village life. The streamlined bedrooms have contemporary furniture and all the comforts you'd expect, including private bath. Singles range from 220 AS ($11.70) to 330 AS ($17.56), while doubles cost between 190 AS ($10.11) and 275 AS ($14.63) per person, with breakfast included. Prices depend on the season and the accommodation.

TRAUENKIRCHEN: Built on a peninsula out into the Traunsee on the western shore is this little summer resort village, once the support facility for a Benedictine abbey at the peninsula's tip. After the Benedictines, the Jesuits occupied the abbey until the 17th century.

If time permits, visit the baroque **pfarrkirche** (parish church). Its pulpit is shaped like a sailing vessel, sculptured figures depicting the catching of fish by Christ's disciples. Nearby is the 17th-century **Chapel of St. Michael.**

Food and Lodging

Hotel Post (tel. 307) is a friendly, balconied hotel with a ground-floor series of rounded arches which lead onto a popular daytime café terrace. Painted a pale yellow to set off the weathered balconies and the gray and white illustrations, the hotel sits on the main square of the village. Heinz and Renate Gröller are the attractive couple who run this spacious establishment. The public rooms are tastefully furnished, and the simple bedrooms have modern furniture, wall-to-wall carpets, and private baths. With half board included, per-person rates in doubles range from 420 AS ($22.34) to 445 AS ($23.67). Singles pay a daily surcharge of 50 AS ($2.66).

Hotel am Stein (tel. 203) is a rambling white hotel which sits beside a lakeside road about a mile outside the village. It has its own private beach, as well as the kinds of facilities which allow you to enjoy the sunshine with a cup of coffee or a drink. A Victorian-style pub in an English format of massive wood detailing and wrought-iron tables is one of the hotel's social gathering places, as well as a colorful dining room with Oriental rugs, forest-green walls, and a high orange ceiling. Per-person rates run from 330 AS ($17.56) daily, with breakfast included. Half board is offered for another 90 AS ($4.79) per person daily. Evelin H. Rabl is your congenial host.

NEUKIRCHEN: This little hamlet is not on any lake, but it lies in a northwesterly direction from Trauenkirchen between two bodies of water of the Salzkammergut, the Traunsee and the Attersee. This strategic location might make it an ideal center for exploring both lake areas, especially if you lodge at the following recommendation.

Pension International (tel. 258) looks like an intelligently renovated farm building. It rambles in a two- and three-story format across a long expanse of greenery, with rustic balconies stretching across the white-painted facade. On the premises is a covered swimming pool. The comfortable bedrooms are filled with autumnal colors, occasional touches of pink, with big glass doors giving access to the outside. A sauna is on the premises. Singles rent for around 265 AS ($14.10), while doubles go for around 550 AS ($29.26).

GMUNDEN: This is one of the most popular summer resorts in the Salzkammergut, perched on the northern rim of the Traunsee with pine-green mountains as a backdrop.

Chestnut trees line the mile-long, traffic-free **Esplanade,** the town's chief attraction. You can walk from the **Rathausplatz** (town hall square) to the **Strandbad** (the lakeside beach), watching the many majestic swans glide serenely along the lake. In days of yore emperors and kings and members of the aristocracy strolled along the Esplanade and in the town's park, just as you can do today. The Welfen from Hannover, Württembergs, Bourbons, and diverse archdukes of Austria favored Gmunden as a pleasure ground, as did Franz Schubert, Friedrich Hebbel, and Johannes Brahms, among others.

The lake beaches are some of the best in the whole area, and in summer you can enjoy the varied lakeside activities, such as watching folkloric performances, dancing in discos, or relaxing in a cozy wine tavern or at an outdoor café. You can also bathe in the open-air swimming pool. Sailing, windsurfing, waterskiing, riding, and tennis are all available here. Perhaps you'd like to go mountaineering in the vicinity of this gemütlich town.

Gmunden, former center of the salt trade, has long produced Gmundner ceramics, and you'll see artistic work in faïence and green-flamed pottery.

A curiority of the town is the **Orth Schloss,** or Palace of Orth, built on the Roman foundations of a small artificial island in the lake, connected to the town by a breakwater. Photographs of this palace are the most characteristic pictures taken of Gmunden, and one always graces the covers of tourist brochures luring visitors to the area. The gatehouse of the schloss, now the headquarters of an Austrian forestry school, is crowned by an onion-shape dome. To reach the schloss, you walk across a 140-yard-long wooden bridge. Once there, you go into an inner courtyard flanked by arcaded galleries.

The palace got its name from its occupant, Johann Orth, the assumed name of Archduke Salvator, nephew of Emperor Franz Joseph. Growing bored with the court life in Vienna, the archduke came here in 1878 to take up life as Johann Orth. Johann or Salvator, whichever, he died mysteriously off the coast of South America in 1891.

The **parish church** *(pfarrkirche)* of Gmunden was built in the 15th century and given the inevitable baroque overlay in the 18th century. Thomas Schwanthaler carved the main altar with scenes of the Three Kings of Orient (the Magi) in 1678.

From Gmunden you can go by cableway in 12 minutes to the top of the **Grünberg,** where you have a view down the Traunsee which has a fjord-like look at its southern end, with limestone rock faces rising almost vertically. The Dachstein completes the view. In winter, ski lifts, runs, and slopes on the Grünberg are easily reached. Also, curling, ice skating, and winter walks along the lake are available in Gmunden.

Food and Lodging

Parkhotel am See (tel. 4230) is a long, low-lying building capped with a red tile roof and an illuminated sign telling the name of the hotel. Between it and the lake someone has planted a rose garden and lots of begonias. The antiques inside include polychrome sculptures, painted double armoires, and gilt-covered 19th-century scroll-back chairs covered in pink satin.

One of my favorite rooms is the spacious lakeside restaurant, where you can sit either indoors or on the covered balcony where the first thing you'll see above your head is a verdant canopy of ivy. Management maintains swimming facilities off a private pier. A Victorian-style bar is on the premises, where you might want to drink after returning from a five-minute walk to the center of town.

With full board included, singles rent for 565 AS ($30.06) to 790 AS ($42.03), while doubles cost between 500 AS ($26.60) and 730 AS ($38.84) per person, depending on the plumbing, the season, and the accommodation.

Freisitz Roith (tel. 4905) sits on a hill overlooking the lake. Its design looks like a combination of a baroque private house and a Victorian-style hotel. Its dozens of architectural oddities include a crenellated tower with tall arched windows, wrought-iron window bars, and jutting parapets over many of the balconied windows, and a stone terrace built into the slope of the grass-covered hill.

The interior has been renovated and today incorporates lots of modern building materials with the older stone-accented design. However, many of the original vaulted ceilings remain. The hotel closes every October for the winter, but during the rest of the year singles rent for 550 AS ($29.26) to 680 AS ($36.18), while doubles go for 480 AS ($25.54) to 585 AS ($31.12) per person, with half board included. On cold days during the spring and early autumn the Prechtl family requires an additional 60 AS ($3.19) per day per room for heat.

Seehotel Schwan (tel. 3391) is a beautifully detailed 19th-century hotel on the main square of town at the edge of the water. Its neoclassical design includes arched pediments above many of the windows, a gabled roof, and château-style corner towers. Painted white, like the bird it's named for, the hotel has a private mineral bath and a sauna on the premises. The well-furnished bedrooms are comfortable, and usually offer good views of both the town and the lake. Singles range from 310 AS ($16.49) to 550 AS

($29.26), while doubles cost between 245 AS ($13.03) and 465 AS ($24.74) per person, with breakfast included. Prices depend on the plumbing and the season.

Waldhotel Marienbrücke (tel. 4011) is a large, hip-roofed chalet with gables, balconies, and a pleasing facade of wood and stucco. Many of the clients are fishermen who spend part of their days angling for trout in the nearby river. Per-person rates, with half board included, are around 445 AS ($23.67) per person.

Pension Haus Magerl, 18 Ackerweg (tel. 3675), has a long elegant facade with white full-length shutters which embellish a double row of balconied french windows. It sits in a grassy meadow with a view overlooking the lake. The clean and attractively simple public rooms have big, sunny windows and rustic wall coverings. On the premises are a sauna, an indoor pool, and a TV room. Per-person rates range from 310 AS ($16.49) to 450 AS ($23.94), with half board included.

Sonnenhof und La Punta (tel. 3884) lies in the center of town in a historic building with arcades. The inside is filled with dark paneling and lots of dimly lit niches, ideal for intimate conversations. By candlelight you read the menu, which offers one of the best assortments of food at the resort. Specialties include fresh lake fish, game, alpine lamb dishes, and a combination of old Austrian recipes and modern cuisine: oysters with mushrooms, butter, and onions, along with a host of regional specialties. Some of these feature savory and well-prepared meat dishes such as chateaubriand for two, medallions of pork in cream sauce, veal steak Luzern, and tournedos with a cognac cream sauce. Desserts include a range of warm sweets, such as banana flambé with chocolate sauce and walnut ice cream with plum-flavored whipped cream. Full meals cost from 185 AS ($9.84). The restaurant is open every day for lunch and dinner, except Monday between the months of October and May.

GRÜNAU IN ALMTAL: It's not on the Traunsee, but Grünau in Almtal, lying to the east of that lake, with good accommodations and restaurants as well as a wildlife park, might be a good stopover for you. It's often less crowded in summer than resorts on the Traunsee, and it occupies a beautiful position in the Alm Valley.

The wide valley lies about 9½ miles east of our last stopover, Gmunden. To reach Grünau, you will pass through **Scharnstein,** which has a 17th-century castle housing the Austrian Museum of Criminal Law. About five miles southward, you come to this summer holiday resort. You'll find the celebrated **Kremsmünster Abbey** to the northeast, if you'd like to make a day's excursion.

Cumberland Wildlife Park (tel. 205) lies four miles south of Grünau. Here you'll see otters, beavers, brown bears, and other animals. There's a restaurant at the park, plus a museum devoted to forestry.

If you continue on south along the Alm Valley, you'll reach Almsee, a lake at 2810 feet.

Food and Lodging

Romantik Hotel und Restaurant Almtalhof (tel. 204) offers a fairytale setting which should appeal to nostalgics around the world. The four-story solidly built chalet has masses of live flowers covering the window boxes and decorative flowers painted onto the regional furniture scattered throughout the hotel. The decor is romantic, charming, and worthy of an extended stay. The intimate bedrooms offer coffered ceilings, elaborate wrought-iron chandeliers, and pink bedding that contrast with the light-grained pine of the wall paneling. The Leithner family charges between 400 AS ($21.28) and 480 AS ($25.54) for a single and between 340 AS ($18.09) and 445 AS ($23.67) for a double, with breakfast included.

The large and elegant dining room has well-polished slats of vertical paneling, stained-glass window medallions, and a collection of old pewter and hunting trophies. Menu items are traditional and Austrian. They include schnitzels, roast beef, roast pork, pork cutlets with apples, a selection of wild game, and an unusual salad with a dressing of yogurt and marinated cabbage. À la carte meals range from 130 AS ($6.92) to 300 AS ($15.96), while fixed-price dinners cost from 155 AS ($8.25) to 360 AS ($19.15). Both the hotel and restaurant are closed between early October and about a week before Christmas and from mid-January until the end of March.

Gasthof Deutsches Haus (tel. 332) is a small, green-shuttered family-run hotel with two floors of cozy bedrooms. The ground-floor dining room has alpine-style furniture and a green tile oven under the beamed ceiling. The sun terrace looks out over a small lake, which is set in a quiet and restful location six miles from the nearest village. The restaurant serves home-style meals, with freshly caught lake trout prepared in several different ways. With half board included, per-person rates are around 240 AS ($12.77) per day. The hotel is open from the first of May until the end of September.

Pension Hochhaus (tel. 241) offers 25 modern and comfortable bedrooms, all of which are maintained by members of the Schiefermayr family. Guests have free use of the large garden and its adjoining terrace. Per-person rates, with half board included, range from 215 AS ($11.44) to 285 AS ($15.16), depending on the season and the plumbing.

Gasthof Seehaus (tel. 366) occupies an idyllic lakeside spot ten miles from the center of Grünau, which gives local residents the perfect excuse to make a midsummer excursion. The building is a long elegant construction that offers only one apartment to visitors, priced at 240 AS ($12.77) per person nightly, including breakfast. The rest of the time the Seehaus is mainly a restaurant, featuring gutbürgerlich regional fare served in generous portions, with meals costing from 250 AS ($13.30).

7. Wels

A flourishing town in Roman times, Wels lies on the left bank of the Traun River in the center of a large farm belt and is known today for its agricultural fairs. It can be reached by heading north from Gmunden after your visit there. It's also an easy drive southwest from Linz. Wels is most often used as a base for exploring the hinterlands, although it has some attractions of its own. In about 1½ hours you can walk through the town, seeing its chief sights.

THE SIGHTS: The **Stadplatz** is considered one of the most architecturally harmonious town squares in Austria, with beautifully decorated facades of old houses and an intricately carved fountain. It is broad and cobbled. Most of the houses date from the 16th to the 18th centuries. The baroque-style

Rathaus (town hall), built in 1748, is one of the most ornate buildings in the old town. The **Ledererturm,** dating from 1618, is the only tower remaining of those that once studded the town walls. Many homes or shops in the old town are held up by arches and passageways with vaulted ceilings.

Emperor Maximilian I died in Wels in 1519, stricken as he was traveling from the Tyrolean country to Wiener Neustadt. The house in which he died is called the **Kaiserliche Burg.** On Burggasse, it has been turned into a museum of minor importance. You can see the room in which the emperor breathed his last.

The **Stadtpfarrkirche** (town parish church) has a 14th-century Gothic chancel and three stained-glass windows from that same century. The entire church was once Gothic until baroque architects went to work on it. The Romanesque inner doorway is surmounted by a tower with a bulbous dome, dating from 1732.

Across from the church stands the **Salome Alt house.** She was the mistress and mother of the dozen children of Prince-Archbishop Wolf Dietrich who is encountered so frequently in Salzburg history. Following the disgrace and overthrow of this ecclesiastic, he retired to Wels.

On the Ringstrasse you can see what is left of **Schloss Pollheim,** where, the story goes, the shoemaker-poet Hans Sachs lived. Wagner is said to have based his character in *Die Meistersinger von Nürnberg* on Sachs.

Wels is a town which has moved into the future industrially, as witness its chemical plants, but it also clings to its imperial past.

FOOD AND LODGING: **Hotel Greif,** 50 Kaiser-Josef-Platz (tel. 5361), has a substantial-looking masonry facade in the center of town. The exterior hasn't been embellished in any way other than an occasional balcony, but the dining room inside is a renovated red and white Viennese-style decor of mirrors, crystal chandeliers, and high ceilings. Pleasantly furnished singles range from 225 AS ($11.97) to 465 AS ($24.74), while doubles cost between 390 AS ($20.75) and 790 AS ($42.03) per room, with breakfast included.

Gasthof Bayrischer Hof, 23 Dr.-Schauer-Strasse (tel. 7214), is easy to recognize because of its elegant blue-and-white facade with neoclassical window treatments and a mansard-style tower extending upward from the building's exposed corner. The garden café is an inviting place to spend part of a warm midday. The simple bedrooms usually contain a wooden armoire and bedside tables, as well as an assortment of autumnal colors. Singles rent for 265 AS ($14.10) to 360 AS ($19.15), while doubles cost between 450 AS ($23.94) and 550 AS ($29.26), with breakfast included.

Restaurant Wirt am Berg, 6 Berg (tel. 5059), was established in 1630 and has been in the same family since 1881. Prominent diners have included Field Marshall Göring, a host of Olympic champions, and the royal family of Monaco. Four kilometers outside Wels, the three-story restaurant is painted a deep yellow-orange and opens into a series of rustically decorated dining rooms with lots of hunting trophies.

On warm days you might prefer to eat under the chestnut trees on the brick-covered terrace. Wild game might be the most popular item on the menu in hunting season, although at any time of year you can still enjoy an appetizer of terrine of wild deer with cumberland sauce, quail liver cocktail with vinaigrette sauce, or consommé of pheasant. This could be followed by

Wels, to sites that are among the most outstanding sightseeing attractions of Upper Austria, will take you first to—

Lambach Abbey

In 1056 a Benedictine abbey was founded at Lambach, 10 miles southwest of Wels and about 15 miles north of the Traunsee. It stands at a point where the Traun River meets its tributary, the Ager. The once Romanesque monastery, which stands in the Marktplatz of the old market town, has changed its face since its early days, now showing a splendid baroque exterior. A towering marble gateway from 1693 leads into the first courtyard.

In the so-called ringing chamber, you can see one of the major attractions of the abbey, Romanesque frescoes from the 11th century. These works of art were once hidden but later discovered. They were restored in 1968 and put on public view, an event hailed by the Austrian press. The frescoes may be seen only on a guided tour May through mid-October from 9 to 11 a.m. and from 2 to 5 p.m. (opens an hour later on Sunday). Off-season hours are 10 a.m. to noon and 3 to 4 p.m. (again opens an hour later on Sunday). Admission is 15 AS (80¢).

The abbey's other attractions include a richly embellished library and a rather sumptuous refectory from the 18th century. There's also a painting gallery with, among other works, some notable pictures by Kremser Schmidt.

The abbey church was built in the 1650s, and its main altar is believed to have been designed by the celebrated baroque architect J. B. Fischer von Erlach. The only surviving monastic theater in Austria, built in 1746, is reached by a stairway.

Kremsmünster Abbey

Near Bad Hall, between the emerging hills of the Alps and the Danube River, overlooking the Valley of Krems, this Benedictine abbey was founded in 777. Two domed towers of the abbey church dominate the local skyline. This abbey, lying 22 miles southwest of Linz, was founded by order of Tassilo III, a Bavarian duke whose son Gunther was killed by a wild boar during a hunt. The abbey was erected to honor the memory of the duke's son. It was, of course, Romanesque, but in the 17th and 18th centuries the old abbey was given the baroque treatment.

The most outstanding feature of a tour through Kremsmünster is the **Fischbehalter,** or fish pond, built by the noted architect Carlo Antonio Carlone. It has five basins, each encircled by arcades, with statues that spout water. Figures depict everybody from Samson to Neptune.

In the cluster of abbey buildings the **Kaisersaal,** or hall of the emperors, has a collection of portraits of sovereigns of the Holy Roman Empire, painted by Altomonte at the end of the 17th century. One of the most outstanding works of art is a *Crucifixion* by Quentin Massys. The abbey still owns the chalice of Tassilo that was presented to the monks by the founding duke. It's the most ancient piece of goldsmith's work in either Austria or Bavaria, the duke's home. In the library is a celebrated manuscript, the *Codex Millenarius,* an eighth-century translation of the gospels.

A curious observatory tower rising nearly 200 feet has an exhibition of materials associated with astronomy and other sciences. This observatory has been called the first skyscraper in Europe.

Gasthof/Pension Goldener Adler, 4 Kirchenplatz (tel. 2372), is composed of a historic central building and a modern annex. The older section has long rows of shuttered windows, a tile roof, and a weinstube, while the new part contains all the modern comforts in a balconied format with window boxes. Singles rent for 360 AS ($19.15) to 435 AS ($23.14), while doubles cost between 600 AS ($31.92) and 870 AS ($46.28), with full board included. Prices depend on the plumbing.

Hofwirt, Hehenberg (tel. 2274), is a pleasantly rustic restaurant with a traditional menu of tried-and-true favorites. It's hard to go wrong here, since everything is freshly prepared and cooked with finesse. You might try one of three kinds of trout, one of the many meat courses, perhaps salmon, and most definitely one of the savory soups. À la carte meals range from 60 AS ($3.19) to 180 AS ($9.58). You'll also get a chance to view many of the local residents, some of whom seem to come here practically every night.

8. The Southeast Corner

After visiting the renowned Kremsmünster Abbey and Bad Hall, you can head south along the Steyr River into an area little known to North Americans—the southeast corner of Upper Austria, bordering Styria. This section where many discoveries await you is known as **Pyhrn-Eisenwurzen.**

If you're ready for lunch, you might want to stop at either Molln or Klaus, coming up.

MOLLN: After traveling along the Steyr River, you can veer southeast off Route 140 at Leonstein to the little hamlet of Molln and this very fine restaurant.

Restaurant Martinsklause (tel. 216). The specialties here are numerous, served in generous quantities and delicately flavored. They include pâté of trout with toast, homemade spiced ham with apple horseradish, veal medallions with fresh tarragon, salt pork "Upper Austria" with bread dumplings, apple dumpling with nuts in an apple wine sauce, and many different kinds of strudel. Average meals cost from 110 AS ($5.85) to 155 AS ($8.25). Warm food is served from 11 a.m. to 1:30 p.m. and from 6 to 8 p.m., although the place is open from 8 a.m. to midnight for drinks and snacks.

KLAUS: In the heart of the Pyhrn-Eisenwurzen district, Klaus is a village set in the midst of some of the most splendid scenery in Upper Austria.

The hamlet, just north of the Klauser See, a beautiful lake, has developed into a popular resort since construction of the reservoir for the hydroelectric power station Klaus. Now a paradise for wild-water enthusiasts and also for canoeing more quietly along the river, Klaus has a special school for kayaking and paddling.

Food and Lodging

Hotel Schinagl (tel. 261). The painted illustration on the front of this partially balconied chalet is of a regionally dressed man and woman courting one another. The friendly ambience inside might encourage you to do exactly the same. On the premises is a rustically paneled stand-up bar, lots of big-windowed panoramas, and a series of comfortable chairs grouped into conversational units. Sporting facilities of the region will be described by Eva Hoheneder. Per-person rates range from 345 AS ($18.35) to 525 AS ($27.93), with half board included. Prices depend on the accommodation, the plumbing, and the season. An evening in the cellar bar is often devoted to live dance music.

VORDERSTODER: After passing by the Klauser See, you can make a detour into the high mountain valley known as **Stodertal.** It lies directly east of the Totes Gebirge mountain range. The upper part of the Steyr River flows through this scenic valley. You'll pass by the Stromboding Waterfall, which drops some 85 feet.

Along the way, you'll find a scenic stopover at the following recommendation:

Pension/Restaurant Stockerwirt (tel. 8214) is beautifully situated on the slope of a hill with a view of the snow-covered mountains. The roof has a long expanse of interconnected gables, with a covering of red tile. The portico covering the entrance is fashioned of burnished sheet metal, hammered into graceful curves. The hotel on this site has been in the same family since 1664, although the format today has been significantly updated. You'll find a covered swimming pool on the premises, an immaculately clean kitchen serving well-prepared meals in a panoramic setting, and a vaulted entrance hall with lots of paneling. Per-person rates, with half board included, range from 280 AS ($14.90) to 360 AS ($19.15), in either a single or a double room.

HINTERSTODER: The Steyr River wends its way through Hinterstoder, the valley's chief resort, which is so remote it has no through traffic. It's about four miles from the principal Linz/Graz artery. Lying directly under the Totes Gebirge massif, the town has combined with Windischgarsten (coming up) and Spital am Pyhrn to become a newly emerging ski resort area in Upper Austria. Hinterstoder has the widest range of accommodations, but if you're selecting a hotel, you might want to consider the possibilities of the other two villages, since the three resorts are within easy reach of one another.

Hinterstoder, which is both a summer and a winter holiday village, has a good ski school. A chair lift will transport you to Hutterer Böden (4550 feet), the middle station on the ascent, where you'll find several ski lifts as well as a hotel. From here you can take a chair lift to Hutterer Höss (6230) feet, where there's a mountain restaurant.

Another ski area, the Dietlgut-Bärenalm, lies about two miles from Hinterstoder at the far end of the valley. In winter a ski bus connects it to the center of the resort area. Once there you can take a double-chair lift to Bärenalm (3950 feet), where you'll find another mountain restaurant.

Food and Lodging

Berghotel (tel. 54210) is shaped like a gently sloping pyramid, with flowered rows of parallel balconies in front of oversize bedroom windows. The hotel lies above Hinterstoder at the middle station of the chair lift, which shuts down every day at 5 p.m. You can get there by car, but I don't recommend it in winter. The hotel offers many sports and fitness facilities, including a gym, a sauna, and an indoor pool. Most of the private accommodations front a southern exposure and contain private baths, balconies, and a view of the well-maintained lawn that many of the guests use for midsummer sunbathing. The disco-keller, if it were located in your hometown, might become one of your preferred hangouts. The Jungreithmair family are the attractive and considerate owners of this hotel. They charge between 500 AS ($26.60) and 820 AS ($43.62) per person, with half board included. Prices depend on the season and the accommodation.

Sporthotel Stoderhof (tel. 5266) is the major hotel in the village, right in the center in a rambling modern format of white walls and a gently sloping gabled roof. A glass-walled greenhouse-type construction extends toward the sun terrace, behind which is an indoor swimming pool. Ilse and Erich Fruhmann might be the best loved innkeepers in Hinterstoder, and many guests believe that Ilse is certainly the most gracious hostess in the entire valley. She'll certainly do all she can to make your stay enjoyable. At the same time her husband Erich is considered the best chef in the village. The hotel lies only a short distance from the chair lifts. The good-size rooms are comfortably furnished. With half board included, the per-person rates in a double range from 445 AS ($23.67) to 490 AS ($26.07). Occupants of a single pay another 50 AS ($2.66) per day.

Pension Dietlgut (tel. 5248) consists of one house with a series of adjacent outbuildings. The style is unabashedly romantic, with steep roofs, exposed cross-timbering, and an idyllic setting in a grassy area at the foot of a rocky cliff. It lies at the end of the valley. If you stay here it's best to have a car because of its distance from the village. The pension is known for its collection of hunting trophies which cover the walls of one of the antique-filled public rooms. In one of the sitting rooms the amber-colored paneling is arranged in an unusual and attractive pattern of random vertical and horizontal lines. The well-kept bedrooms rent for 400 AS ($22.88) to 550 AS ($29.26) in a single and between 400 AS ($21.28) and 530 AS ($28.20) per person in a double. These prices include half board and depend on the plumbing and the season. The owners do much to make you comfortable.

WINDISCHGARSTEN: This resort lies in a sunny valley at an elevation of about 1960 feet, about a half-hour drive from Hinterstoder, just visited. It's a typical Austrian village, with much old-fashioned charm and character, unspoiled so far by the inroads of modern tourism.

Skiing is limited in winter, as this is only an emerging ski resort. A single chair lift goes to the highest station at 2800 feet. The aprè-ski life here is unpretentious and not highly organized, but some does exist, especially in the cellars of the hotels. However, if you'd like a change of pace you can take a bus ride and be deposited at Spital am Pyhrn (coming up) in just 18 minutes.

With a lovely church spire piercing the winter sky and a blanket of snow covering the entire village for much of the winter, Windischgarsten is starkly picturesque, but I still prefer it in summer when the valley is green, the sun reflects off the russet-colored roofs, and the towering, snow-capped mountains form a dramatic background.

Food and Lodging

Hotel Bischofsberg, 31 Edlbach (tel. 455), is a graceful collection of chalet-style buildings set on the side of a hill with a view over the mountains. On the downhill side of the hotel you'll find a rose garden flanking an outdoor pool. From the front you'll notice the summertime café terrace and the painted embellishments around each of the windows. The inside is imaginatively decorated with enough rusticity to make anyone feel at home. In the center of one of the sitting rooms, a stucco and ceramic tile oven gives off wintertime heat below the heavy beams of the paneled ceiling.

The light from the big windows against one wall of the spacious restaurant not only illumines the pink and white napery on your table, but nourishes the potted trees growing in the center of the room. The Löger family (which has so many members that it's almost like a village in itself) are the owners and managers of this attractive hotel. With half board included, per person rates range from 400 AS ($21.28) to 575 AS ($30.59), depending on the season. All rooms contain private bath, and there's also an indoor swimming pool.

Sporthotel Baumschlager (tel. 8282) is a pretty chalet directed by Hans and Gerda Baumschlager, who rank among the region's most experienced hoteliers. Part of the establishment's ground floor is accented with an arched arcade, the roof of which supports a popular café terrace. The third- and fourth-floor balconies are festooned with flowers that are reflected in the glass of the doors leading into the attractive bedrooms. On the premises is a swimming pool, plus an outdoor tennis court, a sauna, a solarium, a bar, and a restaurant, the latter specializing in venison, fish, and regional recipes. In season it serves such delights as fresh asparagus and strawberries. Rates average 420 AS ($22.34) per person daily, with half board included.

Hotel/Pension Schwarzes-Rössl (tel. 311) is a long-established hotel in the center of town. It's housed in an elegantly symmetrical gray building with a gabled roof, an arched entrance, and cleverly painted *trompe-l'oeil* embellishments around each of the rectangular windows. Inside, many of the ceilings are vaulted or timbered, with a scattering of painted antiques and a restaurant—one of the best in town—filled with alpine-style furniture.

The Baumschlager family are your gracious hosts. In addition to owning another well-recommended establishment nearby (the Sporthotel), Mr. Baumschlager was once a ski champion. With half board included, per-person rates average around 320 AS ($17.02) per day.

Food items in the restaurant are usually prepared in a temptingly old-fashioned style and served in big portions. Specialties include schnitzels in cream sauce with noodles, marrow soup, and an array of grilled meats and fish. Fixed-price meals range from 80 AS ($4.26) to 155 AS ($6.12), while à la carte dinners cost between 90 AS ($4.79) and 220 AS ($11.70). The restaurant shuts down for most of November.

Hotel Blaue Sense (tel. 329) is a friendly, well-managed guest house in a modern format that was probably designed in the late 1950s. The interior has stone detailing, arched and vaulted ceilings, and lots of colorful contrasting patterns. The raised sun terrace is a popular place to eat. With half board included, the per-person rates are about 370 AS ($19.68).

Hotel/Restaurant Sperlhof (tel. 430) is a four-story chalet with prominent regional designs in gold and black paint below the big windows of the facade. The hotel covers a large ground area in a series of wings that stretch off to the side. A ski lift, a sauna, an outdoor pool, and a tennis court are on the premises. With full board included, rates are around 350 AS ($18.62) per person in a single or double, all of which contain private baths. The Gössweiner family are your hosts.

SPITAL AM PYHRN: Spital was known as a stopover a long time ago on the ancient toll road that led over the nearby Pyhrn Pass on the road to Graz in Styria. The village, at 2625 feet, lies close to Windischgarsten (see above).

In winter many skiers are attracted to Spital, where you can take a ski bus for about a mile to the foothills of the Pyhrn. There you board a mountain railway heading up Wurzeralm mountain and disembark at the Bergstation. The ride takes only eight minutes and the train can carry some 1000 passengers per hour. The top station is at a lofty 4700 feet. From Bergstation it's possible to go even higher, taking a double-chair lift to a height of 6140 feet.

The **Alpenrose** is the center of most après-ski action. Otherwise attractions are limited, but you can always go over to Windischgarsten, just recommended. Chances are, however, that you'll visit Spital am Pyhrn in summer when it's at its most beautiful.

This village used to be the site of an abbey, and the **Stiftskirche** (abbey church) is well known. Work on it started in 1714 and continued for 16 years. Its baroque exterior is flanked by two towers. Kremser Schmidt did the paintings on the altarpieces of the side altars, and Altomonte painted some of the work on the colonnades in the then-fashionable *trompe-l'oeil* style.

Food and Lodging

Hotel Alpenrose (tel. 225) is a well-established modern hotel with a two-story addition extending to the side of the main house. The public rooms are paneled and sunny, while the simple bedrooms are clean and filled with cheerful colors. An indoor swimming pool is five minutes away on foot. The Wesselitsch family are your hosts. Half-board rates (which in winter include free transportation from the hotel to the ski lifts) range from 265 AS ($14.10) to 310 AS ($16.49) per person, depending on the season, plumbing, and room assignment.

Gasthof Vogel Händler (tel. 282) is a balconied chalet with painted illustrations on the facade as well as lots of flowers. It lies within a ten-minute walk of the train station. The unpretentious interior is paneled throughout many of the public rooms, while the bedrooms have big windows, clean sheets, and simple furniture. In summer a sun terrace offers a place to sit outside. A covered swimming pool and tennis courts are a few minutes away. Per-person rates, based on double occupancy, range from 250 AS ($13.30) to 300 AS ($15.96), with half board included. The supplement for a single is another 25 AS ($1.33) per day. Ingeborg Frech, the convivial owner, is happy to tell you about the sports facilities of the village.

9. Steyr and Enns

For another look at Upper Austria, we'll leave the southeast corner, heading north again via a route which, if followed on, would lead to Linz. Instead, however, we'll detour along the Enns River to visit two of the most ancient patrician cities of Austria.

These cities bear the names of the rivers that flow through the area, known as the Donau-Raum. The first such city to which I'll introduce you is Steyr and the second is Enns.

STEYR: The old town of Steyr was built on a tongue of land that juts out between the Enns and the Steyr Rivers. Three gates and a tower survive from the days when walls surrounded the town. The city's spread since its early days has taken it mainly along the Enns River. The boating crowd likes to visit here in summer, as this is the point of origin for many trips along both rivers.

Because of its name, visitors sometimes think that Steyr is in Styria, but even though that province also took its name from the Steyr River, the city is still very much in Upper Austria.

Steyr is the home of the well-known Steyr-Puch motorbike, and BMW trucks and bicycles are assembled here. But despite the factories, this is no grim industrial town. In its heyday it was considered a rival of Vienna, and the old town, particularly the major square which has many houses from the baroque era, makes it worth a stopover.

The Sights

The **Stadtplatz** (town square) is one of the best preserved in Upper Austria and the city's most attractive feature. The street takes the shape of a plaza, and you'll see arcades as well as several balconied houses in both the Gothic and Renaissance styles. Most outstanding are the **Rathaus** (town hall) at no. 27 and the **Bummerlhaus** at no. 32. Construction on the rococo town hall, crowned by a slender tower, began in 1765. The Bummerlhaus was a private mansion built in the Gothic style. If possible, you should try to see inside some of the courts which were built as a part of these magnificent houses.

The **Dominikanerkirche,** or Dominican church, has a rich baroque interior, but it merits only a passing look. More intriguing is a street near the church, the colorful **Eisengasse,** which winds down to the Enns River.

The **Stadtpfarrkirche** (town parish church), on Pfarrgasse, dates from the middle of the 15th century, built in the Gothic style by the architect who designed St. Stephen's in Vienna to which it bears a resemblance. The church has some quite old stained glass. You'll see many ancient gravestones nearby in the **Pfarrhaus** (parish house), where Anton Bruckner composed his Sixth Symphony. A room in the house honors him.

You may also visit **Christkindl** (Christ Child), two miles west of Steyr, a well-known pilgrimage church in Austria. The celebrated baroque architects, Carlone and Prandtauer, designed Christkindl, which is painted a pinkish mauve. At Christmastime, children all over the world send letters to the *Wirtschaft,* a Christmas post office. If you send a self-addressed, stamped envelope, you'll receive a reply if your letter is addressed to Christkindl.

Food and Lodging

Hotel Minichmayr, 1-3 Haratzmüllerstrasse (tel. 23410). Views from the sun terrace of this old-world hotel encompass the confluence of two rivers and much of the old town. The hotel offers friendly service, excellent food, and comfortable bedrooms (the best of which have been renovated) in a sunny format of taste and style. With breakfast included, singles cost between 360 AS ($19.15) and 480 AS ($25.54), while doubles range from

275 AS ($14.63) to 340 AS ($18.09) per person, with breakfast included.

The Viertler family also direct the items served in the pleasant dining room. Specialties include fresh local river fish, a range of grilled and flambé-style meats, roasts, an excellent oxtail soup, and an array of solid, regionally inspired recipes. Fixed-price meals range from 90 AS ($4.79) to 185 AS ($9.84), while à la carte dinners cost between 95 AS ($5.05) and 300 AS ($15.96).

Linzerhaus (tel. 237) is a rustic hotel with a gently sloping roof and red and white striped shutters. You can reach it by cable car, which might be a good idea since it lies at an elevation of some 4620 feet. The cozy interior offers the kind of rustic accommodations which you might appreciate after a strenuous day outdoors. Robert and Maria Danklmaier, your hosts, charge from 250 AS ($13.30) per person, with half board included.

Restaurant Ulrichsklause, at St. Ulrich (tel. 23459), would make a pleasant excursion from Steyr, particularly on a warm day when the view from its terrace encompasses the river and everything on the other side. In a satellite of Steyr, the restaurant serves specialties of venison, asparagus, mushrooms, and strawberries. You could begin your meal with puff pastry filled with ragoût, a portion of smoked ham, or a variety of fresh salads. Main courses include chipped veal in a wine and cream sauce with mushrooms and potatoes, filet of pike-perch, or charcoal-grilled steaks and cutlets. Dessert could be sweet cheese dumplings rolled in buttered breadcrumbs, served with stewed prunes. Full meals range from 95 AS ($5.05) to 180 AS ($9.58), with hot dinners served from 11:30 a.m. to 2 p.m. and from 6 to 10 p.m. every day (except Sunday evening and all day Monday). The restaurant is closed for the first two weeks in February and for the first two weeks of August.

Café Rahofer, 9 Stadplatz (tel. 24606), is an attractive modern café in the center of Steyr. Serving pastries, wine, coffee, and snacks, it's a popular hangout for shoppers, lovers, and just about everyone else in town. Coffee and pastries average around 18 AS (96¢) apiece.

ENNS: The oldest town in Upper Austria, Enns stands on what was once the site of a Roman camp and later was the Roman city of Lauriacum, on the left bank of the Enns River, a short distance from where its water flows into the Danube. Enns was granted its charter in 1212. The **Rathaus** displays many artifacts from the Roman days of the town.

The **Stadtturm** (town tower), constructed in 1564 on orders of Emperor Maximilian II, still stands on the principal plaza, along with several old patrician houses in the baroque style. From the tower you have an excellent view over the old town and the river.

The **Pfarrkirche** (parish church) is Gothic with a double nave flanked with only one aisle. Pillars divide it into two sections, then into a trio of sections.

To the north of the town stands **Ennsegg Castle,** dating from the 16th century. Some five miles to the west of Enns lies the renowned Augustinian Abbey of St. Florian. (For information, refer to the sights in the environs of Linz.)

Food and Lodging

Hotel Lauriacum, 5-7 Wiener Strasse (tel. 2315), presents a distinguished contemporary facade to a busy street in the center of Enns. The public rooms are filled with a combination of modern and rustic accessories, which include a ceramic tile oven, a coffered ceiling, and a collection of farm implements in one of the restaurants. Other rooms are invitingly contemporary, especially the plant-filled bar area where the stools look like oversize pin cushions set onto chrome columns. Management pays careful attention to its cuisine as well as to the well-being of its guests. The spacious and colorful bedrooms rent for 500 AS ($26.60) in a single and for 780 AS ($41.50) in a double, with breakfast included. Each of the accommodations has a private bath, and a sauna is on the premises.

Restaurant Rahofer, at Kronstorf (tel. 303), is a gemütlich restaurant housed in a former farmhouse in the environs of Enns, about eight kilometers from the center. The dining room looks exactly the way an old-fashioned Austrian inn should, with heavy timbers and lots of paneling. Cuisine sticks faithfully to the tried-and-true recipes that have been prepared for generations in these regions. The seasonally adjusted menu includes an array of grilled meats, pork medallions with cabbage, and a satisfying collection of stews, salads, and soups. À la carte meals range from 115 AS ($6.12) to 340 AS ($18.09). The restaurant is closed on Sunday after 3 p.m. and all day Monday, and reservations are suggested.

10. Stops Along the Danube

Many of the major stopovers along the Danube, including Linz, have been explored in other parts of this guide. Other sections on the great river have been visited in Lower Austria (Chapter V) and in Vienna. However, the Danube offers several rewarding stopovers, besides Linz, in Upper Austria, including the following towns and villages.

Assuming you are picking up this trail at Passau, a border city of West Germany, and driving through the Danube Valley, I'd recommend a visit first to—

ASCHACH: This Danube town has associations with Dr. Faust. (See the description of Faust Schlössl below, where you can order a meal or spend the night—if you dare.) A bridge in the town spans the Danube, and you may be able to see from your bedroom window steamers plying the river. Aschach has many baroque houses from the 18th century.

Directly south of Aschach, you can visit the small town of **Eferding,** which was mentioned in the *Nibelungenlied.* Eferding has one of the finest restaurants in the area.

Food and Lodging

Faust Schlössl (tel. 245). This medieval castle was used by tollkeepers of the powerful Schaumberg family, and later by a revolving series of noble families. The behavior of the residents so frightened the populace that it was soon rumored that the castle was not only haunted, but that it had been built by the devil for Dr. Faustus in a single night. In 1966 it was converted into a hotel with 50 rooms, each of which was designed with a private bath.

The arena of what had been a Roman theater was converted into the basin for an outdoor swimming pool. If you approach the castle from the river it will appear more massive and foreboding than it actually is, although the many wings, arcades, towers, and balconies certainly make an impressive combination of yellow stucco and red tiles.

The interior is surprisingly unpretentious, with few of the original furnishings remaining. The decor is simple, modern, and streamlined, except for an occasional rustic touch. Per-person rates are from 235 AS ($12.50) in a single or double, with breakfast included.

Gasthof Sonne (tel. 308) offers a limited number of comfortable and inexpensive bedrooms, which are usually priced at 300 AS ($15.96) per person, with an excellent half board included. Alfreda Lackner, the friendly mistress of the house, speaks limited English, but makes up for it with personalized service and a well-prepared local cuisine specializing in freshly caught fish.

Restaurant Dannerbauer, Brandstatt (tel. 471), in the suburb of Eferding, is a popular restaurant which many locals drive long distances to reach. On weekends it gets so crowded you may have to wait for both a table and a waitress. The setting is gemütlich, and there's a view of the Danube.

If you like to drink, you might begin your meal with a taste of the local schnapps, which should certainly stimulate conversation at your table. Specialties include a Hungarian fish soup, perch filet in a Riesling sauce, a delicate filet of sole, and a range of well-prepared meat and game dishes. À la carte meals range from 120 AS ($6.38) to 325 AS ($17.29), while fixed-price dinners cost between 145 AS ($7.71) and a whopping 630 AS ($33.52). The restaurant is closed Monday and Tuesday and from mid-January until the end of the first week of February. Reservations are suggested.

Bypassing Linz and Enns, already visited, I recommend that you drive along the Danube to the far eastern border of Upper Austria. Here it's time for another stopover, this one in—

GREIN: Much of the economy of Grein, which lies on the left bank of the Danube, depends on shipping along the river. **Greinburg,** a schloss sheltering the Austrian Shipping Museum, stands to the west of the port. The castle, dating from the 15th century, has an inner court in the Renaissance style, with arcades.

In the **Stadtplatz,** a rococo theater from 1791, seating only about 150 spectators, has been preserved. This is the oldest known theater in Austria. Also on the Stadtplatz are several turreted houses. The **parish church** of Grein has an 18th-century altarpiece by Altomonte.

A Coffeehouse

Kaffeesiederei Blumenstraussl, 6 Stadtplatz (tel. 380), offers two separate dining rooms, both of them decorated in a glowing Biedermeier style. In summer the outdoor coffee garden is popular with almost everyone in town. The establishment lies close to the Rathaus, behind a well-preserved baroque facade. One of the rooms has a massive billiard table, a shiny ceramic stove, Empire-style hanging chandeliers, and country Biedermeier-style banquettes. You'll know when strawberries are in season by the wide range of pastries made with them as a primary ingredient. The Mozart torte is luscious, as well as the array of hot soups to warm up a cold day. Coffee costs between 20 AS ($1.06) and 45 AS ($2.39), while pastries range from 15 AS (80¢) to 30 AS ($1.60) apiece. The café is closed all day Monday, until 2 p.m. on Tuesday, and during the month of October. The establishment also serves drinks, ice cream, and sandwiches.

ST. NIKOLA: On both banks of the Danube near the point where it enters Lower Austria is this 800-year-old town, about two hours by autobahn from Vienna. It's a good base for visiting Melk, the Wachau, and many castles, churches, and medieval towns in the general area, all about an hour's drive from St. Nikola.

Food and Lodging

Hotel zur Post (tel. 412) is composed of the union of a 17th-century central building with a small onion dome attached to the corner tower, plus a modern balconied extension. Practically none of the original furnishings or detailing remains, but the furnishings inside are tasteful, clean, and rustic, and set in a pleasing combination of white plaster walls and horizontal paneling. The Danzer family are your hosts, charging 470 AS ($25) per person in a single or double, with half board included. All units contain private bath.

Donau Hof (tel. 26107). The service and attitude of the Aigner family make this an especially attractive starting point for touring this part of Austria. Parts of the simple white hotel with the red tile roof and the modern extension are more than 400 years old. The public rooms are attractively furnished with painted armoires, chalet-style chairs, and rustic timbers. The bar area stocks practically everything from homemade wines to vintage cognacs. It has a comfortable 1950s-style decor, with round porthole-style windows cut into one of the walls.

The bedrooms are comfortable enough to spend time in, and sometimes they have provocatively dark walls to accent the imaginative color scheme. On the premises are a sauna, exercise room, and a garden terrace overlooking the Danube.

The in-house restaurant bakes many of its own pastries fresh every day, while the menu items include both Austrian and international specialties. Guests are welcome to fish in the hotel-owned waters or in the Danube, and if they catch anything, the hotel will prepare it for supper. Per-person rates in a double are 275 AS ($14.63), while singles cost 310 AS ($16.49) apiece, with breakfast included.

11. Schärding and Braunau

From the far-eastern border of Upper Austria, most visitors will go on into Lower Austria, following the Danube until it reaches Vienna. However, since that territory has been explored previously, we'll jump across the province to highlight some stopovers along its western border before going into the Tyrolean country.

Some towns and villages that merit exploration in this section include—

SCHÄRDING: Because of its beautiful old buildings—painted in pastels of gold, pink, yellow, and turquoise—Schärding is often called the romantic city of the baroque. It lies above the Inn River, about 11 miles south of the West German city of Passau on the Danube, in a region of Upper Austria called the **Innviertel.** The Danube flows in the north, but in the west are the Inn and Salzach Rivers.

If much of the area in and around Schärding reminds you of Bavaria, it's no wonder. The Innviertel was part of Bavaria until it was ceded to Austria in 1779.

Schärding was once a fortified town, and remnants of the old walls stand today, along with some gates and towers. Its **parish church** *(pfarrkirche)*, like virtually every other old church in Austria, was once in the Gothic style but received a baroque overlay.

Food and Lodging

Scheurecker (tel. 265) is a charming old house with a view over the buildings of the central square of the village. It used to be called Zum Goldenen Löwen. The cozy bedrooms are attractively simple, renting for 310 AS ($16.49) to 340 AS ($18.09) in a single and between 600 AS ($31.92) and 670 AS ($35.64) in a double. English is spoken.

Forstinger's Wirthaus, 3 Unterer Stadtplatz (tel. 2302), is an authentically rustic hotel with comfortable accommodations in a country-style setting. Doubles rent for 325 AS ($17.29) per person, including breakfast. The inn's restaurant is known throughout the region for its gutbürgerlich fare. The dining room is intricately crafted, and the service is friendly enough.

READERS' DINING SELECTION: "We discovered this family-run café and winehouse just as we were about to leave Upper Austria. We stopped for a quick lunch, but stayed longer, chatting with the considerate owners, Franziska and Günther Höltzel. Their place has a wood-paneled elegance, and we very much enjoyed the beer, wine, and wholesome, generously served food. Lunch costs about 130 AS ($6.92) apiece, with a drink included. We decided not to spend the night, but learned that singles rent for 200 AS ($10.64), while doubles cost 400 AS ($21.28), with breakfast included" (Susan and Bradford Donohue, Towson, Md.).

ST. MARTIN: As an alternative to staying in Schärding, you might drive deeper into the Innviertel to seek food and lodging in the hamlet of St. Martin, about 19 miles south of Passau. This little health resort in Upper Austria lies near the Inn River, close to the border of Bavaria and Austria. This section of Austria lies between the Danube plain and the Salzkammergut.

St. Martin is known for its hot springs, in which you can bathe while enjoying the brisk air of the alpine foothills. There are several sports facilities here, including swimming, horseback riding, and fishing.

Schlosspension St. Martin (tel. 702). The first record of this castle dates back to 1084. It changed hands several times until a member of the Trenbacher family became Bishop Urban of Passau (1561–1598) and led his district through the Counter-Reformation. In 1865 an English lord married a member of the von Arco family in the barque chapel. The then prime minister of Britain, Lord Gladstone, traveled to the ceremony. Today the residential quarters of this palace have been converted into a hotel. Each of the rooms is decorated with individuality and good taste. The cost of staying in a double room with breakfast is from 425 AS ($22.61) per person nightly.

BRAUNAU AM INN: Lying on the right bank of the Inn River, Braunau, a very old town with several buildings from the Middle Ages still standing, has always been a frontier or border town. If you cross the bridge over the Inn you'll have to clear Customs, as you'll be in the small Bavarian village of Simbach.

The burghers' houses in Braunau date in part from the 16th and 17th centuries, but the most outstanding architectural treasure is **St. Stephen's Church,** with a large square tower rising 315 feet, the third-tallest tower in Austria. Inside you can visit the 15th-century Gothic chancel. In an adjacent chapel is the tombstone of a Passau bishop who died in 1485. See also its 16th-century baker's altar.

Braunau am Inn has the dubious distinction of being the birthplace of Adolf Hitler, although his name was Adolf Schicklgruber then. His father, Alois Schicklgruber, had been made a Customs inspector in Braunau in 1875. You'll find nothing in the town commemorating that 1889 event, and chances are you won't read about it in any tourist literature.

However, the town of Braunau was to be in the limelight much later in connection with its native son. When the Nazis were applying pressure on Austria before their complete takeover of the country, one of the most unlikely proposals made was that Braunau, because it was *Der Führer's Geburtsort* (native town), be ceded to Germany. Vague plans were in the air to turn it into a monument honoring the dictator's nativity scene.

After his takeover of Austria, Hitler made a "sentimental journey" to Braunau. He ordered his driver to take him to the Pommer Inn in which he had been born, but his caravan had a difficult time reaching the building because of cars full of onlookers which jammed the road. Historians recorded that when his car reached Braunau, "a jubilant crowd struggled to touch the vehicle as if it were some religious relic."

Food and Lodging

Hotel Gann, 23 Stadtplatz (tel. 3206), is a distinctive-looking town house on the central square of the village. Its facade is painted a pearl gray-blue, while the heavy moldings around the neoclassical-style windows are pure white. The cellar bar is one of the most memorable places in town, partly because of the stone vaulting that soars over the gaily striped chairs and partly because of the patronage of many of the locals. The bedrooms have high ceilings and lots of cozily renovated comforts. Singles cost 260 AS ($13.83), while doubles rent for 475 AS ($25.27), with breakfast included.

Chapter X

INNSBRUCK AND TYROL

1. Innsbruck
2. Igls and the Environs
3. The Stubai and Wipp Valleys
4. Seefeld
5. Resorts Around the Zugspitze
6. The Lower Inn Valley
7. The Achen Valley
8. The Ziller Valley
9. The Alpbach Valley
10. The Kitzbühel Alps
11. The Kaisergebirge
12. The Upper Inn District
13. The Ötz Valley
14. The Paznaun Valley
15. The Arlberg
16. Lienz and East Tyrol

LAND OF ICE and mountains, of dark forests and alpine meadows where wildflowers bloom in the spring, of summer holidays and winter sports . . . that's Tyrol. Those intrepid tourists, the British, discovered its delights for holiday-makers and made it a fashionable destination for travelers in the last century. Now, however, the principal visitors are the Germans. Munich is only a few hours away, and even though Bavaria is itself one of the major tourist attractions of Europe, even the Bavarians head for Tyrol when they want a change of scenery.

Tyrol and its capital, Innsbruck, had an imperial heyday at the end of the Middle Ages, when the Habsburg, Maximilian I, often called "the last of the knights," was the Holy Roman Emperor. Castles dotted the countryside, many now only ruins.

With a population of about half a million Austrians occupying some 4822 square miles, Tyrol was a much larger district at the turn of the century, until South Tyrol was lost to Italy in 1919. The lost portion was a large wine-growing area, considered the wealthiest part of Tyrol. This loss was a great blow for the Tyrolean people who remained in Austria, as it separated many of them from relatives, friends, and sometimes livelihood.

By the same post–World War I treaty, East Tyrol, whose capital is Lienz, was separated from its sister, North Tyrol, of which Innsbruck is capital. The two are separated by a protuberance of the portion of Tyrol given to Italy which connects with a strip of Land Salzburg border. To the east of North Tyrol, the far larger portion of the split province, lies Land Salzburg. On its west is the Austrian province of Vorarlberg (to be visited in Chapter XI), to the north is Bavaria, West Germany, and to the south, Italy and a small part of Switzerland. East Tyrol is bordered by Carinthia on the east, Land Salzburg on the north, and Italy everywhere else.

Tyrol lies at the junction of several transcontinental links. The Valley of the Inn River, which I've divided into two sections, cuts across the northern part of the province. Many side valleys are offshoots of the major artery. The province is also known for its deep-blue alpine lakes, such as the Achensee and the Walchsee. The Drau River, rising in the Höhe Tauern Alps, runs through East Tyrol.

Tyrol is a province known for its folklore and colorful folk customs, including schuhplatter dancing, brass bands, and yodeling. It's also known for its Tyrol dress. Traditional garb topped off with tall hats (less common nowadays) used to be a special feature for both men and women, with the men being the more elaborately attired.

Today Tyrol is one of the most popular tourist regions of Europe, especially favored by Americans, who have to an extent supplanted the once firmly entrenched British holiday crowds. It didn't become a mecca for American tourists until shortly before World War I when rail magnate J. Pierpont Morgan spent time in Innsbruck and publicized the area when he returned home. Since World War II, the resorts of this province have made it a popular destination for American skiers.

Tyrol is the most frequented winter playground in all Austria. Many prefer its ski slopes to those of Switzerland. It has also produced great skiers, and names such as Toni Sailer have become household words. Skiers flock here for many months, but especially from mid-December until the end of March, reservations are at their tightest at the most fashionable resorts.

Glacier tours around May and June are a big attraction, with mountain climbers appearing in the summer months. Trout fishermen work the waters until the first sniff of autumnal air. July and August bring the most visitors to the province, many of them North Americans, so reservations are essential.

I recommend a private car for getting around, if you can afford it, but only for spring, summer, and fall. If you're not an experienced alpine driver, the other months of the year—especially at some of the remote places—can be hazardous. However, the province is well served by rail and bus connections.

1. Innsbruck

The Tyrol capital, Innsbruck (elevation 1880 feet and population nearly 150,000), is considered one of the most beautiful cities of Europe. It has long been a center of commerce and traffic, as it lies at the junction of two important routes across the central Alps—a north-south and an east-west highway. It's easily reached by rail, air, or road.

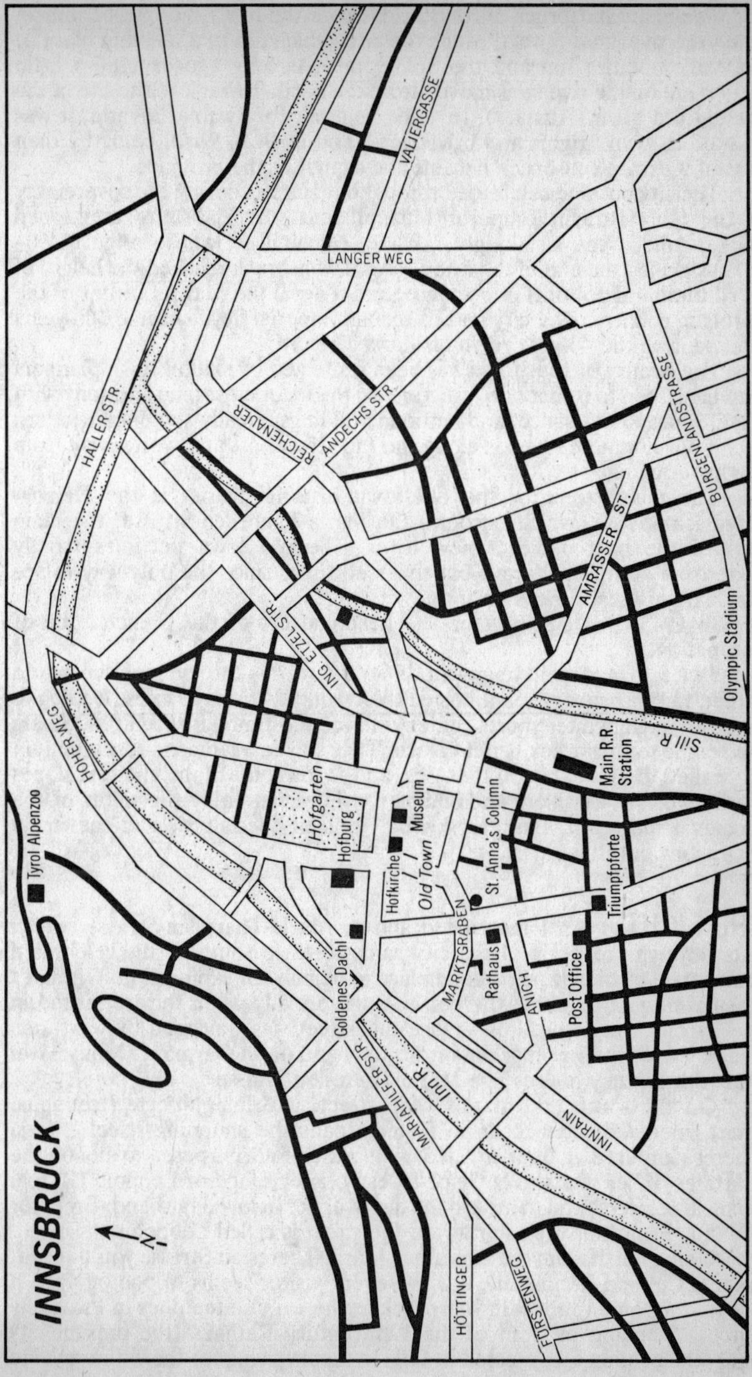
INNSBRUCK
N
HALLER STR.
LANGER WEG
VALIERGASSE
REICHENAUER
ANDECHS STR.
ING. ETZEL STR.
AMRASSER ST.
BURGENLANDSTRASSE
Olympic Stadium
Sill R.
Main R.R. Station
HOHER WEG
Tyrol Alpenzoo
Hofgarten
Hofburg
Hofkirche
Museum
Old Town
St. Anna's Column
MARKTGRABEN
Rathaus
ANICH
Post Office
Triumpfpforte
Goldenes Dachl
MARIAHILFER STR.
Inn R.
INNRAIN
HÖTTINGER
FÜRSTENWEG

The name Innsbruck means "bridge over the Inn," the Inn, of course, being the river that flows through the city, which lies at a meeting place of the Valley of the Inn and the Sill Gorge. As long ago as 1180 a little settlement on the river was moved from the northern bank to the site of the present old town (Altstadt). In 1239, as a part of Swabia Bavaria, it was granted its own "rights and privileges," and in 1420, Tyrol being by then part of Austria, Innsbruck became the capital of the province.

The city became celebrated throughout Europe during the sovereignty of the Holy Roman Emperor Maximilian I, the Habsburg mentioned above, called "the last knight." Under Maximilian, whose reign (1490–1519) signaled the end of the Middle Ages, Innsbruck reached the height of its cultural and political importance, and it's still the cultural center of the Tyrolean country. The city had its second imperial heyday some 300 years later, during the 40-year reign of Maria Theresa.

The beauty of Innsbruck has been protected by skillful town planners who have seen to it that new structures in the inner city are in harmony with the Gothic, Renaissance, and baroque buildings already standing. Modern urban development spreads along the Inn River east and west, away from the historic areas.

The main street of the old town historic district is the **Herzog-Friedrich-Strasse,** which becomes the Maria-Theresien-Strasse, the main axis of the post-medieval new town. The old town becomes strictly pedestrian after 10:30 a.m., but that's all right, since the only way to see that part of Innsbruck is on foot.

In 1945, this city became the headquarters of the French zone of occupation.

Twice in a dozen years—in 1964 and 1976—the eyes of the world turned to Innsbruck when it hosted the Olympic Winter Games, leading to its becoming a winter sports center with the most modern facilities. Skiers who come to Innsbruck benefit twice: They stay in a fantastic cosmopolitan city called the jewel city of the Alps, and ski on some of the choicest slopes of the world. Nonskiers and summer visitors can enjoy the sights of the medieval old town, the shops with Tyrolean specialties, and the many excursions into the environs.

THE SIGHTS: As I mentioned above, **Maria-Theresien-Strasse,** which cuts through the heart of the city from north to south, is the celebrated main street of Innsbruck, a good place to begin your exploration. Often it's fascinating just to watch the passersby, especially when they're attired in the Tyrolean regional dress. Once this street was traversed by wayfarers heading over the Brenner Pass from Italy and on to Germany. Many 17th- and 18th-century houses line Maria-Theresien-Strasse.

On the south end of this wide street, a **Triumphpforte** (triumphal arch), modeled after those in Rome, spans the shopping street. Maria Theresa ordered it built in 1765 with a two-fold purpose: to honor the marriage of her son, the Duke of Tuscany (later Emperor Leopold II), to a Spanish princess, and to mourn the death of her beloved husband, Emperor Franz I. From this arch southward the street is called Leopoldstrasse.

Going north from the arch along Maria-Theresien-Strasse you'll see **St. Anna's Column** (Annasäule), which every visitor seems to photograph. It enjoys the same renown in Innsbruck as the Eros statue does in Piccadilly Circus. Standing in front of the 19th-century Rathaus (the present city hall), the column was erected in 1706 in thanksgiving for the withdrawal in

1703 of Bavarian invasion armies during the War of the Spanish Succession. On top of this Corinthian column a statue of the Virgin Mary stands on a crescent moon, with statues of the Saints Cassianus, Virgilius, George, and Anna surrounding the base.

Not far north of the Annasäule, the wide street narrows and becomes the Herzog-Friedrich-Strasse running through the heart of the **Altstadt** old town), the medieval quarter. This street is arcaded and flanked by a number of well-maintained burgher's houses with a jumble of turrets and gables. Look for the multitude of dormer windows and oriels. Most of the buildings here are overhung with protective roofs to guard them against snowfalls.

Hofburg, 1 Rennweg, to the east of the Aldstadt, is the 15th-century imperial palace of Emperor Maximilian I, rebuilt in rococo style in the 18th century on orders of Maria Theresa. Later it was to hold sad memories for the empress, as it was here that her husband died in 1765. The palace, the exterior of which is colored Maria Theresa ochre (a yellow which the empress favored) and flanked by a set of domed towers, is a fine example of baroque secular architecture. The structure has four wings and a two-story Riesensaal (giant's hall), painted in white and gold and filled with portraits of the Habsburgs. The rooms recall the power and heyday of that ruling family.

You can visit the state rooms and the Riesensaal on guided tours, lasting about half an hour, daily from 9 a.m. to 4 p.m. It's closed Sunday from mid-October to mid-May. Admission is 20 AS ($1.06).

The **Hofkirche,** 2 Universitätsstrasse, is a Gothic-style church built in 1553 by Ferdinand I. Its most important treasure is the cenotaph of Maximilian I, although his remains, alas, are not in this elegant marble sarcophagus glorifying the Roman Empire. He was never brought here from Wiener Neustadt where he was entombed in 1519. The sarcophagus, a great feat of the German Renaissance style of sculpture, has 28 bronze 16th-century statues of Maximilian's real and legendary ancestors and relatives surrounding the kneeling emperor on a tomb with 24 marble reliefs on the sides depicting scenes from his life. One of the statues is based on a design by Dürer. Tyrol's national hero, Andreas Hofer, is entombed here.

The Hofkirche has a lovely Renaissance porch, plus a nave and a trio of aisles in the Gothic style. One gallery contains nearly two dozen statues of the saint protectors of Innsbruck. The wooden organ, dating from 1600, is still operational.

Another chapel, the Silberne Kapell, or silver chapel, was constructed between the church and the palace in 1578 on orders of Archduke Ferdinand II of Tyrol as the final resting place for him and his wife, Philippine Welser. The chapel takes its name from a silver Madonna. Silver reliefs on the altar symbolize the Laurentanian Litany. Alexander Colin designed the sarcophagi of Ferdinand and Philippine.

The Hofkirche and chapel are open from the first of May until the end of September from 9 a.m. to 5 p.m.; otherwise from 9 a.m. to noon and from 2 to 5 p.m. Admission is 20 AS ($1.06).

The **Hofgarten,** a public park containing lakes and many shade trees, including weeping willows, lies north of Rennweg. Concerts are often presented at the Kunstpavillon in the garden during the summer months.

The **Goldenes Dachl,** or Golden Roof, is perhaps Innsbruck's greatest tourist attraction, certainly its most characteristic landmark. It's a three-story balcony on a house in the old town, the late Gothic oriels capped with 2657 gold-plated tiles. It was constructed for Emperor Maximilian I to serve as a royal box where he could sit in luxury and enjoy tournaments in the square below. Completed at the dawn of the 16th century, the Golden Roof was built in honor of Maximilian's second marriage, to Bianca Maria Sforza of Milan (Maximilian was a ruler who expanded his territory not by conquest but by marriage). Not wishing to alienate the allies gained by his first marriage, to Maria of Burgundy, which was ended by her death, he had himself painted on this balcony between the two women. But he is looking at the new wife, Bianca.

Inside the building you can visit the **Olympic Museum,** where video films are shown of Innsbruck and the most interesting scenes from the 1964 and 1976 Olympic Winter Games in English, plus exhibits from the Winter Olympics and an international Olympics stamp collection. The museum is open daily from 9:30 a.m. to noon and from 2 to 5 p.m.

Take a look at Helblinghaus, on Herzog-Friedrich-Strasse opposite the Goldenes Dachl. It's a Gothic structure to which a rococo facade was added.

Dom zu St. Jakob (the Cathedral of St. James), on the Domplatz, was rebuilt from 1717 to 1722 from designs by Johann Jakob Herkommer, a baroque architect. It has a lavishly embellished baroque interior, part of it done by the Asam brothers, and is roofed with domes. The church was heavily damaged in Allied bombing raids in World War II. One of the chief treasures of the cathedral is *Maria Hilf* by Lucas Cranach the Elder, on the main altar. In the north aisle, look for a 1620 monument honoring Archduke Maximilian II, who died in 1618. The church is open from 6 a.m. to noon and from 2 to 5 p.m. It's closed Friday and Sunday morning.

The **Stadtturm,** or belfry, is seen at the old Rathaus (town hall) on the east side of Herzog-Friedrich-Strasse. It rises 190 feet high, and from it you'll have a good view of the city and its environs. Originally built as a watchtower in the 14th century, the Stadtturm has undergone many changes over the centuries. It's open daily from the first of April until the end of October from 9 a.m. to 6 p.m., to 7 p.m. in July and August. Admission is 20 AS ($1.06).

The **Tiroler Volkskunstmuseum** (Tyrol Museum of Popular Art), 2 Universitätsstrasse, houses one of the largest and most impressive collections extant of the artifacts of life in Tyrol, ranging from furniture, often painted, to regional garb.

The museum, adjoining the Hofkirche on its eastern side, is in the **Neues Stift,** or New Abbey, dating from the 16th and the 18th centuries. Rooms on three floors are filled with exhibits. A collection of Tyrolean mangers, or Christmas cribs, contains some from the 18th century. The Stuben (the finest rooms) are on the upper floors. Displays include a range of styles from Gothic to Renaissance to baroque, as well as a collection of models of typical Tyrolean houses. The museum is open from 9 a.m. to 5 p.m., to noon on Sunday. Admission is 20 AS ($1.06).

Ferdinandeum Tyrol Museum (Tiroler Landesmuseum Ferdinandeum), 15 Museumstrasse (tel. 2-20-03), has a celebrated gallery of Flemish and Dutch masters. This museum also traces the development of popular art in the Tyrolean country, including much Gothic art. You'll also see the original bas-reliefs used in designing the Goldenes Dachl. The museum is open from the first of May until the end of September from 9 a.m. to 5 p.m., closing at noon on Sunday. The rest of the year the hours are 9 a.m. to noon and 2 to 4 p.m., closing all day on Sunday. Admission is 18 AS (96¢).

The **Alpenzoo Innsbruck-Tirol,** 37 Weiherburggasse (tel. 3-67-75), lies on the southern slope of the Nordkette below Hungerburg plateau. It contains only those animals indigenous to the Alps, plus alpine birds, reptiles, and fish. The zoo is open daily from 9 a.m. to 6 p.m., to 5 p.m. in winter. Admission is ($2.66).

HOTELS: Always arrive with a reservation, as Innsbruck is said never to be out of season. Accommodations are scarce from June until the end of summer and from about mid-December to mid-April.

The Deluxe Category

Hotel Europa Tyrol, 2 Südtiroler Platz (tel. 35571). The facade of this elegant hotel was bombed in World War II and later rebuilt into the simple modern format you'll see today as you leave the train station. Now it's part of the Steigenberger chain and has been renovated into what is often considered the best hotel in Innsbruck.

The lobby is a high-ceilinged, formally paneled room with an English-style bar at one end and accents of green marble. The upholstery on many of the chairs is made of green leather, set off by the many valuable Oriental rugs. This is a very formal but friendly hotel, with a public image so important that Queen Elizabeth II used it during her stay in Innsbruck.

The uniformed staff is helpful in every way and will usually be willing to show you the heavily ornate yellow and white Barock Saal whose lunette paintings are worth a second look. A. Kurz is the experienced manager of this place.

The 166 rooms rent for 1050 AS ($55.86) to 1380 AS ($73.42) in a single and between 1380 AS ($73.42) and 2280 AS ($120.30) in a double. Breakfast is not included.

Holiday Inn, 15 Salurner Strasse (tel. 36501), offers clean American-style accommodations in a typical Holiday Inn format. While this might not be the charming Tyrolean-style hostelry you'd fantasized about, it is nonetheless convenient, especially for motorists who find parking difficult in the inner city. The hotel has a garage and lies only two blocks from the central train station. Each accommodation is equipped with two double beds, a private bath, radio, phone, TV, and air conditioning. An indoor pool and sauna are on the premises, as well as several theme restaurants. Rates for one person in a double range from 1140 AS ($60.65) to 1670 AS ($88.84), while tariffs for two persons in a double go from 1920 AS ($102.14) to 2700 AS ($143.64), breakfast not included.

Hotel Innsbruck, 3 Innrain (tel. 34511), is a deluxe hotel in the center of the city near the Congress Center. Its facade is painted a vivid tangerine in a contemporary format of windows and op-art trim accenting the vertical rows of bay windows. The lobby has a marble floor and modern-style paneling and cluster chandeliers. On the premises are a big swimming pool, a bar, and a good restaurant. Per-person rates in the handsomely furnished bedrooms range from 600 AS ($31.92) to 960 AS ($51.07), with breakfast included.

First-Class Choices

Hotel Goldener Adler, 6 Herzog-Friedrich-Strasse (tel. 26334). Even the phone booth near the reception desk of this 400-year-old hotel is outfitted in an antique style, concealed behind an old panel. This hotel contains only 16 rooms in a family-run format of leaded windows with stained-glass inserts, travertine floors, ornately carved Tyrolean furniture, and chandeliers where human figures are carved from ram's horns. The reception desk is on the first floor, above the heavy stone buttresses of the street level.

Famous guests have included Goethe, the brother of Marie Antoinette (Joseph II, who arrived incognito in 1777), King Gustav III of Sweden (1783), the violinist Paganini, who cut his name into the windowpane of the room, and in 1573, Duke Albert V of Bavaria who arrived with his son and a retinue of 416 people.

Rooms are handsomely styled and furnished, costing between 840 AS ($44.69) and 1200 ($63.84), while singles range between 600 AS ($31.92) and 840 AS ($44.69), with breakfast extra.

Hotel Central, Am Sparkassenplatz (tel. 24867), is one of the most unusual hotels in town. It's housed in a super-hi-tech format of textured concrete with windows whose edges are beveled into angular glass and steel rectangles. The lobby floor is covered with hand-set mosaics of colored paving blocks arranged into pastel-colored circles. Above your head, it looks as if the bubble-making machine on the Lawrence Welk show went crazy. Thousands of glass balls hang from the high ceiling on golden strands of metal wire.

The management is friendly and capable, and on the premises you'll find one of the popular discos in town, along with an indoor pool, a sauna, and in total contrast to the rest of the hotel, a romantically baroque café with marble columns, sculptured ceilings, large gilt-and-crystal chandeliers, and a collection of international newspapers. The comfortable rooms evoke an almost Japanese sense of simplicity. Doubles range from 575 AS ($30.59) to 800 AS ($42.56), while singles cost between 900 AS ($47.88) and 1200 AS ($63.84), with breakfast included. Prices depend on the season.

Hotel Maria Theresa, 31 Maria-Theresien-Strasse (tel. 35616), is the best known hotel on this famous street a few blocks away from the winding alleys of the oldest parts of Innsbruck. A striking oil portrait of the empress herself hangs in the reception area, which you'll reach by taking a department store–type elevator to the building's second floor. The friendly staff will do everything it can to make you feel comfortable. You may run into members of a tour group, who tend to make this a base. Singles range from 450 AS ($23.94) to 1060 AS ($56.39), while doubles cost between 900 AS ($47.88) and 1680 AS ($89.38), with breakfast included.

Hotel Roter Adler, 4 Seilergasse (tel. 21069), is a dramatically renovated first-class hotel inside a 500-year-old house in the old part of town. In the lobby, modern orange banquettes curve around the antique stone arches that support the vaulted ceiling. The rest of the establishment has lots of exposed wood and cozy corners. Per-person rates in the well-furnished rooms range from 500 AS ($26.60) to 760 AS ($40.43), with breakfast included. The staff is attractive and friendly.

Hotel Grauer Bär, 5-7 Universitätsstrasse (tel. 34531), lies on a street lined with baroque buildings. Its lobby is big enough to park a bus in, with a high ceiling, Oriental rugs, and a small baroque statue of a cherub flying against one wall at eye level. To the side of the lobby is a large persimmon-colored dining room with an ornate ribbed and vaulted white ceiling supported by a central stone column. The attractively rustic bedrooms rent for 600 AS ($31.92) to 720 AS ($38.30) in a single, and for

470 AS ($25) to 600 AS ($31.92) per person in a double, with breakfast included. Prices depend on the plumbing and the season.

The Middle Bracket

Hotel Schwarzer Adler, 2 Kaiserjägerstrasse (tel. 27109), is one of Innsbruck's oldest hotels. Five minutes from the train station, it has an antique-style facade of beige-colored stucco, black shutters, and a big-windowed tower extending upward from the building's corner. Inside you'll find all the vaulted ceilings, aged paneling, and gemütlich clutter you'd expect from such a historic building. Singles cost between 600 AS ($31.92) and 720 AS ($38.30), while doubles range between 480 AS ($25.54) and 600 AS ($31.92) per person, with breakfast included. Half board is offered for 180 AS ($9.58) per person extra.

Hotel Maximilian, 7-9 Marktgraben (tel. 37577). Built in 1982, this inner-city hotel rates as one of the most attractive and up-to-date in Innsbruck. It sacrifices little of the antique charm of yesterday in its willingness to provide modern and convenient accommodations. The woodwork in the lobby is a beautifully crafted example of fine carpentry, while the reception desk is staffed with a bevy of attractive and helpful people.

The 40 rooms are modern and comfortable. The most desirable ones look out over the back, where you'll have a closeup view of the shingled onion dome of the oldest church in Innsbruck (now used as the headquarters of a company which makes keys). Each of the rooms has an attractive modern bath and comes with breakfast included. Compact singles range from 620 AS ($32.98) to 720 AS ($38.30), while doubles cost between 1100 AS ($58.52) and 1250 AS ($66.50).

Villa Blanka, 8 Weiherburggasse (tel. 37771), is a balconied contemporary hotel designed in a big-windowed rectangular format looking out over a well-planted park. It lies about 20 pedestrian minutes from the center of the city. The inside is filled with contoured leather chairs, big modern paintings, and a series of paneled rooms with coffered ceilings ranging from the dramatically contemporary to the rustically conservative. The long sun terrace is set on a balcony above the ground floor, with a view over the rare trees of the hotel's landscaping. Singles range from 620 AS (32.98) to 650 AS ($34.58), while doubles cost around 550 AS ($29.26) per person, with breakfast included.

Hotel Mozart, 15 Müllerstrasse (tel. 23038), is a renovated hotel with a central location and a pleasant series of spacious bedrooms. Comfortably furnished singles rent for 530 AS ($28.20) to 600 AS ($31.92), while doubles cost between 780 AS ($41.50) and 930 AS ($49.48), with breakfast included. All units contain private bath.

Clima Hotel, 7 Zeughausgasse (tel. 28361), is a modern hotel with a saffron-colored facade with an evenly spaced series of protruding white-framed windows. In the center of town, it offers a view of the mountains from many of its lighthearted bedrooms, some of which have abstractly patterned window curtains that could have been designed by Jackson Pollack. On the premises is a dance bar with a big curved serving area, plus a rustic farmer's-style restaurant. Singles range from 540 AS ($28.73) to 635 AS ($33.78), while doubles cost between 850 AS ($45.22) and 1030 AS ($54.80), with breakfast included. All accommodations contain private bath. The hotel is part of a European chain.

Hotel Greif, 3 Leopoldstrasse (tel. 27401), is a five-story building with a desirable location near Innsbruck's arch of triumph and a light-brown facade. The vertical neon sign bolted to the side of the building illuminates the neoclassic pediments above each of the big windows. The modernized interior is filled with comfortable furniture, warm colors of beige, white, and crimson, along with adaptations of chalet chairs. The carpeted bedrooms are partially paneled and rent for around 640 AS ($34.05) per person, based on double occupancy, with breakfast included. The supplement in a single is another 150 AS ($7.98) per day.

Hotel Mondschein, 6 Mariahilfstrasse (tel. 82784), is a peach-colored hotel with a double row of vertical bay windows running from the ground to the fifth floor. A wrought-iron bracket extending over the sidewalk announces that the hotel was built in 1473, although it was tastefully renovated in 1982. One of the best aspects of this place is its location on the banks of the river. On the premises is a restaurant with an old vaulted ceiling and lots of wrought iron, as well as a lobby area with tile floors and Oriental rugs. The colorful and comfortable bedrooms rent for 480 AS ($25.54) to 720 AS ($38.30) in a single and between 840 AS ($44.69) and 1080 AS ($57.46) in a double.

Hotel Royal, 16 Innrain (tel. 26385), is a modern hotel with a riverside location convenient to everything in the city. Of interest to motorists, it has enough parking to give you a free spot (usually). Each of the spacious and comfortable bedrooms is simply and attractively furnished, with its own private bath, small TV, phone, and radio. The sunny dining room is pleasingly filled with burnt-orange carpeting and sunflower-colored walls. Doubles cost around 960 AS ($51.07), while singles rent for 620 AS ($32.98), with breakfast included.

Tourotel Breindössl, 12 Maria-Theresien-Strasse (tel. 24165), lies behind an unusual blue-green facade on a major street of Innsbruck. It's covered with flowered loggias and gently protruding bay windows. The inside is tastefully woodsy, with lots of hanging cloth lamps in the paneled restaurant, welcome touches of wrought iron and regional sculpture in the rustic restaurant, and attractively modern furniture in the comfortable bedrooms. Singles range from 500 AS ($26.60) to 600 AS ($31.92), while doubles cost between 800 AS ($42.56) and 935 AS ($49.74), with breakfast included. All accommodations contain private bath, phone, radio, and (upon request) TV.

The Budget Range

Gasthof-Hotel Weisses Kreuz, 31 Herzog-Friedrich-Strasse (tel. 21890), lies on a street in the old town which has changed little since 13-year-old Wolfgang and his father, Leopold Mozart, stayed here in 1769. The hotel's old facade is relieved with an extended bay window which stretches from the second to the fourth floor. The ground floor is pierced with an arcade, while naïve stencils adorn the white stucco of the upper stories. A wrought-iron sign extending over the sidewalk holds the symbol of the hotel, a white cross.

You'll have to climb past two restaurants and a series of hand-painted ceramic plates set into the stucco of the stairwell before arriving at the third-floor reception area. There you'll be pleasantly surprised by the carved stone columns, a TV room with an arched wood-covered ceiling, a collection of massive Tyrolean chests, and a carved balustrade worn smooth by the palms of generations of visitors.

The staff at the efficient and friendly reception desk charges between 275 AS ($14.63) and 500 AS ($26.60) in a single and between 500 AS ($26.60) and 800 AS ($42.56) in a double, with breakfast included. The informal ground-floor restaurant has been renovated into a modern format of terracotta floors, hanging lamps, and a paneled wall covered with color photographs of food that arc almost guaranteed to makc you hungry.

Hotel/Restaurant Goldene Rose, 39 Herzog-Friedrich-Strasse (tel. 22041). The multifaceted eating areas include a quick-service snackbar with red leatherette banquettes, rock music, and lots of young people sitting under the stone and stucco arches. There's also a ground-floor bar area. The more desirable restaurant is up a short flight of steps. Its ambience is definitely old world, divided into several intimate rooms separated by a corridor lit with wall sconces.

Ceramic tile stoves accent two of the rooms, while much of the paneling is covered with rustic carving. Set meals range from 115 AS ($6.12), including many Italian specialties such as a sole in white wine sauce, saltimbocca, and a long list of Tyrolean dishes such as sauerkraut with smoked pork dumplings. The tempting variety of food here was praised by *Gourmet* magazine.

The hotel also rents simply furnished bedrooms, charging 500 AS ($26.60) in a single and 730 AS ($38.84) in a double, breakfast included.

Pension Stoi, 4 Südtirolerplatz (tel. 25434), is an unpretentious pension across from the train station. The modern masonry-trimmed ground floor contains a coffeeshop with reasonably priced food and drink. Simply furnished singles rent for 300 AS ($15.96), while doubles cost 430 AS ($22.88), with breakfast included.

Gasthof Goldener Löwe, 8 Seilergasse (tel. 22127). This place is centrally located in the old city and might be considered run-down by everyone except the adventerous. You climb a stairwell to what was probably used as a large private home, which has been converted into a warren of small rooms that haven't been painted in a while. The German-speaking management is friendly, and the prices are right: 220 AS ($11.70) in a single and 450 AS ($23.94) in a double. The facade is an elegant combination of gray and white baroque detailing.

Hotel Gasthof Goldene Krone, 46 Maria-Theresien-Strasse (tel. 26160), has a pastel green-and-white facade looking over the traffic on this baroque street. The bedrooms are modern and clean, with concealed reading lights above the built-in beds and big windows. On the premises are a Tyrolean-style paneled restaurant with an alpine atmosphere and a lighthearted café with a long narrow format stretching into a series of hideaway banquettes perfect for intimate talks. Singles range in price from 275 AS ($14.63) to 385 AS ($20.48), with doubles going for 235 AS ($12.50) to 290 AS ($15.34) per person.

Staying at Hungerburg

Hotel Bellevue, Hochinnsbruck/Hungerburg (tel. 36965), is a large and rambling white-walled building with a well-maintained series of flowered balconies and grassy lawns. My favorite room has a red and blue-black Persian carpet with a high ceiling of honey-colored beams and brass chandeliers. On the premises are an indoor pool, a sauna, a restaurant, café, and the kind of bar you'd like to spend time in. From the windows of the spacious modern bedrooms you'll have a view of the mountains and the city of Innsbruck. Doubles range from 1080 AS ($57.46) to 1320 AS ($70.22), while singles go for 600 AS ($31.92) to 780 AS ($41.50), with breakfast included. Rates depend on the location of the units, each of which contains a private bath.

Hotel Pension Zur Linde, Hungerburg (tel. 37103), is a Tyrolean-style hotel with a complicated hipped and gabled roof covered in red tiles, plus a central slate-covered tower capped with a weathervane which usually points to the nearby mountains. Many of the rooms contain private balconies, which look down onto the pleasant outdoor sun terrace. On the premises are a café and a wine restaurant where you might want to order a meal. The Patscheider family are your agreeable hosts. Per-person rates, with breakfast included, range from 290 AS ($15.34) to 360 AS ($19.15). Prices depend on the season and the plumbing.

Gasthof/Pension Klamm, Hungerburg (tel. 36770), is a quiet family-run chalet at the edge of the woods with a view over the city. Its pleasant balconies get lots of sunlight. It takes ten minutes to get to the center of Innsbruck, either by car or via the cable car a few steps away. The interior is appealing. The restaurant has a hospitable bar studded with hunting trophies, while the adjoining dining room has a large arched fireplace, lots of pewter and antique rifles, and a beamed and paneled decor that's very Tyrolean. You might make this the goal of an excursion from town just to have coffee on the sun terrace. Doubles cost 600 AS ($31.92), while singles rent for 350 AS ($18.62) apiece, with breakfast included.

Café/Pension Alpina, Hungerburg (tel. 36989). Botanists will love naming the varieties of flowers that grow from the windowboxes attached to the three floors of balconies of this family-run hotel. Guests often choose to sit under the parasols on the pleasant lawn, sipping coffee and planning their next excursion to Innsbruck. The interior is paneled in light-grained pine, with alpine-style stools around the bar. The accommodating designer of this place surrounded the ceramic oven in the restaurant with a banquette. The Mair family prepares homemade pastries fresh every day in the café. The pleasant bedrooms rent for 335 AS ($17.82) in a single and between 265 AS ($14.10) and 335 AS ($17.82) per person in a double, with breakfast included. Prices depend on the plumbing and the room assignment.

Lodging at Amras

Hotel Kapellar, 96 Philippine-Welser-Strasse (tel. 43106). You'll notice several pieces of polychrome church art scattered throughout the public rooms here, as well as a stone- and wood-trimmed decor of well-crafted rusticity. The in-house restaurant is comfortable, pleasant, and clean, while the rest of the hotel is totally satisfactory and above-average in every way. With breakfast included, singles cost 720 AS ($38.30), while doubles go for around 1050 AS ($55.86). You'll find this hotel near the church in the center of the village.

WHERE TO DINE: This is never a problem in Innsbruck, as this alpine town has more than 150 restaurants, inns, and cafés, some of which offer entertainment at night. I suggest that if you're only going to be in Austria for a short time, you should stick to original Tyrolean specialties. However, if that doesn't suit you, you'll find an array of international cookery as well.

The Leading Restaurants

Belle Époque, 6 Mariahilferstrasse (tel. 82327), is considered the finest restaurant in Innsbruck. It's one floor above ground level in a waterside hotel across the river from the old town. Established about a decade ago, it has a terracotta floor of round tiles, maroon upholstery, pink tablecloths, and an upper-crust decor of exposed wood, wrought iron, and sprays of pink flowers against the simple stucco walls.

This is a French specialty restaurant, serving, among other dishes, feuilleté de ris de veau (sweetbreads), escargots bourguignonne style, oysters, lobsters, entrecôte provençale, gigot d'agneau (lamb), filet of sole, braised turbot, and lotte in champagne. The restaurant is open daily except Sunday from 6:30 p.m. to 1 a.m. À la carte meals begin at 150 AS ($7.98), going up to 310 AS ($16.49) and beyond, plus the cost of your wine.

Domstuben, 3 Pfarrgassee (tel. 33353) is located, as its German name implies, near the cathedral of St. Jakob. You can choose between the ground-floor or the upper-level restaurants, both of them rustically and tastefully filled with lots of wood and handcrafted details. The lower level has a vaulted ceiling. Hors d'oeuvres often come from a well-stocked buffet. If you're in the mood for a non-Austrian dish, the beef Wellington comes with a flaky crust and just the right amount of seasoning, while the filet in cream sauce with noodles complements the wide range of healthy-looking salads. À la carte meals range from 260 AS ($13.83). The restaurant is closed on Sunday, and reservations are suggested.

Restaurant Jörgele, 13 Herzog-Friedrich-Strasse (tel. 26469). Alexander and Jolanda Lochs are the proprietors of this attractive, historic restaurant brimming with atmosphere and a rustic Tyrolean decor. The friendly staff works hard to create a pleasant ambience, and many of the diners seem to return frequently. You climb a short flight of steps before ordering such food items as pepper goulash, wine soup, parmesan cutlet, pork cutlet with zucchini, and a range of other well-prepared and beautifully served dishes. À la carte meals begin at 160 AS ($8.51), going up to 345 AS ($18.35) and beyond. The restaurant is open daily except Sunday, and reservations are suggested.

Restaurant Goldener Adler, 6 Herzog-Friedrich-Strasse (tel. 26334), is the kind of Teutonic establishment that has a firm reputation and a loyal following. Visitors from other Austrian cities often plan ahead to eat here, in the same way that Goethe did when he visited Innsbruck so long ago. In the Goethe Stube, the menu is attractively old-fashioned, specializing in such Tyrolean dishes as braised beef, veal Tyrolean style, noodles with sauerkraut, cabbage soup with bacon, and a superb tafelspitz. There's also fondue, and in the evening there's live music which hopefully will still be playing when you order, for dessert, Salzburger nockerl. Full meals average about 300 AS ($15.96). There's another room, the Adler Bar, on the premises where meals are cheaper.

Churrasco, 2 Innrain (tel. 26398), is an attractive, warmly decorated pizzeria housed in a pink stucco building at the riverside. Inside you'll see an airy and comfortable decor which includes a copper sculpture composed of vertical pipes of varying sizes welded together above the bar. You can sit in one of several rooms. You climb antique stairs to the second floor to reach the pizzeria, La Mamma. There you can enjoy such specialties as game alla carbonara, a mixed fish roast, and at least 16 pasta dishes, and at least seven different meat specialties. In summer the management places tables outside at the edge of the river. Full meals range from 180 AS ($9.58) to 315 AS ($16.75), depending on what you order. Specialties on the ground floor are the same, except for the emphasis on grilled meats.

Moby Dick, Adamgasse (tel. 33580), near the train station, has a dimly lit ambience and a nautical theme, as its name would suggest. Although having little to do with historic Innsbruck, it's still a relaxing place to drop into for a drink, a snack, or a seafood dinner. The decor includes a horseshoe-shape bar and lots of ship's lanterns and polished brass. Menu items run to quick lunches and all the seafood dishes you'd expect. Full meals range from 180 AS ($9.58) to 315 AS ($16.75).

Moderate to Budget Dining

Stiftskeller, 31 Burggraben (tel. 23490). This unpretentious restaurant is housed in an 18th-century yellow-and-white palace, whose baroque detailing can be admired from the streetside beer garden. At night the garden is illuminated by powerful lights attached to the verdant shade trees.

You can, of course, in cold weather dine inside. There, a crucifix of a tormented Christ hangs with other pieces of sculpture under a high wooden ceiling in one of the simple rooms. If you find that too gruesome, there are several other seating possibilities down some of the tiled corridors.

This place can get rowdy at night, but the management works hard cleaning up the next day to prepare for another onslaught. Simple meals are posted on a blackboard, and they usually include soup, a main course, and dessert for around 125 AS ($6.65). The cellar is open daily from 9 a.m. to midnight.

Stiegl-Bräu, 25 Wilhelm-Greil-Strasse (tel. 24338), is a likeable beer hall near the Holiday Inn in the center of town. Popular with locals because of its well-prepared homemade food, the restaurant offers three different wood-paneled rooms, plus copious amounts of wine and beer if you want that. Fixed-price meals range from 115 AS ($6.12) to 170 AS ($9.04). The house specialty includes chicken, veal, and pork on the same platter, accompanied by vegetables and french fries. This is easily big enough for a meal in itself, costing 280 AS ($14.90) for two persons. Franz Dengg is the agreeable owner, opening an outdoor sun terrace for 80 diners in summer.

Heuriger, Hotel Weisses Kreuz, 31 Herzog-Friedrich-Strasse (tel. 21890), advertises itself as an inner-city heurige. From the country atmosphere generated by the painted antique-style facade and the happily cluttered, rustic interior, it's easy to imagine you're in a rural locale. No one will mind if you stop in just for a beer, which seems to go well with the live Tyrolean music.

If you want food, you can choose from simply prepared inexpensive fare, including farmer's platters, wienerschnitzel, rumpsteak with french fries, grilled chicken, and a selection of pasta dishes. Full meals range from 130 AS ($6.92), but snacks and toasts are available too, costing from 40 AS ($2.13) to 75 AS ($3.99). It's open daily from 6 p.m. to midnight.

Restaurant Ottoburg, 1 Herzog-Friedrich-Strasse (tel. 34652). Dating from the 13th century, this restaurant is almost completely covered in wood and has green and red brocaded chairs, pretty waitresses, and Tyrolean music playing softly from near the well-stocked bar area. Beer comes in tall clear glasses without handles, costing around 25 AS ($1.33) for a big one.

Upstairs is a well-known restaurant, separated into four rooms on two different floors, each having the same menu. They have names such as

Maximilian Stube anad Herzogstube. Each room holds a maximum of five tables in a setting that might be called "19th-century Gothic." The decor includes paneling grown smoky with time, carefully notched ceiling beams, and irregular floor plans which create intimate nooks and out-of-the-way crannies for intimate dining.

A daily menu is offered for 110 AS ($5.85). Specialties include venison stew, a special mixed grill, pork chops with rice and carrots, and fried trout, the latter priced by the gram. The chef will also do a veal shank for two persons. The international menu emphasizes Tyrolean specialties, best seen in the dessert list, which offers two kinds of strudel and several other pastries. An average meal will cost around 180 AS ($9.58).

Bräustuben Zipfer (Delevo), 9 Maria-Theresien-Strasse (tel. 28088). You enter this 18th-century beer hall from the busiest street in the inner city, which helps to make this one of Innsbruck's most popular gathering places. The clientele is gemütlich, and at a few tables they appear to be exchanging gossipy tales of long ago. Two anterooms have arched ceilings and golden-grained paneling. Farther on, a high-ceilinged bar area is usually filled with lots of beer drinkers and is accented with blue tiles and medieval sculpture. What you'll see on the ground floor is only a fraction of the total area available to guests here.

Down a flight of steps is a dimly lit cellar with blue-checked tablecloths. Upstairs, an open gallery permits a view of the bar and opens into another drinking area, at the end of which is a round table under a conical ceiling. Even the beams of this place are painted with pithy sayings (one of them, translated, means "old wine makes old hearts young again").

The beer is priced from 20 AS ($1.06) and is served in ceramic mugs, while the food is classically Teutonic, including liver and noodle soup, pork roast with sauerkraut, and apple strudel. Meals are priced at around 170 AS ($9.04), with an exotic touch offered in the pasta dishes from Italy. An inexpensive selection of Austrian wines is available.

Alt Innsprugg, 16 Maria-Theresien-Strasse (tel. 23953). The elaborately ornate facade of this restaurant was crafted in 1577. It has a kind of intricately provincial stonework that would make any modern-day mason beam with pride, plus a series of double-paned arched windows looking out over the main street of town. The second-floor bay windows contain statues of medieval knights that are visible from the street below, while the view from the inside offers a look at the monument of the empress through a screen of geranium-packed window boxes.

The restaurant has two floors, the upper of which is usually sunnier, and a decor that includes murals of Teutonic gods, wrought-iron chandeliers, alpine-style chairs, and woven tablecloths. If you prefer Austrian-style art nouveau, head for the upper room. Open every day but Sunday, the restaurant presents a large menu, with prices for simple meals costing from 80 AS ($4.26) to 125 AS ($6.65). If you order à la carte you might end up spending from 250 AS ($13.30). The menu is standardized Austrian fare, including various kinds of schnitzel, rumpsteak, omelets, goulash soup, smoked meats, and apple strudel.

Hirschstuben, 5 Kiebachgasse (tel. 22979). The old-style decor of this Tyrolean restaurant encompasses two rooms, one with a beamed and one with a vaulted ceiling. You'll see hand-chiseled stone columns, brocade chairs, and a large stainless-steel bar dividing the two rooms. You'll have to go down a few steps from street level, but once you're there you can select an array of daily specials that might include fish soup, trout meunière, sliced veal in cream sauce Zurich style, veal steak with morels and cream sauce, beef Stroganoff, peppersteak, and for dessert, either Austrian crêpes or Salzburger nockerl. Fixed-price meals range from 115 AS ($6.12) to 175 AS ($9.31), white à la carte dinners cost from 90 AS ($4.79) to 300 AS ($15.96). Reservations are suggested.

Altstadtstüberl, 13 Riesengasse (tel. 22347), provides a pleasant destination point after a walk through the old town. In one of Innsbruck's most historic sections, the restaurant offers an uncomplicated decor well suited to the presentation of the simply prepared and generous portions of the Austrian and Tyrolean specialties. These included Tyrolean-style liver, meat and marrow soup, tafelspitz, grilled pork, beef, and chicken, along with potatoes smothered in cheese sauce. Fixed-price meals range from 65 AS ($3.46) to 190 AS ($10.11), while à la carte dinners average 280 AS ($14.90). The restaurant is closed on Sunday.

Restaurant Basco, 12 Anichstrasse (tel. 20149), is a friendly local restaurant whose clientele is likely to know one another by sight. The specialties are more exotic than you'd expect, and include ratatouille cream soup, poached halibut in a Riesling sauce, impeccably fresh vegetables (sometimes covered with a tart hollandaise sauce), and a marvelous dessert concocted from pastry, pistachio ice cream, and nougat cream. The restaurant is open every day, serving à la carte meals ranging from 95 AS ($5.05) to 260 AS ($13.83).

Weisses Rössl, 8 Kiebachgasse (tel. 23057). You'll enter this time-honored place through a stone archway opening onto one of the most famous streets of the old town. At the end of a flight of stairs, with a crucifix at the top, you'll find two rooms with red-tile floors and about the most extensive set of stag horns (complete with the initials of the hunter and the date of the shooting) in Innsbruck. The simple menu offers daily specials and typical Tyrolean dishes usually served with pommes-frites. Specials include saftgulasch with polenta, a grilled plate "alt insprugg" served for two persons, and a variety of schnitzels. Service is friendly, and meals range from 60 AS ($3.19) to 100 AS ($5.32). The restaurant is closed on Sunday and for all of November.

Wienerwald, 12 Maria-Theresien-Strasse (tel. 24165). This chain might be called the Howard Johnson's of Austria. It offers chain-restaurant gemütlich, generous portions, and hours that are usually longer than those of many smaller restaurants, including on Sunday. This particular branch is on one of the main inner-city streets of town. It offers a cavernous beer hall with a high ceiling, plus several smaller rooms which you may or may not pick. The simple and wholesome food includes six kinds of soup, three kinds of salad, five kinds of chicken, and six kinds of schnitzel, along with a sampling of beef and pork dishes. A children's menu is also offered. Beer and wine are served by the glass. The menu is in both English and German, and a meal usually ranges between 75 AS ($3.99) and 160 AS ($8.51), depending on what you order.

Some Leading Cafés

Café Munding, 16 Keibachstrasse, on a quiet corner in the old town, is a comfortable-looking house built in 1720 in a baroque format of frescoes, carved bay windows, and lots of Tyrolean detailing. The interior has been severely modernized, offering an interconnected series of simple rooms, one of which has a discreetly ornate plaster ceiling and an abstract mural. The first thing you'll see when you enter is an immaculately clean pastry and chocolate shop. Food is served in the inner rooms, which in addition to coffee priced from 15 AS (80¢), includes pizzas from 50 AS ($2.66), soups and toasts from 25 AS ($1.33), plus wine by the glass. The waitresses wear black dresses and frilly blue aprons.

Stadtcafé, 2 Rennweg (tel. 26869). Between sips of your coffee, priced from 14 AS (75¢), you can admire the attending nymphs and deities supporting the base of the equestrian statue in front of the elegantly modern café. It has a tall ceiling with starburst chandeliers, warmly tinted brown and tangerine-colored banquettes, and large photographs of theatrical scenes from the nearby Landestheater. It's open from 9 a.m. to midnight, with hot food served from 11 a.m. to 3 p.m. and from 5 to 11 p.m. In addition to just coffee and pastries, you can also order full meals here, including grilled pork, veal, rumpsteak with poppyseed noodles, pasta, Tyrolean soups, and ham and cheese sandwiches. A menu of the day costs 110 AS ($5.84).

Dining in the Environs

Gasthof Wilder Mann (tel. 77387) at Lans. If you appreciate architecture, you'll enjoy studying the stucco tower attached to the corner of this elongated building with the half-timbered triangular section just under the sloping roofline. The interior is pleasantly spacious and rustic, with good service and a series of well-prepared traditional specialties such as wine soup, venison pâté with cumberland sauce, filet steak in a pepper cream sauce, and something called Wilde Mann Platte, which is an assorted collection of several kinds of savory meat with french fries and fresh vegetables for two persons. Dessert could be a Salzburger nockerl. Meals average about 275 AS ($14.63). The restaurant is open daily except from mid-January until the beginning of February. Alois and Paula Schöpf are the gracious owners of this place.

Restaurant Kapeller, 96 Philippine-Welser-Strasse (tel. 43106) at Amras, is set in a beautiful decor of modernized chalet chairs, Oriental rugs, and a tasteful and well-constructed combination of stone, stucco, and wood. Menu items are imaginativeley light, including salads made with generous amounts of radiccio, avocados, mushrooms, and gorgonzola. If you like soup, try the cream of fennel, and if you're looking for fish, sample the John Dory in white wine sauce or the fresh trout. Meat courses include venison in season, tafelspitz, filet of roast hare, and many veal and pork specialties. Fixed-price meals range from 180 AS ($9.58) to 420 AS ($22.34), while à la carte dinners cost from 135 AS ($7.18) to 385 AS ($20.48). The restaurant is closed on Sunday and for all of January, and reservations are strongly suggested.

SHOPPING: On their home turf, you can purchase such Tyrolean specialties as the famed lederhosen, dirndls, leather clothing, woodcarving, Loden cloth, and all sorts of ski and mountain-climbing equipment. You can stroll around such streets as the Maria-Theresien-Strasse, the Herzog-Friedrich-Strasse, and the Museumstrasse, ducking in and making discoveries of your own, perhaps finding some treasured gift or souvenir.

Here are a few of my recommendations if you're seeking something special:

Tiroler Heimatwerk, 2 Meraner Strasse (tel. 22320), is one of the best stores in Innsbruck for such handcrafted Tyrolean-style items as sculpture, pewter, textiles, woolen goods, hand-knitted sweaters, lace, and bolts of silk for do-it-yourselfers. You can purchase regionally inspired fabrics and dress patterns which you can whip into a dirndl (or whatever) as soon as you get home. Also for sale are carved chests, mirror frames, and furniture. The elegant decor includes ancient stone columns and old, well-maintained vaulted ceilings. The friendly saleswomen wear regional dresses.

Gmunder Keramik, 15 Wilhelm-Greil-Strasse (tel. 23152), is the Innsbruck outlet of this famous ceramic house whose headquarters are in Gmunden. Its merchandise includes lidded beer mugs in a variety of colorful, hand-worked patterns, plus complete dinner or coffee services.

At the same address, **Lanz,** 15 Wilhelm-Greil-Strasse (tel. 23105), is a bright and efficient clothing store where the staff wears regional dresses and where the inventory includes everything you'd need to look authentically Tyrolean. Specific items include dresses, sweaters, dirndls, stockings, handkerchiefs, lederhosen, hand-knit sweaters, leather belts, sport coats, and overcoats. The store carries children's clothing and apparel for men too.

Handwerkskunst, 15 Wilhelm-Greil-Strasse (tel. 23152), also at the same address, stands near the Bozner-Platz. This shop sells an attractive selection of handmade objects, such as pewter tankards, vases, candlesticks, boxes of all shapes, silver and Tyrolean garnet jewelry, crystal, textiles, brass antique-style vessels, and porcelain hand-painted breakfast services.

Lodenbaur, 4 Brixner Strasse (tel. 20911). This is the closest address you'll find to a department store in Innsbruck devoted to regional Tyrolean dress. Most of the goods are made in Austria, including a full array of lederhosen, coats, dresses, dirndls, and accessories for men, women, and children. Be sure to check out the basement as well.

Haidegger, 21 Wilhelm-Greil-Strasse (tel. 21443), is one of the best stores for children's toys and clothing. Many of the items are handmade. Clothes here fit children from newborns to 14 years old, including Tyrolean outfits, dirndls, lederhosen, and accessories. The staff is friendly and charming, trying to maintain a lighthearted and airy ambience that children will enjoy.

AFTER DARK: Innsbruck is more lighthearted about its nightlife than is Vienna. If you're in luck you'll get to attend a summer concert in the park or perhaps take in an operetta at the theater. You might retire to a beer hall to listen to brass bands and yodeling or be lulled by zither music at a restaurant.

Why not stroll through the Aldstadt and, if it's a summer night, meander through the Hofgarten, which is lit? Perhaps you'd enjoy taking the funicular to Hungerburg for an overview of the night lights of Innsbruck, where many of the historic buildings and fountains are illuminated. Best of all, you can attend a Tyrolean folkloric evening or retreat to a typical local wine tavern offering entertainment.

The average drink here costs from 50 AS ($2.66) to 75 AS ($3.99), except in the strip clubs which often charge more. Likewise, you almost never have to pay a cover charge except in one of the "erotic" clubs.

It's wise to check with the Tourist Office as to current offerings, both theatrical presentations and folkloric ones. For example, in summer there's often a parade of a Tyrolean brass band in costumes, with a concert at the Goldenes Dachl. There are also likely to be concerts at Ambras Castle, ecclesiastical music at Wilten Basilica, organ concerts at the Igls parish church, and so on. Summer is the active season for this type of public entertainment.

If you want casino action, you have to drive to the resort of Seefeld (see attractions coming up), where the **Spiel-Casino** there offers roulette, baccarat, blackjack, or whatever from 5 p.m. There's also a restaurant, **Locanda,** on the premises.

Many of the restaurants, in addition to food, offer Tyrolean evenings. That way, your dining choice also becomes your nightclub for the evening, which is a lot cheaper than going to a restaurant, then a separate nightclub.

Typical among these is the **Stiftskeller,** 31 Burggraben (tel. 23490), already recommended as a restaurant. It presents a Tyrolean evening, beginning at 8. The folklore program offers an evening of country music, songs, yodeling, zither playing, hackbrett, xylophon, alphorn, singing saws, raffele, folk dancing, and the famous schuhplatteln.

Tyrolean entertainment is also featured at the **Heuriger** at the Hotel Weisses Kreuz, 31 Herzog-Friedrich-Strasse (tel. 21890). In the wine tavern, open to midnight, you can order legs of pork and crisp chicken while enjoying the music.

Club Central, Hotel Central, Am Sparkassenplatz (tel. 20310), is the elegantly futuristic disco inside one of the most architecturally innovative hotels in town. An over-30 crowd gathers here under festive lights in a comfortably padded and upholstered room which occasionally offers live music. There's no dress code, although many of the clients tend to "dress up." Entrance is free, and it's open till 3 a.m. every day of the week.

Café Club Filou, 12 Stiftgasse (tel. 215412), is a popular dance bar housed in a vaulted building with stone columns in the old city. In addition to the disco, the ground floor offers drinks, coffee, and grilled specialties, with the spillover in summer spreading into the garden. The café is open from 5 p.m. to 2 a.m., the garden restaurant from 5 to 10 p.m., and the dancing club from 9 p.m. to 3 a.m.

Tiffany, Rhombergpassage (tel. 34927), is a popular dance bar which accepts credit cards and serves an international cuisine. It's open from 8:30 p.m. to 4 a.m. every night of the week. The clients range from the relatively conservative to a smattering of punk rockers, but Tiffany is generally acknowledged to be one of the city's more interesting clubs.

Highlife Club, 2 Seilergasse (tel. 22163), has a higher percentage of gay clients than any other nightclub in the city. It's small and often gets very crowded. The place is owned by an enterprising couple called Seigfried and Werner. If you decide to go, you'll notice flowers on the wood bar, a cramped gold and metallic dance floor, and a light show visible through branches and paper flowers. Drinks cost between 45 AS ($2.39) and 65 AS ($3.46), and on Saturday night there's a cover charge of 40 AS ($2.13). The club is open seven days a week from 8:30 p.m. to 4 a.m., but doesn't start to fill up until after 10 p.m.

Queen Anne Club, 6 Amraserstrasse (tel. 35155), has a high ceiling, lots of colored lights, and a stage for the musical acts that sometimes appear here. You'll find plenty of places to sit, plus a nearby pub under the same management (Paulis Pub), where a more sedate crowd talks quietly in a warmly masculine ambience of wood and olive-colored velvet.

Nightclub Lady-O, 2 Bruneckerstrasse (tel. 26432), near the train station, offers voyeuristic clients a collection of charming female artists. On one recent occasion they included Speedy Gonzales (erotic acrobatics), Brigitte Varga ("black magic"), and Willy Mexiko (trained pets and striptease). You might also have caught Carlos Nepopo and his Brazilian carnival collection of women's clothing. Entrance fee is 40 AS ($2.13), while the first drink costs 100 AS ($5.32). The club is open daily from 8 p.m. to 4 a.m., with shows beginning at 10:30 p.m.

Goethe-Stube, Restaurant Goldener Adler, 6 Herzog-Friedrich-Strasse (tel. 26334). Aside from the good food (see my restaurant recommendation), this place offers a nightly program of Tyrolean music and "jodlers." It's open between 8 p.m. and 1 a.m.

Scotch Club, 5 Museumstrasse (tel. 25411), is open every day from 8:30 p.m. to 3:30 a.m. This trendy nightclub, which has disco music for dancing, welcomes a wide range of clients of all persuasions. It accepts credit cards, and contains a restaurant serving an international cuisine.

Club Innsbruck

Visitors who stay in Innsbruck at least three days automatically become members of Club Innsbruck, which meets every Monday at 7:40 p.m. at the Hotel Grauer Bar, 5 Universitätsstresse. You'll get a membership card at your accommodation when you check in for the necessary length of stay, assuring you of a surprising number of advantages. The card is also available at the Tourist Office or at the hotel reservation desk at the Central Railway Station (see below under "Practical Facts").

Hotel and restaurant owners and the staff of the Tourist Office welcome you at the club meeting, give you a drink, and dispense information and advice to make your vacation better. You'll be shown slides by mountain guides. Hiking and mountaineering tours are arranged, and badges are awarded for participation.

Your membership card entitles you to free rides on the Innsbruck Mountain Bus daily from 9 a.m., leaving from the Kongresshaus (convention center), and participation in the Innsbruck mountaineering program, with free mountain guides. You get a 50% reduction in admission price at the Museum of Tyrolean Folk Art, the Hofkirche, and the Ferdinandeum State Museum, plus a 20% reduction on fares on the Nordkette, Patscherfofel, and Muterer Alm cable cars and lifts, and a 10% reduction on fees at some tennis courts and greens fees at golf courses.

For further information, ask at the Tourist Office (see below).

EXPLORING IN THE ENVIRONS: Many of the satellite resorts such as Igls (coming up) can properly be considered day trips from Innsbruck. Therefore for the moment I'll highlight, only those attractions on the most immediate outskirts of the city.

Hungerburg

Hungerburg mountain plateau (2860 feet) is considered by many to be the most beautiful spot in Tyrol, affording the best view of Innsbruck, especially on a summer night when much of the city, including fountains and historic buildings, is floodlit. Some of the most scenic hotels in the Innsbruck environs are here, several of which I have recommended above.

You can drive to the plateau or else take the funicular, which departs about four times on the hour from 9 a.m. to 8 p.m., then about every 30 minutes until 10:30 p.m. There's an 11 p.m. funicular on Friday and Saturday night. Round-trip fare is 35 AS ($1.86).

From the plateau, the Nordkette cable railway quickly takes you up to the Seegrube and the Hafelekar (7655 feet) for a sweeping view of alpine peaks and glaciers. This is the starting point of high mountain walks and climbing expeditions. In summer the cable railway runs every hour between 8 a.m. and 6 p.m. A round-trip costs 165 AS ($8.79).

Schloss Ambras

This medieval castle, two miles southeast of the heart of Innsbruck on the edge of the Mittelgebirgsterrace, is divided into a lower and an upper castle, the latter a fortress in the Middle Ages, subsequently much renovated. Archduke Ferdinand II, regent of Tyrol who died in 1595, had Schloss Ambras reconstructed as a Renaissance palace. It was his favorite residence and the center of the cultural life of his court.

The castle has a fine arms and armor collection, particularly jousting equipment, as well as an array of tapestries, antiques, frescoes, and a gallery of imperial portraits from the 15th to the 18th centuries. The Spanish Hall, built in 1570, is a highlight of Ambras, one of the first German Renaissance interiors. Visitors can see this as well as private rooms where Ferdinand lived with his beloved wife, Philippine Welser. Even her bathroom is shown on tours. Unfortunately, Vienna (the Kunsthistorischesmuseum, in particular) made off with most of Ferdinand's rich collections of objets d'art.

Schloss Ambras is open from the first of May until the end of September daily except Tuesday. Admission is 15 AS (80¢). To visit the upper castle you must go on a guided tour, lasting more than an hour and costing another 15 AS (80¢). Tours start at 10 and 11 a.m., noon, and 2, 3, and 3:30 p.m.

After viewing the interior, you can take a leisurely stroll through the castle grounds.

The Wilten Basilica

The southern district of Innsbruck where the Sill River emerges from a gorge, Wilten is one of the most dramatic landscapes in the environs of the city. It's an ancient spot that was once the Roman town of Veldidena.

Its parish church, constructed from 1751 to 1755, became a basilica in 1957. Built in a rich rococo style with twin towers, this is considered one of the most splendid houses of worship in the Tyrolean country. It's noted for its stucco work by Franz Xaver Feichtmayr. Matthaus Gunther is responsible for the frescoes on the ceiling. A sandstone figure depicting "Our Lady of the Four Columns" has been the subject of pilgrimage since the Middle Ages.

Across from the basilica is a cluster of baroque buildings which are the outgrowth of an abbey founded there in 1138. The abbey church, dating from the 1650s, merits a visit. It has a porch guarded by two stone giants and a grille from 1707 found in the narthex. This church was damaged by World War II Allied bombing.

Bergisel

If you're driving, head out the Brenner road to Bergisel (2450 feet), a lovely wooded section in the environs ideal for leisurely strolls in the warm months. It lies near the gorge of the Sill River on the southern outskirts of Innsbruck, about a 20-minute walk from the Wilten Basilica. Here you'll see the ski jumps built for the 1964 and 1976 Olympic Winter Games. You'll have splendid views from the jumps.

The hill here is a historic site, scene of the 1809 battles in which Andreas Hofer led some Tyrolean peasants against French and Bavarian forces. He was later shot to death in Mantua on orders of Napoleon. Below the ski jump, on the north side, is the Andreas Hofer monument erected in 1893 to commemorate the battle. Tyroleans speak of this as their "field of remembrance," and it's filled with memorials and visitors. However, heroic though the local deeds may be, they may not interest North Americans. I recommend that you visit here just for the views and the relaxing walks.

PRACTICAL FACTS: The **Tourist Office** (Städtisches Verkehrsbüro), 3 Burggraben (tel. 25-7-15), will courteously supply you with a wealth of information to ensure that you enjoy your Innsbruck and Tyrol visit. It's open Monday to Friday from 8 a.m. to noon and from 2 to 5:30 p.m., on Saturday from 9 a.m. to noon. If you have children with you, ask for the special guide book for the young.

Hotel information is available at the Central Railway Station (Hauptbahnhof) (tel. 23-7-66).

For **emergency** needs, you should know the following numbers: police—133; fire—122; ambulance—144; mountain rescue service—194.

For emergency medical service, call the **University Hospital,** 35 Anichstrasse (tel. 26-7-11).

The **Lost Property Office** is at the police station (Bundespolizeidirektion), 7 Kaiserjägerstrasse (tel. 26-7-21).

You can **exchange money** at banks in all parts of town Monday to Friday from 7:45 a.m. to 12:30 p.m. and from 2:30 to 4 p.m.; at the Tourist Office; and at the Central Railway Station (7:30 a.m. to 8:30 p.m. daily).

The **American Express** office, 3 Brixnerstrasse (tel. 22-4-91), is open Monday to Friday from 9 a.m. to 5:30 p.m. and on Saturday from 9 a.m. to noon.

The **Central Post Office** (Hauptpostamt), 2 Maximilianstrasse (tel. 26-7-61), is open 24 hours a day Monday to Saturday. The post office at the Central Railway Station, 1-3 Bruneckerstrasse, is open Monday to Saturday from 6:30 a.m. to 9 p.m.

SPORTS: Ski areas around Innsbruck are excellent for winter activity or for summer mountain walks and viewing. Five sunny snow-covered, avalanche-free areas around the capital of Tyrol are served by five cableways, 44 chair lifts, and ski hoists. More detailed information on skiing areas will appear later in this chapter.

In winter, the city is also known for bobsled and toboggan runs and ice-skating rinks.

In summer in Innsbruck you can enjoy tennis at a number of courts, golf on either an 18-hole or a nine-hole course, horseback riding, mountaineering, gliding, swimming, hiking, and shooting.

TRANSPORTATION: A network of three tram and 25 bus lines covers all of Innsbruck and its close environs. Tickets for single rides in the central area are 12 AS (64¢). A book of 5 tickets costs 42.50 AS ($2.26); 10 tickets, 81 AS ($4.31); and 25 tickets, 195 AS ($10.37).

Postal Buses leave from the Central Bus Station, next to the Central Railway Station, heading to all parts of Tyrol.

Taxi stands are in all parts of town, or you can call a radio cab (tel. 2-77-11 or 4-55-00).

You can take a ride in a **fiacre** (horse-drawn carriage) from in front of Tiroler Landestheater, Rennweg.

Parking: If you elect to use your own car for transportation in Innsbruck, you need to know something about parking. The fee for parking in the city center's short-term parking zones (marked by special signs) is 5 AS (26¢) for 30 minutes. The maximum length of time you can stay in one spot is 1½ hours. Parking vouchers can be bought in all post offices, at most tobacconists, and at the Tourist Office.

There are several multistory and underground car parks in Innsbruck.

TOURS: Sightseeing tours of Innsbruck, lasting about an hour, leave by bus from the Hofburg at 10:15 a.m., noon, and 2 and 3 p.m.

A special two-hour bus tour leaves from Maria-Theresien-Strasse, the Central Railway Station, and Bozner Platz at 10 a.m. and 2 p.m.

Daily bus excursions from Innsbruck to the most beautiful part of Tyrol—Zillertal, Alpbach, and Kühtai—and to the favorite places in neighboring Italy and Germany and other parts of Austria, can be arranged at your hotel, a travel agency, or the Tourist Office.

2. Igls and the Environs

This section, site of many of the Olympic Winter Games of 1964 and 1976, might be called "Olympic Innsbruck." It consists of a cluster of resorts, the best known of which is Igls, all lying within easy reach of the Tyrol capital, often with a commuting time of only half an hour. Each of these resorts perched on the slopes where the Olympics took place could be an alternative to staying in Innsbruck, which is often crowded.

A complete system of lifts opens up alpine scenery to everybody, from the beginner to the most advanced skier—or to the sightseer in warm weather.

IGLS: Lying on a sunny plateau in the alpine foothills at an elevation of 2875 feet, Igls is the resort choice of many people who prefer to stay here—in either winter or summer—and commute to Innsbruck, three miles north. Although its number swells greatly with winter and summer visitors, the town has a population of fewer than 2000 souls. Because it's so popular, Igls is certainly not the cheapest resort in Tyrol.

A streetcar from the Berg Isel station in the city will deliver you to Igls, 1000 feet higher than the capital, in about 30 minutes. Buses on route "J" leave every 30 minutes on the hour and half hour from Igls and the main railway station in Innsbruck. The local train on the no. 6 line leaves Innsbruck at a quarter past each hour and Igls at a quarter to.

The outdoor air at Igls, long known as the "sun terrace" of Innsbruck, is never likely to be too hot, even on the hottest day in Austria. In fact it feels air-conditioned outside even in summer. Although much of its world renown has been based on winter sports, this is a popular summer resort too, a place to rest or wander along alpine trails, to play golf on an 18-hole or a nine-hole course, to enjoy tennis, or whatever.

This is the favorite place for Innsbruckers to come to ski, and they're joined by throngs of visitors. Igls shared the Winter Olympics festivities and sporting competition with Innsbruck, and following the success of the 1976 event, this small resort town can boast a thrilling bobsled and toboggan run that enjoys great renown among the sporting crowd flocking here in winter—both Americans and Europeans.

The major excursion from here is to take a cable car up to **Patscherkofel,** at an elevation of 6430 feet, a ride covering about 2½ miles and taking about 18 minutes. Patscherkofel is the mountain that gives Innsbruck its celebrated vista. Many long ski descents from the mountain are possible.

A small kindergarten for children is in a romantic log cabin in the Kurpark, a lovely, natural wooded area near the center of the village.

Food and Lodging

Sporthotel Igls (tel. 77241) is a fancifully designed hotel built in a style that's a cross between a baroque castle and a mountain chalet. Some of the details include jutting bay windows, at least three hexagonal stone-trimmed towers with ornate detailing, and rows of flower-covered balconies. The spacious interior is dotted with antiques and conservative furniture, with plenty of gemütlich corners and sunny areas, both indoors and out.

The hotel has two restaurants, an à la carte grill room, two elevators, a bar, and a big indoor/outdoor swimming pool, plus a range of health and cure facilities. Horseback riding, golf, and tennis are close at hand. In winter the hotel offers a daily five o'clock tea dance. With half board included, rates in a double range from 480 AS ($25.54) to 1440 AS ($76.61), depending on the room and the season. Singles pay a daily supplement of 140 AS ($7.45), and a nearby annex holds the overflow from the main hotel.

Hotel Alpenhof (tel. 05222) is a tastefully furnished chalet with a view of the mountains. Victorian-style armchairs fill the big-windowed main salon, while other facilities include a warmly inviting bar area and a sunny terrace where Victor and Tilly Hittler maintain well-prepared buffets. The hotel was completely modernized in 1980. The carpeted and comfortable bedrooms rent for 510 AS ($27.13) to 770 AS ($40.96) in a double and between 620 AS ($32.98) and 850 AS ($45.22) for a single. All rates are per person with half board included, and vary according to the room and the season.

Agidihof (tel. 7108) is a rambling chalet-style building near the Kurpark and the ski lifts. The interior has lots of hand-worked details, such as antique armoires set into niches designed especially for them, wrought-iron window bars and lighting fixtures, heavily beamed ceilings, and Oriental rugs. The Skardarasy family, your hosts, charge between 360 AS ($19.15) and 840 AS ($44.69) for a single and between 250 AS ($13.30) and 700 AS ($37.24) per person for a double, with breakfast included. Prices depend on the season, the accommodation, and the plumbing.

Hotel Bon Alpina (tel. 7219) is a tastefully designed chalet, with cedar shingles and stucco over part of its brown, white, and yellow-trimmed facade. In the center of the village, a ten-minute walk from the ski lifts, the hotel has a cozy restaurant, a scattering of antiques in the public rooms, and comfortable, simple bedrooms which rent for between 415 AS ($22.08) and 610 AS ($32.45) per person, based on double occupancy, with half board included. Singles pay a daily supplement of 115 AS ($6.12).

Hotel Astoria (tel. 77481) is a wood and white-painted chalet near the center of Igls. The interior is darkly furnished with heavy wooden ceilings, autumnal colors, and hanging brass lamps. On the premises are a padded bar and a small swimming pool. The light-colored bedrooms have private baths, southern balconies, telephone, and TV. The hotel is near the cable cars and a three-minute walk from the public tennis courts. Doubles range from 440 AS ($23.41) to 565 AS ($30.06) per person, with breakfast included.

Hotel Batzenhäusl (tel. 77104). The ornate paneling in the tavern is carved from what the locals call "stone pine," the glow from which beautifully complements the flowered carpets, leaded windows, and hand-worked lamps. The other sections of this comfortable hotel are crafted in a more modern style, still appealing and intimate, with ample use of heavy ceiling beams, flagstone floors, and Oriental rugs. The hotel is an antique chalet with a recently built addition more or less in the same style as the original intricately carved building. Dietrich Arnold and his attractive family, the owners, charge between 480 AS ($25.54) and 840 AS ($44.69) per person, based on double occupancy. Singles pay a daily supplement of 110 AS ($5.85), and all tariffs include full board. See a separate restaurant recommendation for this hotel.

Waldhotel (tel. 77272) is a wood and stucco chalet with red shutters. It's in a flowering garden which members of the Maier family work hard to maintain throughout the summer. Facilities include an indoor swimming pool, a sauna, and a fitness room, as well as a sunny restaurant with immaculate napery, a cozy bar, and a flagstone-covered sun terrace. With half board included, doubles rent for 490 AS ($26.07) to 600 AS ($35.11) per person, while singles range between 590 AS ($31.39) and 730 AS ($38.84), depending on the season. Each of the comfortable rooms has its own bath.

Hotel Tirolerhof (tel. 77194) has one of the prettiest facades in Igls. Designed in a rambling format of Tudor-style half-timbers, gabled red tile roofs, and a long expanse of greenery rising on every side, the hotel offers apartment accommodations for between two and eight persons, as well as standard hotel rooms. In a wooded area four minutes from the center of town, the hotel charges between 280 AS ($14.90) and 400 AS ($21.28) for a single and between 250 AS ($13.30) and 325 AS ($17.29) per person in a double, with breakfast included. An apartment for three persons costs 840 AS ($44.69) to 1020 AS ($54.26), with breakfast included, plus a one-time cleaning charge of 300 AS ($15.96).

Restaurant Batzenhäusl, in the Hotel Batzenhäusl (tel. 77104). "Gemütlich" is a word to describe this carefully paneled antique-style dining room, where the chalet chairs are intricately carved and the service is relaxed and friendly. The well-prepared food includes Austrian specialties such as three kinds of meat on the same platter (covered in a mushroom cream sauce), apple strudel, and a series of savory meat-flavored soups. You might prefer the outdoor veranda or the garden in summer, although the dining room inside is most attractive. Fixed-price meals range from 85 AS ($4.52) to 300 AS ($15.96), while à la carte dinners cost from 95 AS ($5.05) to 420 AS ($22.34).

PATSCH: This small village above Igls lies on the sunny western slope of the Patscherkofel, with a panoramic view of the Stubai Glaciers. Lying on the old Roman road below the Patscherkofel peak, Patsch is only a short distance from the mountain's Olympics slopes.

In winter you'll find facilities here for skiing, including cross-country runs, ice skating, and curling. There's a ski school in the village. Horse-drawn sleighs take you along snow trails.

In summer you can go on hikes, swim, or play golf and tennis. Summer skiing is possible on the Stubai Glacier.

Food and Lodging

Hotel Altwirt (tel. 77409) enjoys a quiet location and an excellent view of the Stubai Glaciers. It was recently built around a carefully planned design incorporating heavy timbers, lots of wood, terracotta floor tiles, and colorful accents of well-chosen textiles. The simple bedrooms have big baths, often tiled in attractively somber tones of grays and blues, plus secluded balconies. The large indoor pool has sweeping views over the snow-covered mountains which you can enjoy from the comfort of the heated water. Singles range from 445 AS ($23.67) to 575 AS ($30.59), while doubles cost between 385 AS ($20.48) and 540 AS ($28.73) per person, with half board included. Children under 6 stay free in their parents' room, while youngsters aged 6 to 11 pay 20% of the adult rates.

Grünwalderhof (tel. 77304), once the private hunting lodge of the counts of Thurn and Taxis, is today operated by members of the same family. The hotel stands on the site of an ancient Roman road. Proudly housed in one of the prettiest chalets in town, it has a pleasant relief of natural-grained lattice under the slope of its gabled roof, striped shutters, and a modern extension stretching out the back toward the secluded outdoor swimming pool. Inside, the ceiling vaults are covered with an artist's rendition of regional wildflowers, while the decor includes a scattering of antiques, lots of paneling, and a spacious and comfortable dining room filled with leather upholstered chairs. On the premises are a small indoor pool, a sauna, and a tennis court. With half board included, doubles cost between 335 AS ($17.82) and 600 AS ($31.92) per person, while occupants of singles pay a supplement of 95 AS ($5.05) per day. Prices depend on the season and the room.

Hotel Bär (tel. 77504) is an amply proportioned hotel that towers five stories above the alpine meadow where it sits a few hundred yards from the center of the village. The inside is covered with paneling tinted the same brown color as the hide of the animal the hotel is named after (a bear). It includes lots of attractive touches, such as big panoramic windows looking over the mountains, a carefully prepared buffet, an antique-style ceramic stove surrounded by a warming bench, an indoor pool, warmly appealing restaurants, and a bar. The cozy and well-furnished bedrooms cost between 430 AS ($22.88) and 565 AS ($30.06) for a single, and between 265 AS ($14.10) and 540 AS ($28.73) per person in a double, with half board included. Prices depend on the plumbing and the season.

Hotel Eschenhof, 1-3 Dorfstrasse (tel. 77472). Ideal for sports enthusiasts, this modern chalet maintains its own tow lift a few steps away from its wood and stucco facade. The modern and comfortable bedrooms are contained in a rambling, big-windowed extension behind the hotel. On the premises are several sunny lawn areas, an indoor pool, a sauna, a tennis court, and a big sun terrace for mid-morning coffee. The simple bedrooms have private baths and wood detailing, renting for 390 AS ($20.75) to 465 AS ($24.74) per person, based on double occupancy, with half board included. Occupants of a single pay another 35 AS ($1.86) per day. The Ostermann family are the owners.

MUTTERS: On a sunny southern plateau above Innsbruck, Mutters is just 6½ miles from the Tyrolean capital. You can drive to the center of the city from here in about 15 minutes, or get there via the Stubaital railway in just 20 minutes. The village is separated from Innsbruck by a wide green forest belt which lies above the city and the Inn Valley.

Mutters is in the skiing and recreation area of the Mutterer Alm and the Axamer Lizum, which were the central base for the sites of the 1964 and 1976 Olympic Winter Games. Mutterer Alm is the place for easy-going skiers. It can be reached by cableway.

Food and Lodging

Hotel Sonnhof, 12 Burgstall (tel. 33747), is a recently constructed stucco chalet in a quiet country location a few minutes' walk from the center. The simple streamlined interior has big windows, colorful accessories, and includes an indoor pool, a sauna, and access to a flagstone-covered outdoor terrace. The Ullmann family maintains the rustically modern bedrooms in top-notch condition, making every effort to perfect the savory cuisine served in the airy and attractive restaurant. With half board included, singles cost between 650 AS ($34.58) and 820 AS ($43.62), while doubles range from 575 AS ($30.59) to 790 AS ($42.03) per person, depending on the plumbing and the season.

Hotel Altenburg, 4 Kirchplatz (tel. 27053). The ground-floor entryway of this pretty flowered chalet is sheltered with a three-arched arcade, which serves as an attractive backdrop for the summertime café set up on the pavement outside. The interior is covered with horizontal planking, long ago sanded smooth and beautifully finished, while many of the ceilings are beamed and timbered and set with recessed pin lights. The elegant restaurant is filled with upholstered banquettes and conservative furniture, with big windows overlooking the mountains. Per-person rates, with half board included, range from 360 AS ($19.15) to 400 AS ($21.28) per person. The hotel is closed from the end of September until Christmas. The Wishaber family are your genteel hosts.

Muttererhof (tel. 27491) has a gabled roof and a dignified chalet-style facade within a few minutes' walk of the village center. Its balconies are covered with flowers. On the premises are a covered swimming pool with sliding glass doors that remain open in summer, an elegantly carved and paneled restaurant filled with carved chairs, leaded windows, and antique artifacts, plus a big lawn area with summertime café tables. Per-person rates range from 460 AS ($24.47) to 540 AS ($28.73) in a double, and singles pay a daily supplement of 40 AS ($2.13). Prices depend on the season.

AXAMER LIZUM: This resort was created for the 1964 Olympic Winter Games. It's about a half-hour drive, 11 miles southwest from Innsbruck. The highest station on the system of funicular and lifts is at Hoadl (7665 feet). You can also take a chair lift to Birgitzköpfl (6700 feet).

In summer you can take pleasure in hiking on alpine footpaths and attending folkloric evenings. Winter brings the opportunity to participate in sports for the whole family. A variety of tracks and ski runs, a natural ice rink, and ski-bob runs are here, plus the longest natural toboggan run in Tyrol. Three chair lifts and four ski tows serve the skiers who come here. Experts find some of the slopes at Axamer Lizum especially challenging.

Food and Lodging

Hotel/Sportpension Lizumerhof (tel. 8244) is an elongated, mountain-style building set on a forested hill within sight of the rocky bluffs of the mountains around it. Near the ski lifts, the hotel is family-run, cozy, unpretentious, and an attractive destination for summertime and winter-time lovers of sports. The dining room has colorful napery, lots of sunshine, and what looks like an 18th-century group portrait. My favorite room has a sloped ceiling and an onion-shape brick-and-plaster fireplace in the center. The Schäfermeier family are eager to be of service to their guests. They charge between 335 AS ($17.82) and 480 AS ($25.54) in a single and between 310 AS ($16.49) and 575 AS ($30.59) per person in a double, with half board included.

Gästehaus Pepi Kapferer (tel. 8739) is an unpretentious chalet directly in front of the ski lifts. In addition to offering simply furnished but comfortable rooms, only some of which contain private bath, the hotel maintains a ski school and a restaurant. With breakfast included, the per-person rates range from 280 AS ($14.90) to 310 AS ($16.49), depending on the season and the plumbing.

3. The Stubai and Wipp Valleys

One of the most beautiful valleys in Tyrol is the Stubaital, a 25-mile-long area with an endless vista of glacier tops and alpine peaks, some 10 miles from Innsbruck. From the Brenner Road you can fork off at Schönberg into the Stubaital, where you'll find little villages such as Fulpmes and neighboring Neustift which are both summer and winter playgrounds.

One of the first hamlets you'll encounter, and one of the most charming, is **Mieders** (3120 feet). From here a chair lift goes up to Kopeneck at 5350 feet.

If you decide to lodge in one of these little-known resorts, you'll find the prices favorable to your pocketbook. However, it's possible to stay in Innsbruck and drive through the valley, either by private car or on a bus, in a day. It's also possible to take a narrow-gauge electric train. If you travel by rail, you can only go as far as Fulpmes. After that, you must continue by bus.

The Wipp Valley, or Wipptal, is the valley of the Sill River, stretching from Innsbruck to the Brenner Pass. An autobahn—a great engineering feat—pierces the valley right on the outskirts of Innsbruck, going over celebrated **Europabrücke** (Europe Bridge), 625 feet high and 900 yards long. As you travel over it you'll literally feel that you're driving on a highway in the sky.

The **Brenner Pass,** known as the lowest gap in the major alpine chain, has been used since Roman times—and probably before. The pass marks the boundary between Italy and Austria.

Your first stopover in this section might be—

FULPMES: The major resort and the most ancient hamlet in the Stubai Valley is Fulpmes, surrounded by high mountains. Mention of a village here goes back to a document of 1344. The resort lies about halfway up the valley. Serles Mountain, to the south of Fulpmes, rises to a height of 8900 feet. You might enjoy an excursion up to Telfes, slightly more than a mile by road above Fulpmes.

Most visitors see the Stubaital on day trips from Innsbruck, but the resort, a spot to visit in both summer and winter, offers a wide range of excellent hotels charging moderate prices, a winning combination. In summer there's an indoor, heated swimming pool between Fulpmes and Telfes. Chair lifts operate in both summer and winter, one going from Fulpmes to Froneben at 4430 feet and one to Kreuzjoch, at 6900 feet.

If you're here at the right time you might enjoy a historical play presented about Tyrol's hero, Andreas Hofer, who led Bavarian and Tyrolean peasants against Napoleon and freed Tyrol from the French emperor's domination.

Food and Lodging

Sporthotel Alphof, Herrengasse (tel. 3164), is a four-story chalet on a quiet lane a short distance from the center of the village. Run by a family, it has an interior with lots of rustic details, such as a green ceramic stove, knotty-pine paneling in one of the dining rooms, and a restaurant with more formal chairs upholstered in mountaintop colors of evergreen and persimmon. On the premises is a sauna, and both indoor and outdoor tennis courts are close at hand. Doubles, with half board included, cost between 760 AS ($40.43) and 1000 AS ($53.20). Singles range from 420 AS ($22.34) to 540 AS ($28.73), also with half board included.

Hotel Pension Auenhof (tel. 2763). The lobby of this chalet has gently arched ceiling beams, lots of carved wood, and white plaster walls dotted with antique farm utensils. The salon has an unusual country baroque armoire with four different portraits painted on its double doors, and a wood-trimmed fireplace that curves toward one of the conversational areas. On the premises are a sauna and an attractive restaurant, and access is possible to lots of ski and hiking trails. A ski bus makes frequent stops at the hotel on its way to the slopes. With half board included, per-person rates, based on double occupancy, range from 360 AS ($19.15) to 480 AS ($25.54), except at Christmastime when rates go up about 100 AS ($5.32) per person. Singles pay a daily supplement of 60 AS ($3.19).

Sporthotel Cristall (tel. 3424) is a big-windowed chalet with four floors of attractively furnished, wood-paneled bedrooms. The in-house restaurant has a corner green ceramic oven, turquoise curtains, and a wholesomely alpine decor of wooden walls and ceilings. An intimate bar on the premises provides an attractive place to meet people. A summertime outdoor café is cantilevered above the slope of the hill into which this hotel is built, with an outdoor swimming pool visible from many of the flowered balconies. There's a sauna on the premises, as well as access to a host of sporting facilities. With half board included, doubles rent for 480 AS ($25.54) to 740 AS ($39.37) per person, while singles range between 500 AS ($26.60) and 780 AS ($41.50). Prices depend on the accommodation and the season.

Alpenhotel Tirolerhof (tel. 2422). My favorite part of this beautifully embellished double chalet is the central fireplace near the reception desk. It looks like something that a witch in an enchanted forest used to lure Hansel and Gretel into her house on a cold night. Its design of roughly applied stucco is curved around a widely splayed grate and fanciful andirons, and in winter it's usually kept burning most of the day. The rest of the hotel has dozens of elegantly rustic touches, such as the rich carving on some of the ceilings and the many rural artifacts strewn tastefully around the intimately lit interior. On the premises are an indoor pool, a hot whirlpool, a sauna, and access to the many nearby sports facilities. The well-furnished bedrooms rent for 465 AS ($24.74) to 660 AS ($35.11), with breakfast included. Singles pay a daily supplement of 40 AS ($2.13).

Hotel Pension Utzinger (tel. 3135). This four-story chalet has one of the prettiest facades in the region. The few windows without balconies are embellished with painted country baroque designs around their borders, while those windows with balconies look through a screen of burgeoning pink blossoms onto a view of the alpine hills. The reception area inside has a gently arched ceiling of honey-colored panels, while the rest of the hotel is tastefully filled with adaptations of chalet chairs, blazing fireplaces, and cozy niches. A sauna is on the premises, and management doesn't seem to mind if you mix up the sexes. The sunny bedrooms cost between 435 AS ($23.14) and 480 AS ($25.54) in a single and between 375 AS ($19.95) and 490 AS ($26.07) per person in a double, with half board included. Prices usually depend on the season.

Hotel Holzmeister (tel. 2260) has dozens of architectural details which a team of craftsmen probably took months to complete. Many of the vaulted ceilings are embellished with painted regional designs, while the woodwork on the walls and ceilings is painstakingly polished and elegantly ornate. The balustrade on the stairwell leading to the upper floors is appropriate to the style of architecture, while each bedroom is a unique statement of comfort and rural charm. On the premises are a sauna and a solarium, and there's access to the many sports facilities of this alpine village. With half board included, per-person rates range from 480 AS ($25.54) to 575 AS ($30.59), depending on the season. Each of the accommodations has a private bath.

Sporthotel Brugger (tel. 2870) is a traditionally maintained four-story chalet with a recently built combination of wood balconies, stucco walls, and a cozy interior with all the modern conveniences. In one of the restaurants someone has arranged a colorfully embroidered collection of cowbells on the wall, while in the main dining room the wood of the freshly upholstered chairs matches the amber-colored paneling on the walls. The spacious and comfortable bedrooms rent for 400 AS ($21.28) to 625 AS ($33.25) per person in a double, with half board included, and for 465 AS ($24.74) to 685 AS ($36.44) in a single, also with half board included. Prices depend on the season. Otto Bacher and his family maintain this establishment, along with a nearby pension whose rates are slightly less expensive. With half board included, tariffs at the pension range from 300 AS ($15.96) to 480 AS ($25.54) per person, depending on the season.

NEUSTIFT: The name of this village means "new monastery" or "new church," and in fact it's a few centuries more recent than, say, the 12th-century *New* Forest in England. But Neustift dates back to 1505, when Emperor Maximilian I did some hunting here and had a chapel built, called "das neue Stift." This village and others in the Stubai Valley have been in the tourist business since the 19th century, when mountain climbers discovered the area and made it accessible.

Neustift, about 3000 feet above sea level, is surrounded by extensive hiking trails for summer visitors, leading up to the glaciers of the Stubai Alps. The Stubai Glacier lift will take you to a dizzying 10,050-foot height, where year-round skiing is pursued.

There are baby slopes here, served by T-bars, or you can take a chair lift from Neustift to Elferberg, a favorite with advanced skiers. Elferberg is also known for its panoramic view and long toboggan runs.

Food and Lodging

Sporthotel Neustift (tel. 2509) is a pleasant wood and stucco chalet with heavy ornamental eaves and painted country baroque patterns around the windows. The cozy interior has all the paneled rusticity you'd expect, as well as wintertime fireplaces which illuminate the well-prepared cuisine in the mountain-style dining room. The Pfurtscheller family are the owners of this engaging hotel, which charges between 550 AS ($29.26) and 765 AS ($40.70) for a single and between 400 AS ($21.28) and 570 AS ($30.32) per person in a double, with half board included. Prices depend on the season, and apartments are available for between two and four guests. Each room has a private bath, a mini-bar, radio, and TV (upon request). A tennis court, fitness room, and sauna are on the premises.

Restaurant Hoferwirt (tel. 2201) is housed in a tastefully up-to-date building which blends easily into the style of the structures around it. The simple interior has immaculate napery and white walls which act as a good foil for the cuisine served by a staff of efficient local residents. Specialties include grilled steak Mexican style, a platter containing three kinds of filet with a brown sauce, an array of pork dishes, some of them rather complicated, and a dessert list that includes flaky crusted cream-filled strudel. Reservations are suggested. Fixed-price meals range from 95 AS ($5.05) to 145 AS ($7.71), while à la carte dinners average 110 AS ($5.85) to 265 AS ($14.10).

STEINACH IM WIPPTAL: This little resort lies at the head of the Gschnitztal, another lovely valley cutting through the Stubai massif. Gschnitztal is most often visited from Steinach. If you take a fast train out of Innsbruck, you can be in Steinach im Wipptal in about half an hour. Be specific as to where you want to go, as there's another Steinach in Austria.

With well-tended ski trails and excellent runs, Steinach is attractive to winter visitors, but it may be that summer tourists have the best of it here, with the beauties of two valleys to explore.

From here you can travel to **Gries am Brenner,** along the Sill River. Some 15 miles from Innsbruck and 8 miles from the Brenner Pass, Gries, at an altitude of 3810 feet, sits at the foot of the Padauner Kogel. This village too is both a summer and a winter resort. In the vicinity is the Brennersee, a lovely lake.

To reach Gries you must go up a steep road. Roman soldiers marched along this route in ancient times, as it was their road to the colonies of Rome in the north. The railway line from here cuts deep into dark tunnels, piercing the Alps until it reaches the border of Italy.

Food and Lodging

Hotel Steinacher Hof (tel. 6241) is a big elegant hotel loosely designed like a cross between a chalet and a private villa. The facade is assembled from weathered planking and white-painted stucco. Architectural details include a row of arched windows stretching toward the rear gardens, plus a large curved extension containing a sunny and light-colored attractive dining room which often has live music. The hotel has installed sun terraces on top of two of the building's low-lying extensions, although guests are free to roam through the gardens if they wish.

On the premises is a big indoor swimming pool, with a nearby cafè, an outdoor tennis court, an intriguing bar painted an eye-catching cerulean blue, and a Tyrolean-style restaurant with knotty paneling carved into neoclassical designs. With half board included, singles range from 555 AS ($29.53) to 620 AS ($32.98), while doubles cost between 445 AS ($23.67) and 590 AS ($31.39) per person. Prices depend on the season and the room, and all accommodations contain private baths.

Hotel Weisses Rössl (tel. 6206). In many ways this hotel is the center of social life in the village. From one side the hotel presents a lime-green neoclassical facade with white detailing and newly installed weatherproof windows. The older section has such antique details as vaulted ceilings, regional memorabilia, and a collection of weapons and hunting utensils from another era. In the chalet-style addition that stretches off the back, members of the Jakober family have installed cozy alpine-style bedrooms, with lots of custom-made carpentry and private baths. A stone-walled room on the premises contains an indoor pool with a nearby sauna and fitness room.

The dining room is large and sunny, and welcomes passing visitors as well as hotel guests. Per-person rates in a double, with half board included, range from 365 AS ($19.42) to 720 AS ($38.30). Singles pay a daily supplement of 50 AS ($2.66). Prices depend on the season and the room, and all units contain private baths.

4. Seefeld

Seefeld, 15 miles northwest of Innsbruck, is the third member of Austria's Big Three of international rendezvous points for winter sports crowds, the other two being Zell am See and Kitzbühel. This fashionable resort lies some 3450 feet above sea level on a sunny plateau.

Seefeld was the site of the Nordic ski competitions in the 1964 and 1976 Olympic Winter Games, to which it owes much of its renown. Skiers are served with 16 cable cars and lifts, 50 miles of prepared *langlauf* (Nordic skiing) tracks, and other cross-country ski trails. The major ski areas are Seefelder Joch and the Härmelekopf, with runs for those of varying degrees of proficiency, from novice to expert.

Other winter activities offered here include curling, horse-drawn sleigh rides, indoor and outdoor skating, horseback riding, and indoor tennis.

Summer visitors can enjoy swimming in either a heated, open-air pool or the lake, fishing, tennis, golfing on the largest 18-hole course in Austria, or walking on the 25 miles of well-tended paths.

Whatever time of year it is, you can try your luck at the **casino,** where roulette, baccarat, blackjack, and slot machines are played.

While you're based in Seefeld, it's relatively easy to explore parts of Bavaria in West Germany. You may or may not get to see little **Wildmoos Lake.** It can and does sometimes vanish all in a day or so, and then there may be grass and grazing cows on what has become meadowland. However, it will suddenly come back again, and if conditions are right, it will become deep enough for swimmers. Wildmoos Lake comes and goes more frequently than Brigadoon.

The little German town of **Mittenwald**, one of the highlights of Bavaria, can easily be explored on a day trip from Seefeld.

THE RESORT HOTELS: **Hotel Klosterbräu** (tel. 2621) is the most unusual and most elegant hotel in town. Constructed around a 16th-century cloister, the hotel combines so many architectural features that it's sometimes hard to believe that the view from the different angles are actually of the same building. The dramatic entrance is under a thick stucco arch which is only slightly wider than the rest of the arches which run along the ground floor. The interior contains soaring vaults supported by massive columns of the same kind of porous stone that built Salzburg (you can still see prehistoric crustaceans embedded in the stone).

Someone has taken pains to add plush accessories such as thick carpeting, Oriental rugs, intimate lighting, a scattering of antiques, and acres of beautifully furnished paneling, some of it carved into intricate designs. The modern sections blend discreetly into the older ones and give the added allure of, for example, a dome-shaped fireplace that juts gracefully into one of the well-furnished public rooms, as well as sweeping staircases and an occasional piece of old sculpture.

The bedrooms are encased in a towering chalet behind the front entrance. The windows look out over the midsummer buffet set up near the outdoor sun terrace.

In the evening the chicly dressed clientele often drop in at the Die Kanne nightclub, whose showgirls, comedians, and musical revues provide a high spot in the nightlife of the village. A daily afternoon tea dance in winter allows the hotel guests to meet one another. The big indoor swimming pool has a cafè area nearby, while an outdoor pool is visible from the sunny balconies of the well-furnished bedrooms, where you can enjoy breakfast if you want. Golf, tennis, mountain climbing, and skiing facilities are all within walking distance.

Rates for such a luxurious hotel are not cheap: singles rent for 1700 AS ($90.44) to 2150 AS ($114.38), while doubles cost between 1180 AS ($62.78) and 1780 AS ($94.70) per person. These tariffs include half board in the hotel's renowned restaurant, and prices vary according to the season and room.

Restaurants on the premises include a country-style Bräukeller with simple furniture and live music, a rustically elegant Tyrolean-style room with carved ceiling beams, pewter candelabrum on each table, and impeccable service, plus a more formal dining room where guests sit on wooden chairs upholstered in alpine patterns below ancient ceiling vaults.

Specialties include cream of broccoli soup, duck in orange sauce, sumptuous salads dotted with breast of marinated chicken, and a host of international and Austrian specialties. The person at the next table might be a vacationing celebrity from Germany traveling incognito. Fixed-price meals range from 215 AS ($11.44), while à la carte dinners average between 120 AS ($6.38) and 420 AS ($22.34). Reservations are suggested.

Hotel Astoria (tel. 2272) is a luxurious double chalet with a panoramic view of the Alps. Managed by Herman Schneeweiss, the hotel takes care to maintain the flowered terraces and the gardens in good condition, and offers an array of conservatively furnished public rooms, bars, and a well-known restaurant to its guests. An indoor swimming pool has tall windows looking out over the forest, with a sauna and exercise room nearby. An evening dance band complements the good international cuisine served in the dining room. Hotel guests have access to an 18-hole golf course, fishing, riding, tennis courts, and a wide selection of nearby mountain paths. The well-dressed clientele come from around the world, and pay between 1160 AS ($56.39) and 1600 AS ($85.12) for a single and between 970 AS ($51.60) and 1660 AS ($88.31) per person in a double. These prices, which vary according to the accommodation and the season, include full board.

Karwendelhof (tel. 2655) is one of the most elegant hotels in the Tyrol. It's constructed in a chalet format with two distinct sections, the exterior walls of which are painted in painstakingly applied regional designs. The 100-year-old Tyrolean-style parlors have parquet floors, heavily beamed ceilings, and lots of antique accents. The bedrooms are elegantly simple, often with at least one of the walls constructed of massive natural-grained planks.

The K-Keller nightclub is one of the social centers of the village, while a casino in an adjoining building opens at 5 every night.

Fritz and Elisabeth Wilberger are the engaging owners. Per-person rates, with half board included, range from 360 AS ($19.15) to 1300 AS ($69.16) in a double and between 410 AS ($21.81) and 1320 AS ($70.22) in a single. Prices vary according to the season and the accommodation.

The hotel restaurant, called Alt Stube, is completely covered in old paneling by now burnished to a rich mellow glow. Menu items include beef, veal, and pork dishes, usually accompanied by fresh vegetables, and followed by regional cheeses and home-baked pastries. Fixed-price meals cost around 180 AS ($9.58), while à la carte dinners average from 120 AS ($6.38) to 465 AS ($24.74). Reservations are suggested.

Schlosshotel Seefeld (tel. 2658). The location of this luxurious chalet is so superb that a legendary nobleman named Oswald decided to build a castle on the site in 1384. Little remains of what historical records say was a gray stone fortress, although today the fine appointments and modern-day comfort of this family-run establishment would tempt even a knight on horseback. The salons have Oriental rugs, an unusual full-length mural, and carefully constructed paneled ceilings.

The spacious bedrooms are simple and comfortable, and give a woodland aura because of the large amounts of exposed wood used to decorate them. A sunny flagstone-covered terrace looks out over the swimming pool in the garden. Half board costs between 750 AS ($39.90) and 1150 AS ($61.18) per person in a double, while singles range from 920 AS ($48.94) to 1160 AS ($61.71), depending on the season and the accommodation.

Grandhotel Hohe Munde (tel. 2191) is an inner-village chalet with six floors of big windows and flowered balconies. At night the lights from the café, bar, and graciously furnished restaurant shine through the big plate-glass windows onto the street outside. The rest of the hotel is conservatively and tastefully furnished with comfortable chairs and vivid colors. In winter the management hosts a five o'clock tea dance, and on the premises is a huge bar area, surrounded by dozens of upholstered stools. Per-person rates, with half board included, range from 455 AS ($24.21) to 900 AS ($47.88), depending on the season and the accommodation. Good food accompanied by live zither music is available in the Klause restaurant.

Hotel Lärchenhof (tel. 2383). The salons of this graciously appointed luxurious hotel are big and sunny, permitting a wide vista from almost any point within. You'll never need to worry about privacy, however, because of the intimate conversational groups scattered throughout the paneled interior. The wood-trimmed bedrooms often have curtained dividers between the sleeping areas and the sitting areas, as well as private baths and all the modern comforts. Guests are given ample chances to leave the shelter of their rooms for quiet moments on the flowered sun terraces which stretch over wide expanses of the second floor as well as over the hotel's grassy lawns. An indoor pool is on the premises. Singles range from 550 AS ($29.26) to 1080 AS ($57.46), while doubles go from 550 AS ($29.26) to 1400 AS ($74.48) per person, with half board included.

Alpenhotel Lamm (tel. 2464). The overhanging eaves of this elaborate hotel are supported by heavy beams that extend at an angle from the second floor to the outer edge of the roofline. The corners are rounded into protruding towers decorated with regional illustrations and designs, many of which are clearly visible from the village church next door. The cozy interior has ceiling beams, as well as an intimate bar, a scattering of rural artifacts and baroque sculpture, a dance bar, a sauna, a steambath, and a hot whirlpool. The most expensive bedrooms are fairly elegant and spacious. Singles cost between 650 AS ($34.58) and 1170 AS ($56.92), while doubles range from 550 AS ($29.26) to 1070 AS ($56.92) per person, with half board included. Prices depend on the season and the accommodation. The Seyrling family are your conscientious hosts.

Hotel Eden (tel. 2259) is a sprawling modern chalet with a facade covered with wooden balconies, a single painted illustration, and a wood and stucco extension jutting out from the front. An outdoor café contained within the natural windbreak of the hotel does a thriving business, both winter and summer. The simple interior has unadorned paneling, stone floors, big windows, and all the essential ingredients for the provision of comfort without excessive frills. You'll probably enjoy at least one drink at the curved wooden bar, or on one of its U-shaped banquettes, before retiring to one of the brightly colored bedrooms. These rent for 570 AS ($30.32) to 1000 AS ($53.20) per person, with half board included. The hotel is open only from December until April.

Hotel Post (tel. 2201) is an imposingly tall chalet with two peaked roofs and evenly spaced rows of dark-toned balconies. You'll probably be greeted in the paneled reception area by a member of the Schneider family, each of whom contributes to keeping this hotel running smoothly. The public rooms contain richly upholstered furniture and the kinds of soft lighting that will put you at ease. On the premises are a hotel disco, a shaded garden, two restaurants, and comfortably and invitingly attractive bedrooms. These rent in high season for 600 AS ($31.92) to 960 AS ($51.07) in a single and between 600 AS ($31.92) and 970 AS ($51.60) per person in a double, with half board included.

Strandhotel Seespitz (tel. 2218) has a large, welcoming design that usually reminds everyone who sees it of the perfect vacation house. Designed like an oversized chalet, with lots of interesting angles and corners, it's separated from the lake only by a well-maintained lawn and a barrier of water-loving plants. The inside is heavily beamed, airy, and filled with light from the big panoramic windows. Paula and Theo Faustmann are the congenial owners of this unpretentious hotel. They charge between 530 AS ($28.20) and 935 AS ($49.74) per person, with half board included. Prices depend on the season and the accommodation.

Hotel Wetterstein (tel. 2938). There's a delicacy to the wraparound balconies of this unusual hotel that can't be found anywhere else in Seefeld. The hipped roofs of the original gray and white-trimmed core rise above a well-planned addition containing the oversize arched windows of the public rooms. The overall effect is appropriate to its location as the village's best viewpoint over the nearby tennis courts, which are transformed into a skating rink in winter. The sun terrace is popular in all seasons.

The interior of the hotel is outfitted with a kind of no-nonsense masculinity which is unpretentious, friendly, and appealing. Parts of the bedrooms are usually covered with horizontal planking, while all of them contain private baths. Doubles are charged between 400 AS ($21.28) and 830 AS ($44.17), with half board included. Occupants of a single room pay 10% more daily.

Dreitorspitze (tel. 29510) is a six-story peak-roofed chalet whose comfortable bedrooms enjoy dramatic views of the mountains. The interior has a warmly appealing combination of honey-colored woods and subtle shades of red, which are contained both in the furniture's upholstery and in the vivid patterns of the dozens of Oriental rugs scattered throughout the public rooms. The hotel has an elevator, plus an indoor swimming pool, a sauna, a sun terrace, and a large garden with a putting green for outdoor golf practice. Per-person rates range from 515 AS ($27.40) to 1250 AS ($66.50), depending on the season and the plumbing. Prices include full board, which is personally supervised by the hotel's owners, Inge and Ludwig Morasch.

Hotel Tyrol-Alpenhof (tel. 2221) is a modern adaptation of a chalet, with four floors of white concrete shielded by wooden shutters and balconies. The main dining room has Empire-style crystal chandeliers, black and gold patterned carpeting, and white and gold Louis XVI–style armchairs. A less formal restaurant is darkly paneled and rustically intimate, with cozy lighting and a woodsy kind of elegance. On the premises are both an indoor and outdoor pool, a hot whirlpool, a disco bar, and at least one wintertime fireplace throwing off welcome heat. Per-person rates range from 560 AS ($29.79) to 1450 AS ($77.14), with half board included. Prices depend on the accommodations and the season.

Hotel Schönegg (tel. 2375) is a simple and functional chalet with an interior decor of conservatively modern furniture. A bar, restaurant, and a sauna are on the premises, as well as warmly contemporary paneling and furnishings. Close to the village center, the hotel is managed by the Schwenniger family, who charge between 390 AS ($20.75) and 815 AS ($43.36) per person, depending on the season, with half board included.

Sporthotel Stern (tel. 2235) is a simple chalet with green shutters, a red roof, and the friendly management of Hermine Schatz and Olga Wanner. On the premises you'll find a cozy bar area padded with leather, plus a paneled restaurant filled with rustic mementos. In winter there's disco dancing in the bar. With half board included, per-person rates in a double range from 335 AS ($17.82) to 420 AS ($22.34), depending on the season and the plumbing. Singles pay a daily supplement of 40 AS ($2.13).

Hotel Marthe (tel. 2505) is a generously sized chalet with golden-brown wooden balconies and shutters, plus a woodsy location a few minutes' walk from the center of the resort. Inside you'll find a heated indoor pool, a bar where you're likely to encounter a genteel member of the Hans Marthe family, an informal restaurant, and cozy bedrooms accented with lots of wood. Singles range from 420 AS ($22.34) to 840 AS ($44.69), while doubles cost between 360 AS ($19.15) and 840 AS ($44.69) per person daily, with half board included. Prices depend on the season and the room.

Hotel Christiana (tel. 2553) is a comfortable, contemporary chalet, with lots of exposed wood and a rustic, homey character. It has an indoor pool accessible through big glass doors in the cellar, thanks to the hotel's location on the slope of a hill. It also has a simple restaurant. Five pedestrian minutes from the center, the hotel charges between 300 AS ($15.96) and 550 AS ($29.26) per person, based on double occupancy, the prices depending on the season. Breakfast is included, and all units have private baths (many of them contain balconies as well).

WHERE TO DINE: Most guests book into a Seefeld hotel on the half- or full-board plan. But at least once you'll want to escape your hotel dining room, perhaps to try one of the recommendations described below.

Restaurant Locanda (tel. 2655) is a wood-covered Tyrolean restaurant with a sweeping view, handcrafted wooden banquettes, lots of mountain rusticity. Menu items include "seadevil" with chive sauce, fresh zucchini baked with cheese, several leafy salads, vealsteak Parma with buttered noodles, and a wide range of Austrian and Italian cheeses, pastries, and wines. Fixed-price meals range from 150 AS ($7.98) to 500 AS ($26.60), while à la carte dinners cost between 200 AS ($10.64) and 400 AS ($21.28). The restaurant is closed on Monday through the spring, summer, and autumn.

Sir Richard (tel. 2093) creates an elegant aura of year-round Christmastime because of its masses of flowers, dozens of burning candles, and the immaculately pressed linen that covers the wood tables. Whether the menu items prepared by the chefs are Italian or Austrian, they are presented on delicate china with attentive service. You might begin your meal with watercress soup, followed by one of a variety of lamb, veal, or fish dishes, often accompanied by masterful sauces. Even the fresh leafy salads have just the right degree of tartness. Fixed-price meals range from 145 AS ($7.71) to 840 AS ($44.69), while à la carte dinners can be anywhere from 200 AS ($10.64) to 455 AS ($24.21). Your meal will probably be accompanied by live Tyrolean music in a style which Austrians appropriately call "evergreen." Reservations are suggested, and the restaurant is closed on Monday between June and November. It's also closed for all of May and from mid-November until December 1.

Birklstüberl (tel. 2322) is a straightforward restaurant serving Austrian specialties in a rustically traditional environment. Specialties are well prepared and include fresh meats and vegetables, soups, cheeses, and homemade desserts. À la carte meals range from 95 AS ($5.05) to 265 AS ($14.10). Reservations are suggested.

Café Columbia (tel. 2448) is one of the best places in town for midafternoon tea or midmorning ice cream. The bentwood chairs are upholstered in vivid colors of deep maroon, which rest on a patterned carpet. You can sit outside under a striped awning if you want, or inside if the mood suits you better. Menu items include a wide range of pastries as well.

APRÈS-SKI: Seefeld in season bustles with typical wine and beer cellars, along with nightclubs and discos. Drinks in most places range from 50 AS ($2.66) to 75 AS ($3.99).

However, the major nighttime attraction is the **Spiel-Casino Seefeld,** at the Hotel Karwendelhof, already recommended. It opens at 5 p.m., offering baccarat, blackjack, and roulette. The casino is so popular that many visitors drive here from Innsbruck, 20 minutes away by auto. The Karwendelhof might be your entire stop for the evening, as it contains the

Alte Stube, a good restaurant, and a nightclub, K-Keller, that often presents shows with international artists.

The **Hotel Klosterbräu,** also recommended previously, is the center of the most sophisticated nightlife on the après-ski circuit in Seefeld. Its nightclub, Kanne, presents an international orchestra and a floor show during its hours of 9 p.m. and 3 a.m. In winter the club also opens at 5 p.m. for a tanz-tee (tea dance). The hotel also features international specialties in its restaurant, Ritter Oswald Stube, and a gemütlich atmosphere in its Bräukeller, open from 10 a.m. to midnight, presenting Stimmung music after 8 p.m.

Nachtexpress, inside the Hotel Columbia (tel. 2448), has a big dance floor, lots of colored lights, and a Tyrolean-style decor that's popular in midwinter.

Bar Tenne, inside the Hohe Munde (tel. 2191), offers a huge rectangular bar, rustic country-style decor, and plaid carpeting for an après-ski crowd who usually meet and mingle easily.

LEUTASCH: If for some reason you don't wish to anchor for the night in Seefeld, you can drive northwest through the Valley of Leutasch (Leutaschtal), which is one of the most scenic valleys in northern Tyrol. It runs under the Wettersteingebirge to the border of Bavaria.

Among the villages in this valley, Leutasch has the best food and accommodations.

Food and Lodging

Hotel Kristall (tel. 6441) has elegant two-toned designs embellishing the outside window frames and long rows of flowered balconies. The interior is outfitted with amber-colored paneling, stone detailing, and a combination of traditional and rustically contemporary furniture. The gemütlich restaurant usually has live music, while the hotel bar is a popular rendezvous spot. On the premises are an indoor pool, a sauna, an exercise room, a solarium, along with Ping-Pong and pool tables. The Bader family charges between 465 AS ($24.74) and 755 AS ($40.17) per person in a double and between 515 AS ($27.40) and 790 AS ($42.03) in a single. Half board is included, and tariffs depend on the season.

Hotel Leutascherhof (tel. 6208) is a three-story chalet with a big extension stretching out the back, plus a rounded bay window jutting out from one of the corners. The paneled interior is intimately lit, especially in the cozy bar and the dining room, where small framed pictures are scattered around for visual interest. The hotel was almost completely rebuilt in 1976, with private bathrooms added to each of the comfortable bedrooms. Per-person rates in a double range from 515 AS ($27.40) to 780 AS ($41.50), while singles cost between 580 AS ($30.87) and 825 AS ($43.89), with breakfast included. Prices depend on the season.

5. Resorts Around the Zugspitze

The Zugspitze, part of the Wetterstein Alps, is a frontier mountain separating West Germany from Austria. The highest peak, almost 9700 feet high, is in the neighbor country but can easily be seen from Tyrol. Its principal resorts are Garmisch-Partenkirchen in West Germany and Lermoos in Austria.

If you're exploring in this area, it's always wise to have your passport with you, as you'll cross the frontier if you follow my recommendations for this section of Tyrol.

Chances are, most readers of this guide will approach the Zugspitze from the Austrian side. If so, you can take a cableway, the Tiroler Zugspitzbahn, from Ehrwald-Obermoos, circling in a half moon through the Bavarian resort, Garmisch, and coming back to where you started. You can also take the trip by cog rail from Garmisch, perhaps departing from there, going up one side of the mountain and down the other, landing in Austria.

EHRWALD: With the most resort facilities of anyplace in the Tyrol section at the foot of the Wetterstein Alps, Ehrwald is popular in all seasons. It's one of a trio of resorts which includes Lermoos and Biberwier, sharing the same attractions (see below).

Bavaria, to the north, can easily be reached using Ehrwald as a base. Most visitors, however, just pass through Ehrwald to take the cable car for the ascent to the **Zugspitze,** one of the major attractions to be found in the west of Austria.

To reach the cable car, drive west from Ehrwald until you see a sign indicating Talstation Obermoos. Or you can take a bus from Ehrwald to that point. Here you board the Tiroler Zugspitzbahn, which will take you to the mittelstation at Gamskar (6610 feet). From that point you go to the Zugspitzkamm station (9203 feet), which had to be blasted out of the mountain rock. Your next stop is the summit of the Zugspitze, arriving at Zugspitzwestgipfel, 9680 feet above sea level.

A busy restaurant at the summit has windows with one of the greatest panoramic views in all of Europe. From here you can see Grossglockner, the Dachstein, and the Bavarian Alps. To the north you're able to see as far as the Starnberger See, a celebrated lake in Bavaria.

This cable car is at its busiest during the summer months. Service is hourly from 8 to 11:30 a.m. and 1 to 5 p.m. Round-trip fare is 350 AS ($13.30).

Food and Lodging

Hotel Schönruh (tel. 2322). From the flagstone-covered terrace on one of the upper floors, guests have a sweeping view of the fertile valley. This well-run hotel looks almost like a Mediterranean villa because of its curved walls, bay windows, and ornamental tower. Once you're inside, however, you'll know you're in a Tyrolean country house because of the crossbeam timbering, the roughly finished plaster walls, the ceramic stoves, and the mountain-style decor. Peter and Heinz Kotz take special care with the cuisine, which is served on immaculate napery in one of the two dining rooms. In winter, depending on the season, comfortable rooms rent for 430 AS ($22.88) to 650 AS ($34.58) per person in a double and between 400 AS ($21.28) and 685 AS ($36.44) in a single. These prices include half board.

Hotel Alpenhof (tel. 2345). The big chimneys visible from the outside let you know that wintertime fires will probably be throwing off a welcome heat indoors. The main salon has a bar, a fireplace, a coffered ceiling, and a welcoming color scheme of ambers, beige, and white which are appealing. Throughout this hotel you'll find charmingly rustic touches, such as the ceramic stove in the alpine-style Stuben restaurant, the acres of paneling, and the thick walls sometimes set with leaded glass. There's also a more formal pink-upholstered dining room.

In winter the management hosts a five o'clock tea dance with disco music in the café. The facilities include an outdoor tennis court, a sauna, and access to the village swimming pool. Per-person rates range from 380 AS ($20.22) to 720 AS ($38.30), based on double occupancy, with half board included. Tariffs during Christmas and New Year's rise slightly more. Singles pay a daily supplement of 60 AS ($3.19).

Hotel Sonnenspitze, 14 Kirchplatz (tel. 2208). Viewed from the front this 19th-century hotel is charming enough to look almost like an oversize cuckoo clock. It has a symmetrical facade whose entrance you'll reach from a two-sided stairwell rising gracefully from the street-level outdoor café. The ornamental overhang of the eaves is crafted into a baroque curve which shelters the flowers on the wooden balconies.

There is a lot of decorative stonework inside, as well as big arched windows, a warmly inviting color scheme, and a scattering of old armoires and antique pewter. The Leitner family are the owners of this congenial place. They close from mid-October to mid-December every year, but the rest of the time they charge from 480 AS ($25.54) to 575 AS ($30.59) for a bathless single and between 480 AS ($25.54) and 770 AS ($40.96) per person for a double (many of these contain private baths). Full board is included in these tariffs.

Alpenhotel (tel. 2254) is a pleasantly designed chalet-style hotel which has the unusual added benefit of having the terminus for the Zugspitzbahn cable car attached to its side. If you stay here, you shouldn't miss riding to the top for a meal or a snack in what's considered an engineering marvel and a panoramic delight. Back at the bottom, your simply furnished room with half board included will cost between 380 AS ($20.22) and 430 AS ($22.88) per person, depending on the season. All the accommodations contain private baths.

LERMOOS: About a mile to the northwest of Ehrwald is Lermoos, a resort attracting visitors in both summer and winter—and it's not bad in spring and fall, either. It joins with Ehrwald and Biberwier to form a trio of resorts close enough together to allow you to take advantage of the facilities of all three. The threesome is linked by bus, with departures about every 30 minutes.

Warm-weather pursuits, besides going up the Zugspitze (see above), include hiking, mountain climbing, easy strolls through meadows and forests, swimming, mini-golf, boating, fishing, cycling, riding in horse-drawn carriages (fiacres), and more.

When the snow falls, this becomes a white sports arena with, of course, downhill and cross-country skiing, ice skating, curling, tobogganing, winter walks, swimming in covered pools, and sunbathing(!). The carriage ride of summer is exchanged for a horse-drawn sleigh ride along snowy roads. Both Lermoos and Ehrwald have sleigh ranks on their church squares. You can reserve a vehicle for your ride between 10 a.m. and 4 p.m. daily. For more information, phone 28-94 at Lermoos or 27-36 at Ehrwald.

Whatever the weather, after dark you can enjoy Tyrolean evenings, learn to dance Tyrolean style, or just relax in a wine cellar or beer tavern.

Lermoos is well situated, set against the backdrop of the Zugspitze. You can take a chair lift to the side of the Grubigstein station (6500 feet), from which you'll have a magnificent view of the mountain peak. Via the chair lift, you can eventually reach the top station at 7215 feet above sea level.

Food and Lodging

Hotel Drei Mohren (tel. 2362) was built in 1806 and renovated in 1961. Its windows are crowned with regional embellishments, with a three-sided bay window extending toward the street from the white stucco facade. Management encourages its guests to go fishing for the region's legendary trout, pike-perch, and carp. The hotel owns a small lake nearby, where guests can swim. Other facilities include an elegantly simple sitting room, with heavy ceiling beams and lots of exposed stone, a series of inviting public rooms with wintertime fireplaces, and two statues of Moorish attendants waiting in stylized poses beside the elevator doors.

Its 50 rooms rent for 385 AS ($20.48) to 745 AS ($39.63) per person, based on double occupancy, while singles cost between 500 AS ($26.60) and 790 AS ($42.03), according to the season and the accommodation, with full board included.

Freshwater fish is the specialty of the chef, and platters are served in a restaurant appropriately known as the trout room. The menu in season also includes wild game. Fixed-price meals range from 135 AS ($7.18) to 240 AS ($12.77), while à la carte dinners cost between 120 AS ($6.38) and 335 AS ($17.82).

Sporthotel Zugspitze (tel. 2630) is a recently constructed chalet-style hotel, with painted designs around the windows, heavy overhanging eaves, and masses of flowers hanging from the balconies. Guests usually decide to spend some time on the sun terrace, which offers a view of the nearby mountains. The interior has big plate-glass windows, lots of exposed wood, and a rustic, homey feeling enhanced by Oriental rugs and light-grained furniture. In a restfully isolated position a few minutes from the center of the village, the hotel charges high-season rates of 435 AS ($23.14) to 655 AS ($34.85) per person in a double. Singles pay a daily supplement of 55 AS ($2.93).

Hotel Post (tel. 2281). The lobby of this pleasant hotel is decorated with antiques, including a baroque chest-on-chest with unusual legs. The decor includes beamed and coffered ceilings, a scattering of hunting trophies, a working ceramic stove, and a collection of contemporary and alpine-style chairs. The ambience is relaxed and attractively informal. A bar area often features evening dancing with live folkloric music. With half board included, per-person rates in a double are from 450 AS ($23.94) per day, with singles costing 500 AS ($26.60). An indoor swimming pool is on the premises.

Hotel Edelweiss (tel. 2214) is a modern chalet-style hotel with an annex that offers all the up-to-date comforts but also lots of rusticity. Both are near the Grubig chair lift. A large indoor pool is nearby, as well as a children's playroom. Per-person rates in doubles range from 390 AS ($20.75) to 720 AS ($38.30), with half board included. Singles pay supplements of 60 AS ($3.19) to 95 AS ($5.05) daily.

Hotel Tyrol, 10 Oberdorf (tel. 2217), is a hillside chalet with a distinctive design that includes a big sun terrace set on top of a curved glass-walled extension. The warmly tinted decor includes multicolored flagstone floors, panoramic views over the village, and a convivial gathering place near the bar's hanging copper lamps. A few minutes from the train station, near the nursery slopes, the hotel charges between 260 AS ($13.83) and 480 AS ($25.54) per person in a double room, half board included. Prices in the sunny, comfortable rooms depend on the season. Singles pay another 60 AS ($3.19) per day.

Hotel Bellevue (tel. 2151) includes an almost surrealistic illustration of a skier on its stucco facade and a host of balconies angled toward the sun. The place has much cozy comfort, including a rustic stuben-style restaurant, a convivial bar area with persimmon-shaped hanging lamps, and a convenient location near the ski lifts, one minute from the center of the village. Per-person rates range from 345 AS ($18.35) to 565 AS ($30.06) in a double and from 450 AS ($23.94) to 650 AS ($34.58) in a single. These tariffs depend on the season and include half board.

Après-Ski

There's nothing fancy here in the way of nightlife, but Teutonic revelers seem to have a good, often rowdy time. If you like to dance, you might check out the already-recommended **Hotel Tyrol**, which often has a live group playing for your entertainment.

Live groups often play for dancing at the Taverna bar of the also-recommended *Hotel Post*. If there's no live action you're likely to get disco music. The Post is also known for its Tyrolean folkloric evenings in season. Likewise, the Kellerbar at the just-cited Hotel Tyrol also occasionally stages these Tyrolean evenings.

When I was last at the recommended **Hotel Drei Mohren** they were having a beer-drinking competition, and I understand this is a regular feature. Here the action might be more Bavarian than Tyrolean . . . and a lot of fun.

When you return from the slopes after a hard day of skiing, everyone joins the throngs at the **Simon Konditorei** which has the best and most mouth-watering pastries in town, along with Swiss hot chocolate wearing a "top hat" of whipped cream.

Drinks in most establishments range from 50 AS ($2.66) to 75 AS ($3.99).

BERWANG: In the far-northern reaches of the Tyrol country, very close to the West German border and encircled by mountains, is Berwang, an as-yet-unspoiled village with friendly innkeepers. The little resort, at an elevation of 4400 feet, has both an upper and a lower village. In winter people enjoy skiing here with runs at varying stages of difficulty. The ski season usually ends in March.

You can reach Berwang by state road 189 from Innsbruck, or you may prefer to approach it by the main Bavarian highways heading south (for example, departing from Ulm via Kempten). From Garmisch in Bavaria, a good highway takes you here by way of Elbsee, crossing the border at Griessen and Lermoos. If you're traveling by train, the station to look for is Berwang-Bichlbach. Don't forget to bring your passport.

Food and Lodging

Alpenhotel Berwangerhof (tel. 8288) is a large, five-story hotel built in two interconnected sections. The generous balconies look out over the nearby village, the center of which is a few minutes away. The decor of the cozily rustic public rooms ranges from vintage Tyrolean to an up-to-date ambience of red upholstered chairs and vividly patterned carpeting.

Overall, the effect is enhanced with Oriental rugs, wide vistas of accommodating public rooms, massive wood detailing, and lots of alpine flavor. On the premises of the hotel is the largest indoor swimming pool in Austria. Manager Heinz Litt invites guests to a daily five o'clock tea dance, often with live entertainment, after which they can move onto their choice of three bars and several restaurants.

Closed from mid-April to mid-May, and from mid-October to mid-December, the hotel charges between 420 AS ($22.34) and 790 AS ($42.03) per person, with full board included.

The main restaurant in this international hotel offers an intriguing combination of the designs of several different countries, with a tasteful emphasis on honey-colored woods, coffered ceilings, painted embellishments, and unusual accessories. Menu items include lasagne, goulash, cold plates, and a variety of meats. Fixed-price meals range from 95 AS ($5.05) to 155 AS ($8.25), while à la carte dinners cost between 85 AS ($4.52) and 230 AS ($12.24). Reservations are suggested.

Sporthotel Singer (tel. 8181) is an elegant chalet with two interconnected sections, each with symmetrical peaked roofs. The interior has the kind of simple rusticity that gives the feeling that each object was carefully chosen by a skilled decorator. Many of the bedrooms have beamed ceilings, and the public salons are reinforced with massive timbers bolted and pegged into carefully finished paneling. There's also a darkly intimate bar. The Tyrolean-style bedrooms rent for 350 AS ($18.62) to 1150 AS ($61.18) per person, based on double occupancy, with half board included. Singles cost between 385 AS ($20.48) and 660 AS ($35.11), also with half board. Prices depend on the season and the plumbing options. Günter Singer and his family are the sports-minded hosts of this congenial hotel.

Gasthof-Pension Edelweiss (tel. 8223) is one of the loveliest chalets in town, lying at the bottom of the village near the Mulden and Sonnen lifts. It's been run by members of the Sprenger family since 1924, and today offers the same attractive hospitality as it did when it was established. The facade is embellished with designs around each of the windows, while a slightly protruding extension has a tongue-in-cheek illustration of a hardy farmer and his coy companion. The paneling on the interior extends into the comfortable bedrooms. Motorists will find an underground garage at their disposal. Per-person rates in a double range from 320 AS ($17.02) to 465 AS ($24.74), with half board included. Singles pay a daily supplement of 25 AS ($1.33).

Sportappartements Blitz (tel. 8272) is a rustically cozy hotel containing both private rooms and apartments for between two and six persons. The well-furnished apartments offer kitchenettes, but residents can also eat in the woodsy restaurant too. The public rooms are equipped with comfortable furniture, lots of hand-crafted paneling, a well-stocked bar with intimately concealed lighting, a sauna, and a big, tastefully simple reception area. The Hans Blitz family are the young and attractively informal hosts of the place. They charge between 150 AS ($7.98) and 300 AS ($15.96) per person. A big breakfast and half board cost an additional 60 AS ($3.19) and 100 AS ($5.32) respectively.

Après-Ski

The most popular place to go at night is the **Sporthotel Singer,** already recommended. Here a four-man band plays for dancing. Of course there's the usual round of kellers and stüberls. But what makes Berwang a bit exceptional is an array of very varied entertainment staged weekly in season, ranging from torchlit processions on skis to beauty contests to amateur nights.

REUTTE: The capital of the Ausserfern district, Reutte lies in the Valley of the Lech, north of the Fernpass. Its location on the traffic route between Füssen in West Germany, the Fernpass, and the upper part of the Lech Valley brings a lot of summer traffic through the town. Reutte is also served by the same train as Lermoos and Ehrwald.

This is mostly a summer resort, with three nearby lakes popular for swimming in summer, although I find them too chilly for my personal comfort. The largest and most attractive of the three lakes is three-mile-long **Plansee**, a body of emerald-green water lying four miles to the east of Reutte. In the Tyrolean country only the Achensee surpasses this lake in size. A short canal links the Plansee to the Heitenwanter See, one of the most beautiful lakes in Tyrol.

Included in the lake trio are the **Frauensee**, two miles northwest of Reutte, and the **Urisee**, about a mile to the northeast.

Many of the burghers' houses you'll see in Reutte are from the 18th century, most often with oriels and painted gables. The **pfarrkirche** (parish church) dates from 1691.

From Reutte you can explore the Lech Valley, which has developed a winter sports trade.

Food and Lodging

Hotel Urisee (tel. 2301) is a lakeside chalet with wood-trimmed loggias and monochromatic decorations around some of the frontal windows. It's surrounded by a wraparound sun terrace, while the interior has overhead pin lights suspended from crisscrossed ceiling beams and rustically attractive furnishings. The bedrooms are woodsy and outfitted in shades of brown and beige. With half board included, overnight rates are around 430 AS ($22.88) per person. During the peak midwinter holiday season per-person prices are about 75 AS ($3.99) higher. The Turri family are your hosts.

Alpenhotel Ammerwald (tel. 8131) is big on local color. Outside the center, the hotel is composed of two symmetrical sections joined in the middle by a connecting series of public rooms. The facade has big windows, cutout shutters, and a long expanse of white stucco stretching toward the back. The cozy, warmly tinted interior has amber-colored paneling, lots of orange and brown fieldstone detailing, and attractive textiles in autumnal colors of subtle reds and greens.

The quiet and sunny rooms rent for 275 AS ($14.63) to 540 AS ($28.73) in a single and between 275 AS ($14.63) and 475 AS ($25.27) per person in a double, with breakfast included. On the premises are a sauna, a swimming pool, a bowling alley, and a bar which has become a fashionable rendezvous point.

The Fraundorfer family, your hosts, seem to know every colorful character in the region, as well as dozens of international guests. Many of them enjoy the well-known restaurant, whose specialties include roasted hare in pepper sauce, wild venison (in season) with mushrooms, and an array of fresh salads. Fixed-price meals range from 120 AS ($6.38) to 180 AS ($9.58), while à la carte dinners cost from 100 AS ($5.32) to 480 AS ($25.54), depending on what you order. Reservations are suggested.

Hotel Tirolerhof (tel. 2557) seems to be one of the few hotels in the Tyrol not designed like a chalet. It rises five stories above the center of town in a simplified baroque style. The curved roofline is covered in red sheet metal rimmed with fragile ice catchers. The interior has an unpretentious decor of exposed wood, wrought-iron lighting fixtures, and simple, attractive furniture. The comfortable bedrooms rent for 400 AS ($21.28) to 480 AS ($25.54) in a single and between 380 AS ($20.22) and 455 AS ($24.21) per person in a double, with half board included. Prices depend on the plumbing and the season.

Food and Lodging on Lake Heiterwang

Hotel Fischer am See (tel. 29116), at Heiterwang, is a quiet, chalet-style hotel right on the lake. It has facilities for boating, a dock and beach area where guests can swim, and a well-maintained lawn and garden leading down to the water. The decor is rustically sunny, with lots of exposed wood and cozy niches. The Bunte family, the owners, close the hotel from mid-October until mid-December. Per-person rates, with half board included, range from 480 AS ($25.54) to 575 AS ($30.59), depending on the season. The restaurant on the premises serves well-prepared Austrian specialties.

6. The Lower Inn Valley

The Valley of the Inn River, called Inntal in German, goes through Tyrol from the southwest to the northeast, a distance of some 150 miles, separating the Swiss frontier at the Finstermünz and the Bavarian border at Kufstein at the far side. For the purpose of convenience in touring I've divided the Inntal into the Upper Inn district (see below) and the Lower Inn Valley.

The heart of a popular tourist district of Austria is formed by the Lower Inn Valley, the Ziller Valley to the south, the Alpbach Valley, and the Achensee area in the north. The section abounds in villages and small towns with lifts and cableways taking visitors on panoramic trips high in the air with magnificent vistas spread out before them.

If you're planning to overnight or spend a longer time in the Lower Inn Valley, you'll find the widest range—at least the best choice—of accommodations in Kufstein, the last Austrian town on the Inn before it enters Bavaria.

Your first stopover in the lower portion of the Inntal might be—

HALL IN TIROL: This old salt-mining town at the foot of the Bettelwurf massif, five miles along the river valley from Innsbruck, was a prize possession of the princes of Tyrol. No longer enjoying the prosperity of other days, Hall is now trying to make a name for itself as a spa to attract a tourist industry. You'll sometimes see it referred to as "Solbad Hall."

Even if you don't choose to overnight here, you may want to stop off for a view of Hall's **Obere Stadt**, or upper town. You begin your exploration at the center of the lower town, the Untere Stadtplatz. The heart of the old town, the Obere Stadtplatz, has many colorful buildings, often with oriels and grilles. Narrow little medieval streets branch off from the upper town square, which still functions in its age-old role as a marketplace. Two of the most charming of streets to seek out, really no more than cobbled alleyways, are the Sparkassegasse and the Arbesgasse.

The **parish church** (*pfarrkirche*), much improved in the 15th century, is in the late Gothic style, although the interior is rococo. The 15th-century Rathaus (town hall) has an attic like a pavilion.

SCHWAZ: About 17 miles northeast of Innsbruck, the old mining town of Schwaz, on the south bank of the Inn River, is even older than Hall in Tirol, just visited, going back to the 12th century. It came into prominence, however, from the 15th to the 17th centuries when it grew fat and rich from copper and silver mines. Today it produces only mercury.

Many of the burghers' houses remain from the town's time of great prosperity. In the Stadtplatz (town square), you can see the much-photographed, Gothic-style **Fuggerhaus,** with oriels, turrets, and an arcaded courtyard.

A Franciscan church, **Franziskanerkirche**, completed in 1515, has both Gothic and rococo touches and three naves. You can visit the cloister, which is pure Gothic. Here the church's treasure, nearly two dozen wall paintings depicting scenes from the Passion of Christ, is displayed.

The 15th-century **pfarrkirche** (parish church) of Schwaz is considered the largest Gothic hall church in Tyrol. It has a roof of some 15,000 plates of copper, worth a vast fortune. Inside you'll see a quartet of aisles and two parallel chancels. Seek out the altar dedicated to St. Anne in the south side aisle.

KUFSTEIN: A settlement at this site on the Inn River has existed for many centuries. Kufstein was first mentioned in a document near the end of the eighth century, and a Bavarian fortress was established here in 1205. In 1393 the settlement was raised to the status of a town by its ruling duke, Stefan III of Lower Bavaria. Emperor Maximilian I wrested the fortress from the Bavarians in 1504 and added Kufstein to the Austrian domain of the Habsburgs.

The old frontier fortress town has often suffered the ravages of hostilities between Bavaria and Austria through the centuries. The town was put to the torch in 1703, losing most of its early medieval character but not its fortress, which, although much added to and altered since the 13th century, still dominates the town, the last outpost of Austria in the Inn Valley.

Today only the memories of its turbulent past linger in this peaceful little holiday resort town, about 1650 feet above sea level, surrounded by woods and lakes with fields green in summer and snow-blanketed in winter. Much traffic between Bavaria and Tyrol passes through here, and it's a convenient touring point for the Kaisergebirge, the limestone range of the Alps.

A promenade runs along the waterfront in the lower part of Kufstein. An outstanding attraction of the town is the **Heldenorgel** (the organ of heroes) in the Burgerturm. This is the world's largest open-air organ, having 4307 pipes, and honors the Austrian and German troops who died in the two World Wars. In summer at noon and again at 6 p.m. recitals are given on the organ, which can be heard some eight miles away.

The **Festung** (fortress) contains a Heimatmuseum (local museum) in which you can see artifacts from primeval life in the Inn Valley and a display of illustrations depicting the war-torn history of the castle and the town. Highlight of guided tours is the Kaiserturm, or emperor's tower, a massive edifice finished in 1522. You can visit cells in which prisoners were held captive. The fortress served as a state prison as late as 1867.

Tours, each lasting more than an hour, are conducted through the apartments and cells of the castle from the first part of April until the end of October, starting at 9:30 and 11 a.m. and at 1:45, 3, and 4:30 p.m. (more frequently upon demand in peak season). The fortress is closed on Monday in April, May, June, and October. Admission is 22 AS ($1.17).

For the best view of Kufstein, visit either Pendling, a mountain across the Inn River, or else Heldenhügel (Mountain of Heroes), where you'll see a memorial dedicated to Andreas Hofer, the Austrian patriot who led a band of peasants made up of Bavarians and his fellow Tyroleans against the forces of Napoleon in 1809.

One of the most interesting excursions from Kufstein is to take the **Ursprungpass Road** which runs along for more than 15 miles, connecting Kufstein to Bayerischzell in West Germany (bring your passport). From Bayerischzell, you can begin your tour of the Bavarian Alps (see *Dollarwise Guide to Germany*).

Another excursion can be made to **Thiersee**, a tiny lake at the foot of a mountain. The lakeside village presents a Passion Play somewhat similar to the world-renowned one staged at Oberammergau in Bavaria.

Erl, another little town that merits a visit, lies about seven miles down the Inn Valley from Kufstein, near the West German–Austrian border. A Passion Play is presented here every five years, the next one coming up in 1988. This play originated here in 1613, but its production was abandoned for many years until its revival in 1959.

Food and Lodging

Hotel Andreas Hofer, 8 Pirmoserstrasse (tel. 3281), named after the famed Austrian patriot, is a modern building in the center of town. Its big auditorium is sometimes used for civic functions, but the hotel adjoining it is clean, comfortable, and contains features such as an informal café and beer hall with a wooden ceiling and a wall constructed from smooth river rocks, a four-lane bowling alley, a beamed restaurant with mountain-style chairs and medieval-style wall murals, a convivial red-upholstered bar area, and comfortable air-conditioned bedrooms. A big parking garage is on the premises. Rates range from 200 AS ($11.70) to 390 AS ($20.75) per person, depending on the plumbing and the room, with breakfast included.

Berghotel Pfandl (tel. 2460). A more outdoorsy place would be hard to find, especially since the only way you reach it is by hiking for around 40 minutes along a well-marked mountain trail. The hotel will arrange for transportation of your luggage from the garage where you'll park your car (called the Pfandel Garage und Parkplatz, it's indicated on signs from the center of Kufstein). If you're coming by train, a taxi will take you from the station to the garage, from which point you'll begin your climb. Both the excursion and the hotel itself are worth the effort.

At Kaisertal, the hotel was initially constructed in the 13th century. It's been under the direction of the same family since 1788. It has a covered cupola for a stork's nest, natural-grained cutout wooden balconies, and an elegantly formal interior with polished paneling and lots of well-constructed furniture. On the premises is an indoor pool, plus two restaurants serving savory Tyrolean specialties. Members of the Schwaighofer family charge between 420 AS ($22.34) and 540 AS ($28.73) per person, with full board included. It would be wise to phone before you begin your climb.

Hotel/Restaurant Goldener Hirsch, 19 Unterer Stadtplatz (tel. 4504), is a forest-green and white building with a baroque trim and a prominent storefront on the ground floor. Arno and Wolfgang Brandt, the owners, have installed a streamlined modern decor under the high coffered ceiling of the formal dining room. The functional bedrooms are furnished with slightly dated pieces, patterned wallpaper, and comfortable beds. Per-person rates, in a single or double, begin at 190 AS ($10.11), with breakfast included.

Hotel Post, 2 Unterer Stadtplatz (tel. 4524), offers simple rooms, friendly service, and what turns out to be a great bargain. At the edge of the lake, the hotel was once an elegant villa, now painted a vivid avocado green and considerably streamlined. The big-windowed restaurant extends in a modern addition on the ground floor. Monika Stecher, the owner, charges from 180 AS ($9.58) in a single and from 360 AS ($19.15) in a double, with breakfast included.

Gasthof Alpenrose, 47 Weissachstrasse (tel. 2122), is a modern stucco building designed like a chalet without balconies. It has a boxy extension partially trimmed with wooden planking, stretching off to one side. The alpine-style dining room is tastefully outfitted with a forest-green patterned carpet and a ceiling composed of wooden beams and detailing of the same color as the carpet. The hotel was built in 1971 in the center of town. Per-person rates, based on double occupancy, range from 445 AS ($23.67) to 540 AS ($28.73), and singles pay a daily surcharge of 85 AS ($4.52). Half board is included in the room price, which varies according to the season and the plumbing.

Zipfer-Keller (tel. 2396) is a vaulted cellar near the river. Its ceilings are painted with depictions of rural personalities and country designs, and the furnishings are unmistakably regional. The well-prepared specialties include tafelspitz with fresh horseradish, bacon-flecked sauerkraut, and a well-stocked salad bar that comes free with your meal, plus an array of Austrian favorites. À la carte meals range from 100 AS ($5.32) to 335 AS ($17.82). Reservations are suggested, and the cellar is closed Wednesday.

7. The Achen Valley

One of the most celebrated lakes in Austria and the largest in Tyrol—some say the most beautiful too—is the **Achensee**. This body of water, usually a light-green color, is 5½ miles long and about three-quarters of a mile wide, surrounded by coniferous forests with the majestic peaks of the Sonnwendgebirge and the Karwendelgebirge as a backdrop.

In summer the entire Achen Valley becomes virtually a holiday resort, with its little villages connected by a steamer which runs from one to another. This is of course the best way to see the lake. You'll notice lots of anglers trying their luck at fishing in the Achensee.

Although it's mainly known as a summer resort, the valley also attracts skiers in winter, with good snow conditions from December to April and five lifts with superb facilities for alpine skiing. More than 30 miles of well-tended cross-country courses take ski trekkers through woods and pastures into the Karwendel valleys. There are also cleared paths for long walks and rides in horse-drawn sleighs. Curling, skating, indoor tennis, bowling, and some minor après-ski activity make for a happy winter holiday.

How to get to the Achen Valley? It's not too difficult. At some point midway in your exploration of the Inn Valley you came to the town of

Jenbach, on the north bank of the Inn. From there it's possible to take a cog railway up to the lake. If you're driving you can head north from Jenbach along a road that winds around a lot at first, until it reaches Achensee. A bus also follows this route. If you're traveling by train you will be deposited at Maurach, at the southern tip of the lake.

Should you be seeking food and lodging, you'll find the most desirable accommodations in—

PERTISAU: This little village on the west side of the lake lies about three miles northwest of Maurach. It's the most frequented resort on the lake in summer, also doing a minor business in winter, attracting those who prefer a holiday in the snow.

Food and Lodging

Hotel Kristall (tel. 5490). During high season this tastefully decorated chalet is almost like a village within the village. Its public rooms are filled with the kinds of ornamentation that gives a rich, full look to the elegant room. Details include old polychrome sculpture, lots of paneling, gracefully curved wrought iron, and touches of brasswork and flickering candles. The richly decorated bedrooms rent for 515 AS ($27.40) to 720 AS ($38.30) per person, based on double occupancy, with half board included. Singles pay a daily surcharge of 95 AS ($5.05). Prices charged by the Adolf Rieser family vary according to the room and the season. There's also an outdoor swimming pool on the grounds.

Hotel/Pension Christina (tel. 5424) is a cozy hotel attached to one of the most attractive cafés in town (see below). The paneled rooms are outfitted with all the modern comforts, renting for 360 AS ($19.15) to 540 AS ($28.73) per person, based on double occupancy, with half board included. Singles pay a daily surcharge of 95 AS ($5.05). The hotel arranges for guests to take breakfast at the nearby Kristall, under the same management, and if they wish, to use its swimming pool and sauna.

Café Christina (tel. 5361), attached to the hotel, has Oriental rugs, green marble floors, upholstered bentwood chairs, and a rustically elegant decor of hanging potted flowers, well-polished wood, and pink napery. You can select a richly decorated pastry from the glass countertop, or order snacks and coffee at one of the tables. Coffee costs from 14 AS (75¢); pastries, from 20 AS ($1.06).

Hotel Rieser (tel. 5251) is a big chalet-style hotel surrounded by low-lying buildings which contain a pool, a sauna, a two-lane bowling alley, a table-tennis room, and a solarium. The public rooms of the main building are richly filled with Oriental rugs, comfortable wood-framed chairs, heavy ceiling beams, and a scattering of carefully inlaid antique reproductions. The color scheme throughout is woodsy and warmly tinted, especially in the dining room where the chef prepares generous portions of savory veal steak with pungent sauce, thick cuts of beef, and tasty regional specialties. Fixed-price meals range from 85 AS ($4.52) to 140 AS ($7.45), while à la carte dinners cost from 90 AS ($4.79) to 300 AS ($15.96), depending on what you order. Service is friendly and efficient.

Hotel Karlwirt (tel. 5268) is a five-story, antique-style chalet with sun-bleached wood balconies, country-style wood trim around the windows, and an interior decor filled with high ceilings, heavy beams, and cozy sitting areas (some of them near a stone fireplace). Franz Joseph came here on a hunting trip about a year before he was crowned emperor. The comfortably rustic dining room has elegant combinations of white plaster and light-grained wood, immaculate napery, and efficient service.

The best part about the comfortable bedrooms is the large areas of light-grained wood which usually cover at least one wall and part of the ceiling. In a nearby building, under ownership by the same family, is a popular restaurant, the Langlauf Stüberl, the tables of which are grouped around a central fireplace whose smoke rises through a metallic funnel.

With full board included, per-person rates range from 565 AS ($30.06) to 720 AS ($38.30) in a single and from 435 AS ($23.14) to 620 AS ($32.98) in a double. The hotel is a few minutes' walk from the center of town.

Wiesenhof (tel. 5246) is a pretty chalet whose dimensions are much deeper than they are wide. In addition to the long expanse of balconied bedrooms stretching to the back of the flowered facade, the hotel has a low-lying extension containing a rustically sunny restaurant, as well as an indoor pool and a solarium. The hotel is pleasantly located in the middle of a big grassy area, slightly removed from the buildings around it. Each of the tasteful and simple rooms has a private bath and lots of comfort. The Entner family charges between 370 AS ($19.68) and 530 AS ($28.20) per person, based on double occupancy, with half board included. Singles pay a daily surcharge of 40 AS ($2.13).

As an alternative to staying in Pertisau, you can drive north to—

ACHENKIRCH: A marvelously engineered road runs along the eastern shore of the Achensee, going through tunnels and affording delightful views of the lake which you might otherwise miss unless you get to take the lake steamer that runs in summer. If you take this road north you'll find the village of Achensee lying at the north end of the lake of the same name.

If you're seeking a good and inexpensive place for a lakeside holiday, go on northwest from the village of Achensee for about two miles, which will bring you to Achenkirch. This little resort has a number of moderately priced hotels serving good, hearty food.

If you continue north from here for about six miles, you'll be at the Achen Pass and the Bavarian border.

Food and Lodging

Sporthotel Achenseehof (tel. 6348). Aside from the evenly spaced windows, the only irregular feature on the facade of this hotel is its arched entrance and the single narrow opening which illuminates the interior's stairwell. The shutters are painted in stripes of red and white, and many of the ground-floor windows are protected with decorative ironwork. The establishment sits in a park-like area whose edges form a gentle curve extending like a peninsula into the lake.

The woodsy interior has lots of paneling, big windows, several fireplaces, and light-grained, heavily beamed ceilings. Josef and Karin Reiter, the friendly owners, charge between 370 AS ($19.68) and 430 AS ($22.88) in a single and between 300 AS ($15.96) and 420 AS ($22.34) per person in a double, with half board included. Prices vary according to the plumbing and the season.

Achentalerhof (tel. 392). The Waldhart family will gladly tell you about the dozens of mountain trails that abound around this pleasant chalet. On the grounds, guests appreciate the outdoor pool, the giant chess board, and the summer hammock attached between a tree and a flagpole. The interior has simple paneling, hanging lamps, and patterned tile floors. A bar area sometimes has live music in winter. With half board included, per-person rates range between 370 AS ($19.68) and 625 AS ($33.25), depending on the season. Each of the attractive bedrooms has a private bath.

Sporthotel Imhof (tel. 6309) is a pleasant chalet surrounded with an alpine meadow whose grasses are carefully trimmed in summer. The inside has a regional theme of masonry fireplaces, a beamed and paneling ceiling (sometimes in contrasting types of wood), and attractively simple bedrooms, usually with lightly finished horizontal planking over parts of their surfaces. The Kellerbar is a wine cellar with candles stuck into bottles, a bar area covered with a decorative roof of cedar shingles, and rush-bottomed chairs painted the color of a fire engine. On the premises are a sauna and a good restaurant. Each of the rooms has its own bath, and costs between 420 AS ($22.34) and 550 AS ($29.26) per person in high season, with half board included.

8. The Ziller Valley

Back at Jenbach in the Lower Inn Valley, from whence I suggested setting out northward to explore the Achensee Valley, I'll now take you south through the **Zillertal** (the German name for the celebrated Ziller Valley) east of Innsbruck, a resort mecca in summer and a playground for lovers of winter sports.

Some say this is the most beautiful valley with the most rewarding scenery in all the Tyrolean country. You may wonder about this claim as you go through the first stretches of the Zillertal, but don't turn back. It gets more impressive the deeper you penetrate into the valley.

When you first enter the Zillertal, you'll pass rich meadowlands where cows are grazing (if it's spring, summer, or autumn), looking as sleek and healthy as those in Switzerland. On your west will be the Tux Alps and on the east the Kitzbühel Alps, to which I'll devote space later on in this chapter. As tempting as it may be to head for these alpine areas, I advise continuing for the time being deeper into the Ziller Valley, which will suddenly grow narrower, the scenery becoming more dramatic.

The people of the Zillertal are said to be the finest singers in Austria, generation after generation of valley families having inherited magnificent voices and making use of their talent.

I always pass through the first of the little villages and resorts, since in my opinion better ones are ahead.

The first town that merits a stopover is—

ZELL AM ZILLER: Don't confuse this resort with Zell am See in Land Salzburg. Zell am Ziller is the major town of the lower section of the Ziller Valley.

Once it was a goldmining town, but those days are long gone. Today any gold mined here is from summer and winter visitors—but that's not meant to suggest that the resort is overpriced. Quite the contrary. Inns here are most reasonable in their prices, making Zell am Ziller a good choice for those seeking a budget holiday.

Like comparable Austrian villages, Zell has a **parish church** (*pfarr-*

kirche), this one dating from 1782. Constructed on an octagonal design, it's surmounted by a huge dome.

The best possible time to be in Zell am Ziller is on the first Sunday in May, when the residents of the Zillertal come together for one of the great folk events of Europe, the **Gauderfest**. This heavily attended occasion is like some huge May Day bash, honoring the ushering in of spring.

The glorious voices mentioned above fill the valley with song. It's very *Sound of Music*, and you expect to see Julie Andrews come prancing over some hill or meadowland at any time. At this centuries-old Maytime festival you not only hear the people of the valley sing, you also get to watch and listen as they play their musical instruments, particularly harps and zithers.

Music isn't all that goes on at the Gauderfest. The beer drinking rivals that at the Oktoberfest in Munich. Just for this occasion, a powerful (I say lethal) malt drink, Gauderbier, is brewed and lavishly imbibed.

Once this village was known only as a summer holiday site, but in recent times it has become a winter sports resort as well. In 1978 the Kreuzjoch area was opened to skiers, and Zell am Ziller took its place on the tourist ski maps of Europe. In season a free ski bus stops at the major hotels to transport guests to these slopes.

You can go by gondola to a restaurant with a view of the **Gründalm** (3350 feet), and then continue by chair lift to **Rosenalm** (5775 feet), where you'll find another restaurant, this one with a panoramic view. From Rosenalm, a drag lift can take you to a lofty citadel 7430 feet above sea level.

Another ski area, the **Gerlosstein**, more than three miles from Zell am Ziller, also has bus service, but not as frequently. From the bottom station, a cableway will lift you to 5400 feet where, if you wish to go on, you can take a chair lift up to 6020 feet.

If you're coming directly to Zell am Ziller, you can fly to the nearest international airport, Munich, in West Germany, and arrange your further transportation there. A narrow-gauge railway runs from Jenbach in the Lower Inn Valley up the Zillertal to Zell.

Food and Lodging

Hotel Tirolerhof (tel. 2227) is a five-story chalet with prominent balconies and a desirable location in the center of the village. On the premises is a Tyrolean-style disco with thick wood walls and lots of rustic detailing, as well as an intimate country-style restaurant. Local residents are likely to gather in the evening for some serious beer drinking, and no one seems to mind if you join them.

The cozy bedrooms have concealed lighting, comfortable beds with thick blue-gray quilts, and all the modern comforts. The hotel is an attractive choice for a stopover. On one night at least you're likely to be entertained by the Schuhplätter. A member of the Waidhofer family will quote you a price ranging from 340 AS ($18.09) to 415 AS ($22.08) per person, depending on the season and the accommodation. Singles pay a daily surcharge of 35 AS ($1.86).

Hotel Bräu (tel. 2313) is a five-story chalet with no frontal balconies. Instead its buff-colored facade is embellished with baroque *trompe-l'oeil* corniches around some of the window frames and heraldic symbols under the eaves. The elegant bedrooms have plenty of exposed wood to reflect the sun streaming through the big windows and well-chosen alpine furniture. Facilities include some very old furniture against the carved paneling of the public rooms, a flowering sun terrace near the well-kept lawns, and a gemütlich restaurant with immaculate pink and white napery and well-prepared food. With half board included, rates range from 315 AS ($16.75) to 425 AS ($22.61) in a single and between 290 AS ($15.34) and 400 AS ($21.28) per person in a double, depending on the season and the plumbing.

Berghotel Zellerhof (tel. 2614) looks like two or maybe three chalets joined together into a balconied format of exposed wood and white-painted stucco. In the center of the village, the hotel has an attractively woodsy decor which includes a big-beamed ceiling, a scattering of rustic artifacts, and cozy bedrooms with parquet floors and patterned area rugs. All of them are equipped with private bath.

Members of the Kröll family often provide a dance band which performs in a big room adjoining the main dining room. They also host a weekly barbecue in the cellar. Per-person rates, based on double occupancy, range from 460 AS ($24.47) to 510 AS ($27.13). Singles pay a daily surcharge of 45 AS ($2.39). Half board is included in these tariffs, which vary according to the season and the accommodation.

MAYRHOFEN: The road divides at Zell am Ziller, and to reach the next destination I've selected, you take the southwest route to the popular resort of Mayrhofen. After a visit there, I recommend that you return to Zell and then go southeast to Gerlos in the other direction.

But first, Mayrhofen.

This resort, standing at 2075 feet, enclosed by towering alpine peaks and lying at the foot of the glaciers crowning the adjacent Alps, is a premier summer holiday spot and winter playground, the finest in the valley in terms of facilities and accommodations. Some of the best food you'll find in the area is served here.

For decades Mayrhofen has drawn summer holiday crowds with its endless opportunities for rambling and mountaineering, hang gliding, shooting, tennis, fishing, swimming in a heated outdoor pool, mini-golf, cycling, and even summer skiing in the Hinterlux glacier area at the top of the valley.

However, in recent years the resort village has come more and more into the picture as a ski center. Starting from scratch, you can learn to ski at the school run by Riki and Ernst Spiess. The children's ski training is especially good here, and there's also a kindergarten, making this an ideal family resort.

Skiing is possible in the Penkenjoch section to the west of Mayrhofen, with a cableway taking you to nearly 6000 feet. Mayrhofen has always offered good skiing for beginners and intermediates, but now, with new Penken terrain, there's more for the experts. From the belvedere here you'll be rewarded with one of the most spectacular views you'll see of the Zillertal alpine range. There's a restaurant here too.

You can also ski in the Ahorn area, to whose 6250-foot height you're lifted by cableway departing from the south of Mayrhofen. At the top, five drag lifts wait to serve you. Also at the top station you'll find—guess what?—a restaurant with a panoramic view.

A wealth of other winter activities is available, including sledging on a natural toboggan run, alpine curling, ice skating, horse-drawn sleigh rides, horseback riding, and sports in an indoor arena.

Mayrhofen is a mecca for mountain climbers during nonskiing seasons, and you can find enjoyable nighttime entertainment ranging from tea dances to fondue evenings all year. You can also hear some of that famous Ziller Valley singing at folk festivals in July and August. The dates are different each year, so check at the tourist office.

Mayrhofen is reached by the Zillertal railroad, and one of the most popular diversions in summer is to take a ride on the narrow-gauge steam train between Zell am Ziller and Mayrhofen.

From here you can also embark on some important excursions into the Alps around the Zillertal, where you'll be rewarded with some of the most spectacular scenery in Tyrol. By the time you reach Mayrhofen, the trail through the Zillertal which you've been following will have split up into four different parts, each one tempting. These valleys radiate off the Zillertal like blades of a big fan, reaching into the Alps. Three of them have the suffix *grund* (the German word for ground) on their names: the Stillupgrund, the Zemmgrund, and the Zillergrund. The latter takes its name from the alpine range.

You may not have time to explore all these valleys, but if you can make time for one, I suggest you make it the fourth of the quartet, the **Tuxertal**, or Tux Valley, the loftiest one, which cuts like a deep slash through the mountains. This valley comes to its terminus at several glaciers, including the Olperer, 11,400 feet high. You can take a bus from Mayrhofen to either the village of Lanersbach or on to Hintertux, both in the Tuxertal. The road runs west from Mayrhofen for some 13 miles to the end of the valley from which ski lifts branch off in several directions.

You come first to **Lanersbach**, the largest village in the Tuxertal, lying in a sunny, sheltered spot. From here you can take a chair lift to the Eggalm plateau where there's a restaurant at 6560 feet. One of the most scenic panoramas of the Ziller Alps stretches before your eyes at this point.

Hintertux is at the top of the valley, which of course is your ultimate destination. Once in this village you're virtually on the doorstep of magnificent glaciers. There are views in every direction. Because of thermal springs, Hintertux also enjoys a reputation as a spa. You may want to buy some woodcarvings here, as the craftsmen in the valley are well known for their skill.

You can ski on the glaciers in summer. A chair lift or a gondola from Hintertux will transport you to Sommerbergalm (6800 feet). Once there, you can take a drag lift west to Tuxer-Joch Hütte (8300 feet).

Food and Lodging at Mayrhofen

Elisabethhotel (tel. 2929) is the most luxurious hostelry in town. The chalet-style facade has carefully detailed balconies, heavy overhanging eaves, a rounded stone entryway, painted designs, and a simple tower extending up from the center of the roof for whatever stork should build a nest there. The spacious and elegant interior is one of those tasteful places which only the right combination of money, taste, and skilled woodworkers can create. The bar area is a favorite rendezvous point, while the restaurant is outfitted in Zillertal-style decor which includes a gently arched wooden ceiling. On the premises are a marble-covered steamroom, a sauna, a solarium, a fitness center, and an indoor pool with half-timbered walls and a massively beamed ceiling.

Each of the rooms has a mini-safe for the storage of your family gemstones, as well as a private bath, TV, radio, and all the modern conveniences. High-season rates range from 950 AS ($50.54) to 1130 AS ($60.12) per person in a double and from 1000 AS ($53.20) to 1200 AS ($63.84) in a single, with half board included.

Alpenhotel Kramerwirt (tel. 2615) is a well-run hotel built Tyrolean style in the heart of the village near the church. There's been a hotel on this spot for the past 300 years, although the building you'll see today dates from around 1900. Its facade has stone trim around some of the windows, green shutters, a painted illustration of a medieval figure, and a tower-like construction high above the roofline. The rustic interior is paneled with dozens of examples of good woodwork, along with a scattering of Oriental rugs and antique painted chests.

Some of the romantic bedrooms have four-poster beds and big marble-covered baths. On the premises is a small indoor pool, plus a sauna and a Turkish bath. A gemütlich nightclub, the Andreas Keller, is—obviously—in the celler, containing exposed masonry, massive ceiling beams, checked tablecloths, and live musicians entertaining the drinkers and diners.

With half board included, per-person rates in a double range from 570 AS ($30.32) to 790 AS ($42.03), depending on the season and the plumbing. Singles pay a daily surcharge of 60 AS ($3.19).

Hotel Neuhaus (tel. 2203). Someone has lavished money and attention on the balconied exterior of this traditional hotel in the center of town. The forest-green shutters are well painted, while decorative talismans hang vertically from the slope of the slate-covered eaves. The hotel is actually a collection of large houses, all in the same style, connected together with passageways and walkways. The interior has both old and new sections, with a decor that includes both deep-relief carving in the 19th-century hardwoods and contemporary fireplaces built into the outside angle of a wall in the sitting room.

The dining room has an arched wooden ceiling, while the bar area might be a relaxed place for a drink before dinner. The spacious double bedrooms rent for 420 AS ($22.34) to 515 AS ($27.40) per person, with breakfast included. Singles pay a daily surcharge of 30 AS ($1.60). Half board is another 240 AS ($12.77) per person daily. Josef Moigg is the proprietor.

Hotel St. Georg (tel. 2794) has, as you'd expect, a painted illustration of the dragon killer himself on the chalet-style facade. The interior includes an indoor pool, lots of paneling, and attractively simple furniture. The balconied rooms rent for 550 AS ($29.26) per person at the height of the winter season (slightly less in summer). Half board is included in the price, and singles pay a daily surcharge of 50 AS ($2.66).

Hotel Neue Post (tel. 2131). The older of the two buildings which form this hotel was built in 1626. It has a romantically paneled weinstube with an elaborately coffered ceiling and lots of atmosphere. The newer part contains comfortable bedrooms, lots of big, sunny windows, and much modern comfort. Skiers tend to gravitate to the Tenne nightclub, which in winter becomes one of the most popular places in the village. There is friendly, efficient service, against a rustically attractive decor. There's also an underground parking garage in the building. Depending on the plumbing and the season, half-board tariffs range from 320 AS ($17.02) to 460 AS ($24.47) per person.

Gasthof Zillergrund (tel. 2377) is near a clear spring-water stream about a five-minute drive (or a 30-minute walk) from the center of the village. The impressive entrance hall is accented with lots of wood and an intricate Oriental rug, while the dining room has a ceramic stove and lots of exposed fieldstone. Rudolf Pfister is the congenial owner of this chalet-style hotel. He charges around 380 AS ($20.22) per person in a double, with half board included. Singles pay a daily surcharge of 15 AS (80¢). A large outdoor café sometimes serves as a destination point for visitors who want to make the trek up from the village.

GERLOS: It's not for the St. Moritz crowd, but Gerlos, a tiny resort in the Alps offering year-round pleasure, has its own special brand of warmth, hospitality, and fun which brings repeat visitors, people who are not seeking the international limelight. Gerlos is in fact a secret which its devotees rather hope will stay that way. For majestic mountain scenery, Gerlos is hard to beat, set against a backdrop of the Kreuzjoch, looming over the resort from its 9020-foot height.

To reach the resort, lying in a secluded, sunny valley at an elevation of 4065 feet, you take a winding mountain road from Zell am Ziller. If you drive to here in winter you'll need snowchains on your tires, but remember —no chains on the autobahn. If you're coming from Innsbruck, 48 miles away, for instance, you can get your chains put on as soon as you reach Zell. There's also a bus service from Zell am Ziller, the ride taking about 45 minutes, depending on road conditions. You should proceed cautiously on a drive to Gerlos even in warm weather, as the steep, winding road may be crowded with motorists.

Gerlos is a good ski resort, with runs ranging from beginners' slopes to those which challenge experts. You can take the Isskogel double-chair lift up to 5500 feet, where you can see a sweep of five valleys, glaciers, and peaks of the Alps.

Summer visitors find a broad choice of pleasures, from hiking on the mountain trails to sailing, windsurfing, and fishing in the waters of the mammoth Durlassboder reservoir just outside the village. Horseback riding is offered in summer or winter, and when trails are snowy you can take a sleigh ride.

If you continue along the road to the east you'll reach the Gerlos Pass and the Krimml waterfalls already visited in Chapter VIII on Land Salzburg. This Gerlos Pass road is one of the most scenic in Austria, linking the Ziller Valley with the upper Pinzgau region of Land Salzburg.

Food and Lodging

Hotel Gaspiner Hof (tel. 5216) consists of three large chalet-style buildings, each connected by underground passages and stairways. They're filled with antiques from the countryside, ranging from spinning wheels to grandfather clocks to just about the most beautiful painted armoires in the region. In one of the public rooms you might even stumble across a harp, and you'd be hard-pressed to avoid the polychrome crucifix hanging from a corner of the sunny restaurant.

On the premises you'll find an indoor pool, a sexually mixed sauna, and romantically rustic bedrooms. The manager, Franz Hörl, is also the chef, having trained in such places as New York and London. He's aided by his three sisters along with his helpful and vivacious mother.

With full board included, per-person rates in high season range from 400 AS ($21.28) to 840 AS ($44.69) in a double, with singles paying an additional 10%. An annex holds the overflow, and costs less than the main building. Per-person rates there, with half board included, range from 370 AS ($19.68) to 480 AS ($25.54), depending on the season.

Hotel Glockenstuhl (tel. 5217). The Eberl family are the owners of this wood and stucco chalet with the overhanging eaves and the neobaroque painting around some of the windows. A big-windowed café on the ground floor might be a worthwhile resting place for coffee and snacks, while the rustic bar area has daily live music in winter. The dining room is spacious and outfitted with a large crucifix against one wall. The spacious bedrooms have simple and attractive furniture along with comfortable beds. Per-person rates in a double range from 290 AS ($15.35) to 565 AS ($30.06), with singles paying a daily surcharge of 35 AS ($1.86). Half board is included in these tariffs, which vary according to the season and the plumbing.

Gasthof Pension Hubertus (tel. 218) is a hillside chalet whose three upper floors are covered with aged wooden planks and relatively ornate balconies. The two bottom floors are made of white-painted stucco, with an arched entrance, big windows, and a wide veranda covered with a rustic porch. The interior has a yellow-and-white ceramic tile stove, vividly painted antique furniture, and country-style curtains and ceiling beams. The spacious bedrooms have lots of exposed light-grained wood, renting for between 300 AS ($15.96) and 400 AS ($21.28) per person, with half board included.

Après-Ski

For such a small village the nightlife in Gerlos is surprisingly sophisticated, although it can be folkloric as well. Yodelers in lederhosen are likely to appear in any bar anytime, and chances are you'll definitely be entertained by a concert on an electric zither before you leave.

Gerlos has about eight clubs and dancing bars, each charging from 50 AS ($2.66) for a typical drink. Most of the nightlife activity takes place in the hotels, principally the already-recommended **Hotel Glockenstuhl** and the **Hotel Gaspingerhof.** Often you might find yourself dancing next to a visiting celebrity, including, on one occasion, Margaux Hemingway, traveling incognito of course.

9. The Alpbach Valley

To tour another alpine valley, this one much smaller than the Zillertal, you can take the road north again, branching off to the east north of Schlitters and heading east again to Reith. Once there you can cut southeast to one of the most delightful and undiscovered valleys in the Tyrolean country. Thomas Wolfe wrote home to his mother of the Alpbachtal that "the valley has some of the most beautiful mountains and villages" he'd ever seen.

ALPBACH: One of the smallest valleys branching off from the Inn set among rich meadows, dark woods, rivers, and mountains, this was a copper- and goldmining area ruled by the Fuggers in medieval times. The little settlement of Alpbach developed during that time. The town now enjoys minor renown as a meeting place of intellectuals, being the headquarters of the European Forum, an organization founded in 1945. Under its auspices, scientists, politicians, artists, and economists meet here to discuss the problems of the world.

From the village you can wander through meadows and forests to centuries-old farmhouses, nestling near high mountains, and enjoy warm hospitality and folkloric evenings in this tradition-steeped valley.

From nearby Brixlegg, a cableway will take you to the Grosser Galtenberg, a mountain standing 7960 feet high.

Food and Lodging

Hotel Böglerhof (tel. 5227) has a history almost as old as that of the town itself. Built in 1470 as the home of a bowmaker, it became a hostel, a courthouse, and later a prison for the errant miners of the region. In 1936 Thomas Wolfe stayed here in what was at the time a farmhouse. The owner between 1945 and 1979 was the mayor of Alpbach, and he did everything he could to restore it to its rustic glory.

Today what you'll see is two symmetrical chalets with sun-bleached wooden balconies and elegantly embellished ground-floor windows. In summer thousands of geraniums and petunias virtually seem to set the chalet on fire because of their vivid colors. The interior has lots of old detailing such as massive ceiling beams, exposed carved stone, shiny paneling, and in the bedrooms romantically carved and painted furniture.

On the premises is a double-level disco, plus an outdoor sun terrace, several bar areas, an indoor pool, and cozy restaurants where fresh-baked bread is a matter of course.

Per-person rates range from 600 AS ($31.92) to 1000 AS ($53.20) in a single and from 575 AS ($30.59) to 925 AS ($49.21) per person in a double, with half board included. Prices depend on the season and the facilities. Tennis players will be glad to know about the nearby outdoor courts.

Alphof (tel. 5371) is surrounded by light-colored wooden balconies, above which the heavy decorative eaves support a nesting tower for a stork's nest. The Jenewein family maintain their hillside hotel (a short distance from the center of the village) in top-notch condition, and eagerly respond to the inquiries of their satisfied guests. The interior decoration is cozy and rustic, and although the bedrooms tend to be somewhat small, guests usually amuse themselves at the big indoor pool, the public tennis courts, the sauna, the sun lawn, or in one of the restaurants or at the horseshoe-shape bar. There's usually a fire blazing in one of the fireplaces in the public rooms in winter. Per-person rates in a double range from 540 AS ($28.73) to 985 AS ($52.40), depending on the season. Singles pay a daily surcharge that can range from 75 AS ($3.99) to 265 AS ($14.10), depending on the season. Half board is included in these tariffs.

Hotel Post (tel. 5203) is a Tyrolean-style chalet surrounded by two tennis courts, a big outdoor pool, and masses of flowers. The interior contains a pub-style bar area popular with the après-ski crowd. The public rooms are filled with painted doorways and antique-style chests, along with lots of paneling and invitingly rustic detailing. A sauna offers a place to relax after a cold day outside. The Silberberger family, your hosts, charge between 500 AS ($26.60) and 685 AS ($36.44) per person, based on double occupancy, with half board included. Singles pay a daily surcharge of 120 AS ($6.38).

Hotel Alpbacherhof (tel. 5237). There's something streamlined and elegant about the simple interior of this hotel, almost as if the decorator wanted a lighter effect than is usually found in chalet-style hotels. Nonetheless the design retains the rustic beauty of exposed wood. The main fireplace is flanked with red marble and built into a manorial-style format with a gently tapering plaster-covered chimney. The Andreas Bischofer family, the owners, have installed both an indoor and an outdoor pool, along with modern baths in all the comfortable bedrooms. With full board included, per-person rates range from 780 AS ($41.50) to 900 AS ($47.88), depending on the season.

Haus Angelika (tel. 5339) is a super-bargain. Built in 1970, it's a comfortable alpine-style pension serving breakfast in a rustically paneled room with red and black accents. In the sitting room you'll often find a blazing fire. No meals other than breakfast are served here, but overall it's a comfortable and well-managed place to spend the night. It's in the center of the village, not too far from the local church. Per-person rates range from 210 AS ($11.17) to 290 AS ($15.34), depending on the season. The Steinlechner family are your hosts.

REITH IM ALPBACHTAL: If you're seeking something more luxurious than tiny Alpbach offers, you can drive back to Reith and stay at the four-star hostelry recommended below.

Hotel Kirchenwirt (tel. 2648) is a modern chalet with sunny windows and flowered balconies. The ceilings of the interior are elegantly geometrical and rather ornate, sometimes finished in attractive combinations of light and dark woods. Even the big indoor pool has a crossbeamed covering. In the sitting room the smoke from the central fireplace is funneled up through a bonnet hanging from above. The Rieser family are your hosts, charging from 455 AS ($24.21) to 765 AS ($40.70) per person in a double and from 635 AS ($33.78) to 815 AS ($43.36) in a single, with half board included. Prices depend on the season and the plumbing. On the premises are a sauna, a table-tennis and exercise room, and a children's playroom.

The neighboring town to Reith is—

RATTENBERG: This small border town of some 2000 residents, once part of Bavaria, merits a stop just to look around the old quarter. Rattenberg, annexed by Maximilian I to be part of the Habsburg imperial holdings, was once a mining town, but the industry died out in the 17th century.

The old quarter still looks very much a medieval and Renaissance town. Many of the burghers' houses are from the 15th and 16th centuries, their oriels supplying the householders with a view of the comings and goings on the streets (a pursuit which has been replaced by television). Many of the old houses are coated with stucco, and a lot of the doors and some windows are framed in pink marble.

The same pink marble was used for finish in construction of the *pfarrkirche* (parish church) which dates from 1473. The two naves were later given the baroque decorating treatment.

As you walk down Hauptstrasse (main street) to see the old houses, you might also like to go on a shopping expedition, to purchase some of the glassware and local handicrafts for which Rattenberg is known.

You may want to go to the **Burg**, the fortified castle built on orders of Maximilian I when he confiscated the town from the Bavarians. The castle is in ruins, and it's about a half-hour walk from the town, but visitors go for the panoramic view of the area. Sometimes dramas are presented at the castle in summer.

10. The Kitzbühel Alps

Hard-core skiers and what is euphemistically called "the colorful people of the international leisure set" are attracted to this ski region. The Kitzbühel Alps are covered with such a dense network of lifts that they now form the largest skiing area in the country, with a series of superlative runs. The action centers at the town of Kitzbühel, but there are many satellite resorts that are much less expensive, such as St. Johann in Tirol.

Kitzbühel is, in a sense, a neighbor of Munich, 81 miles away, whose municipal airport is used by most visitors who frequent the Kitzbühel Alps in wintertime.

KITZBÜHEL: Edward, Prince of Wales (you may remember him better as the Duke of Windsor), may have put Kitzbühel on the international map of fashionable ski resorts with his "discovery" in 1928 of what was then a town of modest guest houses. Certainly, his return a few years later with Mrs. Simpson caused the eyes of the world to focus on this town, and the "upper crust" of England and other countries began flocking here, placing a stamp of elegance and sophistication on Kitzbühel.

At the time of this 20th-century renaissance, however, Kitzbühel was already some eight centuries old by documented history, settlement having been here much, much longer than that. Archeological finds have shown that during the Bronze Age and until the ninth century B.C. copper was mined and traded in nearby mountains. The settlement "Chizbuhel" is first mentioned in documents of 1165, the name being derived from the ruling family of Chizzo. Kitzbühel was a part of Bavaria until 1504, when it came into the hands of Holy Roman Emperor Maximilian I of Austria and became a part of Tyrol.

A second mining era began in Kitzbühel in the 15th century, this time gold and silver being the products, and the town became fat and prosperous for many decades. Numerous buildings from the mining days are still here, as are remnants of the town walls and three of the gates. In what used to be the suburbs of Kitzbühel you'll see some of the miners' cottages still standing.

What to See and Do

The town has two main streets, Vorderstadt and Hinterstadt, and unlike St. Moritz where all the buildings are of modern vintage, Kitzbühel has preserved its traditional style of structures, at least in its core along these streets. You'll see three-story stone houses with oriels and scrollwork around the doors and windows, heavy, overhanging eaves, and Gothic gables.

The **parish church** (*pfarrkirche*) was built from 1435 to 1506 and renovated in the baroque style in the 18th century, restored again in 1951. The lower part of the **Church of Our Lady** (Liebfrauenkirche) dates from the 13th century, the upper part from 1570. Between these two churches stands the **Ölberg Chapel** (Ölbergkapelle) with a 1450 "lantern of the dead" and frescoes from the latter part of the 16th century.

In the **Heimatmuseum** (local museum), 34 Hinterstadt, you'll see artifacts from prehistoric mining times in Europe and of the north alpine Bronze Age; a winter sports section with trophies of Kitzbüheler skiing greats and displays showing the development of skiing here; and exhibits detailing the town's history. At one time this building was the town granary, built on the site of an early medieval castle. The center of the building is from the 13th century. The museum is open daily from 9 a.m. to noon.

In winter the emphasis in Kitzbühel, 2300 feet above sea level, is on skiing, and facilities are offered for everyone from novices to experts. The ski season starts just before Christmas and goes on until the beginning of April. With more than 50 lifts, gondolas, and mountain railroads on five different mountains, Kitzbühel has two main ski areas, the Hahnenkamm and the Kitzbüheler Horn. Cable cars are within easy walking distance, even in ski boots.

The linking of lift systems on the Hahnenkamm provides the celebrated **Kitzbühel Ski Circus,** which makes it possible to ski downhill for more than 50 miles, with runs that suit every stage of proficiency. Numerous championship ski events are held here, one being the World Cup event each January, when top-flight skiers pit their skills against the toughest downhill course in the world, a stretch of the Hahnenkamm especially designed and prepared for maximum speed. A ski pass entitles the holder to use of all the lifts that form the Ski Circus.

Skiing became a fact of life in Kitzbühel as long ago as 1892, when the first pair of skis was imported from Norway and intrepid daredevils began to slide down the snowy slopes at breakneck speeds. Many great names in skiing have since been associated with Kitzbühel, perhaps the most renowned being Toni Sailer, a native of the town, who was the triple Olympic champion in the 1956 winter games.

Of course there are many other winter activities offered: curling, ski-bobbing, ski jumping, ice skating, tobogganing, hiking on cleared trails, and hang-gliding, as well as such indoor activities as tennis, bowling, and swimming. The children's ski school provides training for the very young. And don't forget the après-ski, with bars, nightclubs, and discos rocking from tea time until the wee hours.

Kitzbühel has summer too, with activities including walking tours, visits to the Wild Life Park at Aurach (about two miles from Kitzbühel), tennis, horseback riding, golf, squash, brass band concerts in the town center, cycling, and swimming. For the latter, there's an indoor swimming pool, but I recommend going to the Schwarzsee (Black Lake). This *see,* about a 15-minute walk from the center of town, is a peat lake and has bathing establishments, boats to rent, fishing, a waterski school, and restaurants.

In either summer or winter, you can take the cable car which leaves for Kitzbüheler Horn (6550 feet) every half hour, costing 110 AS ($5.85) per person.

Kitzbühel is not a cheap place to stay, but to make things easier on your pocketbook, the Tourist Office, 18 Hinterstadt, has come out with a

Guest Card for summer visitors. This card is valid after being stamped by your hotel or guest house and entitles you to reductions, some of them quite substantial, on the price of many activities, plus some freebies.

Where to Stay

Although there's a wide range of hotels in Kitzbühel, reservations are absolutely mandatory in the high-season months, particularly the peak ski times such as February. As for Christmas in Kitzbühel, someone once wrote, "It's best to make reservations at birth."

Deluxe Living: The core of **Hotel Schloss Lebenberg** (tel. 4301) is a medieval knight's castle whose simple walls and turrets have been covered with a smooth layer of unblemished stucco. A modern extension looking vaguely like a cross between a villa and a chalet has been added nearby. The entire complex sits on a hill looking over the village, with dozens of mountain paths originating at its door. Very little of the castle's original decor has survived the passage of the years, and the interior is filled with wall-to-wall carpeting and modern furniture. Nonetheless the hotel is comfortable and inviting, with a large indoor pool, a range of health and cosmetic facilities, a big sun terrace, and an energetic social program. The breakfast buffet in the elegant dining room is lavish. The hotel charges between 545 AS ($28.99) and 1400 AS ($74.48) per person, based on double occupancy; singles pay a daily surcharge of 120 AS ($6.38). Half board is included in the price.

Parkhotel (tel. 4395) is an elegantly sprawling mountain-style villa with a half-timbered upper section and a solid lower section of thick gray stone. It stands in a large park slightly removed from the center of town, and has been known for years as one of the resort's most important hotels. The interior has an appealing combination of high beamed ceilings, wood floors, and thick plaster walls which virtually kill the noise between the rooms.

On the premises are outdoor tennis courts, an outdoor pool, an indoor fitness center with a hot whirlpool, a sauna, a solarium, and a café. The après-ski bar often has live music, especially during the winter, and an engaging crowd of chic habitués. Doubles cost between 530 AS ($28.20) and 1150 AS ($61.18), depending on the season and whether or not the accommodation has a private balcony. Singles pay a daily surcharge of 100 AS ($5.32). Half board is included in the room price.

Hotel Maria Theresia (tel. 4711) is a modern chalet with six stories of carefully applied decoration on its face and an interior where much effort has been spent on creating a woodsy and quality-oriented decor. On the premises are a large bar area, a stone-trimmed lobby with an open fireplace, a sauna, a Turkish bath, a Viennese café, and dining facilities. Much of the paneling is darkly tinted, even in the comfortable bedrooms. Per-person rates in a double, all of which contain a private bath, range from 540 AS ($28.73) to 1020 AS ($54.26), with half board included. Prices vary widely according to the season. Singles pay a daily surcharge of 40 AS ($2.13).

First-Class Choices: The ancestor of the **Hotel Goldener Greif** (tel. 4311) was built in 1271, and parts of it probably still remain buried within the massive walls of this well-known hotel. It was completely modernized in 1954, and the facade has a vivid series of *trompe-l'oeil* baroque frescoes which give a realistic illusion of depth to the windows. From another angle the hotel is pure chalet style, with lots of balconies and red and white shutters. Owner Josef Harisch likes unpretentious charm with a good dose of luxury thrown in.

In the heart of the old town, next to the Spiel-Casino, this hotel is a traditional favorite for lots of vacationers who'd prefer never to stay anywhere else. The vaulted interior contains open fireplaces, comfortable furniture, and a free-form swimming pool. With half board included, per-person rates range from 550 AS ($29.26) to 1200 AS ($63.84) in a double, with singles paying a daily surcharge of 60 AS ($3.19).

Romantikhotel Tennerhof (tel. 3181) looks a lot like a Tyrolean hunting lodge. A 15-minute walk from the center in a quiet and sunny park, the hotel is filled with regional antiques and carefully constructed paneling. Some of the public rooms have dramatically multicolored flagstone floors, ceramic tile stoves, well-placed hunting trophies, and a collection of elegantly comfortable chalet-style chairs. The view from the hotel's grassy outdoor café encompasses the pool and all of the village. Tennis courts are on the premises. Per-person rates, with breakfast included, range from 865 AS ($46.02) to 1320 AS ($70.22) in a single and from 700 AS ($37.24) to 1020 AS ($54.26) in a double. Prices depend on the season and the plumbing.

The Moderate Range: Schlosshotel Münichau (tel. 2962) is a 14th-century hunting lodge with red and white chevron shutters, at least three slate-roofed towers, and a severe design that could only be medieval. Lying four kilometers from the center of Kitzbühel, the hotel commands an impressive view of the mountains from its location in the center of lush alpine meadows. An outdoor pool and a few medieval buildings are visible from the windows of the individually decorated bedrooms. The public rooms are embellished with unusual engravings and covered with vaulted ceilings. You'll find at least three open fireplaces, as well as a rustically elegant restaurant. Per-person rates in winter range from 480 AS ($25.54) to 1280 AS ($68.10), depending on the plumbing. The cheaper units are in a comfortable modern annex a few steps away from the main building. Summer rates are slightly cheaper.

Hotel Jägerwirt (tel. 4281). The name of this place means "Hunter's Inn," and even if you don't like to chase and kill wild animals, you should love the blazing fires and the mellow paneling of this rustically attractive hotel. Designed like two small chalets joined with a central section, the hotel has a bar area with hewn overhead beams and friendly service, as well as spacious bedrooms with lots of exposed wood.

On the premises, a nightclub, the Halali, has an octagonal dance floor with dining tables set up around it and a timbered ceiling radiating out from the center like the spokes of a wheel. The Bartenstein family, the owners, charge from 360 AS ($19.15) to 1100 AS ($58.52) per person in a double and from 420 AS ($22.34) to 1150 AS ($61.18) in a single, with half board included. Prices vary widely according to the season. Both indoor and outdoor tennis courts are near the hotel.

Hotel Weisses Rössl (tel. 2541) is outside the town gate in an imposing L-shaped building with a flagstone-covered rooftop terrace that shelters a small swimming pool, a fountain, and swinging settees. Views from the balconies adjoining the well-furnished bedrooms encompass much of the surrounding countryside. The public rooms include a round dance floor with the hotel's insignia, a white horse, inlaid into its center, two dining rooms, and a sitting room with a formal fireplace and an Oriental rug. Winter rates range from 470 AS ($25) to 840 AS ($44.69) per person, based on double occupancy, with half board included. Singles pay a daily surcharge of 70 AS ($3.72). The overflow from the main building spills over into the nearby annex, whose rooms fall at the lower end of the price structure. Summer rates are slightly cheaper.

Hotel Zur Tenne (tel. 4444) might be considered one of the most popular hotels in town, frequented by a jet-set clientele who seem to return year after year, often asking for the same room. The simple facade is painted terracotta and buttercup, with a glass extension stretching toward the street in the center of town. The interior contains old Tyrolean artifacts, attractively mellowed paneling, open fireplaces, and an unpretentiously rustic collection of furniture. On the premises is a hot whirlpool, plus a health center area, along with a big nightclub/restaurant combination where guests look down on the dancing from two levels of balconies. Singles range from 670 AS ($35.64) to 1040 AS ($55.33), while doubles go between 1100 AS ($58.52) and 1850 AS ($98.42), with breakfast included. Half board is available for an additional 170 AS ($9.04) per person daily.

Hotel Tyrol (tel. 2468) is an attractively scaled chalet with five balconied stories and an open-sided wooden tower which the owners hope will eventually contain a stork's nest. In the center of town, the hotel has a simple decor and functionally practical bedrooms. On the premises is a large, somewhat bare dining room with clean linen and a wood-paneled bar area. Per-person rates range from 240 AS ($12.77) to 410 AS ($21.81), with breakfast included. Prices depend on the season and the plumbing.

Hotel Schweizerhof (tel. 2735) is a well-designed cross between a chalet and a mountain villa. It has a hipped tin roof, lots of balconies, and an exterior which looks like a different building from practically every direction you observe it. The interior has some attractive antiques, Oriental rugs, and lots of beamed and paneled ceilings. The hotel is close to the departure point for the Hahnenkamm cable car. Singles rent for 480 AS ($25.54) to 985 AS ($52.40), while doubles range anywhere from 540 AS ($28.73) to 900 AS ($47.88) per person, with half board included.

Hotel Klausner (tel. 2136), eight minutes from the center of town, is an ochre-colored twin-roofed building with a big parking lot and a quiet location. The interior has lots of stone detailing, both on its floors and in an occasional column supporting the wood and plaster ceilings. The attractively simple bedrooms have high ceilings and functional furniture. A big garden with a sun terrace is close to the rear entrance. Per-person rates, with half board included, range from 450 AS ($23.94) to 840 AS ($44.69) in a double, with singles costing between 500 AS ($26.60) and 900 AS ($47.88). Prices depend on the accommodation and the season.

Hotel Die Postkitsche, 30 Ehrenbachgasse (tel. 3291), has the kind of quiet good taste and generous use of space that only an elegant hotel can provide. The 18th-century entrance hall has chiseled stone columns supporting the vaulted ceiling, red stone flooring, and a gracefully curved stairwell sweeping past wrought-iron balconies to the upper floors. You'll recognize this place by the yellow and black chevron shutters, the baroque painting around some of the windows, and the elaborate wrought-iron sign arching over the street. Guests will find a bar, a weinstube with old paneling, and a beamed dining room serving French specialties. Each of the charming bedrooms has its own individual decor and much comfort. Per-person rates in a double range from 420 AS ($22.34) to 660 AS ($35.11); singles pay a daily surcharge of 80 AS ($4.26). These prices, which vary according to the season, are for bed and breakfast only.

Sporthotel Bichlhof (tel. 4022). Slightly more than two miles south of the center of the resort, this hotel offers panoramic views over most of the valley. Its tasteful chalet format includes a big covered swimming pool in a separate building, as well as a discreet decor of exposed paneling and patterned carpeting. The simple and spacious bedrooms sometimes have geometric grid patterns of dark wood against white walls that look almost Japanese in their simplicity. With breakfast included, per-person rates in both single and double rooms range from 635 AS ($33.78) to 800 AS ($42.56), depending on the season.

Hotel Tiefenbrunner (tel. 2141) is a generously proportioned five-story building with a modern facade of recessed balconies and two-tone trim. Inside this elegant place the management has built a large swimming pool, a sauna, and massage and exercise facilities. The first thing you'll see is a large, comfortably furnished entrance area, with discreetly patterned orange carpeting and lots of plaster arches. The dining room has a beautifully coffered ceiling and handsome modern chairs, while the bar area is intimate. This is a good choice for a stopover in Kitzbühel, especially since it's in the center of town, close to everything. With half board included, per-person rates range from 550 AS ($29.26) to 1330 AS ($70.46), based on double occupancy, depending on the season and the accommodation. Singles pay a daily surcharge of 100 AS ($5.32).

Mainly Pensions: About a mile from the center of town, close to the Schwarzsee, is **Bruggerhof** (tel. 2806), a countryside chalet with orange awnings covering its outdoor sun terrace. The interior has massively scaled ceiling beams, some of them carved into alpine patterns, and a warmly burning corner fireplace whose smooth stucco contrasts handsomely with the paneling around it. The dining room has geometrically patterned wooden ceilings and wrought-iron chandeliers, while another section has gracefully ornate stucco columns supporting the full-grained ceiling. Josef Reiter and his family are the owners, charging between 500 AS ($26.60) and 790 AS ($42.09) per person in a double, with half board included. Singles pay a daily surcharge of 60 AS ($3.19).

Hotel Hahnenhof (tel. 2582) is an old-fashioned villa at the foot of the Hahnenkamm. Its interior has fresh colors, lots of wall-to-wall carpeting, a scattering of antiques, and exposed ceiling struts composed of heavy beams. The hotel is a gracious place to stay, very quiet because of its isolation from the village, which is about ten minutes away. Per-person rates in doubles range from 420 AS ($22.34) to 625 AS ($33.25) and in a single between 515 AS ($27.40) and 745 AS ($39.63), depending on the season, with half board included.

Hotel Pension Alpina, 4a Hahnenkammstrasse (tel. 2731), is a graciously sprawling chalet with baroque ornamentation painted around the windows of its white facade. The interior is warmly furnished with lots of knotty pine and an assortment of autumnal colors. It has an indoor pool, modern bedrooms with only a few unnecessary frills, and an indoor pool. On the edge of a park, the hotel has a sweeping view of the valley. The Venlet family charges between 310 AS ($16.49) and 930 AS ($49.48) per person, based on double occupancy, with half board included. Prices vary according to the season, and singles pay a daily surcharge of 50 AS ($2.66).

Hotel Ehrenbachhöhe (tel. 2152) is an attractively isolated hotel at Hahnenkamm. Its chalet-style facade looks out over a wide vista of mountains, while from the warmth of the interior you can swim in the indoor pool, enjoy good cuisine in the warmly paneled dining room, or a few beers under the massively cross-timbered ceiling of the bar area. The attractively detailed bedrooms rent for 650 AS ($34.58) to 900 AS ($47.88) per person, based on double occupancy, and singles pay a daily surcharge of 60 AS ($3.19). These prices include full board and vary according to the season.

Gasthof Eggerwirt (tel. 2455) presents a beige-and-brown, traditionally designed facade to the street. The borders of the windows are embellished with country baroque paintings, while the modernized bedrooms have chalet-style furniture and colorful accessories. Toni and Frieda Hechenberger are the owners, charging winter rates of 250 AS ($13.30) to 385 AS ($20.48) per person, with breakfast included.

Where to Dine

Most guests stay at Kitzbühel on the half-board plan. It's also fashionable to dine around, checking out the action at the various hotels. With one or two exceptions, most notably the Unterberger Stuben, all the best restaurants are in hotels.

Wirtshaus Unterberger-Stuben (tel. 2101) is a preferred hangout for the rich and famous who come every year to Kitzbühel. In addition to an occasional German-speaking film star (or whatever), you'll also find a scattering of athletes, urbanites, entwined couples, and hunters. Overall, the ambience is authentically Tyrolean.

The owner, Mr. Unterberger, is the son of the town's most appreciated cook. Having learned to cook at his mother's stove, he and his wife decided to open this country-style inn in what had been his old family home.

In a setting of old paintings and rustic paneling, you are likely to be served one of your finest meals in the Tyrol. Try, if you see it on the menu, a poppyseed soufflé, or any of the specialties of the many countries which once belonged to the Austrian Empire. The fresh fish and the game are well prepared and savory. Dessert will probably feature (in summer) the succulent mountain berries of the region, or you might order the poached apples filled with white chocolate mousse.

An average meal will cost around 400 AS ($21.28), although it could conceivably rise or fall 200 AS ($10.64), depending on what you order. Reserve ahead and please be on time for your appointment. The restaurant is open from 9 a.m. to midnight, with warm meals served only between noon and 1:30 p.m. and between 6:30 and 10 p.m. The chef takes off during all of June and all of November and on Tuesday between March 15 and June 30 and from December 1 to 20.

Tennerhof (tel. 3181). You'll walk a short distance from the center of town before reaching the restaurant contained in this well-run hotel that looks like a balconied hunting lodge. The restaurant has a multicolored flagstone floor, a heavy beamed ceiling, and fern-green walls and tablecloths. Your attention will probably be directed toward the huge windows, whose view might give you pause between courses.

Specialties of the house include pungent lamb medallions, trout dishes, and a range of Tyrolean specialties. You'd better phone ahead for a table, since many of the guests staying at the hotel tend to fill up the dining room. Fixed-price meals range from 195 AS ($10.37) to 310 AS ($16.49), while à la carte dinners go from 200 AS ($10.64) to 360 AS ($19.15).

Restaurant Zur Tenne (tel. 4444). Even if you don't stay at this fashionably sporty hotel attached to this three-tiered restaurant, you'll at least want to stop in for a drink or a meal. The ambience is improved by the attitude of the young waiters who do everything they can to be helpful.

Scattered with antiques, the restaurant looks down on a floor that later in the evening is filled with dancers.

Menu items include steaks (which are sometimes grilled right at your table on a hot slab of stone) and Tyrolean specialties. Don't forget to stop for a nightcap at the adjoining bar area. Fixed-price meals range from 145 AS ($7.71) to 215 AS ($11.44), while à la carte dinners cost from 145 AS ($7.71) to 400 AS ($21.28). Reservations are important.

Schloss Lebenberg (tel. 4301). The royal family of Monaco has graced the dining room of this hotel. If the elegantly upholstered Louis XVI chairs and the discreetly striped wallpaper are not to your liking, you'll find three other dining areas nearby, all sharing the same menu. Fresh bread and butter are *de rigeur,* and specialties include cream of tomato soup with gin, calf liver Tyrolean style, and a tempting array of fresh desserts, many of them made (in summer only) with whatever mountain berries are in season. Fixed-price meals range from 215 AS ($11.44) to 310 AS ($16.49), while à la carte dinners cost from 145 AS ($7.71) to 385 AS ($20.48). The restaurant is closed from early April til mid-May and from early October until the beginning of December.

Goldener Greif (tel. 4311). The floor of this elegant restaurant is covered with a series of Oriental rugs, the white napery is spotless, and the ceiling is a webbed network of crossbeam panels. The effect looks like the inside of a hunting lodge. Specialties include a fresh cream soup made with brains, an array of schnitzels, and simple desserts. The menu is rather limited, although the ambience is warm and inviting. Fixed-price meals range from 90 AS ($4.79) to 145 AS ($7.71), while à la carte dinners cost from 90 AS ($4.79) to 300 AS ($15.96).

Stamperl (tel. 2555). Popular with the hardy locals who seem to survive in Kitzbühel even when the tourists leave for the season, this gemütlich restaurant is filled with old wood and lots of atmosphere. Marikka Lichter was a well-known popular singer in the German-speaking world, before she came here to direct the honest and savory food coming from the kitchen. Specialties include liver noodle soup, tafelspitz with roast potatoes and homemade horseradish, and an array of what is said to be the best ice cream in Kitzbühel. À la carte meals range from 120 AS ($6.38) to 335 AS ($17.82).

READER'S SHOPPING RECOMMENDATION: "I was fascinated by a shopping note in *Gourmet* magazine in an article by Lillian Langseth-Christensen. She lured me to the studio of **Leni Kuborn-Grothe** at 4 Franz-Reisch-Strasse, who makes embroidered jewelry. Unfortunately, since I cannot improve upon the words of Mrs. Langseth-Christensen, I'll quote her instead: 'Her [meaning Leni Kuborn-Grothe] embroidery is reminiscent of gold-encrusted peasant caps, and she designs everything from enchanting spangled hearts to royal tiaras. The tiaras weigh as little as a feather and look as though they come from the Tower of London.' I heartily concur with this recommendation. Most ski resorts often sell a lot of junky souvenirs, but not this place. Give it a try" (Reba Lowe Frazer, New York, N.Y.).

Après-Ski

Kitzbühel has about the best après-ski life in the Tyrolean country. Even before the approach of night the activity has already begun in the mad dash for a seat at the **Praxmair,** Vorderstadt (tel. 2646). This is one of the most famous pastry shops in Austria, and it's known for its florentines. Later on the Praxmair Keller pulsates with life, especially if the owner, Toni Praxmair, stages one of his Tyrolean evenings, complete with zither music and yodelers. Inevitably, the woodcutter's folk dance will be presented. But if it's still five o'clock, the item to order is hot chocolate with a "top hat" of whipped cream.

At the average place drinks cost from 50 AS ($2.66), rising to 75 AS ($3.99) in the more expensive establishments.

The biggest after-dark attraction is the **Spiel-Casino** (tel. 2300), in the already-recommended Hotel Goldener Greif. Opening at 7 p.m., it has a restaurant and a bar, in addition to offering roulette, blackjack, and baccarat. Its summer season is from July 1 to mid-September, and its winter season lasts from Christmas until the end of March.

One of the most popular places in town is **Zur Tenne,** Vorderstadt (tel. 4444). Usually the best live groups in town appear here, and dancers gyrate on the large floor. Every February "Miss Austria" is selected by a jury here. For example, Eva Rueber-Steier went on to become "Miss World."

Currently the chicest disco is **Drop-In,** Hinterstadt (tel. 2270). The **Alt Wien,** Vorderstadt (tel. 4746), also has a dance bar with a band.

If you want to escape overcrowded bars in the middle of the season, gallop over to the **Happy Horse,** a bit out of town at Ehrenbachgasse (tel. 3018). This disco is open only in winter.

Since most of the clubs of Kitzbühel are likely to be expensive, you might try the **Heurigenstadt Goldene Gams,** Vorderstadt (tel. 2611). The decor is neo-Grinzing, and you can order both hot and cold food here. You're even allowed to grill your own steak. A zither player is likely to be on hand to play *The Third Man* theme.

Try also the après-ski bar at the previously recommended **Park Hotel.** The ambience is atmospheric, and you're likely to be entertained by a singer accompanied on an electric organ.

If it's an English pub you seek, try **The Londoner,** Franz-Reisch-Strasse (tel. 3318), which lately has been very popular, drawing a chic crowd. There's another pub, also called **The Londoner,** Im Gries (tel. 4740), which is in the British pub style as well.

ST. JOHANN IN TIROL: St. Johann does not have the chic reputation of Kitzbühel, but neither does it have the high prices. Many "dollarwise" visitors stay here, taking advantage of the lower tariffs, and go to Kitzbühel, six miles to the south, to enjoy the facilities there.

This village, lying between two mountains, the Wilder Kaiser and the Kitzbüheler Horn, is both a summer holiday center and a winter ski resort. In summer it has a busy, open-air swimming pool, and in winter, good ski runs appeal to both beginners and experts. A ski school and ski kindergarten, plus cross-country ski trails, add to the attractions. Bars in the snow are popular.

Many old-style Tyrolean houses fill the little town with charm, and some of the old inns have frescoed exteriors.

The Kaisergebirge, near St. Johann, draws many European mountain climbers.

Food and Lodging

Hotel Fischer (tel. 2332) is a well-built chalet in the center of the village, with a copper-colored tree and hanging vines flanking the sun terrace, plus evenly spaced rows of wooden balconies. The sunny bedrooms are comfortable (albeit somewhat small), and they have private baths and wouldn't mind taking a short excursion to a restaurant with a vaguely South American theme, this might be the place for you. The thick cuts of meat are grilled any way you prefer, and they're seasoned properly for a maximum tenderness. Menu items include several kinds of soup (for instance, lobster bisque), roast beef Créole style, shrimp, frog legs, and a wide range of salads. Martha Erös, the wife of the owner and chef, is likely to be on hand to welcome guests to this popular restaurant. À la carte meals range from 140 AS ($7.45) to 315 AS ($16.75). The restaurant is closed all day Wednesday and for lunch on Thursday, and reservations are suggested otherwise.

WAIDRING: A Tyrolean village in the region where Tyrol, Bavaria, and Land Salzburg meet, Waidring is a popular holiday resort in summer and winter.

Summer visitors find 33 miles of well-tended walking paths, as well as high-altitude hiking trails on **Steinplatte** (6000 feet). In winter, Steinplatte offers ideal skiing conditions from December to mid-April, with a good lift system. You can go up the local mountain on the Waidring-Steinplatte mountain road if you prefer, although that's probably a better summer pursuit.

A ski school, illuminated natural toboggan run, curling, cross-country skiing, Tyrolean folklore evenings, and moonlight tobogganing add to the attractiveness of Waidring.

Food and Lodging

Sporthotel Tiroler Adler (tel. 5311) is a large balconied chalet in the middle of the village. Its balconies are covered in summer with masses of flowers, which contrast attractively with the weathered planking of parts of the facade. The interior has a woodsy contemporary decor that includes an elegant dining room and a slightly less formal restaurant with upholstered bar stools and light-grained paneling. Per-person rates in doubles range from 400 AS ($21.28) to 530 AS ($28.20), with singles costing an additional 50 AS ($2.66) per day. Half board is included in these tariffs, which vary according to the season.

WESTENDORF: This charming, friendly Tyrolean village lies at an elevation of 2575 feet on a sunny plateau in the Brizental (Brixen Valley) of the Kitzbühel Alps, undisturbed by through traffic. It's easily accessible by car, however, via the Inn Valley motorway to Wörgl and then the B70 Brixental road—but you'd better have heavy-tread tires on your car. You can also come here by train on the Innsbruck–Salzburg–Vienna railway.

Westendorf is surrounded by wooded mountains with walking and cycling trails, and summer visitors can ride the lifts up to the heights for views of the countryside.

For winter visitors the village has about 25 miles of prepared ski runs in use from the first of December until the middle of April, supervised by a well-organized mountain rescue service. Some 80 ski instructors are on hand to teach you how. Even tiny tots can learn to ski. The resort offers 15 chair lifts and T-bars, for which you need only one ski pass. There are good runs for both novice and intermediate skiers.

Other winter activities include sleigh rides, tobogganing, ice skating, curling, cross-country skiing, and after that, Tyrolean evenings complete with yodeling and whatever.

Food and Lodging

Hotel Briem (tel. 6310) sits quietly in a sunny meadow a few minutes away from the village center. It's designed in an attractively formal chalet format of recessed balconies, clean white stucco, and lots of painted ornamentation around the weatherproof windows. The interior is appropriately rustic, with a simple dining room and a lounge/bar area. Singles range from 375 AS ($19.95) to 415 AS ($22.08), while doubles cost between 420 AS ($22.34) and 465 AS ($24.74) per person in high season, with half board included.

Sporthotel Jakobwirt (tel. 6245). The Ziepl family are the owners of this charmingly traditional alpine-style hotel. The decorated building angles itself around an arcaded outdoor sun terrace with café tables and waitress service. The public rooms have massive ceiling beams, some of them carved, a hospitably rustic bar area, a scattering of antiques, and geometrically patterned tile floors in natural colors. Partly because of its location in the center of the village, the hotel's restaurants are popular throughout the year. These include an attractively formal dining room with pink-upholstered chairs and a woodsy weinstube with green and white tablecloths. High-season prices range from 500 AS ($26.60) to 540 AS ($28.73) per person, based on double occupancy, and singles pay a daily surcharge of 60 AS ($3.19). Half board is included in these tariffs.

Hotel-Pension Haus Veronika (tel. 6207). André Stöckl is the charming and hospitable owner of what turns out to be one of the most enjoyable guest houses in the village. Its painted and flowered facade is adorned with country baroque illustrations around the windows, with a slightly recessed ground floor whose entrance is sheltered by the overhang of a row of gently curving stone arches. The simple restaurant is immaculately clean and is covered with a pleasing combination of glowing woodwork and white plaster. The bedrooms are outfitted Tyrolean style, with painted headboards and alpine floral motifs. With half board included, per-person rates range between 240 AS ($12.77) and 450 AS ($23.94), based on double occupancy, with singles paying a daily surcharge of 40 AS ($2.13). All units contain private baths, and the owners speak well-modulated English.

11. The Kaisergebirge

This nature reserve of Tyrol is known popularly by its nickname, "Kaiser." Lying to the north of the Kitzbühel alpine range (see above) and to the east of the Inn River, this is a land of coniferous forests and meadowlands filled in warm weather with contented-looking cows, a land of much beauty, ideal for hikers and climbers. It has towering mountain peaks and gorges of untamed beauty.

The Valley of the Kaiser connects with the Valley of the Inn at Kufstein. It divides the 6560-foot-high Zahmer Kaiser (tame emperor) from the Wilder Kaiser (wild emperor), which has a jagged peak rising to 7690 feet. Essentially, the Kaisergebirge is a limestone mountain range.

I will have two stopovers in this district, one in the southern part at Ellmau and another in the far-northern section, Walchsee, a lake-district retreat close to the Bavarian border. St. Johann in Tirol (see above) technically falls within this area, but because of its situation as a moderately priced resort near high-priced Kitzbühel, I included it in the district just visited.

ELLMAU: This holiday resort stands at 2500 feet at the base of the Wilder Kaiser mountain and is considered the most beautiful spot in the valley. It lies in a triangle formed by Munich, Salzburg, and Innsbruck, within easy commuting distance of Kitzbühel. You can, of course, drive here. If you come by train, go to Kufstein, and from there a taxi will bring you to Ellmau.

In summer the little resort has an excellent hiking area and offers open-air concerts and Tyrolean evenings. It's also possible to take a cable car, the Hartkaiserbahn, for a panoramic sweep into the mountains.

Winter brings skiers to Ellmau, which has 10 lifts and well-maintained slopes. In addition, there are 52 more lift facilities in the surrounding area. In snow time you can participate in ice skating, curling, horse-drawn sleigh rides, cross-country skiing on well-kept courses, and of course, those Tyrolean evenings again.

Food and Lodging

Hotel Bär & Tyrol (tel. 2395) is a winning combination of at least six different buildings clustered together in an isolated position a few minutes' walk from the village church. The furnishings of the interior run the gamut from rustically modern (in the Hotel Bär) to 19th-century conservative (in the Hotel Tyrol), although the two styles compatibly merge with one another to the delighted approval of repeat guests.

On the premises you'll find flagstone floors, Oriental rugs, comfortable settees, cafés, bar areas, and romantically furnished dining rooms. Everything is outfitted with taste and gemütlich comfort, with lots of visual stimuli to tease your aesthetic palate.

In a separate building is a pizzeria serving attractive food in an informal setting. An outdoor pool is a short distance away, as well as an array of both summer and winter activities. Hotel guests have access to the tennis courts and golf course in nearby Kitzbühel. Also on the premises are a wide range of massage, beauty, and physical therapy facilities. Management works hard to organize camping outings and social events.

Each of the upper-crust bedrooms is decorated individually, with ample use of rustic planking and tastefully unusual colors. Lorette and Karl-Heinz Windisch are the hard-working owners here. Accommodations come in a wide variety of single or double rooms, including private outbuildings and apartments, some of them very luxurious. Per-person rates range from 660 AS ($35.11) to 2000 AS ($106.40) based on double occupancy, half board included. Singles pay a daily surcharge ranging between 120 AS ($6.38) and 180 AS ($9.58). Tariffs depend on the season and the room assignment.

Some critics say that the best food in the province is served on the pink or green napery of this elegant restaurant. Americans will be flattered to see that the menu includes wines from California as well as Austria. Management invites guests to look into the kitchen, where an army of uniformed chefs prepares such specialties as cream of crayfish soup, delicate salads of watercress, crayfish meat, and morels, as well as salmon steaks in a mustard and cucumber sauce, or rack of veal in a marsala sauce with leafy spinach. Desserts could include such delicacies as walnut ice cream with honied sour cherries. Prices for elegant repasts served here range between 210 AS ($11.17) and 660 AS ($35.11). Reservations are important.

If you're traveling with children, a day counselor named "Aunt Jola" will take care of them in winter and summer, involving them in an array of healthy outdoor sporting activities.

Hotel Hochfilzer (tel. 2501). The entrance to this lovely hotel is under an archway painted around its edges with intricate designs of vines and flowers. Above that is a depiction of a handsome peasant and his pretty wife flanked by flowered balconies and tastefully monochromatic paintings. The facade is only a hint of the kinds of personalized attention and detailing available in this rambling hotel. The friendly staff does everything it can to serve you at the thick-walled bar or in the cozy restaurant. The hotel has been owned by the Hochfilzer family since 1840. A modern chalet-style extension with lots of weathered wood and yellow shutters was added in 1973. Today the comfortable bedrooms rent for 550 AS ($29.26) to 800 AS ($42.56) per person in high season, with half board included. The supplement in a single, and also for use of the covered garage, is 75 AS ($3.99) a day.

Berghof Ellmau (tel. 2723) is a modern building with an unusual amount of big-windowed exposure toward the direct rays of the sun. About ten minutes from the center of the village, the hotel is efficiently managed by Mrs. Refle, who charges between 360 AS ($19.15) and 625 AS ($33.25) per person, based on double occupancy, with singles paying a daily surcharge of 95 AS ($5.05). These tariffs include half board.

Alpenhof (tel. 2692) is a pleasant chalet a few minutes from the center of the village, close to the ski school and many of the chair lifts. Its facade looks like twin houses adjoining one another, with evenly spaced rows of delicate balustrades set at the edge of the wooden balconies. The rustic interior contains comfortable bedrooms priced from 350 AS ($18.62) to 420 AS ($22.34) per person, with half board included. Tariffs depend on the season.

Sporthotel Ellmau (tel. 2721) has a gently sloping roof and long horizontal rows of balconies. Its elegantly sporty interior has massive wooden posts supporting heavy ceiling beams, blazing fireplaces set into stucco niches, and a big comfortable dining room. There is an indoor pool and a sauna, as well as a dance bar. Per-person rates range from 400 AS ($21.28) to 755 AS ($40.17) daily, depending on the season and the plumbing. Half board is included in these tariffs. Singles pay a daily surcharge of 35 AS ($1.86).

Hotel Kaiserblick (tel. 2230). *Blick* means "view" in German, and that's exactly what you'll get from the windows of this comfortable hotel. The sun terrace and the balconies are angled toward the village church, all of the Ellmau Valley, and the knife-edged mountains beyond. If you turn away from the scenery you'll see a hotel that is tastefully rustic, outfitted with clean napery, pleasant autumnal colors, and lots of well-polished paneling. An outdoor pool is set onto the lawn outside, maintained in good condition by the owners Johann and Paula Vötter. A gracefully curved stairwell leads up to the cozy bedrooms. Per-person rates, based on double occupancy, with half board included, range from 290 AS ($15.34) to 400 AS ($21.28). Singles pay a surcharge of 25 AS ($1.33) per day, and tariffs depend on the plumbing and the season.

WALCHSEE: Both a lake and a village lying close to the West German–Austrian border bear the name Walchsee. This is one of the most remote corners of the Tyrolean country, and although known to Austrians and Bavarians, is little known to the average North American traveler. The lake, one of the largest and most beautiful in Tyrol, is set against a backdrop of alpine meadows and dark forests. In summer the Walchsee has many facilities for water sports. To reach the lake, you can drive or take a bus from St. Johann in Tirol or else from Kufstein.

The little resort village has excellent accommodations and food at moderate prices, which helps explain its popularity with European visitors.

If you develop "lake fever," you can also go to the smaller **Hintersteiner See,** facing the Wilder Kaiser at an elevation of 2925 feet. However, the road to Lake Hinterstein is very poor.

Food and Lodging

Hotel Panorama (tcl. 5661) is one of the most pleasant hotels in the region. It sits on a hillside, affording good views from behind the flowers covering the dozens of balconies. A parasol-dotted sun terrace has been set up just outside the eight-foot arches of the ground floor, which are ringed with intricate two-toned designs. The inside is elegantly woodsy, with lots of exposed wood and much detail. On the premises is a hospitable bar area, plus an indoor pool which leads into a form of stone grotto. There are plenty of health facilities, as well as friendly, attractive personnel. High-season rates range from 530 AS ($28.20) to 730 AS ($38.84) per person, half board included. Tariffs vary according to the room assignment.

Hotel Schick (tel. 5331). The facade of this unusual hotel angles in a gentle curve toward an inner-village street. Sections of the white stucco are painted with soft shades of pink and blue into geometric regional designs. The interior has original uses of natural-grained pine, which acts both as a divider for the tables in one of the airy restaurants and as a warmly hospitable wall covering. Some of the decor includes half-timbered beams set into plaster walls, a round enclosure surrounding an open hearth which funnels smoke up from the center of one of the sitting rooms, and lots of soft lighting. The hotel maintains an indoor swimming pool, a wide range of health and beauty treatments, and access to nearby tennis courts with professional instruction. Per-person rates, based on double occupancy, range from 450 AS ($23.94) to 860 AS ($45.75), with half board included. Prices depend on the season, and singles pay a surcharge of 60 AS ($3.19). All units contain private baths.

12. The Upper Inn District

I've already introduced you to the Inn Valley that lies to the east of Innsbruck. Now on a much different excursion we'll go west from the Tyrolean capital in the direction of the remote western province, Vorarlberg. Along the way will be many detours and offshoots through valleys. At Landeck we'll depart from the westward trek, swinging directly south along the Inn, stopping off at the summer and winter resorts of Serfaus and Nauders as we head for the Italian frontier. Along the way, large mountains such as the Ötztal Alps rise on either side.

Heading west from Innsbruck, your first stopover might be—

ZIRL: Although Zirl, eight miles to the west of Innsbruck, is usually visited as a luncheon stopover, the town does a busy tourist business, lying as it does at the crossing point of the main roads from Munich, the Brenner Pass, and Innsbruck.

Food and Lodging

Goldener Löwe (tel. 2329) is a small and high-quality hotel whose 200-year-old alpine format was recently renovated into an attractively woodsy style of simple, comfortable rooms, each of which has a private bath. There's nightly Tyrolean dancing in the Löwengrube restaurant. If that doesn't appeal to you, there are also two rustic weinstubes. The Plattner family works hard supervising and preparing the specialties in the restaurant, which include freshly caught trout with chives and wild mushrooms, a host of regional specialties prepared with wild berries and natural ingredients, and excellent and imaginative desserts. Meals range from 120 AS ($6.38) to 290 AS ($15.34). Reservations are suggested.

Each of the comfortable rooms has a private bath. They rent for 500 AS ($26.60) to 565 AS ($30.06), and singles pay a surcharge of 110 AS ($5.85) daily. These tariffs include half board. The hotel also has some apartments available for up to four persons, and there's a garage on the premises.

KÜHTAI: From Zirl you can make an interesting scenic detour, leaving the Valley of the Inn for a while. Head first for Kematen, a village at the entrance of the Sellrain Valley and then west along the Melach Gorge. You'll pass through the valley villages of Sellrain and Gries, which I don't view as meriting a stopover, although Innsbruckers like to escape the city in winter and come here to enjoy the mountain air. After passing another village, St. Sigmund, you'll be on your ascent to the plateau at Kühtai, a high-up summer and winter holiday center.

This village, on the land register of the counts of Tyrol in the 13th century, was later a resort of emperors. Maximilian I acquired the shooting rights in Kühtai in 1497, and an imperial hunting seat was built beginning about 1622, by Archduke Leopold. The Jagdschloss, or hunting lodge, remains from that time and is now one of the most delightful accommodations in this section of the guide (see below).

Kühtai offers winter recreation, including ski slopes for all stages of expertise, cross-country tracks, and ski-bobbing, with snow "guaranteed" from November to May. A ski school and ski kindergarten add to the attractions, with après-ski enjoyment provided.

From Kühtai the road continues into the Ötz Valley, which I will treat separately in an upcoming division. For the purposes of this section, however, I'll take you northwest from the town of Ötz to Imst, another major stopover along the Upper Inn region.

Food and Lodging

Jagdschloss Kütai (tel. 201). The charming and aristocratically elegant grandson of Kaiser Joseph, Count Stolberg-Stolberg, is the owner of this former hunting lodge, parts of which date from 1450. Archduke Leopold ordered a more recent version built on this site, incorporating parts of an older building. What you see today is a solidly constructed chalet with red and white chevron shutters and a stunning view over the countryside. Many of the massively paneled and timbered public rooms contain vaulted ceilings and furnishings dating back to the 17th century. These include very old chests, glistening brass chandeliers, antique engravings, and carefully grouped hunting trophies. Rates range from 540 AS ($28.73) to 1040 AS ($55.33) per person, with half board included. The rooms at the cheaper end of the price scale are sometimes located in the comfortable annex nearby.

The cozily rustic restaurant has the kind of paneling you'd want in your own home. Everything about this place reeks of atmosphere and style. The chefs use the best quality meats to produce their specialties. The beef Stroganoff is heavenly. The leafy salads appear to have been picked minutes ago, and the desserts are richly satisfying combinations of chocolate, pastries, and fruit. Meals range from 160 AS ($8.51) to 340 AS ($18.09). Unfortunately for summer visitors this hotel is closed between May and November.

Hotel Mooshaus (tel. 277) is a homey, family-run hotel, Tyrolean style, which stands in the heart of the village not far from the ski lifts. Its public rooms include gently arched beamed ceilings, as well as wrought iron accents dividing the congenial bar area from the rest of the establishment. The 48 rooms have all the conveniences, such as a private bath and phone. Some of the units also contain private balconies. On the premises you'll find a sauna, a solarium, and a sun terrace. In the Zirbenholzbar you'll be entertained by once-a-week dancing and special dinners.

High-season rates range from 445 AS ($23.67) to 815 AS ($43.36) per person, based on double occupancy, and from 565 AS ($30.06) to 850 AS ($45.22) in a single, with half board included. If you visit at Christmas, however, there's a surcharge.

Specialties in the rustically appointed restaurant are perfect for appetites sharpened by a day outdoors. They include pork medallions in a mushroom cream sauce with spätzle, veal steak with mushrooms, and an unusual collection of ice creams, crème caramels, and special coffees (some of them mildly intoxicating). Meals range from 110 AS ($5.85) to 340 AS ($18.09). Reservations are suggested.

Hotel Tyrol (tel. 208). There's something starkly dramatic about the balconied facade of this mountainside hotel. The enormous sun terrace butts against the masonry-covered side of the building and looks out over a richly romantic view of the mountains. The wooden balconies are vertically interconnected with angled struts which originate at the building's base and eventually rise to support the heavy overhang of the eaves.

On the premises you'll find an indoor swimming pool with big-windowed views over the countryside, a pleasant dining room, a fitness room, table tennis, and a sauna. High-season rates range between 480 AS ($25.54) and 755 AS ($40.17) in a single and between 400 AS ($21.28) and 755 AS ($40.17) per person in a double, with full board included. Prices depend on the time of year and the plumbing. Disco-holics will find dancing in the basement. The owners are Josef and Traudl Härting. Some bed-sitting rooms are available housing two to five persons.

IMST: An old market town on a terrace above the river, Imst, at the mouth of the Gurgl Valley, is used as an overnight stop for many motorists as it lies at the junction of the Innsbruck-Landeck route. This is a good center for exploring the Pitz Valley and the Ötz Valley.

Imst is divided into an upper town (Oberstadt) and a lower town. If you're rushed, skip the lower one and visit Oberstadt. Its 15th-century **pfarrkirche** (parish church) was reconstructed after being swept by fire in 1822. The steeple of this large edifice is the highest in Tyrol, 300 feet. A large statue of St. Christopher stands outside the church. St. Michael's Chapel, next to the parish church, is a war memorial, with monumental frescoes by local artists inside.

Imst is especially known for its **Schemenlaufen** (Ghost Walk), a Shrovetide festival presented every four years (next time is in 1988). Schemenlaufen is a masked Fasching (carnival) procession held on the Sunday before Shrovetide, which of course culminates in Shrove Tuesday, the day before Ash Wednesday. Revelers wear carved masks, such as those of witches looking like the opening act of *Macbeth,* many of which are more than a century old. If you're not around at carnival time, you can see a collection of these masks in the local museum **(Heimatmuseum)** at 1 Ballgasse.

Food and Lodging

Hotel Post (tel. 2554) is an enormous hotel composed of a 15th-century core and a more recent addition. The two main buildings are angled at 90 degrees from one another and are set in the midst of a pleasant park. The older of the two has an onion-dome tower and a steeply sloping gabled roof, as well as elegantly painted monochromatic embellishments. The Singer family maintain a full-fledged array of sporting activities around the hotel, including a covered swimming pool whose sliding glass doors open onto a view of the valley. The interior has an impressive collection of country antiques, wrought-iron doors, and carved paneling. With full board included, rates range from 530 AS ($28.20) to 720 AS ($38.30) in a single and from 480 AS ($25.54) to 720 AS ($38.30) per person in a double. Tariffs depend on the season.

Alpenhotel Linserhof (tel. 2415) is composed of two alpine chalets set in a meadow between a forested hillside and a small lake. The interior is rustically outfitted with wrought-iron accents and lots of exposed wood. On the premises is an indoor pool, plus a friendly staff and a pleasant restaurant with a mellow patina covering its paneled walls. This is a hospitable place to spend the night. Hermann Linser, the owner, charges between 400 AS ($21.28) and 670 AS ($35.64) per person, with full board included. These tariffs include accommodations in apartments as well as in hotel rooms.

Hotel Stern (tel. 3342) is a recently constructed simple chalet, with a sunny location on a grassy lawn and a rustically woodsy interior. The public rooms are dotted with an informally cluttered collection of hunting trophies, cooking utensils, and rustic artifacts. With half board included, the pleasant bedrooms cost between 530 AS ($28.20) and 590 AS ($31.39) per person.

Terrassenhotel Linser (tel. 2860) has an up-to-date exterior which includes flat roofs and big windows. The interior is attractively rustic, most of it covered with horizontal planking and regional accessories. From the grassy front lawn guests can look out over the mountains. On the premises is a sauna, plus a big indoor pool, a well-managed restaurant, and a bar. The hotel sits in the middle of a meadow somewhat removed from the center of the village. With breakfast included, per-person rates in doubles range from 425 AS ($22.61) to 460 AS ($24.47), while singles pay between 405 AS ($21.55) and 460 AS ($24.47).

Hotel Eggerbräu (tel. 2460) is a large, severely designed modern building with an abstract multicolored mural decorating one side. The interior is more rustic than you'd guess by looking at the outside. In addition to its tastefully decorated restaurant, it has a hospitable bar area and cozy, well-furnished bedrooms. Per-person rates in a double range from 430 AS ($22.88) to 460 AS ($24.47), with half board included. Singles pay a daily surcharge of 60 AS ($3.19).

ARZL: The Pitz Valley is certainly not the most spectacular in Tyrol, but it's quite suitable if you're seeking a tranquil mountain valley like that which so delighted Thomas Wolfe decades ago. Arzl lies a short drive southeast of Imst on the south bank of the Inn River. From here you can continue your exploration by taking a curvy road that pierces the Pitztal (Pitz Valley), which runs south into the Ötztal Alps, lying between two other valleys—Ötztal on its eastern side and Kaumertal in the west.

If you take the road all the way to the end of the valley, passing through the hamlets of Trenkwald and Plangeross, you'll arrive at **Mittelberg** at the head of the valley. For your effort and time you'll be rewarded with a splendid view of the Mittelberg Glacier. The main town in the Pitztal through which you'll pass is St. Leonhard.

Food and Lodging

Hotel Post (tel. 3111) is a pleasant chalet. Its interior is filled with all the accoutrements you'd probably want in an alpine hotel, including a green ceramic stove, lots of paneling, and an open fireplace. Renovated in 1972, the hotel charges between 240 AS ($12.77) and 480 AS ($25.54) per person in a double, with half board included. Singles pay a daily surcharge of 40 AS ($2.13).

LANDECK: Back on the main road after a detour into the Pitz Valley, continue your westward journey through the Upper Inn district, coming to a stop at Landeck, 15 miles west of Imst, lying at an elevation of 2675 feet. Landeck is an industrial town, and hardly the most attractive one in the Inn Valley, but it's a convenient stopover choice.

The old town was built at the junction of the Inn and Sanna Rivers, and also the junction of the roads from the Reschen Pass and from Arlberg. It's on the rail line that leaves Innsbruck going toward the far western Austrian province of Vorarlberg and points in eastern Switzerland. Landeck lies south of the Lechtal alpine range.

Burg Landeck, a 13th-century castle, dominates the town and houses a local museum. However, its most striking feature is the view that unfolds from here. The 1471 **pfarrkirche** (parish church) stands on a terrace almost as if it were at the foot of the schloss. It's one of the best known Gothic-style buildings in the province. Inside, note the altarpiece from the 16th century. The winged altarpiece is in the late Gothic style.

In season, some of the hotels in Landeck present Tyrolean folkloric evenings.

Food and Lodging

Hotel Schrofenstein (tel. 2396) contains an elegantly antique entrance area, complete with an old beamed ceiling, marble floors, and Oriental carpets. The bedrooms are more modern, possessing all the comforts. On the premises is a rustic wine cellar plus an attractive restaurant. With breakfast included, singles cost 420 AS ($22.34), while doubles rent for 770 AS ($40.96).

Hotel Schwarzer Adler (tel. 2316) has an unusual facade painted with rustic alpine designs around the windows. The sunny interior gives off a well-established feeling of security and tradition. With half board included, this family-run hotel charges 335 AS ($17.82) per person daily.

FISS: Fiss and its neighboring hamlet, Ladis, on the east side of the Inn River, may be reached by car or by taking the train to Landeck and going on by bus. Secure snow conditions, long ski runs, and concomitant winter activities are available here with the hustle and bustle of larger ski centers. Fiss has retained much of the originality of a Tyrolean mountain village.

Food and Lodging

Schlosshotel Fiss (tel. 6557) looks like an updated version of a medieval fortress. Part of this effect is because of the square tower whose ground floor is pierced by an arched passageway, allowing cars to pass below it. The rest of the establishment stretches into the slope of a hill, which a guest can climb thanks to a series of flagstone steps flanked with carriage lamps. The rustic interior has massive ceiling beams, a scattering of antiques, and a pleasant dining room. The cozy bedrooms are outfitted with autumnal colors and lots of horizontal planking. With half board included, per-person rates in a double range from 480 AS ($25.54) to 800 AS ($42.56). Singles pay a daily surcharge of 60 AS ($3.19).

SERFAUS: Lying on the west bank of the Inn River, Serfaus is a convenient stopover between Landeck (see above) and Nauders (see below), if you're touring. This was once a farm village, but has been turned in recent years into a colorful summer holiday retreat and winter sports resort set against a backdrop of peaks crowned with icy white hoods. It has an exceptional range of good hotels at moderate prices.

Sunny slopes in an extensive skiing area span three mountain valleys and have cable car, chair lift, and surface lift transport. You'll find intermediate and beginner ski runs, cross-country trails, and other winter sports facilities.

Summer visitors can walk to centuries-old mountain farms, listen to brass bands, swim, and find perfect relaxation in this hospitable spot.

The town is known for its two churches from the Middle Ages—one from the 14th century and the other from the dawn of the 16th century. Many buildings here still bear testimony to the ancient Rhaeto-Romanic cultural traditions of the area.

Food and Lodging

Hotel Cervosa (tel. 6211) is an eight-minute walk south from the center of the village. It's a large double chalet with lots of balconies. The hotel contains many facilities for the amusement of both summer and winter guests, including a restaurant with blue upholstery and pink napery, a paneled weinstube with lots of hunting trophies and wrought-iron lighting fixtures, a sun terrace with chaise longues and waitress service, a hospitable bar, and a host of well-furnished public rooms.

On the premises is a big indoor swimming pool, plus a sauna, and a wide choice of massage and beauty facilities. The Westreicher family, the hosts, charge between 515 AS ($27.40) and 1200 AS ($63.84) per person, based on double occupancy, and between 625 AS ($33.25) and 1320 AS ($70.22) for a single, with half board included. Tariffs vary widely according to the season. The most expensive accommodations included in the range of these prices are apartments suitable for up to four persons.

Hotel Alpenhof (tel. 6274) is an alpine chalet a four-minute walk from the center of the village. The interior has some of the most charming detailing around, much of it finished from light-grained knotty pine, well sanded, with a mellow glow. On the premises are dozens of charming extra touches, along with an indoor pool, plus an accommodating and friendly service performed by the Karl Schuler family. High-season rates range from 780 AS ($41.50) to 1050 AS ($55.86) in a single and from 745 AS ($39.63) to 1140 AS ($60.65) per person in a double, including half board.

Hotel Furgler (tel. 201) is a large modern chalet in the center of the village. Its public rooms contain lots of heavy ceiling beams, attractively furnished horizontal planking, and a blazing fireplace within a tapering plaster chimney. On the premises is a well-maintained dining room filled with thick stucco walls and lots of light, plus an indoor swimming pool with table tennis, chaise longues, and big windows. The rustically comfortable bedrooms rent for 430 AS ($22.88) to 1140 AS ($60.65) per person, and singles pay a daily surcharge of 75 AS ($3.99). Half board is included in these prices, which vary according to the season and the accommodation. There's a garage on the premises.

Tirolerhof (tel. 6236) is a pretty inner-village chalet with beige and terracotta accents placed attractively across its stucco facade. The Tschuggmall family, the good-natured owners of this place, frequently dress in Austrian regional costume and do everything they can do to be helpful to their guests. You'll enter a reception area that's beautifully covered with light-grained pine, some of it carved into alpine motifs. A tastefully rustic restaurant serves well-prepared Austrian specialties. On the premises is a paneled weinstube, a cozy sitting room accented with fieldstone masonry, and immaculately wood-trimmed bedrooms filled with fresh colors. High-season rates range from 600 AS ($31.92) to 720 AS ($38.30), with singles paying a daily surcharge of 25 AS ($1.33). A generous half board is included in these tariffs.

Hotel Löwen (tel. 204) is an attractively painted stone-trimmed chalet with gray and terracotta designs around its wood-framed windows. The balconies are cut from wood that has been weathered by time. Inside, the hotel has lots of horizontal planking, a beamed dining room, a bar, a swimming pool, a sauna, and a billiard room, plus a flowered sun terrace. Per-person rates in a double range from 400 AS ($21.28) to 1260 AS ($67.03), while singles pay from 515 AS ($27.40) to 1240 AS ($65.97), with half board included. Rates vary widely according to the season and the accommodation. The Tschiderer family are your hosts.

Hotel Schwarzer Adler (tel. 491) is a five-story, square-based chalet with wood and regional designs accenting its facade. The interior has all the rustic touches you'd expect, including heavy timbers and lots of light-grained paneling. On the premises is a health center containing a sauna, a whirlpool, a Turkish steambath, and a fitness center. The Karl Lugger family take special care of the cuisine they serve. Summer rates range from

385 AS ($20.48) to 430 AS ($22.88) per person in a double. Winter tariffs are much higher, going from 850 AS ($45.22) to 875 AS ($46.55) per person in a double. Depending on the season, singles range from 465 AS ($24.74) to 935 AS ($49.74). These prices include half board. In addition to the dining room, there's also a pleasant wine cellar.

Après-Ski

The hotels already recommended dominate this form of activity. The kellers and taverns of the hotels charge from 50 AS ($2.66) for drinks in most cases. In the peak season the **Hotel Cervosa** brings in live groups that entertain while patrons dance. The **Hotel Furgler** is also likely to provide the same type of nighttime diversion.

NAUDERS: This village of narrow streets, at an elevation of 4585 feet, is known for its location near the Swiss, Austrian, and Italian frontiers, which has made it an international gathering place with some excellent hotels, charging reasonable prices.

About 12 minutes from the heart of Nauders you can take a drag lift to Stables (6400 feet), then on to Stableschochboden (7352 feet). There's also a chair lift to the west of the resort, called the Mutzkopf lift, going up to Rialsch at more than 6000 feet. A restaurant with a panoramic terrace and a good view lies here on a belvedere.

For the most exalted view of all, you can take a trip by a gondola to **Bergkastel,** which rises some 2625 feet from its point of origin at the Reschen area to the east of Nauders. From there drag lifts go to the Bergkastel summit at 8530 feet.

Some four miles from Nauders you come to the Reschen Pass at 4955 feet and the Italian border.

Food and Lodging

Hotel Astoria (tel. 310) is a pleasant balconied chalet set in the middle of town. On the premises, directed by the Ernst Wiestner family, is a cozy collection of public rooms embellished with brass chandeliers, well-finished wood paneling, and an attractively formal dining room and a slightly less formal weinstube. Everywhere here the colors are reminiscent of a woodsy mountaintop house, even though the establishment is set in the middle of the village. On the premises is an indoor pool, plus a sauna, a solarium, and a dancing bar where the management sometimes presents live musical entertainment. Per-person rates in a double range from 385 AS ($20.48) to 755 AS ($40.17), with half board included. Rates depend on the room and the season, and all the accommodations contain private baths.

Hotel Almhof (tel. 222). Herr Kröll turns out to be a delightful host at this tastefully rustic chalet with an arched entryway and generously proportioned balconies. The interior is a winning combination of plush Oriental rugs, massive ceiling beams, attractive lighting, and elegantly chosen accessories. Taking great pride in their establishment, the Kröll family have even had their name carved into one of the well-finished ceiling beams in the dining room. You'll find a country-style weinstube, a hospitable bar, an indoor pool with a sauna, and a choice of health facilities, along with a children's playroom.

Although the hotel is in the center, the ski run comes almost to its doorstep. In high season the comfortable bedrooms rent for 525 AS

($27.93) to 1150 AS ($61.18) per person in a double or an apartment, and between 700 AS ($37.24) and 1000 AS ($53.20) in a single. These prices vary according to the time of year and include full board.

Hotel Margarete Maultasch (tel. 236) is a rustic hotel with lots of innate charm. Its stucco and shingle facade is composed of a pleasing series of curves and angled lines. The interior is a tasteful collection of mellow paneling and massive ceiling beams, some of which are arranged like spokes of a wheel around the top of a circular fireplace in one of the cozy sitting rooms. The facilities include an indoor swimming pool, a sauna, a solarium, and a table-tennis room. The Senn family are the owners, charging wintertime rates of 625 AS ($33.25) to 925 AS ($49.21), based on double occupancy. Singles pay a daily surcharge of 35 AS ($1.86). Prices are slightly lower in summer and vary according to the room assignment.

Hotel Schwarzer Adler (tel. 254) is a well-constructed chalet with a prominent restaurant on the ground floor. The real appeal is on the inside, where some of the heavily timbered ceilings and walls are reinforced with angled crossbeams and accented with a happily cluttered ambience of contrasting fabrics and rustic details. You'll find an occasional antique blanket chest, as well as a blazing fireplace with a carved mantelpiece and a tapering chimney. The Tschiggfrey family are your hosts, charging between 360 AS ($19.15) and 730 AS ($38.84) per person in a double and from 400 AS ($21.28) to 720 AS ($38.30) in a single. Prices vary widely according to the season and include half board. Breakfast is lavish enough to be called brunch.

Hotel Post (tel. 202) has been owned by members of the same family since the 17th century. The present hotel is divided into an old and a new section, which offer all the modern comforts. The older part has been enveloped in an unblemished layer of unadorned stucco, emphasizing even more clearly the jutting bay windows whose bases are covered with seasonal flowers. Parts of the interior still contain some old paneling and a scattering of antique alpine chests and chairs.

There's a restaurant on the premises, as well as a weinstube. The Baldauf family owns fishing rights in a section of the nearby stream and lake, which guests are free to use if they wish. Per-person rates in a double range from 360 AS ($19.15) to 515 AS ($27.40), with singles paying a daily surcharge of 35 AS ($1.86). Half board is included in these rates, which vary according to the season. At Christmas, tabs rise 10%.

Hotel Erika (tel. 240) is capably managed by Essat and Ilse Mangalify, who do much to make a guest feel at home in their attractively rustic modern chalet. The public rooms have benefited from the lavish attention of carpenters, who added built-in cabinets and wooden accents throughout the hotel. The bedrooms have lightly finished wooden planks covering the ceilings, as well as comfortable beds and private baths. Well-prepared Austrian specialties are served in the elegantly woodsy dining room. Per-person rates in a double range from 360 AS ($19.15) to 450 AS ($23.94), including half board. Singles pay a daily surcharge of 35 AS ($1.86).

Sporthotel Tirolerhof (tel. 431) is a six-story chalet which is slightly taller than the other inner-village buildings surrounding it. From the upper-floor sun terrace and from the balconies guests can look down on the outdoor swimming pool. Some of the beams and timbers of the interior are interrupted by a brick-and-plaster exposed chimney which provides winter heat to the comfortable chairs clustered around it. The furnishings of the tasteful public rooms include attractive woodsy pieces and lots of autumn-colored Oriental rugs. An indoor swimming pool is on the premises, and other features include a hospitable bar, an attractively paneled weinstube, and a big sun terrace. Much of the clientele tends to be mildly athletic and sports loving. The Senn family are your hosts, charging from 565 AS ($30.06) to 910 AS ($48.41) per person in high season, based on double occupancy, with half board included. Singles pay a daily surcharge of 85 AS ($4.52).

Après-Ski

It's not especially organized but relaxed and casual, the way most skiers prefer it.

Guests of the previously recommended **Hotel Almhof** are likely to be entertained by zither music in the late afternoon when they return from the slopes. A feature of the establishment is a grill room where you can cook your own meats to your desired perfection, just as you do back home.

One of your most elegant evenings with chic, convivial company is likely to be spent at the four-star **Hotel Astoria,** also recommended previously. It draws a fun-loving crowd to its bar, and later on guests can arrange to go on horse-drawn sleigh rides in the winter's night, returning in time for a body-warming glass of Kirsch.

The **Hotel Margarete Maultasch,** also recommended before, has a nightclub, Lady M, with music for dancing, and on occasion it also has fondue evenings.

Drinks at all of the establishments recommended above begin at 50 AS ($2.66).

13. The Otz Valley

This next excursion into the Ötz Valley is actually an offshoot detour that can be made before you reach the midpoint of your tour of the Upper Inn district. Following the Valley of the Inn, you head west from Innsbruck, but before reaching Imst you can take a good but winding road (no. 186) south toward the Italian border. Along the way you'll find many worthy stopovers, each town or village offering good food and hotels, again at reasonable prices.

The Ötztaler Ache flows through the valley which extends for about 35 miles from the south bank of the Upper Inn. The mouth of the valley is at Ötz (spelled *Oetz* on some maps). Along the road you'll see many waterfalls as you ascend. I hope you'll be there on a sunny day, to marvel at the glaciers and peaks of the Ötztal Alps spreading before you. The valley cuts deep into the heart of some of the highest peaks in the eastern alpine range and leads into the midst of what has been called the "Tyrolean arctic," a glacier region of ethereal beauty. The mountain villages have glacier lifts for extensive skiing. Glacier skiing is possible from spring through fall on the gigantic Rettenbachferner.

This long valley has good skiing in its lower and outer reaches, but if it's summer and you're here just for the sightseeing, the inner or mid part is the most spectacular.

Our first stopover is at—

ÖTZ: Ötz (also spelled Oetz) is reached by going three miles south from the junction of the Inn River and the Ötztaler. A holiday center in both winter and summer, the resort, noted for its mild climate, is perched 2695 feet high on a sunny slope. Ötz has many old buildings, often with traditional oriels and painted facades. A Gothic **pfarrkirche** (parish church) dates from the 14th century, although it was enlarged centuries later.

Just two miles southwest of the town is a warm body of water, **Piburger Lake** (3000 feet), which is popular in summer.

From Ötz, you can also make a 5½-mile trek south to the hamlet of **Umhausen,** the oldest village in the valley, now a holiday resort.

Food and Lodging

Sporthotel Habicherhof (tel. 6248) has a strikingly modern design based loosely on an alpine chalet. A six-story central section rises above rambling extensions containing the public rooms and a sun terrace, as well as a woodsily futuristic building with enormous windows and an indoor pool. The building blends attractively into the slopes of the hillside into which it is built. The high-ceilinged interior contains lot of smooth planking and coffered ceiling panels, as well as a bar area with alpine stools, cozy restaurants, and sitting rooms. The multilingual staff, directed by the Haslwanter family, creates a homey, informal atmosphere. The hotel sits on the main road leading into town, in the heart of the valley, surrounded by abundant snowfields. With full board included, per-person rates range from 435 AS ($23.14) to 575 AS ($30.59).

Alpenhotel Oetz (tel. 6232), in the center of the village, is built on a stone foundation pierced with big arched windows. Visitors enjoying the view from the raised sun terrace are sheltered from the wind by the balconied bulk of the hotel rising behind them. The interior has softly shining wood and parquet floors, paneled ceilings, and sunny colors—lots of homey comfort. Solid, traditional cookery, usually well prepared, is available in the dining room. The Falkner family charges between 325 AS ($17.29) and 445 AS ($23.67) per person for lodging in a single, double, or triple room, with half board included. Prices depend on the season, and each of the comfortable units contains a private bath.

Hotel Drei Mohren (tel. 6301) might be the most distinctive building in the village. Dating from the turn of the century, the building is a baroque fantasy of onion domes, medieval towers, and hipped roofs, with dozens of arched windows piercing through the thick white walls. Most of the grandly paneled bedrooms have private balconies and carved headboards. The chalet-style restaurant here is dotted with old engravings and beautifully finished paneling. With half board included, per-person rates run 440 AS ($23.41) in a double. The management is friendly, providing a lighthearted touch. On the premises are an outdoor tennis court and a covered garage.

Gasthof zum Stern, 6 Kirchweg (tel. 6323). Parts of this pleasant inn date from 1611. Today the facade is opulently covered with bay windows painted with country baroque designs and an army of courtiers helping to support the window frames. You'll recognize the hotel by the gilt and wrought-iron bracket hanging over the sidewalk, just below the cascades of summertime geraniums. The paneled interior is filled with charm and rustic details, including a ceramic stove with green cylindrical indentations. The Griesser family are the accommodating owners of this place. They charge around 290 AS ($15.34) per person, based on double occupancy, with singles paying a daily surcharge of 25 AS ($1.33). These prices include half board and vary according to the season.

Heiner (tel. 6309). In high season this café and pastry shop has an avid collection of last year's fans waiting for a table. The family who runs this place is so well known that some of the locals simply call the establishment by the family name, which happens to be Hald. Aside from a wide collection of coffees and teas, the establishment sells eight combinations of yogurt, six kinds of refreshingly flavored milk, eight kinds of milk-shakes (one of them with red wine), at least ten kinds of flavored egg-nog, and about 40 different concoctions that include ice cream in some way.

If you don't like sweets, you'll find about 15 kinds of carafe or bottled wine, as well as cognac. If dinner or lunch is on your mind, you can enjoy oxtail soup flavored with sherry, a crab cocktail, a host of omelets, and there are also children's platters. More filling are the various kinds of veal, beef, and pork dishes (wild game in season), served with tasty salads. The price for meals varies widely. However, some specials are offered ranging in price from 100 AS ($5.32) to 210 AS ($11.17), while à la carte meals begin at 130 AS ($6.92), going up to 265 AS ($14.10). It's open daily except from mid-November to mid-December.

Continuing up the valley, your next stopover might be—

LÄNGENFELD: This major tourist resort, attracting both winter and summer visitors, is in the heart of the Ötz Valley, at the mouth of the Sulz Valley. The Fischbach torrent splits Längenfeld into two distinct parts. For miles around you can see the 240-foot high spire of the **pfarrkirche** (parish church) in upper Längenfeld.

If you base here, you might enjoy an excursion north to the **Stuibenfälle,** or Stuiben Falls, about two miles southeast of Umhausen. Perhaps the single most outstanding natural attraction of the Ötz Valley, the falls plunge down some 500 feet under a natural rock bridge. Wear your hiking shoes, as it's about a 20-minute walk from the road.

Food and Lodging

Gasthof zum Hirschen (tel. 5201) has been under the direction of the Gstrein family since 1860. Its chalet-style facade is embellished with stone detailing and a painted depiction of a jousting tournament. The interior is especially attractive. There's more paneling than you could literally shake a stick of knotty pine at. Nestled under some of the well-maintained plaster vaults, an alpine chest or a weathered crucifix appears. This is a pleasant place from which to explore the local foot trails. Per-person rates, with half board included, range from 400 AS ($21.28) to 455 AS ($24.21), based on double occupancy. Singles pay a daily surcharge of 60 AS ($1.60), and tariffs vary according to the season.

Hotel Edelweiss (tel. 5206) has a large L-shaped floor plan that was created when a modern wing was added to an existing chalet. The simple interior is a combination of authentically rustic decor (as reflected by the weinstube) and a slightly more contemporary format of painted panels set between areas of natural-grain wood. The Engelbert Kuen family, the owners, charge between 275 AS ($14.63) and 360 AS ($19.15) per person, with half board included, for their comfortable but simple bedrooms.

SÖLDEN: The capital of the inner Ötz Valley, Sölden, about 4400 feet above sea level, draws visitors to this valley in summer, to the woods in spring and autumn, and to the heights in winter.

Sölden is the best known village in the valley, linked by road, cable car, and ski lift to its higher sister village, **Hochsölden** (6800 feet), a much more compact resort. Often winter visitors to Sölden on the half-board arrangement take lunch in Hochsölden when they visit it for the day. There's a ski kindergarten at Sölden.

You can take a cable car from Sölden, passing over glacial fields to some 10,000 feet on the **Geislacherkogel,** where from the upper station you'll be rewarded with a panoramic sweep of the Ötztal Alps. The Geislacherkogel from Sölden is the highest in Austria. A tunnel through the glacier connects the summer glacier resort of Rettenbachferner with the Tiefenbachferner, a large, recently developed summer ski resort.

Sölden is also the beginning of the **Ötztal Glacier Road** (Ötztaler Gletscherstrasse), one of the loftiest roads in the Alps, rising to some 9250 feet. Toll on this road is 175 AS ($9.31) per passenger.

Food and Lodging

Hotel Central (tel. 2260). This riverside chalet is designed around two big interconnected sections. The establishment has an interior constructed from high-quality building materials which include large quantities of beautifully grained timbers, big stucco arches, glowing wooden floors, and regional monochromatic detailing on some of the walls.

The comfortable furnishings include leather-covered settees, Oriental rugs, and woodcarvings prominently displayed on some of the vertical supporting beams. The spacious bedrooms are tasteful, opulent, and spacious, all of them containing a private bath.

On the premises you'll find a bar with live Tyrolean music and a rustically intimate restaurant with excellent service and specialties. They include an array of light-textured international dishes such as calf liver in a chanterelle cream sauce. Garnishes for some of the main courses are unusual and tasty. They include ginger crêpes, for example, or a sweet chestnut parfait in a Calvados and grape sauce. Prices in the restaurant range from 190 AS ($10.11) to 695 AS ($36.97).

Guests of the hotel in high season pay from 1140 AS ($60.65) to 1680 AS ($89.38) for a single and from 1020 AS ($54.26) to 1560 AS ($82.99) per person, based on double occupancy, with prices rising higher at Christmas.

Hotel Solderhof (tel. 2317) is a contemporary chalet whose facade has maintained the rustic painted detailing of the region. The main salon contains a big curved bar, an attractively coffered ceiling, comfortable chairs and banquettes, and a collection of Oriental rugs covering the tile floor. On the premises is an informal stube as well as a more formal, elegantly appointed dining room. A hot whirlpool and sauna are part of the health facilities. In high season doubles range from 540 AS ($28.73) to 720 AS ($38.30) per person, while singles go from 625 AS ($33.25) to 800 AS ($42.56). These prices include half board and vary according to the season.

You can drink at one of three bars and listen and dance to a live band at the already-recommended **Hotel Central,** the best spot for nightlife in Sölden. Chances are, you'll get to hear lederhosen-clad music-makers. At times, if the house count is right, the place takes on a carnival-like atmosphere.

The **Hotel Sonne** brings in live bands to play for dancing, and once a week the staff here stages a Tyrolean evening.

The other leading hotel for nightlife is the recommended **Hotel Bergland,** which on my last visit had the best band in Sölden.

Young people are fond of the Alm Bar in the **Hotel Tyrolerhof** (tel. 2288), a modern hotel in the center of the resort.

Drinks in most places begin at 50 AS ($2.66).

HOCHSÖLDEN: This upper-level resort (6800 feet), towering over just-visited Sölden, lies on a sunny alpine plateau and attracts visitors in both summer and winter. At first Hochsölden may not seem like a village at all, being more a cluster of modern hotels. It's connected to its lower sister by road, cable car, and ski lift. Because of the easy communication between the two resorts, the much larger facilities of Sölden, including the après-ski life, are available to guests at the Hochsölden hotels.

Its higher elevation makes it possible to ski at Hochsölden longer than at Sölden. Rettenbachferner and Tiefenbachferner, summer glacier skiing areas, are easily accessible to both resorts (see above).

Food and Lodging

Hotel Edelweiss (tel. 2641) is an impressively designed hotel among a handful of other hostelries on the bleak alpine meadows near the top of the mountain ridge. Except for a curving glass-walled extension and a low-lying building containing a swimming pool, the structure looks like an oversize chalet. The paneled interior has lots of heavy beams and comfortable couches. On the premises are a bar and a restaurant, usually filled with an enthusiastic crowd of skiers. The woodsy bedrooms are accented with exposed planking. They rent for 550 AS ($29.26) to 1080 AS ($57.46) per person, based on double occupancy, and between 550 AS ($29.26) and 1060 AS ($56.39) in a single. These prices vary widely according to the season and include full board. Visitors who are not hotel guests have access to the timbered nightclub through a separate door on the ground floor. Herbert and Anni Fender are your hosts.

Sporthotel Schöne Aussicht (tel. 2403) is one of the handful of chalet-style hotels in this ski village. This one has a popular day bar, a scattering of blazing fireplaces, a big health and fitness area with a sauna and solarium, a hairdressing salon, and simple, comfortable bedrooms. Overnight rates range from 405 AS ($21.55) to 840 AS ($44.69) in a single and between 360 AS ($19.15) and 780 AS ($41.50) per person, based on double occupancy. Half board is included.

Alpenhotel Enzian (tel. 2505). On sunny days in late winter you're likely to see dozens of visitors stretched out on chaise longues on the big sun terrace of this elegant alpine hotel. Designed with curved corners, gables, and honey-colored exterior planking, the Enzian contains a no-frills modern interior with lots of exposed wood. On the premises are a billiard room, a bar and restaurant, a sauna, and simple, modern bedrooms. The Riml family charge between 265 AS ($14.10) and 755 AS ($40.17) per person in a double, with half board included. Singles pay a daily surcharge of 35 AS ($1.86).

Hotel Alpenfriede (tel. 2227) is a six-story wooded chalet with angled bay windows extending out from the ground floor. The interior has a sunny, airy kind of decor that's attractively uncluttered. On the premises is a paneled sitting room and a warmly tinted bar area with heavy ceiling timbers, plus a sun terrace, TV room, and table-tennis room. With half board included, high-season rates range from 385 AS ($20.48) to 780 AS ($41.50) per person, based on double occupancy, with singles paying a daily surcharge of 30 AS ($1.60). The Lengler family are your hosts.

Après-Ski

As mentioned, you can avail yourself of the more active nighttime diversions of Sölden, down below, but you'll also find plenty of informal nightlife on your doorstep if you're based in a hotel in Hochsölden. Naturally, most of the après-ski nightlife centers around the major hotels, which charge from 50 AS ($2.66) for a drink in most places.

Even if you have your ski boots on, you can join the dancing throngs at the **Hotel Hochsölden** (tel. 2229), which comes alive just as soon as skiers return from the slopes for the day and darkness falls. That means that this tea dance is going strong by 4:30 p.m.

The **Hotel Edelweiss,** previously recommended, is one of the liveliest places on the after-dark circuit, with a live band playing for dancing.

More disco unfolds live at the also-recommended **Schöne Aussicht.** The dress here is wide-ranging—some men dress up in jackets and ties, others preferring sweaters.

OBERGURGL: This village with the funny-sounding name is part of a three-resort complex which includes Hochgurgl (see below) and Untergurgl. Obergurgl, lying less than two miles upstream from Untergurgl, is one of the loftiest villages in Austria, 6322 feet, and the second-highest parish in Europe. This is where the Swiss physicist and aeronaut, Dr. Auguste Piccard, landed in his celebrated balloon.

This district is one of the major ski centers of the Tyrolean country. It's not well known among American skiers, although if you stay here you'll be virtually on the doorstep of the Ötztal Alps, surrounded by towering peaks and glistening glaciers. Some of the ski runs end right in the village. A two-stage chair lift, leaving from the center of Obergurgl, services the principal ski area, the Gaisberg-Hohe-Mutt.

Food and Lodging

Hotel Austria (tel. 314). Hans Steiner and his family are the congenial hosts of this pleasantly balconied chalet whose angled facade—located a short distance above the resort—provides lots of sunny terrace space. The tasteful interior is covered with beautifully grained panels and carved timbers, along with coffered ceilings, thick Oriental rugs, and lots of well-crafted architectural extras. On the premises are a sauna, a solarium, a hot whirlpool, and a Turkish steambath, as well as a bar area, a nightclub, and a baronial fireplace giving off wintertime heat. There's also an elegant restaurant with a subdued color scheme of pink, blue, and knotty pine. The comfortably rustic bedrooms rent for 660 AS ($35.11) to 1380 AS ($73.42) for a single and between 530 AS ($28.20) and 1080 AS ($57.46) per person, based on double occupancy. These tariffs vary widely according to the season, and half board is included.

Hotel Edelweiss & Gurgl (tel. 224) has been owned for many years by members of the Scheiber family. Designed like a contemporary chalet, with lots of balconies angled toward the sun, the hotel is close to the center of the village, but has lots of space around it for a peacefully secluded feeling. The public rooms have much paneling and rustic comfort. On the premises are a big conference room, a day bar, and a farmer-style restaurant. High-season rates range from 720 AS ($38.30) to 1020 AS ($54.26) in a single and from 660 AS ($35.11) to 960 AS ($51.07) per person, based on double occupancy. Full board is included in these rates, which vary according to the season.

Fitnesshotel Gotthard (tel. 335) is an attractive chalet sitting a five-minute walk above the center of the resort. The interior has carefully crafted wooden walls and ceilings, some of them rather elaborate, a Tyrolean-style collection of architectural extras such as a ceramic stove surrounded by a warming bench, a well-rated restaurant with panoramic views over the countryside, a bar, a fitness room, and a big indoor pool covered with an impressive set of timbers. The rustically cozy bedrooms—each with a modern bath—rent for 430 AS ($22.88) to 1080 AS ($57.26) in a single and between 455 AS ($24.21) and 1020 AS ($54.26) per person, based on double occupancy. Here, as in every other hotel in the village, prices vary widely according to the season. Half board is included.

Hotel Hochfirst (tel. 232), near the Festkogel chair lift, is one of the biggest hotels in town. Designed like an enormous slope-roofed chalet whose facade is tastefully divided into several different planes, the establishment benefits from a raised sun terrace and a jutting extension containing the indoor swimming pool. The pleasant interior has furniture upholstered in soft colors, half-timbered walls, heavy ceiling beams, and lots of paneling. On the premises are several restaurants and a bar, plus all the comforts you'd expect. Rates range from 460 AS ($24.47) to 1280 AS ($68.10) in a single, while doubles go from 420 AS ($22.34) to 1140 AS ($60.65) per person, with half board included. The wide price ranges are because of seasonal differences, the winter being the more expensive season.

Hotel Josl (tel. 205) is a pleasant chalet with a big sun terrace and a gently sloping alpine-style roof. A minute's walk from the center of the village, its simple and rustic interior welcomes guests in both summer and winter. The Sport Café inside is popular with skiers and outdoors lovers. Per-person rates range from 600 AS ($31.92) to 720 AS ($38.30), with half board included. Tariffs depend on the season. The establishment is conscientiously managed by the Gstrein family, who maintain another hotel a short distance away. Called the Sporthotel Sonnberg, it usually has room for guests when the Josl is fully booked.

Hotel Alpina (tel. 296) is a six-story chalet with lots of wooden balconies angled toward the sunlight. The paneled interior has much regional detailing, including a green ceramic stove in the rustic knotty-pine–covered restaurant. A cozy bar and a formal dining room with pink napery are also on the premises. In high season, with half board included, per-person rates range from 565 AS ($30.06) to 995 AS ($52.93), based on double occupancy. Singles pay a daily surcharge of 110 AS ($5.85). Rates are slightly lower in summer, and special wintertime tariffs are available for clients staying a week or more.

Berg Gasthof Gamper (tel. 317), owned and managed by Josef Gamper and his family, is a tastefully designed chalet lightly embellished with regionally inspired painted illustrations. Near the Gaisberg lift, slightly away from the center of the village, the hotel has public rooms containing a crackling fireplace constructed from large gray stones, along with comfortable banquettes and a well-finished collection of ceiling panels which give the establishment a cozily rustic feeling of well-being. The simple bedrooms have various kinds of wood, including light-grained knotty pine covering some of the walls. With half board included, wintertime rates range from 470 AS ($25) to 815 AS ($43.36) per person. These prices are slightly lower in summer.

Hotel Burger (tel. 333) has a stone foundation and a pleasant chalet design. In a quiet open meadow on a hillside above the village church, the hotel offers good views of the glacier and the nearby mountains. The interior is simple, rustic, and comfortable, with lots of country-style accessories mingling happily with the streamlined design. High-season rates, with half board included, range from 530 AS ($28.20) to 720 AS ($38.30) in a single and from 430 AS ($22.88) to 700 AS ($37.24) per person in a double. Prices vary according to the season, with summer rates being cheaper.

Après-Ski

There's quite a bit of après-ski life in Obergurgl, most of it relaxed and casual, with drinks costing from 50 AS ($2.66) in most places.

After you return from the slopes you might want to join your fellow skiers for drinks in the Sport Café at the already-recommended **Hotel Josl.** This is a popular rendezvous spot, at least to begin your evening festivities.

The disco at the also-recommended **Hotel Austria** is one of the most sophisticated and expensive places for nighttime diversions.

There are not only two bars but frenetic dancing to disco music at the recommended **Hotel Hochfirst.** Often Tyrolean evenings are presented at this hotel, and if so, you should reserve a table, as they're very popular.

Local folk music evenings are also presented at the **Hotel Josl,** but with no particular regularity. You'll have to inquire locally.

HOCHGURGL: If Hochgurgl (7050 feet) were actually a village, it would take the "loftiest village in Austria" title away from other claimants. However, Hochgurgl is really little more than a cluster of hotels, whose owners anxiously await the first snowfall each year. You can approach Hochgurgl from the Timmelsjoch Alpine Road. A ski bus runs back and forth between Hochgurgl and Obergurgl.

This is an area for dedicated skiers who want access to some of the highest peaks of Europe. A three-section chair lift, leaving from Untergurgl, just outside Obergurgl, will transport you to Wurmkogl at some 10,000 feet. At this lofty elevation skiing is possible all year. From a restaurant at Wurmkogl you have a magnificent view of the Italian Alps.

Food and Lodging

Hochgurgl Hotel (tel. 266) is an elegant chalet which glows at night from the many lights illuminating its rustically contemporary facade. The interior contains handsomely appointed apartments and private rooms, many of them filled with hand-worked paneling and comfortable furniture.

The Tyrolean-style weinstube inside is filled with old paneling and rustic accessories, and has about the coziest ambience in town. The house specialty here is a savory roasted leg of venison, stuffed with bacon, onions, mushrooms, and lots of spices. This is elegantly served with a cream sauce made from apple schnappes, juniperberries, and raspberries.

The other facilities at this accommodating hotel include a fitness center, a sauna, a massage room, a hairdresser, a dance bar, an elevator, and a big indoor pool. You'll also find a ski boutique on the ground floor. Rates for doubles range from 935 AS ($49.74) to 1550 AS ($82.46) per person in high season, with half board included. Singles pay a daily surcharge ranging from 240 AS ($12.77) to 480 AS ($25.54). The luxurious apartments are even more expensive.

Hotel Alpenrose (tel. 249) is a tastefully designed chalet with white walls and darkly contrasting wood trim. Riders on the nearby chair lift can clearly see the regional designs painted around the windows on part of the facade. The pleasant interior has much modern comfort and a paneled and simply furnished collection of clean rooms. The Egger family charges between 530 AS ($28.20) and 700 AS ($37.24) per person in a double in high season, while singles pay a daily surcharge of 60 AS ($3.19). These prices include half board.

Sporthotel Ideal (tel. 290) is a simple chalet set in a slightly isolated, sunny position just outside the village. On the premises is a well-stocked ski store and a pleasantly woodsy decor of horizontal planking, paneled and coffered ceilings, tastefully vivid colors, and comfortable furniture. Facilities include a sauna, a bar, a dining room, a weinstube, and a reading room. Winter rates range from 565 AS ($30.06) to 730 AS ($38.84) in a single or double, with half board included. Prices vary widely with the seasons. In summer, half-board rates are around 300 AS ($15.96) to 350 AS ($18.62) per person, depending on the accommodation.

Hotel Riml (tel. 261) might have the most contemporary design in town. With its gently sloping roof and an emphasis on restful horizontal lines, the hotel has big windows that open into pleasantly woodsy bedrooms. The public rooms are covered with large amounts of light-grained paneling in an airy, sunny format. A restaurant, a bar, a sauna, and a bowling alley are on the premises. The Riml family are your hosts, charging between 450 AS ($23.94) and 875 AS ($46.55) per person in a single or double, with half board included. Prices depend on the plumbing and the season, and children under 14 receive a discount.

Berghotel Angerer Alm (tel. 241) is an attractive wood-trimmed chalet built into the side of a sloping meadow. It required a team of careful craftspeople to complete the richly paneled interior, which was embellished with such details as an unusual masonry fireplace that funnels its smoke through a beaker-shaped copper canopy built into the wall. Some of the furnishings of the public rooms include rustic alpine chests scattered among comfortable armchairs. On the premises are a warmly intimate bar area, a chalet-style restaurant, an indoor swimming pool, a popular sun terrace, and a Ping-Pong room. The comfortably rustic bedrooms rent for 550 AS ($29.26) to 1080 AS ($57.46) per person, with half board included. Room prices vary according to the season. Members of the Scheiber family are your hosts.

Alpenhotel Laurin (tel. 227) has an attractive boxy design with most of the elements of a traditional chalet. Built into a hillside, the hotel does a thriving business on its raised sun terrace and in its comfortable, tastefully decorated restaurant. Here, in a room walled with panoramic windows, you'll dine on simple wooden chairs upholstered in brown and beige tweeds, on napery of the same colors. Many visitors to Hochgurgl wouldn't consider not eating here at least once. Menu items include all the regional and Austrian specialties, such as a collection of imaginative salads, schnitzels, simple but well-prepared vegetables, and fruited desserts. À la carte meals range from 100 AS ($5.32) to 300 AS ($15.96), although they'll be included in your hotel bill if you stay here and opt for half-board plans. These range over the course of the year from 540 AS ($28.73) to 890 AS ($47.35) per person, depending on the season and the exposure.

VENT: This is the end of the valley—the end of the road, so to speak. Vent is small and unspoiled, and many discriminating visitors prefer it to Obergurgl and Sölden, which are likely to be overrun at the height of the ski season.

Driving south from Sölden, you go first to the hamlet of Zwieselstein. There you fork in a southwesterly direction, proceeding for about eight miles, passing through the Venter Tal, or Valley of Venter, with its magnificent alpine scenery, until you reach this mountain village (about 6200 feet above sea level). If you don't want to drive, you can take a bus from Zwieselstein to Vent in summer, a favorite season for mountain climbers. Vent has not only a weather station but also a glacier observatory.

A wickedly steep mountain road, with gradients up to 30%—more suitable for mountain goats than for vehicles—will take you to **Rofenhöhe,** which at 6606 feet is one of the loftiest villages in Austria with year-round residents. To the north is the **Wildspitze,** the tallest peak in the north Tyrolean country, at 12,375 feet. **Kreuzspitze,** 11,340 feet, looms on the right, and to the south is **Thalleitspitze,** 11,175 feet.

If you come to Vent to ski, a drag lift will transport you to the top station (8850 feet).

Food and Lodging

Hotel Similaun (tel. 8104) presents a simplified chalet design—with many concessions to late 20th-century building techniques—to a panoramic view of the Alps. This is the most contemporary hotel at the resort. It has an interior decoration that is light and airy, with ample use of exposed wood. Horbert Gstrein, the owner, charges between 385 AS ($20.48) and 525 AS ($27.93) in a single or double, with half board included. The most expensive seasons, whose figures are included in these rates, are Christmas, Easter, and spring carnival. Mr. Gstrein is the headmaster of the local ski school and speaks excellent English.

Hotel Post (tel. 8119). Directed by the Pirpamer family, this wood and white-painted chalet has a big-windowed restaurant visible from the ground floor. Near the chair lift, the hotel contains a covered swimming pool, sauna, solarium, and elevator. Each of the pleasant bedrooms has a private bath, and rents for 200 AS ($10.64) to 575 AS ($30.59) per person, depending on the season, with breakfast included.

14. The Paznaun Valley

In this snowy valley 56 miles from Innsbruck, the postcard-pretty views are a dime a dozen, the snowland being a valley about 22½ miles long lying between Landeck and Galtür. The Trisanna River is its waterway. To reach the Paznaun, head west from Innsbruck, then take a southwesterly route as signposted. At the head of the valley at Galtür is the impressive Fluchthorn mountain peak.

Few Americans have discovered the Paznaun Valley so far, yet it offers superb skiing. The main village is Ischgl, which has put together a ski circus spilling over with runs and lifts across the border into Switzerland. Galtür, the second most important village, has lots of terrain on Ballunspitze and Seinisjoch. The valley is a choice starting point for ski mountaineering tours in the Silvretta glacier region and among the peaks of the Samnaun Alps.

You can even get a touch of the "winter wonderland" experience in summer by taking a highly recommended excursion deep into the Blue Silvretta mountain range, with towering peaks and glaciers as a backdrop.

ISCHGL: The major town of the Paznauntal is both a summer resort and a winter ski center, near the border of Switzerland. A most attractive village, Ischgl lies about halfway along the valley where the Trisanna Valley branches off. The resort, built on terraces at 4600 feet, is about a half-hour drive from Landeck. It can also be reached by bus from Landeck. Ischgl is well worth a visit.

In the west of town, you can take the Silvrettabahn cableway up to **Idalpe** (7600 feet). The panoramic view from the lofty station is among the most impressive in the Austrian Alps. From the east part of Ischgl you can take yet another cableway to the Pardatschgrat station at 8600 feet.

Food and Lodging

Hotel Elisabeth (tel. 5411), one of the most elegant hotels in the region, has a monumental curved facade covered with balconies, all of which face south. The well-appointed interior contains an attractively somber color scheme which is brightened with flashes of color from the many Oriental rugs and well-chosen upholstery fabrics. In the center of it all, skillful masons have installed an open fireplace, with a conical chimney tapering gracefully up toward the ceiling.

On the premises are a rustic nightclub with live music, a café and pastry shop, a bar, a pizzeria, a covered pool and fitness center, and spacious, luxuriously equipped bedrooms. These have all the modern comforts, including a big color TV, a mini-bar, balconies with southern exposure, and a host of extras. In high season they rent for 900 AS ($47.88) to 1730 AS ($92.04) per person, with half board included. Singles pay a daily surcharge of 180 AS ($9.58).

The Marend restaurant has lots of space between its beautifully decorated tables and a soft color scheme of dusty rose, muted grays, and wood tones. Specialties are well prepared and ideal for an appetite whetted by mountain air (the roast beef is very tasty). À la carte meals range from 130 AS ($6.92) to 335 AS ($17.82).

Hotel Madlein (tel. 226). If you look at it from a certain angle you can count three wood-covered chalets which interconnect to form this well-situated hotel. Near the center of town, convenient to the cable cars, the hotel contains a swimming pool, lots of fitness facilities, and a cozy series of public rooms. These include a nightclub (which sometimes attracts well-known musical groups), two attractive restaurants, and a sitting room with an open fireplace built into a wall composed of massive gray rocks. High-season rates range from 960 AS ($51.07) to 1440 AS ($76.61) per person in a double, from 1120 AS ($59.58) to 1240 AS ($65.97) in a single, with half board included. A wide range of apartments suitable for up to four persons is also available.

Hotel Post (tel. 5233) is an imposingly sized chalet-style hotel in several different sections. The interior has rustic accents which include lots of paneling, geometrically ornate ceilings, a central fireplace whose smoke rises through a stucco funnel, and a well-appointed dining room. The cozy bedrooms rent for 470 AS ($25) to 960 AS ($51.07) per person in a double, with singles paying daily surcharges ranging from 35 AS ($1.86) to 95 AS ($5.05). These tariffs include half board, and vary widely with the time of year and the plumbing assigned you.

Hotel Christine (tel. 5346) is a pleasant chalet with a rustic interior which includes a bar, a restaurant, a pool, and a central fireplace surrounded by banquettes. Rates in high season, with breakfast included, range from 360 AS ($19.15) to 700 AS ($37.24) per person, based on double occupancy. Singles pay a daily surcharge of 70 AS ($3.72) to 95 AS ($5.05). Prices vary according to the time of year, and all accommodations contain private bath.

Gasthof Goldener Adler (tel. 5402). No one knows exactly when this inn was built, but it was mentioned in a legal document in 1640. Later it served as the region's courthouse in the 17th and 18th centuries. Today it sits behind a six-story pastel-colored facade, with white trim and a solidly prosperous kind of ambience. The carved entrance is set with stained glass, while the panels of the interior range from full-grained natural wood to those painted in light colors with regional designs. You'll find lots of rustic details and much modern comfort.

Johann Kurz and his family are the owners. In high season they charge between 540 AS ($28.73) and 830 AS ($44.17) per person, based on double occupancy, and between 590 AS ($31.39) and 935 AS ($49.74) in a single, with half board included. Some apartments are available for two to four persons, ranging up to 1120 AS ($59.58) per person in high season, with half board included. The gasthof is closed between early October and the end of November. It contains a Tyrolean-style restaurant serving well-prepared local specialties. A la carte meals range from 100 AS ($5.32) to 325 AS ($17.29).

Alpenhotel Ischglerhof (tel. 5331) is a comfortable hotel owned and managed by the Ludwig Kurz family. Its combination of different alpine styles includes a conical tower whose windows are surrounded with pink borders. The rambling surfaces of the rest of the hotel are covered for the most part with wooden balconies. The public rooms are elegantly decorated with what probably adds up to an acre of paneling, crafted from both light and dark woods. A rustic and comfortable bar area has darkly intimate lighting and dance music, while one of the sitting rooms contains a hospitably inviting open fireplace. Per-person rates range from 570 AS ($30.32) to 850 AS ($45.22), with half board included. Prices vary widely according to the time of year.

Après-Ski

The après-ski lift begins early with a "tea dance" at the already-recommended **Hotel and Café Christine.** Here the owners, Rudolf and Anna Wolf, welcome not only their own guests but visitors from the other hotels to a lively atmosphere.

The **Hotel Elisabeth,** also recommended previously, has one of the most intimate and romantic candlelit atmospheres on the après-ski circuit.

In season a live band is brought in to play music for dancing and your entertainment.

One of the most elegant places to gather at night is the **Hotel Madlein,** also recommended, which has dancing and music. At the Madlein, head for the Almbar with its wooden beams, whitewashed brick, and attractive young patrons.

Drinks at all the establishments in town begin at 50 AS ($2.66).

GALTÜR: At the head of the Paznauntal and at the foot of the Silvretta Pass (closed to winter traffic) is Galtür, near the Swiss border and about an 18-minute drive from Ischgl, just visited. This relatively unspoiled resort, perched at a rather exalted 5800 feet, has been well known for decades as a ski mountaineering center and a popular summer resort, attracting mountain climbers.

It has become better known in recent years for its downhill and its Nordic, or *langlauf,* skiing. You can purchase the Silvretta ski pass which entitles you to use the lifts at Ischgl as well as chair and drag lifts to take you from Galtür to the highest station at 7260 feet. The Silvretta ski pass, incidentally, opens up a total of nearly 50 lifts. Snow is good here from December to April.

There's a bus link between Galtür and Landeck, some 25 miles away.

Food and Lodging

Hotel Ballunspitze (tel. 214). The creative architect who designed this attractive hotel began with a clapboard house to which he added a modern balconied extension that ended up being about four times as big as the original house. The genteel family who direct it, the Leo Walters, make guests feel at home. Their public rooms have been carefully paneled and filled with comfortably rustic furniture.

The hotel sits at the edge of the village, within walking distance of most everything. Per-person rates, with half board included, range from 325 AS ($17.29) to 720 AS ($38.30), based on double occupancy, and singles pay a surcharge ranging from 60 AS ($3.19) to 110 AS ($5.85) daily.

Two simple chalets are nearby, both of them owned by the same family. They are the **Pension Leo Walter** and **Haus Hoamatl.** They charge about 60% less than their parent hotel in accommodations considerably more spartan.

Hotel Fluchthorn (tel. 300) is a tall alpine-style chalet whose form is slightly more streamlined than the others around it. It has monochromatic paintings around some of its windows and a warmly rustic interior. Fixtures include heavy ceiling beams, some of them carved, along with brass chandeliers, ceramic stoves, and comfortable easy chairs. On the premises are a dancing bar, a Tyrolean-style restaurant, and a sauna, as well as covered tennis courts and an indoor pool just a few steps down the street. The hotel is closed between the first of October and mid-December. High-season rates range from 700 AS ($37.24) to 910 AS ($48.41) in a single and between 500 AS ($26.60) and 900 AS ($47.88) per person, based on double occupancy. Half board is included, and tariffs are considerably cheaper in summer.

Hotel Pazmauner Hof (tel. 333) has been owned and directed by members of the Lorenz family for the past century. Designed in a typical Tyrolean style with lots of balconies, this attractively unpretentious hotel has been expanded to include a collection of rustically paneled rooms with chalet-style furniture and lots of cozy comfort. The big-windowed dining room serves tasty, well-prepared Austrian specialties. High-season prices range from 535 AS ($28.46) to 610 AS ($32.45) per person, with half board included.

Almhof (tel. 253) is a modern hotel with big windows and lots of balconies. It's built into the side of a hill, with a collection of tastefully rustic bedrooms (often with Tyrolean-style furniture) and paneled public rooms that include a hot whirlpool, a sauna, and a restaurant. The hotel was recently built by the Huber family. High-season rates range between 575 AS ($30.59) and 840 AS ($44.69), with half board included.

The same management runs the **Hotel Wirlerhof** (tel. 346), a recently expanded chalet, with a decor that includes an updated kind of rusticity. On the premises is a curved bar with intimate lighting, along with two restaurants and a café dance bar. With half board included, per-person rates range from 600 AS ($31.92) to 935 AS ($49.74) in high season.

Gasthof Landle (tel. 213) is set between an alpine creek and a treeless mountain. The unusual design of this hotel includes a conservative chalet joined at its side to a larger, more innovative addition. The Zangerle family, the owners, prepare tasty specialties for the cozy restaurant and make their guests feel welcome. The simple bedrooms are attractive and clean. In high season, singles range from 350 AS ($18.62) to 565 AS ($30.06), while doubles cost between 300 AS ($15.96) and 530 AS ($28.20) per person, with half board.

Hotel Alpenrose (tel. 201) is an attractive modern chalet whose simplified exterior sits against a backdrop of craggy mountains. The streamlined interior has taste and all the modern comforts, one of them being a well-recommended restaurant where the old-fashioned cookery honors butter, cream, and rich dishes as dietary stables. After a day in the mountains this might be exactly what you want. You'll enjoy the braised beef with onions or the chef's special brochette. Meals range from 100 AS ($5.32) to 335 AS ($14.82).

Per-person rates in the hotel in high season go from 325 AS ($17.29) to 540 AS ($28.73), with half board included. The location is a few minutes' walk from the center of the village.

Berghaus Franz Lorenz (tel. 328) is a modern chalet a few minutes' walk from the center. Named after its helpful and friendly owner, the hotel serves generous and well-prepared meals, including a buffet breakfast. With half board included, per-person rates in high season range from 550 AS ($29.26) to 815 AS ($43.36), based on double occupancy, with singles paying a surcharge of 50 AS ($2.66) per day.

Après-Ski

For such a small ski village the nightlife is more extensive and sophisticated than one might imagine.

The early evening begins with a tea dance at the already-recommended **Hotel Wirlerhof-Almhof.** The ski crowd here—still wearing their boots—arrive right from the slopes. Coffee, hot chocolate, beer, and tempting pastries are downed in a lively atmosphere of smoke, drink, and good times.

More in the center of town, the place to go is the also-recommended **Hotel Fluchthorn,** where there's a lively dance bar in the cellar that at some point seems to draw every skier in town.

Drinks in most places begin at 50 AS ($2.66).

15. The Arlberg

There's no such thing as a sacred ski mountain—so far as I've ever heard—but if there were it would have to be the Arlberg, the mecca of the serious skier. Alpine skiing went out from here to conquer the world. On the east side of the Arlberg, 63 miles west of Innsbruck, is what's known as the cradle of alpine skiing. Here were born the names and the legends known to all dedicated skiers: the Ski Club Arlberg, the early Kandahar races, Hannes Schneider and his Arlberg method.

The Arlberg, with peaks that top the 9000-foot mark, lures skiers with its vast network of cableways, lifts, runs stretching for miles, a world-renowned ski school, and numerous sporting amenities. Runs begin at the intermediate level, reaching all the way to the "nearly impossible."

The Arlberg, the loftiest mountain in the Lechtal range, marks the boundary between the settlers of the Tyrolean country and the Vorarlbergers who live in the extreme western province of Austria. One of the Arlberg's most celebrated peaks is the Valluga, at 9220 feet.

In 1825 a road was opened allowing vehicular traffic to travel to the Arlberg Pass. A six-mile-long rail runnel was opened in 1884, linking Tyrol and Vorarlberg, and finally in 1978 a new road tunnel linked the two provinces. Toll for the highway tunnel is 160 AS ($8.51). The road tunnel is the third longest in Europe. If you're not driving, you'll find the area serviced by the well-known Arlberg Express rail link.

ST. ANTON AM ARLBERG: Alpine skiing is no longer in the cradle, having come of age to the point where St. Anton is now more the citadel of this winter sport, for a modern resort has grown out of the old village on the Arlberg Pass which was the scene of ski history in the making. This is a center for a ski area that is considered among the finest in the Alps.

It was at St. Anton (4225 feet) that Hannes Schneider, born here in 1890, evolved modern skiing techniques as a very young man and started teaching tourists how to ski in 1907. The Ski Club Arlberg was also born here, in 1901. In 1911 the Arlberg-Kandahar Cup competition came into being with donation of a valuable trophy to be awarded annually to the best alpine skier. The cup took its name from the donor, British Field Marshal Lord Roberts of Kandahar, and one of the earliest British skiers, Sir Arnold Lunn, chose his favorite Tyrolean village, St. Anton am Arlberg, for the competition. Formerly held every year at St. Anton, the event is now alternated among German, French, and Italian resorts, coming home every fourth year.

Before his death in 1955 Schneider saw his ski school rated as the world's finest. Today the ski school, still at St. Anton, is one of the world's largest and best, with about 300 instructors, the majority of whom speak English.

The snow in this area is considered perfect for skiers, and the total lack of trees on the slopes makes the situation ideal. The ski fields of St. Anton stretch over a distance of some six square miles. Beginners stick to the nursery slopes down below, and for the more experienced skiers there are the runs from the Galzig and Valluga peaks. A cableway will take you to **Galzig** (6860 feet), where there's a self-service restaurant. You go from here to **Ballugagrat** (8685 feet), the highest station reached. The peak of the

Hotel Bergland (tel. 2234). The architect of this striking hotel incorporated a chalet format with steep rooflines over an assembly of trapezoids, rectangles, and cubes. The result is a pleasing hotel where guests are pampered. The upper-level sun terrace with its dozens of pink parasols is one of the most popular places in town on a sunny day. Set just at the edge of the village, this family-run hotel has a gracefully elegant interior covered with well-finished paneling below heavy ceiling beams.

The public rooms contain a scattering of antique alpine chests, as well as beautifully appointed restaurants and bars (two of each). On the premises is a dancing bar with live music, an indoor pool, a sauna, and an engaging, friendly staff.

The bedrooms are warmly intimate and are usually accented with well-finished planking. Singles range from 575 AS ($30.59) to 1240 AS ($65.97), while doubles cost between 500 AS ($26.60) and 1120 AS ($59.58) per person, with half board included. Prices vary according to the season.

Hotel Sonne (tel. 2203) is an attractive, modernized chalet with an attentive management by members of the Gurschler family. Next to the chair lift to Hochsölden, the hotel has a rustically mellow interior filled with well-finished paneling, regional accessories, and all the modern comforts. On the premises is an attractive restaurant with pink and white napery, an intimately lit bar area, and cozy paneled bedrooms. High-season rates are 660 AS ($35.11) per person in a double and around 720 AS ($38.30) in a single. Prices depend on the season, and all accommodations contain private bath. Half board is included in the price, which rises over Christmas.

Hotel Alpina (tel. 2202). Built into the slope of a hill and flanked by towering conifers, this pleasant hotel rises five stories above the alpine path running alongside it. Its windows are embellished with painted borders, and its attractively simple interior has lots of paneling and all the modern comforts. High-season rates range from 540 AS ($28.73) to 720 AS ($38.30) per person, based on double occupancy, and between 590 AS ($31.39) and 770 AS ($40.96) in a single. Half board is included in these rates. A sauna, a Turkish steambath, and a hot whirlpool are on the premises.

Gasthof Waldcafé (tel. 2319) is a pleasant chalet on the side of the mountain practically in the path of most of the major ski runs. On the premises is a congenial restaurant, as well as simple bedrooms. Burkhard Riml, the owner, charges between 460 AS ($24.47) and 575 AS ($30.59) per person, based on double occupancy, and single rooms cost an additional 60 AS ($3.19) per day. Half board is included in these tariffs.

Café/Restaurant Hermann (tel. 2335). An alpine stream runs nearby, and the air couldn't be fresher than it is from the balconies of this pleasant chalet. Set some distance above the village, the hotel is capably directed by Jermann and Edith Fender, who make visitors feel welcome. The interior is accented with big windows looking out over the forest, lots of paneling, and regionally inspired detailing. The bedrooms have attractively wood-trimmed formats and all the modern comforts. Per-person rates range from 310 AS ($16.49) to 550 AS ($29.26) in a double; singles pay a daily surcharge of 25 AS ($1.33). Half board is included in these rates.

Après-Ski

There's quite a lot of nightlife, centering customarily around the major hotels. If you get bored, you can take the cableway up to **Hochsölden** and check out the more casual nightlife there.

Valluga at 9220 feet commands a sweeping panoramic view. St. Christoph (see below) is the mountain annex of St. Anton.

In addition to the major ski areas I just mentioned, there are two other important sites attracting followers of the sport: the **Gampen/Kapall** and the **Rendl.**

St. Anton am Arlberg in winter is quite fashionable, popular with the wealthy and occasional royalty, a more conservative segment of the jet set than you'll see at other posh ski resorts. There are many other cold-weather pursuits than just skiing, including ski jumping, mountain tours, curling, skating, tobogganing, and sleigh rides, plus après-ski on the quiet side.

There's so much emphasis on skiing here that few seem to talk of the summertime attractions. In warm weather you'll find St. Anton tranquil and bucolic, surrounded by meadowland. A riot of wildflowers blooming in the fields announces the beginning of spring.

Food and Lodging

Hotel Schwarzer Adler (tel. 2245). There's been a hotel here for the past 100 years, although the building itself dates from 1570 when it was constructed from stones taken from the ruins of nearby Arlen Castle. The hospice became known for its hospitality to travelers crossing the Arlberg mountain, and today the hotel maintains the same time-honored tradition. Its painted facade is striking, especially the ornate sundial.

The furnishings include some antique armoires painted in regional designs, an occasional ceramic stove, and comfortable chairs. On the premises is a well-liked café, the Tschol, as well as a disco bar reached through a ground-floor door leading into a modern addition.

In the center of the village, the hotel charges high-season prices ranging from 880 AS ($46.82) to 1440 AS ($76.61) in a single and from 840 AS ($4.69) to 1400 AS ($74.48) per person, based on double occupancy, with half board included. Prices depend on the season.

The in-house restaurant is a friendly and well-run establishment, with many of the specialties coming from the region. The schnitzels and Sacher torte taste as good as they do in Vienna. Meals range from 150 AS ($7.98) to 335 AS ($17.82). Both the hotel and restaurant are closed in October and November.

Hotel Arlberg (tel. 2248), owned by the Ennemoser family, is a big, attractively styled hotel with dramatic sweeping lines in the construction of its wood and stucco facade. The richly paneled interior gives off a warmly hospitable tinge to the clients who appreciate the bar and restaurants. There's a wintertime disco, as well as comfortable bedrooms with plenty of exposed wood tones. A tennis court, covered swimming pool, Turkish bath, and sauna all belong to the hotel. Rates range from 800 AS ($42.56) to 1200 AS ($63.84) in a single, and from 720 AS ($38.30) to 1380 AS ($73.42) per person in a double, some of which include small suites. Half board is included.

Hotel Mooserkreuz (tel. 2730) is a generously sized mountain inn on the sunniest part of the slopes above the village. This hotel stands on the road to the Arlberg Pass. The Opitz family will help to make your stay pleasant. Guests have free use of their indoor pool as well as the sauna, and the hotel bus makes frequent runs to the center of town and to the ski lifts. High-season rates range from 880 AS ($46.82) to 1180 AS ($62.78) in a single and from 830 AS ($44.17) to 1120 AS ($59.58) per person, based on double occupancy, with half board included.

Hotel Tyrol (tel. 2340). When you enter the reception area of this attractive chalet you'll see a sweeping staircase rising from the lobby to the upper floors. Near the edge of the village, the hotel has an attractively decorated series of cozy public rooms, a restaurant, and comfortable bedrooms. Rates in high season range from 635 AS ($33.78) to 1180 AS ($62.78) per person in a double and from 720 AS ($38.30) to 1140 AS ($60.65) in a single, with half board included. The public tennis courts are a three-minute walk from the hotel.

Sport Hotel (tel. 3111) is just three pedestrian minutes from the begining of the chair lifts. On the premises of this hotel are a café, a steakhouse, a tavern, and a formal restaurant, as well as a cocktail bar and nightclub with dancing. There's also an ozone-enriched swimming pool with a water cascade, a fitness center with a sauna, and intimately cozy bedrooms with TV, radio, phone, and private bath. Erich Kuen and his family are the owners of this place, which is pleasantly paneled and well furnished throughout. In a single, rates range from 960 AS ($51.07) to 1440 AS ($76.61). Based on double occupancy, the per-person rate goes from 720 AS ($38.30) to 1320 AS ($70.22). Breakfast is included in these high-season rates, and half board is available for another 180 AS ($9.58) per person daily.

Gasthof Montjola (tel. 2302) is a rustically appealing Tyrolean-style guest house with green and white striped shutters, lots of exposed wood, and an interior that has much charm. Throughout, you'll see heavy ceiling beams, a stone-rimmed fireplace, rustic knickknacks, and immaculately set dining room tables. Fondue is a specialty, and it's usually prepared by a member of the Nohl family. In summer rates are 240 AS ($12.77) per person daily, with breakfast included. In winter guests book in here mainly on the half-board plan, costing from 580 AS ($30.87) to 865 AS ($46.02) per person, based on double occupancy. Singles pay a daily surcharge ranging from 50 AS ($2.66) to 90 AS ($4.79).

Hotel Rosanna Stüberl (tel. 2011) is an attractively designed chalet with long rows of balconies and big windows. The interior has well-finished paneling, as well as a gently arched ceiling over one of the restaurants. The reception area has especially intricate beams, carved into geometric patterns. A rustic bar area might be a relaxing place for a drink. Food served in the restaurant includes raclette, fondue, homemade specialties, and a wide assortment of tortes. Your meal will usually be accompanied by live music, sometimes on a zither. Overnight rates, with half board included, range from 480 AS ($25.54) to 1130 AS ($60.12) per person, based on double occupancy. Tariffs depend on the season.

Après-Ski

St. Anton's after-dark lights are among the most glittering in the Tyrol. However, it's likely to be expensive, with drinks beginning at 50 AS ($2.66) but likely to cost from 75 AS ($3.99) in most of the better places. Hopefully you'll like your fellow skiers, as in season it's likely to be elbow-to-elbow (or whatever) in most places.

The chic rendezvous of the resort is the already-recommended **Hotel Arlberg.** Its Kellerbar is one of the liveliest in St. Anton.

The **Hotel Tyrol,** also recommended previously, enlivens the nightlife scene with its nightclub and live band.

At the **Hotel Rosanna Stüberl,** also recommended, the Stüberl offers live music after dark.

One of the most popular discos in St. Anton is at the **Hotel Schwarzer Adler,** also recommended previously.

Yet another center is the **Sport Hotel,** also recommended before. Its Taverna offers live music, and if disco is still your scene, then there is "Drop-In."

ST. CHRISTOPH: The mountain annex of St. Anton, St. Christoph (5850 feet), is linked to the St. Anton terrain by a cableway at Galzig. It's on the road to the Arlberg Pass and has essentially the same ski facilities available at St. Anton, only here you're closer to the action than at that village. However, St. Anton is the place to go for après-ski activity if you're staying at St. Christoph.

If you're not driving your own car, take the train to St. Anton, then go either by bus or taxi to St. Christoph.

A hospice, long ago destroyed by fire, was built on this spot in the 15th century, serving stranded travelers rescued from avalanches or caught in snowdrifts.

Food and Lodging

Arlberg Hospiz (tel. 26110) is a prosperous-looking, white-walled building whose steep gabled roof looks strong enough to support even the heaviest blanket of snow. This establishment was built on the site of the medieval hospice that burned down. A chapel still stands next door, commemorating the lives of those who died crossing the pass. Memories of that historic inn live on through the service offered by the Werner family.

The interior is loaded with rustic comfort, including beautifully finished paneling, gently vaulted ceilings, a scattering of wintertime fireplaces, and a big bar area in an even larger sitting room.

Rates range from 755 AS ($40.17) to 1120 AS ($59.58) in a single and between 635 AS ($33.78) and 1430 AS ($76.08) per person in a double. These tariffs include an excellent half board in a restaurant classified as a Relais de Campagne.

Food served is a far cry from what was offered to the wandering monks of the Middle Ages. Specialties include tempting salads, wine soup, marinated herring hausfrau style, a range of Austrian specialties (often with an unusual twist), game dishes with spätzle, and an array of desserts, many of which in summer make use of the fresh berries grown in the surrounding mountains. Meals range from 240 AS ($12.77) to 700 AS ($37.24). It's closed during all of May and for most of October and November.

16. Lienz and East Tyrol

East Tyrol is like an afterthought—of but not actually in Land Tyrol. When Italy won South Tyrol in 1919 in the aftermath of World War I, East Tyrol was like a refugee child separated from its mother and not reunited with her. This part of Tyrol was cut off from the rest of the province by a narrow projection of Italian land which connects to Land Salzburg.

Italy, including what used to be South Tyrol, lies to the south and west of East Tyrol, with Land Salzburg to the north and Carinthia to the east. The little subprovince, of which Lienz is the capital, is cut off from its neighbors on the north by seemingly impenetrable Alps. East Tyrol is known as Osttirol in German.

Because of its isolated position, East Tyrol tends to be neglected by the average North American tourist, which is a shame. The grandeur of its scenery and the warm hospitality of its people make it worth visiting. It's crowned by the magnificent peaks of the Hohe Tauern, the Grossvenediger, and the Grossglockner, and to the south lie the Lienz Dolomites, which invite exploration. The scenery along the Drau and the Isel Valleys is spectacular. These two main valleys have many little side hollows worth exploring, especially the Virgental. You'll see a lot of alpine pastureland, meadows, relatively undiscovered valleys, and beautiful lakes.

The Romans occupied East Tyrol in ancient times. Later, the Slavs moved into the area as settlers and made it a section of Carinthia. It has known many rulers, from the Bavarians to the French. Even Great Britain had a hand in running things here, when the Allies made East Tyrol a part of the British-occupied sector of Austria from 1945 to 1955.

Since 1967 it's been possible to reach East Tyrol by taking the three-mile-long Felbertauern Tunnel, a western route through the Alps. If you're driving, you can come from the east or the west. From the Grossglockner Road, you take the Felbertauern Road and the tunnel. If you're driving from the north to Lienz, the East Tyrol capital, you can take the Falbertauern Road from Land Salzburg, passing through the tunnel. In summer you may want to take the celebrated Grossglockner Road and the Iselberg Pass. This road runs along the boundary between East Tyrol and Carinthia.

It's also possible to take a train from Italy to East Tyrol. Corridor trains also operate between Innsbruck and Lienz. As you pass through Italy on this trip, the trains are locked and you don't have to show your passport or clear Italian Customs.

Woodcarving, long a pursuit in East Tyrol, is still practiced in tranquil chalets during the long winter months. You might like to shop for some pieces while you're here.

LIENZ: Don't confuse this city with *Linz,* the capital of Upper Austria. Lienz with an *e* serves as the capital of East Tyrol. It lies at the junction of three valleys—the Isel to the northwest, the Puster to the west, and the Drau to the east. The old town of Lienz stretches along the banks of the Isel River, with **Lieburg Palace,** a 16th-century building now the seat of local government, overshadowing the Hauptplatz (main square).

The sights of Lienz are easy to see, taking no more than about 1½ hours. One of the main attractions is **Schloss Bruck** (Bruck Castle) with its **Osttiroler Heimatmuseum** (Museum of East Tyrol). This was the fortress of the counts of Görz, who held sway over vast estates until they fell prey to the Habsburgs at the beginning of the 16th century. The castle stands at the head of the entrance to the Valley of Isel, less than a mile from the center of Lienz.

In the museum, much has been preserved of the life and times of the people of East Tyrol, including handicrafts and peasant dress. The Rittersaal (knight's hall) shows how the castle looked in the Middle Ages. The most important feature of the museum is the Albin Egger-Lienz gallery, containing a magnificent collection of the art of this outstanding native painter, who died in 1926. Most often, he took the Tyrolean country and its people as his subjects. Another section displays artifacts unearthed at the archeological site of the Roman town of Aguntum (see below).

The museum is open daily from around Easter until the end of October from 10 a.m. to 5 p.m. Off-season it's closed Monday. Admission is 30 AS ($1.60), and there's a restaurant at the schloss.

If you have time, visit **St. Andrä** (Church of St. Andrew), the outstanding feature of which is the collection of 16th-century tombstones carved of marble quarried outside Salzburg. The last of the counts of Görz is buried here. The church, consecrated in 1457, was restored in 1968, having fallen into a sad state of disrepair. During the restoration workmen uncovered murals, some dating from the 14th century. The nave is in the late Gothic style, and the church is considered the finest example of Gothic architecture in East Tyrol. A memorial chapel honors Lienz war dead. The renowned painter, Albin Egger-Lienz, mentioned above, is entombed here.

In winter Lienz, at an elevation of 2850 feet, attracts skiers to its two major ski areas: the **Hochstein** and the **Zertersfeld,** serviced by chair and drag lifts. The height of the top station is 7225 feet.

In summer the town fills up with mountain climbers, mainly Austrians, who come to scale the Dolomites. This is a good base for many excursions in the area. For example, from Schlossberg, you can take a chair lift up to **Venedigerwarte** (3335 feet). You can also explore the excavations of **Aguntum,** the Roman settlement, three miles east of Lienz. You can bathe in **Lake Tristacher,** three miles south of the city.

The **Dolomites,** actually the northwestern part of the Gailtal alpine range, lie between the Gail Valley and the Drau Valley. Their highest peak is the Grosse Sandspitze at more than 9000 feet.

Food and Lodging

Hotel Traube (tel. 2552). The location couldn't be more ideal, in the very center of town on a street lined with verdant shrubbery and decorative trees. The distinctive facade is painted a vivid red, with forest-green shutters and a striped canopy covering part of the ground-level café. The interior reflects the general sophistication of the staff.

Furnishings in both the public rooms and the bedrooms are elegant and comfortable. On the roof is a covered swimming pool, while in the cellar a vaulted disco (often with live music) provides evening entertainment.

This hotel has been owned for many generations by members of the Vergeiner family, who charge between 500 AS ($26.60) and 685 AS ($36.44) for a single and between 590 AS ($31.39) and 710 AS ($37.77) per person in a double, with breakfast included. Half board, depending on the season, ranges from 120 AS ($6.38) to 240 AS ($12.77) per day.

The restaurant is housed in one of the town's most elegant rooms and benefits from its designation as a Relais de Campagne. À la carte meals range from 125 AS ($6.65) to 360 AS ($19.15). The hotel and restaurant are closed from early November until mid-December.

Hotel Sonne (tel. 3311) is an up-to-date hotel with all the modern comforts. Many of the bedrooms have cozy accents which usually include light-grained planking and tastefully cheerful colors. On the premises is a bar set a short distance away from a baronial modern fireplace whose tapering chimney is accented with decorative chains. On the premises are a sauna, a fitness room, a roof garden with a sun terrace, and an underground garage.

Rates range from 540 AS ($28.73) to 590 AS ($31.39) in a single and from 470 AS ($25) to 515 AS ($27.40) per person in a double, including breakfast. Half board costs another 170 AS ($9.04) per person daily.

The in-house restaurant serves excellent cuisine to an international clientele. Specialties include rosemary-flavored ham with melon slices, pork filet in a cabbage sauce, succulent meats, and crispy salads. Meals range from 125 AS ($6.65) to 445 AS ($23.67). Both the hotel and restaurant are closed between early October and mid-December.

Hotel Post (tel. 2505). On the main square of town, this Mediterranean-style building has a décor that might be called flirtatious. Its inspiration seems to come from points south of the (Austrian) border. Examples of this Italian charm include the ribbed awnings stretching over the entrance and the rococo gilt mirror and small bandy-legged tables in the vaulted reception area. The Lederer family are the friendly owners. With half board included, singles range from 490 AS ($26.07) to 540 AS ($28.73), while doubles cost between 445 AS ($23.67) and 480 AS ($25.54). Prices depend on the season and the accommodation.

Gasthof Pension Haidenhof (tel. 2440) looks like an appealing cross between an alpine chalet and a Mediterranean villa. The windows of the hotel's central section are bordered with painted Tyrolean designs, while on either side symmetrical wings with strong horizontal lines stretch toward the surrounding forest. Views from the balconies of the simple bedrooms encompass most of Lienz. On the premises is a sun terrace, along with a series of pastel-colored vaulted ceilings, plus a paneled restaurant. Per-person rates range from 360 AS ($19.15) to 375 AS ($19.95), with half board included. You'll be about 20 minutes from the center of town.

Hotel Glöckturm, 2 Pfarrgasse (tel. 04852), is a sprawling old-fashioned hotel set in a wooded area beside the river. The facade looks as though three different buildings were welded into a single unit, all of them painted a baroque yellow with red and sea-green trim. The interior is simple and attractive, albeit with a decor probably inspired around 1962. Christian Gasser, the owner, charges around 290 AS ($15.34) per person in a double and 325 AS ($17.29) in a single, with breakfast included.

Gasthof Goldener Fisch (tel. 2132), about two minutes by car from the center of town, offers views of different mountains from practically every room in the house. The prosperous-looking facade is painted beige with brown shutters, which tends to accent the jutting bay windows festooned in summer with flowers. The interior has lots of exposed paneling, a ceramic stove, and a hospitable bar and restaurant. The Egon Vergeiner family, the hosts, charge 245 AS ($13.03) for a single and 480 AS ($25.54) for a double, with breakfast included.

Food and Lodging at Oberlienz

If you have a car, you might prefer to stay at Oberlienz or "Upper Lienz," which is at the Zettersfeld cable-car station.

Hotel Haus Stocker (tel. 2766) is an L-shaped chalet in a sunny location near the Zettersfeld cable car. Benefiting from a panoramic view over Lienz and the Dolomites, the hotel is a few minutes' drive from the center of town. On the premises is an outdoor pool, as well as a collection of attractively paneled sitting rooms and dining rooms. There's a sauna on the premises, plus a big lawn for sunbathing and occasional nighttime musical entertainment. Per-person rates, with breakfast included, range from 300 AS ($15.96) to 325 AS ($17.29) per day.

Berghaus Pepi Stiegler (tel. 4788) is a contemporary chalet built into a hillside with a view of the mountains. Set within sight of the T-bar ski tow, the hotel has a streamlined attractive interior with few unnecessary frills. It also has a farmer's-style bierstube and a big indoor pool, a sauna, a children's playroom, a bar, and a restaurant. Per-person rates in high season range from 275 AS ($14.63) to 500 AS ($26.60), with half board included.

MATREI IN OSTTIROL: A winter sports resort and summer holiday retreat, Matrei in East Tyrol has much charm. From its location, winter visitors can avail themselves of two ski regions with well-prepared descents from above the 7500-foot mark as well as interesting tracks for cross-country skiing and ski hiking. There are reliable snow conditions in the newly developed Goldried ski area (more than 6500 feet) and at the runs near Matrei Tauernhaus (see hotel recommendations) and the Venedigerblich mountain railway.

In summer this is a choice spot for mountain climbing, walking, horseback riding, and tennis.

To reach Matrei by train, you can go to Lienz via Spittal or Innsbruck. From Lienz there's a Postal Bus connection. Of course you can also come here by car. Just don't confuse Matrei in East Tyrol with another Matrei which you may have passed through in your exploration of the Wipp Valley.

Food and Lodging

Hotel Rauter (tel. 311) has an attractive modern facade. It looks like a combination of a beach resort house and an alpine chalet. The most distinctive feature is the huge simplified adaptation of an arched window from a Gothic church set into a curved area above the front entrance. Inside, some of the structural elements seem to have roots in the 1930s, including the irregular columns rising into an expanding series of disks, the uppermost of which contains verdant green plants. The bedrooms have lighthearted elements that might be Japanese, art deco, or modified Gothic, depending on your whim.

This is definitely a year-round hotel, containing facilities geared to sports of all seasons. These include a big indoor pool and a summer outdoor pool, as well as both in- and outdoor tennis courts. Horseback riding is nearby, and the hotel bus makes frequent winter runs to the ski slopes. Anglers will find rich fishing areas close to the hotel.

The Obwexer family charges between 455 AS ($24.21) and 800 AS ($42.56) per person in a wide variety of accommodations, with half board included. A comfortable annex holds the overflow from the main hotel. The restaurant is tastefully outfitted with accessories. Specialties include medallions of spring lamb with a calvados cream sauce and parsley apples and sweet corn. Meals range from 135 AS ($7.18) to 360 AS ($19.15).

Pension Alpengasthof Tauernhaus (tel. 8801) is a rustic complex of at least three buildings clustered in an alpine meadow about nine miles from the center of Matrei. Technically it's up in the Tauerntal at about 5000 feet. You can reach it by bus from Matrei if you want to spend some time in this quiet isolated place. The accommodations house anywhere from one to six persons in simple bedrooms accented with lots of wood. Otto Brugger, the owner, along with his family, charges around 220 AS ($11.70) per person in a single or double, with breakfast included.

Gästehaus Schönblick (tel. 420). About ten minutes from the center of the village, this modern hotel benefits from a quiet location and a view of the mountains. Capably managed by Juliana and Franz Schwöller, the hotel serves only breakfast to an outdoor-loving clientele. The decor includes lots of homey touches, such as an open fireplace and a pleasant contemporary decor of big windows and vivid colors. Per-person rates, with breakfast, in a double cost from 210 AS ($11.17); singles pay a surcharge of 20 AS ($1.06) per day.

Gasthof Hinteregger (Weisses Rössl) (tel. 287). The entrance to this attractive hotel is marked with a metal sculpture of a white horse rearing up on its hind legs. The facade is painted a tasteful blue-gray with attractive detailing and prominent bay windows. In the center of the village, the hotel has a pleasantly rustic interior accented with lots of exposed wood and old-fashioned architectural details that add considerable amounts of charm. On the premises are a restaurant and a weinstube. Rates range from 400 AS ($21.28) to 450 AS ($23.94) per person, based on double occupancy, with half board included. Singles pay a surcharge of 25 AS ($1.33) daily.

Gasthof Panzlwirt, 4 Tauerntalstrasse (tel. 218), offers Tyrolean-style hospitality in a recently enlarged and modernized chalet. The house might be one of the most decorative in the village, accented with regional designs around many of the windows and wooden balconies weathered from the sun. The hotel is owned and managed by members of the Panzl family, who are descendants of Johann Panzl, a fierce soldier and noted eccentric who fought for the freedom of the Tyrol in the wars against the French in the early 19th century. He probably would have appreciated the rustic comfort of the hotel. The Panzlwirt contains a bowling alley, a café, a restaurant, an underground garage, and a series of pleasantly furnished public rooms. With breakfast included, per-person rates range from 290 AS ($15.34) to 335 AS ($17.82). Each of the rooms has a private bath, and many of them contain balconies.

VIRGEN: This village in the Virgental (Valley of the Virgen) lies to the west of Matrei in Osttirol, visited above. The road through the valley is stunning, stretching for slightly less than 12 miles. Along it you pass through gorges and tunnels. Eventually you can see the 11,480-foot-high Dreiherrenspitze.

Food and Lodging

Gasthof Sonne (tel. 5204) is a comfortable hotel built up on a terrace on the side of a hill in the center of the village. The main section has a hipped roof over white walls and a restaurant filling most of the big glass-walled extension on the first two floors. The interior has lots of rustic detailing and well-finished paneling. The Duregger family, your hosts, charge rates ranging from 240 AS ($12.77) to 400 AS ($21.28) per person for an overnight stay.

SILLIAN: The highest village in the Valley of Puster (Pustertal), Sillian lies in the Dolomites a short distance from the Italian border. It's sunny and fog-free, even in winter, and has good snow conditions from December to March. Skiers will find the area serviced by chair and drag lifts. This unique landscape attracts nonskiers and summer visitors with its many beautiful walks.

On the outskirts of Sillian are the ruins of the 13th-century **Heimfels Castle,** once occupied by the powerful counts of Görz.

Food and Lodging

Atzwanger (tel. 6205) is a white building with light-grained balconies stretching across the straight lines of its four-story facade, Recently built, it has an interior decor accented with simple rustic furniture, lots of paneling, and an occasionally blazing winter fireplace. The hotel stands slightly downhill from the village church, and is operated by a family with the same name. Per-person rates range from 170 AS ($9.04) to 240 AS ($12.77) in a double, and singles pay a daily surcharge of 25 AS ($1.33).

Pension Adelheid (tel. 6280) is an unpretentious white-walled house with a prominently hipped and gabled red tile roof. A modern extension shoots out from the side of the main building, which has an interior decor of light-grained paneling and simple furnishings. Per-person rates, with half board included, range from 250 AS ($13.30) to 290 AS ($15.34).

OBERTILLIACH: A short distance from Sillian, this little hamlet near the Italian frontier might be an ideal stopping place in summer if you're gulping down all the beautiful scenery in the area, or in winter if you'd like to ski in the Lienz Dolomites.

Food and Lodging

Gasthof Weiler (tel. 202) has attractive proportions and simple lines. You'll reach it by climbing a curved stone staircase which ends at a stone-flanked sun terrace. The well-furnished interior is filled with warmly tinted colors and lots of exposed paneling, while the cozy contemporary bedrooms are outfitted with simple furniture and different shades of various earth colors. On the premises are a bar and restaurant, serving regional cooking. Rates in singles range from 275 AS ($14.63) to 435 AS ($23.14), while per-person charges in a double go from 260 AS ($13.83) to 425 AS ($22.61), with half board included. Prices depend on the season.

Chapter XI

VORARLBERG

1. Bregenz
2. The Bregenz Forest
3. Feldkirch and Dornbirn
4. Bludenz and Its Valleys
5. The Brand Valley
6. Little Walser Valley
7. The Montafon Valley
8. Arlberg—the West Side

THE WESTERNMOST PROVINCE of Austria, and the smallest one other than Vienna, is Vorarlberg, a land of mountain villages and lakes, of deep valleys and meadowlands. This province is known for its natural beauty and scenery. In autumn, for example, one of the most beautiful spots on the European continent is the plain of the Rhine Valley near Dornbirn.

This is where Central Europe meets Western Europe, the Arlberg massif separating Vorarlberg from Tyrol. Essentially this province lies between Lake Constance and the Arlberg mountains. Local legend has it that this—not Mount Ararat in the Middle East—is where Noah landed with the ark after the flood waters had receded.

Of all the provinces of Austria, Vorarlberg is the most like Switzerland. In fact at the end of World War I it almost became part of that neighbor country. Vorarlbergers speak the Alemannic dialect of German, which is more closely related to the language of the Swiss just across the border to the west than it is to that spoken elsewhere in Austria.

Bregenz, the province's capital, opens onto Lake Constance, which Austria shares with both West Germany and Switzerland.

Vorarlberg is supported by tourism and industry, mostly textiles. Outside its best known tourist centers, such as Zürs and Lech, prices in the province are quite reasonable, especially in gasthof-type accommodations.

This is the most highly industrialized province of Austria—after Vienna, of course—but industry rarely pollutes the air and somehow seems to blend in with nature for the most part. For instance, one of its major industries is hydroelectric installations in the mountains.

If you're traveling by train from Innsbruck, my last stopover (Chapter X), you can reach Bregenz in Vorarlberg in about 3½ hours.

1. Bregenz

The capital of Vorarlberg province, Bregenz, once the Roman town of Brigantium, sits on terraces rising above the water at the eastern end of Lake Constance (Bodensee, in German). One of the major tourist goals in the province, Bregenz is really a small, "two-in-one" place—a modern town along the shore of the lake with a traffic-free old town towering over it. In summer the promenade along the shoreline is popular.

On lake vessels, you can travel the Bodensee district, venturing into West Germany and Switzerland, which share Lake Constance with Austria. For a panoramic view of the lake and the town, with Switzerland looming in the background, take the cable-car ride to Pfänder (see below).

Bregenz is at its liveliest in July at the time of its celebrated **music festival,** an event that rivals the festival at Salzburg. Many concerts are given, some open-air and some at the Festspiel-und-Kongresshaus. Most exciting are the elaborate productions of operas, operettas, and musical comedies presented on a large stage floating on the lake, with the audience watching from an amphitheater which seats 6500 persons. You'll see ornate barges arriving with elaborately dressed actors and singers. The stage is on a series of islands anchored by pillars driven into the lake bottom. Tickets for these stage productions cost from $8 to $75.

The Unterstadt, or the **Lower Town,** is the shopping district, with traffic-free malls along the lakeshore. In spring the quays of the Unterstadt blaze with color from flowerbeds as in some lakeside Swiss towns.

The **Vorarlberger Landesmuseum** (Vorarlberg Regional Museum) on the Kornmarkt is a rich repository of the artifacts and culture of the province. Exhibits are to be seen from the prehistoric days of the province, as well as Roman artifacts. You'll see a storybook of history with Romanesque and Gothic ecclesiastical works of art which come from churches in the district. See, in particular, a portrait of the Duke of Wellington by Angelica Kauffmann, who died in 1807. The museum is open from 9 a.m. to noon and from 2 to 5 p.m. daily except Monday, charging 10 AS (53¢) for admission.

The **Upper Town** is called both Oberstadt and Altstadt. Once the stronghold of the counts of Bregenz and Montford, it's of interest to the lover of antiquity. If you're driving, head up the Kirchestrasse, the Thalbachgasse, and the Amstorstrasse. Park and stroll back into the Middle Ages as you go along the quiet squares and narrow streets of the old quarter. Before the Upper Town was Roman Brigantium, this was the site of a Celtic settlement.

Among Oberstadt's attractions is **Martinsturm,** or the Tower of St. Martin, from the 13th century. A museum with local artifacts is on the upper floor of the tower. **St. Martin's Chapel,** founded in 1363, at the base of the tower, contains some murals from the 14th century. Far more interesting than any art, however, is the view of the surrounding area to be seen from the top of the tower.

See, if possible, the **Pfarrkirche** (parish church) dedicated to St. Gall. This 15th-century sandstone structure has a sunken nave from the 18th century.

The most important excursion in the environs is to **Pfänder,** to the east of Bregenz, reached by traveling 7½ miles by a narrow little twisting road through the mountains. To get there, head out of Bregenz along the road to Lindau, in West Germany, turning right in the direction of Lochau, where you pass a parish church. Make a right turn onto a secondary road leading to Pfänder. You'll come to a car park from which you go by foot to the Schwedenschanze belvedere, at nearly 3500 feet. From the terrace you'll have a fine view of the town and the lake.

If you don't go by car, you can get to Pfänder from Bregenz by cableway. Go to the lower station, which is about 500 yards east of the Kornmarkt. It takes about seven minutes to reach the summit. The cableway usually runs from 8:30 a.m. to 8 p.m., but in peak season, July and August, the run continues until 10 p.m. while the sky is still pierced with light. A round-trip ticket costs 75 AS ($3.99) per person. Allow about an hour and 45 minutes for this excursion.

If you're in Bregenz the second half of June any year, you might drive south of the town to the hamlet of **Hohenems,** which is about 11 miles from Lake Constance. The little town has a well-attended music festival, but don't count on staying at a hotel here. Accommodations for festival time are fully booked a year in advance. However, you might call the Hohemens Tourist Office (tel. 23-01), where a member of the staff will try to get you an accommodation in a private home.

The festival consists of compositions by Franz Schubert, although Schubert, who died at the age of 31, had no connection with Hohenems. It was selected as the site for the festival, called the Schubertiade Hohenems, by the noted German baritone Hermann Prey when he launched the event in 1976. The festival is presented in two rather small concert halls, the larger one seating only 475 persons.

For tickets to the festival, you can write to the **Schubertiade Hohenems,** Postfach 100, A-6845 Hohenems, Austria. Tickets for most performances range from $8 to $40.

Where to Stay

Schwärzler Hotel, 9 Landstrasse (tel. 22422), lies within two minutes by car from the center of town and is by all accounts the best hotel in Bregenz. Such noted visitors as Arthur Ashe, Leonard Bernstein, José Carreras, Richard Claydermann, and Birgitt Nilsson have all stayed behind the terracotta walls of this elegant hotel. The hotel offers well-furnished bedrooms with private balcony and a view of the mountains. On the premises are a restaurant, a covered swimming pool, a flowered sun garden, a bowling alley, and a host of extras. Rates in a single range from 480 AS ($25.54) to 755 AS ($40.17), while per-person prices in a double go from 420 AS ($22.34) to 480 AS ($25.54), with breakfast included.

Hotel Weisses Kreuz, 5 Römerstrasse (tel. 22489), is a graciously proportioned baroque building with a green and white facade and a steeply pitched roof with three tiers of gables. Completely renovated in 1983, the interior is filled with painted armoires, elegant antiques, and conservative furniture. In the center of town, the hotel is a popular gathering place for local residents. There's an à la carte restaurant on the premises. In comfortably furnished bedrooms, rates range from 455 AS ($24.21) to 660 AS ($35.11) in a single and from 720 AS ($38.30) to 950 AS ($50.54) in a double, with breakfast included. Prices depend on the season.

Berghof Fluh, 7 Fluherstrasse, Bregenz-Fluh (tel. 24213), is a comfortable modern hotel designed almost like a spacious private home. Lying in Fluh, a small village just outside town, the hotel has a long flowered sun terrace with a view of the Swiss Alps. You'll also find a series of rustic public rooms, many of which are paneled, and a German-style tavern with a beamed ceiling, a handsome wooden bar, and an occasional visit by a local rock band. The sunny and cheerful bedrooms rent for 460 AS ($24.47) for a single and 780 AS ($41.50) for a double, with breakfast included. Half board costs another 155 AS ($8.25) per person daily. The in-house restaurant is often visited by German, Swiss, and Austrian urbanites who willingly make the trip here. A friendly waiter will present you with a small handwritten menu which will usually have an assortment of fish, game, and crispy salads from both the Austrian and international repertoire of fine cuisine. À la carte meals range from 135 AS ($7.18) to 325 AS ($17.29). It's closed Monday.

Gasthof Adler, Mehrerauerstrasse (tel. 31788), is a long horizontal structure with a steeply pitched red tile roof set above two floors of red-shuttered windows. Part of the facade has been covered with modern planking, although the rest of the hotel looks much older. The cozy interior contains a restaurant, a bar, and a coffeeshop, as well as a sauna. The bedrooms are furnished with painted furniture and lots of exposed wood. Per-person rates range from 180 AS ($9.58), with breakfast included. None of the rooms has a private bath, but the facilities in the hallways are adequate.

Hotel Heidelberger Fass, 30 Kirchstrasse (tel. 22463), is an unusual baroque hotel in the center of town. Its facade is crowned with a big rococo gable with elaborately curved sides, including an adaptation of that design above some of the windows. The interior has lots of well-finished paneling, crisscrossed ceiling beams, and country-style accessories. The attractive restaurant serves well-prepared Austrian specialties. Singles cost 410 AS ($21.81), while doubles go for 325 AS ($17.29) per person, with breakfast included.

Where to Dine

Zoll, 118 Arlbergstrasse (tel. 31705), is a discreetly elegant restaurant which has become one of the stars of Austrian nouvelle cuisine. Ingredients are ultra fresh and perfectly attuned to the seasons. The handwritten menu lists imaginative recipes made from hare, quail, and fresh fish from the lake. Specific dishes include venison schnitzel with spinach spätzle, cheese ravioli made in house, zander filet with optional seaweed garnish, a savory tafelspitz with homemade horseradish, and an excellent wine list (the steward will make an honest selection for you if the names are a bit confusing). The restaurant is closed for two weeks in January and June, and on Thursday during the rest of the year. À la carte meals range from 125 AS ($6.65) to 520 AS ($27.66), while fixed-price meals cost from 420 AS ($22.34) to 720 AS ($38.30).

Burgrestaurant Gebhardsberg (tel. 22515). There's a marvelous view of Bregenz, the lake, and the Rhine Valley from the flowered terrace of this castle restaurant. If you've dreamed about being fêted by a team of waiters in the upper floors of a Teutonic castle, this is the place for you. The terrace is built on an observation platform above the main gate. The entire complex, which includes a 14th-century church, is built high on a rocky bluff above the lake.

The eating areas inside are comprised of several tastefully decorated rooms, and the menus for all of them include roast beef, an array of lake fish, a well-stocked fresh salad buffet, and a host of Austrian specialties. Fixed-price meals range from 140 AS ($7.45) to 250 AS ($13.30), while à la carte dinners jump from 100 AS ($5.32) to 360 AS ($19.15). The restaurant is closed Tuesday and during the winter between November and Easter.

Mandolino, 20 Kaiserstrasse (tel. 22883), is a likeable Italian restaurant, which does a popular local trade. Vegetables are properly prepared here, with just the right amount of crispy freshness, while the salads have several tasty varieties of lettuce. A specialty is the flambéed maccheroncini with pepperoni and parmesan, savory lamb chops, cannelloni, and a tasty lasagne. Portions are generous and might be followed, if you're in the mood, by homemade ice cream. À la carte meals range from 155 AS ($8.25) to 325 AS ($17.29). Reservations are suggested, and the restaurant closes on Sunday.

After Dark

If you're in Bregenz on a summer night you don't need nightlife, for few smoke-filled clubs could compete with a walk along the lakeshore and a visit to a café. However, if you seek richer divertisements, you can visit the **Spiel-Casino Bregenz,** 2 Römerstrasse, where roulette, baccarat, and blackjack are played from 4 p.m. daily. The parking garage at the casino is free.

2. The Bregenz Forest

From Bregenz you can make one of the most interesting scenic excursions in Vorarlberg—or in Austria, for that matter—deep into the Bregenzerwald, or Bregenz Forest. It's not as well known as the Black Forest of West Germany, but in my opinion it has just as much charm and character as its sister *wald* to the north.

The forest takes up the northern part of the Vorarlberg alpine range. A state highway splits the valley of the Bregenzer Ache River, making motoring easy, but the true charm of the forest lies off the beaten path in the little undiscovered valleys cut by tiny tributaries of the river. In spring the beautiful alpine meadows burgeon with wildflowers. In the background you can see the towering Alps.

Don't expect a proliferation of trees in the Bregenz Forest. The Austrians have cleared a lot of the woodlands to make meadows, where you'll see contented cows grazing, reminiscent of Switzerland.

One of the most frequented areas for sports and recreation is the **Bödele,** lying between the Valley of the Ache (don't you love that name?) and the Valley of the Rhine. Skiers are drawn to the highlands in winter.

The people who live in the forest are strong on keeping the old customs alive. If you're passing through the valley on a Sunday, you'll probably see Vorarlbergers going to church in their traditional garb. The headdress of the women is often striking, ranging from small crowns to wide-brimmed black straw hats. Unlike most of the rest of Europe the people of this area wear white for mourning rather than black.

BEZAU: The best known village of the Bregenz Forest, Bezau is surrounded by a landscape that's beautiful in both winter and summer. In the spring, summer, and autumn, you can hike, go mountaineering, swim, fish for trout, and play tennis or mini-golf.

In winter there's alpine skiing with the Hinterbregenzerwald ski ticket covering a range of more than 50 lifts and cable railways. There are some 25 miles of cross-country ski trails. You can also go tobogganing or play tennis at one of the three courts inside a hall.

A cableway from here will take you to the Baumgartenhöhe at 5350 feet.

Food and Lodging

Kur Sporthotel Post (tel. 2207) is one of the loveliest hotels in the region. It's composed of two tin-roof chalets covered with cedar shingles and flowery balconies. An elaborate wrought-iron sign extends over the driveway leading up to the hotel's location between a collection of houses and a big open field. This establishment was founded in 1850 as a link in the Austrian postal services. Shortly afterward, an enterprising member of the Natter family established a restaurant on the premises.

The elegantly decorated hotel you see today is still managed by a descendant of the original founder. Renovated in 1976, the hotel contains a blazing fireplace open to view on four sides, lots of rustic beams, tastefully discreet lighting, and a collection of alpine-style antiques.

The bedrooms are country-style luxurious, and have many rustic details as well as modern baths and up-to-date comforts. On the premises is a heated indoor pool whose ceiling is a skillfully crafted wood-beamed marvel. Per-person rates in a double range from 650 AS ($34.58) to 890 AS ($47.35). Singles pay a daily supplement of 60 AS ($3.19).

Gasthof Gams (tel. 05514) is a dignified-looking hotel which rambles across a big lawn a few buildings away from the village church. The facade is an appealing combination of cedar shingles, white stucco, steeply pitched gables, and recessed balconies. Although the core of the hotel was built in 1648, guests find all the modern comforts, particularly in the well-heated outdoor pool whose entrance is through a low opening on the inside of the hotel (the water is so warm, according to management, that many guests enjoy swimming even during snowstorms). Also on the premises are two outdoor tennis courts, a hot whirlpool, a sauna, a big garden, and several rustically antique-style sitting rooms. The wood-paneled bedrooms range from 400 AS ($21.28) to 675 AS ($35.91) per person, with half board included. Prices depend on the season, the accommodation, and the plumbing.

The restaurant is outfitted in an appealing style which originated years ago in the region. The establishment specializes in seafood, such as a well-prepared filet of sole, along with filet steak, curry dishes, and desserts which include a variety of fresh mountain berries. Full meals cost from 145 AS ($7.71) to 345 AS ($18.35).

DAMÜLS: This is one of the leading ski centers for winter sports in the Bregenz Forest, at an elevation of 4680 feet. One skier who goes here every year describes it as being for connoisseurs. Hotels organize weekly après-ski programs, so check to see what the action is during your stay here. The village is small, so it's easy to get to know your fellow visitors well.

Damüls is an area of great scenic beauty, making a summer visit pleasant. This is the loftiest village in the forest.

Food and Lodging

Hotel Damülser Hof (tel. 210) is a peacefully isolated collection of modern chalets interconnected with covered passageways. All of them sit in a sloping alpine meadow a short walk from the village church. The elegant interior has enough variety in its decor to please most guests. Each of the cozy public rooms is crafted from such top-quality materials as exposed bricks, carved and painted wooden ceilings, and intricately crafted wrought iron. There are plenty of intimate niches, lots of soft lighting, and several blazing wintertime fireplaces. On the premises are a friendly bar area, an indoor pool, a sauna, a good restaurant, a bierstube/café, a dance bar, a sporting goods store, a bowling alley, and a big sun terrace.

The bedrooms are romantically paneled, renting in high season for between 530 AS ($28.20) and 650 AS ($34.58) per person in a double and between 575 AS ($30.59) and 830 AS ($44.17) in a single, with half board included. Rates at Christmastime rise around 300 AS ($15.96) per person higher. The Klauser family are your accommodating hosts.

Hotel Hohes Licht (tel. 201) is a pleasant modern chalet at the edge of a loosely grouped cluster of other buildings. Its facade is decorated with red shutters and patterned balconies, with an awning sheltering the windows of the ground-floor public rooms. On the premises is an indoor swimming pool, as well as a sauna and a tastefully decorated restaurant which seems to give off an amber glow from the exposed wood and pink curtains. The simple bedrooms rent for 480 AS ($25.54) to 610 AS ($32.45) per person, with half board included.

Hotel Mittagspitze (tel. 211), a short distance away from the village church, is a pleasingly designed chalet with an angled facade of alternate areas of white walls and weathered planking. The attractive decor emphasizes lots of amber-colored paneling, simple furniture, and tasteful accessories. Many of the rooms have private balconies, renting for 515 AS ($27.40) per person in units holding from one to three persons. Apartments for four or more cost around 590 AS ($31.31) per person. These prices include half board. The in-house restaurant serves tasty and well-prepared food accompanied by excellent service from a team of uniformed waiters.

MELLAU: One of the most charming and relatively unknown resorts in the Bregenz Forest is Mellau, a hamlet set against gently rolling mountains with plenty of woodland for walking, if you center here. Trout fishermen find excitement and rewards in the Bregenzer Ache with its fast-flowing waters. Canoeing from here in the river's rapids is a thrilling sport. The village has a large, heated outdoor swimming pool.

Many folkloric evenings give visitors the chance to be entertained by groups wearing the traditional dress of the valley.

Food and Lodging

Hotel Pension Kreuz (tel. 2208) is a modern, five-story hotel with two distinct sections, each with a symmetrically peaked roof and lots of big-windowed balconies. The pleasant interior is dotted with rustic accessories, such as a stone-rimmed fireplace, heavy beams, hunting trophies, and brass chandeliers, while the attractive, up-to-date dining room has chairs upholstered in red and lots of space. On the premises is an ozone-enriched swimming pool, plus a sauna, a collection of bar areas, a bowling alley, a dance hall, a reading room, and a daytime café with its own bakery. Ernst and Hedwig Metzler, the owners, charge from 360 AS ($19.15) to 960 AS ($51.07) per person, with half board included. Their bedrooms are romantically woodsy. Prices vary according to the season and the accommodation.

Hotel Engel (tel. 2246). The oldest members of the Rogelböck family remember when their hotel was housed in a much older building whose picture you can see inside the modern chalet that replaced it. The cozy interior is accented with warmly designed textiles, blazing fireplaces, sunny and well-decorated restaurants, and a big indoor pool. Per-person rates, with half board included, range from 375 AS ($19.95) to 480 AS ($25.54) in a double, and singles pay a daily supplement of 50 AS ($2.66).

3. Feldkirch and Dornbirn

Up to now I've assumed that you might enter Austria from Lake Constance if you're coming from either Switzerland or West Germany or directly from the Bavarian section of the latter country. However, you might also approach from another part of Switzerland, coming into Feldkirch. After visiting Feldkirch, I'll introduce you to the largest city of Vorarlberg, Dornbirn, which is even bigger than the provincial capital, Bregenz.

FELDKIRCH: This old town, considered "the gateway to Austria," is nearly halfway between Paris and Vienna, lying on the road through the Arlberg. If you're traveling by rail from Switzerland, Feldkirch will be your first town in Austria. Unfortunately, many people rush on to other destinations, but it will be worth your time to get off the train and explore this town that goes back to medieval days.

Feldkirch was once a fortified town which grew up at the "heel" of Schattenburg Castle on a tributary of the Ill River, becoming known for its classical Latin school. The old town, which can be explored in about an hour, is the tourist attraction, the new town lying to the northeast.

The heart of the old town is **Marktgasse** (market street), a rectangle with arcades. Many of the old-style houses are graced with oriels and frescoed facades. A popular wine festival is held here in July, with the town filling up with revelers.

Among the curiosities of the old town is the **Katzenturm,** or tower of the cats. The cats in this case were actually lions. The tower was named for a defense cannon here adorned with lion heads. The **Churertor,** or Chur Gate, is another Feldkirch landmark. Sights include the **Domkirche** (cathedral church), known for its 15th-century double nave. See the *Descent from the Cross,* a 1521 painting by Wolf Huber of the Danube school.

Schattenburg Castle, once a defense fortress and now a museum and restaurant, can be reached by car by heading up Burggasse, or you can climb the steps by the Schlosssteig. Parts of the castle were built at the turn of the 16th century. From the castle precincts you have a view of the Valley of the Rhine.

The **Heimatmuseum** (local museum) in the castle exhibits a wealth of furnishings of the region, ranging from those that filled a farmer's shack to pieces that graced the hall of a nobleman. Also displayed are a large collection of art and an armor collection. The museum is open from 9 a.m. to noon and from 1 to 5 p.m. daily except Wednesday. Admission is 15 AS (80¢).

Food and Lodging

Hotel ILL-Park, 2 Leonhardsplatz (tel. 24600), has the most strikingly contemporary facade in town. The drama of its format is enhanced by its location on a brick-covered square at the edge of the old quarter. The 92 tastefully decorated bedrooms have private bath, mini-bar, TV, and radio. On the premises is a cafeteria, plus a beer cellar with an adjoining bowling alley (the perspective of which looks like a time tunnel from some space war), a dance bar, and an indoor swimming pool. Except for the rustic beer hall the decor is contemporary, with pin lighting and lots of attractively muted colors.

With breakfast included, doubles cost 950 AS ($50.54) while singles rent for 660 AS ($35.11). The international menu in the restaurant features week-long specials from many different countries. When I was last there the emphasis was on Provence, and the food items included a well-prepared Mediterranean fish soup. Meals range from 120 AS ($6.38) to 480 AS ($25.54). Reservations are suggested.

Central Hotel Löwen, 15-19 Neustadt (tel. 2207), has an ochre facade with an entrance beneath an arched street-level arcade. The interior is outfitted with a simple collection of rococo-framed mirrors, eclectically grouped chairs, and simple accessories, including what look like family portraits. The Furtenbach sisters, the owners, charge between 385 AS ($20.48) and 515 AS ($27.40) for a single and between 325 AS ($17.29) and 430 AS ($22.88) per person in a double, with half board included.

Hotel Hochhaus, 177 Reichsstrasse (tel. 23369), a minute's walk from the train station, is in two separate balconied sections, one of which rises almost twice as high as the other. The hotel is painted a pastel yellow with neutral-toned balconies. On the premises is a ground-level sun terrace, and the comfortable bedrooms have big windows and contemporary furniture. Rates range from 215 AS ($11.44) to 455 AS ($24.21) for a single and from 200 AS ($10.64) to 390 AS ($20.75) per person in a double, with breakfast included.

Restaurant Lingg, Am Marktplatz (tel. 22062). This restaurant has a good local reputation, and many of the town's lunches take place here. The dining section is one floor above ground level in an old structure on the main square, whose medieval buildings are visible from the windows. You could begin your meal with melon with shrimp, served in a homemade mayonnaise sauce, and then follow with one of several well-prepared meat, fish, or game specialties from the Austrian kitchen. Full set meals range between 80 AS ($4.26) and 215 AS ($11.44), or from 95 AS ($5.05)—if you're dining very simply—to a high of 320 AS ($17.02) if you order à la carte. It's closed Monday, and reservations are suggested.

DORNBIRN: The "city of textiles," Dornbirn lies in the heart of Vorarlberg province, of which it is the largest town and the commercial center. A trade fair in mid-July ties in with the Bregenz Festival. Dornbirn, only seven miles from the provincial capital, is at the outskirts of the Bregenz Forest on the edge of a broad Rhineland valley.

The city center is the Marktplatz (market square), graced by a 19th-century parish church in neoclassical style and by the **Rotes Haus** (Red House), a 1639 building which is now a restaurant.

The most exciting excursion in the environs is to **Karren** (3200 feet), about 1½ miles from the heart of town. The sturdy of foot and shank will make the climb in about two hours, but you can take a cable car and get there in five minutes. For your trouble, you'll be rewarded with a magnificent view. From here you can hike down to the Rappen Gorge, with the Ache River flowing through it.

Food and Lodging

Parkhotel, 6 Goethestrasse (tel. 62692), is an elegant modern hotel in a park area in the heart of town. A hotel of international standards in both comfort and cuisine, it serves as the preferred rendezvous point for the area's political and industrial leaders. The rather grand decor is conservative and contemporary, with lots of wood accents and big windows looking out over the lawns. On the premises are tennis courts, a sauna, and an indoor pool.

The hotel has one of the town's best known restaurants, whose clientele is rather solidly conservative and whose food is good. Called the Jägerstüble, it serves snails, crispy asparagus in spring, and a specialty with lamb, onions, and saffron rice. The chef occasionally features dishes from Provence or Italy. À la carte meals range from 145 AS ($7.71) to 355 AS ($18.87). Rates in one of the comfortably furnished bedrooms range from 330 AS ($17.56) to 525 AS ($27.93) per person, with breakfast included.

Hotel Zum Verwalter, 1 Schlossgasse (tel. 62579), belongs to a family that has run the hotel for the last two centuries. The hotel is composed of a beautiful ochre house with green shutters and a steeply pitched roof, plus an attractive balconied addition stretching out into the well-maintained lawn. The interior provides the kind of simple, high-quality decor which many of you will find loaded with charm. My favorite room is the paneled Schützenstüble, whose artifacts and lace-trimmed tablecloths handsomely complement its regional specialties.

The comfortable bedrooms have paneled ceilings, gracefully curved headboards, and warm colors. They rent for around 400 AS ($21.28) for a single and for around 325 AS ($17.29) per person in a double, with breakfast included. These prices vary according to the season, the exposure, and the accommodation. The Herburger family are the friendly owners.

Sport & Tagungshotel Rickatschwende, Bödelestrasse (tel. 65350), is a sprawling modern hotel built onto an older shingle-sided house. Tennis courts, an indoor swimming pool, and a sauna are on the premises, as well as a paneled series of public rooms. The hotel sits at the edge of a grassy field at the edge of town. The cozy bedrooms have warm colors, lots of exposed wood, and big sunny windows. They rent for 750 As ($39.90) in a single and 650 AS ($34.58) per person in a double, with half board included. A garage on the premises charges 60 AS ($3.19) per day to shelter your car.

Katharinenhof, 2 Felder-Strasse (tel. 62577), is a flat-roofed contemporary hotel with turquoise and white designs painted below some of the windows and a ground-floor extension stretching toward the street. Serving only breakfast, the hotel has both a covered swimming pool and a sauna on the premises. Rates range from 450 AS ($23.94) to 515 AS ($27.40) in a single and from 330 AS ($17.56) to 350 AS ($18.62) per person in a double, with breakfast included. Some triples are available for 815 AS ($43.36) to 865 AS ($46.02). The Zumtobel family are your hosts.

Krone (tel. 62720). The solidly constructed dining room is large enough to hold many hungry diners. The chef is skillful at his craft, as were the carpenters who worked to build the place. Choices from the kitchen include avocado with crabmeat, which might be followed by a ragoût of venison with fresh spätzle. Your dessert might be an array of fresh sorbets or a praline soufflé with ice cream. Full meals range from 105 AS ($5.59) to 310 AS ($16.49). The Krone is closed Wednesday and for part of Saturday.

Rotes Haus (tel. 62306) was constructed in 1639 and has today one of the best decorated facades in town. It's been known for many years as a bastion of conservative, high-quality traditional cookery. A glance at the menu will reveal a modified nouvelle cuisine. Items on the menu—designed like a page from an old-fashioned newspaper—include lamb with mint sauce, blue trout in butter sauce, osso buco, and a salad buffet that's crispy and well stocked. Full meals range in price from 125 AS ($6.65) to 385 AS ($20.48). Reservations are suggested, and it's closed during most of November.

4. Bludenz and Its Valleys

This little alpine town, at an elevation of about 2000 feet, is at exactly the halfway point between Paris and Vienna on the main highway connecting the capital of the province, Bregenz, with the capital of the country, Vienna. Some of the houses in the town were here in the Middle Ages.

Bludenz is the gateway to five major mountain valleys: the **Klostertal,** the **Montafon,** the **Brandnertal** (Brand Valley), the **Grosswalsertal,** and the **Walgau.**

The Klostertal goes toward the east where lies the internationally renowned skiing territory of the Arlberg. The Montafon leads southward to the Silvretta alpine road, power stations, dams, artificial lakes, and the Silvretta-Nova ski center. The beautiful Brand Valley to the southwest has as a highlight the Lünersee, the largest lake in the eastern Alps. These three valleys are visited below.

Of less interest to tourists is the Grosswalsertal to the north and east, and Walgau to the northwest.

Motorists pass through here, traveling the route from Lake Constance to the Arlberg and the Montafon Valley. Because of the valley's attractions, a variety of excursions are offered originating in Bludenz, including trips to some of Austria's finest skiing centers.

Besides the heavy tourist business engendered here, Bludenz also has an industrial side, with chocolate factories rivaling those of Switzerland, plus the textile plants.

The town is surrounded by mountains, some of which reach a height of about 9800 feet. Directly north of the town you can take a cableway to **Muttersberg** (4635 feet), called the sun terrace of Bludenz.

FOOD AND LODGING: **Schlosshotel,** 5 Schlossplatz (tel. 3017), in the center of town, is built high up on the same rocky bluff as the castle and the baroque church. The hotel design is solidly conservative, with recessed balconies, red shutters, and a sprawling L-shaped format which includes more than a few modern building materials. The establishment encompasses well-maintained bedrooms in both the main building and the rambling annex a few steps away.

The interior decor has massive timbers, ornate chandeliers, and warmly textured colors. You might enjoy at least one meal on the terracotta tiles of the sun terrace, or under the gently arched ceiling of the dining room. A bowling alley is on the premises, as well as a children's playroom and a putting green. The in-house café serves ice creams and pastries, while the restaurant offers well-prepared Austrian specialties. The Dörflinger family charge between 500 AS ($26.60) and 600 AS ($31.92) per person in a double and between 600 AS ($31.92) and 750 AS ($39.90) in a single, with half board included.

5. The Brand Valley

Often visited from Bludenz (see above), the Brand Valley (Brandnertal in German) is one of the most scenic valleys in Austria, a place of rare beauty surrounded by glaciers, with many side valleys. Romantic little villages and lush pastureland are set against a panoramic alpine backdrop. This is a valley with a wealth of inns and hotels, especially at Brand (coming up).

Skiers are attracted to the mountain ranges here, namely Niggenkopf and Palüd. The valley runs for almost ten miles before reaching Brand.

BRAND: A few centuries ago exiles from the Valais in Switzerland settled this village at the mouth of the Zalimtal near the Swiss border. At an elevation of 3400 feet, Brand has long been a popular mountain health resort spread out along a mile stretch at the base of the Scesaplana mountain range. It's now a much-visited winter sports center, the main resort of the Rätikon district of Vorarlberg.

You can take a cableway to the top of the Tschengla at 4095 feet, as well as a chair lift to Eggen at 4165 feet. From there, you can make connections to Niggenkopf at 5235 feet.

A cable car also goes to the glacial **Lünersee** (Lake Lüner), a rather austere body of water which is the largest lake in the eastern Alps. It has been dammed and a reservoir created. The trip to Lünersee takes about two hours, 12 minutes of which is by cable car which runs from June until mid-October. If you're at the lower station by 8 a.m. you can catch the first car, but you must leave by 5 p.m. The round-trip fare is 65 AS ($3.46) per person.

Food and Lodging

Hotel Scesaplana (tel. 221) has a tasteful chalet-inspired design of wood accents, accommodating sun terraces, and balconied extensions angling out from the peak-roofed core. The hotel, skillfully managed by Ruth and Helmut Schwärzler, is in the center of the resort and has an attractively paneled interior totally in keeping with the alpine spirit of the town. A few steps away is an indoor swimming pool, as well as both indoor and outdoor tennis courts, a sauna, a solarium, two restaurants, a bar, and a disco. A range of other sports is within easy access, including riding, fishing, skiing, and carriage drives (many of them cost an additional fee). Clients on the half-board plan receive a wide choice of specialties included with the evening meal. Per-person rates on that half-board plan range from 675 AS ($35.91) to 1200 AS ($63.84) in a double, and singles pay a daily supplement of 50 AS ($2.66).

Hotel Walliserhof (tel. 241) is a solidly built hotel with rows of recessed balconies and big windows looking out over the village church on one side and a long expanse of fields on the other. The public rooms are rustic, dotted with heavy timbers and well-maintained paneling. On the premises is a covered pool, plus a sporting goods store and a sauna. Both indoor and outdoor tennis courts are nearby. The Meyer family, your hosts, charge from 770 AS ($40.96) to 930 AS ($49.48) per person in a double and from 830 AS ($44.17) to 985 AS ($52.40) in a single, with full board included. Prices depend on the season and the room assignment.

Hotel Colrosa (tel. 225) is a popular stopover point for families and athletes, set in a quiet location on a forested hillside, not far from the center of town. Designed like a chalet, the hotel contains rustically pleasant rooms capped with beamed and paneled ceilings and accented with wintertime fireplaces. Capably managed by the Heinz Beck family, the hotel charges between 480 AS ($25.54) and 905 AS ($48.15) per person daily, with half board included. Prices depend on the season and the room assignment.

Hotel Hämmerle (tel. 213), owned by a family of the same name, is a wood-trimmed chalet with a modern extension added on to a much older core. In the center of town, the hotel offers a big sun terrace, lots of grass-covered lawns for children's games or for playing, and a pleasantly paneled interior illuminated by brass chandeliers sometimes accented by a depiction of a double-headed eagle. Many of the cozy bedrooms have private balconies and views over the mountains. With half board included, per-person rates in a double range from 500 AS ($26.60) to 600 AS ($31.92) in high season. Singles pay a daily supplement of 25 AS ($1.33).

Hotel Lagant (tel. 285) is a simple chalet-style hotel at the edge of the village, near the Niggenkopf chair lift. Built in 1970, the establishment contains an indoor swimming pool, an elevator, a big sun terrace, and cozily attractive public rooms filled with a rustic ambience. On the premises is a hospitable bar and a restaurant serving well-prepared Austrian specialties. Per-person rates in high season range from 500 AS ($26.60) to 700 AS ($37.24), with singles paying a daily supplement of 120 AS ($6.38). These tariffs include half board.

Après Ski

Nightlife is very casual but fun at Brand, especially in the peak of the season. Drinks begin at 50 As ($2.66) in most places.

The Scesa Taverna nightclub at the already-recommended **Hotel Scesaplana** is the major rendezvous point in town and has the most sophisticated entertainment. Tea dances usually get under way here at 4:30 p.m., and the Irish coffee is said to be the best in town. You'll also want to sample their fine draft beer later in the evening.

Special folkloric Vorarlberg evenings are also organized in season (ask at the tourist office to see what's featured at the time of your visit).

6. Little Walser Valley

The Kleinwalsertal (Little Walser Valley) is not to be confused with the Grosswalsertal (Big Walser Valley), mentioned above. Both take their name from the exiles who settled here from the Valais section of Switzerland.

Little Walser lies in Vorarlberg, but is separated from the rest of the towns and hamlets of the province. The Allgäu Alps cut it off completely from the rest of Austria, so that although it's technically a part of this country, it's governed by West German customs and uses the West German mark instead of the Austrian schilling as the coin of its realm. As German appearing as this valley may seem, however, you're reminded that you're still in Austria when you mail a letter, as Austrian stamps are necessary.

To say "completely" cut off isn't quite accurate, since Little Walser

Valley *can* be reached directly from the rest of Austria, but you'd have to take a mountain goat trail to make the journey. Otherwise, to enter the valley you start at Oberstdorf at the border between West Germany and Austria.

The Breitach River runs through this broad valley, which is surrounded by limestone mountains. The valley is rich in tradition, and most of the old folk customs and dress are still kept alive by its people.

Little Walser Valley is both a summer and a winter resort. People come in summer to enjoy the pure mountain air, and they retreat here in winter for the snow.

REIZLERN: This is the biggest hamlet in the valley, at the head of the Schwarzwassertal, or Black Water Valley. One of its most popular attractions is its **Spiel-Casino Kleinwalsertal.** Germans flock over the border to play roulette, baccarat, and blackjack from 5 p.m. The casino also has a restaurant and a bar. It's open from Christmas until the end of January and from April to December 23.

South of the hamlet, you can take a cableway, called the Kanzelwandbahn, to a mountain perch at 6555 feet.

Food and Lodging

Hotel Stern (tel. 5208) is an attractive chalet, with heavy eaves and regional decorations painted around the borders of the windows. Built in 1936, the hotel has dozens of handcrafted extras you'll only find in an older building, including thick wall paneling, oversize beams, and a scattering of fireplaces. On the premises is a Swiss-style restaurant, plus a gemütlich bierstube, a dancing bar, a bowling alley, a sauna with massage facilities, a children's play area, and a covered swimming pool. Per-person rates range from $23 to $52 in a single and from $20 to $43 in a double, with half board included. Prices depend on the season and the plumbing. Meals in the sympathetic dining room are often accompanied by zither music.

Gasthof Traube, 56 Walserstrasse (tel. 5177), is a contemporary chalet with an attractively simplified facade which still retains such oldtime accents as overhanging eaves and long wood-trimmed balconies. The hospitable interior includes dozens of ceiling beams and lots of rustic paneling. The hotel charges between $25 and $32 per person in summer and between $32 and $36 per person in winter, with half board included. The Hugo and Christl Fischer family, your sports-loving hosts, do much to make your stay comfortable.

HIRSCHEGG: If you blink you'll have passed through this hamlet. You can take a chair lift from here to the top station of the Heuberg at 4500 feet, but the main reason for stopping in Hirschegg is the excellent accommodation described below.

Ifen-Hotel (tel. 5071). Built in 1936, this hotel is approved by at least five European hotel associations, including the prestigious Relaix et Châteaux. Seen from a distance, the place looks like a pleasing marriage between a Mediterranean villa and a Teutonic piece of art deco. Architectural features include gently curving walls and distinctive struts extending at an angle from the exterior walls to the edge of the overhanging eaves.

Views from the dozens of balconies encompass most of the village and the valley it sits in.

The elegant public rooms are filled with heavy beams, big windows, and rustic accessories, all in the framework of luxurious comfort. On the premises are four outdoor tennis courts, three indoor tennis courts, a covered swimming pool, and a wide range of sports and fitness facilities. A team of chefs prepare elegant meals for the restaurants, which often feature live folkloric music. Otto and Renate Simon, the sophisticated hoteliers, welcome an assortment of guests from around the world. They charge between $27 and $70 in a single and between $27 and $80 per person in a double, with half board included. Prices are based on the season and the plumbing.

7. The Montafon Valley

Montafon is a high alpine valley known for its powdery snow and sun. It stretches some 26 miles at the southern tip of Vorarlberg, with the Ill River flowing through on its way to join the Rhine. The valley, filled with mountain villages and major winter recreation areas, is encircled by the mountain ranges of Rätikon, Silvretta, and Verwall.

Montafon has been called a "ski stadium," so designated because it's a vastly integrated ski region. One ski pass covers unlimited use of 70 cable cars, chair lifts, and T-bars in all four main ski areas of the valley, as well as transportation between the resorts.

Hochjock-Zamang has fine skiing in the back bowls and down the front, and is the main mountain at Schruns of Hemingway fame (see below). Tschagguns has Grabs-Golm for some easier runs. Silvretta-Nova at Gaschurn and St. Gallenkirch is a superb ski circus on several mountains, and the Schafberg of Gargellen is secluded in a side valley.

SCHRUNS/TSCHAGGUNS: These hamlets are so close together that they can be treated as one, being only about three-quarters of a mile apart. Schruns is the major town of the Montafon, lying on the right bank of the Ill River. Tschagguns, a smaller resort than Schruns, is on the left bank. Although celebrated for winter sports, both are also popular in summer.

At Schruns you can go by cableway to the already-mentioned Hochjoch-Zamang. First, you go to Kapell at 6025 feet, where you'll find its renowned restaurant. On the sun terrace here, people do everything from making love to getting an alpine suntan. A chair lift will take you from Kapell up to Sennigrat at 7550 feet. It's finally possible to take a so-called Hochjoch taxi (really a lift) from Sennigrat to Kreuzjoch.

From Tschagguns you can take a chair lift to Grabs-Golm at 4550 feet. You'll also find a restaurant here. After that, you can go by drag lift to Hochegga at 5202 feet.

About Schruns, where he spent winters while he worked on *The Sun Also Rises,* Hemingway said that he preferred to go where the rain became snow.

Food and Lodging at Schruns

Hotel Alpenhof Messmer (tel. 2664) presents a generously sized modification of a chalet to a view of the valley and the mountains. Dieter and Charlotte Messmer have taken care to landscape this pleasant hotel into the hillside on which it sits, a short distance from the center of town. This has involved planting grass and shrubs on top of one of the hotel's low-lying extensions, which increases the natural attraction of the sunny terrace.

The interior has rustic accessories as well as an indoor pool (whose ceiling is supported by massive timbers), a hot whirlpool, and several open fireplaces. The bedrooms are a monochromatic delight of textiles whose color comes close to matching the amber-tinted paneling. They usually contain color TVs, private baths, and phones. Rates in doubles range from 575 AS ($30.59) to 1100 AS ($58.52) per person, depending on the season and the accommodation, with half board included. Occupants of singles pay an extra 75 AS ($3.99) to 290 AS ($15.34) per day.

Sport-Hotel Alpenrose (tel. 2655) is a contemporary chalet, with lots of wood-accented balconies, stone retaining walls, and big windows. From the downhill side you'll notice a streamlined wood-and-glass extension looking out over the valley. The interior is loaded with rustic accessories, knotty paneling, and leather armchairs. On the premises are an indoor pool, a sauna, massage facilities, a children's playroom, a hospitable bar area, a reading lounge with an open fireplace, and a ceramic tile oven with its own warming bench. Ten minutes from the center, the hotel charges between 455 AS ($24.21) and 865 AS ($46.02) per person, with half board included. Prices vary widely according to the time of year and the accommodation.

Löwen-Hotel Schruns, Silverttastrasse (tel. 3141). The creative designers of this hotel decided to give guests the best of both worlds. They set a pleasantly rambling chalet on top of a big lawn area in the center of town. The shrub-dotted lawn in front is actually poised on the top of the roof of an ultramodern steel, glass, and concrete construction which contains an Olympic-size swimming pool.

This is in many ways a social center of the town, and except for outdoor recreation, it provides almost everything you need for a vacation. On the premises are five restaurants, an attractive bar accented with flowered patterns which contrast nicely with the exposed wood, a popular disco with live acts, and an attractive and hospitable female manager, Irma-Marie Ritter. Among the restaurants, the most appealing is the French restaurant and the Montafoner Stüble, where meals range between 120 AS ($6.38) and 400 AS ($21.28).

The imaginatively designed bedrooms attract an international clientele who frequently return every year. With half board included, per-person rates in a double range from 700 AS ($37.24) to 1320 AS ($70.22), while singles pay a daily surcharge of 180 AS ($9.58) to 215 AS ($11.44). The hotel is closed from mid-October until a few days before Christmas.

Hotel Krone (tel. 2255) is a peach-colored baroque building with white trim, black shutters, stone edging, and a hipped roof with at least one pointed tower. Owned by members of the Mayer family since 1847, the hotel has a shaded beer garden, a collection of charmingly rustic artifacts, and ornate paneling whose rich glow is reflected in the leaded windows. Management takes special care of its cuisine, which is well prepared and beautifully served. Per-person rates, based on double occupancy, with half board included, range from 445 AS ($23.67) to 540 AS ($28.73), with singles costing another 60 AS ($3.19) per day. Prices vary according to the season. Each of the pleasant bedrooms has a private bath.

Feuerstein (tel. 2192) is the best known place in town for ice cream and pastries. Housed in an antique-style building above the town, the establishment provides a breathtaking view in addition to its attractively decorated pastries. Some of them are miniature works of art. Both coffee and pastries average around 21 AS ($1.11) apiece.

Food and Lodging at Tschagguns

Cresta Hotel (tel. 2395) looks like a skillfully blended collection of modern additions gradually added on to an older architectural core. The entrance is under a soaring concrete arch supported at one end by a masonry column. You can have a drink at the bar or a meal near the green tile stove in the Taverne. Here, daily specials include grilled veal steak, asparagus in season, a whole array of fresh salads, and desserts such as Viennese strudel. Meals range from 90 AS ($4.79) to 300 AS ($15.96) and include both fixed-price and à la carte selections. The bedrooms are often paneled with light-grained wood, and all are comfortable. High-season rates, with half board included, range from 360 AS ($19.15) to 600 AS ($31.92), based on double occupancy. Singles pay a daily surcharge of 60 AS ($3.19). Prices depend on the season, the plumbing, and the accommodation.

Sporthotel Sonne (tel. 2334) is an attractive chalet, half of whose facade is decorated with gray-green shutters and the other half with wood-trimmed balconies. An older building, for some visitors even more charming, is connected to the new one with a covered passageway. The interiors are filled with pleasing variations of soft reds, russets, and wood-grained colors, with big windows that flood the public rooms with sunlight. The bedrooms have lots of space and rustic furnishings, some of them painted with floral designs. A covered swimming pool and a sauna are both on the premises. In high season, Heidi and Hubert Schöpf, the pleasant owners, charge between 400 AS ($21.28) and 685 AS ($36.44) for a single and between 410 AS ($21.81) and 660 AS ($35.11) per person in a double. These prices include full board. Tariffs vary depending on the season and the room assignment. The cheaper units are usually in the older section.

Alpenparkhotel (tel. 2557). Warm and intimate are the first impressions a visitor usually has when he or she enters this family-run hotel on a hillside above the village. A few minute's walk from the center, the hotel is designed like a chalet with wood-trimmed balconies, big panoramic windows, and a raised sun terrace. The furnishings graciously complement the paneling and the autumnal colors, while the well-equipped bedrooms are most comfortable. On the premises are a hospitable bar and an attractive restaurant. In high season, the Pobitzer family charges between 420 AS ($22.34) and 500 AS ($26.60) for a single and between 360 AS ($19.15) and 600 AS ($31.92) per person for a double. These prices include breakfast, and half board is offered for another 170 AS ($9.04) per person daily.

Après Ski

You can resort-hop, going back and forth between Schruns and Tschagguns, checking out whatever action appeals to you. Drinks begin at a reasonable 50 AS ($2.66) in most establishments.

At Schruns, the already-recommended **Hotel Alpenrose** brings in a band every Saturday night in season to play for dancing. It also sponsors *schuhplättler* nights about twice a week.

The **Kurhotel Montafon,** which is the leading spa hotel of this resort, already recommended, also presents a one-man band in its Taverne where music is played until after midnight.

The **Löwen Hotel,** also recommended, had the liveliest band on my last visit. Disco action is in the Löwen-Grube. Occasionally you can see folkloric shows here, as well as international shows. It's probably your best bet in town.

Tschagguns also is lively after dark in season. The moment they return from the slopes, skiers pile into the previously recommended **Cresta Hotel** and the **Sporthotel Sonne** for drinks, either hot chocolate or beer. Later, as the evening progresses, both of these places have dancing.

If you'd like a stube for some gemütlich fun and reasonable meals, try the **Gasthof Löwe** (tel. 2247), run by the Tschohl family.

GASCHURN: This resort, reached by bus from either Bludenz or Schruns, lies at an elevation of 3230 feet and is the starting point for the Silvretta-Nova winter sports arena. Gaschurn and the smaller resort, **Partenon,** are similar in position to Schruns and Tschagguns. In summer, visitors can fish for trout in the Ill River (not to be confused with the Ache River—or its source).

A chair lift from Gaschurn takes you into one of the most beautiful ski regions in Austria, the **Silvretta-Nova.** Visitors can ride on the world's largest gondola lift, carrying six persons. In addition there are seven chair lifts and 20 T-bar lifts. This extensive lift system enables you to use the 50 miles of well-kept slopes, ranging from nursery runs to the most sophisticated slopes and touring routes. The ski school offers single and group lessons as well as cross-country skiing, and there's a ski kindergarten.

From the Silvretta-Nova section, a drag lift will take you to the Gampabinger Berg at 7210 feet.

Not only is the Silvretta-Nova a major ski area, the **Versettla** is as well. It's reached by a two-stage chair lift. The top station is at 6590 feet. In about 18 minutes you can rise 3310 feet.

Food and Lodging

Sporthotel Epple (tel. 251) is a first-class vacation hotel, designed in a contemporary format. The decor is luxurious, conservatively modern, and rustic, with lots of exposed wood and comfortable furniture. A covered swimming pool, a sauna, and tennis courts are on the premises. In the center of town, the hotel charges between 1000 AS ($53.20) and 1300 AS ($69.16) in a single and between 800 AS ($42.56) and 1300 AS ($69.16) per person in a double, with half board pension included. Prices depend on the season and the accommodation.

Zum Fässle, the adjoining restaurant, offers a friendly welcome to visitors, as well as a varied menu specializing in Swabian specialties. These include a juicy roast beef with onions, an array of crispy salads, homemade spätzle, and desserts such as tasty strudels. Full meals range in price from 145 AS ($7.71) to 345 AS ($18.35). Both the hotel and the restaurant are closed from mid-April to mid-December.

Posthotel Rössle (tel. 331). The older section of this 100-year-old hotel has a weathered shingle facade, green shutters, white trim around the graceful windows, and a gently sloping gabled roof. In 1966 the Kessler family added a bigger chalet-style addition with all the modern comforts. These include both an indoor and outdoor pool, whose waters flow into one another, and a massive structure with soaring lintels and curved walls whose roof supports a comfortable sun terrace.

The public rooms inside are universally rustic and accented with well-finished paneling, although the older section contains units you might find more colorful. Also on the premises are a sauna, a bowling alley, and an open fireplace. The 85 beds rent for 385 AS ($20.48) to 800 AS ($42.56) per person, in a double, with half board included, depending on the season, the room assignment, and the plumbing. Singles pay a daily surcharge of 120 AS ($6.38).

Apart-Hotel Versettla (tel. 233) is a solidly built chalet with a gently sloping roof which connects with the eaves of a smaller chalet covered with shingles and aquamarine shutters. It's convenient for skiers because of its location on the slopes, which enables athletes to almost jump from their beds into their ski boots. The attractive interior is more up-to-date, yet includes rustic accessories, warm colors, and soft lighting. On the premises are an après-ski bar, a restaurant, a sauna, and a big sun terrace. The comfortable wood-trimmed apartments are available for up to four persons. They rent for 480 AS ($25.54) to 760 AS ($40.43) per person, and usually contain private bath, phone, color TV, and balcony. Prices depend on the season.

Hotel-Pension Sonnblick (tel. 662) is a contemporary chalet set at the edge of the village near a steeply rising hill. The accommodating sun terrace is flanked with stone retaining walls, while the interior is outfitted in a kind of alpine modern, with an open fireplace, brass chandeliers, and rustic accessories. The bedrooms are somewhat on the small side, but are sunny and comfortable, sometimes giving a view of the village church and the hills beyond it. On the premises are an indoor pool, a sauna, a café, a day-bar, and an elevator. An older section is connected to the new section by a passage. Rates range from 310 As ($16.49) to 700 AS ($37.24) per person, with half board included. Prices depend on the season and the plumbing.

Restaurant Alt Montafon (tel. 232), covered throughout its two dining areas with thick panels and 19th-century farm implements, offers about as much local flavor as you're likely to find in the region. The owner of this restaurant is an avid hunter, and the menu understandably attracts the "antlered fruits" of the region. In addition the homemade noodles are sometimes laced with pungent cheese, the garden vegetables are fresh and crispy, and the house specialty is roasted veal. You get a satisfying menu choice after a strenuous day outdoors. Be sure to reserve a table because in winter this is one of the most popular places around. Meals cost from 200 AS ($10.64) to 550 AS ($29.26), and it's closed on Monday.

Après Ski

Once a week the tourist office issues an information sheet to keep guests informed about what's going on in and around Gaschurn. That way you won't miss out on any of the folkloric evenings, with traditional song and dance, along with special dinners, picture and slide evenings, and lots more. Drinks in most places begin at a reasonable 50 AS ($2.66). Occasionally the town sponsors a dual slalom in the evening, which is floodlit.

The best place for après-ski life is the Taverne of the already-recommended **Sporthotel Epple,** where in chic, snug surroundings you can enjoy zither music and dancing on most nights every week in season.

The **Hotel Versettla**, also recommended, has disco action twice a week.

At the **Hotel Verwall** (tel. 206), run by the hospitable Durig family, you can dance to live music in the "Design Bar."

GARGELLEN: This is a charming mountain village at the end of the valley, with no through traffic. To reach the hamlet of Gargellen, you turn to the southwest—the road is marked—before you approach St. Gallenkirch. Gargellen lies between the Silvretta alpine range and the Rätikon. If you don't have a car, you can reach this resort by taking a bus from Schruns, after leaving St. Gallenkirch. You go five miles southwest through the Valley of the Gargellen to the village of Gargellen (4675 feet).

Mountaineers flock to this well-patronized summer holiday resort. Trout fishing in the many fast-flowing mountain streams in the environs is another lure. You might enjoy a dip in the heated open-air swimming pool or taking a horseback ride.

In winter this is a ski place, with an extended ski area. Lifts link well-prepared runs for both beginners and experienced skiers. You'll also find a well-known ski school, a ski kindergarten, and cross-country slopes.

You can be transported to the resort's highest station, at 7600 feet.

Food and Lodging

Sporthotel Bachmann (tel. 6316) has an attractive chalet-style format constructed on top of a modern swimming pool set into the hillside. The interior is intimately cozy, combining lots of polished knotty paneling, ceramic tile stoves, open fireplaces, and rustically comfortable furniture. The dining room has massive beams supporting the ceiling and soft red upholstery covering the straight-backed chairs. Also on the premises are an outdoor pool, a sauna, and tennis courts with a teacher. You have access to a host of wholesome alpine activities. High-season rates range from 480 AS ($25.54) to 890 AS ($47.35) per person, with half board included. Prices vary according to the season and the accommodation. Singles pay a daily surcharge of 25 AS ($1.33).

Hotel Silvretta (tel. 4088) is built on a hillside manor whose scattered farms and houses you can see from inside. The interior is accented with decorative stone walls, blazing fireplaces, weathered timbers, and thick plank-covered walls. On the premises are a double-lane bowling alley, a sun terrace, a restaurant, and a sauna with massage facilities, plus a music bar from which you can watch the activities in the indoor pool. The Schaper family, your hosts, charge between 325 AS ($17.29) and 500 AS ($26.60) for a single and between 355 AS ($18.87) and 670 AS ($35.64) per person in a double, with half board included. Prices depend on the season.

Alpenhotel Heimspitze (tel. 6319) is a farmer's-style chalet with an interior filled with a kind of heavy grace and dozens of handcrafted extras. Some of the ceiling beams look hand hewn, and the knotty paneling attractively complements the autumnal colors of the finely patterned carpeting. You'll notice a scattering of carved alpine chests and polychrome statues, as well as soft lighting and a big fireplace trimmed with river rocks.

The bedrooms sometimes contain flowered upholstery with white backgrounds, lace-trimmed tablecloths, and big sunny windows. The hotel is popular for both its rooms and its paneled restaurant whose walls glow with a mellow sheen. Rates in high season range between 480 AS ($25.54) and 840 AS ($44.69) for a single and between 420 AS ($22.34) and 840 AS ($44.69) per person in a double, with full board included.

Skiers and hikers will be glad to know that lunch on this plan can be taken either in the main hotel or in the Schafberg restaurant at the top of one of the chair lifts. The Thöny family are your hosts. A children's playroom is on the premises, as well as a country-style restaurant whose tables are often decked with alpine roses. Specialties include fresh salads, tafelspitz, pork filet with buttered spätzle, and a wide choice of pastries. Full meals range from 165 AS ($8.79) to 335 AS ($17.82). The restaurant is closed on Monday, and both the hotel and the restaurant are closed between early May and mid-June and between early October and mid-December.

Hotel Feriengut Gargellenhof (tel. 6274). The oldest sections of this weathered chalet are built almost completely of different kinds of wood, both inside and out. Even the newer sections offer old-fashioned comfort in a tastefully designed format of rustic detailing and polished paneling. On the premises you'll find blazing fireplaces, leaded windows set with dozens of rounded panes of glass, cascading flowerboxes, and a scattering of painted regional antiques. The town's outdoor pool, tennis courts, and the Schafberg's ski lifts are a short distance away.

The mountain-style bedrooms offer lots of comfort, costing between 430 AS ($22.88) and 925 AS ($49.21) per person in high season, based on double occupancy, with half board included. Singles pay a daily surcharge of 60 AS ($3.19).

Many visitors to this area make an excursion to one of the two in-house restaurants, both of which offer impressive mountain views. Specialties include homemade liver spätzle soup, Vorarlberg-style sauerbraten, a savory array of juicy meats, and heavenly desserts, all served in big portions to an enthusiastic crowd of regular customers. Whether you eat in the dining room or on the sun terrace, the establishment serves the kind of hearty, well-prepared food that goes well with the mountain air. Meals range from 145 AS ($7.71) to 445 AS ($23.67). Both the hotel and the restaurant are closed in May, June, October, and November.

Hotel Edelweiss (tel. 6317) is a well-maintained chalet with a gabled roof and four floors of comfortable bedrooms. A few steps from the village church, in a cluster of other chalets, the hotel is administered by the Drexel family. The hotel has only 30 beds, renting for 265 AS ($14.10) to 360 AS ($19.15) per person in a double, with half board included. Singles pay a daily surcharge of 55 AS ($2.93). The hotel is about a three-minute walk from the ski lifts.

Hotel Alpenrose (tel. 6314) is a tastefully symmetrical chalet built into the side of an alpine meadow. Its facade is appealingly covered with weathered planking, and its interior provides rustic comforts, including a panoramic dining room with a woodsy decor, an agreeable bar area, a sauna, a whirlpool, a children's playroom, and physical fitness facilities. Per-person rates in a double in high season range from 540 AS ($28.73) to 840 AS ($44.69), while singles cost between 660 AS ($35.11) and 780 AS ($41.50), with half board included.

Après Ski

It's a tiny village, but there are some nocturnal stirrings, with drinks priced from 50 AS ($2.66).

British skiers, in particular, like to drop in at the already-recommended **Hotel Edelweiss** for one of the best teas in town, with delicious pastries.

The four-star **Hotel Madrisa** (tel. 6331) is probably the most popular spot for nightlife. Its band plays for dancing couples every night, and it's also been known to present fondue evenings, as in Switzerland, and to stage fashion shows.

The **Hotel/Café Dörflinger** (tel. 6386) is a modest, family-run place, but its bar is a major rendezvous point for the skiing crowd.

At the **Hotel Silvretta,** just recommended, you can enjoy drinks at the bar beside the swimming pool.

Perched high on a mountain terrace, the **Hotel Vergalden** (tel. 6530), run by the Braunger family, brings in a local band once a week for dancing and rowdy fun in general. After a night's festivities here many guests take a thrilling toboggan ride back to their own domicile.

8. Arlberg—the West Side

The east side of Arlberg was visited in Chapter X on Innsbruck and Tyrol, so it's time for me to tell you the "west side story" of this massif which separates Vorarlberg from Tyrol.

This part of Austria is one of the major meccas for winter sports in Europe. Leading resorts on the celebrated Arlberg massif, the highest mountain range in the Lechtal Alps, include Lech and Zürs, and there's also rustic, tiny Stuben, with its own north-facing snow-catcher, the mighty Albona. An Arlberg ski pass allows the holder to use the 70 ski tows, chair lifts, and cable cars in the entire Arlberg region.

Up through the Flexen Pass, you come to Zürs, a chic, elegant, refined resort with skiing at Trittkopf and Mahdloch. Lech is larger, with easier skiing on Kriegerhorn and Mohnenfluh.

LECH: Founded in the 14th century by emigrés from the Valais district of Switzerland, Lech, on the northwestern flank of the Arlberg mountain range, still has its original **Pfarrkirche** (parish church) from that era. This archetype of a snug alpine ski village is practically joined to Oberlech, a satellite resort a little farther up the mountain. Lech stands at 4730 feet; Oberlech, at 5600 feet.

Zürs, a sister village to Lech, is considered slightly more fashionable, but Lech has its own claim to fame: it has played host to Prince Charles and Princess Diana.

Lech is 8½ miles from Landen, and you can reach it and Oberlech by bus from St. Anton am Arlberg. Lech also lies on a major rail route.

In summer, visitors like to come here to tour the Upper Lech Valley, which stretches for about 35 miles to a lovely vale lying between the Lechtal and the Allgäu Alps.

Lech, Oberlech, and Zürs are linked by about 70 lifts, making for a magnificent ski circus. Snow is advertised as guaranteed from the end of November until the end of April. Oberlech has a pedestrian zone with frequent cable-car connections. Lifts and runs are close together. It's possible to ski between Lech and Zürs. A cable car, whose last run is at 1 a.m. connects Oberlech to the heart of Lech. You can take the Rüfikopf cable car from the heart of the resort to Rüfikopf (7635 feet).

Regardless which resort you stay in, I suggest you go to Oberlech if the day is sunny and find yourself a spot in one of the big sun-terrace restaurants there.

Food and Lodging at Lech

Hotel Arlberg (tel. 2134) is a sprawling chalet well equipped for an alpine vacation. In addition to a well-maintained lawn area, the grounds contain an outdoor pool, tennis courts, and a flowered sun terrace where waiters serve meals on well-ironed tablecloths. The interior contains beautiful regional antiques, some of them painted, carefully crafted paneling, and elegant accessories. Guests appreciate the intimate lighting in the bar after a day in the brilliant sunshine of the surrounding mountains, and also enjoy the warmth from the sitting room's baronial fireplace.

The food served in the richly outfitted dining room is as generous as the decor itself. The Schneider family directs a team of chefs who prepare a daily specialty from one of three or four European culinary traditions, as well as a consistently available array of Austrian-inspired foods which includes a wide array of game and fish dishes, cream-flavored goulash, and cream schnitzels. Meals range from 160 AS ($8.51) to 420 AS ($22.34). Hotel tariffs go from 650 AS ($34.58) to 2350 AS ($125.02) per person, with full board included. Prices vary widely throughout the course of the year.

Hotel Almhof Schneider (tel. 601) is a huge building roughly designed like several chalets clustered together. The interior is luxuriously outfitted with textured plaster, blazing fireplaces (including one beside the indoor pool), painted alpine cupboards, richly tinted fabrics, and polished stone. The international clientele who come here spend lots of time on the sun terrace and value the hotel's location near the ski lifts.

The well-furnished bedrooms rent for 1260 AS ($67.03) to 3250 AS ($172.90) per person per day, with full board included. The most expensive accommodations in this price range are small apartments. Clients who decide to drop in over Christmas pay an additional 1900 AS ($101.08) per day.

Specialties in the elegant Walliser Stuben are written discreetly on a limited menu, whose every item uses impeccably fresh ingredients. It emphasizes unusual recipes, some strongly influenced by nouvelle cuisine. Suggestions include medallions of venison in an orange pepper sauce, exotic salads, and an international array of fish and meats. Dinners range in price from 180 AS ($9.58) to 480 AS ($25.54).

Hotel Jagdhaus Monzabon (tel. 2104) is a tastefully decorated four-star hotel in the center of town. Designed like a chalet, it has public rooms that are conservatively outfitted with heavy beams, hunting trophies, comfortable chairs, and accents of wrought iron. On the premises are a beauty salon, an indoor swimming pool, a sauna, billiard tables, a bar, a café, and a restaurant. Willy Schneider and his family are the owners, charging between 1180 AS ($62.78) and 1340 AS ($71.29) per person in a single or double, and between 1490 AS ($79.27) and 2000 AS ($106.40) per person in apartments sleeping up to four. Half board is included in these high-season rates.

Gasthof Post (tel. 22060). Queen Beatrix of the Netherlands is a frequent visitor to this establishment. But even without royal clientele it's still called the noblest hotel in town. Designed as a Romantik-Hotel, the chalet-style facade is ornamented with trompe-l'oeil murals. This hotel long ago served as a postal station, and today guards many of the accessories that might have been used a century ago, including alpine painted chests, acres of blond paneling, furniture that could have come from a wealthy farmer's house, and a scattering of baroque sculpture.

Clients fortunately get the best of the 20th century during their use of the indoor pool, the nearby tennis courts, the beauty and massage facilities, or any of the convivial gathering places, which include a popular sun terrace and several bars.

The Moosebrugger family have installed all the modern conveniences in the bedrooms, which sometimes have elaborately painted headboards and refrigerators concealed in old chests. Accommodations include some units which are vast. Depending on the time of the year, singles range from 840 AS ($44.69) to 2040 AS ($108.53), while doubles cost between 660 AS ($35.11) and 2400 AS ($127.68) per person daily, with half board included.

The restaurant is a member of Relais et Châteaux, and serves food worthy of that designation. The menu includes dozens of Austrian classics, especially game dishes, while the tafelspitz served here will help you understand why it was Franz Joseph's favorite dish. Other delicacies include blue trout, rabbit pâté, and an impressive dessert list. Fixed-price meals range from 180 AS ($9.58) to a peak 1000 AS ($53.20) if you really shoot the works. À la carte meals go from 210 AS ($11.17) to 550 AS ($29.26). Reservations are suggested.

Hotel Krone (tel. 2551). This building became a hotel when it was acquired by a member of the Pfefferkorn family in 1865. The ceiling in the bar dates from about a century earlier (1741, to be exact). Today the hotel sits in a favored position between the village church and the river, with an expanded contemporary format containing 100 beds. The interior is attractively woodsy, containing ceramic tile stoves, beamed ceilings, paneled accents, and comfortable fireside chairs.

On the premises is an ultramodern fitness center covered with circular orange tiles. It contains a sauna, a solarium, massage facilities, a hot whirlpool, and a Turkish steambath. The timbered restaurant has a panoramic view and a well-prepared menu with big portions. Specialties include fish soup Provence style, roast veal in a chicken liver sauce, and several regional recipes. Meals range from 135 AS ($7.18) to 390 AS ($20.75). Occupants of the hotel enjoy the evening dance bar, which is in an adjoining wing to avoid disturbing sleepers in the pleasant bedrooms. Per-person rates in a double range from 590 AS ($31.39) to 1630 AS ($86.72), depending on the season. Half board is included. The comfortable accommodations in the nearby annex are slightly cheaper than those in the main building.

Tannbergerhof (tel. 202) is an attractive shingled chalet with green shutters and lots of interior space. The atmosphere is conducive to helping athletes and nonathletes appreciate sports and outdoor activities, although there's certainly enough inside to distract even the most ardent sportsperson. The public rooms are accented with well-finished paneling, a ceramic tile stove with a warming bench, soft lighting, and blazing fireplaces. On the premises is a popular evening disco, plus a lounge bar, and a restaurant serving specialties such as paprika goulash and an array of veal dishes. With full board included, per-person rates range from 700 AS ($37.24) to 1640 AS ($87.25), depending on the season. Meals in the restaurant cost from 200 AS ($10.64) to 550 AS ($29.26), and reservations are suggested. In a separate chalet, a three-minute walk from the hotel, the management maintains a covered swimming pool, a hot whirlpool, and a sauna.

Hotel Pension Lech (tel. 289). The Grabher family are the owners of this pleasant hotel comprised of two chalets, five minutes away from the ski lifts. The interiors are handsomely paneled and accented with soft lighting and forest colors. On the premises are a sauna, a bowling alley, a casino-bar, and a warmly paneled evening steakhouse. In high season, the comfortable bedrooms rent for 670 AS ($35.64) to 960 AS ($51.07), with half board included.

Hotel Pension Solaria (tel. 2214) is a partially shingled green-shuttered chalet set on a hillside at the edge of the village, a few minutes' walk from the center. The simple interior has attractively finished wood accents, lots of cozy comforts, and easy access to the village's sporting facilities, including the nearby ski lifts which you can reach by skiing a short distance downhill from the front door. The pleasant bedrooms rent for 315 AS ($16.75) to 1060 AS ($56.39) per person, based on double occupancy, and singles pay a daily surcharge of 50 AS ($2.66). Half board is included in these prices, which vary according to the season. The Ender family, your hosts, will arrange to have breakfast served in your room if you wish.

Hinterwies (tel. 2320) is a white-walled chalet with wood-grained shutters and baroque-style embellishments painted around three of the windows. The simple interior is tastefully outfitted with lots of exposed wood, country-style furniture, and light colors. One of my favorite parts is the flagstone-covered back terrace which leads up to the tapering chimney of a brick fireplace protected by the overhang of the upper floors. The uncluttered bedrooms have lots of personalized and appealing touches. They cost between 850 AS ($45.22) and 1350 AS ($71.82) per person, based on double occupancy. Singles pay a daily surcharge ranging from 95 AS ($5.05) to 155 AS ($8.25) daily. These prices include half board, and differences are based on the season.

Food and Lodging at Oberlech

Sonnenburg (tel. 2147) is a large double chalet with symmetrically peaked rooflines and alternating areas of white walls and wood-trimmed balconies covering the modern facade. In front the management has constructed a sun terrace looking down the hillside, while indoors the decor is warm, intimate, and woodsy. Many of the walls are accented either with brick or horizontal planking, with a scattering of regional antiques to augment the mellow glow from the paneling.

On the premises is an indoor pool with a panoramic view, plus a kindergarten, two restaurants, and a collection of well-maintained bedrooms with all the modern comforts. A short distance away an annex (called Hohe Welt) charges slightly less than the main building for the pleasantly furnished rooms. Within the two buildings, per-person rates range from 750 AS ($39.90) to 1480 AS ($78.74) in a double, with singles paying a daily surcharge ranging from 105 AS ($5.59) to 120 AS ($6.38) per day. Prices depend on the room and vary according to the season.

Hotel Montana (tel. 2460), above the village, has a large sun terrace looking out over Lech. It's designed like a light-grained chalet and has a stylish interior, making ample use of fuschia and pink as the appealing colors, which contrast well with the ruddy paneling. The in-house swimming pool is backed by an abstract mural, while the café/bar area is an attractive place for a midafternoon drink. The owner, Guy Ortlieb, an expatriate Frenchman, organizes weekly farmer buffets and cocktail parties, and does what he can to make his guests feel at ease in the sporty ambience of this pleasant hotel. Full-board rates in high season range from

925 AS ($49.21) to 1560 AS ($82.99), based on double occupancy. Singles pay a daily surcharge of 100 AS ($5.32).

The hotel's Zur Kanne has been elected to several prestigious rankings, including the Chaine des Rôtisseurs. It's known for serving the best fish in the valley, including salmon in saffron sauce, Provençale frog legs, and Alsacian wine soup. At the tables the waiter will present a woman (if accompanied by a man) a menu with no prices indicated. In case she wonders, a full meal ranges from 225 AS ($11.97) to 480 AS ($25.54). In high season, with full board included, rates range from 925 AS ($49.21) to 1560 AS ($82.99) per person in a double, with singles paying a daily surcharge of 100 AS ($5.32).

Après Ski

Lech has perhaps the finest après-ski life in Vorarlberg, and if you ever get bored here, you can also check out the action at the satellite resorts or go over to Zürs.

Dedicated skiers always head for the Scotch Bar of the **Hotel Kristberg** (tel. 288), which is owned and run by Egon Zimmermann, a former Olympic racer.

The evening begins even earlier, however, with a tea dance at the **Hotel Tannbergerhof** (tel. 2202), where Hilde Jochum welcomes you for a good time. Later in the evening you can dance to disco music.

The Stüberl of the **Hotel Berghof** (tel. 2635) is deserving of its popularity. The Burger family make you feel most welcome, and you can stick around enjoying their fine cuisine later on if you wish.

The **Hotel Krone** (tel. 2551) has dancing to a resident band in the evenings. Run by the Pfefferkorn family, this hotel is centrally located and has two bars and a hot whirlpool bath if you're interested.

Drinks at most places range from 50 AS ($3.66) to 75 AS ($3.99).

Dining at Zug

Rote Wand (tel. 2758). If you decide to try this appealing restaurant, you can feel safe in knowing that both Prince Rainier of Monaco and King Hussein of Jordan have tried it also. A specialty of the house is spätzle with cheese, which many diners enjoy almost as much as the roast veal and pork, the warm cabbage salad, or the tafelspitz. Some diners say that the real attraction, however, is the fondue bourguignonne or chinoise, which you could precede with a soup made from a purée of venison. If you're up for dessert, the hot curd strudel is heavenly.

Reservations are suggested for meals which range between 230 AS ($12.24) and 600 AS ($31.92). The interior includes massive ceiling beams over a rustically attractive alpine-style decor. The restaurant is next to the onion dome of the village church. Josef and Hildegard Walchare are the hard-working owners of this superior establishment. In winter they'll arrange for a horse-drawn sleigh to pick you up in Lech, if you telephone and arrange for it. They're open from December 1 until around April 20 and again from July 1 until the end of September.

Auerhahn (tel. 9854) is an old room in a building at the edge of the village. The furnishings are vintage farmer's style, and the ambience is friendly, warm, and woodsy, with a likeable kind of hubbub coming from the crowded tables inside. Specialties include fondue, liver noodle soup,

Provençale-style lamb, and an array of pork dishes. Dessert might be a traditional strudel smothered in vanilla sauce. À la carte meals range from 150 AS ($7.98) to 360 AS ($19.15). Reservations are suggested, and the restaurant is closed in May and October.

ZÜRS: An immaculate resort lying about 2½ miles from Lech in a sunny valley, Zürs (about 5600 feet) consists of half a mile of typical white stucco Vorarlberger buildings, with carved wood balconies. The resort, really a collection of hotels, is reached via the magnificent Flexen Road.

Unlike most of the places we've visited, Zürs is strictly a winter resort, and nearly all the hotels close in summer. This mountain village has an abundance of "guaranteed" snow. In fact, once Pierre Trudeau, the prime minister of Canada, was snowed in and missed a summit meeting. Because of its location Zürs is avalanche prone, but these potential snowslides do not deter the loyal habitués of Zürs. The snow here has been compared to talcum powder.

Zürs (pronounced "Seurs") is a favorite of monarchs and film stars. More formal than Lech, it's considered one of the most elegant resorts in the world, far more select than St. Moritz or Gstaad, although lacking their ostentation. The resort has 130 ski instructors. Many of the wealthy guests, often from South America, have their own personal teacher.

A drag lift east of Zürs takes you to **Hexenboden** (7700 feet). From there a cable lift goes to **Trittkopf** (7875 feet), where you'll find a mountain restaurant and a sun terrace.

In the west, a chair lift will take you to **Seekopf** (7175 feet). From the windows and terrace of the restaurant here, you can see the frozen Zurser Lake. From Seekopf a chair lift goes to the top station at 8035 feet.

Food and Lodging

Hotel Zürserhof (tel. 182). Five separate chalets combine forces in the shelter of an alpine valley to create this most luxurious of mountain refuges. This is the establishment that put Zürs on the tourist map, and is the preferred choice of King Hussein and his American-born queen, as well as the playground of VIPs from around the world. It grew from a house erected by the Count and Countess Vallay Tattenbach in 1927, when they began to accept paying guests. When Hitler took over Austria, the Tattenbachs sold it and emigrated to Costa Rica. In 1955 the establishment was taken over by Ernst Skardarasy.

The accommodations usually consist of private apartments, many of which have stone fireplaces, lots of space, and opulent comforts. The public rooms are decked out with old panels, antiques, and Persian carpets. There's music almost every night in the cellar bar, and a wide assortment of even the most esoteric sports (an indoor driving range for golfers, for example). A tennis player's admirers can watch him or her volley on the indoors courts from the security of a café area and relax later in the sauna or whirlpool.

Specialties in the elegant restaurant are a lighter version of the traditional Austrian cuisine, with the freshest ingredients used. There's an emphasis on buffets. À la carte meals range from 190 AS ($10.11) to 560 AS ($29.79). Singles and apartments for one person range from 1560 AS ($82.99) to 2900 AS ($154.88), while doubles and apartments cost from

1400 AS ($74.48) to 3700 AS ($196.84) per person, with full board included.

Sporthotel Lorunser (tel. 2254). Princess Grace of Monaco used to send her children here, and today you're likely to spot two or three Princess Caroline look-alikes at the hospitable bar of this luxurious hotel. Rustically designed with lots of cedar shingles and regional paintings around the windows, the hotel has intricately carved ceiling beams, open fireplaces, well-finished paneling, and dozens of elegant accessories and furnishings, as well as comfortable wood-trimmed bedrooms. Per-person rates in a double range from 1200 AS ($63.84) to 2450 AS ($130.34), depending on the accommodation and the time of year. Singles pay from 85 AS ($4.52) to 145 AS ($7.71) additional. Full board is included in these tariffs.

Central Sporthotel & Villa Edelweiss (tel. 2662). The imposing facade of this large hotel incorporates white walls, cedar shingles, and painted embellishments. This is the oldest hotel in Zürs, although you'll find it hard to believe after looking at the brightly painted bedrooms which seem to come in a rainbow assortment of vivid colors. The public rooms include open fireplaces, a small bar, a popular disco, a white dining room with occasional gilt accents, and a French restaurant painted an eye-catching forest green with a glowing set of Biedermeier straight-backed chairs.

Specialties include a roast pork filet stuffed with ham and cheese and covered with a thick mushroom cream sauce. Meals range from 155 AS ($8.25) to 420 AS ($22.34), whereas accommodations cost from 1300 AS ($69.16) to 1800 AS ($95.76) in a single and from 1150 AS ($61.18) to 1620 AS ($86.18) per person in a double. These prices include full board. Tariffs vary according to the accommodations, and rooms in the annex are slightly cheaper.

Thurnher's Alpenhof Sporthotel (tel. 2191). This distinctive-looking chalet has vertical timbers running in uninterrupted lines from near the ground floor to the eaves. The attractive effect is almost like looking at a weathered gridwork stretched across the white facade. The interior is a tasteful collection of carved panels, polished wood, and warmly textured fabrics. The dining room is crowned with timbers almost big enough to be railroad ties, and is furnished with elegant upholstered chairs.

On the premises are an indoor swimming pool, a fitness room, a big sun terrace, and a sauna. Each of the bedrooms has a private bath and all the modern comforts. They range in price from 1350 AS ($71.82) to 2400 AS ($127.68) per person in a double, with full board included. Apartments are available for up to 2700 AS ($143.64) per person daily. Singles pay daily surcharges ranging from 190 AS ($10.11) to 250 AS ($13.30). Elfi and Oskar Thurnher, your hard-working hosts, do everything they can to make your vacation pleasant.

Hotel Hirlanda (tel. 145) is a pleasant chalet with a rustically cozy interior dotted with an open fireplace, a farmer-style restaurant, a bar, and a collection of livable bedrooms. These usually have dark wood accents, chalet-style furniture, and white walls. They rent for 1080 AS ($57.46) to 1350 AS ($71.82) per person, with full board included. A sauna and a covered garage are on the premises. Oswald Wille and his family are your hosts.

Hotel Enzian (tel. 242) is a pleasantly symmetrical chalet with lots of wood accents and muted orange shutters. The interior is a tasteful combination of wood walls, coffered ceilings, warmly tinted upholsteries, and open fireplaces. On the premises are two dining rooms, a bar, a sun terrace with waiter service, and a sauna. The Elsensohn family, your sports-loving hosts, do everything they can to create a relaxed ambience. The hotel is at the edge of the village near the cable-car station. Per-person rates, with half board included, range from 815 AS ($43.36) to 1300 AS ($69.16), depending on the accommodation, the season, and the plumbing.

Hotel Maria (tel. 2644). The Hartinger family are your hosts at this simple chalet with its wood-paneled interior. Accents inside include lots of wrought iron, some with vines growing over it, vertical planking on the walls of the intimate bar, and soft lighting. Per-person rates in double rooms with half board included range from 780 AS ($41.50) to 1070 AS ($56.92). Singles pay a daily surcharge of 95 AS ($5.05). Each of the pleasant accommodations has a private bath, mini-safe, phone, and refrigerator.

Hotel Albona (tel. 2341) is a contemporary chalet with big panoramic windows and a dramatic contrast between the light and dark areas of its facade. The interior is comfortably filled with velvet banquettes pulled around an open fireplace, rustic ceiling beams, and polished wood. On the premises are a range of health facilities (sauna, steambath, massage, and jet shower), indoor golf equipment, a cozy series of sitting rooms, a carefully decorated restaurant which exudes warmth, a popular farmer's-style bar and disco, and dozens of charming accents. Rates in a single range from 1560 AS ($82.99) to 1840 AS ($97.89), while the per-person tariff in a double goes between 1440 AS ($76.61) and 1620 AS ($86.18), depending on the season and the accommodation.

Après Ski

With its newly opened **Casino,** Zürs has a very fashionable nightlife, what there is of it. Naturally the hotels dominate the action, and drinks tend to be expensive, in the 75-AS ($3.99) range.

The most luxurious and elegant place to be seen at night is the already-recommended **Hotel Zürserhof** where there's dancing to a live band.

However, if you like more informal action, you'll gravitate to the also-recommended **Hotel Edelweiss** in the heart of the resort, where there's also dancing at night.

For discos (which I've usually found empty), check out those at the **Hotel Albona** and the **Hotel Mara,** both previously recommended.

STUBEN: This little hamlet and winter resort is almost a suburb of Lech, lying on the northern fringes of the larger village, on the west side of the Arlberg Pass. Stuben can be reached by bus, but the most romantic way to go from Lech is by horse-drawn sleigh.

The tiny hamlet has been a way station for alpine travelers for many centuries, but in recent years it has become a modern ski area, with its own lift station on Albona. Stuben does not enjoy the chicdom that Zürs does, but its prices are much more reasonable, and it's in a fine location for skiers, having links with St. Anton in the Tyrol as well as with Lech and Zürs in the Arlberg region. In fact the Arlberg ski pass mentioned above is valid for lifts and cars linking Stuben, St. Christoph, St. Anton, Zürs, and Lech.

Stuben is especially geared for family enjoyment, with children's ski courses, special meals, and hosts who help the smallfry feel at home.

This was the birthplace of Hannes Schneider, the great ski instructor.

Food and Lodging

Hotel Mondschein (tel. 721) is a 250-year-old country house with cascading window boxes and forest green shutters. The interior is more contemporary, although the hospitality inside is pure old-fashioned Austrian. The hotel offers much comfort, and facilities include a pleasant restaurant, a bar, and an indoor swimming pool. Per-person rates range from 800 AS ($42.56) to 890 AS ($47.35) in high season, with half board included. Low-season rates are about 15% less. Werner Walch is the friendly host.

Hotel Post (tel. 761). When it was built in 1608 this hotel served as a shelter for tired mail-coach travelers. Today it welcomes more up-to-date visitors in its rustically attractive public rooms with lots of exposed wood and heavy timbers. Most of the public rooms have been designed in an attractively contemporary format of great comfort, which include open fireplaces and deep-seated chairs. On the premises are a restaurant and bar, both of which offer welcome refreshment after a day outdoors. Just at the edge of the village, the hotel charges between 620 AS ($31.92) and 770 AS ($40.96) for a single and between 600 AS ($31.92) and 720 AS ($38.30) per person in a double, with half board included. Prices vary according to the season and the accommodation. Rooms at the nearby "Hunting Lodge Post" cost about 20% less than units in the main hotel.

Hotel Albona (tel. 712) is an attractive chalet with wooden shutters. On a narrow street in the center of the village, the hotel is outfitted with lots of exposed wood, simple furniture, and sunny colors. On the premises are a hot whirlpool, a dancing bar, a restaurant, and a collection of comfortable wood-trimmed bedrooms. Per-person rates in a double in high season range from 620 AS ($32.98) to 810 AS ($43.09), while singles cost from 750 AS ($39.90) to 810 AS ($43.09), with half board included.

Chapter XII

CARINTHIA

1. Klagenfurt
2. Lake Wörther
3. Lake Ossiacher
4. Villach
5. Spittal an der Drau
6. Lake Millstätter
7. Bad Kleinkirchheim
8. Lake Weissen
9. The Möll Valley and Mallnitz
10. The Gail Valley
11. Lake Klopeiner
12. The Vellach Valley

THE SOUTHERNMOST PROVINCE of Austria, Carinthia (Kärnten, in German) has been generously endowed by nature. Encircled by high mountains which give it fairly well-defined borders, it has been compared to a gigantic amphitheater, cut across by the Drau River (which becomes the Drava when it enters Yugoslavia). This province consists of mountainous Upper Carinthia in the west and the Lower Carinthian basin region in the east. Because of its warm and sunny weather and lakes, which attract bathers and water sports enthusiasts who don't go to ocean shores, a section of Carinthia is known as the Riviera of Austria. The Carinthian climate is the country's mildest.

Villach, to be previewed later, is the biggest road and rail junction in the eastern Alps, and Klagenfurt is the capital of Carinthia.

This is an ancient province, archeological discoveries in the area showing that it was known to the human race far back in unrecorded time. The Romans did not overlook it, their legions marching in to conquer alpine Celtic tribes of the kingdom of Noricum and establishing it as a Roman province.

For centuries this home of ethnic groups from Slovenia belonged variously to the kingdom of Germany and Avar-dominated Slavs from the east. Eventually the populace, hoping to fend off invasions, invited Bavaria to become Carinthia's protector. Thus it came to be ruled by Bavarians and was a part of the Holy Roman Empire. Bavarian settlers gradually assimilated with the Slav population.

When the Habsburgs took Kärnten as a part of their rapidly expanding empire, it was a duchy of the Holy Roman Empire under the Bohemian aegis, a situation resolved finally when Ferdinand I of Habsburg, soon to become emperor, married the heiress to Bohemia and made Carinthia an imperial duchy, later to be designated a province of Austria.

Yugoslavia claimed southern Carinthia after World War I, and in that confused time some of the territory was ceded to that country and more to Italy. All this land was later restored, and in 1920, after the collapse of the Habsburg Empire, a plebiscite was taken and a Slovenian minority in the south, along the Yugoslav border, voted to remain with Austria. A sizable minority of Carinthia's population of 600,000 today is Slovenian, but the majority of it is German.

The sunny weather and numerous idyllic lakes that are scattered among gentle hills and steep mountains make Carinthia mostly a summer tourist center. If you like water sports or just lazing in the sun, then a summer visit to this province might be in order. It's little known to or visited by North Americans, yet it's an ideal stopover point if you're heading south to Yugoslavia or Italy. The scenery is varied, and there is much beautiful countryside to be explored.

If you're athletic you can climb the gentle *Nocks* or else seek out the more demanding steep mountains. Fishing is a popular sport in this province, both in the lakes and the colder mountain streams. The region boasts more than 200 warm, clean lakes of varying sizes.

The "Carinthian Riviera" is the name given to the main lake area, including Wörther See, not far from Klagenfurt, the provincial capital. There are also Lake Ossiacher and Lake Millstätter. Weissensee, the fourth big lake, is less well known than the other three, but there are those who consider it the most beautiful. The best way to see the lakes in summer is to take one of the boats operating from April until the middle of October.

The best season to visit Carinthia if you want to enjoy the beauty and pleasure of the lakes is from the middle of May until the end of September, although the first two weeks in October are also ideal most years. In July and August tourists flock in, so if you plan to visit then, be sure you have reservations.

Although the warm lakes are the main drawing card for Carinthia, the province is making an increasing attempt to attract skiers to its mountains in winter. Skiing lasts from December until March, not April as in some parts of Austria farther north. As a ski center this province is much less expensive than Tyrol or Land Salzburg.

1. Klagenfurt

The provincial capital of Carinthia, Klagenfurt is a university town dating from 1161. Its charter was granted in 1252. The city lies only 38 miles from Italy and less than 19 miles from Yugoslavia. It is the cultural center of Carinthia.

Klagenfurt was destroyed by fire in 1514, but it was rebuilt and designated as the capital of the duchy in 1518. It was then a walled city, but the walls were torn down during the Napoleonic invasions in 1809. The center of the city is in quadrangular shape with four so-called rings, which are streets laid out along the former city walls. The center of this quadrangle and of the modern city is **Neuer Platz,** presided over by a fountain in the shape of a ferocious dragon called *Lindwurm,* the city's symbol.

It can get very hot in Klagenfurt in the peak of summer, but if you're there, do as the Klagenfurters do—retreat to nearby Wörther See (Lake

Wörther) in the western sector of the city and linked to it by a man-made canal.

THE SIGHTS: A major sight is the **Landesmuseum,** or provincial museum, on Arnulfplatz. On the grounds you can see Roman artifacts, including votive stones, gleaned from the excavations in Carinthia. The museum exhibits art and artifacts of the province from prehistoric times to the present. The most outstanding feature is a display of ecclesiastical art, much of it dating from the 15th and 16th centuries. Also on view is a scale model of Klagenfurt as it was at the dawn of the 19th century. See the skull of a rhinoceros which is said to have been a model for the renowned Dragon Fountain in the Neuer Platz.

The museum is open May until October from 9 a.m. to 4 p.m., from 10 a.m. to noon on Sunday and holidays. It's closed on Monday. Admission is 20 AS ($1.06).

The **Alter Platz,** both a broad thoroughfare and a square, is lined with many baroque mansions, some from the 16th century. It is the center of the Altstadt (old town) and is a pedestrian zone. Many crooked, narrow little streets and alleys open off the square.

The **Landhaus,** originally an arsenal, later Carinthian state headquarters, and now the offices of the provincial government, stands on the Alter Platz. The building was begun in 1574 and completed in 1590. A moated castle once stood on this site. The courtyard of the present building has two-story arcades. A set of staircase towers has bulbous caps. Its Grosser Wappensaal, or Great Blazon Hall, dating from 1739, was handsomely decorated by Joseph Ferdinand Fromiller, who died in 1760. The ceiling painting of the hall is in trompe l'oeil. It has 665 heraldic shields.

The state hall may be visited from April until the end of September from 9 a.m. to 5 p.m. It's closed on Sunday and Monday. Admission is 10 AS (53¢).

The **Trinity Column** in the Alter Platz is from 1681. One of the most interesting buildings on the square is **Altes Rathaus** (old city hall) from the 17th century. It has a three-story arcaded courtyard. The **House of the Golden Goose** (Haus zur Goldenen Gans) on the Alter Platz is from the final year of the 16th century.

The **Domkirche** (cathedral) of Klagenfurt lies to the southeast of the Neuer Platz. Construction on this building began in 1578. The interior is richly adorned in stucco and has ceiling paintings from the 18th century.

If you have children with you, take them by the **Minimundus,** a world in miniature, lying 2½ miles from Klagenfurt on Lake Wörther (see below). This mini-town has building models which are 1/25th of their actual size, including not only castles but also the Eiffel Tower.

Here you'll also find boat landing stages for trips on the lake in summer. There's a mini-golf course in nearby Europa-Park.

WHERE TO STAY: **Romantik Hotel Musil,** 14 Oktoberstrasse (tel. 511660), is by many accounts the most elegant and romantic hotel in town. A pastry shop greets you on the left as you enter. The sunny dining room does a thriving business, and well it should. The well-furnished bedrooms, loaded with atmosphere, rent at 1400 AS ($74.48) for a double and 900 AS ($47.88) for a single, with breakfast included. The hotel is part of a cluster that also includes the Hotel Porcia and the Hotel Moser-Verdino, recommended below.

Hotel Moser-Verdino, 2 Domgasse (tel. 57878). The café and restaurant in this old-fashioned hotel are the gathering place for groups of friendly acquaintances. The pink facade is accented with a big glassfront facing the street. The decoration is luxurious and restrained, and the hotel, owned by a prominent family of innkeepers, is considered a good choice for a stay in Klagenfurt. Doubles cost 1140 AS ($55.33), while singles rent for 700 AS ($37.24), with half board included.

Hotel Porcia, 13 Neuerplatz (tel. 511590), the third sister of the group, offers comfortable but small rooms and a limited number of parking places. Doubles range from 1050 AS ($55.86), while singles cost 650 AS ($34.58), with breakfast included.

Hotel Europapark, 222 Villacher Strasse (tel. 21137), is designed in a low horizontal format that blends pleasingly into the landscaped garden around it. The sunny interior is filled with simple imaginative furniture, with a warmly appealing collection of modern abstractly patterned fabrics. The Meschnig family, your congenial hosts, charge between 580 AS ($30.87) and 625 AS ($33.25) for a single and between 815 AS ($43.36) and 890 AS ($47.35) for a double, with breakfast included.

Hotel Goldener Brunnen, 14 Karfreitstrasse (tel. 55868), on the cathedral square in the heart of the city, is a peach-colored building with an arcaded courtyard filled with burgeoning plants. The management sets café tables there in summer. The comfortable bedrooms rent for 480 AS ($25.54) to 660 AS ($35.11) for a single and 840 AS ($44.69) to 1020 AS ($54.26) for a double.

Hotel Sandwirt, Pernhartgasse (tel. 56209), is a comfortable, centrally located hotel owned by Paul Jamek. The proud possessor of a long tradition, the hotel has upper-floor windows with elegant neoclassical borders, although the ground-floor facade has been severely modernized. More than one Austrian president has stayed in the well-furnished bedrooms. Singles rent for 420 AS ($22.34) to 720 AS ($38.30), while doubles cost between 660 AS ($35.11) and 1150 AS ($61.18), with breakfast included. Half board is another 180 AS ($9.58) per person daily. Specialties in the hotel's restaurant include an array of schnitzels, zander filet, and French desserts. Full meals range from 100 AS ($5.32) to 330 AS ($17.56).

Kurhotel Carinthia, 41 8-Mai-Strasse (tel. 422399), is a severely modern hotel with six floors of two-tone concrete facing and big glass windows. The conservatively furnished bedrooms include flowered fabrics and an occasional 19th-century antique. Centrally located, and very quiet, the premises contain a sauna, a hairdresser, a café, and a full range of health and massage facilities. Each of the pleasant bedrooms has a private bath, and rents for 635 AS ($33.78) in a single, from 815 AS ($43.36) in a double, and from 1140 AS ($60.65) in a triple.

Hotel Garni Blumenstöckl, 11 Oktoberstrasse (tel. 67793), is a very old hotel whose best features might be the arcaded central courtyard. From there you can sip drinks or coffee while watching the begonias grow from the ornate wrought-iron balconies supported by chiseled stone columns. Centrally located, the hotel offers peaceful and calm rooms, each of which has a private bath and shower. Per-person prices are around 360 AS ($19.15), with breakfast included. The hotel is closed during part of September and October.

Hotel Wörthersee, 338 Villacher Strasse (tel. 21158), looks like a cross between an Edwardian villa and a Teutonic castle. Sitting directly at the edge of the lake, its facade is an imaginative mixture of pointed gables, medieval-style towers, stone-trimmed arcades, and half timbering. Built in 1840, the hotel has been modernized into a simple wood-trimmed format retaining a few of the original details in the public rooms, such as a ceramic stove in the paneled dining room as well as dozens of hunting trophies. The streamlined and cozy accommodations (some of which are apartments) rent for 315 AS ($16.75) to 640 AS ($34.05) per person, based on double occupancy, with half board included. Singles cost about 30% more per day.

WHERE TO DINE: **Rôtisserie Ascot,** 9 Kramergasse (tel. 57171), is the best restaurant in the entire province. You'll find this elegant dining establishment in a pedestrians-only zone near the center of town. The French-oriented menu includes such specialties as snail soup, fish soup, lamb consommé with truffled dumplings, entrecôte with fresh cabbage, fresh salmon, blini with salmon caviar, and a succulent calf liver with white pepper sauce. Lamb dishes are also a specialty, and they're most often prepared à la Provençale with plenty of herbs. Dessert might be a kiwi sherbet or a choice of more filling and richer concoctions. Meals range from 160 AS ($8.51) to 360 AS ($19.15). It's closed on Sunday.

Hotel Dermuth, 52 Kohldorferstrasse (tel. 21247). The decor is solidly traditional, with all the rustic accessories that might be found in a regional farmhouse. The elegantly printed menu of this hotel, however, lists a series of specialties considerably more up to date. These include roast beef, schnitzels, and combinations of ingredients such as tender cuts of beef served with fennel and grated cabbage. À la carte meals range from 90 AS ($4.79) to 185 AS ($9.84).

Restaurant Stadtkrug, 7 Theatergasse (tel. 86355), prepares a succulent variety of fish, many of them imported from France. Specialties include a swarm of fresh- and saltwater fish and crustaceans, such as sauteed shrimp, as well as such meat items as veal schnitzel in madeira sauce, fresh vegetable soups (try the tomato), and various kinds of fruited desserts. Full meals range from 130 AS ($6.92) to 310 AS ($16.49). You'll have to choose between a meal in the sunny courtyard or in one of the intimate interior rooms.

Restaurant Maria Loretto, at Loretto (tel. 24465), is a rustically appealing antique-style house whose oversize balcony offers a peaceful view of the lake. Your first course here might be goose liver or an asparagus and leek soup, which could be followed by a seafood risotto. If you prefer meat, the tournedos are juicy and cooked the way you prefer them. The restaurant is closed on Monday and during November. Meals range from 140 AS ($7.45) to 550 AS ($29.26) on the fixed-price menu, and between 120 AS ($6.38) and 290 AS ($15.34) on the à la carte.

Weinstube Kanzian (no phone), at Kardinalplatz, attracts a collection of amiable citizens who gather near the potted palms, chattering at tables separated from one another by screens. Specialties include wienerschnitzels that are so big they hang over the edge of the plate, and an array of juicy meats with french fries. Your first course could be one of several kinds of soup, while the meal might not be complete without a piece of homemade torte for dessert. There's a wide selection of beer and wine as well. Dinners cost from 180 AS ($9.58).

Knödelstube, 11 Villacher Strasse (tel. 511774), is a likeable weinstube in the center of town. The ambience is like that of an inner-city heurige, while the food is solidly wholesome and traditional. Of the many recipes on the menu, the most popular are the noodles, which are prepared with meats, cheeses, vegetables (such as sauerkraut), or as the base of several kinds of soup. Dessert might be apple-flavored noodles with cider sauce (which is appropriate to the name of the restaurant, "The Noodle Stube"). A la carte meals range from 65 AS ($3.46) to 180 AS ($9.58).

Wiery, Tessendorfer Strasse (tel. 43239), is a popular restaurant accommodating all kinds of local citizens, who appreciate the rich beer and savory food. Specialties include roast pork in a pungent sauce, soups, salads, and tortes. Full meals cost from 80 AS ($4.26) to 230 AS ($12.24). It's closed in October and every Saturday.

Café Musil, 10 Oktoberstrasse (tel. 511660), inside the well-known hotel of the same name, is the best café in town. Patterned after a Viennese coffeehouse, the establishment serves a filling breakfast and an array of tortes and pastries which usually come fresh from the oven. Coffee and pastries cost between 14 AS (75¢) and 25 AS ($1.33).

EXCURSIONS FROM KLAGENFURT: **St. Veit an der Glan** was the capital of Carinthia from 1170 until yielding the honor to Klagenfurt in 1518, the dukes of Carinthia holding power when the province was an imperial duchy before the Habsburg takeover. The town was surrounded by high walls in the 15th century.

In the rectangular Hauptplatz (main square) at the center of town is a Trinity Column, dating from 1715, erected to mark the town's deliverance from the plague. Also on this square is the fountain called Schüsselbrunnen. The bottom part of this fountain is believed to have been excavated at the old Roman city of Virunum. A bronze statue crowning the fountain is a depiction of a miner from the 16th century, which St. Veit has adopted as its symbol.

The Rathaus (town hall) has a baroque exterior, but the building is from 1468. It has a lovely arcaded courtyard. Guided tours are conducted through the great hall of the Rathaus from 8 a.m. to noon and from 1 to 4 p.m., except Wednesday afternoon. It's also closed Saturday and Sunday from November to April.

The pfarrkirche (parish church) is Romanesque with a Gothic choir. A circular *karner* (charnel house) is nearby. The baronial castle here served as an arsenal in the 16th century but has now been turned into a regional museum displaying artifacts of the area.

St. Veit an der Glan stands at the center of the most castle-rich section of Austria, with more than a dozen of the fortress complexes lying within a 6½-mile radius of St. Veit.

The best known and most visited is **Hochosterwitz Castle,** about six miles to the east of St. Veit, first mentioned in documents of 860. In 1209 the ruling Spanheims made the Osterwitz family hereditary royal cupbearers, owners and occupants of Hochosterwitz as a fiefdom. When the last of that line was a victim of a Turkish invasion, the castle reverted to Emperor Frederick III and was subsequently passed by him to the governor of the area, Chrishof Khevenhüller. In 1570 Baron George Khevenhüller, also the governor, purchased the citadel and fortified it against the Turks, providing it with an armory and adding the gates, a task completed in 1586. Since that time the castle has been the property of the Khevenhüller family, left to them by Baron George, as shown on a marble plate in the yard dated 1576.

The castle, standing in a spectacular spot on a lonely, isolated hilltop

530 feet above the valley, gives an eagle's-eye view of the area around. It's considered the most striking castle in the country. To reach it, you go up a 16th-century approach ramp and through a total of 14 fortified gates. You can visit a number of rooms that have been opened to the public by the Khevenhüller family to show off the armor collection. In the private rooms you can also see a portrait gallery of the ancestors of the present owners.

Visits are possible from Easter until the end of September from 9 a.m. to 6 p.m. for an admission of 30 AS ($1.60). There's a regional-style café and restaurant in the inner courtyard open to the public.

You can also strike out from St. Veit heading south again on the main road back to Klagenfurt. If you turn left after four miles and travel east, you'll reach the celebrated Ausgragungen, or **excavations at Magdalensberg,** at a distance of about nine miles from St. Veit.

Magdalensberg was a Celto-Roman settlement site and is considered the oldest Roman habitation north of the Alps. It is known that the Romans built a town here when they came this way to trade in the final century before the birth of Christ. In 1502 a farmer made the first discovery of a settlement here when he found a bronze statue, now called the *Magdalensberg Youth* (on display in Vienna).

However, it was not until the late 19th century that excavation work began. Even then collectors were mainly interested in discovering valuable Roman art objects. Serious archeologists began to work the site during the Allied occupation of Austria. As you explore the ruins, you can see the foundations of a temple as well as public baths and some mosaics. Tours lasting about 1½ hours are conducted through the site May to October from 8 a.m. to dusk, costing 20 AS ($1.06).

A celebrated pilgrimage, known as the "Four Hills Pilgrimage," starts from here every April. Complete with burning torches, the pilgrims race over four hills, and the run must be completed within 24 hours. It's a rather pagan event—at least pagan in origin.

At the summit of the mountain the Austrians have erected a pilgrimage shrine honoring two saints: Mary Magdalene and Helen. From it a beautiful panoramic view of the encircling mountain range, including the Klagenfurt basin, unfolds before you.

Returning once more to St. Veit, you can head northeast along Route 83, which becomes the E7. When you reach the junction with 93, turn west along the upper Gurk Valley road, passing through the hamlet of **Strassburg,** which was a walled town in the Middle Ages.

Here there is a pfarrkirche (parish church) in the Gothic style, which you might want to visit if you have time. The Heilig-Geist-Spital Church, dating from the 13th century, has some lovely frescoes. Dominating the village is a castle built in 1147 but much changed over the centuries. Once this was the headquarters of the powerful prince-bishops of Gurk. It has been turned into a Heimatmuseum (local museum).

The major goal of every pilgrim, however, lies two miles to the west—the **Cathedral of Gurk,** principal feature of the little market town in which it stands. From 1072 until 1787 this was the see of a bishop.

The dom (cathedral) is a three-sided basilica erected from the mid-12th century to the beginning of the 13th, considered one of the most splendid examples of Romanesque ecclesiastical architecture in the country. A set of towers with onion-shape domes rises nearly 140 feet.

The cathedral is rich in artwork, including the Samson doorway, an excellent example of Romanesque sculpture dating from 1180; some

16th-century carved panels which tell the story of St. Emma, an 11th-century countess who was canonized in 1938; the main 17th-century altar with dozens of statues; and a 1740 baroque pulpit. In the bishop's chapel you can see Romanesque murals which, other than the main altar, are the most important art objects in the cathedral.

The dom can be visited from the first of April until the first of November from 7:30 a.m. to noon and 1 to 5 p.m. On Saturday and Sunday it opens for visits at 11 a.m. In the off-season it's open from 7:30 a.m. to noon and 1 to 4:40 p.m., opening at 10 a.m. on Saturday and Sunday.

After visiting the Cathedral of Gurk, you can take the same road going east and back through Strassburg. Back on the E7, and depending on your time and interest, you can either turn north to visit the town of **Friesach** or else go south again, passing through St. Veit en route to Klagenfurt.

If you opt for the Friesach detour, you'll find an interesting old town worth exploring. Friesach may have been your gateway to Carinthia if you came here from Vienna. You enter Friesach after going through Styria. This is an ancient town, whose first mention in historic annals occurred in the mid-ninth century. It was once a property of the prince-archbishops of Salzburg, who held onto it until the beginning of the 19th century. Lying in the broad Valley of Metnitz, this was once a major stopover for traders between Venice and the capital of Austria.

Some of medieval Friesach survives, including part of the town walls which date from the early 12th century. In one section of town you can see the remains of a moat. The Romanesque Stadtpfarrkirche (town parish church) building, noted for its stained glass in the choir, was constructed in the 13th century. The town has a number of other interesting buildings, including a Dominican monastery from 1673, built on the site of a much older structure and containing a 14th-century church. In summer, open-air plays are performed at the monastery. You can also visit the 13th-century Heiligblutkirche (Church of the Holy Blood) south of the Hauptplatz, the main square of the town.

West of Friesach, a mile-long road or footpath takes you to the hill, **Petersberg,** on which is the Church of St. Peter, dating from the 10th century. Here you can visit a watchtower to see 12th-century frescoes. You can also see the ruins of a castle that belonged to those prince-archbishops of Salzburg. North of the town on another hill is a second castle, partially reconstructed but still much in ruins. Standing on Geiersberg, this schloss is from the 12th century.

I have no accommodations to recommend in Friesach, but you can travel up the Valley of the Melnitz some 24 miles to the mountain summer resort and winter ski area of **Flattnitz** (4560 feet). It has a circular church in the Gothic style, dating from 1330, built on the site of an earlier Romanesque house of worship.

Flattnitz has some fine hotels with good rooms and excellent food, everything at moderate costs.

Food and Lodging at Flattnitz

Hotel Eisenhut (tel. 27119) is a sprawling chalet set at the base of a forested hillside. On the premises are a small indoor pool, a sauna, a bar, and a friendly staff directed by the Rothenpieler family. The simple bedrooms rent for 435 AS ($23.14) to 515 AS ($27.40) for a single and between 265 AS ($14.10) and 500 AS ($26.60) per person in a double. These tariffs include full board.

Alpenhotel Ladinig (tel. 30113) is a generously sized country baroque hotel next to a 12th-century church in an isolated alpine meadow. The renovated interior contains wide hallways with massively handcrafted stairwells and a scattering of simple furniture and paneled walls and ceilings. The Ladinig family, who acquired this building from the diocese in 1917, charge between 350 AS ($18.62) and 400 AS ($21.28) per person, depending on the room assignment and the plumbing, with full board included.

A Side Trip to Maria Saal

In the immediate vicinity of Klagenfurt you can visit the pilgrimage church of **Maria Saal,** standing on a hill overlooking the Zollfeld plain, some 6½ miles north of the provincial capital near what was once the Roman city of Virunum, capital of Noricum province.

Maria Saal is a major pilgrimage church of the province. A house of worship was first built here by Bishop Modestus around the mid-eighth century. The present church, with its twin towers made of volcanic stone dominating the valley, dates from the early part of the 15th century, when a defensive wall was constructed to ward off attacks from the east. In the latter part of that century the Magyars had a try at taking the fortress-church but were not able to conquer it, nor were the Turks in later years.

One of the church's most outstanding features is a "lantern of the dead" in the late Gothic style at the south doorway. There are some marble Gothic tombstones on the church grounds. See also the *karner* (charnel house), which is octagonal in shape and Romanesque in style, with two tiers of galleries. The church has many objets d'art, but it is the 1425 image of the Virgin inside that has made it the subject of pilgrimage.

An interesting excursion to take from Maria Saal is to the **Herzogstuhl,** or Carinthian ducal throne, one mile to the north. A double throne on this ancient site was constructed from Roman stones found at Virunum. The dukes of Carinthia used it as a location from which to grant fiefs in medieval days.

2. Lake Wörther

The biggest alpine lake in the province is Wörther See, or Lake Wörther, ten miles long, lying to the west of Klagenfurt and linked to the city by a man-made channel, mentioned above. In summer it's a mecca for devotees of water sports. In spite of its being an alpine lake, the waters of Wörther See are amazingly warm, its temperature often going above 80° Fahrenheit in midsummer. Beginning in May, Austrians go swimming here, a most unlikely occurrence in most other alpine lakes of other provinces.

The little villages around Wörther See are flourishing summer resorts, especially such centers as Maria Wörth and Velden. Leaving Klagenfurt, we'll go first along the northern perimeter of Lake Wörther, stopping off in the little village of—

KRUMPENDORF: This is just a small stopover along the road, but it contains some moderately priced hotels serving good food. It's also well equipped for water sports. A city bus from Klagenfurt will deliver you to Krumpendorf. This safe, pleasant resort does a thriving family business. Its hotels are spread out, vying for choice spots along the Wörther See.

Food and Lodging

Seehotel Koch (tel. 522) is one of the most appealing hotels on the lake. In a small park area, its central building contains a rustically paneled weinstube originally built in 1496. A newer building, constructed in 1972, accommodates the overflow from the older section. The public rooms are tastefully decorated with lots of hewn wood, sunny colors, and well-upholstered furniture. Facilities include a lakeside pier, a beachside bar, a hotel bar, a breakfast terrace, a swimming pool, tennis courts, and a mini-golf course. The sunny bedrooms, each of which has a private bath, rent for 360 AS ($19.15) to 590 AS ($31.39) for a single and between 355 AS ($18.87) and 600 AS ($31.92) per person for a double, with full board included.

Strandhotel Habich (tel. 607), set in a park-like garden at the edge of the lake, is administered by members of the Habich family. The exterior looks like a well-appointed private house, and the homey atmosphere inside contributes to that feeling. On the premises are five outdoor tennis courts, a lakeside swimming area with piers for boating, a covered swimming pool, a flowered breakfast terrace, a children's play area, and a rustically paneled interior with lots of woodsy appeal. Per-person rates, with full board included, range from 390 AS ($20.75) to 615 AS ($32.72), depending on the season and the room assignment. The hotel is open from the first of May until the middle of October.

PÖRTSCHACH: Known for its promenade along the lakeside, Pörtschach, where many lavish villas have been constructed, is the major resort along the north shore of Lake Wörther and one of the premier resorts in Carinthia. A section of the town juts out on a tiny peninsula, and in summer the promenade is a blaze of flowerbeds. Pörtschach is a sports-oriented resort, with waterskiing, sailing, riding, and golf available.

To the southwest of the resort stands Leonstein Schloss, and in the surrounding area you can take many nature walks or go on scenic drives.

Food and Lodging

Hotel Schloss Leonstein (tel. 2816). A century ago Johannes Brahms composed one of his violin concertos here. What you'll see today is a 14th-century, once-fortified castle whose public rooms are tastefully filled with well-chosen furniture. Throughout the establishment are wrought-iron accents, old terracotta tiles, stone detailing, and a cozy set of vaulted ceilings. On the premises are tennis courts, massage and beauty facilities, an assortment of water sports, and cozily elegant bedrooms, some of them duplexes. Per-person rates, with full board included, range from 480 AS ($25.54) to 1020 AS ($54.26) for a double while singles cost from 650 AS ($34.58) to 1050 AS ($55.86).

The restaurant offers a candlelit ambience which many Austrians travel long distances for. Either served in the courtyard or inside, the food is consistently good, including filet of trout, Valencian fish soup, veal cutlet with cream sauce, and zander filet. The imaginative salads complement the homemade desserts, which are often accompanied by live music. Full meals range from 180 AS ($9.58) to 360 AS ($19.15). Reservations are suggested.

Hotel Schloss Seefels (tel. 2377) is a lakeside collection of elegantly ornate buildings that curve along the shoreline just behind a screen of trees. On the premises are quays sheltering a small flotilla of motorboats, as well as facilities for tennis (four outdoor courts), swimming (both indoor and outdoor pools whose waters interconnect), and fitness. The elegant and cozy bedrooms are freshly outfitted with decorator colors, discreetly flowered fabrics, and well-polished antiques. My favorite of the luxurious sitting rooms contains a massively ornate ceramic stove dripping with laurel garlands, an ornate chandelier, and comfortable chairs upholstered in light-colored fabrics.

You'll find dozens of sporting locales, including a sauna with a built-in TV, as well as a handful of bars and an à la carte restaurant where an unusual dessert might be a pistachio parfait. Full meals range from 275 AS ($14.63) to 490 AS ($26.07). Room prices go from 760 AS ($40.43) to 1380 AS ($73.42) for a single and from 635 AS ($33.78) to 1600 AS ($85.12) for a double, with half board included. Prices vary widely with the season and the accommodation.

Parkhotel (tel. 2626) is a modern concrete-and-glass cube jutting up from a peninsula extending into the lake. The hotel is surrounded with a large tree-dotted park, which makes the area quiet and peaceful. The spacious public rooms are streamlined of any excess flamboyance, yet maintain a kind of restrained contemporary dignity, especially with their high ceilings and big windows. Facilities include a supervised kindergarten, a private beach with an outdoor pool for children, a host of water sports, an indoor swimming pool, and a range of massage and beauty facilities. Open from May until September, the hotel charges 685 AS ($36.44) to 1100 AS ($58.52) per person, with half board included. Prices depend on the accommodation.

Seehotel Werzer-Astoria (tel. 2231) is a resort-style hotel scattering into several buildings of varying ages. One of the most unusual is the 19th-century bathhouse, which extends into the lake, crowned with a latticed tower. On a peninsula jutting out into the lake, the hotel offers big lawns, a private beach, sauna and massage facilities, a host of boat-oriented water sports, and eight outdoor tennis courts. On the premises are spacious public rooms, with big windows and lots of sunlight. These include a wine tavern, a lakeview restaurant, and a terrace with waiter service. Management plays host at Carinthian buffets and dinner dances. With full board included, per-person rates range from 350 AS ($18.62) to 1000 AS ($53.20) in a single and from 310 AS ($16.49) to 1050 AS ($55.86) in a double.

Hotel Sonnengrund (tel. 31526) has peach-colored walls, wooden balconies, and a pleasant 1950s-style design in a quiet location surrounded by trees. Under a willow tree on the big flagstone-covered sun terrace the management has set up dozens of outdoor tables. Inside, the decor has lots of exposed wood and simple furniture. A private beach is reserved for hotel guests within a two-minute walk from the front door. Open from the end of April till the end of September, the hotel charges between 505 AS ($26.87) and 935 AS ($49.74) for a single, while doubles cost anywhere from 470 AS ($25) to 865 AS ($46.02) per person, with full board included.

Seehotel Wallerwirt (tel. 2316) is a tastefully designed hotel with strong accents of black and white covering its elongated facade, and a flat roof looking out over a lawn area leading up to a private beach. On the premises are three floodlit tennis courts, a host of water sports, and instruction for many of the outdoor activities. Per-person rates in comfortable rooms range from $22 to $47 for a single and from $22 to $50 per person in a double, with full board included. Rooms in the nearby annex are slightly less expensive.

Hotel Rainer (tel. 2300) is scattered among four houses set at the edge of the lake. The older buildings have lots of architectural embellishments including towers, gables, and porches, that only the 19th century could have produced. Set on a big, well-maintained lawn, the houses look out over the hotel piers and the private beaches. On the premises is a collection of four outdoor tennis courts, water sports facilities (often with instruction), and a range of accommodating public rooms. Per-person rates range from 410 AS ($21.81) to 1550 AS ($82.46) per day, with half board included.

The hotel is closed from mid-October until the end of April. You'll walk through a dramatic black entryway before reaching the Lucullus restaurant, which might be the main reason for staying here. The walls are ornamented with dozens of such elegant knickknacks as antique keys and hand-hammered pieces of utilitarian ironwork. Your meal might include salmon, mussel soup, fresh shrimp, and an array of such unusual desserts as kiwi sherbet. Fixed-price meals cost 455 AS ($24.21). The Lucullus is closed on Sunday and Monday. Barbara and Gerhard Rainer are the hard-working owners.

Hotel Savoy (tel. 2658) is a contemporary balconied hotel set in a green area with an outdoor swimming pool. One of the exterior walls is covered with an abstract design of a dragon, skillfully painted in blues and grays. Per-person rates range from 600 AS ($31.92) to 755 AS ($40.17) in rooms or apartments, with breakfast included. These tariffs are for double occupancy. Singles require an additional 95-AS ($5.05) surcharge per day. The Trübswasser family are your hosts.

Haus Seefried (tel. 2391) is an elegant yellow-painted building with a design that might be Edwardian. Its steeply pitched gables protect an appealing collection of arcades, shutters, and porches, all of which look out over the water and the lawns leading up to it. On the premises are outdoor tennis courts with a trainer and water sports facilities. The Semmelrock-Werzer family are the obliging and intelligent hosts of this attractive hotel. The hotel is actually an annex of a larger hotel, the **Österreichischer-Hof,** in the center of the village, about a four-minute walk away. With half board included, rates in the Haus Seefried range from 350 AS ($18.62) to 685 AS ($36.44) per person, while tariffs in the main hotel cost between 400 AS ($21.28) and 850 AS ($45.22) per person, also with half board included. Rates vary with the season and the plumbing.

Gasthof Joainig, 4 Kochwirtplatz (tel. 2319), is a graceful country house with a hipped and gabled roof, louvered wooden shutters, and masses of summertime flowers clustered in the burgeoning flowerboxes. On the premises is a big sun terrace, while the interior contains a pleasantly simple collection of wooden furniture and a large bar/café/pastry shop. The bedrooms are trimmed with wood, except for their smallish formats, and are comfortable. Per-person rates range from 280 AS ($14.90) to 420 AS ($22.34), based on double occupancy, with half board included. Singles cost another 25 AS ($1.33) per day.

La Bohème (tel. 3191) is a popular and elegant restaurant with a Paris-inspired decor where specialties include seafish soup, braised stuffed mushrooms, filet steak La Bohème in a delicate cabbage and mushroom sauce, and an array of desserts such as raspberry or lemon sorbets. À la carte meals range from 240 AS ($12.77) to 480 AS ($25.54). Reservations are suggested.

MOOSBURG: This little village two miles northeast of Pörtschach nestles on a southern mountain slope with magnificent views. It's not actually on the lake, but many prefer to stay here because of the accommodation recommended below.

Moosburg has a castle dating from the 16th century. It is believed that the German ruler Arnulf was born in a Carolingian castle that stood on this spot. Only the ruined tower of that ancient structure remains.

Landhaus Coester (tel. 7177) is a family-run pension offering a sunny patio and several balconies, as well as a view of the mountains to the south. Per-person rates range from 280 AS ($14.90), with a fortifying breakfast included.

VELDEN: Considered the most sophisticated resort in Carinthia, at the western end of the Wörther See, Velden is called the heart of the Austrian Riviera. The resort has many beautiful parks sweeping down to the lakeside, and from most of the hotel bedrooms you'll have views of the sparkling blue lake with the peaks of Karawanken in the background, marking the Yugoslav and Italian borders.

Naturally, the big attraction here is water sports, ranging from bathing in the warm alpine lake to waterskiing and surfing. Instruction is available in water activities. The long swimming season begins the first of May and continues until the end of October. You can also play golf at a course 2¼ miles from Velden on the south bank of the lake, and many of the resort hotels have tennis courts.

Most guests spend their days bathing in the lake and later enjoy dancing. Five o'clock tea dances are popular, and you can also trip the light fantastic to the music of orchestras on lake terraces. Summer festivals are often staged in Velden, and balls and beauty contests keep the patrons of the resort amused. Also, this is a fine center for motoring, with good roads taking you on many scenic routes.

In addition, Velden has a well-patronized **casino**, with a restaurant and bar. The casino, offering blackjack, baccarat, and roulette, opens at 7 p.m.

Food and Lodging

Hotel Schloss Velden (tel. 2655) was built as a home for one of the local aristocrats in 1603. The owner, of course, is long dead, but the ornate towers at each of the building's four corners and the neoclassical extension stretching toward the lake are still painted an ochred yellow, much the way he built them originally. A Renaissance archway capped with no fewer than three obelisks flanks the entrance to the gardens, while a long L-shaped extension with steeply pitched roofs sweeps off to one side.

On the premises is a modern annex connected to the main building, built roughly in the same style (although vastly simplified), as well as outdoor tennis courts, a musical bar with live music, an elegant red-walled restaurant, a cozy weinstube, and several terraces, some of them with outdoor bars. Water sports are available at the lakeside. The well-furnished rooms are equipped with modern comforts, while the public rooms are filled with luxurious old furniture and elegant accessories. Singles cost between 480 AS ($25.54) and 1060 AS ($56.39), while doubles range in price between 480 AS ($25.54) and 960 AS ($51.07) per person, with half board included. The hotel closes for the winter at the end of September, opening again at the beginning of May.

Seehotel (tel. 2020), in the center of Velden, is a conservatively styled building with frontage on the lake. An awning stretches from the building out over a pleasant sun terrace, while the rooms inside are a lighthearted mixture of slightly dated furniture, bright colors, and lots of exposed wood. The hotel has a dancing terrace at the edge of the water and stages a five o'clock tea dance every afternoon in summer. On the premises is a Viennese-style café, a bar, a grill room, and all the modern comforts. Per-person rates range from 385 AS ($20.48) to 875 AS ($46.55), with full board included. Prices depend on the season and the accommodation.

Hubertus Hof (tel. 2676) is a symmetrically designed, three-story house with a dignified, restrained facade that emphasizes the curved wrought-iron balconies and its gracefully hipped roof. The simple and dignified interior contains comfortable furniture and lots of cozy niches. An equally pleasant second building in the garden accommodates the overflow from the lakeside house and also contains a café and a big sun terrace. On the premises are a swimming beach, a restaurant, an array of sporting activities, and a small library. Per-person rates in both singles and doubles range from 380 AS ($20.22) to 890 AS ($47.35), with half board included. Prices depend on the season and the plumbing. The Kenney family are your hosts.

Seehotel Europa (tel. 2197) is a white-walled hotel built in a contemporary format in a tree-dotted area at the edge of the lake. Its pier area contains water sports, plus a private bar. The nearby tennis courts are floodlit at night for round-the-clock volleying. On the premises are a dancing bar, a big sun terrace covered by an awning, and a modern dining room with angular chairs. A comfortable annex nearby holds the overflow from the main hotel. Per-person rates, in a single or double, range from 500 AS ($26.60) to 865 AS ($46.02), with half board included. Prices depend on the plumbing and the season.

Hotel Alte Post–Wrann (tel. 2141) is a friendly hotel partially concealed behind well-positioned plantings in the center of town, close to the casino. Its facade is pierced with stone-trimmed arched windows leading into the pleasant bedrooms. A private beach maintained by the hotel is a two-minute walk from the front door. On the premises is a rustic wine tavern called the Reblaus, whose outdoor entrance is marked by massive beams that probably came from a wine press. There's also a paneled restaurant dotted with hunting trophies, a ceramic tile stove, and chandeliers fashioned from deer antlers. Rates range from 430 AS ($22.88) to 625 AS ($33.25) in a single, while doubles cost between 300 AS ($15.96) and 580 AS ($30.87) per person, with half board included. Tennis courts are nearby. Prices depend on the season and the plumbing.

The hotel also has the Wrann restaurant (same phone), in a verdant summertime location in a garden, whose entrance is also marked by those massive beams. Under a canopy of trees you can order schnitzels, curried rice, veal in cream sauce, and a range of traditional Austrian and regional recipes, many of them served with homemade spätzle. Open only in the warm months, from May to September, the restaurant suggests that reservations be made. Full meals range from 120 AS ($6.38) to 265 AS ($14.10).

MARIA WORTH: Part of this village, on the southern side of the lake across from Pörtschach, juts out into the Wörther See on a rocky peninsula, providing a good view of the surroundings. From Maria Wörth you can patronize the golf courses in the nearby hamlet of Dellach.

The village's pfarrkirche (parish church) is Gothic with a baroque interior, and to confuse its styles even more, a Romanesque crypt. It's noted for its main altar, dating from the 15th century. The circular *karner* (charnel house) in the yard, with a round tower, was built in 1278. The church is a pilgrimage sanctuary.

Nearby is another noted church, the Rosenkranzkirche, from the 12th century, often referred to as "the winter church." It has some 11th-century Romanesque frescoes of the apostles.

Food and Lodging

Hotel Astoria (tel. 2279) is an attractively designed hotel built in several interconnected sections with a pointed tower jutting upward from the center. It sits at the neck of a peninsula extending into the lake, with its own marina and bathing beach as well as two big piers, one of which is covered with deck chairs. The elegant public rooms have lots of sunny space and a scattering of Oriental rugs. On the premises are an indoor pool, a sauna, a masseur, a garage, a bierstube, and two restaurants. Per-person rates in summer range from 500 AS ($26.60) to 1020 AS ($54.26), double occupancy, with singles paying a daily surcharge of 75 AS ($3.99). These prices include half board.

Schlosshotel Maria Wörth (tel. 2235) has an ornate baroque facade facing the lake. The hotel is set at the end of a peninsula extending into the lake, separated from the mainland by a verdant forest coming almost to the hotel walls. The elegantly spacious interior is trimmed with polished wood and Oriental carpets, while the updated bedrooms have simple furniture and modern comfort. Per-person rates in a double range from 265 AS ($14.10) to 560 AS ($29.79), with half board included. Singles pay a daily surcharge of 40 AS ($2.13).

Hotel Wörth (tel. 2276) is a balconied chalet set on a hillside sloping steeply down to the lake. Guests enjoy the sun terrace, the rustically beamed dining and sitting rooms, and the attractively streamlined bedrooms, many of which provide private balconies and a view of the village church a short distance away across the blue waters of a small inlet. The hotel has an attractive beach area and a convenient location in the center. Summer rates range from 445 AS ($23.67) to 875 AS ($46.55) per person, double occupancy, with singles paying a 75 AS ($3.99) daily surcharge. Half board is included in these tariffs.

Strandhotel Harrich (tel. 2228) is a lakeside hotel whose wood-trimmed balconies stretch across a generous expanse of shoreline. The building sits amid a well-planned garden, with an abstractly shaped sun terrace cantilevered above the slope of the hillside. There's also a lakeside grassy area with a scattering of deck chairs. On the premises are an indoor pool, a sauna, a fitness room, and conscientious management by the Harrich family. The accommodations include apartments and bungalows. Per-person rates range from 600 AS ($31.92) to 1320 AS ($70.22) for the apartments (each of which has two bedrooms), and between 445 AS ($23.67) and 700 AS ($37.24) in a double. Singles cost about 15% more per day. These tariffs include half board.

Eschenhof (tel. 2260) is a likeable restaurant near the center of town which serves traditional dishes to a local crowd of residents. Menu items include zander (fish filet) and several veal dishes, with desserts ranging from simple confections to flaming crêpes suzette. À la carte meals range from 180 AS ($9.58) to 445 AS ($23.67).

LAKE KEUTSCHACHER: On the way down from the mountain, you might visit Keutschacher See, as Lake Keutschacher appears on your map, stopping first at Keutschach, the chief village on the route. It has a little pfarrkirche (parish church) in the Romanesque style. To the south of the hamlet is the brilliant-green Lake Keutschacher, one of the warmest alpine lakes.

Lodging at Keutschach am See

Strandpension Brückler (tel. 2384) is a homey kind of pension at the edge of the lake. Guests are housed in one of three buildings, all clustered near one another. The main building is beautifully decorated, chalet style, with painted embellishments and vivid green shutters. The interior is simple and contemporary, while the cuisine features produce grown on the nearby farm. With breakfast included, per-person rates in a double range from 170 AS ($9.04) to 325 AS ($17.29), with singles costing another 45 AS ($2.39) per day.

REIFNITZ: This is really just a smaller version of Maria Wörth, slightly more than a mile directly east of that resort on the road back to Klagenfurt. From here you can take a road up to a hill known as the **Pyramiden Kogel** (nearly 3000 feet), where there's a lookout tower and a restaurant. If the day is sunny you'll have an excellent view of Carinthia.

On the way down from the hill you might stop off at **Keutschach** with its little Romanesque-style parish church and a castle in the baroque style. To the south of this village is Lake Keutschacher, with brilliant emerald-green water.

Parkhotel Sekirn (tel. 2225) is a gracefully proportioned four-story building with a red tile roof, gables, wood detailing, and cream-colored walls. Set in a large park, the hotel offers personalized service and a pleasing collection of simply decorated public rooms. With half board included, per-person rates go from 530 AS ($28.20) to 700 AS ($37.24) in a double. Singles pay a daily surcharge of 145 AS ($7.71).

3. Lake Ossiacher

For the next journey, we'll head west from Klagenfurt, passing through Moosberg, already visited, and going on to Feldkirchen. Before long I'll introduce you to Lake Ossiacher (Ossiacher See, in German), third-largest lake in the province, some seven miles long. Its water temperature in summer is only minutely cooler than that of Lake Wörther—a comfortable 79° Fahrenheit.

The lake is ringed with little villages that have been turned into resorts attracting summer visitors, mainly Austrians, who come here to bathe and enjoy water sports.

FELDKIRCHEN: Our first stopover, Feldkirchen, is an old town that was once the property of the Bamberg bishops. At a major crossroads, Feldkirchen grew and prospered from traders passing through the area. (It is not to be confused with the Feldkirch in Vorarlberg.)

Segments of the Middle Ages live on in Feldkirchen, especially in its patrician houses and narrow streets. Visit the old quarter to see the Biedermeier facades added in the first part of the 19th century. The village has a pfarrkirche (parish church) in the Romanesque style but with a Gothic choir. If you go inside you'll be rewarded by a look at some frescoes from the 13th century.

In the vicinity of the town are some small lakes worth a visit if time permits.

Hotel Rainer, 1 Eppensteinerstrasse (tel. 2097), is an imaginatively designed modern hotel with a flat roof, lots of exposed wood, and a pleasingly geometric format that looks almost Bauhaus. The bedrooms are filled with comfortably angular lines and streamlined furniture. On the premises are a big sun terrace and a hospitable dining room. Per-person rates are around 360 AS ($19.15) a day.

OSSIACH: This resort on the south side of the lake is small (pop. of 650) but it's still the biggest settlement on the Ossiacher See. It has a Benedictine abbey originally built in the 11th century but reconstructed in the 1500s. The monastery was dissolved a century or so ago. Now special events of the Carinthian Summer Festival take place here. On several occasions Leonard Bernstein has conducted the orchestra.

Gasthof Schlosswirt (tel. 347) is a simple house with an upper floor trimmed with wood. The interior has knotty paneling and a rustic contemporary format of no-frills comfort. The Pribernig family charge 350 AS ($18.62) per person in a double and 385 AS ($20.48) for a single, with half board included.

SATTENDORF: On the north shore of the lake, Sattendorf, both a summer and a winter resort, is well equipped with good hotels to receive guests. In summer you can breathe the pure mountain air and wander across alpine meadows and deep into the forest. There's bathing both in indoor pools and in Lake Ossiacher.

From the lake you can go on several easy excursions, including one on the Kanzelbahn cable car, 10 minutes away, and a 20-minute run by car to either Italy or Yugoslavia (if you have a visa). You can also make day shopping trips to either Klagenfurt, already visited, or Villach (see below).

Food and Lodging

Sonnenhotel Zaubek (tel. 2713) is a contemporary hotel with wide balconies and a flat roof. The interior is filled with wood detailing, heavy ceiling beams, wrought-iron touches, and lots of sports and health facilities. On the premises are a small indoor pool, a sauna, a pleasantly airy restaurant, and a bar with evening dancing. The Zaubek family, your conscientious hosts, charge between 360 AS ($19.15) and 815 AS ($43.36) per person, with half board included. Prices depend on the size of the accommodation and the season.

Hapotel Diana (tel. 2381) is a large hillside hotel with a generously sized format of big windows, wide balconies, and pleasantly contemporary furniture. On the premises is a big indoor pool with an arched ceiling supported by boomerang-shaped timbers of laminated wood, plus a warmly tinted bar and restaurant, a sauna, and a sun terrace. There is easy access to the nearby hiking trails. Per-person rates range from 310 AS ($16.49) to 455 AS ($24.21), with half board included, in one of the double rooms. Singles pay a daily surcharge of 95 AS ($5.05).

Sporthotel Alpenrose (tel. 2220) is a balconied chalet partially surrounded by a raised sun terrace dotted with summertime parasols. Built into a hillside, the hotel has two levels of big-windowed public rooms facing guests as they approach the downhill side. The warmly tinted interior is dotted with exposed wood, autumnal colors, and comfortable lounge chairs. On the premises are an indoor pool, a sauna, a restaurant, a dance bar, and several open fireplaces set into attractively textured masonry walls. With full board included, singles cost between 410 AS ($21.81) and 700 AS ($37.24), while doubles go for 400 AS ($21.28) to 675 AS ($35.91) per person, with prices varying according to the season and the plumbing.

ANNENHEIM: This little lakeside resort which rarely gets an American visitor is quite inexpensive, a good place to have a budget holiday, especially at the accommodation listed below. Annenheim is on the north side of Ossiacher See, near the end of the lake.

From here a cable car, the Kanzelbahn, will take you to Kanzelhöhe at 4880 feet. Here you will find an observatory tower from which you can view the surrounding country.

Pension Haus am See, 9 Seeuferstrasse (tel. 2746), is a four-story contemporary house built practically at the water's edge. A two-story extension juts out to one side, with a big sun terrace coming down to the waterside. A sauna is part of the facilities, as well as a garage. This quiet hotel charges between 170 AS ($9.04) and 360 AS ($19.15) per person, depending on the season and the accommodation.

4. Villach

In the center of the Carinthian lake district, Villach is the gateway to the south. If you get bored, you can always drive over into Yugoslavia (visa required) or Italy for the day. Or if you're heading south already, this would make a good stopover.

An industrial town, Villach, the second-largest town in Carinthia, lies in a broad basin of the Drau River. There was a settlement here in Roman times, and later Villach was the property of the bishops of Bamberg, a distant see near Nürnberg, Germany, from the 11th century until Maria Theresa acquired it for the Habsburgs.

At the center of the **Aldstadt** is the Hauptplatz (main square) at the north end of which is a bridge over the Drau. On the southern part is a **pfarrkirche** (parish church) dedicated to St. Jacob. It has three aisles and a mixture of styles, with a baroque altar and Gothic choir stalls. Like most towns of its size, Villach has a **Trinity Column** dating from 1739, commemorating deliverance from the plague.

Theophrastus Bombastus von Hohenheim, Swiss-born chemist and physician better known as Paracelsus, lived here as a youth while his father practiced medicine.

From the heart of the old town it's a 2½-mile drive to **Warmbad-Villach,** known for its thermal swimming pools and mineral springs. This spa, on the southern fringe of Villach, whose waters are said to counteract the aging process, is the only such place where visitors can swim at the source of thermal waters.

In the **Schillerpark**, on Peraustrasse in Villach, you can see a large panoramic relief of the province which might be helpful before you set out on a tour. It is called *Relief von Karnten.* You can see the relief from the first of May to mid-October except Sunday and holidays from 9 a.m. to noon and from 2 to 5 p.m. Admission is 10 AS (53¢)

Villach is a good center from which to explore the Carinthian lake district, including the Villacher Alpe, an 11-mile journey via a toll road that costs 150 AS ($7.98) per car in summer. There are panoramic views in many directions, the best spots for viewing being marked.

At the end of the road it's possible to travel up to the summit of Dobratsch (7100 feet), going partway by chair lift and then by foot. The round-trip chair-lift ride costs 55 AS ($2.93). This is one of the most celebrated views in Austria. Allow about 2¾ hours for this excursion.

FOOD AND LODGING: Romantik Hotel Post (tel. 26101) was built in 1500, incorporating many of the rich vaulted ceilings that you'll still see today. The facade is a Teutonic fantasy of carved stone detailing, Ionic columns, and intricately patterned wrought iron. Between 1548 and 1629 this was the town palace of one of the richest families in Carinthia. During that period the building hosted an emperor, a king, an archduke, and later an empress (Maria Theresa). Later the nephew of Napoleon I dropped in and signed a registration slip which still belongs to the hotel.

On the premises of this historic place are a baronial fireplace, plus an arcaded courtyard shielded from the sun with an ancient collection of chestnut trees, and a host of elegantly furnished bedrooms. The establishment pays special attention to its cuisine, much of which is heavily laced with cheese, butter, and cream, following recipes similar to those used in aristocratic homes 200 years ago. These include tafelspitz, schnitzels (sometimes stuffed with cheese and ham), and recipes made from local venison, including soups, pâtés, and stews. Fixed-price dinners in the vaulted restaurant range from 90 AS ($4.79) to 540 AS ($28.73), with à la carte meals costing between 95 AS ($5.05) and 290 AS ($15.34). Reservations are suggested. There's also a less formal bierstüberl on the premises. Singles range from 420 AS ($22.34) to 610 AS ($32.45), while doubles cost from 325 AS ($17.29) to 500 AS ($26.60) per person, with breakfast included.

Hotel Europa (tel. 26766) is an elegantly detailed street-corner building in the center of town. The three-story hotel is painted a pale yellow and is accented with white trim and restrained neoclassical detailing. The renovated interior is filled with conservative furniture and pleasing tones of grays, reds, and browns. A Viennese-style coffeehouse is on the premises. Singles range between 515 AS ($27.40) and 600 AS ($31.92), while doubles cost between 780 AS ($41.50) and 910 AS ($48.41), including breakfast.

Brauhof, 8 Bahnhofstrasse (tel. 24222). Some of the items on the varied menu of this colorful place have origins in Italy, including the lasagne and the array of pasta dishes. But the main focus is on the type of wholesome and simple cuisine centering around grilled steaks in several different variations, as well as liver noodle soup, veal cutlets, and well-seasoned sauces. Many of the clients will be drinking beer with their meals, but good wines are available too. Full dinners range from 100 AS ($5.32) to 215 AS ($11.44). It's open all day.

Food and Lodging at Warmbad-Villach

Kurhotel Karawankenhof (tel. 25503) is a large modern hotel with a flat roof and long rows of symmetrical balconies. It maintains a battery of health facilities on the premises, as well as being connected by underground passageway to the spa facilities. These lie just on the other side of the huge outdoor pool, whose waters, heated by underground springs, are warm enough even for wintertime bathing. Set in the midst of a flowering garden, the hotel offers modern comfort to a conservative clientele who appreciate the bar, the open fireplaces, and the in-house restaurant. Rates in singles range from 480 AS ($25.54) to 850 AS ($45.22), while doubles cost between 515 AS ($27.40) and 755 AS ($40.17) per person, with half board included.

Kurhotel Josefinenhof (tel. 25531) is a sprawling contemporary hotel with evenly spaced rows of big windows and metal balconies. A sun terrace stretches toward the well-maintained lawn area, while a comfortably simple collection of public rooms offers warmly tinted resting places. On the premises are an open fireplace, an indoor pool, a bar, several restaurants, and a host of health and beauty regimes, including facilities for hydrotherapy. Singles range from 535 AS ($28.46) to 970 AS ($51.60), while doubles cost between 430 AS ($22.88) and 900 AS ($47.88) per person, with half board included.

Warmbaderhof (tel. 25501) is a large and elegant hotel closely linked to the town's cure facilities. On the premises is a large heated pool with a ceiling shaped like a continuous barrel vault covered with wood strips and an abstract mural at the far end. The lush gardens are visible from the streamlined balconies leading into the comfortable rooms. An angular outdoor pool connects with the waters of the indoor pool. A wide range of sporting activities, many of them organized, are close at hand, including tennis, horseback riding, and walking tours. The management sometimes has evening dances on the big sun terrace. Two restaurants on the premises serve well-prepared food. Prices range from 770 AS ($40.96) to 1000 AS ($53.20) in a single and from 575 AS ($30.59) to 1400 AS ($74.48) per person in a double, with half board included.

LAKE FAAKER: If you're in Villach in summer, you may want to drive over to Lake Faaker (Faaker See, in German), a small body of water that is nonetheless popular with swimmers and devotees of sports such as waterskiing. This is quite a warm lake, with water temperatures in July and August reaching 79° Fahrenheit. Campers like to come here.

If you'd like to stay at the lake, you'll find—

Food and Lodging at Faak am See

Inselhotel Faakersee (tel. 2145) is a summertime hotel at the edge of the lake. Its attractive facade has evenly spaced rows of recessed balconies, masses of flowers, and oversize windows. The decor inside is tastefully contemporary, with stone-flanked open fireplaces, accents of wrought iron, a simple restaurant serving well-prepared food, and a bar. The hotel is set on an island in the middle of the lake. A motorboat will pick you up at the mainland pier and redeposit you if you want a break on shore. Closed from the end of September until the third week of May, the hotel charges between 530 AS ($28.20) and 1230 AS ($65.44) per person, according to the season and the plumbing, with full board included.

Strandhotel Fürst (tel. 2115) is a simple and attractive modern hotel at the edge of the water near a sandy beach. A flagstone-covered path stretches past a collection of lawnchairs on its way to the lake. The public rooms are airy, spacious, and filled with comfortable contemporary chairs. Per-person rates in a double range from 335 AS ($17.82) to 635 AS ($33.78), with singles paying a daily surcharge of 30 AS ($1.60). Half board is included in these tariffs.

Da Luciano Unteraichwald (tel. 3122) is an Italian restaurant decorated with hanging fish nets and Mediterranean memorabilia vaguely reminiscent of Naples. Menu items include sardines marinated in cabbage and olive oil (guaranteed to appeal to both Austrian and Italian tastes), minestrone, an array of pasta dishes, and a savory veal schnitzel in madeira sauce. You can also try the grilled lobster, which goes well with the crispy array of salads. Desserts might be marinated in Grand Marnier. Meals range from 115 AS ($6.12) to 500 AS ($26.60).

5. Spittal an der Drau

Lying west of Lake Millstatter, Spittal, like Friesach in the east, is another "gateway" to Carinthia. It is not to be confused with Spital in Tyrol or Spital am Pyhrn in Upper Austria. This city on the Drau River is one of the leading centers of Upper Carinthia. It's at the foot of the Goldeck, which rises more than 7000 feet and is reached by cableway.

THE SIGHTS: Spittal is noted for the **Porcia Schloss,** really an Italian palazzo rather than an Austrian castle. It sits next to a park. It was constructed between 1533 and 1597 and is considered the most impressive Italian Renaissance building in the country. Its most striking architectural feature is the courtyard designed in the Italianate style with three-story galleries enclosing three sides.

The **Bezirksheimatmuseum** (regional museum) is on the second floor of the castle. Exhibited here are artifacts of the Drau region, local handicrafts, and regional costumes. It is open mid-May until the end of September from 9 a.m. to 5:30 p.m., charging an admission of 25 AS ($1.33).

In the environs, you can visit Teurnia-Ausgrabungen, the **excavations at Teurnia,** three miles northwest of Spittal at the village of St. Peter im Holz. The village grew up on the site of a Celtic settlement and, later, Romans lived here, as evidenced by excavation of a forum that was destroyed by the Slavs in the seventh century.

A museum here displays artifacts dug up right before World War I, from the cemetery of a fifth-century church, including mosaics bearing early Christian symbols. The museum is open May to October from 9 a.m. to noon and 1 to 5 p.m. Admission is 15 AS (80¢).

FOOD AND LODGING: **Hotel Ertl** (tel. 2048) is designed in a long, three-story format of cream-colored stucco with detailed trim around the windows. The hotel sits almost on the street, although there's a verdant garden with a sun terrace stretching off to the back, as well as a few café tables set up on the side. The dining room inside is attractively set up with pink napery, coffered ceilings, and brass chandeliers, while the warmly tinted bedrooms are cozy and appealing. An outdoor pool and a mini-golf area are on the premises. With half board included, per-person rates are 400 AS ($21.28) daily.

Hotel Alte Post (tel. 2217) is a simply decorated hotel with a streamlined collection of furniture. In the center of town, the hotel has some rooms which are comfortably furnished and spacious. With breakfast included, per-person rates range from 250 AS ($13.30) to 480 AS ($25.54), depending on the season.

6. Lake Millstätter

The second-largest lake in the province, the blue Millstätter See to the east of Spittal, is eight miles long, one mile wide, and 460 feet deep. This beautiful lake is set against a backdrop of the forested Seerücken (2840 feet) to the south and Nockberge to the north. Reflected in the lake are the peaks of the Reisseck and Kreuzeck in the far distance.

MILLSTATT AM SEE: Lying about midway along the northern rim of the lake, Millstatt rivals Seeboden as the principal Lake Millstätter resort.

The average hotel here is open only during the warm months. The highest prices are charged in July and August, when reservations are mandatory at this popular resort. Prices are often reduced in late spring and early autumn, and it's usually easy to find a room at those times. An organ music festival is held here in August.

Millstatt's main sight, other than the lakeside location, is the **Stift** (abbey), founded in 1080 as a Benedictine monastery but taken over by the Jesuits near the end of the 16th century. Part of its buildings has been used as a hotel since 1773, Hotel Lindenhof, once the mansion of the Grand Master of the Knights of St. George.

In the abbey courtyard stands a 1000-year-old "Judgment" lime tree. The cloister, which has Gothic vaulting and Romanesque arches, is reached from the east side of the court. The abbey contains a fresco of the Last Judgment, considered a masterpiece of Austrian Renaissance art. The abbey church (Stiftskirche) has a Romanesque doorway that is the major architectural attraction of the complex.

Food and Lodging

Stiftshotel Lindenhof (tel. 2101), a former abbey, is today an imposing hotel designed like a Teutonic castle, with two massive peak-roofed towers rising above a gabled center section. On the premises are a few linden trees that the management says are 1000 years old, along with an outdoor pool and a lakeside beach area. The bedrooms are decorated farmer's style, containing private baths and modern comforts. The big garden makes an ideal resting point or a play area for children. The Wolf family are the proud owners. Per-person rates, double occupancy, range from 410 AS ($21.81) to 425 AS ($22.61), with singles costing another 25 AS ($1.33) per day.

Hotel am See Die Forelle (tel. 2050) is an attractive yellow hotel with a simple facade which includes clean lines and black shutters. The lakeside terrace is sheltered with chestnut trees, while the interior contains bright, light-colored rooms, attractively uncluttered public areas, a bar, and a sunny restaurant. The conservatively furnished bedrooms are filled with tasteful objects and comfortable furniture. On the premises is an outdoor pool plus a big, well-maintained lawn area. The Aniwanter family are the owners of this appealingly streamlined hotel. They charge between 490 AS ($26.07) and 925 AS ($49.21) for a single and between 475 AS ($25.27) and 1000 AS ($53.20) per person for a double, with full board included. Prices vary with the season.

Hotel Post (tel. 2108), constructed around 1900, looks much older. Designed like a baroque country villa, it has ochre walls, black shutters, and neoclassical trim around the windows. The interior is a pleasing mixture of Victorian-era and contemporary furniture. There's an open fireplace plus a restaurant with well-polished knotty-pine paneling and massive chandeliers. The renovated bedrooms are simple and comfortable. They rent for 335 AS ($17.82) to 700 AS ($37.24) per person in a double and between 530 AS ($28.20) and 700 AS ($37.24) in a single, with full board included. The Sichrowsky family are the owners of both this hotel and the nearby Hotel Postillion which is more expensive.

Strandhotel Marchetti (tel. 2075) is an elongated yellow-walled hotel with dark shutters and a lakeside position. Flanked by well-trimmed chestnut trees, the establishment has a lakeside terrace sheltered with sun parasols and a collection of simply furnished public rooms bathed in vivid sunlight. A range of sporting activities are within walking distance. The Marchetti family charge from 350 AS ($18.62) to 625 AS ($33.25) per person in a double and from 340 AS ($18.09) to 455 AS ($24.21) in a single, with half board included. Also on the premises are a small library and an elevator.

Hotel Gasthof Seewirt (tel. 2110) is a modern hotel with recessed balconies, big windows, and an asymmetrical design. The sunny interior is rustically up to date and includes a simple restaurant. Per-person rates, based on double occupancy, range from 310 AS ($16.49) to 565 AS ($30.06), with singles paying a daily surcharge of 50 AS ($2.66). These tariffs include half board.

Gasthof Hubertusschlössl (tel. 2110) is technically described as an annex of the more banal Hotel Seewirt, but it's the architectural gem of the village. Designed with a steeply pitched terracotta roof, Romanesque porches, a soaring octagonal tower capped with a wrought-iron weather vane, and lots of baroque embellishments, it's almost a lakeside fantasy. The simple interior contains unpretentious bedrooms, renting for between 265 AS ($14.10) and 455 AS ($24.21) per person in a double. Singles pay a daily surcharge of 50 AS ($2.66).

Hotel Annenhof (tel. 2031) is an elaborately pretty chalet with gables, an arched loggia, and a two-tone facade of light yellow paint and dark-grained wood. Separated from the water only by a willow tree and a row of verdant shrubbery, the hotel contains sunny and spacious bedrooms which are simply furnished in appropriate good taste. On the premises are a rustic restaurant and bar with exposed stone and structural supports made from stripped saplings and rough planking. The sunny terrace offers a good view of the lake. A full array of sports activities are within walking distance. A sauna is available to guests, who pay between 300 AS ($15.96) and 470 AS ($25) per person daily, based on double occupancy, with singles paying a daily surcharge of 35 AS ($1.86). Half board is included in these rates. Karl and Herta Beisel are the good-natured hosts.

Pension Silberhof (tel. 2171) is an elegant 19th-century house with dozens of interesting architectural details, including a vertical row of bay windows and half-timbering across the upper floors. The renovated interior is graced with enormous picture windows which offer a view of the nearby village and the lake. Set a short distance above Millstatt, the hotel is managed and directed by the conscientious Maria Silbernagl. Per-person rates, with breakfast, in a room with private bath, are 240 AS ($12.77) daily.

Kärntner Stub'n, at Obermillstatt (tel. 2161), is a homey restaurant housed in a modern chalet with a big sun terrace. The interior has big windows, sheer curtains, and a beamed ceiling. The Propenter family is the owner of this pleasant café and restaurant, which prepares savory combinations of venison, veal, and pork with fresh vegetables. Specialties include venison ragoût, a saddle of venison in spicy gravy with chanterelles and dumplings, filet of venison house style (served with red cabbage), and typical Carinthian recipes such as fleischnudel (pastry filled with spiced meat). You can also order a Schlachtplatte, a platter of smoked meats, black pudding, cabbage, and dumplings. If you want to precede your meal with soup, you might try the garlic cream or the caraway cream. Full meals, fixed price, range upward from 110 AS ($5.85). It's open all year.

SEEBODEN: Many prominent Austrian families have summer villas at this resort on the western side of Millstätter See, using it the way some French families do the Côte d'Azur. Seeboden is quite popular in summer with water sports enthusiasts who enjoy skiing and boating on the lake.

The most popular excursion to take from here is along a narrow road for about six miles to the Hansbaueralm at 5635 feet. This is the lower station from which a cable car will take you to the Tschiernock mountain (6850 feet).

Food and Lodging

Sporthotel Royal Seehof (tel. 81714) is composed of two modern buildings set in the same grassy park at the edge of the lake. A few steps away, guests enjoy access to six outdoor tennis courts, a sandy beach area, a glass-walled indoor pool that looks somewhat like a big greenhouse, and three indoor tennis courts, each with a sliding roof for ventilation on hot days. The simple and well-furnished interior contains a bar and a restaurant. The Santner family are your hosts, charging between 490 AS ($26.07) and 980 AS ($52.14) per person in a double, with singles paying daily surcharges ranging from 110 AS ($5.85) to 130 AS ($6.92). Half board is included in these rates, which vary according to the season and the plumbing.

Strandhotel Koller (tel. 81245) is a lakefront hotel constructed in two interconnected sections on a well-maintained lawn. Many of the comfortable rooms have balconies looking over the water, and within view of the old-fashioned cabana and bathing pier. The simple and woodsy interior has plenty of rustic accents, including open fireplaces, comfortable wooden furniture, and a pleasing combination of warm colors. On the premises is a big-windowed restaurant, an indoor pool, a sauna, and a café/weinstube. A range of sporting facilities is within walking distance. The hotel is open only from Easter until mid-October. It charges between 420 AS ($22.34) and 700 AS ($37.24) per person in a double and between 490 AS ($26.07) and 710 AS ($37.77) in a single, with full board included.

Hotel Pension Klein (tel. 81218) is a modern chalet-style construction with a few regional designs painted across its wood-trimmed, big-windowed facade. Set on a grassy lawn, the hotel charges between 380 AS ($20.22) and 500 AS ($26.60) per person, with half board included.

RADENTHEIN: You reach this village three miles east of the lake by taking the road to Turracher Höhe (refer to Bad Kleinkirchheim, below). If you stay here you can head west to Lake Millstätter or east to Bad Kleinkirchheim, and you'll enjoy a reasonably priced accommodation at either place.

Hotel Metzgerwirt (tel. 2052) is designed like a concrete cube pierced with modern windows. This pleasant hotel is unpretentiously filled with wood accents, open fireplaces, and home-style decor. On the premises is a rustic restaurant serving well-prepared dishes, along with cozy sunny bedrooms renting for 250 AS ($13.30) to 500 AS ($26.60) per person in a double and between 310 AS ($16.49) and 500 AS ($26.60) for a single, with half board included. Prices vary widely with the season and the plumbing.

TREBESING: Going north from Seeboden on the way to Gmünd you find this hamlet, which is off the beaten path but lies in an area of great scenic beauty. It attracts both summer and winter visitors.

Hotel Trebesinger Hof (tel. 2350) is a pleasantly designed contemporary chalet set on top of a covered swimming pool whose waters are visible through the plate-glass windows on the ground floor. Sunk into the lawn area in front of the hotel, a reflecting pool contains a roughly hewn sculpture looking vaguely like some pagan emperor's crown magnified to hundreds of times its original size. The Neuschitzer family are the accommodating hosts, keeping their pleasantly rustic public rooms in tip-top condition. On the premises are a sauna, a bar, massage facilities staffed by the owner himself, and a woodsy restaurant serving well-prepared food made from fresh ingredients. Independent of the board plan, meals range from 75 AS ($3.99) to 340 AS ($18.09), while per-person rates, with full board included, go from 425 AS ($22.61) to 530 AS ($28.20) in doubles and between 425 AS ($22.61) and 600 AS ($31.92) in singles. Prices depend on the season and the accommodation.

GMÜND: This small town is in the lower region of the Lieser Valley, at the start of the Malta Velley. It's not on the lake but lies northwest of Seeboden on the road to Salzburg, an easy commute to the Millstätter See. Austrians use it as headquarters for exploring the Nock sector of Carinthia, which lies to the southeast of the town and is visited by mountain climbers in summer and skiers in winter.

The **Altstadt** (old town) of Gmünd still has defensive walls pierced by gates erected in the 16th century. Its Old Castle from the 15th century is now mainly in ruins.

A popular excursion from Gmünd is through the **Malta Valley,** taking a toll road beginning to the northwest of the town. This is one of the most enchanting valleys in the country and considered the loveliest in Carinthia. The scenery consists of waterfalls and newly developed artificial lakes along with a nature reserve.

Food and Lodging

Gasthof Kohlmayr, 7 Hauptplatz (tel. 2149), presents a peach-colored facade with restrained white trim to the main square of town. The decor inside is conservative and pleasant, with lots of rustic accessories and exposed wood. Per-person rates, in a single or double, with half board included, are 325 AS ($17.29) per day.

Gastehaus-Pension Alte Mühle (tel. 2257) is a beautifully detailed chalet with elegant balconies and charmingly old-fashioned embellishments standing out in monochromatic low relief. The interior contains lots of rustic accessories and an open fireplace. Open year round, the pleasant hotel offers rooms priced at 200 AS ($10.64) per person, based on double occupancy, with singles paying a daily surcharge of 35 AS ($1.86). All units contain private bath and come with breakfast included.

Pension Platzer, 26 Vorstadt (tel. 2745), is a low-lying hotel set at the edge of a small freshwater lake. A garden with well-maintained roses stretches off to the back, while the interior is pleasantly decorated with lots of exposed wood, coffered ceilings, and conservative furniture. The pleasant bedrooms range from 270 AS ($14.36) to 320 AS ($17.02) per person, based on double occupancy, with half board included. Singles pay a daily surcharge of 35 AS ($1.86).

Stadtschänke, 27 Hauptplatz (tel. 2218), is about as rustically folkloric a restaurant as you'll find in the region. Decked with light-grained banquettes and lots of old-fashioned artifacts, the restaurant specializes in the kinds of traditional cuisine for which Austria is famous. These include pork, veal, and beef dishes, many of them served with spätzle. The waitresses wear dirndls. Closed Monday in winter, the restaurant serves full meals ranging in cost between 80 AS ($4.26) and 240 AS ($12.77).

7. Bad Kleinkirchheim

A seven-mile drive to the east of Lake Millstätter you'll come upon Bad Kleinkirchheim, once just a popular summer spa but now a thriving winter ski area as well. Since World War II this resort in the Carinthian Nock mountains has become a mecca for skiers of the not-too-demanding variety. It's about fourth in popularity among Austrian ski resorts, with Tyrol, Land Salzburg, and Vorarlberg centers in the lead. Its winter season is also shorter than those of loftier alpine areas.

Cross-country skiing and winter hiking are popular here, with long runs and even gradients. The Kaiserburg chair lift takes skiers to the upper station at 6250 feet. The satellite resort of St. Oswald, 2½ miles north of the spa, has some good hotels.

Visit the hot springs of Bad Kleinkirchheim, Katharinenquelle, and the pilgrimage church of St. Katharina, which is known for its carvings.

FOOD AND LODGING: Kurhotel Ronacher (tel. 366). Built in 1908 as an elegant way station for clients who came for the cure at the adjacent spa, this hotel offers a thermal indoor swimming pool, a log-cabin sauna, many physical therapy techniques, a first-class restaurant, and a café. The interior is luxuriously furnished with pine paneling, ceramic stoves, and open fireplaces, along with comfortably rustic furniture. The bar area affords a rendezvous point, while frequent buffets provide a lavish spread of delicacies. Helga and Günther Ronacher do everything they can to provide a restful environment for their guests. A range of both organized and freely scheduled sporting events is available. Per-person rates, with full board included, range from 700 AS ($37.24) to 1590 AS ($84.59) in a double and from 755 AS ($40.17) to 1120 AS ($59.58) in a single. Prices vary with the season and the room assignment.

Hotel St. Oswald (tel. 591) is an imaginatively designed alpine chalet with an unusual roofline which angles at several different directions. The interior is luxuriously furnished with wooden ceilings, a scattering of open fireplaces, antique pewter, hand-painted antiques, and brass chandeliers. On the premises are a sunny indoor swimming pool, an accommodating bar with a hand-painted wooden ceiling, dozens of intimate nooks, and a full range of indoor and outdoor sporting facilities. The Scheriau family, the attractive owners, with their young children, do everything they can to make a vacation pleasant. They often stage organized dances with Carinthian music, as well as activities for children, including painting, handicrafts, and short trips. Singles range from 710 AS ($37.77) to 960 AS ($51.07), while doubles cost between 600 AS ($31.92) and 850 AS ($45.22) per person, with full board included. Prices depend on the season and the accommodation.

Hotel Pulverer (tel. 289) is a carefully designed collection of several chalet-style buildings arranged into a hotel and athletic complex near the ski lifts. Guests have a wide choice of elegantly decorated public rooms, some of which have gently vaulted wood ceilings, big windows, plaid carpeting, and ceramic tile stoves (the chimney of one of these rises more than two stories under a cathedral ceiling in the reception area). There's also a scattering of open fireplaces, along with cozy dining nooks, alpine style, with hunting trophies and antique art objects. Elegance and comfort, all with a woodsy rusticity, are trademarks here. On the premises are an indoor pool and a range of health and beauty regimes. There's also access to lots of sporting facilities. Rates range from 745 AS ($39.63) to 1140 AS ($60.65) for a single and from 700 AS ($37.24) to 1020 AS ($54.26) per person in a double, with full board included. Prices vary according to the season and the accommodation.

Hotel Alte Post (tel. 212) is a rambling hotel which makes a gentle curve around a manicured lawn with an outdoor pool set at the far end. Nearby are several outdoor tennis courts, while indoor courts are a few steps away. The interior is rustically filled with heavy beams, stippled plaster, and open fireplaces. The in-house bar is a warmly decorated hideaway, while the dancing bar is a rendezvous point for dozens of vacationers. The facade is a fancifully detailed ensemble of blue and white paint around arched entrances and rounded windows. Singles range from 600 AS ($31.92) to 765 AS ($40.70), while doubles run between 455 AS ($24.21) and 865 AS ($46.02) per person, with half board included. Prices vary with the season and the room.

Hotel Prägant (tel. 452), near the Römerbad thermal swimming pool and lift station, is a balconied chalet just downhill from the village church. Decorated over part of its surface with regional-style paintings, the hotel is covered with cascades of flowers in summertime. The cozy interior is decked out with lots of exposed wood, open fireplaces, and an indoor pool. On the premises are a sauna as well as massage facilities. A wide range of indoor and outdoor sporting possibilities are within easy reach. In high season, per-person rates range from 720 AS ($38.30) to 800 AS ($42.56), with half board included. Franz and Irmgard Prägant are the owners.

Hotel Kirchheimerhof (tel. 278) is a hillside chalet with recessed latticework balconies and a low-lying extension cantilevered above the sloping lawn. The view from the sun terrace takes in most of the village, while on a sunny day you might see farm animals grazing not far from the foundations. On the premises is an indoor pool, plus a dancing bar with a high ceiling, along with a cozy series of public rooms (some with open fireplaces) outfitted with rustic paneling and plenty of well-chosen accessories. The Hinteregger family charge between 660 AS ($35.11) and 700 AS ($37.24) in a single and between 600 AS ($31.92) and 780 AS ($41.50) per person in a double, with half board included.

Hotel Römerbad (tel. 8234) is a well-designed chalet with prominent balconies and attractive contrasts of light and dark detailing. The interior is rustically appropriate for its forested hillside location. It has an open fireplace, wrought-iron detailing, lots of exposed wood, a warmly appealing bar area, and big panoramic windows looking out over the forest. A range of sporting facilities is within easy walking distance of this pleasant hotel, which is efficiently directed by its good-natured owners, Walter and Ingrid Putz. Rates in singles range from 530 AS ($28.20) to 910 AS ($48.41), while per-person tariffs in doubles run from 455 AS ($24.21) to 815 AS ($43.36), with half board included. Prices depend on the season and the room assignment.

Sonnalm (tel. 5070) is a pleasant chalet with strong horizontal lines and regionally inspired painted illustrations bordering the outside of the panoramic windows. The sunny interior, which looks out over verdant lawns, has a beamed and paneled interior with lots of carved detailing. An open fireplace is outlined by a rounded travertine arch and capped by an abstractly shaped plaster dome. The emphasis throughout this hospitable place is on comfort. The spacious bedrooms have private balconies. They rent for 540 AS ($28.73) to 720 AS ($38.30) in a single and between 500 AS ($26.60) and 710 AS ($37.77) per person in a double. The Burgstaller family are the owners.

NEARBY RESORTS: From Bad Kleinkirchheim you can either stay at or just visit two satellite resorts in the area.

Feld Am See

This tiny resort lies on the shores of Lake Feld (Feldsee, in German), a diminutive lake that's one of the most idyllically situated in Carinthia.

To reach it, drive east from Döbriach, passing through Radenthein (see above). At that village, turn on a secondary road which will take you to Feld am See, where you can enjoy a lakeside holiday or else explore either Brennsee or Afritzersee, two lakes immediately south of Feldsee. The road skirts the shores of both these little lakes. The area is one of the most charming and undiscovered spots in the province.

Hotel Lindenhof (tel. 2274) is the attractive establishment belonging to the Nindler family. One of the entrances is below a rectangular plaque set with regional designs in colors of terracotta and white, while another is set into an old-fashioned facade with country baroque detailing around the shuttered windows. The interior is warmly outfitted with high ceilings, many of them paneled with well-finished boards, tartan-patterned carpeting in autumnal colors, wrought-iron detailing, and lots of cozy comfort. On the premises is a wood-covered bar area illuminated with forgiving light, as well as a restaurant and sauna. Per-person rates range from 335 AS ($17.82) to 515 AS ($27.40) in a double, while rates in a single run from 410 AS ($21.81) to 510 AS ($27.13), with half board included. Prices vary with the season.

Turracher Höhe

From Bad Kleinkirchheim, take a road northeast to reach this popular spot at an elevation of 5785 feet, at the pass leading over the Gurktal alpine range into Carinthia. This is sought out as a ski resort in winter and is much visited in summer for its scenic views. You'll be in the vicinity of two lakes, the Schwarzee (black lake) and the Turracher See.

A chair lift will transport you to Kornock (6560 feet). Mountain climbers are drawn here in summer to scale the peaks in the Nock area. Turracher Höhe is on the border of the province of Styria.

Hotel Hochschober (tel. 8213). Barbara and Peter Leeb set the tone of this lakeside resort, where casual clothes are the order of the day and where the sporting facilities include an indoor pool, a sauna, massage, bowling, indoor shooting, and where activities feature musical programs in the music room and a disco in the basement. Three mountain lakes in the immediate vicinity provide destination points if you want to go walking. Built in 1929, the hotel looks like the ideal kind of place for a country vacation. The interior is rustically paneled, containing woodsy accessories and open fireplaces, along with plenty of comfortable lounge areas, a bar, and a supervised children's play area. The warmly decorated restaurant serves simple food priced between 120 AS ($6.38) and 300 AS ($15.96) for a full meal. Per-person rates in the hotel range between 625 AS ($33.25) and 880 AS ($46.82) per day, with full board included.

8. Lake Weissen

The fourth-largest lake in Carinthia, Lake Weissen (Weissensee, in German), is also one of the loveliest and least known. On its shores are a few hamlet-size resorts, and more hotels are being built, but tourism is in the infancy stage here. The lake's major resort is Techendorf (see below). Neusach is another small holiday hamlet.

Of the major lakes visited so far, the Weissensee, southwest of Spittal an der Drau (see above) is the highest. It's about seven miles long and rather narrow, about 550 yards across. Its waters are warm in summer, more than 75° Fahrenheit.

It's not possible to drive around Lake Weissen. Visitors usually walk to it, although you could get there by boat.

TECHENDORF: As mentioned above, this is the major resort on Lake Weissen, perched on the northwest shore. A bridge spans the lake from here. If you take the bridge you'll find a chair lift to take you up to the Naggler Alm (4382 feet), which is gaining popularity as a ski area.

Food and Lodging

Sporthotel Alpenhof (tel. 2107) is a contemporary chalet with wood-trimmed balconies and low-lying wings stretching off to one side. Built in 1976, with special emphasis on the view available from the panoramic windows, the hotel contains a simplified kind of rusticity, with warm colors and exposed wood detailing. An adjoining building houses massage and health facilities, which you may not have time for because of the many sporting possibilities within easy reach. The Zöhrer family maintain the pleasant bedrooms, charging between 490 AS ($26.07) and 755 AS ($40.17) per person in a double and between 430 AS ($22.88) and 600 AS ($31.92) in a single, with half board included. Prices vary according to the season and the plumbing.

Strandhotel Weissensee (tel. 2219) is a lakeside chalet whose wood-and-stucco facade is accented with green shutters, patterned balconies, and masses of summertime flowers. Set in the midst of a well-maintained garden, the hotel has a pleasant sun terrace, a range of nearby water and land sports, a sauna, a bar, an appealing restaurant with a ceramic tile stove and heavy beams, and elegantly simple bedrooms. These often have decorative arches separating the sleeping from the sitting areas, big windows with balconies, and attractively contemporary furniture. Per-person rates, in a single or double, range from 420 AS ($22.34) to 960 AS ($51.07), with full board included. Prices vary with the season and the room.

Hotel Enzian (tel. 2221) is an imposingly old-fashioned chalet behind a set of stone columns flanking the path to the main street. Designed with weathered balconies and an attractively hipped roof, the hotel contains simple and attractive accommodations outfitted with warm colors and all the modern comforts. On the premises are an outdoor tennis court, a big lawn leading up to the lake, a rustic bar, and a simple restaurant serving well-prepared Austrian specialties. Rates range from 335 AS ($17.82) to 635 AS ($33.78) for a single and between 320 AS ($17.02) and 650 AS ($34.58) per person in a double, with half board included.

9. The Möll Valley and Mallnitz

Called Mölltal in German, this valley was known in the days of the Romans, with legions passing through it often during their long reign in Carinthia. This is still a much frequented route, as it is now the southern gateway to the celebrated Grossglockner Road described in the Land Salzburg section (see Chapter VIII). The valley contains the remains of several castles from the Middle Ages.

The resorts of Heiligenblut and Döllach, described below, lie roughly between Zell am See in Land Salzburg and Lienz, the capital of East Tyrol. Also in this section, I'll take you on a detour north of Obervellach to visit the ski resort of Mallnitz, which lies directly to the south of the well-known Badgastein of Land Salzburg, although there's no road to there through the towering alpine ranges.

KOLBNITZ: The first stopover I recommend in the Möll Valley, Kolbnitz, is a sunny hamlet set against a mountain backdrop. To reach it, drive northwest from Spittal. This can be the center for many day excursions, either into the Carinthian lake district or to the Grossglockner area. You can even have your car loaded on the train at Mallnitz to go through the tunnel to Badgastein in Land Salzburg. But the main reason for stopping here is the hotel recommended below.

Hotel Marhof (tel. 243) played an important role in the feudal politics of the region when it was built in 1150. The founding fathers of this hotel proudly called themselves "free peasants" (as opposed to the masses of serfs in the region), in exchange for which they paid annual revenues to the ruling aristocrat. Much later, when Franz Joseph tried to bestow a title upon a former owner, Joseph Walter, the "free farmer" proudly refused, saying that he preferred the title of his ancestors.

Today the family seat of all this is a prosperous-looking hip-roofed building with a stucco facade and green and white chevron shutters. Transformed into a hotel in 1967, the building has a simple wood-accented interior, unpretentious furniture, an outdoor pool, and a big lawn area for sunbathing. Heinz Walter, the owner, will welcome you into the cozy dining room, where specialties include tafelspitz, beef soups, and Viennese-style food which, of course, means schnitzels. Full meals range from 80 AS ($4.26) to 215 AS ($11.44). Rates in the hotel range from 360 AS ($19.15) to 455 AS ($24.21) per person, based on double occupancy, with half board included. Singles pay a daily surcharge of 35 AS ($1.86).

OBERVELLACH: Most of the castles in the Möll Valley are centered around this little village, which also has a late Gothic church known for its 1520 altarpiece by Jan van Scorel, one of the Dutch masters. The artist was a great admirer of Dürer, as evidenced by his works. In the Middle Ages, Obervellach was a gold-mining town.

Among the medieval castles near this village are Oberfalkenstein from the 15th century and Groppenstein from the 12th and 15th centuries.

MALLNITZ: Before you continue your exploration of the Möll Valley, I recommend a detour to Mallnitz, which is both a summer and a winter ski resort. Lying directly north of Obervellach, a five-mile drive up a steep road, this is a great bargain resort at any time of year, the prices being quite reasonable since Mallnitz is neither fashionable nor well known.

At an elevation of 3900 feet, it's so high up that the mountains around it wear permanent ice caps. In summer hikers go on mountain expeditions from this resort, a cable car taking passengers to Elschesattel (8600 feet). There are several ski lifts and horse-drawn sleigh rides are popular in winter.

Mallnitz lies at the southern end of the Tauern railroad tunnel. Since you can't drive directly from here to Land Salzburg, why not have your car loaded on the train? Otherwise, if you want to go north to that province you'll have to take a long and circuitous highway route.

Food and Lodging

Alpenhotel Mallnitz (tel. 262) is an attractive chalet hotel set in the hollow of a rocky valley. The service is especially relaxed and friendly, thanks almost entirely to the tone set by the Alber-Berlinger family, who, with their two children, do everything they can to be helpful. Built in 1905, the hotel has richly textured paneling, big windows, lots of rustic accessories, and an impressive collection of hunting trophies. Meals in one of the warmly appealing restaurants could include an array of veal or beef dishes, many of them grilled and covered with savory sauces, tasty soups, cold marinated herring, and homemade desserts. Full meals range from 85 AS ($4.52) to 300 AS ($15.96). The pleasant bedrooms rent for 350 AS ($18.62) to 600 AS ($31.92) for a single and between 320 AS ($17.02) and 555 AS ($29.53) per person in a double, with half board included. Prices vary with the season.

Hotel 3 Gemsen (tel. 396) is a pleasant chalet-style building with four floors of shutters, balconies, wood trim, and regionally inspired designs. Just to the left of the front entrance someone has stenciled three deer between the painted dates of both the year of founding and the year of renovation, which are 1758 and 1979 respectively. Inside, the decor is covered with vaulted or beamed ceilings, rustically home-style furnishings, and lots of warm colors. On the premises are an alpine-style bar, a simple restaurant, and lots of cozy comforts. The Peter Sterz family, the hosts, charge 310 AS ($16.49) per person in a single or double, with half board included.

WINKLERN: This little resort, 19 miles to the west of our stop in Obervellach, stands at an elevation of 3100 feet. It's north of Lienz, the capital of East Tyrol, and Iselberg. From here you can enjoy a view of some of the highest mountains in Austria.

Winklern has a pfarrkirche (parish church) with a watchtower from the Middle Ages.

Hotel Defreggerhof (tel. 252) is an attractively embellished four-story house with gables, balconies, and sunflower-colored illustrations around the borders of its windows. The hotel is a convenient starting point for walks through the surrounding hills. On the premises are a heated indoor pool and a sauna. There is easy access to the village's sporting facilities. Per-person rates range from 360 AS ($19.15) to 420 AS ($22.34), based on double occupancy, with singles paying a surcharge of 60 AS ($3.19) per day. Half board is included in these tariffs.

DÖLLACH: A gold- and silver-mining center in the Middle Ages, Döllach is now a small Möll Valley resort, its reasonable prices attracting visitors in both summer and winter. Lying six miles from Heiligenblut, our next destination, Döllach is at a 3360-foot elevation, set in an area of some beautiful waterfalls.

The Grosskirchheim Castle has artifacts from the town's mining days preserved in a regional museum.

Food and Lodging

Hotel Schlosswirt (tel. 411), one of my favorite hotels in the region, is a well-proportioned chalet with flowered balconies, weathered siding, and a desirable location at the edge of the forest. All the outdoor sports are available within a few minutes' walk. The interior has a kind of unpretentious elegance that comes mainly from fine woods and careful craftsmanship. The spacious bedrooms have comfortable furniture and lots of horizontal planking. On the premises are an attractive bar area and one of the best restaurants in the region. Your meal might begin with cream of trout soup and fresh chives, followed by a juicy pork filet stuffed with gorgonzola. Dinners range between 85 AS ($4.52) and 250 AS ($13.30), and reservations are suggested. The Sauper family are your conscientious hosts, charging per-person rates, with half board included, of 430 AS ($22.88) to 600 AS ($31.92) in a double. Singles pay a daily surcharge of 60 AS ($3.19).

Hotel Post (tel. 205) is the traditional spot in town, offering lots of rustic detailing and a choice of comfortable rooms. The English-speaking staff is friendly and accommodating, preparing a savory cuisine served in a woodsy dining room. The per-person rate in a single or double is 500 AS ($26.60), with half board included.

HEILIGENBLUT: If you enter the Möll Valley from the north, coming from Zell am See along the Grossglockner Road, this is the first important little resort you'll reach. It lies at the foot of the southern slope of the Grossglockner. Because of its location there's a lot of traffic through here in summer.

The steeple of the 15th-century pfarrkirche (parish church), backgrounded by the lofty mountain, is a much-used subject for illustrations and photographs.

In summer Heiligenblut is the headquarters for a well-known mountain climbing school. In winter skiers take over.

Food and Lodging

Hotel Glocknerhof (tel. 2244) is built dramatically on a sloping hillside a stone's throw from the beautifully severe lines of the village church. The hotel's exterior walls are covered with weathered balconies. The interior is rustic, warm, cozy, elegant, and alluring, all at the same time. On the premises are a covered swimming pool, with big windows looking out at a sweeping panorama, an inviting bar, a sauna, a sun terrace, a children's playroom, an open fireplace, a dancing bar, and a host of organized activities which include *schuhplatter* evenings, dinner dances, and buffet cookouts.

Per-person rates range from 475 AS ($25.27) to 1110 AS ($59.05) in a double and from 600 AS ($31.92) to 1060 AS ($56.39) in a single, with half board included. Prices vary according to the season. The most expensive accommodations within this price range are small, tastefully furnished apartments. The overflow from the main hotel is housed in one of three annexes.

Hotel Post (tel. 2242) is a pleasant chalet with wrap-around balconies. A wide sun terrace offers a sunny resting place. The paneled interior is accented with wrought-iron chandeliers, warmly tinted fabrics, big windows, and alpine colors of red and forest green. On the premises are a bar area with lots of massive timbers and a restaurant serving well-prepared local specialties. Each of the comfortable bedrooms has a private bath, as well as a private balcony, radio, and phone. Doubles range from 410 AS ($21.81) to 565 AS ($30.06) per person, while singles go for 470 AS ($25) to 540 AS ($28.73), with half board included. The Eder family are your hosts.

Haus Senger (tel. 2243) is a weathered double chalet, with recessed balconies and a covering almost completely fashioned from wood planks. The cozily rustic interior has massively hewn vertical supports, open fireplaces whose plaster chimneys are crafted into abstract shapes, stone detailing, and lots of cozy niches. The comfortable bedrooms rent for 265 AS ($14.10) to 600 AS ($31.92) per person, with half board included. Prices depend on the plumbing and the season.

10. The Gail Valley

A lovely valley running parallel to the Valley of the Drau, the Gailtal, as the German-speaking people call it, lies between the Carnic alpine range and the Gail Valley Alps. A trip here will take you into the deepest southern fringes of Carinthia along the Italian border. You'll find the resorts here to be largely undiscovered, unpretentious, and modestly priced.

HERMAGOR: This is the major town in the Gail Valley, lying to the west of Lake Presseger which gives it some claim to being a summer resort. Its pfarrkirche (parish church) is from the 15th century. In summer Hermagor is popular with hikers and climbers who head for the hills.

Food and Lodging

Hotel Wulfenia and **Hotel Sonnenalpe** (tel. 421 and 425) are two sprawling chalets connected to one another by a raised tunnel stretching over the parking area between them. These massive hotels have many facilities, including all the usual sporting equipment, as well as comfortable public rooms outfitted with softly glowing paneling, open fireplaces, stone detailing, panoramic windows, and rustically contemporary furnishings.

On the premises are a full range of health and beauty facilities, as well as an indoor pool, whirlpool, sauna, and Turkish steambath. A bowling alley and outdoor tennis courts are also available. Clients appreciate the bars, disco, restaurants, and the organized entertainment arranged by the vivacious hosts, the Pucher family.

With full board included, per-person rates range between 565 AS ($30.06) and 1020 AS ($54.26) in a double and between 670 AS ($35.64) and 1030 AS ($54.80) in a single. These prices vary with the accommodation and the season.

KOTSCHACH-MAUTHEN: With a name like that for your vacation site, no one will know where you're going if you tell them, but you'll know that this resort is in the upper part of the Gail Valley. *Mauthen* refers to the toll that was once collected here. The town has a 16th-century pfarrkirche (parish church), known as the "cathedral of the valley."

This little resort is at a major road junction through which you go heading south to the Plöcken Pass, with Italy as your ultimate destination. From Kötschach-Mauthen you can go south to the pass for a distance of just under nine miles, but it's a narrow, twisting road with gradients of 14%. I consider it suitable only for skilled alpine drivers who don't mind the numerous hairpin curves. The Italian motorists coming north don't seem to mind!

Food and Lodging

Kürschner Gesundheits-Hotel (tel. 259), painted a pale yellow with white trim, contains an elegant vaulted reception area, comfortable bedrooms, and virtually every kind of massage, acupuncture, and nutritional care available in Austria. On the premises are a big garden with a heated swimming pool, a tennis court, and a friendly management who frequently organize walking tours, garden parties, and group activities. Singles range from 490 AS ($26.07) to 745 AS ($39.63), while doubles go for 460 AS ($24.47) to 755 AS ($40.17) per person, with full board included. Prices vary with the season, the accommodation, and the plumbing.

Kellerwand, at Mauthen (tel. 269), is one of the most elegant restaurants in the region. You'll be greeted by the sounds of classical music as soon as you enter. You'll probably want a drink at the small, well-appointed bar area before you're led to a beautifully set table where fresh flowers, silver candlesticks, and painted porcelain along with fresh bread are de rigeur. Menu items include strips of sauteed calf liver with leaf spinach, trout dumplings, chicken in burgundy sauce, cream of mushroom soup, and veal in a sherry sauce. If you're interested in a dessert after all that, it could be a vanilla ice cream confection with a Grand Marnier sauce. Closed between mid-October and mid-December, the restaurant requests reservations and charges between 105 AS ($5.59) and 455 AS ($24.21) for full meals.

11. Lake Klopeiner

The waters of Klopeiner, the warmest lake in Carinthia, can reach 82° Fahrenheit in summer. The lake, surrounded by woodlands and shaped like an amphitheater, lies to the south of the market town of Völkermarkt. Lake Klopeiner is fairly small—only 1¼ miles long and less than half a mile wide at its broadest point. In summer it's thronged with fun-loving Austrians. The government does not permit motor-powered craft on the lake, endeavoring to keep its sky-blue waters free of pollution.

The resorts that ring the lake are part of the commune of St. Kanzian.

FOOD AND LODGING AT ST. KANZIAN: **Strandhotel Obir** (tel. 2223) is a contemporary lakefront hotel painted white and pastel yellow. Its big white balconies look down on a lawn area dotted with sun parasols. The simple interior contains a kind of no-frills comfort, big windows, and modern furniture. With half board included, per-person rates range from 355 AS ($18.87) to 630 AS ($33.52), the prices varying according to the season.

Hotel Klopeinersee (tel. 2294). Between the road and the edge of the lake, this pleasant hotel has blue shutters, white walls, and long rows of simple balconies. On the premises are a sun terrace with pretty wrought-iron chairs, a bar, lots of panoramic windows, and a restaurant. Many clients enjoy swimming off the hotel pier. Per-person rates, with full board included, range from 445 AS ($23.67) to 780 AS ($41.50), depending on the season. The hotel is open from early May until the end of September.

Strandhotel Marolt (tel. 2321) is an imposing-looking hotel whose different sections are joined together like a series of balconied cubes stretching along the lakeshore. The wood-trimmed facade contains big sliding windows that open into the well-furnished bedrooms, each of which has a private bath. On the premises are a covered swimming pool, several outdoor tennis courts, a bathing pier, a dancing terrace for outdoor parties, and a pleasant restaurant. On the spacious grounds around the hotel are a series of at least three annexes which hold the overflow from the main building. Singles cost between 385 AS ($20.48) and 625 AS ($33.25), while doubles run between 335 AS ($17.82) and 625 AS ($33.25) per person, with full board included. Prices vary according to the room and the season.

12. The Vellach Valley

Southeast of Klagenfurt, the Carinthian capital, the Vellach Valley leads to the Yugoslav border. It's a place well known in history. Your fellow visitors to this area are likely to be Yugoslavians.

The major stopover in the valley is—

EISENKAPPEL: This town is also known by its Yugoslav name, Selezna Kapla. It lies at the foot of Karawanken, 24 miles from Klagenfurt, or Celovec, as you're likely to hear it called in this valley, the home of a Slovenian ethnic group. Eisenkappel is only 10 miles from the Jezersko Pass, at the Austro-Yugoslav border.

The town is surrounded by centuries-old forests and mineral springs, and it has many cultural and historical curiosities, owing to its position as a frontier town. The southernmost of all the market villages of Austria, Eisenkappel is known both as a summer tourist center and a winter ski resort.

There are many sky-blue lakes and white mountain peaks nearby. Lake Klopeiner, to the north of this town, is the warmest lake in Carinthia, as described above. Five miles to the southwest you'll see the celebrated Trögerner Gorge.

Food and Lodging

Hotel Schlosspark (tel. 455). Set among a copse of lakeside trees, this striking chalet is a simplified version of something you'd find in the mountains. Its facade is painted an appealing orange yellow with dark shutters. A ground-level sun terrace stretches almost up to the water's edge. The streamlined interior is unpretentiously filled with simple furniture, much of it plushly upholstered, sometimes in attractively vivid colors. On the premises are a dancing bar, an indoor pool, outdoor tennis courts, a bierstube, and a formal restaurant with Louis XVI–style chairs. The uncluttered bedrooms rent for 420 AS ($22.34) to 480 AS ($25.54) per person in a double. Singles pay a daily surcharge of 60 AS ($3.19), and prices vary according to the season.

Hotel Obir (tel. 382) is a strikingly dramatic hotel constructed of red brick with black-framed windows set into its many outside angles. In the center of town close to the thermal baths, the hotel has a big airy format and a simplified interior decor much in keeping with the modern exterior. The simple bedrooms rent for 290 AS ($15.34) to 360 AS ($19.15) per person, with half board included. In winter the management charges an additional 35 AS ($1.86) per room for heat.

Chapter XIII

STYRIA

1. Graz
2. Bad Gleichenberg
3. Leoben
4. Murau
5. Turracher Höhe
6. Dachstein-Tauern
7. From Tauplitz to Altausee
8. Bruck an der Mur
9. Aflenz Kurort
10. Mariazell

THE "GREEN HEART OF AUSTRIA," Styria (Steiermark, in German) is so called because forests cover about half the land mass, with grassland and vineyards blanketing yet another quarter. The second-largest province in the country after Lower Austria, Styria has many neighbors. It borders not only Yugoslavia and Hungary but also the Austrian provinces of Burgenland, Lower Austria, Upper Austria, Land Salzburg, and Carinthia. Part of Styria takes in the alpine ranges of the Salzkammergut, and some of it (the eastern part) resembles the steppe country of the great Hungarian plain.

This land of valleys and rivers, mountain peaks and glaciers, was long an area bitterly fought over, being greedily attacked through the ages by Huns, Hungarians, and Turks, among others. But not all of its suffering from the depredations of battle were in previous centuries. Great damage was inflicted in World War II, particularly in East Styria.

Even in Celtic times the mountains of Upper Styria were known as a prime source of the iron ore on which the tribes depended for their weapons and other valuable implements. The Romans exploited the rich deposits, and the Crusaders used armor made from Styrian iron to fight the "infidel" in the east. Iron resources shaped the economy of Styria, and today it is Austria's leading mining province. Nine-tenths of all the iron ore produced in Austria comes from Erzberg, which means "ore mountain."

Styria is steeped in tradition, more so than any other Austrian province. The distinguishing costume often worn by Styrian men is a case in point. Derived from an original peasant costume, it's made of stout greenish-gray cloth with Styrian green material being used for the lapels and as a stripe down the outside of the pant legs.

Styria is one of the bargain provinces of Austria. Even its top hotels charge prices that would be in the moderate range in most of the major cities of Europe. You can take the train here from either Salzburg or Vienna, and state bus service links all the towns and villages of the province. I think, however, that the ideal way to travel here is by car, since you'll want to be adventurous and head up an unknown valley or drive right up to some castle-fortress.

You'll find good hunting country in Styria. In fact a lot of the game you see on those hunter's menus throughout Austria ran wild in Styrian woodlands during its lifetime. In summer you can fish for trout in the Enns and other rivers. Mountain climbing is another popular summer activity.

In the last decade or so Styria has been entering the winter holiday scene as a ski area, but it still has a long way to go before it will have the facilities of Land Salzburg or Tyrol. Likewise, its après-ski life is not yet nearly on a par with that of already-flourishing Austrian ski centers.

Graz, the capital of Styria, is the second-largest city in the country. In the imperial heyday it was best known as the place to which state officials retired. It even acquired the nickname "Pensionopolis" (City of the Retired) from this fact.

1. Graz

Graz, capital of the iron-rich province of Styria, combines a modern way of life with historical architecture to achieve a harmonious blend of past and present. Its history as a settlement probably dates back to prehistoric times, brought about by its location at the base of a hill at a ford across the Mur River, an important facet of transportation in the beginning of civilization. Romans, Slavs, and Bavarians all took their turn in the development of a town on the northern edge of a plain where the Mur leaves the wooded mountains of central Styria.

Early settlers, fearing flooding, established fortifications on the steep dolomite hill overlooking the river's ford site. The name of the city is derived from the Slavic word *gradec,* meaning "little fortress." This little castle was built on the hill which is now the Schlossberg in Graz. The town is first mentioned in historical documents from early in the 12th century. Graz has come under many governments, among them Germany, Bohemia, Hungary, Babenbergs, Habsburgs—you name it.

The medieval town developed at the foot of the Schlossberg, and some buildings of the late Gothic period remain, constructed when Emperor Frederick III used Graz as a capital after being forced out of Vienna by the Hungarians. The Burg (castle) and the cathedral of that era, houses that seem to huddle together, narrow-gable roofs, and arcaded courtyards contribute to the city's charm today.

Life wasn't always kind to the people of Graz. In 1480 they must have felt that fate was being extra cruel. In that year of the "Plagues of God," the little town was afflicted by locusts, the Black Death, the Turks, and a threat from the Hungarians.

When the Habsburg inheritance was divided in 1564 into Austrian and Spanish branches, Graz became the capital of "Inner Austria," the residence of Archduke Carl, who ruled Styria, Carinthia, and Italian Habsburg patrimonial lands. Graz was again prosperous. Carl had the town's fortifications strengthened on Italian designs, with bastions and moats.

A Jesuit College and Lutheran foundation school were both active by the end of the 16th century. Johannes Kepler, who gained renown for his mathematical and astronomical knowledge, began his teaching career at the Lutheran school. Fine arts and commerce flourished in Graz, bringing honor and riches to the city, as reflected in palaces and mansions of that period, although when Ferdinand II became emperor, he moved his court to Vienna in 1619. The influence of Italian baroque architects made its impact during this period.

The city walls were demolished in 1784, and the area they occupied, the *glacis* (slopes), was planted with trees. Napoleon's armies made three appearances here when he was trying to take over all of Europe, and the defeat of Austria at the Battle of Wagram in 1809 resulted in a treaty which forced Graz to level the battlements of the Schlossberg, in retaliation for the failure of the French troops to seize the citadel earlier that year. Only the Uhrturm (clock tower) and the bell tower were saved, rescued by payment of a high ransom by the citizens of Graz. Schlossberg was transformed into the beautiful park on that site today.

World War II saw much destruction by bombers, and the early entry of Russian troops into the city continued the devastation. However, during the occupation Graz was allotted in 1945 to the British and reconstruction began, so that today you can enjoy warm hospitality in the "Garden City" of Austria.

Graz is a city of some quarter of a million inhabitants at present, with such thriving industrial enterprises as breweries, machine factories, trading companies, and service industries. The Graz Fair is a commercial and industrial event of great importance in southeast Europe. Three universities, an opera house, a theater, museums, concert halls, and art galleries are the center of cultural life for Lower Styria.

If you're in the vicinity in the fall of the year, you might want to attend the Steierischer Herbst (Styrian Autumn) festival, which features contemporary art, music, and literature.

WHERE TO STAY: Accommodations range from luxury hotels to camping sites. There are many reasonably priced family hotels and inexpensive lodgings, and even the top hotels will strike many as being easy on the pocketbook. I'll lead off with the more expensive choices, and then preview a selection in the middle and budget range.

Hotel Steirerhof, 12 Jakominiplatz (tel. 76350). An unpretentious reception area leads into the public rooms of one of the best hotels in Graz. This is the traditional, conservative favorite, lying near the Opera on a large inner-city square. It's been severely modernized into a contemporary decor. On the premises are a piano bar and a restaurant, plus a courtyard with café tables. Singles range from 840 AS ($44.69) to 1430 AS ($76.08), while doubles cost between 1150 AS ($61.18) and 1760 AS ($93.63), with breakfast included.

Hotel Daniel, 1 Europaplatz (tel. 911080), has a boxy urban look with a flat roof and a sprawling design of concrete and glass. The contemporary interior is filled with upholstered banquettes and modern accessories, and is often frequented by business people from other cities. On the premises are a popular bar area and an elegantly efficient restaurant. A short walk from the old city at the station plaza, the hotel charges between 830 AS ($44.17) and 975 AS ($51.87) in a single and from 1150 AS ($61.18) to 1500 AS ($79.80) in a double or suite. All units contain private baths and all the modern comforts, and breakfast is included in the tariffs.

City Hotel Erzherzog Johann, 3–5 Sackstrasse (tel. 76551), stands near the pedestrian zone in the old city. This elegant hotel arranges some of its rooms around a skylit atrium surrounded by gracefully curving wrought-iron balconies and verdant plants. There's an array of attractive facilities on the premises, including a contemporary bar area with vivid accents of black and brass, along with a formal restaurant and spacious high-ceilinged bedrooms. Reached from the street through a chiseled stone archway set with elaborate ironwork and transparent doors, the hotel charges between 335 AS ($17.82) and 720 AS ($38.30) for a single and from 575 AS ($30.59) to 1070 AS ($56.92) for a double, including a breakfast buffet. Prices vary according to the plumbing.

Hotel Wiesler, 4 Grieskai (tel. 913241), has a history that goes back to 1603, and has been under the ownership of the Wiesler family since 1870. This is one of the best known hotels in town. Directly on the quay, the hotel offers renovated bedrooms and a baronial collection of high-ceilinged public rooms. Singles cost between 370 AS ($19.68) and 800 AS ($42.56), while doubles range between 735 AS ($39.10) and 1150 AS ($55.86), depending on the plumbing.

Hotel Weitzer/Goldener Ochs, 15 Griesgasse (tel. 913801), has been in the same family for four generations. (It's not to be confused with the previously recommended Hotel Wiesler.) Standing on the river, it consists of two buildings connected by a glass overhead tunnel. The Weitzer itself is the more formal of the two, with large, old-fashioned, and spacious rooms; whereas accommodations in the Goldener Ochs tend to be small and boxy. However, the whole hotel (or hotels) is well run and modernized with much contemporary comfort. Depending on the plumbing, singles range from 400 AS ($21.28) to 975 AS ($51.87) and doubles cost from 385 AS ($20.48) to 750 AS ($39.90). The Restaurant Kasserolle on the ground floor is considered by some residents to be the best in town. Furnished in a modern, warmly tinted style, with formally dressed waiters even at lunchtime, the establishment offers an elegant salad bar with an array of greens, cold marinated vegetables, and varieties of lettuce including the deluxe mache. The chef's tafelspitz is especially good. Meals average around 150 AS ($7.98).

Schlossberg Hotel, 30 Kaiser-Franz-Josef-Kai (tel. 82557). Housed behind a beautifully embellished cerulean-blue facade, this 15th-century country baroque inn is my favorite hotel in Graz. Renovated from a decrepit rooming house in 1982 by a former race car driver, Helmuth Marko, the hotel is now one of the most unusual and most charming hostelries in town. It was personally decorated by the owner's wife, with choice 19th-century furniture (she has her own antique business as well as excellent taste). The hotel offers 43 beds in individually designed rooms, each of which combines the thick original walls with dozens of modern comforts. There's an early Biedermeier ceramic stove in the bar area and several pieces of baroque sculpture are set into well-placed niches. There's also a courtyard with a lion's head fountain. Per-person rates range from 560 AS ($29.79) to 680 AS ($36.18) in a single and from 920 AS ($48.94) to 1040 AS ($55.33) in a double.

Parkhotel, 8 Leonhardstrasse (tel. 33511), is a large hotel rambling across a gently angled corner of a street near the Opera, the City Park, and the university. The interior is a pleasing combination of baronial accessories (suits of armor and hanging tapestries in the beamed dining room) and modern comforts. An in-house garage will solve your parking problems. For rooms with bath, radio, and TV, the Florian family charge 750 AS

($39.90) for a single and 1060 AS ($56.39) for a double, with breakfast included.

Hotel Gollner, 14 Schlögelgasse (tel. 72521), the preferred choice of the city's visiting opera stars, is across the street from the Opera House. Its renovated interior has a kind of 1950s simplicity, with a no-nonsense contemporary decor and spacious bedrooms. On the premises is an unpretentious restaurant serving wholesome food. Singles cost between 310 AS ($16.49) and 720 AS ($38.30), while doubles range from 600 AS ($31.92) to 1180 AS ($62.78), with breakfast included.

Hotel Mariahilfe, 9 Mariahilferstrasse (tel. 913163), is a four-story stucco building with a red tile roof, prominent gables, and modified neoclassic detailings around the windows. Centrally located, the hotel has unpretentious public rooms with an elevator, red leather chairs, brass chandeliers, and tiny flags of most of the major countries of Europe clustered on a radiator stand. The cozy weinstube offers Styrian specialties. With breakfast included, rooms with bath cost 660 AS ($35.11) for a single and 900 AS ($47.88) for a double. Bathless rooms go for 325 AS ($17.29) in a single and 600 AS ($31.92) in a double.

Hotel Drei Raben, 43 Annenstrasse (tel. 912686), near the train station, not far from the old city, is a contemporary hotel, offering all the modern comforts. Well-furnished bedrooms rent for 430 AS ($22.88) in a single and from 690 AS ($36.71) in a double, with breakfast included.

Pension Süd, 10 Stemmerweg (tel. 281860). Ten minutes by car from the center of town, heading south, this simple white-walled pension offers a kind of no-frills accommodation with lots of peace and quiet. On the premises are an indoor pool and a sauna. Singles cost between 545 AS ($28.99) and 580 AS ($30.87), while doubles range between 675 AS ($35.91) and 720 AS ($38.30), with breakfast included.

Hotel Grazerhof, 10 Stubenberggasse (tel. 79824), in the center of town, offers simply furnished bedrooms which you'll reach by crossing through the marble-covered ground-floor area. The format is turn of the century, but simple and unpretentious. The 26 rooms rent for 500 AS ($26.60) in a single with bath and 650 AS ($34.58) in a double with bath, including breakfast.

On the Outskirts

Gastehaus/Café Zum Kreuz, 451 Kärntnerstrasse (tel. 29-2436), is an ochre-colored guesthouse which has been run by the same family for more than a century. In a suburb south of Graz, the establishment contains only a dozen rooms, as well as a popular restaurant that's often the destination for people from the city who come here for the Styrian wines and the homemade gutbürgerlich cookery. Homemade sausages are a specialty in September and March. Singles cost 360 AS ($19.15) while doubles go for 515 AS ($27.40), with breakfast included. A four-lane bowling alley is close by.

Hotel/Restaurant Pfeifer Zum Kirchenwirt, Graz-Mariatrost (tel. 391112), in an agricultural suburb seven kilometers from the center of Graz, is an ochre-colored hotel which has comfortable rooms—some of them very modern—and a gutbürgerlich restaurant with lots of wood trim. On the premises are a sauna and lots of thoughtful details. The hotel's exterior is an appealingly old-fashioned combination of country baroque detailing, hipped roofs, and exposed stone. The Pfeifer family charge between 335 AS ($17.82) and 480 AS ($25.54) in a single and between 480 AS ($25.54) and 650 AS ($34.58) in a double, with breakfast included.

WHERE TO DINE: The variety of restaurants is enormous, ranging from first-class establishments to beer halls to student hangouts. Prices in even the top restaurants are moderate, and among the low-cost dining establishments are surprisingly low. You can dine in the hotels (which have some of the best food in town) or in cozy pubs and intimate bistros.

My recommendation, for the most part, is to skip the typical international cuisine when possible and concentrate on genuine Styrian specialties. These include wurzelfleisch, a kind of stew, or the different kinds of sterz, a dish made of buckwheat or corn. The homemade sausages in all their infinite varieties are generally excellent. Vienna is noted for its hendl (chicken) dishes, but Graz chefs also do chicken extremely well.

The art of beer brewing is particularly cultivated in Graz. For the local Puntigam or Reininghaus beers, as well as for the Gösser beer, which is brewed in Upper Styria, the people of Graz have a special predilection.

Or you may want to try Styrian wine which grows on steep slopes exposed to the sun. Important varieties such as Welschriesling, Muskat-Sylvaner, Traminer, but also the Schilcher, which grows only in a limited area in West Styria, have received international recognition.

Many of the wine restaurants of Graz provide background music in the evening.

Hofkeller, 8 Hofgasse (tel. 82439), has a gilt-edged reputation in town as a haven for gourmets who appreciate well-cooked traditional foods. The restaurant, which was formerly a simple wine and beer tavern, has been transformed into an elegant room with refreshing touches of vivid green. The tables are covered with fine napery, good silverware, and beautiful porcelain. The limited menu is augmented by a list of daily specials, whose appearance is heavily dependent on the availability of the ingredients. Your meal might include seafood salad in walnut oil, artichoke hearts stuffed with goose liver and mushrooms, a wide selection of fish, and a savory lamb cut flavored with thyme. Full meals range from 80 AS ($4.26) to 300 AS ($15.96). Reservations are suggested.

Victorian Steakhouse, 15 Burggasse (tel. 79139). Aside from its restaurant, this place also shelters one of the hottest bars in town, frequented by an attractive crowd of well-dressed youth. The bar area is a dimly lit, horseshoe-shaped rendezvous point where you'll be lucky to get a seat. You can eat at the bar if you wish, although the Victorian-style steakhouse might be more appealing.

The decor includes depictions of everybody from voluptuous nudes to the Queen of England, as well as John Bull flanked by two Union Jacks, cut red-velvet wallpaper, impeccably dressed waiters, and a pianist playing classical music or American jazz.

When I was last there they were having a British week, with a special menu featuring steak-and-kidney pie, beef Wellington, and grilled lamb cutlets. However, they always have an array of steaks, chops, and cutlets, along with fish dishes, cooked the way you want them. Mixed drinks are available, and the wine list contains a brief history of the building. Steaks cost from 120 AS ($6.38), and full meals go for around 250 AS ($13.30). There's a popular disco in the basement, called "Downstairs."

Gambrinuskeller, 6-8 Färbergasse (tel. 700243). The decor, like the menu, combines elements from rustically conservative Austria with overtones from the Middle East and the Balkans. In addition to lots of exposed wood, the dining rooms contain Oriental rugs which cushion the unyielding surfaces of the banquettes. A large oil painting of a Balkan peasant girl in native headdress dominates one end of the room, while a stainless-steel deli-style case separates the busy kitchens from the dining areas. The unusual menu offers Brazilian, Persian, and Italian foods as well. You might enjoy cevapcici, churrasco of pork, Iranian-style kebabs, Italian pasta dishes, grilled steaks, and kebabs. Dessert could be anything from baklava to apple strudel. Full meals average around 130 AS ($6.92) with a wide variation of possibilities on either end.

Restaurant Goldene Pastete, 28 Sporgasse (tel. 73416), is housed inside the oldest inn in Graz, constructed in 1571. It's owned by Walther Patterer and his family, who have run it for more than a quarter of a century. The restaurant is housed in a five-story Renaissance inner-city building of pink stucco with green shutters and lots of windowboxes. The waiters, each dressed in regional garb, are kept busy running from the kitchens to the three dining rooms, which are set on three different floors. In addition to 140 places inside, the summer garden holds an additional 60 diners. Open from 10 a.m. to midnight every day but Saturday and Sunday, the restaurant serves gutbürgerlich food to all walks of life. The international menu contains an occasional Yugoslav dish, such as cevapcici, but mainly it offers Austrian specialties, including zander (a fish), several noodle dishes, grilled veal, steaks, pork roast in a pepper cream sauce, and schnitzel Cordon Bleu. Full meals range from 85 AS ($4.52) to 240 AS ($12.77). It's closed for the last two weeks in August.

Landhaus-Keller, 9 Schmiedgasse (tel. 80276). A dimly lit corridor extends past at least three rustic and authentically Teutonic dining areas (there are four if you count the nooks and crannies). It eventually opens onto a series of outdoor tables behind the restaurant. This outdoor area, surprisingly, opens onto a neighboring courtyard with flowers and a view of the arcade of a baroque church. A sign in the window advertizes "delicacies from lakes, rivers, and streams," as well as a wide selection of veal, beef, pork, and both roast and fried chicken dishes.

Specialties are usually from Styria, based on old recipes. You might begin with sour cream soup with burnt polenta, meatballs with sauerkraut, Styrian cheese dumplings in beef broth, and browned omelets with blueberries. It's open from 10 a.m. till 1 a.m. every day but Sunday and holidays. Meals average around 115 AS ($6.12). The original building was constructed in the early 16th century, and hosted such famous guests as Metternich, Franz and Eduard Sacher, Field Marshall Esterhazy, and the Duke of Wellington.

Kepler Keller, 6 Stempfergasse (tel. 72449), is probably the best known evening wine tavern in Graz. Named after the Renaissance mathematician and astrologer Johannes Kepler, who used to live there, the establishment has during its lifetime served a glass of wine or beer to practically everyone in Graz. The interior is cozily welcoming, done up in a pleasingly authentic decor of thick paneling and rustic accessories, but my favorite area is the candlelit courtyard, whose outdoor tables are flanked with a three-story arcade whose repeating arches are supported by chiseled Doric columns accented with cascading flowerboxes.

Live music is usually part of the evening's entertainment. In addition to simple meals, such as schnitzels, pork, steaks, omelets, cheeses, and salads, the establishment serves carafes of the local wine. The specialty of the house is a Styrian rosé called Schilcher, whose grape only grows south of Graz. The restaurant also serves copious quantities of the Styrian beer called Gösser. It's open from 5 p.m. till 2 a.m. every day, with live music after 9 p.m. (the last meal is served at 1 a.m.). The restaurant is closed on Sunday. Full meals average between 100 AS ($5.32) and 210 AS ($11.17), although simple platters can be had for less.

Krebsenkeller, 12 Sachstrasse (tel. 79377), near the Hauptplatz, is about the closest establishment to a total entertainment complex available in Graz. You enter a covered passage which ends in an enclosed courtyard, one side of which has a beflowered loggia. Café tables are usually set up under a grape arbor, although you can choose between an underground "keller," a ground-level stüberl, or a gemütlich restaurant, each of which has different entrances from the courtyard. This labyrinthine arrangement of rooms was built in 1538 by a local official and his wife. Simple fixed-price meals are a real bargain. They cost between 65 AS ($3.46) and 95 AS ($5.05), although the more expensive à la carte items can go much higher. Menu items include grilled specialties of varying degrees of spiciness, a full range of soups, salads, fish, and game dishes.

Restaurant Spinnrad'l, 7 Dietrichplatz. Once you're past the vestibule you'll be in a high-ceilinged square room almost entirely built of exposed brick, which is fairly rare in Graz. There are many nooks and crannies for intimate dining, with a large bar area, a wood-beamed ceiling, modern crystal chandeliers, and a collection of nautical art objects. A marble-top display case contains a selection of wines. The menu offers many Austrian dishes as well as many well-prepared salt- and freshwater fish dishes. You can also try calamari, filet goulash Stroganoff, pepper steak Brazil, onion soup, tafelspitz, Spanish paella, lobster, and salmon steak. Warm meals, beginning at 150 AS ($7.98), are served from 11 a.m. to midnight.

Restaurant Stadtkeller, 3 Andreas Hofer Platz (tel. 73354). Housed in a stucco building with primitive flying buttresses, this gutbürgerlich restaurant can be found on a busy traffic circle near the river. Inside, hanging glass lamps, timbered ceilings, and stenciled wall murals combine with an unpretentious menu to create a typical Styrian ambience. A former Austrian president was born in a building on this site in 1774. Fixed-price meals range from 90 AS ($4.79), although you can eat here at virtually any price level, from economy to upper bracket. Menu items come from both the Austrian and the international kitchen, and include a wide variety of pizzas, the most interesting of which is made from "fruits of the sea." There are also Italian pastas, Hungarian dishes, and typically Styrian platters. The terrace overlooks the river and often accommodates a wide variety of local residents, a good sign.

THE SIGHTS: The **Old Quarter** of Graz is, in great part, preserved in its original state, and a tour through it is a must for visitors (see "Tours," under "Practical Facts," below). Major sights include the **Hauptplatz** (main square) in the heart of the city, surrounded by ancient houses with characteristic brown-tile roofs with narrow gables. The most notable is the House of Luegg at the corner of Sporgasse, known for its arcades and facade dating back to the 17th century.

A few steps down Herrengasse, the wide shopping and business street, is the **Landhaus,** seat of the provincial government, a Renaissance masterpiece completed in 1565 by an Italian architect, Domenico dell'Allio.

Above the main gate a window is especially highlighted, intensifying the effect of the gate. The arcaded courtyard is bounded on the south by an arched arcade transversing the court. The arched Renaissance-style well was poured in bronze near the end of the 16th century.

After that, the next major site is the **Landeszeughaus,** or armory, next to the Landhaus. Being the capital and main city of the province, Graz was militarily important in earlier times, and for more than two centuries it was a bulwark against the ever-invading Turks. The armory, built from 1642 to 1645 by Anton Solar, dates from the time of the Turkish wars. Its early baroque gate is flanked by statues of the war deities, Mars and Bellona, the work of Giovanni Mamolo. The four floors of the building are separated by the original strong wood-beamed ceilings.

Now a museum displaying three centuries of weaponry, the Zeughaus contains some 30,000 harnesses, coats of mail, helmets, swords, pikes, muskets of various kinds, pistols, arquebuses, and other implements of war. In 1749 Empress Maria Theresa, in recognition of Styrian military service and strategic significance, allowed this arsenal to remain when others in her empire were destroyed.

You can visit the armory, April to October, Monday to Friday from 9 a.m. to 4 p.m. It closes at noon on Saturday and Sunday. Admission is 15 AS (80¢).

Paulustor, or Paul's Gate, between the remnants of the former rampart of Graz, dates from the time of the fortification of the city by Italian architects. The side of the gate facing the city is plain, the exterior being decorated with large coats-of-arms of Archduke Ferdinand and his first wife, Anne of Bavaria.

Another major attraction is the **Landesmuseum Joanneum,** which has departments at different locations. The natural history displays are at the old Joanneum building, 10 Raubergasse. The collections of the Old Gallery and of the arts and crafts department are in the new Joanneum building at 45 Neutorgasse. Here you'll see stained glass, altarpieces, and important art from the Middle Ages, some going back to the 12th century.

The New Gallery on the third floor of the former Herberstein town house, 16 Sachstrasse, shows art from the 19th century to the present. The Styrian Museum of Folklore is at 13 Paulustorgasse. At the Eggenberg Palace (see below) you'll find the department of prehistory and early history, including an extensive collection of Roman stones in an open-air pavilion in the park, the Münzenkabinett, a coin collection, and the Styrian Hunting Museum.

Most Joanneum exhibits are open Tuesday to Friday from 9 a.m. to 4 p.m., to noon on Saturday and Sunday. Admission is 15 AS (80¢).

The **Domkirche** (cathedral), between Burgergasse and Burggasse, was originally the Romanesque Church of St. Aegydius, a fortified church outside the town walls, first mentioned in a document in 1174. In the 15th century Frederick III had it converted into a spacious three-bayed city parish church in the late Gothic style, although instead of a Gothic spire the structure later acquired a wooden turret. Archduke Carl of Inner Austria attached the church to his residence, the Burg (castle), and later entrusted it to the Jesuits. After the dissolution of that order it became the cathedral church of the bishops of Seckau. Inside you'll see two shrines, circa 1475, made in Mantua, and a baroque high altar, the 18th-century creation of Father Georg Kraxner.

Next door on Burggasse is the **Mausoleum of Emperor Ferdinand I,** one of the most remarkable buildings of Graz. Started in 1614 and completed in 1638, it was intended as the tomb of the emperor and his first wife. The church, crowned by a crossing cupola with the tomb chapel also cupola vaulted, is regarded as the best example of mannerism in Austria. The high altar is an early work of J. B. Fischer von Erlach, done from 1695 to 1697. The central sarcophagus of the tomb intended for Ferdinand's parents contains only the remains of his mother. His father, Archduke Carl of Inner Austria, was interred elsewhere.

Other than the cathedral, the most important church in Graz is **Mariahilferkirche** (Church of Our Lady of Succor), 3 Mariahilferplatz, built for the Minorite brothers on the right bank of the Mur River. Pietro de Pomis carried out reconstruction of the church in the early 17th century and painted the celebrated altarpiece depicting St. Elizabeth interceding with the Virgin Mary. This painting made the church a place of pilgrimage. Originally the now double-spired church had only one spire.

Overlooking Graz, **Schlossberg,** the formerly fortified hill, rising to a height of 1550 feet above sea level, is an island of quiet. As I mentioned above, the fortifications were leveled in 1809 by terms of a treaty Napoleon dictated to a defeated Austria. You can take a cable railway to the restaurant on top or climb the winding stairs. From the top you'll be able to look down on the city and its environs. Guided tours of the citadel are given daily (except in the winter) on the hour from 8 a.m. to 5 p.m., starting from the bell tower opposite the upper station of the cable railway.

The **Clock Tower** (Uhrturm) on the citadel is a curiosity above the walls of the former Citizens' Bastion. It acquired its present appearance in 1555–1556, when the original Gothic tower was given Renaissance treatment, resulting in a circular wooden gallery with oriels and four huge clock faces.

The **Burg** (castle) northeast of the Hauptplatz in the Old Quarter is distinguished by its unique double-spiral staircase constructed in 1499 for Emperor Maximilian I.

About two miles from the city, you can visit **Schloss Eggenberg** (Eggenberg Palace), a square 17th-century building with towers on its four corners and an accentuated facade over the main gate. The palace sits in a large park now used as a game preserve. The four wings of the baroque-style structure surround a large court with arched arcades and two smaller courts separated by the palace church. You can take guided tours of the baroque state apartments on the second floor from the first of April until the end of October from 9 a.m. to 1 p.m. and 2 to 4 p.m. (time of last tour departure). Admission is 15 AS (80¢).

The ground floor of the south wing houses the Landesmuseum Joanneum's department of prehistory and early history mentioned above, with a good collection of Styrian antiquities. Visits are possible from the first of February until the end of November from 9 a.m. to 5 p.m. for 15 AS (80¢) admission.

The Styrian Hunting Museum, another part of the Landesmuseum Joanneum collections, is on the first floor of the palace, with the same visiting hours and admission charge.

A major attraction in the environs is about ten miles north of Graz, at Stübing, the **Austrian Open-Air Museum** (Osterreichisches Freilicht-museum), set in a wooded valley branching off from the Valley of the Mur. Here you'll see rustic buildings from all the Austrian provinces, some as much as 300 years old. The 60 authentic structures include a smokeroom house (Rauchstubenhaus) from East Styria of a type also seen in Land

Salzburg, and circular, triangular, and rectangular houses. The museum is open from the first of April to the end of October daily except Monday from 9 a.m. to 4 p.m. Admission is 35 AS ($1.86).

SHOPPING: You might begin your shopping expedition at the Hauptplatz, which is the main square in the center of town. The major shopping streets, including Herrengasse, branch off from here. Of course the major item to buy, if the dress should appeal to you, is Styrian clothing in the famous Styrian grays and greens, a style of dress that has spread all over Austria. You'll find a good selection of dirndls and hats in particular, as well as local handicrafts and leather clothing.

Steirisches Heimatwerk, 4 Paulustorgasse (tel. 77106), is a large, many-roomed store selling cookbooks, shoes, dirndls, a big selection of regional blouses, dresses, coats, silk, wool, and cotton fabrics, as well as objects made from glass, ceramics, and wood. Every item is made in Austria. Some of the more unusual items include hand-painted depictions of the local saints in small wooden frames. The sales personnel are helpful. The store is part of the local folklore museum.

Brühl and Söhne, 8 Stubenberggasse (tel. 71048), sells Styrian-style clothing for men, women, and children. The antique cash register here is a minor work of art, and the personnel are helpful and friendly. Their inventory includes dirndls, coats, skirts, hats, vests, suits, and accessories.

Anton Pichler, 28 Herrengasse (tel. 79562), sells hats of all kinds in a simple store lined with glass cases. The varieties range from Tyrolean and Styrian traditional designs to more updated versions, including golfing and hunting hats. The elegant chrome and marble-trimmed exterior opens to reveal a wood-paneled rectangle with hundreds of hats covering the paneled walls.

THE CAFÉS OF GRAZ: **Café Glockenspiel,** 4 Glockenspielplatz (tel. 80291). On a quiet baroque square, this ground-floor café is housed in a lime-colored, ornately embellished building with blue and white café tables set up in front. A formally attired waiter will take your order for coffee, light snacks, and sandwiches. The interior is comfortably upholstered with serpentine banquettes, blue-flecked upholstery, and mahogany paneling and tables. Original paintings and lithographs are displayed amid a crowd of people who can be either jet set or vintage dowager, depending on the time of day. Coffee and pastries cost from 20 AS ($1.06) to 30 AS ($1.60) each. It's closed on Sunday.

Café am Tummelplatz, 8 Hans-Sachs-Gasse (tel. 71588), is an elegant, recently built coffeehouse attracting an upbeat clientele, many of them fairly young. Coffee and tea are served in fragile porcelain, with polite service. Coffee averages 21 AS ($1.11), with pastries costing from 16 AS (85¢). It's closed on Sunday.

Café Leinich, 4 Kaiser-Josef-Platz (tel. 80586). Perfect on a summer day, with a view looking over the activity in the open-air market, this popular institution serves good coffee and homemade pastries. Devotees of the rich concoctions, where fresh fruit and berries are used in abundance, include students, workers, and a handful of retired people (some of whom plan their afternoon around the time spent here). Coffee and pastries each range from around 15 AS (80¢) to 25 AS ($1.33). It's closed in August.

Katharine, 32 Sporgasse (tel. 77263), is the kind of catch-all rendezvous point that includes students doing their homework, advocates of low-budget radical chic, and an occasional tourist who wanders in for a cup of coffee. The long narrow rooms are outfitted with a tongue-in-cheek format of American football posters, sheet music from *Carmen,* a violin in a display case facing the street, and pinball machines. There's also an Italian ice cream stand and a pizza oven. Pasta and pizzas range upward from 45 AS ($2.39). It's open from 8 a.m. to 10 p.m.

GRAZ AFTER DARK: Sometimes restaurants combine dancing with disco action and nightclub shows, so at one address you might make an evening of it. The cafés often have music as well. Because of the university in Graz, many of the after-dark haunts are heavily frequented by young people.

The **Opernhaus** (opera house) at the Opernring presents both opera and ballet (phone 76451 for information about programs and tickets). The building was built "in the style of Fischer von Erlach" at the end of the 19th century.

In summer you can often hear concerts in the **Stadtpark,** or city park, which adjoins the northeast side of the citadel.

The **Styrian Autumn,** an arts festival, takes place during parts of September and October. It has a reputation for being avant-garde, presenting everything from jazz to mime.

Haus Gottinger, Strassgang (tel. 281850), is a formal disco for the over-30 crowd. You'll need a car to get here because it's about a 20-minute ride from the center of Graz. When rock groups come for special appearances the cover charge is slightly more than the regular entrance fee of 35 AS ($1.86). There's a restaurant as well. It gets popular on weekends, and is open from 7 p.m. to 4 a.m.

"Downstairs," Victorian Steakhouse, 15 Burggasse (tel. 79139), is the basement addition to one of the most popular bars and restaurants in town (see my dining recommendations). You reach it by descending a worn flight of stone steps from the bar area upstairs, where you might want to stop first for a drink. Covered with brick vaulting, the disco contains slot machines, a small dance floor, a long rectangular bar area, and a vaguely Dickensian decor of dark banquettes and old English beer ads. There's no cover charge, and drinks cost from 50 AS ($2.66) to 60 AS ($3.19). The disco is open from 8 p.m. to 2 a.m. However, it's closed on Sunday and holidays.

PRACTICAL FACTS: For information, check with the **Graz Tourist Office** (Fremdenverkehrsbüro der Stadt Graz), 25 Kaiserfeldgasse (tel. 76591).

Emergency services are available by telephoning as follows: **police**—133; **fire**—122; **ambulance**—144; **medical**—190; **drugstore**—18.

To find out about the **weather,** phone 16.

A **Lost and Found Office** is at police headquarters, 8 Paulustorgasse (tel. 76531).

The main **post and telegraph office** is at 46 Neutorgasse (tel. 9800). There's also a post office next to the main railroad station (Bahnhof).

For information on **air travel,** call Thalerhof Airport, south of the city (tel. 291541), or the AUA (Austrian Airlines) city office, 16 Herrengasse, Landhaus (tel. 79641). Lufthansa also has a city office, at 6 Herrengasse (tel. 72583).

If you're traveling by **car,** Graz is connected to the European superhighway system, via roads to the southbound and the Pyhrn autobahns as well as to the main road through the Mur and Mürz Valleys. The city offers all necessary services to motorists. Ask about this courtesy at the Tourist Office (see above).

Postal Bus information is available at Postverkehrsbüro Graz, 19 Andreas-Hofer-Platz (tel. 71525), if you want to travel to outlying areas by this means.

TRANSPORTATION IN GRAZ: **Graz City Transport** operates streetcar and bus service throughout the city. Jakomini Square in the city center is the point of intersection of all streetcar lines. To use the network of bus lines, starting points are at Jakomini Square or from terminals of the streetcar lines. For information on any phase of the transport system, telephone 78931.

Radio **taxi** service is available by phoning 983 or 2801.

TOURS: **Guided tours** are offered daily June 1 to September 9, except Saturday, Sunday, and holidays. You'll be taken past the Schlossberg (Citadel), the city park, the Hilmteich, and the university, through Paul's Gate to the cathedral, the Burg (castle), the mausoleum of Emperor Ferdinand II, and the opera house. The tour ends at Eggenburg Palace, where you can visit the state rooms and the park. Tours leave at 3 p.m. from the Grazer Congress (Graz Convention Center), Landhausgasse at Raubergasse, and end about 5:15 p.m. in the Renaissance courtyard of the Landhaus.

An electric cable railway will take you in three minutes some 1550 feet up from the lower station at 38 Kaiser-Franz-Josef-Kai to the upper station at the Schlossberg Restaurant. This run is made about every 15 minutes.

A free **walking tour** will take you through the Old Quarter in about two hours. You meet in front of the main entrance of the city hall (Rathaus) on the main square at 3 p.m. Your guide will show you the Landhaus, the Burg, the cathedral, and other points of interest.

Many other tours are offered, by foot, bus, streetcar, car, cable, and even swimming in Graz and its environs. Ask at the Tourist Office (see above).

2. Bad Gleichenberg

The most important summer spa in South Styria, Bad Gleichenberg, lies southeast of Graz near the border of Yugoslavia, in a setting of rolling hills and vineyards. This is one of the most interesting—but little known—parts of Austria to explore. Untersteiermark, or Lower Styria, where this spa is located was a lot larger in the days of the Habsburgs. Much of its territory was lost to Yugoslavia following the breakup of the empire after World War I.

Bad Gleichenberg's setting is a lovely valley opening to the south. In the area's magnificent parks, you'll see exotic plants, including the giant sequoia. You can partake of the mineral waters of the Emma, Konstantin, and Johannisbrunnen springs and even take a bottle home with you. The spa has an interesting entertainment program, plus special tours in the environs.

You can drive to Bad Gleichenberg, take an express train from Vienna, or a bus from Graz or Vienna.

FOOD AND LODGING: **Hotel Austria** (tel. 2205) is a prosperous-looking white-walled villa with gray shutters and a raised sun terrace. The light coming in from the big old-fashioned windows floods the interior. On the premises is an informal bar area covered with a brick vaulted ceiling, and a collection of public rooms is filled with comfortable furniture in distinguished combinations of white and dark colors. Rates range from 400 AS ($21.28) to 600 AS ($31.92) per person in a double and from 370 AS ($19.68) to 600 AS ($31.92) in a single. These prices vary with the season and include full board.

Hotel Gleichenbergerhof (tel. 424) is a pleasant contemporary chalet set in a forested area with a masonry sun terrace stretching below the white and dark-colored facade. The simple interior has lots of rustically modern accessories, including a piano bar and an open fireplace. The Kaulfersch family charge 460 AS ($24.47) per person, based on double occupancy, with half board included. Singles pay a daily surcharge of 35 AS ($1.86), and all units contain private bath, balcony, and phone.

KAPENSTEIN: As an alternative to staying in Bad Gleichenberg, you can drive east to this little hamlet and its schloss hotel near the Yugoslav border.

Schloss Kapfenstein (tel. 202) is a solidly built castle with a hipped roof and a curving extension that's almost as old as the main building itself. Set in the middle of verdant forests and rich fields, the castle accepts paying guests in rooms filled with antique furniture and all the modern comforts. Singles cost 385 AS ($20.48), while doubles rent for 600 AS ($31.92), with breakfast included. Half board is available for another 85 AS ($4.52) per person daily.

The hotel is closed between mid-December and early March. You can eat on the castle's terrace if you wish, as it offers a view of the village below. Every Thursday the Winkler-Hermaden family presents a Styrian buffet; otherwise specialties are based on regional recipes such as roast hen, homemade blutwurst and sausages, and apple strudel. À la carte meals cost between 80 AS ($4.26) and 200 AS ($10.64), while fixed-price meals run between 75 AS ($3.99) and 120 AS ($6.38).

3. Leoben

In 1797 Napoleon signed a peace treaty in Leoben in Upper Styria, a town built on a loop of the Mur River northwest of Graz and known for its ironworking industries and lignite mining. In fact it's the seat of a mining college. But because it's industrial, don't assume that the town is without attractions.

The **Altes Rathaus** (old city hall) stands on the Hauptplatz (main square) of Leoben. The **pfarrkirche** (parish church) of the town has two towers dating from the latter 17th century. The **Mautturm,** or toll tower, called the "mushroom tower," is Leoben's most distinguishing landmark, dating from 1615.

If possible, visit the 14th-century **Church of Maria Waasen,** which has some excellent stained glass in the choir. One of its windows depicts the

Passion of Christ. This church is west of the town, near the bridge spanning the Mur.

A popular excursion is to **Göss,** 1¼ miles south of Leoben, where the celebrated Göss beer is produced. The brewery took over what had once been a nunnery, dating from the 11th century. It's considered the oldest nunnery in Styria and still has a Gothic church and a Romanesque crypt.

FOOD AND LODGING: Hotel Baumann (tel. 42564). In the center of town, this French-style mansion rises five ornate floors across the street from a small park. The interior has been drastically remodeled into a comfortably modern format of exposed wood and simple furniture. The comfortable bedrooms have big windows and attractively muted color schemes. On the premises are a dancing bar, a restaurant, and a formal sitting room. Doubles range from 575 AS ($30.59) to 925 AS ($49.21), while singles cost between 460 AS ($24.47) and 535 AS ($28.46), with breakfast and free use of the sauna and gym room included. The hotel is open from the first of May until the end of October.

The hotel's restaurant, S'Reindl, offers Styrian specialties as well as international food served in a rustically decorated restaurant. Lines of copper pots as well as a series of spoked wheels decorate the plaster walls of this wood-trimmed restaurant. Specialties ordered from the handwritten menu on any given day will cost between 75 AS ($3.99) and 275 AS ($14.63).

Hotel Kindler, 7-11 Straussgasse (tel. 43202), incorporates a richly decorated older building with a strikingly contemporary big-windowed building just next to it. A few doors away from the antique civic buildings in the center of town, the hotel is comfortably decorated with simple modern furniture and tasteful colors. Singles range from 130 AS ($6.92) to 290 AS ($15.34), while doubles cost between 110 AS ($5.85) and 230 AS ($12.24) per person, depending on the season and the plumbing.

The Iron Road, no. 115, northwest from Leoben leads to the old market town and ski area of—

VORDERNBERG/PRÄBICHL: The market town of Vordernberg lies at the foot of the Präbichl Pass in the heart of Upper Styria. On its east is the Hochschwab mountain range and on the west the Eisenerz (iron ore) Alps with the romantic Gesäuse canyon. Its alpine location makes this area attractive either as a summer resort or a winter holiday center. Vordernberg is the oldest center of the Styrian iron industry. Iron mining here is ancient, having been a pursuit of the Celts and the Romans.

On the town's Hauptplatz (main square), you can visit the **Iron Works Museum** (wheel works no. 4). The 17th-century **Pfarrkirche** (parish church) has in its graveyard tombs of former hammermill and wheel works owners. The town's **Laurentius Church** is from the 15th century. The **Rathaus** (town hall) still has its original tower and stucco ceiling. A richly decorated wrought-iron fountain dates from 1668. There are many splendid burghers' houses in Vordernberg.

The Präbichl, with its Polster and Grubl skiing areas, is well known as an important ski center in Styria. A number of ski lifts lead up to the skiing grounds, with their well-prepared, avalanche-free slopes which allow skiing until April. A ski school, cross-country tracks, toboggan runs, curling and ice-skating rinks, and cleared footpaths are all part of the winter holiday scene.

Summer visitors can take mountain walks and climbs in the Hochschwab area and the Alps, to see the rich alpine flora. From May to October, guests can visit the Styrian Erzberg (ore mountain) on guided inspection tours.

Hotel Hubertushof, 36 Hauptstrasse (tel. 214), is a contemporary chalet built into a gently sloping meadow. The cozy interior is comfortably filled with conservative modern furniture, lots of paneling, and rustic accessories. Per-person rates, with breakfast included, range from 230 AS ($12.24) to 265 AS ($14.10), depending on the season. All accommodations have private baths. Every Saturday and Sunday the management provides live music at a late afternoon "tea dance."

4. Murau

Lying on both sides of the Mur River at the foot of the Stolzalpe, which rises to nearly 6000 feet, the old town of Murau is a winter ski region and also the center of many a summer excursion. It's easily reached from Salzburg via the Tauern motorway, as well as from Carinthia, Vienna, and the rest of Styria.

Murau's **pfarrkirche** (parish church) of St. Matthew dates from the 13th century. Note the "lantern of the dead," a late Gothic sculpture in front of the church. Remnants of the medieval walls of the town can be seen.

Summer visitors enjoy high alpine tours. Two chair lifts will take you through the Murau recreation area. Skiers come here in winter, especially for the fine cross-country tracks. The Murau center is a good place for rest and relaxation at any time of the year. It advertises itself as "not intended for the masses." It's a good family vacation spot.

In summer you can take a ride on an old steam-engine train on the narrow-gauge Murtal railway which goes through the Mur Valley on its run to Tamsweg in the neighboring province of Land Salzburg.

The 900-year-old **Stift St. Lambrecht** (convent of St. Lambrecht) with fine collections of ecclesiastical art and artifacts is nearby, as is the little romantic village of **Oberwölz.** Both are worth a visit. You can go also a short distance to **Wildbad Einöd** for thermal baths.

FOOD AND LODGING: **Hotel Brauhaus** (tel. 2437) is a solid-looking building set in front of a reflecting pool surrounded by seasonal flowers. Comfortable and unpretentious bedrooms rent for 220 AS ($11.70) in a single and for around 275 AS ($14.63) per person in a double. These prices include a breakfast buffet; otherwise, half board is another 75 AS ($3.99) per person daily. The establishment is better known for its restaurant, serving well-prepared meals on a flagstone-covered terrace or inside in a vaulted dining room. Directed by the Lercher family, the hotel includes a sauna. The location is within an easy walk of the village's sporting facilities.

Gasthof Lercher (tel. 2431) is a pleasantly designed, sunflower-colored building with white trim and a generously rambling design that includes several different sections. In the center of town, the hotel is directed by the Lercher family, who carefully maintain the flagstone-covered entrance hall and the rustically accommodating bar area. Singles cost 350 AS ($18.62) per day, while doubles rent for 310 AS ($16.49) per person, with breakfast included.

5. Turracher Höhe

A section of Turracher Höhe was previewed above in the chapter on Carinthia (Chapter XII), but part of it is also in Styria, at the western end of the province on the pass over the Gurktal alpine range that leads into Carinthia. This is both a summer tourist center and a winter ski area.

The mountains surrounding the plateau (5785 feet) on which Turracher Höhe is situated are excellent for hiking. The Turrachersee (Lake Turrach) is ideal for fishing, windsurfing, sailing, and rowing.

The Nock mountain range (7875 feet) has wide, carefully prepared ski slopes, cross-country tracks, and marked winter hiking trails. T-bars and chair lifts are available, as is a ski school.

Seehotel Jägerwirt (tel. 8257) looks like a collection of lakeside chalets carefully joined together with low-lying reception areas and public rooms. The interior is filled with recreational facilities such as a sauna, a children's play area, tennis courts, bars, and restaurants, all of them mixed with a scattering of open fireplaces and rustic furniture. A lakeside terrace covered with flagstones provides a place for pleasant outdoor dinners in summer. The Brandstätter family are the accommodating hosts, charging from 535 AS ($28.46) to 825 AS ($43.89) per person in a double, with singles paying daily surcharges ranging from 35 AS ($1.86) to 50 AS ($2.66). These prices include full board and use of the sauna and indoor swimming pool. The hotel is open from June 10 until October 15 and from December 20 until April 25.

6. Dachstein-Tauern

In northwest Styria you'll find the major ski area in the province. The Dachstein, in the Salzkammergut, is a gigantic alpine mountain range cutting across Land Salzburg, Upper Austria, and Styria, with mammoth glaciers lying between its peaks. The Enns River separates the Dachstein and the Tauern massifs. This is the site of championship ski races and also the place for powder skiing.

The principal Styrian ski resorts, Schladming and Ramsau, are previewed below.

RAMSAU: At the foot of the mighty Dachstein massif, which reaches a height of nearly 10,000 feet, Ramsau is an emerging ski resort, rivaling but not yet surpassing Schladming (see below). The prices here are, in general, lower than those at Schladming.

Ramsau lies on a high plateau to the north of Schladming.

Food and Lodging

Sporthotel Matschner (tel. 81721) is a double chalet whose identical wings are separated by a collection of flowered balconies. On the premises are an indoor swimming pool and supervised tennis courts with a resident coach. The hotel provides easy access to the many nearby sporting facilities. The Knaus family does what it can to make your stay comfortable. Rates range from 500 AS ($26.60) to 840 AS ($44.69) per person, with half board included, depending on the season and the accommodation. All rooms have private bath, radio, and balcony, and rates include participation in the organized sporting activities.

Alpengasthof Peter Rosegger (tel. 81223) is a pleasant chalet surrounded by larches and a grassy field, with a cozy interior of rustic furniture, country-style chintz, and exposed paneling. Fritz and Barbara Walcher are the young and attractive owners of this place, charging between 530 AS ($28.20) to 550 AS ($29.26) per person in high season, with a Styrian-style half board included. On the premises are a sauna, a fitness room, table tennis, and a paneled gaststube with a ceramic stove dating from 1667. There's also a summertime terrace.

Almfrieden Hotel (tel. 81753) is a contemporary chalet with two symmetrical wings joined by an interconnecting section. Set at the base of a rock-strewn mountain, the hotel looks out over a grassy meadow and a nearby sun terrace covered with parasols. The interior is rustically paneled with pine boards and dotted with open fireplaces and mountain-style chairs. With full board included, per-person rates range from 350 AS ($18.62) to 385 AS ($20.48) in bathless rooms and from 455 AS ($24.21) to 660 AS ($35.11) for units with private bath. Prices depend on the season and the accommodation.

Hotel Post (tel. 2708) is an attractively detailed chalet with summertime flowerboxes, heavy overhanging eaves, and an oversize format that contains an interior decor of rustic accessories and lots of paneling. On the premises are an indoor pool, a sauna, an elevator, a nearby cinema, and a restaurant and bar with an open fireplace. The Lackner family are your hosts, charging from 305 AS ($16.23) to 455 AS ($24.21) per person in a double and from 385 AS ($20.48) to 490 AS ($26.07) for a single, with half board included. Prices vary according to the season and the plumbing.

Pension Ennstalerhof (tel. 81080) is a simple and attractive chalet with flowered balconies, a pleasant garden, and a warmly rustic interior with autumnal colors, Oriental rugs, big windows, and open fireplaces. In high season the simple and practical rooms rent for 455 AS ($24.21) per person, with half board included.

Hotel Restaurant Pehab Kirchenwirt (tel. 81732) is a rambling balconied building in the shadow of the village church in the center of the village. The pleasantly furnished interior is filled with warm colors, lots of paneling, open fireplaces, and wrought-iron accents. On the premises are a bar, two restaurants, and a sauna. There is easy access to the nearby public indoor swimming pool and the ski facilities. The comfortable well-furnished rooms rent for 420 AS ($22.34) to 505 AS ($26.87) per person, based on double occupancy, with half board included. Singles pay an additional 75 AS ($3.99) per day.

Hotel Alpenrose (tel. 81414) is a pleasantly balconied chalet with an isolated position in a sunny meadow and a comfortably rustic interior filled with wood paneling and regional flowered fabrics. Alfred Pilz and his family arc your congenial hosts, charging from 420 AS ($22.34) to 480 AS ($25.54) per person, with half board included. Prices depend on the season.

SCHLADMING/ROHRMOOS: This skiing center is in the Dachstein-Tauern recreation and winter sports area on highway no. 308 and the Vienna-Bruck/Mur-Graz rail line, making it easy to reach. The Planai (6235 feet) and the Hochwurzen (6070 feet) have fast downhill runs and ski slopes, equipped with a cableway, five double-chair lifts, a connectable three-seat chair lift, ski buses, and 15 ski hoists, at all altitudes. Some 22,000 persons per hour can be transported.

The Dachstein-Südward cableway makes skiing at 8865 feet possible in summer. There are ski schools, and you can leave small children at the kindergarten, which has a children's ski hoist.

Miles of winter footpaths make for good, invigorating walking. You can also enjoy horse sleighing, tobogganing, ski-bobbing, curling, game feeding trips, and many other winter activities. Cafés and bars offer lively après-ski, as do the hotels.

In summer you'll enjoy mountaineering, swimming, tennis, bowling, and a lot of top-quality entertainment, along with warm Styrian hospitality.

Schladming is an ancient town lying in the upper valley of the Enns River between Dachstein to the north and Schladminger Tauern to the south. It was a silver- and copper-mining town in medieval times. Old miners' houses can still be seen in the town. The pfarrkirche (parish church) is late Gothic. An 1862 church in town is the largest Protestant church in Styria.

Food and Lodging at Schladming

Sporthotel Royer (tel. 23240), opened in 1975, offers a gracious and contemporary place to stay, with a large collection of sporting facilities. Conceived in a daringly modern design of recessed balconies and dramatically angled rooflines, the hotel has a big indoor as well as a heated outdoor swimming pool, tennis courts, and children's play facilities. There's easy access to the many outdoor ski and hiking trails in the vicinity. On the premises are a comfortably appointed bar area and a rustic restaurant, as well as a more formal dining room. The warmly furnished bedrooms rent for 740 AS ($39.37) to 985 AS ($52.40) per person, based on double occupancy, with half board included. Singles pay a daily surcharge of 140 AS ($7.45).

Romantik Hotel Alte Post, 10 Hauptplatz (tel. 22571). The first records of this historic restaurant in the center of town date from 1618. The facade is the kind of symmetrical chalet you'd expect in the hills nearby, with a round arched door and dark shutters. The renovated interior, in addition to being a popular restaurant, offers rooms priced from 465 AS ($24.74) to 660 AS ($35.11) per person, based on double occupancy, with half board included. Singles pay a daily surcharge of 100 AS ($5.32) per night. The restaurant includes a high-ceilinged formal dining room and a rustically outfitted salon—which might be considered older and more regional—called the Knappenstube. Specialties include a well-prepared collection of wienerschnitzels, salads, and fish dishes. Meals range from 75 AS ($3.99) to 305 AS ($16.23), depending on what you order.

Haus Barbara, 553 Coburgstrasse (tel. 22077), is an attractively decorated three-story chalet with a picture of a female saint wielding a sword and carrying a chalice painted onto the facade. A short walk from the village, just opposite the Planai cable car, the hotel includes a bar with an open fireplace and a collection of pleasant rooms, each of which has a private bath, phone, and radio. Many of them also contain balconies. No meals are served other than breakfast, which is included in the price of 215 AS ($11.44) to 335 AS ($17.82) per person in a double and between 250 AS ($13.30) and 370 AS ($19.68) for a single. Prices depend on the season.

Steirische Rauchkuchl (tel. 2529) is a pleasantly rustic restaurant contained within the paneled walls of a stone and stucco house whose exterior is festooned with flags from a dozen or so different countries. The multilevel interior contains a contemporary fireplace whose smoke is funneled up through a metal chimney, and an amusingly comfortable bar area where clients sip their drinks from swings hanging from a beamed ceiling. In winter, daily dance bands provide evening entertainment from 8:30 until 2 a.m. Food items include regional and Austrian specialties, such as grilled meats, fish, and game (in season). Dinners are priced between 140 AS ($7.45) and 250 AS ($13.30). Closed for part of October, the restaurant is open daily between 11 a.m. and 1:30 a.m.

Food and Lodging at Rohrmoos

Gasthof Waldfrieden (tel. 61487). Built by the Stocker family in 1964 and renovated in 1976, this hotel is a pleasantly sprawling chalet with festoons of summertime flowers hanging from its wooden balconies and gracefully painted decorations around many of its windows. Each of the 40 rooms has its own private bath, balcony, and phone. The in-house restaurant is pleasantly beamed, with pink napery and lots of wooden accents. A flagstone-covered terrace provides a mountain vista in summer, while sports lovers will appreciate the many skiing and hiking facilities in the vicinity. High-season rates, with half board included, range from 370 AS ($19.68) to 470 AS ($25) per person, double occupancy. Rooms in a nearby annex (none of which has private bath) are less expensive, renting for 290 AS ($15.34) to 360 AS ($19.15) per person, double occupancy, with half board included. Singles pay a daily surcharge of 50 AS ($2.66).

Gasthof Sonneck (tel. 61232) is a simple balconied chalet with white walls, big windows, and wooden balconies. A flagstone-covered terrace provides a relaxing place for a midafternoon cup of coffee. The interior is pleasantly paneled and rustically outfitted with glowing pine and tasteful furniture. The simple rooms look out over the mountains, and cost between 335 AS ($17.82) and 385 AS ($20.48) per person, double occupancy, in high season, with half board included.

Hotel Rohrmooserhof (tel. 61455) is an attractively proportioned chalet with long rows of wrap-around balconies and big windows to let sunlight stream into the simply furnished bedrooms. Set into the slope of an alpine hillside, the hotel has an outdoor pool, a pastry and confectionary shop, and a collection of public rooms accented with lots of wood paneling. Tennis courts and a wide range of sporting activities are close at hand. Depending on the season, per-person rates range from 360 AS ($19.15) to 500 AS ($26.60), with half board included, in a double room. Singles pay a daily surcharge of 85 AS ($4.52).

Schwaigerhof (tel. 61422) is an attractively embellished five-story chalet with a prominent aerie for a stork's nest jutting above the gently sloping roof and a hillside location with a view of the mountains. The interior contains an indoor swimming pool, lots of pine paneling, a bar, and two restaurants. Each of the simple bedrooms has its own bath, and a host of sporting facilities are available nearby. The Stocker family charge between 320 AS ($17.02) and 480 AS ($25.54) per person, based on double occupancy, with half board included, depending on the season. Singles pay a daily surcharge of 40 AS ($2.13).

PICHL-MANDLING: Another well-known winter sports center is comprised of Pichl and its neighboring villages of Mandling, Gleiming,

Preunegg, and Vorberg. In the Enns Valley, the center has the same accessibility by car, bus, or train as does Schladming/Rohrmoos (see above).

Pichl has avalanche-proof, prepared skiing grounds for users from beginners to experts, a cabin cableway, two double-chair lifts, and nine ski hoists. You'll find natural toboggan runs, curling rinks, a ski school, and a ski kindergarten. Nonskiers will enjoy walks along the cleared footpaths, folkloric events, and sleigh rides. The area is also a lure for summer visitors, who can explore the mountains on foot, swim, and make trips to surrounding attractions.

Alpengasthof-Hotel Pichlmayrgut (tel. 305) is one of the most distinctively styled hotels in the region. It stretches over a sprawling expanse of alpine hillside in various wings, one of which looks like a medieval castle with chevron shutters. A more recent addition is built in roughly the same style, with big windows, a rounded watchtower, and lots of stone masonry. On the premises are an indoor pool, 130 beds, a sauna, a bar, a café, two restaurants, and a host of additional facilities. Doubles range from 480 AS ($25.54) to 515 AS ($27.40), while singles cost 550 AS ($29.26), with half board included.

7. From Tauplitz to Altaussee

The Styrian Salzkammergut, a section the province shares with both Upper Austria and Land Salzburg, is one of the most beautiful regions of Styria. In the northwest part of the province and long a summer holiday center, this is rapidly developing as a winter ski resort area as well. Prices here are much lower than you'll find at the more chic resorts of Land Salzburg.

This area is just to the southwest of the celebrated Land Salzburg lake district.

TAUPLITZ/TAUPLITZALM: Ranking among the most popular winter sports centers and recreation areas in Austria, Tauplitz and its pasture and lake district, Tauplitzalm, are also good for summer holidays.

The Tauplitzalm can be approached from Tauplitz by chair lift, and the scenic mountain area is a fine country for hiking. You can enjoy swimming, tennis, mini-golf, folkloric entertainment, and dancing, plus 5 p.m. tea. The Tauplitzalm can also be reached from Bad Mitterndorf (see below) on the Tauplitzalm alpine road.

In winter the flying ski jump on the Kulm near Tauplitz is a constant attraction. The two places account for more than a dozen ski lifts, ski schools with special children's courses, and long-distance running schools for walking on skis. This is a training center for domestic and foreign national ski teams.

Food and Lodging at Tauplitz

Berghotel Tauplitzalm (tel. 325) is a four-story, symmetrically designed mountain hotel with a sun terrace in front and long rows of horizontal balconies and big sliding windows facing the valley. Most guests arrive by cable car from Tauplitz, the better to be close to the ski slopes on the following day. The interior is rustically cozy and attractively unpretentious. A collection of ski trophies adorns a wall in the dining room, and the simple bedrooms are tastefully decorated. Doubles cost between 505 AS ($26.87) and 720 AS ($38.30), while singles range between 565 AS ($30.06) and

720 AS ($38.30), depending on the season. These tariffs include full board.

Gasthof/Pension Horst Hechl (tel. 268) is an imposingly Teutonic-looking building set in front of an outdoor tennis court, with an outdoor swimming pool in back. The gabled and hipped roof contains a series of attractively decorated bedrooms, which rent for 260 AS ($13.83) to 450 AS ($23.94) per person, with half board included. On the premises are a sauna, a bar, and salons with wintertime fireplaces and lots of paneling.

Pension/Café Sonnenuhr (tel. 256) is a generously proportioned alpine-style house with a gabled roof, four stories of wood-framed windows, and lots of encircling balconies. A low-lying extension off to one side has a big terrace on top. The interior is filled with contrasting patterns and colors and big-windowed views of the surrounding mountains. Rates range from 315 AS ($16.75) to 380 AS ($20.28) per person daily, double occupancy, with half board included. Singles pay a daily surcharge of 25 AS ($1.33).

Food and Lodging at Tauplitzalm

Sporthotel Kirchenwirt (tel. 306) is a sprawling balconied chalet built into the side of a mountain. Many of the walls are covered with cedar shingles, while the interior is a cozy combination of knotty-pine paneling, freshly imaginative colors, and rustic accents. On the premises are a covered swimming pool, a sauna, a day bar, a sun terrace, and tastefully simple rooms costing between 455 AS ($24.21) and 625 AS ($33.25) per person daily in high season, with half board included. Prices vary with the plumbing and the season.

BAD MITTERNDORF: Long renowned as a health spa in the Salzkammergut, Bad Mitterndorf's proximity to Tauplitz has made it a major ski center as well. Lying in the southern foothills of the Totes Gebirge, Bad Heilbrunn, 1¼ miles to the south, is a satellite of Bad Mitterndorf. Salza-Stausee, a lake, is south of the village.

Food and Lodging

Kur und Sporthotel Bad Heilbrunn (tel. 2486) is a striking modern hotel complex that rises abruptly from the forested hillside into which it was built. On the premises are both an indoor and an outdoor swimming pool, plus a wide range of physical therapy and spa facilities. Many of the contemporary bedrooms have private balconies and baths, along with all the modern conveniences. Singles range from 620 AS ($32.98) to 1100 AS ($58.52), while doubles run from 705 AS ($37.51) to 1100 AS ($58.52) per person, depending on the exposure, the accommodation, and the season. These prices include full board.

Hubertushof (tel. 2595) is a well-designed chalet with four floors of balconies, big windows, and wood trim. The tasteful interior is outfitted with gracefully rustic furniture, wood ceilings, and earth colors. Per-person rates with half board included range from 310 AS ($16.49) to 385 AS ($20.48), double occupancy. Singles pay a daily surcharge of 25 AS ($1.33).

Hotel-Pension Schmidt (tel. 453) is a balconied chalet with a tastefully rustic interior which includes a gently sloping stairwell accented with curves of wrought iron. The furnishings are tastefully rustic, including splashes of vivid colors. Per-person rates range from 420 AS ($22.34) to 455 AS ($24.21), with half board included.

Hotel Kogler (tel. 2325) has a chalet-style facade and a T-shaped floor plan. Its balconies are usually draped with summertime flowers, while a verdant garden stretches away from the big windows of the ground-floor reception area. Per-person rates, based on double occupancy, range from 385 AS ($20.48) to 430 AS ($22.88), depending on the season. Prices include half board, and singles pay a daily surcharge of 50 AS ($2.66).

Pension Lord (tel. 2553) is an attractively simple chalet whose uncomplicated design includes wooden balconies stretching across part of the facade and a big picture window piercing through a section of the ground floor. Five minutes on foot from the center of the village, the hotel offers an indoor pool, lots of mountain views, and a rustically modern interior filled with comfortable furniture. The Lord family are your accommodating hosts, charging from 360 AS ($19.15) per person in a single or double, with half board included. The hotel is closed during October, November, and parts of April.

Grimmingwurz'n (tel. 3132) is an elegantly rustic restaurant which draws a steady stream of loyal local diners. The menu ranges from regionally inspired to international. Food items include cream of snail soup, plus an array of fish, ragoûts, and meat, particularly veal. Desserts feature a range of seasonally adjusted fruited pastries and sorbets. À la carte meals range from 130 AS ($6.92) to 360 AS ($19.15), while fixed-price meals cost between 335 AS ($17.82) and 700 AS ($37.24). It's closed from mid-April until the first of May and from mid-November to mid-December.

IRDNING: Instead of staying at Tauplitz or Bad Mitterndorf, you might want to take a secondary road leading to one of the most beautiful hotels in Europe, where guests can find facilities for rest and recreation.

Hotel Schloss Pichlarn (tel. 2841). Some parts of this sprawling castle are more than 800 years old. Other sections are undeniably modern, including the up-to-date amenities in the comfortable rooms. The entrance is through an arched door covered with chevron designs. The interior is accented with soaring arches, ornate chandeliers, and thick Oriental carpets. The bedrooms are filled with fine antiques and tasteful colors, while on the premises are an elegant dining room, an accommodating bar area, an outdoor terrace, and a range of sporting facilities including an indoor and outdoor pool, a sauna, massage facilities, and a beauty salon. Many other attractions lie a short distance away. Per-person rates range from 1140 AS ($60.65) to 1740 AS ($92.57) in a single and between 1080 AS ($57.46) and 1560 AS ($82.99) in a double, depending on the accommodation and the season. Full board is included in these tariffs.

BAD AUSSEE: Surrounded by lake, mountains, and woods, Bad Aussee is an old market town and spa in the "green heart" of the Salzkammergut. It lies in the Valley of Traun, with the Totes Gebirge and the Dachstein massif visible in the distance. The ideal time to visit this salt- and mineral-spring spa is in June, when fields of narcissus burst into bloom, one of the most spectacular signs of spring coming to Europe.

Bad Aussee, at the confluence of a pair of upper branches of the Traun River, is considered the capital of the Styrian section of the Salzkammergut. Only three miles to the north is Lake Altaussee, with the spa town of Altaussee (see below) on its shore.

In summer this is a good center for walking and climbing in one of the most beautiful sections of Austria. Although Bad Aussee has long been known as a summer spa resort, it has also developed into a winter ski center, with the location of several ski lifts nearby making it attractive to ski enthusiasts.

Bad Aussee's most celebrated association is with Archduke Johann of the House of Habsburg. In 1827 he married the daughter of a local postmaster, an occurrence that in that era and within the empire was a *cause célèbre* that rivaled the romance of the Duke and Duchess of Windsor. A statue of the "Prince of Styria," Johann, can be seen in the Kurpark.

Incidentally, the Bad Aussee Glaubersalt spring is said to be particularly effective for losing weight, but I can't vouch for the truth of that claim.

Food and Lodging

Eurotel Erzherzog Johann, 62 Kurhausplatz (tel. 2507), is a conservatively designed, lemon-colored building with stone detailing, forest-green trim, and an arched entranceway in the center of town. The rustic interior offers a handful of wintertime fireplaces, beamed ceilings, and comfortably up-to-date furniture, as well as easy access to the area's sporting facilities. The spa facilities are connected to the hotel by a covered passageway. Twin-bedded rooms rent for 600 AS ($31.92) to 700 AS ($37.24) per person, while singles go for 1000 AS ($53.20). These prices include half board and vary according to the season.

Pension/Villa Kristina (tel. 2017) is a regionally styled villa about five minutes on foot from the center of town. The steep-roofed, wood-trimmed house is loaded inside and out with dozens of handcrafted details, a scattering of antiques, and all the modern amenities. Surrounded by a flowering park, the hotel offers shaded terraces as well as balconies adjoining some of the pleasantly furnished rooms. The Raudaschl family, your obliging hosts, charge between 420 AS ($22.34) and 475 AS ($25.27) in a single and from 435 AS ($23.14) to 500 AS ($26.60) per person in a double, with full board included. Prices vary slightly according to the season.

Hotel Wasnerin (tel. 2108) was established in 1860 as a hotel for visiting nature lovers, although the building you see today was constructed in 1934 by the grandmother of the Steinbichler family, who still run it today. Built with generously rambling proportions, in a gabled and hip-roofed style with lots of exposed wood and elegantly arched windows looking out on a raised sun terrace, the hotel offers simply decorated bedrooms for 275 AS ($14.63) to 360 AS ($19.15) per person, double occupancy, with half board included. Singles pay a daily surcharge of 50 AS ($2.66). Prices depend on the season and the plumbing.

Lewandofsky (tel. 2571) welcomes a loyal crowd of clients into its old-fashioned dining room which serves a wide range of strictly Austrian pastries along with coffee. The summertime garden area adjoins the city park and offers a view over the central square of town, as well as of the people flocking to the spa facilities for "the cure." Coffee costs from 17 AS (90¢) to 22 AS ($1.17), and pastries average 22 AS ($1.17).

ALTAUSSEE: This is a more tranquil spot for a stopover than Bad Aussee nearby. It also lies in the Styrian section of the Salzkammergut. Lake

Altaussee, facing the Totes Gebirge, is one of the most beautiful bodies of water in Styria. It's about two miles long, with rowboats for rent so that you can explore its area. For many decades Altaussee was only a lakeside summer resort, but because of the nearby ski region of Mount Loser (4995 feet), it now does a winter ski trade as well.

From Altaussee trips can be arranged in summer to the **Aussee Salt Mines,** two miles to the northwest. Conducted tours, lasting about an hour and 25 minutes, are offered from 9 a.m. to 4 p.m. daily, costing 75 AS ($3.99). The mines, called Salzbergwerk, were used by the Nazis to store valuable art to prevent its destruction by Allied bombing raids.

From Altaussee you can see the Dachstein glacier.

Food and Lodging

Landhaus Elisabethpark am See, 38 Fischerndorf (tel. 7205), is a three-story, wood-trimmed chalet with a hipped and gabled roof. It sits in a garden area with frontage on the lake and a backdrop of forested hills. The interior has a ceramic tile stove, hanging iron chandeliers, and a collection of comfortable chairs and wooden tables. Peter Lowatschek is the friendly director of this establishment, which charges per-person rates, breakfast included, of 360 AS ($19.15) daily.

Hotel am See (tel. 71361) is a rambling white villa set between the village church and the lake, with pleasant sun terraces, lots of contemporary comfort, and a friendly management by the Frischmuth family. The simply decorated interior is filled with attractively functional furniture. Rates range from 400 AS ($21.28) to 780 AS ($41.50) in a single and from 360 AS ($19.15) to 690 AS ($36.71) per person in a double, with half board included. The hotel is closed every year from the end of September until Christmas.

Hotel Pension Seevilla, 60 Fischerndorf (tel. 8102), is a romantic villa with arched windows, hipped roofs, and lots of exterior detailing. The interior contains deeply coffered ceilings, exposed wood, and a gracefully curving stone stairwell with an elaborate wrought-iron balustrade leading to the tastefully masculine bedrooms. On the premises are a bathing beach and an indoor pool, and there is access to a wide range of nearby sporting facilities. Each of the units has a private bath, balcony, mini-bar, radio, and TV hookup. The Maislinger family are the owners, charging from 540 AS ($28.73) to 690 AS ($36.71) per person for a double and from 610 AS ($32.45) to 930 AS ($49.48) for a single, with half board included. In winter a hotel bus will carry skiers to the nearby slopes.

Hotel Kitzer (tel. 71227) is a beautifully detailed chalet with a Viennese-style restaurant on the ground floor. Visitors will find a popular sun terrace dotted with parasols in summer, as well as a tastefully paneled interior with lots of accessories, including a dome-topped ceramic stove. The Berndl family are the conscientious owners, charging between 300 AS ($15.96) and 410 AS ($21.81) per person, with half board included. Prices vary slightly with the season.

Gasthof zum Loser, 80 Fischerndorf (tel. 7373), is one of the best restaurants in the region, with a body of local folklore to fill a volume and a loyal clientele that includes actors and poets from as far away as Vienna and California. Many of the fish served here are caught in the nearby lake, and some of the best ones are smoked in the restaurant's own smokehouse nearby. Every Thursday owner Hans Glaser hosts a musical evening, which is the most fun event in town. Glaser himself plays the bass-fiddle. His wife Heidi and their children are a visible presence at the restaurant. Framed on the walls of the restaurant are signed photographs of satisfied clients, including U.S. naval officers.

In addition to the smoked fish, specialties include wild game dishes, saddle of venison, wild mushroom soup, Styrian-style pork in cabbage, and homemade spätzle. The restaurant is closed the last week in March until mid-April and between the first of October and December 20. À la carte meals cost between 125 AS ($6.65) and 400 AS ($21.28), while fixed-price dinners range from 120 AS ($6.38) to 170 AS ($9.04).

8. Bruck an der Mur

A while back, at Leoben we headed west to take in the resorts and attractions of West Styria. If we had continued north along the Mur River instead, I would have brought you to Bruck an der Mur, at the point in the Styrian alpine range where the Mur and the Mürz flow together. The ruined fortress of Lanskron looks down on the bustling industrial town of Bruck, where factories process iron ore.

THE SIGHTS: The main attraction of the principal plaza (Hauptplatz) of the town is the **Eiserner Brunne,** a lacy wrought-iron well, done in 1626, one of the finest existing examples of Styrian ironwork.

Also on the Hauptplatz stands the most impressive building in Bruck, the 15th-century **Kornmesserhaus.** Some of it is in the flamboyant Gothic style, while other architectural parts are based on designs of the Renaissance. It has a splendid loggia and arcades.

The **pfarrkirche** (parish church) is on the Kirchplatz (church square). Its major treasure is a sacristy door which, like the fountain just visited on the Hauptplatz, is of wrought iron, circa 16th century.

FOOD AND LODGING: **Hotel Bauer** (Zum Schwarzen Adler) (tel. 51331), dating from 1683, is better known as the inner-village restaurant than as a hotel, although it does offer a limited number of rooms to guests who willingly choose to eat in the restaurant as well. The smallish but well-furnished double rooms usually have modern baths and all the comforts. Doubles cost 625 AS ($33.25), while singles rent for 375 AS ($19.95), with breakfast included. The restaurant is host to a swelling crowd of local diners, who sit either in the main dining room or in the rustically decorated stüberl. Specialties include venison pâté with cumberland sauce, an array of roast meats with noodles, and homemade pastries, some of them richly covered with whipped cream. À la carte meals range from 85 AS ($4.52) to 270 AS ($14.36).

Hotel/Restaurant Bayer, Hauptplatz (tel. 51218), next door to the Rathaus, offers friendly service, comfortable rooms, and good food, right in the heart of town. The bathrooms and many of the furnishings have recently been remodeled or replaced, under the direction of the owners, Sepp and Helga Bayer. Doubles range from 530 AS ($28.20) to 700 AS ($37.24), with singles going for 325 AS ($17.29) to 530 AS ($28.20), breakfast included. Half board in the family-style restaurant is another 115 AS ($6.12) per person.

Kalte Quelle (Koller) (tel. 52872). Residents of the town often say that the terrace of this restaurant, in a valley just south of town with a view of the mountains, is about the best place to be on a hot day in summer. The Koller family directs this pleasantly paneled restaurant with a rustic decor and attractive table settings. Specialties include veal cutlets with green noodles, liver noodle soup, filet of beef in a mustard sauce, and a temptingly fresh strudel. À la carte meals cost between 85 AS ($4.52) and 250 AS ($13.30).

KAPFENBERG: If you don't want to stay in Bruck, you can visit its sister town, nearby Kapfenberg. This town is mainly modern, but it has a schloss hotel which might interest you.

Burghotel Kapfenberg, 1 Schlossberg (tel. 22531). You won't find many baroque embellishments on the outside of this fortress-like hotel which towers over the town. The walls of this castle are as impenetrable today as they were when parts of the foundations were built 1000 years ago. Of course the interior has been modernized and redecorated, although you'll probably enter through the narrow gate, placed at the bottom of a watchtower that looks positively medieval, into a brick and stone courtyard whose niches are set with crucifixes and trailing ivy. The accommodations, which are efficiently supervised by members of the Mayerhofer family, are apartments with private baths and sitting rooms, along with bedrooms. They rent for 840 AS ($44.69) per person. The hotel is open all year.

FROHNLEITEN: South of Bruck an der Mur you'll come to an Austrian golfing center with an 18-hole international championship course. Long before it discovered golf, however, Frohnleiten was already an ancient town. It has a pfarrkirche (parish church) with rococo embellishments, and to the southwest of town stands a castle from the Middle Ages, **Rabenstein Castle.** It was constructed on the foundations of a Roman fort, and when the baroque craze swept Austria, the castle was not spared.

The town also has an **alpine garden** stretching across 22 acres and exhibiting more than 10,000 species from nearly all the continents of the world where plants grow.

Food and Lodging

Golfclub Murhof (tel. 2228) is an attractively isolated collection of several buildings, many of them painted a light yellow with black shutters and stone trim. All of them are clustered in the center of an 18-hole golf course, with fairways of several degrees of difficulty. On the premises are an indoor pool, a small lake, two tennis courts, an elegantly accommodating bar and sun terrace, a sauna, a restaurant, and lots of extra facilities. The entire facility is almost completely encircled by two rivers which eventually join near putting green no. 10.

Per-person rates range from 565 AS ($30.06) to 670 AS ($35.64) in a double, with full board included. Singles pay a daily surcharge of 60 AS ($3.19). Golfers will be charged greens fees of around 215 AS ($11.44) per day. All of the facilities are open to paying members of the outside community as well as to hotel guests.

Weissenbacher (tel. 2334), on the road to Graz, serves well-prepared and traditional Austrian food such as fresh asparagus in season, ham, cheese, beef, and chicken dishes to a loyal crowd of clients who appreciate the large portions and the rich desserts. À la carte meals range from 60 AS

($3.19) to 215 AS ($11.44). Members of the Weissenbacher family are usually in attendance.

WEIZ: If you're seeking reasonable accommodations in the area, you can drive east from Frohnleiten along a twisting secondary road until you reach Weiz. This is a typical Styrian town—clean and neat, the new blending harmoniously with the old and mountains forming a backdrop.

Weiz is often visited by Austrians who like to ride on its narrow-gauge railway, running on Saturday from July to September. The twin-towered church here was built in the 1600s as a fortress against Turkish invaders from the east.

Romantik-Hotel Modersnhof (tel. 3747) looks like an enlarged private house with big arched windows on the ground floor and a long row of cutout wooden balconies. It actually has a history of at least 250 years, and the well-furnished public rooms offer dozens of cozy seating areas with views over the quiet landscape around it. A curving iron staircase leads up to the simply furnished bedrooms, which rent for 780 AS ($41.50) to 900 AS ($47.88) per person, with full board included.

The intimately decorated dining room offers a menu with a small but well-chosen selection of specialties which include cream of tomato soup, trout filet, veal filet "house style" (with rosemary, mushrooms, and hollandaise sauce), and an array of fresh salads and homemade desserts. À la carte meals range from 175 AS ($9.31) to 375 AS ($19.95), while fixed-price meals cost between 300 AS ($15.96) and 500 AS ($26.60). The restaurant is closed Monday, and reservations are suggested.

9. Aflenz Kurort

This is one of the best bases you can find if you want to go mountain climbing in the Hochschwab. It has a reputation as both a summer resort and a winter sports site. Aflenz Kurort (5095 feet) can be reached from Kapfenberg in about half an hour.

In winter the attraction is the chair lift to Bürgeralm, which has a ski tow. In summer the chair lift is used by climbers exploring the Hochschwab mountains.

FOOD AND LODGING: **Aflenzer Hof** (tel. 2245). The oldest part of this hip-roofed stucco house was built in the 15th century, although since then it has been considerably modernized to include 1960s-style accessories and vivid colors which complement the thick walls and the vaulted ceilings. Guests who prefer more up-to-date accommodations can stay in the nearby annex, built in a big-windowed modern style with lots of wood trim and pleasant landscaping in a flowered garden. The Schaffenberger family charge between 300 AS ($15.96) and 325 AS ($17.29) per person in a single or double with private bath, including breakfast.

Hubertushof (tel. 2231) is a dignified stucco house with flowerboxes and green shutters at the windows, as well as a gabled roofline looking out over stately shade trees. The interior is a colorful assemblage of recently built furniture covered with contrasting patterns and country-style accessories. Per-person rates range from 275 AS ($14.63) to 360 AS ($19.15), based on double occupancy, with singles paying a daily surcharge of 25 AS ($1.33). Prices vary with the season and include half board.

Specialties in the restaurant include all kinds of Austrian-style sausages, served with black bread, and the kinds of caloric desserts that will send you jogging the next morning. Meals cost between 80 AS ($4.26) and 180 AS ($9.58).

Alpengasthof Gollner (Bürgeralm) (tel. 2426). In winter this attractive alpine hotel can only be reached by chair lift, although if you don't have a car you'll enjoy the ride up even in summer. The interior is simply furnished with unpretentious taste by a member of the Gollner family, who do everything they can to make guests feel at home. None of the rooms has a private bath, but toilets and showers are easily accessible. Per-person rates, with half board included, are 250 AS ($13.30) daily.

10. Mariazell

Mariazell is the most celebrated pilgrimage center in Austria, in addition to being a winter playground and a summer resort.

The object of pilgrimage is a church dating from the dawn of the 13th century, with three prominent towers. It was originally constructed in the Romanesque style then fashionable, and a Gothic choir was built on in the latter 14th century. The bulbous domes are baroque, a style laid on most of Austria's churches in the 17th century. Fischer von Erlach, both senior and junior, baroque architects by now familiar to readers of this guide, aided in the Mariazell transformation.

In the treasury are votive offerings accrued over some 600 years. The **Chapel of Grace** is considered the national shrine of Austria. Miracles are attributed to its statue of the Virgin, giving rise to fame that spread all over Europe. The statue is mounted on an altar designed by the younger von Erlach. In summer large groups gather on Saturday night for torchlit processions to the church.

The treasury is open from the first of May until the end of October from 10 a.m. to noon. Admission is 15 AS (80¢).

Over the years Mariazell has attracted much royalty, some of the Habsburgs, in particular, being fond of this village.

Many fathers take their sons to Mariazell to teach them how to ski, a generations-old tradition. Here are all the appurtenances of a modern winter sports and recreation center: avalanche-proof grounds for skiers of all skills, a cableway, a chair lift, numerous ski hoists, a natural toboggan run, a skating rink, a ski school, and a ski kindergarten. Mariazell is a winter holiday center for the whole family.

Its high altitude and good, brisk climate make this a favored summer vacation site, with a multitude of recreational pursuits to choose among. You can go walking on about 125 miles of footpaths, mountaineering, swimming, rowing, sailing, windsurfing, canoeing, fishing, horseback riding, glider flying, and camping, or you can play tennis or golf.

For one of the most dramatic views in the area, take a cableway to the Gemeindealpe (5335 feet) where you'll have a panoramic view of the Ötscher mountain range. The lift operates daily from 9 to 11:30 a.m. and 1 to 4:30 p.m. (on weekends only from Easter until the first of June and during October). It's closed in winter. The round-trip fare is 85 AS ($4.52).

FOOD AND LODGING: **Hotel Feichtegger** (tel. 2416) is a centrally located, flat-roofed, five-story hotel with evenly spaced rows of recessed balconies. The angularity of the facade is relieved with masses of flowers in the window boxes. Inside you'll find an open fireplace trimmed with roughly hewn stone, a rustically modern bar area, a restaurant, a paneled tavern, and sunny, simply decorated bedrooms. With breakfast included, rates range from 205 AS ($10.91) to 335 AS ($17.82) in a single and from 215 AS ($11.44) to 325 AS ($17.29) per person in a double.

Hotel Goldenes Kreuz (Hotel Scherfler) (tel. 2309). The ground-floor facade of this hotel near the basilica has been severely modernized, but the upper stories still retain the rococo detailing and white trim of the year they were built. The interior has lots of elegant accessories, two restaurants (one modern and one regionally paneled), and attractively furnished rooms filled with provincial designs painted on the comfortable furniture. With half board included, the per-person rate in a double is 455 AS ($24.21), with singles paying a daily surcharge of 25 AS ($1.33).

Hotel Goldene Krone (tel. 2583) is an old Styrian house with substantial proportions, stone trim, and a steeply pitched gabled roof next to the basilica. Most of the solidly constructed furniture was added when the hotel was remodeled. On the premises is a contemporary bar area with decorative masonry accents, plus a simple restaurant and comfortable bedrooms. These rent for 290 AS ($15.34) to 360 AS ($19.15) per person in a double, with half board included. Singles pay a daily surcharge of 25 AS ($1.33). The Moser family are the helpful managers.

Chapter XIV

HUNGARY

HUNGARY IS A SMALL COUNTRY—not quite as big as the state of Indiana. Its neighbors are Czechoslovakia on the north, Austria on the west, Yugoslavia on the south, and Roumania and the U.S.S.R. on the east. The Danube River is a main artery of communications for the country, forming the Czech-Hungarian border from the point at which the river flows in from Austria until it makes its turn south at the Danube Bend to go on to Yugoslavia. To the east of the Danube after its turn is the Great Plain, the Alföld, and the northern middle hills, while to the west lie the Small Plain and Transdanubia. The only important mountain range of the country stretches southwest to northeast, a part of the Carpathians. Transdanubia is a region of small, barren hills, extinct volcanoes, and sloping downs. Both the Great and Small Plains are fertile regions. Hungary is a land of forests, meadows, and a temperate climate. This is an agricultural country, but efforts are succeeding to achieve a better balance with industrial expansion.

The official name of the country, a socialist nation, is the Hungarian People's Republic, and its capital, Budapest, is ideally situated on the Danube. Budapest was formed by joining two towns which, in their early days, developed separately—Buda on the hilly west bank and Pest on a plain on the eastern side of the river. They were united in 1873 to make the country's leading city (see below). The largest provincial cities in Hungary are Miskolc, Debrecen, Szeged, Györ, and Pécs.

In Hungary you'll discover a Communist country that has managed to achieve a healthy economy, with a fair measure of freedom for its people and a foreign policy based on peaceful coexistence. It's a contemporary country with a diversified economy, but it doesn't forget its history, preserving architecture, folk music, dancing, arts, and crafts of its past, together with relics of historic riches.

Visit Hungary's freshwater inland sea, Lake Balaton. Enjoy the many thermal baths throughout the country. Sample the special Hungarian cuisine, and toast your friends in *barack* and Tokay wine. Hungary is a land of hospitable people, but you must never forget that Soviet power is a fact of life here. Obey the laws and regulations of this country, however, as of any other country you visit, and you can enjoy a happy holiday.

1. Getting Acquainted

THE PEOPLE: When I was in Hungary preparing this book and checking on some statistics, I ran across a printed statement by a Hungarian writer which said that the land comprising the country "had never been uninhabited." If the reference was to habitation by mankind, the statement was probably fairly accurate. The discovery in the 1960s at Vértesszöllös of relics of prehistoric man dating back 500,000 years seems to indicate that human beings have been here a good long time. However, the region became demonstrably inhabited when Celts settled along the Danube some 1000 years B.C.

After the coming of the Christian era there were Romans, Huns, Avars from Asia, Greeks, Germans, and Slavs—and probably a few more—who moved in, but the major impact was the coming of the Magyars in the ninth century A.D. The actual origin of the Magyars is long hidden in the mists of prehistoric time, but they probably came from the Ural mountains most recently, and their language is not of the Indo-European derivation as are other Western European tongues but is Finno-Ugric. That may not mean much to you, but it's the reason Hungarian differs so greatly today from the language of its neighbors. So many Magyars moved in that they rather quickly assimilated the remnants of their predecessors, so that now the language and customs of the country are firmly entrenched.

Of the almost 11,000,000 inhabitants today, 98% are Hungarian, with a smattering of Germans, Slovaks, Gypsies, and Croatians. The country is predominantly Catholic, 55% (both Greek and Roman), with another 20% following Calvinism and the rest being variously accounted for, some of course being Jewish. Hungarian Jews were not ignored by the Nazis. In 1944, 600,000 of them were rounded up and shipped to concentration camps, where thousands died. Today there are only about 20,000 Jews outside Budapest, with some 80,000 in the capital city.

Traditionally, Hungarian society is male dominated. Women are honored, but mainly their place is considered to be in the home, or at least secondary to that of males in the marketplace. In rural areas, even quite near large cities, and in villages, women still hand down to their daughters age-old skills in embroidery, spinning, and household chores. This is slowly changing in the large towns, but it's an important facet still of the Hungarian temperament. With the long, long history of warfare in the Carpathian Basin it's no wonder that the concept of man as the protector of his women and children has survived.

THE HISTORY: Just as it reads throughout Europe—in Switzerland, Germany, Austria, and wherever—that after the Celtic tribes came the Romans, so it was in the region that is now Hungary. It was a part of the Roman province of Pannonia, and excavations have unearthed a vast

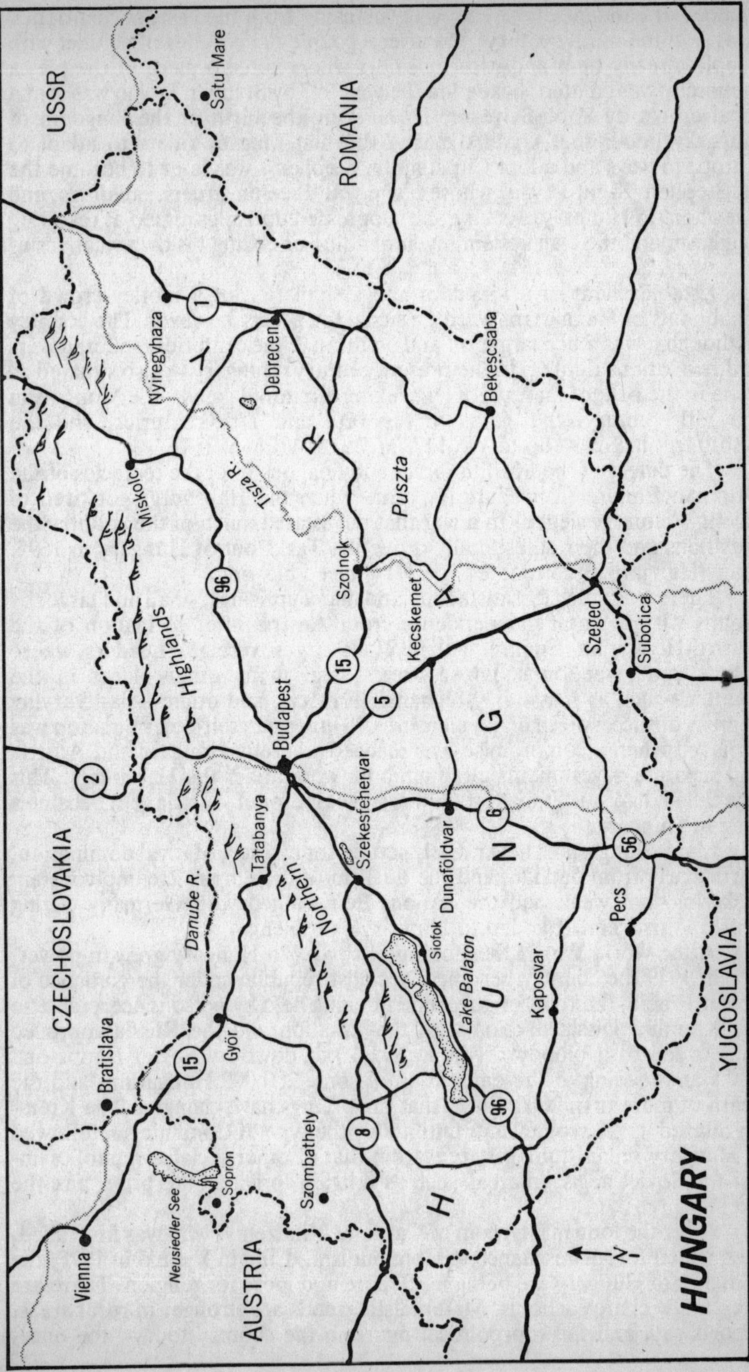
HUNGARY
USSR
Satu Mare
ROMANIA
CZECHOSLOVAKIA
AUSTRIA
YUGOSLAVIA
Vienna
Bratislava
Neusiedler See
Sopron
Szombathely
Györ
Danube R.
Tatabanya
Budapest
Northern
Highlands
Szekesfehervar
Siofok
Lake Balaton
Kaposvar
Pecs
Dunaföldvar
Kecskemet
Szolnok
Szeged
Subotica
Bekescsaba
Puszta
Tisza R.
Debrecen
Nyiregyhaza
Miskolc
H
U
N
G
A
R
Y
1
2
5
6
8
15
56
96
N

number of Roman relics. The Magyars came from the east, as mentioned above, in the ninth century, and after a couple of centuries of conflict with people already here and with outsiders who wanted a piece of the pie, a monarchy was created, headed in the year 997 by Stephen I, who was sent a royal crown by Pope Sylvester II, marking the birth of the kingdom of Hungary under the Árpád dynasty, the first Magyar rulers to adapt to European ways and adopt Christianity. Stephen I was later to become the St. Stephen (Szent István) whose name you'll see on streets, buildings, and elsewhere in Hungary. As king, he suppressed uprisings aimed at restoring paganism and the clan system, even blinding or exiling his own relatives as necessary.

Establishment of a kingdom and assimilation of a motley crowd of inhabitants as Hungarians wasn't a signal for peace, however. The country (although it was much larger off and on through the centuries) suffered wars and revolutions right up to the present century. Hungary was so situated as to be in the path of many peoples seeking territorial gains—the Mongols in the 13th century, the Turks in the 16th and 17th centuries, and the Habsburgs in 1686—up to World War I and World War II.

The defeat of the Muslim forces and final ouster of the tentacles of the Ottoman Empire from Hungary came when the Habsburgs got tired of having Vienna besieged. In a war that devastated much of the country the Austrians and their allies finally drove the Turks out of Hungary in 1699. Many Hungarians considered it a very mixed blessing.

There was much dissatisfaction and many uprisings, small and large, by groups wishing total independence from Austria after formation of the Austro-Hungarian Empire with a Habsburg sovereign. Leaders whose names you'll see on squares, streets, and many other places in the country—such as Kossuth, Széchenyi, Rákóczi, and others—had varying degrees of success. Finally, a measure of Hungarian self-determination was achieved when a compromise was reached whereby Hungary and Austria had separate governments although both were under the Habsburgs. This was called dualism. Franz Joseph was still emperor of Austria, but became a king in Hungary.

Many Hungarians never really settled for any sort of royal domination, particularly from outside, and the dualism of the empire created constant bickering that weakened the nation. Being allied with Germany during World Wars I and II added to Hungary's problems.

After World War II the Communist party in Hungary grew in power, and in 1949 the country became a socialist republic under the guidance of Soviet Russia, the reins of government being held by persons acceptable to the Kremlin. Dissatisfaction with the situation and the Russia-approved leaders led to a bloody revolt in 1956, put down by Soviet troops and tanks and leading to the emigration of some 200,000 Hungarians and the death of more than 2000. Since that time things have changed. The Kremlin relaxed its grip somewhat, until today the type of Communism followed in Hungary seems quite different from that of other socialist republics under the Soviet aegis, in areas such as religion, private enterprise, and the like.

After the long martyrdom of Cardinal Mindzenty, who was first jailed, then exiled for his resistance to Communism, dying in Vienna in 1975, the churches of Hungary are being used more and more for religion. There are even a few church schools. Materialistic trends are stronger in rural areas, reports say, and the top political figure in the country today—the oncefeared János Kadar, Hungarian Socialist Workers' party first secretary—is now seen as a patriot who has achieved the goal of liberalizing life in Hungary.

GOVERNMENT: The highest organ of state power is the unicameral National Assembly, with a Presidential Council exercising the functions of the head of state. Executive power is the province of the 14-member Council of Ministers, headed by the prime minister and responsible to the National Assembly. The leading political force is Kadar's Socialist Workers party. The seat of government is in Pest.

SPORTS: Hungary is a sporting nation, football, fencing, and swimming being the most popular branches in both spectator and participant activities. Budapest has a fine, new sports arena, and provincial towns such as Győr, Szombathely, Székesfehérvár, Debrecen, and Eger, have modern stadiums and racing grounds.

Water plays a major role in Hungary's sports scene, with such activities as sailing, windsurfing, rowing, motorboat cruising, swimming, and fishing being popular pursuits.

Sailing vessels are rented in Budapest and at 34 resorts in the Balaton district and around Lake Velence. Windsurfing is also an activity at the two lakes, Balaton and Velence.

All over the country you can find waters good for rowing, canoeing, and kayaking, with facilities for renting the boats and instruction courses being offered. It's also possible to go rafting on the Tisza River. Motorboating is available everywhere except on Lake Balaton, Lake Velence, and the Soroksár branch of the Danube.

Swimming pools and beaches will be found all over the country, many open all year.

Fish are abundant in Hungarian waters, which are much less polluted than those in Western Europe, so that the fish have a chance to thrive. Foreign visitors may purchase a fishing permit, usually issued by local water agencies, on presentation of a passport. At Lake Balaton you can get a permit from travel offices, at your hotel, or from a local fishing association at most settlements. They will also advise you as to restrictions on size and quantity of an allowable catch. You can catch bream, carp, pike-perch, silure, balin, and other varieties in the well-stocked lakes and rivers. There are closed seasons on some fish, and angling is forbidden in Lake Balaton from April 20 to May 20.

Hiking is a popular pursuit in Hungary, with many people going on long walking trips, camping along the way rather than trying to find a hotel. When you're equipped with good hiking boots and a rucksack, you can set forth to see the country's grass roots. One-day excursions are recommended, as there is not an overabundance of tourist accommodations along hiking routes. You can get information, advice, maps, and even help in finding lodgings at the travel offices in county towns.

Horseback riding is big in Hungary, and cross-country riding tours can be arranged by tourist agencies and travel offices. There are also riding schools where you can learn the basics. You are responsible for supplying your own boots and riding breeches.

Both Hungarian and foreign sports hunters find red deer, roe deer, wild pigs, and fallow deer plentiful, with some game birds also popular targets. If you're interested in this sport, you should get in touch with the Hungarian Game Trade Cooperative Enterprise (MAVAD), 39 Uri útca (tel. 122-667), in Budapest before you go to the country with that in mind.

Tennis, mini-golf, and bowling have been gaining in popularity in Hungary in recent years.

Snow and ice come to Hungary too, although not of the quantity or length of stay found in Austria. Winter sports include skiing, sledging, bobsledding, ice skating, and ice sailing (a popular sport on Lake Balaton), plus riding in an old-fashioned *fakutya,* a chair-like skating sledge.

For information before you go to Hungary on all these sports possibilities, check with **IBUSZ Hungarian Travel Bureau,** 630 Fifth Ave., Rockefeller Center, Suite 520, New York, NY 10111 (tel. 212/582-7412 or toll free 800/367-7878).

NATURE: Hungary is serious about environmental protection and nature conservation. "Museums of nature" have been created over vast areas, with 5% of the country's territory coming under the law to conserve natural resources. More than 100 national and nearly 600 local reserves and 28 protected areas are open to visitors. There are three national parks whose protection is a priority by Hungarian law, both to conserve and to display their valuable features. People with a wide range of interests are attracted to the cave systems, wildfowl reserves, and botanical gardens.

The national parks are Hortobágy, a flat plain between the Tisza River and Debrecen; Kiskunság, between the Danube and Tisza Rivers; and Bükk, in the northern highlands.

Hortobágy National Park covers about 104,000 acres of woods, fishponds, meadows, marshland, and villages, where thousands of birds either live or visit during migrations. The trees, flowers, and animals of the steppe flourish here. One of the six sections of the 15,000-acre Kiskunság National Park is visited in Part 9 of this chapter, the Great Plain and Puszta. The heart of Bükk National Park, some 70,000 acres, is the Bükk plateau, an unequalled region of caves and symbiotic plants.

Gemenc, visited below in Part 8, "Southwest Hungary," is the country's largest wildlife reservation, but there are other conservation areas, among them one at Sopron and one at Tihany. Arboretums with exotic plants, rare flowers, and primeval trees are found all over the country, including at Budapest.

SPAS: Hungary has an abundance of thermal springs, which were being enjoyed some 2000 years ago. The Romans built baths at Aquincum, the capital of Pannonia province. These baths were segregated—not by sex but by civilian or military status. During the turbulent times following Roman domination the baths were destroyed, and today there are only relics, such as beautiful mosaic floors, to recall the former glory.

In the Middle Ages fleshly pleasures were frowned on, but slowly, over a few centuries, baths regained respectability, mainly because of their healing powers. In the 18th and 19th centuries major spas began to develop in Budapest and elsewhere in Hungary. The baths of the capital are visited in Part 4 of this chapter.

Today several hundred baths and beaches invite visitors, providing entertainment, relaxation, and recuperation. Some are used mainly for treating the sick. No thermal spring bath should be entered without a doctor's approval. Most of the thermal waters have high concentrations of dissolved minerals which are beneficial to sufferers from a range of illnesses, either through being dunked in or drunk.

Besides the Budapest baths, thermal waters are found at the following spas: Balatonfüred, Bükfürdő, Eger, Gyula, Hagdúszoboszló, Hárkany, Héviz, Parád, and Zalakaros.

CULTURE: More than 500 important cultural events are held in Hungary annually, with visitors being attracted by interpretation of the work of world-renowned Hungarian composers Franz Liszt, Béla Bartók, and Zoltán Kodály; by concerts at Keszthely and Martonvasár; by the series of programs of the Budapest Art Weeks or the Szeged Open-Air Festival; and by the summer cultural events at the Sopron Festive Week, the Gyula Castle Festival, the Szentendre Theater, or the open-air theater on Margaret Island.

In the more than 500 museums of varying sizes you can see art from ancient to modern, including ecclesiastical works.

Well-known foreign theatrical companies and celebrated guest artists regularly appear on Hungarian stages and at concert halls. Hungarian dance art is known throughout Europe.

Rock concerts, carnivals, balls, and equestrian displays attract many visitors as well as local people.

FOLK ART: In Hungary you can see something of the relics of the old life of the peasantry as well as contemporary folk art. The different styles that developed in the architecture, costumes, dancing, handcrafts, and customs in different eras and among people of different ethnic backgrounds are still evident. Of course the oldest original objects of folk art are preserved in museums and other collections, but in folk art shops you'll find a wide variety of fine items of the art which can be purchased.

Tourists in Hungary find many-colored popular art. In different regions artisans carry on time-honored occupations handed down through generations. For instance, they do embroidery in Mezökővesd, lacework in Kiskunhalas, and fine pottery and dishes in Mezőtúr.

Visitors can participate in occasions like those of the past where forms of folk art originated. You might take part in a Matyo wedding ceremony, a vintage fun gathering, or attend a masked fancy-dress ball. Think what a memorable time you can have enjoying the frolic of a harvest festival to usher in the new bread!

CUISINE: In Hungary today you can eat better than you can in the other Communist countries of Eastern Europe, where you often experience difficulty getting fed at all! The Hungarians have been called "born eaters." It might be conceded that they are restaurateurs as well, and many of them have gone west to establish citadels of the gourmet cuisine in such places as New York and London. Most restaurants in Hungary are state-run these days, but there are those good souls still around whose parents remember what the food was like under the Habsburgs, when the cuisine of Hungary apparently reached rarefied heights of excellence.

Hungarian cuisine has been able to preserve much from the old, however, even from ancient times, and it has assimilated influences which have reached it in the course of time from immigrant ethnic groups and from abroad. Hungarian cooking has preserved the rich vegetable garnishings as well as several desserts introduced from Renaissance Italy, Turkish spices, and sauces and layered pastries created in Austrian and German kitchens. Many dishes from the surrounding Slavic peoples have been incorporated into Hungarian cookery, while French, Greek, Arab, English, and Indian specialties have added further variety.

Basically, you'll find in Hungary a cuisine in which beef, fish, chicken, pork, or whatever is cooked in lard. Sour cream, onions, and garlic, of course, are tossed in to give the mixture its flavor. The foundation of modern Hungarian cooking is the use of lard, onions, and paprika, and the favorite ingredient is sour cream.

Paprika, often called "the soul of Hungarian cooking," has probably only been in use here since the 16th or 17th century, maybe not that early. Where it came from is uncertain, some authorities believing that the invading Turks introduced it along with other Oriental spices. The Turks did leave behind bags of coffee which launched the Vienna coffeehouses in Austria, so perhaps they also left behind, after 150 years of rule, bags of the peppers which have become the hallmark of the Hungarian cuisine. However they got here, the handed-down agricultural know-how and the climate have combined to create the paprika industry in the southern part of the Great Plain, east of the Danube. Hungarian cooks use the sweet, brilliant red paprika in many dishes—used sparingly by the better chefs.

Just as the Spanish gave the world paella, so Hungary contributed **goulash,** or *gulyás* in Hungarian, a dish that seemingly every other housewife in America knows how to make, at least in some version. Chefs never seem to agree on how to concoct it, each having an individual interpretation.

Gulyás is a folk dish descended from the Magyars, a belly-warming stew known to have been a menu item in the ninth century. The ingredients could be dried and later prepared out in the open by shepherds and plainsmen. Its basis is cubes of rib or shoulder beef, cooked with finely chopped onion, diced potatoes, and salt, with modern additions of paprika and caraway seeds. Other meats are used by some cooks, even chicken, but true gulyás almost never has sour cream in it.

There are three other categories of Hungarian paprika dishes: pörkölt, paprikás, and tokány. **Pörkölt** is usually made of veal, although beef, mutton, pork, game, goose, or duck may be used. **Paprikás** goes best made with veal or chicken, but lamb, duck, or even fish is sometimes used. Sweet or sour cream is always stirred in. **Tokány,** the fourth of the notable stews of the country, comes in as many varieties as goulash, and the meat of which it is made ranges from beef to sausage.

Paprika-flavored stews aren't all that Hungarian cooks produce. **Stuffed cabbage** is another favorite, the leaves most often containing bacon, pork, rice, and herbs. Golden-brown suckling pig, chicken fried in bread crumbs, and soups are worth sampling. Another excellent dish is **fogas,** a freshwater fish from Lake Balaton, mild tasting and with a firm texture, somewhat like pike-perch. (It appears on German menus as zander.)

One of the finest products of Hungarian cooking is the sweet pastries that compete with Vienna's best. Try the strudel, called **rétes** in Hungary,

A variety of fillings provides you with many taste treats. In the provinces they still produce jam-filled **barátfüle,** the **kürtöskalács** (cream horns), and the acclaimed carnival doughnuts, or **fänk.**

DRINK: Hungary has plenty of **coffee** today, after a long scarcity a few decades ago, and the tradition of offering guests a small glass of espresso in homes and offices has been revived. The coffeehouses are back in business. Young and old alike gather again in the innumerable espresso cafés to sip, talk, and make friends. The coffee, however, may not suit you unless you like it strong and thick.

Hungarians are proud of their country's **wines,** the most celebrated being, of course, Tokay, from the village of Tokaj (see below). It's considered the only great wine made east of the Rhine. One type, Tokaji Aszú, is a syrupy, sweet-tasting wine said to be produced, like a notable sauterne, from "noble mold." Other Tokays vary from sweet to dry.

Egri Bikavér (so-called bull's blood of Eger) is a popular heavy red table wine. Often today this wine is not Hungarian at all but comes from places such as North Africa. I suggest you try the home-grown version while you're here. Exceptional favorites are the Pinôt Noir from Pécs and a burgundy-like wine called Villányi Burgundi from the southernmost city of Hungary, Villány. On the shores of Lake Balaton a grape is grown that is used to produce a rich white wine, Keknyelu (meaning blue stem).

A popular apéritif is **barack,** which is considered the best apricot brandy made in Europe. You may find it too sweet to drink before a meal, but I like a glass of it after dinner. Maybe you will too. Other brandies you may want to sample are plum, cherry, or even rose-hip.

If you don't wish to order an alcoholic drink, you might enjoy one of the country's mineral waters or a native brand of **beer.** One of the most popular brand names is Kinizsi.

2. Traveling to and Within Hungary

Traveling to Eastern Europe, especially Hungary, is easier than it's been in years. Hungary is eager to attract the Western visitor, and restrictions have been relaxed in recent years. You can either visit Hungary on a package deal or else as an independent traveler. First, I'll discuss the easiest means of—

GETTING THERE: The only international airport in Hungary is in Budapest, and the only carrier that flies there from the United States is **Pan American,** one of the world's leading carriers. There's simply no easier way to get to Hungary than on this particular route which, to the thousands of passengers who have already traveled with Pan Am, offers competitive prices and efficient transfers to Budapest from all parts of North America.

Evening flights on a well-inspected 747 leave for Budapest either two or three times a week, depending on the season, from New York's JFK Airport. Clients make a quick plane change at up-to-date airports in either Frankfurt or Munich before continuing on a 737 to Budapest. Pan Am sets it up so that the transfer will be as simple and efficient as possible, and your baggage will be automatically transferred through to your final destinations.

Return flights leave Budapest at 8:30 a.m. either two or three times a week, again depending on the season, landing at around noon in New York. This includes a rapid plane change in either Frankfurt or Munich where again your luggage will be automatically transferred to your final destination.

Prices fall into a wide range of categories, but your cheapest fare will be an APEX ticket in low season, which ranges from September 15 to May 14. This type of ticket is one of Pan Am's most popular for vacationers, and it requires that tickets be purchased at least 14 days in advance, with a minimum sojourn in Hungary of between seven days and one year. This same fare is available in high season, which lasts from May 15 until September 14, although it will invariably cost more.

Another fare influenced by the season in which you fly is called an excursion fare. It requires no advance purchase, and you can leave the date of your return open, although you're required to stay over for between 10 and 90 days.

The other fare possibilities on Pan Am are not influenced by seasonal price changes. They include regular Cabin Class, Clipper Class, and First Class. Clipper Class offers seating as comfortable as the First Class seating on many other airlines, a free movie, free headset, complimentary bar, separate check-in facilities, and upgraded food and service.

First Class is the preferred choice of anyone who wants to arrive at his or her final destination in as well-rested a condition as possible. First Class, of course, offers all the specialized attention and facilities of Clipper Class, as well as seats that convert into almost horizontal sleepers and a wide variety of sophisticated extras.

Specific fares on all of the transatlantic routes are subject to change without notice, particularly in the event of a fare war over the Atlantic. This would only be to the traveler's advantage, so the best bet is to call your travel agent or Pan Am's toll-free number, available from directory assistance in your area. There you will learn about specific departure times and connections as you prepare for your eventual flight.

VISAS: In order to enter Hungary, United States and Canadian citizens must have a valid passport *and* a visa. Visas may be obtained from the Hungarian Embassy, 3910 Shoemaker St. NW, Washington, DC 20008, or the Hungarian Consulate General, 8 East 75th St., New York, NY 10021. In Canada the Hungarian Embassy is at 7 Delaware Ave., Ottawa, ON K2P OZ2.

Visas are also issued at the Budapest Airport and at the border if you're traveling by car. However, I advise you to get yours before you leave home if you know you're coming to Hungary. You cannot get a visa at the border if you're traveling by train nor at the pier if you're coming in by boat or hydrofoil. Visas are valid for six months from the date of issue, for a stay of up to 30 days.

Your travel agent can handle the details of securing a visa for you, or if you have questions about obtaining it yourself, get in touch with IBUSZ Hungarian Travel Bureau, whose New York toll-free number is 800/367-7878.

TRAVELING WITHIN HUNGARY: Now you're in Hungary. If you came by any means other than by private vehicle, chances are you're in Budapest, and now you're wondering how best to get around the country. I'll deal first with things you should know if you're going to be doing your own driving, and then introduce you to the various means of public transport available in this country.

By Car

In Hungary you drive on the right, and the rules of the road used in most of continental Europe are observed. You do not—repeat *not*—drive in this country if you have had a single drink of alcoholic beverage, even a beer. It's also strongly recommended that you not drive after taking a strong tranquilizer or a painkiller before the effects have worn off. Police in Hungary keep a close eye on drivers. The Hungarian Highway Code prescribes that using three-point safety belts in the front seat is required, and children under 6 must ride in the back seat.

On Hungarian roads, with the exception of motorways and limited-access roads, horse-drawn carts, bicycles, and pedestrians are part of the traffic. In the country and on roads through villages you may find livestock using the road too. Although regulations say that horse carts and bicycles must have lights at night, many fail to obey the law, so it's in your own best interest to drive especially carefully after dark. Headlights are required to be on low beam from dark until daylight.

The speed limit on motorways is 75 miles per hour. On other roads outside built-up areas it's 60 miles per hour, and in congested sections, 35. You must yield to pedestrians at zebra-striped crossings and when turning at a road junction.

Accidents must be reported within 24 hours or on the first work day to the **State Insurance Company,** International Department, in Budapest, 60 Hanzsabégi út, or to the County Directorates of the State Insurance Company. If someone is injured, notify the police immediately. If you are stopped for a traffic offense, the police can give you a warning on the spot or impose a fine ranging from 10 Ft. (22¢) to 200 Ft. ($4.45). Believe me, it's better to admit you were at fault and pay up, as otherwise you'll face a long, involved process that may result in a fine which could go to 5000 Ft. ($111.35) and lose you valuable time.

Gas stations: The red color and the Áfor emblem of the state-owned Hungarian motor fuel stations can be recognized from a long way off. In addition you'll find Shell, BP, and AGIP stations. Stations are usually open from 6 a.m. to 10 p.m.; in Budapest and on motorways and other busy roads, they're open 24 hours.

Cost of gasoline: 86 octane is 6.40 Ft. (14¢) a liter; 92 octane, 8 Ft. (18¢) a liter; and 98 octane, 9.60 Ft. (22¢) a liter.

For help on the road, the **Hungarian Automobile Club** provides a large number of services. Its headquarters is at 4/a Rómer Flóris út in Budapest, open weekdays from 8 a.m. to 5:30 p.m., on Saturday from 8 a.m. to 12:30 p.m. You can get information in English from the club's Technical Service, 2 Boldizar út in Budapest (tel. 850-722). There are several technical service stations at larger towns throughout the country.

If you have a breakdown in Budapest, call 260-668 between 7 a.m. and 7 p.m. In the country, the "yellow angels," the breakdown fleet of the automobile club, will come to your rescue. This service is free for club members, with nonmembers being charged. When you enter the country or visit the Hungarian Automobile Club headquarters, ask for an emergency card. If your car breaks down, just hand the card to a passing motorist, who will deliver it to the "yellow angels."

Car Rentals: As it does in Austria, **Budget Rent-a-Car** maintains offices in Hungary, making car rentals almost as easy as picking up a phone. The type of car and the pricing structure are slightly different from those across the border in Austria, but North Americans will quickly get the hang of the new system.

When you arrive at the airport in Budapest, there is a Budget counter to help you pick up your car and to fill out the necessary forms. All major credit cards are accepted. Equally acceptable are a minimum cash deposit of $150 or a cash payment of the estimated rental of a car. If you're arriving in Budapest by train, a representative of Budget will pick you up anywhere in the city (at the train station, your hotel, whatever), and take you to their downtown office at 16 Vaskapy Utca (tel. 142-819).

All you need to rent a car in Hungary is to present a driver's license which has been valid for one year prior to the date of rental. You must also be between the ages of 21 and 70. The Hungarian government does not charge tax for car rentals. Liability insurance is included in Budget's rates, although many clients (including myself) choose to purchase optional accident insurance, which costs $4 per day or $24 per week. Without the purchase of such additional insurance the driver is responsible for 10% of the actual damage, up to a maximum of $400 should an accident occur. A surprising advantage of the Hungarian insurance laws allows drivers to buy optional accident insurance for $1 per week. While collecting an eventual settlement might involve you in a lengthy bureaucratic process, the policy in theory gives additional coverage to the driver in case of *any* personal accident he or she should suffer while in possession of the car (even, I was told, for slipping in a bathtub). The policy will also cover accidents affecting a driver's passengers, but only for mishaps directly related to the car.

The cheapest car available is a Czech-made Skoda 120L with manual transmission, two doors, and enough room to hold four passengers plus their luggage. Per-day rates, with unlimited mileage included, are about $37 for one to three days, $29 per day for four to seven days, and $25 per day for eight or more days.

In the "slightly larger" category are a Lada 1200 or a Dacia 1310, both with manual transmission, four doors, and a more comfortable format. These rent for $47 per day for one to three days, $40 per day for four to seven days, and $35 per day for eight days or more. Just a little more expensive would be a Lada 1500, suitable for five passengers with their luggage.

Finally, if you want to tour Hungary in as much bourgeois opulence as possible, you can rent a sporty Mazda 929 for approximately $110 per day for one to three days, $88 per day for four to seven days, and about $72 per day for eight days or more.

As a final extra, luggage racks are available on special request for an additional $1 per day.

Any of the personnel at Budget's toll-free number will be happy to give further details and reserve a car for you in advance. From points throughout the United States, call 800/527-0700 and ask for the international department. In Canada, call 800/268-8900 (in Toronto, 482-0222, in British Columbia, 112-800/268-8900; and in Québec, 800/268-8970).

By Train

Hungary has an extensive, well-developed railway network, with 38 modern express trains daily, linking the larger towns and the capital. Railway tickets may be purchased at the ticket office of any railway station, at IBUSZ Hungarian Travel Bureau ticket offices, or at the **Hungarian State Railways** (MÀV) central public service office in Budapest, 35 Népköztársaság útja (tel. 228-049). Since Hungarian State Railways belongs to the European railways reservation system, you can book passage on the trains here from elsewhere.

For a good look around the country, you may want to buy a **go-as-you-please ticket** valid on all lines and available for 10, 20, or 30 days. You purchase these tickets from an IBUSZ office (see "Information," in this section). The Inter-Rail concession ticket for young people is also valid in Hungary. These are for persons up to the age of 26. In Budapest and at some provincial towns you can buy your tickets from an automatic dispenser at the railway station.

It's wise to get your tickets for the whole journey before you start. Seat reservations should be made well in advance, especially during the peak summer season. You can break your journey at any point in Hungary without formalities.

There are restaurants and snackbars at railway stations where you can have a hot meal and a choice of drinks. There is dining- and buffet-car service on domestic fast and express trains. On long-distance passenger trains, the first-class carriages and dining cars are in the middle of the train. Sleeping cars are only on international trains.

By Bus

Every day, the **Volán** company makes 38,000 intertown and 40,000 local bus runs within Hungary. Practically all villages and towns of more than 200 inhabitants with no rail link have a Volán bus service. Season tickets, usually for a 20% reduction from the regular price, can be bought for one, three, and ten days. You can purchase your tickets at IBUSZ offices or other large travel agencies.

For travel information, get in touch with the International Bus Terminal in Budapest on Engels tér (tel. 172-966 or 182-122).

By Boat

Mahart, the Hungarian Shipping Company, operates a hydrofoil service between Budapest and Vienna, a five-hour journey. IBUSZ will provide you with information about this trip in Vienna, 26 Kärtnerstrasse (tel. 52-78-79), or 4 Krugerstrasse (tel. 52-92-60). In Budapest, you should inquire at the Mahart international boat station, 2 Belgrád-rakpart (tel. 181-953) or at the IBUSZ office at 3/a Tanács körút (tel. 423-140).

At Lake Balaton there are boat services across the lake and excursion boats as well as ferries carrying cars between Tihany-rev and Szántód-rev from May 29 to September 25 every 40 minutes from 6:20 a.m. to midnight. This is reduced to 6:20 a.m. to 8 p.m. in spring and autumn. The fare is 4 Ft. (9¢) per passenger or 30 Ft. (67¢) for a private car and driver.

There are regular Mahart boats from Budapest to the Danube Bend. In summer sightseeing boats leave daily from Vigadó tér in Budapest (see "Tours in Budapest," below).

By Plane

It's simple. You can't travel by air to any Hungarian location except Budapest. **Malév,** Hungarian Airlines, operates service from Ferihegy

Airport in Budapest between the nation's capital and 39 cities in 26 countries—but none within Hungary.

Malév does provide some special tours and excursions within the country. Especially popular are gastronomic, musical, and professional programs. Malév Airtours' central office is at 2 Roosevelt tér in Budapest (tel. 186-614). The Malév number at Ferihegy Airport is 570-033.

3. The ABCs of Hungary

Plunging into Hungary, with its language and its government both being totally foreign to the average North American, can be mind-blowing. However, it should help to ease your adjustment to have a few of the basic ABCs of the country at your fingertips.

CAMPING: There are more than 100 campsites in Hungary, mainly open from the beginning of May to the end of September, most accommodating only camping vehicles, although some rent out tents. Tourists can get information and reserve places in advance from the travel office of the Magyar Camping and Caravanning Club in Budapest, 6 Üllői út (tel. 336-563).

CIGARETTES: Nearly all the major hotels will sell you cigarettes and other tobacco products. In addition to that, all cities and towns have tobacco shops called *Trafik* or *Dohánybolt.* If you want some hard-to-find foreign brand and your hotel doesn't stock it, chances are you can purchase it at an Intertourist shop, for which you will have to pay "hard currency" (that is, Western).

CLIMATE: The country has a temperate climate with continental, Mediterranean, and Atlantic Ocean influences. The annual mean temperature is 50° Fahrenheit. The coldest month is January, with 14° to 30° temperatures, and the hottest is July with about 71° Fahrenheit. The number of hours of sunshine is high—close to 2000 per year in most of the country.

CLOTHING: In summer, a lightweight jacket, wrap, or sweater may be necessary in the evening. In winter, a moderately heavy coat is advisable.

CREDIT CARDS: Sometimes they're better than having Hungarian currency to pay with. In the larger hotels and restaurants and in certain shops and department stores, American Express, VISA, Carte Blanche, MasterCard, Diner's Club, and Eurocard are accepted. However, don't count on being able to use one of the cards in small villages.

CRIME: Violent crime such as rape and murder is rather rare in Hungary. (Hungarians kill themselves more by suicide than they kill each other.) However, that doesn't mean that you should lower your guard. Protect your valuables in the sensible way that you would when traveling anywhere in Western Europe. Even if the Hungarians are a fairly honest people, they are flooded with millions of visitors every year, dozens of whom are arrested by the police for stealing.

CURRENCY: There are no restrictions on the amount of foreign currency you can bring into Hungary, and it's wise to keep plenty of dollars on hand, because they won't take their own money for IBUSZ tours or hotel accommodations! They take credit cards (see above) or U.S. currency only. Keep your exchange slip in case you need to trade back when you're leaving the country, as you can't leave with more than 100 **Forints,** the currency of Hungary, which must be in coins, not banknotes. The current rate is 44.9 Forints (Ft.) to $1 U.S.

Foreign currency can be exchanged only at officially designated places: banks, National Savings Bank branches, travel offices, hotels, and camping sites. Private exchange of currency is forbidden.

One Forint equals 100 **fillérs.** There are banknote denominations of 10, 20, 50, 100, and 500 Forints, and coins worth 1, 2, 5, and 10 Forints, as well as 10-, 20-, and 50-fillér pieces.

CUSTOMS: You can bring goods into Hungary duty free for your own use—in reasonable amounts, of course. If you're over 16, you can carry with you 250 cigarettes or 50 cigars, two liters of wine, and one liter of spirits. Articles of value, such as tape recorders, radios, and cameras, should be declared on entering the country so you can be sure of not being charged duty on them when you leave. You may bring in small gift items worth up to 5000 Ft. ($111.35). When you leave the country you may take only 3000 Ft. ($66.81) worth of goods out as personal luggage without special permission. You may bring 100 Ft. ($2.23) into the country with you, and it must be in coins.

Narcotics, antisocialist literature, pornographic literature or film, explosives, and firearms are prohibited. Sports guns and ammunition and two-way radios require a special entry permit.

ELECTRICITY: Electric current in Hungary is 220 volts AC, 50 cycles.

EMERGENCY PHONE NUMBERS: Throughout Hungary, the numbers to call in an emergency are the same. They are: ambulance—04; police—07; and fire—05.

FIRST AID: All foreign visitors are entitled to first aid, which any hospital or medical consulting room will provide.

HITCHHIKING: Since public transportation in Hungary is relatively inexpensive, there may not be much need to hitchhike. However, it is possible to do so, although the car picking you up is likely to be from some other European country. One American student told me he was picked up by a former German SS officer who had many a story to relate! The government of Hungary does not forbid hitchhiking, but I get the impression that they view it with a lack of enthusiasm.

HOLIDAYS: National holidays are observed in Hungary on January 1, Easter Monday, April 4, May 1, August 20, November 7, December 25, and December 26.

INFORMATION: When you visit a country with a language barrier as forbidding as the Hungarian tongue may seem to you at a glance, it's wise to have sure sources of information beforehand and to know where to get answers in English once you're there. If you have any questions on touring Hungary when you're planning your trip, write to the **Tourist Information Service** (Idegenforgalmi Tájékoztaló Szolgálat), H-1440 Budapest, VII. 52 Rákóczi út (tel. 228-649).

Either in or outside of Budapest, the **IBUSZ Hungarian Travel Bureau** can usually help you. With scores of branch offices, they can supply you with information and services. Its New York address is: IBUSZ Hungarian Travel Bureau, North American Division, 630 Fifth Ave., Rockefeller Center, Suite 520, New York, NY 10111 (tel. 212/582-7412 or toll free 800/367-7878). They'll do all they can to plan all details of your Hungarian trip. The English-speaking staff, headed by the talented Hungarian director, Peter Gomori, will offer you brochures, maps, advice, information—virtually everything you'll need for a safe and insightful journey to one of Europe's most interesting countries. This is probably the single most abundant source of information, aside from this book, that a tourist can tap before a trip, especially since the materials IBUSZ provides are in English and are usually free. In Budapest the main office of IBUSZ is at 3/C Tanács körút (tel. 423-140). You'll find IBUSZ offices all over Hungary.

Other sources of information in Hungary are:

Express, 16 Szabadság tér, Budapest (tel. 111-430).

Cooptourist, 13-15 Kossuth tér, Budapest (tel. 116-683).

Budapest Tourist, 5 Roosevelt tér, Budapest (tel. 173-555).

Volántourist, 13 Oktober 6 útja, Budapest (tel. 123-410).

Malév Airtours, 2 Roosevelt tér, Budapest (tel. 186-614).

Each major town in Hungary has a travel agency bureau and local office of tourism, but you may have difficulty in smaller places getting understandable information in English.

One of the very best sources of information for tourists is the **Tourinform Bureau** in Budapest (see "Practical Facts" in the Budapest section of this chapter).

NEWSPAPERS AND MAGAZINES: Don't think you'll be cut off from news from the West during your tour of Hungary. The *International Herald Tribune* is widely sold in Budapest but much less available in the provinces. Likewise, American news magazines, such as *Time* and *Newsweek,* are for sale at major kiosks, particularly at leading hotels. There's also a bilingual newspaper (in German and English) called the *Daily News,* which is often slipped under your hotel door every morning free. It's decidedly pro-Soviet, however.

POST OFFICE: Most city post offices are open from 7 a.m. to 8 p.m. Monday to Saturday. At most post offices you can make phone calls and send telegrams. Unlike Western Europe, it is not customary to send your mail poste-restante or general delivery. It's better to have your mail forwarded directly to the hotel where you'll be staying.

REGISTRATION: Citizens of the United States and all other nonsocialist countries must be registered at the local police station within 24 hours of their arrival in Hungary, but you do not need to worry about having to do it yourself if you're staying in a hotel or pension. The management will arrange registration for you. However, if you're staying at a noncommercial accommodation, such as at the home of friends, then be sure to sign in within the allotted time. The head of the family can register for everybody.

STORE HOURS: Consumer-goods shops are open normally from 10 a.m. to 6 p.m. (to 8 p.m. in Budapest and other cities), till 2 p.m. on Saturday. Food shops open earlier and close later. Generally, business offices are open from 8 or 8:30 a.m. until 4:20 or 5 p.m.

TELEPHONE AND TELEGRAM: I have read in many sources that calls to the West are "almost impossible" to make from Hungary. However, on one recent trip I was able to reach both New York (repeated calls) and Paris and London numbers after a wait of anywhere from 5 to 20 minutes. Try to call at slow periods of the day. If you want to inquire about phone problems, telephone 172-200 in Budapest and an English-speaking operator will come on to assist you. If you're making long-distance calls, either within Hungary or to the West, it's best to go through your hotel switchboard or else use the phone facilities at the post office.

Otherwise, you can go to the international telecommunications center in Budapest, where you can not only make phone calls, but send telegrams and Telex messages. It is at the corner of Petőfi Sándor utca and Martinelli tér, and is open from 7 a.m. to 8 p.m. Monday to Friday. On Saturday it closes at 7 p.m. On Sunday and holidays it's open only in the morning.

In Budapest you'll see a number of phone booths, most characteristically in green and yellow. Inside, easy-to-follow instructions are given about how to make a local phone call.

TIME: The clocks of Hungary operate seven hours ahead of Eastern Standard Time in the United States. However, sometime in April the country goes on its own central European summer time, which puts it only six hours ahead of Eastern Standard Time, which of course only lasts until the last Sunday in April, when it becomes Eastern Daylight Saving Time, making seven hours' difference again. However, Hungary goes off the summer time in September, so until clocks in the United States are turned back to standard time on the last Sunday in October there's only the six-hour difference from Eastern time. Understand all that?

TIPPING: Despite attempts in certain parts, no one has succeeded in wiping out this custom. Tipping is firmly entrenched and appreciated.

Everyone expects a tip, even the filling station attendant. Don't overtip, but certain gratuities are appreciated, even when service has been included. For special requests, gypsy violinists expect at least 100 Ft. ($2.23). Otherwise, give them from 20 Ft. (45¢) to 50 Ft. ($1.11). Maids usually get 50 Ft. ($1.11), but the poor lavatory attendant only gets 2 Ft. (4¢). If your hotel has a doorman and he hails you a cab (or performs some other service), tip 10 Ft. (22¢). Porters get 10 Ft. (22¢) per bag. Hatcheck girls get 10 Ft. (22¢). Taxi drivers, hairdressers, whomever, generally expect about 15% of the bill.

TOILETS: All major Hungarian cities and towns have public conveniences. They are found in public parks, museums, metro stations, and in train and bus terminals. Pictures on the door indicate whether the toilet is for men or women. If not, know that *férfi* means men and *női* is for women.

4. Budapest

The lights are brighter, the people have more joie de vivre in Budapest, the most romantic city I've found in Eastern Europe—and I've traveled all the countries except Albania. The Hungarian capital, "pearl of the Danube" as it's been named by people who have traveled the entire 1700-mile length of the river, is a bustling city of some 2.1 million inhabitants. Its architecture ranges from that left by the Romans to that of the present day. The Buda Castle District alone has been called an open-air museum, with buildings and historic monuments that seem to be an inexhaustible treasury. You see structures of historic character standing on streets with a medieval atmosphere—but you also see modern, well-planned, attractive housing estates and commercial buildings developed in harmony with the legacy of the past.

The ancient city of Buda lies on the gentle wooded slopes of the right (west) bank of the Danube, with the busy, modern metropolis of Pest on the left (east) bank, spread out on the plain.

As in many other parts of the temperate sections of Europe, especially along rivers and lakes, Celtic tribes had settlements on the Danube at this site, and then the Romans moved in. The legions of the Caesars and Romans who followed them settled in Pannonia, today's Hungary, in the first century of the Christian era, building the Pannonia capital, Aquincum, where Buda stands today.

In 896 when the Magyars occupied the country where they live today, one of their strategic settlements was established on one of the islands here in the Danube, Csepel. During the early Middle Ages a new fortified royal town was founded on the hill of Buda, where at the turn of the 14th century the Hungarian kings set up the seat of government that had formerly been based in the ancient coronation town of Székesfehérvár (see the description at the end of Part 6 on Lake Balaton).

The Turkish army slashed its way to power in Hungary in the middle of the 16th century, holding sway until they were driven out a century and a half later, bleeding Buda of its wealth, even converting the largest church, known today as the Matthias Church, into a mosque. After the ouster of the followers of Mohammed, the city was reconstructed under a strong baroque influence in the architecture and decoration.

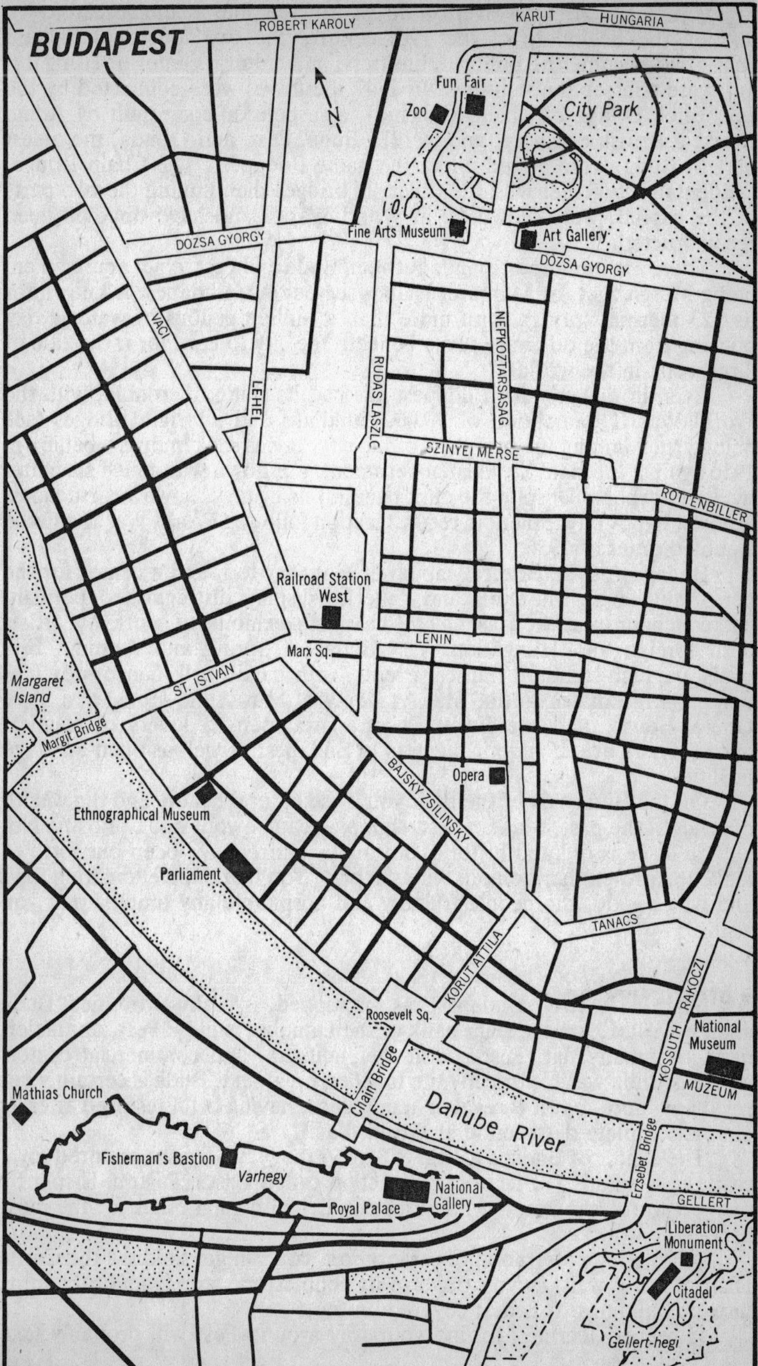
BUDAPEST
ROBERT KAROLY
KARUT
HUNGARIA
N
Fun Fair
Zoo
City Park
Fine Arts Museum
Art Gallery
DOZSA GYORGY
DOZSA GYORGY
VACI
LEHEL
RUDAS LASZLO
NEPKOZTARSASAG
SZINYEI MERSE
ROTTENBILLER
Railroad Station West
LENIN
Marx Sq.
ST. ISTVAN
Margaret Island
Margit Bridge
Opera
BAJSKY ZSILINSKY
Ethnographical Museum
Parliament
TANACS
KORUT ATTILA
RAKOCZI
Roosevelt Sq.
National Museum
KOSSUTH
MUZEUM
Chain Bridge
Danube River
Mathias Church
Fisherman's Bastion
Varhegy
National Gallery
Royal Palace
Erzsebet Bridge
GELLERT
Liberation Monument
Citadel
Gellert-hegi

Pest, just across the river on the plain, grew into a commercial town, and by the beginning of the 19th century the two towns—Buda and Pest—had become the political, business, and cultural center of Hungary, but were still separate entities. In 1849 the towns were connected by the celebrated Bridge of Chains (lánchid), a suspension span built by Adam Clark, a British engineer; and in 1873 Buda, Pest, and Óbuda, the oldest part of Buda, were united under the name Budapest. The Chain Bridge, incidentally, together with the other six bridges then linking the two parts of the capital, were blown up in World War II and have since all been reconstructed.

There are numerous islands between Buda and Pest, chief among them being Margitziget, or Margaret Island (see below). Budapest is known for its 123 thermal springs, with more than a million gallons of water a day pouring from the dolomite strata beneath the city to earn for it the title of largest spa in the world.

Even in this century Budapest has had its share of trouble, with the World War II demolition of 33,000 buildings and all eight bridges (see below) then linking the two parts of the city. It was shaken by a rebellion in 1956 against the rigid Socialist government, put down with much slaughter by Soviet troops. Despite the dark pages of its history, however, Budapest is now a happy city. Splendid reconstruction followed World War II and the troubled times of 1956.

Budapest is the cultural capital of Hungary too, and a center for the performing arts. Museums and galleries display distinguished permanent collections, as well as having changing exhibits of work by artists both foreign and Hungarian. The Budapest Spring and Autumn Festivals are high-standard musical events, with ballet, folk dance presentations, opera, and operetta. The Academy of Music, the Hungarian State Opera House, and the Erkel Theatre are open to lovers of classical music. There are 25 indoor theaters in Budapest as well as open-air stage facilities.

On the Buda side of the river you'll see natural beauty and the wealth of relics of the past, while in Pest, shopping can be your no. 1 priority. Not all you'll see is old and historic, but major efforts have been put forth to make the present harmonious with the past. You'll find the Hungarian food and wines good, the people friendly and hospitable any time of year you visit.

AN ORIENTATION: Budapest, as mentioned, is really two cities, Buda and Pest. Buda, on the right bank of the Danube, is hilly; Pest, on the left bank, is mainly flat. Pest is still the industrial and commercial center; whereas Buda was historically the fortified royal seat. Buda is certainly not royal any more, but it is regal in appearance, having been restored after its almost complete destruction in World War II.

The center of Buda is **Castle Hill** or Várhegy, where the restored royal castle now stands. To its north, a section called Castle District is split by many colorful old streets which run parallel with each other for the most part.

After a long afternoon of exploration, you can get to know the Castle District fairly well, as you traverse its cobblestone streets and take in its historic buildings. It is best covered on foot.

However, learning to find your way around Pest will probably take more time than you plan to spend in Hungary. Most of Budapest's ancient monuments lie within the "Inner City" of Pest, including many of the leading hotels, night clubs, and restaurants, along with the major government buildings such as Parliament.

The **Nagykörút** or "Great Boulevard" forms a half moon in Pest, stretching for nearly four miles. It takes in all of Pest from Margaret Bridge to Petőfi Bridge, and, along the way, it changes its name four times (at one point, it is called Lenin Körút).

The other major avenue of Pest (and I don't expect you to learn to pronounce it right away) is **Népköztársaság** útja, which was patterned after the Champs-Elysées. It stretches from the Inner Boulevard to the Municipal Park.

Pest also has a pedestrian-only shopping street, called **Kígyo utca,** which is laid out between Váci utca (also good for shopping) and Felszabadulás tér or "Square of Liberation."

In the center of the Danube lies Margaret Island, a spa garden 1½ miles long.

HOTELS: As part of the government's energetic program to develop tourism, a glistening collection of elegant hotels has replaced the 19th-century dinosaurs that used to front the Danube. Many of the new hotels are affiliated with chains in the West, including Hilton, Inter-Continental, and Novotel.

However, in spite of this, shortages are reported every season from the first of May until early in the autumn. Therefore it's always imperative to secure a reservation. There are many hotels in Budapest which charge far cheaper prices than those I've cited here. The catch is, they're almost always fully booked in spring, summer, and autumn by Soviet-bloc tour groups. Therefore it's pointless to describe them because, chances are, you wouldn't get in any way.

All the hotels, including the deluxe and upper bracket ones, are reasonable in price when compared to those in Western capitals.

Deluxe Choices

Hilton Hotel, 1-3 Hess András tér (tel. 853-500). Few hotels have created the kind of attention in the design and architectural world that greeted the opening of the Hilton in Budapest in 1977. Critics hailed it as an intelligent and tasteful blend of one of the most historic sections of medieval Buda with a gleaming modern hotel, and a quick walk through its public rooms will show you why. The 700-year-old walls of a 13th-century Dominican church were incorporated into the design, as well as the restored baroque facade of a 17th-century Jesuit university. It is this ornate facade, covered with draping laurel garlands, which a guest sees first, as he or she walks or drives through the narrow cobblestone streets of Castle Hill.

The hotel is next door to the most potent symbol of the Hungarian nation, the Matthias Church, and just above the neo-Gothic Fishermen's Bastion. Views across the Danube from the windows of the well-furnished bedrooms—which correspond to the high standards of Hiltons everywhere—encompass sweeping panoramas of the Hungarian Parliament and 19th-century Pest. As you walk through the sunny public rooms of this hotel you can look directly into the partially rebuilt nave of a 13th-century church, which is used as the setting for summertime operas, ballets, and musical concerts which you can watch from the huge windows of the glittering lounge area.

Each of the 323 guest rooms contains a color TV set with in-house movies, as well as all the accessories and extras you'd expect from a deluxe modern palace. On the premises are three restaurants, several bars, and a breakfast buffet so plentiful you could skip lunch. There's also a nearby disco, plus the only gambling casino in Budapest.

Guests who want to go swimming have free access to the pool at the Thermal Hotel Margitsziget, which is connected by hotel bus. Rates range from $63 to $99 daily in a single and from $86 to $120 in a double. Prices vary with the season and the view. For more information, see my restaurant and nightlife recommendations.

Hotel Duna Inter-Continental, 4 Apáczai Csere János Utca (tel. 175-122), in the heart of downtown Pest, was built on a desirable riverfront location affording dramatic views of Castle Hill and the stream of the Danube's traffic. This is perhaps the best established of the new palaces along the river. It was built in 1969 as one of the first modern hotels, and changed the face of tourism in Budapest. Three older hotels were demolished to make room for this silver-and-glass 12-story building with views from its thousands of oversize windows. Since that time it has housed presidents, visiting dignitaries, pop stars, and film celebrities. Elizabeth Taylor celebrated her 40th birthday here while filming *The Blue Bird.*

The side of the hotel facing away from the Danube, toward Pest, is an enormous expanse of stressed concrete, a design which permits each room to have a view of the river. The big lobby area is flooded with sunlight from large windows and has gold-tinted rugs, pin lighting, and lots of plants. It leads into what might be my favorite bar in Budapest, the Gypsy Bar. This has a soothing collection of dark fabrics, stone walls, lots of intimate niches, and a remarkable collection of hooked tapestries covered with geometric figures and mythological beasts cavorting against vivid splashes of color.

The conservatively tasteful bedrooms have all the necessary accessories and up-to-date amenities to satisfy the constantly flowing stream of international clients. Singles cost 2400 Ft. ($53.45) and 3350 Ft. ($74.61), while doubles range from 3300 Ft. ($73.49) to 4050 Ft. ($90.19).

On the premises are four restaurants, two bars, all kinds of boutiques, a beauty parlor, a florist, and an in-house movie system. In addition, the Business Center will handle many of the services a visiting business person will need, with available secretaries, photocopying services, and multilingual translators.

Atrium Hyatt, 2 Roosevelt tér (tel. 383-000), is built right on the river in a rectangular design of vertically interconnected rows of jutting bay windows fashioned of bronze-colored metal. As its name implies, its lobby is set up around a soaring atrium design, with what looks like the hanging gardens of Babylon trailing from the nine floors of balconies leading into the unpretentiously comfortable bedrooms. To reach your room you'll step into a glass elevator that will glide silently up an exposed channel. The soaring effect of the many rows of balconies ends in a corrugated steel roof supported with girders and trusses. From the ceiling hangs a full-size wood-and-canvas replica of the first Hungarian-made airplane, which you can study from the lobby's decor of fountains, plants, and comfortable

($17.82). Reservations are strongly suggested. The restaurant is closed on Sunday.

Café-Restaurant Hungária, 49 Lenin Körút (tel. 228-668), is the most famous restaurant in Hungary, a riot of rococo decor on a busy avenue in downtown Pest. The reproduced signatures on the front cover of the menu have been called a "time-machine celebrity register," since they contain the names of what were once some of the most important literary and artistic figures in the world, including Charlie Chaplin and Thomas Mann. This is the last of the approximately 30 coffeehouses that between the wars hosted virtually every liberal thinker in Hungary, and provided a setting where much of the Hungarian literature of the 20th century was written.

It also provided a place for dandified members of the leisure class to while away endless hours gossiping and staring into the leering faces of the satyrs that support the globe lights of the entranceway.

Christened Café New York because of its home in the branch office of an American insurance firm, the establishment's name was changed to the Hungária by one of the state catering firms in 1954. It was closed again by the socialist regime, which claimed that some of the seeds of the 1956 revolution were fermented here. The German and Russian bombs which rained down on this part of town in 1945 and 1956 destroyed the ornate tower that was rebuilt twice in the same obelisk-capped style.

The Hungarian government has spent a vast sum restoring the marble and gilt interior. You can still order fiery goulash, or a waldorf salad, fish cocktail, fried strips of carp, paprika chicken, sauteed chicken marengo style, ribsteak in paprika sauce, sponge cake with chocolate sauce, or pancakes Gundel.

There are dozens of places to sit, many below the beige, marble, and gilt-covered capitals that are still emblazoned "NY," but the best place to dine is in "Deep Water." This is the lowest part of the café, reachable via a wide carpeted stairwell, where vested waiters offer attentive service and where dancers from all parts of Hungary and Gypsy musicians provide evening entertainment. Note that it's customary to palm a small compensation, around 100 Ft. ($2.23), to the smiling leader as he comes to your table to ask for musical requests. With drinks included, a full meal will cost around 500 Ft. ($11.14). It's open daily from 7 a.m. to 10 p.m.

Gundel Restaurant, 2 Állatkerti út (tel. 221-002). From the flowered terrace of this landmark restaurant, built near the city zoo in 1873, you can hear the lions roar. In fact as you approach the symmetrically ornate facade you'll be able to make out the sculpted animal heads emerging from the stonework. A uniformed doorman will usher you into a high-ceilinged reception area surrounded with beautifully etched glass and porphyry trim. The sunny and somber dining room is flooded with sunlight from the big windows and accented with red marble columns, potted palms, and photos of Budapest between the World Wars.

The most famous owner of this restaurant was one of Hungarian gastronomy's most important contributors. Dubbed the Hungarian Escoffier, he invented pancakes Gundel, that chocolate-covered flambéed dessert which now appears so often on menus throughout Hungary. Although long gone from the premises (which are now directed by a state catering firm), the restaurant is still highly regarded. In fact the meals for Mrs. Thatcher's 1984 state visit to Budapest were cooked in the kitchens of this establishment.

If you show up any day of the week between noon and 4 p.m. and from 7 p.m. to midnight, you too can taste Hungarian specialties that are reputed to be among the best in Budapest. The items, served on the gold and white china, include pheasant pie with cumberland sauce, crêpes stuffed with fowl, Hungarian mushroom soup, Serbian-style carp, filet of goulash, a stew of prawns and mussels cooked in "the sailors' way," goose breast with a goose-giblet risotto, braised quails, and rosemary-flavored roast of lamb. Count on spending about 700 Ft. ($15.59). The restaurant is closed for Sunday supper in winter. To reach it, take bus 1 or 4 or trolley 72.

Restaurant Kalocsa, Hotel Hilton (tel. 853-500). If you like provincial patterns of flowers and hearts along with formal, impeccably organized service, you'll gravitate to this dimly lit restaurant. It takes its motif from the town of Kalocsa, one of the most important folkloric regions of the country. It's there that the women apply patterns to practically everything in sight, including the walls, furniture, and even the napery.

A formally dressed waiter will offer you a traditional apéritif of apricot brandy, followed by a choice of a dozen or more appetizers. This will probably include a tray of cold hors d'oeuvres wheeled up to your table. Dessert too is wheeled in on a tray, as are the cheeses and liqueurs. All of this will be accompanied by music from one of the best Gypsy bands in Hungary.

Perhaps most important, beyond the nostalgic folklore of the decoration you'll have a stunning view of the far side of the Danube, with Parliament's hulk sitting almost directly opposite your table. Menu specialties include stuffed cabbage, stuffed leg of goose, carp soup, calf brains in beer batter, fish paprika Kalocsa, and poppyseed cake. Open from noon to 4 p.m. and from 7 p.m. to midnight, the restaurant charges about 500 Ft. ($11.14) for a full meal.

Mathias Keller (Mátyás Pince), 7 Március 15 tér (tel. 181-650), was built in 1910, close to the river, near Elisabeth Bridge. This turn-of-the-century restaurant has become a Budapest landmark. It was conceived in a labyrinthine format of stained glass, lots of detailed woodwork, graceful wooden chairs, and a series of wall frescoes of scenes taken from the life of King Matthias Corvinus. You'll enter a glass door from the sidewalk into a spacious vestibule area and leave your coats with the attendant before heading down a long hallway decorated with green and beige illustrations from the adventures of Bacchus.

The brasserie is on the left and the restaurant on the right, either one of which might strike your fancy. Hungarian music comes from behind a carved zither in a half-paneled area covered with green baize, which you'll enjoy while being waited on by a small army of uniformed waiters. You'll have many rooms to choose from, including an inner sanctum with round wooden columns capped with neo-Romanesque capitals painted in somber colors.

The Hungarian specialties include crisp roast knuckle of pork, bridegroom's soup, stewed sirloin cutlet with goose liver Budapest style, fisherman's soup in a kettle, quail with bacon, and roast pork with cabbage, which could be followed by chocolate pancakes flambé or a cold raspberry strudel. Full meals begin at 300 Ft. ($6.68). The brasserie is open continuously from 11 a.m. until 1 a.m., and the restaurant serves between noon and 4 p.m. and from 7 p.m. until 1 a.m. seven days a week.

Kárpátia, 4 Károly Mihály (tel. 173-503). The decor of this unusual restaurant is almost like that of a secularized church. In fact it combines many of the best features of medieval architecture with good food and attentive service. You'll be ushered through a vestibule into a Gothic fantasy of stenciled walls, ornate hardwood thrones, immaculate sea-green napery, and gilded capitals carved into patterns of grape leaves and animal heads. The high vaulted ceilings are embellished with leaf and vine patterns of red, green, and gold, while the wrought-iron globe lights are fanciful combinations of white glass and black metal. Even the floor is crafted from a combination of black and pink mottled stone, accented with ornate brass trim, which tends to complement the masses of stained glass set into the windows and into the tops of the carved Gothic banquettes.

The restaurant as you see it was constructed in 1925 by a well-known caterer named Charles Spolarich. His culinary standards live on both in the brasserie, near the front door, and in the spacious restaurant leading off to the back. Menu items include fried carp, boiled blue trout, sauteed goose liver Hungarian style, assorted strudels, crisp roast duck, pancakes Gundel style, braised beef with game sauce and bread dumplings, stuffed cabbage, and smoked leg of pork with beans. All of this you can enjoy every day of the week for lunch or for dinner (when Hungarian music is provided) for around 450 Ft. ($10.02) per person.

Grand Hotel Royal, 47-49 Lenin Körút (tel. 421-120), is a large square room with a 1950s-style decor that's among the best of its era. The hotel was rebuilt after World War II bombings and is a fine example of postwar modernism. The airy, spacious dining room allows lots of space between the immaculate tables. The impeccable service is performed by a well-trained, uniformed staff. The chandeliers look like inverted umbrellas with a Chinese twist of hanging circles within circles, with tinges of gold, plus marble accents in the wall fixtures that repeat the circular theme.

Inside the lobby of the hotel the restaurant serves such items as Hortobágy crêpes, three kinds of fish, stuffed sour cabbage, tournedos Budapest style, paprika chicken with dumplings, and Gundel-style crêpes. Meals average from 300 Ft. ($6.68) to 350 Ft. ($7.80), and the restaurant is open seven days a week from 7 a.m. to 10 a.m., noon to 3 p.m., and 6 to 11 p.m.

Vigadó Café/Beerhall, 1 Vigadó Utca (tel. 181-598). Near Vörösmarty Square on the Pest side of the Danube in the newly built Vigadó Concert Hall, this elegantly modern inner-city restaurant, despite its name, is more of a light and airy restaurant than a beerhall. The seating is divided among semi-private modern compartments formed from wood, starched burlap, and rattan accented with brass nails. Although the restaurant is large, you'll get the feeling of being in a much more intimate space thanks to the secluded seating arrangements.

The tables are butcher-block constructions, each two inches thick, and will ultimately hold such simple specialties as fogas Orly style, roast pork with asparagus, chicken in a basket, and smoked pig's leg with horse-radish, along with pork Kodály style and rumpsteak with roquefort sauce. Dessert might be a poppyseed parfait or one of three or four other pastries homemade in the kitchen. Meals range upward from 210 Ft. ($4.67).

Régi Országház Vendéglö (Old Parliament Restaurant), 17 Országház (tel. 160-225). A plaque outside the front door of this yellow baroque house on Castle Hill announces that the building was constructed on the foundations of a medieval house in 1700. You'll enter one of two forest-green doors and walk into a labyrinthine arrangement of rustically decorated rooms, the first of which has about the biggest stucco-domed stove you're likely to see. The ambience is one of candlelit intimacy among local residents, whose faces are dimly lit amid the regional-style plaster walls and the crudely vaulted ceilings. Throughout your meal a wandering musical trio with a surprisingly operatic soprano wanders gypsy-style throughout the rooms. The outdoor terrace might be a summertime oasis.

The vested waiters usually speak English and serve such specialties as Russian blinis with caviar, cold grape soup, roast trout, deer filet with bread dumplings, Serbian salad, green pepper salad, stuffed cabbage with dill sauce, larded wild goose (for two only), roast goose liver with madeira sauce, rumpsteak Gypsy style, and turkey breast Kiev. The restaurant is open for lunch, although its real flavor can only be appreciated at night. Expect to spend from 400 Ft. ($8.91) to 450 Ft. ($10.02) here. It's open daily from 11 a.m. to 1 a.m.

La Bodega, Hotel Flamenco, 7-10 Tas vezér Utca (tel. 252-250), is at the bottom of an elegant Plexiglass and polished hardwood stairwell leading down from the lobby of this hotel. The restaurant's vestibule is covered with depictions of jungle plants and birds, and eventually leads through an elegantly simple pair of beveled glass doors into an intimate copper-trimmed enclave of Spanish food, top government officials, and local artists. A central column supports a fanciful lotus-like copper sculpture which almost envelops the warmly textured restaurant. The decor includes hanging carriage lamps, blue and white tiles, comfortable yoke-like chairs, and lots of Spanish portraits. If you don't mind making this cross-cultural changeover, you'll probably enjoy this restaurant, ordering cocido madrileño (the famous stew of Madrid), gazpacho, garlic soup with egg, paella, mussels in almond sauce, sangría, and a medley of octopus, squid, and shrimp in wine sauce. The restaurant stays open later than almost any other in town (in the true Spanish tradition), and it most often will have one of the local university's visiting Iberian students playing a guitar. A full meal will cost around 500 Ft. ($11.14).

Halászbástya Restaurant, Fishermen's Bastion (tel. 853-500), adjoins the Hilton Hotel on Castle Hill. You might consider this an unlikely place for a restaurant, but actually the neo-Gothic fantasy called Fishermen's Bastion contains enough interior space to shelter a restaurant, and even a disco (see the nightlife recommendations) within its thick stone walls. One of the most charming places in town is the summertime terrace, open for lunch only. The management has set up tables under the stone vaulting of what looks almost like the ambulatory of a cloister. One side is open to a view of the Hilton and the Matthias Church, while the other looks out over the Danube and virtually everything on the far side of the river.

As you lunch you'll even be sheltered from the river breezes by glass inserts set into the pointed arches of the Gothic parapet. Of course if you prefer to dine inside, there's an attractively decorated restaurant at the bottom of a flight of winding stone steps inside the largest of the bastion's towers. Each of the curved banquettes is covered with sheepskin cushions, and you'll think you've suddenly been transported to the Great Hungarian Plain. The lighting is concealed behind copper wall fixtures, and there's even a scattering of puszta-style antiques placed throughout the labyrinthine arrangement of rooms inside. Menu specialties include beefsteak Budapest style, fish soup, bean soup, Danish caviar, two kinds of zander, and fogas meunière. Expect to pay between 350 Ft. ($7.80) and 600 Ft. ($13.36) for an average meal. The indoor restaurant is open daily for dinner from 7 p.m. to midnight. The colonnade terrace serves lunch in summer from noon to 3 p.m.

Fehér Galamb (White Pigeon), 9-10 Szentháromság Utca (tel. 160-809). On Castle Hill, not far from the Hilton, this pleasant restaurant faces a medieval-style square with an equestrian statue of Andras Hadik. The glass door from the street will pivot on a silent central hinge, leading into a small entrance vestibule. This rather startling debut to your experience is the result of the massive restorations that followed war bombings. The cellar, which today can be reached down a winding stone staircase past walls that were once part of the medieval fortress, was one of Budapest's last resistance points before the Soviet takeover. Today you can sit at one of the lower level's small tables and reflect on the horror that took place here. The ground floor is filled with vivid sunlight, lots of plants, and a huge black iron stove shaped like the cap of a witch. Big enough to roast an entire pig, it serves mainly as decoration.

The same menu is offered on both levels. Specialties include veal paprika, tournedos Rossini, filet of red deer, zander, jokai bean soup, Hungarian fish soup, Hungarian fruit soup, chicken soup, roast suckling pig, grilled pig's liver, fried slices of goose, roast pigeon, braised haunch of venison, boiled trout in red wine, and a dessert of, for example, sour cherry strudel. The friendly vested staff performs an excellent service, and your meal will be serenaded by Gypsy musicians who, of course, will probably deserve a 100-Ft. ($2.23) tip. Expect to pay from 350 Ft. ($7.80) for a full meal. The ground-floor restaurant is open from 11 a.m. till midnight every day of the week. The wine cellar is open from 4 p.m. to midnight every day except Sunday.

Hármashatárhegy Restaurant, Hármashatárhegyi út (tel. 888-780), offers a summertime terrace perched high on a hill which many Budapesters consider the most scenic vantage point for the entire city. In fact it's about 1650 feet above sea level, and if you're not dizzy from the altitude, you will be from the Hungarian wines and Gypsy music. Popular in both summer and winter, it offers a choice of such Hungarian specialties as potato soup, venison goulash, and a range of schnitzels and international dishes. It's open from noon to midnight every day but Tuesday. An average meal will cost around 450 Ft. ($10.02). You can reach it by taking bus 65 on Kolozsi Square.

Restaurant Plantan, Hotel Thermal Margitsziget, Margitsziget (tel. 111-000), is the glistening and spacious restaurant named after the rows of plantain trees that had to be cut down for its construction in 1979. In summertime clients can eat on the outdoor terraces with a view of the adjacent botanical gardens. A huge buffet usually simmers under copper domes on the big central table. The chandeliers are made of modern crystal, the napery is elegant, and the service is excellent. During the course of any particular meal the music might come from a team of Gypsy musicians partially concealed behind a wooden screen. The menu features six Hungarian specialties, including stuffed cabbage, veal paprika, frog legs, or filet steak Budapest style (with chicken liver and letcho). If these don't appeal to you, try the pheasant with apple purée, or one of seven kinds of fish. A meal here will cost between 400 Ft. ($8.91) and 500 Ft. ($11.14).

Fortuna Haz, Hess András tér (tel. 160-270), was doing a brisk business in the 18th century in a building which was partially built in the 14th century. Today, greatly restored, this popular restaurant sits across the square from the Hilton behind a stone-trimmed yellow baroque facade. There are several different aspects to this establishment, including a vaudeville and girlie show beginning at 12:30 a.m. It also has a Gothic-style restaurant serving good food. The dining section is reached through a carpeted hallway lined with pointed stone arches whose stonework has been pitted with time. The somber decor is accented with a big stained-glass window, iron chandeliers, and a coffee machine trimmed with Dresden-style china from Pecs. Menu items include carp paprika style with dumplings, crêpes Hortóbagy (stuffed with meat), pâté de foie gras, and paprika chicken with gnocchi. At lunch a tourist menu is offered for only 85 Ft. ($1.89). However, at dinner expect to pay around 700 Ft. ($15.59). The restaurant is open from noon to 4 p.m. and 7 p.m. till 1 a.m. every day of the week. The bar is open from 10 p.m. till 4 a.m. every day but Wednesday. The location is on Castle Hill.

Pest-Buda Restaurant, 3 Fortuna út (tel. 360-768), near the Hilton Hotel on Castle Hill, dates from 1880. It was already a celebrated restaurant by the turn of the century, catering to the "carriage trade" who came from as far away as Vienna. Today the tile-roofed building which houses it is marked with an ornate wrought-iron bracket hanging over a chiseled archway that serves as an entrance. Old-fashioned music accompanies your meal at this first-class restaurant. Menu items include such classic Hungarian and Viennese dishes as goulash and wienerschnitzel, along with excellent rich desserts. This is best as a dinner choice, but it's also open for lunch if you're touring in the Castle Hill district. Expect to pay between 500 Ft. ($11.14) and 600 Ft. ($13.36) for an evening meal.

Restaurant Százéves (Hundred-Year-Old Restaurant), 2 Pesti Barnabás Utca (tel. 183-608), is the oldest restaurant in continuous operation in Budapest. It adopted its name on the 100th anniversary of its establishment, and even though a more accurate statement of its age would be 150, no one seems to want to change the name of an already-proven success. The cream-colored walls are dotted with copper vessels and rustic bric-a-brac, and much of the service and some of the cookery are performed on a rolling cart close to your table. Menu items include Transylvanian specialties as well as trout, roast pheasant, venison stew with mushrooms, goose liver Hungarian style, and lobster soup. It's open daily from 11:30 a.m. to midnight. Meals range upward from 450 Ft. ($10.02).

Ménes Csárda, 15 Apáczai Csere János Utca (tel. 170-803). The simple interior is ringed with huge photographs of stallions racing across the puszta and accented with wooden beams and immaculate napery. This relatively new restaurant is in Pest, near the riverside hotel palaces that have begun to change the face of Budapest. Meals served below the vaulted ceilings include such Hungarian specialties as stuffed spiced quail, goulash of filet of pork, Hungarian ragoûts prepared at the table, sour cherry strudel, and a full array of Hungarian wines. It's open seven days a week from noon to midnight, serving meals which range upward from 450 Ft. ($10.02). The waiters wear regional costumes, and the musical entertainment comes from an ancient instrument called a zymbalon.

Duna-Corso, 3 Vigadó tér (tel. 186-362). You'll enter from a discreet door covered with white lace curtains which face the red obelisk at the side of the Inter-Continental Hotel. A horseshoe-shaped copper-topped bar near the coatroom is the first thing you'll see, where a changing collection of disco music plays softly. The attractive restaurant is covered with soft red and white wallpaper, a stone floor cut into geometric patterns of the same colors, and immaculate napery. You'll be only a stone's throw from the opera and the operetta house, although the clientele is strictly middle-class Hungarians who come here for the good value of the inexpensive and well-prepared food. This includes fish soup, zander (fish) filet, oxtail soup, trout, goose liver with mushrooms, medallions of veal Budapest style, half a roast hen with french fries, nine kinds of salad, and six kinds of liver, including baked goose liver with potatoes. For dessert, try a cheese concoction, vargabeles, which originated in Transylvania, or a strudel made with morello cherries. Fixed-price meals go for an unbelievable 40 Ft. (89¢), while à la carte can range from anywhere from 60 Ft. ($1.34) to 180 Ft. ($4.01).

Restaurant Borkatakomba, 64-67 Nagy Tétényi Utca (464-859). One hundred years ago the stone vaults cut into the limestone here were used as wine catacombs. Today they're the most famous in the city, and have been transformed into a rustic and unpretentious restaurant where you can sit on wooden casks and taste the most recent (or one of the older) vintages. The location is at Budafok, a suburb southwest of Budapest. The caves have been gaily decorated in a regional style, and the food is full-bodied Hungarian. It's good fun, inexpensive, and is frequently accompanied by Gypsy music entertainment in the evening. Meals range upward from 300 Ft. ($6.68), but this does not include a 100-Ft. ($2.23) tip for the musicians, which you should discreetly give to the leader when he comes up to your table. It's open every day except Tuesday from 5 p.m. to midnight.

Bajkál Restaurant, 1-3 Semmelweis Utca (tel. 176-839). On the ground floor of the House of Soviet Culture and Sciences, near a busy street corner in the heart of commercial Pest, is an outpost of Soviet decor, food, and culture in the middle of the inner city. You'll be greeted near the door by the sight of a huge bronze samovar whose polished sides dimly reflect the vivid patterns of provincial-inspired colors decorating the walls. The menu reflects recipes from all parts of the Soviet Union. It includes a series of unpronounceable names, the most easily recognizable of which will be "borscht" and "shashlik," although the waiter will probably be able to help guide you through in his faltering English. Meals range upward from 450 Ft. ($10.02), and the restaurant is open from 10 a.m. to 10 p.m. every day but Sunday and holidays.

Restaurant Napoletana, 3 Petöfi tér (tel. 185-714), kittycorner from the Hotel Inter-Continental, is an Italian-style pizzeria with a trendy decor of potted palms, orange plastic chairs, and orange tablecloths. It also has lots of Hungarian touches—uniformed waiters, white marble floors, wine glasses in modern designs, and rock music performed by a live band in the evening. It may be confusing to spot this place, since the words for Italian restaurant are emblazoned in red, green, and white letters on three different picture windows in three different languages (none of them English). The menu is written in misspelled Italian and correctly spelled Hungarian, and includes four kinds of pizza, ten kinds of pasta, and a wide array of veal and beef dishes, including veal cutlet milanese. You can also order a selection of cold antipasti, Sicilian cassata, and a large selection of salads, minestrone, Italian bean soup, and many more items. Light meals cost upward from 120 Ft. ($2.67), while full meals will go for twice that. It's open seven days a week from 10 a.m. to midnight, to 2 a.m. in summer.

THE CAFÉS OF BUDAPEST: Most of the famous old cafés that were so talked about between the wars are gone. Café life is not as important as it used to be in the pre-television era; however, some of it still flourishes, as reflected by the recommendations below.

Café Vörösmarty, 7 Vörösmarty tér (tel. 181-708). This old-world establishment, when it was known as the Gerbeaud, was famous through Europe as a sort of twin sister to the celebrated Demel in Vienna. Now nationalized, it is considerably more proletarian than when it was founded in 1858. It caters to a diverse crowd of old women in fur hats, wealthy

Austrian tourists, and diverse students from around Europe and the Middle East. But every afternoon it produces the kind of gossip and semi-chaotic hubbub that seems to mirror the inconsistencies of Budapest itself. The decor includes marble tables and parquet floors in a long railroad-style layout of at least four separate sitting areas, all of them painted in shades of beige, pastel reds, and greens below reproduction gold and white ceilings. The establishment is known for its excellently brewed coffee. Always celebrated for its chocolate, it turns out a chocolate and marzipan royal torte that's positively sinful. Coffee ranges from 20 Ft. (45¢) to 28 Ft. (62¢); tortes, from 16 Ft. (36¢) to 28 Ft. (62¢); and marzipan, from 10 Ft. (22¢) to 16 Ft. (36¢).

Café Ruszwurm, 3 Szentháromsag (tel. 161-431). The government has declared this 17th-century coffeehouse a historic monument. The café on Castle Hill is within an easy walk of Matthias Church, and in summer is mobbed with clients wanting a taste of what is reported to be the finest pastry in Hungary. In tourist season the least crowded time of the day is between 2 and 3 p.m., when you might find a chance of a seat on one of the fragile Biedermeier chairs or on one of the gracefully curved striped settees.

The café comprises only two intimate rooms, the first of which contains inlaid antique cabinets holding a tempting array of chocolates and pastries, all of which are freshly baked on the premises. In the second room, a waitress whose frilly blouse is trimmed with the same lace as that hanging in the windows will bring you pastries from 18 Ft. (40¢) and coffee from 12 Ft. (27¢). If you're in doubt as to what you should order, try the sour cherry strudel. The café is open daily from 10 a.m. to 8 p.m.

Café Pierrot, 14 Fortuna Utca (tel. 161-229). The trademark of this place is the face of a clown miming an allure made popular in Paris at the turn of the century. It's owned by Ilona Zsidai, who was once the head of press and publicity for Hungar Hotels. Along with her husband, who discovered what had been an abandoned bakery in a house more than 600 years old, she painstakingly created an avant-garde enclave in the middle of old Buda.

The decor includes Philippine-style cane chairs bent into graceful art-nouveau patterns, a well-polished samovar, and an antique oven now painted white. The marble-top tables rest on cane bases, the grand piano is covered Mata Hari style with an Oriental rug, and the walls are dotted with pen-and-ink drawings vaguely reminiscent of Picasso. Above the bar a stuffed effigy of Pierrot, the French clown, hangs under one of the plastered ceiling vaults. In addition to the masses of chrysanthemums, you'll be greeted by Elton John's music and a sophisticated crowd.

Whether you sit inside or on the summer terrace, you'll enjoy the coffee (dispensed from an Italian espresso machine), a Hungarian brandy, Irish coffee, and such specialties as Sacher torte, goose liver sandwiches, rolls with Tokay wine cream, and an array of crêpes stuffed with such goodies as chestnut chocolate and whipped cream or a combination of nuts, sultanas, punch sauce, and whipped cream. Mixed drinks range from 60 Ft. ($1.34) to 75 Ft. ($1.67); crêpes, from 45 Ft. ($1) to 60 Ft. ($1.34); and Irish coffee, from 85 Ft. ($1.89).

Café Korona, 16 Dísz tér (tel. 161-591), is considered one of the watering holes of the literati. This might be a pleasant destination point after a walk through old Buda. A few steps from the city ramparts, on your way back from the museums inside the Royal Palace, this clean and unpretentious coffeeshop offers Hungarian poetry readings as well as illuminated display cases of cakes and pastries, many of them incredibly fancy. My favorite was a chocolate bundt cake with a confectioner's cross on the top. The shop is fairly new, and a bigger room off to the side of the vestibule has false marble tables resting on bentwood bases. The pretty waitresses will serve a simple selection of whiskies and wines from a well-dusted rack if you want them to. Cakes range upward from 15 Ft. (33¢) and hard drinks, from 55 Ft. ($1.23). It's open from 10 a.m. till 9 p.m. every day of the week.

Café Margaréta, Hilton Hotel, 1-3 Hess András tér (tel. 853-500), is one of the nicest places in old Buda for a midsummer cup of coffee. Its entrance is at the rear of the Hilton, the side that faces the Danube. Its interior is a warmly inviting blend of well-worked paneling in two kinds of wood, modern crystal chandeliers, shield-back upholstered chairs, and peach-colored upholstery. The best part, however, is the summertime practice of setting up tables in the semicircular depression between the hotel and the neo-Gothic arches of Fishermen's Bastion.

Sheltered by the windbreak created by the architecture around you, you'll surely want to spend time savoring a puszta cocktail, a mixed drink, or a glass of wine, perhaps a beer, which might be accompanied by one of the cold snacks or a delicious strudel. It's open from 9 a.m. to 9 p.m. in winter, to 2 a.m. in summer. Count on spending from 100 Ft. ($2.23) or a lot more.

Különlegességi Café, 70 Népköztarsaság útja (tel. 111-870), is a turn-of-the-century café that was established by one of Hungary's most famous pastry chefs, Sándor Lukács. You'll be greeted by a huge display case as you enter from the busy commercial street in Pest where it's located. My favorite place to sit is in the "white chamber" on the upper floor, whose gold-trimmed decor has been classified as a national monument. All the pastries you could think of, as well as coffee, are available for 18 Ft. (40¢) to 28 Ft. (62¢). It's open from 8 a.m. to 9 p.m.

Művész Café, 29 Népköztarsaság útja (tel. 224-606), offers a quiet refuge from the activity of this busy street near the Opera House. Many of the clientele tend to be actors and musicians. The front room is usually more crowded than the back room, so you can choose the ambience you prefer. The walls of this establishment are covered in green silk, and the chairs are cane-backed baroque. Coffee and tortes range from 18 Ft. (40¢) to 28 Ft. (62¢). It's open every day from 8 a.m. to 9 p.m.

THE SIGHTS OF BUDAPEST: Don't go looking for skyscrapers in the Hungarian capital—there aren't any. But there are architectural treasures preserved from many eras of the city's history for you to see, as well as beautiful parks and streets, and many museums with displays to intrigue almost everybody.

Hours for the museums in Budapest and throughout Hungary are usually 10 a.m. to 6 p.m. All museums are closed on Monday. Admission is free on Saturday. Other days, the charge ranges from 5 Ft. (11¢) to 10 Ft. (22¢).

Castle Hill

Várhegy, or Castle Hill, a long narrow plateau, is the core of the Buda of the Middle Ages. The streets are still cobbled, and many gardens and courtyards are hidden away along the narrow alleys. Small palaces, mansions, many in the baroque style, and medieval churches have been restored after suffering massive damage in World War II. The Nazis staged the last defense of Budapest in the Castle and Gellért Hill districts, and as a consequence, were shelled and bombed by advancing Soviet troops. The district is surrounded by ramparts and once-fortified walls.

In the midst of much controversy, a Hilton Hotel was built right in the center of Castle Hill, the first (and it may well remain the only) hotel in the world incorporating and built around a 13th-century church. This gives the Hilton the unique advantage of being not only a hotel but a sightseeing attraction listed in guidebooks (see my hotel recommendation above).

The major attractions of Várhegy include the **Matthias Church** (Mátyás-templon), which was founded in the 13th century by King Béla IV. It was given the name it bears today after the wedding here of King Matthias and Beatrice of Aragón in the 15th century. The church, originally named Church of Our Lady, has been reconstructed many times since it was built, and the gold tile-roofed structure shows traces of varying architectural eras.

The Turks, during their 150-year stay in Hungary in the 16th and 17th centuries, converted the church into a Gothic-style mosque. In the Loreto Chapel you'll see a marble statue of the Virgin. The Turks tried to destroy it, but it was too big, so they just sealed it up and apparently forgot it. In the siege of 1686, however, the walls covering the statue fell down. The troops of the pasha considered this sudden emergence of the "Holy Lady" a miracle and did not try to do her further harm.

An important event here was the crowning in 1867 of Emperor Franz Joseph I as king of Hungary. Liszt composed the Coronation Mass for this great occasion. The last coronation in this church was that of the last Habsburg emperor, Charles (Karl) IV in 1916, after the death of Franz Joseph in the middle of World War I.

The church has an interesting treasury museum, with many sacred relics and stone carvings from the Middle Ages, replicas of the crown jewels of Hungary, vestments, and Renaissance chalices. Part of the museum is in the crypt. A baroque column outside the church is dedicated to the Trinity in token of deliverance from the plague.

High mass in the "coronation church" is held Sunday at 10 a.m.

Fishermen's Bastion (Halászbástya, in Hungarian), at the eastern end of Castle Hill, gets its name from the fishermen of the Middle Ages who were assigned the job of protecting the north side of the Royal Palace during any siege that might occur. At the turn of the century builders duplicated a Romanesque version of these ramparts and turrets. The walls were built over an old fishermen's village. No longer used for defense, the bastion provides one of the most dramatic places in Budapest today to take a walk if you're seeking a panoramic view of the Pest side of the Danube embankment. In front of the bastion is an equestrian statue of St. Stephen.

The **Royal Palace** is where the Nazis held sway in Budapest in World War II. The palace had been the headquarters of the controversial Admiral Horthy, but the Führer's occupation forces made it their command post. The Soviets reduced it to rubble in their push against the Nazis.

World War II was not the first time the palace was destroyed. Its construction was ordered by King Béla IV in the 13th century, and it was the ancient seat of the Hungarian kings, called Budavári palota, or Buda royal palace. In the siege of 1696 the Turks razed it, and it was rebuilt in baroque style following the liberation of the city from the Muslim yoke by Prince Eugene of Savoy. Today an equestrian statue of the prince stands on the terrace in front of the neo-baroque structure, completely rebuilt since 1945 with a healthy respect for its history.

The palace houses two of the most important museums in Hungary: the Historical Museum of Budapest and the Hungarian National Gallery. Before you enter the palace, walk to the edge of the terrace for a panoramic view of the city.

The **Historical Museum of Budapest** (Budapesti Történeti Múzeum) is in the south wing of the palace, 2 Szent György tér (tel. 160-607), accessible from Szarvas square. Here you'll find displays tracing 1000 years of the turbulent history of Budapest from Roman times forward. Magyar saddles and weapons evoke the ancestors of today's Hungarians. Many artifacts and pictures from the Turkish occupation can be seen.

Medieval passageways and fortifications discovered in the war-damaged building are now incorporated into the museum, together with much medieval sculpture. Of interest is the display of the construction of the Royal Palace. Among the furniture, ceramics, and porcelain treasures, outstanding in the Great Gothic Hall are white marble reliefs from the closing years of the 15th century, showing King Matthias and Queen Beatrice. One of the most stunning parts of the museum is the Hall of the Knights. The former royal gardens in their present layout are from the 15th century.

The **Hungarian National Gallery** (Magyar Nemzeti Galéria) (tel. 160-030) occupies the heart of the Royal Palace. This museum is devoted solely to the works of Hungarian painters and sculptors from medieval times to the 20th century, the major collection showing the panoramic sweep of the work of Hungary's top talent.

If you don't have much time to spend here, I suggest that you seek out the works of the celebrated painter of the 19th century, Mihály Munkácsy, who lived from 1844 to 1900. Of many of the country's artists who went on to national acclaim, Munkácsy seems to have gained the widest audience. See also the impressionistic landscapes of Paul Szenyei-Merse (1845–1920).

Gellért Hill

Gellért-hegy, as it's called in Hungarian, overlooks the Danube from a height of 770 feet above sea level, offering a magnificent vista of both Pest and Buda. The hill was named for St. Gerard who converted the country to Christianity and was martyred in 1046 by being tossed off this hill into the Danube by pagans who resented his efforts. Gellért Hill, to the south of Castle Hill, is one of the most beautiful parklands in Budapest.

The **Citadel** (or citadella), constructed by the Habsburg forces during Hungary's struggle for freedom from its link with Austria in 1849, crowns the hill site. The Germans staged a last-ditch effort here before the fall of Budapest to advancing Soviet troops late in World War II, and the fortress had to be reconstructed after the war ended. Its walls are more than nine feet thick. Today it houses a well-known restaurant, the Citadella, 11 Gellért-hegy (tel. 451-362), which was restored in 1984, with a terrace offering a panoramic view of the city and river, plus dinners such as steaks cooked over an open fire.

Visible from almost anywhere in Budapest is the **Liberation Monument,** called Hungary's Statue of Liberty. The monument honors the "heroic Soviet liberators" who freed the city from Nazi occupation, although those liberators have yet to go home themselves. The names of the soldiers of the Red Army who died in the battle are engraved on the monument.

Aquincum

An important Roman city with some 100,000 inhabitants at the peak of its power and prestige, Aquincum was the capital of Rome's province of Pannonia. Its name means "ample waters." It stood on the right bank of the Danube, about four miles upstream from the heart of Buda, at the place where Óbuda (Old Buda) was later built. Outside of Italy, the excavations here, begun in the 1930s, have developed into one of the major discoveries of a Roman urban sector.

The **amphitheater,** which dated from the second century A.D., has been reconstructed on the foundations of the old walls. Larger than the more celebrated Colosseum in Rome, the Aquincum stadium could seat 16,000 bloodthirsty spectators. Gladiators were sent up from Rome to amuse the legionnaires stationed at this frontier outpost of the Roman empire and the civilian populace. A fortress was later built on the site of the Roman city, and long after that houses were built where the amphitheater had stood.

Some of the artifacts found here are displayed in the **Roman Camp Museum,** 103 Szentendrei út (tel. 687-650). You can even see remains of the plumbing and heating system used by the Romans.

Margaret Island

Now a resort with two major hotels and a recreation area, Margitsziget, as the Hungarians call Margaret Island, lies in the middle of the Danube and can be reached from both the right and the left banks by the Margaret Bridge. The bridge, by the way, was reconstructed after being blown up in World War II—not by Allied bombs but when Nazi demolition charges went off accidentally in 1944, at a time when the bridge was in heavy use.

The island, 1½ miles long and only a few hundred yards wide at its midsection, was once the domain of the elite of the Roman empire, lying midway between where Pest is and the Pannonia capital, Aquincum.

The government has turned the island into the biggest park in Budapest, with a big city-owned swimming pool that can accommodate as many as 20,000 persons, a zoo where you can see peacocks and deer, and a well-known rose garden, with many other flowers flourishing in summer. A long-established spa draws people seeking the curative effects of warm thermal waters, which were first brought to the surface in 1866. Summer restaurants are popular here. Busts of some of Hungary's outstanding authors and painters have been placed in the woodlands.

At an open-air theater in the center of the island, theatrical performances, opera, ballet, concerts, and sporting events are likely to be presented during your stay if you're here in summer.

Close by the theater are the ruins of a 13th-century Dominican convent. Margaret, daughter of King Béla IV, was enrolled in the convent at the age of 11 and devoted her life to it. She was later made a saint, and the island was named for her.

A Franciscan church once stood on Margitsziget, but it is now only a lonely archeological "dig." The Premonstratensian Chapel near the Grand Hotel is a modern reconstruction of a 12th-century church. It contains the oldest bell in Hungary in its tower, one that somehow escaped destruction during the Turkish occupation.

The island is closed to cars, but if you're driving, you can cross the Árpád Bridge in the north and go as far as the car park of the Thermal Hotel. Better yet, travel there by public transport.

St. Stephen's Basilica

The two tall spires of Szent István Bazilika, on Bajcsy-Zsilinszky út, dominate the skyline of Pest. Work on construction of this church, the largest in Budapest, holding up to 8000 persons, went on from 1851 to 1905, with restoration being necessary after World War II. The 315-foot-high dome collapsed in 1868 and had to be rebuilt.

The hodgepodge of architecture of this church, dedicated to St. Stephen, formerly Hungary's first king, Stephen I, ranges from Renaissance to neoclassical. Two frontal towers grace this architectural mélange, and a bust of St. Stephen, made from Carrara marble, is over the major gate. Leading Hungarian painters and sculptors helped with the decoration.

Actually, St. Stephen's Basilica is a parish church—not properly a basilica, although that's what the people of Budapest call it.

Parish Church of the Inner City

Speaking of architectural mélanges, take a look at this, the oldest church in Pest, called Belvárosi-templon in Hungarian. The parish church, at the Pest end of the Elisabeth Bridge at 15 Március tér, dates from the 12th century. It even has a Muslim prayer niche.

A 12th-century Romanesque church was originally built here, but it was rebuilt in the 14th century in Gothic style. Two Renaissance alcoves were added in the 16th century. The Turks added their bit when they turned it into a mosque during Ottoman rule in Hungary. During the liberation from the Turks by the Habsburgs the church was damaged, and after it was gutted by fire in 1723 the baroque architects took over.

Hungarian National Museum

The oldest and most important museum of Budapest is the Hungarian National Museum, 14-16 Múzeum körút (tel. 134-400), Magyar Nemzeti Múzeum to the Hungarians. It even has the oldest relic on display to be found in almost any museum—the skull found at Vértesszőlős which has been placed in time at about a half million years ago, although one of my sources says 50,000 years. It's old, anyway.

The museum displays the historical and archeological wealth of a much-ravished and looted country. It's like a storybook of the history of Hungary, with its ancient jewelry and weaponry, a piano owned by Beethoven, and even a 17th-century tent from the Turkish occupation. A major exhibit is a perfectly preserved mosaic floor of a Roman house from the third century B.C. A gold teaspoon that belonged to Empress Maria Theresa and Franz Liszt's gold baton are displayed.

The royal regalia of Hungary is the most outstanding and sought-out exhibit, displayed in the Hall of Honor. In 1945 the retreating Hungarian army, fearful that the royal treasures would fall into Russian hands, turned the regalia, consisting of coronation robes, scepter, gilded 14th-century orb, and crown, over to the advancing U.S. Army.

The royal regalia rested at Fort Knox in the United States until it was returned to Hungary in 1978. The crown, said to have been worn by St. Stephen, the country's first king, is the symbol of national pride in Hungary and is often depicted in paintings. Latter-day experts consider that the crown dates from the 12th century and so could not have been the one used for the coronation of Stephen, but this doesn't diminish the Hungarians' pride in it.

The main collections here date back to 1802, although the building now housing them was constructed between 1837 and 1847. The neoclassical-style structure with Corinthian columns is surrounded by a spacious garden.

Museum of Applied Art

Since 1896 the Museum of Applied Art (Iparművészeti Múzeum for short), 33-37 Üllői út (tel. 175-222), has operated in this highly decorative, domed mansion of brick and ceramic tile near the southern end of the Grand Boulevard (see below). The displays give the history of ceramics in Hungary. There is also a collection of Italian-Renaissance textiles, Turkish carpets, clocks, ivory carvings, antiques, and 17th-century Flemish tapestries. Some of the work of gold- and silversmiths dates from the 15th century. Much 18th- and 19th-century English furniture is exhibited.

Parliament

The domed, neo-Gothic Parliament building (Országház) on the Pest side of the river may remind you of the Houses of Parliament in London, except that here the building looks out over the Danube rather than the Thames. *And* it's crowned by a red star. Standing at Kossuth Lajos tér, the Parliament edifice, constructed between 1884 and 1902, evokes the grandeur of the Austro-Hungarian Empire. It was one of the largest buildings in the world at the time it was erected. The dome is the same height as that of St. Stephen's Basilica, 315 feet.

There are 27 gates, 10 courtyards, and 29 stairways, along with 88 statues—a parade of historical figures of Hungary, from kings to generals. Out front is an effigy of Mihály Károlyi, who was president of Hungary during the short-lived republic formed after World War I. (Károlyi was forced into exile in 1919.)

Individual visitors to the Parliament building are not permitted, but travel agencies arrange group tours for foreign visitors.

Ethnographical Museum

Housed in an ornate 19th-century building at 12 Kossuth Lajos tér is the Ethnographical Museum (Néprajzi Múzeum), the country's most important collection of Hungarian folk art. Included are costumes, daily utensils, decorative objects, tools, textiles, religious icons, and many naïve country paintings. You can also see a collection of the art of Oceania.

The building, completed in the 1890s, was designed as headquarters of the Supreme Court of Hungary. Its main hall has been compared to a railway station.

The Grand Boulevard

The street signs read Nagykörút, but calling it the Grand Boulevard probably works better if you're a North American. It's also known as the "Big Ring." Street planners in the 19th century, heavily influenced by Haussmann's boulevards in Paris, laid out this three-mile thoroughfare, the heartbeat of Pest, to form a half moon, stretching from both ends of the big loop made by the Danube. Road construction was completed in 1896. The boulevard, which traverses one of the most densely populated parts of Pest, is divided into four different sections: Szent István körút, Lenin körút, Jozsef körút, and Ferenc körút.

Long celebrated in song and story, this is a land of theaters, cinemas, and apartment houses, as well as of elegant cafés and nightclubs. As you stroll along the boulevard, much will catch your eye, including a monument to Engels and Marx. You'll pass the Western Railway Station, the renowned Hungaría Café and Restaurant (see my dining recommendations), and the buildings housing the press organs of the Hungarian Socialist Workers' party.

People's Republic Road

This broad avenue, considered the most attractive and elegant in Pest, has witnessed much of the turbulent history of Hungary during the some 11 decades of its existence. Laid out in the 1870s and taking the Champs-Élysées as its role model, the avenue goes from the Inner Boulevard to City Park, a distance of almost two miles.

I defy you to pronounce the name of the road as it appears on the street signs, unless you're Hungarian. It's Népköstársaság útja now, but it has had many names over the years. Once it was called Radial Avenue, or Sugár út. Then for a long time it was known as Stalin Avenue, and for a brief period during the 1956 Hungarian uprising it was called Avenue of Hungarian Youth. The Gestapo once hung out at building no. 60, which later became the headquarters of the Soviet secret police.

The buildings along the People's Republic Road are an architectural hodgepodge, although most of them are described as neoclassical. They're interesting, often with a mosaic or a frieze on the exterior, perhaps a courtyard with a fountain. The State Opera House, constructed from 1878 to 1884, is on this avenue, and the first underground (metro) system in Budapest, dating from 1896, runs under the roadway.

Heroes' Square

At the end of the People's Republic Road is Heroes' Square (Hősök tére) begun in 1896 to celebrate the millennium of Hungary. A semicircular colonnade, divided by a 118-foot column topped by a winged figure rising in the center, exhibits a pantheon of Hungarian historical figures, including St. Stephen. Seven equestrian statues of ancient Magyar chieftains surround the column. Work on the monument was not completed until 1929.

A stone tablet in front of the Millennial Monument is the simple Hungarian War Memorial on which Margaret Thatcher, the first British prime minister ever to visit Hungary, placed a floral wreath.

Fine Arts Museum

On the northern side of Heroes' Square, at 41 Dózsa György út, stands the Museum of Fine Arts (Szépművészeti Múzeum), where you can see everything from the art of ancient Egypt and Roman vases up to the pictures of European masters, such as Goya, Rembrandt, and Murillo. Some 600 old masters can be seen at any one time.

Here are excellent works from the Italian Renaissance period, seven El Grecos, and works by Zurburán, Hans Memling, Dürer, and Vermeer. The museum is rich in works by French impressionists and post-impressionists, including Renoir, Pissarro, Cézanne, Gauguin, and Monet. See *The Slaughtered Ox* by Rembrandt and Titian's *Portrait of the Venetian Doge Trevisan.* Among English pictures, you'll see art by Hogarth, Reynolds, and Constable. A celebrated painting is *Esterházy Madonna* by Raphael, and *Sermon of St. John the Baptist* by Pieter Brueghel the Elder is worth seeking out.

Many of the paintings were shipped by rail freight to Germany in 1944, when the Nazi hierarchy was engaged in "collecting" valuable artworks from wherever. Miraculously, somehow the collection from Hungary was spared and sent back.

The building is right at the entrance of the City Park.

City Park

Northeast of Heroes' Square lies the Városliget, or City Park, a popular recreation center occupying some 250 acres of land. Budapest denizens flock here in summer to enjoy the big boating lake, open-air swimming pools, and the triple-domed Széchenyi Baths, one of the largest medicinal bath complexes in Europe. The botanical garden in the park has a wealth of Hungarian and exotic plant life. The zoo, one of the oldest in Central Europe, open since 1866, has some 4000 live animals and a monkey island in the artificial lake.

A fantasy castle, the **Castle of Vajdahunyad,** is a reproduction of a castle that once existed in Transylvania, in that part of the world which Hungary was forced to yield to Roumania. Housed in the castle is the Hungarian Agricultural Museum, in which the histories of farming, hunting, and fishing are traced. You can also visit a recreated wine cellar.

A most astonishing nearby sight, at least in Eastern Europe, is a statue of George Washington. It was erected by donations of Hungarian emigrés to the United States.

An amusement center, **Vídam Park,** roller-coaster and all, adjoins City Park. It's styled after Luna Park in Berlin and the Tivoli in Copenhagen.

The Danube Bridges

In an act of dubious military value, the Nazis blew up all the bridges of Budapest in their ignominious retreat from the city. This flagrant destruction took its place among such achievements as blowing up the historic bridges across the Arno in Florence. Before this devastation, Budapest looked with as much pride on its bridges as Londoners take in those spans crossing the Thames or Parisians in the bridges across the Seine.

After the war, Hungarians set about rebuilding the historic spans, and today they form one of the most beautiful sights along the Danube. In the course of your exploration of Buda and Pest you will doubtless cross them many times.

Budapest's two parts are linked by eight bridges, two of them being railway spans. They include:

Margaret Bridge (Margit hid): Built to French designs from the 1870s, it crosses the southern tip of Margaret Island.

Chain Bridge (also called Széchenyi lanchid, named for a Hungarian hero): The first permanent stone bridge linking Pest and Buda, it was originally built by Adam Clark, a British engineer, in 1849.

Árpád Bridge (Árpád hid): A spur of this bridge leads to the northern tip of Margaret Island. It's the longest of the Budapest bridges, about 1.3 miles, and connects the industrial suburbs of Óbuda and Ujpest.

Petőfi Bridge (Petőfi hid): Originally built in the 1930s, this links the Pest and Buda sides of the Grand Boulevard. It was named for a Hungarian hero-poet.

Liberty Bridge (Szabadság hid, in Hungarian): Once named for the Austrian emperor/Hungarian king, Franz Joseph, this bridge was constructed beginning in 1894. The first span rebuilt after World War II, it was renamed Liberty Bridge.

Elisabeth Bridge (Erzsébet hid): This bridge is not a duplicate of the more ornate one constructed at the turn of the century. When it was opened in 1903, it had the widest span of any bridge in the world.

Excursions

The wooded **Buda Hills** rise to the west of the Danube. You can take the cog railway of the public transport system to Széchenyi-hegy and to Szabadság-hegy (Liberty Hill). The train leaves from the terminus across the street from the Budapest Hotel. The journey takes you through beautiful scenery. On Széchenyi-hegy, you can take the Pioneer Railway on which, except for the engine driver, all posts are filled by schoolchildren—conductors, switch persons, telegraph operators, and traffic managers. The 1¼-mile train trip takes you across beautiful country to Hűvösvölgy.

You can also take a cable chair lift in summer, soaring about a mile, from Zugliget to János-hegy (John's Hill). You can get to either Zugliget or János-hegy by public transport from Moskva tér. The chair lift trip comes to an end near the top of János-hegy. From there, a few minutes' walk will take you to the summit where there's a lookout tower at 1735 feet, providing a panorama of Budapest. If the weather's right you can see for a distance of some 45 miles. The hills are popular for excursions.

Beethoven fans may want to take a trip to Martonvasár, some 20 miles from Budapest on Route 70. Here you'll find **Brunswick Castle,** once the home of the Brunswick family whose most celebrated visitor was Ludwig von Beethoven. The castle was originally built in the 18th century, but what you see now is a neo-Gothic structure into which it was reconstructed in the 19th century.

Music historians say that a number of Beethoven's compositions are connected with the castle and the park. Josephine Brunswick was rumored to have been his "immortal beloved," the woman to whom he wrote his famous love letters. The composer dedicated the *Appassionata* Sonata to the Brunswick family, and it's said that he composed the *Moonlight* Sonata at the castle. A bust of Beethoven is found on a tiny island in a lake.

In the castle on the ground floor a few rooms have been made into a Beethoven Museum, with relics and documents relating to the composer displayed. The rest of the castle is now occupied by an agricultural institute. The museum is open only on Saturday and Sunday.

In summer, open-air Beethoven concerts are given under the trees in the park surrounding the castle.

TRANSPORTATION: If you fly to Budapest you'll land at **Ferihegy Airport.** This is the only commercial airfield in the entire country, as there are no domestic flights. This is a well-equipped airport, and you can exchange currency here, as well as book hotel rooms or rent a car. Allow about 30 minutes to travel between the airport and one of the hotels in the center of the city. An airline bus makes the trip for only 10 Ft. (22¢), but you might prefer the comfort of a taxi, which will cost about 150 Ft. ($3.34), plus tip.

Budapest has three main **railway stations.** The main one, (and, chances are, you will arrive here from Vienna) is the east station or Budapest Keleti, 10 Baross tér (tel. 224-052). The terminus of the west station, Budapest-Nyugati, 111 Lenin körút (tel. 315-346), is the point from which trains head north to such cities as Prague and Berlin (that part of it which is the capital of East Germany). If you're heading for Lake Balaton, go to the south station or Budapest-Déli, 37 Krisztina körút (tel. 351-512). Trains also depart here for Yugoslavia and such points in Italy as Trieste and Venice. For information about train service in general, telephone 227-860.

If you're **driving** your own vehicle, be warned that traffic is very heavy in peak times in Budapest, between 6 and 9 a.m. and between 2 and 6 p.m. During those times you might prefer to leave your vehicle in one of the car parks you'll find by the underground stations or at any of the parking places in town and use public transport. You'll always be near a bus, tram, or underground line, and they go fast. It's almost impossible to park in downtown Budapest. You'll be more comfortable and get to your destination more quickly (and cheaply) via public transport.

Public Transport

All public transport in Budapest is handled by the Budapest Transport Company—on buses, trams, the suburban railway HÉV, the underground, trolleybuses, the cog-wheel railway, the chair lift, and riverboats. Most tram, trolleybus, and underground lines run from 4 a.m. to midnight, a few main lines having all-night service. Buses usually run from 5 a.m. to 11 p.m.

Tram and trolleybus tickets (yellow) and bus tickets (blue) must be purchased in advance, at tobacconist shops, train and bus terminals, railway stations, season ticket offices, terminals of the cog-wheel railway, travel offices, and from automatic machines. There are no conductors on public transport vehicles. You punch your own ticket when you go on board.

The yellow ticket, costing 1 Ft. (2¢), can be used on trams, trolleybuses, the underground, and the suburban railway to the city limits. The blue bus ticket costs 1.50 Ft. (3¢) and it's valid from one end of the route to the other. If you want to transfer you must get a new ticket. To use the underground, put a 1-Ft. piece in the automatic turnstile. If you're staying in Budapest you can save money by buying season tickets, good for one month.

Up to the age of 6, children are allowed to travel free on practically all public transport vehicles when accompanied by an adult. On riverboats they can travel free up to the age of 2, for half fare up to age 10.

You can get information on travel by public transport at the terminal of the suburban railway HÉV in Batthyány tér (tel. 370-716); at Déli pályaudvar (Southern Railway Station) (tel. 153-287); or at 2 Szabó Ervin tér (tel. 183-583). You can also get information concerning travel by public transport 24 hours a day by calling 17-80-80.

If you lose something on a public transport conveyance, you can ask about it at 18 Akácfa Utca (tel. 226-613). This office is open on Monday, Tuesday, and Thursday from 7:30 a.m. to 3:30 p.m., on Wednesday and Friday from 7:30 a.m. to 6:30 p.m.

Taxis

In Budapest, taxis can be ordered by calling 222-222 or 666-666. The vehicles are clearly marked with a "Taxi" sign. The meter shows 8 Ft. (18¢) when you start your trip, with 2 Ft. (4¢) added for about every three-tenths of a mile. To arrange in advance for a taxi to pick you up at a certain time, phone 188-888.

SHOPPING IN BUDAPEST: The Budapest shopping center consists of the Grand Boulevard, the "Big Ring," with its four parts (sometimes also referred to as rings): Szent Ist ván körút, Lenin körút, Jozsef körút, and Ferenc körút. Department stores and shops line both sides of the streets, with a broad selection of merchandise. The real downtown shopping however, is on Kigyó út, Petőfi út, Sándor út, and Váci út. There are three shop networks, Intertourist, Utastourist, and Konsumtourist, which have shops selling goods particularly in demand by foreigners for convertible currency.

Wherever you do your buying, keep any receipt or bill of sale you get here, since it will also serve as your permit to take your purchases out of the country.

Among items you may want to take home with you are hand-embroidered peasant blouses and other handmade goods, dolls in provincial costumes, leather riding whips from the plains, packages of hot paprika, and sheepskin jackets. You'll find albums and tapes of Hungarian and Gypsy music. Also offered here are items from Czechoslovakia and Russia which you don't find in the U.S.

Food shops are generally open from 6 or 7 a.m. to 6 or 7 p.m. Other stores usually open at 10 or 11 a.m. and close at 6 or 7 p.m. The larger shops and department stores are open until 8 p.m. on Thursday. On Sunday, only a few sweet shops, florists, and tobacconists are open, mainly in the morning.

Népművészet, 14 Váci Utca (tel. 185-844), offers a huge array of native handicrafts from virtually every region in Hungary. The inventory includes tablecloths, pottery, carved boxes, patterned furniture, and a wide selection of handmade rugs. The store is massively staffed with an army of pleasant saleswomen, few of whom speak English. Their selection is about the best in town.

Mintaterem Folklore Shop, 12 Regiposta Utca (tel. 185-143), sells a wide variety of textiles, provincial style embroideries, tablecloths, and pillows.

Fimcoop Stúdióbolt, 7 Apáczai Csere János Utca (tel. 183-912), is a consumer outlet for several of Hungary's lesser known porcelain factories. It sells regional pottery, as well as an entire dinner service of elegant bone china. There's also some etched and engraved crystal, plus a collection of Bohemian colored wine stems. They do not mail purchases, but they do a good job of wrapping whatever you buy. The store is conveniently located behind the Inter-Continental Hotel.

Fókusy, 32 Váci út (tel. 182-718), is an international bookstore operating out of a vaulted series of rooms in a commercial section of Pest. The art book selection is especially good, although they also sell books on Hungarian cookery (in English, of course) as well as guides to Hungarian architecture.

BATHS: Geneticists say that all of us are descendants of sea creatures, and biologists suggest that we are 90% water. If that's so, it isn't surprising that the natives of a landlocked country such as Hungary should savor their hours in the public baths. Bathing in the mineral-rich waters so abundant in this region are as old as the Roman Empire. Tiberius Nero ordered the first wells dug, and the baths he created were enjoyed and expanded by virtually every conquering race afterward. That includes the Turks who built—what else—Turkish baths at the water sources.

During the heyday of Hungarian nationalism in the 19th century the opulence of the baths rivaled that of private palaces throughout the rest of Europe. The widespread belief that the waters were good for everything from respiratory ailments (by breathing the fumes) to urinary and digestive disorders (by drinking the waters) to rheumatic and arthritic complaints became even stronger.

Today Budapest is still a city of therapeutic baths, with 123 thermal springs surfacing here, the waters containing large quantities of calcium, magnesium, hydrocarbonates, sulfate ions, and hydrosulfates. The springs from under Gellért Hill are radioactive.

Whether or not you decide to go bathing (and many hygiene-conscious Westerners have given up bathing in public places altogether), you might still want to walk into the neo-Byzantine mystery of the baths. The baths at the **Hotel Gellért,** 1 Szent Gellért tér (tel. 460-700), are perhaps the most photographed water spa in the world, and with good reason. Brilliantly colored mosaics cover the soaring vaulted ceilings, and the thermally heated waters churn into the swimming areas from the mouths of sea monsters skillfully crafted into dream-like expressions of grotesquerie. You'll see hundreds of people suffering from all kinds of real and imaginary ailments waiting in turn for what is supposed to be the beneficial action of the mineral-rich waters. The entrance fee is only 30 Ft. (67¢)—the same for the others—and the entrance is on the opposite side of the hotel which faces the Danube.

The **Széchenyi Baths,** 11 Allatkerti (tel. 221-220), is one of the largest in Europe. It's combined with open-air swimming pools. This complex of medicinal baths stands in a big park in the heart of the capital. It has a water rich in calcium, magnesium, hydrocarbonates, chlorides, sulfates, and various alkalines, which are said to be beneficial in the treatment of degenerative locomotor disorders.

The **Császár Baths,** 35 Frankel Leo (tel. 159-850), contains a beautiful thermal bath built by the Turks in the 16th century and a 300-bed rheumatological hospital for patients. The medicinal courtyard of the baths—surrounded by a classicist-style horseshoe-shaped building—is cool in summer as it's shaded by huge plane trees.

TOURS: IBUSZ Hungarian Travel Bureau operates tours in Budapest as well as in the rest of Hungary. A **City Tour** takes you on a three-hour sightseeing bus trip to top attractions, including Heroes' Square, Matthias Church, Fishermen's Bastion, Castle Hill, and the Citadel on Gellért Hill. This tour is given year-round at 9:45 a.m. From May to August there are tours at 9:45 and 10:45 a.m. and at 1:45 and 2:45 p.m. In April and September the times are 9:45 a.m. and 1:45 p.m. The price is $5.50 (U.S.).

A **Goulash Party** is a must when you're visiting Budapest. This is an evening tour with Hungarian food and wine, plus a spectacular show. They are available every night at 8 from May 1 through October 31, except that there's no Sunday party May 15 to June 15 and October 1 to October 31. The price is $17 (U.S.) per person.

See **Budapest by Night** in a five-hour tour including dinner with floor show, dancing, wine tasting, and Gypsy music. This fun evening is available at 7:30 p.m. May 1 to October 31, on Wednesday and Saturday the rest of the year. The price for all this? Just $25 (U.S.).

Tour **Parliament and the National Gallery** in Buda Castle year-round on Wednesday and Friday at 10:30 a.m., with a trip available at 1:30 p.m. from May 1 to October 31. (Some tours may be canceled because of Parliament functions.) The charge is $4.50 (U.S.).

If you're not going to the **Danube Bend** on your own, IBUSZ has a fine half-day tour by bus on the right bank of the Danube. You'll go to Esztergom, the early church center; Visegrád, with its medieval castle with impressive fortifications; and Szentendre, where you'll see the National Village Museum. In good weather lunch is served outdoors. The trip is offered starting at 9 a. m. on Tuesday and Friday from May 1 to October 31, on Saturday from November 1 through April 30. The price of this tour is $21 (U.S.).

A full-day excursion to **Lake Balaton,** Hungary's inland sea, by bus leaves at 8 a.m. on Monday and Thursday May 1 to October 31. You'll have lunch in the beautiful lake region and go sightseeing among the little villages. This trip costs only $25.50 (U.S.).

One of the most interesting tours from Budapest is a full-day excursion to a world-famous **stud farm** where you'll see a horse show and go riding in a carriage. You can even take a horseback ride if you choose. Lunch at a csárda (inn) will be accompanied by Gypsy music. This trip is available at 8:30 a.m. on Wednesday and Sunday from May 1 to October 31, on Sunday only from November 1 to April 30, at a cost of $26.50 (U.S.).

IBUSZ can book you on an exciting **hydrofoil trip** between Budapest and Vienna from April 1 to October 31 for $26 (U.S.) per person one way, $43 round trip. You leave Budapest from Belgrád-rakpart and Vienna from Mexicoplatz. The days of scheduled trips vary so make your reservations with IBUSZ as soon as you know when you wish to travel on the Danube—at high speed.

It's wise to arrange to take any of these tours before you go to Hungary, in order to be sure of having an English-speaking guide. Get in touch with IBUSZ Hungarian Travel Bureau, North American Division, 630 Fifth Ave., Rockefeller Center, Suite 520, New York, NY 10111 (tel. 212/582-7412 or toll free 800/367-7878). The main IBUSZ office in Budapest is at 3/C Tanács körút (tel. 423-140).

Another **hydrofoil tour** is available on the Mahart line, with service several times a day to show you the panoramic cityscape of Budapest from the water. For information and tickets, phone Vigado tér pier at 181-223 or Bern Jozsef tér pier, 354-907.

If you'd like a more leisurely **cruise along the Danube,** ask your travel agent about a trip aboard the new *M.V. Danube Princess,* a ship designed for special cruises. This ship of the P&O Cruises line travels from Passau in West Germany, stopping at Durnstein, Bratislava in Czechoslovakia, Budapest, Esztergom, Vienna, Melk in Austria, and back to Passau. You can luxuriate in good food, wine, music, and service while you pass along through the beautiful heart of middle Europe.

NIGHTLIFE: Budapest is the liveliest capital in Eastern Europe. Unlike the capitals of Western Europe, its nightlife is also inexpensive.

Maxim Varieté, 4 Batthyány tér (tel. 351-113), is the most opulent and most professional cabaret/floor show in the Hungarian capital. You'll be ushered into a large vestibule area whose entrance is illuminated by a Las Vegas–style neon sign above a dark street in commercial Pest. A series of hostesses will lead you to a cloakroom, and after a short wait you'll descend a red-carpeted stairwell to a well-appointed bar area (see the Casanova piano bar in a separate writeup), and ultimately to your seats.

The plushly upholstered semicircular seating area offers multitiered views of the round stage. Service is honest and polite, with a rigid supervision by the Pannonia hotel chain. Guests in the audience can include a wide variety of patrons, from vacationing Soviet military personnel (discreetly dressed in business suits) to Austrian businessmen on an off-the-record weekend.

The show is a nostalgic reminder of nightlife in Old Budapest, and includes the somewhat predictable assortment of dance routines, magic acts, trained animals, and a dazzling array of ever-changing costumes. Reservations can be made at tourist offices or at most of the bigger hotels. The entrance fee—which you can pay for in advance in exchange for a voucher—is around 200 Ft. ($4.45) per person, after which your first drink costs 250 Ft. ($5.57). If you want to order dinner the charge is 700 Ft. ($15.59), including half a bottle of champagne. There are shows every day except Sunday at 8 p.m. and again at 11 p.m.

Casanova Piano Bar, 4 Batthyány tér (tel. 351-113), is a warmly accommodating piano bar whose historic premises were said to have been visited by Casanova himself, as well as Emperor Joseph II. The piano has a bar built around it, and the music ranges from Latin rhythms to folkloric Teutonic. It's open from 6 p.m. to 4 a.m. every day. Beer costs from 55 Ft. ($1.23) and scotch from 180 Ft. ($4.01). The establishment is contained within the walls of the previously recommended Maxim Varieté.

Budapest Casino, Hilton Hotel, 1-3 Hess András tér (tel. 853-500), is the only casino in Budapest. In the tower of the Hilton, the casino insists that non-Hungarian currency be used as a medium of exchange. The 5-DM ($1.95) entrance fee must be paid in West German marks, and there's a change booth on the premises. The polite English-speaking staff is young and attractive, and games include French and American roulette, boule, blackjack, baccarat, and slot machines (which take only DMs). Winnings are not taxable and may be taken out of the country. Presentation of a passport is required at the door, and members of socialist countries, including Yugoslavia, are not admitted.

Bellevue, Hotel Inter-Continental, 4 Apáczai Csere János (tel. 175-122), high on the top floor of one of the best hotels in town, offers incomparable views of the Danube, which might be best enjoyed on a summertime weekend when the monuments are illuminated. The clientele tends to be a conservative older crowd, who enjoy the international dance bands and the changing array of food. The walls are crimson, and dancing takes place under a red felt canopy trimmed with gold braid. Depending on the week of your visit the cuisine might be Hungarian, Portuguese, Italian, Indian, Greek, or Indonesian. It's open from 7 p.m. to 2 a.m., and reservations are suggested. You'll spend from 800 Ft. ($17.82) and up.

Nightclub Havana, Thermal Hotel Margitsziget, Margitsziget (tel. 111-000), offers a little bit of Cuba in the middle of the most historic island in Hungary. In fact this is one of the top nightclubs in town. If you've always wanted to hear Havana-style music and didn't know where to find it, this is the place for you.

Housed on the lower level of the Thermal Hotel Margitsziget, the club is reached by going down an elegant marble-walled staircase with mirrors and brass trim into a scarlet vestibule whose doors open into one of the most colorful rooms in Budapest.

Curved rows of horseshoe-shaped banquettes with small round tables and quasi-art deco chairs are angled toward the small stage area, which serves as a focal point for the Latin music and the dance floor. It's open from 10 p.m. until 4 a.m. every night except Sunday. Hours on Sunday are 6 p.m. until midnight, when only recorded music is played. The entrance fee is 180 Ft. ($4.01) on Friday and Saturday, and 130 Ft. ($2.90) Monday through Thursday.

Halászbástya, Fishermen's Bastion (tel. 853-500). This youth-oriented disco, part of the Hilton complex, will offer what might be your only chance to dance under the vaulted ceiling of a stone-ribbed monument whose origins go back more than a thousand years. It's on the upper floor of the biggest tower in Fishermen's Bastion, and might be an amusing stopover point after a late-night walk on Castle Hill. Several side rooms—one of which contains a bar—lead off into medieval-style chambers, whose comfortable settees are often filled with trendy members of Budapest's under-25 crowd. An overhead crystal chandelier accompanies the flashing pin lights, while the music is up to date, danceable, and fun. Two beers cost 110 Ft. ($2.45). There's no cover charge.

Gellért Bar, Hotel Gellért, 1 Szent Gellért tér (tel. 460-700). The average age of the guests is between 35 and 60, and many of them argue that this is the best place in town to hear big-band and jazz music. The decor is undeniably 1950s, and although just a tiny bit run-down, it might evoke memories of another era with its leatherette chairs, diagonally patterned harlequin-style marquetry walls, maroon accents, and a big bar at the far end of the room. Even the ceiling is covered with a sculpture. The bar is open from 10 p.m. to 4 a.m. daily except Sunday. The club is reached through a separate entrance from the street, near the main entrance to the hotel. There's no cover and, once inside, you'll find mixed drinks costing from 140 Ft. ($3.12).

Horoszkop, Buda-Penta Hotel, 41-43 Krisztina körút (tel. 250-060), is probably the most popular and perhaps the biggest nightclub in Budapest. It's conceived in a labyrinthine arrangement of black-accented, dramatically lit, and plushly decorated rooms. Scattered throughout this elegant place are highly imaginative brass plaques depicting the 12 signs of the zodiac. Trying to find the representation of your particular star sign will give you the chance to explore the entire establishment, even that section with a view of the hotel's indoor swimming pool. The big dance floor stays open from 10 p.m. to 4 a.m. seven days a week, although there's never a show on Sunday. Admission is 100 Ft. ($2.23). A beer costs 60 Ft. ($1.34), and a scotch goes for 145 Ft. ($3.23).

Club 1,2,3,4, Hotel Asotira, 19 Kossuth Lajos Utca (tel. 173-411), is an old-fashioned strip and girlie show, with local maidens dressed in spangles and feathers, with an occasional magic act. The entrance fee is 80 Ft. ($1.78), and the show is popular with visiting tourists from Eastern bloc nations.

Das Durstige Krokodil (The Thirsty Crocodile), 10 Országház Utca (tel. 160-933). Johnnie Rae sings "Cry" on the tapes, but you'll also hear jollier American songs. This small neighborhood bar on Castle Hill attracts the staff from the nearby Hilton, as well as a smattering of low-key locals who enjoy the dimly lit tongue-in-cheek ambience, the mirrored shelves holding an array of liquors, and the off-duty Budapesters celebrating a free evening. Beer costs from 55 Ft. ($1.23), and hard drinks begin at 80 Ft. ($1.78).

PRACTICAL FACTS: Tourist information is plentiful in Budapest from the same sources listed under "Information" in "The ABCs of Hungary" (see above). The **Tourinform Office** in Budapest is at 17-19 Petőfi Sandor út (tel. 179-800). Here you can get answers in English to questions about travel, accommodations, transport programs, and other tourist information. It's open weekdays from 7 a.m. to 9 p.m., on Saturday to 8 p.m., and on Sunday from 8 a.m. to 1 p.m.

Emergencies? For help call: **police**—07; **fire**—05; **ambulance**—04.

Budapest **Police Headquarters** may be reached for other than emergency situations by calling 123-456.

The **U.S. Embassy** in Budapest is at 12 Szabadság tér (tel. 124-224).

Need a **babysitter?** This can be a problem not only in Budapest but throughout the country. There's likely to be a language barrier even if you're lucky enough to find someone to leave with the small fry. Deluxe and first-class hotels often arrange for sitters. Otherwise, you have to do some mighty fine negotiating at your hotel desk—and hope the clerk will have a kindly mother.

5. The Danube Bend

The Danube River flows generally eastward across Austria and between Hungary and Czechoslovakia on its long journey to the Black Sea. A short way north of Budapest in the heartland of Hungary, however, the great river makes a sudden elbow bend, cutting through the Börzöny and Pilis Mountains after it leaves the Czech border, to become a southward-flowing waterway. Steeped in history, the Danube Bend, framed by the medieval towns of Esztergom and Visegrád, is a little piece of geography that reflects the turbulent past of the Hungarian kingdom. The banks of the bend are lined with hills hovering over quiet riverfront towns and glorious with blossoming fruit trees in spring. Sheep graze on the slopes in the shade of 1000-year-old castles brooding over the Danube.

The river, a major transportation artery from prehistoric times, has seen mighty armies marching along its banks since Roman times. Empire builders of the Caesars established a heavily fortified defensive system at the important outpost, the Danube Bend. Good roads linked Pannonia with the rest of the Roman Empire, providing passage for traders and troops. A military road connected the military camps and forts along the Danube between Aquincum (a part of modern-day Budapest) and Esztergom. The roads they built served the Romans and also their successors in peace and in war.

Visit both banks of the Danube Bend if you have time, but if not, then you'll find the right bank of greater interest. The major towns to see include Szentendre, Visegrád, and Esztergom. On the left bank, the primary town to seek out is Vác.

The most popular tour of this historic region is from Budapest to Esztergom, moving toward the Czech border. Motorists should follow Route 11 along the right bank (the west bank out of Budapest), but don't expect to find any bridges in the bend area. You cross the river by ferry.

One of the most romantic ways to explore the area is by boat. In summer a boat departs at 7:30 a.m. from the Vigadó tér at Budapest, heading for Esztergom. A one-way ticket costs 80 Ft. ($1.78). The regular boat trip takes about 5½ hours. However, on Saturday and Sunday you can make the trip to Esztergom and Visegrád by hydrofoil in two hours. To find out about these trips, call **Dunatours,** 17 Bajcsy Zs út (tel. 314-533). (Duna is the Hungarian name for the Danube.) To vary the trip, after you leave the boat you can take a bus to Szentendre and there take a suburban train, known as HÉV, back to Budapest.

You can visit the Danube Bend in one busy day while you're centered in Budapest, and this is the common method for usually rushed foreign visitors. However, for those with more time, there are a few hotels that merit a stopover or a longer stay.

SZENTENDRE: A resort town some 12½ miles from Budapest, Szentendre lies at the southern gate of the Danube Bend, on the west side after the river turns southward. The Romans built a fortress, Ulcisia Castra, here. Then in the late 14th century Serbian settlers, pushed up the river by the Turks, moved in and founded the town. Szentendre Island is one of a number of islands in the Danube from the bend to Budapest. The town, with its Mediterranean ambience, has long been a favorite with artists, many of whom have galleries in their homes and shops.

The heart of the town is Karl Marx tér, which seems like a somewhat inappropriate name for a square flanked by baroque houses, mainly from the 18th century, built by rich Serbian merchants. Szentendre is one of the most colorful towns on the river, with medieval houses and shops painted in pinks, greens, and yellows. Castle Hill is the most storied part of the historic town.

Ferenczy Károly, the renowned Hungarian artist (1862–1927), lived here for a long time. You can see several paintings by this impressionist artist at the **Károly Ferenczy Museum,** 6 Karl Marx tér. Works by his two children are also displayed.

The work of my favorite Hungarian artist is shown at the **Kovács Margit Museum** at Washtagh Gy út. Sculptures and ceramics by Margit Kovács, who was born in Györ in 1902, are prized by connoisseurs throughout the world. Many of her bright clay and ceramic figurines are here. The artist left this house, in which she lived to the age of 75, to the state. Admission to the museum is 5 Ft. (11¢). For 7000 Ft. ($155.89) you can often get a copy of Margit Kovács' work.

You can also visit the **Serbian Museum of Ecclesiastical History** at 6 Engels út, where art from the 18th-century is displayed. The museum also has a superb collection of icons, some from the 16th century, and rare books.

There are seven Greek Orthodox churches in Szentendre. The first stone church built in the town was a 13th-century structure, now the most treasured historic monument here. **Pozharevachka Church** on Kossuth Lajos Utca is a baroque building with a Louis XVI tower. Inside is an 18th-century iconstasis (a partition on which icons are hung, separating the sanctuary from the nave). **Blagosestenska Church** on Görög Utca is a fine baroque building with 18th-century furnishings. The **Greek Orthodox Episcopal Church** on Alkotmány Utca has as its main attraction the rococo wrought-iron gate. The large decorated iconstasis is from 1777 to 1781.

A cultural festival is held in Szentendre every summer, with art and drama highlighted.

Food and Lodging

Restaurant Görög Kancso (Greek Pot), Görög Utca (no phone). This unpretentious restaurant serves simple Greek meals in a stucco and stone-trimmed format of friendly service and low-key residents. A coal-burning pot-bellied dragon stove is the sole source of heat. You'll find this restaurant at the bottom of a cobblestone street that runs toward the river. You'll recognize it by the iron doors which close like shutters over the stone arch of the entranceway. One of the many Serbian restaurants in town, this one serves pork liver, paprika chicken, and beefsteak with egg. Meals usually cost between 70 Ft. ($1.56) and 90 Ft. ($2).

The **Hubertus Pension** (no phone) is a family boarding house in a tranquil location at the end of a road winding through the Szentendre hillside. It's a modest 1930s-style structure with wrought-iron grillwork on the windows and a balustraded terrace over a one-story section. A huge painting, *Hunting Trophies,* in the lounge gave rise to the pension's name, St. Hubert being the patron saint of hunters. This room, with red velvet curtains and a piano with candles and flowers; has a homey atmosphere which guests enjoy. The hostess, Mrs. János Wahr, decorated the house herself, selecting antiques and suitable materials to make the place attractive. There's a small bar for drinks and a dining area decorated with antlers, where guests can savor Mrs. Wahr's good Hungarian cuisine. Try her potato scones.

The bedrooms, with their old-fashioned furnishings, are immaculate, the bathrooms attractive. Giant copper candlesticks and tile coal stoves contribute to the coziness of the rooms. What about charges in this comfortable pension? A room with bath is from 300 Ft. ($6.68) to 600 Ft. ($13.35) per person per night. That includes a full breakfast, kind words from the hostess, and, of course, peace and quiet.

VISEGRÁD: It's only a village today, but Visegrád, 28 miles from Budapest and once the site of a Roman fort, was for a few centuries the seat of Hungary's kings. It's about ten miles up the river from Szentendre. After the conquest of the country by the Magyars, Visegrád became the major center of the Danube Bend, and a **royal citadel** was built on the hill by the

Angevin kings in the 13th century as a defense against the Mongols who kept pressing from the east and the north. The citadel keep housed the coronation insignia of the Hungarian kings.

This fortress stood for 500 years until it was bombed by the Austrians in the 18th century when Hungarian rebels sought to throw off the Habsburg yoke. The ramparts have been reconstructed, and from them you have a magnificent view of the Danube Bend. You can reach the citadel by bus or by climbing the steep slopes.

It was in this citadel that King Matthias Corvinus was born in 1458. When he grew up to be sovereign, Matthias had a royal palace erected on the river down the hill from the fortress, a 15th-century Renaissance concoction that's impressive even in ruins. This palace was called a paradise on earth, its glory becoming a legend across Europe after it was razed by the Turks. Until digging started, many historians discounted the splendors which have been proved true.

The main attraction of the palace ruins is the parade ground with the donjon (the massive inner tower), built around 1250, in the center. Called **Solomon's Tower**, this structure houses some artifacts found in the ongoing excavations. The remains of an original red marble fountain, an outstanding relic of Hungarian Renaissance sculpture, are here.

Food and Lodging

Hotel Silvanus (tel. 136-063). You'll see this hotel as you drive up toward it from the bottom of a hill. It rises in a modern format of cement, glass, and tile, an attractive contrast to the ruins of the historic fortress a hillock (and a five-minute walk) away. Built in 1971, the hotel has a marble-trimmed lobby with lots of exposed wood, a combination bowling alley and coffeeshop in the basement, and a view of the Danube from the sunny terrace outside. In high season you'll probably find hordes of children and blaring video games as well, but the isolated position and the surrounding woods offer plenty of peace and quiet nonetheless.

There's also a self-service coffeeshop, plus a disco bar, tennis courts, and a brasserie. Doubles range between $17.50 and $31, with an obligatory breakfast costing another $3 per person. The in-house restaurant is an elegantly paneled room with huge wrought-iron chandeliers fashioned in a design that's solid, heavy, and very Hungarian. Since this is one of the most famous hunting regions in the country, venison is featured on the menu, as well as leg of lamb with tarragon and steamed barley, ground braised beef with mushrooms in white wine, stuffed pike, roast wild boar, and roast wild goose, along with larded pheasant and game stew. An average meal costs 300 Ft. ($6.68) without wine.

On the Outskirts

Restaurant Szöke Forrás (tel. Dömös 9), at the village of Dömös, is a pleasant modern restaurant which lies at the southernmost point of the bend of the Danube, some 10 kilometers from Visegrád and 15 kilometers from Esztergom. It serves as an attractive stopover for clients sightseeing in the region for the day. Its unusual design includes a sloping roof built in several distinctly separated sections, a raised terrace cantilevered above the ground, and large expanses of window walls looking out onto a secluded flat area.

The stone floor is laid in small rectangular slabs, while the soaring ceiling is fashioned of heavy blond beams. The simple menu includes pork cutlet Holstein, rumpsteak with mushrooms, chicken paprika with noodles, and apple strudel. Meals range from around 300 Ft. ($6.68). It's open seven days a week, with music and folk dancing in the evening.

ESZTERGOM: A small city 40 miles upriver from Budapest, Esztergom is across the Danube south from Czechoslovakia, a short distance west from where the river begins its fairly sharp right turn. There was once a bridge across to Czechoslovakia, but it was destroyed by bombs in World War II and has never been rebuilt. A ferry is the only link today.

Esztergom was a significant fortress in Roman days, and it was in this vicinity that Marcus Aurelius, Stoic philosopher, worked on his *Meditations* before he became Roman emperor in A.D. 161. The town became the capital of Hungary in the tenth century, and it was here that Stephen I of the Árpád dynasty was born and was crowned. Considered the cradle of Hungarian Christianity, this is today the seat of the cardinal-primate of Hungary. King Stephen (later St. Stephen) founded an archbishopric here and ordered construction of a basilica on a hill dominating the town.

Esztergom flourished, having its golden age in the 12th century, but it was totally destroyed by the Turks and was not really revived until the 19th century. The present cathedral was built between 1822 and 1860 on the site selected by St. Stephen on Castle Hill, called Várhegy.

The **cathedral,** 390 feet long and the largest church in Hungary, is in the classicist style, with a massive dome. In fact a prototype of the dome alone was made into a church a short distance away. One of the highlights of the basilica is the **Archepiscopal Treasury,** so rich that the cathedral is called "the Vatican of Hungary." It contains, among other exhibits, golden crosses from the 13th century and royal drinking horns from the 15th century. A celebrated work is the golden Calvary cross of King Matthias Corvinus. Admission to the treasury is 5 Ft. (11¢).

The southern side of the cathedral, the so-called **Bakócz Chapel,** was built between 1506 and 1511 and survived the Turks. During the construction of the present basilica, it was taken apart and its 1600 numbered pieces built into the side of the new cathedral. Franz Liszt, Hungarian composer, conducted a mass he had written for the occasion at the consecration of the splendid house of worship.

The remains of the **royal palace** are side by side with the basilica. Although these digs are only partially worked, Roman and medieval relics are displayed in an open-air lapidarium here. In the palace is the oldest 12th-century living room in Hungary. The most ornate part of the palace is the Royal Chapel. From the reconstructed battlements you get a fine view of the city and the Danube, even looking into Czechoslovakia on the north bank.

The **Museum of Christianity** (Kereztény Múzeum), in the Primate's Palace at 2 Berenyi Zsigsmond út, is the finest such collection outside Budapest. You'll see many Italian and Hungarian paintings from the Middle Ages, as well as Flemish and French tapestries. The Italian artworks, dating from the 12th to the 15th centuries, include paintings by Lorenzetti, Duccio, and Giovanni di Paolo. One of the most remarkable treasures is a 15th-century altar from Garamszentbenedek, a work of Tamás Kolozsváry.

The **Archepiscopal Library** is on Bajcsy-Zsilinsky út in an early eclectic building housing 200,000 volumes of the country's oldest library. Among the contents are more than 700 incunabula. The Water Town Parish Church on the same street is an Italian baroque building erected between 1728 and 1738.

In the midst of all its historic memorabilia, Esztergom is a lively, developing town, the cultural and industrial center of the region. You can enjoy the thermal baths here after strolling through the old streets.

6. Lake Balaton

The "Hungarian Sea," Lake Balaton, is the summer playground of the nation, with interest in winter activities on the increase. Since Hungary has no seacoast, this lake, 62 miles southwest of Budapest, is the country's Riviera. The Romans knew of the medicinal spas around the shores of the lake, but it took until the 19th century for the sport of swimming to catch on. Since then Lake Balaton has drawn hordes of people to frolic in summer—both Hungarians and thousands of foreign visitors. The waters of the lake and its spas have been praised by all comers, including Rabindranath Tagore, the celebrated Indian poet and Nobel Prize winner, who wrote: "I have seen nearly all the world, but nowhere else have I found the wonderful beauty of sky and water more enchanting than here."

Balaton is the largest lake in Central Europe, some 50 miles long, with a shoreline of some 120 miles. It's slightly larger than Lake Geneva, but unlike that deep body of water, this Hungarian lake averages only about ten feet in depth. On the southern shore the water is shallow, with velvety sands, while in the north the lake's bottom is flat and pebbly, and the water deepens abruptly. The lake is surrounded by plains and vineyards. Blossoming fruit trees draw visitors in spring for drives along the shore, which is studded with small villages where you'll see old churches and thatched cottages. The northern shore is dotted with long-dead volcanoes.

Lake Balaton is almost completely ringed with summer resorts and lakeside houses. The state has taken over many once-private villas as well as some hotels, turning them into holiday homes for workers from throughout the country who look forward eagerly to their summer retreat here. Cutting deep into the lake is the Tihany peninsula, perhaps one of the most scenic parts of the lake. The two shores are connected by ferry service between Szántód and Tihany.

Swimmers prefer the waters off the north shore, although with increasing crowds of vacationers you'll find them everywhere. So many bathers go into the lake that there's a danger of pollution from too much suntan oil!

Motorboats are not allowed on the lake, but it's filled with sailboats. A large program of water sports includes windsurfing and rowing. The lake is rich in fish, and even if you don't want to catch your own, as many people do, you can enjoy fish dishes in the *csárdas* (inns) along the lake. The most characteristic fish served here is fogas, a kind of pike-perch. Some fogas as large as 21 pounds have been caught in the lake.

In July and August Lake Balaton is vastly overcrowded. Never arrive then without a hotel reservation unless you plan to visit just for the day, returning to Budapest at night. Fast trains from the capital make frequent runs in summer, carrying carloads of holiday-makers, many of whom begin the party as soon as the train leaves the station heading for the lake. I recommend that you go in the late spring or early fall. The water is cooler then, but the conditions are less crowded.

Lake Balaton is not only a summer resort, although that is its main thrust into tourism. In winter parts of the lake ice over, and winter sports enthusiasts take over.

Sledging, ice skating, and a winter version of windsurfing called ice sailing are popular. Also, the old-fashioned *fakutya,* a chair-like skating sledge, has made a comeback in recent years. Fishing through holes cut in the ice has a following too.

Tourist information on Lake Balaton is available from four adjacent counties—Fejer, Veszprém, Somogy, and Sala. **Tourist Information Bureaus** are:

Feger County, 6 Szabadság tér, 8001 Szekesfehvarar (tel. 12-494).

Veszprém County, 3 Münnich F. tér, 8200 Veszprém (tel. 13-750).

Somogy County, 6 Szabadság tér, 8600 Síofok (tel. 10-900); Budapest office: 26 Wesselényi út, 1075 Budapest (tel. 226-080).

Zala County, 4 Kovács Károly tér, 8900 Zalaegerzeg (tel. 11-443).

I'll begin our journey on the north shore of the Balaton, heading west until I have eventually introduced you to the whole lake district.

BALATONALMÁDI: Among the major resorts of Lake Balaton is Balatonalmádi, about 70 miles from Budapest, lying on a bay and surrounded by hills studded with villas dating from the 1880s. You can reach this resort by car on the M7 and on road 71. The center of the little town is to the south of the high road, with an extensive park from which the quay reaches out into the lake.

This is an ideal resort choice for families with children, since the water here is shallow, unlike that at other Balaton holiday centers. Scheduled and charter boats operate regularly from the landing stage, providing transport to other points on the lake.

Roman artifacts have been found in the Almádi area.

Food and Lodging

Hotel Auróra, 14 Bajcsy Zsilinszky út (tel. 38090), is a 12-story glass-and-concrete hotel built on a slight hill above the lake. The interior benefits from the many big windows which flood the earth-colored furniture with light. On the premises are a tennis court, a sauna, a bowling alley, a rose garden, a vaulted tavern called the Kakas Csárda (see the recommendation coming up), a restaurant, and a nightclub. The hotel's private beach will rent windsurfers, and there's a swimming pool on the premises. Built in 1969, the hotel charges between $38 and $60 for a double room, with prices varying with the season.

Hotel Tulipán, 1 Marx tér (tel. 38084), is a small comfortable hotel whose facade angles itself around a street corner in the center of town. Its unusual design includes a central tower and symmetrically hipped roofs. Hungarian specialties are offered in its restaurant. Guests have free use of the private beach of the nearby Hotel Auróra, a five-minute walk away. With half board included, rates range from $35 to $38 per person daily.

Kakas Csárda, 14 Bajcsy-Zsilinszky út (tel. 38090). It's hard to believe that such a modern hotel could have such an antique tavern in its cellar, but that's exactly the case with this vaulted restaurant in the basement of the Hotel Auróra. A large part of the inner room is devoted to a trio of 300-liter wine barrels, although there's still plenty of room for the sky-blue tables, hand-woven napery, and a chattering crowd of vacationing Budapesters. The outdoor terrace includes facilities for barbecuing, as well as tables overlooking the park. Meals range upward from 400 Ft. ($8.91). The restaurant serves food from 4 p.m. till midnight every day of the week between May and September.

Muskátli Restaurant, 4 Marx tér (tel. 38154), is a rustically contemporary restaurant whose walls are encircled with well-finished pieces of vertical planking, cut into graceful semicircular curves. Even the ceiling is crafted from strips of the same wood, which produces a decor that is both imaginative and uniquely Hungarian. A manicured garden with thriving summertime roses surrounds the building. You might enjoy a drink in the cocktail lounge before heading in for dinner. Specialties are often prepared right at your table, and they feature recipes from different parts of the country. Full meals range from 450 Ft. ($10.02). It's open every day from 6 p.m. to midnight.

BALATONFÜRED: This is one of the oldest and best known resorts on the north shore, as well as being a first-class spa of international renown, with nearly a dozen medicinal springs. It's situated some 80 miles from Budapest and is accessible by either car or train. An old town with narrow, twisting streets, Balatonfüred's outlying country is one of the major wine-growing districts of Hungary. A promenade along the lake is lined with poplars. The heart of the resort is Gyógy tér, the spa square.

Rabindranath Tagore, the Nobel Prize-winning Indian poet, came here to recover from a heart attack in 1926, and to commemorate his stay in Balatonfüred he planted a tree that still flourishes in a little park here. The tree-planting started a tradition, which was followed by another Nobel Prize winner, the Italian poet Salvatore Quasimodo. Balatonfüred has long been a mecca for persons suffering from cardiac diseases.

The most popular excursion to take from here is to the Tihany peninsula, coming up.

Food and Lodging

Hotel Annabella, 25 Beloiannisz Utca (tel. 40110), has a pleasantly contemporary design of strong horizontal lines and evenly spaced rows of panoramic balconies. Its six stories include simply furnished, comfortable bedrooms, each with private balcony and bath. Some of the suites have wall-size photographs of autumnal forests and separate sleeping alcoves. On the premises are both an indoor and an outdoor swimming pool, a coffeeshop, disco, and a colorful and sunny Hungarian restaurant that is said to be the largest in the country. Open from May till October, the 384 comfortably furnished bedrooms rent for $39 to $62 apiece and are designed for two persons.

Hotel Marina, Széchenyi Utca (tel. 40810), is perhaps the best known and most up-to-date hotel at the resort. It consists of a tower building which soars up above the hilly landscape around it, and a low-lying section which contains balconied rooms with views over the tree-dotted beach and the rose garden. The enormous lobby area has beige and brown tartan carpeting and a modern airy design of wood paneling and big windows. On the premises you'll find a bowling alley, a large and beautiful swimming pool, an oval bar in an adjoining snackbar and brasserie, and a wide variety of kiosks and services. This hotel is open from May until October, during which period it's one of the most popular on Lake Balaton. Half board for two persons is $42 daily in the off-season, rising to $60 for full board during the peak season (from the last week of June until the last week of August).

Hotel Margaréta, 29 Széchenyi út (tel. 40821), sits in an isolated field a few minutes' walk from the lake. A three-story covered atrium extends over some of the comfortable and functionally furnished public rooms. This simple and unpretentious hotel is a good choice if you prefer a smaller hotel. The bedrooms have good mattresses, private kitchenettes, private balconies, big bathrooms in vivid colors, four-channel TVs, and three-band radios, all encased in red plastic covers. Uniformed waiters with impeccable manners serve ham, cheese, salami, crusty rye bread, and croissants with black coffee for breakfast, in a sunny dining room with gold napery and white-painted wooden ceiling cutouts. This is one of the few hotels in the region to remain open all year. Clients have access to the big indoor pool at the nearby Hotel Marina. The 52 bedrooms rent for $25 to $43 per day and can conceivably hold between two and four persons.

Baricska Csárda (tel. 40209) might be the most popular restaurant on the north shore of Lake Balaton. It sits in the center of rolling hills, within view of the lake. It has a vine-covered terrace for diners who prefer a view of the stars, although the beamed tavern and the vaulted cellars offer traditionally decorated intimate spots for dining in high Hungarian style. The big wine press dates from 1833 and serves as a sort of symbol of the establishment. It's open from April until the end of October from 11 a.m. till 11 p.m. every day. Meals range from 400 Ft. ($8.91).

Hordó Csárda, Baricska dűlő (tel. 40867). Among rolling vine-covered hills, this low-lying building was once used to store wine. It was also a place to barbecue sausages. A few years ago it was redecorated and expanded into a tastefully colorful restaurant which serves as a focal point of social life on the north shore of the lake. Every evening the management presents a floor show that you can enjoy while tasting such specialties as bean soup with cabbage and pork, goulash stew, fish soup, and strudel with poppyseed and pumpkin. The restaurant is open April till October from 11 a.m. until 11 p.m. every day. It's opposite the Hotel Marina. Full meals cost from 400 Ft. ($8.91).

Balaton Restaurant, 5 Tagore sétány (tel. 40266), built in 1962, is a large and airy restaurant with a high ceiling, potted palms, and a big abstract mural of boats sailing on the lake. A dance band plays in the evening for any guests who might care to trip the light fantastic on the dance floor. Service is polite and efficient, and specialties are typically Hungarian. It's open from 11:30 a.m. to midnight. Meals cost from 400 Ft. ($8.91).

Kedves Café, 7 Blaha Lujza Utca (tel. 40273), offers a quick stand-up coffee bar, a snackbar on the upper floor, and a more formal café whose decor takes advantage of the building it is housed in, which dates from 1795. The management hosts a Sunday morning puppet show for children, although many adults seem to enjoy it more. There are regularly scheduled literature readings presented by popular artists and actors (but, alas, only in Hungarian). In the heart of town, the café has a verdant sun terrace whose wicker chairs are a rendezvous point for visiting urbanites and their friends, all of whom seem to enjoy the brilliant sunshine. The coffee costs 21 Ft. (47¢), and pastries begin at 18 Ft. (40¢).

TIHANY: The most beautiful spot of the entire Lake Balaton region is usually conceded to be Tihany peninsula. This finger of land stretching three miles into the lake and containing some 90 acres, is a wildlife reserve.

Its cone-shaped geyser hills are covered with poplar and acacia trees, and there's a forest of lavender. The main village, also called Tihany, is on the hillside at the top of the peninsula, but the entire area is now a resort. It even has its own little lake, Lake Belső. You can fish in it as well as in Lake Balaton.

The twin-spired abbey, dating back some nine centuries, distinguishes the skyline of Tihany. The Romanesque crypt is all that remains of the building launched by King Andrew I in the 11th century, but I suppose that's enough for him: that's where he's buried. The present church and its adjoining monastery are baroque, resulting from work started in 1719. The abbey is known for its organ, used in summer for concerts.

The monastery houses a museum, and there's also an open-air ethnographic display which is a popular feature of Tihany. Summer is always active on the peninsula—and not just on the lake.

You can reach Tihany by car, but if you're traveling by train you'll have to get off at Balatonfüred and take a bus the short distance to the peninsula.

Food and Lodging

Hotel Tihany, Tihany-Rév (tel. 44091), looks like a tastefully designed balconied cube raised up on concrete stilts above the verdant garden around it. Near the ferryboat at the tip of the Tihany peninsula, the hotel is part of a resort complex of shady trees, tennis courts, mini-golf facilities, snackbars, and its own restaurant. Also on the premises are a disco, three bars, and a terraced coffeeshop with a sweeping view of the lake. The 138 rooms are open from the end of April to the end of September. During that period doubles with shower cost between $38 and $41 apiece per day, with half board included for both occupants. During high season, which is from the last week of June until the last week of August, the management requires that guests take full board for $61 daily per couple.

Sport Restaurant, Fürdőtelep (tel. 44016). If you dine in this circa-1920 house, you can choose between a seat near the panoramic windows overlooking the lake or a perch near the colorful wall murals painted into regionally inspired patterns by the women of Kalocsa. In good weather a series of simple tables are set up near the boat landing under the partial shade of a canopy. In the evening part of the establishment becomes a disco. Simple meals, featuring fish soup and other Hungarian specialties, range from 400 Ft. ($8.91). It's open from Easter until the end of September, serving daily from 10 a.m. until 1 a.m.

Rege Café, 38 Batthyány út (tel. 44017), near the abbey on the hilltop above the lake, is open all year long. The terrace might be the most popular part of this traditional coffeehouse, where menu items include drinks, coffee, and pastries. Coffee runs from 21 Ft. (47¢) and pastries from 18 Ft. (40¢).

KESZTHELY: The largest town on Lake Balaton, Keszthely is a place of many charming buildings and old streets. Dating from prehistoric times, this town, lying on the northwestern corner of the lake, attracted the Romans of course, and it was a flourishing market town in the Middle Ages. Its position as a bathing resort was established long, long ago. The first agricultural academy in Europe was founded here in 1797 by György Festetics, who also founded a library.

The most magnificent building in town is the **Festetics Palace,** its southern wing dating from 1750. In the latter 19th century many additions were made to the structure until now it contains some 100 rooms. The Helikon Library, with more than 50,000 volumes, is housed here. Much of the art that once graced the palace walls has been carted off, but some still remains to give the visitor pleasure. The museum of the palace, with a collection of antiques and documents, is of at least passing interest.

I most enjoy, however, a walk in the park around the palace, where many sculptures and ornamental planting please the eye. Summer music concerts are presented here. Much of the aura of the past century still lingers in the park along the pier.

Food and Lodging

Hotel Helikon (tel. 11330). On the water less than a mile from the center of town, this eight-story balconied hotel curves gracefully around its own private beach. The big windows of the lobby look out over a winding staircase which leads directly from an upper floor of the hotel onto the center of a small private island a short distance from the shoreline. The interior has red porphyry floors, low-slung leather couches, and an attractive English-speaking staff. In winter the management closes two of the floors, but stays in business despite the reduced flow of clients. On the premises are a restaurant with Gypsy music, a dance café, a big sun terrace, two bars, and a nightclub. Doubles range from $23 to $39 per day, with breakfast included. Singles occupying a double room pay a daily surcharge of $2. Full meals in the restaurant cost an additional $5.50.

Restaurant Hungária, 34 Kossuth Lajos Utca (tel. 12265). The most impressive part about this brasserie is the nine-foot-tall arched windows set with gold and white stained glass. Each of them is painstakingly set with heraldic shields and depictions of medieval cities. This is a Hungarian/Austrian restaurant, where Gösser beer is a specialty. The color scheme is tastefully wood paneled and sunny, and the banquettes are comfortably upholstered. A large central bar area with immaculate beer taps curves through the center of this popular restaurant, while an additional country-style room stretches out in back. The service is polite, and the other diners tend to be good friends and workers. Menu items include Serbian bean soup, chicken liver risotto, beef on a skewer, pork filet with mushrooms and rice, and an array of simple meats. Dessert might be a well-prepared cheese strudel. Full meals cost around 225 Ft. ($5.01).

Now, I'll make a short detour northwest from the shores of Lake Balaton to—

HÉVIZ: The most celebrated spa in Hungary, Héviz, only four miles from Lake Balaton, draws many visitors to Lake Héviz, the largest warm-water thermal lake in Europe and second largest in the world (the only other such lake, the larger one, is in New Zealand). The summer temperature of Lake Héviz is 96° Fahrenheit, while in winter it drops to 80°. The sulfide water is radioactive, and the bottom of the lake is covered with a layer of peloid containing mineral and vegetable components. The mud and the lake water both are said to be beneficial to sufferers from a number of ailments, including rheumatism.

Because this is a medicinal lake, one should not go into the water without first checking with a doctor. This is especially true for pregnant women or those persons suffering from heart diseases.

To reach the resort spa, you can travel by car from Sopron, via Route 84. The nearest railway station is Keszethely, from which buses leave every 20 minutes for Héviz.

A variety of excursions and entertainment is available in the vicinity.

Food and Lodging

Thermal Hotel Héviz (tel. 11190), built near one of the most famous thermal springs in the country, opened in 1976. Because of its wide-ranging spa facilities, it has more than a 90% occupancy rate year round, with 85% of the clients coming for some form of medical treatment, usually from places outside Hungary.

The maroon facade adjoins a collection of communal spa hotels which service the needs of Hungarian workers sent by their unions for recuperative therapy.

The elegant decor includes a series of marble-floored public rooms with leather armchairs, a plush restaurant with modern upholstered versions of medieval chairs and gypsy music, a brasserie with handmade ceiling panels of red and black patterns over natural grained woods. My favorite is the coffeeshop, whose end wall has a wood marquetry mural showing a dramatic version of a seminude charioteer in many different kinds of European hardwood.

The 203 rooms are attractively furnished with well-upholstered furniture and all the modern conveniences. They rent for $26 to $34 daily in a single and between $37 and $47 for a double, with breakfast included. Full meals in the restaurant cost $6.50. Prices of the rooms cited include only the most basic water treatments; additional therapy will cost more. The gracefully curving roof construction above the thermal pool is an awesome piece of craftsmanship, entirely built of laminated struts and beautifully grained wood planks.

By the time of your visit the management should have opened an in-house casino.

Back on the Lake Balaton trek, the next stopover is—

SÍOFOK: The largest and most important resort on the lake is Síofok, where an estimated 10,000 bathers can be comfortably accommodated on the beach daily. It was the long, sandy beach, in fact, that was responsible for the early popularity of Síofok. This resort has the best tourist facilities and hotels, as well as the beach, to be found on Lake Balaton. In summer you can attend performances at an open-air theater in Dimitrov Park.

Nearly all visitors come to Síofok for the beach and water, but in case of rain you might want to visit the Beszédes József Museum near the Sío bridge. The history of hydroengineering in Hungary is traced here, and you can see relics relating to the history of the town, plus fishing implements.

Every day passenger boats set out on scheduled journeys from Síofok's harbor to other lake resorts. For instance, you can take a ferry to the Tihany peninsula on the north shore (see above) without having to drive around the entire lake, thus avoiding the slow-moving, congested summer traffic. There are opportunities for rowing, sailing, or going on paddle-tandems on the lake. At the Sío channel near Síofok harbor, you can watch the action of the sluice gates, an interesting spectacle.

An Excursion

The most important excursion from Síofok is to Ságvár, 5½ miles to the south, where the remains of a primitive settlement more than 17,000 years old were discovered, as well as artifacts from the Roman village of Tricciana, which was part of the province of Pannonia. Clay pipes and mosaic floors once used in Tricciana were unearthed. The results of the excavations form a museum.

Food and Lodging

Hotel Neptun, Balatonföldvár-Park (tel. 40388), is the most modern hotel on the south shore of Lake Balaton. Equipped with a full range of recreational facilities, the dramatically angular skyscraper contains 210 balconied rooms, each with phone and radio. On the top floor there's a panoramic nightclub. The hotel also contains tennis courts and a restaurant and bar, and offers free admission to the beach. Doubles range from $52 to $63 in high season (June 23 to August 25) when full board is included for both occupants. Half board is offered in the rates charged in the interim season (from May 26 to June 23) and from August 24 until September 8), when doubles range from $32 to $40 daily. The hotel was built in 1977.

Hotels Europa (tel. 11400), **Balaton** (tel. 10655), **Hungária** (tel. 10677), and **Lido** (tel. 10633), 9-15 Petőfi sétány, consist of four modern hotels, all looking somewhat alike, set side by side along the lake. Each has long rows of balconies, big windows, and comfortably furnished unpretentious bedrooms, a total of 550 rooms. In high season, with full board included, doubles at all the hotels range from $22 to $69 daily. The assorted restaurants, bars, nightclubs, and cafés scattered among the four hotels are, of course, open to the clients of all of them.

From Lake Balaton, you may want to take some excursions "inland," exploring two of the most historic cities of Hungary. Alternatively, these cities could be explored on your way to the lake from Budapest.

SZÉKESFEHÉRVÁR: Halfway between Budapest and Lake Balaton lies the town of Székesfehérvár, which celebrated its millennium in 1972. For centuries this town, now an industrial center, played an important role in the history of Hungary, and you can see some monuments of historic interest here. The Romans were here of course, and their name for the settlement at this locale was a little simpler than the present-day appellation. They called it Alba Regia.

Before the Turks came in 1526 with fire and sword, Székesfehérvár was the site of the coronation and burial of Hungarian kings. It was the capital of Hungary during the Árpád dynasty which produced King Stephen I, later St. Stephen. An impressive 11th-century basilica stood here, built between 1016 and 1038, where 38 Hungarian kings were crowned over five centuries, with 18 kings being entombed here also. It was the resting place of St. Stephen until the Turks destroyed his grave. The Ottoman hordes left only the foundations of the basilica.

You can visit an open-air museum on the ruins of the former coronation cathedral east of the main square, Szabadság tér. In the Istán Király Museum (King Stephen Museum), at the corner of Népoztársasag and Gagarin tér, archeological finds and folkloric exhibits may be seen.

The Turks destroyed most of the medieval buildings, and the town was mainly rebuilt in the 18th century. The Bishop's Palace, dating from 1790, and the Town Hall are on the main square. You can see the rococo furnishings of the Fekete Sas (Black Eagle) pharmacy, the oldest one in the country dating from 1758, now a pharmacy museum.

Budenz-House on Arany János Utca, named for one of the founders of the Finno-Ugrian comparative linguistics institute, has in its cellar the only brick wall in town which dates back to the Árpád dynastic period.

Food and Lodging

Hotel Alba Regia, 1 Rákóczi Utca (tel. 13484). The name of this concrete-and-glass hotel is the same as the ancient Roman name for the town itself. The facade is dotted with evenly spaced rows of oversize glass windows, which flood the simple bedrooms with light. On the premises are a popular restaurant, a nightclub, and an open-air terrace. Doubles cost between $27 and $35, depending on the plumbing and the season. The hotel is in the center of town near the ancient ruins.

Excursions

Lake Velence, about seven miles east-northeast from Székesfehérvár, just off the M7, has some good beaches and docks along its southern shore, and facilities for water sports are available. Part of the lakeshore is thick with reeds, but you can see its rich bird life from a boat which passes through channels cut into the dense, reedy marshland.

The village of **Tác,** some eight miles south of Székesfehérvár on the M7, is worth a visit to see the remains of the Roman town of Gorsium, an important Pannonian communication center excavated in 1958. The nucleus of Gorsium was a Roman military camp built in the first century. Nearby, a Roman burghers' town developed and prospered until the fifth century. An open-air museum displays stone finds, reliefs, excavated sections of streets, commercial buildings, a large villa, an early Christian basilica, and ornate fountains. The cemetery from the fourth and fifth centuries is also interesting.

VESZPRÉM: Not actually on Lake Balaton but lying only a few miles from its north shore is Veszprém, Castle District, the capital of the Bakony mountains. This local cultural center is an industrial and university town, some 25 miles to the west of Székesfehérvár.

A town built on five hills, Veszprém is rich in historic monuments, with many narrow streets and dozens of baroque buildings from the late 18th century. The citadel was a favorite residence of Stephen, Hungary's first crowned king, and parts of the one-time royal castle were used in the **Episcopal Palace,** on Tolbuhin marsall út, built between 1765 and 1776. The first Hungarian bishopric was founded here. Next to the Episcopal Palace is the 13th-century early Gothic Gisella Chapel.

A written record from 1002 actually mentions the cathedral at Veszprém, **St. Michael's.** Originally a Romanesque building consecrated in 1060, it was destroyed many times, making a comeback in different eras in Gothic style, then baroque, and finally, at the beginning of the 20th century, as a neo-Gothic cathedral.

Next to its northern part are the ruins of the 10th-century **St. George's Chapel.** It was rebuilt in Romanesque style in the 12th and 13th centuries. This is the oldest structure (or remains of a structure) in Castle District. You can also see **Calvary Hill** with its 11th-century cemetery and remains of the St. Nicholas Church, which was built in the 13th century.

The baroque Town Hall of Veszprém stands on Szabadság tér, the so-called Liberty Square which is the center of town.

7. Western Border Region

This section of Hungary wears the most varied face in the country. It has historical small towns, spas, flowery villages, botanical gardens, forests on the eastern foothills of the Alps, medieval castles, and special folklore. Activity ranges from intensive agricultural production in the river valleys to rapidly developing industry in the large towns. This is an area rich in natural beauty spots and man-made masterpieces. The region embraces three counties, Győr-Sopron, Vas, and Zala, and is bordered by three countries, Austria, Yugoslavia, and Czechoslovakia.

The Hungarians often call this section Transdanubia, which means, roughly, that part of the country lying to the west and south of the Danube. This was a portion of the province of Pannonia in the days of ancient Rome's domination and contains more Roman remains than any other section of Hungary. In this area of rich farm country, vineyards, and orchards, you'll find more medieval, baroque, and Renaissance buildings than anywhere else in the country.

Chances are you'll enter Hungary from Austria. If you leave Vienna heading east, you'll probably go through your border formalities at the little town of Hegyeshalom (another important crossing is farther south at Sopron, coming up later). If you do come in on the major artery from Vienna, your first stop in Hungary might be at Györ. Even if you're en route to Lake Balaton or Budapest, this section is easily visited along the way and well merits a stopover.

GYŐR: A county seat and rapidly developing industrial town 80 miles from Budapest on the M1 motorway, Győr is reached about midway in your journey if you're traveling between Vienna and the Hungarian capital. It's called "town of the waters" because it lies at the confluence of the Danube, Rábá, Rábca, and Marcall Rivers. Győr, which was the town of Arrabona in Roman days, is attractive to visitors today in spite of its heavy industry. Its old core shows a strong baroque influence, and it is known for the Győr Ballet Company.

The **Székesegyhiz** (cathedral), on Martinovics tér, was founded in the 11th century, but many builders have had a hand in working on it in its long and turbulent history. In the 17th century its architects were imbued with the spirit of the baroque, but two centuries later neoclassicism was preferred. The structure suffered much damage in World War II. One of the most ancient parts of the cathedral is the Hédervâry Chapel, where you'll see a masterpiece of the medieval Hungarian goldsmith's art, the reliquary of St. Ladislas. The Püspökvar (bishop's castle) also originated in the 11th century.

Also of note is the Carmelite Church at Köztársasag tér (Republic Square), an early 18th-century baroque edifice. The Town Hall on Szbadság tér is a U-shaped, neobaroque, turreted building.

Food and Lodging

Hotel Rábá, 34 Árpád út (tel. 15533). You'll find yourself in the pleasant interior of an anonymous white stone and aluminum building that looks out over a parking lot beside a busy commercial street. Nonetheless the interior is unpretentious and filled with lots of comfort. The restaurant on the premises has two rooms, high ceilings, modern chandeliers, and a polite staff wearing forest-green suits. An average meal costs around 250 Ft. ($5.57), and rooms range from $10 to $14 daily in a single and from $17.50 to $36 for a double, with breakfast included. Prices depend on the plumbing and the accommodation. This is Hungary's largest hotel outside Budapest, with 195 rooms.

Vaskakas (Iron Cock), 2-4 Köztarsaság (tel. 22655). During the Middle Ages residents of Győr used to hide under the vaults of this medieval cellar to avoid the Turkish bombardments that used to shake the city ramparts. Today one of the city's most unusual restaurants lies behind the arched facade whose entrance is marked with a statue of a rooster. In the evening the stone vaults will be pierced with the sound of Gypsy music, which echoes happily off the white marble floors. The tables are covered with blue and white cloths, and flanked with rustically modern chairs which I was told are an adaptation of a medieval design. You'll find this place on a baroque square near the Rábă River.

The formally dressed waiters will bring well-flavored dishes laced with paprika and pickled vegetables. These include pork goulash, a Parisian-style schnitzel, veal medallions Hungarian style, and an array of roast meats. For dessert, try not to miss the Gundel crêpes, covered with chocolate sauce and flamed in cognac at your table. Meals range from 250 Ft. ($5.57), and the restaurant is open from 11:30 a.m. to midnight.

Jerván Kioszk, 1 Tolbuhin sétany (tel. 12686). Considered more a snackbar than a traditional restaurant, this popular establishment sports brick walls, hanging lamps, and a long bar area. Clients take meals on gold tablecloths; Menu items include foods from Armenia, Bavaria, Slovakia, and Thuringia, as well as traditional Hungarian favorites. A coffee bar with a big tree-shaded terrace is on the upper level. Meals cost from 180 Ft. ($4.01), and it's open from 11 a.m. every day.

PANNONHALMA: About 13 miles southeast of Győr on Route 82 sits a centuries-old Benedictine abbey and abbey church. This has been the center of the Benedictine order in Hungary for some 1000 years. The first Benedictine monks came here and took up habitation on the hill site in A.D. 996, building the first stone church in 1137. Construction of the abbey began in the 13th century. It was rebuilt in baroque style during the centuries, but the foundations of the original cloisters remain, a legacy of the Árpád dynasty which ruled the kingdom of Hungary in its infancy.

One of the most important libraries in the country is at the abbey. With 320,000 volumes laboriously assembled over the centuries, it houses a priceless object, the foundation deed of an abbey on the Tihany peninsula overlooking Lake Balaton, dating from 1055. What makes it significant is that it's the first document extant which contains Hungarian words inserted into the Latin text. The library, largest in the world in the hands of a single religious order, is adorned by 150 carved cherrywood bookcases and a balconied upper level.

The abbey church, which was transformed into a mosque when the Turks occupied Hungary, is all that remains of the early Gothic churches of the country. It was rebuilt in the 19th century on medieval foundations. The three-nave Romanesque crypt is the oldest part, dating from around 1200. It's said that the abbot's chair in the crypt contains slivers of wood from the chair used as the throne by St. Stephen, the first crowned king of Hungary. The king's coronation robes are in a glass case at the far end of the library. A bronze statue in the courtyard is of Astrik, the man who carried the crown from Pope Sylvester II in Rome to Hungary for the crowning of Stephen.

One section of the monastery, a barracks during the Turkish period, is filled with Benedictine memorabilia. There is a rich collection of paintings, including a masterpiece, *Fête in Brussels,* by David Teniers, 14th-century works by Fra Angelico, and some polychromed religious statues.

Stephanie, who was the wife of Crown Prince Rudolf of Austria when he allegedly committed suicide at Mayerling for love of another woman, is buried in the crypt here. She and her second husband came to Pannonhalma in 1945, fleeing the Russians and bearing more than 8000 rare books and dozens of manuscripts. Before she died she willed this treasure to the monastery.

Of interest too are some stone carvings set into a tunnel inside the complex leading under one of the buildings. These are from the Forum in Rome, the gift of the Italian foreign minister under Mussolini. A museum displays Bronze and Stone Age implements, Roman amphorae, and ancient glass jewelry, plus some Bronze Age hair clips and bracelets, as well as a grisly collection of swords and halberds.

Today in this severe-looking complex of old and new buildings, reminiscent of Mont St-Michel on its hilltop with steeply buttressed walls looking out over a sweeping valley, some 300 students are housed, and a home for old people is maintained. Concerts are held in the basilica from spring to autumn.

You can visit the establishment daily except Monday from 8:30 a.m. till 4 p.m. The entrance fee is 8 Ft. (18¢), but monastery rules require that you be accompanied by a guide, who costs 120 Ft. ($2.67) and will probably not speak English (perhaps German). Half the money collected goes to the monastery and half to the tourist office. An additional tip of 100 Ft. ($2.23) for the guide is quite acceptable.

Where to Eat

Restaurant Pannonhalma, 1 Szabadság tér (tel. 70175), is a local working-class restaurant which you might want to drop into after a tour of the monastery. Behind a fieldstone facade at the bottom of the road leading up the hill to the monastery, the restaurant serves lunches every day of the week and dinner every day except Monday. With wine included, you can dine here for around 110 Ft. ($2.45). Your meal might include goulash, a pork dish, fish soup, paprika chicken, and other Hungarian recipes.

TATA: Before going on to Budapest, I'd like to veer south on Route 100 for another stopover—Tata, a well-known baroque spa town and equestrian headquarters on the shores of a lake. Called the town of old watermills and springs, Tata, once the scene of royal hunting parties, lies between the Gerecse and the Vértes Mountains, with other lakes nearby. The town reached its heyday in the 15th century, with King Sigismund rebuilding the royal castle near here. The Diet met at Tata under King Matthias in 1510.

Jakob Fellner, an architect known throughout Europe, lived and worked here in the 18th century for a long time and was responsible for the reconstruction of the town with the use of baroque and rococo styles for many of the buildings. An example of his work is the parish church on the Kossuth tér. The Esterházy Palace on November 7 tér was also designed by Fellner, this one in Louis XVI style.

About 1½ miles to the north of Tata is the **Fenyes spa,** where you can bathe in sulfurous, slightly radioactive spring water. The lakes of the area are popular recreation spots. A national park surrounds the lake of Tata, and a riding school here is known throughout the country.

Another historic castle, **Öregvár,** lies on the shore of a lake. After destruction by both the Turks and the Habsburgs, it was reconstructed in a romantic style.

Food and Lodging

Hotel Diana (tel. Tata 715) occupies the former Esterházy mansion, which since its 1971 conversion into a hotel has added a nearby annex. The building includes an angular brick-trimmed tower extending off to one side from the main building and a pleasant exterior of baroque yellow with red-tile roofs. On the premises are a first-class restaurant, a tennis court, and dozens of walking paths. Many of the bedrooms in the main building still retain their baroque furniture. Doubles range from $18 to $43 daily, depending on the season and the accommodation. Open all year, the hotel is about three miles from the center of town.

SOPRON: Lying right on the old Hungarian-Austrian border, Sopron, once the capital of the province of Burgenland, is one of the most history-rich cities of the western border region of Hungary. When the Austro-Hungarian Empire was split up after World War I, a plebiscite was taken and Sopron, then called Ödenburg, voted to be part of Hungary, while the rest of the Burgenland province chose to be part of Austria (see Chapter VI). Sopron today is one of the best preserved cities of Hungary, with much work being carried out to protect national monuments and fewer problems with devastation from outside.

Sopron, known to the Romans as Scarbantia, is between Lake Fertő (Neusiedlersee or Lake Neusiedl in Austria) and the Sopron Mountain, 125 miles from Budapest, 44 miles from Vienna, and 5 miles from the Austrian frontier station, Klingenbach. It's an important holiday resort town of Hungary.

The inner city, enclosed by the medieval city wall, has as its landmark the **Fire Tower** (Tűztorony, in Hungarian), where 125 steps take you up to an observation level. The lower part of the tower is in Romanesque style, the midsection in Renaissance, and the upper portion in baroque. Next door to the tower is a museum of Roman artifacts.

The main square of town is Fö tér, where you are literally surrounded by historic buildings. In the middle of the square is **Trinity Column,** constructed at the beginning of the 18th century. Its three-tier spiral columns decorated with angels make it an outstanding example of Hungarian baroque sculpture. The Town Hall looks more like a national theater. On this square also is the Patika Museum, at no. 2, a pharmacy with all the old paraphernalia.

The once Gothic Benedictine **Kecske-templom,** called the Goat Church because of the goats carved into the crests on the structure, was built on the square between 1280 and 1300. Its tower is from the 14th century. The church is known for its rococo main altar and altarpieces around the pulpit.

At no. 8 on the square, the **Storno House** is a beautiful Renaissance structure built in the 15th century. A rare private collection of paintings and other treasures of the Storno family are on display here. Everybody from King Matthias to composer Franz Liszt has stayed here.

At 16 Szent György Utca is Erdődy Palace, a flamboyant rococo-style building. Two medieval synagogues stand at 11 and 22 Új Utca, from the 14th and 13th centuries. St. Michael's Church, Szentmihály út, is a Gothic building from the Middle Ages, with beautiful interior sculptures and paintings. In the churchyard at the back is the oldest building of the town, the Romanesque-Gothic St. James's Chapel, built in the mid-13th century.

The names of celebrated musicians are known here, and important events in the town's music life are connected with the name of Franz Liszt. The composer made his piano debut here as a child prodigy. Liszt fans will gravitate to the Liszt Ferenc Museum, Május 1 tér (First of May Square), where many fine arts and handicrafts displays may be seen. The museum also traces the history of Sopron over the years.

Two other composers of note who spent time in Sopron were Franz Joseph Haydn and Johann Strauss. Haydn, who was a protégé of the Esterházy princes (see below), often stayed at what was then the White Horse Inn on the main street of Sopron at no. 55. The street is now Lenin Körút. Strauss composed a section of his "One Night in Venice" during a stay in this city.

A popular recreation area in the vicinity is the **Lövérek,** an extension of the Alps with a subalpine climate, rich in woods and pine forests. On the north shore of Lake Fertő, 5½ miles from Sopron, in the underground halls of the monumental limestone quarry at Fertorákos, classical music concerts are held and old Greek tragedies performed in summer.

Good red wines are produced from grapes grown on the hills around Sopron, the best known being the Kékfrankos.

Food and Lodging

Hotel Lövér, 4 Várisi Utca (tel. 11061). Many Austrians from across the nearby border retreat here for weekends. The hotel is built in the middle of the Sopron forest, in a dramatically modern format of several different wings extending at different angles from a central core. The lobby is a sunny, high-ceilinged expanse of carefully crafted stone and woodwork, with comfortable chairs for reading and an attentive staff ready to assist you in whatever way it can. On the premises are a swimming pool, a fitness room, a sauna, a fine restaurant, a bar, and a sporting center with tennis courts less than a kilometer away. The hotel was recently renewed and enlarged to contain 203 bedrooms, which are furnished with simple attractive pieces and mini-bars. Singles range from $23 to $30 daily, while doubles go from $32 to $40, with a buffet breakfast included. Open all year, the hotel maintains a wintertime ski lift.

Hotel Palatinus, 23 Út Utca (tel. 11395), presents a simple white facade to one of the city's best preserved historic squares. The interior is a simple blend of modern textiles and wooden furniture. In summer a terrace offers a place to sit outdoors. The in-house restaurant is open from 7 a.m. to 11 p.m. The comfortable bedrooms rent for $10 to $18 daily in a single and between $22 and $35 for a double, with breakfast included. Prices vary with the season and the plumbing.

Cézár Wine-Cellar, 3 Hátsókapu Utca (tel. 11337), dating from the 17th century, is outfitted inside with soaring vaulted ceilings, some of which are trimmed with stone, along with massive sections of an antique wine press. The menu is well known for its good selection of local wines, as well as its simple Hungarian foods. You'll sit on three-legged stools at tables set against the whitewashed plaster of the plain white walls. You'll recognize the restaurant by its location inside a centrally located baroque building whose facade is painted a refreshing pastel green. Tabs average about 200 Ft. ($4.45), and it's open every day from 9:30 a.m. to 9:30 p.m.

Generális Café-Snack Bar, 7 Fő tér (tel. 14841), on the main square of town, is a 17th-century baroque building with an inner courtyard filled with Gothic relics. This building hosted enough high-ranking military officers in its time to merit the name "the General's House," although the clientele you'll see today will be lunching local residents. A coffeeshop is in the first room, while an informal restaurant with high plaster arches and a visible grill are located toward the rear. The house specialty is a regional recipe for pork chops. Light meals are available for around 180 Ft. ($4.01), and it's open from 7:30 a.m. to 9:30 p.m. daily.

Hungária Snack Bar, 60 Lackner Kristóf Utca (tel. 14036). Just after crossing the border, many Austrian tourists profit from the attractive prices both at this warmly contemporary restaurant and at the adjacent Shell gasoline station. There's no reason why you shouldn't do the same thing. The glass building offers tourist services as well as currency exchange offices. The restaurant serves a wide variety of Hungarian and international foods in a decor of barrel chairs upholstered in autumnal colors, curved ceiling panels, and hanging amber-colored lights. Light meals range upward from 180 Ft. ($4.01).

FERTŐD: The major excursion from Sopron is 17 miles to the southeast to the **Esterházy Palace at Fertőd.** It's the most outstanding (also the most mammoth) baroque palace in the country and has been called "the Versailles of Hungary." The horseshoe-shaped palace suffered damage in World War II, since repaired. What became a 126-room imperial palace was a hunting lodge until Miklós Esterházy, a prince of the Holy Roman Empire, effected the change. Construction on the transformation started in 1760 and lasted a decade.

As mentioned in the chapter in this book on Burgenland, Haydn was conductor for the court of the Esterházy family. When the noble court was in residence at Fertőd, the composer lived in the baroque-style Music House which was part of the palace complex, conducting concerts in the three-story gilt concert hall. You can see the concert hall and Haydn's Music House, preserved as a memorial to the composer, on guided tours.

In summer, concerts are given in memory of Haydn in the baroque concert hall or in the magnificent gardens of the palace.

KŐSZEG: The old walled town of Kőszeg has been a border outpost throughout its long history, standing today only a few miles from the Austria border station of Rábafüzes. A holiday resort enjoying a subalpine climate, Kőszeg was inhabited as far back as the Avar times in the sixth and seventh centuries, long before the coming of the Magyars.

The town was often embroiled in conflicts between the armies of Austria and Hungary. Its "finest hour" came in 1532 when the people of the town staged a heroic defense against the invading Turkish hordes. The odds were, at a rough estimate, 200,000 Turks to 1000 defenders. Kőszeg held out for some 22 days, delaying the western sweep of the Ottoman Empire, and, it is believed in these parts, thus saving Vienna. The Wellington-like hero was Capt. Miklós Jurisich. The central square of the town bears the name of the valiant captain.

Jurisich tér (Jurisich Square), once defended by walls and watchtower, has preserved its medieval townscape to the present day. The square has a number of notable buildings, including the Town Hall and a 17th-century baroque church, St. Emerich's, as well as St. James's Church. Although St. James's dates from as recently as the 19th century, it stands on the site of an early Minorite church from the 13th century, one of the most significant Gothic historic monuments in the country. A baroque altarpiece is from 1693. There are many historic churches in Kőszeg.

The 14th-century Kőszeg castle played an important role in the battles against the Turkish invaders. It has two towers left from the Middle Ages, and the western wing has a decorative Renaissance row of windows from the 15th century. The eastern wing houses the Jurisich Miklós Museum, where you can see much weaponry, some from the 17th century, and many antiques. Over the centuries architects have used varying styles for the castle, including Gothic, Renaissance, and baroque. Reconstruction work has been under way since 1958.

SZOMBATHELY: There's been a town at the site of Szombathely on the Rábá River for a long, long time. In fact this is said to be the oldest town in Hungary. It may well be, since it apparently was something more than a village when the Romans made it the capital of their province of Upper Pannonia. They called the town Savaria. It was an important trading center at the time, situated on the Amber Road, a busy trade route used by the Romans. Remnants of the road are visible in the **Garden of Ruins** discovered here in 1938.

Szombathely has yielded many archeological treasures. The Garden of Ruins mentioned above, between the present-day school and the cathedral, was named for Istvá Járdányi Paulovits who led excavations carried out here. You can see the remains of the one-time imperial palace with its 20-yard mosaic floor, a significant relic of fourth-century Pannonia.

The Basilica of St. Quirinus was the largest Christian building in Pannonia.

The **Isis shrine,** on Rákóczi út, is the largest sanctuary of the Isis cult, a religion of Egyptian origin, unearthed in Pannonian territory. It was restored in the 1960s. Every August opera performances are presented at the shrine, and there's a small museum here of Roman artifacts.

On a more recent note, a Franciscan church on Savaria tér (square) was rebuilt in the baroque style in the 17th and 18th centuries. The Dominican church on Talbuhin út is a baroque structure dating from about 1670, its interior being from the 17th and 18th centuries.

The **cathedral** on Berzsenyi Dániel tér, one of the most significant Louis XVI–style buildings in Hungary, can hold 5000 persons. Construction on it began at the end of the 18th century, with destruction being inflicted heavily in a U.S. Air Force bombing raid in 1945. However, it has been restored.

The largest town in western Transdanubia, Szombathely is one of the main tourist centers of West Hungary. It's 137 miles from Budapest and 12½ miles from Kőszeg, just visited.

On the northern edge of this city lies the village of Kámon, where you can visit the **Arboretum** with its 2000 shrubs and trees, including a rose garden with flowers named for such "goddesses" as Sophia Loren.

Food and Lodging

Hotel Cladius, 39 Bartók Béla körút (tel. 13760), in the center of the resort, has evenly spaced rows of curved borders encircling the big glass windows of the five-floor facade. Each of the comfortable rooms has its own balcony, a view of the surrounding park area, as well as a decor that tries vaguely to evoke the region's connections with ancient Rome. On the premises are two restaurants, a coffeeshop, and a nightclub. The 98 rooms are equipped with mini-bar, phone, radio, and an occasional TV. Tennis courts and a sauna are on the premises. Doubles range from $27 to $50 daily, depending on the season and the accommodation.

Hotel Isis, 1 Rákóczi Utca (tel. 14990), rises like a streamlined cube from its location in the heart of town, near the site of the Isis shrine. Its glass-covered facade is accented with wide black bands stretching horizontally across the front, while the entryway is under a heavy concrete parapet built off to one side. The simple and colorful interior contains a bar, a restaurant with Gypsy music, and a coffeeshop that doubles as a disco in the evening. Singles cost between $10 and $13 daily, while doubles range between $17 and $26, with breakfast included. Prices vary with the plumbing and the season.

Excursion to Ják

Some ten miles southwest of Szombathely is the abbey church of Ják, a masterpiece of Hungarian Romanesque architecture and one of the oldest churches in the country. It was built in the first half of the 13th century as a church with basilica-type nave and aisles. Two towers flank its facade, and rich sculptures decorate the portal.

8. Southwest Hungary

The Celts liked it, the Romans liked it, and through the centuries Southwest Hungary, once a part of the Roman province of Pannonia, has been a plum which numerous territory-hungry plunderers have tried to gobble up. The vicissitudes of war and migration have left their mark on the area. The Magyars came here too, when they moved westward and took over a broad swatch of what is now Hungary. However, during the Turkish conquest the Hungarian population dwindled, and Yugoslavs and Germans settled in the region in the 17th century. After World War II Moldavians and Slovakian Hungarians moved in.

To this day a significant number of the inhabitants here speak German, with people of other nationalities and ethnic groups using the language and carrying on the traditions and folk art of their ancestors. You can see how the celebrated colorful Sárköz embroidery with its many motifs is produced and visit the folk art cottages in Decs and Sióagard. In Bátaszék and Ófalu, German folk art predominates, while in South Baranya, a section of Southwest Hungary, women still weave Yugoslavian designs. Presbyterian churches in Kóros, Kovácshida, and Drávaiványy have fine examples of Ormánság fold art.

The Mecsek region of Southwest Hungary, lying mainly to the south of Lake Balaton, has one of the mildest climates in the country. Rivers and streams slice the terrain, and the shores of its lakes and the depths of the woodlands are quiet and serene. Many Yugoslavs view Mecsek as their vacationland.

Southwest Hungary is a good place to sample dishes from a cookery that is a result of many ethnic specialties.

PÉCS: The Mecsek region is the site of my favorite provincial city in all of Hungary, Pécs, the largest city in the district and fourth largest in the country, 125 miles from Budapest. Its warm climate gives it a Mediterranean aura.

Pécs is 2000 years old, although that hasn't always been its name. The Romans built a town on the slopes of the Mecsek mountain, naming it Sopianae and using it as the capital of eastern Pannonia province. This area was ruled by the Romans for four centuries. By the time the Magyars appeared in Transdanubia, the town was no longer called Sopianae but was referred to in a ninth-century document as "Quinque Basilicae," the town of five churches. It's believed that the churches alluded to were really memorial chapels from Roman times.

The oldest architectural relics of Pécs are the fourth-century tombs found in the Roman cemetery whose center is where Cathedral Square (Dom tér) was built in the Middle Ages. Some of the tombs are frescoed vaults with chapels erected over them. Those on the higher ground of the Mecsek slopes which survived the Dark Ages probably looked like churches to travelers approaching the city. Evidence has been found of four of these chapels for which this must have been true. An entrance has been opened in the eastern buttress of the Dom tér so that you can see one of the wall-painted chapel crypts, the decoration of which shows that it was the burial place of a Roman Christian family. The town's atmosphere today shows a heavy influence of Mediterranean culture, and the only other similar painted crypts are in Italy.

In the Middle Ages the city walls of Pécs encircled a larger area than that of contemporary Vienna. One of the most valuable medieval historic monuments in Hungary is the four-spired Romanesque **cathedral,** founded in the 11th century by St. Stephen, the country's first king, in the Dom tér. It has since seen many rebuilders and restorers, but the spatial concept has been preserved through the centuries. The five-nave undercroft is part of the original construction. The spire-capped towers date from the 11th and 12th centuries. The cathedral is rich in frescoes and carvings by outstanding Hungarian ecclesiastical artists. During Turkish rule, 1543–1686, the cathedral was turned into a mosque and storehouse, a stain removed when the area was returned to Christian sovereignty.

The **bishop's palace** stands on the west side of the Cathedral Square, near where Christian catacombs were found. This palace originated in the Middle Ages but received its present look in the mid-19th century.

The first university in Hungary, founded in Pécs in 1367, made the town a citadel of humanism in the 15th century, a situation that was greatly changed by the Turkish occupation. After a 17-year siege the followers of Mohammed moved in as rulers in 1543, staying for 143 years and leaving their indelible mark on Pécs. The main square of the town, Széchenyi tér, is a curious cultural mélange, with many historic buildings of varying provenance.

Here you'll see the **Pasha Kasim Mosque,** the largest building in Hungary from the Turkish era, now used as the inner-city parish church. Its minaret was demolished in the 18th century. Restorers of the mosque have uncovered some of the calligraphy on the walls, but a crucifix now occupies the former Muslim *mihrab,* or prayer niche.

Also on this square is the archeological collection of the **Janus Pannonius Museum.** In seven rooms of exhibits, you see artifacts dating from the Stone Age to the Magyar takeover of the country in the ninth century. The glass cases of the museum, named for the 15th-century humanist scholar and renowned poet Janus Pannonius, occupy five other buildings in the town besides the one on Széchenyi tér.

All visitors to Pécs will want to see the **Eosin Fountain,** symbol of the town, in front of the one-time Ignorantine Church dating from the 1720s. This fountain was donated by the well-known Zsolnay Porcelain Factory, founded here in 1870. A **Zsolnay Museum** with 8500 items on display occupies the oldest house in Pécs, a former private home at 2 Káptalan Utca from pre-Turkish days. The house survived the Muslim occupation because it was chosen by the Turkish chief mufti as his private quarters. Displays in the museum include what may well be the most sophisticated porcelains in Central Europe, plus ceramic sculptures, pottery, and tiles.

You can see the only surviving mosque-minaret combination in Hungary at the **Yakovali Hasan Mosque,** built in the 16th century and now housing a museum. The mosque has been restored to its original atmosphere, and the museum shows a cross-section of life and culture of the Hungarian Turkish period. You'll see a collection concerning the life of dervishes who had a monastery nearby. After the Turks were driven out in 1686, Bishop Nesselrode had the mosque rebuilt (1702–1732) for use as a chapel and hospital. You may visit the museum and mosque for an admission of 8 Ft. (18¢).

All Saints Church, Tettye Utca, built on the Tettye plateau outside the city walls, survived the Turk occupation. Constructed as a one-nave

Romanesque church in 1157, it was given three naves in a 15th-century restoration.

Art lovers will seek out the **Csontváry Museum,** 11 Janus Pannonius Utca, and **Vasarely Museum,** 3 Káptalan Utca, both art museums. The work of Tivadar Csontváry Kosztka, the "Rousseau of the Danube," and other Hungarian artists, including modern ones, is shown at the first address. The Káptalan structure, birthplace of Victor Vasarely, shows his work as one of the founding fathers of kinetic art and a pop art practitioner. Admission to the art museums is 5 Ft. (11¢).

Pécs is an important cultural center of Hungary, with a summer theater program in July, including opera, ballet, pantomine, drama, and concerts.

A short journey will take you to the Tettye plateau from which the road leads through the Mecsekkapu (gateway of the Mecsek) to a zoo and pioneer railway, then up to Missinatető, where the **television tower** is a major attraction. You can take an elevator to its lookout terrace and café from which you have a magnificent view of the Mecsek, the city of Pécs, and the Zsolnay eosin tiled roof of the post office, and even as far as to the fortress of Siklós (see below) and Harkány, a thermal resort.

Food and Lodging

Hotel Pannónia, 3 Rákóczi út (tel. 13322). The jutting porch of this hotel is angled into a series of zigzag lines that are repeated in the design of the decorative tiles on each of the balconies. Inside, the simple bedrooms are carpeted and sometimes offer unusual views over the old city. Built in 1976 in the center of town, the hotel offers two bars, a spacious wood-paneled restaurant with an evening dance band, a summer terrace, and a nightclub. Rates in its 108 well-furnished rooms range from $30 to $50 for two persons, with breakfast included. The higher tabs are for suites.

Hotel Nádor, 15 Széchenyi tér (tel. 11477), is the grand dowager hotel of Pécs. Built on the main square of town in 1845, it faces one of the most important mosques in Hungary. The hotel's blackened facade is designed in an ornate style of floor-to-ceiling windows and grandly proportioned frontal arches. Inside you'll find what might be the most popular restaurant in town, as well as a less formal beer hall with evening entertainment which sometimes includes a Spanish singer and guitarist. Doubles, depending on the plumbing and accommodation, range from $17 to $36 daily, with breakfast included.

The Nádor's restaurant offers a high-ceilinged dining room with light paneling and hunting trophies. A huge oval of wrought iron dotted with metal sculptures of deer hanging from links serves as a rustic lighting fixture. The service is efficient and alert, bringing well-prepared food on red, white, and gold porcelain made in the nearby factories. Specialties include a wide range of venison, a selection of poultry, pork cutlets with green beans and sour cream, rumpsteak with spicy butter, roast meat on a spit, and a good selection of cheese, along with homemade strudel or crêpes Gundel. An average meal runs around 300 Ft. ($6.68).

Excursion to Mohács

One of Hungary's largest river docks is on the Danube in the Baranya County town of Mohács, about 25 miles west-southwest of Pécs, where the

Hungarians lost a bloody battle against the Turks in 1526. This was a prelude to the 143-year occupation of the country, dating from 1543. You can see the **Mohács Historical Garden of Monuments** with carved grave posts and wooden statues.

Medieval times are brought back to life here each year with springtime festivals called *busójárás,* which originated from the Sokác Slavonic ethnic group.

SIKLÓS: The fortress town of Siklós, about 20 miles south of Pécs, is another settlement dating back to Roman times. It lies in Villány, the major wine-producing district of Southwest Hungary. The fortified castle, built here after the Mongol invasion of 1241, escaped the fate of other such castles in the country which ended as ruins. This remnant of the Middle Ages, **Siklós Fortress** (Siklós Var) was remodeled somewhat in the 15th century and then was almost in ruins in 1686 when the Turks abandoned it. It was given by the Austrian emperor to one of his generals, who rebuilt it in the 18th century and installed his coat-of-arms above the narrow entranceway leading up a hill into the inner courtyard. The 18th-century look was retained in a 1969 restoration.

Aside from a hotel built into one of the oldest parts and an underground restaurant (see my hotel and restaurant recommendations, below), the fortress has an unusual church, a torture chamber, a summertime café on the ramparts, a museum, and a gift shop.

The austere chapel is the only intact Gothic structure in south Transdanubia. You'll see a "web net" ceiling of chiseled stone ribs and a private balcony leading directly into the living quarters of the lord and lady of the castle. The holy water near the chapel door is contained in a basin which the occupying Turks also used as a font. Near the entrance is a gift shop, selling handmade jewelry, textiles, and a striking variety of black porcelain with flowers done in shiny black paint against a black matte background. In summer you may hear Gregorian chants emanating from a recording played in the chapel.

Inside the castle look for a small wooden door braced with iron that leads down to the torture chamber, equipped with uniquely Hungarian instruments of torture. In another underground cellar that used to house the guards who defended Siklós, a local cooperative operates the restaurant described below. The living quarters of the noble owners can be visited. You can almost circumnavigate the ramparts in good weather, looking out over the vineyards surrounding this ancient brick and stone stronghold.

The most memorable woman to live here as lady of Siklós Var was Dorothy Kanizsai, who is much celebrated in Hungarian legend. It was she who shouldered the grisly and unhappy task of burying the dead after the disastrous battle of nearby Mohács in 1526 when the Turks slaughtered the Hungarian troops. With a handful of serfs helping, she laid to rest the bloodied bodies of the Hungarian dead in the graveyard at Satorhely, today a memorial park (see above).

Siklós hosts an annual ceramic symposium and exhibition, Castle Festival and Brass Band meetings, and a summer cultural program.

Food and Lodging

Hotel Tenkes, Siklós Fortress (tel. Siklós 6), is built into the stone superstructure of the castle itself. The entrance through the courtyard leads into an airy, stone-floored lobby with a high ceiling and a riserless stairway climbing dramatically to the simple rooms of the upper floors. Many of these ring the exterior wall of the fortress, offering views of the ramparts and the vineyards beyond. The 30 bedrooms are attractively simple, almost beautifully severe. Many of them have 15-foot ceilings, simple stucco walls, big closets, and lots of plants. Some of the larger rooms have interior stairwells leading to sleeping lofts. Double rooms cost $25 daily with breakfast, $27.60 with half board, and $38 with full board.

Even if you can't stay here, you might want to patronize the Restaurant Tenkes. The guard quarters used to be under the vaults of this brick and stucco cellar with a red stone floor. Today it's a pleasant restaurant where Hungarian specialties are served on elegantly fragile green and white Herend china. Gypsy music plays every evening to an appreciative crowd of local community members and visiting tourists. Meals average 300 Ft. ($6.68).

SZEKSZÁRD: This is the capital of the county of Tolna, which is about 95 miles from Budapest and almost 40 miles from Pécs in Southeast Hungary, its eastern border formed by the Danube River. People have inhabited the site of Szekszárd for many centuries. The Roman town of Alisca sat on what is now Béla tér (Béla Square), where King Béla I established a Benedictine abbey in 1061. Roman ruins are on view here.

The County Hall on Béla tér is worth seeing. It was built between 1828 and 1832 in the classicist style. Interesting houses stand on the Geray tér. The archeological and ethnographical collections at the Béri Bologh Ádám Museum are particularly rich.

The hill region around Szekszárd and Bálazék, another Tolna County town, produces some excellent wines, most celebrated of which are red Kadarka, Bull's Blood, and Cabernet.

Food and Lodging

Hotel Gemenc, 1 Mészáros Lázár Utca (tel. 11722), is a modern balconied hotel built out of reinforced concrete and glass. A minute's walk from the center of town, it offers comfortably simple bedrooms and a big sunny restaurant with stone floors, black tile accents, immaculate napery, and an impressive collection of hunting trophies. The formally dressed waiters bring Hungarian specialties from behind a screen of potted palms. An average meal usually costs 300 Ft. ($6.68). Doubles range between $20 and $30 daily, with an obligatory breakfast costing an additional $3 per person.

Excursions

The **Sötét Valley,** between the townships of Szekszárd and Kakasd, is a nature reserve of 2471 acres, with footpaths, benches, and a rowing pond, a popular spot for quiet and relaxation.

The **Gemenci Forest,** eight miles from Szekszárd, is a national nature reserve situated in a former flood area of the Danube called Sárköz. In the 25,000 acres is almost every species of Hungary's birds and wild animals, as well as lush grass and leafy trees. Rare and valuable animals can be seen in their natural habitat or at the Hunter's Lodge. Guided tours, with English commentary, of the game reserve are possible from Szekszárd in summer, going by miniature railway or by boat on the backwaters of the Danube. Trips are arranged by the **Tolna County Tourist Office,** 19 Széchenyi út (tel. 12-428) in Szekszárd.

DECS: One of the biggest villages in the Sárköz, Decs (don't confuse it with Pécs, a city) is known for the **Sárközi tájház** (cooperative crafts store), 35 Kossuth út (tel. 3), a combination museum and crafts store in the middle of a farm community. Here you can purchase local crafts products, especially needlepoint.

The museum contains artifacts which would have been in a puszta farmer's house 100 years ago. They include a collection of small, thick-walled rooms filled with furniture, photos of poker-faced wedding couples in all their hand-embroidered finery, cooking utensils, and decorative china.

You can visit every day except Monday from 10 a.m. to noon and 1 to 6 p.m., but this place isn't easy to find—the entrance is on a bleak street and isn't very distinctive.

KALOCSA: About four miles east of the Danube, lying to the northeast of Szekszárd, is Kalocsa, the folkloric capital of Hungary, noted for its paprika and its "painting women," who are especially known for their wall painting. In fact Kalocsa has a **Paprika Museum** (a first for me!), on the Marx tér, across from an open-air fruit and vegetable market. The tiny museum traces the history of paprika (pepper) farming and the process by which it is turned from a vegetable into the spicy red powder.

The historic heart of the town, which was rebuilt in the 18th century, is Szabadság tér, where you'll see a baroque cathedral from the time of the rebuilding, the fourth house of worship on that spot. A three-story archbishop's palace is also on the square.

One of the interesting sights in town is the **Károly Viski Museum** at Istvan út. In various rooms, the life of the region around Kalocsa is recreated. Of more recent vintage is the **Nicholas Schőffer Memorial House,** created in the birthplace of the well-known artist who now lives in Paris.

If it's folklore you came here for, head for the **Kalocsa Folk Art Cooperative,** which has both a small museum with farm implements and antiques, and a gift shop selling the renowned pottery and flower-embellished embroidery of the area.

9. The Great Plain and Puszta

Hungary's Great Plain and puszta region takes up about half the country, beginning almost at the outskirts of Budapest and reaching the frontiers of Yugoslavia and Roumania. The Tisza River divides the plain, a nearly flat expanse which is considered the most typical Hungarian landscape—or at least the best known.

This is a land of legend, celebrated in poetry and song. It's known for its *csikós,* or riders, of the Great Plain and their magnificent horses. In the puszta areas you can get glimpses of ancient Hungarian shepherd traditions.

Many of the sleepy little villages are still living happily in the past, enjoying the untouched simplicity of peasant life.

In days of yore the Great Plain was almost like the American prairie, a wild, untamed land, except that back then it consisted mainly of swamplands and puszta. The sand of the plain was driven by the wind for centuries, until the peasants tied it down with acacias and made it fertile. Now vineyards grow on the reclaimed acres, and cattle graze on meadowland.

Two major routes are followed in the exploration of the plain—one southwest to Szeged, going via Kecskemét, and the other directly to the east of Budapest all the way to Debrecen, not too far from the Roumanian border.

KECSKEMÉT: Once a quiet farm town, Kecskemét has been irrevocably altered by progress. For a long time the town was charmingly intact (and much of it still is), as it was never bombed in any wars, although it did suffer many medieval fires. During recent years the single-story houses of the old town have been replaced by modern housing estates, and industry has gained a leading role in the town's economy. Two squares—Kossuth tér and Szabadság tér—join to form the core of the town. In the center of the region between the Danube and Tisza Rivers, 55 miles southeast of Budapest, Kecskemét was a settlement at the time of the Magyar invasion of Hungary in the late ninth century.

There's still much of the old town to be seen, including three churches opening onto Kossuth tér. Oldest is the **Franciscan church,** which has wall pillars dating from the 13th to the 15th centuries. It was later remodeled in the baroque style. The **Calvinist** (Protestant) **church** is from the 17th century. The **"Old Church,"** a neoclassical Catholic house of worship, was begun in 1774. A synagogue, built in 1862 in neo-Byzantine style on Szabadság tér, is now occupied by the House of Technology.

Kecskemét was the native town of the 20th-century composer Zoltán Kodály, who pioneered in the field of music education. The International Kodály Seminar is held here every two years (in the odd years) at the beginning of August. The **Zoltán Kodály Institute of Music Education** is housed in the former monastery of Franciscan friars.

Late in the 19th century Hungary wanted to create a typically Hungarian architectural style, and a country-wide competition was held. The winning design was what you see today at the three-story **Town Hall,** a style designated Hungarian art nouveau or Hungarian Secessionist. This gaudily painted, vaulted fantasy has dozens of architectural details, many incorporating Kecskemét's symbol of a standing goat, but the structure looks more Gothic revival than anything else. The ceremonial hall on the second floor, used now for an occasional wedding ceremony, is graced with frescoes done by Bertalan Székely in 1896. The entire room is covered with peasant-inspired designs in beige, pink, and green pastels. In the center ceiling hangs what may be the most magnificent chandelier you'll see in Hungary.

Two other buildings of the Hungarian Secessionist school of architecture are the **Cifra Palace** and **Kecskeméti Galeria,** 1 Rákóczi út. The latter contains a good collection of 19th-and 20th-century Hungarian art, plus 20th-century works on the ground floor. The gallery keeps standard museum hours, with the last ticket sold at 5:30 p.m. Entrance is 5 Ft. (11¢) daily, free on Saturday.

The **József Katona Museum**, named for the playwright who was born in Kecskemét, houses a rich local, historical, archeological, and ethnic collection. **Theater Katona József,** also honoring the native son who died in 1967, is used for concerts and plays. It's baroque yellow with a red tile roof and has decorative urns on its corners. Michael York has performed here, and filmmakers have for decades used it for scenes in movies, including *The Phantom of the Opera.* It was used in the European TV series on the lives of Berlioz and Wagner, in which Richard Burton played Wagner.

You might want to go shopping in Kecskemét, and I recommend trying the Hungarian Intourist shop, the Zoltán Kodály book and music store, and the Amphora glassware, china, and ceramics emporium for good buys. Of course there are lots of souvenir shops throughout the town. Kecskemét is in the center of an apricot growing region that turns out one of the most celebrated of all Hungarian drinks, *barack,* an apricot brandy you may want to sample and take home.

Food and Lodging

Hotel Aranyhomok, 3 Széchenyi tér (tel. 20011), is a six-floor rectangular hotel in the center of town near the yellow baroque church. In Hungarian its name means "Golden Sands." If you're sightseeing you might want to stop for a snack in the ground-level café. On the premises is an upstairs bar with a solid wall of stained glass, plus a nearby two-level restaurant with enormous windows, lots of plants, Gypsy music, and a slanted ceiling studded with chrome detailing and hanging lamps that look vaguely Chinese.

Menu items include fried filets of goose liver, medallions of pork Hungarian style, Russian salad, crêpes stuffed with pork and served with a paprika sauce, Hungarian beef stew in red wine, and a dessert that might be crêpes Gundel or else a strudel. You can eat a full meal for less than 250 Ft. ($5.57). Each of the pleasant bedrooms has a private balcony looking out over the inner-city park at the edge of which the hotel is located. Doubles range from $15.50 if bathless up to $40 for a suite.

Dining on the Outskirts

Szélmalom (Windmill) **Csárda** (no phone). You'll notice the vanes of this transplanted windmill from far across the plain as you drive from Kecskemét toward Szeged on the E5 highway, near kilometer stone 91. The interior is a round room with thick wooden tables arranged like the spokes of a wheel, each radiating toward a circular bar area in the center. Each seating area has its own small arched window of double-paned glass, a bouquet of flowers, and puszta-style furniture which is pegged, not nailed, together. A vested waiter will place a red and black hand-woven mat in front of you, on top of which will be served such specialties as "drunken piglet with sauerkraut," or bean soup with sour cream. Meals range from 120 Ft. ($2.67). The restaurant, which is run by a local agricultural cooperative, opens an upper level when it's busy.

Erdőkert Csárda (no phone) lies in a forested area close to Highway 44, about 15 kilometers outside Kecskemét. Built in a former farmhouse, the red-tiled building has a paneled interior decor of warmly finished pine, with hanging animal skins, embroidered napery, and antique farm implements hanging from sections of the simple white plaster. Both the recipes and the crockery that they're served on come from the Hungarian Plain. Open from 7:30 a.m. to 9:30 p.m. every day in season, it serves meals that average around 300 Ft. ($6.68).

Excursions in a National Park

The most important excursion you can take from Kecskemét is to the **Bugacpuszta,** the most frequently visited of the six separate regions of the Kiskunság National Park. The park contains some 100 square miles of landscape set aside by the government for protection. Much of it is windswept desert, with sandstorms in early spring sometimes enveloping Kecskemét, 15 miles away. In the Bugac you'll find tiny salt lakes, marshes, dense forests, sand dunes, and wildflower meadows. Featured is the Pásztormuzeum (peasants' museum), showing relics of the Bugac peasant life.

The traditional rigid animal husbandry is pursued today as a tourist attraction. The ancient Hungarian gray forked-horn cattle, twisted-horn Racka sheep, "mangalica" pigs with curly bristles, and the renowned Hungarian half-breed horses will be found here. Besides the flora and fauna, the Bugac farmsteads are of interest.

Tours can easily be arranged at the tourist office in Kecskemét or at the leading hotel, Aranyhomok. Visitors go first to the Bugac Csárda, a wayside inn, from which they're taken by horse carriages along dirt roads. Along the way you'll get to see some cowboys, puszta style, called *pasztorok,* wearing baggy white trousers.

The excursion ends back at the Bugac Csárda, where local specialties and wine from the grapes produced in the sandy soil are served.

SZEGED: Sweet paprika, salami, fish soup, and the summer theater festival are major productions of Szeged, the economic and cultural center of Hungary's southern Great Plain. On the banks of the Tisza River, this was the first planned city in Hungary, others just growing up haphazardly. Szeged in its early days may have done just that, but when the town was destroyed by flood in 1879, Franz Joseph, emperor of Austria and king of Hungary, personally visited here and ordered the town redesigned and rebuilt. The inner boulevard bears the name of Lenin, but the outer ring uses names of the various cities that contributed to the rebuilding, such as Paris, Vienna, and Rome.

The main square of the town, Széchenyi tér, is like a municipal park, one of the country's finest greet squares, occupying about 12 acres. There's also a Roosevelt tér (square) in Szeged, honoring the American wartime president. This may not, at first thought, seem unique, but it's most unusual in a Soviet-bloc country.

The most celebrated landmark of the town is the **Votive Church** on Dom tér (cathedral square), a neo-Romanesque, a two-towered church completed in 1930. Its attraction is an organ with five manuals and 10,180 pipes, the second largest such instrument in Europe after that of the Milan Cathedral. Beside the Votive Church stands the medieval **St. Demetrius Tower.** When construction started on the new church in 1913, the builders tried to blow up the old tower to make way for the new edifice. They failed, and the people of the town considered this divine intervention, so the tower was allowed to remain.

The **Greek Orthodox Serb Church** behind the Votive Church is a richly ornamented baroque building with a Louis XVI steeple. Inside there's a Byzantine-style iconostasis (a partition on which icons are hung, separating the sanctuary from the rest of the church). The **Lower Town Parish Church** on Mátyás Király tér (square) is a valued historic building with a sacristy from the 15th century.

Szeged draws many visitors in summer to its celebrated Open-Air Theater Festival, held annually in July and August, when Hungarian and international opera and drama are presented by native and foreign stars. Performances are on Cathedral Square on a stage before the Votive Church.

You can go boating on the Tisza in summer and swim in a cold-water pool or the open-air facility in the park. Both holiday visitors and locals go to the hydropathic establishment on Kálvin Square where they can bathe in thermal spring water.

Szeged is a convenient and pleasant place to stop if you're on your way to Transylvania, once a part of Hungary but now in Roumania, or else to Belgrade in Yugoslavia.

Food and Lodging

Hotel Hungária, 2 Komócsin Zoltán tér (tel. 10855), is a modern ten-story hotel on the bank of the Tisza River. It has a uniformed staff and a fire-engine-red corner bar just off the big lobby area. Its huge dining room might happen to be hosting a tour group from Siberia during your visit, although the ambience created by the musical group playing 1940s-style big-band music lightens the mood considerably. Next to the Szeged National Theater, the hotel charges between $27 and $48 daily for a double room with breakfast included. The higher price is for a suite.

Hotel Tisza, 1 Wesselényi Utca (tel. 12466), the oldest hotel in town, has an elegantly ornate 19th-century facade painted lime green with white trim. Parts of the interior have been drastically renovated with little of the original detailing left. The big skylit dining room is a pleasant oasis, with oversize windows flooding part of the interior with sunlight and huge wall murals with stylized human figures covering two opposite walls. Bela Bartok used to perform in the concert hall on the ground floor of this historic place. With breakfast included, the old-fashioned single rooms range from $9 to $18 daily, while doubles cost from $17 to $36. The higher double tariff is for a suite.

Hotel Royal, 1 Kölcsey Utca (tel. 12911), is a centrally located medium-size hotel (110 rooms) near many of Szeged's architectural treasures. This is a satisfactory and unpretentious stopover in the center of town, with a streamlined interior covered with reddish slabs of polished stone. Most of the facade is old, ochred, elaborately 19th century (and slightly in need of repair), but that doesn't influence the comfort of the simple rooms or the friendly treatment by the English-speaking staff. The section of the facade just above the entryway is more modern. Singles range from $12 to $15 daily, while doubles cost between $22 and $50 (a suite), with breakfast included. Each of the units has a radio and phone. The in-house bar leading off the lobby has a dimly lit decor of high ceilings and modern stained-glass ceiling lamps.

Restaurant Alabárdos, 13 Oskola Utca (tel. 12914). The bronze panels on the front door facing the street depict mythological scenes that will make you search through your memory of ancient religions. An inner set of doors glows with carefully set stained glass. You'll enter a vestibule and find a pleasant brasserie with a vaulted ceiling off to the right. There will usually be students from the nearby university talking quietly in a good-natured ambience of darkly lit intimacy. If you turn left after entering, you'll see a long series of vaulted rooms whose walls are hung with medieval weapons that almost make you shudder.

You'll quickly forget your fears when you see the fragile Herend china, the fine crystal, and the elegant cutlery, along with the simple wildflowers clustered in vases. In one of the rooms a large millstone topped with a mound of multicolored candle drippings and a single burning taper gives a Gypsy-like aura of the puszta. No lunch is served, but in the evening a Gypsy band provides music as you are served such specialties as mixed fish soup of Szeged, paprika chicken with sour cream and dumplings, pork goulash with noodles, fried goose liver with tartar sauce, "robber's meat" on a spit, sauteed frog legs, and Hungarian veal stew. Expect to spend from 300 Ft. ($6.68) to 450 Ft. ($10.02).

The brasserie is open every day except Tuesday from 2 p.m. to 10 p.m., and the restaurant is open Monday to Thursday from 6 p.m. to midnight, from 6 p.m. to 2 a.m. on Friday and Saturday (to 11 p.m. on Sunday).

Virág Café, 1 Klauzál tér (tel. 11459). In summer a terrace extends into the baroque square in front, although in winter you'll have to sit amid the dozens of old-world details that fill this Central European–style coffeehouse. The furniture is from the turn of the century, including pink marble tables and cambriole-legged chairs. The crystal chandeliers are each slightly different, my favorite being a brass-trimmed art nouveau fantasy. As long as you're looking around, be sure to notice the porcelain-trimmed coffeemaker from Pécs. Come here for ice creams, coffee, and the best pastries in town. Pastries cost upward from 10 Ft. (22¢), with beverages priced from 18 Ft. (40¢). It's open from 7 a.m. to 10 p.m. every day of the week.

DEBRECEN: The cultural and economic center of eastern Hungary, near the Roumanian border, is Debrecen, a largely industrial city which is nevertheless an up-to-date resort. Already the third-largest city in Hungary, Debrecen is one of the country's most rapidly developing towns. The main thoroughfare is the Vörös Hadsereg útja.

This site must be a good place to live. Evidence shows that there were people here in the Stone Age, and in the 14th century Debrecen was a bustling market town on an important trade route. It has long been a seat of learning and culture, known for its **university** in Memorial Gardens. The seat of learning was established in the Middle Ages, the present building being from the early 19th century. Its library contains one of the biggest public collections in the country.

The largest Calvinist Church in Hungary is here. **The Great Church** on Kossuth tér (square), the heart of the city, is one of the finest examples of Hungarian classicist architecture in the country. It has a colonnaded facade and tall twin towers, the tower on the left containing a five-ton bell, the largest in Hungary. St. Anne's Church on Béke út is a baroque structure erected between 1719 and 1746.

You might also visit the **Déri Museum** on Múzeum Utca, which is rich in East Asian artifacts and also has some Etruscan items. Many 19th- and 20th-century works of art are on display. See *Ecce Homo* by Mihály

Munkácsy, one of Hungary's most outstanding artists. The museum also has a recreation of a typical East Hungary peasant room, complete with four-poster bed.

The Csókonai Theater on Liszt Ferenc Utca is one of the most important examples of 19th-century Romantic eclecticism built outside Budapest.

Debrecen has long been known for its fierce spirit of independence. Groups formed here in 1849 to oppose the Habsburgs and again in 1944 to fight the Nazis.

Food and Lodging

Arany Bika (Golden Bull), 11-15 Vörös Hadsereg Utca (tel. 16777), is a historic hostelry. Art nouveau in style, it's celebrated for its cuisine, said to be the best outside Budapest. The hotel stands diagonally across from the "Great Church" in the heart of town. Dating from 1699, it has as its principal dining room an area rich in nostalgia. Here excellently prepared food is served, with meals costing from 250 Ft. ($5.57) to 400 Ft. ($8.91), which make them great bargains considering the quality of the cuisine.

Chandeliers hang from a stained-glass ceiling three stories high. The Golden Bull takes its name from an innkeeper who had a sign put up in memory of the former owner, János Bika. The sign depicted a golden bull.

The hotel was completely modernized and made ready for occupancy in 1914, just in time to catch the beginning of World War I. Depending on the plumbing, singles range from 400 Ft. ($8.91) to 800 Ft. ($17.82), with doubles costing from 580 Ft. ($12.92) to 850 Ft. ($18.93).

10. Northern Highlands

This is the section of Hungary perhaps least explored by North Americans, yet it's one of the most rewarding in terms of natural sightseeing attractions. In the northeastern section of the country, the highlands border on Czechoslovakia and Russia. Occasionally you'll see a ruined castle standing on top of a hill, a reminder of all the conquering hordes who have passed through this part of Hungary.

Parts of the highlands are heavily forested with beech, hornbeam, pine, and oak trees. The area contains some state game reserves, where you may chance to spot a wild boar. Certainly you'll see herds of deer. The Hungarian eagle also still lives in these parts.

The highest mountain peak in Hungary, 3300 feet, is at Kékestető. The Hungarians use this area for winter sports, although many cross the border into Czechoslovakia to ski where the mountain ranges are much higher. Most Western visitors will enjoy the highlands more in summer, exploring the many vineyards, caves, and lakes. The major wine-producing regions are Tokaj, Eder, and Gyöngyös.

EGER: This city, northeast of Budapest, lies on the banks of the little Eger River at the meeting point of the Mátra and Bükk Mountains. Celebrated for its thermal springs and baths and its wines, Eger is rich in historic monuments. It was already an old town when the Mongols invaded in 1241, with a bishopric founded by St. Stephen, the first king of Hungary, who donned the crown in A.D. 1000.

The Mongols and later the Turks were particularly cruel to the people of Eger, but the cruelty bred heroism among the townsfolk. Eger Castle was built after the Mongol invasion, and it played its most important role against the Turks. Every Hungarian knows of the heroic defense of the castle in 1552 by István Dobó and Gergely Bornemissza who, with a handful of men, defeated the massive Turkish army, thought before that to be invincible.

However, some 34 years later the Turks came back, this time capturing the town and turning it into one of the regional capitals of the Ottoman Empire. For almost a century Eger was the northernmost outpost of Muslim might. The Turks erected mosques, baths, and the **Kethuda Minaret,** which has been restored in recent years. This 14-sided, 130-foot-high Turkish building, now one of the small city's main attractions, stands on Dobó István tér, the square named for the commander who led the successful 1552 defense of Eger. The mosque of Knézich Károly beside which the minaret was originally built was torn down in 1841.

The **castle-fortress** has been much restored, with little remaining from the original 15th-century edifice, but it's worthwhile having a look at the vast system of subterranean casemates, and the view from here is the best in Eger. The material excavated from the underground of the old castle is displayed in the Castle Museum, which occupies a Gothic building of the former episcopal palace. Exhibited is a lot of weaponry from both sides in the 1552 siege. The town was reclaimed for the kingdom of Hungary in 1687.

The **Minorite Church,** on Dobó István tér, is an 18th-century baroque building colored pink and ivory with green-topped towers. The **Cathedral of Eger,** on Szabadság tér, the second-largest church in the country, is of Greek temple style, built between 1831 and 1836. On its facade a tympanum rests on a Corinthian column.

You don't really need to be directed to specific sights in the old town of Eger, as this baroque city has much of interest for you to discover just by walking around through the little winding streets at the foot of the castle. The most interesting street is Kossuth Lajos Utca, filled with buildings in the baroque and rococo styles.

As a curious side note to your touring, take a look at the 18th-century Lyceum, now a secondary school for girls. It's called the Ho Chi Minh Teachers' Training College. This is the largest baroque building of its type in the country, complete with a museum on the upper floor and an astronomical observation tower.

Wine connoisseurs will want to sample the renowned wine, **Egri bikavér,** or bull's blood, product of the valley of Szépasszony. You'll find this wine in many old taverns in the heart of town.

Food and Lodging

Hotel Eger, 1-3 Szálloda Utca (tel. 13233), is a balconied L-shaped hotel set at the foot of the castle, close to the cathedral. It has 172 unpretentious modern bedrooms, which look out over balconies onto a view of the historic city itself. The facade is embellished with an unusual series of curved panels set between the windows, giving the impression that the window panes are eyes staring through holes in evenly spaced masks. On the premises are a tennis court, an indoor swimming pool with a view of the terrace outside, a restaurant, and a bar. Depending on the accommodation, a single rents for $9 to $27 daily, while doubles cost between $17 and $50 (a suite), with a breakfast buffet included.

Hotel Park, 8 Klapka Utca (tel. 13233), is the oldest hotel in town, with a certain style not found in newer buildings. Its arched and hip-roofed exterior is expanded with a series of extensions which maintain the style of the original building. The entire hotel contains only 39 rooms, which might be appropriate if you prefer smaller, more personally run hostelries. The restaurant has a big terrace and serves the regional wines as well as Hungarian specialties, which are accompanied in the evening by Gypsy music. Per-person rates range from $9 to $11 daily in a single and from $17 to $30 in a double, with breakfast included.

Fehér Szarvas Csárda (White Stag), 8 Klapka Utca (tel. 13233, ext. 28), in the cellars of the Hotel Park, has an intimately rustic ambience of coffered ceilings, warmly tinted paneling and exposed brick, along with an impressive collection of hunting trophies. The overall effect is almost like that of a hunting lodge, especially with the evening Gypsy music. As you'd expect, the house specialty is venison in many different forms, ranging from soups to stews to roasts. You'll also find wild boar soup served with sour cream and various forms of poultry cooked on a spit. Meals begin at 300 Ft. ($6.68). It's open from 6 p.m. to midnight every day but Tuesday.

Dobos Café, 6 Széchenyi Utca (tel. 13335), is a city landmark which also offers the best pastries in town. Established by one of Hungary's leading confectioners of the 19th century, who named the establishment after himself, it is now a popular rendezvous point. The elegantly colorful decor includes red stone floors set into differently shaped rectangular slabs, marquetry paneling, and cambriole-legged chairs upholstered in olive-green velvet. The crystal chandeliers and wall lights date from the age of Maria Theresa.

The specialty of the house is a richly caloric dessert called Dobos cake, although there are also ice cream and coffee drinks. Pastries range upward from 10 Ft. (22¢); drinks begin at 18 Ft. (40¢). It's open every day from 7:30 a.m. to 10 p.m.

AGGTELEK: This village stands at the western end of one of the biggest and loveliest systems of caves in all of Europe—the **Baradla Caves,** the greatest natural phenomenon in Hungary. The whole passage stretches a distance of some 14 miles, part in Czechoslovakia. However, you don't need to show your passport to explore the caverns. Bones found deep inside show that prehistoric bears and Stone Age man inhabited these subterranean chambers—but probably not at the same time.

The so-called Hall of the Giants is one of the largest caverns in Europe. In summer, concerts and operas are presented here. One formation is fancifully called "The Leaning Tower of Pisa." The "Observatory" is one of the biggest stalagmites in the world. A lake formed in the caves can be crossed by rowboat.

The caves were once torchlit, which must have made exploration pretty spooky. Now professional guides take you through, and a good lighting system lets you see the full beauty of the grottoes. Tours are of varying length, depending on a party's stamina and interest. It's possible to take a short tour, lasting one hour, beginning at Aggtelek. Dress warmly and wear good, sturdy walking shoes. The temperature inside is around 50° Fahrenheit even in midsummer. The caves are closed on Monday.

TOKAJ: The best known little town in Hungary is Tokaj, but its product—"the wine of kings and the king of wines"—is **Tokay,** renowned since the

Middle Ages. Tokaj lies some 30 miles east of Miskolc, Hungary's second-largest city (but of little interest to most visitors), at the confluence of the Bodrog and Tisza Rivers, in the heart of one of the great wine-growing regions of the country. The ideal time to visit in the countryside around Tokaj is in autumn at harvest time.

No other country, including France, has been able to produce Tokay wine successfully. This vintners' pride has been enjoyed by such personages as Maria Theresa, Voltaire, Goethe, Beethoven, and Frederick the Great, and in the wine cellars of Tokaj you can discover what all the excitement is about.

The most exciting cellar to visit is Rákóczi cellar, said to contain some 450,000 gallons of wine. The entrance is at 13 Kossuth tér. Built centuries ago, the cellar has more than two dozen labyrinthine passageways and a total length of almost a mile. In the country's fight for independence from the Habsburgs in the 19th century, this cellar was often the scene of secret partisan meetings.

You can also visit a wine museum which has been installed in a former wine cellar. You will see, among other exhibits, a 19th-century grape press.

SAROSPATAK CASTLE: Finally, you can visit one of the most outstanding castles in the area, Sárospatak Castle, considered one of the greatest monuments in Hungary. To reach it, you take Route 37 from Miskolc.

Construction on this fortified castle, which lies in a park near the Czech border, spread across the centuries, but the oldest part is the red tower, rising six floors, dating from the latter part of the 15th century. Many Italian architects worked on the building.

Guided tours are conducted through the fortress, during which you'll see a display of religious art and a system of cellars. See, in particular, loggia from the 1640s, a shining example of Renaissance art in Hungary. You can visit one of the largest Gothic hall churches in East Hungary, the core of which is from the 14th century.

Like all other historic monuments in Hungary, the castle is closed on Monday.